Contemporary Authors®

ISSN 0010-7468

Contemporary Authors®

A Bio-Bibliographical Guide to Current Writers in Fiction, General Nonfiction, Poetry, Journalism, Drama, Motion Pictures, Television, and Other Fields

volume 208

GALE®

THOMSON

GALE

Detroit • New York • San Diego • San Francisco • Cleveland • New Haven, Conn. • Waterville, Maine • London • Munich

Contemporary Authors, Vol. 208

Project Editor
Scot Peacock

Editorial
Katy Balcer, Sara Constantakis, Anna Marie
Dahn, Alana Joli Foster, Natalie Fulkerson,
Arlene M. Johnson, Michelle Kazensky, Julie
Keppen, Jennifer Kilian, Joshua Kondek, Lisa
Kumar, Thomas McMahon, Jenai A. Mynatt,
Judith L. Pyko, Mary Ruby, Lemma Shomali,
Susan Strickland, Anita Sundaresan, Maikue
Vang, Tracey Watson, Denay L. Wilding,
Thomas Wiloch, Emiene Shija Wright

Research
Tamara C. Nott, Sarah Genik, Nicodemus Ford,
Michelle Campbell

Permissions
Lori Hines

Imaging and Multimedia
Dean Dauphinais, Robert Duncan, Leitha
Etheridge-Sims, Mary K. Grimes, Lezlie Light,
Dan Newell, David G. Oblender, Christine
O'Bryan, Kelly A. Quin, Luke Rademacher

Composition and Electronic Capture
Carolyn A. Roney

Manufacturing
Stacy L. Melson

LIBRARY OF CONGRESS CATALOG CARD NUMBER 62-52046

ISBN 0-7876-5201-6
ISSN 0010-7468

Printed in the United States of America
10 9 8 7 6 5 4 3 2 1

Contents

> **Indexing note:** All *Contemporary Authors* entries are indexed in the *Contemporary Authors* cumulative index, which is published separately and distributed twice a year.
>
> **As always, the most recent Contemporary Authors cumulative index continues to be the user's guide to the location of an individual author's listing.**

Preface

Contemporary Authors (*CA*) provides information on approximately 115,000 writers in a wide range of media, including:

- Current writers of fiction, nonfiction, poetry, and drama whose works have been issued by commercial publishers, risk publishers, or university presses (authors whose books have been published only by known vanity or author-subsidized firms are ordinarily not included)

- Prominent print and broadcast journalists, editors, photojournalists, syndicated cartoonists, graphic novelists, screenwriters, television scriptwriters, and other media people

- Notable international authors

- Literary greats of the early twentieth century whose works are popular in today's high school and college curriculums and continue to elicit critical attention

A *CA* listing entails no charge or obligation. Authors are included on the basis of the above criteria and their interest to *CA* users. Sources of potential listees include trade periodicals, publishers' catalogs, librarians, and other users of the series.

How to Get the Most out of *CA*: Use the Index

The key to locating an author's most recent entry is the *CA* cumulative index, which is published separately and distributed twice a year. It provides access to *all* entries in *CA* and *Contemporary Authors New Revision Series* (*CANR*). Always consult the latest index to find an author's most recent entry.

For the convenience of users, the *CA* cumulative index also includes references to all entries in these Gale literary series: *Authors and Artists for Young Adults, Authors in the News, Bestsellers, Black Literature Criticism, Black Literature Criticism Supplement, Black Writers, Children's Literature Review, Concise Dictionary of American Literary Biography, Concise Dictionary of British Literary Biography, Contemporary Authors Autobiography Series, Contemporary Authors Bibliographical Series, Contemporary Dramatists, Contemporary Literary Criticism, Contemporary Novelists, Contemporary Poets, Contemporary Popular Writers, Contemporary Southern Writers, Contemporary Women Poets, Dictionary of Literary Biography, Dictionary of Literary Biography Documentary Series, Dictionary of Literary Biography Yearbook, DISCovering Authors, DISCovering Authors: British, DISCovering Authors: Canadian, DISCovering Authors: Modules* (including modules for Dramatists, Most-Studied Authors, Multicultural Authors, Novelists, Poets, and Popular/Genre Authors), *DISCovering Authors 3.0, Drama Criticism, Drama for Students, Feminist Writers, Hispanic Literature Criticism, Hispanic Writers, Junior DISCovering Authors, Major Authors and Illustrators for Children and Young Adults, Major 20th-Century Writers, Native North American Literature, Novels for Students, Poetry Criticism, Poetry for Students, Short Stories for Students, Short Story Criticism, Something about the Author, Something about the Author Autobiography Series, St. James Guide to Children's Writers, St. James Guide to Crime & Mystery Writers, St. James Guide to Fantasy Writers, St. James Guide to Horror, Ghost & Gothic Writers, St. James Guide to Science Fiction Writers, St. James Guide to Young Adult Writers, Twentieth-Century Literary Criticism, 20th Century Romance and Historical Writers, World Literature Criticism,* and *Yesterday's Authors of Books for Children.*

A Sample Index Entry:

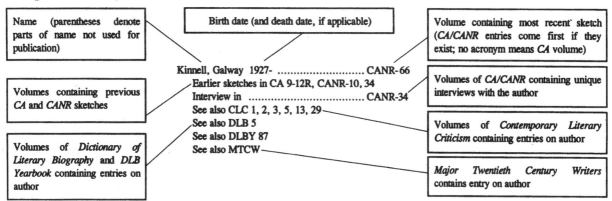

How Are Entries Compiled?

The editors make every effort to secure new information directly from the authors; listees' responses to our questionnaires and query letters provide most of the information featured in *CA*. For deceased writers, or those who fail to reply to requests for data, we consult other reliable biographical sources, such as those indexed in Gale's *Biography and Genealogy Master Index*, and bibliographical sources, including *National Union Catalog, LC MARC*, and *British National Bibliography*. Further details come from published interviews, feature stories, and book reviews, as well as information supplied by the authors' publishers and agents.

An asterisk (*) at the end of a sketch indicates that the listing has been compiled from secondary sources believed to be reliable but has not been personally verified for this edition by the author sketched.

What Kinds of Information Does An Entry Provide?

Sketches in *CA* contain the following biographical and bibliographical information:

- **Entry heading:** the most complete form of author's name, plus any pseudonyms or name variations used for writing

- **Personal information:** author's date and place of birth, family data, ethnicity, educational background, political and religious affiliations, and hobbies and leisure interests

- **Addresses:** author's home, office, or agent's addresses, plus e-mail and fax numbers, as available

- **Career summary:** name of employer, position, and dates held for each career post; resume of other vocational achievements; military service

- **Membership information:** professional, civic, and other association memberships and any official posts held

- **Awards and honors:** military and civic citations, major prizes and nominations, fellowships, grants, and honorary degrees

- **Writings:** a comprehensive, chronological list of titles, publishers, dates of original publication and revised editions, and production information for plays, television scripts, and screenplays

- **Adaptations:** a list of films, plays, and other media which have been adapted from the author's work

- **Work in progress:** current or planned projects, with dates of completion and/or publication, and expected publisher, when known

- **Sidelights:** a biographical portrait of the author's development; information about the critical reception of the author's works; revealing comments, often by the author, on personal interests, aspirations, motivations, and thoughts on writing

- **Interview:** a one-on-one discussion with authors conducted especially for *CA*, offering insight into authors' thoughts about their craft

- **Autobiographical essay:** an original essay written by noted authors for *CA*, a forum in which writers may present themselves, on their own terms, to their audience

- **Photographs:** portraits and personal photographs of notable authors

- **Biographical and critical sources:** a list of books and periodicals in which additional information on an author's life and/or writings appears

- **Obituary Notices** in *CA* provide date and place of birth as well as death information about authors whose full-length sketches appeared in the series before their deaths. The entries also summarize the authors' careers and writings and list other sources of biographical and death information.

Related Titles in the *CA* Series

Contemporary Authors Autobiography Series complements *CA* original and revised volumes with specially commissioned autobiographical essays by important current authors, illustrated with personal photographs they provide. Common topics include their motivations for writing, the people and experiences that shaped their careers, the rewards they derive from their work, and their impressions of the current literary scene.

Contemporary Authors Bibliographical Series surveys writings by and about important American authors since World War II. Each volume concentrates on a specific genre and features approximately ten writers; entries list works written by and about the author and contain a bibliographical essay discussing the merits and deficiencies of major critical and scholarly studies in detail.

Available in Electronic Formats

GaleNet. *CA* is available on a subscription basis through GaleNet, an online information resource that features an easy-to-use end-user interface, powerful search capabilities, and ease of access through the World-Wide Web. For more information, call 1-800-877-GALE.

Licensing. *CA* is available for licensing. The complete database is provided in a fielded format and is deliverable on such media as disk, CD-ROM, or tape. For more information, contact Gale's Business Development Group at 1-800-877-GALE, or visit us on our website at www.galegroup.com/bizdev.

Suggestions Are Welcome

The editors welcome comments and suggestions from users on any aspect of the *CA* series. If readers would like to recommend authors for inclusion in future volumes of the series, they are cordially invited to write the Editors at *Contemporary Authors*, Gale Group, 27500 Drake Rd., Farmington Hills, MI 48331-3535; or call at 1-248-699-4253; or fax at 1-248-699-8054.

Contemporary Authors Product Advisory Board

The editors of *Contemporary Authors* are dedicated to maintaining a high standard of excellence by publishing comprehensive, accurate, and highly readable entries on a wide array of writers. In addition to the quality of the content, the editors take pride in the graphic design of the series, which is intended to be orderly yet inviting, allowing readers to utilize the pages of *CA* easily and with efficiency. Despite the longevity of the *CA* print series, and the success of its format, we are mindful that the vitality of a literary reference product is dependent on its ability to serve its users over time. As literature, and attitudes about literature, constantly evolve, so do the reference needs of students, teachers, scholars, journalists, researchers, and book club members. To be certain that we continue to keep pace with the expectations of our customers, the editors of *CA* listen carefully to their comments regarding the value, utility, and quality of the series. Librarians, who have firsthand knowledge of the needs of library users, are a valuable resource for us. The *Contemporary Authors* Product Advisory Board, made up of school, public, and academic librarians, is a forum to promote focused feedback about *CA* on a regular basis. The seven-member advisory board includes the following individuals, whom the editors wish to thank for sharing their expertise:

- **Anne M. Christensen,** Librarian II, Phoenix Public Library, Phoenix, Arizona.

- **Barbara C. Chumard,** Reference/Adult Services Librarian, Middletown Thrall Library, Middletown, New York.

- **Eva M. Davis,** Youth Department Manager, Ann Arbor District Library, Ann Arbor, Michigan.

- **Adam Janowski, Jr.,** Library Media Specialist, Naples High School Library Media Center, Naples, Florida.

- **Robert Reginald,** Head of Technical Services and Collection Development, California State University, San Bernadino, California.

- **Katharine E. Rubin,** Head of Information and Reference Division, New Orleans Public Library, New Orleans, Louisiana.

- **Barbara A. Wencl,** Media Specialist, Como Park High School, St. Paul, Minnesota.

International Advisory Board

Well-represented among the 115,000 author entries published in *Contemporary Authors* are sketches on notable writers from many non-English-speaking countries. The primary criteria for inclusion of such authors has traditionally been the publication of at least one title in English, either as an original work or as a translation. However, the editors of *Contemporary Authors* came to observe that many important international writers were being overlooked due to a strict adherence to our inclusion criteria. In addition, writers who were publishing in languages other than English were not being covered in the traditional sources we used for identifying new listees. Intent on increasing our coverage of international authors, including those who write only in their native language and have not been translated into English, the editors enlisted the aid of a board of advisors, each of whom is an expert on the literature of a particular country or region. Among the countries we focused attention on are Mexico, Puerto Rico, Germany, Luxembourg, Belgium, the Netherlands, Norway, Sweden, Denmark, Finland, Taiwan, Singapore, Spain, Italy, South Africa, Israel, and Japan, as well as England, Scotland, Wales, Ireland, Australia, and New Zealand. The sixteen-member advisory board includes the following individuals, whom the editors wish to thank for sharing their expertise:

- **Lowell A. Bangerter,** Professor of German, University of Wyoming, Laramie, Wyoming.

- **Nancy E. Berg,** Associate Professor of Hebrew and Comparative Literature, Washington University, St. Louis, Missouri.

- **Frances Devlin-Glass,** Associate Professor, School of Literary and Communication Studies, Deakin University, Burwood, Victoria, Australia.

- **David William Foster,** Regent's Professor of Spanish, Interdisciplinary Humanities, and Women's Studies, Arizona State University, Tempe, Arizona.

- **Hosea Hirata,** Director of the Japanese Program, Associate Professor of Japanese, Tufts University, Medford, Massachusetts.

- **Jack Kolbert,** Professor Emeritus of French Literature, Susquehanna University, Selinsgrove, Pennsylvania.

- **Mark Libin,** Professor, University of Manitoba, Winnipeg, Manitoba, Canada.

- **C. S. Lim,** Professor, University of Malaya, Kuala Lumpur, Malaysia.

- **Eloy E. Merino,** Assistant Professor of Spanish, Northern Illinois University, DeKalb, Illinois.

- **Linda M. Rodríguez Guglielmoni,** Associate Professor, University of Puerto Rico—Mayagüez, Puerto Rico.

- **Sven Hakon Rossel,** Professor and Chair of Scandinavian Studies, University of Vienna, Vienna, Austria.

- **Steven R. Serafin,** Director, Writing Center, Hunter College of the City University of New York, New York City.

- **David Smyth,** Lecturer in Thai, School of Oriental and African Studies, University of London, England.

- **Ismail S. Talib,** Senior Lecturer, Department of English Language and Literature, National University of Singapore, Singapore.

- **Dionisio Viscarri,** Assistant Professor, Ohio State University, Columbus, Ohio.

- **Mark Williams,** Associate Professor, English Department, University of Canterbury, Christchurch, New Zealand.

CA Numbering System and Volume Update Chart

Occasionally questions arise about the *CA* numbering system and which volumes, if any, can be discarded. Despite numbers like " 29-32R," " 97-100" and "207," the entire *CA* print series consists of only 252 physical volumes with the publication of *CA* Volume 208. The following charts note changes in the numbering system and cover design, and indicate which volumes are essential for the most complete, up-to-date coverage.

CA First Revision
- 1-4R through 41-44R (11 books)
  Cover: Brown with black and gold trim.
  There will be no further First Revision volumes because revised entries are now being handled exclusively through the more efficient *New Revision Series* mentioned below.

CA Original Volumes
- 45-48 through 97-100 (14 books)
  Cover: Brown with black and gold trim.
  101 through 208 (108 books)
  Cover: Blue and black with orange bands.
  The same as previous *CA* original volumes but with a new, simplified numbering system and new cover design.

CA Permanent Series
- *CAP*-1 and *CAP*-2 (2 books)
  Cover: Brown with red and gold trim.
  There will be no further Permanent Series volumes because revised entries are now being handled exclusively through the more efficient *New Revision Series* mentioned below.

CA New Revision Series
- CANR-1 through CANR-117 (117 books)
  Cover: Blue and black with green bands.
  Includes only sketches requiring significant changes; **sketches are taken from any previously published CA, CAP, or CANR volume.**

If You Have:	You May Discard:
CA First Revision Volumes 1-4R through 41-44R and *CA Permanent Series* Volumes 1 and 2	*CA* Original Volumes 1, 2, 3, 4 Volumes 5-6 through 41-44
CA Original Volumes 45-48 through 97-100 and 101 through 208	**NONE:** These volumes will not be superseded by corresponding revised volumes. Individual entries from these and all other volumes appearing in the left column of this chart may be revised and included in the various volumes of the *New Revision Series*.
CA New Revision Series Volumes *CANR*-1 through *CANR*-117	**NONE:** The *New Revision Series* does not replace any single volume of *CA*. Instead, volumes of *CANR* include entries from many previous *CA* series volumes. All *New Revision Series* volumes must be retained for full coverage.

A Sampling of Authors and Media People
Featured in This Volume

Janet Burroway

Burroway is an award-winning novelist and playwright. She is notable for the meticulous research she puts into such novels as *Raw Silk,* the story of the ill-fated marriage of an American woman to an English businessman, and *Cutting Stone,* which is set against the backdrop of U.S.-Mexican relations in the years before World War I. She is also the author of the play *Hoddinot Veiling,* which was Britain's independent television entry at the Monte Carlo festival in 1970. An autobiographical essay by Burroway is included in this volume of *CA.*

Amanda Davis

Davis, a young author who garnered critical recognition for the short story collection *Circling the Drain* and the novel *Wonder When You'll Miss Me,* was killed in a plane crash in 2003 while on a national book tour. Davis was the winner of *Story* magazine's annual short story contest in 1997 and was awarded fellowships from the prestigious MacDowell Colony, Bread Loaf Writer's Conference, Wesleyan Writers Conference, and Corporation of Yaddo. Her work has been noted for its lyricism and memorable characters.

Raymond Federman

Although French-born novelist and poet Federman physically escaped the horrors of the Holocaust that claimed his family, his work continues to grapple with the experience of death and survival that marked the author when he was young. His fiction, experimental in form, questions the validity of autobiography and fiction alike by becoming autobiographical fiction, written in a language, English, that Federman learned as an adult. His first book of poems, *Among the Beasts/Parmi les monstres,* is the earliest literary version of his Holocaust experience. An autobiographical by Federman is included in this volume of *CA.*

Glen David Gold

Gold is a journalist and screenwriter whose first published novel, *Carter Beats the Devil,* received excellent reviews. Gold's protagonist is none other than Charles Carter, a.k.a. Carter the Great, an illusionist whose skill rivaled that of Henry Houdini's. The story begins in 1923, a time when people in the United States were obsessed with magic acts, as U.S. President Warren G. Harding appears as a participant in Carter's show. Critics applauded Gold for his artful sleight-of-hand in telling a complex and historically rich tale of intrigue.

Doris Humphrey

A key figure in the creation of modern dance, Humphrey rebelled against the methods of her teachers to create a new style of dance reflecting personal experience. One of her most important contributions to modern choreography is the development of the fall-and-recovery concept, which involves the loss of equilibrium and its emotional impact. Near the end of her life, Humphrey wrote what would become a standard text on choreography, *The Art of Making Dances.* Other writings by Humphrey appeared in *New Dance: An Unfinished Autobiography,* which was later completed by Selma Jean Cohen as *Doris Humphrey: An Artist First.*

sean o huigin

During the 1980s and early 1990s, Canadian poet and writer o huigin made a name for himself by writing popular children's poetry collections. The majority of his poems deal with dark topics lightened with humor. Written for middle-grade readers, *Scary Poems for Rotten Kids* depicts the various monsters that may inhabit a child's room and nightmares. Stylistically, o huigin's poetry resembles that of e e cummings in its use of little or no punctuation and few capital letters. He is also the author of the 1983 narrative poem *The Ghost Horse of the Mounties.*

Matthew Pearl

Pearl's first novel, *The Dante Club,* reached eleventh place on the *New York Times* bestseller list within weeks of its publication. The actual "Dante Club" met in Cambridge, Massachusetts, in the mid-nineteenth century to translate and study Italian poet Dante Alighieri's works, and its members included poets Henry Wadsworth Longfellow and James Russell Lowell, publisher J. T. Fields, and Harvard scholar Oliver Wendell Holmes, Sr. The club provides the background for Pearl's fictional invention, a murder mystery in which the killer's methods are based on the punishments that Dante describes for sinners in the *Inferno.*

Fred Russell

Russell, considered one of the most beloved sportswriters in the South, was a man who literally never retired and wrote more than 12,000 columns for four generations of fans. He won many awards for his accomplishments, and Vanderbilt University's Grantland Rice sports writing scholarship, established in the name of another great sportswriting alumni in 1956, was renamed the Fred Russell-Grantland Rice sports writing scholarship in 1986. Among his titles are *Funny Thing about Sports* and *Bury Me in an Old Press Box: Good Times and Life of a Sportswriter.*

Acknowledgments

Grateful acknowledgment is made to those publishers, photographers, and artists whose work appear with these authors' essays. Following is a list of the copyright holders who have granted us permission to reproduce material in this volume of *CA*. Every effort has been made to trace copyright, but if omissions have been made, please let us know.

Photographs/Art

Janet Burroway: All photos reproduced by permission of the author.

Raymond Federman: All photos reproduced by permission of the author, except as noted: portrait of Federman (shirt and jacket), by Steve Murez; photo of Federman receiving U.S. citizenship papers, © U.S. Army. All reproduced by permission.

Élisabeth Vonarburg: All photos reproduced by permission of the author, except as noted: portrait of Vonarburg (face in hands), by Robert Laliberté; portrait of Vonarburg (curly hair and glasses), by Jacques Robert. All reproduced by permission.

A

ABRAMS, Nita 1953-

PERSONAL: Born 1953, in Baltimore, MD.

ADDRESSES: Office—1730 New Brighton Blvd., Suite 104-313, Minneapolis, MN 55413. *Agent*—Donna Bagdasarian, Vigliano Associates, 584 Broadway, New York, NY 10012. *E-mail*—nita@nitaabrams.com.

CAREER: Writer. Also teacher of nonfiction writing classes.

MEMBER: Romance Writers of America.

WRITINGS:

A Question of Honor (fiction), Zebra (New York, NY), 2002.
The Exiles (fiction), Zebra (New York, NY), 2002.
The Spy's Bride, Zebra (New York, NY), in press.

SIDELIGHTS: Nita Abrams is the author of historical romance novels that take place in the early nineteenth century. With settings that range from England to Austria, she spins stories of women who are willing to go against social restraints for their commitment to family and country. In Abrams' 2002 novel *The Exiles,* her protagonist risks her life by disguising herself as a young man to spy for England in the drawing rooms of Viennese society, where both danger and romance await. Abrams told *CA:* "I fell into writing fiction by accident. I had been teaching and writing nonfiction for some time, and I'd always enjoyed historical novels. One day a scene popped into my .head. I wrote it down. Next thing I knew I had eight chapters—then twenty. I've enjoyed becoming a part of a different world, a world where you can be paid to daydream!"

Abrams' first book, *A Question of Honor,* takes place in England in 1813 as Napoleon Bonaparte wages war against the rest of Europe. When a war-weary captain leaves the field of battle to visit his sister in England, the beguiling but mysterious family governess quickly catches his attention. *Library Journal* reviewer John Charles praised Abrams' "polished writing" and dubbed *A Question of Honor* "superb."

BIOGRAPHICAL AND CRITICAL SOURCES:

PERIODICALS

Library Journal, February 15, 2002, John Charles, review of *A Question of Honor,* p. 129.

OTHER

Kensington Books Web site, http://www.kensington books.com/ (March 12, 2003).

*   *   *

ABT, Jeffrey 1949-

PERSONAL: Born February 27, 1949, in Kansas City, MO; son of Arthur and Lottie (Weinman) Abt; married Mary Paquette (a university lecturer), July 16, 1972; children: Uriel, Danya. *Education:* Drake University,

B.F.A. (with honors), 1971, M.F.A. (with honors), 1977; attended Hebrew Union College-Jewish Institute of Religion, 1971. *Religion:* Jewish.

ADDRESSES: Office—Department of Art and Art History, 150 Art Building, Wayne State University, Detroit, MI 48202; fax: 208-545-7268. *E-mail*—j_abt@wayne.edu.

CAREER: Teacher of adult education classes at public schools in Des Moines, IA, 1973-77; Wichita Art Museum, Wichita, KS, curator of collections, 1977-78; Billy Hork Galleries Ltd., Chicago, IL, general manager, 1978-80; University of Chicago, exhibitions coordinator at university library, 1980-86, assistant director, 1986-87, then acting director of David and Alfred Smart Museum of Art, 1987-89; Wayne State University, Detroit, MI, associate professor of art and art history, 1989—, member of advisory board for Humanities Center, 1993-94. Artist, with paintings and drawings exhibited throughout the Midwest and represented in public collections; sculptor, with work commissioned by Waldinger Foundation and Iowa Jewish Guild. Wayne State University Press, member of editorial board, 1990-96, board chair, 1996-2001. Ragdale Foundation, trustee, 1985-96, member of national advisory council, 1996—; Detroit Institute of Arts, member of education advisory board, 1992-94; Detroit Artists Market, member of board of directors, 1994-2000, board chair, 1999-2001.

MEMBER: American Association of Museums, Association for Museum History, College Art Association, Committee on Museum Professional Training.

AWARDS, HONORS: Grants from National Endowment for the Humanities, 1991, 1993, Rockefeller University, 1992, Reva and David Logan Foundation, 1998, and Kaufman Memorial Trust, 1998; Award of Merit, publication category, Historical Society of Michigan, 2002, for *A Museum on the Verge: The Detroit Institute of Arts, 1882-2000.*

WRITINGS:

(Illustrator) Alice Ryerson Hayes, *Water: Sheba's Story* (poetry), Bookwrights Press (Charlottesville, VA), 1997.
A Museum on the Verge: The Detroit Institute of Arts, 1882-2002, Wayne State University Press (Detroit, MI), 2001.

Author of exhibition catalogues. Contributor of articles and reviews to periodicals, including *Visual Resources, Art History, Chronicle of Higher Education,* and *Journal of the American Research Center in Egypt.* Editor, *Book and Paper Group Annual,* 1985-86.

WORK IN PROGRESS: A Humanist's Science: James H. Breasted and His Historical Laboratory, 1895-1935.

BIOGRAPHICAL AND CRITICAL SOURCES:

PERIODICALS

Detroit News, January 22, 2002, Joy Hakanson Colby, review of *A Museum on the Verge: The Detroit Institute of Arts, 1882-2000.*

*   *   *

ADAM, David 1936-

PERSONAL: Born October 18, 1936, in Alnwick, England; son of Norman Leslie and Mary Adam; married Denise Macaulay, July 1, 1960; children: Dawn Louise, Sharon. *Education:* Attended Kelham Theological College, 1954-59. *Politics:* "Radical." *Religion:* Christian. *Hobbies and other interests:* Song writing, Celtic history and spirituality, photography, birdwatching, walking.

ADDRESSES: Home and office—Vicarage, Holy Island, Berwick-upon-Tweed TD15 2RX, England.

CAREER: Anglican vicar. National Coal Board, Northumberland, England, coal miner, 1951-54; ordained Anglican priest, 1959, serving in Auckland, England, 1959-63, West Hartlepool, England, 1963-67, and Danby, England, 1967-90; Holy Island, Berwick-upon-Tweed, England, vicar, 1990—. Conductor of religious retreats; lecturer and broadcaster. National Coal Board, chaplain; Danby Agricultural Show, vice president; Holy Island Charities, chair.

WRITINGS:

The Edge of Glory: Prayers in the Celtic Tradition, illustrated by Peter Dingle and others, SPCK (London, England), 1985, Morehouse-Barlow (Wilton, CT), 1988.

The Cry of the Deer: Meditations on the Hymn of St. Patrick, illustrated by Peter Dingle and Jenny Pearson, Morehouse-Barlow (Wilton, CT), 1987.

Tides and Seasons: Modern Prayers in the Celtic Tradition, Triangle (London, England), 1989.

The Eye of the Eagle: Meditations on the Hymn "Be Thou My Vision," Triangle (London, England), 1990.

(With James Douglas) *Visions of Glory for Voices* (music), Eschenbach Editions, 1990.

Border Lands: The Best of David Adam's Celtic Vision, illustrated by Jean Freer and others, SPCK (London, England), 1991, Sheed & Ward (Franklin, WI), 2000.

Power Lines: Celtic Prayers about Work, Triangle (London, England), 1992, Morehouse Publishers (Harrisburg, PA), 2000.

Fire of the North: The Illustrated Life of St. Cuthbert, SPCK (London, England), 1993.

The Open Gate: Celtic Prayers for Growing Spiritually, illustrated by Jean Freer, Triangle (London, England), 1994, Morehouse Publishers (Harrisburg, PA), 1995.

The Rhythm of Life: Celtic Christian Prayer, illustrated by Jean Freer, SPCK (London, England), 1996, published as *The Rhythm of Life: Celtic Daily Prayer,* Morehouse Publishers (Harrisburg, PA), 1997.

(Compiler and author of introduction) *The Wisdom of the Celts: A Compilation,* W. B. Eerdmans (Grand Rapids, MI), 1996.

A Celtic Daily Prayer Book: A Compilation, Marshall & Pickering, 1997, published as *A Celtic Book of Prayer,* Roberts Rinehart (Boulder, CO), 1997.

Flame in My Heart: St. Aidan for Today, illustrated by Jean Freer, Triangle (London, England), 1997, Morehouse Publishers (Harrisburg, PA), 1998

Clouds and Glory: Prayers for the Church Year; Year A, SPCK (London, England), 1998, Morehouse Publishers (Harrisburg, PA), 2001.

On Eagles' Wings: The Life and Spirit of St. Chad, Triangle (London, England), 1999.

Traces of Glory: Prayers for the Church Year; Year B, Morehouse Publishers (Harrisburg, PA), 1999.

Forward to Freedom: A Journey into God, Darton Longman & Todd, 1999, published as *Forward to Freedom: From Exodus to Easter,* Upper Room Books (Nashville, TN), 2001.

A Desert in the Ocean: God's Call to Adventurous Living, Triangle (London, England), 2000, published as *A Desert in the Ocean: The Spiritual Journey according to St. Brendan the Navigator,* Paulist Press (New York, NY), 2000.

Glimpses of Glory: Prayers for the Church Year; Year C, Morehouse Publishers (Harrisburg, PA), 2000.

Landscapes of Light: An Illustrated Anthology of Prayers, photographs by David Cooper, Paraclete Press (Orleans, MA), 2001.

(Compiler) *A Celtic Psaltery: Psalms from the Celtic Tradition,* Triangle (London, England), 2001.

Island of Light: An Illustrated Collection of Prayers, SPCK (London, England), 2002.

Walking the Edges: Celtic Saints along the Roman Wall, SPCK (London, England), 2003.

WORK IN PROGRESS: Psalms and Songs for Today, for the five-stringed harp.

SIDELIGHTS: A vicar of the Church of England whose parish is located on Holy Island, or Lindisfarne, a three-mile-long peninsula of the coast of northern England that is transformed into an island at high tide, David Adam is the author of a number of books of prayer and reflection that are rooted in the Celtic Christian tradition. Adam told *CA:* "A love for the mystery and wonder of creation inspires most of my writing, along with the Celtic saints and peoples with their poetry, prayers, and songs. Included in the Celtic peoples are modern writers such as Teilhard de Chardin, especially his *Hymn of the Universe* and *Milieu Divin.*

"I have a day-to-day diary in which I write something each day—a poem, a few paragraphs, or a prayer—in reaction to the circumstances and people I meet. Most of the diary writing comes through contact with people and the created world. I prefer to write by hand and only later transfer portions to the computer.

"My early inspiration for writing came from working among teenagers who needed to discover their own ways of prayer. We used as a guide book *The Poems of the Western Highlanders.* Since then I have read the lives and works of Celtic saints. The island I live on was founded as a church by St. Aidan, and this gives me great inspiration.

"I believe there is a great need for people to open their eyes, ears, and hearts to what is going on around them and in the world. We need to re-sensitize ourselves to the great mysteries around us."

BIOGRAPHICAL AND CRITICAL SOURCES:

PERIODICALS

Publishers Weekly, February 18, 2002, review of *Landscapes of Light: An Illustrated Anthology of Prayers,* p. 64.

OTHER

SPCK Publishing Web site, http://www.spck.org.uk/ (March 12, 2003).

* * *

ADAMS, Jody 1957-

PERSONAL: Born March 26, 1957, in Pittsfield, MA; daughter of Thomas R. (a rare books librarian) and Virginia M. (a librarian) Adams; married Kenneth Michael Rivard, February 22, 1986; children: Oliver Maxwell, Roxanna Simone. *Ethnicity:* "White, Anglo-Saxon Protestant." *Education:* Brown University, B.A., 1980.

ADDRESSES: Office—Sapphire Restaurant Group, 20 University Rd., Cambridge, MA 02138.

CAREER: Chef. Worked variously as an assistant chef at restaurants, including Seasons and Hamersley's Bistro, Boston, MA; Michela's (restaurant), Cambridge, MA, executive chef, 1990-94; Rialto (restaurant), Cambridge, MA, partner and chef, 1994—; Red Clay (restaurant), Chestnut Hill, MA, partner and chef, 2001—.

AWARDS, HONORS: Named "Rising Star" by Restaurant Hospitality, 1992; featured among "America's Ten Best New Chefs," *Food and Wine,* 1993; Perrier-Jouet Best Chef Award, James Bear Foundation, 1997; Fine Dining Hall of Fame inductee, *Nation's Restaurant News,* 2000.

WRITINGS:

In the Hands of a Chef: Cooking with Jody Adams of Rialto Restaurant, William Morrow (New York, NY), 2002.

SIDELIGHTS: Acclaimed chef Jody Adams is the co-owner and chef at several Boston, Massachusetts-area restaurants, as well as the author of 2002's *In the Hands of a Chef: Cooking with Jody Adams of Rialto Restaurant.* Adams commented on *StarChef.com:* "If you're going to work in the restaurant business, you have to love it. The Stress is high, the hours are long and the pya is nominal. The reward is the culture. It's full of interesting, creative people who excel in the art of performance and making people happy. I can't imagine doing anything else."

BIOGRAPHICAL AND CRITICAL SOURCES:

OTHER

StarChefs.com, http://starchefs.com/ (March 12, 2003), "Jody Adams."

* * *

AGARD, John 1949-

PERSONAL: Born 1949, in British Guiana (now Guyana); immigrated to England, 1977. *Education:* Attended Roman Catholic secondary school in Georgetown, British Guiana (now Guyana).

ADDRESSES: Agent—c/o Author Mail, Candlewick Press, Inc., 2067 Massachusetts Ave., Cambridge, MA 02140.

CAREER: Writer. Commonwealth Institute, London, England, touring lecturer; South Bank Centre, London, writer-in-residence, 1993; British Broadcasting Corp., writer-in-residence for Windrush project. Also worked as an actor and a performer with a jazz group.

AWARDS, HONORS: Poetry prize, Casa de la Amèricas (Cuba), 1982; Other Award, Children's Rights Workshop, 1986, for *Say It Again, Granny! Twenty Poems from Caribbean Proverbs.*

WRITINGS:

JUVENILE AND YOUNG ADULT POETRY

I Din Do Nuttin and Other Poems, illustrated by Susanna Gretz, Bodley Head (London, England), 1983.

Say It Again, Granny! Twenty Poems from Caribbean Proverbs, illustrated by Susanna Gretz, Bodley Head (London, England), 1986.

The Calypso Alphabet, illustrated by Jennifer Bent, Henry Holt (New York, NY), 1989.

Go Noah, Go!, illustrated by Judy Brown, Hodder & Stoughton (London, England), 1990.

Laughter Is an Egg, illustrated by Alan Rowe, Viking (London, England), 1990.

(Editor) *Life Doesn't Frighten Me at All,* Heinemann (London, England), 1989, Henry Holt (New York, NY), 1990.

(With Grace Nichols) *No Hickory, No Dickory, No Dock: A Collection of Caribbean Nursery Rhymes,* Viking (London, England), 1991, published as *No Hickory, No Dickory, No Dock: Caribbean Nursery Rhymes,* illustrated by Cynthia Jabar, Candlewick Press (Cambridge, MA), 1994.

Grandfather's Old Bruk-a-down Car, illustrated by Kevin Dean, Bodley Head (London, England), 1994.

(Editor, with Grace Nichols, and contributor) *A Caribbean Dozen: Poems from Caribbean Poets,* illustrated by Cathie Felstead, Candlewick Press (Cambridge, MA), 1994, published as *A Caribbean Dozen: A Collection of Poems,* Walker Books (Boston, MA), 1995.

(With others) *Another Day on Your Foot and I Would Have Died,* illustrated by Colin McNaughton, Macmillan (London, England), 1996.

(Editor) *Why Is the Sky?,* illustrated by Andrzej Klimowski, Faber & Faber (London, England), 1996.

We Animals Would Like a Word with You, illustrated by Satoshi Kitamura, Bodley Head (London, England), 1996.

Get Back, Pimple!, Viking (London, England), 1996.

From the Devil's Pulpit, Bloodaxe Books (Newcastle upon Tyne, England), 1997.

Hello New! New Poems for a New Century, illustrated by Lydia Monks, Orchard (London, England), 2000.

Points of View with Professor Peekaboo, illustrated by Satoshi Kitamura, Bodley Head (London, England), 2000.

Come Back to Me, My Boomerang, illustrated by Lydia Monks, Orchard (London, England), 2001.

(Editor, with Grace Nichols) *Under the Moon and over the Sea: A Collection of Caribbean Poems,* illustrated by Christopher Corr, Candlewick Press (Cambridge, MA), 2002.

Einstein, the Girl Who Hated Maths, illustrated by Satoshi Kitamura, Hodder Wayland (London, England), 2002.

CHILDREN'S FICTION

Letters for Lettie and Other Stories, illustrated by Errol Lloyd, Bodley Head (London, England), 1979.

Dig away Two-Hole Tim, illustrated by Jennifer Northway, Bodley Head (London, England), 1981.

Lend Me Your Wings, illustrated by Adrienne Kennaway, Little, Brown (Boston, MA), 1987.

The Emperor's Dan-Dan, illustrated by Alison Forsyth, Hodder & Stoughton (London, England), 1992.

Oriki and the Monster Who Hated Balloons, illustrated by Jenny Stowe, Longman (Harlow, England), 1994.

The Monster Who Loved Telephones, illustrated by Jenny Stowe, Longman (Harlow, England), 1994.

The Monster Who Loved Cameras, illustrated by Jenny Stowe, Longman (Harlow, England), 1994.

The Monster Who Loved Toothbrushes, illustrated by Jenny Stowe, Longman (Harlow, England), 1994.

(With Korky Paul) *Brer Rabbit, the Great Tug-o-War,* Barron's Educational Series (Hauppauge, NY), 1998.

Some of Agard's work has been translated into Welsh.

OTHER

Shoot Me with Flowers (poetry), illustrated by Marilyn Agard, privately printed (Guyana), 1974.

Man to Pan: A Cycle of Poems to Be Performed with Drums and Steelpans, Casa de las Américas (Havana, Cuba), 1982.

Limbo Dancer in the Dark (poetry), privately printed, 1983.

Limbo Dancer in Dark Glasses (poetry), Greenheart, 1983.

Livingroom, Black Ink Collective (London, England), 1983.

Mangoes and Bullets: Selected and New Poems, 1972-84, Pluto Press (London, England), 1985.

(With others) *Wake Up, Stir About: Songs for Assembly* (traditional tunes), arranged by Barrie Carson Turner, illustrated by Peter Kent, Unwin Hyman (Cambridge, MA), 1989.

Lovelines for a Goat-born Lady (poetry), Serpent's Tail (London, England), 1990.

A Stone's Throw from Embankment: The South Bank Collection (poetry), Royal Festival Hall (London, England), 1993.

The Great Snakeskin (children's play), illustrated by Jill Newton, Ginn (Aylesbury, England), 1993.

(Editor) *Poems in My Earphone*, Longman (Harlow, England), 1995.

Weblines (poetry), Bloodaxe Books (Newcastle upon Tyne, England), 2000.

Work represented in anthologies, including *Border Country: Poems in Progress*, edited by David Hart, Wood Wind Publications (Birmingham, England), 1991; and *Grandchildren of Albion*, edited by Michael Horovitz, New Departures (Piedmont, Bisley, Stroud, Gloucester, England), 1992. Contributor of poetry to periodicals, including *Poetry Review*.

SIDELIGHTS: John Agard's writings are infused with the Caribbean rhythms of his homeland in South America. Agard was born and raised in what is now Guyana, east of Venezuela, near the southeastern edge of the Caribbean Sea. He had completed high school when he relocated to England in 1977, where he now makes his home. Agard is highly regarded as a performance poet whose work is most powerful when read aloud but, with numerous volumes of poetry and prose to his credit, he has earned a solid readership as well.

Many of Agard's published writings are children's verse collections or stories. His vocal rhythms, combined with an affinity for word play, puns, and jokes, are appealing to children of all ages. Agard's stories are sometimes retellings or revisions of folk tales and are enlivened by his own sense of the comic and his appreciation for the absurd. His poems concern the elements of everyday life common to children everywhere, made unique by the poet's tendency toward Caribbean dialect and whimsical humor. Agard often writes of Anancy, the trickster spider of folk tradition, and Agard himself has been likened to a trickster of the spoken word.

For beginning readers Agard created *The Calypso Alphabet,* a book full to the brim with exotic new words and concepts embedded in the musical ambience of Caribbean idiom and illustrated by Jennifer Brent with colors, people, and landscapes which epitomize life in the West Indies. *I Din Do Nuttin and Other Poems* retains the idiomatic flavor of Agard's verse, while his rhymes describe the ordinary events and people common to all children. Agard's poems

also demonstrate his talent for seeing the adult world through the eyes of a child, according to Robert Protherough in the *St. James Guide to Children's Writers,* and reveal Agard's cleverness at what Protherough described as the "lively turning upside-down of conventional phrases," a device that can be as thought-provoking as it is amusing. Another collection, *Grandfather's Old Bruk-a-down Car,* explores the relationships between people and the objects they hold dear. Wherever they live, children know someone who would not feel complete without a special object, whether it is a car, a violin, or even a body part. *Laughter Is an Egg* contains rhymes and riddles for the young reader who welcomes the challenge of a mystery. Solving some of the riddles and untangling the word plays may not be as easy as one might think.

Lest a reader presume that Agard's sole objective as a poet is to entertain, a *Junior Bookshelf* reviewer of *Laughter Is an Egg* emphasized that Agard's poetry reveals "a serious man" dedicated to the often difficult art of crafting exceptional poetry. Even in rhymes intended for children Agard uses his work as a vehicle for his thoughts on topical issues and trends. *No Hickory, No Dickory, No Dock: A Collection of Caribbean Nursery Rhymes,* which Agard wrote with fellow Guyanese poet Grace Nichols, contains poems compelling in their musicality, according to a *Kirkus Reviews* contributor. The selections, both original verse and Caribbean-style parodies of traditional Mother Goose rhymes, are intended for the very young, yet one of Agard's contributions, "Baby-K Rap Rhyme," is a lament for the ecological damage humans have inflicted from one end of our planet to the other. In *We Animals Would Like a Word with You* he questions in lyrical rhyme the way people treat the world's animals. In his review of the book for the *Times Educational Supplement,* Josephine Balmer commented that Agard "subverts and invents," ultimately producing "the best that poetry can offer."

For older students, *Points of View with Professor Peekaboo* addresses a range of contemporary issues, from the majesty of the natural world to the increasing degradation of the environment to the question of genetic identity. Though some reviewers faulted the volume for its uneven poetic quality, in the *Times Educational Supplement* John Mole cited the work as an "often funny, inventive" collection.

For the more mature teenager, Agard has produced *From the Devil's Pulpit,* wherein he ruminates about the hedonistic, self-centered nature of modern society from the devil's point of view. He addresses a panorama of the world's ills as many perceive them: sex, religion, politics, art, and gambling, to name a few, along with genuine horrors such as the carnage in Bosnia and the civil war in Northern Ireland. In more than a hundred poems Agard demonstrates his versatility with poetic form, syncopating verses with his trademark lilting idiom and indulging his propensity for jokes, puns, and playful humor. In *School Librarian* Susan Elkin called *From the Devil's Pulpit* "spiky, rude, clever, irreverent and, often, very funny." In her review for the London *Observer,* poet Helen Dunmore called Agard "one of the most eloquent contemporary poets." Bruce King, in a review for *World Literature Today,* pointed out that Agard as Lucifer is neither a proponent of sin nor a moralist, but "more a social satirist," and that *From the Devil's Pulpit,* while addressing some of the more controversial issues of contemporary times, is by no means an exploration of depravity or a defense of misbehavior. King suggested that the volume reflects the philosophy that "life consists of balance, opposites, temptations, curiosity, excitements, pleasures; every god needs a devil, every order needs a disorder, every established hierarchy needs skeptical mockery." Elements of this philosophy can be seen throughout the body of Agard's work.

Agard has also written stories for children. *Dig away Two-Hole Tim* is set in Guyana, and introduces young readers to the colorful English dialect of the West Indies. More a captioned picture book than a continuous narrative, it tells the story of an unintentionally mischievous boy preoccupied with holes: digging, cutting, exploring, or simply pondering holes. *The Emperor's Dan-Dan* is a Caribbean-style versification of the story of the emperor's new clothes, replete with appropriate dialect and featuring the trickster Anancy as the emperor's tailor. Another of Agard's stories is *Brer Rabbit, the Great Tug-o-War,* in which the great American trickster matches wits with Rhino and Hippo, luring them into a competition that none can win.

In addition to his prolific and successful career as an author for all ages, Agard has also worked toward popularizing Caribbean poets, especially among young readers of England and North America. With Grace Nichols he compiled *A Caribbean Dozen: Poems from Caribbean Poets,* in which they introduce the work of thirteen Caribbean poets from around the world,

amplifying their poems by adding photographs and personal background narratives from each poet included. The collection was well received by critics, including John Mole, who reported in the *Times Educational Supplement:* "Even the weakest of [the selections] . . . are joyously enthusiastic." "Most of the entries here speak directly to the child's own world," Bettina Berch noted in *Belles Lettres.* In *Books for Keeps* Morag Styles called *A Caribbean Dozen* "a great treat," even for readers as young as primary school students.

Agard also edited a thematic collection titled *Why Is the Sky?* that addresses the sometimes imponderable questions children ask. "It is a richly seasoned stew," wrote a *Junior Bookshelf* reviewer, drawn from every corner of the world and from the ages. The poetry comes from Shakespeare and from the Bible; also represented are twentieth-century poets such as Langston Hughes and Helen Dunmore. The selections are intended for young readers, though adult poetry is included as well. Linda Saunders described *Why Is the Sky?* in *School Librarian* as "an excellent collection of poetry. . . . There is something here for every child."

BIOGRAPHICAL AND CRITICAL SOURCES:

BOOKS

St. James Guide to Children's Writers, 5th edition, St. James Press (Detroit, MI), 1999, pp. 8-9.

PERIODICALS

Belles Lettres, summer, 1995, Bettina Berch, review of *A Caribbean Dozen: Poems from Caribbean Poets,* p. 45.

Black Scholar, winter, 1993, Denise de Cairnes Narain, review of *Lovelines for a Goat-born Lady,* pp. 36-38.

Booklist, March 15, 1991, review of *Life Doesn't Frighten Me at All,* p. 1742; May 1, 1995, Hazel Rochman, review of *No Hickory, No Dickory, No Dock: A Collection of Caribbean Nursery Rhymes,* p. 1576.

Books for Keeps, January, 1988, review of *Say It Again, Granny! Twenty Poems from Caribbean Proverbs,* p. 16; July, 1991, review of *Laughter Is an Egg,* p. 11; November, 1992, review of *Go Noah, Go!,* p. 17; May, 1993, review of *The Calypso Alphabet,* pp. 8-9; September, 1994, Morag Styles, review of *A Caribbean Dozen,* p. 88; March, 1997, M. Styles, review of *We Animals Would Like a Word with You,* p. 23; May, 1997, review of *Another Day on Your Foot and I Would Have Died,* pp. 24-25; January, 1998, review of *Why Is the Sky?,* p. 20; May, 1998, Elaine Moss, review of *Brer Rabbit, the Great Tug-o-War,* p. 6; March, 2001, review of *Points of View with Professor Peekaboo,* p. 24.

English Journal, April, 1991, Elizabeth A. Belden and Judith M. Beckman, review of *Life Doesn't Frighten Me at All,* p. 84.

Growing Point, March, 1983, review of *I Din Do Nuttin and Other Poems,* p. 4040; July, 1986, review of *Say It Again, Granny!,* p. 4654.

Instructor, August, 2001, "Jump into Shape Poetry," p. 54.

Journal of Commonwealth Literature, August, 1992, review of *Lovelines for a Goat-born Lady,* p. 200.

Junior Bookshelf, June, 1980, review of *Letters for Lettie and Other Stories,* p. 123; February, 1982, review of *Dig away Two-Hole Tim,* p. 12; August, 1983, review of *I Din Do Nuttin and Other Poems,* pp. 156-157; August, 1990, review of *Laughter Is an Egg,* p. 172; April, 1991, review of *Go Noah, Go!,* pp. 53-54; February, 1993, review of *The Emperor's Dan-Dan,* p. 9; February, 1995, review of *Grandfather's Old Bruk-a-down Car,* p. 14; August, 1996, review of *Get Back, Pimple!,* p. 153; October, 1996, review of *Why Is the Sky?,* pp. 189-190.

Kirkus Reviews, April 15, 1989, review of *Lend Me Your Wings,* p. 619; May 15, 1995, review of *No Hickory, No Dickory, No Dock,* p. 706; April 15, 2001, review of *Weblines,* pp. 550-551.

London Review of Books, December 5, 1985, Blake Morrison, review of *Mangoes and Bullets: Selected and New Poems, 1972-84,* pp. 14-15.

Observer (London, England), October 26, 1997, Helen Dunmore, review of *From the Devil's Pulpit,* p. 15.

Publishers Weekly, November 24, 1989, review of *The Calypso Alphabet,* p. 70; June 5, 1995, review of *No Hickory, No Dickory, No Dock,* p. 64; July 23, 2001, review of *Weblines,* p. 69.

School Librarian, February, 1991, Pauline Long, review of *Go Noah, Go!,* p. 17; November, 1992, Celia Gibbs, review of *The Emperor's Dan-Dan,* p. 138; November, 1994, Vivienne Grant, review

of *Grandfather's Old Bruk-a-down Car,* p. 160; February, 1997, review of *Why Is the Sky?,* p. 41; November, 1997, review of *From the Devil's Pulpit,* p. 220; autumn, 1998, Vivienne Grant, review of *Brer Rabbit, the Great Tug-o-War,* p. 129; spring, 2001, review of *Points of View with Professor Peekaboo,* p. 42.

School Library Journal, September, 1982, Marilyn Payne Phillips, review of *Dig away Two-Hole Tim;* July, 1989, Carolyn Caywood, review of *Lend Me Your Wings,* p. 61; April, 1990, Marilyn Iarusso, review of *The Calypso Alphabet,* p. 86; August, 1990, Annette Curtis Klause, review of *Life Doesn't Frighten Me at All,* p. 166; August, 1995, Barbara Osborne Williams, review of *No Hickory, No Dickory, No Dock,* pp. 131-132.

Times Educational Supplement, February 16, 1990, Gerard Benson, review of *Life Doesn't Frighten Me at All,* p. 67; July 13, 1990, Kevin Crossley-Holland, review of *Laughter Is an Egg,* p. 28; June 14, 1991, Charles Causley, review of *No Hickory, No Dickory, No Dock,* p. 25; February 5, 1993, James Riordan, review of *The Emperor's Dan-Dan,* p. R10; November 11, 1994, Gillian Clarke, review of *Grandfather's Old Bruk-a-down Car,* p. R7; December 2, 1994, John Mole, review of *A Caribbean Dozen,* p. A14; September 22, 1995, J. Mole, review of *Poems in My Earphone;* March 8, 1996, p. X; Jill Pirrie, review of *Get Back, Pimple!,* p. II; December 13, 1996, Josephine Balmer, review of *We Animals Would Like a Word with You;* January 19, 2001, J. Mole, review of *Points of View with Professor Peekaboo,* p. 20.

Times Literary Supplement, January 18, 1991, Giles Foden, review of *Lovelines for a Goat-born Lady,* p. 18; July 27, 2001, Paula Burnett, review of *Weblines,* p. 23.

Wilson Library Bulletin, November, 1990, Cathi Mac-Rae, review of *Life Doesn't Frighten Me at All,* p. 129.

World Literature Today, spring, 1998, Bruce King, review of *From the Devil's Pulpit,* pp. 438-439; summer-autumn, 2001, Bruce King, review of *Weblines,* p. 118.

OTHER

Roots and Water (videotape series), Films for the Humanities and Sciences, 2000.*

ALLENBAUGH, Kay

PERSONAL: Married second husband Eric Allenbaugh (an author and leadership consultant); children: four sons.

ADDRESSES: Home—612 Cabana Lane, Lake Oswego, OR 97034. *Agent*—c/o Author Mail, Simon & Schuster, 1230 Avenue of the Americas, New York, NY 10020.

CAREER: Writer and conference speaker.

WRITINGS:

COMPILER; "CHOCOLATE" SERIES

Chocolate for a Woman's Soul, Simon & Schuster (New York, NY), Volume 1: *Seventy-seven Stories to Feed Your Spirit and Warm Your Heart,* 1997, Volume 2: *Seventy-seven Stories That Celebrate the Richness of Life.*

Chocolate for a Woman's Heart: Seventy-seven Stories of Love, Kindness and Compassion to Nourish Your Soul and Sweeten Your Dreams, Simon & Schuster (New York, NY), 1998.

Chocolate for a Woman's Heart and Soul, Simon & Schuster (New York, NY), 1998.

Chocolate for a Lover's Heart: Soul-Soothing Stories That Celebrate the Power of Love, Simon & Schuster (New York, NY), 1999.

Chocolate for a Mother's Heart: Inspiring Stories That Celebrate the Spirit of Motherhood, Simon & Schuster (New York, NY), 1999.

Chocolate for a Woman's Spirit: Seventy-seven Stories of Inspiration to Lift Your Heart and Soothe Your Soul, Simon & Schuster (New York, NY), 1999.

Chocolate for a Teen's Soul: Life-Changing Stories for Young Women about Growing Wise and Growing Strong, Simon & Schuster (New York, NY), 2000.

Chocolate for a Woman's Blessings: Seventy-seven Heartwarming Stories of Gratitude That Celebrate the Good Things in Life, Simon & Schuster (New York, NY), 2001.

Chocolate for a Teen's Heart: Unforgettable Stories for Young Women about Love, Hope and Happiness, Simon & Schuster (New York, NY), 2001.

Chocolate for a Woman's Dreams: Seventy-seven Stories to Treasure as You Make Your Wishes Come True, Simon & Schuster (New York, NY), 2001.

Chocolate for a Teen's Spirit: Inspiring Stories for Young Women about Hope, Strength, and Wisdom, Simon & Schuster (New York, NY), 2002.

Chocolate for a Woman's Courage, Simon & Schuster (New York, NY), 2002.

Chocolate for a Teen's Dreams: Heartwarming Stories about Making Your Wishes Come True, Simon & Schuster (New York, NY), 2003.

Author's works have been translated into Spanish.

ADAPTATIONS: Author's writings have been adapted for audio cassette.

SIDELIGHTS: Kay Allenbaugh had what she calls a "mountain-top experience" one day while combing her hair in front of the bathroom mirror. A voice that she said was God told her to write a book for women. Despite her self-proclaimed shyness and fear of book signings and interviews, Allenbaugh wrote *Chocolate for a Woman's Soul,* the first in what would become the best-selling "Chocolate" series.

Allenbaugh described her reaction to hearing the voice: "For an hour, my creativity soared. I knew exactly what I would do. And then as quickly as euphoria arrived it departed, and my fear took over. God must surely have a good sense of humor." Allenbaugh admitted to feeling in over her head. "Because of our mind-body-spirit connection, my physical body reacted to my emotional fear," she explained on *soulfulliving. com.* Allenbaugh spent two years writing *Chocolate for a Woman's Soul,* unable to sit down due to severe back spasms, and so completed the book standing at her computer.

Chocolate for a Woman's Soul was so well received that Simon & Schuster contracted with Allenbaugh for a series, and Allenbaugh began addressing not only adult females, but teens as well. Of *Chocolate for a Lover's Heart,* *School Library Journal* reviewer Cynthia J. Rieben said, "The stories don't gloss over the rough spots in relationships; instead, they show love shining through in spite of illness and death, unfaithfulness or abandonment, misunderstandings and dashed hopes." Dana Vance, reviewer for *Voice of Youth Advocates,* called *Chocolate for a Teen's Soul* "a good choice for classroom read-alouds or for reluctant readers."

The "Chocolate" series books generally contain sixty-nine to seventy-seven stories contributed by women of all ages.

BIOGRAPHICAL AND CRITICAL SOURCES:

PERIODICALS

Booklist, June 1, 2001, Linda Zeilstra, review of *Chocolate for a Teen's Heart: Unforgettable Stories for Young Women about Love, Hope and Happiness,* p. 1801.

Library Journal, June 15, 1998, Nancy R. Ives, review of *Chocolate for a Woman's Heart: Seventy-seven Stories of Love, Kindness and Compassion to Nourish Your Soul and Sweeten Your Dreams,* p. 122; October 15, 2000, Barbara Hoffert, review of *Chocolate for a Woman's Soul: Seventy-seven Stories to Feed Your Spirit and Warm Your Heart,* p. 53.

Publishers Weekly, April 28, 1997, review of *Chocolate for a Woman's Soul,* p. 68; August 20, 2001, "Bittersweet Tales for Teens," p. 82; November 5, 2001, review of *Chocolate for a Woman's Dreams: Seventy-seven Stories to Treasure as You Make Your Wishes Come True,* p. 55.

School Library Journal, August, 1998, Catherine Charvat, review of *Chocolate for a Woman's Heart,* p. 198; July, 1999, Cynthia J. Rieben, review of *Chocolate for a Lover's Heart: Soul-Soothing Stories That Celebrate the Power of Love,* p. 115.

Voice of Youth Advocates, April, 2001, Dana Vance, review of *Chocolate for a Teen's Soul: Life-Changing Stories for Young Women about Growing Wise and Growing Strong,* p. 59.

OTHER

Chocolate for Women Web site, http://www.chocolate forwomen.com/ (April 16, 2002).

Soulfulliving.com, http://www.soulfulliving.com/ (May 3, 2002), Kay Allenbaugh, "It's All about Trust."*

ALLISON, Amy 1956-

PERSONAL: Born February 3, 1956, in Philadelphia, PA; daughter of Steve (a radio talk show host) and Wanda (a dancer and dance teacher; maiden name, Hilliard) Allison; married Dave Edison. *Education:* University of California—Santa Barbara, B.A. (summa cum laude), 1977; Pacific School of Religion, M.Div., 1986. *Hobbies and other interests:* Yoga, myth and folklore, art (fine, folk, and popular).

ADDRESSES: Home and office—North Hollywood, CA. *Agent*—c/o Author Mail, Chelsea House Publishers, 1874 Sproul Rd., Suite 400, Broomall, PA 19008. *E-mail*—tsotskelah@aol.com.

CAREER: Writer. Also works as copy editor, proofreader, and teacher.

MEMBER: Society of Children's Book Writers and Illustrators.

WRITINGS:

Machu Picchu, Lucent Books (San Diego, CA), 1993.

Shakespeare's Globe, Lucent Books (San Diego, CA), 1999.

Life in Ancient China, Lucent Books (San Diego, CA), 2000.

Roger Williams: Founder of Rhode Island, Chelsea House Publishers (Philadelphia, PA), 2000.

Antonio Banderas, Chelsea House Publishers (Philadelphia, PA), 2001.

John Leguizamo, Chelsea House Publishers (Philadelphia, PA), 2001.

Edwin Stanton: Secretary of War, Chelsea House Publishers (Philadelphia, PA), 2001.

Gargoyles on Guard, Richard C. Owen (Katoneh, NY), 2002.

Luis Alvarez and the Bubble Chamber, Mitchell Lane Publishers (Bear, DE), 2002.

Contributor of poetry to periodicals, including *Turtle* and *Cricket.*

WORK IN PROGRESS: Honeycomb, a young-adult novel.

SIDELIGHTS: The scope of children's author Amy Allison's nonfiction is not limited to a single topic or academic field. Two of her books are part of the "Latinos in the Limelight" series published by Chelsea House Publishers for the elementary and middle school audience. *John Leguizamo* and *Antonio Banderas* offer brief overviews of the lives and achievements of these contemporary celebrities, beginning with a look at the highlights of their years as children and adolescents. Allison also documents their professional careers, including film (and, in the case of Leguizamo, stage) appearances. Each book is illustrated with photographs and includes a bibliography of sources for the reader who seeks more detailed information.

Allison also writes about historical figures. *Roger Williams: Founder of Rhode Island* is not only a biography, but also an exploration of the times in which Williams came to prominence. Allison discusses the historical framework of early colonial America, the political and other issues that affected the lives of the colonists, and the contemporaries of Williams who had an impact on his life. The book contains illustrations depicting the people, places, and events of which she writes, as well as brief background notes with supplementary information about selected key topics.

Other writings focus on historical places, in one instance a specific architectural site. *Shakespeare's Globe* is the history of a theater, from its origins in Elizabethan England through its reconstruction in the 1990s. Allison's focus is on the architecture of this historic building and the relationship of the building's structure to the dramas presented within its walls. However, she also provides an array of anecdotal information about the composition of Shakespeare's audience, the technical aspects of staging plays at the Globe, and the historical, cultural, and social events that surrounded the theater in its heyday. According to reviewer Sally Margolis in *School Library Journal*, one highlight of *Shakespeare's Globe* is a "handy time line" Allison constructs to position the history of the Globe within the context of other historical events and social trends.

Allison once told *CA:* "What I relish about writing nonfiction is immersing myself in research. I become a detective, searching out clues to pivotal truths about people and events. I try to write nonfiction that is as spellbinding as fiction in its pacing and arresting detail.

"For me, reading has always felt like riding a magic carpet. Now, as a writer, I myself weave together words that transport others through time and space."

BIOGRAPHICAL AND CRITICAL SOURCES:

PERIODICALS

School Library Journal, February, 2000, Sally Margolis, review of *Shakespeare's Globe,* p. 128; August, 2001, Edith Ching, review of *Roger Williams: Founder of Rhode Island,* p. 191; April, 2002, Tim Widham, review of *John Leguizamo,* p. 162.

*   *   *

AMMACHI
See AMRITANANDAMAYI, Mataji

*   *   *

AMRITANANDAMAYI, Mataji 1953-

PERSONAL: Original name, Sudhamani; born September 27, 1953, in Kerala, India; father, a fisherman.

ADDRESSES: Agent—c/o Author Mail, Mata Amritanandamayi Center, P.O. Box 613, San Ramon, CA 94583. *E-mail*—mam@amritapuri.org.

CAREER: Operated as a trance medium until the late 1970s; Mata Amritanandamayi Center, Kerala, India, founder and Hindu spiritual teacher. Also affiliated with a center named after her in San Ramon, CA; conducted a world tour, 1987, including travel across the United States; United Nations Millennium Peace Summit, invited participant, 2000. Sometimes uses the name Ammachi.

WRITINGS:

For My Children: Spiritual Teachings of Mata Amritanandamayi, Mata Amritanandamayi Mission (Kerala, India), 1986.
Awaken, Children! Dialogues with Sri Sri Mata Amritanandamayi (originally published as *Amritanandamayi sambhashanangal*), two volumes, trans-

lated and adapted by Swami Amritaswarupananda, 2nd edition, Mata Amritanandamayi Mission Trust (San Ramon, CA), 1990, 3rd edition, 1992, revised edition, Mata Amritanandamayi Center (San Ramon, CA), 1998.

Eternal Wisdom: Upadeshamritam, compiled by Swami Jnanamritananda Puri, translated from Malayalam by M. N. Namboodiri, Mata Amritanandamayi Center (San Ramon, CA), 1999.

SIDELIGHTS: Mataji Amritanandamayi, also known as Ammachi, has been a spiritual teacher in the Hindu tradition since the late 1970s. She was first a trance medium in south India, but she gradually gained devotées. Amritanandamayi's father eventually gave her the family land to establish a spiritual center and community in what is now known as Amritapuri, India. She has since undertaken tours and established the Mata Amritanandamayi Center in San Ramon, California, and her birthplace in India is the headquarters of her worldwide spiritual mission.

"[Amritanandamayi] is a highly respected spiritual teacher of countless people, from all walks of life, all over the world," wrote a contributor to *Skipping Stones* in a preface to Amritanandamayi's keynote address to the United Nations Millennium Peace Summit in August, 2000. Amritanandamayi has published a small number of writings that present her spiritual teachings, of which devotion is the centerpiece. Her Web site conveys her insistence "that all of the residents [of my communities]. . . have a thorough grounding in spiritual practices like meditation, devotional singing, yoga and scriptural study. This will give them the necessary stability and inner peace to deal with the unavoidable ups and downs of life."

BIOGRAPHICAL AND CRITICAL SOURCES:

BOOKS

Chaitayna, Bramacharya Amritatma, *Mata Amritanandamayi: Life and Experiences of Devotees,* Mata Amritanandamayi Mission Trust (Kerala, India), 1988.
Religious Leaders of American, 2nd edition, Gale (Detroit, MI), 1999.

PERIODICALS

Hinduism Today, July, 1987, "Holy Woman Brings the Mother Spirit to the West: Mataji, 35, of Kerala Inspires Thousands with Devotion and Vedantic Truths during USA Tour," pp. 1, 15.
Skipping Stones, January, 2001, "United Nations Millennium Peace Summit," p. 28.

OTHER

Mataji Amritanandamayi Center Web site, http://www.ammachi.org/ (April 25, 2002).*

*   *   *

AUCH, Mary Jane

PERSONAL: Born in Mineola, NY; married Herm Auch (a graphic artist and cartoonist), 1967; children: Ian, Kat (daughter). *Education:* Skidmore College, B.A. (art); Columbia University, degree in occupational therapy.

ADDRESSES: Home—Rochester, NY. *Agent*—c/o Holiday House, 425 Madison Ave., New York, NY 10017. *E-mail*—jmauchwebsite@aol.com.

CAREER: Worked as an occupational therapist at a children's hospital, and as a designer, graphic artist, and illustrator for *Pennywhistle Press.*

WRITINGS:

SELF-ILLUSTRATED PICTURE BOOKS

The Easter Egg Farm, Holiday House (New York, NY), 1992.
Bird Dogs Can't Fly, Holiday House (New York, NY), 1993.
Peeping Beauty, Holiday House (New York, NY), 1993.
Monster Brother, Holiday House (New York, NY), 1994.
Hen Lake, Holiday House (New York, NY), 1995.
Eggs Mark the Spot, Holiday House (New York, NY), 1996.
Bantam of the Opera, Holiday House (New York, NY), 1997.

Noah's Aardvark, Golden Books (New York, NY), 1999.

The Nutquacker, Holiday House (New York, NY), 1999.

(With husband Herm Auch) *Poultrygeist,* Holiday House (New York, NY), 2002.

(With husband Herm Auch) *The Princess and the Pizza,* Holiday House (New York, NY), 2002.

NOVELS

The Witching of Ben Wagner, Houghton Mifflin (Boston, MA), 1987.

Cry Uncle!, Holiday House (New York, NY), 1987.

Mom Is Dating Weird Wayne, Holiday House (New York, NY), 1988.

Pick of the Litter, Holiday House (New York, NY), 1988.

Glass Slippers Give You Blisters, Holiday House (New York, NY), 1989.

Angel and Me and the Bayside Brothers, illustrated by Cat Bowman Smith, Little, Brown (Boston, MA), 1989.

Kidnapping Kevin Kowalski, Holiday House (New York, NY), 1990.

A Sudden Change of Family, Holiday House (New York, NY), 1990.

Seven Long Years until College, Holiday House (New York, NY), 1991.

Out of Step, Holiday House (New York, NY), 1992.

The Latchkey Dog, illustrated by Cat Bowman Smith, Little, Brown (Boston, MA), 1994.

Journey to Nowhere, Holt (New York, NY), 1997.

I Was a Third-Grade Science Project, illustrated by Herm Auch, Holiday House (New York, NY), 1998.

Frozen Summer (sequel to *Journey to Nowhere*), Holt (New York, NY), 1998.

The Road Home (sequel to *Frozen Summer*), Holt (New York, NY), 2000.

I Was a Third-Grade Spy, illustrated by Herm Auch, Holiday House (New York, NY), 2001.

Ashes of Roses, Holt (New York, NY), 2002.

ILLUSTRATOR

Sara Pennypacker, *Dumbstruck,* Holiday House (New York, NY), 1994.

Vivian Vande Velde, *Troll Teacher,* Holiday House (New York, NY), 2000.

ADAPTATIONS: The Easter Egg Farm and *Peeping Beauty* and were adapted for audiocassette by Live Oak Media (Pine Plains, NY), 1995, as was *Eggs Mark the Spot,* 1997. *The Witching of Ben Wager* was made into a film by Leucadia Film Corp. and released by Films for Families (Murray, UT).

SIDELIGHTS: Author, illustrator, and poultry fan Mary Jane Auch has written contemporary and historical novels as well as humorous picture books. Many of her picture books feature Auch's favorite feathered friends—chickens—which she renders in brilliant, heat-dried oil paints. Among her titles are the juvenile novels *Journey to Nowhere, I Was a Third-Grade Science Project,* and *A Sudden Change of Family.*

Auch's interest in art and poultry came early. Because she was an only child and wished she were part of a larger family, she exercised her imagination freely, filling notebooks with drawings of characters having conversations via dialog balloons. At her Web site Auch remembered, "I loved to draw from the time I was able to hold a pencil or crayon. I used to fill notebooks with my sketches, often drawing the same characters on page after page." The year she attended second grade many families kept their children home from school because a dangerous polio epidemic was raging and vaccinations had not yet been instituted. Auch's mother, a former second grade teacher, taught her daughter to read, and when classes finally resumed at mid-year, Auch was reading several grade levels ahead of her class. "By the end of the school year, I had learned that reading was magic," the author/illustrator noted on her Web site. "Though I didn't know it then, the writer in me was probably born the year that I almost missed second grade."

Auch majored in art at Skidmore College, but because she found graphic art work unrewarding, she went on to earn a second degree in occupational therapy. After working for a few years at a children's hospital in Connecticut, Auch met her future husband, graphic artist and editorial cartoonist Herm Auch. After getting married, Herm Auch went to work for a Rochester, New York newspaper while Auch raised their son and daughter on a small farm.

Despite enjoying her role as a mother, Auch yearned to get back into the art field and found herself a job creating illustrations for the children's newspaper *Pen-*

nywhistle Press. At the suggestion of friends, in 1984 she also took a week-long workshop on writing for children, which turned out to be a revelation. Realizing that writing books for children was what she wanted to do, she went to work. After writing four novels and racking up thirteen rejections, she sold her first book, *The Witching of Ben Wagner,* about newcomer Ben, who befriends friends a mysterious girl. Several reviewers commended the work for its characterizations, including *Booklist* reviewer Carolyn Phelan, who also commented on Auch's inclusion of "satisfying touches of humor and insight."

During the late 1980s and early 1990s Auch honed her skills. She published at least one, but often two, novels per year. In these contemporary novels although families struggle with real challenges, Auch handles her plots with a light touch, often employing slapstick humor. In *Cry Uncle!,* which a *Kirkus Reviews* contributor dubbed "an auspicious debut," a boy deals with not only moving to a new town but also having his great uncle move in with the family. In *Mom Is Dating Weird Wayne* a daughter whose parents are divorced resists liking her mother's new boyfriend. Reviewers commented favorably about *Mom Is Dating Weird Wayne,* particularly the humor injected into its plot that, according to *Booklist* critic Denise M. Wilms, compensates for "some occasionally forced characterizations."

Auch's novel *Pick of the Litter* recounts a teen's feelings as she adjusts to her mother's pregnancy, while *The Kidnapping of Kevin Kowalski* shows how two boys deal with the physical limitations of an injured friend. Writing in the *Bulletin of the Center for Children's Books,* Roger Sutton acknowledged Auch as an established writer of children's books due to her "practiced" hand at telling a good story: "believable characters" and an interesting plot.

After writing nine books for older children, Auch took on a new challenge. Rekindling her interest in oil painting, she wrote and illustrated with cartoonish paintings her first picture book, *Easter Egg Farm,* about a peculiar hen named Pauline whose eggs are anything but plain. Pauline returns in Auch's 1996 offering, *Eggs Mark the Spot.* In this tale Pauline visits an art museum, thwarts art robbers, and renders her own versions of famous masterpieces.

With the success of the "spirited yarn" featuring Pauline, to quote *Booklist* contributor Stephanie Zvirin, Auch was on a roll, and has gone on to write a

steady stream of books about multitalented chickens involved in such pursuits as acting, dancing, and singing. Tongue-in-cheek titles include *Peeping Beauty, Hen Lake, Eggs Mark the Spot, Bantam of the Opera, The Nutquacker,* and *Poultrygeist.*

But why chickens? Chickens were a fond part of Auch's childhood, and both of her grandmothers raised them. One grandmother had a large chicken farm and sold eggs to stores throughout Long Island, while the other had a small flock housed in an area dubbed "Hen Park," where Auch liked to watch them. As she noted on her Web site, "After watching the hens go about their business for a while, I discovered that they had real personalities, just like my class in school There was the bossy one, the shy one, the hard worker, the lazy one, and even the class bully!" Because of their personalities, chickens seemed ideal fictional characters; for example, in *Peeping Beauty* a hen named Poulette aspires to become a ballerina, creating in *Booklist* reviewer Ilene Cooper's view a "delightful new twist" on the old chicken-fox tale. Full of puns, ballet terms, and boldly colored paintings, *Peeping Beauty* garnered praise, *School Library Journal* critic Joy Fleishhacker remarking on the "lively" language and "positive message" while a *Publishers Weekly* critic dubbed it a "snappy tale."

Auch's enthusiasm for her feathered friends has inspired feathered farces based on famous theatrical works: The ballet *Swan Lake* has become *Hen Lake,* as Poulette competes for stardom against a snooty peacock. In the same way, *Phantom of the Opera* has become *Bantam of the Opera,* in which the rooster Luigi, tired of crowing, seeks a more exalted role. Although young readers might miss the theater-based jokes, the books possess other appealing qualities. *Booklist* contributor Stephanie Zvirin described the illustrations for *Hen Lake* as "delightfully silly," while Kay Weisman noted in the same periodical how the artwork for *Bantam of the Opera* suits the story's "exaggerated humor."

When Auch decided to try her hand at historical fiction, she delved deep into the history of western New York during the early 1800s. *Journey to Nowhere, Frozen Summer,* and *The Road Home,* which form the "Genesee" trilogy, portray the unsuccessful attempt by a Connecticut family to homestead in Genesee County, New York. It is told from the point of view of the eldest daughter, Mem, who shoulders increasing responsibility as the tale progresses. Upon publication of the first volume of the trilogy, *Journey to Nowhere,* reviewers recognized Auch's desire to present a realistic and un-romanticized portrait of pioneer life, while at the same time telling a good story. According to *Horn Book* contributor Mary M. Burns, Auch has been largely successful, providing readers with "fascinating details" and "insight" into local customs. Furthermore, Elizabeth Bush noted the "refreshingly believable portrait" of Mem's family in her *Bulletin of the Center for Children's Books* review, while *School Library Journal* critic Allison Trent Berstein praised the book's "appealing characters."

Auch continues her trilogy with two more novels. In *Frozen Summer* Mem's family combats crop-killing weather, the birth of another baby, and her mother's death from post-partum depression. Although Carol A. Edwards of *School Library Journal* found the plot somewhat implausible, a *Kirkus* reviewer praised the novel as "refreshing" and "highly realistic." *Booklist* contributor Kay Weisman praised Auch's characterizations, particularly that of Mem's fallible father. In *Voice of Youth Advocates,* Evelyn Butrico applauded *Frozen Summer* overall as "an excellent piece of historic fiction." Mem's efforts to return to Connecticut with her siblings are the focus of *The Road Home.* Again, the work was praised for its characterizations and descriptions. While *Horn Book* critic Mary M. Burns found the ending "contrived," this weaknesses was outweighed by the book's merits.

In yet another creative turn, during the late 1990s Auch and her husband teamed up to create intermediate chapter books about a reluctant science-fair trio, among them *I Was a Third-Grade Science Project* and its sequel *I Was a Third-Grade Spy.* In the former, Josh, best friend Brian, and reluctant teammate Dougie try to hypnotize Brian's dog, but accidentally hypnotize Josh instead, with surprising results. *I Was a Third-Grade Spy,* which Piper L. Nyman called a "perfectly silly sequel" in *School Library Journal,* recounts how the boys use the dog, who can now speak English, as a spy. Reviewers praised both works for their humor, pace, and choice of language. Reviewing the first volume in *School Library Journal,* Lucy Rafael pointed out the "funny, clever ending," while in *Publishers Weekly* a critic commended Auch's use of "flippant dialogue and clever one-liners." Supplementing such humor were Herm's line-drawn illustrations. After Herm retired from newspaper work in 2000, The couple planned more joint writing and illustrating projects.

BIOGRAPHICAL AND CRITICAL SOURCES:

PERIODICALS

Book Links February 15, 1991, review of *Kidnapping Kevin Kowalski,* pp. 1214-1215.

Booklist, November 15, 1987, Carolyn Phelan, review of *The Witching of Ben Wagner,* p. 560; June 15, 1988, Denise M. Wilms, review of *Pick of the Litter,* p. 1732; January 1, 1989, D. M. Wilms, review of *Mom Is Dating Weird Wayne,* p. 782; January 15, 1990, D. M. Wilms, review of *Angel and Me and the Bayside Bombers,* p. 996; March 1, 1992, Stephanie Zvirin, review of *The Easter Egg Farm,* p. 1278; January 15, 1993, Leone McDermott, review of *Out of Step,* p. 905; March 1, 1993, Ilene Cooper, review of *Peeping Beauty,* p. 1234; October 15, 1993, Stephanie Zvirin, review of *Bird Dogs Can't Fly,* p. 448; February 1, 1994, Kay Weisman, review of *The Latchkey Dog,* p. 1005; November 15, 1994, Janice Del Negro, review of *Monster Brother,* p. 610; August, 1995, S. Zvirin, review of *Hen Lake,* p. 1954; March 1, 1996, Nancy McCray, review of *The Easter Egg Farm,* p. 1190; March 15, 1996, S. Zvirin, review of *Eggs Mark the Spot,* p. 1268; April 15, 1997, Kay Weisman, review of *Journey to Nowhere,* p. 1428; October 1, 1997, K. Weisman, review of *Bantam of the Opera,* p. 335; October 15, 1997, Donna Miller, review of *Eggs Mark the Spot,* p. 423; March 15, 1998, John Peters, review of *I Was a Third-Grade Science Project,* p. 1243; January 1, 1999, K. Weisman, review of *Frozen Summer,* p. 874; November 1, 1999, Marta Segal, review of *The Nutquacker,* p. 537; April 1, 2000, Ilene Cooper, review of *The Road to Home,* p. 1476; November 15, 2000, M. Segal, review of *Troll Teacher,* p. 650; May 1, 2001, Gillian Engberg, review of *I Was a Third-Grade Spy,* p. 1678.

Bulletin of the Center for Children's Books, January, 1989, Roger Sutton, review of *Mom Is Dating Weird Wayne,* pp. 115-116; May, 1990, R. Sutton, review of *Kidnapping Kevin Kowalski,* p. 207; April, 1994, Betsey Hearne, review of *The Latchkey Dog,* p. 250; November, 1994, Susan Dove Lempke, review of *Monster Brother,* p. 79; June, 1997, Elizabeth Bush, review of *Journey to Nowhere,* p. 350.

Childhood Education, June, 1988, Tina L. Burke, review of *Cry Uncle!,* p. 309.

Children's Book Review Service, October, 1993, review of *Bird Dogs Can't Fly,* p. 13; December, 1995, review of *Hen Lake,* p. 37.

Horn Book, March, 1989, Nancy Vasilakis, review of *Glass Slippers Give You Blisters,* p. 207; March, 1990, Anita Silvey, review of *Angel and Me and the Bayside Bombers,* p. 198; July-August, 1997, Mary M. Burns, review of *Journey to Nowhere,* p. 449; January, 1999, review of *Frozen Summer,* p. 57; July, 2000, M, M. Burns, review of *The Road to Home,* p. 450.

Kirkus Reviews, October, 1987, review of *Cry Uncle!,* p. 1511; February 1, 1988, review of *Pick of the Litter,* p. 198; October, 1988, review of *Mom Is Dating Weird Wayne,* p. 1523; November, 1992, review of *Out of Step,* p. 1372; December, 15, 1993, review of *The Latchkey Dog,* p. 1586; March 15, 1996, review of *Eggs Mark the Spot,* p. 455; March 1, 1998, review of *I Was a Third-Grade Science Project,* p. 334; November 15, 1998, review of *Frozen Summer,* p. 1664.

Language Arts, January, 1994, Miriam Martinez and Marcia F. Nash, reviews of *The Easter Egg Farm* and *Peeping Beauty,* pp. 56-57.

Publishers Weekly, November 27, 1987, review of *Cry Uncle!,* p. 82; November 16, 1990, review of *A Sudden Change of Family,* p. 57; April 27, 1992, review of *The Easter Egg Farm,* p.267; April 12, 1993, review of *Peeping Beauty,* p. 62; November 22, 1993, review of *The Latchkey Dog,* p. 63; April 4, 1994, review of *Dumbstruck,* pp. 80-81; November 14, 1994, review of *Monster Brother,* p. 67; September 11, 1995, review of *Hen Lake,* p. 85; February 12, 1996, review of *Eggs Mark the Spot,* p. 77; May 12, 1997, review of *Journey to Nowhere,* p. 77; July 28, 1997, review of *Bantam of the Opera,* p. 74; March 23, 1998, review of *I Was a Third-Grade Science Project,* p. 100; December 7, 1998, review of *Frozen Summer,* p. 60; September 27, 1999, review of *The Nutquacker,* p. 59; January 28, 2002, review of *The Princess and the Pizza,* pp. 289-290.

School Library Journal, October, 1987, Lucy Hawley, review of *The Witching of Ben Wagner,* p. 124; November, 1987, Sylvia S. Marantz, review of *Cry Uncle!,* p. 102; May, 1988, Trev Jones, review of *Pick of the Litter,* p. 95; November, 1988, Phyllis Graves, review of *Mom Is Dating Weird Wayne,* p. 110; February, 1989, Katherine Bruner, review of *Glass Slippers Give You Blisters,* p. 80; March, 1990, Tom S. Hurlburt, review of *Angel and Me and the Bayside Bombers,* pp. 184-185; May, 1990, Katharine Bruner, review of *Kidnapping Kevin Kowalski* p. 102; December, 1990, Trev Jones, review of *A Sudden Change of Family,* pp.

97-98; October, 1991, Connie Tyrrell Burns, review of *Seven Long Years until College,* p. 119; April, 1992, Heide Piehler, review of *The Easter Egg Farm,* p. 86; September, 1992, Janet M. Bair, review of *Out of Step,* p. 250; April, 1993, Joy Fleishhacker, review of *Peeping Beauty,* p. 90; December, 1993, Nancy Mendali-Scanlan, review of *Bird Dogs Can't Fly,* p. 78; January, 1994, Jana R. Fine, review of *The Latchkey Dog,* pp. 112-113; May, 1994, Rebecca O'Connell, review of *Dumbstruck,* p. 118; October, 1994, Leah Hawkins, review of *Peeping Beauty,* p. 75; November, 1994, Lauralyn Persson, review of *Monster Brother,* p. 72; October, 1995, Teresa Bateman, review of *The Easter Egg Farm,* p. 80 and Steven Engelfried, review of *Hen Lake,* p. 96; May, 1996, Betty Teague, review of *Eggs Mark the Spot,* p. 84; May, 1997, Allison Trent Bernstein, review of *Journey to Nowhere,* p. 128; August, 1997, Judith McMahon, review of *Eggs Mark the Spot,* p. 63; October, 1997, Ann Cook, review of *Bantam of the Opera,* p. 88; May, 1998, Lucy Rafael, review of *I Was a Third-Grade Science Project,* p. 106; December, 1998, Carol A. Edwards, review of *Frozen Summer,* p. 118; October, 1999, Lisa Falk, review of *The Nutquacker,* p. 65; July, 2000, Sharon Grover, review of *The Road to Home,* p. 100; October, 2000, Gay Lynn Van Vleck, review of *Troll Teacher,* p. 140; July, 2001, Piper L. Nyman, review of *I Was a Third-Grade Spy,* p. 72.

Stone Soup, September, 1999, Cathrina Altimari-Brown, review of *Frozen Summer,* p. 34.

Voice of Youth Advocates, April, 1988, Mary L. Adams, review of *The Witching of Ben Wagner,* p. 21; June, 1992, Carmen Oyenque, review of *Seven Long Years until College,* p. 91; August, 1999, Evelyn Butrico, review of *Frozen Summer,* p. 182.

OTHER

Poultry in Motion: About Mary Jane Auch, http://www.mjauch.com (March 4, 2002).*

*   *   *

AYALA, Francisco (de Paula y Garcia Duarte) 1906-

PERSONAL: Born March 16, 1906, in Granada, Spain; son of Francisco and Luz (Garcia Duarte) Ayala; married Etelvina Silva Vargas, 1932; children: one daughter. *Education:* University of Madrid, LL.B.,

1929; studied in Germany, 1929-30; University of Madrid, doctorate in law, 1932.

ADDRESSES: Agent—c/o Clan Libros, Nicaragua, 17, 28016 Madrid, Spain.

CAREER: Essayist, novelist, short story writer, critic, and journalist. *Revista de Occidente,* critic, 1927-30; editor of *Revista de Occidente* and *La Gaceta Literaria;* University of Madrid, Madrid, Spain, professor of law, 1932-35; counsel to Spanish Parliament, c. 1933-36; Spanish Republic's ambassador to Czechoslovakia, 1937; University of Puerto Rico, professor, 1950-56; professor at various universities in the United States, including New York University, University of Chicago, Bryn Mawr College, and Rutgers University, 1956-76; New York University, New York, NY, King Juan Carlos I of Spain Professor of Spanish Culture and Civilization, 1987-88. U.S. representative to the United Nations Educational, Scientific, and Cultural Organization (UNESCO).

MEMBER: Spanish Royal Academy.

AWARDS, HONORS: National Critic's Prize, 1972; National Literature Prize, 1983; National Prize for Spanish Letters for overall literary achievement, 1988; Miguel de Cervantes National Literary Prize, 1991; nominee for the Nobel Prize for literature and the Juan Rulfo Prize.

WRITINGS:

Tragicomedia de un hombre sin espíritu, Industrial Gráfica (Madrid, Spain), 1925.

Historia de un atardecer, Industrial Gráfica (Madrid, Spain), 1926.

El boxeador y un ángel, Cuadernos Literarios (Madrid, Spain), 1929.

Indagación del cinema (title means "Inquiry into Cinema"), Mundo Latino (Madrid, Spain), 1929.

Cazador en el alba, Ulises (Madrid, Spain), 1930.

El derecho social en la constitución de la república Española, Minuesa de los Rios (Madrid, Spain), 1932.

Los derechos individuales como garantía de la libertad, Minuesa de los Rios (Madrid, Spain), 1935.

El pensamiento vivo de Saavedra Fajardo, Losada (Buenos Aires, Argentina), 1941.

El problema del liberalismo, Fondo de Cultura Economica (Panuco, Mexico), 1941.

Oppenheimer, Fondo de Cultura Economica (Panuco, Mexico), 1942.

Historia de la libertad, Editorial Atlantida (Buenos Aires, Argentina), 1943.

(With Renato Treves) *Una doble experiencia política: España e Italia,* Colegio de México, Centro de Estudios Sociales (Mexico City, Mexico), 1944.

Ensayo sobre la libertad, Colegio de México, Centro de Estudios Sociales (Mexico City, Mexico), 1944.

El hechizado (title means "The Bewitching"; also see below), Emecé Editores (Buenos Aires, Argentina), 1944.

Histrionismo y representación: ejemplos y pretextos, Editorial Sudamericana (Buenos Aires, Argentina), 1944.

Los politicos, Editorial Depalma (Buenos Aires, Argentina), 1944.

Razón del mundo: Un exámen de conciencia intellectual, Losada (Buenos Aires, Argentina), 1944.

Jovellanos, Losada (Buenos Aires, Argentina), 1945.

Tratado de sociología, Losada (Buenos Aires, Argentina), 1947.

La cabeza del cordero, Losada (Buenos Aires, Argentina), 1949.

Los usurpadores (short stories; includes "El Hechizado"), Editorial Sudamericana (Buenos Aires, Argentina), 1949, translation by Carolyn Richmond published as *The Usurpers,* Schocken (New York, NY), 1987.

La invención del Quijote: Discurso leído en la fiesta de la lengua española celebrada en la Universidad de Puerto Rico el día 24 de abril de 1950, Editorial Universitaria (Rio Piedras, Puerto Rico), 1950.

Ensayos de sociología política: En qué mundo vivimos, Instituto de Investigaciones Sociales, Universidad Nacional (Mexico City, Mexico), 1951.

Introducción a las ciencias socials, Instituto de Investigaciones Sociales, Universidad Nacional (Mexico City, Mexico), 1952.

Derechos de la persona individual para una sociedad de masas, Editorial Perrot (Buenos Aires, Argentina), 1953.

Historia de macacos, Revista de Occidente (Madrid, Spain), 1955.

Breve teoría de la traducción, Obregón (Mexico City, Mexico), 1956.

El escritor en la sociedad en masas, Obregón (Mexico City, Mexico), 1956.

La crisis actual de la enseñanza, Editorial Nova (Buenos Aires, Argentina), 1958.

La integración social en América, Editorial Perrot (Buenos Aires, Argentina), 1958.

Muertes de perro (novel), Editorial Sudamericana (Buenos Aires, Argentina), 1958, translation by Joan Maclean published as *Death as a Way of Life,* Macmillan (New York, NY), 1964.

Tecnología y libertad, Taurus (Madrid, Spain), 1959.

Experiencia e invención: (Ensayos sobre el escritor y su mundo), Taurus (Madrid, Spain), 1960.

El fondo del vaso (sequel to *Muertes de perro*), Editorial Sudamericana (Buenos Aires, Argentina), 1962.

El as de bastos, Editorial Sur (Buenos Aires, Argentina), 1963.

De este mundo y el otro, E.D.H.A.S.A. (Barcelona, Spain), 1963.

La evasión de los intelectuales, Centro de Estudios y Documentación Sociales (Mexico City, Mexico), 1963.

Realidad y ensueño, Editorial Gredos (Madrid, Spain), 1963.

España a la fecha, Editorial Sur (Buenos Aires, Argentina), 1965.

Mis páginas mejores, Editorial Gredos (Madrid, Spain), 1965.

El rapto, La Novela Popular (Madrid, Spain), 1965, English edition edited by Phyllis Zatlin published as *El rapto,* Harcourt Brace (New York, NY), 1971.

Cuentos, Anaya (Salamanca, Spain), 1966.

De raptos, violaciones y otras inconveniencias, Alfaguara (Madrid, Spain), 1966.

Hacia una semblanza de Quevedo, Bedia (Santander, Spain), 1969.

Obras narrativas completas, Aguilar (Mexico City, Mexico), 1963.

El cine: arte y espectáculo, Universidad Veracruzana (Xalapa, Mexico), 1966.

Reflexiones sobre la estructura narrativa, Taurus (Madrid, Spain), 1970.

El jardín de las delicias, Editorial Seix Barral (Barcelona, Spain), 1971.

El Lazarillo: Nuevo exámen de algunos aspectos, Taurus (Madrid, Spain), 1971.

Confrontaciones, Editorial Seix Barral (Barcelona, Spain), 1972.

Los ensayos: Teoría y crítica literaria, Aguilar (Mexico City, Mexico), 1972.

Hoy ya es ayer, Moneda y Crédito (Madrid, Spain), 1972.

Cervantes y Quevedo, Editorial Seix Barral (Barcelona, Spain), 1974.

La novela: Galdós y Unamuno, Editorial Seix Barral (Barcelona, Spain), 1974.

El escritor y el cine, Ediciones del Centro, (Madrid, Spain), 1975.

El escritor y su imagen (Ortega y Gasset, Azorín, Valle-Inclán, Antonio Machado), Ediciones Guadarrama (Madrid, Spain), 1975.

(Editor) *Dictionario Atlantico,* Editorial Sudamericana (Buenos Aires, Argentina), 1977.

Galdós en su tiempo, Universidad Internacional Menéndez Pelayo (Santander, Spain), 1978.

De raptos, violaciones, macacos y demás inconveniencias, Editorial Seix Barral (Barcelona, Spain), 1982.

De triunfos y penas, Editorial Seix Barral (Barcelona, Spain), 1982.

Recuerdos y olvidos: 1. Del paraíso al destierro, Alianza (Madrid, Spain), 1982.

Palabras y letras, Edhasa, (Barcelona, Spain), 1983.

Recuerdos y olvidos: 2. El exilio, Alianza (Madrid, Spain), 1983.

La estructura narrativa y otras experiencias literarias, Editorial Crítica (Barcelona, Spain), 1984.

La retórica del periodismo, Real Academia Espanola (Madrid, Spain), 1984.

La imagen de España: continuidad y cambio en la sociedad española: (papeles para un curso), Alianza (Madrid, Spain), 1986.

El jardín de las malicias, Montena (Madrid, Spain), 1988.

Mi cuarto a espadas, El Pais (Madrid, Spain), 1988.

Las plumas del fénix: Estudios de literatura española, Alianza (Madrid, Spain), 1989.

El escritor en su siglo, Alianza (Madrid, Spain), 1990.

Relatos granadinos, Alianza (Madrid, Spain), 1990.

El tiempo y yo; o El mundo a la espada, Alianza (Madrid, Spain), 1992.

Contra el poder y otros ensayos, Ediciones de la Universidad (Madrid, Spain), 1992.

El regreso, Editorial Juventud (Bacelona, Spain), 1992.

Relatos, Editorial Bruño (Madrid, Spain), 1992.

Narrativa completa, Alianza (Madrid, Spain), 1993.

De mis pasos en la tierra, Aguilar (Madrid, Spain), 1996.

En qué mundo vivimos, Aguilar (Madrid, Spain), 1996.

Cuentos imaginarios, Libros Clan (Madrid, Spain), 1999.

Un caballero granadino y otros relatos, 1999.

SIDELIGHTS: Prolific Spanish writer Francisco Ayala's career began at a young age. He began writing poetry at eight, and his first novel, *Tragicocomedia de un hombre sin espíritu,* was published when he was only eighteen. He went on to become a critic for philosopher José Ortega y Gasset's prestigious journal, *Revista de Occidente,* by the time he was twenty-one. During these years, Ayala was also studying law at the University of Madrid; he received his law degree in 1929 and a Ph.D. in law in 1932, and subsequently became a professor of law and a counselor to the Spanish parliament.

Ayala published several more novels and short story collections in the 1920s and early 1930s, but in the mid-1930s he turned his attention to nonfiction works, writing a study of the new constitution of the Spanish Second Republic and other books on law and philosophy. With the outbreak of the Spanish Civil War in 1936, Ayala became the Republic's ambassador to Czechoslovakia. His father was executed by General Francisco Franco's forces during the war, and when the Republic was defeated Ayala went into exile in the Americas. He first settled in Argentina, working as a translator and continuing to write. Then, when the right-wing government of Juan Perón came to power in Argentina, Ayala left the country for Puerto Rico, and later for the United States, where he taught for many years. Ayala did not visit Spain again until 1960, although he moved back to the country to live after the death of Franco in 1975. In 1983 he was elected to the Spanish Royal Academy and was awarded the National Prize for Spanish Literature, and in 1991 he won the Miguel de Cervantes National Literary Prize, winning out over Nobel Prize laureates Camilio José Cela, Gabriel García Márquez, and Mario Vargas Llosa. The Cervantes Prize, Spain's highest literary award, recognizes a body of work "which has conspicuously enriched the literary patrimony of the Spanish speaking world."

Ayala's best-known book in the English-speaking world may be *Los usurpadores,* published in English as *The Usurpers.* This collection of short stories, written while Ayala lived in Argentina, is set in the Spain of the Middle Ages. Possibly the most-lauded tale from the collection is "The Bewitched," in which a man spends his life fighting the Spanish bureaucracy, trying to gain an audience with the king. When this man is finally permitted see the king, he finds himself in the presence of Carlos II, the monarch who was so severely mentally and physically handicapped that he could not even speak coherently, let alone rule. This story was dubbed "the gem of the . . . collection" by a *Kirkus Reviews* contributor, and called "a masterpiece of Hispanic literature" by famed writer Jorge Luis Borges, according to a critic for *Publishers Weekly.* Another notable story in the collection is "The Inquisitor," in which a former Jewish Grand Rabbi turned Catholic is so zealous in his prosecution of the Inquisition that he does not even have mercy on his only child. In the prologue to the book, Ayala explains the theme that binds the stories together: "power exercised by man over his fellow man is always a usurpation."

Many critics noted that, though *Los usurpadores* is set in the past, it is actually intended to critique illegitimate usurpations of power on the part of Franco and others in contemporary times. A similar critique is at the heart of Ayala's most famous novels, *Muertes de perro* and its sequel *El fondo del vaso.* Both stories are set in the same fictionalized Latin American nation, the former under the rule of a petty dictator, the latter after his fall. Although Ayala refused to identify the country that was his models for these books, they have generally been identified with Argentina and Perón.

Charles L. King, who wrote about Ayala in *Encyclopedia of World Literature in the Twentieth Century,* concluded: "[Ayala's] profound reflections on man's moral nature as well as on his relation to society and to the cosmos distinguish his work and provide it with an underlying and continuing unity. In Ayala, the artist and the concerned intellectual . . . fuse in rare and brilliant equilibrium."

BIOGRAPHICAL AND CRITICAL SOURCES:

BOOKS

Bieder, Maryellen, *Narrative Perspective in the Post-Civil War Novels of Francisco Ayala,* Department of Romance Languages, University of North Carolina Press (Chapel Hill, NC), 1979.

Costa, Luis, Richard Critchfield, Richard Glosan, and Wulf Koepke, editors, *German and International Perspectives on the Spanish Civil War: The Aesthetics of Partisanship,* Camden House (Columbia, SC), 1992.

Del Pino, Jose M., *Montajes y fragmentos: Una aproximacion a la narrativa española de vanguardia,* Rodopi (Amsterdam, Netherlands), 1995.

Encyclopedia of World Literature in the Twentieth Century, St. James Press (Detroit, MI), 1999.

Irizarry, Estelle, *Francisco Ayala,* Twayne (Boston, MA), 1977.

Julia, Mercedes, editor, *Historicidad en la novela española contemporanea,* Universidad de Cadiz (Cadiz, Spain), 1997.

Novela española actual, Fundacion Juan March & Catedra (Madrid, Spain), 1977.

Reference Guide to Short Fiction, 2nd edition, St. James Press (Detroit, MI), 1994.

Sanchez Trigueros, Antonio, and Antonio Chicharro Chamorro, editors, *Francisco Ayala, teorico y critico literario,* Diputacion Provincial de Granada, Biblioteca de Ensayo (Granada, Spain), 1992.

Vazquez, Medel, and Manuel Angel, editors, *El universo plural de Francisco Ayala,* Alfar (Seville, Spain), 1995.

PERIODICALS

American Hispanicist, Volume 4, numbers 30-31, 1978, Janet Diaz and Ricardo Landeira, "'El tajo' de Francisco Ayala: Un caso de conciencia," pp. 7-12.

Anales Cervantinos, Volume 32, 1994, p. 207.

Anales de la Literatura Española Contemporanea, 1994, p. 165.

Choice, November, 1987, E. H. Friedman, review of *The Usurpers,* p. 482.

Cuadernos Hispanoamericanos, Volumes 329-330, 1977, Andres Amoros, "Algunos articulos olvidados de Francisco Ayala, hace cincuenta anos," pp. 236-259, Manuel Andujar, "Francisco Ayala en signos de admiracion," pp. 288-289, Mariano Baquero Goyanes, "Cervantes y Ayala: El arte del relato breve," pp. 311-326, Estelle Irizarry, "Autor y lector ficcionalizados en obras de Francisco Ayala," pp. 327-340, German Gullon, "Degradacion y dictadura en *Muertes de perro,* de Francisco Ayala," pp. 329-330, Ildefonso-Maneul Gil, "Donde amistad y admiracion confluyen (homenaje a Francisco Ayala)," pp. 281-287, Jose L. Cano, "Francisco Ayala," pp. 276-280, Monique Joly, "Francisco Ayala: Ensayo de interpretacion de su obra narrativa posterior a la guerra," pp. 366-383, Rosario Hiriart, "Francisco Ayala: Vida y obra,"

pp. 262-275, and "Metamorfosis de una anecdota: 'Incidente,' de Francisco Ayala (un comentario de texto)," pp. 387-402, Erna Brandenberger, "Francisco Ayala y Alemania," pp. 308-310, Ricardo Gullon, "Francisco Ayala, critico literario," pp. 347-355, Agnes Gullon, "Francisco Ayala, professor," pp. 302-307, William M. Sherzer, "Ironia y nerismo en *El inquisidor,*" pp. 477-480, Carolyn Richmond, "La complejidad estructural de *El jardin* de las delicias vista a traves de dos de sus piezas," pp. 403-413, Janet W. Diaz and Ricardo Landeira, "La 'historia dentro de la historia' en tres cuentos de Francisco Ayala," pp. 481-494, Nelson R. Orringer, "La mano y el centro en *Los usurpadores,* de Ayala," pp. 495-510, Thomas Mermall, "La pseudo-racionalidad del discurso en la narritiva de Francisco Ayala," pp. 341-346, Gonzalo Sobejano, "Lectura de el doliente," pp. 449-468, Manuel Duran, "Notas sobre Francisco Ayala, *El rapto* y el mito del eterno retorno," pp. 329-330, Dionisio Canas, "Objectable representacion de Francisco Ayala," pp. 300-301, Emilio Orozco Diaz, "Palabras de saludo a Francisco Ayala en su presentacion publica en Granada," pp. 290-299, Ignacio Soldevida-Durante, "Para una hermeneutica de la prosa vanguardista espanola (a proposite de Francisco Ayala)," pp. 329-330, Galvarino Plaza "Un relato de Francisco Ayala: Realidad imaginada o soledad intransferable," pp. 429-440; April, 1993, Francisco Ayala, Rosa Chacel, Rafael Alberti, Jose Bello, and Luis Garcia Mankro, roundtable discussion of the Generation of '27, p. 514; June, 2001, David Vinas Piquer, article on Francisco Ayala, p. 79.

Dactylus, Volume 12, 1993, p. 14.

Discurso Literario: Revista de Temas Hispanicos, spring, 1989, Naomi Lindstrom, "Creation in Criticism, Criticism in Creation: Four Ibero Exemplars," pp. 423-444.

Hispania, March, 1969, Janet Winecoff Diaz, review of *La Cabeza del cordero,* p. 70; May, 1974, John J. Staczek, review of *El rapto,* p. 398; September, 1971, Robert Hatton, review of *El rapto,* p. 613; May, 1980, Gary Eugene A. Scavinicky, review of *Dictionario Atlantico,* p. 447; May, 1985, Estelle Irizarry, review of *La estructura narrativa y otras experiencias literarias,* p. 304; May, 1987, "The Ubiquitous Trickster Archetype in the Narrative of Francisco Ayala," pp. 222-230.

Hispanic Journal, spring, 1989, Raymond Skyrme, "Substance and Shadow: The Anatomy of Self-Reflection in *La cabeza del cordero,*" p. 95.

Hispanofila, September, 1991, Daniel E. Gulstad, "Homecoming and Identity-Quest in Ayala's *La cabeza del cordero,*" pp. 1-15.

Insula, January, 1999, p. 625; June, 1993, p. 23.

Kirkus Reviews, April 15, 1987, review of *The Usurpers,* p. 572.

Letras de Deusto, Silvia Rurunat, "Francisco Ayala y el monologo interior: Un recuento," pp. 189-194.

Letras Peninsulares, spring, 1990, Mary Vasquez, "Homenaje a Francisco Ayala y Rosa Chacel," Robert Lima, "With Francisco Ayala at NYU," pp. 95-99, Janet Perez, "Francisco Ayala: The Art of Literary Recycling," pp. 139-148; Nelson R. Orringer, "Historicity and Historiography in F. Ayala's *Los usurpadores,*" pp. 119-137.

Modern Age, summer, 1991, Noel Valis, review of *The Usurpers,* p. 401.

Modern Language Journal, February, 1972, Ana Maria Fagundo, review of *El rapto,* p. 102.

Monographic Review/Revista Monografica, Nelson R. Orringer, "The Baroque Body in Francisco Ayala's *El rapto,*" pp. 46-59.

Neophilologus, July, 1997, p. 381.

New York Times Book Review, June 21, 1987, William Ferguson, review of *The Usurpers,* p. 22.

New York Times, June 19, 1983, p. 30.

Ojancano: Revista de Literatura Espanola, October, 1993, Nelson R. Orringer, "Missteps of the Comic Body in Francisco Ayala's *El fondo del vaso,*" pp. 69-88; October, 1997, analysis of short story technique of Francisco Ayala, p. 241; April, 1998, Manuel L. Abellan, comparison of Francisco Ayala and Ramon Sender, p. 19.

Perspectives on Contemporary Literature, Volume 1, number 1, 1975, Charles Olstad, "Alienation: Theme and Technique in Francisco Ayala," pp. 96-104.

Publications of the Modern Language Association of America, Volume 84, 1969, Keith Ellis, "Cervantes and Ayala's *El rapto:* The Art of Reworking a Story," pp. 14-19.

Publishers Weekly, May 8, 1987, review of *The Usurpers,* p. 61.

Razon y Fe, July, 1999, p. 61.

Revista Canadiense de Estudios Hispanicos, autumn, 1981, Raymond Skyrme, "The Divided Self; The Language of Scission in 'El tajo' of Francisco Ayala," pp. 91-109; winter, 1990, Raymond Skyrme, "Analysis of the Visual Mode in *La cabeza del cordero,*" pp. 293-314; fall, 1996, Francisco Ayala, article on the language of Spanish literature, p. 5; fall, 1992, Rosalia Cornejo-Parriego, analysis of the work of Francisco Ayala, p. 31.

Revista de Estudios Hispanicos, 1978, Nelson R. Orringer, "The Hand and the Scepter in *Los usurpadores* by Francisco Ayala," pp. 113-134; Volume 12, 1998, p. 113.

Revista Hispanica Moderna, December, 1997, p. 241.

Romance Languages Annual, 1996, p. 528.

Salina, November, 1998, Rosa Navarro Duran, review of *Los Usurpadores,* p. 137.

Siglo XX/20th Century, p. 25.

Spanish Royal Academy, Francisco Ayala, discourse on the lexicography and importance of the Spanish language, p. 57.

Suplemento Literario La Nacion (Buenos Aires, Argentina), April 26, 1992, Francisco Ayala, acceptance speech for the Cervantes Prize, p. 1.

Suplementos Anthropos: Materiales de Trabajo Intelectual, September, 1993, p. 3.

USF Language Quarterly, Volume 17, number 1-2, 1978, Antonio Martinez, "Dos parabolas de nuestro tiemps: 'Muertes de perro' y 'El fondo del vaso,'" pp. 48-50.

World Literature Today, summer, 1983, J. Schraibman, review of *Recuerdos y Olvidos,* p. 437; autumn, 1983, L. Larios Vendrell, review of *Triunfos y Penas,* p. 615; autumn, 1990, Terry O. Taylor, review of *Las plumas del fénix: Estudios de literatura española,* p. 613; spring, 1993, John Crispin, review of *El tiempo y yo o El mundo a la espada,* p. 339; winter, 1995, Susana Rivera, review of *El rapto,* p. 102.

OTHER

El poder de la palabra, http://www.epdlp.com/ (May 3, 2002).

Francisco Ayala Web site, http://www.mcu.es/ (May 3, 2002).

New York University Web site, http://www.nyu.edu/ (May 3, 2002), "Holders of the King Juan Carlos I of Spain Professorship in Spanish Culture and Civilization."

Premio Cervantes Web site, http://www.terra.es/ (May 3, 2002).

Terra, http://teleine.ole.com/ (May 3, 2002).*

AZÚA, Felix de 1944-

PERSONAL: Born 1944, in Barcelona, Spain.

ADDRESSES: Agent—Editorial Anagrama, S.A. Pedró de la Creu, 58. 08034 Barcelona, Spain.

CAREER: Professor of aesthetics, newspaper columnist, and novelist.

AWARDS, HONORS: Herralde Prize, 1987, for *Diary of a Humiliated Man.*

WRITINGS:

El lenguaje y la búsqueda de la verdad, EDHASA (Barcelona, Spain), 1971.
Las lecciones de Jena, Seix Barral (Barcelona, Spain), 1972.
Lecture y crítica, La Gaya Ciencia (Barcelona, Spain), 1975.
Las ciencias ornamentals, La Gaya Ciencia (Barcelona, Spain), 1976.
(With Javier Marias and Vincente Molina-Foix), *Tres cuentos didácticos,* La Gaya Ciencia (Barcelona, Spain), 1977.
Concer Baudelaire y su obra, Dopesa (Barcelona, Spain), 1978.
Las lecciones suspendidas, Alfaguara (Madrid, Spain), 1978.
La paradoja del primitivo, Seix Barral (Barcelona, Spain), 1983.
Mansura, Editorial Anagrama (Barcelona, Spain), 1984.
Historia de un idiota contada por él mismo, o, El contenido de la felicidad, Editorial Anagrama (Barcelona, Spain), 1986.
Cambio de bandera, Editorial Anagrama (Barcelona, Spain), 1991.
Venecia de Casanova, Planeta (Barcelona, Spain), 1993.
Demasiadas preguntas, Editorial Anagrama (Barcelona, Spain), 1994.
Dictionario de las artes, Planeta (Barcelona, Spain), 1995.
Diario de un hombre humiliado, Editorial Anagrama (Barcelona, Spain), 1987, translation by Julie Jones published as *Diary of a Humiliated Man,* Lumen Editions (Cambridge, MA), 1996.

El aprenizaje de la decepción, Editorial Anagrama (Barcelona, Spain), 1996.
Salidas de tono, Editorial Anagrama (Barcelona, Spain), 1996.
Lecturas compulsivas: una invitación, Editorial Anagrama (Barcelona, Spain), 1998.
La invención de Caín, Alfaguara (Madrid, Spain), 1999.
Momentos decisivos, Editorial Anagrama (Barcelona, Spain), 2000.
Baudelaire: y el artista de la vida moderna, Editorial Anagrama (Barcelona, Spain), 2000.

POETRY

El velo en el rostro de Agamenón, (1966-1969), Ediciones Saturno (Barcelona, Spain), 1970.
Edgar en Stephane, Lumen (Barcelona, Spain), 1971.
Lengua de cal, A. Corazon (Madrid, Spain), 1972.
Poetas españoles postcontemporáneos, El Bardo (Barcelona, Spain), 1974.
Poesía (1968-1978), Ediciones Peralta (Madrid, Spain), 1979.
Pasar y siete canciones, La Gaya Ciencia (Barcelona, Spain), 1979.
Ultima lección, Legasa (Madrid, Spain), 1981.
Farra, Hiperion (Madrid, Spain), 1983.
Los discípulos en Sais, Hiperion (Madrid, Spain), 1988.
Poesía (1968-1988), Hiperion (Madrid, Spain), 1989.

Author of prologue to the Catalan literary collection *Herois i Heroïnes* by Jodi Gabarro, to various translations of works by Samuel Beckett and Alain Robbe-Grillet, and to a translation of *El lenguaje y la búsqueda de la verdad* titled *Language and the Pursuit of Truth,* by John Wilson.

SIDELIGHTS: Felix de Azúa is a highly respected Catalan novelist and essayist. His first novel to be translated into English, *Diary of a Humiliated Man,* was described as "mordantly funny, at times horrifying, [and] always invigorating," by a *Publishers Weekly* contributor. It has received many other excellent reviews as well, and has been compared to some of the great twentieth-century novels of ideas, particularly nineteenth century Russian writer Fyodor Dostoevsky's novel *The Underground Man.*

Azúa's protagonist, much like that of *The Underground Man,* decides to go underground and live like a stranger in his own city, Barcelona, as he pursues the most banal life possible. "The narrator is a sardonic commentator on his times," Steven Moore wrote in a review for the *Washington Post Book World.* "It is an original treatment of age-old questions on the nature of sin, good vs. evil, human vs. animal." Eric Howard praised the narrator in a review for *Library Journal,* commenting that he "is unpretentious, witty without being stagy, and tenderly satiric."

In a conversation with Jordi Gracia in *Cuadernos Hispanoamericanos,* Azúa said that in order to bring his contemporary Spain and Catalonia to the page he decided to look to the way that James Joyce, in created a gigantic poetic artifice that was a literary Ireland, is capable of shining light on the historical Ireland that he knew and wanted to convey. Azúa told Gracia that he thinks that the novel form has the same literary possibilities as drama or poetry, but that the novel is also able to reflect a historical, as well as universal experience.

BIOGRAPHICAL AND CRITICAL SOURCES:

BOOKS

Perez, Magallon Jesus, editor, *Luz vital: Estudios de cultura hispanica en memoria de Victor Ouimette,* Department of Hispanic Studies, McGill University (Toronto, Ontario, Canada), 1999.
Toro, Alfonso de, editor, *La Novela española,* Kassell (Reichenberger, Germany), 1995.

PERIODICALS

Booklist, October 15, 1996, review of *Diary of a Humiliated Man,* p. 404.
Choice, May, 1997, review of *Diary of a Humiliated Man,* p. 1503.
Confronto Litterario, Volume 8, 1992, p. 189.
Cuadernos Hispanoamericanos, October, 1999, Jordi Garcia, interview with Felix de Azua, p. 93.
El Mundo, April 11, 2000, Pilar Maruell, review of *Momentos decisivos.*
Insula, March, 1997, Jenaro Talens, analysis of the work of Felix de Azua, p. 7.
Kirkus Reviews, August 1, 1996, review of *Diary of a Humiliated Man,* p. 1503.
Library Journal, October 1, 1996, Eric Howard, review of *Diary of a Humiliated Man,* p. 126.
Publishers Weekly, August 26, 1996, review of *Diary of a Humiliated Man,* p. 90.
Quimera, February, 1988, interview with Felix de Azua, p. 16; May, 1992, reviews of *Cambio de bandera,* p. 60.
Washington Post Book World, December 22, 1996, Steven Moore, review of *Diary of a Humiliated Man,* p. 9.
World Literature Today, autumn, 1988, Joseph Schaibman, review of *Historia de un idiota contada por el mismo o El contenido de la felicidad,* p. 635.

OTHER

Que Leer, http://www.queleer.navegalia.com/ (July 14, 2002), Mauricio Bach, review of *Momentos decisivos.**

B

BAGLEY, Mary (C.) 1958-

PERSONAL: Born March 11, 1958, in St. Louis, MO; daughter of Robert E. (a mechanical engineer) and Harriet E. (an editor) Bagley; children: Jeremiah, Sarah. *Ethnicity:* "White." *Education:* University of Missouri—St. Louis, B.A., 1980, M.A., 1982; St. Louis University, Ph.D., 1994. *Religion:* "Southern Baptist." *Hobbies and other interests:* Photography.

ADDRESSES: Home—12539 Falling Leaves Ct., St. Louis, MO 63141. *Office*—Department of English, Missouri Baptist College, One College Park Dr., St. Louis, MO 63141. *Agent*—Robin Vent, P.O. Box 154001, St. Louis, MO 63141. *E-mail*—Robin@galaxy5.com.

CAREER: Missouri Baptists College, St. Louis, MO, professor, 1983—. *America Alive!* (cable program), St. Louis, MO, writer and broadcaster, 1983-85; Save the Ambassador Theatre, president; lecturer, editor, and broadcaster.

MEMBER: Modern Language Association, National Council of Teachers of English, Sigma Tau Delta.

AWARDS, HONORS: Key to the City of St. Louis, MO, 1984; William Barnaby Faherty Award, 1990.

WRITINGS:

The Front Row: Missouri's Grand Theatres, Gateway (St. Louis, MO), 1984.
Handbook for Professional and Academic Writing, Copley Books (La Jolla, CA), 1988.

Professional Writing Types, Tapestry, 1989.
Selected Readings in Nineteenth- and Twentieth-Century Literature, Harcourt (New York, NY), 1994.
Poetics of Realism, Forbes, 1994.
Willa Cather's Myths, American Heritage (New York, NY), 1996.

Also author of *The Art of Writing Well,* 1987; *Business Communications;* and *Art of Business Writing.* Contributor of more than five hundred articles and short stories to journals and other periodicals.

WORK IN PROGRESS: A mystery story for *Mary Higgins Clark* magazine; research on contemporary literature and comparative literature.

SIDELIGHTS: Mary Bagley told *CA:* "I've always written about things I've liked such as the old movie palaces. They're fascinating—enchanting. They inspire my imagination by their exotic design. I tend to write also as therapy. It helps me escape many of life's sad things. I recently lost my mother and brother within three months of each other. My form of catharsis is expressing my feelings in a short story, and the words seem to flow so easily."

*   *   *

BAHR, Alice Harrison 1946-

PERSONAL: Born July 24, 1946, in New York, NY; daughter of Arthur (a railroad worker) and Charlotte M. (a waitress; maiden name, Waterstradt) Harrison; married Robert A. Bahr (a writer and publisher),

February 14, 1971; children: Keith, Aimee. *Ethnicity:* "Caucasian." *Education:* Temple University, B.A., 1968; Drexel University, M.L.S., 1972; Lehigh University, M.A., 1975, Ph.D., 1980. *Hobbies and other interests:* Scuba diving, reading.

ADDRESSES: Home—Mobile, AL. *Office*—Library, Spring Hill College, 4000 Dauphin St., Mobile, AL 36608. *E-mail*—bahr@shc.edu.

CAREER: Lehigh University, Bethlehem, PA, assistant reference librarian, 1970-74; Cedar Crest College, Allentown, PA, adjunct faculty member, 1978-82; Libraries at Cedar Crest and Muhlenberg Colleges, Allentown, project librarian, 1980-88; Spring Hill College, Mobile, AL, director of library, 1988—, adjunct member of English faculty, 1989, associate professor, 1993-99, professor, 1999—. Institute for Legal and Ethical Issues in the New Information Era, participant, 2000.

MEMBER: American Library Association, Association of College and University Libraries (chair of research for college librarianship committee, college libraries section, 1998-2000), Network of Alabama Academic Libraries.

WRITINGS:

Book Theft and Library Security Systems, 1978-79, Knowledge Industry Publications (White Plains, NY), 1978, 2nd edition published as *Book Theft and Library Security Systems, 1981-82,* 1981.
Microforms: The Librarian's View, 1978-79, Knowledge Industry Publications (White Plains, NY), 1978.
Automated Library Circulation Systems, 1979-80, Knowledge Industry Publications (White Plains, NY), 1979.
(Editor) *Future Teaching Roles for Academic Librarians,* Haworth Press (New York, NY), 2000.
(Editor) *InPrint: A Directory of Publishing Opportunities for College Librarians* (Internet publication), Association of College and Research Libraries, 2001.

Contributor to books, including *The Library and Information Manager's Guide to Online Services,* edited by Ryan E. Hoover, Knowledge Industry Publications (White Plains, NY), 1980. Contributor of articles, poems, and short fiction to library journals and other periodicals, including *White Rock Review, Wind/Literary Journal, Parade, Pennsylvania English, Skylark, Alabama Librarian, Library Trends,* and *Technical Services Quarterly.* Founding editor and editor-in-chief, *College and Undergraduate Libraries,* 1990-99; guest editor, *Library and Archival Security,* 1991.

WORK IN PROGRESS: An assessment of the quality of coauthored papers; short stories.

SIDELIGHTS: Alice Harrison Bahr told *CA:* "Every English major has some instinct for writing, albeit sometimes only the desire exists, not the talent. As a librarian, I've had ample opportunity to write. Much of that writing was the result of combating day-to-day problems. Just as a fiction writer's feelings speak for others, I knew that local problems had a national audience. As a result of that activity and as a long-term commitment to the contributions that smaller academic institutions make to the quality of individual lives and to education as a whole, I have become passionate about encouraging college librarians to publish.

"On a daily basis, college librarians solve practical problems in innovative ways: rethink organizational structure as a way of life, creatively do more with less, and often play a major role in the lives of their institutions, teaching, chairing committees, leading in the merger of computer and library services. Unfortunately, the workloads of college librarians prevent wide circulation of their accomplishment and leave research unique to their institutions undone."

*   *   *

BAILIN, George 1928-

PERSONAL: Born May 10, 1928, in Brooklyn, NY; son of Herman (a grocery store owner) and Marion (a salesclerk; maiden name, Blesofski) Bailin; married; first wife's name Marilyn (divorced); married Daryl Whatley (an instructor), January 31, 1987; children: Jill, Michael. *Education:* City University of New York, B.A. (English), 1949; Manhattan College, M.A. (counseling psychology), 1970; Sarah Lawrence College, M.F.A. (creative writing), 1980. *Hobbies and other interests:* Writing, exercise.

ADDRESSES: Home—P.O. Box 298, Harriman, NY 10926-0298. *Office*—Sacred Orchard Corp., P.O. Box 298, Harriman, NY 10926-0298. *E-mail*—dgbailin@warwick.net.

CAREER: New York City Public School System, New York, NY, English teacher, 1955-83; Westchester Community College, Valhalla, NY, adjunct English professor, 1985-88; Bergen Community College, Paramus, NJ, adjunct English professor, 1988—. Evander Childs High School, dean of men. Yoga Society of New York, board member; Sacred Orchard Corporation, founder. *Military service:* New York State National Guard, 1965-67, became private first class.

MEMBER: Yoga Society of New York, United Federation of Teachers.

WRITINGS:

POETRY; UNLESS OTHERWISE NOTED

Collapsing Spaces, Tilting Times, Stone Country Press, 1980.
Counterculture, Seaport Poets & Writers Press, 1981.
Dead Reckoning, Dragonsbreath Press, 1984.
Evening News Report, Seaport Poets & Writers Press, 1985.
First Strike, Seaport Poets & Writers Press, 1987.
Sage of Ananda (spiritual teachings), Seaport Poets & Writers Press, 1993.

Contributor of literary criticism to periodicals, including *South and West, Puckerbush Review,* and *University of Maine Review;* contributor of poetry to *Colorado Quarterly, Prairie Schooner, Beloit Poetry Journal, Kansas Quarterly,* and other national publications.

WORK IN PROGRESS: Meditator's Newsletter, a monthly publication available in hard copy or online at http://www.sacredorchard.org; a sequel to *Sage of Ananda.*

SIDELIGHTS: George Bailin told *CA:* "Having met a liberated sage, I turned all my energies in that direction."

BAIRD, Alison 1963-

PERSONAL: Born in Montreal, Quebec, Canada; daughter of Donal (a fire-fighting consultant) and Violet (a nurse; maiden name, Morgan) Baird. *Education:* University of Toronto, B.A. (with honors), 1986, M.A., 1990. *Hobbies and other interests:* Watercolor painting, amateur theater, travel.

ADDRESSES: Home—Ontario, Canada. *Agent*—Sternig & Byrne Literary Agency, 3209 South 55th St., Milwaukee, WI 53219.

CAREER: Writer.

MEMBER: Canadian Society of Children's Authors, Illustrators, and Performers.

AWARDS, HONORS: Regional winner, Silver Birch Award, 1996, for *The Dragon's Egg;* Canadian Children's Book Centre choice, c. 1999, for *The Hidden World* and *White as the Waves: A Novel of Moby Dick;* Best of 2001 selections, *Resource Links,* for *The Wolves of Woden;* IODE Book Award nomination, Violet Downey National Chapter, for *White as the Waves.*

WRITINGS:

The Dragon's Egg, illustrated by Frances Tyrrell, Scholastic Canada (Markham, Ontario, Canada), 1994.
White as the Waves: A Novel of Moby Dick, Tuckamore Books (St. Johns, Newfoundland, Canada), 1999.
The Hidden World, Puffin Books (Toronto, Ontario, Canada), 1999.
The Wolves of Woden, Puffin Books (Toronto, Ontario, Canada), 2001.
The Witches of Willowmere (first novel in "Chronicles of Willowmere"), Penguin Books Canada (Toronto, Ontario, Canada), 2002.

Work represented in anthologies, including *What If . . . ? Amazing Stories,* selected by Monica Hughes, Tundra Books, 1998; and *Wonder Zone: Stardust,* Trifolium, 2001. Contributor of short stories to magazines, including *On Spec.*

ADAPTATIONS: Baird's short story "Moon Maiden" was recorded on compact disk, Prentice-Hall.

WORK IN PROGRESS: An epic adult fantasy series for Warner Books.

SIDELIGHTS: Canadian writer Alison Baird's novels reflect her fascination with fantasy, drawing as they do upon the author's knowledge of myth and folklore from around the world. She creates imaginary worlds that blend elements of disparate legends and tales into a single world of her own design, one that reviewers have found to be solid and believable. Sometimes Baird creates a parallel contemporary world, equally realistic, and sends her protagonists back and forth from one realm to the other in their quest for solutions to epic dilemmas. In the 2002 work *The Witches of Willowmere*, Baird combines history, magic, and the supernatural in a story about a modern teen forced to confront her own destiny against a malevolent power. Reviewing the novel in *Resource Links*, K. V. Johansen praised Baird's teen protagonist as "a believably strong and resilient, yet unhappy and troubled young woman," and the novel's storyline "briskly-paced." Dubbing *The Witches of Willowmere* a "metaphysical mystery" *Hamilton Spectator* critic added of this first series installment: "And, of course, Baird's writing is as excellently crafted as ever."

In Baird's 1999 novel *The Hidden World*, Maeve O'Connor's real world is the rugged Avalon peninsula in southeastern Newfoundland, Canada, where the unhappy teenager has been sent to visit relatives. No happier there than in her native Toronto, Maeve immerses herself in a book written by her grandmother about a modern girl who mysteriously finds herself in the mythical Avalon of King Arthur. When Maeve experiences a similar supernatural transportation her first response to the eery event is denial, followed by resistance. Eventually she is drawn into a medieval land replete with fairies, strange mythical creatures, and, of course, an adventurous quest. *Quill & Quire* reviewer Philippa Sheppard noted with favor the vivid splendor of Baird's fantasy world and her realistic depiction of contemporary Newfoundland, a landscape unfamiliar to many American—and even Canadian—readers.

The Wolves of Woden is another novel of parallel worlds, set in the Avalon peninsula prior to the events of *The Hidden World*. In the midst of the anxiety cre-

ated by World War II, teenager Jean MacDougall finds herself unexpectedly in the exotic other-world of Annwn. There she finds ancient ancestors of twentieth-century Newfoundlanders engaged in a war of their own. It is a fierce battle indeed, pitting primitive Celts against Viking invaders, and druids and fairy folk against the evil witch Morgana and even the mythical god Woden himself. Jean embarks on a quest for the legendary Spear of Lugh, which she believes has the power to save both worlds. In this ambitious epic, Baird displays her knowledge of many myths. She weaves strands of real and imaginary, contemporary and ancient, history and fantasy, gods and men to build a story that "actually improves upon its predecessor [*The Hidden World*]," according to Laurie McNeill in *Quill & Quire*, "creating an exciting and often truly magical narrative." Baird fills her story with people who are, in the opinion of a *Hamilton Spectator* reviewer, "wonderful, fully believable characters in both worlds." *Resource Links* contributor Krista Johansen recommended *The Wolves of Woden*: "The action is gripping, the blending of Celtic and Norse mythology, the Arthurian legends, and fairy lore deftly handled, and the conflicts complex."

Baird's novel *The Dragon's Egg* takes place in contemporary Toronto and features an imaginative nine-year-old protagonist. Ai Lien is different: her name and ethnicity mark her as an outsider at her new school. She is ridiculed for her superior intelligence and subjected to the taunts of bullies who are all older than she is. Ai Lien needs a friend who can accept her as she is. She finds him in a special stone that becomes her "dragon's egg." When the egg hatches, Ai Lien's invisible friend becomes her companion and ally against the world. In *Quill & Quire* Ken Setterington recommended *The Dragon's Egg* to fans of dragon stories, noting especially "the magic and majesty of Chinese dragons" as Baird depicts them.

Baird is also the author of *White as the Waves: A Novel of Moby Dick,* an adaptation of Herman Melville's classic as seen through the eyes of the whale. She tells the story of the whale—named White as the Waves—from birth, surrounding him at times with friends, accompanying him on his more solitary travels through the seas, experiencing with him the assaults of the whalers who repeatedly threaten his life. To accomplish this narrative, Baird creates a complex undersea world, paying careful attention to every detail of its landscape, culture, and inhabitants. *Quill & Quire* reviewer Teresa Toten noted a disruptive amount of explanation in this long novel, to the detriment of the story itself, but she cited the story of White as the Waves and his relentless pursuit of Captain Ahab as an "original" and "intriguing adventure."

Baird once told *CA:* "I am one of those people who always intended to be writers from an early age. I was given my first library card when I was four years old, commencing a lifelong love affair with books. Nathaniel Hawthorne's *A Wonder Book,* a retelling of classical Greek myths, was one of my favorites; I also devoured the works of E. Nesbit, C. S. Lewis, and J. R. R. Tolkien. With the passing years the longing to be a writer myself took hold. At the age of twelve I wrote a collection of poems, four of which were ultimately published in various magazines and anthologies. With this encouragement, I continued to write through high school and university. My first short stories were published in 1993, my first book the year after.

"Of all genres, I am most drawn to fantasy fiction, enjoying the absolute free rein it grants to the imagination. Children's fiction is also attractive to me because, despite the label's implied exclusivity, it is in fact ageless. A well-written 'children's' book can be a source of delight for the adult reader as much as for the child: like a myth or folk tale it transcends age boundaries. This is the kind of book which, as a child and as an adult, I always longed to write."

BIOGRAPHICAL AND CRITICAL SOURCES:

PERIODICALS

Canadian Book Review Annual, 1999, review of *White as the Waves: A Novel of Moby Dick,* pp. 481-482.
Canadian Children's Literature, summer, 1997, review of *The Dragon's Egg,* p. 54.
Hamilton Spectator (Hamilton, Ontario, Canada), July 14, 2001, review of *The Wolves of Woden* September 14, 2002, review of *The Witches of Willowmere.*
Quill & Quire, October, 1994, Ken Setterington, review of *The Dragon's Egg,* p. 43; March, 1999, Philippa Sheppard, review of *The Hidden World,* p. 70; May, 1999, Teresa Toten, review of *White as the Waves,* p. 37; August, 2001, Laurie McNeill, review of *The Wolves of Woden,* p. 32.
Resource Links, October, 2001, Krista Johansen, review of *The Wolves of Woden,* p. 36; October, 1999, Connie Hall, review of *White as the Waves,* p. 24; winter, 2002, K. V. Johansen, review of *The Witches of Willomere,* p. 24.

*   *   *

BAKER, Ernest W., Jr. 1926-

PERSONAL: Born October 20, 1926, in Sedalia, MO; son of Ernest W. (a business owner) and Sara Elizabeth (Staples) Baker; married September 4, 1948; wife's name Joan E. (a homemaker; deceased); children: Robert, Michael. *Ethnicity:* "Caucasian." *Education:* University of Missouri, B.J., 1948. *Politics:* Republican. *Religion:* Lutheran. *Hobbies and other interests:* Farming.

ADDRESSES: Home—2441 Cedar Key Dr., Lake Orion, MI 48360. *E-mail*—erniewbaker@msn.com.

CAREER: Zimmer-Keller, Inc. (advertising agency), employee, beginning 1948; E. W. Baker, Inc. (advertising agency), Troy, MI, founder and chief executive officer, 1964-89; BBDO Detroit, Troy, MI, executive vice president, 1990-2000; writer, 2000—. *Military service:* U.S. Army, Infantry during World War II; served in the South Pacific.

MEMBER: Veterans of Foreign Wars, Adcraft Club of Detroit.

AWARDS, HONORS: D.Sc., Cleary College.

WRITINGS:

A Fifty-Year Adventure in the Advertising Business, Wayne State University Press (Detroit, MI), 2000.

WORK IN PROGRESS: A novel.

SIDELIGHTS: Ernest W. Baker, Jr. told *CA:* "I began my fifty-two-year career in the advertising business with the Zimmer-Keller, Inc. advertising agency in 1948. I founded the E. W. Baker, Inc. advertising agency in 1964 and was responsible for guiding that agency through twenty-six years of operation. The agency was acquired by DDB Needham Worldwide in 1990, but in 1993 the agency's parent corporation, the Omnicom Group, transferred the accounts and staff to BBDO Detroit.

"During my career in the advertising business I handled the advertising for companies in a variety of business categories. Some of these companies I was involved with for many years—two of them for more than forty years. They include Standard Federal Bank, Stroh's Beer, the Detroit Tigers baseball team, Better Made Potato Chips, Awrey's bakeries, Little Caesars, Michigan Apples, Huron Cement, Hardees, Howard Johnson's Restaurants, Vernor's ginger ale, and several divisions of the Stanley Tool Works. I retired December 31, 2000. My career is described in the book *A Fifty-Year Adventure in the Advertising Business.*"

*　　*　　*

BALDINI, Antonio 1889-1962

PERSONAL: Born October 10, 1889, in Rome, Italy; died November 6, 1962, in Florence, Italy. *Education:* Studied literature and philology at University of Bologna.

CAREER: Journalist, dramatist, poet, and editor. *Military service:* Italian Army, 1915-18, served as an officer.

WRITINGS:

Nostro Purgatorio: fatti personali del tempo della guerra italiana. 1915-1917, Fratelli Treves (Milan, Italy), 1918, reprinted, Università degli studi di Trento, Dipartimento di scienze filologiche e storiche (Trento, Italy), 1996.

Salti di gomitolo, Vallecchi (Florence, Italy), 1920.

Umori di gioventu, 1911-1915, Vallecchi (Florence, Italy), 1920.

La strada delle meraviglie, Montadori (Milan, Italy), 1923, reprinted, Einaudi (Turin, Italy), 1974.

Michelaccio, La Ronda (Rome, Italy), 1924.

Galleria: rivista mensile del Corriere italiano, serial publication Le Monnier (Florence, Italy), 1924.

Armando Spadini, La terza pagina (Rome, Italy), 1924.

Le più belle pagine di Agnolo Firenzuola, Fratelli Trevies (Milan, Italy), 1925.

Le più belle pagine di Lodovico Ariosto, Fratelli Trevies (Milan, Italy), 1928.

La dolce calamità, overo la Donna di nessuno. Quatro racconti, L'Italiano (Bologna, Italy), 1928, published as *Beato fra le donne,* Mondatori (Milan, Italy), 1940, reprinted, Sellerio (Palermo, Italy), 1992.

La Signorina Elsa, Modernissima (Milan, Italy), 1929, reprinted, Dall'Oglio (Milan, Italy), 1967.

La Italia e gli italiani del secolo XIX, Le Monnier (Florence, Italy), 1930.

Amici allo spiedo, Vallechi (Florence, Italy), 1933, published as *Italia di bonincontro,* La Nuova Italia (Florence, Italy), 1941.

L'Ottava d'oro, Mondatori (Milan-Verona, Italy), 1933.

Ludovico della tranquillità, Mondatori (Milan, Italy), 1933.

La vecchia dal Bal Bullier, L'Italiano (Rome, Italy), 1934.

Cuore d'una volta, V. Bompiani (Milan, Italy), 1935.

Poesie di Giovanni Pascoli, Mondatori (Verona, Italy), 1939.

Cattedra d'occasione, La Nuova Italia (Florence, Italy), 1941.

Il sor Pietro, Cosimo Papareschi e Tuttaditutti, Le Monnier (Florence, Italy), 1941.

Buoni incontri d'Italia, Sansoni (Florence, Italy), 1942.

Strada maestra: antologia italiana per la scuola media, Perella (Rome, Italy), 1942.

Viaggio pittorico e sentimentale sul Reno, Le Monnier (Florence, Italy), 1942.

Bertoldo, Bertoldino e Cacasenno, Colombo (Rome, Italy), 1943.

Diagonale 1930, Parigi, Ankara; note di viaggio, Mondatori (Milan, Italy), 1943.

Se rinasco. . . . , Tumminelli (Rome, Italy), 1944.

Rugantino, er commedione (sonnets), Colombo (Rome, Italy), 1944.

Da Montecavallo alle Tuileries con la prigionia nel forte di Finestrelle, 1809-1813, Colombo (Rome, Italy), 1944.

De Amicis, Garzanti (Milan, Italy), 1945.

Il libro delle 40 novelle, dei migliori scrittori italiani e stranieri, O. E. T. Bottega dell'antiquario (Rome, Italy), 1946.

La Toscanina; pagine dell'800, Colombo (Rome, Italy), 1946.

Fine Ottocento, Le Monnier (Florence, Italy), 1947.

Pastoso, Garzanti (Milan, Italy), 1947.

La monaca di Monza, Universale Economica (Milan, Italy), 1950.

Melafumo; quindici variazioni, Edizione Radio Italiana, 1950.

(With Leonetta C. Pieraccini) *Visti di Vicino,* Vallecchi Editore (Florence, Italy), 1952.

Il libro dei buoni incontri di guerra e di pace, Sansoni (Florence, Italy), 1953.

(Editor, with Calogero Fazio) *Buoni incontri: antologia italina e pagine di scrittori stranieri ad uso del Ginnasi superiori e del Licel Scientifici,* Montadori (Milan, Italy), 1953.

VII (i.e. Settimo) quadriennale nazionale d'arte di Roma, novembre 1955-Aprile 1956, De Luca (Rome, Italy), 1955.

Italia sottovoce, Sansoni (Florence, Italy), 1956.

Quel caro magon di Lucia; microscopie manzoniane, R. Ricciardi (Milan, Italy), 1956.

Il Doppio Melafumo, Edizione Radio Italiana (Turin, Italy), 1957.

Simpatia di Roma, Almanacco Torrioni (Milan, Italy), 1957.

Romana per lettori e veditori, Fratelli Lega (Faenza, Italy), 1957.

Michelaccio; Racconti, Mondatori (Verona, Italy), 1958.

Ariosto e dintorni, S. Sciascia (Rome, Italy), 1958.

Studi pascoliani, Stab. Grafico F. Lli Lega (Faenza, Italy), 1958.

VIII quadriennale nazionale d'arte di Roma; Dicembre 1959-aprile 1960, Mondatori (Verona, Italy), 1959.

Nuovi racconti italiani, Nuova Accademia esitrice (Milan, Italy), 1962.

Gente di Trastevere, Mondatori (Verona, Italy), 1963.

Poesie, Mondatori (Milan, Italy), 1965.

Un sogno dentro l'altro, Mondatori (Milan, Italy), 1965.

Sole di febbraio, U. Mursia (Milan, Italy), 1967.

La Scala di servizio; introduzione al libro e alla lettura, R. Ricciardi (Milan, Italy), 1971.

Il lettore in pantofole, M. Bulzoni (Rome, Italy), 1971.

Tastiera, Fratelli Palombi (Rome, Italy), 1977.

Michelaccio; e, Rugantino, Longanesi (Milan, Italy), 1981.

Carteggio: 1911-1954, Edizioni scientifiche italiane (Naples, Italy), 1984.

Ricerche sulla storia di Eunapio di Sardi: problemi di storiografia tardopagana, CLUEB (Bologna, Italy) 1984.

Avvenimenti e discorsi, Pàtron (Bologna, Italy), 1985.

Il Sor Pietro, l'Antologia e la Nuova antologia, Le Monnier (Florence, Italy), 1989.

Carteggio: 1915-1960, Edizioni scientifiche italiane (Naples, Italy), 1984.

Carteggio: 1929-1961, Edizioni di storia e letteratura (Rome, Italy), 1992.

Carteggio: 1933-1962, Le Monnier (Florence, Italy), 1992.

Galleria: una revista di Soffici e Baldini sotto il fascismo; gennaio-maggio 1924, Le Monnier (Florence, Italy), 1992.

Carteggio: 1912-1962, Edizioni di storia e letteratura (Rome, Italy), 1993.

Carteggio: 1915-1962, Edizioni di storia e letteratura (Rome, Italy), 1997.

Carteggio: 1915-1955, Edizioni scientifiche italiane (Naples, Italy), 1997.

Storie Perdute: III secolo d.C., Pàtron (Bologna, Italy), 2000.

Author's works have been translated into French.

SIDELIGHTS: Antonio Baldini was an Italian neoclassicist writer, poet, and critic whose work, full of humor and fantasy, spanned five turbulent decades. He was born into a well-to-do Roman family on October 10, 1889, about thirty years after Italy had achieved its unification, and studied literature and philology at the University of Bologna.

In the years leading up to Italy's entry in World War I, Baldini worked as a journalist for *La Voce* magazine while associating with a closed circle of young intellectuals in Rome. In 1914 he published his first novel, *Pazienze e impazienze di Maestro Pastoso,* which could be seen as a summing up of Baldini's intellectual formation during his early years. Between 1915 and 1918 he served as an Italian army officer in the first world war and upon returning home he published *Nostro Purgatorio,* an acclaimed memoir of his military experience that was among the earliest chronicles of the heroism and disillusion in that war. After a short period of working as a businessman in Upper Silesia, he threw himself into journalism and became one of the founders of *La Ronda.* He was also an active member of a group of intellectuals who frequented the "terza saletta" of Rome's Café Aragno. These young men, who could be seen as forerunners to the Paris café society of the 1920s, debated on everything from the growing industrialization and rigid conformism of Italian society (ultimately to culminate in fascism) to the influence of classical literature on their rapidly changing world.

In 1920, Baldini published *Salti di gomitolo.* This was the first in a series of works characterized by a desire to confront serious issues behind a mask of humor, fantasy, and fragmentary allusions that owed much to the classical tradition. The book is broken into two parts, "Echi del Nostro Disfattismo," and "Lavori di Striglia, Rasoio. E di Gomma." The second part is a blend of poetry, prose, and fantasy that focuses on liberation from the self and the fragmentary world Baldini inhabited. His criticism of other works in the book ultimately relates back to himself, this type of criticism becoming an aspect of all of Baldini's later writing.

In 1923 came *La strada delle meraviglie,* a work based around three sisters and their fairytale-like desire to marry a king's baker, cook, and son respectively. Complete with a wicked queen and a witch, the book revolves around sorcery, magic, and the good sisters' actions, with all eventually finishing well. A year later Baldini published the partly autobiographical *Michelaccio,* perhaps his most famous work. This book humorously traces the life of its titular hero, "a scamp blessed with a down-to-earth attitude and fantastic good luck," wrote Luigi Scanzo in *Encyclopedia of World Literature in the Twentieth Century.* Through the 1920s, Baldini continued to contribute to newspapers such as *Corriere della Sera* and *La Tribuna,* finally becoming editor of *Nuova Anthologia* in 1931 while remaining prolific as a writer. In 1929 *La dolce calamità* appeared, paying homage to women Baldini loved, both in the real world and that of his fertile imagination. Particularly notable is the fairytale "Il gigante Paolone e la piccola Mabruca." In *Amici allo spiedo,* published in 1932, Baldini used his well-honed wit to gently make fun of intellectual/artistic contemporaries such as Chirico, Spadini, and Croce. While the sketches are well defined and often humorous, they never resort to nastiness. Continuing on the theme of remembering intellectual colleagues, Baldini published *La vecchia dal Bal Bullier,* a memoir of his experiences in Paris café society during the 1920s. Baldini's heart, however, always remained in Rome, and the visions of his native city were central to the work he created. In 1942, with Italy at war and seriously divided, he produced one of his most important works in *Rugantino.* Using many of the same techniques of blending fantasy and reality used in *Michelaccio,* Baldini paid homage to the Rome he loved and its transformation through the centuries.

Although none of Baldini's works gained widespread popularity—his fragmentary style was appreciated mostly by intellectually sophisticated readers—he stayed busy to the end of his life. Some of his later works include *Se rinasco, Melafumo, quindici variazioni, Italia sottovoce,* and the posthumously released *Un sogno dentro l'altro.* He also continued editing books of poetry and literature by leading Italian figures such as Giovanni Pascoli and others. Baldini died in Florence on November 6, 1962. Although Baldini's Italy had been devastated by two world wars and twenty-one years under fascism, his colorful and often humorous visions were frequently in open contrast to the violent years in which he wrote.

BIOGRAPHICAL AND CRITICAL SOURCES:

BOOKS

Di Biase, Carmine, *Antonio Baldini,* Mursia (Milan, Italy), 1973.

Di Biase, Carmine, *Lessico di Antonio Baldini,* Sansoni (Florence, Italy), 1974.

Fleishmann, Wolfgang Bernard, editor, *Encyclopedia of World Literature in the Twentieth Century,* Frederick Ungar Publishing Co. (New York, NY), 1965.

Orioli, Giovanni, *Lettura di Baldini,* 1st di Studi romani (Rome, Italy), 1965.

Zennario, Silvio, editor, *Dante nella i etteratura italiana del Novocento,* Bonacci (Rome, Italy), 1979.

PERIODICALS

Alla Bottega, Volume 8, 1970, Carmine Di Biase, "La grande guerra in Baldini e i suoi contemporanei," pp. 5-8.

Arcadia, Accademia Letteraria Italiana, Volume 4, 1963, Emerico Giachery, "Ricordo di Antonio Baldini," pp. 102-104.

Aspetti Letterari, Volume 30, 1970, pp. 19-27.

Baretti, Volume 3, 1962, Giuseppe Toffanin, "Ricordo di Antonio Baldini," pp. 21-23.

Brigata, Volume 18, 1973, Antonio Gallo, "Tre saggisti meridionali per Dante, Baldini e Febonio," pp. 12-15.

Capitolium, Volume 38, 1963, Livio Jannatoni, "Baldini, figlio pacioso di una roma ottocentesca," pp. 22-24.

Carovana, Volume 12, 1962, Filiberto Mazzoleni, "Profilo di Antonio Baldini," pp. 219-221.

Citta di Vita, Volume 25, 1970, Carmine di Biase, "La Roma Visita di Baldini," pp. 45-54.

Convivium, Volume 31, 1963, Mario Cincinnati, "Antonio Baldini," pp. 72-74.

Giornale d'Italia, Volume 21-22, 1972, Luigi Pasquini, "Ricordo di Antonio Baldini," p. 3.

Idea, Volume 26, 1970, Carmine Di Biase, "Confessioni e impegno d'uomo in Echi del nostro disfattismo," pp. 52-58; Volume 28, 1972, Carmine Di Biase, "Antonio Baldinia nel 1920," pp. 51-54.

Italia che Scrive, Volume 45, 1962, Massimo Grillando, "Antonio Baldini," pp. 213-217.

Lettore di Provincia, August, 1993, Manuela Ricci, "Baldini-Panzini: Un percorso tra le carte del fondo 'A Baldinia' della Biblioteca Comunale di Santarchangelo di Romagna," pp. 27-34; December, 1994, "Lettere di Antonio Baldini," pp. 63-74.

Letture, Volume 18, 1963, Luigi Cattoretti, "Antonio Baldini stillista prezioso," pp. 163-176.

Martinella, Volume 17, 1963, Luigi Pasquini, "Antonio Baldini, ovvero buonicontri e buonumore," pp. 277-286; Volume 26, 1972, Nello Vian, "Antonio Baldinia, Giovanni Beltrami e l'amor del libro," pp. 291-296.

Narrativa, Volume 9, 1964, Gino Raya, "Diciannove lettere di A. Baldini," pp. 55-62.

Nuova Antologia, Volume 98, 1963, "Omaggio ad Antonio Baldini."

Osservatore Political Letterario, Volume 8, 1962, Giovanni Titta Rosa, "Baldini e Melafumo," pp. 29-32; Volume 10, 1964, Mariano Moretti, "Mezzo Secolo con Baldini," pp. 63-69; Volume 16, 1970, pp. 73-82.

Rassegna della Letteratura Italiana, Volume 83, 1979, Umberto Carpi, "Il Primo Baldini," pp. 307-315.

Silarus, September-October 2001, Filberto Mazzoleni, "Antonio Baldinia e il suo amore per Roma," pp. 16-19.

Studi Romani, January, 1984, Eugenio Ragni, "Rileggiamo (Meglio) Antonio Baldini," pp. 49-60.

Vita e Pensiero, Volume 45, 1962, Pina Romagnoli Robuschi, "Antonio Baldini," pp. 823-826; Volume 52, 1969, Carmine di Biase, "Lavori di striglia, di rasoio e di penna di Antonio Baldini," pp. 919-928.*

BALMUTH, Daniel 1929-

PERSONAL: Born June 20, 1929 in New York, NY; son of Martin (a salesman) and Betty (a homemaker) Balmuth; married Rita Jackmow (a social worker), June 27, 1953; children: Susan, David, Michael. *Education:* City College, B.S.S., 1950; Cornell University, M.A., 1951, Ph.D., 1959. *Politics:* Democrat. *Religion:* Jewish.

ADDRESSES: Home—17 Marion Place, Saratoga Springs, NY 12166. *E-mail*—dbalmuth@skidmore.edu.

CAREER: State University of New York at Plattsburgh, assistant professor of history, 1956-58; Skidmore College, Saratoga Springs, NY, assistant professor, then professor of history, 1958-98.

MEMBER: American Association for Slavic Studies.

AWARDS, HONORS: Fulbright Award for travel to Finland, 1961-62; IREX grant for study in the Soviet Union, 1966; Malt Endowment Summer Seminars, 1983, 1994.

WRITINGS:

Censorship in Russia, 1865-1905, University Press of America (Lanham, MD), 1979.
The Russian Bulletin, 1863-1917, Peter Lang (New York, NY), 2002.

Contributor of book reviews to *Choice,* 1969—.

SIDELIGHTS: Daniel Balmuth told *CA* that his primary motivation for writing is "to offer a knowledge of Russian history that will enable the reader to understand contemporary Russia. In addition, I was interested in the viewpoint of Russian liberalism in the period before the Bolshevik Revolution."

*   *   *

BARRETT, Kim E(laine) 1958-

PERSONAL: Born June 21, 1958, in London, England; daughter of Peter William (a master builder) and Kathleen (an administrative assistant; maiden name, McNally) Barrett; married Philip Bonomo, July 2, 1988 (divorced, May, 1992); married Peter Henderson

Pierce (a career naval officer), November 16, 2002. *Ethnicity:* "Caucasian." *Education:* University College, London, B.Sc. (with honors), 1979, Ph.D., 1982. *Hobbies and other interests:* Cooking, theater, dance, British contemporary literature, film, academic career development.

ADDRESSES: Home—San Diego, CA. *Office*—School of Medicine, University of California—San Diego, 8414 Medical Center, 200 West Arbor Dr., San Diego, CA 92103; fax: 619-543-6969. *E-mail*—kbarrett@ucsd.edu.

CAREER: National Institutes of Health, Bethesda, MD, visiting fellow, 1982-85; University of California—San Diego, La Jolla, CA, assistant professor, 1985-92, associate professor, 1992-96, professor of medicine, 1996—, vice chair for research at School of Medicine, 1999—.

MEMBER: American Gastroenterological Association (chair of intestinal disorders section, 2001-03), American Physiological Society (member of council, 2001-04), Gastroenterology Research Group (president, 1998-2000).

AWARDS, HONORS: Young Investigator Award, American Gastroenterological Association/Gastroenterology Research Group, 1994; Bowditch Award, American Physiological Society, 1996; McKenna Lectureship, Canadian Association of Gastroenterology, 2003.

WRITINGS:

(Editor, with others) *Neuroimmunophysiology of the Gastrointestinal Mucosa,* New York Academy of Sciences, 1992.
(Editor, with others) *Gastrointestinal Transport,* Academic Press (Orlando, FL), 2001.

Contributor to more than eighty books. Contributor of numerous seventy articles to scientific journals, including *American Journal of Physiology.* Editor-in-chief, *American Journal of Physiology-Cell Physiology,* 1996-2002.

WORK IN PROGRESS: Gastrointestinal Physiology, a textbook; research on epithelial biology, signal transduction, inflammatory bowel diseases, cystic fibrosis, and infectious diarrhea.

SIDELIGHTS: Kim Barrett told *CA:* "I write to communicate—to students, colleagues, and other scientists. My goal is to convey complex technical information in a way that is accessible even to the uninitiated. My inspiration for my current work in progress, a textbook for first-year medical students, is to aid me in teaching them more effectively and instill in them an abiding interest in intestinal physiology."

*   *   *

BEAVER, Harold (Lothar) 1929-2002

OBITUARY NOTICE—See index for *CA* sketch: Middle name is sometimes spelled "Lowther"; born Helmut Lothar Bibergeil, June 27, 1929, in Dessau, Germany; died of a heart attack June 9, 2002. Literary scholar, educator, and author. Beaver left his native Germany as a child, before the outbreak of World War II. He was educated in England at Oxford University, then pursued graduate studies in the United States at Harvard University. When he returned to England, Beaver devoted himself to the promotion of American literature in England. He began as an editor for Oxford University Press and contributed frequently to the *Times Literary Supplement.* Eventually Beaver accepted a position at the University of Warwick, where innovative programs in American studies and comparative literature were beginning to emerge as respectable approaches to interdisciplinary research. Beaver's approach to literary interpretation diverged from the conventions of his day, and the subjects of his attention were often authors whose writings also challenged convention. Beaver was lauded for his heavily annotated edition of Herman Melville's *Moby Dick* in 1972, but a journal article he published eleven years later on homosexual allusions in the novel provoked a certain amount of controversy. The method of analysis employed by Beaver for that article was deconstruction, also controversial at the time; his article on *Moby Dick* has since been cited as a factor in the continuing popularity of deconstructionism as a tool for gender research. Beaver produced literary editions of other authors as well: Edgar Allan Poe, Lewis Carroll, and Mark Twain. His 1987 study of *Huckleberry Finn* included an early interpretation of Twain's treatment of the issue of slavery. Beaver moved to the University of Amsterdam in the 1980s to head a new American literature program there. In Amsterdam he wrote *The Great American Masquerade,* in which he commented on a wide range of cultural figures from colonial days to the twentieth century. He spent his final years in Thailand.

OBITUARIES AND OTHER SOURCES:

PERIODICALS

Times (London, England), July 23, 2002, p. 28.

*   *   *

BELBEL, Sergi 1963-

PERSONAL: Born May 29, 1963, in Terrasa, Spain. *Education:* Studied French and Romance philology.

ADDRESSES: *Office*—Dept. of Dramatic Literature, Institut del Teatre de la Disputaciò de Barcelona.

CAREER: Autonomous University of Barcelona, Barcelona, Spain, created theater course, 1983; Institut del Teatre de la Disputaciò de Barcelona, professor of theater literature, beginning 1988; translator, playwright, and director.

AWARDS, HONORS: Marquès de Bradomin Prize, 1985, for *A.G./V.W. Calidoscopios y faros de hoy.*

WRITINGS:

PLAYS

A.G./V.W. Calidoscopios y faros de hoy (first performed c. 1985), Centro Nacional de Nuevas Tendencias Escénicas (Madrid, Spain), 1986.

Dins la seva memòria, Edicions 62 (Barcelona, Spain), 1988.

Elsa Schneider, Institut del Teatre de la Diputació de Barcelona (Barcelona, Spain), 1988.

En companyia d'abisme: i altres obres, Edicions 62 (Barcelona, Spain), 1990, translation of title play by John London published as *Deep Down* in *Modern International Drama,* State University of New York (Binghamton, NY), 1993.

(And director) *Tàlem* (first produced at the Teatre Romea, Spain, 1990), Editorial Lumen (Barcelona, Spain), 1992, translation by Sharon G. Feldman published as *Fourplay* in *Contemporary Catalan Plays,* edited by David George and John London, Methuen (London, England), 2000.

Carícies, Edicions 62 (Barcelona, Spain), 1992, translation by John London published as *Caresses* in *Spanish Plays,* edited by Elyse Dodgson and Mary Peate, Nick Hern Books (London, England), 1999.

(With Miquel Górriz) *Minim'mal show,* E. Climent (Valencia, Spain), 1992.

Després de la pulja, Editorial Lumen (Barcelona, Spain), 1993, translation by John London, Xavier Rodriguez Rosell, and David George published as *After the Rain* in *Klaus Chatten and Sergei Belbel: Sugar Dollies and After the Rain,* Methuen (London, England), 1996.

Morir: Un moment abans de morir, Tres i Quatre (Valencia, Spain), 1995.

(With Òscar Roig and Jordi Sànchez) *Sóc lletja: Un musical antiestètic,* Edicions 62 (Barcelona, Spain), 1997.

Criatures, Edicions 62 (Barcelona, Spain), 1998.

La Sang, Edicions 62 (Barcelona, Spain), 1998.

El tiempo de Planck; La sangre, La Avispa (Madrid, Spain), 2000.

Ivern, Empúries (Barcelona, Spain), 2002.

Has also translated the works of several other dramatists into Catalan; his own works have been translated into several languages, including Spanish, French, German, and English.

ADAPTATIONS: *Carícies* has been adapted as a film by director Ventura Pons.

SIDELIGHTS: Sergei Belbel was born in the Catalan region of Spain in 1963. After studying the philology of Romance languages, he created the theater course at the Autonomous University of Barcelona in 1983. Belbel's first major work of experimental theater, *A.G./V.W. Calidoscopios y faros de hoy,* garnered him the Marquès de Bradomin Prize in 1985. Though this play, which puts together the characters of French writer André Gide and English novelist Virginia Woolf, originally appeared in Spanish, Belbel has written most of his ouvre in his native Catalan. He has continued to cultivate the experimental in his dramas; indeed, Eduardo Galán in *Primer Acto: Cuadernos de Investigacion Teatral* stated that Belbel is not interested in telling stories in his plays, but rather in showing moments of human conflict. Galán further noted that Belbel's plays are difficult, closed, complicated, and aimed at a small, intellectual audience. The critic did not mean this in a negative sense, and went on to praise Belbel's 1990 effort *En companyia d'abisme* for its perfect structure. Belbel's plays have been translated into several languages, including Spanish, French, English, and German. He has also served as a translator himself, making the works of many international dramatists available in Catalan.

One of Belbel's best-known plays is *Després de la pulja,* which has been translated into English as *After the Rain. Després de la pulja* is set in the surreal environment of an office rooftop, where everyone goes to smoke in secret because smoking has been banned. This illicit refuge also becomes the scene of burgeoning romances and office politics. The characters include three secretaries who look exactly alike except for their hair color.

Belbel's other plays include *Tàlem,* in which a husband and wife buy a newly designed bed and insist that their friends make love in it first before they themselves use it. *En companyia d'abisme* is even more experimental, in that it consists of two characters who must remain completely motionless except for a few special maneuvers that are excruciatingly painful when executed. *Carícies* is another of Belbel's better-known pieces. The play, which features a variety of different couples in scenes of severe miscommunication, has been adapted as a film by director Ventura Pons.

BIOGRAPHICAL AND CRITICAL SOURCES:

PERIODICALS

Assaig de Teatre, September-December, 1998, Sharon G. Feldman, "Dos conversaciones con Sergi Belbel," pp. 219-237.
Estreno, fall, 1998, David George, "The Reception of Sergi Belbel's *Despres de la pluja,*" pp. 50-57.
Lletra de Canvi, March, 1989, Joan Casas, "Sergi Belbel: Faedor de teatre," pp. 7-11.
New York Times, June 8, 1999, Anita Gates, "Big Brother Wants You to Quit Smoking," p. B5.
Primer Acto, March-April, 1990, Eduardo Galán, "Sergi Belbel artifice de la renovacion escenica," pp. 82-88; November-December, 1997, Irene Sadowska, "Tres españoles en Francia," pp. 143-145.
Vanidad, April, 1997, Javier Cortijo, review of *Morir,* p. 129.

OTHER

Rutgers University Web site, http://www.rci.rutgers.edu/ (March 21, 2002), "Sergi Belbel."
Terrassa, http://www.terrassa.org/ (May 7, 2002), "Sergi Belbel."*

*　　*　　*

BELL, Alan P(aul) 1932-2002

OBITUARY NOTICE—See index for *CA* sketch: Born January 18, 1932, in Newark, NJ; died of a stroke May 13, 2002, in Bloomington, IN. Psychologist, minister, educator, and author. Bell was responsible for groundbreaking research in the study of homosexuals, holding that homosexuality was the result of biology rather than improper socialization. Bell's education was diverse; he received a bachelor's degree in philosophy from the University of the South in 1952, a master's degree in divinity from General Theological Seminary in 1955, and a Ph.D. in counseling from Columbia University in 1967. During the late 1950s, he was an Episcopal minister and cofounded a parish in Denville, New Jersey. His interest in counseling people, however, led to his study of psychology; and his interest in problematic sexual habits came when he helped counsel a sex offender at the Veterans Administration hospital in New York. This resulted in his first book, written with Calvin S. Hall, titled *The Personality of a Child Molester: An Analysis of Dreams* (1971). After receiving his doctorate, Bell taught at Indiana University, Bloomington, becoming a professor of education in 1974. He also became a senior research psychologist at the Kinsey Institute, where he was vice president for twelve years. While at the institute Bell became involved in a study of homosexual men living in San Francisco, with the goal of discovering the root cause of homosexuality. Contrary to popular belief at the time, Bell concluded that homosexuality was not the result of how someone is raised but, rather, it was caused by a biological predisposition for this behavior. Written with Martin S. Weinberg, Bell's 1978 work *Homosexualities: A Study of Diversity among Men and Women* contains the conclusions to this study. It was followed by two other books on the subject: *Sexual Preference: The Development in Men and Women* (1981), written with Weinberg and Sue Kiefer Hammersmith, and *The Mind and Heart in Human Sexual Behavior: Owning and Sharing Our Personal*

Truths (1997). Although Bell's ideas about homosexuality were initially quite controversial, over time they gained wide acceptance within the scientific community.

OBITUARIES AND OTHER SOURCES:

PERIODICALS

Los Angeles Times, May 26, 2002, p. B21.
New York Times, May 24, 2002, p. C11.
Washington Post, May 28, 2002, p. B6.

* * *

BENJAMIN, Lois
    See GOULD, Lois

* * *

BENNETT, Paul Lewis 1921-2002

OBITUARY NOTICE—See index for *CA* sketch: Born January 21, 1921, in Gnadenhutten, OH; died of cancer May 28, 2002, in Granville, OH. Educator, poet, and author. Bennett joined the faculty at Denison University in 1947 and taught English there for approximately forty years; he was appointed to the Lorena Woodrow Burke Chair of English in 1978 and was designated poet-in-residence at Denison in 1986. In 1953 Bennett founded a writing program at the university; it was one of the first college writing programs in the United States that was open to undergraduate students. Bennett was himself a writer. His poetry collections include *A Strange Affinity* and *The Eye of Reason.* In the 1990s he wrote *Appalachian Mettle* and *Max: The Tale of a Waggish Dog.* Bennett also worked as a film writer and contributed to various literary journals and other magazines.

OBITUARIES AND OTHER SOURCES:

PERIODICALS

Atlanta Journal-Constitution, May 31, 2002, p. C7.
Chronicle of Higher Education, June 14, 2002, p. A39.
Houston Chronicle, May 31, 2002, p. 42.

BENTLEY, James 1937-

PERSONAL: Born March 9, 1937, in England; son of James (a miner) and Dorothy (a homemaker) Bentley; married, 1962; wife's name Audrey W.; children: Joanna Davson, Emma-Jane Debat. *Education:* Oxford University, M.A. (history), 1959, M.A. (religion), 1962; University of Sussex, D.Phil., 1980. *Politics:* "Passionate on issues but not a party member." *Religion:* Church of England.

ADDRESSES: Home and office—Turnac, 24250 Domme, France; fax: 0044553281553.

CAREER: Thames & Hudson, London, England, travel writer. *Military service:* Territorial Army (Great Britain), became major, awarded Territorial Decoration.

WRITINGS:

Ritualism and Politics in Victorian Britain: The Attempt to Legislate for Belief, Oxford University Press (New York, NY), 1978.
Cry for God: The Survival and Mission of the British Churches, Bowerdean Press (London, England), 1978.
Between Marx and Christ: The Dialogue in German-speaking Europe, 1870-1970, NLB (London, England), 1982.
(Reteller) *Children's Bible,* illustrated by Colin and Moira Maclean, F. Watts (New York, NY), 1983.
(With Warwick Rodwell) *Our Christian Heritage,* G. Philip (London, England), 1984.
Martin Neimöller, 1892-1984, Free Press (New York, NY), 1984.
Restless Bones: The Story of Relics, Constable (London, England), 1985.
A Guide to the Dordogne, Penguin (New York, NY), 1986.
Secrets of Mount Sinai: The Story of the World's Oldest Bible—Codex Sinaiticus, Doubleday (Garden City, NY), 1986.
A Calendar of Saints: The Lives of the Principal Saints of the Christian Year, Facts on File (New York, NY), 1986.
Life and Food in the Dordogne, New Amsterdam (New York, NY), 1987.
A Guide to Tuscany, Viking (New York, NY), 1987.

Languedoc, photographs by Charlie Waite, Salem House (Topsfield, MA), 1987.

The Rhine, photographs by Charlie Waite, Salem House (Topsfield, MA), 1989.

Albert Schweitzer: The Doctor Who Gave Up a Brilliant Career to Serve the People of Africa, G. Stevens (Milwaukee, MN), 1989.

Dare to Be Wise: A History of the Manchester Grammar School, James X James (London, England), 1990.

Alsace, Penguin (New York, NY), 1990.

(With Patricia Lantier) *Albert Schweitzer: The Doctor Who Devoted His Life to Africa's Sick,* G. Stevens Children's Books (Milwaukee, MN), 1991.

Albert Schweitzer: The Enigma, HarperCollins (New York, NY), 1992.

(Editor) *Some Corner of a Foreign Field: Poetry of the Great War,* Little, Brown (Boston, MA), 1992.

A Guide to Eastern Germany, Viking (New York, NY), 1993.

Fort Towns of France: The Bastides of the Dordogne & Aquitaine, photographs by Francesco Venturi, Tauris Parke Books (London, England), 1993.

The Most Beautiful Villages of Tuscany, photographs by Hugh Palmer, Thames & Hudson (New York, NY), 1995.

The Most Beautiful Villages of the Dordogne, photographs by Hugh Palmer, Thames & Hudson (New York, NY), 1996.

(Editor) *The Tongues of Men & of Angels: Inspirational Poetry & Prose from the Renaissance to the Restoration,* Little, Brown (Boston, MA), 1996.

To Live in France, photographs by Michael Busselle, Thames & Hudson (London, England), 1997.

The Most Beautiful Villages of Burgundy, Thames & Hudson (New York, NY), 1998.

The Most Beautiful Villages of England, Thames & Hudson (New York, NY), 1999.

The Most Beautiful Villages of Brittany, Thames & Hudson (New York, NY), 1999.

The Most Beautiful Villages of the Loire, Thames & Hudson (London, England), 2001.

The Most Beautiful Country Towns of Tuscany, photographs by Alex Ramsay, Thames & Hudson (New York, NY), 2001.

SIDELIGHTS: James Bentley is an experienced travel writer who specializes in European villages. *The Most Beautiful Villages of the Dordogne,* for instance, introduces readers to the French region named for the river that flows through it. *Booklist*'s Brad Hooper

praised the "buoyant text" that describes the area's local cuisine and dramatic history, while *The Most Beautiful Villages of Tuscany* allows for "incomparable vicarious travel," according to Hooper. *To Live in France* takes the reader beyond Paris to travel from village to village. As Hooper declared in another *Booklist* review, the book "beckons us to stay a while to appreciate the geographical and cultural diversity that is la belle France."

BIOGRAPHICAL AND CRITICAL SOURCES:

PERIODICALS

Biblical Archaeologist, March, 1989, review of *Secrets of Mount Sinai: The Story of the World's Oldest Bible—Codex Sinaiticus,* pp. 40-41.

Booklist, March 15, 1992, Gilbert Taylor, review of *Albert Schweitzer: The Enigma,* p. 1325; November 15, 1995, Brad Hooper, review of *The Most Beautiful Villages of Tuscany,* p. 533; October 1, 1996, Brad Hooper, review of *The Most Beautiful Villages of the Dordogne,* p. 317; January 1, 1998, Brad Hooper, review of *To Live in France,* p. 767.

Book Report, November-December, 1992, Sharon Howell, review of *Albert Schweitzer: The Enigma,* p. 49.

Commonweal, February 24, 1984, Cornel West, review of *Between Marx and Christ: The Dialogue in German-speaking Europe 1870-1970,* p. 124.

Contemporary Review, February, 1998, Richard Mullen, review of *God's Representatives: The Eight Twentieth-Century Popes,* pp. 104-105.

First Things, October, 1998, Thomas F. X. Noble, review of *God's Representatives,* pp. 34-41.

Geographical Magazine, June, 1999, review of *The Most Beautiful Villages of England,* p. 92.

Journal of Church and State, autumn, 1983, John H. Hallowell, review of *Between Marx and Christ,* p. 571-574.

Library Journal, March 15, 1992, Eric D. Albright, review of *Albert Schweitzer: The Enigma,* p. 94.

New Catholic World, January-February, 1988, Neil J. McEleney, review of *Secrets of Mount Sinai,* p. 58.

New Statesman, June 11, 1982, Donald Soper, review of *Between Marx and Christ,* pp. 24-25; August 17, 1984, Geoffrey Best, review of *Martin Neimöller, 1892-1984,* pp. 23-24.

Progressive, February, 1985, review of *Martin Neimöller,* p. 45.

Publishers Weekly, March 30, 1984, "Neimöller Biography Due from Free Press," pp. 34-35; December 6, 1985, Genevieve Stuttaford, review of *Secrets of Mount Sinai,* p. 66; January 6, 1992, review of *Albert Schweitzer: The Enigma,* p. 54.

RQ, summer, 1987, W. Keith McCoy, review of *A Calendar of Saints: The Lives of the Principal Saints of the Christian Year,* p. 509.

School Library Journal, January, 1988, Anne Douglass, review of *A Calendar of Saints,* p. 98; November, 1989, Jean H. Zimmerman, review of *Albert Schweitzer,* pp. 116-117.

Science Teacher, January, 1990, Ronald N. Giese, review of *Albert Schweitzer: The Doctor Who Devoted His Life to Africa's Sick,* pp. 86-88.

Wilson Library Bulletin, March, 1987, James Rettig, review of *A Calendar of Saints,* p. 63; March, 1991, Patty Campbell, review of *Life and Food in the Dordogne,* p. 125A.*

* * *

BLIVEN, Bruce, Jr. 1916-2002

OBITUARY NOTICE—See index for *CA* sketch: Born January 31, 1916, in Los Angeles, CA; died January 2, 2002, in New York, NY. Writer. Bliven was a respected nonfiction author who wrote a number of popular history books about New York City and state. A 1937 graduate of Harvard University, he was also the son of the managing editor of the *New Republic.* He began his career as a writer and editor for magazines and newspapers, including the *New Yorker, New York Post, New Republic,* and England's *Manchester Guardian* during the 1930s. He later became a freelance writer. Bliven's first book was a history of the typewriter, *The Wonderful Writing Machine,* published in 1954. His focus then moved on to writing books on military history—Bliven was a U.S. Army captain who served during World War II and took part in D-Day—and the history of New York state, where he lived most of his life. Several of these books, including *The Story of D-Day, June 6, 1944* (1956), *The American Revolution* (1958), *From Pearl Harbor to Okinawa* (1960), and *From Casablanca to Berlin* (1965), were written for children. His other books are for adults and include *Battle for Manhattan* (1956), *Under the Guns: New York 1775-1776* (1972), *The Finishing Touch* (1978), and *New York: A History* (1981).

OBITUARIES AND OTHER SOURCES:

BOOKS

Who's Who in America, 55th edition, Marquis (New Providence, NJ), 2001.

PERIODICALS

Los Angeles Times, January 16, 2002, p. B11.
New York Times, January 14, 2002, p. A14.
Washington Post, January 16, 2002, p. B8.

* * *

BLIVEN, Naomi 1925-2002

OBITUARY NOTICE—See index for *CA* sketch: Born December 28, 1925, in New York, NY; died January 14, 2002, in New York, NY. Journalist. Bliven made her name as a prolific contributor of book reviews to the *New Yorker.* A 1945 graduate of Hunter College in New York, she joined the staff of the *New Republic* right out of college. From 1949 to 1954 she was an editor for the New York-based publisher Random House before becoming a book reviewer for the *New Yorker* in 1958, a position she held for the rest of her life. During her career she wrote over two thousand reviews for the *New Yorker.* In addition, she published two books: *New York: The Story of the World's Most Exciting City* (1969), which she wrote with her husband, Bruce Bliven, Jr., and a 1989 novel titled *On Her Own.*

OBITUARIES AND OTHER SOURCES:

BOOKS

Who's Who of American Women, 22nd edition, Marquis, 2000.

PERIODICALS

Los Angeles Times, January 21, 2002, p. B9.
New York Times, January 19, 2002, p. A13.

BODGER, Joan
    See MERCER, Joan Bodger

*   *   *

BRENNER, Michael 1964-

PERSONAL: Born January 4, 1964, in Weiden, Germany; son of Hermann and Henny (Wolf) Brenner; married Ilana Zahavi, August 10, 1988; divoced, 1999; children: Simone. *Education:* Attended Hebrew University, 1987-88; Heidelberg College of Jewish Studies, M.A., 1988; Columbia University, Ph.D., 1994. *Religion:* Jewish.

ADDRESSES: Office—Abteilung für Jedische Geschichte und Kultur, Historisches Seminar, Universität München, Geschwister-Scholl-Platz 1, 80539 Munich, Germany.

CAREER: Indiana University, Bloomington, IN, visiting assistant professor of Jewish history, 1993-94; Brandeis University, Waltham, MA, assistant professor of modern Jewish history, 1994-97; Tauber Institute for the Study of European Jewry, assistant director, 1995-97; University of Munich, Munich, Germany, professor of Jewish history and culture, 1997—.

AWARDS, HONORS: Oldenburg Youth Book Prize, 1983.

WRITINGS:

Am Beispiel Weiden: Jüdischer Alltag im Nationalsozialismus, Arena (Würzburg, Germany), 1983.
Nach dem Holocaust: Juden in Deutschland, 1945-1950, C. H. Beck (Munich, Germany), 1995, translated as *After the Holocaust: Rebuilding Jewish Lives in Postwar Germany,* Princeton University Press (Princeton, NJ), 1997.
The Renaissance of Jewish Culture in Weimar Germany, Yale University Press (New Haven, CT), 1996.
(Coauthor) *German-Jewish History in Modern Times,* Volume 2: *1780-1871,* edited by Michael A. Meyer, C. H. Beck (Munich, Germany), 1996, Columbia University Press (New York, NY), 1997.

(Editor, with Derek Penslar) *Circles of Community: Collective Jewish Identities in Germany and Austria, 1918-1932,* Indiana University Press (Bloomington, IN), 1998.
(Editor, with Derek Penslar) *In Search of Jewish Community: Jewish Identities in Germany and Austria, 1918-1933,* Indiana University Press (Bloomington, IN), 1998.
(Editor, with Rainer Liedtke and David Rechter) *Two Nations: British and German Jews in Comparative Perspective,* M. Siebeck (Tübingen, Germany), 1999.
(Editor, with Yfaat Weiss) *Zionistische Utopie, israelische Realität: Religion und Nation in Israel,* C. H. Beck (Munich, Germany), 1999.
(Editor, with Stefan Rohrbacher) *Wissenschaft vom Judentum: Annäherungen nach dem Holocaust,* Vandenhoeck & Ruprecht (Göttingen, Germany), 2000.
Zionism: A Brief History, translated by Shelley Frisch, Markus Wiener Publishers (Princeton, NJ), 2002.

WORK IN PROGRESS: Modern Jewish historiography.

SIDELIGHTS: Michael Brenner once told CA: "I began writing history when I was a high school student in Germany and composed an essay on Jewish life during the Nazi period in the small Bavarian town where I grew up after the war. This essay, which won a national award, became my first book before I graduated from high school, and it certainly influenced my later career in a most crucial way. I was immediately fascinated with both research and writing, having in the process also discovered details about the fate of my own family during the Holocaust. I went on to study history and Jewish Studies, and continued to write. Over the years, I have gained more distance to my topics, but in some way I always feel it rather advantageous for engaged writing to have a personal relation to one's subject matter."

*   *   *

BRETT, Philip 1937-2002

OBITUARY NOTICE—See index for *CA* sketch: Born October 17, 1937, in Edwinstowe, England; died October 16, 2002, in Los Angeles, CA. Musicologist, educator, and author. Brett is credited with bringing an awareness to musical scholars of the importance of sexual identity in the works of musical composers. A graduate of King's College, Cambridge, where he earned his Ph.D. in 1965, he was an assistant lecturer at Cambridge before joining the faculty at the University of California at Berkeley in 1966 as a music professor. During the 1960s, as people became more aware of the issue of homosexuality, Brett spent a period of self-examination that led to his realization that he was gay. He then began to wonder about the sexual orientation of various musical composers and how this affected their works. Of great interest to him was the English composer Benjamin Britten, who was known to many to be homosexual although the issue was never openly discussed. When Brett published a paper about Britten and the influence of his homosexuality on his opera *Peter Grimes* it caused a great deal of controversy in the musical community. Despite suffering some criticism for this piece, however, Brett held on to his post at the university and built a reputation for writings now classified as the "new musicology," the branch of study that links music with feminism, homosexuality, and other gender and ethnic issues. Brett edited numerous books on the subject, including *Benjamin Britten: "Peter Grimes"* (1983) and the coedited book *Cruising the Performative: Interventions into the Representation of Ethnicity, Nationality, and Sexuality* (1995). He also contributed scholarly essays to journals and music encyclopedias and was general editor of *The Byrd Edition*. In 1991 Brett left Berkeley to join the faculty of the University of California at Riverside; in 2001 he moved to the University of California, Los Angeles. In addition to his teaching and writing, Brett was also a musician, playing the harpsichord and a type of Renaissance organ; he received a Grammy nomination in 1991 for a recording of his performance of "Susanna" by Handel.

OBITUARIES AND OTHER SOURCES:

BOOKS

Directory of American Scholars, tenth edition, Gale (Detroit, MI), 2002.
Who's Who in Entertainment, third edition, Marquis (New Providence, NJ), 1997.

PERIODICALS

Los Angeles Times, October 27, 2002, p. B22.
Times (London, England), November 4, 2002.

BREWSTER, Benjamin
See RODNEY, Lester

* * *

BROSNAHAN, Leger (Nicholas) 1929-

PERSONAL: Born December 11, 1929, in Kansas City, MO; son of Earl F. (a contractor) and Helen Rose (Mottin) Brosnahan; married Irene Teoh, November 7, 1967; children: Leger Nicholas, Jr., Jennifer Ru-chiau. *Ethnicity:* "Irish-French." *Education:* Georgetown University, A.B., 1951; Harvard University, M.A., 1952, Ph.D., 1957. *Politics:* "Conservative." *Religion:* Roman Catholic. *Hobbies and other interests:* Travel, gardening, reading.

ADDRESSES: Home—400 Augustine Way, Normal, IL 61761-3118. *Office*—Department of English, Illinois State University, Normal, IL 61790-4240; fax: 309-438-5414. *E-mail*—lnbrosna@ilstu.edu.

CAREER: Northwestern University, Evanston, IL, instructor in English, 1957-61; University of Hawaii at Manoa, Honolulu, assistant professor of English, 1961-63; University of Maryland at College Park, assistant professor of English, 1965-68; Illinois State University, Normal, began as associate professor, became professor of English, 1968—. Worked as a foreign expert in China, 1980-82. *Military service:* U.S. Army, 1952-54; became sergeant.

MEMBER: Mediaeval Academy of America, Modern Language Association of America, National Association of Scholars, American Association of University Professors, Association of Literary Scholars and Critics.

AWARDS, HONORS: Fulbright grants for France, 1963-65, Japan, 1968-70, and Russia, 1992-93.

WRITINGS:

Around the World in English, Kenkyusha, 1974.
Japanese and English Gesture, Taishukan, 1988.

Chinese and English Gesture, Beijing Language and Culture University Press, 1988.

Standard American English Behavior, Dongwang Munhwasa, 1998.

Contributor of book reviews to periodicals, including *Speculum.*

WORK IN PROGRESS: Korean and English Gesture; research on Spanish and English gesture.

SIDELIGHTS: The author of several books intended to benefit students of English as a second language, Leger Brosnahan told *CA* that he was inspired to write after he made a trip to China without being able to speak Chinese.

*   *   *

BULL, Schuyler M. 1974-

PERSONAL: Born November 13, 1974, in Stamford, CT; daughter of Sheppard M. Greene; stepdaughter of Sherman M. and Peggy Ann (Risom) Bull; married William D. Minckler, October 5, 2002. *Education:* Trinity College (Hartford, CT), B.A., 1997; Boston College, J.D., 2002. *Hobbies and other interests:* Horseback riding, running with her dogs, needlepoint, gardening.

ADDRESSES: Home—Norwalk, CT. *Office*—1055 Washington Blvd., 10th Floor, Stamford, CT 06902. *E-mail*—sky@minckler.org.

CAREER: Soundprints (publisher), Norwalk, CT, editorial assistant, 1996-97; Grosset & Dunlap (publisher), New York, NY, editorial assistant, 1997-98; Office of Paul Hastings (law practice), Stamford, CT, associate attorney, 2001—.

MEMBER: American Bar Association, Connecticut Bar Association, American Horse Show Association, Phi Beta Kappa.

AWARDS, HONORS: Parents' Choice Award for *Through Tsavo: A Story of an East African Savanna.*

WRITINGS:

Through Tsavo: A Story of an East African Savanna, illustrated by Paul Kratter, Soundprints (Norwalk, CT), 1998.

(Adaptor) *The Nutcracker,* illustrated by Jerry Smath, Grosset & Dunlap (New York, NY), 1999.

Along the Luangwa: A Story of an African Floodplain, illustrated by Alan Male, Soundprints (Norwalk, CT), 1999.

WORK IN PROGRESS: A novel about three women, a mother and two daughters; research for a book about a family in the midwest.

SIDELIGHTS: Schuyler M. Bull told *CA:* "According to my mother, I have always been a writer. I have been creating stories and characters in my head for as long as I can remember and have journals covering my life since I was ten years old.

"For me, writing has always been like laughing, singing, or going for a walk—just something I do to enjoy myself. I never wrote for an audience—I wrote because characters in my head demanded to be put on paper.

"My published writings grew out of an internship I did in college. I was working as an editorial assistant at a small publishing house in Connecticut when a writer broke a contract to do a book. The publisher was going crazy trying to fill the slot, and I asked if I could submit some work for consideration. The rest is, as they say, history. *Through Tsavo: A Story of an East African Savanna* led to *Along the Luangwa: A Story of an African Floodplain,* and hopefully, one day, will lead to more books.

"Regardless of whether these other books get published, I know I will always write. There are too many stories waiting to be told."

*   *   *

BURCE, Suzanne Lorraine 1929-
(Jane Powell)

PERSONAL: Born April 1, 1929 (some sources cite 1928), in Portland, OR; daughter of Paul (a malt shop owner) and Eileen Burce; married Geary Anthony Steffen, Jr., November 5, 1949 (divorced August 6, 1953);

married Patrick Nerney, November 8, 1954 (divorced, 1963); married James Fitzgerald, June 27, 1965 (marriage ended); married David Parlour, October 21, 1978 (divorced, 1981); married Dick Moore (a public relations executive and former child actor), May 21, 1988; children: (first marriage) Geary, Suzanne; (second marriage) Lindsay.

ADDRESSES: Agent—Michael Hartig Agency Ltd., 156 Fifth Ave., Suite 820, New York, NY 10010.

CAREER: Actress and singer. Film appearances include *Song of the Open Road,* United Artists, 1944; *Delightfully Dangerous,* United Artists, 1945; *Holiday in Mexico,* Metro-Goldwyn-Mayer, 1946; *A Date with Judy,* Metro-Goldwyn-Mayer, 1948; *Luxury Liner,* Metro-Goldwyn-Mayer, 1948; *Three Daring Daughters,* Metro-Goldwyn-Mayer, 1948; *Nancy Goes to Rio,* Metro-Goldwyn-Mayer, 1950; *Two Weeks with Love,* Metro-Goldwyn-Mayer, 1950; *Rich, Young, and Pretty,* Metro-Goldwyn-Mayer, 1951; *Royal Wedding,* Metro-Goldwyn-Mayer, 1951; *Small Town Girl,* Metro-Goldwyn-Mayer, 1953; *Three Sailors and a Girl,* Warner Bros., 1953; *Athena,* Metro-Goldwyn-Mayer, 1954; *Deep in My Heart,* Metro-Goldwyn-Mayer, 1954; *Seven Brides for Seven Brothers,* Metro-Goldwyn-Mayer, 1954; *Hit the Deck,* Metro-Goldwyn-Mayer, 1955; *1955 Motion Picture Theatre Celebration,* 1955; *The Girl Most Likely,* Universal, 1957; *The Enchanted Island,* Warner Bros., 1958; *The Female Animal,* Universal, 1958; *That's Entertainment!,* 1974; *Tubby the Tuba,* 1976; *Marie,* Metro-Goldwyn-Mayer/United Artists, 1985; *That's Dancing!,* 1985; *Picture This,* 1999; and *Broadway: The Golden Age, by the Legends Who Were There,* 2002.

Appearances on television series include *Turn of Fate,* NBC, 1957-58; *Loving,* ABC, 1985-86; and *Growing Pains,* 1988-91. Host of the series *The Musicals.* Appearances on TV miniseries include *Perfect Murder, Perfect Town,* CBS, 2000. Appearances on TV movies include *Mayday at 40,000 Feet!,* CBS, 1976, and *The Sandy Bottom Orchestra,* Showtime, 2000. Appearances on TV specials include *Ruggles of Red Gap,* NBC, 1957; *Standard Oil Anniversary Show,* NBC, 1957; *Give My Regards to Broadway,* NBC, 1959; *Meet Me in St. Louis,* CBS, 1959; *The Victor Borge Show,* NBC, 1960; *The Victor Borge Special,* NBC, 1960; *Hooray for Love,* CBS, 1960; *Feathertop,* ABC, 1961; *The Jane Powell Show,* NBC, 1961; *The Danny*

Thomas Special, NBC, 1967; *The Night of 100 Stars II,* ABC, 1985; *The 11th Annual Circus of the Stars,* 1986; *Happy Birthday, Hollywood!,* ABC, 1987; *An Evening with Alan Jay Lerner,* CBS, 1989; *Burt Reynolds's Conversations With . . . ,* The Nashville Network, 1991; *Nelson and Jeanette,* PBS, 1992; *Real Memories: Jane Powell,* Turner Classic Movies, 1995; *The Making of "Seven Brides for Seven Brothers,"* 1997. Appearances on episodic television include *Toast of the Town,* 1954; *Alcoa/Goodyear Theatre,* NBC, between 1957-1958; *The Andy Williams Show,* 1964; "The Jitterbug," *The Judy Garland Show,* 1964; *Fantasy Island,* ABC, 1978; *The Love Boat,* ABC, 1981; "Old Habits Die Hard," *Murder, She Wrote,* CBS, 1987; *As the World Turns; The Dick Powell Show,* NBC; and *The June Allyson Show,* CBS. Other television appearances include *Wheeler and Murdoch,* 1970, and "The Andersons: Dear Elaine," *The Letters,* ABC, 1973.

Stage appearances include *Irene,* Minskoff Theatre, New York City, 1973; *I Do! I Do!,* Pantages Theatre, Los Angeles, 1980; *The Night of 100 Stars II,* Radio City Music Hall, New York City, 1985; *Ancestral Voices,* George Street Playhouse, New Brunswick, NJ, 2000; *Avow,* Century Theatre, New York City, 2000; *70, Girls, 70,* York Theatre Company, New York City, 2000; and *Nothing like a Dame 2000,* Richard Rodgers Theatre, New York City, 2000. Appeared in the solo show *The Girl Next Door and How She Grew* (see also below); also appeared in *Cinderella,* New York City Opera; in *AfterPlay,* off-Broadway production; and in *Chapter Two, Marriage-Go-Round,* and *Same Time, Next Year.* Major tours include *Carousel!, My Fair Lady, Oklahoma!, Peter Pan, The Sound of Music,* and *South Pacific.*

Recordings include the video *The 1950s: Music, Memories, and Milestones,* 1988. Also appeared in *Fight Back with Fitness,* an exercise video for arthritis sufferers. Also recorded the album *Change Partners,* 1994. Singles include "Ride on a Rainbow" and "I Have You to Thank," both released by Verve.

AWARDS, HONORS: A star on the Hollywood Walk of Fame.

WRITINGS:

AS JANE POWELL

The Girl Next Door . . . and How She Grew (autobiography), Morrow (New York, NY), 1988.

Also author of monologue *The Girl Next Door . . . and How She Grew.*

SIDELIGHTS: Born Suzanne Lorraine Burce, Jane Powell appeared in her first film, *Song of the Open Road* (1944), when she was just fifteen years old. Her big break came in 1951, when she replaced June Allyson (who had become pregnant) and Judy Garland (who was ill) in *Royal Wedding.* Performing dances choreographed for Allyson and Garland, with steps she had not had an opportunity to sufficiently practice, Powell nevertheless made a name for herself in her role.

Throughout the 1950s, Powell's career in Hollywood flourished, and she associated with the likes of Elizabeth Taylor, with whom she was so close that each served as a bridesmaid at the other's first wedding. Powell sang at President Harry S Truman's inaugural ball in January 1949, and reached the pinnacle of her success with her performance as Milly in *Seven Brides for Seven Brothers* (1954). But as the bottom began falling out of the studio system that had prevailed during the golden age of Hollywood, and as the big-budget, lush musicals that had proliferated since the 1930s became a thing of the past, Powell's career as a starlet of the silver screen abruptly faded. She was not yet thirty years old.

In the decades that followed, Powell made a name for herself on stage and the small screen. She also created a one-woman act based on her life, calling it *The Girl Next Door . . . and How She Grew.* The title also became the name of her autobiography, published in 1988. Talking with Marian Christy of the *Boston Globe,* Powell said of her own life, "I've changed. I'm not so frantic, so nervous. Sometimes I express ideas I never knew. I used to be a person who felt held down. All I ever heard was: 'You can't!' 'You shouldn't!'. . . . I've gotten better as I've gotten older. I used to have highs and lows. Now my attitude is more steady. I used to worry if I wasn't worried. As I've gotten older, I don't have anxieties." More than a decade later, in 2000, Simi Horwitz of *Back Stage* found the septuagenarian actress still going strong, and appearing off-Broadway in Bill C. Davis's *Avow.*

BIOGRAPHICAL AND CRITICAL SOURCES:

BOOKS

Contemporary Theatre, Film, and Television, Gale (Detroit, MI), Volume 34, 2001.
Powell, Jane, *The Girl Next Door . . . and How She Grew,* Morrow (New York, NY), 1988.

PERIODICALS

Back Stage, August 4, 2000, Simi Horwitz, "From MGM's Girl-Next-Door to Modern Mom" (interview), p. 31.
Boston Globe, July 27, 1988, Marian Christy, "Confidence Finally Arrives" (interview), p. 73.
Publishers Weekly, June 17, 1988, Genevieve Stuttaford, review of *The Girl Next Door . . . and How She Grew,* p. 52.
USA Today, May 20, 1987, Nanci Hellmich, "Jane Powell at Fifty-eight: Time for Savoring" (interview and profile), p. D4.*

*   *   *

BURROWAY, Janet (Gay) 1936-

PERSONAL: Born September 21, 1936, in Phoenix, AZ; daughter of Paul M. (a tool and die worker) and Alma (a speech teacher; maiden name, Milner) Burroway; married Walter Eysselinck (a theatre director), March 18, 1961 (divorced, 1973); married William Dean Humphries, 1978 (divorced, 1981); married Peter Ruppert, 1993; children: (first marriage) Timothy Alan, Tobyn Alexander; Anne Lindsay Ruppert (stepdaughter, third marriage). *Education:* Attended University of Arizona, 1954-55; Barnard College, B.A. (cum laude), 1958; Cambridge University, B.A. (with first class honors), 1960, M.A., 1965; additional study at Yale School of Drama, 1960-61. *Politics:* Liberal.

ADDRESSES: Home—240 DeSoto St., Tallahassee, FL 32303. *E-mail*—jburroway@english.fsu.edu.

CAREER: During her school years, worked for Young Men's Hebrew Association, *New Yorker,* and for UNICEF in Paris, France; supply teacher in Binghamton, NY, 1961-63; regional director, New York State Expansion Program for Young Audiences, Inc., 1962-63; University of Sussex, Brighton, England, School of English and American Studies, 1965-70, began as assistant lecturer, became lecturer; University of Illinois at Urbana-Champaign, special assistant to the writing laboratory, 1971; Florida State University, Tallahassee, associate professor, 1971-77, professor, 1977-2002, McKenzie Professor of English literature and writing, 1986-95, Robert O. Lawton Distinguished Professor, 1995-2002, professor emerita, 2002—.

Janet Burroway

Costume designer, Belgian National Theater at Ghent, 1965-70, and Gardner Centre for the Arts, University of Sussex, 1965-71.

AWARDS, HONORS: Pulitzer Prize nomination in literature, 1970, for *The Buzzards;* AMOCO award for excellence in teaching, Florida State University, 1974; National Endowment for the Arts creative writing scholarship, 1976; runner-up for National Book Award, 1977, for *Raw Silk;* Florida Fine Arts creative writing grant, 1983-84; Florida State University Distinguished Teaching Award, 1992; Lila Wallace-*Reader's Digest* fellow, 1993-94; Reva Shiner Playwrighting Prize, Bloomington Playwright's Project, 1997; finalist, Playwrights' Center of San Francisco Annual Dramarama Competition, 1998 for *Sweepstakes;* Lawrence Foundation Award, *Prairie Schooner,* 1999; Arts & Letters Playwrighting Prize, 2001, for *Division of Property*; Pushcart Prize, 2002.

WRITINGS:

FICTION

Descend Again (novel), Faber (London, England), 1960.
The Dancer from the Dance (novel), Faber (London, England), 1965, Little, Brown (Boston, MA), 1967.

Eyes (novel), Little, Brown (Boston, MA), 1966.
The Buzzards (novel), Little, Brown (Boston, MA), 1969.
Raw Silk (novel), Little, Brown (Boston, MA), 1977.
Opening Nights (novel), Atheneum (New York, NY), 1985.
Cutting Stone (novel), Houghton Mifflin (Boston, MA), 1992.

PLAYS

Garden Party, produced at Barnard College, 1958.
The Fantasy Level, produced at Yale University School of Drama (New Haven, CT), 1961, produced at Brighton Festival, (Brighton, England), 1968.
The Beauty Operators, produced at Gardner Centre for the Arts, 1968, produced by Thames Television, London, England, 1970.
(Contributor) Palmer Bovie, editor, *Five Roman Comedies,* Dutton (New York, NY), 1970.
Hoddinott Veiling, produced by ATV Network Television (London, England), 1970.
Due Care and Attention, produced by ATV Network Television (London, England), 1973.
(Contributor) Palmer Bovie and David Slavitt, editors, *Complete Roman Drama Series,* Johns Hopkins University, 1995.
Medea with Child, produced at Bloomington Playwrights' Project (Bloomington, IN), 1997.
(Adaptor, with Charles Olsen) *Opening Nights,* National Public Radio, 1997.
Sweepstakes, produced by the Actors Repertory Theater of Tallahassee, 1999; staged reading at Playwrights' Center of San Francisco, 1998, and the Royal National Theatre Studio, London, England, 1999.

Also author of *Division of Property* and texts for dance performed by the Florida State University Dance Repertory Company: *Text/Tile,* 1991, *The Empty Dress,* 1994, *Yazoo City Station,* 1998, and *Quiltings,* 2000.

OTHER

But to the Season (poems), Keele University Press, 1961.
The Truck on the Track (juvenile), J. Cape (London, England), 1970, Bobbs-Merrill (Indianapolis, IN), 1971.

The Giant Jam Sandwich (juvenile), J. Cape (London, England), 1972, Houghton Mifflin (Boston, MA), 1973.

Material Goods (poems), University Presses of Florida (Tallahassee, FL), 1980.

Writing Fiction: A Guide to Narrative Craft, Little Brown & Co. (New York, NY), 1982, sixth edition, Longman (New York, NY), 2003.

Embalming Mom: Essays in Life, University of Iowa Press (Iowa City, Iowa), 2002.

Imaginative Writing: The Elements of Craft, Longman (New York, NY), 2003.

Contributor of poetry to anthologies, including *New Poems by American Poets No. 2,* Ballantine, 1957, *The Guinness Book of Poetry,* Putnam, 1961, and *Sound and Sense,* Harcourt, 1973. Contributor of essays to anthologies, including *A Certain Age,* Virago, 1993, *Minding the Body,* Anchor, 1994, *The Day My Father Died,* Running Press, 1994, *We Are What We Ate,* Harcourt, 1998, *Between Mothers and Sons,* Scribner, 1999, and *Letters to a Fiction Writer,* Norton, 1999. Contributor of articles to periodicals, including *Mademoiselle, Seventeen, Yale Review, Story Quarterly, Chronicle of Higher Education, Utne Review, World and I,* and *Prague Review.* Fiction reviewer, *New Statesman,* 1970-71 and 1975, and *New York Times Book Review,* 1991—; columnist, *New Letters,* 1994—.

SIDELIGHTS: "Janet Burroway is a writer of wide range and many voices," wrote Elizabeth Muhlenfeld in *Dictionary of Literary Biography.* "[Her] themes are universal—love, death, the implications of choice, human culpability—and in the broadest sense, her novels are profoundly moral. She creates a determinedly realistic world, a *comedie humaine* with tragic implications, where evil is most often the result of blindness."

Burroway is noted for the meticulous research she puts into her novels; her best-known work, *Raw Silk,* was a seven-year project. The story of the ill-fated marriage of an American woman to an English businessman, *Raw Silk* is narrated by the wife, Virginia Marbalestier. Virginia is "an engaging character; she speaks with wry intelligence and rare honesty, and she fastens onto the details of her life with a characteristic humor even when she is suffering most deeply," according to Muhlenfeld.

While Burroway "is not saying anything radically new in *Raw Silk,*" as Anatole Broyard pointed out in the *New York Times Book Review,* nevertheless "what makes [the novel] better than just another contemporary document are the good lines, like a form of personal attractiveness, which enliven its pages." Similarly, Mel Watkins, writing in the *New York Times,* found that what sets *Raw Silk* apart "is Janet Burroway's superb stylistic gifts. . . . By focusing on the nuances of marital erosion, the silences, the minute fissures and crevices that go unnoticed until they become permanent breaches, [the author] has fashioned an affecting latte of ennui and dissolution."

In Burroway's 1992 novel, *Cutting Stone,* the author presents to readers an ambitious work of historical fiction, in the opinion of *New York Times Book Review* contributor Angeline Goreau. Set against the backdrop of U.S.-Mexican relations in the years before World War I, Baltimore blueblood Eleanor Poindexter has followed her banker-husband to the small Arizona town of Bowie to make a new home. While initially characterizing Burroway's protagonist as "a rehash of one of the most sentimental clichés of American frontier literature," *Times Literary Supplement* contributor John Clute went on to explain that the novelist's "conception has a redeeming intensity; she presents Eleanor as a figure whose responses to the world around her are almost preternaturally sensitive. Her twelve-month transformation—from spoiled and fainting wife into toughened optimist—reads like the metamorphosis of some transcendent, not entirely human creation. By the end of the novel she has become a kind of saint." Adapting to her new environment, the fictitious Eleanor eventually confronts actual history in the form of Mexican revolutionary leader Pancho Villa, who, according to historical record, camped out in Bowie in August of 1914.

While Richard Eder expressed a less positive view of Eleanor in his *Los Angeles Times Book Review* critique of *Cutting Stone,* the reviewer found "passages of persuasive writing" throughout the novel, particularly as Burroway describes the harshly beautiful landscape of Arizona, and the transformation of Sam, a vulnerable Chinese-American youth, who learns self-reliance through living off the land. Burroway's depiction of the character of the Mexican servant Maria and her energetic pursuit of a better life occasions "the best writing in the book," in Eder's view. While noting that her prose is sometimes hampered by a "lack of control or malfunction" with regard to the use of detail, Joseph Parisi praised Burroway's body of work in *Contemporary Novelists,* concluding that Burroway "has incisive power to reveal the moral ambiguities, contradictions, and rationalizations of her characters, especially the women."

Burroway's play *Hoddinot Veiling* was Britain's independent television entry at the Monte Carlo festival in 1970. The author's manuscripts and working papers are collected at the Strozier Library, Florida State University, in Tallahassee.

Embalming Mom: Essays in Life, is an intimate portrait of the author's life in essay form. The book is "alternately clever, humorous, lively, sad and charming," according to Pam Kingsbury of the *Library Journal. Embalming Mom* is a collection of sixteen essays which delve into Burroway's childhood, explore the similarities of the author with that of the poet, Sylvia Plath, follow her career aspirations, and humorously describe the asperity of failed marriages, child rearing, death, and other self-evolving experiences. Frank Bentayou, a writer for the *Plain Dealer,* depicted Burroway's informal writing style as "intimate as an after-dinner chat." Lynn McWhirter of The Review of Arts, Literature, Philosophy, and the Humanities RALPH noted "With writing like this, Burroway wins our hearts—and by the time she gets past the pools, and the cats and the writer worrries—she has us whole, has us entire."

AUTOBIOGRAPHICAL ESSAY:

Janet Burroway contributed the following autobiographical essay to *CA:*

This is the first thing I know about myself: My mother said, "When she was born, I was horrified to see she had coal-black hair an inch long that stuck out all over her head like an Indian." I must have heard this several hundred times; it was the opening sentence of the anecdote about the seventy-odd temporary "permanents" I had before I left home for college.

If it were the first sentence of a novel, I would set an exam on it. What expectations for female children are indicated? What attitude toward nonwhite races is implied? What does the choice of language tell us about the character of the mother? Which of the daughter's later problems and concerns can be traced back to the attitudes here exhibited?

Once when I came home from England, dandling a cherub on my knee, a wife, a published novelist, a university lecturer, a fashionable resident of the cultured country of my choice—a model candidate therefore for "seeing my mother as a person"—I said to her, breezily, "It must have been hard on you to have a stocky, straight-haired daughter."

"Oh," my mother said. "It was *terrible. Terrible.*"

If I had four hundred pages instead of forty to spend at the typewriter, I might give full space to the Samson story, the fight against the cutting of my hair. I might tell the story of the ugly duckling, the stories of my coming to understand the power of bigotry, of the unwilling feminist, the addictive personality in a temperance family, the story of the search for home—all of which figure in my fiction as subject matter. But this is a "literary autobiography," so I will concentrate on the portions of those stories that suggest a writing life.

*

My perfectly adequate but problematic body came into the world on September 21, 1936, in Tucson, Arizona, and was transported at some time before my memory begins to be raised in Phoenix.

My parents were both ex-Ohioans, of whom there were a plethora in the desert in those days. My mother had come about 1909, *her* father having been diagnosed as consumptive and having therefore left the bank in Lorain to take on the managership of a remote marble quarry in the mountains above Rowie. After a few years the quarry went broke—but not before my mother had learned the loneliness of being the only white child in Marble Camp, sitting on a rock watching the games of Mexican children with whom she was not allowed to play.

My father's father was a fishmonger and factory foreman in Canton, Ohio, and when my dad was six his mother died giving birth to his younger sister Jessie—after which my grandfather married his former wife's best friend.

The two households, rustic in Arizona and working class in Canton, were I believe models of Methodist moral rectitude, but my mother's mother had a flash of giggling madness in her that made for both more merriment and more angst. My mother herself was "frail," diagnosed at eighteen as having an ulcer. When she was of marriageable age it became obvious that Bowie, Arizona, offered her no match, and she went to Ohio to visit relatives, returning with my father as prize.

They were married in 1924 in the Little Church Around the Corner in New York, this being one of the titillating facts of their romance, since they had to travel from Ohio to New York unchaperoned before they faced the preacher. Their first house in Bowie was a barber shop, converted by railway-tramp laborers at a dollar a day during the Great Depression. In 1932 my brother Stanley was born in Tucson.

After my birth we moved to Phoenix, and my first three years were spent in "the house on Twenty-fourth Place." There I learned to "read," probably when I was two, because the occasion of it was my brother's difficulty learning in first grade (a manifestation of his resistance to being turned into a performer—truly another story). My mother therefore made flashcards, and since there was nothing in particular to do with me while Stanley practiced them, I was set on the couch beside him. I remember only two of the cards—a "Mexico" with a sombrero set askew on the *M,* and a "look" of which the two *o*'s were long-lashed eyes—and it's perfectly possible that these are the only two cards I then recognized, but all the same I was trotted out for company and presented as precocious. Why my brother didn't murder me I don't know; it was years later that he broke my finger, and then for some lesser transgression.

I remember being freshly dressed for Sunday School, holding my father's hand and looking up to see beyond him the fronds of an awesomely tall palm tree, and beyond that the searing blue Arizona sky. In my first novel I gave this memory a more specific character, but really it is an image of religious awe.

Shortly after my third birthday we moved into an L-shaped stucco bungalow of my father's own design and making at 322 E. Alvarado Street. My father was a *moral* builder (I have tended to understand, and to render in print, true-caulked joints as the touchstone of

Father, Paul Burroway, 1923

good men) and the house still announces its modest solidity while many later jerry-buildings are desert dust. But the trouble with it in 1939 was that the street was newly scratched out of the sand, mostly bare lots, grudging to grass or a new hedge.

Arizona was too spare and barren for me. The real seemed bald. On our street there were few trees and small; behind us was a vast vacant lot (later a baseball field) powdery most of the time and slimy with mud in the rare rains. The farthest I could walk on my own was to the MacAlpine Drug Store across Seventh Street for a nickel ice cream cone that melted as I ate it. My bare feet got horn-hard on the hot dirt while I dreamed of being a ballerina. I seemed to have an instinctive distaste for western music and rodeo gear. Later I understood these attitudes as snobbery, and felt abashed before writers like Tom McGuane and Tom Robbins, who had the strength of spirit to celebrate American folk rubbish—but how did I conceive such a snobbery in the first place? By the time I was eight I had an entrenched conviction that the real world was elsewhere than Arizona, and I have never entirely changed my mind.

The significant legacy of those early judgments was not that I should find my home elsewhere but that I should never entirely find my home. It is the sense of *no, not here* that is my familiar. When my five-year-old son, transplanted to America, vowed that he would return to live in England where he was born, I never doubted him. I envied him rather, that such a passion, so early conceived, should be a longing rather than a rejection.

In the meantime the things that seemed "real" to me were the things that I would now describe as heightened, striking, technicolor. Christmas, for instance. My family had a true hedonistic talent for Christmas—a heritage I have tried to pass on, rigorously defending it against all charges of consumerism and commercialism.

Movies especially represented the world as it ought to be, and this passion was shared by all the family. We went perhaps twice a week to the Deco-decorated Fox or to the Orpheum with its Spanish courtyard and clouds moving across the plaster sky. I must have been aware even in the earliest days that the point of my mother's curling and steaming and twisting-round-her-finger of my hair, was that I should look as much as possible like Shirley Temple—which was also my heart's desire.

I was allowed dance lessons from the age of four or so, ballet and tap, later adagio, acrobatic, and—finally!—toe. I got to be measured for the tiny tutus or tap ruffles of Mr. Scholl's recitals. I watched, backstage, the annual painting for the same recital of the lady who went nude except for her leaf of gilt. It perplexed and dazzled me that this and only this particular public nudity seemed to be allowed.

More thrilling still was the Phoenix Little Theatre production of *Guest in the House* for which I understudied and, once, performed the youngest role. Whenever I see mothers defend, and toddlers mouth their enthusiasm for, public performance and beauty contests, my knee-jerk reaction is that the kids are being used, but my memory tells me I was stagestruck of my own accord, and a stage mother was the mother I most wanted.

Most thrilling, held out like a promise of every year's completion, was the trip to California, to eat in the green-lit plaster grottos of the Waldorf Cafeteria, to buy a winter coat and a storybook doll at the May Company, to ride the merry-go-round and later the bumper cars at the greasy glorious Pike, and to be tumbled in the cold and terrifying wonderful Pacific surf.

Jumping, jumping in the surf; the water jumps so I jump, with every wave. It is a jumping competition. The sea smacks me in the face, upends me, drags on whatever part of me is nearest the ocean floor. I am towed under. I fight, right myself, stand and face the next wave, jump. Salt surges backward through my nose into my throat; coughing makes the membranes above my palate sting. I don't want to get out, I never want to get out. I ignore my parents' calling. Only exhaustion will finally shove me shoreward, dump me on the sand, because even if I feel "in my element," there is something I don't have in common with the ocean, that it goes on tireless, never pulls a muscle, heaves for breath, dizzies with churning head over gritty heels in the salt wet.

California also magically contained an extended family, a score of people one way or another connected to my grandmother, Gamie. With these people we had wonderful beach reunions. The most interesting family was that headed by my mother's cousin Walter Pierce, whose daughter Martha Anne lived in a beruffled attic bedroom in their Riverside house. Surf and trees were exotic enough, but stairs in a private house seemed like something out of books, and dormer windows . . . ! I envied Martha Anne for most of my childhood.

The Pierces were connected to Louisa May Alcott by a route I could never trace. My grandmother claimed to be Louisa May's second cousin, and one of the Pierce sisters was named Premilia, supposedly after a Premelia Alcott—but Uncle Walter and I have searched in vain for corroboration. The real connection doesn't matter, of course; the important thing is that the family believed it, and had no difficulty crediting anybody's literary ambitions—indeed, always had an eye out for them. Gamie's brother, Uncle Ernie, was the author of a "privately published" book of poems called *Infiniverse*. Uncle Ernie was considered to be "a little cracked," and in later life no doubt he was—though I never felt as certain as my mother that I would be harmed by listening to his theories about the

Mother, Alma Milner, 1923

moon and the menstrual cycle. And I liked his explanation of his book's title: "One evening I was sitting around the dinner table with my sons, and one of them mentioned the universe. I thought, Why universe?! Doesn't it go on forever? Why not *Infiniverse?*" This idea thrilled me almost as much as it seemed to thrill Uncle Ernie—I particularly liked the throwaway part, "mentioned the universe"—but I don't know whether he felt any particular affinity for his great-niece poet.

California was also "real" of course because it was where the movies were made, and my parents were as excited as I to step in the cement feet at Grauman's Chinese, collect autographs on Hollywood and Vine, get free tickets to the broadcasts of "Stella Dallas" or "Amos 'n' Andy," and expensive ones to live shows. Once we saw a striptease by mistake, and once by more profound mistake my parents took me to a performance of A *Streetcar Named Desire*, which disturbed me in a way I could articulate to no one.

Much later I noted this irony: My mother had wanted to be an actress, and had been prevented from it "by

her health," which dictated that she could not leave Arizona for the Emerson School of Oratory in Boston. I always knew that her own parents were somewhat relieved not to have to make a decision against the theatre on moral grounds, but they felt, and my mother passed on to me, a conviction that actresses were wicked. They were wicked for three clearly delineated reasons: they smoked, they drank, and they had a lot of husbands. In my late forties, when I sat to contemplate the shape of my life, I realized that my adolescent rebellion had taken some very obvious forms; I had then already given up a couple of husbands, and now I undertook to give up the drink and the cigarettes. As a friend had pointed out to me, there are two ways to let your parents rule your life: by doing as they say, and by doing the opposite.

*

I suppose everyone has a first memory of being able to write. What characterizes my memory is a sense of fraud. I remember being at a little table looking onto the quarter-circle of backyard from my room in the house on Alvarado Street. I had not yet started to school, but I knew my alphabet and could make all the letters. I could already form *Janet,* and didn't consider this being able to write; it was like being able to make a cat out of two circles with ears and tail; mere *drawing.* I practiced these letters on cheap slick manila paper with turquoise lines. Then I called to my mother asking her how to spell *Burroway,* and as she slowly called out the letters from another room, I formed them. I copied them several times, then demanded that she look and see if I had it right. She must have praised me, but I don't remember. I remember writing the letters over and over again with a sense of breathless power. And then suddenly I was self-suspicious. *I* had not really done anything. Mom had spelled the name. I had only copied down letters I already knew. I was somehow taking credit for something not my own.

This odd sense dogged me. When as a teenager I won a dress-designing competition I was thrust into a despairing sense of fraud, confessed to my mother that I had taken a sleeve style from one dress, neckline from another, skirt shape from a third; the only original thing I had done was to add the applique of the fish and bubbles. Mom laughed. What did I think designing *was?* I caught the sense in the character of Miguel in my first novel, *Descend Again.* Miguel translates a

Spanish lullaby, not understanding that translation is something different from plagiarism. But writing about it did not exorcize the tendency, which plagues me in the classroom: These students think I have done something for them, but it's only a fraction of what they could get from reading the books I've read.

I have learned to tell my writing students that in the world as we know it nothing is made or destroyed, only rearranged; and that the process of creation is selection and arrangement. I know this to be true. But somewhere the stubborn enemy in me does not believe it.

My mother liked to make stories of her children's accomplishments, and would assure anyone who would listen that I wrote my first poem at the age of five. Consequently, I seem to remember doing so, bringing my headful of lines out to my mother on the little red concrete front porch where purple verbena grew in a huge turquoise pottery vase, and I do remember the poem.

> There once lived a man on the street.
> He was sixty years old at that time,
> And before he was ninety-nine
> He prayed to the Lord: Lord, do not let me die
> For I am the shepherd of your sheep.
> Then he went outside, and a rope hanging from
>   the sky.
> He took hold of it, and up and up he went
> Until he was in the sky.
> Then he knew who he was.
> He was Jesus, God's shepherd.

I've written worse. I still rather like the idea of Jesus not knowing who he was even though he declared it with conviction. But I also think that this effort could be duplicated by most of the first graders in a Poets in the Schools program, and that my mother's assigning it a prophetic character may in fact have been a *cause* of my later poetry.

No more poems were caused, however, until about the seventh grade, and I probably cared less about the first one than about my mother's praise. A slightly later memory marks for me the urgent connection I feel to language.

"Gakie and Gamie," Dana T. and Maud Pierce Milner, mid-1950s

In this memory I seem very young and small, but it is crucial that I was able to write a letter, so I will put it at the summer between first and second grades.

I had been left to spend a week with my grandparents in Wilcox. At Gamie's house—it was never spoken of as my grandfather's, Gakie's; I suppose the bank was his place and the home hers—as in California, things were in sharper focus than at home, and in sharper color: the huge black and white squares of the checkerboard kitchen floor, the drawer filled with shining, miniature but real, pots and pans; Weedy the golden Pekingese who spent his waking hours padding across the checkerboard after my grandmother. The grass in the ample backyard was of some vivid apple green that we could not achieve in Phoenix. A black china cat slept on the hearth and a glass-fronted cupboard displayed a whole set of *black* dishes! The ceilings of the bedrooms were plastered in ochre over blue, and the blue shapes could be read as clouds can be, but they did not change, and became familiar: the hatted lady, the pig, the coolie hat. Over my iron bedstead in the guest room Gramma Pierce, Gamie's mother, stared stern and life-sized out of an oval frame, over the window seat and out the window, into the garden at the weeping willow—and I never hear the expression "piercing gaze," without remembering this private etymology.

Every day I walked the half-dozen blocks to the Valley National Bank where my grandfather was manager (it was my first experience of that heady female pleasure, Prestige by Association), and Gakie gave me a shiny dime, which I was then allowed to take to the Vandercamp Emporium and spend at once. Fifteen cents a week was my standard allowance; a dime a day was wealth. No one told me to save a part of it or to spend it wisely. I could buy a little frame, a book of paper dolls, a ball and jacks—anything! Back at Gamie's house I could go next door to the vacant lot and dance on a slab of concrete unaccountably laid as if for my private stage. Or I could poke into the old tool shed, sniff in the musty smell that I never otherwise encountered in my childhood, Arizona being so dry. As I recount this it seems to me a memory of longer ago than the 1940s, and I realize that part of the magic of Gamie's house was that even then, compared to the flat harsh light of home and its boxy houses, Wilcox had the feel of more graceful "olden times."

I loved the place. But one afternoon when I had been there for several days I was standing at the window seat in "my" bedroom sifting through a box of old Christmas cards. I looked up from the cards, out the window like Gramma Pierce, at the gently tossing ribbons of green willow—and I was struck a blow in the stomach of physical and yet not-physical pain. It was at once empty and lead-heavy, as if emptiness had been made lead-heavy in me. I had never felt anything like it and I could not take in the force of it. I gaped out the window, astonished, immobilized. I stood for a moment trying to breathe, and when I caught my breath I began to cry—not merely from the eyes or nose, but with desperate expulsions as if I could send the thing away, extrude it from my stomach with my breath.

Gamie came to me. "What is it, Dolly!"

I said, gasping astonishment, "I don't *know. . . !*"

She put her arms around me. "Oh, Dolly, you're homesick."

I believe that my need for words, my anxious and largely misplaced trust in definition, stems from that moment. The pain still choked me but its name had put it in the world. My grandmother knew what it was. It had been before.

My memory does a "cut to" here, to the fold-down writing desk beside the bed. "Dear Mom," I wrote, "I am . . ." I asked Gamie to spell the word and I painstakingly wrote it out. ". . . *homesick.*" I was impressed at the length of it. It still sounded alien to my ears. My letters were blurry with tears, and now that I knew the pain was connected with the thought of home, the thought of home brought on the pain. But I knew what it was called and I could write it down. I could define myself by it. I was homesick. It was a mortally grown-up thing to be.

Let me not distort the meaning of this memory to me. The void is very large and the pride is scarcely a pebble. When I have lost a mother, child, marriage, lover, home—"homesick" is how I feel it. When I hurt, it is with that pain I hurt, and thousands of words must be thrown into the void before it begins to contract around them. I have been able to understand the concept of "black hole" only in emotional terms. But if my particular sort of pain took its form in that moment, so did the puny power to face it off.

*

Mom gave "elocution" lessons, and had striking success correcting the speech defects of stammerers, split palates, and at least one girl with Down's syndrome. Most of her pupils, however, learned to "say pieces."

All through grammar school I took lessons from Mom, but she tended to be impatient with me; so I invented a game in which I left the house, toured the block, rang the doorbell, and presented myself as "Brenda." My mother approved this ruse, and on the whole she was successful in pretending that she must treat me with the politeness due a stranger's child.

I learned to recite "My Darling Little Goldfish" with appropriate inflections, and I advanced to prose, to monologue and dialogue situations in which a mother

With brother Stanley, 1938; "the first of an unconscionable number of studio portraits"

tried to telephone the grocer while keeping three small children out of trouble, or the salesgirl lost track of how much lace she was measuring as she complained about her job. There were relaxation exercises that I have since learned are yoga, and which I still use.

The goal then was that I should stand up, at intervals of perhaps two months, at Friday night socials of the Central Methodist Church, and bring glory on myself, my mother, Methodism, and the American Way of Life.

Understand that I fully concurred in this desire. Nevertheless I sweated and wished to die. From four o'clock on the relevant Fridays I sank into a stupor of dread and prayed that the cross should be lifted from me. I sweated. After supper I dressed—in yokes with Peter Pan collars, dirndles with ruffles, pinafores with rickrack trim, in peplums, puffed sleeves, peasant blouses, scallops—and sweated.

In the church basement I sat and watched while Mrs. Logan rendered "Mighty like a Rose" and the Robinson twins did their tap routine. I smiled and applauded, my heart banging without rhythm against my breast-

less fat. I strode forward with the appearance of nonchalance through the metal-backed folding chairs, paused, faced the crowd, gulped a breath, and spoke.

Afterward, four flower-hatted women and, if I was lucky, a middle-aged man, would tell me how talented I was, how charming, how to be proud of!

Do not suppose that I suspected some imbalance between the effort and the praise. I learned the lesson of my life. Praise and relief! Praise and to be done with it! Even now, when many thousand facings of a lecture hall have dimmed the anxiety, when I am free of the Peter Pan collars and my heart no longer pounds—even now, every time I speak I feel the atavistic pattern: dread, discipline, praise, relief.

On the knickknack shelf in the living room was a trophy that Stanley had won at the age of four or five in a KOY radio station competition, reciting "Moo Cow Moo" or "Nice Mr. Carrot." Shortly thereafter, however, he retired from public life and never to my knowledge acquired, desired, or competed for a trophy until, at the age of thirty-eight, as he left the *Oakland Tribune* for the *Los Angeles Times,* he was offered a slug from the press etched with the signatures of his fellow newsmen.

At the age of ten or twelve he decided to become a writer. He asked for a typewriter for Christmas and installed a lock on his door. He began to write for the *Emerson Herald,* the newsletter of our grammar school, and in the eighth grade became its editor. He went to North Phoenix High School with the intention of becoming editor of the *Mustang Roundup,* which he duly did. With two friends, he founded, wrote, and drew cartoons for the *Fadical Tower,* a sort of early Arizona cross between the *Village Voice* and the April Fools' issue of a campus rag.

My relationship with my brother went through the usual sibling changes, but I think it was quite early for a younger sister that I began, mostly secretly, to idolize him. A few of our California summers were spent in a trailer on the shore at Seal Beach, and when the hours got long, the swimming and the Monopoly grew old, Stan used to beguile the time with stories of stunning invention. A favorite series was called "A Penny for Luck," in which a sequence of characters down, out, desperate, or dying for lack of money briefly and ignorantly held in their hands a priceless collectors'-item penny, which at the end of the story each would spend for something tragically insignificant. I begged for these stories so often that Stan finally tired of them and had one of the characters flip the penny into a river. Once when I marvelled at his skill Stan invented a spur to my own invention: he asked me to name any three objects and then he wove them into a plot; then he named three and I had to make up the story about them. It was a literary version of our favorite drawing game, in which one person drew a quick scribble and the other had to turn it into a face.

These brotherly attentions were confined mostly to vacations, though, and when Stan was with his high-school friends I became the younger-sibling *persona non grata*. I suffered accordingly. I sat outside the door where the mysteries of *Fadical Tower* were being plotted, invented excuses to wander through, tried with singular lack of success to invent the sort of joke that would make Stan, Wes, and Fred laugh the way they did over their cartoons.

I don't know whether this forlorn adoration had anything to do with my eventually becoming a writer—certainly I wavered and moiled over my choice of profession, a far cry from Stan's early and absolute commitment. I do know that it had something for good and ill to do with my conception of love, both the clarity of the feeling in myself, and the anxiously low expectation of return. Having said that, I should also say that as adults my brother and I have become easy good friends, and we still carry on a bantering rivalry, begun when he was in high school and I in grammar school. When *Material Goods* came out in 1980, he sent me a poem that ended:

> Awed by slim volumes, what am I to say?
> (My headlines growing cold, type going gray);
> Just this: *Three million readers, kid, TODAY!*

About the seventh grade I began to write poems again. I was by this time thick of torso, my straight hair hidden under a fizz of home perm, my feet like my nose too large, my despair constant that I could never expect to look like Adena Wolf nor be the beloved of beautiful Vernon Godbehere—and in such self-dissatisfaction I took the path more travelled by and became the teacher's pet.

Our literature teacher was a Mr. Allsworth, blandly aging, slightly slow, with a head full of beautiful white hair. He was inclined to praise my efforts with a mild, not altogether satisfactory, benignity. One day we read a story about a defenseless wild animal—I think it was a rabbit—who defended her young against a vicious lone dog, and succeeded in some dramatic way that left the dog dead. I thought it peculiarly one-sided. How could we be so sure that the dog was a villain? (I think I was predisposed to like dogs better than underdogs at the time.) I therefore concocted my first experiment in point of view—with no notion that is what I was doing—and brought Mr. Allsworth a new version of the story in which the dog was trying to save his injured master by feeding him until help could arrive. In my version the dog also died (so did the master), but tragically, hearing in his doggy brain a voice from the heavens pronouncing that his was a job well done. A little more satisfactorily than usual, Mr. Allsworth appeared to be startled.

Then I made a wonderful discovery. In our family there had always been two capitalized *I*'s besides the ego's name. My father was in favor of anything that could be called an Idea. My mother had a mystical affection for Inspiration. I now discovered the value of the latter, for although bedtimes were considered absolute, and if I were caught under the covers with a Sylvia Seaman mystery and a flashlight I would be sharply reprimanded, it turned out that in my mother's opinion Inspiration was not subject to schedule but would come will-you nil-you, early or late, and there was nothing that a mortal could do about it. My muse suddenly declared herself to be of the midnight variety. In the space of a few months I wrote a couple of dozen after-hours poems, which made their way into the hands of Mr. Allsworth.

Now Mr. Allsworth did a much more satisfactory thing: he kept me after school on Thursday afternoons for a whole semester teaching me prosody. Dimeter. Rich rhyme. Spondee. Caesura. *Envoi*. (Every once in a while, when my job as a teacher seems routine and fruitless to me, I remember how profoundly those Thursday sessions have affected my life, how the iamb miraculously mirrored the rhythm of blood beat, how those Arabs folded their tents and in irregular anapests silently stole away.)

This was my first "workshop." I knew its purpose was to make me a better writer, not ever suspecting it was also a way to make a living. Later, lecturing on prosody to two or three hundred students at the University of Sussex, I observed (and have had no reason since to revise the observation) that grammar and high-school teachers somehow always seem to think you'll get the poetic feet later, and college teachers to assume you've had them, and unless somebody takes the effort to make sure, you'll miss a fundamental pleasure of poetry.

Mr. Allsworth reviewed my weekly efforts and made the following pronouncement: "I think the world may have found in you another Margaret Fishback." I have never learned who this lady was.

One of the poems I wrote, called "A Bundle for Britain," celebrated the birth of Bonnie Prince Charlie, and at Mr. A's urging I sent it to Buckingham Palace. I received in return a typed letter under the seal of the palace, signed by a lady-in-waiting to Her Majesty Princess Elizabeth. I was briefly famous. The letter was later stolen out of a collection of my poems at the Emerson Grammar School Hobbies Fair, and I always suspected Adena Wolf. I don't know why, unless it represents some sort of ineffable logic that the girl I so envied for her beauty should return my envy for the one thing I had.

By the eighth grade I had entered pubescent misery and more or less forgot about poetry. Much later I tried to track Mr. Allsworth down to thank him, but I was unable to do so. Many of my regrets concern not what I've done, but the failure to let people know how much they mattered to me.

I wrote one last sentimental parting poem for the *Emerson Herald,* then a valedictory address of equal and largely unfelt nostalgia. I was anxious to get on to high school where things had to get better.

*

They did and didn't. There was a lot more of the same—starring in English class and standing on the sidelines at the basketball dance—and I may have been so busy doing what was then called "discovering boys" that I failed to notice I was also discovering friendship and kinds of competence.

Marilyn Lane was lanky, limber, and had a faulty muscle in one eyelid that produced an involuntary wink—usually when she was about to say something

witty. I had never known a witty girl before. It was the myth of our friendship that we had begun as enemies, each finding the other conceited, which I believe was the only flaw that anybody was ever accused of. But I don't remember disliking her, only that we had a wonderful time assuring everyone that such dislike had occurred. Marilyn's parents were divorced, and she lived with her father and was good pals with her stepmother, all of which was vaguely shocking. Worse, she had a homosexual uncle she liked a lot. In my family such things were never admitted to.

"Mere" and I were both "good at English" and competed for grades and assignments on the *Roundup,* eventually in our senior year sharing its editorship, one semester each. The competition was real—neither of us ever pulled punches—but it also went along without in the least damaging our affection. I knew what the phrase "friendly rivalry" was all about (from both Stan and Mere) and later when I heard about the famous competition among females I thought what a fine thing it was.

Mere and I shaved our legs, ignoring my mother's admonitions about how we would regret it (we never did), jointly owned (this being a way to stretch our allowances) the largest collection of outsized earrings at North High, shopped for fabrics together, pored over dress designs, and taught each other to alter commercial patterns to our pleasure. Once Mere cleaned out the Baptist library and discovered a book of sex advice for Sunday schoolers. We learned horrific things from this book, and were both eager to assure each other of the truth, that we'd never *heard* of self-abuse. We figured out what it was. The close of one chapter admonished us to "Remember to take Jesus Christ with you in your sex life," and this became our secret greeting. "Remember. . . ." When, in my junior year, my brother introduced me to his college roommate and friend Bob Pirtle, and Bob and I started dating, Bob introduced me to his brother Dave, I introduced Dave to Marilyn, and we made up a foursome. All the others in this daisy chain are far-flung, but Dave and Marilyn have been married for thirty years.

Through these years I wasn't sure that I wanted to write; both dress design and acting looked more glamorous to me, and although I spent more time in the journalism room, I enjoyed drawing and silk screening, oratory and acting much more. The drama coach suggested that I become a theatre critic, but that seemed dull to me.

By my junior year I felt myself to be in a crisis of indecision over my life's work. I clerked summers and weekends for a dress shop, also designing felt skirts for them which my mother made (sequins one by one on sea horses, hundreds of tiny hand stitches on the surrey with the fringe on top). I was cast as one of the sisters in *Uncle Harry* (a middle-aged dowager; just what I thought of myself and obviously what everybody else thought of me). But as a senior I failed to be cast as the Shrew for the taming thereof, and had to settle for designing the set—a bitter second best.

The *Shrew,* however, was to be directed by my English teacher Dee Filson, and I was in love with him. He was tall, graying, horn-rimmed, and intense. His classes left me breathless. It was my first experience of the connection between eroticism and the intellect. Mr. Filson insisted that we think of ourselves as adults. When we discussed family relations we were to "relate" to our potential children rather than our soon-to-be-abandoned parents. One day when one of the students used the word "Communist" in a sneering tone, Mr. Filson said: "Hey, whoa! Would you like to define Communism for us?" (This was still the early fifties.) He then spent the rest of the hour on Marx, comparing ideological communism to the practice of the Soviet government and also to various forms of Western democracy. He concluded, "When you look at it this way, Jesus Christ was the first Communist. And *tomorrow* . . . one of your mothers is going to call the principal to tell him I said so."

Rapt, I raced home to impart to my Republican parents, who had surely somehow missed all this inspiring information and explication, what Mr. Filson had said. My mother called the principal.

Now Mr. Filson somewhat took the sting out of my failure by deploring the practice of student committee casting, saying that if it was up to him I would have had the part of Kate. I set to designing (with no experience and no training), and came up with an elaborate and barely adequate series of castle rooms for the cumbrous turntable we were using. But for the road to Padua I was inspired, and adorned it with a single tree in the form of a variegated pink cloud impaled on a black prong. Dee Filson later told me that this tree was used, repainted, in North High Players productions for the next ten or fifteen years.

By this time I was involved in public speaking, though I was too self-conscious to be good at impromptu debate, and made the best showing where I could write

and memorize my lines. The Knights of Pythias Oratorical Contest (do they still have that?) was just the ticket. The subject: *Motoring Courtesy and How to Promote It.* My gimmick: pretending to forget my lines and grinning foolishly at the audience to elicit a return grin, thereby proving that friendliness was contagious. Arrgh.

But I won in the city, in the state at Globe (occasion of my first television appearance: I bored my eyes into the screen during evening news, deciding that after all I didn't look that bad), and then went to Nogales for the regional contest. Dee Filson drove, the debate coach, Mr. Harvey, sat up front with him, my mother and I sat in the back; I won, we drove back, and when we arrived home my mother lashed out at me, shocked and shouting, outraged, scandalized, that married Mr. Filson and I had been flirting the whole way.

She was, I now realize, in pain. And she was right. I may then have scoffed at her, but I have since seen a dozen marriages founder on such attraction, and have myself married a student. It is always serious. The erotic bond between teacher and student is a kind of sanctioned incest.

For the opening night of *The Taming of the Shrew* I designed and made a dress in variegated pinks to match the tree, and Mr. Filson told me that I was beautiful. It seems to have been the first time I'd been told that, and certainly the first time I believed it. The next year when I was a freshman at the University of Arizona Dee came to see me two or three times, took me to lunch and for long walks in the mountains, told me that he was divorcing, and asked me to marry him. I was too terrified even to give it serious consideration. I can't think that there is anyone alive who would mind my recording this, but I don't underestimate the seriousness of the offer, to him or me. Years later I realized the sensitivity and restraint he had shown toward a virginal Methodist adolescent; and the gift he offered, which was the first dim sense that my intellect and my femininity were not each other's enemies.

When Gakie retired from the little bank in Wilcox, Daddy had built him and Gamie a home only a few doors away from ours. Now as I finished high school Gakie was finishing his life. It suddenly occurred to me that I took him very much for granted. Two memories from his dying time stay with me. In one I am sitting on the floor beside the living-room couch watching the first television set to make its way into our lives. Gakie lies on the couch and we are holding hands. I know that what I'm about to say is dangerous because it acknowledges his dying. But the urge is strong, and I have never shied from drama. I say, "I wish I had got to know you better." He squeezes my hand, pats it. He says, "It's all right. It's all right."

Some days later I had a phone call saying that I had won an Elks or Rotary scholarship, and my mother and grandmother did a dance of distress, agitatedly asking each other whether they dared tell Gakie—he'd be so excited it might give him another heart attack! It was perfectly clear they were going to tell him, and eventually they did. I stood across the room from where gaunt white-haired Gakie was propped in bed while Mom bore the dangerous tidings. Gakie listened, grinned at me. He said, calmly, "It's starting, Sissy." My grandfather's name was Dana T. Milner, and he was known as Dana T. Remember that; it comes up later.

My brother had transferred to Stanford School of Journalism in his senior year and was now on his way to being a newspaperman. Stanford was the college generally considered coolest among my peers, and it was really the only one that interested me, but to go there I would have to get a serious Stanford scholarship. Once my grandfather had owned Sunnyslope Mountain north of Phoenix; he'd bought it for $500, but sold it soon after, with a princely profit, for $2,000. Dad's home designs were being used to build 500 tract houses at a time, but because he had no architect's license they belonged to the architect whose stamp they bore, and Dad made nothing from them. Besides, he has confided in me since, he thinks it builds character to put yourself through college.

I didn't get the Stanford scholarship. Wait-listed meant that I would have to go to the University of Arizona at Tucson. I had so wanted, for so long, to leave Arizona. My brother's friend Fred Mendelsohn, who went to Harvard (when asked he would only say "I go to school in the East"—a measure of sophistication that the East imparted), urged me to try to get into Radcliffe or Barnard, but like Dee Filson's proposal, this seemed to me to require a leap into the void.

*

Having lived nearly all my life in the same place, with the same people—and for a dozen years with a room

of my own—it was hard to share a dorm cubicle with a stranger, a bouncy, horsey, good-natured blond Hawaiian who collected snake skins and mynah bird feathers. It was hard for a night person to make it to a 6:40 class five days a week, to be barked at by a grizzled prof: *"Papa va aller à Amiens!"* It was hard to face up to how much history had already occurred, and how many names and numbers there were attached to it. At the University of Arizona I was homesick a lot of the time, and ashamed of being homesick because I had made such a production of wanting to leave home.

I "rushed," pledged Kappa Kappa Gamma, got the lead in a play, dated beer-tasting boys on frat excursions to nearby mountains, got ceremonially pinned to a Phi Gam majoring in Range Grasses; and about all of this felt anxiously grateful but slightly askew to my center—something for which it took me many years to find a name: inauthentic.

But there were also moments that prefigured deeper excitement. University of Arizona had a surprising, superior faculty, some of them asthmatics held in the desert for health's sake. In spite of myself I began to care about history (Luther was dethroned from sainthood for me in one brilliant half-hour lecture), and then—science!

One morning I exited from a botany class, my notebook page covered with fresh diagrams of vascular bundles (a term of which I had lived in happy ignorance until that morning), broke a leaf off a magnolia tree, turned it stem-end-up—and saw the organic double of my diagram. It was the first time it had occurred to me that science had anything to do with my world. I performed the only sort of homage I knew how, and hotfooted it after an A in the course. Later, in *Raw Silk,* I gave Virginia Marbelestier the same sort of rudimentary love of that single science. I gave her the vascular bundles, too.

Mademoiselle magazine, Patrick McCarthy, and Helen McCann got me out of Arizona. I was actively pursuing the *Mademoiselle* College Board Contest, doing assignments from each month's issue of the magazine, now in writing, now in design, now in merchandising, trying to impress the editors with my nouveau Renaissance quality, hoping to get brought back to New York for the month of June, all expenses paid *and* salaried.

I was spurred on by my English teacher Pat McCarthy, one of the trapped asthmatics, a Columbia graduate, an energetic teacher for all the breath it cost him; a brilliant good guy. I wrote a piece for him about the excessive thinness of the theatre types, of which he said, "If I didn't know better, I would assume that this were written by a fat person." So far as I know this is the only time anyone ever managed to salve my secret wound while praising my writing. In one of his classes I demanded, "Doesn't it (writing) get easier?" to which he replied, "It doesn't get easier. It gets *better.*" It was also in one of his classes that I disgraced myself over Keats's urn. McCarthy asked, "Why does he say 'O Attic shape'?" and I replied, "Where else would you find a Grecian urn except in an attic?" He thought this witty, but I was too slow, too drearily trained in Methodist honesty, not to admit I'd meant it. I was too dashed to open my mouth for a few weeks after that, and only realized in graduate school that I'd had a couple of genuine perceptions about the urn.

McCarthy urged me to start with Plato and read, read; I'd never heard of Plato. He gave me *Catcher in the Rye* and I thought it was a test—a dirty book; would I dare tell him it was trash? He urged me to apply to Columbia; I thought he meant Stevens College in Columbia, Missouri (very high prestige among the sorority sisters).

But one day I happened to notice an article in the local paper that a Miss Helen McCann, Registrar of Barnard College, was in the area recruiting from private girls' schools. There were only half-a-dozen hotels in town, so I called them until I found her. She came out to the university and bought me lunch. I have no memory at all of what I said to make her champion my cause at Barnard. But I do remember that she said to me, "It's not easy to be poor in New York, but everything in the city is at the end of a ten-cent subway fare."

I applied for admission and an alumni scholarship at Barnard. I wrote an article on bigotry called "Color Blind" for the *Mademoiselle* contest. It won the prize for that month's entries, which meant that I was going to New York as a contest winner, which meant that I could be at Barnard for the crucial interview.

New York, June 1959. I didn't know that my arrival was a classic. I followed from the airport, carefully mimicking a trim and confident young beauty with a chic hatbox on which I saw, as she descended from the bus at Grand Central, an Ames, Iowa, address. I stood on the curb there waiting for the cabdriver to come around and open the door for me. When his irritation had passed he recognized a rube, and on the way to the Barbizon told me, Bronx accent, "New Yawk is like a gigantic ice cream sundae. Y'eat it all at once y'get sick to y'stomach. Y'spoon it up a little bit at a time, kid, y'never get enough."

It was the year after Sylvia Plath's spot on the *Mademoiselle* College Board junket, though of course none of us would so have dated anything then. Twenty college girls—some greener than others and I the greenest; also the only freshman—gathered in a room whose walls were partly mirrored, partly papered in Victorian newspaper clippings full of bustles and parasols. Joan Didion was one of the twenty, so was Gael Greene (of *Blue Skies, No Candy),* Adri Steckling who now designs under her own label; and Jane Truslow—laidback, compassionate, the one I felt closest to and would most have liked to know, though our paths only once crossed again. Betsy Talbot Blackwell, with a cigarette holder that *seems* in my memory to have been a foot long and rhinestone studded, in any case certainly announced, "We believe in pink this year."

I was assigned to advertising, taken out of it to do the editorial, sent to an afternoon or two on an article about Sylvia Plath, who had just won the Mount Holyoke Intercollegiate Poetry Competition ("Guest Editor Makes Good"), taken off of that, photographed in my frizzy curls, sent to fashion shows and cocktail parties and home to the Barbizon Hotel.

One of the perks of the contest was that each of us was to be allowed to interview for the August issue the celebrity of our choice. As a recent convert, I had given as my three choices, "J. D. Salinger, J. D. Salinger, and J. D. Salinger." The editors knew about J.D.'s reclusiveness, and as I was the only one of us who showed a particular interest in the theatre, had decided that I would interview the Swedish actress Viveca Lindfors, then starring in *Anastasia* on Broadway. I'd never heard of her. The only info I'd been able to find on her in Arizona was in the *New Yorker* blurb about the play. *Mademoiselle* required an advance list of questions I was going to ask her so, jaded, I went to the box office, picked up a playbill, and turned the "Who's Who in the Cast" notes into questions.

It happened that mine was to be the first interview. I had not seen *Anastasia* and my editor had not suggested I do so—probably because an excursion to that play was planned for the College Board the following week.

I was squeamish about the whole business, not less so when I realized that I was to be accompanied by a sinewy little photographer with a fast mouth, and a gum-chewing secretary who would take notes for me and therefore effectively remove my one device for hiding angst. I wore a blue linen suit I had made myself, a little white pique hat with a veil. Miss Lindfors' agent had forgotten to tell her about the interview, and when she nevertheless graciously let us into her cramped dressing room, she was in full fur-and-wool costume from the matinee, exhausted, sweating furrows in her greasepaint, and monumentally, breathtakingly beautiful. The secretary sat on her dressing table, chewing, swinging a leg. The photographer kept shoving my chair closer to Lindfors, my knees into hers, saying, "Cheat to the camera, baby; cheat to the camera."

Embarrassment, irritation, jadedness, angst—suddenly transformed themselves to a fist around my throat. I could scarcely squeak out my first banal question. I couldn't hear the answer at all. I sweated in the bank of dressing lights. I thought I would vomit, faint. The secretary saw that I had blanked and (chewing gum, swinging leg) prompted, "Janet!" Her panic deepened mine.

"Cheat to the camera, baby."

After perhaps the third question Viveca Lindfors handed me a copy of the playbill and said, "I think you will find all the answers to your questions in here." At perhaps the fourth she turned a dark appraising eye on me and said (with perfect justice), "You don't listen, do you?"

Chew, chew, swing. "Janet?"

"Cheat to the camera, baby."

Now I would not vomit or faint but would die. Nevertheless, somehow, perhaps to assuage her own boredom by saying something interesting, Viveca Lindfors began to talk. I could hear little, remember less, but I remember her saying, "You Americans are

all so concerned with happiness. Happiness is not the most important thing. The most important thing is the work." This, no doubt, is the one thing I remember because it was so outrageous an idea. I could hear my mother saying, "All I want is your happiness, honey," which certainly meant that I was falling from virtue somehow and would pay for it, but beyond that certainly assumed (I assumed, Americans assumed, doesn't everybody assume?) that happiness, its pursuit, *was* the main thing, the *summum bonum.* At the moment, my personal pursuit was in disarray.

Outside the stage door, the photographer took me by the shoulders and shook me hard—he was so short that he had to reach up to do it. "If the others ask you, it went fine, hear? It went fine!"

The next week, though, things did go better. My editorial was accepted. At the ball on the roof of the St. Regis I met a young poet who kissed me in a hansom cab. I recovered somewhat. Who was Viveca to me or I to Viveca? I wrote her a thank-you note in which I shamelessly played on my own naivete (first trip to New York, first trip backstage, etc.).

But then we went to see *Anastasia.* Lindfors blew me away. She was dazzling, superb, powerful. When, in the second act, Eugenie Leontovich acknowledged Anastasia as her granddaughter, I experienced for the first time what is meant by a "recognition scene." I began to cry—for Anastasia, but also that *I* had not been recognized—and I continued off and on through the third act, to the quizzical embarrassment of my peers.

I couldn't let it go. When the show was over I left the others and shouldered my way to the entrance at the side of the stage. A hoarse-voiced, horse-faced woman blocked my passage, but when I blubbered out my story she opened the door a crack and whispered, "I didn't see you, hear?"

Lindfors had her maid and her little boy with her. She sent them away.

"When I got your letter I thought I had been hard on you," she said.

My words tumbled. "I told myself it didn't matter, but I hadn't seen you act. You're a *great* actress. I couldn't let you think all that of me. It isn't true I want to be an actress. I want to write. They had me say that. I'm sorry . . ." and so forth. I began to cry again, and Viveca Lindfors, statuesque in velvet and fur, began to cry with me! Then we sat and talked, and I could listen, and when I left she said, "You go out and write with all the sincerity you feel now, and you will be a *greeeat* writer, and I will buy your books!"

Eyes streaming, I sailed from the backstage door and hailed a cab. All the way to the Barbizon I cried while the driver clucked his tongue and suffered for me: "Broadway's tough, kid; Broadway's a heart-breaker."

The young poet asked me out again. His parents invited me to dinner. After a couple of weeks they invited me to vacation with them in the Adirondacks. I got my scholarship to Barnard and gave the pin back to my Arizona aggie.

I had no sense whatever of myself as representative of a historically experimental generation, no sense of myself as having a Hollywood-distorted view of romance and love. I certainly saw myself as engaged in a search for the right man to marry, and assumed that eventually to find such a person was my inalienable right. I had no sense that this particular holy grail required certain tests and qualities in the seeker's self, nor that I was, however virginally, embarking on a life of serial monogamy.

I did know that there was a painful discrepancy between what I felt and what I felt I ought to feel. After the somehow trying glamour of the Adirondack vacation, when my poet had gone off to England in a Fulbright batch with Sylvia Plath, I felt trapped and frightened. I had discovered the Philip Larkin poem that begins:

> No, I have never found
> The place where I could say:
> This is my proper ground,
> Here I will stay,
> Nor met that special one
> Who has an instant claim
> On everything I own
> Down to my name . . .

In the days before the Barnard dorm opened I lay in a hotel room monotonously reciting it, unable to make myself go out.

*

But my three years at Barnard were a watershed. As soon as I arrived I went to Rosalie Colie, the Milton scholar on the Barnard faculty and a friend of my University of Arizona English teacher, told her that I was horrifically uneducated, and asked her to make a reading list for me. She began by assuring me that I overestimated my ignorance, ended by being amazed at it. Barnard students were mainly New Yorkers and it would not have been possible to grow up in New York as innocent of great works as I was. Armed with my list I went to library and bookstore, thence to the Cloisters, where—in suitable setting, I thought—I sat slogging through the *Dialogues,* then Aristotle, Sophocles, Aeschylus. I signed up for a masterpieces course, and began to get a little direction from S. Palmer Bovie, whose combination of erudition and irreverence helped ease me into my place in the world of books. (Bovie was, is, a fearsome fearless punner: years later when I wrote him from a Florida apartment on Pensacola Street he shot back: *Is that the drink that makes you think?* Boyle also taught me that the true goal of a pun is not a laugh but a groan.)

I lived with graduate and other transfer students in Johnson Hall, and in those days we walked freely along Morningside Drive and sat in Morningside Park to study. I could take a subway safely back from a party in the Village in the middle of the night. The racking homesickness passed after a few weeks or months, and I found another witty woman for friend in Judy Kaye, with whom I learned the routine and irreplaceable pleasure of the six-hour dorm talk.

I joined the Columbia Players, failed once more to get a part, but since my backward background had netted me the unusual ability to sew, I made myself indispensable by designing costumes. In the Players I made friends with Bruce Moody, who for introduction bit my knee, surely a paradigm of Bohemian behavior. (Once my grandmother came to New York. On the bus downtown to hear Norman Vincent Peale I spotted a bearded man with an earring and a woman in high heels and pedal pushers. "Look, Gamie!" I said. "Bohemians." "Oh, yes," she replied. "Or maybe Serbians.") Bruce also, when I protested that I couldn't go to a theatre party because I didn't drink, came to pick me up carrying a quart of milk and a two-quart brandy snifter.

Early in my first, sophomore, year at Barnard, something happened that had the feeling of portent as it occurred. I was one evening shoulder-deep in the tub in the dank dorm bathroom, spacey with having read a whole volume of Ogden Nash at a sitting, and an idea for a poem occurred to me. I hadn't written a poem for at least four years. "Dear Reader, I have no complaint, / As Long as you peruse my verse, / Concerning what you are or ain't. . ." It was a silly piece of Nashian verse, but my heart was racing in iambs, the rhymes kept leaping up into place, I could see the outline of the whole three-part thing and hung onto it round the edges of my mind while I filled in the center like strokes of a crayon in a coloring book, going back over and back over the lines from the beginning because I didn't have a pencil and didn't dare jar it out of my head by getting out of the now tepid water and going to my room before it was all filled in. Flinging on my robe, I went. I had enough of it memorized to be able to finish the rest, dogged, soggy, slogging. The funny thing about this verse was that, as the point of it was that the reader should *not* read a whole volume of me at one sitting, it only made sense if I went on to write at least a volume's worth of poems. I was excited in a way that has since become familiar. First cousin to my mother's old *Inspiration-capital-I,* this is the moment an idea demands to become a thing.

My alumni scholarship paid tuition, room, and board, and my folks were sending me thirty dollars a month for books and spending money. It wasn't going to be enough. I went to the Young Men's Hebrew Association and applied there to be part-time secretary to John Kolodney, who ran the Poetry Center. I lied about having shorthand, but anyway Kolodney interviewed by the original expedient of having me write a letter to Edwin Arlington Robinson inviting him, in spite of his deceased condition, to read at the Center.

Thereafter for two or three afternoons a week, for seventy-five cents an hour, I bused from class to Ninety-second and Lexington, made sketchy notes of Kolodney's dictation, and invented the letters I thought he intended to write. We got along fine.

One of the duties of my job was to make the coffee and the onion dip for the Young Poets' Reading Series, so I got to meet a dozen of these enviable creatures. Once when the recent Lamont winner Donald Hall was scheduled to read, I raced in before onion-dip time to the Doubleday's on Fifth Avenue and demanded a copy of *Exiles and Marriages.* "Say again?" the slow clerk asked, whereupon a personable young man behind him held up a copy of the book. "It looks like this."

"Where'd you get that?" I said. "Will you sell it?"

"I wish I could, but I'm afraid I have to read from it tonight. I'm Donald Hall.

"And," he added, "I can't tell you how often I've dreamed of walking into a bookstore and hearing a lovely young coed ask for my poetry."

Another of my jobs was the first screening of the Center's new contest, which was to result in publication by Harper and Row. I found this task grim and long; I was not daunted by the *bad* poetry, but the floor-to-ceiling piles of the mediocre threatened me. It was clear from the most amateur and superficial reading that the best manuscript by far was *The Hawk in the Rain* by a young Englishman, Ted Hughes—so clear that I was only glancingly pleased that the final judges agreed with me.

Contests and readings were in those days extremely rare, and the Center may have much to answer for. Also relatively rare was the practice of offering writing workshops, which both Barnard and the Center, however, did. I was gluttonous for workshops, and over the three years I spent in New York I sampled nearly a dozen teaching styles, learning something (*usually*) about writing) from each. I studied with George Plimpton, Hortense Calisher, Walker Gibson, Louise Bogan. Marianne Moore was a fellow classmate in one workshop. The worst teacher was W. H. Auden, who, often drunk, always bored, sat reminiscing about the *tramontana* or reciting Dante in Italian, swinging a loafer on the end of his argyled toe. The best was Rolfe Humphries, who, inventive with exercises in rhyme scheme, vowel length, consonant clusters, and stanza form, ensured that we tune our ears by forbidding us to make sense for the first half of the semester.

In my senior year I took a playwrighting workshop with Howard Teichmann at Barnard, and he helped me to get a production of my play *Garden Party,* directed by Dolph Sweet, with Barnard women and (out-of-work) professional men. The play featured a God wearing Dacron (modern miracle) and a Satan who turned Eden into a subdivision called Paradise Lots. I described it as "a rewrite of Milton from a woman's point of view," though I had not heard of feminism, and my irritation at Milton's misogyny seemed unconnected to anything in my own life.

The experience of play production was excruciating. The actors *would* not get the lines right. The second act was crushingly dull. The director had no notion what I was up to. The longer they rehearsed, the more puerile the whole thing seemed. But on opening night I sat listening to lit humans talk words *I* had written, surrounded in the dark by others who responded, laughed, sighed. There's nothing like it. Fan letters for a novel are remote by comparison, posthumous praise of a creature long dead to me. I thought then, and I think now, that writing for the theatre would suit me best. Unfortunately, my best ideas have come as novels and would not yield their form.

As a result of this play, I got an agent at MCA. I also got a poem in the *Atlantic,* a summer as a junior assistant at the *New Yorker,* the Elizabeth Janeway Prize at Barnard, and the Intercollegiate at Mount Holyoke. I also got deflowered, drunk, entangled with a married man, and mononucleosis. I won a Marshall Scholarship to Cambridge, but, exhausted, I wandered into Palmer Bovie's office one afternoon feeling that I didn't feel what I ought to feel, and wailed (I had started reading Henry James), "I'm not sure I *want* to go to England."

"Life is a question of alternatives," Palmer reasonably pointed out.

*

By the time I left New York I could not imagine why anyone would want to live anywhere else. Culture shock hit me again in England. I spent the first year at Cambridge always cold, often irrationally frightened, and sometimes suicidal. This is true even though I was active and excited by the beauty and the intellectual richness around me.

I had first seen Sylvia Plath at a Fulbright reception my first fall in New York. I had worked on an article about her poetry for *Mademoiselle,* I had later pretended jealousy of her to my poet at Oxford, and he flirted back by mail that her name was really Plass, but she had a lisp; later he'd written that she was engaged to Ted Hughes, whose manuscript I'd read for the Poetry Center. Now I found that I was to live in the same room she'd inhabited at Cambridge, in the Whitstead House annex to Newnham College—a room occupied in the interim by poet Lynne Lawner, and which therefore had a tradition to keep up.

In England, 1965

On the Marshall Scholarship application I had been asked why Cambridge was my first choice of British university. I had no real reason. Of course I was going to choose Oxford or Cambridge, and I'd been told that Cambridge was prettier. Besides, the poet had gone to Oxford, and that love affair had not worked out. The only thing approaching an intellectual justification was that I admired David Daiches's literary criticism. I put down that I wanted to study with Daiches, assuming, however, that he would not supervise a student outside his own college. Now I was told that Daiches had agreed to take me on, and I went to his tutorial rooms at Jesus College once a week, at the civilized sherry hour, to study the English Moralists ("From Plato to Sartre" as this course was unofficially known). The following term he taught me the period 1880-1910; after that Tragedy, and the second year the Moralists again; I shared supervisions this time with Margaret Drabble, of whom I was intellectually in awe.

I was and am convinced that the accidental pattern of my studies—the American format, with fifteen class hours a week, constant assignments and frequent exams; followed by the English tradition, a week of constant reading culminating in a paper and a single hour of class—was an ideal way to cure my Arizona academic innocence. The freedom at Cambridge certainly added to my terror, but it also stretched me. I remember that one day Daiches said, "I think Forster this week. Yes, read E. M. Forster."

"What of Forster's?"

"Oh, there isn't much of Forster."

I wasn't one to defy authority. That week I read *all* of Forster. Another week I read seven novels of Henry James, huddled over a shilling-meter gas fire so close that the fingers outside my book turned red while my thumbs on the inside were still numb with cold.

The lectures at Cambridge, attendance voluntary, ran the gamut from sublime to bathetic, and I attended my share, but it is also true that most of the learning was not done in the classroom. In New York the social unit had been the couple. Men and women were not allowed in each other's rooms, so there had to be somewhere to go and a reason to go there—a "date." At Cambridge the social unit was the group, and there was always a group to join, for morning coffee, afternoon tea, evening wine, Sunday sherry. It was 1959, and the debate raged over C. P. Snow's *Two Cultures and the Scientific Revolution.* Opera, for some reason, was also a hot topic. So was Spain. I felt myself flourish, and then suddenly I would feel myself a fraud, a cowgirl in sheep's wool.

Once more I acted, designed costumes, wrote poetry and fiction for the literary magazine *Granta,* which was edited by the American triumvirate of Richard Gooder (still at Cambridge), Andre Schiffrin, and Roger Donald (now editors at Pantheon and Little, Brown, respectively). In theatre and writing there was so much talent that I believed the British were inherently superior, never mind their superior school system. I was convinced of this for all the six years until I came back to live in England, by which time it was both news and common knowledge that my particular years at Cambridge were phenomenal for talent. My colleagues in the theatre and literary groups, for instance, were Jonathan Miller, Dudley Moore,

Peter Cook, Corin Redgrave, Ian McKellen, Derek Jacobi, Eleanor Bron, Margaret Stimpson, Margaret Drabble, Clive Swift, Bamber Gascoigne, Andrew Sinclair, Simon Gray, A. C. H. Smith, Jonathan Spence. . . . David Frost was given the editorship of *Granta* as I was leaving, but was generally recognized as an entrepreneurial, second-rate mind.

For spring vacation that year Andre Schiffrin, Lena de la Iglesia, Roger Donald, and I drove down to La Napoule on the French Mediterranean and rented a yellow stucco house overlooking the sea, eighty dollars for the month. I had begun my first novel in my senior year at Barnard, and had believed I would make it my first priority at Cambridge. But I'd made no headway. Now I threatened to spoil the vacation for myself, sitting in the courtyard in the sun, my typewriter on the paving stones, blocked, hating every word that managed to transfer itself to the page. I remember feeling that, having found writing a solace, I now found it the very cause of the depression it was meant to relieve.

Nevertheless, I managed to write a scene or two of *Descend Again.* Lena—full name Maria Elena de la Iglesia—one afternoon trilled, "Oh, put my name in your novel!" so I obliged by naming an Arizona Mexican schoolgirl after her. I think it helped me write the scene. Lena was delighted—"Oh, put my name in *all* your novels!" I have done so, freely translating her into Mary Helen Church, Lena Fromkirk, Ellen Chiesa, and so forth. Lena and I see each other once a year at most, but the private joke is a powerful bond.

That summer Roger, his mother, and I did the American race through Europe—approximately one country, seven cathedrals, and twenty thousand calories a week—too rich for my budget, as was the running-water sort of hotel we chose—so that by the time they left me in Paris and flew for home, I was flat broke. I had not yet learned or decided that the middle class never starves, and I spent a worried week until I was taken on as a temporary secretary by UNICEF's office at Neuilly—which later became the setting of my second novel.

Meantime I had got my European sea legs, and this two months alone in Paris, renting a room from a kind, motherly *petit bourgeois* woman in the eighteenth *arrondissement* (so that I was playing house, not touristing) passed in a kind of exalted energy. I contracted the myth that I could *write* in Paris, and although I now had a full time job, I began to write lunch hours, evenings, and weekends—managing all the same to see plenty of the Seine and the Left Bank. I wrote all but a couple of chapters of *Descend Again,* and finished those as soon as I returned to Cambridge. When I had a letter from Charles Monteith at Faber and Faber that he would publish it, I literally fell, hard on the left kneecap, on the stone kitchen floor.

I went down to London to meet Monteith in the old Faber offices in Russell Square. In my mind's eye I see myself wearing the same white piqué hat and veil with which I had confronted Viveca Lindfors, but that is hardly possible; it must have less to do with sartorial fact than with the quality of the apprehension. Monteith had told me he wanted to discuss a few changes, and I was convinced he would say, "The male hero doesn't live. Make him live." I *knew* about that, and knew nothing to do about it.

However, Monteith's suggestions were minimal, practical, and possible. He himself sat monumental in a swivel chair, shining of dome and fob (twenty years later he looked not a day older to me), and said, "Miss Burroway, I don't think *either* of us is going to make a fortune—or indeed a living—out of this book."

I had been in England for over a year by then, and I neatly translated how positive a remark this was. If he proposed to print a book with which he expected to make no money, it meant he wanted to buy into my future.

Monteith was editor to both Hughes and Plath, and through Faber I finally met them. Anthony Smith at Cambridge had introduced me to the Indian poet Zulfikar Ghose, who was going to publish a slim—emaciated—volume of my poems at the University of Keele; and Zulfi and I went to dinner with the Hugheses at their flat just behind the London Zoo aviary.

Sylvia and I acknowledged how oddly our lives had touched without our having met before. But what I mainly remember of the evening is Sylvia's hassled handling of the few-months-old baby while she cooked. I awkwardly offered to help but she refused; I recognized the anxious inability to discommode a

guest. Finally she came out to the living room and handed the baby to Ted, who held the bundle in a simian crook of arm, his body in alien relationship to the swinging bundle as he described how he lay awake at night and listened to the animals in the zoo. That second year in Cambridge I lived with three other women in a little terrace house, mine the attic bedroom with the four-poster bed. I acted less, wrote more, had a gentle romance, and in general a gentler time than the first frenetic year. In the final term I managed to "gear up" for the tripos, had some serious luck in the exam questions (this is not modesty; on the night before I sat the exam for the English Moralists I noticed quite by chance that Plato used "love" as a verb, Paul as a noun. The exam next day asked, "Compare the concept of love in Plato and Paul")—and I sailed back to America with a First in my fist.

*

It was through Charles Monteith also that I had met Curtis Canfield, dean of the Yale School of Drama, and now I had the NBC-RCA Fellowship in Playwrighting—a one-year award, unrenewable, which meant that I had come to the end of Grant Road. Next year I would have to earn my living.

Bruce Moody drove me up to New Haven from New York with the books and sewing machine he had stored for me while I was at Cambridge, and we painted my second attic apartment. Always a nester, I made what was by then the half-dozenth set of curtains and bedspread for a college room.

Yale was a disappointment after Cambridge, a regression from the self-discipline of the tutorial system, and my seventh year of college was my poorest and least (though I think we didn't use the word yet) "motivated." I could not seem to make myself memorize dates and proper nouns for Theatre History. John Gassner, who taught the playwrighting course, was a brilliant critic, a vast repository of knowledge about American realism, and a warm, sweet person; but he'd been left behind by the Absurd and had no way of dealing with the plays his most interesting students were writing then. I was trying to be "experimental" myself, and was very bad at it, and Gassner could not help me.

So it was not a profitable year for me as a writer. What unexpectedly opened up was the world of costume design. It was the rule at the drama school that everyone must take a turn at every aspect of production. I was a seamstress (I had been given a naked doll at five, and a hank of calico; by high school I made all my clothes) and an experienced amateur costume designer, so I was more useful than Frank Bevans's crews expected of a playwright.

They put me to work, got me excused from stage shifting and prop crews, gave me the most intricate pleating and pintucking to oversee, taught me to make wigs, strand by strand of polyester glued on buckram head forms. By the end of the year I had barely passed four courses and had written a consummately mediocre play, but I knew how to run a costume room from sketch to strike. As with Mr. Allsworth's prosody, I loved the learning and never supposed it was a possible profession.

But the profession of wife had meanwhile presented itself as an alternative to going back to New York next year as a secretary. John Gassner's assistant was Walter Eysselinck, a Fulbright scholar from Belgium, a director as well as a playwright, a graduate in Germanic philology from the University of Ghent (native language Flemish but equally at home in French and English), a wine connoisseur, and gourmet cook.

I think we were ready to marry—he on the verge of his Ph.D. and I facing the employment void. I also think we had so many genuine interests in common that it masked the fact we differed in some basic values. My friend Julia Kling years later observed that Walter and I would have made a fine *arranged* marriage—if only we hadn't had to believe we were in love. I remember asking Walter one day in New Haven if he was "glad" that I was American. What I meant was that I was glad he was European; it seemed to expand my own scope (Prestige by Association). Walter, no doubt understanding exactly what I meant, angrily said, "Not at all!" However, he was glad I was American.

It was a nervous business, telling my parents I was marrying a foreigner, but made easier by the accident of his name. There were Walters all up and down the ranks of the cousins Pierce. If I had been marrying his brother Hans, it would have seemed more foreign altogether.

More serious was the issue of my parents' fanatical anti-tobacco/alcohol stance. I had been smoking and drinking for five years, but I now thought that if I didn't say so, my parents would later blame these mortal sins on my new husband. I think this was a sound impulse, but my mother accused me (not, to my shame, altogether inaccurately) of wanting champagne at my wedding rather than her—and she and dad decided not to come. On the eve of my wedding day I received from my father a forty-eight-page closely handwritten letter on the evils of smoke and drink, connecting these two habits to every known sin from uncleanliness to prostitution. I felt immensely righteous on the receipt of this letter (the second I had ever received from him)—and worldly, and sorry for my father that he was such a hick. I don't know why I carried the letter around the world for twenty years after that, unearthing it in my mid-forties to discover that it was full of sense, and love, and impeccable advice.

Walter and I were married by William Sloane Coffin at the Yale chapel. I was "given away" by John Gassner, our reception was held at the Canfields' home, and in a car borrowed from a generous former boyfriend (and in which, God help me, I taught Walter to drive on our honeymoon) we traveled to Vermont where we spent a week not alone but in the excellent company of Walter's Bennington friends the Gils and the Mamises.

The following summer we bought a two-year-old Dodge, all chrome and fins, and took off on a 9,000-mile camping trip. We had a flawless attitude toward camping. We carried no tent, only blankets and blowup mattresses. If it rained we had to go to a motel. With a shower and a mattress-night's sleep, by this expedient, every three or four days, we made our way across the Northern states, down the West Coast, and back across the South, visiting my relatives all along the way. My parents turned out to like Walter a lot, though my father did warn me that it would be "hard to live with a European" in ways that I "didn't yet understand." Again I pitied his provinciality.

We spent three weeks in New Orleans recording and photographing Walter's octogenarian jazz musician friends and holding the kitty at Preservation Hall; then we headed north to New York and Walter's first job on the theatre faculty of Harpur College, SUNY Binghamton.

We spent two years in Binghamton, one in the third-floor apartment of a molding clapboard house (Salvation Army furniture and Sears pots), the second in a plastic and polyester dorm apartment as counselors. I began to learn something about the petty politics of university life. Nesting in earnest now, I also began to learn how easy it was, without any academic pressure or expectation, to dawdle through the day's minimal housework and fail to make it to my typewriter at all.

I took a job in the continuing education department at Harpur, teaching the masterpieces course to secretaries and tool and die workers from Ansco, IBM, and Endicott shoes. I liked the students and the classroom, but I hardly felt I had a career; it had always been clear to me that I didn't want to *teach.*

I also costumed for Walter, mounting one show in which two assistants and I produced fifty-six costumes and twenty-three wigs. I had immediate pleasure of any day spent in the costume room, but paid for it in guilt that my second novel was not progressing.

Toward the end of the first year Walter was warned that he would be deported under Public Law 555, which decreed that Fulbright scholars could not trade their student visas for resident status until they had spent two years in their country of origin. Under this particular statute his marriage to an American made no difference, and in fact the customs officials several times tried to trick him into saying he had married me for citizenship. The law made a general kind of sense, since Fulbrights were often given to law and medical students from third world countries. But Flanders was not hurting for another playwright/director.

My mother, who had only reluctantly transferred her Republican loyalties from Taft, now wrote Barry Goldwater in the U.S. Senate, and Goldwater introduced a bill "For the Relief of Walter Eysselinck." This bill had not a hope of passing, and the deportation orders continued to arrive every month, but as long as the bill was pending, the orders did not have to be obeyed.

We moved into the dorm to save money, and I went to work for Young Audiences, Inc., a non-profit organization that provided chamber-music ensembles to rural schools throughout the state. I was hired for this job by Sue Winston, a woman with a silver upsweep and a golden soul. When I explained (that Arizona honesty) the tenuousness of our situation, Sue pulled her glasses down on her nose and peered over them. "My dear. Do you really think you can go through life beholden to Barry Goldwater?"

Probably not, and after half a year of it, it became obvious that we didn't want to go through life under deportation orders either. Walter began applying for Belgian jobs. In the late spring he was hired as a director by the Flemish division of Belgian National Television. I was two months pregnant when we left for Ghent.

*

If the lack of academic structure had been bad for my writing, depriving me of the English language was good for it. Walter and I spoke English at home on Vaderlaanstrasse, and friends, relatives, and waiters were always anxious to practice their English on me, but the topics were pretty well confined to food, tourism, and my Expectation. I became fluent in French on these three topics with my mother-in-law, and I began a rudimentary Flemish vocabulary with the shopkeepers and wives. But the theatrical conversations that interested me were in fast Flemish, and exclusively conducted by males. I had no one with whom to talk literature. The bookstores stocked almost no English fiction. The local library had all of Hemingway, Faulkner, and Jane Austen; I read or reread those. And I wrote. In the two years we spent in Belgium I finished my second novel and wrote the third.

We lived in the striking grey stone *bas haus* that Walter's architect father had designed in the thirties. Under the contrasting tutelage of Walter (more butter, more spice!) and his mother (more subtle, more vitamins!) I got to be a pretty fair gourmet cook, although a first pregnancy is not the best time to acquire this skill.

On the other hand, Ghent was a wonderful place to have a baby. "Natural" childbirth was in full vogue, and I took a tram weekly to classes in "kinesthetic training," monthly to an extraordinary clinic staffed by nuns and lorded over by a mammoth doctor who had no "second," never took a vacation, never got sick, delivered two or three dozen babies a week with hands each as big as a newborn. When Timothy Alan was born I was attended by this doctor, my familiar kines-thetician, my husband, and several nuns; and Tim was brought to me in a white lawn smock I had designed and made—fifteen minutes old in a button-down collar. I shared a semiprivate with a young woman who translated my Flemish into gutteral Ghentenaar for her mother, and with a parade of visitors to both of us, bearing azaleas and candied violets, whom the nuns offered beer and champagne.

Adjustments, I may have mentioned, come hard for me. For the first few months after Tim's birth I fought postpartum depression. Tethered to a hawk's cry by a small metal ring in the pit of my gut, I walked my diminished round. I had pushed myself hard to finish *The Dancer from the Dance* before Tim was born, and Faber was to publish it, but *Descend Again* had never found an American publisher, and now my New York agent Phyllis Jackson reported little success with this one. By the time Tim was five months old it became alarmingly apparent that he was going to walk early. I felt that I had lost any identity outside of "Tim's mom," and that if I didn't write a novel before he walked, I would never write another. I had an outline for a tight twenty-four-hour story, so I set a schedule and went at it, piling the desk with playpen toys that I handed down one after the other through the morning. *Eyes* was finished in five months, and accepted together with *Dancer* by Al Hart at Little, Brown.

Meanwhile Walter and I had left Tim behind with "Gramma Belgium" for a short Irish vacation, and on the way had visited my old tutor David Daiches in his new job as director of the School of English and American Studies at the University of Sussex. Daiches had banteringly offered me a teaching job, which I refused on the grounds that I had a husband. "Well," he said, "we're looking for a director for the arts centre . . ."

Whenever I am introduced in a lecture hall by someone reading through my *curriculum vita,* I have the impulse to point out that, as I die by drowning, this is *not* the life that will pass before my eyes. At fifty, I find that I am mainly interested in my child-hood and, of adulthood, what's going to happen in the next year or so. I'm also conscious that many authors have written their autobiographies only up to the point that they began to write other books: *A Childhood: One Writer's Begmnings.* Childhood contains all our mystery; adulthood only secrets.

As I lived the events of 1965 to 1971 in England, life's changes seemed most marked by the acquisition of a house, the birth of a second son, the loss of a third baby, domestic violence, the decision to leave the marriage. Work was what happened every day. If I was lucky some of the work was at the typewriter. I had come firmly to identify myself by the activity of writing, but a mother/teacher/writer inevitably deals with the claims of those professions in that order: the baby's cry/the class preparation/the chapter.

Nevertheless, as I look back on it, it was the commit-ment to writing that steadily deepened and changed its nature in those years. My first novel had come out in England to the kind of clattering acclaim that makes promises to the writer it dubs promising. *The Dancer from the Dance* had a cool reception, *Eyes* was praised but without any exclamation points attached. In America, both of these novels fell into the critical void. When Walter produced two of my short plays, *The Fantasy Level* and *The Beauty Operators,* for the Brighton Festival, one London paper treated me to the experience of rapier attack.

I had always known that I did not write for money—that was easy. Now between the publication of my first novel and my fourth, a total of ten years, I came to understand that, my childhood lessons notwithstand-ing, I did not write for praise. Writing is very hard for me, I'm very slow, and a lot of the time I simply hate doing it. Nevertheless that labor and the love of that labor are who I am. The work is the reward.

The Gardner Centre for the Arts was lavishly conceived and, in the years we were there, ambitiously pursued. Walter oversaw the construction of a theatre designed by Sean Kenny, cleverly transformable from an intimate round to a full proscenium, with several sorts of stage between. The building also had artists' studios, a scene shop, and a costume room.

It seems very odd to me now that I organized this room, equipped it, found crews, and designed the first couple of shows, without its ever occurring to me that this was the sort of work one should get paid for. I did not think of myself as a professional costumer, and it would be true to say that at the time I costumed mainly in the capacity of the director's wife. Later I got a small fee for shows at the Gardner, of which I costumed eight or ten, and also at the National Theatre of Belgium, where Walter continued to direct from time to time.

There are advantages to not being a professional, though. I always felt detached from the work, which meant that I could take an easy and immediate pleasure in it. I would be incapable of saying, "Isn't my new novel wonderful?" But I could perfectly well rush backstage with an armful of brocade or patched leather and demand, "Isn't this terrific? Didn't this turn out great? *Look* at this!"

I spent long hours in the costume room at the Gardner Centre, including many long nights, and some of my well-wishers deplored the loss of my writing time. But, unlike teaching, costuming exercises mainly the hand and eye, which is both a relief from the typewriter and an important teacher of sense detail. The costume crew offered me the richest camaraderie of my life, too—a relief from the solitude of writing. And then, one never knows where a novel is going to come from. Most of the plot and setting, and all of the professional detail, of my most recent novel, *Opening Nights,* came out of the hacking, tacking, binding, blind-hemming, and breaking-down of those days in the Gardner Centre basement.

The first year Walter, Tim, and I lived in a drearily modern rented bungalow, but the second year, with immense trepidation, we borrowed twelve thousand pounds for a brick box surrounded with two acres of garden under the Sussex Downs at Westmeston near Ditchling. This house was called "Green Hedges," which seemed both boring and untrue (in winter the hedges were brown, in spring leaf red), and for Walter's love of jazz we renamed it "Louisiana," which made us very unpopular with the neighbors.

We could not see the neighbors, however: roses, daffodils, orchards, and vegetable beds surrounded us; sheep fields and downs stretched to the horizon on every side. The house had been built in 1939 for the farm bailiff of the local manor. It had an entrance hall eighteen feet square with a manorial fireplace and a skylight thirty feet overhead. It had a living room twenty by thirty, a scullery, butler's pantry, wine cupboard, "box room" (I never did find out what that was; I kept boxes in it)—as well as seven bedrooms of which two comprised the "staff flat." The house had been lived in since the Second World War by two aging women who had retreated to one downstairs corner of it. Nothing had been painted in that time. The spiders and mice had flourished. There were a hundred and eight broken window panes. I was seven months pregnant when we moved in.

If Belgium was a good place to have a first baby, Sussex was a magical place to have a second. The British assumption is that, after a normal first pregnancy, the second child will be born at home. I was therefore scheduled on the regular rounds of the district midwife, who instructed me in filling biscuit tins with cotton wool and baking them at rice pudding temperature, and so forth. She was, however, appalled at the condition of the house, which had one temporary electrical source and no heat, and suggested that I might want after all to consider hospital. I argued her down, feeling more like a pioneer than I ever had in Arizona.

I picked the smallest bedroom, gave it yellow eyelet curtains and a two-bar electric fire, and my second boy was born in a storm on Guy Fawkes Day with the celebratory fireworks bursting over Lewes six miles to our east. The midwife cheered me on, Walter mopped my brow with cologne; five minutes before the birth our four-month Irish setter *Eh La-Bas* wandered in and jumped on the bed.

"On the whole," said staid Dr. Rutherford, "I don't think we want that dog in here." He ushered the puppy out and washed his hands again. The midwife said, "Just pick a spot on the picture rail, aim the head for that, and *push.*" Dr. Rutherford positioned his hands to receive the baby that I, of my labor alone, joyfully delivered. (Like the vascular bundles, I later gave this experience in slightly altered form to Virginia Marbalestier of *Raw Silk.*)

But I had expected a girl. "Ah," I gasped. "We'll have to have another," to which Dr. Rutherford replied that he couldn't recall ever hearing the suggestion *quite* so soon before.

For two days this creature of the unexpected gender had no name. I am by profession a namer of things, and this was very painful for me. When Tim was born, I had tried to sell Walter on the idea of "Dana" as a name, after my grandfather, for either a girl or a boy, either first or middle. He would have none of it. Now I tried again to convince him, but Walter simply didn't care for the sound. Finally we agreed that we both liked "Toby," but not "Tobias." The *Oxford Etymological Dictionary of Names* yielded "Tobyn," and we concurred in the choice of Tobyn Alexander Eysselinck.

I telegraphed my parents in relief that the decision had been made. A week later I had a letter from my mother. How odd, she said. Did I remember that Gakie was always called Dana T.? The T. stood for Tobin, which was his mother's maiden name. But he had always hated the Tobins, and had pretended that it stood for Timothy.

I have slim patience for astrology and related pseudosciences. But I do believe that much of what we call ESP is simply memory and intuition imperfectly understood, and that telepathy probably has less in common with magic than with radio waves. The naming of my sons is one of half-a-dozen striking instances in my life of my having made a connection I am not quite willing to attribute to coincidence. Or, as I put it in the mouth of Galcher in *The Buzzards,* the novel I was then about to write, "coincidence comes from God."

*

While Toby and the Gardner Centre were being born, I started teaching at Sussex, sometimes full-time, sometimes half. Even half-time teaching allowed me to hire a nanny, to repaint a few walls, and replace a few window panes. Earning my own nanny was important to me—I knew that it was necessary for me to "waste" innumerable hours at the typewriter, and that I could not be beholden to Walter for the time that, as W. H. Auden observed, you don't know "whether you are procrastinating or must wait for it to come." I also wanted to teach for the experience itself, and for the comradeship of the faculty. I taught the basic courses on a modified tutorial system—usually two students at a time, occasionally small seminars—and, as at Harpur College, I enjoyed both the students and the sense that the dormant actress in me was getting exercised. But I cared less about it than about house, boys, theatre. Until I came to Tallahassee, teaching presented itself to me as a job, not a *metier.*

Occasionally I gave a university-wide lecture, and these always filled me with the terror of the early elocution student, so that I prepared heavily and long for them. The very first of these lectures was to be on Aeschylus' *Oresteia,* which had been a work of signal importance to me since the days of Palmer Bovie's great-books course.

We had begun the refurbishing of our ramshackle house with the "staff flat"—in order to rent it, in order to pay the gardener; and our first tenants were two

With Tim and Toby, at "Louisiana," 1970

male American graduate students. One of these—I'll call him R.—had until a few months before been engaged to Valerie Percy, daughter of the senator from Illinois. It was not long after he moved into our house that Valerie Percy was stabbed in her bed in a house full of sleeping family members. R. went home to the funeral.

When he returned he needed to talk, frequently and often late into the night. He was particularly haunted by the realization that now, at Sussex, he was *popular* because of the murder. His connection to celebrity-tragedy meant he could date any girl he wanted. He had not much liked Senator Percy, but he now identified grimly with the sense that Percy, who was up for reelection and would certainly win, would never know whether his victory resulted from the murder of his daughter.

So there I was, in the evening solacing this troubled student, in the daytime writing a lecture about a king who must have his daughter killed in order to make war on Troy. The plot fell on me: an American politician who must risk his daughter for his career. I had never seen myself writing a political novel, and I was afraid of the size of it; but Goldwater had run for the presidency by then, and at the distance of four thousand miles from Arizona I had often felt that the people I grew up with were peculiar aliens. This plot was one I needed to explore, in order to make some connections between the cowgirl and the lady of the English manor.

For more than a year, though, I costumed, mothered, and taught, only daydreaming this book as I drove over the downs each day to the university.

My American editor at Little, Brown helped me by sending me dozens of press handouts of speeches from Percy, Goldwater, Rockefeller, and Robert Kennedy, until I got the feel of the rhetoric. I was determined that, although there was a reference to the *Oresteia* on virtually every page, the story would be coherent to someone who had never heard of any Greek but Spiro Agnew. (I succeeded all too well, and no one—agent, editor, critic, scholar—has noticed my arduous theft until I point it out.)

The Buzzards came out in 1970 in both London and Boston, and although it was nominated for a Pulitzer in America, its real success was in England. I think I had been away from home for long enough that the perspective I had of America was detached. I don't mean by this that it was untrue; on the contrary. My journalist brother, when he first read the novel, responded that I didn't realize how dirty American politics were. When he read it again ten years later, he told me that I had "invented Jimmy Carter."

Meanwhile, the rapier attack notwithstanding, *The Beauty Operators* had been produced by Thames Television, and I had written a television play (which ended up with the dreadful title of *Hoddinott Veiling)* that was taken to the Monte Carlo Festival as British Independent Television's entry.

I could now make, if not a living, at least my nanny's living writing television plays, and I quit the university. I had also written a children's book, *The Truck on the Track,* and after a long search for an illustrator I more or less literally stumbled (he and I being stumblers both, of the amiable sort) into John Vernon Lord. John's painstaking detail and sharp colors reflected two of my own work methods (his wife describes it as "knitting"), and his vivid pictures helped sell the book to Jonathan Cape, afterwards to Bobbs-Merrill. In the last year in England I set John Vernon Lord's story *The Giant Jam Sandwich* into verse. After the publication of *The Buzzards,* I reviewed fiction regularly for *New Statesman* magazine. Once a month a stack of thirty books would arrive; I'd skim them, read eight or ten, pick four or five to review. I could get in bed at nine at night, curl up with a novel and call it work—my kind of job!—except that it was no living wage either.

The vogue in my early-mothering years was for natural childbirth and permissiveness. In the same period in my mother's life it had been for a germfree environment—with the consequence that I hadn't had the usual complement of childhood diseases. During the costuming of *A Doll's House* at the Gardner Centre I got the mumps. I remember sitting in bed miserably hemming a skirt with fourteen yards of ruffle, wondering why I had *ever* put so much energy into such an endeavor. Now, when Toby was about a year-and-a-half old, I lost a third pregnancy to rubella.

The Gardner also hit rough times. A British recession strapped the university for funds, and the arts appeared among the expendable expenses. Walter ran afoul of the students, who resented the Centre's professional orientation. The fine English actor Patrick Wymark, then dying of alcoholism although we didn't know it, failed to learn his lines and put the audience through an excruciating opening night. He fully redeemed himself by his performance the following season in Eduardo Manet's *Nuns* (and by bringing into my life his friend Bernie Hopkins, who later sustained me and the children through difficult months)—but that production, the happiest I ever took part in, was a harbinger of disaster for all its participants. Wymark and the theatre designer died of heart attacks, another actor hanged himself, a third was institutionalized for a breakdown, the set designer died of leukemia—all within a year.

Walter and I separated. One way of describing this is that I started to write a comic novel about a couple impossibly at odds; and as I wrote, it became less funny.

The novel began as *Warp,* was eventually published as *Raw Silk.* I had chosen the textile industry as background because I figured that I knew enough about cloth to have a head start on the research. I had no intention of writing an academic novel, and in any case it is my practice to write from autobiographical *feelings,* housing them in fictional characters and events. (In the case of *Raw Silk* this turned out to be no favor to Walter; readers accurately picked up on the feelings and inaccurately assigned Oliver Marbalestier's rape and assault to him.)

I had by that time noticed that several themes, unchosen, had chosen me; each of my novels contained a parent in some way abandoning his or her children (a thing I could never do), a suicide or attempted suicide, and a strong older man/younger woman relationship. I resolved this time to choose the unchosen, and to face these themes head on. "This morning I abandoned my only child . . ." the book began.

There was another thing that I wanted very much to accomplish. Richmond Lattimore, in his introduction to the *Oresteia,* had opened up for me the secret of Aeschylus' use of interconnected image patterns. In *The Buzzards,* which drew heavily on the *Oresteia,* I had taught myself how to do this by building on the *same* symbol complex—the net, the web, wild birds and animals, their eggs and young, etc.—that Aeschylus had used. In the new book I wanted to create a complex of original symbols, "interweaving" images of cloth, water, travel, plant life, and balance.

The research for the novel took me into East Anglia, to textile mills in country I hadn't seen since I was a student at Cambridge; and then to Japan, the first time I had been on my own since before my marriage. Japan would not have been my choice of a new country to explore—the novel plot dictated it—so the intensity of my pleasure took me by surprise. I was humbled by my illiteracy and proud of nevertheless being able to manoeuver, from Tokyo to Nikko, Takayama, Osaka. I felt clarified by the clarity of Japanese sounds and colors, calmed by the patterns of gardens, temples, paintings, cloth. And, surprised by how much at home I felt, I was also startled at how much I loved being alone.

Years before in Binghamton, Walter and I had made friends with Blair and Julia Kling, and it had turned out to be a friendship that could survive transatlantic separation. We had all met again in Ghent, London, Sussex—and Julia and I discovered that we could take up a conversation mid-sentence after a three-year hiatus. Blair taught history at the University of Illinois, and Julia had in the interim become a family counselor there.

In December of 1971 I brought the children and returned to America. Tim was then eight, Toby five. Though I left England in manic spirits, high on freedom, it must in some dim corner of my brain have been clear to me that I was going to need my best friend and a family counselor, and so we went to Illinois.

First, though, I took the children home to Phoenix for Christmas, arriving with mystical appropriateness four hours after the death of my grandmother, so that I was able to arrange the funeral while my mother took care of the boys. Mom had for years now been subject to heart failure, and lived with an oxygen tank beside the bed while Dad cared for her and learned to give her the life-saving mercury shots. It is another of the coincidences I cannot explain, that while I arranged for the burial of her mother, and was myself unknowingly on the verge of miscarriage, I was able to offer Mom the happy distraction of Tim and Toby, their suitcase of Christmas presents to wrap. She was not, however, fooled by my blow-softening version of our surprise visit. "You've left him, haven't you?"

The next eight months in Illinois were traumatic in every way that I have since come to understand as normal, but which felt at the time as if I had invented some entirely new form and depth of pain. Luckily, I was totally ignorant of the sad state of American academic budgets, and I presented myself so persistently to the University of Illinois that they actually found me a job.

I was to teach freshman composition in a Special Opportunities Education program to students from "disadvantaged Chicago high schools." The pay was barely livable, but we got a bargain in a beautiful rental on a lake, and for as long as my freedom-high lasted, it seemed to me the best possible way to come home to America.

When classes began, I learned that the black students did not want to be taught white literature and did not want to be taught black literature by me. The two Chicanos wanted Lorca. The militants were articulate, quick, and ashamed of being at the University of Illinois at all; the moderates were cowed and quiet. Many of the students wrote well, a couple of them brilliantly, in a hip style it was my duty to destroy in order that they could produce term papers for history. They knew all this. I walked into the situation believing I would teach them Yeats. I am not sure to this day what was learned on either side.

My own emotional state so deteriorated that I could no longer write—or even cook and sew. In paralytic lassitude I tried to choose a pattern or operate a pair of scissors. I had a hundred and fifty pages of the novel done, but the only thing I could write was a journal that seemed to me to say nothing but "Help! Help!" (Actually it's not so bad, and has taught me how much of competence operates on automatic pilot, how much we misperceive our own performance or effect.) I relied heavily on Julia, both of us aware that the imbalance in this new relationship threatened our friendship. And I relied heavily on Gail Godwin, who was teaching at Illinois that year on leave from Iowa, and who lent me her house and her tough understanding when I needed them.

I knew I had to have a real job. The only appropriate opening in the graduate office listings was an associate professorship in creative writing at Florida State University in Tallahassee. I didn't know much about my future at that point, but I knew for sure I wasn't going to *Florida.*

I had bought a rattletrap station wagon. In the spring break I loaded Tim, Toby, and three students who would pay the gas, and went back to New York to seek help from the Barnard employment office. Tim had chicken pox on the way to New York (Toby on the way back). We ran out of gas in the middle of the night in the middle of Pennsylvania. When I left England, I had left everything of my own behind except one suitcase of my favorite clothes and jewelry. We'd been in New York a half hour or so when the car was broken into and this suitcase stolen. I went to Barnard in the jeans and sweater that were now the only clothes I owned. I felt as if, having left most of myself behind by choice in Sussex, the rest had been snatched away. There was no job to be had, and there was no me.

I did not see how I could live in *northern Florida,* a regression and in any case a contradiction in terms; and after I'd got the job I could see it even less. I told Julia that I was failing to cope with the children and would have to give them up to their father, but she was no help. She said, "Did they have breakfast this morning? Did they catch the school bus? Did they have lunch money? You're coping." I told a colleague in Illinois that I was going to have to commit myself, but he was no help. He said, "How many hours a day do you think there are in a mental institution?" I decided that I would give up and go back to the marriage, but I thought that perhaps it would be better to try teaching at Florida State first, to prove that I couldn't do it; otherwise I might always wonder if I could have.

I have elsewhere written of my arrival in Tallahassee, my conviction that it was a possible place to die but not to live, my abortive search for an apartment with a gas stove, my slow reemergence as a functional self. Though I have now been here fifteen years, longer than any other place except the place where I was raised, the Tallahassee episode is ongoing, and seems to have been brief, and I can't clearly tell which are its most significant passages.

In my first year here, my mother died in Arizona. For two years I made no progress on *Raw Silk.* I had conceived it as a comedy; now it seemed both tragic and melodramatic. When I was able to see it as both funny and painful, I wrote again.

But I wrote looking out onto an asphalt parking lot. At best, Tallahassee seemed no better than a stopgap, and the stages of my reconciliation came slowly one by one.

First I discovered it was a wonderful place for raising children. Mine, having had earaches and adenoidal infections from October to March in England, now lived all year outdoors and never got sick. Then it dawned on me that Florida State was an extraordinarily congenial place to work, my colleagues supportive and disinclined to politicking, my students as badly educated, and as eager, as I had been at their age. For the first few years I felt trapped in a corner of America ("You can get to hell from here, but you have to change in Atlanta"), but after the publication of *Raw Silk* I began to be asked to speak in places far and near, large and small, by people who sent me tickets to get there. I got a dog and bought a house, and then a bigger dog, and a bigger house.

I taught narrative techniques until I figured out how to do it, and then wrote a textbook, *Writing Fiction.* The British production of *The Nuns* continued to haunt me until I found a way to wrench it around into a plot, and wrote *Opening Nights.* I began to think about my mother's childhood in the marble quarry, and am at work on a first historical novel, *Cutting Stone.*

For four years from 1978 I was married to Bill Humphries, a.k.a. Lazlo Freen or, to his friends, The Freen; a painter, a gentle person, a former student of mine, eighteen years my junior. I have also told that

The author's father on the beach at Alligator Point, Florida, 1983

story elsewhere, and will tell it again. Though the marriage ended, I came out of it warmly in favor of the older-woman—younger-man liaison; Freen and I came out of it the best of friends. This is a phenomenon I would not believe if I hadn't lived it, so I'll leave it to later fiction to try to be convincing.

My boys have grown up here, so different from each other that it seems impossible they were raised under the same effort of Spock and spaghetti. Tim is twenty-three, Episcopalian, Republican, polite, a sharp dresser, a gourmet, and a second lieutenant in the U.S. Army. Toby is twenty, a radical feminist, a left-wing anarchist, and an actor, busking around Piccadilly Circus in a mohawk and shredded jeans.

But he no longer goes by that name. Like his great-grandfather before him he rejected the Tobyn. He was eight, straight-haired and stocky, inclined to suffer in the shadow of his older brother, and to believe that anyone who praised his blue eyes meant that he was fat. He came to me and said, "Toby is a round name, isn't it?"

"Why yes," I said. "That's very clever."

"Tim is a straight-up-and-down name."

A couple of days later he announced that he had taken his middle name, and every time I got it wrong for the next two years—every time—he said, "My name is *Alex.*"

We have traveled, together and separately, the boys to Belgium, Pittsburgh, Bavaria; I to France, Italy, India; and all of us to England, where Alex at seventeen made good his promise to take up residence. Florida State University has a London program on which I teach from time to time, so that I have been able to put back into my life the friends I left behind in Cambridge and Sussex in the total of ten years there.

Of the dozens of stories about people under the illusion that they are short-term sojourners *(Magic Mountain* comes to mind, and *It's A Wonderful Life),* my favorite is about the boy Krishna traveling with the godhead. He leaves his companion resting under a tree while he crosses the field to fetch the god a ladle of water from the farmhouse on the opposite side. The ladle is brought by a young woman with waterblue eyes that remind him of the eyes of the god. He forgets why he came. He marries the woman with the water-blue eyes, brings the farm to fruit, nurtures the animals, and fathers many children. When the woman dies he is an old man. He remembers his errand, fills the ladle, and carries it across the field. The god sits under the tree. He drinks. "Thank you," he says.

Ten years ago I moved, smack in the middle of the capital city of Florida, into a patently English house. It is white brick with forest green shutters, climbing ivy, a picket fence. The only thing that I added to the garden at Sussex was a magnolia tree; here my acre wears magnolias as its natural right; I have added the roses and the daffodils.

Spring and fall I often borrow a cottage on the beach at Alligator Point an hour away. I take a typewriter and my dogs Shirley and Pushkin. I sit and write looking out over the dunes, the sea oats, and the sand, to the Gulf of Mexico. The water doesn't jump or tumble here; it is not a competition. I am at peace, of a piece with the sand, grass, sea. I have never found the place where I could say: This is my proper ground. But I can look out at the waterblue gulf and up through the fronds of a palm tree at the searing sky, and it reminds me quite a lot of having a home.

Autobiographical notes after 1986:

In retrospect, the eighties seem a narrowing and thinning time. Tim left home for college, first for a year with his father at the University of Michigan, then transferring to the University of Florida at Gainesville. My second marriage ended in 1981, and when Alex and I spent a semester on the FSU London program in 1983, he stayed behind to finish first school and then college (and has been in London ever since). That same year I gave up drinking and two years later, with more difficulty, smoking; alcohol had been an abusive lover, nicotine a false friend.

In May of 1986 my father was diagnosed with lymphoma, and the chemo proved too brutal for his heart. It was clear that our stepmother, Gladys, was by that time in the early stages of Alzheimers and could not take adequate care of him; my brother and I flew to Arizona at least monthly, he from California and I from Florida, for the next seven months. It's worth remarking that when Dad and Gladys had visited us in Tallahassee for what proved to be his last Christmas, I had urged him to write an autobiography, and he (thorough, intense, and dogged, as always), had complied on the sort of yellow legal pad familiar from my childhood. He sent his memoir to Tallahassee in chapters that I typed on the computer and returned; he proofed them and sent them back to me for correction—so that by the time I sat with him in hospice in Sun City, I was able to read him his life from a bound copy of his "book."

If this wearing and grieving period had a positive side, it was that my brother and I discovered we could be generous, supportive friends. At one point Stan called, touched to find how thoroughly Dad had arranged his insurance so that we would not be burdened with his last bills. "What he's leaving us," he said, "is Gladys," and we solemnly vowed that, she being childless and without relatives, we would also share her care (she lived another ten years). In October Aunt Jessie, Dad's sister, came to spend the last few weeks in hospice with him. Dad died in November; Stan and I acknowledged the fearful strangeness of being orphans.

The author's oldest son, Tim Eysselinck, 1986

In many ways I welcomed living alone, though I had a feeling that the children's portion of the house lacked ballast and might lift off suddenly one night. From time to time unhappily married women I met at conferences or reading gigs wistfully told me how lucky a life I had. When I went to Alligator Point to write, what I felt was not freedom so much as pleasurable awe, born of solitude at the edge of the ocean. I was conscious of being unable to imagine ever again sharing my space and time with someone else. Loneliness, however, came and went. Involuntarily and inveterately verbal as I am, sometimes the best experiences seemed incomplete without a shared critique. I spent a delightful six weeks at Yaddo in the "little-season" with like-minded artists, and then a significantly less delightful summer session full of brat packers and agent-talk. The novel *Cutting Stone* ground along slowly at the center of my life, and I realized that when art is all there is, it can matter absurdly out of all proportion whether it's going well or badly.

Since the London semester in 1983 I had toyed with the idea of buying a flat in London. Now in 1988 (in the all-time peak for real estate, the worst time for

Youngest son Toby (now Alex) Eysselinck, 1986

such an undertaking) I used my small inheritance as down payment on a "studio," a single 15x20 room with a closet-sized kitchen and a bath, in the Ladbroke Grove neighborhood near Portobello Road. *Writing Fiction,* by then in its third edition, would cover the mortgage payments. I had reestablished many old, and contracted new, friendships in England, and it suited me wonderfully to write during the day and go to the theatre in the evening. My idea was that if I spent the academic year in Tallahassee and four-month summers in London, I would have the ideal writing life, and enough of both city and sun.

Almost immediately I fell in love with Peter Ruppert, who had a three-year-old daughter in Tallahassee and could not share such a schedule.

Peter and his wife Jeanne had been friends for all eighteen of my years at FSU. We had (we later figured out) arrived on the same day in 1972; Peter and I had met that first winter on a Ph.D. orals and immediately disagreed about Brecht; we three had been part of a social-intellectual group that evolved over the years to study German expressionist film and literary theory, celebrate major holidays together, and play cutthroat games of Risk and Trivia at the beach. As editor of the FSU press, Jeanne had edited my poetry collection *Material Goods.* Peter, a film, comparative literature and Utopian scholar in modern languages, often served as outside member on theses and dissertations in the writing program. When Peter and Jeanne adopted Anne in 1986, she had become part of the group, and once at Thanksgiving at our house, while Tim made gravy at the stove, I had famously dandled her on my knee, saying, "Don't you want to bring me one of these?" It did not then cross my mind that Anne herself would be "brought" to me.

Peter divorced Jeanne in 1989, and after a while he and I began going to movies together, then to dinner, where I apparently admonished him that we were "out as friends, not on a date." The truth is that I was prone to anxiety-ridden infatuation and had never before experienced a deepening, ripening friendship. By 1991 we were, however, "living together in two houses" and vacationing together in my London flat; in 1992, when *Cutting Stone* was published by Houghton Mifflin, we drove six thousand miles cross country for the publicity tour, and I showed him all the haunts of my childhood; in '93 we spent a semester in Italy on the FSU Florence program. Late that year we invited our friends to Saturday brunch, sneaked off on the Tuesday to Tortola, were married in St. Thomas on the Thursday, back on Friday. We put a white bow on the door by which our brunch guests entered: all the women got it; none of the men did. Anne, seven by now, and not entirely reconciled to this turn of events, nevertheless proudly showed off the iridescent purple party dress I had made her.

Home life became rich and easy; in the professional sphere things somewhat soured. My colleague Jerome Stern, who had for many years brilliantly directed the writing program, died, like Dad, but far too early, of lymphoma, and for a few years the program floundered. The University seemed to me, like the arts and the English-speaking world in general, money-mad, bureaucratically burdened, and caught up in corporate *newspeak.* For four years I worked on a novel called *Paper,* set in a Georgia paper mill I had thoroughly researched. I had a plot, a theme, and a device I loved—surely a bad sign—but the characters would not deign to come alive. Even their deaths were a yawn. One point-of-view character was a writer who couldn't write, and when he did, wrote more badly than I intended. I went to the desk each morning (or, more often, afternoon) leaden and trapped, only wishing for my pages to be done or the hours to end. When I had about two hundred pages I showed them to my agent Gail Hochman and my editor at Houghton Mifflin, Janet Silver. Janet came down to Tallahassee. She asked, "What do you *love* about this novel?" and I knew instantly that the answer was: not enough. I scrapped it. This was a fearful thing to do. I had never not finished a book I had begun, and superstition ineluctably suggested that if I didn't finish this one I would never finish another.

Nor do I believe that when one door closes another inevitably opens. But it must happen sometimes. My anger at university paperwork generated a short story that would, though I didn't immediately know it, provide the seed of the next novel. After the publication of *Cutting Stone,* I had begun writing regularly for the *New York Times Book Review.* Now in 1995 Bob Stewart at *New Letters* magazine called to ask if I would write a quarterly essay column—anything I wished to comment on re life or lit. I said no, not possible; my load was already heavy with teaching and recalcitrant fiction. But Peter said: why not? We generated, he pointed out, more than enough material over coffee at morning "mucky talk" (*mucky* being Anne's word for blanket). And with misgivings that now seem bizarre, I said all right, then, and set my hand to the unfamiliar genre of the "personal essay." Almost at once I discovered the relief and pleasure, given my heavy academic commitment, of being able to *finish* something and see it in print (—what's more, exactly as I had written it. Almost alone among editors, the guys at *New Letters* fix the typos and allow great latitude in matters of quirk and style.)

Meanwhile Lynda Davis in the superb FSU dance department involved me in texts for dance. This began modestly enough with a colloquy on the subject of inspirational sources with choreographer Nancy Smith-Fichter, then as a few exchanges of fiction and choreography classes. Eventually I was using writing exercises as "problems" for her choreographers to solve in dance while I held a microphone and fed back images their bodies suggested in a rough poetry-patois that the dancers dubbed "white lady rap." We publicly

With husband Peter Ruppert, Cambridge, England, 1991

performed an homage to John Cage, "Dadadata," then a more ambitious "memory quilt" called "Text/tile," and a comedy, "The Empty Dress." We began doing annual performances, choreographed and written anew each time, for the annual quilt show at the R. A. Gray museum And there began to stir in me the long-dormant love of theatre.

As long ago as Cambridge and the Yale School of Drama I had believed that playwriting would be my major form, but for many reasons I had not written a play since I came to Tallahassee. Tallahassee was part of it—not a theatrical metropolis, and although the Drama department was good and getting better, there was the usual academic insularity between English and Theatre. I was also, after painful experience as the wife and chief feather-smoother of a temperamental director, to some extent relieved to operate in a more solitary venue. Most importantly, since my failure to write *Cutting Stone* as a film script in 1976, I had come to believe that my best subject matter was psychological, and that often I couldn't even *find out* what the story was until I entered—the entrance that playwriting denies you—my characters' thoughts. But now I started to itch for the communal, externalized, and energetic genre of spectacle. I remembered that my friend Eleanor Bron had, as a Cambridge undergraduate, once mentioned Medea as the part she most wanted to play. Our friendship had renewed and flourished with my London stays, and I now promised her a *Medea*. FSU awarded me a semester's grant to work in London, and with the help of an undergraduate improvisational crew, trying to use the "choreographic" methods of writing I had learned from Lynda Davis, I sat down every afternoon to produce a scene or a monologue without any preconception of who the

Stepdaughter Anne Lindsay Ruppert with "Chelsea," 2001

ing under her direction, and was later produced by the Bloomington Playwright's Project, where it won the Reva Shiner Prize in the late nineties.

While I was at work on this play, my first husband and my boys' father, Walter Eysselinck, became ill. The boys visited him in both Egypt, where he had taught for a number of years, and in Belgium, where he died in the winter of 1996. Apart from the natural sympathy for Tim and Alex, each of whom separately grieved to me, "I always thought I would get to know my father"—apart from that, I had a curious reaction to Walter's death, which was disbelief mixed with the jolting sense: *now the theatre is open to me again.* I could not have foreseen, and could perhaps not have invented, such an impulse. With it, I recognized how clearly I had repudiated the theatre with the repudiation of that marriage.

Stepmother Gladys died in 1997, and I had meanwhile become the primary caretaker (at long distance) of the last family member of that Burroway generation, my father's only sister, beloved Aunt Jessie. Jessie's mother had died a day after she was born premature in 1910; she was not expected to survive (though in fact she lived to a vigorous ninety-two years). She had never married, had become the first Burroway Democrat and academic (historian), and had lived for forty years, in Oklahoma and then Missouri, with colleague Winifred White, in an old-fashioned sort of maiden-friendship—patently a marriage but never a love affair. Fearful that her money would run out before her life did, in her eighties Aunt Jessie had let herself get hooked on mail-in sweepstakes, her house full to bursting with boxes of china figurines, video and audio tapes, "semi-precious" jewelry, and kitchen gadgets. It took me, Stan, the attorney general of Missouri, and the collusion of the postman to put a stop to her shameless exploitation by Publishers Clearinghouse, U.S. Purchasing, Reader's Digest, and sundry other scams. Eventually we got back some of her money, and eventually Jessie saw she had been conned. In the meantime, with a sense not entirely free of my own corruption, I was inspired to use her plight in a further play, *Sweepstakes,* which I never showed her, but which was read at the Playwrights' Center of San Francisco as a finalist in the 1998 Dramarama and, through the help of actress Brenda Blethyn, at the National Theatre Studio in London. Charles Olsen, director of the Actors' Repertory Theatre of Tallahassee, had suggested and collaborated with me on the

characters were, when or where the drama took place, or what would happen. In these sessions I "danced it through," that is, continued to write dialogue in the conviction that with repetition and exercise, something would eventually happen. All I knew about the plot was this: daddy falls in love with a younger woman, and mommy says it's okay, but then she murders the young woman and the kids. It turned out to be a plot with which *all* of my student volunteers could one way or other identify. At the end of the semester, I had some hundred and fifty scenes from which I set about to shape the (stylized and anachronistic, however) *Medea with Child.* Eleanor has never (yet) had a chance to play the role, but it had a fine London read-

adaptation for radio of *Opening Nights,* which the company recorded in 1997. Now over a period of nearly a year they rehearsed and helped me with the *Sweepstakes* script, producing it in 1999. They also spent a winter's Sundays in helpful improvisation for a play that I have yet to write. In the meantime I revived an old idea in a one-act, *Division of Property,* which was selected by Lanford Wilson for the Arts & Letters 2000 prize and produced there and at the Stella Adler in Los Angeles. My London agent, who does not handle plays, dubiously and almost wistfully, asked, "Are you determined to be a playwright and novelist both?" A commercial indiscretion, clearly, to which the answer is by now a clear and commercially unviable *yes.*

Through their thirties, my wild boys steadied and settled. Alex found his partner in red-headed British Tricia Howard, and went to work first for the University of Wisconsin and later for the London Underground, putting his money where his mouth was—in the working class. His college degree would have allowed him to start in management, but he preferred to work his way up from station assistant one exam and promotion at a time, focusing on worker conditions and the necessity of public transport. Tricia gave birth to Eleanor Janet in 1994 and Holly Katherine in 1996, and they live in Morden, south London.

Tim put in a stint as security guard in Cameroon, joined the Army Reserves, and was sent from his base in Frankfurt to Bosnia, Republic of Congo, and Namibia, where he ran a de-mining operation. When this operation was privatized, he was hired to continue in the job he had done as a soldier. In Namibia he met and married Birgitt Coetzee, a third-generation colonial (German and Afrikaans) with a ten-year-old son— thereby becoming a stepparent like his mom. In 2001 they gave birth to a daughter Thyra; the next year Tim's Namibian job was completed and they were transferred to Ethiopia for the same sort of operation. If you had told me ten years ago that one of my sons would be running a humanitarian de-mining team in Africa, and the other Supervisor of London Underground's Oxford Circus Station, I would certainly have guessed wrong which would be which.

With our children spaced out among Florida, England, and Africa, Peter and I are happily forced to travel. In 1998 we sold the Ladbroke Grove flat and moved to a three-bedroom in Maida Vale, where we now spend

"The London granddaughters," Holly (left) and Eleanor, 2002

two months every summer writing and playing with the granddaughters, taking side trips to Africa and the continent. I'm grateful to Peter for bringing me a daughter, and to my sons for having produced three girls, all of which makes up for the deprivation of a daughterless youth. Eleanor and Holly in particular would rather have costumes than clothes, so my old profession of costumier has an easy amateur outlet.

I've said almost nothing of the university to which I was beholden for my living, and that smacks of an ingratitude of which I am no doubt guilty. I have been enriched and perhaps kept young by my students, of whom a few have become close friends. I value my colleagues, who infuse my social as well as my professional life, and though teaching has always been my job, writing my work, the university treated me well. No one ever asked if I might rather have time than money, but I was granted a McKenzie Professorship in the late eighties (McKenzie being my paternal grandmother's maiden name, this was a matter of considerable excitement, for me and especially Aunt Jessie), given a Distinguished Teaching Award in 1992, and made a Robert O'Lawton Distinguished Professor in 1995. Nevertheless at some point in the mid-nineties I realized that I had stopped learning from my students—the graduates could still surprise me, but I had read every undergraduate short story I was likely to receive—and at the earliest opportunity, which was 1998, I chose "phased retirement," which meant teaching one semester instead of two.

A little to my surprise, greatly to my relief, I discovered that I had not been lying all these years, and that I write more when I teach less. The short story "Report

With step-grandson Neal and granddaughter Thyra, 2001

on Professional Activities" expanded by fits and starts into a novel, *Time Lapse,* near completion. A self-contained section of it, "Deconstruction," was published in *Prairie Schooner,* where it won the 1999 Lawrence Foundation award. An aborted chapter became a short story, "The Mandelbrot Set," which appeared in *Five Points* and was reprinted in *Pushcart Prize XXVII.* The fifth edition of *Writing Fiction* appeared. Several of the essays I had written for *New Letters* and other magazines and anthologies suggested the shape I had perceived in my life, of diminishment and re-burgeoning: loss of mother and father, departure of the children, then love, marriage, stepmotherhood, and grandmotherhood. I collected these under the title *Embalming Mom,* and this book was published by the University of Iowa Press in spring 2002 as the launch volume of a new non-fiction series, "Sightline." That summer the sixth edition of *Writing Fiction* also appeared, along with a new across-the-genres text book, *Imaginative Writing,* which I had balked at writing but in which I enjoyed having my say about poetry, drama, and the essay as well as fiction. I retired in May.

It's forty years since I published my first novel, and it's inevitable that I'm aware of vast changes in the publishing business, which is more efficient, savvy, and international; also trashier, more cutthroat, and less welcoming to experiment. On the plus side, whereas I started out being "discovered" (more often and for more years than could feel comfortable) by older men editors; now I am aided, edited, and encouraged by younger women. On the other side, the accountants and the money managers make ever more of the publishing decisions, which implies and dictates a swing to the political right.

I know no serious writer who does not grieve at the arbitrary nature of the twenty-first-century Pub Bizz. The star system makes for ludicrous imbalance between quality and reward, and all of us are tainted by the scramble for advances, publicity, puffs, and prizes. My agent is the best in New York, but the nature of agenting has changed; in the fifties, the agent was a cheerleader for her clients; now her job is often to act as buffer between the realities of the market and the unrealistic expectations of art. I've been extraordinarily lucky in the intellect and goodwill of my editors, who, however, are also increasingly shackled to the bottom line. It's easy to see how a totalitarian state censors its writers through threat and bodily harm; it's less evident, but also insidious, how capitalism silences those who don't particularly suit themselves to Mammon.

All of this has left me with a double vision: my relationship to the language is full of joy, my doings in the public sphere mired in the ancient angst. The exception is public reading—perhaps because the readers' audience is self-selected, and we have a mutually vested interested in the pleasure of the word.

Aging, I find, gives with one hand what it takes with the other, balancing diminished looks with diminished vanity, offering concentration in the place of vigor, replacing lived melodrama with strange invention. At this writing, still polishing the manuscript of *Time Lapse,* I find myself with a second wind or, perhaps, a third act. I've written a new children's book, the first since *Giant Jam Sandwich,* which is still in print. I'm ready to write a memory play set in Arizona in the forties, *Parts of Speech,* and have a further novel heavy in my head (born out of the dregs of the abandoned *Paper,* and in answer to the question "What do you *love* about this novel?") I'm going to write a musical!—if I can get the rights to the novel I want to adapt; and in any case Peter and I, having more or less settled our disagreement about Brecht, will write a version of *The Caucasian Chalk Circle* set in the Civil War during the burning of Atlanta.

After that . . . but maybe I'd better not tempt the Gods.

BIOGRAPHICAL AND CRITICAL SOURCES:

BOOKS

Dictionary of Literary Biography, Volume 6: *American Novelists since World War II,* Gale (Detroit, MI), 1980.

PERIODICALS

Booklist, April 15, 1992, Alice Joyce, review of *Cutting Stone,* p. 1500; March 1, 2002, Donna Seaman, review of *Embalming Mom: Essays in Life,* p. 1082.

Christian Science Monitor, May 28, 1992, Susan Miron, review of *Cutting Stone,* p. 11.

Glamour, July, 1985, Laura Mathews, review of *Opening Nights,* p. 116.

Library Journal, June 15, 1985, Mary K. Prokop, review of *Opening Nights,* p. 71; April 1, 1992, Charles Michaud, review of *Cutting Stone,* p. 145; June 15, 1993, Suzan Connell, review of *Cutting Stone,* p. 128; March 1, 2002, Pam Kingsbury, review of *Embalming Mom: Essays in Life,* p. 98.

Los Angeles Times, June 23, 1985, Richard Eder, review of *Opening Nights,* p. 3.

Los Angeles Times Book Review, June 23, 1985, p. 3; March 3, 1992, pp. 3, 7; April 11, 1993, p. 1.

Ms., August, 1977; June, 1985, Jennifer Crichton, review of *Opening Nights,* p. 67.

New Statesman and Society, August 12, 1977; July 31, 1992, Robert Carver, review of *Cutting Stone,* p. 36.

Newsweek, April 4, 1977; July 8, 1985, Walter Clemons, review of *Opening Nights,* p. 70B.

New Yorker, July 1, 1985, review of *Opening Nights,* p. 97.

New York Times, June 22, 1977; June 23, 1985, Jennifer Dunning, review of *Opening Nights,* p. 20.

New York Times Book Review, April 10, 1977, Anatole Broyard, review of *Raw Silk,* p. 14.; March 18, 1979, review of *Raw Silk,* p. 37; June 23, 1985, Jennifer Dunning, review of *Opening Nights,* p. 20; June 7, 1992, Angelina Goreau, review of *Cutting Stone,* p. 11.

Observer (London, England), July 14, 1985, p. 21.; June 7, 1992, Angeline Goreau, review of *Cutting Stone,* p. 11

Plain Dealer, June 9, 2002, Frank Bentayou, "Lively Ideas, Homey and Professorial," p. J9.

Publishers Weekly, April 26, 1985, Sybil Steinberg, review of *Opening Nights,* p. 70; March 23, 1992, review of *Cutting Stone,* p. 62.

School Library Journal, January 1991, Sharron McElmeel, review of *The Giant Jam Sandwich,* p. 61.

Times Literary Supplement, October 14, 1977; May 22, 1982; August 14, 1992, John Clute, review of *Cutting Stone,* p. 18.

OTHER

Review of Art, Literature, Philosophym, and the Humanities Web site, http://www.ralphmag.org (summer, 2002), review of *Embalming Mom: Essays in Life.*

C

CALLADO, Antônio 1917-1997

PERSONAL: Born January 26, 1917, in Niterói, Brazil; died 1997. *Education:* Studied law.

CAREER: Novelist, essayist, playwright, and journalist. British Broadcasting Corporation, staff member, beginning 1941; worked in radio in France, 1944-47; *Jornal do Brazil,* Rio de Janeiro, Brazil, journalist, c. 1950s-60s.

AWARDS, HONORS: Golfinho de Ouro; Premio Brasília; Goethe Institute Prize, 1982, for *Sempreviva.*

WRITINGS:

Esqueleto na lagoa verde: um senaio sôbre a vide e o sumiço do coronel Fawcett, Ministério da Educacão e Saude (Rio de Janeiro, Brazil), 1953, new edition, 1961.

A cidade assassinada (three-act play), J. Olympio (Rio de Janeiro, Brazil), 1954.

Assunção de Salviano (novel; title means "The Assumption of Salviano"), J. Olympio (Rio de Janeiro, Brazil), 1954, reprinted, Nova Fronteira (Rio de Janeiro, Brazil), 1983.

Retrato de Portinari, Museu de Arte Moderna do Rio de Janeiro (Rio de Janeiro, Brazil), 1955, reprinted, Paz e Terra (Rio de Janeiro, Brazil), 1978.

Frankel (three-act play), Ministério da Educacão e Cultura (Rio de Janeiro, Brazil), 1955, English translation, Servico de documentacão (Rio de Janeiro, Brazil), 1956.

Pedro Mico, zumbi do catacumba (play; also see below), Dramas e Comédias (Rio de Janeiro, Brazil), 1957, reprinted, Nova Fronteira (Rio de Janeiro, Brazil), 1996.

O colar de coral, Dramas e Comédias (Rio de Janeiro, Brazil), 1957.

A Modona de cedro (novel; title means "Cedar Madonna"), J. Olympio (Rio de Janeiro, Brazil), 1957, reprinted, Nova Fronteira (Rio de Janeiro, Brazil), 1994.

Os industriais da sêca e os "Galileus" de Pernambuco: aspectos da luta pela reforma agrária no Brasil, Civilizacão Brasileira (Rio de Janeiro, Brazil), 1960.

O tesouro de Chica da Silva (two-act play; also see below), Sociedade Brasileira de Autores Teatrais (Rio de Janeiro, Brazil), 1962.

Forro no Engenho Cananêia, Civilizacão Brasileira (Rio de Janeiro, Brazil), 1964.

Tempo de Arraes, padres e comunistas na revolução sem violência, J. Alvaro 80, 1964.

Enciclopédia Barsa, Encyclopaedia Britannica (Rio de Janeiro, Brazil), 1964.

Quarup (novel), Civilizacão Brasileira (Rio de Janeiro, Brazil), 1967, reprinted, Nova Fronteira (Rio de Janeiro, Brazil), 1990, translation by Barbara Shelby, Knopf (New York, NY), 1970.

64 D.C., Tempo Brasileiro (Rio de Janeiro, Brazil), 1967.

Vietnã do norte: advertência aos agressores, Civilizacão Brasileira (Rio de Janeiro, Brazil), 1969.

Bar D. Juan (novel), Civilizacão Brasileira (Rio de Janeiro, Brazil), 1971, translation by Barbara Shelby published as *Don Juan's Bar,* Knopf (New York, NY), 1972.

Djanira: 5 estudios de casa de Farinha, Cultrix (São Paulo, Brazil), 1972.

Censorship and Other Problems of Latin-American Writers, Centre of Latin American Studies (Cambridge, England), 1974.

Reflexos do baile, Paz e Terra (Rio de Janeiro, Brazil), 1976, 5th edition, Francesco Alves (Rio de Janeiro, Brazil), 1997.

Passaporte sem carimbo, Avenir (Rio de Janeiro, Brazil), 1978.

Sempreviva (novel), Nova Fronteira (Rio de Janeiro, Brazil), 1981, English translation, 1988.

Antônio Callado, Abril Educação (São Paulo, Brazil), 1982, 2nd edition, Nova Cultura (São Paulo, Brazil), 1988.

Expedição Montaigne, Nova Fronteira (Rio de Janeiro, Brazil), 1982.

(Editor with Alfredo Bosi) *Machado de Assis,* Atica (São Paulo, Brazil), 1982.

A revolta da cachaça: teatro negro (plays; contains *O tesouro de Chica da Silva, Pedro Mico,* and *Uma rede para Iemanjá*), Nova Fronteira (Rio de Janeiro, Brazil), 1983.

Concerto carioca (novel), Nova Fronteira (Rio de Janeiro, Brazil), 1985.

Entre o deus e a vasilha: ensaio sobre a reforma agrária Brasileira, a qual nunca foi feita, Nova Fronteira (Rio de Janeiro, Brazil), 1985.

Um Escritor na biblioteca, Setor de Editoração da Biblioteca Pública do Paraná (Curitiba, Puerto Rico), 1985.

(With Roger D. Stone) *Sonhos da Amazônia,* Buanabara (Rio de Janeiro, Brazil), 1986.

Memórias de Aldenham House (autobiographical novel), Nova Fronteira (Rio de Janeiro, Brazil), 1989.

(With others) *Amazon expo* (in Portuguese and English), Armanaka'a Amazon Network (Brazil), 1992.

O homem cordial e outras histórias, Atica (São Paulo, Brazil), 1993.

(With Marilia Martins and Paulo Robert Abrantes) *3 Antônios & 1 Jobim: histórias de uma geração,* Relume Dumará (Rio de Janeiro, Brazil), 1993.

Viagem inteligente: as mais belas cidades do mundo na visão de sete autores Brasileiros, Geração (São Paulo, Brazil), 1994.

(Editor) Francisco de Mello Franco, *Reino da estupidez,* Giordano (São Paulo, Brazil), 1995.

(Translator) Gabriel García Marquéz, *O amor nos tempos do cólera* (Portuguese translation of *Love in the Time of Cholera*), Record (Rio de Janeiro, Brazil), 1995.

Contos para um Natal Brasileiro, Relume Dumará (Rio de Janeiro, Brazil), 1996.

(With Darcy Ribeiro) *Mestiço é que é bom!,* Revan (Rio de Janeiro, Brazil), 1996.

(With Martha Vianna) *Crônicas de fim do milênio,* F. Alves (Rio de Janeiro, Brazil), 1997.

(Author of text) *Candido Potinari: Proyecto Cultural Artistas del Mercosur* (in Spanish), Banco Velox (Buenos Aires, Argentina), 1997.

Callado's works have been translated into Italian, Spanish, English, and German.

ADAPTATIONS: Callado's play *O tesouro de Chica da Silva* was adapted as the film *Xica,* directed by Carlos Diegues.

SIDELIGHTS: One of the more influential Brazilian writers of the late twentieth century, Antônio Callado enjoyed "a typical middle-class upbringing," according to Naomi Hoki Moniz in an essay for *Encyclopedia of World Literature in the Twentieth Century.* As a young man he studied law but began his career as a journalist, working in England and France for the British Broadcasting Corporation. Though he enjoyed his European sojourn, according to Moniz Callado "felt a profound longing for Brazil and a deep desire to return and rediscover his own country." Callado did so by becoming a writer for *Jornal du Brazil,* where his activism landed him in and out of jail. Callado parlayed that experience into a career in journalism, criticism, fiction, and drama.

In his writings, Callado sought to build upon Brazil's national identity; "thus his novels are a kaleidoscopic voyage across Brazil, in a effort to portray what he found to be its multiple and genuine realities," Moniz said. One of the first of Callado's books to receive wide attention was the novel *Quarup.* Its title taken from an Indian death ritual, *Quarup* portrays realistically the conflicting ideologies and contrasting cultures of Brazil's indigenous people and the imperialist upper classes of European descent as seen through the eyes of a fallen priest. *Quarup* was widely embraced in Brazil, but its translation from Portuguese to English drew some mixed notices. Ronald Christ of *Commonweal* interpreted the novel as a fictionalization of actual events that touches on "social and economic oppression, exploitation and extermination of the Indians, military repression leading to brutal, calculated torture of opponents of the government." While commending Callado's intent, Christ was less impressed with the author's style, labeling the novel's characters "cardboard constructions or weirdly frivolous, fatuously grotesque caricatures" and *Quarup* "a book that never jells into a consistent vision of the inner or outer life of Brazil." *New York Times Book Review* contributor David Gallagher likewise noted that "it is a pity that so absorbing a novel could be marred by a clumsy technique and by a flat unfertile style." *New Republic* contributor Joseph Page found Callado to be "at his best in catching the mood and style of his *carioca* characters, and at his worst trying to evoke the regional setting for the events in *Quarup*."

In the political novel *Bar D. Juan*, Callado "juxtaposes the plans of a group of inept Brazilian dreamers with the actualities of guerilla action in [Che Guevara's] Bolivia," according to Dorothy Nyren in *Library Journal*. The titular tavern is in Rio de Janeiro, where the affluent young gather to indulge in revolutionary fantasies. The plot thickens when the young people are "galvanized into a suicidal project by an emissary of Castro's," as Martin Levin explained in the *New York Times Book Review*. This "funny, cynical, seductive" novel, noted a *Time* critic, "is virtually a textbook on how not to run a revolution."

By the time the award-winning novel *Sempreviva* was published, Callado had established himself as "certainly the greatest Brazilian political novelist of today," according to Wilson Martins in *World Literature Today*. Martins described the author as "not a politician who writes novels, but a novelist who sees in politics the matter of novels." *Sempreviva* dramatizes Brazil's cultural issues through an exiled character, Vasco, who returns to his homeland to find his beloved Lucinda murdered by military terrorists who are also depleting the country's panther population, torturing and killing the animals for their pelts. At first bent on bloody revenge, Vasco decides instead to expose the terrorists to international scorn. "However, such is not to be," as Malcolm Silverman noted in *Modern Language Review*. "Both he and his nemesis die in unconscious servitude—one amid amorous nostalgia, the other amid naturalistic perversity." Silverman went on to describe *Sempreviva* as "a novel of ideas whose spontaneous exposition of polemics is revealed through a prose often poetic in its imagery."

BIOGRAPHICAL AND CRITICAL SOURCES:

BOOKS

Encyclopedia of World Literature in the Twentieth Century, 3rd edition, St. James Press (Detroit, MI), 1999.
Latin American Lives, Macmillan Library Reference (New York, NY), 1996.

PERIODICALS

Brasil-Brazil, Volume 1, number 1, Christina-Ferreira Pinto, "Mito e realidad politica em *Sempreviva* de Antônio Callado," pp. 7-16.
Choice, October, 1970, review of *Quarup,* p. 1047; September, 1972, review of *Don Juan's Bar,* p. 820.
Commonweal, October 9, 1970, Ronald Christ, review of *Quarup,* p. 51.
Library Journal, February 15, 1972, Dorothy Nyren, review of *Don Juan's Bar,* p. 698.
Luso-Brazilian Review, summer, 1997, Thomas P. Waldemer, "Revenge of the Cannibal: Surrender and Resistance in Antonio Callado's Nativist Novels," pp. 113-123.
Modern Language Journal, spring, 1982, Malcolm Silverman, review of *Sempreviva,* pp. 108-109.
New Republic, July 4, 1970, Joseph Page, review of *Quarup,* p. 25.
New York Times Book Review, June 14, 1970, David Gallagher, review of *Quarup,* p. 4; April 9, 1972, Martin Levin, review of *Don Juan's Bar,* p. 42.
Time, April 17, 1972, review of *Don Juan's Bar,* p. 92.
World Literature Today, spring, 1982, Wilson Martins, review of *Sempreviva,* p. 315; spring, 1984, Leland Guyer, review of *A revolta da cachaça: teatro negro,* p. 249; spring, 1990, Irwin Stern, review of *Memórias de Aldenham House,* p. 284.

OBITUARIES:

PERIODICALS

Independent (London, England), February 1, 1997, p. 18.*

CAPMANY (FARNES), Maria Aurèlia 1918-1991

PERSONAL: Born 1918, in Barcelona, Spain; died 1991, in Barcelona, Spain; daughter of Aureli Capmany (a Catalan folklorist). *Education:* Attended University of Barcelona.

CAREER: Novelist, playwright, essayist, feminist, literary critic, and cultural attaché. Founder of Adrià Gual School of Dramatic Art; university professor. Cultural counselor of the city of Barcelona.

AWARDS, HONORS: Joanot Martorell Prize for Catalan narrative, for *El cel no és transparent;* Sant Jordi Prize for Best Catalan Novel, 1968, for *Un lloc entre els morts.*

WRITINGS:

Necessitem morir (novel; title means "We Must Die"), Aymà (Barcelona, Spain), 1952.

Com una mà, Ediciones Moll (Palma de Mallorca, Spain), 1952.

L'altra ciutat (novel; title means "The Other City"), Selecta (Barcelona, Spain), 1955.

Betúlia, Selecta (Barcelona, Spain), 1956.

Tana o la felicitat (novel; title means "Tana, or Happiness"), Ediciones Moll (Palma de Mallorca, Spain), 1956.

Vés-te'n, ianqui! o, si voleu, traduit de l'americà (novel; title means "Yankee Go Home; or, If You Prefer, Translated from the American"), Laia (Barcelona, Spain), 1959.

El gust de la pols (novel; title means "The Taste of Dust"), Ediciones Destino (Barcelona, Spain), 1962.

La pluja als vidres (novel; title means "Rain on the Windowpane"), Club Editor (Barcelona, Spain), 1963.

El desert dels dies (play; title means "The Desert of Days"), Occitania (Barcelona, Spain), 1966.

La dona de Catalunya: Consienca i situacio (nonfiction), Edicions 62 (Barcelona, Spain), 1966.

Un lloc entre els morts (novel; title means "A Place among the Dead"), Nova Terra (Barcelona, Spain), 1967.

Dia si, dia no: Apunts sobre la nostra societat actual, Llibres de Sinera (Barcelona, Spain), 1968.

Felicment, jo soc una dona (novel; title means "Fortunately, I Am a Woman"), Nova Terra (Barcelona, Spain), 1969.

Vitrines d'Amsterdam (novel; title means "Showcases of Amsterdam"), Nova Terra (Barcelona, Spain), 1969.

Pedra de toc I (collected essays; title means "Cornerstone I"), Nova Terra (Barcelona, Spain), 1970.

(With Carmen Alcalde) *El feminismo ibérico* (title means "Iberian Feminism"), Oikos-Tau (Barcelona, Spain), 1970.

Anna, Bel I Carles, Lumen (Barcelona, Spain), 1971.

Quim/Quimà (novel), Estela (Barcelona, Spain), 1971.

Cartes impertients (title means "Impertinent Letters"), Ediciones Moll (Palma de Mallorca), 1971.

Salvador Espriu, DOPESA (Barcelona, Spain), 1971.

El jaqué de la democracia (novel; title means "The Dinner Jacket of Democracy"), Plaza & Janés (Barcelona, Spain), 1972.

Pedra de toc II (collected essays; title means "Cornerstone II"), 1973.

Carta abierta al macho ibérico (title means "Open Letter to the Iberian Macho"), Ediciones 99 (Madrid, Spain), 1973.

El feminisme a Catalunya (nonfiction; title means "Feminism in Catalonia"), Nova Terra (Barcelona, Spain), 1973.

L'alt rei en Jaume (play; title means "Old King James"), Aymá (Barcelona, Spain), 1977.

Liberación de la mujer: ano cero (title means "Women's Liberation: Zero Hour"), 1977.

Dona, doneta, donota (title means "Woman, Little Woman, Big Woman"), EDHASA (Barcelona, Spain), 1979.

Coses I noses, La Magrana (Barcelona, Spain), 1980.

Angela I els viut mil policies, Laia (Barcelona, Spain), 1981.

Dietari de prudéncies (title means "Prudent Diaries"), Hogar de Libro, Nova Terra 20 (Barcelona, Spain), 1982.

El malefici de la reina d'Hongria, Barcanova (Barcelona, Spain), 1982.

La color mas blau (novel; title means "The Bluest Color"), Planeta (Barcelona, Spain), 1982.

(With Jaume Vidal Alcover) *Ca, barret!* (play), Ediciones Moll (Barcelona, Spain), 1984.

El cap de Sant Jordi, Planeta (Barcelona, Spain), 1988.

Also the author of numerous plays, including *Tu i l'hipòcrita,* 1960, and *Vent de garbí i una mica de por,* 1968. Author of radio and television scripts. Contributor to periodicals, including *Serra d'Or* and *Presencia.*

SIDELIGHTS: Maria Aurèlia Capmany was a woman of many talents. She studied philosophy at the University of Barcelona and taught at the university for a time before she founded a drama school and became an actor, director, and playwright. Her best-known contributions, however, are in the field of feminism. Capmany wrote several books on the subject that are considered foundational works for Iberian feminism, including *La dona a Catalunya, El feminismo ibérico,* and *El feminisme a Catalunya.*

Capmany also authored fictional works in support of feminism that often use irony as a weapon. In *Cartes impertinents,* she combined twenty-seven fictional letters written to women by women. These women come from all age groups and social classes, but their letters share a common thread of social criticism as well as a sense of irony.

Lo color més blau is also told through fictitious letters, but in this instance most of the letters are written by two women: Oliva and Delia, childhood friends who are separated by the Spanish Civil War at the age of fifteen. Delia, the child of communists, spends her life in exile in Europe and South America while Oliva, the child of wealthy parents, remains in Barcelona. Despite their parentage, by the end of the book Delia has joined the bourgeoisie and Oliva has become an activist.

Another book that uses humor to make a feminist point is *Dona, doneta, donota,* described by Janet Pérez in *Contemporary Women Writers of Spain* as "a satiric illustration of women's perennial fight to achieve their rightful place in society." In other works, including *Feliçment, jo sóc una dona, El gust de la pols,* and *Un lloc entre els morts,* Capmany directs her piercing irony to mocking hypocrisy in society, especially the hypocrisy of bourgeois and Catholic values.

In addition to her feminist treatises and her novels, Capmany also wrote plays and radio and television scripts, and, noted Pérez in *Contemporary Women Writers of Spain,* she was "an outstanding literary critic and essayist on sociopolitical subjects."

BIOGRAPHICAL AND CRITICAL SOURCES:

BOOKS

Pérez, Janet, *Contemporary Women Writer of Spain,* Twayne (Boston, MA), 1988.

PERIODICALS

Estreno, spring, 1986, L. Teresa Valdivieso, "A proposito de la version castellana de 'Tu i l'hipòcrita,'" pp. 9-10.
Explicacion de Textos Literarios, Volume 24, numbers 1-2, Genaro Pérez, "La poética feminista del género *noire:* Pottecher, Ortiz y Capmany," pp. 149-158.
Letras Femeninas, spring, 1986, Barbara Dale May, p. 103.
Catalan Review, Volume 7, number 2, 1993, pp. 11-18, 41-56, 57-69, 71-90, 91-103, 105-114, 215-129.
Estreno, spring, 1986, pp. 9-10.
Explicaciones de Textos Literarios, Volume 24, 1995, p. 149.*

OTHER

El Poder de la Palabra, http://www.epdlp.com/ (March 21, 2002).
Fundació Maria Aurèlia Capmany, http://www.fmac. org/ (March 21, 2002).*

*   *   *

CAREY, Jacqueline 1964-

PERSONAL: Born 1964, in Highland Park, IL. *Education:* Lake Forest College, B.A. (psychology and English).

ADDRESSES: Home—Douglas, MI. *Agent*—Jane Dystel Literary Management, One Union Square West, Suite 904, New York, NY 10003. *E-mail*—Contact@ jacquelinecarey.com.

CAREER: Writer.

MEMBER: Science Fiction and Fantasy Writers of America; Novelists, Inc.

AWARDS, HONORS: Locus award for best first novel, 2002; *Romantic Times* Reviewer's Choice award for best fantasy novel, 2002.

WRITINGS:

Angels: Celestial Spirits in Art and Legend, Metro-Books (New York, NY), 1997.

Kushiel's Dart (novel), Tor Books (New York, NY), 2001.

Kushiel's Chosen (novel), Tor Books (New York, NY), 2002.

Kushiel's Avatar (novel), Tor Books (New York, NY), 2003.

Contributor of essay to *Lamidi Olonade Fakeye: A Retrospective Exhibition and Autobiography* (exhibition catalogue); author of short stories and essays; story "Jazznight" published in *I-94: A Collection of Southwest Michigan Writers;* contributor of articles and reviews to *Salon.com.*

WORK IN PROGRESS: *Elegy for Darkness* (novel).

SIDELIGHTS: Jacqueline Carey's first novel, *Kushiel's Dart,* was hailed in *Publishers Weekly* as a "brilliant and daring debut" that places Carey "immediately [in] the top rank of fantasy novelists." Set in a world resembling that of Renaissance Europe, the book introduces heroine Phedre no Delaunay, who plays the role of courtesan and spy among the political elites of her people. A red spot in her eye shows that Phedre is an "anguisette," an individual chosen by the chastising angel Kushiel for her ability to receive sexual pleasure through the experience of pain—a fact that critics found integral to Phedre's complex and unusual character. Replete with sexual intrigue and adventure, the novel "blends Christianity and paganism with fascinating results," according to *Booklist* reviewer Paula Luedtke.

In the sequel, *Kushiel's Chosen,* Phedre is now Comtesse de Montreve, bound to serve and protect Queen Ysandre of Terre d'Ange from the evil clutches of Melisande Shahrizai. A writer for *Publishers Weekly* considered the book a slight disappointment. But Luedtke, in a *Booklist* review, wrote that *Kushiel's Chosen* "fulfills every promise made by *Kushiel's Dart.*" In particular, Luedtke admired Carey's skill in creating an "unforgettable" heroine and a story with "tremendous emotional punch."

BIOGRAPHICAL AND CRITICAL SOURCES:

PERIODICALS

Booklist, July, 2001, Paula Luedtke, review of *Kushiel's Dart,* p. 1991; February 1, 2002, Paula Luedtke, review of *Kushiel's Chosen,* p. 931.

Library Journal, July, 2001, Jackie Cassada, review of *Kushiel's Dart,* p. 131.

Publishers Weekly, May 14, 2001, review of *Kushiel's Dart,* p. 58; February 18, 2002, review of *Kushiel's Chosen,* p. 80.

OTHER

Jacqueline Carey Web site, http://www.jacquelinecarey. com (September 5, 2002).

*   *   *

CARTER, Charles Frederick 1919-2002

OBITUARY NOTICE—See index for *CA* sketch: Born August 15, 1919, in Rugby, Warwickshire, England; died June 27, 2002, in Glasgow, Scotland. Statistician, economist, educator, administrator, and author. Carter will be remembered as the founding vice chancellor of the University of Lancaster. Though he was trained as a statistician and economist, Carter was deeply involved in the planning and building of the new university in 1959 and in its administration until his retirement in 1978. He maintained a wide range of other activities as well. Carter was the coauthor of several books that addressed problems of technical progress in England in the 1950s, among them *Industry and Technical Progress* and *Investment in Innovation.* He also served as chair of the British Post Office review committee, which group initiated substantial innovation in British telecommunications. Later in his career Carter wrote about economic uncertainty and policies for economies under pressure. One of his intense interests was Northern Ireland. He taught economics at the Queen's University in Belfast in the 1950s, chaired the Northern Ireland Economic Development Council for ten years, and coauthored the book *The Northern Ireland Problem.* Carter was made an honorary member of the Royal Irish Academy and was awarded several honorary degrees from universities in both Ireland and Northern Ireland. In 1960 he authored *The Science of Wealth,* and followed it with *Wealth,* in which he argued that the happiness and well-being of a society cannot be equated to the level of its economic prosperity. He contributed much of his time to philanthropic and civic endeavors, including those devoted to broadcasting, social policy, international trade, and educational development. In retirement Carter chaired the research committee of the Policy Studies Institute in London, and he served as co-president until 1997. Carter was a fellow of the British Academy and the International Academy of Management. He was knighted by Queen Elizabeth II in 1978.

OBITUARIES AND OTHER SOURCES:

PERIODICALS

Independent (London, England), July 20, 2002, obituary by Grigor McClelland, p. 20.
Times (London, England), July 10, 2002, p. 32.

*   *   *

CARTER, Mike 1936-

PERSONAL: Born September 12, 1936, in London, England; son of Thomas and Ethel Carter; married Diana Pountney, August 12, 1960; children: Robin, Sally. *Education:* University of Sheffield, B.A. (with honors), 1961. *Hobbies and other interests:* Drama, soccer, para-gliding, plays mandolin in an Irish band.

ADDRESSES: Home—Te Kohanga Rd., Onewhero, R.D. 2 Tuakau, Auckland, New Zealand.

CAREER: Secondary school teacher, 1961-89; writer, 1989—.

MEMBER: Drama Club, Soccer Club, Microlite Club.

WRITINGS:

Biggest Pool of All, Wendy Pye (New Zealand), 1995.
Space Games, Lothian (Port Melbourne, Victoria, Australia), 2001.

Contributor of short stories and articles to periodicals, including *New Zealand School Journal* and *School.*

ADAPTATIONS: Some of Carter's short stories have been broadcast by New Zealand Radio.

WORK IN PROGRESS: Writing about chicken farming, a boy with a powered parachute, and a girl with a guardian angel.

SIDELIGHTS: New Zealand author Mike Carter told *CA:* "I cannot remember a time when I couldn't read. Of course those were the days before television. (We still don't own one.) Words I've found fascinating—and writing gives me time to get them right. Raising a family and full-time teaching (ages eleven through seventeen years) didn't allow much energy or time for writing more than skits and articles for newspapers. I retired from full-time teaching in 1989 and since then have had a number of short stories published.

"I've used personal experience as a basis for most stories—teaching, parachuting, para-gliding, soccer, animals—then I've added a fictional component or twist. A writer creates his/her own world, although often the characters take on a life force of their own and hove off in a completely unanticipated direction. Maybe God feels that way about us.

"Writing is an enjoyable hobby. As I walk or drive I have a host of chaacters talking, performing in my mind. I'm never alone if I unleash my imagination. At the moment I'm sifting through ideas about chicken farming, guardian angels, and flying."

*   *   *

CASSILL, R(onald) V(erlin) 1919-2002

OBITUARY NOTICE—See index for *CA* sketch: Born May 17, 1919, in Cedar Falls, IA; died March 25, 2002, in Providence, RI. Educator, editor, and author. Cassill was a respected novelist, short story writer, and editor who, through his classes at the University of Iowa's Writers Workshop and at Brown University and with his textbook *On Writing,* inspired many others to follow his footsteps. A graduate of the University of Iowa, where he earned a B.A. in 1939, Cassill served in the U.S. Army during World War II before returning to his university to receive his master's degree in 1947. Cassill then earned a living through a combination of writing, teaching, and editing. From 1946 to 1948 he was an instructor at Monticello College before returning to the University of Iowa as a writing instructor from 1948 to 1952 and again during the early 1960s. Between stints in Iowa, he lectured at such universities as Columbia and the New School for Social Research (now New School University), concluding his career at Brown University where he was an English professor from 1966 until 1983, and a professor emeritus thereafter. Cassill also worked as a book reviewer for such publications as the *Chicago Sun Times* and *Book Week,* was an editor for *Collier's Encyclopedia* during the mid-1950s, and for *Dude* and *Gent* magazines in 1958. As a writer, Cassill's work ranged from sexy potboilers to more complex studies of moral dilemmas, with his most acclaimed novel being *Doctor Cobb's Game,* which was loosely based on the Profumo sex scandal in England. At his best, Cassill was compared by some critics to such luminaries as Norman Mailer, and even his less ambitious work demonstrates a marked sensitivity to his craft and a strong moral sensibility. His oeuvre contains two dozen novels, including *The Eagle on the Coin, A Taste of Sin, My Sister's Keeper, The President, Flame,* and *After Goliath,* six short-story collections, including *The Father, and Other Stories* and *Collected Stories,* and edited publications such as *The Norton Anthology of Short Fiction* and *The Norton Anthology of Contemporary Fiction.* Cassill put writing aside in 1985, believing he had "used up" his gift. In addition to his writing, Cassill was also an artist who had his work displayed at such exhibits as the Eleanor Smith Galleries in Chicago and the Wickersham Gallery in New York City.

OBITUARIES AND OTHER SOURCES:

BOOKS

Writers Directory, 16th edition, St. James Press (Detroit, MI), 2001.

PERIODICALS

Chicago Tribune, April 2, 2002, section 2, p. 9.
New York Times, April 1, 2002, p. A21.
Times (London), April 7, 2002.

*   *   *

CASTELAO, Alfonso (Daniel) R(odriguez) 1886-1950

PERSONAL: Born January 29, 1886, in Cabo de Vila (Rianxo), Spain; died January 7, 1950, in Buenos Aires, Argentina. *Education:* Graduated from University of Compostela, Santiago de Compostela, Spain.

CAREER: Political activist and writer.

MEMBER: Real Academia Galega.

WRITINGS:

As Cruces de Pedra na Bretaña, Semianario de Estudos Galegos (Santiago de Compostela, Spain), 1930.
Galicia martir: estampas, Committee to Aid Spanish Democracy (Toronto, Canada), 1937.
Galicia mártir, Ediciones Españolas (Madrid, Spain), 1937.
Castilla no es España, es la anti-España, Biblioteca Catalana (Mexico D.F., Mexico), 1944.
Estatuto de autonomía pra Galicia, 1936, Akal (Madrid, Spain), 1948.
Os vellos non deben de namorarse, farsa en tres actos con un prólogo e un epílogo, Galaxia (Vigo, Spain), 1953.
Cousas, Galaxia (Vigo, Spain), 1961, translation by Kristy Hooper published as *Things,* Planet (Aberystwyth, Wales), 2001.
Retrincos, Celta (Madrid, Spain), 1962.
Escolma possible, Galaxia (Vigo, Spain), 1964.
El Pensamiento político de Castelao, Ruedo ibérico (Paris, France), 1965.
Os dous de sempre, Galaxia (Vigo, Spain), 1967.
Galicia y Valle-Inclán. [Conferencia leída en la Habana en enero de 1939], Celta (Lugo, Spain), 1971.
Cousas da morte: antoloxía, Castrelos (Vigo, Spain), 1973.
Prosas recuperadas, Celta (Lugo, Spain), 1974.
Cuatro obras: teatro, relatos, fantasía macabra, ensayos, Cátedra (Madrid, Spain), 1974.
Narrativa e teatro, Akal, (Madrid, Spain), 1975.
Nós, Akal (Madrid, Spain), 1975.
Cousas, terceiro libro, Castrelos (Vigo, Spain), 1975.
Castelao, prosa do exilio, Patronato da Cultura Galega (Montevideo, Uruguay), 1976.
Homenaxe a Castelao, Universidad de Santiago (Santiago, Chile), 1976.
Sempre en Galiza, Akal (Madrid, Spain), 1976.
Diario 1921, Galaxia (Vigo, Spain), 1977.
Discursos parlamentarios (1931-1933), Castro (La Coruña, Spain), 1978.
Coroa poetica para Castelao: 187 poemas, de 1911 a 1987, Castro (La Coruña, Spain), 1978.

Cincoenta homes por dez reás, Galaxia (Vigo, Spain), 1978.

Castelao, Galaxia (Vigo, Spain), 1979.

Un ollo de vidro: memorias d'un esquelete, Rueiro (La Coruña, Spain), 1980.

Narracións e outras prosas, Galaxia (Vigo, Spain), 1982.

El problema de les nacionalitats ibèriques: antologia de "Sempre en Galiza," Edicions 62 (Barcelona, Spain), 1983.

Castelao, 1886-1950, Ministerio de Cultura (Madrid, Spain), 1986.

Castelao para nenos, La Torre (Madrid, Spain), 1988.

Cadernos (1938-1948): escolma, Galaxia (Vigo, Spain), 1993.

175 debuxos de Castelao, Fundación Caixa Galicia (Santiago de Compostela, Spain), 1996.

Diario 1921. Revista Nós. Do meu diario. Cubismo. Apéndices, Galaxia (Vigo, Spain), 2000.

Introducción. Escritos políticos. Varia, Galaxia (Vigo, Spain), 2000.

SIDELIGHTS: Although known as an accomplished artist and author, Alfonso R. Castelao considered himself first and foremost a political activist for political autonomy for Galicia. Castelao was born in Spain, but his family moved to Argentina in 1886 and then returned to Galicia four years later. Castelao earned a medical degree but practiced medicine for a very short time deciding to devote himself entirely to art, literature, and Galician politics. In 1923 he enrolled in the Semanario de Estudos Galegos, devoting himself to the ethnographic and cultural history of the Galician people in Iberia. In 1926 he was accepted into the Real Academia Galegaand, and five years later he was the elected representative from the Province of Pontevedra as a separatist candidate and founded the Partido Galeguista. During the elections of 1936 he was the most popular candidate of the Frente Popular and the most outstanding voice for Galician autonomy.

During the years of the Spanish Civil War Castelao was an active participant for the Republican cause as well as the creation of the "estamps" or drawings, that brought world-wide attention to the plight of the Spanish people and to him as an artist. In 1940 he went to Buenos Aires as a self-proclaimed exile, and he lived there for many years creating his art and his writing as well as creating the Partida Galeguista in Argentina.

Castelao's work can be divided into four categories: graphic arts, literary criticism, fiction and poetry, and political writing.

The most important collections of Castelao's drawings and other graphic art are *Cousas da vids,* Cincuenta homes por dez reás, *Album Nós,* and *Galicia martír.* His prose fiction works include *Un ollo de Vidro, Cousas, Retrincos,* and *Os vellos no debn namorarse.* His most influential and published political writing are *Sempre in Galiza, Discursos parlamentarios, O Estatuto de Galiza,* and *Antecentes e comentarios,* while his literary criticism is best represented by *As cruces de pedra na Galiza, As cruces de pedra na Bretaña,* and *O galeguista no arte.*

BIOGRAPHICAL AND CRITICAL SOURCES:

BOOKS

Modern Spanish and Portuguese Literature, Continuum (New York, NY), 1988.*

*　　*　　*

CHAMPOURCIN, Ernestina de 1905-

PERSONAL: Born July 10, 1905, in Vitoria, Spain; married Juan José Domenchina (a poet and secretary), November 7, 1936 (deceased, 1959). *Education:* Attended Catholic schools in Spain.

ADDRESSES: Agent—c/o Author Mail, Ediciones Torremozas, Apartado de correos: 19032, 28080 Madrid, Spain.

CAREER: Poet and novelist; translator in Mexico, c. 1936-73.

WRITINGS:

En Silencio: Poesias (poetry; title means "In Silence"), Espasa-Calpe (Madrid, Spain), 1926.

Ahora (poetry; title means "Now"), [Madrid, Spain], 1928.

La Voz en el viento: 1928-1931 (poetry; title means "The Voice in the Wind"), Compañia General de Artes Graficas (Madrid, Spain), 1931.

La Casa de enfrente (novel; title means "The House across the Street"), Signo (Madrid, Spain), 1936.

Cántico inútil (poetry; title means "Useless Canticle"), M. Aguilar (Madrid, Spain), 1936.

Presencia a oscuras (poetry; title means "Presence in Shadows"), Rialp (Madrid, Spain), 1952.

El Nombre que me diste (poetry; title means "The Name You Gave to Me"), 1960.

Cárcel de los sentidos, 1953-1963 (poetry; title means "Prison of the Senses"), Ecuador (Mexico), 1964.

Hai-Kais espirituales (poetry; title means "Spiritual Haikus"), A. Finistre (Mexico), 1967.

Cartas cerradas (poetry; title means "Closed Letters"), Ecuador (Mexico), 1968.

(Editor) *Dios en la poesía actual,* Biblioteca de Autores Cristianos (Madrid, Spain), 1970.

Poemas del ser y del estar (title means "Poems of Being and Becoming"), Alfaguara (Madrid, Spain), 1972.

Primer exilio (poetry; title means "First Exile"), Rialp (Madrid, Spain), 1978.

La Ardilla y la rosa: Juan Ramón en mi memoria (correspondence; title means "The Squirrel and the Rose: Juan Ramón in My Memory"), Libros de Fausto (Madrid, Spain), 1981.

La Pared transparente (Madrid, 1979-1980) (poetry; title means "The Transparent Wall"), Libros de Fausto (Madrid, Spain), 1984.

Huyeron todas las islas, Caballo Griego para la Poesia (Madrid, Spain), 1988.

Antologia poética (title means "Poetic Anthology"), Torremozas (Madrid, Spain), 1988.

Poesía a través del tiempo (title means "Poetry across Time"), Anthropos (Barcelona, Spain), 1991.

Del Vacío y sus dones (poetry; title means "Emptiness and Its Gifts"), Torremozas (Madrid, Spain), 1993.

Also author of the novel *María de Magdala,* 1943.

Contributor to Gerardo Diego's 1934 anthology *Poesía española contemporáneos;* also translated works by many different authors into Spanish.

SIDELIGHTS: Ernestina de Champourcin is considered to be the most important female poet of Spain's famed literary "Generation of 1927." Born in Vitoria, Spain, in 1905, she followed the guidance of her fellow countryman and poet Juan Ramón Jiménez and "quickly achieved notoriety," in the words of Joy B. Landeira in the *Encyclopedia of World Literature in the Twentieth Century.* Champourcin's first collection of poetry, *En Silencio,* appeared in 1926. Two years later, she produced *Ahora,* which Landeira felt "plunges into the modernist and surrealist traditions with vibrant language, complex metaphors, and lush exoticism." The critic went on to explain that *Ahora,* along with Champourcin's 1931 collection *La Voz en el viento,* "insured her inclusion in the lively Madrid literary scene where she was granted exclusive book contracts and named among the Generation of 1927." Champourcin's poetry also appeared in the definitive anthology of that literary group, Gerardo Diego's *Poesía española contemporáneos.*

In 1936, Champourcin married another poet associated with that group, Juan José Domenchina. The wedding took place the day before fascist General Francisco Franco moved his troops into Madrid during the Spanish Civil War; because Domenchina served as secretary to Republican leader Manuel Azaña, the newlyweds fled the country immediately. They stopped in Toulouse, France, for a brief period before going on to Mexico, where Domenchina died in 1959. Champourcin stayed in Mexico until 1973.

Before leaving Spain, however, Champourcin managed to publish her first novel, *La Casa de enfrente.* The story centers on the life of a young girl from her childhood through her first love. Champourcin also managed to get out her fourth volume of poetry, *Cántico inútil.* Landeira praised this work as "arguably the finest in all her production and certainly the best of her early writing."

After Champourcin and her husband arrived in Mexico, she used her early training in French and English to work as a translator. During this time, she translated the works of many different authors, ranging from sociology texts to mysteries by Dorothy L. Sayers. Occasionally, she and Domenchina translated a book together. Until 1952, her translation work apparently kept Champourcin so busy that she did not write or try to publish poetry. When she did return to the poetic scene, her poetic style and motivation had changed, revealing the influence of Domenchina's attitude toward his own art. As Landeira put it: "No longer did she experiment with exuberant metaphors or focus on carefully crafted structure. All of her poetry from 1952 through 1974 adhered to the thematic credo that 'God is in all poetry,' a theme shared by her husband who believed that the poet's only life was to dialogue with God." Landeira noted further that Champourcin's work during these years was "deeply felt and reliant on biblical themes." Collections in this vein include 1960's *El Nombre que me diste* and 1964's *Cárcel de los sentidos, 1953-1963.*

Champourcin's next major poetical shift seems to coincide with her return from Mexican exile to Spain in 1973. Since this personal event, her poetry has lost its emphasis on religious matters and deals more with the struggle to remain a poet in the face of the difficulties of old age. According to Landeira, the poet presents herself as "desperate for communication and increasingly frustrated by a lack of human contact and the loss of sight and hearing." As a poet, Champourcin thus "seeks transcendence through nature, awareness of the world around her and the consolation of poetic memory."

In 1981 Champourcin published *La Ardilla y la rosa: Juan Ramón en mi memoria,* a collection of her correspondence and memories of her poetic mentor, Jiménez. Interestingly, the primary title means "The Squirrel and the Rose." One of Champourcin's more recent poetry volumes is 1993's *Del Vacío y sus dones.* The title means "Emptiness and Its Gifts," a further reference to the decline of the poet's physical senses and the means by which she is able to compensate for it. *Del Vacío y sus dones* received a great deal of praise from Birute Ciplijauskaite in *World Literature Today.* He noted that the collection consists primarily of free verse, "except for a few poems in rich alexandrines." Ciplijauskaite mentioned Champourcin's poetic evolution towards a more "retrospective focus . . . and a more philosophical stance," but then went on to conclude that "this spiritual self-portrait whose originality and authenticity of voice rest on unshaken faith offers hope and transpires deep, bliss-bringing religiosity elevated to its purest essence."

BIOGRAPHICAL AND CRITICAL SOURCES:

BOOKS

Encyclopedia of World Literature in the Twentieth Century, 3rd edition, St. James Press (Detroit, MI), 1999.

PERIODICALS

Letras Femeninas, spring-fall, 1991, Catherine G. Bellver, "Tres poetas desterradas y la morfologia del exilio," pp. 51-63.

Ojancano, October, 1988, Andrew P. Debicki, "Una Dimensión olvidada de la poesía española de los '20 y '30: La Lírica visionaria de Ernestina de Champourcin," pp. 48-60.
Review Interamericana, spring, 1982, Rafael Espejo-Saavedra, "Sentimiento amoroso y creación poética en Ernestina de Champourcin," pp. 133-139.
World Literature Today, summer, 1994, Birute Ciplijauskaite, review of *Del Vacío y sus dones,* p. 539.

OTHER

Entrevista, http://www.ucm.es/ (March 21, 2002), "Ernestina de Champourcin."*

* * *

CHAPMAN, Robert L(undquist) 1920-2002

OBITUARY NOTICE—See index for *CA* sketch: Born December 28, 1920, in Huntington, WV; died January 27, 2002, in Morristown, NJ. Lexicographer, educator, and editor. Chapman was a man of many words. He is best remembered as the lexicographer who brought *Roget's International Thesaurus* into the twentieth century. The thesaurus, first published by Peter Mark Roget in 1852, is notable because it groups words by theme rather than strictly by definition. Chapman edited the fourth edition of the work in 1977, but it was his fifth edition, published in 1992, that expanded the compendium with more than 50,000 new words—including colloquialisms such as "AIDS," "yuppie," "hacker," and "crack" (as in cocaine)—that were unknown in Roget's time. Chapman was reported to be one of the few lexicographers willing to exploit computer databases in his relentless search for new words. Chapman also added several new categories to reflect modern interests and new technologies, such as fitness and exercise, computer science, and substance abuse. Chapman taught medieval English literature at several eastern U.S. colleges, including a stint at Drew University in New Jersey from 1966 to 1986. Previously he had worked as a lexicographer and dictionary editor for the New York City publishers Funk & Wagnalls Company and Holt, Rinehart & Winston. Chapman's other publications included a dictionary and a thesaurus devoted to American slang.

OBITUARIES AND OTHER SOURCES:

PERIODICALS

Florida Times-Union, February 8, 2002.
Grand Rapids Press, February 7, 2002.
Los Angeles Times, February 24, 2002, obituary by Elaine Woo, p. B16.
New York Times, February 5, 2002, obituary by Margalit Fox, p. A23.
St. Petersburg Times (St. Petersburg, FL), February 6, 2002.
Star-Ledger (Newark, NJ), February 6, 2002, obituary by Rudy Larini, p. 31.
Washington Post, February 10, 2002, p. C8; February 25, 2002, p. B6.

*   *   *

CHRISTODOULOU, Anastasios 1932-2002

OBITUARY NOTICE—See index for *CA* sketch: Born May 1, 1932, in Akanthou, Cyprus; died after a stroke May 20, 2002, in Milton Keynes, England. University administrator and author. Christodoulou, as founding secretary of the Open University, was an influential advocate of distance learning and higher education for all. A graduate of Queen's College, Oxford where he earned a master's degree in 1959, his love of the British Commonwealth began with his work for the British Overseas Civil Service in what is now Tanzania. Returning to England in 1962, he joined the University of Leeds as assistant registrar, becoming deputy secretary from 1966 to 1968. His interest in higher education for all citizens, including those in the Commonwealth nations, led to his appointment as secretary of the Open University, which was established in 1969. As secretary, Christodoulou was in charge of finances, administration, and staff, and his leadership helped make the university a resounding success. He left the Open University in 1980 to become the secretary-general of the Association of Commonwealth Universities, where he remained until his retirement in 1996. In this capacity he worked to advocate the improvement of educational opportunities through distance-learning programs. He was recognized for his leadership in education when he was made a Commander of the Order of the British Empire in 1976; he was also the recipient of several honorary degrees. Christo-

doulou's publication contributions include coeditorship of *Commonwealth Universities Yearbook,* including the 62nd edition (1986), and as a contributor to *The Commonwealth Universities: The Story of the Association of Commonwealth Universities, 1963-1988* (1988).

OBITUARIES AND OTHER SOURCES:

BOOKS

Who's Who, 152nd edition, St. Martin's (New York, NY), 2000.

PERIODICALS

Scotsman (Edinburgh, Scotland), June 8, 2002, p. 15.
Times (London, England), May 30, 2002, p. 33.

*   *   *

CHUCK-YIU, Clara Law
See LAW, Clara

*   *   *

CLEWES, Dorothy Mary 1907-2003

OBITUARY NOTICE—See index for *CA* sketch: Born July 6, 1907 in Nottingham, England; died February 8, 2003. Writer. Clewes was a British writer for all ages, best known for her easy-to-read picture books for young children. She studied at Nottingham University, and later became a secretary and worked for her family's doctor in Nottingham while writing in her spare time. Her first novel was published in 1925, but it was not until after marrying Winston Clewes, a prolific writer, in 1932, that Dorothy devoted herself to writing on a full-time basis. Beginning in 1968, Clewes began her most famous series, the adventures of a stubborn four-year-old in the "Willie" books: *Upsidedown Willie, Special Branch Willie,* and *Fire Brigade Willie.* From these popular picture books to teen novels like *Storm over Innish,* her books have pleased both British and American readers with their interesting settings, intriguing subjects, and likeable, well-drawn characters.

OBITUARIES AND OTHER SOURCES:

PERIODICALS

Guardian (Manchester, England), February 25, 2003,
Julia Eccleshare, "Dorothy Clewes: Writer in
Touch with the Imagination of Children."

*   *   *

COHEN, Haim
   See COHN, Haim H(erman)

*   *   *

COHN, Haim H(erman) 1911-2002
   (Haim Cohen)

OBITUARY NOTICE—See index for *CA* sketch: Born
March 11, 1911, in Lübeck, Germany; died April 10,
2002, in Jerusalem, Israel. Attorney, judge, and author.
Cohn was a former Israeli Supreme Court justice who
was a staunch advocate of human rights. He studied at
the universities of Hamburg and Frankfurt, as well as
at the Hebrew University of Jerusalem and Rabinical
College, during the early 1930s. Attending the
Palestine Government Law School, he received his
degree in 1937, the same year he was admitted to the
Bar in Palestine. After graduation Cohn entered private
practice in Jerusalem for ten years. He became a state
attorney in 1948 and was director-general of the
Ministry of Justice from 1949 to 1950 and attorney
general from 1950 to 1960. As a supreme court justice
from 1960 to 1981 Cohn became noted for his
insistence that Israeli law be based on secular, not
religious, principles. His desire that justice apply to
everyone equally sometimes resulted in his unpopular
siding with Arabic people; he was often in the minor-
ity opinion regarding such things as the right of
extremist Arab party members to run for office. Cohn
also defended Rudolf Kastner, who had been accused
of being a Nazi collaborator but who was later
vindicated, and he opposed the death penalty absolutely, even for convicted Nazi Adolf Eichmann.
Cohn's work was recognized in 1980 when he received
the Israel Prize. He was the author of many books,
including *Jewish Law in Israeli Jurisprudence* (1968),
The Trial and Death of Jesus (1971), *Human Rights in
Jewish Law* (1984), and *Selected Essays* (1992).

OBITUARIES AND OTHER SOURCES:

BOOKS

International Who's Who, 63rd edition, Europa
Publications (London, England), 2000.

PERIODICALS

Los Angeles Times, April 11, 2002, p. B13.
New York Times, April 13, 2002, p. A16.
Times (London, England), April 26, 2002.
Washington Post, April 13, 2002, p. B6.

*   *   *

COLLINS, David (Joseph) 1962-

PERSONAL: Born November 5, 1962, in Detroit, MI,
United States; son of James (an automotive executive)
and Eileen Foley Collins; married Louise Mooney,
April 30, 1994 (deceased November 28, 1997);
children: Robin Ryther (daughter). *Education:* University of Michigan (Ann Arbor), B.A. (English), 1985.
Religion: Catholic.

ADDRESSES: Office—The Gale Group, 27500 Drake
Rd., Farmington Hills, MI 48331-3535. *Agent*—Carol
Mann, The Carol Mann Agency, 55 Fifth Ave., New
York, NY 10003. *E-mail*—dave.collins@gale.com.

CAREER: Writer and editor. Gale Research Co. (now
The Gale Group), Farmington Hills, MI, editor,
1986—. *Military service:* U.S. Marine Corps, 1983;
attended Officer Candidate School (honorable
discharge).

WRITINGS:

My Louise: A Memoir, Ontario Review Press
(Princeton, NJ), 2002.

SIDELIGHTS: David Collins has been called one of a
new breed of writers who aren't afraid to display
emotion. This is evident in his first title, *My Louise,* a

memoir of the struggle of Collins's wife, Louise, as she battled breast cancer, and his own battle against his grief after her death. As Meredith Parets noted in *Booklist,* "[Collins's] account of Louise's courage and his grief in the face of this reality are moving and true, as are his frank depictions of the ravages—both psychological and physical—of her treatments." A critic for *Kirkus Reviews* recognized that "the author's description of slow footsteps on the stairs as his father comes to deliver the news of Louise's death is heartfelt in its simplicity."

A *Publishers Weekly* reviewer described the personal revelations contained in *My Louise* with the observation that "most notable is [Collins's] evolving perspective on parenting, from the subtle and sad transition as he takes over primary care of Robin when Louise is no longer able." But life, not death, is the overriding theme of the book. "The biggest problems seem to solve themselves," Collins concludes in *My Louise.* "I think I'll just point myself in the right direction, fold away this picture of my wife and daughter in my heart, and let the adventure continue."

Collins told *CA:* "While I have written a few stories and some poetry over the years, and have written professionally in my job as a reference book editor, I have always wanted to someday write a 'serious' literary book. *My Louise,* my first published book, details my thoughts and reflections in the months and years immediately following my wife's death from breast cancer in 1997. As such it is not really the book I had imagined writing (I was thinking along the lines of a novel or collection or stories), but it became the book I needed to write at that time. About a year after Louise's death I found myself having a difficult time processing the many emotions of grief (principally anger bordering on rage, but also plenty of sadness too). On top of that I was also struggling to keep my head above water in the raising of our daughter Robin, who was just two-and-a-half years old at the time of Louise's passing.

"In many ways I see a writer's task as being one of bringing an order to chaos—of sifting through a maze of thoughts, feelings, and ideas and bringing them to some kind of sense that is pleasing both intellectually and artistically. I found that in my grief I had all the material I needed for a book that could prove helpful first to myself (as a catharsis) and my daughter (as something for her to read when she is older, to help her understand this important time in her young life). Secondly, I hoped that it could help others who had experienced a similar kind of loss and had not found the means or time to express themselves or otherwise do that important work of finding some resolution to their grief, some meaning or reason to move on. So it was a combination of all these things that motivated me to write *My Louise.*

"While the book has as its focus a woman's tragic death at a young age from breast cancer, I do not really see it as a 'breast cancer book.' I intentionally steered clear as much as possible from clinical details of the disease and treatments, choosing instead to focus on the wreckage that breast cancer leaves behind. I see the book being more about grief than anything else—the ways in which the grieving mind (in this case, mine) uses everything at its disposal—memory, intellect, faith, anger and fear to name but a few—to find the strength and more importantly, a reason to move on.

"Of course, the book is also a tribute to my wife and to her incredible courage. It is about Louise and the loss of Louise and all the ramifications of both. To me breast cancer is what took her away from us—something to be reckoned with certainly, and something to be enlightened about—but to make it the focus of this book would be to give it too much power. While breast cancer took Louise from us, my book was a way to reclaim her memory on terms that we can live with.

"Because the book is about grief, I felt that the central narrative voice had to be distinctly my own. Writing from the point of view of a newly widowed young man, I felt it important to be exactly that—in all of its authenticity and, at times, raw emotion. To help convey the way the mind sifts back and forth from the present moment to memory and back again, I presented the narrative in a very non-linear way. I also thought that by juxtaposing some of the sadder and more personal stories of Louise's illness and death with more immediate tales of my daily struggles as a single father, I could break the story up somewhat and make it more readable and interesting. In that sense I wrote the book in a number of smaller pieces and then wove them together in a way that I thought would be rhythmic and lyrical."

BIOGRAPHICAL AND CRITICAL SOURCES:

BOOKS

Collins, David, *My Louise: A Memoir,* Ontario Review Press (Princeton, NJ), 2002.

PERIODICALS

Booklist, September 15, 2002, Meredith Parets, review of *My Louise,* p. 183.
Kirkus Reviews, August 1, 2002, review of *My Louise,* p. 1088.
Publishers Weekly, August 5, 2002, review of *My Louise,* p. 64.

*   *   *

CONYERS, James L., Jr. 1961-

PERSONAL: Born June 17, 1961, in Jersey City, NJ; son of James L., Sr. (a laborer) and Agnes Conyers; married May 30, 1985; wife's name Jacqueline I.; children: Chad Anthony, Sekou Khalfami, Kamau Abotare. *Ethnicity:* "African American." *Education:* Ramapo College of New Jersey, B.A.; State University of New York—Albany, B.A. and M.A.; Temple University, Ph.D. *Politics:* Democrat. *Religion:* Baptist. *Hobbies and other interests:* Carpentry.

ADDRESSES: Home—7814 Potter Plaza, Omaha, NE 68122. *Office*—Department of Black Studies, AS 184, University of Nebraska—Omaha, Omaha, NE 68182-0041; fax: 402-554-3883. *E-mail*—jconyers@home.com.

CAREER: State University of New York—Cobbleskill, assistant professor of black studies, 1994-96; University of Nebraska—Omaha, professor of black studies, 1996—.

MEMBER: Alpha Phi Alpha.

AWARDS, HONORS: Diop Award for research in black studies; grants from National Endowment for the Humanities.

WRITINGS:

EDITOR

Africana Studies: A Disciplinary Quest for both Theory and Method, McFarland & Co. (Jefferson, NC), 1997.
Charles H. Wesley: The Intellectual Tradition of a Black Historian, Garland Publishers (New York, NY), 1997.
(With Alva P. Barnett) *African-American Sociology: A Social Study of the Pan-African Diaspora,* Nelson-Hall (Chicago, IL), 1999.
(With Alva P. Barnett) *Africana History, Culture, and Social Policy: A Collection of Critical Essays,* International Scholars Publications/University Press for West Africa (San Francisco, CA), 1999.
Carter G. Woodson: An Historical Reader, Garland Publishing (New York, NY), 1999.
Black American Intellectualism and Culture: A Social Study of African American Social and Political Thought, JAI Press (Stamford, CT), 1999.
Black Lives: Essays in African-American Biography, M. E. Sharpe (Armonk, NY), 1999.
African-American Jazz and Rap: Social and Philosophical Examinations of Black Expressive Behavior, McFarland & Co. (Jefferson, NC), 2001.
A Structural Analysis of Enslavement in the African Diaspora, Edwin Mellen Press (Lewiston, NY), 2001.
Black Cultures and Race Relations, Burhham Inc. Publishers (Chicago, IL), 2002.
Afrocentricity and the Academy: Essays on Theory and Practice, McFarland & Co. (Jefferson, NC), 2003.

WORK IN PROGRESS: More books and articles; research for a biography of Charles H. Wesley.

*   *   *

COOTES, Jim E. 1950-

PERSONAL: Born June 17, 1950, in Sydney, New South Wales, Australia; son of Sydney (a foreman electrician) and Ina (a homemaker; maiden name, Gibson) Cootes. *Education:* Kogarah Technical College, trade certificate, 1969. *Religion:* Baptist. *Hobbies and other interests:* Aviculture, aquaculture, growing orchids, playing the guitar.

ADDRESSES: Agent—c/o Author Mail, Timber Press, 133 Southwest Second Ave., Suite 450, Portland, OR 97204. *E-mail*—jecootes@ozemail.com.au.

CAREER: Australian Department of Defense, Sydney, New South Wales, Australia, engraver, 1966-97; Australia Post, Sydney, delivery officer, 2000—.

WRITINGS:

The Orchids of the Philippines, Timber Press (Portland, OR), 2001.

Contributor to orchid magazines in Australia and around the world.

WORK IN PROGRESS: The Orchids of the Philippines, Volume 2; research on the *Bulbophyllinae* family of orchids.

SIDELIGHTS: Jim E. Cootes told *CA:* "I wrote *The Orchids of the Philippines* because of the lack of books on the subject. I grow many orchids native to the Philippines, and there is still much difficulty in trying to identify these plants. I currently have in my greenhouse at least twenty-three unidentified orchid species from the Philippines."

BIOGRAPHICAL AND CRITICAL SOURCES:

PERIODICALS

Choice, January, 2002, L. G. Kavaljian, review of *The Orchids of the Philippines,* p. 903.

*   *   *

CRUMP, William D(rake) 1949-

PERSONAL: Born February 28, 1949, in Nashville, TN; son of William Milton and Mary Frances (Drake) Crump. *Education:* David Lipscomb College, B.A., 1971; University of Tennessee Center for the Health Sciences, M.D., 1974. *Politics:* Conservative. *Religion:* Church of Christ. *Hobbies and other interests:* Playing the organ, literature of the church.

ADDRESSES: Home and office—757 Howse Ave., Madison, TN 37115. *E-mail*—cootum@earthlink.net.

CAREER: Reference Pathology, Nashville, TN, pathologist, 1982-86, 1990-95; Roche Biomedical, Monroe, LA, pathologist, 1986-89; Loyola University, Chicago, IL, fellow at Medical Center, 1989-90; writer. Church organist, 1998-2002.

MEMBER: College of American Pathologists, American Theatre Organ Society.

WRITINGS:

The Christmas Encyclopedia, McFarland and Co. (Jefferson, NC), 2001.

WORK IN PROGRESS: A Christmas quiz book; a Christmas I.Q. test.

SIDELIGHTS: William D. Crump told *CA:* "For *The Christmas Encyclopedia* I originally envisioned a lighthearted quiz book of nearly 1,000 college board-type questions and answers that focused on all aspects of the Christmas season. From Advent to Epiphany, from the Nativity to Santa Claus, from foreign traditions to Scrooge, the Grinch, and 'How the Flintstones Saved Christmas,' readers could test their 'Christmas I.Q.' and explore the highlights of 2,000 years of Christmas. My publisher, on the other hand, felt that readers would better appreciate an encyclopedic approach over a massive quiz. Yet I still foresee a Christmas quiz book or a Christmas I.Q. test on the horizon."

BIOGRAPHICAL AND CRITICAL SOURCES:

PERIODICALS

Booklist, May 15, 2002, review of *The Christmas Encyclopedia,* p. 1628.
Choice, April, 2002, M. E. Snodgrass, review of *The Christmas Encyclopedia,* p. 1387.
Library Journal, January, 2002, Laurie Selwyn, review of *The Christmas Encyclopedia,* p. 83.

D

DAVIS, Amanda 1971-2003

PERSONAL: Born 1971; died in a plane crash near Asheville, NC, March 14, 2003; buried in Carrboro, NC; daughter of James (a physician) and Francie (a librarian) Davis. *Education:* Wesleyan University, B.A.; Brooklyn College, M.F.A. *Religion:* Jewish.

CAREER: Writer. *Esquire* (magazine), New York, NY, fiction assistant, 1997-99; City University of New York, Brooklyn College, adjunct lecturer in English, 1997-98; 92nd Street Y, New York, NY, instructor, 2000; Antioch University, Los Angeles, CA, mentoring instructor, 2002; Mills College, Oakland, CA, assistant professor of English, 2002-03.

MEMBER: Author's Guild, Writer's Room, Associated Writing Programs.

AWARDS, HONORS: Short story prize from *Story* magazine, 1997, for "Prints"; Tara fellow, Heekin Foundation, 1998; fellow, Bread Loaf Writer's Conference, 1997 and 2000, Blue Mountain Center, 1998, MacDowell Colony, 1999 and 2003, Djerassi Resident Artists Program, 2000, Wesleyan Writers Conference, 2000, Tyrone Guthrie Center, 2001, and Corporation of Yaddo, 2002.

WRITINGS:

Circling the Drain (short stories), Rob Weisbach Books (New York, NY, 1999.
Wonder When You'll Miss Me (novel), Morrow (New York, NY), 2003.

Contributor to books, including *Best New American Voices 2001,* Harcourt, 2002, *Burned Children of America,* Minimum Fax, 2002, and *Lit Riffs,* MTV Books, 2003. Contributor of short stories and articles to periodicals, including *Book, Poets and Writers, Black Book, Failbetter.com, Yale Literary Magazine, Bookforum, McSweeney's, Esquire, Seventeen,* and *Story.*

SIDELIGHTS: Amanda Davis garnered critical recognition for her books *Circling the Drain,* a collection of short fiction, and *Wonder When You'll Miss Me,* a novel. Davis was the winner of *Story* magazine's annual short story contest in 1997 and was awarded fellowships from the prestigious MacDowell Colony, Bread Loaf Writer's Conference, Wesleyan Writers Conference, and Corporation of Yaddo.

Davis, who had been writing short stories since junior high school, moved to New York shortly after graduating from college in order to seriously pursue a writing career. She worked at a public relations job for a corporation—a job she hated—and waited tables, but the job that was most helpful was her stint in the *Esquire* fiction department. "It was tremendous—I learned a lot, got to read a lot of great stuff—but so frustrating," Davis told Ron Hogan in *Beatrice Magazine.* "There'd be a two-foot stack of submissions that I'd be looking at, twice a week. And you have to get through it, because there's another stack just like it coming." Davis avoided having her work end up in stacks like that through some lucky timing. She got a scholarship to the prestigious Bread Loaf writer's conference and there met Lois Rosenthal, the editor of *Story.* She sent Rosenthal her story, "Chase," about a girl who kills a boy's horse so that she won't have a rival for his affection, and Rosenthal bought it.

"Chase" is one of the fifteen stories in Davis's 1999 collection *Circling the Drain*. Many of these stories focus on troubled—or troubling—relationships between men and women. In "Red Lights like Laughter," a couple waits out a blizzard in a hotel room. They seem normal enough until Davis reveals the violent act that they are fleeing from. In the title piece of the collection, a woman falls for a man who works at the shoe-rental counter at a bowling alley. He turns out to be a shoe fetishist.

Other of Davis's stories explore different territory. The seventeen-year-old heroine of "The Visit" bonds with a grandfather who's suffering from Alzheimer's disease. "Testimony" tells the tale of a woman convinced that her late brother could actually channel the voice of God. "The Very Moment They're About" focuses on a teenage couple on the last night of summer camp, who are about to experience a first kiss that will mark the dividing line between childhood and adulthood. In one of Davis's most experimental stories, "Faith, or Tips for the Successful Young Lady," a slimmed-down high schooler is stalked by her fat former self—an entity she can actually see and who goads her to take revenge on those who used to taunt her.

Several critics found a gentle, calm quality in Davis's stories. "Amanda Davis writes gently, even poetically, about extraordinary brutality," Mary Elizabeth Williams noted in her review of *Circling the Drain* for the *New York Times Book Review*. "With a calm tone, the sensibility of a Southern writer, and a twinge of magic realism, [Davis] probes the lives of girls and women for whom boys are a painfully enthralling necessity," wrote Touré in the *Village Voice*. "It's amazing how deep Davis's stories run because most of them are as short as a few pages." Other critics remarked on Davis's narrative skill. Polly Morrice in *Salon.com,* for example, found that "in nearly all of these stories . . . things move right along. . . . By combining her talent for narrative with her willingness to take risks . . . Davis might really soar her next time out." "There is nothing groundbreaking here," Gaelle Eizlini admitted in *FFWD Weekly,* "but Davis introduces an edgy voice laced with fear, insecurity, exhilaration and rage. . . . A talented newcomer."

In February of 2003, Davis published her first novel, *Wonder When You'll Miss Me,* the story of a teenaged girl who is raped at her high school, survives a subsequent suicide attempt, and then decides to join the circus and leave her troubled past behind. Faith Druckle also imagines she has an invisible companion, The Fat Girl, her own overweight former self, who goads her into violence. Faith's work at the circus, where she takes on the new name of Annabelle Cabinet, leads her to a kind of psychological healing among the freaks and circus performers. "Davis never lets us assume," Shannon Bloomstran wrote in *Mostlyfiction.com,* "that Faith's . . . new life is perfect. . . . We are left, however, with a measure of hope." The critic for *Publishers Weekly* praised Davis's "tensely lyrical prose and fullbodied characterizations." According to Sarah Rachel Egelman in her review for *Bookreporter.com,* "Davis has created a lucid, compelling page-turner that defies categorization." Meredith Parets in *Booklist* concluded: "This is an astonishing debut: dark, disturbing, and fiercely openhearted."

In March of 2003, while on a national book tour to promote *Wonder When You'll Miss Me,* Davis was killed when the single-engine plane she was flying in crashed into a mountain some eighteen miles from Asheville, North Carolina. Her father, who was piloting the plane, and her mother were also killed in the accident. Janet Holmgren, president of Mills College, where Davis taught, stated in the *San Francisco Chronicle* that Davis was "a talented new voice in American fiction and a highly respected new member of the faculty who brought great energy and passion to her teaching." Davis's friend Heidi Julavitz, in a tribute posted at the *McSweeney's Magazine* Web site, called the writer "one of the funniest, self-effacing, chutzpah-charged and big-hearted human beings anyone could ever hope to encounter."

BIOGRAPHICAL AND CRITICAL SOURCES:

PERIODICALS

Booklist, February 1, 2003, Meredith Parets, review of *Wonder When You'll Miss Me,* p. 971.
FFWD Weekly, July 15, 1999, Gaelle Eizlini, review of *Circling the Drain.*
Kirkus Reviews, December 1, 2002, review of *Wonder When You'll Miss Me,* p. 1714.
Library Journal, May 15, 1999, Christine DeZelar-Tiedman, review of *Circling the Drain,* p. 130.

New York Times Book Review, June 20, 1999, Mary Elizabeth Williams, review of *Circling the Drain.*

Publishers Weekly, May 10, 1999, review of *Circling the Drain,* p. 57; November 18, 2002, review of *Wonder When You'll Miss Me,* p. 40.

Village Voice, October 23, 2002, Touré, review of *Circling the Drain.*

OTHER

Beatrice Magazine, http://www.beatrice.com/ (October 23, 2002), Ron Hogan, "Amanda Davis: 'I Have No Idea What I'm Doing, but I'm Enjoying It.'"

Bookreporter.com, http://www.bookreporter.com/ (March 19, 2003), Sarah Rachel Egelman, review of *Wonder When You'll Miss Me.*

McSweeney's Internet Tendency, http://www.mcsweeneys.net/ (March 21, 2003), Heidi Julavits, tribute to Amanda Davis.

MostlyFiction.com, http://www.mostlyfiction.com/ (January 29, 2003), Shannon Bloomstran, review of *Wonder When You'll Miss Me.*

Salon.com, http://www.salon.com/ (June 7, 1999), Polly Morrice, review of *Circling the Drain.*

Wonder When You'll Miss Me Web site, http://www.wonderwhenyoullmissme.com/ (March 19, 2003).*

OBITUARIES:

PERIODICALS

News-Observer (Charlotte, NC), March 18, 2003, Rah Bickley, "A Life of Letters Cut Short."

New York Observer, March 21, 2003, Joe Hagan, "Amanda Davis, 1971-2003."

New York Post, March 17, 2003, p. 12.

New York Times, March 18, 2003, p. C14.

Register-Guard (Eugene, OR), March 16, 2003.

San Francisco Chronicle, March 18, 2003, p. A22.*

*   *   *

DAVIS, Benjamin O(liver), Jr. 1912-2002

OBITUARY NOTICE—See index for *CA* sketch: Born December 18, 1912, in Washington, DC; died of complications from Alzheimer's disease July 4, 2002, in Washington, DC. U.S. Air Force officer and author. General Davis commanded the famous, all-black Tuskegee Airmen squadron during World War II and is credited with being a major force in integrating the U.S. military. His military career is a long story of breaking down the barriers of prejudice. The first African American to graduate from West Point in 1936, Davis was denied entrance into the U.S. Army Air Corps because of his race and instead completed his first assignment in a segregated infantry unit at Fort Benning, Georgia. After attending infantry school there, he was transferred to the Tuskegee Institute, where he taught military tactics. When President Franklin Roosevelt created an all-black flying unit in 1941, Davis advanced to become a pilot in 1942. As a lieutenant colonel, he was then put in command of the 99th Pursuit Squadron—known as the Tuskegee Airmen—in 1942. During World War II his squadron was sent to Tunisia and then Germany, where their fighter planes protected bombers from German attacks. One of Davis's proudest achievements is that his squadron never lost a bomber. Despite their record, the 99th was at risk of being disbanded until Davis protested and convinced General George Marshall to keep the unit intact. In 1944 and 1945 Davis was put in command of other all-black units: the 332nd Fighter Group, based in Italy, and then the 477th Bombardment Group, based stateside in Kentucky. After the war Davis helped President Harry S Truman draft the order to integrate the U.S. military, and served in the Pentagon and in a variety of overseas posts. In 1965 he was promoted to lieutenant general. He retired in 1970, but in 1998 President Bill Clinton promoted Davis to full general. In his post-military years, Davis worked in the Department of Transportation where, among other duties, he was in charge of the sky marshal program that helps guard planes against hijackers. Davis, a true war hero, was awarded three Distinguished Service Medals, the Silver Star, the Distinguished Flying Cross, three Legions of Merit, an Air Medal with five oak leaf clusters, the French Croix de Guerre with palm, and the Star of Africa. He wrote of his life and his achievements in his 1991 book *Benjamin O. Davis, Jr., American: An Autobiography.*

OBITUARIES AND OTHER SOURCES:

BOOKS

Contemporary Heroes and Heroines, Volume III, Gale (Detroit, MI), 1998.

Who's Who among African Americans, 11th edition, Gale (Detroit, MI), 1997.

Who's Who in American Politics, 16th edition, Marquis (New Providence, NJ), 1997.

PERIODICALS

Los Angeles Times, July 6, 2002, p. B18.
New York Times, July 7, 2002, p. A19.
Washington Post, July 6, 2002, p. B7.

* * *

de SYON, Guillaume 1966-

PERSONAL: Born March 2, 1966, in Paris, France; son of Michel (a psychiatrist) and Joëlle (a tour leader; maiden name, Carpano) de Syon; married Maria Mitchell (an historian).

ADDRESSES: Office—Albright College, 13th and Bern Sts., Reading, PA 19612-5234. *E-mail*—gp_desyon@fandm.edu.

CAREER: Albright College, Reading, PA, teacher of history.

MEMBER: American Historical Association, Society for the History of Technology.

WRITINGS:

(Editor, with others) *The Collected Papers of Albert Einstein,* Volumes 8A and 8B: *Correspondence, 1914-1918,* Princeton University Press (Princeton, NJ), 1998.
Zeppelin! Germany and the Airship, 1900-1939, Johns Hopkins University Press (Baltimore, MD), 2001.

WORK IN PROGRESS: Crossing the Big Divide: Europe and Transatlantic Flying (tentative title), for Texas A & M University Press; research on the history of post-World War II tourism in Germany, French airships, airline advertising, and Switzerland during World War II; research on the cultural history of aviation.

BIOGRAPHICAL AND CRITICAL SOURCES:

PERIODICALS

History Today, November, 2001, Anne Pointer, review of *Zeppelin! Germany and the Airship, 1900-1939,* p. 58; May, 2002, A. D. Harvey, review of *Zeppelin!,* p. 80.
New Yorker, April 22, 2002, Mark Rozzo, review of *Zeppelin!,* p. 42.

DEVAUX, Claudia 1946-

PERSONAL: Born October 28, 1946, in California. *Education:* Lewis and Clark College, B.A. and M.A.T., 1968; California Polytechnic State University, San Luis Obispo, M.S., 1979; University of San Francisco, Ed.D., 1997. *Religion:* Roman Catholic.

ADDRESSES: Home—148 Lake Merced Hill, San Francisco, CA 94132-2935. *Office*—Hewlett-Packard Co., 19111 Penneridge Ave., Mail Stop 46U-01, Cupertino, CA 95014; fax 408-447-0658. *E-mail*—claudia_devaux@hp.com.

CAREER: Hewlett-Packard Co., Cupertino, CA, marketing executive. Minister to separated, divorced, and widowed Roman Catholics; participant in the establishment of a spirituality center in Benin.

WRITINGS:

(Coauthor) *Bamboo Swaying in the Wind,* Loyola University Press (Chicago, IL), 2000.*

* * *

DHOFARI, Temim
    See DJAOUT, Tahar

* * *

DIAL-DRIVER, Emily 1946-

PERSONAL: Born March 6, 1946, in Granite, OK. *Education:* Oklahoma State University, B.S., 1968, M.A., 1971, Ed.D. (higher education), 1991.

ADDRESSES: Home—1702 Meadow Rd., Claremore, OK 74017. *Office*—Department of Communications and Fine Arts, Rogers State University, 1701 West Will Rogers Blvd., Claremore, OK 74017. *E-mail*—edial-driver@rsu.edu.

CAREER: Ohio State University, Columbus, dietary interviewer for Children's Hospital Research Foundation, 1968-69; Rogers State University, Claremore,

OK, instructor, 1971-74, instructor, then professor of English, 1980—, coordinator of ACHIEVE Program and chairperson of curriculum committee, both 1996-99. National speaker on topics related to distance education, educational media, and curriculum development; developer of "telecourses"; also gives poetry readings. Celebration of Books, volunteer, 1993-99. *Military service:* U.S. Army, Ordnance Corps, 1974-78; became captain.

MEMBER: American Association of Community and Junior Colleges, Oklahoma Education Association (president, 1996—), Oklahoma Higher Education Television Association, Phi Kappa Phi, Delta Kappa Gamma, Omicron Nu.

AWARDS, HONORS: Grant from National Endowment for the Humanities, 1989-90; Excellence Award, National Institute for Staff and Organizational Development, 1998; Pixley Excellence in Teaching Award, 1998; Outstanding Professor Award, Oklahoma Leadership Academy, 1999-2000.

WRITINGS:

Composition II: Multiple Learning Opportunities, Rogers State University (Claremore, OK), 1989.
(Editor and author of introduction) Maggie Fry, *The Cherokee Female Seminary Years: A Cherokee National Anthology,* Rogers State University (Claremore, OK), 1990.
(Editor and contributor) *The Competitive Edge II,* Centrilift (Claremore, OK), 1992.
Write Right, EUN (Portland, OR), 1993.
College Writing: Discovering the Writing Spiral, Rogers State University (Claremore, OK), 1994.
A Guide to College Writing, McGraw (New York, NY), 1996.

Plays produced at Will Rogers Theater include *Beauty and the Beast,* 1987; *The Three Little Pigs,* 1988; and *Hansel and Gretel,* 1989. Scriptwriter for television courses. Contributor of articles and poems to periodicals, including *Oklahoma English Journal, Writers and Projects, Executive Educator, Community College Review,* and *Through Magic Glasses.* Poetry editor, *Cooweescooee,* 1995-99.

WORK IN PROGRESS: September-June, May-December: What It Means I Can't Remember, a "novel of manners and murder."

DJAOUT, Tahar 1954-1993
(Tayeb S., Temim Dhofari)

PERSONAL: Born January 11, 1954, in Azeffoun (Greater Kabylia), Algeria; died June 2, 1993, in Algiers, Algeria. *Education:* Attended University of Algiers; University of Paris II, graduate degree (journalism and communications).

CAREER: Worked as a journalist for various French-language publications in Algeria and the United States, sometimes under the pseudonyms Tayeb S. and Temim Dhofari; founded independent newspaper *Ruptures,* January, 1993.

AWARDS, HONORS: Duca Foundation Prize, 1984, for *Les Chercheurs d'Os;* Kateb Yacine Prize, Noureddine-Aba Foundation, 1991, for *Les Vigiles;* Prix Meditérranée, 1991, for *Les Vigiles.*

WRITINGS:

POETRY

Solstice barbelé (title means "Barbed Wire Solstice"), Naaman (Sherbrooke, Quebec, Canada), 1975.
L'arche à vau-l'eau (title means "The Ark Downstream"), Saint-Germain-des-Prés (Paris, France), 1978.
Insulaire et cie, 1980.
L'Oiseau minéral, 1982.
Les rets de l'oiseleur, Enterprise Nationale du Livre (Algiers, Algeria), 1984.
(Editor) *Les mots migrateurs* (title means "Migrating Words"), Office des Publications Universitaires (Algiers, Algeria), 1984.
Perennes (title means "Perennials"), 1993.

FICTION

L'Exproprié (title means "The Expropriated"), Majault (Paris, France), 1981.
Les chercheurs d'os (title means "The Bone-Seekers"), Seuil (Paris, France), 1984.
L'Invention du désert (title means "The Invention of the Desert"), Seuil (Paris, France), 1987.

Les vigiles (title means "The Watchmen"), Seuil (Paris, France), 1991.
Le dernier été de la raison (title means "The Last Summer of Reason"), Seuil (Paris, France), 1999.

SIDELIGHTS: Poet, novelist, and journalist Tahar Djaout, an outspoken critic of repression and religious fanaticism, once wrote in a poem, "If you speak, you die. If you are silent, you die. So, speak and die!" The words were prophetic; Djaout was gunned down in May, 1993 in front of his apartment in Bainem, Alegria and died days later. The author, whose first name means "pure one," dedicated his writing and life to human rights.

Djaout was born into a poor Berber family in the seaside town of Azeffoun in 1954, early in the Algerian nationalist movement. He entered the University of Algiers as a mathematics student, and continued his interests in poetry, which he had begun writing as a teenager. He earned a graduate degree in journalism and communications from the University of Paris II.

At age twenty-one Djaout published his first poetry collection, *Solstice barbelé*. He wrote several collections and edited an anthology of young Algerian poets, *Les Mots migrateurs*. The title represents the freedom and creativity of childhood and independence. Djaout and his generation of writers represented hope and revolution for Algeria, and its quest for independence from French colonizers. "If history, for [Djaout], is a discourse of usurpation, a site of dispossession, poetry is the means by which the habitual order of words and things is subverted, the place where freedom is learned," Danielle Marx-Scouras wrote in the *Encyclopedia of World Literature*.

Despite his burgeoning career as a journalist and his international reputation as a novelist, his real love was poetry. There, Djaout could succinctly express such stunning realities as, "There are cities where it is horrible to be twenty," from his early poem "Birthday." Beginning in the late 1970s, Djaout started writing essays on culture for the weekly Algerian publications *El Moudjahid* and *Algérie-Actualité*. At the same time he was also writing for French and U.S. publications, using the pen names Tayeb S. and Temim Dhofari. Eight years of war, after which the French departed, had left his country in disarray: more than two million Algerians had been left homeless, and the French regime left the Algerians with few professionals or skilled laborers. There was also infighting among the revolutionary leaders, a coup, and fundamentalist rioting against the one-party government.

The Islamic Salvation Front (FIS), whose aim was to change Algeria into an Islamic state, gained significantly in municipal and general elections in the early 1990s. After violent demonstrations, the government outlawed the FIS, further arousing its more militant supporters. They began a campaign of terror which included assassinations of intellectuals, politicians, artists, military officials, and journalists—including Djaout. On May 26, 1993, Djaout was shot in the head three times en route to work at the newspaper *Ruptures*, which he had founded that January. He died without regaining consciousness on June 2.

Djaout's five novels, including the posthumously published *Le dernier été de la raison*, earned him worldwide literary status. His first novel, *L'Exproprié*, is situated in a post-independent Algeria and involves a nomadic Berber trapped between two cultures while seeking his place in his country. David K. Bruner wrote in *World Literature Today*, "*L'Exproprié* mixes poetry and prose to make a bitter statement about an Algerian's search for identity and some semblance of justice and reason in a world which is chaotic, surrealistic, and horrifying. Although Algerian-based, this statement may just as well be made for most places on earth."

Les chercheurs d'os illustrates how war disrupts a small village community. Narrated by a fourteen-year-old boy, *Les chercheurs d'os* reports the "sacred journey" to locate the remains of relatives for customary burial. Djaout contrasts the younger generation, which must fight over its remains (i.e., its history), with the village elders, who stuff themselves with the sacrifices of others. J. D. Gauthier wrote in *World Literature Today*, "The dialectic of continuity in the sun's daily work and the temporary span of life of a man enters the boy's consciousness, and he begins to ponder the great truths: death, life, tradition."

L'Invention du désert investigates the history of the Arab conquest of the Maghreb, a segment of northwest Africa. Djaout, through his characters, reveals his sentiments about religion and its place in society. *L'Invention du désert* "questions the notion of purity at the heart of religious fanaticism in Algeria today," Marx-Scouras wrote. *Les vigiles,* the last novel published in Djaout's lifetime, features a young physics teacher who modernizes his grandmother's weaving loom. But the bureaucracy bogs him down with suspicion and petty concerns. In the face of international acclaim, the government decides it needs a scapegoat for its inaction. It tells a nondescript citizen he must "disappear." Told he is useless ("*peu utile*") to society, he hangs himself. This tale exemplifies Djaout's contempt toward the government's disregard for the individual.

In *Le dernier été de la raison,* a bookseller struggles against rulers who believe the worship of God should be the only artistic expression. He loses his friends, family, and his beloved bookshop, which the state takes over. Often prophetic in his fiction, Djaout, in his final novel, "sounds a warning," wrote James Schiff in *Book,* "about what can happen when religious fundamentalism proliferates." A *Publishers Weekly* reviewer, who read the English version, cited the author's "excellent flair for poetic description."

Though born in a Berber-speaking province, Djaout, as did most Algerian intellectuals, wrote in French. While the government labeled his work foreign literature, in reality, Djaout represented his country's striving for self-definition. "Djaout's great subject," Adam Shatz wrote in the *New York Times Book Review,* "was his country's slow, painful effort to enter modernity, and he examined it with the troubled love of a native son."

BIOGRAPHICAL AND CRITICAL SOURCES:

BOOKS

Encyclopedia of World Literature in the Twentieth Century, St. James Press (Detroit, MI), 1999.

PERIODICALS

Book, January-February, 2002, James Schiff, review of *The Last Summer of Reason,* p. 70.
Booklist, October 15, 2001, John Green, review of *The Last Summer of Reason,* p. 381.

French Review, October, 1978, Josette Bryson, review of *Solstice barbelé,* p. 177; October, 1996, Marie Naudin, "Tahar Djaout: Paysage metaphorique de l'Algérie," p. 81; December, 1996, Patricia Geesey, "Exhumation and History: Tahar Djaout's *Les chercheurs d'os,*" p. 271.
Kirkus Reviews, September 1, 2001, review of *The Last Summer of Reason,* p. 1233.
New York Times Book Review, December 23, 2001, Adam Shatz, review of *The Last Summer of Reason,* p. 18.
Publishers Weekly, October 1, 2001, review of *The Last Summer of Reason,* p. 38.
Research in African Literatures, fall, 1999, Reda Bensmaia, review of *L'Invention du désert,* p. 151.
World Literature Today, winter, 1985, J. D. Gauthier, review of *Les chercheurs d'os,* p. 143; spring, 1992, Evelyn Uhrhan Irving, review of *Les vigiles,* p. 388, David K. Bruner, review of *L'Exproprié,* p. 563; spring, 2000, Jean-Marie Volet, review of *The Last Summer of Reason,* p. 339.

OTHER

Arab.Net, http://www.arab.net/algeria/ (May 16, 2002).
Ruminator Books Web site, http://www.ruminator.com/ (May 15, 2002).

OBITUARIES:

PERIODICALS

New York Times, June 14, 1993.*

*   *   *

DUFTY, William (F.) 1916-2002

OBITUARY NOTICE—See index for *CA* sketch: Some sources cite full name as Christopher William Dufty; born February 2, 1916, in Merrill, MI; died of complications from cancer, June 28, 2002, in Birmingham, MI. Journalist, editor, speech writer, screenwriter, author, and ghostwriter. His skillful navigation along a life-path strewn with fortunate circumstances led Dufty from a reporter's beat at the *New York Post* all the way to Hollywood. It was his first wife, Maely Bartholomew, who introduced Dufty to singer Billie Holiday in New York City. Thus began a close friendship that would last until Holiday's death in 1959. Dufty coauthored Holiday's popular autobiography *Lady Sings the Blues,* which was later adapted as a screenplay starring Diana Ross. Some years later in Paris, Dufty encountered author George Ohsawa, who wrote about the relationship between food, meditation, and spirituality. In 1965 Dufty produced an English-language edition of Ohsawa's writings titled *You Are All Sanpaku.* The book has been described by some as a cult classic, and after its publication Dufty was credited with introducing American readers to the macrobiotic diet. In the late 1960s Dufty attended a conference on the relationship between food and cancer, and there met silent film star Gloria Swanson, who would later become his second wife. Swanson warned Dufty of the dangers of a sugar-laden diet, and in 1975 he published his second book on nutrition: *Sugar Blues.* The publication of *Sugar Blues* led to a reunion with Swanson, and they were married in 1976. Dufty remained devoted to the actress for the rest of her life, assisting her in the composition of her autobiography, *Swanson on Swanson.* Dufty assisted many other celebrities with their memoirs, and it is estimated that he was the ghostwriter of some forty books during his lifetime. He was also a screenwriter, a speech writer for politicians and trade union officials, an editor, and a freelance writer. Dufty's investigative reporting earned him a Page One Award from the Newspaper Guild and a George Polk Memorial Award from Long Island University.

OBITUARIES AND OTHER SOURCES:

PERIODICALS

Chicago Tribune, July 4, 2002, pp. 2-8.
Los Angeles Times, July 4, 2002, obituary by Myrna Oliver, p. B14.
New York Times, July 6, 2002, p. A11.

Times (London, England), August 2, 2002.
Washington Post, July 3, 2002, p. B6.

*   *   *

DURGNAT, Raymond (Eric) 1932-2002

OBITUARY NOTICE—See index for *CA* sketch: Born September 1, 1932, in London, England; died May 19, 2002, in London, England. Film critic, educator, and author. Durgnat was a prominent film critic and film historian with eclectic tastes for all types of cinematic entertainment. He was a sergeant in the Royal Army Education Corps in the Far East before completing his education at Cambridge University, where he earned a B.A. in 1957. Although he worked in the film industry in the late 1950s as a staff writer for Associated British Pictures, Durgnat did not enjoy working directly for a film company and became a freelance writer instead. He also taught film and art history during the 1960s and 1970s at St. Martin's School of Art, Queen's University in Kingston, Ontario, and Columbia University. It was Durgnat's criticism of film published in various magazines, as well as in a number of books, that gained him widespread attention as a quirky observer of the cinematic art form. He wrote about such topics as sexuality in film and the art of comedy. Among his books are *Eros in the Cinema* (1966), *Films and Feelings* (1967), *The Crazy Mirror* (1969), *A Mirror for England* (1971), *Durgnat on Film* (1975), and *WR: Mysteries of the Organism* (1999).

OBITUARIES AND OTHER SOURCES:

BOOKS

Writers Directory, 16th edition, St. James Press (Detroit, MI), 2001.

PERIODICALS

Independent (London, England), May 25, 2002, p. 20.
Times (London, England), May 29, 2002, p. 30.

E

EATON, Jack 1947-

PERSONAL: Born September 24, 1947, in St. Asaph, Clwyd, Wales. *Education:* Clare College, Cambridge, B.A. (with honors), 1969; University of Warwick, M.A.; Cambridge University, Ph.D., 1992.

ADDRESSES: Home—48 Maesceinion, Aberystwyth, Wales. *E-mail*—jke@aber.ac.uk.

CAREER: Vanden Berghs, Bromborough, England, personnel management trainee; Oxford University, Oxford, England, research associate and senior research fellow at St. Edmund Hall, 1971-72; University of Wales, Aberystwyth, lecturer in industrial relations, beginning 1972. Lecturer at other institutions, including University of Cranfield, 2002, North East London Polytechnic, Open University, and University of Nottingham; job analyst for local authorities.

AWARDS, HONORS: Certificate of recognition, Business Association of Latin American Studies Conference, 1989.

WRITINGS:

(With C. G. Gill and R. Morris) *Industrial Relations in the Chemical Industry,* Saxon House (Farnborough, England), 1978.

(With C. G. Gill) *Trade Union Directory: A Guide to All TUC Unions,* Pluto Press (London, England), 1981.

Judge Bryn Roberts: A Biography, University of Wales Press (Cardiff, Wales), 1989.

(With W. Maksymiw and C. G. Gill) *British Trade Union Directory,* Longman (London, England), 1990.

(With M. F. Bott, A. Coleman, and D. Rowland) *Professional Issues in Software Engineering,* 2nd edition, U.C.L., 1994, 3rd edition, Taylor & Francis, 2000.

Globalization and Human Resource Management in the Airline Industry, Avebury (Aldershot, England), 1996, 2nd edition, Ashgate Publishing (Brookfield, VT), 2001.

Comparative Employment Relations, Polity Press (Malden, MA), 2000.

Also author (with Nerys Fuller-Love) of *Rheolaeth Adnoddau Dynol* (distance learning materials; title means "Human Resource Management"), Education Resource Centre, University of Wales (Aberystwyth, Wales). Contributor to books, including *Mondragon: Myth or Model?,* Open University Press, 1982; and *The Current State of Economic Science,* Volume 4, edited by S. B. Dahiya, Spellbound Publications, 1999. Contributor of articles and reviews to periodicals, including *Corporate Communications, Journal of European Business Education, Inter Economics, Anglo Japanese Journal, British Journal of Industrial Relations, Political Quarterly, Personnel Review, Chemistry and Industry, Journal of Modern History,* and *Employee Relations.*

*   *   *

EGAN, Linda 1945-

PERSONAL: Born September 7, 1945, in Las Cruces, NM; daughter of Burl L. (a farmer and electrical and chemical engineer) and Lois M. (a hospital administrator; maiden name, Poole; present surname, Stanford)

Logan; married Michael F. Egan, October 25, 1963 (divorced December 17, 1964); children: Kevin Michael. *Ethnicity:* "Anglo." *Education:* Attended University of Madrid, 1967-68; California State University—Sacramento, B.A., 1968; University of California—Berkeley, M.A., 1970; attended Santa Barbara City College, 1978-80, and El Colegio de México, 1991; University of California—Santa Barbara, Ph.D., 1993. *Politics:* Independent. *Religion:* Episcopalian.

ADDRESSES: Home—7690 Howerton Dr., Sacramento, CA 95831. *Office*—Department of Spanish and Classics, University of California—Davis, 1 Shields Ave., Davis, CA 95616; fax: 530-752-4339. *E-mail*—lindadeeegan@attbi.com and ldegan@ucdavis.edu.

CAREER: High school Spanish teacher at a private school, Santa Barbara, CA, 1970-78; *Santa Barbara News-Press,* Santa Barbara, reporter, 1980-82, editorial page editor, 1983-88; Los Rios Community College District, Sacramento, CA, public information manager, 1982-83; Santa Barbara City College, Santa Barbara, lecturer, 1974-83 instructor in Spanish and chair of journalism department, 1988-90, director of Summer in Salamanca study program, 1999; University of California—Davis, associate professor of Spanish, 1993—. California Polytechnic State University, guest lecturer for editor-in-residence program, 1987; resident Spanish teacher for private tour to Peru, 1989; teaches writing in Santa Barbara area.

MEMBER: Modern Language Association of America, Latin American Studies Association, Santa Barbara/Yalta Sister Cities Association (vice president), Phi Kappa Phi.

AWARDS, HONORS: First place awards, California School Boards Association, 1981, for series on gifted education, and 1984, for editorial on school funding; first place award, Fund for Animals, 1987, for editorial on cougar hunting.

WRITINGS:

Diosas, demonios y debate: las armas metafísicas de Sor Juana, Biblioteca de Textos Universitarios, Equipo Independiente de Investigación y Edición (Salta, Argentina), 1997.

Carlos Monsiváis: Culture and Chronicle in Contemporary Mexico, University of Arizona Press (Tucson, AZ), 2001.

Contributor to books, including *Y diversa de mí misma entre vuestras plumas ando. Homenaje internacional a Sor Juana Inés de la Cruz,* edited by Sara Poot Herrera, Colegio de México (Mexico City, Mexico), 1993; *Vivir del cuento (La ficción en México),* edited by Alfredo Pavón, Universidad Autónoma de Tlaxcala (Mexico City, Mexico), 1995; *El cuento mexicano: homenaje a Luis Leal,* edited by Sara Poot Herrera, Universidad Autónoma Nacional de México (Mexico City, Mexico), 1995; *The Other Mirror: Women's Narrative in Mexico, 1980-1995,* edited by Kristine Ibsen, Greenwood Press (Westport, CT), 1997; and *Cuento y figura (La ficción en México),* edited by Alfredo Pavón, Universidad Autónoma de Tlaxcala, 1999. Contributor of articles and reviews to periodicals, including *Literatura Mexicana, Mexican Studies, Studies in Latin American Popular Culture, Bulletin of Hispanic Studies, Bilingual Review, Revista de Literature Mexicana Contemporánea, Calíope,* and *Revista Canadiense de Estudios Hispánicos.*

WORK IN PROGRESS: A comprehensive analysis of the theme and image of (human) sacrifice in Mexican narrative from the Conquest to the present; research for a book on Sor Juana Inés de la Cruz's so-called "translation" of the language and concepts of accounting into poetic trope and theme, with Sara Poot Herrera; a revised edition of *Diosas, demonios y debate;* an annotated anthology of chronicles of conquest and colony in Mexico and Peru.

SIDELIGHTS: Linda Egan told *CA:* "With respect to writing in general, my primary motivation is the satisfaction of having what seems to be a good idea to communicate and then the pleasure in realizing the expression of the idea. It's a mixed pleasure, to be sure. Even at the height or depth of frustration, when I am in the very throes of creating a text, I am aware that I love this awful undertaking. When it's finally done—cut, condensed, rewritten, and tweaked—I take an unseemly pleasure in the beauty of the words I've put together on paper. An inveterate letter-writer even at age ten, I have probably spilled a debilitating amount of my creative energy into envelopes mailed to friends and family over the last forty-five years. Friends say they hold onto a letter until the family is gathered at the table, and then they read it together for dessert. The other day, a dear friend who felt she was going to die soon handed over two or three bulging sacks full of the cards and letters I had sent her over the years. Fortunately, she has had to open another sack because she is still very much alive, and I am still writing to her.

"That's one motivation for writing. Others include those that spurred me to complete *Carlos Monsiváis: Culture and Chronicle in Contemporary Mexico.* I believed in the project with the fervor of a former editorial page editor and journalism professor. It was my opinion that Monsiváis's thought, and his loyal commitment to writing about the progress of his country toward democratization and modernity, needed to be appreciated among English speakers of the United States and elsewhere. No one had written on his works; certainly there had been no major study such as the book-length project I was working on. I wanted to see in print my study on his writings and, most of all, to watch sales grow as an indication of the meaningful number of readers who would have thus come to understand the transcendent import of a democratic thinker like Monsiváis. Secondly, of course, if I had not published the book, I would not today be an associate professor.

"I don't think of myself as being influenced or 'following' any trend or mentor. But I do believe what theorists suggest: that any new text published is but one more sentence added to an endless dialogue. So, I can say that, when I was thirteen and living on an alfalfa farm in the Mojave Desert, I attempted to write on my portable Smith Corona my version of *Gone with the Wind,* set in Ripley, California, and featuring myself as a Scarlett whose name I no longer recall choosing, and Buzzie Cox as my incarnation of Rhett Butler. I didn't finish the book, but I subsequently spent many long years communing with writers of historical romances and thrillers about serial killers (I've given up on romance, apparently, but I still read good writers on bad people). I have always thought I would write one of those, and I happen to have tucked away a manuscript for a young-adult novel about the California missions. My two published books are on Sor Juana Inés de la Cruz, for which the influence, directly, was the seventeenth-century nun's poetry, drama, and essay, and my fascination with what I saw in her thinking through the window opened by my researches into comparative religions, including Kabbalah, neoplatonism, and gnosticism.

"My book on Carlos Monsiváis was influenced by my prior career as a newspaper reporter and subsequently an editorial page editor, and then as the chair of a journalism program. When I decided to resign, first my post at the newspaper, then my position in the journalism program, I told in-taking administrators at the University of California—Santa Barbara that I wanted to do my doctoral dissertation on the equivalent in Mexico of a Tom Wolfe, Norman Mailer, or Jane Kramer of the U.S. school of 'New Journalism.' I made the acquaintance of many literary journalists of Mexico, including the internationally renowned Elena Poniatowska, but the one who seduced my imagination and sequestered my unflagging loyalty for the ten years it took me to produce the first book on his collected writings is Carlos Monsiváis. He is widely held today to be the foremost intellectual of Mexico, respected throughout Latin America, feted now in Spain, translated by academics in England, sought after for conferences in the United States, and so shy I cannot be entirely sure he has been brave enough as yet even to read the book I wrote about him. I wish he would. His fears would be unfounded, and I'll bet he would learn a lot about himself.

"As a newspaper reporter and editorial writer and editor, I was inspired by a world of problems, challenges, and rare epiphanies that I felt compelled to let my reading public know about. I always wanted to tell the Truth and I wanted to tell it entertainingly and compellingly so that it would make a lasting impression. I was idealistic enough to believe I might inspire the reader to act for peace and justice in a world in which democracy is ever only a good idea unless, daily, people of good will—and a lot of reliable information—get out of their TV chairs and act responsibly to make the ideals of the U.S. Constitution work as a reality. My first assignment was for two weeks writing obituaries; this is apparently an initiation process no beginning journalist can escape. Then I was the education writer for a year. I preferred writing long, in-depth feature stories in which 'immersion reporting' and attention to dramatic detail in writing would not only report the facts of a man's passion for restoring old benches in city parks or a Cuban-Greek woman's reunion after thirty years with an ex-political prisoner from Cuba, but also posit more transcendent, symbolic realities through the suggestion of language itself. People I didn't know picketed the *News-Press* when I was 'promoted' to cover the doings of the city council. When I left that post, the mayor said she would miss reading on my face an instant editorial about arguments and decisions she presided over on the council. I am grateful for Sheila Lodge's humane acceptance of my tell-tale expression, which often enough must have revealed impatience, incredulity, and disgust.

"The same editorial zeal, you might say, inspired me to write about Monsiváis, whose society, like all of ours, is so much in need of fewer fools in office and more humane leaders who can be grateful for the brand of artistically meaningful analysis and implicit advice that this gifted Mexican thinker extends through his literary journalism to statesmen and ordinary citizens alike.

"Similarly, I am inspired to write about Sor Juana because of her comparable courage and will. She is held to be the best writer of the colonial period in Mexico and for long decades after. She exerts a strong influence still today on new writers of Latin America and among Chicana authors of the United States. Feminism is a concept recently invented among women of the Western canon, but Sor Juana could have spelled out its terms for them. In a place and time defined by religious intransigence and profound hostility toward women, the Mexican nun encrypted impertinent social and personal criticisms in her work while risking, because of the fame and acclaim she had earned from Spain to Peru, censure and worse at the hands of the Inquisition. Today scholars believe they have found documentable evidence that her career was, indeed, cut short by threats of more dire punishment than abrupt silencing. I write about her because she's talented, she's smart, she's influential, she's interesting, and she's brave."

*　　*　　*

EICOFF, Alvin M(aurey) 1921-2002

OBITUARY NOTICE—See index for *CA* sketch: Born June 8, 1921, in Lewistown, MT; died of congestive heart failure March 2, 2002, in Highland Beach, FL. Advertising executive and author. Eicoff is often credited as the creator of the television "infomercial" and other advertising innovations. After attending Stanford University and receiving his bachelor's degree from the University of Texas in 1943, Eicoff began his career in marketing as a radio advertiser,

promoting such products as rat poison and fly spray. He then moved on to television in the late 1940s and 1950s while working as an executive for such firms as Grant Co. and Marfree Advertising. In 1962 he became president of Gottschalk & Eicoff, moving on to Wolf, Krautter & Eicoff from 1964 to 1966 before founding his own company, A. Eicoff & Co., that year. Eicoff's theories about advertising proved both unconventional and effective. For example, he worked with telephone company AT&T to establish the toll-free 1-800 system so that customers would be more likely to call in orders. He also believed that consumers are more susceptible to product advertising late at night, thus creating the lengthy infomercial, and declared that advertising during major television events such as the Super Bowl is a waste of time because viewers are more interested in the program than in commercials. Named one of the most important television advertising figures in history by *Advertising Age* in 1995, Eicoff explained his advertising philosophy in the books *Or Your Money Back: Eicoff on Broadcast Direct Marketing* and *Direct Marketing through Broadcast Media: TV, Radio, Cable, Infomercials, Home Shopping, and More.* He served as president of Eicoff & Co. until the firm was purchased by Ogilvy & Mather in 1981. Among other honors, he was named to the Direct Marketing Hall of Fame in 1997.

OBITUARIES AND OTHER SOURCES:

BOOKS

Who's Who in the World, 17th edition, Marquis (Providence, NJ), 2000.

PERIODICALS

Chicago Tribune, March 5, 2002, section 2, p. 7.
Los Angeles Times, March 11, 2002, p. B9.
New York Times, March 9, 2002, p. A14.
Washington Post, March 10, 2002, p. C5.

*　　*　　*

ELSTOB, Peter 1915-2002

OBITUARY NOTICE—See index for *CA* sketch: Born December 22, 1915, in London, England; died July 21, 2002. Businessman, publisher, and author. Elstob was a colorful character who is best remembered as the author of several military history books and as being a controversial officer of the writers organization International PEN. Having a checkered early career, after attending the University of Michigan for only one year he beat a hasty retreat back to England when he got into trouble with the police. Joining the Royal Air Force (RAF) as a pilot, he was kicked out of the service for flying dangerously close to the luxury liner *Queen Mary* to wave at his girlfriend. Next, he went to Spain to fight against the fascists and was arrested on suspicion of being a spy. Although his first wife, Leigh Smith, negotiated Elstob's release, the experience was a horrifying one about which he wrote in his first book, *Spanish Prisoner* (1939). When World War II began Elstob attempted to rejoin the RAF but was rejected, so he enlisted in the Royal Tank Regiment. During the war he saw action in Africa and Europe and was made a tank commander; one of his most successful books, *Warriors for the Working Day* (1960), is about his war experiences. After the war Elstob was involved in a number of business ventures, including running the Arts Theatre Club in London during the 1940s and early 1950s, successfully marketing a beauty masque product, and running an artists' colony in Mexico, where he met the woman who would be his second wife, Barbara Morton. In 1958 Elstob made the news when he financed an unsuccessful balloon voyage across the Atlantic Ocean, and his 1959 book *The Flight of the Small World* tells of this adventure. His next big business venture was Archive Press, a publishing company begun in 1963 that reprinted old historical texts. During the 1960s and early 1970s, Elstob published several noteworthy histories, including *The Armed Rehearsal* (1964), *Bastogne: The Road Block* (1968), *The Battle of the Reichswald* (1970), *Hitler's Last Offensive* (1971), and *Condor Legion* (1973). His writing tapered off as he became increasingly involved in International PEN, first as press officer and later as general secretary and vice president. Under the auspices of this organization he was involved in negotiating the release of a number of authors imprisoned for their political writings, and he became highly controversial for trying to include writers from communist countries in PEN. Elstob's last book, the 1986 novel *Scoundrel,* is about a con artist possessing character traits which led many to believe the book was based on the author himself. In addition to his writings, Elstob edited *A Register of the Regiments and Corps of the British Army* (1972) and *The Survival of Literature* (1979).

OBITUARIES AND OTHER SOURCES:

PERIODICALS

Daily Telegraph (London, England), July 31, 2002, p. 1.
Independent (London, England), August 9, 2002, p. 18.
Times (London, England), July 25, 2002, p. 29.

*   *   *

ENGLAND, Chris 1961-

PERSONAL: Born January 20, 1961, in Oldham, England; son of Alan (a writer and teacher) and Mary (a teacher; maiden name, Blissett) England; married Susan Elvy (a church parish administrator), April 2, 1994; children: Peter William, John Stanley, Michael Christopher. *Education:* Pembroke College, Cambridge, B.A. (with honors), 1983. *Hobbies and other interests:* Football, cricket, the Oldham Athletic Football Club.

ADDRESSES: Home—56 Ellison Rd., London SW16 5BY, England. *Agent*—Peters, Fraser & Dunlop, 34-43 Russell St., London WC2B 5HA, England.

CAREER: Actor, director, playwright, and author. Film roles include an appearance in *Lagaan,* 2002.

MEMBER: Les Raymonds Celebres Football Club, Dusty Fleming International Hairstylists Country Club.

WRITINGS:

(With Arthur Smith) *An Evening with Gary Lineker* (play; produced in London, England), Josef Weinberger, 1992.
(With Nick Hancock) *What Didn't Happen Next,* Andre Deutsch (London, England), 1997.
Bostocki Cup (television movie), London Weekend Television, 1999.
Balham to Bollywood, Hodder Headline (London, England), 2003.
No More Buddha, Only Football, Hodder Headline (London, England), 2003.

Columnist for *Four Four Two,* 1994-98.

SIDELIGHTS: Chris England told *CA:* "I am both an actor and a writer. I began writing while at university in order to generate acting roles for myself. Since the success of *An Evening with Gary Lineker*—a play about the 1990 Football World Cup which I cowrote and appeared in on London's West End—I have been mostly writing on sports-related topics.

"*What Didn't Happen Next* is an alternative history of football (by which I mean soccer); *Bostocki Cup* is a spoof documentary about an under-achieving team and *Balham to Bollywood* is a behind-the-scenes production diary of a film I acted in called *Lagaan,* which picked up an Oscar nomination for best foreign film in 2002. The film is not about football, but cricket—my other great enthusiasm."

* * *

ENGSTER, Daniel (Albert) 1965-

PERSONAL: Born November 11, 1965, in Youngstown, OH; son of David (an independent businessperson) and Helen (a bookkeeper) Engster. *Ethnicity:* "Caucasian." *Education:* Colorado College, B.A., 1988; University of Chicago, Ph.D., 1996.

ADDRESSES: Office—Department of Political Science, University of Texas—San Antonio, 6900 North Loop 1604 W., San Antonio, TX 78249.

CAREER: Tulane University, New Orleans, LA, visiting professor of political science, 1997-98; University of Texas—San Antonio, assistant professor of political science, 1998—.

MEMBER: American Political Science Association.

WRITINGS:

Divine Sovereignty: The Origins of Modern State Power, Northern Illinois University Press (DeKalb, IL), 2001.

* * *

ENSLEY, Eddie

PERSONAL: Male. *Ethnicity:* "Native American." *Education:* Belhaven College, B.A.; graduate study at Loyola Institute of Ministry. *Religion:* Roman Catholic.

CAREER: Writer. Member of Contemplative Brothers.

WRITINGS:

Sounds of Wonder: Speaking in Tongues in the Catholic Tradition, Paulist Press (New York, NY), 1977.
Contemplation and the Charismatic Renewal, Paulist Press (New York, NY), 1987.
Prayer That Heals Our Emotions, HarperCollins (New York, NY), 1988.
Salagi, Credence Audio, 1992.
Visions: The Soul's Path to the Sacred, Loyola University Press (Chicago, IL), 2000.

WORK IN PROGRESS: Visions Journal, for Loyola University Press; research on the history of spirituality, experiences, and visions.

* * *

ESPINA, Concha 1869-1955

PERSONAL: Original name, Concepción Espina de la Maza; born April 15, 1869, in Santander, Spain; died May 19, 1955, in Madrid, Spain; married Ramón de la Serna, 1892 (separated, 1916); children: five.

CAREER: Novelist, dramatist, and short story writer. Middlebury College, Middlebury, VT, visiting professor.

AWARDS, HONORS: Royal Academy Fastenrath prize, 1914, for *La esfinge maragata;* theatrical prize, 1918, for *El jayón;* National Prize for Literature, 1926, for *Altar mayor,* and 1952, for *Un valle en el mar;* named cultural representative to the Antilles by King Alfonso XIII, 1928.

WRITINGS:

NOVELS

Altar Mayor, Renacimiento (Madrid, Spain), 1900.
Llama de cera, Cid (Madrid, Spain), 1900.
Tierra firme, Ediciones G. P. (Barcelona, Spain), 1900.
Mis flores, 1904.

Las mujeres del Quijote, A. Lopez del Arco (Madrid, Spain), 1905.

Trozos de vida, 1907.

La niña de Luzmela (title means "Luzmela's Daughter"), Fernando Fe (Madrid, Spain), 1909.

Despertar para morir (title means "To Awake the Dead"), Renacimiento (Madrid, Spain), 1910.

Agua de nieve, Renacimiento (Madrid, Spain), 1911, translation by Terell Louise Tatum published as *The Woman and the Sea,* R. D. Henkle (New York, NY), 1934.

La esfinge maragata, Renacimiento (Madrid, Spain), 1914, translation by Frances Douglas published as *Mariflor,* Macmillan (New York, NY), 1924.

Al amor de las estrellas, 1916.

La rosa de los vientos, Renacimiento (Madrid, Spain), 1916.

Ruecas de marfil, Renacimiento (Madrid, Spain), 1917.

El metal de los muertos (title means "The Metal of the Dead"), Gil-Blas (Madrid, Spain), 1920.

Dulce nombre, Renacimiento (Madrid, Spain), 1921.

Cumbres al sol, Prensa Gráfica (Madrid, Spain), 1922.

El cáliz rojo, A. Aguado (Madrid, Spain), 1923, translation by Frances Douglas published as *The Red Beacon,* D. Appleton (London, England), 1924.

Tierras del Aquilón, Renacimiento (Madrid, Spain), 1924.

Arboladuras, 1925.

Alta mayor (title means "High Altar"), 1926.

Las niñas desaparecidas, Renacimiento (Madrid, Spain), 1927.

El secreto de un disfraz, Gráfica (Madrid, Spain), 1924.

El goce de robar, Moderna (Madrid, Spain), 1928.

El príncipe del cantar, Figarola Maurin (Toulouse, Spain), 1928.

La virgen prudente (title means "The Wise Virgin"), Renacimiento (Madrid, Spain), 1929.

Marcha nupcial, Atlantida (Madrid, Spain), 1929.

Huerto de rosas, Atlantida (Madrid, Spain), 1929.

Siete rayos de sol, Renacimiento (Madrid, Spain), 1930.

Copa de horizontes, Compañia Ibero-Americana de Publicaciones (Madrid, Spain), 1930.

El hermano cain, Atlantida (Madrid, Spain), 1931.

Singladuras, Compañia Ibero-Americana de Publicaciones (Madrid, Spain), 1932.

Candelabro, Hernando (Madrid, Spain), 1933.

La flor de ayer, Espasa-Calpe (Madrid, Spain), 1934.

Retaguardia, Librería Internacional (San Sebastián, Spain), 1937.

Luna roja, Librería Santarén (Valladolid, Spain), 1938.

Casilda de Toledo, 1938.

Las alas invencibles, 1938.

El desierto rubio, 1938.

Las alas invencibles: novela de amores, de aviación y de libertad, Aldecoa (Burgos, Spain), 1938.

Princesas del martirio, G. Gili (Barcelona, Spain), 1939.

La ronda de los galanes, Católica Española (Seville, Spain), 1939.

Casilda de Toledo, Biblioteca Nueva (Madrid, Spain), 1940.

La tiniebla encendida, 1940.

La otra, 1942.

El fraile menor, Gráfica Informaciones (Madrid, Spain), 1942.

Victoria en América, Nacional (Madrid, Spain), 1944.

La rosa de los vientos, M. Aguilar (Madrid, Spain), 1944.

El más fuerte (title means "The Strongest"), 1947.

Un valle en el mar (title means "A Valley in the Sea"), Exito (Barcelona, Spain), 1951.

Dulce nombre, Gráficas Reunidas (Madrid, Spain), 1952.

Una novela de amor, 1953.

Aurora de España (la virgen prudente), Biblioteca Nueva (Madrid, Spain), 1955.

Also author of *Singladuras, La eterna visita,* and *Dulce nombre.*

OTHER

Mujeres del Quijote (essays), A. Aguado (Madrid, Spain), 1903.

El jayón (play; title means "The Foundling"), [Madrid, Spain], 1918.

Pastorales, Gil-Blas (Madrid, Spain), 1920.

Cuentos (short stories), Gil-Blas (Madrid, Spain), 1920.

Simientes (articles), V. H. Sanz Calleja (Madrid, Spain), 1922.

Talín y otros cuentos (short stories), Knopf (New York, NY), 1927.

Entre la noche y el mar (poetry), Hernando (Madrid, Spain), 1933.

Esclavitud y libertad: diario de una prisonera (title means "Slavery and Liberty: Diary of a Prisoner"), Reconquista (Valladolid, Spain), 1938.

Moneda blanca (plays), Gráfica Informaciones (Madrid, Spain), 1942.

La segunda mies (poetry), A. Aguado (Madrid, Spain), 1943.

SIDELIGHTS: Considered one of the most successful Spanish women writers of the early twentieth century, Concha Espina penned over fifty books, including novels, poetry, and plays. Influenced by post-romantic sentimentalism and realism, Espina eludes identification with any major literary movement. Her early novels, usually set in rural Santander, feature detailed descriptions of the natural world. Although Espina never declared herself a feminist, her focus is on female protagonists, their internal dilemmas contrasting with the social setting they inhabit.

La niña de Luzmela showcases the writer's philosophy that suffering is a fundamental part of human existence. Roger Moore, writing in *International Fiction Review,* noted that the novel—about a *nétigua,* or bird of ill omen—contains a 'second level.' Moore proposed that "the nétigua symbolizes . . . the whole world of witches and witchcraft which it represents in Cantabrian folklore." Moore explained that, "with the death of the nétigua, peace and harmony are restored to [protagonist] Carmen who is free to renew her idyllic life at Luzmela. . . . Clearly there is a thematic link between the nétigua, with all its folkloric meanings, and the less savory characters" of Espina's novel.

Cited by critics as Espina's best and most successful work, *La esfinge maragata* is the story of a young woman, Florinda, who is transported into the forbidding world of the Spanish *Maragatería* and who ultimately sacrifices herself to save her family. According to Judith A. Kirkpatrick, writing in *Hispania,* Espina "draws heavily on the tradition of regionalist and naturalist novels in her carefully crafted descriptions of the harsh Maragatan district." Kirkpatrick noted that "the text also illustrates Florinda's real and metaphorical passage from a world in which woman is primarily a construct of male imagination and language into a female community where women define themselves in terms of their own strengths and concerns." Kirkpatrick concluded, "neither lover, father, nor priest serves as the catalyst for Florinda's self-sacrifice. She remains entrapped in patriarchal society, but she has freed herself [nonetheless]. . . . Women bonding with other women is the key to their survival, and Florinda's

actions directly serve female needs." Brian J. Dendle, writing in *Anales de la Literatura Española Contemporanea,* stated that the descriptions in *La esfinge maragata* "exemplify a fundamental . . . element in Concha Espina's concept of the natural world: her belief that nature is the vessel of the sacred, of a transcendental realm which can be attained by those of superior sensitivity and moral integrity." Places such as "the region of birth, Spain, [and] mountains," Dendle noted, are sacred. The critic continued: "egotism, mediocrity, and materialism are a form of darkness, of absence of light; Espina's central characters transcend the blindness and superficiality of the everyday world in their exercise of moral responsibility and in their devotion to absolute values."

Espina presents an innovative perspective on Miguel Cervantes's classic novel *Don Quixote* in *Las mujeres del Quijote.* In this book, according to *Letras Peninsulares* contributor Roberta Johnson, Espina "sets Don Quixote aside to concentrate on some of the ancillary female figures." Johnson stated, "the book, taken as a whole, projects a more concrete and specific vision of women than the novels and other writings of Espina's masculine compatriots."

Espina's first and most important play, *El jayón,* takes place in rural Spain. According to Mary Lee Bretz, writing in *Estreño,* "some critics have seen *El jayón* as a naturalistic play in which natural selection determines the ultimate survival of the fittest." Bretz noted that "the amorous triangle [between Marcela, Andrés, and Irene] contributes only partially to the dramatic conflict," and added: "Espina combines two codes that are not normally concurrent, the classic-tragic and the naturalistic." "*El jayón,*" stated Bretz, "remains . . . Espina's major contribution to Spanish drama" and represents "a new theatrical tradition in Spain."

According to Judith A. Kirkpatrick in *Hispanic Journal,* in Espina's *La virgen prudente* protagonist Aurora's "situation presents the other side of the literary norm. Traditional marriage is what is precisely harmful although it averts the impeding of the important work of revitalizing Spanish society in order to realize radical changes in the actions that establish womanhood." Kirkpatrick described *La flor de ayer* as "a transitional novel in which change in the direction of Spanish politics is clearly noted. . . . Espina intends to use [protagonist] Victoria as an interlace between the world of the liberated feminists of the

Republic and the world of the masculine control of the [revolutionary Fascist] Falange [movement], but with no escape. The two positions are incompatible and Victoria has to set her hopes with one or the other. Middle ground does not exist."

Writing in *Letras Peninsulares,* reviewer Mónica Jato described *Esclavitud y libertad: diario de una prisonera* as a book "in which Concha Espina records the experiences lived during the first year of civil contentions in the refuge of Luzmela. But the importance of the diary not only resides in character testimony, in the entry, it is owed the receipt of major attention . . . because the pages narrow findings that bind the creative process of [this] novel about the war [in Espina's 1937 novel] *Retaguardia.*" Characterizing the later novel as a "story of love and pain," Yaw Agawu-Kakraba stated in *Romance Notes* that in *Retaguardia* "the action focuses on the Quiroga and Ortiz families, whose respective children, Alicia and Felipe Quiroga, [and] Rafael and Rosa Ortiz, fall in love with each other. These amorous couples, however, experience a rude awakening to the realities and atrocities of the [Spanish] Civil War." According to Jato, "*Retaguardia* always 'manipulates' historical events in order to negatively characterize the enemy [though] during this period no technical explanations are [available] to employ in the written novel." Jato concluded that Espina acts on "a moral obligation to participate in the conflict" through her writing as a means of registering "an individual testimony to protect the collective living experience." The novelist infuses *Retaguardia* with both "fiction and an epic dimension," Jato added.

Although Espina was blind by 1937, she continued to write industriously until her death in 1955.

BIOGRAPHICAL AND CRITICAL SOURCES:

PERIODICALS

Anales de la Literatura Española Contemporanea, 1997, Brian J. Dendle, "Solar Imagery in Three Novels of Concha Espina," pp. 199-209.
Estreño, fall, 1984, Mary Lee Bretz, "The Theater of Emilio Pardo Bazan and Concha Espina," pp. 43-45.
Hispania, May, 1995, Judith A. Kirkpatrick, "From Male Text to Female Community: Concha Espina's *La esfinge maragata,*" pp. 262-271.
Hispanic Journal, spring, 1996, Judith A. Kirkpatrick, "Concha Espina: Giros ideológicos y ha novela de mujer," pp. 129-139.
International Fiction Review, winter, 1980, Roger Moore, "The Role of the 'nétigua' in *La niña de Luzmela,*" pp. 24-28.
Letras Peninsulares, spring, 1996, Roberta Johnson, "Don Quixote, Gender, and Early Twentieth-Century Spanish Narrative," pp. 33-47; fall-winter, 1999, Mónica Jato, "*Retaguardia y Diario de una prisionera,* de Concha Espina: ¿Novela autobiográfica o diario novelado?," pp. 437-454.
Romance Notes, winter, 1996, Yaw Agawu-Kakraba, "Reinventing Identity: Class, Gender, and Nationalism in Concha Espina's *Retaguardia,*" pp. 167-179.

OTHER

El poder de la palabras, http://www.epdlp.com/ (April 22, 2002), "Concha Espina."
Escritoras, http://www.escritoras.com/(April 22, 2002), Ana Coe Snichp, "Concha Espina."*

F

FAGE, John Donnelly 1921-2002

OBITUARY NOTICE—See index for *CA* sketch: Born June 3, 1921, in Teddington, Middlesex, England; died August 6, 2002, in Machynlleth, Wales. Historian, educator, and author. Fage became well known as an historian specializing in African—especially West African—history. He first became interested in the subject while in the Royal Air Force during World War II. After returning to England and graduating from Cambridge University in 1949 with a Ph.D. in history, he moved to Ghana where he took a post as a lecturer in history at the University of Ghana in Accra. He was a professor there from 1955 to 1959 and a deputy principal from 1957 to 1959, after which he joined the faculty at the University of London's School of Oriental and African Studies. In 1963 he moved to the University of Birmingham, where he was a professor and later administrator. After serving as dean of the faculty of arts and as pro-vice-chancellor during the 1970s he was made vice principal in 1981. Fage did not enjoy administrative work, and he retired early to his home in Wales in 1984. Credited with helping to lead the way in making African history an important field of study in England and colonial Africa, Fage authored several important works on the subject, including *An Introduction to the History of West Africa* (1955; third edition, 1962), *An Atlas of African History* (1958; second edition, 1978), *Ghana: A Historical Interpretation* (1959), *A History of West Africa* (1969), and *A History of Africa* (1978; fourth edition, 2001). Just before his death, he also published the autobiography *To Africa and Back*.

OBITUARIES AND OTHER SOURCES:

BOOKS

Writers Directory, 16th edition, St. James Press (Detroit, MI), 2001.

PERIODICALS

Independent (London, England), August 20, 2002, p. 16.
Times (London, England), September 3, 2002.

* * *

FAIRFIELD, Paul 1966-

PERSONAL: Born January 26, 1966, in Brockville, Ontario, Canada; son of James (a chartered accountant) and Eleanor Fairfield. *Ethnicity:* "Caucasian." *Education:* McMaster University, B.A., 1989, Ph.D., 1995; University of Waterloo, M.A., 1991. *Politics:* Liberal.

ADDRESSES: Office—Department of Philosophy, Queen's University, Kingston, Ontario, Canada K7L 3N6. *E-mail*—paulfairfield@hotmail.com.

CAREER: Queen's University, Kingston, Ontario, Canada, adjunct assistant professor of philosophy, 2001—.

MEMBER: International Institute for Hermeneutics (senior associate fellow), Canadian Society for Hermeneutics and Postmodern Thought.

WRITINGS:

(With Gary B. Madison and Ingrid Harris) *Is There a Canadian Philosophy? Reflections on the Canadian Identity,* University of Ottawa Press (Ottawa, Ontario, Canada), 2000.

Moral Selfhood in the Liberal Tradition: The Politics of Individuality, University of Toronto Press (Toronto, Ontario, Canada), 2000.

Theorizing Praxis: Studies in Hermeneutical Pragmatism, Peter Lang (New York, NY), 2000.

Death and Life, Algora (New York, NY), 2001.

The Ways of Power: Hermeneutics, Ethics, and Social Criticism, Duquesne University Press (Pittsburgh, PA), 2002.

(Editor and contributor) *Working through Postmodernity,* University of Ottawa Press (Ottawa, Ontario, Canada), in press.

Contributor to books, including *The Ethics of Postmodernity: Current Trends in Continental Thought,* edited by Gary B. Madison and Marty Fairbairn, Northwestern University Press (Evanston, IL), 1999. Contributor to periodicals, including *Philosophy Today, Business and Professional Ethics Journal, Reason Papers, Eidos,* and *American Catholic Philosophical Quarterly.* Editor, *Symposium: Journal of the Canadian Society for Hermeneutics and Postmodern Thought.*

WORK IN PROGRESS: Public/Private (a monograph); *Why Democracy?* (tentative title), a monograph; "Difference Diagnostics: Postmodern Reflections on Ethical Expertise," to be included in *Ethical Expertise: A Critical Assessment,* edited by H. Tristram Engelhardt and Lisa Rasmussen.

*   *   *

FARNES, Maria Aurèlia Capmany
    See CAPMANY (FARNES), Maria Aurèlia

FEDERMAN, Raymond 1928-

PERSONAL: Born May 15, 1928, in Paris, France; immigrated to United States, September, 1947, naturalized citizen, 1953; son of Simon (a painter) and Marguerite (Epstein) Federman; married Erica Hubscher, September 14, 1960; children: Simone Juliette. *Education:* Columbia University, B.A. (cum laude), 1957; University of California—Los Angeles, M.A., 1959, Ph.D. (French), 1963. *Hobbies and other interests:* Cinema, theater, jazz, golf.

ADDRESSES: Home—12428 Avenida Consentido, San Diego, CA 92128. *Office*—c/o State University of New York—Buffalo, Buffalo, NY 14260.

CAREER: University of California—Santa Barbara, assistant professor of French, 1962-64; State University of New York—Buffalo, associate professor of French, 1964-68, professor of French and comparative literature, 1968-73, professor of English and comparative literature, 1973-90, distinguished professor, 1990-99, Melodia E. Jones Chair of Literature, 1994-99, distinguished professor emeritus, 2000—. University of Montreal, visiting professor, 1970; Hebrew University of Jerusalem, writer in residence, 1982-83; U.S. Information Agency, lecturer in Europe, Asia, Africa, and the Middle East; gives readings from his works. Jazz saxophonist, 1947-50. Fiction Collective, codirector, 1977-80; Fiction Collective Two, member of board of directors; Hallwalls, member of board of directors, 1980-83. New York Council on the Arts, member of literature panel, 1978-81; American Awards for Literature, member of panel of judges, 1995; also fiction judge for Creative Artists Public Service Program, Massachusetts Arts Council, Wisconsin Arts Council, and New York State Foundation for the Arts. *Military service:* U.S. Army, 82nd Airborne Division, 1951-54; served in Korea and Japan; became sergeant.

MEMBER: Modern Language Association of America, Coordinating Council of Literary Magazines (member of board of directors, 1976-79), American Association for the Studies of Dada and Surrealism, PEN American Center, Samuel Beckett Society (honorary trustee), Phi Beta Kappa.

AWARDS, HONORS: Grants from State University of New York, New York State Research Foundation, and the Asia Foundation; Guggenheim fellowship, 1966-

Raymond Federman

67; Frances Steloff Prize, 1971, and *Panache* Experimental Fiction Prize, 1972, both for *Double or Nothing;* Pushcart anthology prize, 1977, 1994; Camargo Foundation fellow in Cassis, France, 1977; Fulbright fellowship to Israel, 1982-83; fiction fellow, National Endowment for the Arts, 1985, and New York State Foundation for the Arts, 1986; American Book Award, Before Columbus Foundation, 1986, for *Smiles on Washington Square;* fellowship for Germany, German Academic Exchange Service, 1989-90; Les Palmes Académiques, Government of France, 1995; Writer's *Union of Romania,* silver medal for life achievement, 2002.

WRITINGS:

POETRY

(Translator) F. Jacques Temples, *Postal Cards,* Noel Young Editions (Santa Barbara, CA), 1964.

(Translator) Yvonne Caroutch, *Temporary Landscapes,* Mica Editions (Venice, Italy), 1965.

Among the Beasts/Parmi les monstres (bilingual), Éditions Millas-Martin (Paris, France), 1967.

Me Too, West Coast Poetry Review Press (Reno, NV), 1975.

Duel-l (trilingual in English, French, and German), Stopover Press (Berlin, Germany), 1991.

Now Then/Nun denn (bilingual; English and German), Editions Isele (Freiburg, Germany), 1992.

99 Hand-written Poems/99 Poèmes-écrits-à-la-main, Weidler Verlag (Berlin, Germany), 2001.

Here and Elsewhere (selected poems), Six Gallery Press (Geneva, OH), 2003.

NOVELS

Double or Nothing, Swallow Press (Chicago, IL), 1971, revised edition, Fiction Collective Two (Boulder, CO), 1991.

Amer Eldorado (in French), Éditions Stock (Paris, France), 1974, revised edition, Weidler Verlag (Berlin, Germany), 2001.

Take It or Leave It, Fiction Collective, 1976, revised edition, Fiction Collective Two (Boulder, CO), 1997.

The Voice in the Closet/La Voix dans le cabinet de débarras (bilingual), Coda Press (Madison, WI), 1979.

The Twofold Vibration, Indiana University Press (Bloomington, IN), 1982, new edition, Sun and Moon Press (Los Angeles, CA), 1995.

Smiles on Washington Square, Thunder's Mouth Press (New York, NY), 1985, new edition, Sun and Moon Press (Los Angeles, CA), 2000.

To Whom It May Concern, Fiction Collective Two (Boulder, CO), 1990.

La Fourrure de ma Tante Rachel, Éditions Circé (Saulxures, France), 1997, translated by the author as *Aunt Rachel's Fur,* Fiction Collective Two (Boulder, CO), 2001.

Loose Shoes: A Life Story of Sorts, Weidler Verlag (Berlin, Germany), 2001.

Mon corps en neuf parties, Weidler Verlag (Berlin, Germany), 2002.

OTHER

Journey to Chaos: Samuel Beckett's Early Fiction, University of California Press (Berkeley, CA), 1965, reprinted, Books on Demand, 1998.

(Editor and translator) Yvonne Caroutch, *Paysages provisoires/Temporary Landscapes* (bilingual), Stamperia di Venizia, 1965.

(With John Fletcher) *Samuel Beckett: His Work and His Critics,* University of California Press (Berkeley, CA), 1970.

(Editor) *Cinq Nouvelles* (collected fiction), Appleton-Century-Crofts, 1970.

(Editor) *Surfiction: Fiction Now and Tomorrow* (essays), Swallow Press (Chicago, IL), 1975, revised edition, Ohio University Press (Athens, OH), 1981.

(Editor, with Tom Bishop) *Samuel Beckett: Cahier de L'Herne,* Éditions de L'Herne (Paris, France), 1976, revised edition, Hachette (France), 1985.

(Editor, with Lawrence Graver) *Samuel Beckett: The Critical Heritage,* Routledge & Kegan Paul (London, England), 1979, also published as *Modern Drama.*

The Rigamarole of Contrariety (fiction chapbook), Bolt Court Press (Buffalo, NY), 1982.

(Translator, with Genevieve James) Michel Serres, *Detachement* (essays), Ohio University Press (Athens, OH), 1989.

Playtexts/Spieltexts (bilingual in English and German; experimental poetry and prose), German Academic Exchange Service (Berlin, Germany), 1989.

Critifiction: Postmodern Essays, State University of New York Press (Albany, NY), 1993.

Eine Version Meines Lebens (autobiography; title means "A Version of My Life"), Maro Verlag (Augsburg, Germany), 1993.

(Editor, with Bill Howe) *Sam Changed Tense* (poetry collection in homage to Samuel Beckett), Tailspin Press (Buffalo, NY), 1995.

The Supreme Indecision of the Writer (essays), Bolt Court Press (Buffalo, NY), 1995.

(With George Chambers) *Penner Rap* (fiction), Suhrkamp Verlag, 1998.

The Line (fiction chapbook), Club of Odd Volumes (Amherst, NY), 1996.

The Precipice and Other Catastrophes (bilingual in English and German; collected plays; includes *The Precipice,* produced in Jyvaskyla, Finland, 1998), Poetry Salzburg (Salzburg, Austria), 1999.

Contributor to numerous books, including *Essaying Essays; Pushcart Prize Anthology II; The Wake of the Wake; Bright Moments;* and *Imaged Words and Worded Images.* Contributor of fiction, poetry, articles, and essays to periodicals in the United States and abroad, including *Partisan Review, Chicago Review, Tri-Quarterly, Paris Review, North American Review, French Review, Modern Drama, Film Quarterly, Comparative Literature,* and *Fiction International.* Coeditor, *MICA,* 1960-63; contributing editor, *American Book Review;* member of editorial board, *Jewish Publication Society* and *Buff.* Several of Federman's books have been translated into Polish, German, French, Greek, Portuguese, Italian, Spanish, Japanese, Chinese, Hungarian, Romanian, Hebrew, Finnish, Turkish, Dutch, and Russian.

ADAPTATIONS: The Voice in the Closet was adapted into a full-length ballet under the title *Project X; Playtexts/Spieltexte* was adapted as a stage production, produced in Cologne, Germany, at Theater Forum, and as a radio play, both 1992; the play *The Precipice* was adapted as a radio play by Deutschland Radio, 1998. All of Federman's novels have been adapted into radio plays and broadcast in German by Bayerischer Rundfunk (Bavarian Radio), Munich.

SIDELIGHTS: According to some critics, Raymond Federman attempts in his novels to redefine fiction, calling the developing form "surfiction." "Building on the work of (James) Joyce, (Louis-Ferdinand) Celine, (Samuel), Beckett, and other twentieth-century masters, his fictions are fascinating constructs that combine a brilliant style, unorthodox typography, and a masterful new approach to the development of characters and literary structure," declared Welch D. Everman in the *Dictionary of Literary Biography Yearbook: 1980.* "Unlike the traditional novel, these works are not intended to be representations of events; they are events in their own right, language events that reflect on their own mode of becoming and that, in effect, critique themselves. . . . Federman questions the very nature of fiction, the fiction writer, and the reality that the writer's language is supposed to represent."

One reality that affected Federman's life strongly was the Nazi Holocaust. In the summer of 1942, the Gestapo entered his family's apartment, taking his parents and his two sisters to the death camps; Raymond, whom his mother hid in a closet, escaped. Although Federman's fiction is called experimental in form, its contents grapple with the experience of death and survival that marked the author while he was young. Questioning the validity of autobiography and fiction alike, Federman creates autobiographical fictions, and does so in a language, English, that he learned as an adult. Federman's first book of poems,

Among the Beasts/Parmi les monstres, is the earliest literary version of his Holocaust experience. His subsequent fictions, according to Everman, rewrite this "original text."

Federman's first novel, *Double or Nothing,* has been described as a multilayered, bleakly comic work whose plot focuses on a young French immigrant who lost his family in the concentration camps. The immigrant's story is told by a would-be author who narrates his own life as well as that of the young immigrant. Comments on the writing process are intertwined with the narrative. At least two additional voices are added to the layering, producing a potentially infinite regression of narrators. Typography is important to the novel, for each page is a complete visual unit. "Humor is one of Federman's key tools," Everman pointed out. "The style is frantic and purposely paradoxical, and often the reader laughs not so much at the antics of the characters as at his own confusion in the face of this convoluted text."

Take It or Leave It, Federman's second novel in English, is an extended reworking of his French novel *Amer Eldorado.* A note on the title page calls it an "exaggerated second-hand tale." The plot concerns a young French immigrant in the U.S. Army, Frenchy, who has thirty days to travel from Fort Bragg, North Carolina, to a ship that will take him to Korea, but who must first travel north to upstate New York to retrieve some crucial army papers. The story is told by a nameless narrator who is interrupted by faceless audience members and literary critics. "*Take It or Leave It* is a text which constitutes, contradicts, and erases itself, as it constitutes, contradicts, and erases the voices which it produces and by which it is produced," Everman said.

The Voice in the Closet/La Voix dans le cabinet de débarras, Federman's bilingual novel of 1979, suggests a shift in the author's work while preserving his preoccupation with form. Federman sets himself a strict form, consisting of twenty pages with eighteen lines per page and sixty-eight characters per line. From this constricted form—which parallels the physical constriction of a closet—emerges the voice of a boy hiding in a closet while the Nazis take away his family. The voice speaks to a writer named federman (with a lowercase "f"), who has repeatedly tried and failed to tell the boy's story. Critic Peter Quartermain, writing in the *Chicago Review,* called *The Voice in the Closet*

"a compelling book indeed. . . . [It] astonishes partly because nothing in Federman's previous work . . . prepares us for the obsessive immediacy of this. This book may be a one-shot, perhaps, but in it Federman has come to do what over a generation ago D. H. Lawrence enjoined readers as well as writers to do: trust the tale."

The English version of *The Voice in the Closet* is part of Federman's 1982 novel, *The Twofold Vibration.* Here, typography and style are more traditional than in most of Federman's earlier work. The setting of the novel is New Year's Eve, 1999. In a self-reflexive style, the narrator, an old man whose history contains many parallels with Federman's, tells the story of his life. Meanwhile, two characters named Namredef and Moinous, who serve as doubles for the narrator, argue about the way the story ought to be told. Reviewing the book for the *Times Literary Supplement,* Brian Morton commented: "For the first time with any success, Federman . . . combines a sense of time and consequence with the spatial concerns of radical postmodernist fiction. . . . If this is not what John Gardner called 'metafiction for the millions,' it is at least an entertaining and salutary journey through the darker and more troubled outlands of contemporary history and fiction."

Smiles on Washington Square once again features a character named Moinous who bears resemblances to Federman. Moinous, a French-born, naturalized American who has served in Korea, is out of work in New York City. At a political rally, he meets—or perhaps does not meet—Sucette, the leftist daughter of a wealthy New England family. Sucette, who is studying creative writing at Columbia University, begins to write stories about a man named Moinous. Two weeks later, they may or may not meet again; indeed, the whole love story may belong to Sucette's creative writing efforts. Alan Cheuse, in the *New York Times Book Review,* commented, "In this new work of fiction [Federman] appears intent on compressing and compacting his story. . . . The result is much more charming and readable than anything else of his in English. . . . Basically, the novel succeeds because of its appealing voice, something resembling Moinous's 'English with a French Accent.'"

Federman once told *CA:* "I write to gain my freedom and hopefully to liberate my readers from all conventions. Anything goes because meaning does not precede language, language produces meaning. There is as much value in making nonsense as there is in making sense; it's simply a question of direction." Of his work, Federman once commented, "My entire writing career has been a Journey to Chaos."

AUTOBIOGRAPHICAL ESSAY:

Raymond Federman contributed the following autobiographical essay to *CA:*

A VERSION OF MY LIFE—THE EARLY YEARS

To Whom It May Concern

I often wonder if being a writer, becoming a writer is a gift one receives at birth, or if it happens accidentally in the course of one's life. I am always envious, and suspicious too, of those who say to me, "I wrote my first poem when I was eight years old, and published my first story when I was fifteen." It makes me feel that perhaps I wasted the first twenty-five years of my life.

Even today, after the millions of words I have scribbled (in English and in French) over the past thirty years, with six novels in print, one more in progress, one abandoned, two volumes of poems, several books of essays and criticism, hundreds of loose pieces of prose and poetry in magazines, and much more still unpublished, I often doubt that I am a writer. Thirty years of trying to convince myself of this fact. Thirty-one years, to be exact, since my first published poem in a college magazine in 1957, a five line poem titled "More or Less." It went like this:

> From Cambrian brain-
> Less algae sprung the ten-ton
> Flesh and bone reptile
> Then man from ape till bodi-
> Less brain shall inherit the earth

A ponderous little poem which certainly does not indicate that I was then or would ever become a writer. Even now I believe I am still working at becoming one, and perhaps I shall die never knowing whether or not I was a real writer. It seems to me that everything I write (and few days pass that I do not sit at my desk

to work) is a preparation for the great book that someday will make of me the real writer. Meanwhile my books are published, reviewed, discussed, analyzed, translated, praised and attacked; a couple received literary prizes; and still I am not sure.

The other day my best fan, my lovely twenty-five-year-old daughter, Simone, on the phone from New York City (collect of course), says to me, oh without malice, lovingly in fact, "Hey Pop, I think I know what your epitaph will be, I mean, you know, what should be written on your tombstone: OUT OF PRINT." What gentle brutality! She's got it right though, there is brutality in what writers do. Writing is such an inhuman thing to be doing, so brutally asocial, unnatural. So much against nature. No wonder writers suffer fits of doubt and despair.

No, I do not think I was born a writer (even though I too can doubt and despair like a true writer), but the accidents of my life may have helped make of me a writer. If I was given a gift at all which forced me to write, it was what happened to me, often in spite of myself, during the first twenty-five years of my life. Much of the fiction I have written found its source in those early years.

In a recent article about my work, the critic Marcel Cornis-Pop states, rightly so I suppose, that "unlike some of his metafictional contemporaries, [Federman] has been blessed (or cursed) with enough biography for several epic cycles, condemned to stringing out the story of his life endlessly in various fictions." In retrospect, the first twenty-five years of my life certainly contained enough drama, enough adventures, misadventures, and misfortunes to inspire several novels. I lived those years oblivious to myself and to the sordid affairs of the world around me, unaware that the experiences I was living, or I should say enduring, would someday make a writer of me. My life began in incoherence and discontinuity, and my work has undoubtedly been marked by this. Perhaps that is why it has been called experimental.

And I Followed My Shadow

I was born in Paris, France, in 1928, May 15, a Taurus, which means one who lives in the world with his feet firmly on the ground and his head in the clouds. But if

Parents, Marguerite and Simon, on their wedding day, c. 1925

this is my official date of birth, it was not until July 16, 1942, that my life really began. On that day, known in France as *le jour de La Grande Rafle,* more than twelve thousand people (who had been declared stateless by the Vichy government and forced to wear a yellow star bearing the inscription *JUIF)* were arrested and sent to the Nazi death camps. That day, my father, mother, and two sisters were also arrested and eventually deported to Auschwitz where they died in the gas chambers. There are records of this. I escaped and survived by being hidden in a closet. I consider that traumatic day of July 16, 1942, to be my real birth-date, for that day I was given an excess of life.

A poem I wrote years ago titled "Escape" opens with these lines: "My life began in a closet / among empty skins and dusty hats / while sucking pieces of stolen sugar." On July 16, 1942, at 5:30 in the morning, while the French militia and the German gestapo were com-

ing up the stairs to our third-floor apartment in Paris to arrest us, my mother pushed me into a little closet on the landing of the staircase. As I sat there in the dark, still half-asleep, wearing only my underwear, I listened to my mother, my father, and my two sisters go down the stairs on their way to extermination.

X-X-X-X, these are the symbols I have used throughout my work to mark that moment. For me these signs represent the necessity and the impossibility of expressing the erasure of my family. I believe I have spent the last thirty years of my life (and will probably spend the remaining years) writing in order to understand my mother's gesture when she hid me in that closet, and in order to decipher the darkness into which I was plunged that day.

Almost everything that precedes "the closet moment," as I have referred to it over the years, seems to have been erased from my memory. The first fourteen years of my life are like a blur. I have only vague, disjointed recollections of what I did with my parents, with my sisters and my cousins, with my school friends, before that fatal day. And I often suspect that some of these recollections are pure inventions. I know certain facts about my parents, their origin and background, and about the place where I was raised. Facts I learned after the war from surviving relatives, and from old family papers and photographs I found in a cardboard box in our apartment. Over the years, I have returned to France many times, and on several occasions went back to the neighborhood of my childhood on the outskirts of Paris to see the apartment building where we lived. I even reentered the closet where I was left to survive, and visited the school where I first learned to read and write, and wandered in the streets where I used to play, but I never found anything there of any significance. No vivid traces of joyful or even unhappy events that took place before the closet moment. Nothing singular that demands to be told. Only facades and facts are what I found there.

I have no remembrance at all of playing with my sisters, of arguing and fighting with them, as brothers and sisters do. I found only one photograph of my sisters in that cardboard box. It shows the three of us at the ages of six, seven, and nine—I was the middle child. My sisters look pretty in that picture. It must have been taken around 1935. Sarah was sixteen when she was deported in 1942, and Jacqueline thirteen. I know nothing of their thoughts, their dreams, their

The author with his sisters, Jacqueline and Sarah, Paris, c. 1935

desires, their ambitions. I cannot remember a single sentence that passed between us. I think Sarah wanted to become a teacher or a scientist, and Jacqueline a ballerina, but I may have invented this about them.

Much of what I know about my parents, and the rest of my family—grandparents, uncles, aunts, and cousins—I gathered after most of them had disappeared. It is in conversations with the few relatives who survived the Holocaust that I learned something of my parents, of my sisters, and of myself too, before the closet moment. I do not mean to suggest that I suffer of amnesia, or that I have a bad memory. On the contrary, I have a terrific memory. Undoubtedly many events of the early years of my life have been blocked, but also lost in the turmoil of World War II, for there is an obvious reason for the ignorance I have of my own childhood.

It was not until I got married, in 1960, and found myself suddenly raising a family (Erica had three young children when I married her, Steve was ten, Jim seven, Robin three, and then our own daughter, Simone, was born in 1962) that I began to understand that we do not really remember our early years, but that these are remembered for us by our parents as they tell us over and over again who we were and what we did when we were little, tell us again and again how happy or unhappy we were, how *smart,* how *cute* we were, especially when they show us photographs of ourselves when we were children. Eventually, as we get older, we take over our own memories, and even take from our parents the photo-

graphs they preserved. But by then these have become secondhand memories. I suppose the reason I know so little of who I was and what I did when I was a child is because my parents disappeared too soon for them to be able to tell me, and continue to tell me, the stories of their lives before I was born and the stories of my early years, and show me the pictures of their childhood and mine. These stories and pictures have vanished with them.

What I know now from vague memories, and from what I managed to gather afterward, is that my parents were poor, very poor. And worse, until their deportation, they were considered foreigners in France—*des étrangers:* Jews who had come from the ghettos of Eastern Europe, and who had never been able to become assimilated in the French culture. My father, Simon, was born in Siedlce, a small town in Poland near the Russian border. He was the second-youngest of nine children. (Only one of my uncles and four cousins on my father's side survived the Holocaust.) My father was eighteen when he came to France in 1922, but he was never able to obtain French citizenship because of political reasons. He was a fanatic Trotskyite. An anarchist, I was told. My mother was born in Paris, but of parents who, in a strange reversed journey, immigrated to Europe in the late nineteenth century from what was known then as Palestine. They went first to Poland for a few years, and after that to France. Their first two children were born in Palestine, then three more in Poland. My mother was the first of eight children to be born in Paris, but she lost the French citizenship she had acquired at birth when she married my father, and like him became stateless. The French have very subtle and complicated laws to protect *la patrie* from being taken over by foreigners. My sisters and I had to be naturalized French citizens even though we were born in France.

Politics was at the center of my father's life. He spent most of his time participating in demonstrations or sitting in cafés arguing with foreigners. I know this because when I was a little boy he sometimes took me (to the despair of my mother) to these demonstrations, to teach me, as he used to say, about the great revolution, or took me to the cafés in Montparnasse where I would sit quietly next to him drinking *une limonade* while he argued with the people there. I could not understand a word of what was being said in these foreign languages, but the arguments were loud and passionate. My father spoke seven languages. But as I learned later, there were other passions and obsessions in his life.

Tall and handsome, with pale grey eyes, he was a great womanizer. This I was told by aunts on my mother's side who did not care much for my father and who described him to me as a "lazy, irresponsible, and irrational man." He was an artist. A surrealist painter who never attained fame and recognition, who "never became anything." Nonetheless, he was an artist, though all his paintings and drawings are lost. Stolen or destroyed during the war. I have searched in many places for traces of my father's work but have failed to find anything. It was suggested to me that perhaps he painted under a different name than Federman. I suppose my father was what used to be called romantically a "starving artist." His work barely brought enough money for his wife and children to survive. During the hard years of the 1930s when my sisters and I were growing up, often my mother shamefully took us to stand in line at the *soupe populaire.* Faithful to the romantic image of the starving artist, my father was also afflicted with tuberculosis, and constantly spat blood. One of his lungs had been collapsed. It was known as a pneumothorax, and every other week he had to have oxygen pumped into his lungs. I think my father suffered a great deal in his short life, physically and intellectually. He was thirty-eight years old when he died at Auschwitz. He was described to me, by the uncle who brought me to America (a brother-in-law of my father who knew him when he was a young man in Poland), as a wild, reckless, but sensitive man. A dreamer. He was also an inveterate gambler. He played the horses, cards, dice, roulette, baccarat.

I have one vivid memory of my father and his gambling. One day he came home to our one-room apartment and emptied his pockets on the table. Stacks of large bills. We had never seen so much money. My mother started crying, but we the children were screaming with joy. My father announced that we were all going on a vacation to the seashore. Deauville, in Normandie. We left by train that very day, and stayed in a hotel which appeared to my sisters and me as a fabulous, unreal palace. We had a two-room suite for the whole family with beautiful furniture and a balcony overlooking the sea. But we didn't stay there very long. The next day we were back on the train to Paris. While my mother sat on the beach watching us children play in the sand, my father was losing the money at the Deauville casino. It was the first time I saw the ocean. I must have been six or seven years old. The next time I saw the sea was when I boarded the boat to America, in 1947.

If I have managed to preserve or reconstruct an image of my father, of my mother I hardly remember anything, except that she was short, wore thick glasses, was plain-looking, always spoke in a soft voice, and that she worked hard all the time doing laundry for other people so she could feed her children. After the war, her brothers and sisters, all of whom managed to survive the Holocaust (they were well-off and found places to hide somewhere in southern France), often referred to my mother as a saint, but of course that's just an expression. *"Pauvre Marguerite,"* they would say, *"elle a tellement souffert."* I think it was a way for them to appease their guilt for not having helped my parents escape as they themselves did. All my aunts and uncles on my mother's side died of old age in their large, comfortable beds.

My mother's father, I was told, died very young, in 1910, of pneumonia, leaving my grandmother with eight children, the youngest only a few months old. Four of the children were placed in an orphanage. My mother was one of them. She stayed in that orphanage for twelve years, until the age of eighteen, when she came out into the world to work. That's all I know of her, except that she had big dark eyes and cried a lot.

The Voice in the Closet

July 16, 1942, is the last time I saw my parents and my sisters. I can almost relate, day by day, everything that happened to me from that moment on. I stayed in the closet all that day and until late into the night. I was afraid to come out because I knew that the people who lived downstairs did not like Jews and they might see me and denounce me. As I look back on the long hours I spent in that closet sitting on a pile of old newspapers, I do not think that I was really scared, but that I was in a state of total incomprehension. I felt that what was happening was temporary, that my parents would soon return and everything would be just as before. I lived with this feeling, this deluding hope, for the next three years until the end of the war, when it slowly became clear that my parents and sisters were never coming back. Eventually I was given documents that confirmed their extinction.

Groping in the dark, I found old clothes piled in a corner of the closet, and behind these a box full of sugar cubes. Sugar probably bought on the black market and hidden there by my mother. I sucked on the sugar when I became hungry during that long day. Later, in the afternoon, I had to defecate, but felt ashamed not to be able to do it in the proper place. Unable to hold back, I unfolded a newspaper, crouched over it holding my penis away from my legs so as not to wet myself, and did it right there. Then I rolled the paper into a parcel and placed it near the door, and when finally it was night outside, and all was quiet in the building, I opened the door of the closet and listened while holding my package of excrement in one hand. The landing was on the top floor of the building, but there was a short ladder that led to a skylight in the roof. I climbed that ladder holding the newspaper away from my face, but feeling its warmth and wetness on my hand, and when I reached the skylight I lifted the glass pane and placed the parcel on the roof. Three years later, when I returned to Paris, this is the first place I went. I wanted to know if my package was still there. Of course, there was nothing on the roof. I have often wondered what happened to this symbolic package in which I had wrapped my fear.

It would take pages and pages to describe in detail what happened from the moment I stepped out of the closet to the day when I returned to see if the parcel I had left on the roof was still there. Briefly then so that I can get on with the story, the story of my life, I must rush through the next three years—the years of wandering and surviving during the war.

It was the middle of night when I tiptoed down the stairs holding in my hands a pair of man's shoes too big for me which I found on the floor of the closet, and wearing one of my father's jackets which had been hanging from a nail in the wall. Underneath the jacket I only had my boy's shorts. I was going down as quietly as I could when I tripped on one of the steps and almost fell. As I slipped I let go of the shoes and they tumbled down the stairs with a frightening noise. A door opened above me and someone shouted, "Who is there!" In panic I ran the rest of the way down and out into the street. At that time there was a curfew every night, and only people with special permits were allowed in the streets. As I was running I heard footsteps around a street corner. I quickly pushed open the door of a building and hid inside a corridor under the staircase. I waited there until morning. Somehow I had the presence of mind to remove from the jacket the yellow star sewn on it. I left it under the staircase with the shoes, which were useless to me. I

knew I had to go to the Marais, the old Jewish neighborhood in the center of Paris, where most of my aunts and uncles lived, and warn them about what had happened. Our apartment was in Montrouge, just outside the city limits. It was a long walk, and of course I had no money to take the metro. Still I had to go and tell my aunts and uncles to get away, and take me with them.

Even though I was walking without shoes, and wearing a jacket so large that it looked like a winter overcoat, no one paid attention to me. It was a nice warm day. The sky clear and indifferent. It took me a long time to reach the Marais, but as I approached I became aware of the frantic activity of the ongoing roundup. Army trucks were parked everywhere, and people wearing yellow stars and carrying suitcases or bags were being led to these trucks by uniformed guards.

I went to my aunt Basha's apartment, at the corner of rue Beaubourg and rue Rambuteau. (I mention the exact location because on the very spot where my aunt's building once stood now stands the Centre Pompidou and the National Museum of Modern Art. Fabulous substitution. The insolence of history replaced by the playfulness of art.) Aunt Basha was my father's youngest sister whom we often visited to play with her children, two boys and one girl about the same age as my sisters and I. I found my aunt, my uncle, and the two boys sitting in the apartment waiting, their suitcases packed. They told me that our other relatives in this neighborhood, all the aunts and uncles and cousins, had already been arrested. The boys had seen them being taken away when they went out to investigate what was going on.

My cousin Sarah, the youngest of the three children, was not at home. She was in the country, my aunt told me, and I learned later that's how she too survived. She stayed at a farmhouse with an old widow who made her work as her servant and took her to church every day. My cousin Sarah and I found each other at the end of the war and for a while lived together until I left for America. She could not come to the United States because she was denied a visa for reasons of health. At the required medical examination at the U.S. Consulate in Paris, the doctor discovered a tuberculous spot on her left lung. Soon after I left France, my cousin Sarah went to Israel. She was seventeen then. She fought in the war of independence of 1948, and afterward joined a kibbutz. She's been living and working on that kibbutz for the past forty years. We were reunited, in 1982, after thirty-five years of separation, when I went to Israel on a Fulbright fellowship to teach at the Hebrew University of Jerusalem. I found a fifty-year-old woman of great strength and unusual character.

Not long after I arrived at my aunt's apartment the police came to arrest them. I had told my aunt and uncle what had happened and how my mother hid me in a closet, and I had pleaded with them that we should all try to get away, but they had explained that they didn't know where to go, and even if there was a place in the free zone, they didn't have the money to go there. Not enough to buy train tickets for all of us, and pay someone to get us through the line of demarcation between the occupied zone and the free zone. Many Jews were deported during the war not because they could not escape (there were many ways one could buy survival, even from the Germans), but because they were poor. The police asked who I was, but since I didn't have a yellow star on my shirt, and my aunt explained that I was just a friend of the boys, not Jewish, they left me alone. Besides, my name was not on their list. I was now wearing one of my cousins' short pants and shirt, and a pair of his espadriles which my aunt gave me when she saw what I had on as I came in. I walked with my aunt, uncle, and cousins to Place des Vosges, that sumptuous historical square with its beautiful arcades, whose entire perimeter was lined with army trucks. I waited with them until it was their turn to go. I kissed my uncle, my aunt, and my cousins good-bye, and then watched them being pushed up into one of the trucks. I have often wondered if that day, when I was left standing there, I had not been chosen so that someday I could tell that story.

Among the Beasts

After the trucks left I walked all the way back to Montrouge. I was still thinking that perhaps my parents and sisters had been sent home. I wanted to make sure. I was standing at a distance from the building where we lived because I didn't want to be seen by the neighbors, when a woman approached me. She was someone with whom my mother washed people's clothes at the nearby *lavoir*. Of course, she knew what had happened, and was surprised to see me standing there. I told her about the closet. She grabbed me by the arm and quickly led me to her apartment, just a

block away. She gave me some food, I remember, a bowl of warm milk and a piece of bread. She kept saying that we had to find a way to hide me. But then after a while she explained that perhaps the best thing to do was for me to go to the police and tell them that I had been left behind. This way, she went on, they would put me with my parents and everything would be fine. She told me she would take me to the militia headquarters herself. I suppose she had realized that she could be in serious trouble if she kept me.

Feeling lost and confused, and tired, too, as I had not slept for almost two days, I agreed with her that it was the best thing to do. We were walking towards the Montrouge police station, on Avenue de la Republique, the woman was holding me by the hand, when suddenly I pulled away from her and started running in the opposite direction from the station. I knew that I could not let this woman take me there. I heard her call behind me, "Where are you going? Come back, they'll catch you." But I kept running until she was out of sight.

The next few days, until I managed to reach the non-occupied zone, unfolded like a wild adventure movie, and I lived every moment totally unconscious of what I was going through. There was the frantic wandering in various neighborhoods of Paris trying to find someone in my family who might still be there and who would take care of me. There were the two days and two nights I spent at the bustling train station hoping to be able to sneak up on a train leaving for the free zone. There was the night when all the men in the station were rounded up and questioned by the Germans and some of them arrested, and I was one of those they questioned but let go. And there was the night when I found myself on a freight train going in the wrong direction, away from the free zone, but when that train stopped in the middle of the night to let another train go by in the other direction, I jumped across the track and managed to force my way inside one of the cars. It was full of huge bags of potatoes. I was so hungry I climbed on top of the bags, tore one open, and for a long time sat there eating raw potatoes until I became sick to my stomach and vomited. Later, when the train slowed down around a curve I jumped off and wandered in the countryside until morning when I was picked up by an old farmer in a horse carriage on his way to the city. I had jumped from the train full of potatoes just a few kilometers from Paris. Again I went to the train station, still hoping to find a

Raymond during World War II

way to get to the free zone, and that night, during an air raid, with two young men from Belgium I met in the station, I hid inside a freight car while all the people were rushing to the shelters. The train must have already been inspected by the Germans because as soon as the blaring sirens announced the end of the air raid it left the station. The next morning I got off near Toulouse in the southwest of France. The two Belgian young men stayed on the train. They were trying to reach Spain and from there North Africa to join the Free French Forces. They thought I should come with them, but I told them that I wanted to stay in France because my parents might come back soon and they would be worried about me.

I have no idea why I got off the train where I did. It had stopped in a small station, and it was so peaceful there, and since no one paid attention to me, I decided to try and find a place to stay until things were back to normal. Later that day, after wandering for a while in the fields, eating fruit from the trees along the way, I found a farm which needed help. It was a time when farms were run by old men and women because most able-bodied men had been taken away to work in German factories. Therefore, when someone came along,

even a clumsy, inexperienced, fourteen-year-old city boy like me, who was willing to work just for food and a place to sleep, no questions were asked. I looked strong and healthy enough to do a good day's work. There were many people wandering about in those days. It was not until the Germans invaded the free zone, late in 1942, that the situation got difficult for those who were hiding in the country or who had joined the French underground.

I stayed on that farm for three years, until France was liberated. I worked hard in the fields and in the barn, from early morning till late evening, except for a few hours on Sundays when the old man who owned the farm, with his daughter and her two small children, would put on their best clothes to go to the village church. They would take me along. Since I was never asked what my religion was, I thought it would be better to not say anything and go with them. And so every Sunday in that church, I mouthed the Latin words of their prayers.

During those three years I became a good farmer, but I was lonely all the time, sad and homesick, and my body hurt constantly from the brutal work. Especially my hands. They were always full of sores, cuts, and blisters. The crude and vulgar mode of existence of the people and animals had gradually taken over my whole being. I was confused, and could not understand the indifferent violence of reproduction and of death which surrounded me. Every day animals were born, died, or were killed. And as I participated in this incessant process of birth and death, I became accustomed to its violence and simplicity. I felt dirty all the time. Prisoner of that dirtiness. Day after day I toiled in the fields or in the barn absent from myself. I did not suffer of hunger for there was plenty to eat on the farm, but some intolerable discontent was at work in my body and it seemed to center on the most immediate organ of contact with nature: my hands. Their physical appearance upset me. On the farm, my hands were always dirty, rough, sore, and red, and I could never get my fingernails clean.

I finally returned to Paris in May 1945, riding all the way on top of an American tank. It was a joyful journey. The German occupation was over, the country was free, people in the little towns and villages were singing "La Marseillaise" and dancing in the streets, and I was convinced that my parents and sisters were already home waiting for me. Of course, no one was there when I arrived.

All this sounds so much like the script of a bad movie. But I suppose, in retrospect, one's life always becomes a series of clichés. Even the most horrendous moments appear banal. After all, many boys and girls were left hidden in closets or abandoned in train stations during the war, and many farmers, kindhearted prostitutes, and nuns took cognizance of these children and saved them, so that ultimately all these stories become trivial.

A few weeks after my return to Paris I was working in a factory, the night shift, making tubes for toothpaste. All my aunts and uncles on my mother's side had also returned from wherever they were hiding, and were quite surprised to find me alive. They held a family council to decide what to do with me, but since they all found reasons for not being able to take care of me, I left in the middle of their gathering. What I wanted most was to go back to school, but that was not possible. I had to earn a living. I was seventeen now and had a huge gap in my education. I took a room in Montparnasse, the neighborhood where my father used to spend most of his time before the war. Since I worked at night, I slept part of the day, and the rest of the time I sat in cafés with the friends I had made in the factory and planned ways to make extra money on the black market.

When I got back to Paris, I spent a lot of time trying to find out what had happened to my parents and sisters. I went from one office building to another, waiting in line with other people who were there to obtain information about their families. Eventually I was given documents which ascertained my parents' and sisters' death at Auschwitz. Still, once in a while I would go to my old neighborhood to see if perhaps my mother or father or one of my sisters had come back. Many whose parents, brothers, or sisters were deported during the war lived with this false hope that one of them had survived and would someday return. It took me years to get rid of this delusion.

Amer Eldorado

One day, the concierge of our old apartment building in Montrouge gave me a letter addressed to my father. It had come from America, but was written in Yiddish. Since I do not know Yiddish, I had someone translate it for me. It was from an uncle I didn't even know existed. His name was David Naimark. I learned later,

when I finally met him in America, that he had married one of my father's sisters back in Siedlce, and was still living there when the war started.

This uncle explained in his letter that he, but not his wife and children, had managed to escape deportation in Poland, and that now safe in America he was anxious to know if my father and his family were well. He had written to the old address. David Naimark was a journalist, and in his letter he told how, in 1939, when the Germans invaded Poland, he was doing a reportage in Russia and got literally locked out of his country. That's how he survived. For the next few years he wandered in Russia, then in China, lived in Shanghai for a while, and finally made it to the United States in 1945. When he wrote to my father, David Naimark was working as a political writer for the *Jewish Daily Forward,* the leading Yiddish newspaper in America.

I immediately wrote to this uncle in America, telling him what had happened, and that I was the only one left from our family. I wrote in French, and he replied in Yiddish. Then he started sending packages with clothes, canned food, cartons of cigarettes, chocolate, most of which I would sell on the black market. Eventually he asked if I and my cousin Sarah wanted to come to America. When we said yes, he made the necessary arrangements for us to obtain immigrant visas. We waited nearly two years before being called to the U.S. Consulate. This is when my cousin Sarah learned that she could not go because of her health. For weeks the two of us agonized whether or not I should go alone. She insisted that I should. I left on the S.S. *Marine Jumper,* an old liberty ship, on August 19, 1947. A few months later, my cousin Sarah went to Israel with a group of young French Zionists. I have often wondered if I made the right decision. Would I have become a writer if I had gone to Israel with my cousin Sarah?

On the boat that was taking me to America, I met a young man my age with whom I had gone to school when I was a boy. He too had managed to survive alone and had discovered an uncle in America. His name was Lucien Jacobson. He became a painter in America, an abstract expressionist of some renown. He appears in my novel *Double or Nothing* under the name of Loulou.

My uncle David Naimark died in 1960. At his funeral in New York, attended by a large number of people, many of them eminent Yiddish writers, I learned that he was one of the most respected political analysts of his generation. All his writing was, of course, in Yiddish. From the moment we met until his death, I was never able to communicate with my uncle. He had arrived in America at a rather advanced age, and since he lived and worked mostly in a Yiddish environment, he barely learned to speak English. I came without any knowledge of the English language, but when I became fluent enough, I discovered that I could not talk with my uncle. I never learned Yiddish, and he did not know French. I have often regretted not to have known who he was.

My uncle met me at the boat. We had sent each other photographs, and were able to recognize one another. We embraced. He was a short, round man. He wore gold-rimmed glasses, and had a big nose. All the years I knew him, he always wore the same wrinkled brown suit with the same striped tie. Most of the money he earned he sent to Europe or Israel to members of his family who had survived. He spoke to me in Yiddish, and I spoke to him in French. I think we understood what we had to say. From the pier where the boat landed my uncle took me to the Bronx by subway to spend a few days with friends of his, Polish Jews who had survived the Holocaust and had recently come to America. When we got into the subway and I found myself surrounded mostly by black people, for a moment I wondered if I had come to the wrong country. I had no idea what America was all about. I only knew what I had seen in the American movies shown in Paris after the war—movies about gangsters, cowboys and Indians. At the time when I arrived, my uncle was the editor of the Detroit branch of the *Jewish Daily Forward*—that branch folded in the 1950s. After a few days in New York, sight-seeing (my uncle took me to see the Empire State Building, the Statue of Liberty, and we even went one afternoon to Coney Island), we left for Detroit by train. Since my uncle lived alone in a one-room furnished apartment, he had reserved a room for me (with kitchen privileges) in the house of a Hungarian family. Two weeks after I arrived in Detroit, I was working on the assembly line at one of the Chrysler factories. I often wondered then why I had come to this great land of opportunity, and what I was doing there, in Detroit. In 1947, Detroit was a rather depressed and depressing city.

Again I worked the night shift, which means that I slept most of the day. Once a week, on Fridays, I would meet my uncle and he would take me for din-ner to a kosher restaurant near his office in the Jewish neighborhood. We managed to exchange a few words. He would ask how I was doing, if I had made friends, if I was saving money. It was a sad, lonely period of my life. Working all night, and sleeping late into the afternoon, I would spend the rest of my time wandering alone in the city, or else reading, mostly adventure novels, in French, since I could not yet manage a whole book in English. It took several months before I dared check out from the public library a novel in English. I chose it at random on the shelves. I remember, it was Thackeray's *Vanity Fair*. I really don't know why I chose this particular book that day. Perhaps its subtitle intrigued me: "A Novel without a Hero." Or else because of the opening sentence of the preface, which I read standing in front of the bookshelves and must have found relevant at the time to my own state of mind: "As the manager of the Performance sits before the curtain on the boards, and looks into the Fair, a feeling of profound melancholy comes over him in his survey of the bustling place." I suppose the expression "profound melancholy" is what attracted me.

I had no idea then that someday I would become a writer, but reading was important to me, and I spent a lot of time at the public library. I had arrived in America with two French books in my suitcase. I still have them: Jean-Paul Sartre's *La Nausée*, and a pornographic novel titled *J'irai cracher sur vos tombes (I Shall Spit on Your Graves)*. The copy I have is by Vernon Sullivan. Some years later, when I was studying French literature at Columbia University, I discovered that it was the pseudonym of Boris Vian, the eccentric existentialist friend of Jean-Paul Sartre. At the time I bought these two books, everyone in France was fascinated by existentialism.

One day, a few weeks after I arrived in Detroit, while wandering in the streets, I noticed the word "HIGH SCHOOL" inscribed on a building. I went in. By then I had enough English to manage to make myself understood (with a rather thick French accent which, I must confess, I have carefully cultivated over the years, "for social and sentimental reasons," as the protagonist of one of my novels says of his own accent). I spoke to the principal, who said that even though at nineteen I was older than most students, he would accept me in his high school. He suggested a program of courses—English, American history, government—and took me around the school to meet

High-school graduation picture, Detroit, 1949

some of the teachers. However, because I worked at night I could only come to class in the afternoon. The principal was very understanding, and made it all possible. The next day I was a student at Northern High School on Woodward Avenue. Most of the students were black, which I discovered on my first day in class.

Double or Nothing

During the two years I spent at Northern High School (I received my diploma in 1949), I was known only as Frenchy. There I not only learned to read and write English, learned about American history and government, but I also learned to play the clarinet and the saxophone. At Northern High School jazz entered into my life.

After class on the first day of school as I was walking out of the building, I heard loud music coming from the auditorium. I opened the door and saw students gathered in small groups in corners of the auditorium, improvising on their instruments. They were playing jazz. I had heard jazz before, in Paris, but I had never heard it played like this. I sat quietly in one of the and

listened. A man, a white man (all the teachers at Northern High School were white), was sitting at a desk on the stage of the auditorium. He was large and chubby, with curly hair, and a very red nose. His name was Mr. Lawrence, the music teacher. After a while he banged loudly on his desk several times with a stick, and all the students gathered around him in a half circle and began to play. Not jazz, but what sounded to me like military music. I remained in my seat and listened. What I didn't know then was that among these students were young men who would someday become leading figures in the world of jazz. Tommy Flanagan was there playing the piano, and Kenny Burrell was playing the guitar, and Frank Foster the tenor saxophone, and the Heath brothers were there too, and Roland Hanna. Eventually I came to know all of them, and when I learned to play my saxophone well enough I joined a small combo they had formed and played in jam sessions with them all over the city. One night, in 1949, Charlie Parker, who was in town for a concert, came into the Blue Bird, a jazz club on Dexter Boulevard where we were jamming, and as he stood next to me asked if he could "blow my horn." That night, Yardbird played my tenor saxophone for forty minutes. I did not wipe my mouthpiece for weeks afterward. I have recalled and fictionalized that unforgettable moment in my novel *Take It or Leave It* in a chapter titled "Remembering Charlie Parker; or, How to Get It out of Your System."

Meanwhile, back in the auditorium on my first day of school. When the band stopped playing I approached Mr. Lawrence and asked if I could learn to play an instrument. He pointed to a room offstage and told me to go in there and choose something I would like to learn. The room was full of musical instruments, most of them broken. I came out with a clarinet. Mr. Lawrence showed me how to put the mouthpiece in my mouth and how to place my fingers on the keys, then he wrote some scales on a piece of paper and told me to practice, and to come back when I had learned these. Every day after school I worked with Mr. Lawrence, and a few weeks later I was playing clarinet with the Northern High School marching band.

My best friend at Northern High School was Ernest Blake. He played the alto saxophone but never became a professional jazz musician. During the Korean War he was drafted into the army and made a career of it as a captain. He was standing next to Mr. Lawrence when I asked if I could learn to play an instrument, and after I got the clarinet, Mr. Lawrence told Ernest to teach me the scales. Later that afternoon we went to Ernest's home to practice. Ernie, as he was known to everyone, noticed my thick French accent (how could he not) and asked all kinds of questions about France, and about me, and how I had come to Detroit. Ernie was the first person I met in America who showed interest in who I was and where I came from and how I felt. When we finished practicing my scales, Ernie asked if I liked jazz. I told him I did but didn't know much about it. We sat on the floor next to his record player and for hours listened to the music of Charlie Parker and Wardell Gray and Dizzy Gillespie and Thelonious Monk and Miles Davis. Ernie explained that this was the new jazz and that it was called "bebop." That day I knew I wanted to become a jazz musician and play bebop.

I never made it as a jazzman. Even though I studied and practiced for long hours, I never became as good as my high-school friends in Detroit. Eventually the tenor saxophone I bought with the money I had saved working as a waiter in the Catskills during the summer of 1948 went into a pawnshop on Sixth Avenue in New York just before I was drafted into the army in 1951. But jazz has given me a great deal of pleasure in my life, and is certainly responsible for the somewhat delirious improvisational quality critics have attributed to my writing.

After I graduated from Northern High School in 1949, I spent one semester studying music at Wayne University, which was at the time just a city college mostly for black students. By then I had stopped working in the factory. I had a job in a grocery store on the east side, in the black neighborhood, where I rented a small room near Ernie's house. But even though I had friends now, and spent most of my time practicing my saxophone, I was unhappy in Detroit. The factories with their promise of a good salary were always there to tempt you, and eventually one always went back to work in one of these, even for a few months, until one was laid off again. The winters were particularly hard and depressing. Finally, in January 1950, with fifty dollars I had saved, I left for New York. There I was reunited with Lucien Jacobson, the childhood friend I had found on the boat to America. Loulou had stayed in New York when I went to Detroit. Together we rented a furnished room in the Bronx, near the Grand Concourse.

Loulou was living a bohemian life, carefree and irresponsible. He was trying to become an artist, and

refused to take a job. He lived off other people, or the little money his uncle gave him whenever he went to visit him in Queens. While Loulou stayed in our room in the Bronx to draw or paint, I would go out in search of a job, any job, to pay the rent and buy food for the two of us. During the winter of 1950, there was a recession in America, and it was almost impossible to find work, and for months we lived only on noodles. Every morning I would check the *New York Times* want ads and then go stand in long lines with other young men until we were told there were no more jobs for that day. Meanwhile, in order to keep going, Loulou and I became regular customers of the New York City pawnshops. Gradually most of my things—my winter overcoat, my first American suit, the new suitcase I had bought in Detroit to move to New York, my wristwatch, and eventually my brand-new saxophone—ended up in a pawnshop. This went on for several months until finally I got a job as a dishwasher in a cafeteria—the Automat on Sixth Avenue. But that job didn't last long. I was fired a few weeks later when I got caught taking food to bring home to Loulou. Eventually Loulou and I were thrown out of our furnished room for not paying the rent. I moved to Brooklyn when I got a job in a lampshade factory (I suppose that's postmodern irony). Meanwhile Loulou left for Florida. He was fed up with New York and starvation. I bumped into him, in 1954, after I got out of the army, on Forty-second Street and Times Square. By then I was studying at Columbia University on the GI Bill. Loulou had just returned to New York. He was with a girlfriend, a woman much older than he, who, he explained to me, was supporting him until he became famous. This was the last time I saw Loulou, but some years later I read in a magazine about a successful show he had in a New York gallery.

Take It or Leave It

While living in the Bronx with Loulou I was taking evening courses at City College of New York, but now that I had moved to Brooklyn I wanted to continue. So after work I would ride the subway from Brooklyn to the Bronx and back. I did a lot of good reading on that subway (novels, political writing, some philosophy), but without any sense of direction. At CCNY I got involved with an anti-McCarthy group and participated in some demonstrations. I was beginning to like living in New York. I had a job, a place of my own, friends, even a girlfriend in Brooklyn, and I was involved in something, but all this ended when, in

March 1951, I was drafted into the army. Since I had applied for U.S. citizenship I was now eligible for military service. The day I was inducted I volunteered for the paratroops, almost in spite of myself, just to get away from the sergeant in charge of the recruits who kept mocking my French accent and referring to me as a "frog." After basic training I was sent to jump school at Fort Benning in Georgia, and then assigned to the 82nd Airborne Division in Fort Bragg, North Carolina. It was my first encounter with the South. Even though I had lived for almost two years in the black ghetto of Detroit, I was unprepared for the kind of prejudice and racial discrimination I discovered in the South, especially among my tough fellow paratroopers, most of whom were barely literate farm boys or hillbillies from the deep South. I have recounted, in my novel *Take It or Leave It,* in a burlesque and ironic fashion, the adventures and misadventures of Frenchy in the 82nd Airborne Division. Frenchy made forty-seven jumps as a paratrooper.

In February 1952, I was shipped to Korea and spent a few months on the front line, near Inchon, until I was ordered to Tokyo, where I was assigned to the 510th Military Intelligence Group as an interpreter for the U.N. French-speaking forces. The army had discovered that I had one useful qualification: I could speak French. It was as though I had been given a new lease on life. In the muddy foxholes of Korea I was convinced that I would be killed one night. But now as a member of the victorious occupying forces in Japan with lots of money to spend which I made on the black market, I had a good life (and a beautiful Japanese girlfriend). So good in fact that I decided to reenlist for one additional year just to stay in Tokyo. I was discharged from the army in 1954.

I became an American citizen in Tokyo, in 1953. That year a new law was passed by Congress permitting foreigners who were serving abroad in the U.S. Army to become citizens on foreign land. I was among the ninety foreigners gathered in the Hardy Barracks Theater in Tokyo who received citizenship papers from Brigadier General Homer Case as he told us what a historical moment this was. Moinous, the antihero of my novel *Smiles on Washington Square,* recounts how he too became an American citizen in Tokyo while serving in the U.S. Army, and how that day he was given a little American flag on which was written "Made in Japan."

It was in Tokyo that I began to write. Short pieces that look like poems, though at the time I had no idea what

As a paratrooper before first jump, Fort Benning, Georgia, 1951

poetry was or how it should be written. These poems were about the prostitutes, the pimps, the transvestites, the hustlers, the black marketeers in the streets of Tokyo. I suddenly felt a need to express and record for myself what I was seeing there. I wrote my first short story on the ship which was bringing me back to the States to be discharged. I was unhappy to go back to America. There was nothing awaiting me. I had tried to find a way to remain in Tokyo, but was told that only if I reenlisted in the army for life could I stay overseas. The story was naively titled "You Can't Go Home Again." During the three years I spent in the army I had read everything Thomas Wolfe had written, but also novels by Hemingway, Faulkner, Fitzgerald, and many others, especially war novels— the classics such as *The Young Lions, From Here to Eternity, The Naked and the Dead,* anything I could find in the Fort Bragg library, or in the Ernie Pyle Recreation Center library in Tokyo.

Receiving U.S. citizenship papers, Tokyo, 1953

After I was discharged in March 1954, I went back to New York. I was broke. I had lost all the money I had made in Tokyo on the black market playing poker on the ship back to the States. A few days after I was a civilian again, I was working as a waiter in a French restaurant on Lexington Avenue. Totally disenchanted with America, I was then seriously considering returning to France and abandoning the Great American Dream. But one day, near Times Square, where I spent a lot of time going to movies after work, I stumbled into an army friend from Tokyo. His name was George Tashima, an American. In Tokyo George often told me that he wanted to become a writer, and that he had started a novel about an American Japanese who, during World War II, when he was still a boy, spent time with his family in an internment camp in Arizona. It was George who told me in Tokyo that I should try to write down my experiences there, that perhaps I too could become a writer.

George was discharged from the army a few months before me, and when I bumped into him he was studying creative writing at Columbia University under the G.I. Bill. He explained that I too could study there since I was also eligible for the G.I. Bill. The next day, George Tashima literally led me to the registrar at Columbia University. I had to take an entrance exam because even though I had a high-school diploma I had been away from school too long. I barely passed that exam (especially the parts dealing with science), but in the fall of 1954, I became a freshman in college. I was twenty-six years old. That year I read Shakespeare for the first time, and for the next three years I

read Homer and Dante, the Romantic poets, all the great Russian novelists, and Flaubert, Proust, Thomas Mann, Joyce, and Kafka, and many others. I majored in comparative literature since after all I was fluent in a foreign language. But more importantly, at Columbia University I studied creative writing and spent much time writing poetry, short stories, and even a novel which was never finished.

As I was going through the course catalog to prepare my first semester's schedule, I came across the description of a poetry workshop offered by Leonie Adams which stated that students needed the instructor's permission to register. When I went to Leonie Adams's office to ask if I could take her course, I had with me some of the things I had written in Japan. Leonie Adams was a tiny woman who always wore purple clothes and whose long grey hair fell over her eyes. I sat next to her desk while she read my poems, shaking her head in apparent approval. Finally she told me that I could come to her workshop. She said that my poetry was quite unusual, especially the subject matter, that it was very realistic and had a curious loose form. Then she added: "You write a bit like Walt Whitman." "Who?" I asked. She repeated the name. I asked her to spell it as I wrote it on a piece of paper. After I left her office, I rushed to the library and took out the complete works of Walt Whitman. I spent most of that night reading *Leaves of Grass* aloud to myself, and though I was fascinated by the beauty and the daring of this poetry, I found little affinity with my own writing.

I learned a great deal about writing poetry from Leonie Adams, who emphasized symbolism and ambiguity, but also from Babette Deutsch, whose poetry workshop I took during my second year at Columbia. From Babette Deutsch I learned about form and discipline. She would often invite me and other students to her apartment to have tea and talk poetry, and I would always leave with a book under my arm which she insisted I should read. Also she started me on translations, saying that it was the best way to learn how to write. As one of the projects for her workshop, I put together a collection of poems I translated from various French poets.

My first instructor in fiction writing was Dick Humphreys (who has published numerous novels). In 1976, when the Fiction Collective published my novel *Take It or Leave It,* Dick Humphreys attended the publica-

With the Buick Special immortalized in Take It or Leave It, *New York, 1954*

tion party. He reminded me of a note he had written on one of the stories I submitted to his class. It said: "There is something totally illogical about the way you write fiction." I had written a story in which the first-person narrator commits suicide in the middle of the story by jumping off a boat and yet continues to tell the story after his death. Dick Humphreys explained that it was not possible, even in a work of fiction, to have a character die and remain the narrator. This had never occurred to me. I had discovered that writing fiction was a way to gain freedom, and therefore thought that anything was possible. It may explain why a critic once referred to me as "a writer who is capable of making a mess out of chaos."

I graduated from Columbia University (cum laude, Phi Beta Kappa) in June 1957, with my head full of books, and boxes full of manuscripts (hundreds of poems, short stories, and one unfinished novel titled *And I Followed My Shadow*). During my senior year, a story I submitted to a contest at a writers' conference held at Columbia won a one thousand dollar prize. The story, called "Young Man Without a Horn," was about

a jazz musician who cannot find the money to retrieve his saxophone from a pawnshop just when he is offered a splendid job. With the prize money I bought a 1951 Pontiac which I drove to California.

I had been offered fellowships to do graduate work at Columbia, Harvard, and the University of California at Los Angeles. I went up to Cambridge for an interview with the people in comparative literature at Harvard. They told me that they would be very pleased to have me in their program and hoped that I would be able to devote all my time to my studies. I replied that I would certainly study hard, but that I had to find some sort of job to support myself because the fellowship I was being offered only covered my tuition and textbooks. I was told, "At Harvard one does not take on spare-time jobs." At Columbia, even though my tuition was covered by the G.I. Bill, I needed three different jobs in order to survive. I turned down the Harvard fellowship, and instead went to California as a teaching assistant at UCLA, where I received my M.A. in 1958, and my Ph.D. in 1963. I wrote the first doctoral dissertation in English on the fiction of Samuel Beckett, and it was published as a book in 1965, under the title *Journey to Chaos*.

The Twofold Vibration

I first encountered the work of Samuel Beckett in 1956, when I saw the Broadway production of *Waiting for Godot* with Bert Lahr, E. G. Marshall, Kurt Kasznar, and Alvin Epstein. I was overwhelmed. I knew I had seen something important even though I did not fully understand what it was. I have not stopped reading and studying the work of Beckett since that day. In 1979, 1 was elected "honorary trustee" of the Samuel Beckett Society. If the Holocaust and the closet experience greatly marked my emotional and psychological life, the work of Samuel Beckett and my personal relationship with the man have deeply marked my intellectual and creative life. From reading Beckett's work and talking with him (we first met in Paris in 1963, and remained in contact until his death in 1989) I learned that being a writer means never to compromise one's work, and that no linguistic utterance, however convincingly representational it may seem, can ever successfully accommodate the chaos of life.

At UCLA, busy taking graduate courses while teaching French to freshmen, I had to set aside the novel I had started at Columbia. After I got my M.A. in 1958,

Family portrait, 1963. Clockwise from left: Raymond, stepson Jim, wife Erica, stepdaughter Robin, stepson Steve, daughter Simone

I decided to return to France and see if, perhaps, I might be able to live and write there. I sold my old Pontiac, some of my clothes, most of my books, even some of my jazz records to buy a plane ticket from Los Angeles to Paris, and left in May 1958. This was my first return to France after eleven years in exile. The three months I spent in Paris that summer were a total disaster. I only found disenchantment and sordid memories there. I was unable to write. I returned to UCLA just on time to register for the fall semester and continue working on my Ph.D., and again abandoned for the time the writing of fiction.

Soon after my return from France, I met Erica at UCLA where she was studying French. She had just gotten a divorce, and had gone back to college while taking care of her three young children. Marrying her is certainly the most successful thing I have ever done. While still working on my dissertation, I found myself suddenly raising children and learning to care for a family. But Erica and the children made me discover that there was laughter in me, and even tenderness. I had lived all the years since I emerged from the closet thinking that life was only unhappiness and loneliness. But now I was surrounded with affection and joy. No one has been more supportive of my work, especially when the writing doesn't go well, than Erica, who is also my best and most severe critic. She reads everything I write, and not a word goes by that she has not carefully scrutinized and questioned. She always cuts where I have the tendency for excess or sentimentality, though sometimes, behind her back, I cannot resist reinserting certain words she has deleted. Together we have enjoyed golf and tennis, of which we are both fanatics, and good food, and good friends, and we have gambled in casinos all over the world. Erica and I have traveled to most European countries (Erica was born in Vienna), but also to Japan, Egypt, India, and Israel.

Our daughter Simone was born on December 7, 1962—Pearl Harbor Day. I finished the final draft of my doctoral dissertation on Beckett two days before her birth. The dissertation is dedicated to Oscar, the name Simone was referred to before she arrived in this world.

From 1959 to 1964, I taught in the French department of the University of California at Santa Barbara. During those five years I not only finished my dissertation, but wrote a lot of poetry, both in English and in French, some of which was published in a bilingual volume in Paris, in 1967, under the title *Among the Beasts*. In Santa Barbara, I founded and edited *Mica*, a literary magazine that has since become a collector's item. Through *Mica* I became acquainted with a number of writers with whom I have remained in contact. At that time I was also doing a lot of translations from the French. Some of these, including prose pieces by Jean Genet and poems by André Breton, Max Jacob, Boris Vian, and others, appeared in issues of *Big Table* and the *Evergreen Review*. In 1965, I published *Temporary Landscapes*, a book of poems by Yvonne Caroutch I had translated from the French. I was suddenly becoming part of the contemporary literary scene, and it was a new experience for me. But now that I had my Ph.D. and was teaching full time in a university, I also had to write and publish criticism.

Though I kept writing poetry, I was anxious to return to fiction, and the novel I had already abandoned several times. I felt torn between the necessity of having to write criticism, and the more profound and personal need to write fiction. Meanwhile, in 1965, my Beckett book, *Journey to Chaos*, was published, and received favorable reviews, including one in the *New York Times*. Suddenly I found myself being recognized as a Beckett scholar.

In 1964, I accepted a position in the French department at the State University of New York at Buffalo. (After my first novel was published, I moved to the English department.) In the sixties, SUNY-Buffalo was an exciting center of literary activities—and it is still. Important writers from all parts of the U.S. and from abroad came to Buffalo, and some settled there. Charles Olson was still teaching in the English department when I arrived, and a number of poets and novelists joined that department in the following years— Robert Creeley, John Logan, Irving Feldman, Carl Dennis, John Barth, and many others. Leslie Fiedler came the same year I did, and we have been friends ever since, even though we have not always agreed about what literature is or should be, and have argued much and passionately during the years we have been together. Buffalo has been good to us. Recently Leslie mentioned that he had written eleven books while in Buffalo. I told him I had written exactly the same number.

In 1966, one year after my Beckett book was published, I was awarded a Guggenheim fellowship to spend a year in France to finish a second book on Beckett and write on contemporary French poetry. We left on the *United States*, in June 1966, and on the boat I began writing notes toward a new novel. Besides finishing the book on Beckett and writing articles, I spent part of the year in Paris working on that novel, which eventually became *Double or Nothing*.

With its pulverized syntax, its wild, exuberant typography, and its outrageous self-reflexiveness, *Double or Nothing*, which was finished in 1970, had difficulties finding a publisher. Richard Kostelanetz, who had read the manuscript, went from one publisher to another for over a year trying to get the book accepted, and though most of them found it original and interesting, they thought it would be too expensive to produce. I was beginning to think that *Double or Nothing* would never be published when Michael Anania, who was then literary editor at Swallow Press, accepted it. The book appeared in 1971, and won two prizes—the Frances Steloff Fiction Prize, and the Panache Experimental Fiction Prize. I was forty-three years old. At the publication party in Chicago, Jerome Klinkowitz, who had already read the novel, suggested that I send a copy to Ronald Sukenick, whose work, he said, I would find interesting and not unlike my own. And indeed, not only did I find Ron's fiction fascinating, but we immediately became friends. Meanwhile Jerome Klinkowitz and Larry McCaffery, whom I met soon after the publication of *Double or Nothing*, have remained my most devoted readers and supporters.

When Ronald Sukenick received the copy of *Double or Nothing* I had sent him, he wrote back saying that he had already gotten the book from the publisher, and in fact had reviewed it for the *New York Times*. In his review Ron wrote of *Double or Nothing*: "It is a considerable achievement, a deliberate and complicated doodle, a perversely trivial book that forces you to take it seriously. And that also opens interesting possibilities for contemporary fiction." Because of this novel which, according to the reviews, "defied all the conventions of fiction with effrontery and laughter," I found myself associated with a group of experimental writers known then as metafictionists, and subsequently as surfictionists (a term I coined in an essay-manifesto published in *Partisan Review,* in 1973, under the title "Surfiction: A Position"). Though greatly discussed and analyzed, and even taught in literature courses, *Double or Nothing* has been regarded, and still is today, as a curiosity. The German translation, titled *Alles oder Nichts,* which appeared in 1986, also won two prizes, and made the list of best books published in Germany that year.

Since 1971, 1 have not stopped writing fiction in order to achieve the vocation of my name—Federman/ *Homme de Plume!* But that's another story. Perhaps, next time, I shall tell that version of the story.

And all will be *Smiles on Washington Square!*

Federman contributed the following update to *CA* in 2002:

ANOTHER VERSION OF MY LIFE

Much has happened, in my life and in my writing, since I wrote the final words of my mini-autobiography in 1989.

The titles I gave to each section of "A Version of My Life" suggest that while writing about my past, I was projecting into the novels I wrote in the future. The title of each section is in fact the title of one of these novels, thus pointing to the relation between life and fiction.

"A Version of My Life" reveals how the past, that is to say history, becomes fiction. The title of that autobiography—"A Version of My Life"—puts into question the veracity of the facts of history. But at the same time it points to the potential fictionality of my past. This is why my autobiography could only be called "A Version of My Life." Other versions were awaiting to be written in the novels.

1. Federman on Federman: Lie or Die

Never trust the artist, trust the tale.

—D. H. Lawrence

If I were a critic (which I was once upon a time) and were asked to discuss (in spoken or written form) Federman's fiction, I would not discuss what Federman has written in his books (those curious books which seem to defy any classification and yet call themselves novels with effrontery), but what he has left unwritten. I mean unwritten not only in terms of substance and content, but also in terms of form and language. His books are full of holes, full of gaps, full of missing elements, to use an oxymoron. And his language too is full of holes, full of missing parts. His books are, in fact, always left unfinished. Federman writes unfinished stories made of unfinished sentences but which pretend to be finished stories made of finished sentences. Look for instance at the ending of *Take It or Leave It*:

> and so he folded himself upon himself like an old wrinkled piece of yellow paper there on that hospital bed as I took leave of him (on the edge of the precipice) closed himself like a used torn book that nobody needs any more a useless book to be thrown in the garbage as he thought of the trip the big beautiful journey he could have made cross country coast to coast and which someday he could have told like a beautiful story or retold with all the exciting details to a friend or to some gathering of interested listeners with all the passion necessary to tell such a fabulous story directly or indirectly but now it was finished canceled and so empty of his last drop of courage and the last words of his story which is now canceled canceled since they were shipping him back to where it all started he said sadly to himself: no need trying to go on no . . . but perhaps next time yes the next time . . . . (so long everybody)

Federman's novel *To Whom It May Concern* also ends on a note of unfinishedness when the narrator-writer declares:

> and so, as I continued to listen to the cousins, their faces fading into darkness, their voices becoming more and more faint, I realized that their story would always remain unfinished . . . .

Therefore, when dealing with Federman's work, one must accept the fact that what makes up his fiction is not necessarily what is there (that is to say what is

Reading from his work with translator Karin Graf, Berlin, 1990

told, what is visible, what is readable, what is present, what is presented, what is represented or appresented), but what is not there (what is not told, what is not visible, not readable, not presented, not represented or appresented). In other words, what is important to notice in Federman's fiction is what is absent.

Indeed, the fundamental aspect, the central theme of his fiction is *ABSENCE*. Federman writes in order to cancel, or better yet, in order to absent the very story he wants to tell. In the same process, he writes to absent, or better yet, to deconstruct the very language he employs.

As the commentators of his work have often noted, Federman has perfected the art of cancellation and absence, and he has done so with cunning and devious stratagems. Therefore, what the critic should discuss in his work are the holes, the gaps, the voids, the empty spaces, the blank pages, and of course the closet, the precipice, and especially the four *X-X-X-X's* that recur throughout the works to designate that absence.

What must be apprehended in Federman's fiction is what is missing, what has been deliberately or perhaps unconsciously left out. But not because what is missing could not be told or written—such as the unspeakability of the Holocaust and the destruction of his family that inform Federman's life and work, and to which he refers in one of his fictions as The Unforgivable Enormity—but because Federman is primarily writing to demonstrate the impossibility and the necessity of the act of writing in the Postmodern/Post-Holocaust/Post-Hitler era. As such he seems to suggest that in order to be able to write under today's moral, social, psychological and political conditions, one must lie, or invent (same thing), one must fill the holes, for if one cannot lie or invent, cannot fill the holes, one will certainly die (as a writer that is).

It is clear then from this central idea that in order to survive (which also means in order to be able to write), one must lie. One must invent what one has not lived, what one has not witnessed. In this respect, one could say that what is missing from Federman's work (since it is presented as a lie) is the truth—the paradoxical truth that says that in order not to die (as a writer) Federman must lie about his life (as a human being). Federman must invent what absence refuses to tell. He must render absence present into words, whether it is in his autobiography or in his novels.

This raises the essential question: *How to replace a life, the experiences of a life, in its context, when in most cases, one has forgotten or falsified the original text?*

*

Fiction writers are often asked (and I am no exception): *Is your fiction autobiographical?* And the writer usually replies, somewhat embarrassed, as if the fact that he used elements of his own life was an embarrassing matter: *Yes, I suppose one could say that my fiction is autobiographical, but I must emphasize that* I have distorted and even displaced many facts in order to achieve a distance from myself . . . *an aesthetic distance,* the writer adds, de-emphasizing the last part of his reply as if unsure of its meaning.

In other words, as suggested throughout "A Version of My Life," fiction and autobiography are always interchangeable, just as life and fiction, fact and fiction, language and fiction; that is to say history and story are interchangeable. And this because, for me, the story always comes first. Or to put it slightly differently: Everything is fiction because everything always begins with language, everything is language.

The great silence within us must be decoded into words

in order to be and to mean . . . .

Paradoxical as it may seem, only fiction is real, only fiction is true, only fiction remains after the facts. The rest cannot be verified for it remains in the domain of absence, in the domain of what has already happened in the past, and the past can never be totally recaptured,

as writers quickly learn in the process of writing fiction or their autobiography. The past is always mediated by memory, or the failings of memory. And so, to a certain extent each of my novel is another version of my life.

2. Reflections on "A Version of My Life"

A few years ago I was approached by the editor of *Contemporary Authors Autobiography Series* to write a mini-autobiography (mini, because from the start I was limited to a 10,000 word text). I told the editor, half-jokingly, that with such a word limitation, I could only give him the story of the first twelve years of my life, especially since these twelve years had been packed with so many dramatic events. This mini-autobiography was to be included in a series of volumes that contain other such "essays in autobiography," as the editor called them, written by various contemporary authors.

At first I was reluctant to accept this offer. I felt that it was somewhat premature for me to write the story of my life, and besides my fiction was already the story of my life—or is it the reverse? But I accepted and wrote what I eventually called: "A Version of My Life—The Early Years." The early years because I chose to deal with moments and events of my life only up to 1971, the year when my first novel, *Double or Nothing*, was published.

My autobiography is not only a written text, but it also contains a dozen or so photographs which illustrate certain moments of my life. The title, of course, immediately throws an element of doubt and duplicity over the text: "A Version of My Life." One could ask, which version? And if there are other versions, which is the true version, the real version, the more reliable version? One could also ask, does that mean that the facts related here may not be correct, and therefore may not be trusted?

The photographs in the text do not lie, at least as far as photographs supposedly freeze the subject in time and space. It is really me that one sees there in various places, at various moments, and with various people (my sisters, my wife, my daughter, friends, fellow-writers, my dog). But the text: can it be trusted? Can the language of the text be trusted? And even less so, the events related by that language? There is no way to verify, no way to ascertain the veracity of what I have written.

The reader of my autobiography can only *take my word[s]* for it. Indeed, the reader of an autobiography can only believe the words the writer has used, even though he knows that these words are deficient and unreliable.

Because of the unreliability of language, I cannot deny nor affirm that the facts related in my autobiography have or have not been distorted from the truth.

Similarly, an artist who paints a self-portrait cannot claim that he has really painted himself since he knows that the medium he uses (paint) only creates an illusion. Autobiographies and self-portraits are always distortions of reality because they are created on the basis of a memory or an image, with words or with paint.

I have often wondered how a painter creates a self-portrait. Does he stand before a mirror, or does he paint himself while looking at another picture (a photograph or a sketch), or does he simply work from memory? But then can the artist trust the image he has of himself—in his mind or in his portfolio? These are very intricate questions that raise the whole problematic of not only self-portraits but autobiographies.

For instance, what was Velasquez looking at when he painted himself in the process of painting the self-reflexive painting that we are looking at the famous "La Meninas"? Even more interesting and problematic is the painting by the Austrian artist, Egon Schiele, entitled "Portrait of the Artist Masturbating." One can only wonder how and when Schiele observed himself in order to be able to paint himself in the process of doing what he has represented?

These are some of the questions that came to my mind when I began writing my autobiography. These forced me to reflect on what I was doing, on the very idea of an autobiography, that is to say, to reflect on the subject I am addressing here now.

An autobiography is never the complete history of the person who writes it. By necessity (of space, of language, of prudishness perhaps, of humbleness even, of time) it must be selective. The autobiographer functions very much like the novelist who obviously selects what he will tell or not tell about his characters.

Right from the start I had to make choices about what I would include in the 10,000 words that were prescribed to write the story of my life. Would I write mostly about my family—my ancestors, my parents, my wife, my children? Or would I write mostly about myself? Should I concentrate on my childhood, my education, my travels, my adventures and misadventures, my love life, or even my sexual life? Should I write mostly about what I am today? In other words, would I write from a civil, a familial, a social, a psychological point of view, or would I write strictly from a personal, self-centered point of view? Would I reveal all—my fantasies, my ambitions, my failures, my qualities and my vices?

Obviously, limited as I was by the number of words assigned to me, I had to limit myself to only certain aspects and certain moments of my life. But then this is also how I write my novels—by a process of selection and cancellation.

I finally decided that I would write about those moments and those events in my life which made of me a writer. That is to say, I would write about those experiences (happy or unhappy, sad or funny as they may have been) which ultimately became my fiction. For this reason, I gave each section of this autobiography a title which happened to be the title of one of my novels. I did this to show clearly the relationship between my fiction and my life—between autobiography and fiction, or vice versa.

What amazed me while writing this autobiography was to what extent I was borrowing from my novels, literally lifting whole passages, paragraphs, sentences. I was plagiarizing myself. My fiction was nourishing the story of my life. It felt as if I were writing not about myself, but about the fictitious life of someone whose name happens to be Raymond Federman. This forced me to reflect further on the notion that a biography is always something one invents after the facts.

In *The Twofold Vibration*, the protagonist (an unnamed Old Man who is to be deported to the space colonies on New Year's Eve 1999) is asked by one of the narrators to tell the story of his life, and the Old Man replies: *I have no story, my life is the story.* But then he changes his mind and says: *No, the story is my life.*

What I finally wrote in my autobiography is not really the story of my life, but the story of how I became a

At the Stuttgart Seminar, 1992. Left to right: Heidi Ziegler, William Gass, Malcolm Bradbury, Ihab Hassan, Raymond Federman, John Barth

writer because of certain experiences I had during the early years of my life. That is why I could only write "A Version of My Life"—a manipulated version.

My life began in incoherence and discontinuity, I wrote then, but I could also have written, *My life began with doubt and uncertainty.* Whatever the case, it is true that my work has been marked by this uncertain, incoherent, doubtful, discontinuous beginning, and that in order to be recorded in history, or better yet in order to be able to record my life in a story, I had to lie—to lie or invent (same thing) so that I could survive, and not die.

My death is behind me, says the Old Man in *The Twofold Vibration,* who is also a survivor of the Holocaust and a novelist.

To lie or to die. That is the writer's dilemma, or rather the writer's paradox. Echoing Zeno's old *Liar's Paradox: All Cretans are liars, I am a Cretan,* I can

say for all writers and for myself too: *All writers are liars, I am a writer,* thus preventing all possibilities of questioning the veracity of my work.

3. If You Don't Believe History Believe the Story

A few years ago at a literary conference in San Francisco, where I was presenting a paper and reading from my fiction, a critic, an antagonistic critic questioned, in public, before a large audience, the truth of the most important and most traumatic moment in my life—of my autobiography. He questioned the truth of what I have called *The Closet Experience,* which is well-known to those who are familiar with my work. That experience is described in "A Version of My Life." No need to repeat it.

But it is true, after all, that there is no way to verify, to prove that what is told really happened to me. No way to ascertain that what I have been recounting over and over really occurred. From an early poem published in 1958, entitled "Escape," to my latest novel-,*Aunt Rachel's Fur*, I have been circling around that closet experience, digging into that obsession, telling the same old story, and yet there is no way to know if it truly happened to me. Here is the poem again. It contains the entire story.

ESCAPE

My life began in a closet
among empty skins and dusty hats
while sucking pieces of stolen sugar

Outside the moon tiptoed across the roof
to denounce the beginning of my excessiveness
backtracked into the fragility of my adventure

Curiosity drove me down the staircase
but I stumbled on the twelfth step and fell
and all the doors opened dumb eyes
to stare impudently at my nakedness

As I ran beneath the indifferent sky
clutching a filthy package of fear in my hands
a yellow star fell from above and struck my
   breast
and all the eyes turned away in shame

Then they grabbed me and locked me in a box
dragged me a hundred times over the earth
in metaphorical disgrace
while they threw stones at each other
and burned all the stars in a giant furnace

Every day they came to touch me
put their fingers in my mouth
and paint me black and blue

But through a crack in the wall
I saw a tree the shape of a leaf
and one morning a bird flew into my head

I loved that bird so much
that while my blue-eyed master
looked at the sun and was blind
I opened the cage and hid my heart
in a yellow feather

No, there is no way to know if I was locked in a closet when I was a little boy, if the moon tiptoed across the roof that night, if I stumbled on the steps while going down the staircase, if the doors opened to stare at my nakedness, if a bird really flew into my head, and so on. And what about the filthy package of excrement left on the roof? Who can believe that? It was dark that night. No one saw the boy. There were no witnesses. And if there were some, by now they must either be lost or dead, or have forgotten the whole sordid affair.

And so, Federman has perhaps been lying about his life, or else he has been inventing for himself an experience so that he could write it. Or better yet, Federman has borrowed that experience from someone else, and has attributed it to himself. Writers often do that, borrow stories from others. After all, Federman has openly stated, on several occasions, that all writers are pla[y]giarizers.

It is even possible that in repeating the same *second-hand story* over and over again—the story of the closet, but also the story of the raw potatoes on the train, the story of the farm, the story of the journey to America, of the factory in Detroit, the story of the noodles, the story of Charlie Parker and the tenor saxophone, and of the Buick Special, and all the other stories he has told—Federman convinced himself of the truth of these fictions.

After all, it is well known that many children were hidden in closets or abandoned in train stations during the Second World War. Therefore, the story of Federman's closet becomes rather common and banal. It could be anybody's story. Everybody's story.

And so, that day in San Francisco, I had no argument, no refutation to offer to that critic who questioned the truth of the experience that nourishes my fiction. No, I had no proofs to convince him of the truth. I only had my fiction—my lies. But then isn't it imagination (or lies—same thing) that fills the holes of absence?

With writer friends Lance Olsen (left) and Larry McCaffery in the Borrego Spring Desert, 2001

However, something important should be added here, important in relation to the questioning of the facts of my life. After having denounced me publicly, the young critic concluded by saying (and this is crucial to our topic): *Mister Federman, I may be suspicious of the facts of your life, I may not trust your biography, but I must admit that I am totally convinced by the stories you tell in your novels. Not only convinced, but deeply moved by them.* I trust your stories.

This was a most unexpected reversal, a most amazing way of concluding his argument. For suddenly he was no longer an antagonistic critic, but a sympathetic reader of my fiction. Of course, what is interesting is that he expressed doubt about the truth of my life, and showed trust in a fiction supposedly based on my life. However, by questioning the veracity of certain facts of my life, he raised the crucial question of the equivocal relationship that exists today between facts and fiction, between biography and fiction, between memory and imagination.

This sudden reversal was important to me because I do not think that I became a writer in order to tell the story of my life. I became a writer in order to tell stories. And I am sure this is true of all those who call themselves writers. If some of the stories I have told happened to be based on my life, finally it is totally irrelevant—especially when it comes to judging the quality, or the efficacity, or even the beauty of my fiction.

The real question then about autobiography as fiction or fiction as autobiography is this: Do we read fiction simply to find out about the life of the author, or because we are interested in people, interested in the human condition? If we are interested only in the life of the author, then why not simply ask the author to tell the story of his life, why not simply read his autobiography. But if he does tell the story of his life, can we trust it? Can we trust him or her? No, I do not believe that we read fiction to learn about the life of the author. If this were the reason for reading novels, or for listening to a writer talk about his work, the entire enterprise of literature would become trivial, boring, derisive, uninteresting.

What is interesting in the relationship between fiction and autobiography is the mechanism by which a writer transforms elements of his life into stories. What is fascinating is the process that makes it possible for a life to become fiction, or vice versa for fiction to make it possible for a writer to have a biography—real or imagined.

I suppose I should now tell what happened to me and what I did after the publication of my first novel, *Double or Nothing*, in 1971, since that is where "A Version of My Life" stopped. But to tell all that would take volumes, and most of it would be uninteresting, repetitious, and banal. Perhaps even boring. The story of how one becomes a writer, or an experimental writer, has been told too many times. The same for the story of how one becomes a Distinguished Professor Emeritus. And besides, the real story of what happened in my life since 1971 is inscribed, one way or another, in the writing I did since then—in the twelve novels I published, in the poems, in the fiction and critifiction, and in the millions of words I scribbled in English and in French. Everything I have written since 1971, in whatever form it may have taken, makes-up "The Other Versions of My Life." To which one must add the versions of my life invented by other people.

For instance, my daughter's version, which she wrote a few years ago for a special occasion.

MY FATHER THE FICTIONEER

Federman may have told you that his daughter is a world renowned director—or a pretty little girl. Actually I am renowned mostly in his mind and I am actually thirty-four, the age he was when our friendship began. When I was very small, my first word was

Raymond and Erica

Mop—an amalgam of Mom and Pop. Mop was the funny man with the big nose and warm eyes (Mom remained Mom for some reason).

My father is a fictioneer. As a child I thought that to be as good as a musketeer. In fact I am sure I was told that. I was told many things. It was then that he began to tell me stories, all sorts of stories—how he was a trapeze artist in the circus; how he tested parachutes and jumped out of airplanes; how he helped Sticky and Palucci steal the Eiffel Tower; how he jumped off a train and broke his nose and escaped the concentration camps; how Tomas Edison and Alexandre Graham Bell were French like him; how he had heard from Sticky and Palucci while I was at school, and they had been on the moon; how he had been in the Olympic trials for backstroke; how he narrowly escaped court marshal when he was dealing on the black market in Japan; how his saxophone was played by Charlie Parker; how his father was a communist, like himself; how God doesn't exist, rather there is Samuel Beckett, who is a personal friend of his.

Sometimes he would tell me these stories when we would drive around in the car, listening to jazz on the radio, while he smoked Gauloises or Gitanes, without filter, with the windows rolled up so that the wind wouldn't mess up his hair; or sometimes it would be at the movies, in the afternoons after school—he'd take me to see Godard or Sergio Leone films, only those, but all of them, over and over; sometimes we would play tennis or golf, and he would say he had taught me everything I know, which is why I am so good. He didn't like it if I won, but he liked it when I got real close. We were real close. He was my best friend.

There was a period when I wanted to know what was true and what was not, but that didn't last long. I guess I only wanted to know so that I could tell my friends the stories, but I soon realized he didn't really know himself, and mostly it really didn't matter. So I tell his stories, pick and choose the ones I like best, embellish them a bit. I introduce my father to my friends and when they meet him, they understand that I am a second generation fictioneer. When I was very sick, nine years ago and we thought I might die, my Pop whispered in my ear, "If I could trade places with you I would." I believed him. I said to him, "You didn't do all that surviving for nothing; we come from a long line of survivors, those that made it." And so here we are. Remember if you hear him tell a story about me, it probably isn't true. Also that there may not be very many, but he isn't the only one called Federman.

[Simone]

BIOGRAPHICAL AND CRITICAL SOURCES:

BOOKS

Contemporary Literary Criticism, Gale (Detroit, MI), Volume 6, 1976, Volume 47, 1988.

Contemporary Novelists, 6th edition, St. James Press (Detroit, MI), 1996.

Cornis-Pope, Marcel, *Narrative Innovations and Cultural Rewriting in the Cold War Era and After,* Pelgrave (New York, NY), 2001.

Dictionary of Literary Biography Yearbook: 1980, Gale (Detroit, MI), 1981.

Erdpohl, Evamaria, *Criteria of Identity: An Comparative Analysis of Raymond Federman and Jasper Johns,* Peter Lang (Frankfurt, Germany), 1992.

Gerdes, Eckhard, *The Laugh That Laughs at the Laugh: Writing from and about the Pen Man Raymond Federman,* Writers Club Press (Lincoln, NE), 2002.

Hartl, Thomas, *Raymond Federman's Real Fictitious Discourses: Formulating Yet Another Paradox,* Edward Mellen Press (Lewiston, NY), 1995.

Kutnik, Jerzy, *The Novel as Performance: The Fiction of Ronald Sukenick and Raymond Federman,* Southern Illinois University Press, 1986.

McCaffery, Larry, Doug Rice, and Thomas Hartl, *Federman from A to X-X-X-X,* San Diego State University Press (San Diego, CA), 1998.

Pearce, Richard, *The Novel in Motion: An Approach to Modern Fiction,* Ohio State University Press (Columbus, OH), 1983.

Sletaugh, Gordon E., *The Play of the Double in Post-modern American Fiction,* Southern Illinois University Press, 1993.

PERIODICALS

American Book Review, March-April, 1981, pp. 10-12; January-February, 1982, pp. 2-3; November-December, 1983, p. 7; September-October, 1986, pp. 22-23; August, 1996, p. 5.
Boundary 2, fall, 1976, pp. 153-165.
Chicago Review, summer, 1977, pp. 145-149; autumn, 1980, Peter Quartermain, review of *The Voice in the Closet/La voix dans le cabinet de débarras,* pp. 65-74.
Chicago Tribune Book World, September 2, 1982.
Fiction International, numbers 2-3, 1974, pp. 147-150.
Los Angeles Times Book Review, February 9, 1986, Allen Boyer, review of *Smiles on Washington Square,* p. 4.
Michigan Quarterly Review, winter, 1974.
Modern Fiction Studies, winter, 1994, p. 857.
New Republic, July 11, 1970, p. 23.
New York Times Book Review, January 23, 1966, p. 4; October 1, 1972, pp. 40-41; September 15, 1974, p. 47; November 7, 1982, pp. 12, 26; November 24, 1985, Alan Cheuse, review of *Smiles on Washington Square,* p. 24.
North American Review, March, 1986, pp. 67-69.
Saturday Review, January 22, 1972, p. 67.
Times Literary Supplement, May 5, 1966, p. 388; October 12, 1973, p. 1217; December 3, 1982, Brian Morton, review of *The Twofold Vibration,* p. 1344.
Yale Review, spring, 1983, pp. 12-13.

* * *

FELDMAN, Alfred 1923-

PERSONAL: Born August 7, 1923, in Hamburg, Germany; son of Joachim and Paula Feldman; married Frances Reed, 1964; children: Suzanne, Philip. *Education:* University of Chicago, M.S. (chemistry), 1956; Johns Hopkins University, M.S. (computer science), 1978.

ADDRESSES: Agent—c/o Author Mail, Southern Illinois University Press, P.O. Box 3697, Carbondale, IL 62902-3697.

CAREER: Chemist and computer systems consultant; retired. Holocaust survivor.

WRITINGS:

One Step Ahead: A Jewish Fugitive in Hitler's Europe (memoir), Southern Illinois University Press (Carbondale, IL), 2001.

BIOGRAPHICAL AND CRITICAL SOURCES:

PERIODICALS

Library Journal, November 15, 2001, Mary C. Bagshw, review of *One Step Ahead: A Jewish Fugitive in Hitler's Europe,* p. 76.
Publishers Weekly, October 15, 2001, p. 55.

OTHER

Southern Illinois University Press Web site, http://www.siu.edu/~siupress/ (March 12, 2003).

* * *

FINKELSTEIN, Norman 1954-

PERSONAL: Born May 30, 1954, in New York, NY; son of Harry (a lumber yard manager) and Dora Grief (an elementary school teacher) Finkelstein ; married Kathryn Wekselman (divorced, 1995); married Alice (a librarian), May 10, 1997; children: Ann, Steven. *Education:* State University of New York at Binghamton, B.A. (English), 1975; Emory University, Ph.D. (English), 1980. *Religion:* Jewish.

ADDRESSES: Office—Xavier University, 3800 Victory Parkway, Cincinnati, OH 45207-4446. *E-mail*—finkelstein.norman@lycos.com; finkel@xu.edu.

CAREER: Xavier University, Cincinnati, OH, professor of English, 1980—.

MEMBER: Modern Language Association, Association for Jewish Studies.

WRITINGS:

The Objects in Your Life (poems), House of Keys/
Atlanta Poetry Collective (Atlanta, GA), 1977.

*The Utopian Moment in Contemporary American Po-
etry* (literary criticism), Bucknell University Press
(Lewisburg, PA), 1988.

*The Ritual of New Creation: Jewish Tradition and
Contemporary Literature* (literary criticism), State
University of New York Press (Albany, NY), 1992.

Restless Messengers (poetry), University of Georgia
Press (Athens, GA), 1992.

Track (poetry), Spuyten Duyvil (New York, NY),
1999.

*Not One of Them in Place: Modern Poetry and Jewish-
American Identity* (literary criticism), State
University of New York Press (Albany, NY), 2001.

Columns: Track, Volume II (poetry), Spuyten Duyvil
(New York, NY), 2002.

WORK IN PROGRESS: Currently at work on *Powers,*
the third and final volume of "Track," a long serial
poem. Researching a book on the contemporary long
poem, to include Robert Duncan, Armand Schwerner,
Ronald Johnson, and Nathaniel Mackey, among others.

SIDELIGHTS: Norman Finkelstein is a poet, literary
critic, and professor of English at Xavier University in
Cincinnati, Ohio. He published his first poetry collection, *The Objects in Your Life,* in 1977. Craig Hill, in
Small Press Review, praised Finkelstein's imagination.
"From the first line to the last this small book of poetry
embodies a large poetic impact."

His next book, *The Utopian Moment in Contemporary
American Poetry,* was of a critical nature. Writing
from a Marxist perspective, Finkelstein analyzes
contemporary American poetry, searching for hints of
the sublime and of "some incorporeal or intangible
state," while remembering his contradictory responsibility to canon formation. Finkelstein seeks a utopian
ingredient beyond the ideological constraints of a
particular age. David Porter wrote in *American Literature,* "Finkelstein usefully groups his poets along a
divide between 'interiorizing and exteriorizing
discourses': the 'Objectivists' Williams, Zukofsky and
Oppen; the New York School of O'Hara and Ashbery,
those 'poets of process, of indeterminacy and open
form' with their 'lingering traces of . . . the Romantic

sublime . . .'; Robert Duncan, Jack Spicer, Helen
Adam, and Ronald Johnson of 'The New Arcady' . . .
and, in the final chapter, William Bronk, a poet track-
ing 'the theme of the self in time,' finding utopian
possibility even in 'historicism's bordello.'"

In *The Ritual of New Creation: Jewish Tradition and
Contemporary Literature,* Finkelstein attempts to
understand the significance of Jewish culture and tradition in postmodern literature, and in an age of fading
traditions. He discusses his encounters with and the
work of contemporary Jewish-American thinkers
Harold Bloom, Gershom Scholem, George Steiner,
Walter Benjamin, poets John Hollander and Allen
Mandelbaum, and the fiction of Cynthia Ozick and
Philip Roth. A *Choice* reviewer said, "The discussion
of these potent cultural figures is as rewarding as it is
demanding, for the author has provided an invaluable
work of intellectual synthesis worthy of its subject."
According to the reviewer, Finkelstein, through these
voices, traces a pattern of discourse, in which the
redemptive past, Jewish heritage, becomes a literary
ideal for some writers, a reference point against
contemporary and future existence.

In an essay-style review of Finkelstein's book,
published in *Jewish Writing and Thought,* Sanford
Pinsker observed, "In less skillful hands, the yoking of
Continental theory to what does, or does not, constitute
Jewish writing might have become so precious,
convoluted, and impenetrable that neither religious
writing nor its secular counterpart would have been
well served; but Finkelstein takes imaginative writing
and intellectual construction with equal seriousness.
Better yet, his own writing is equal to the demanding
task he has set for himself."

Finkelstein's collection of poetry, *Restless Messengers,*
recalls certain themes discussed in *The Ritual of New
Creation:* Symbols of Jewish heritage are used to
construct Finkelstein's own postmodern poetry. Joseph
Donahue, writing in *Multicultural Review,* described
the first poem as centering around a shoemaker
plucked from a story by I. B. Singer, and suggested
that this shoemaker is but one of several guides leading the reader into a building of living memory. In this
structure, Donahue suggested, Finkelstein excavates
what survives today of old European Jewish culture.
Donahue wrote, "But the poetry is also aware of how
readily fact dwindles into fable and how neither fact
nor fable placate the desire for something like truth."

Keith Tuma, reviewing the collection in *Sulfur,* bemoaned what he called the poetry's prosody but commended Finkelstein's meditative wisdom, melancholy yet engaging.

Ohio Review contributor Donald Revell compared Finkelstein's imaginative words to those of Franz Kafka, Schulz, and Isaac Babel. "A poem," Revell suggested, "is first a promise, then a desolation, and finally an uneasy covenant." Revell added, "In *Restless Messengers* . . . Norman Finkelstein endures and understands vision as a continuous diaspora, as a moment of immanence whose force shatters the moment and sends its disparate elements into futurity."

In *Not One of Them in Place: Modern Poetry and Jewish-American Identity,* Finkelstein attempts to understand the connection between the modernist aesthetic of the twentieth century and the aesthetic of twentieth-century Jewish-American poets whose ideas were shaped more significantly by English literature than Hebrew thought. Finkelstein discusses the work of poets Charles Reznikoff, Louis Zukofsky, Allen Grossman, Jerome Rothenberg, Armand Schwerner, Harvey Shapiro, Michael Heller, and Hugh Seidman. He also describes the poets' critical reception at the hands of Harold Bloom and Robert Alter. A *Choice* reviewer said, "Readers will have to determine for themselves whether the American and Jewish literary traditions can be reconciled, but Finkelstein's . . . presentation will greatly enhance the endeavor."

Finkelstein told *CA:* "My poetry has always been something of a scholar's art. Another way to put this is that although much of my poetry, like most lyric poetry, is about the self, what I am moved to declare about that self is mediated by the strong and frequently explicit presence of other texts within the zone of poetic utterance. In short, my poetry is always already a commentary, as much as my criticism is. Regardless of genre, my vehicle of written expression is charged through its contact with other writing; and it is through such contact that I gain access to what I have to say about myself and the world."

BIOGRAPHICAL AND CRITICAL SOURCES:

PERIODICALS

American Literature, March, 1989, David Porter, review of *The Utopian Moment in Contemporary American Poetry,* pp. 146-148.

Choice, September, 1978, review of *The Objects in Your Life,* p. 866; March, 1993, M. Butovsky, review of *The Ritual of New Creation: Jewish Tradition and Contemporary Literature,* p. 1145; December, 2001, M. Butovsky, review of *Not One of Them in Place: Modern Poetry and Jewish-American Identity,* p. 683.

Multicultural Review, April, 1992, Joseph Donahue, review of *Restless Messengers,* p. 74.

Ohio Review, winter, 1992, Donald Revell, review of *Restless Messengers,* pp. 101-118.

Publishers Weekly, December 13, 1991, review of *Restless Messengers,* p. 51.

Salmagundi, summer, 1994, Sanford Pinsker, review of *The Ritual of New Creation,* pp. 225-233.

Small Press Review, January, 1980, Craig Hills, review of *The Objects in Your Life,* p. 13.

Sulfur, spring, 1993, Keith Tuma, "Briefly Tooted," pp. 342-343.

*   *   *

FOX, Laurie (Anne)

PERSONAL: Married D. Patrick Miller (an author).

ADDRESSES: Home—Berkeley, CA. *Agent*—c/o Author Mail, Simon & Schuster Publicity, 1230 Avenue of the Americas, New York, NY 10020.

CAREER: Literary agent in San Diego and San Francisco; writer-in-residence, Los Angeles schools.

WRITINGS:

Sweeping Beauty, Illuminati (Los Angeles, CA), 1985.
Sexy Hieroglyphics: 3,375 Do-It-Yourself Haiku, Chronicle (San Francisco, CA),
My Sister from the Black Lagoon: A Novel of My Life, Simon & Schuster (New York, NY), 1998.

SIDELIGHTS: In her semiautobiographical novel, *My Sister from the Black Lagoon,* Laurie Fox portrays the lives of Lorna and her mentally disturbed sister, Lonnie, as they grow up in California during the 1960s. While Lonnie threw temper tantrums, howled like an animal, and shaved her head, Lorna tried to find her way through high school and college unscathed by this family tragedy. She turned to poetry and acting, which helped her develop independently of her sister.

My Sister from the Black Lagoon caught the attention of critics. Although Susan Hall-Balduf described Fox in the *Detroit Free Press* as a writer of "vivid" prose, she also asserted that Lorna's contention that Lonnie resembled the movie creature from the Black Lagoon and "that she just wants, needs, deserves a life free of analysis and drugs and other people's control," "insults" families in which a member suffers from a mental illness. Myah Evers, writing in *Library Journal*, judged the pace to be too slow in the early chapters, though she found the characters to be "outrageous" yet plausible. *Booklist* reviewer Toni Hyde, however, commented that Fox's clear writing and "conversational tone" make the novel readable. And a *Publishers Weekly* critic praised the novel as a "triumph of storytelling verve, dark humor and unabashed candor."

BIOGRAPHICAL AND CRITICAL SOURCES:

PERIODICALS

Booklist, July, 1998, Toni Hyde, review of *My Sister from the Black Lagoon: A Novel of My Life,* p. 1856.
Detroit Free Press, August 30, 1998, Susan Hall-Balduf, "A Troubled Sister Uses up All the Love Her Family Has to Give," p. 7H.
Library Journal, June 15, 1998, Myah Evers, review of *My Sister from the Black Lagoon,* p. 105.
Los Angeles Times Book Review, April 7, 1985, Jonathan Kirsch, "Paper Weight," p. 9.
Publishers Weekly, June 8, 1998, review of *My Sister from the Black Lagoon,* p. 45.*

*   *   *

FREEBERG, Ernest

PERSONAL: Male; married. *Education:* Emory University, Ph.D. (American history).

ADDRESSES: Office—Humanities Department, Colby-Sawyer College, 100 Main St., New London, NH 03257. *E-mail*—efreeber@colby-sawyer.edu.

CAREER: Colby-Sawyer College, New London, NH, assistant professor of humanities.

MEMBER: American Historical Association, Organization of American Historians.

AWARDS, HONORS: John H. Dunning Prize.

WRITINGS:

The Education of Laura Bridgman: First Deaf and Blind Person to Learn Language, Harvard University Press, 2001.

SIDELIGHTS: In *The Education of Laura Bridgman: First Deaf and Blind Person to Learn Language,* Ernest Freeberg examines the education of seven-year-old Laura Bridgman by educational reformer Samuel Gridley Howe. Howe was director of the first institution for the education of the blind in America.

Howe belonged to a circle of New England reformers which included Horace Mann, Henry Wadsworth Longfellow, and Ralph Waldo Emerson. What bound these men together was their deeply felt belief in the value of doing good works: working for the abolition of slavery, helping the poor, and caring for the infirm. As Natalie Angier wrote in the *New York Times Book Review,* "old Calvinist theories of the inevitability of suffering and of original sin were giving way to theories of the essential beauty and perfectibility of every human being."

In educating young Laura, who had lost her sight and hearing from scarlet fever, Howe hoped to prove that, as Freeberg wrote, "a child's love of learning was not the creation of outside forces of punishment and reward, but was an internal urge so strong that, with the enlightened help of a wide educator, it could overcome the most unfavorable of external circumstances."

Howe also hoped to prove that, if given no guidance about religious matters, Laura would naturally come to believe in a rational and benevolent God, much like the one Howe himself worshipped. But upon his return from a sixteen-month trip to Europe, Howe discovered that Laura had become a Baptist, a choice that bothered him. As Laura grew older, Howe had little to do with her, seemingly losing interest in an experiment that had failed.

"Freeberg places the poignant relationship in the context of their times," Daniel Walker Howe wrote in the *Harvard University Press Online*, "showing the significance that the scientific community attached to Laura's education, as well as why the general public took such a keen interest in her case."

BIOGRAPHICAL AND CRITICAL SOURCES:

BOOKS

Freeberg, Ernest, *The Education of Laura Bridgman: First Deaf and Blind Person to Learn Language,* Harvard University Press (Cambridge, MA), 2001.

PERIODICALS

Library Journal, April 1, 2001, Patricia A. Beaber, review of *The Education of Laura Bridgman: First Deaf and Blind Person to Learn Language,* p. B6.
New Yorker, July 2, 2001, Louis Menad, review of *The Education of Laura Bridgman,* p. 81.
New York Times, May 21, 2001, Richard Bernstein, review of *The Education of Laura Bridgman,* p. B6.
New York Times Book Review, May 27, 2001, Natalie Angier, review of *The Education of Laura Bridgman,* p. 12.
Publishers Weekly, May, 2001, review of *The Education of Laura Bridgman.*

OTHER

Harvard University Press Online, http://www.hup. harvard.edu/ (December, 2, 2001), Daniel Walker Howe, reviews of *The Education of Laura Bridgman.*

Houston Chronicle Online, http://www.chron.com/ (December 2, 2001), Renata Golden, review of *The Education of Laura Bridgman.**

*   *   *

FROST, Shelley 1960-

PERSONAL: Born December 30, 1960, in Redwood City, CA; daughter of Patrick and Nancy (Ruff) Cravalho; married Kevin Frost, July 12, 1986; children: Bret. *Education:* San Jose State University, B.A. *Politics:* Democrat. *Religion:* Roman Catholic.

ADDRESSES: Home—2404 Dekoven, Belmont, CA 94002.

CAREER: Peninsula Humane Society, public relations officer, 1988-89; Pets in Need, Redwood City, CA, manager, 1989-94; Frosting on the Cake Productions, Belmont, CA, director and video producer, 1994—. HEN, judge of essay contest, 1990—; CAPE, founder, member of board of directors, 1993-2000, and volunteer.

MEMBER: Belmont/San Carlos Mothers Club (president, 1995-96).

AWARDS, HONORS: Brady Award, Peninsula Humane Society, 1995; ITA Platinum Video Award, for *Babymugs!*

WRITINGS:

(With Ann Troussieux) *Throw like a Girl: Discovering the Body, Mind, and Spirit of the Athlete in You!,* Beyond Words Publishing (Hillsboro, OR), 2000.

Creator of the videotapes *Babymugs!,* 1994, and *Kidstuff with Dick Clark, Real Girls, Real Sports, Old Friends,* and *Little Patriots.*

WORK IN PROGRESS: Animals in the News, completion expected in 2003.

BIOGRAPHICAL AND CRITICAL SOURCES:

PERIODICALS

Sports Illustrated for Women, January 1, 2001, Meesha Diaz Haddad, review of *Throw like a Girl: Discovering the Body, Mind, and Spirit of the Athlete in You!,* p. 19.

OTHER

Frosting on the Cake Productions Web site, http://www.frostingonthecakevideo.com (July 9, 2002).

G

GAETZ, Dayle Campbell 1947-

PERSONAL: Born August 4, 1947, in Victoria, British Columbia, Canada; daughter of John Laurence (a salesman) and Marjorie Gladys (a bank teller; maiden name, Delf) Campbell; married Gary Clifford Gaetz (in telecommunications), 1969; children: Andrea Ledlin, Brian. *Education:* University of Victoria, B.A. *Hobbies and other interests:* Boating, hiking, visiting museums.

ADDRESSES: Home—1150 North Beach Rd., Salt Spring Island, British Columbia V8K 1B3, Canada. *E-mail*—dgaetz@saltspring.com.

CAREER: British Columbia Tel-Communications, Victoria, British Columbia, Canada, draftsperson; School District No. 64, Ganges, British Columbia, teacher on call; freelance writer and journalist, 1998—.

MEMBER: Writers' Union of Canada, Canadian Society of Children's Authors, Illustrators, and Performers.

AWARDS, HONORS: Our Choice awards, Canadian Children's Book Council, for *A Sea Lion Called Salena, The Golden Rose,* and *Living Freight;* Geoffrey Bilson Award for Historical Fiction for Young People, Red Cedar Award, and Manitoba Young Readers' Choice award shortlists, all for *The Golden Rose;* Geoffrey Bilson Award shortlist, for *Living Freight;* Silver Birch Award nomination, 2002, for *Mystery from History.*

WRITINGS:

JUVENILE FICTION

Grandfather Heron Finds a Friend, Porcépic Books (Victoria, British Columbia, Canada), 1986.
A Sea Lion Called Salena, Pacific Educational Press (Vancouver, British Columbia, Canada), 1994.
The Mystery at Eagle Lake, Michel Quintin (Waterloo, Quebec, Canada), 1995.
Night of the Aliens, Roussan Publishers, Inc. (Montreal, Quebec, Canada), 1995.
Alien Rescue, Roussan Publishers, Inc. (Montreal, Quebec, Canada), 1997.
The Case of the Belly-up Fish, ITP Nelson (Toronto, Ontario, Canada), 1998.
Mystery from History, Orca Book Publishers (Victoria, British Columbia, Canada), 2001.

YOUNG ADULT FICTION

Spoiled Rotten, Maxwell Macmillan (Don Mills, Ontario, Canada), 1991.
Tell Me the Truth, Maxwell Macmillan (Don Mills, Ontario, Canada), 1992.
Heather, Come Back, Maxwell Macmillan (Don Mills, Ontario, Canada), 1993.
The Golden Rose, Pacific Educational Press, Inc. (Vancouver, British Columbia, Canada), 1996.
Living Freight, Roussan Publishers, Inc. (Montreal, Quebec, Canada), 1998.

NONFICTION

The Whale Project, illustrated by Jacqueline Fortin, Quintin Publishers (Waterloo, Quebec, Canada), 1994.

Discover Salt Springs: Funky Facts and Awesome Activities for Kids of All Ages, Moonshell Publishers (Salt Spring Island, British Columbia, Canada), 2000.

WORK IN PROGRESS: Barkerville Villains, a historical mystery; also working on sequel to *The Golden Rose* and *Living Freight,* titled *The Rose and the Ring.*

SIDELIGHTS: Canadian author Dayle Campbell Gaetz told *CA:* "I find it difficult to imagine life without reading. Some of my earliest and best memories involve being read to as a child. My grandmother read in a rather serious fashion but with a clarity that made me aware of every word, the way each word sounded, and how the sound and meaning fitted together to make a story.

"My mother had animated reading style that made it seem as if, at every moment, we were reaching the exciting conclusion, so I needed to listen carefully. At bedtime she read especially quickly, which I once believed meant she could not wait to find out what happened next. I now suspect she was either physically tired or tired of reading the same story for the twenty-first time. Either way, she was in a hurry to reach the end.

"My father often read to us at bedtime. He may have been exhausted after a long day's work, he may have found children's stories mind-numbingly boring, or perhaps he had a diabolical plan to put us to sleep as quickly as possible. I don't know, but I have my suspicions. What he did was insert a yawn at every opportunity with the inevitable result that I fell asleep long before the end of the story. My older sister, Diane, managed to stay awake, though. At least, she claimed she did, even if she always refused to tell me what happened.

"I am grateful to Gram, Mom, and Dad for a precious lifetime gift. The gift of reading. And yes, I thank Diane, too, for encouraging me to use my imagination and provide my own endings to stories. That was my first step toward becoming a writer.

"The day I opened, for the first time, a real, hard-cover book I could read all by myself stands out clearly in my memory. Our first grade reading group gathered on little chairs near the chalkboard, having graduated beyond the thin, soft-covered pre-readers. That feeling of anticipation, of cracking open a brand new book and delving into its mysteries is one that I relive over and over again.

"Although I have always loved to be outside with my friends, riding bikes, climbing trees, building forts and playing on the beach, I have always had a book to return to at the end of the day. As I progressed through school, I also progressed through books, one genre at a time from animal stories to adventure, to mystery, to biography.

"In spite of being a grandmother myself now, my habits have not changed all that much even if I no longer build forts on a regular basis. I still enjoy most of those other pastimes, including, and especially, a good book just waiting to be picked up and enjoyed."

BIOGRAPHICAL AND CRITICAL SOURCES:

PERIODICALS

Books in Canada, December, 1994, Pat Barclay, review of *A Sea Lion Called Salena,* p. 58.
Canadian Children's Literature, winter, 1999, Jason Nolan, review of *The Golden Rose,* p. 79.
Quill & Quire, June, 1994, Linda Granfield, review of *A Sea Lion Called Salena,* p. 50.
Resource Links, October, 2001, Jill McClay, review of *Mystery from History,* p. 13.
School Library Journal, February, 2002, Ann W. Moore, review of *Mystery from History,* p. 130.*

*   *   *

GECÉ
See GIMÉNEZ CABALLERO, Ernesto

*   *   *

GIBRAN, Daniel K. 1945-

PERSONAL: Born November 21, 1945, in Hague, Guyana; father a farmer and mother a homemaker; married Joan M. Harrison (an economist), November 12, 1976; children: Kerstin M., Nicole K. *Ethnicity:* "East Indian." *Education:* University of Kent at Canterbury, M.A. (international relations), 1985; University of Aberdeen, Ph.D., 1990. *Politics:* Democrat; "Liberal with a conservative touch." *Religion:* Seventh-Day Adventist.

ADDRESSES: Home—519 Bluff View Dr., Pegram, TN 37143. *Office*—Tennessee State University, 3500 John Merritt Blvd., Nashville, TN 37209. *E-mail*—dgibran@tnstate.edu.

CAREER: Planning Institute of Jamaica, Kingston, senior political economist, 1987-90; Shaw University, Raleigh, NC, began as assistant professor, became associate professor, 1991-96; Tennessee State University, Nashville, professor, 1996—. Raleigh Seventh-Day Adventist Church, religious liberty leader, 1992-95; Nashville First Seventh-Day Adventist Church, religious liberty leader, 1998-2000.

WRITINGS:

The Exclusion of Black Soldiers from the Medal of Honor, McFarland & Co. (Jefferson, NC), 1997.
The Falklands War: Britain versus the Past in the South Atlantic, McFarland & Co. (Jefferson, NC), 1998.
Leadership and Courage: A Brief History of the All-Black 92nd Infantry Division in Italy during WWII, McFarland & Co. (Jefferson, NC), 2001.

WORK IN PROGRESS: "A major work on the political and social history of Guyana from 1945 to 2000."

SIDELIGHTS: Daniel K. Gibran told *CA:* "I have developed an interest in words from a very early age, and understand their power and utility. Writing does not come to me that easily primarily because I am a perfectionist. But once I get started, the ideas and words flow quite easily."

*   *   *

GILES, Kris
    See NIELSEN, Helen Berniece

*   *   *

GILKES, Cheryl Townsend 1947-

PERSONAL: Born November 2, 1947, in Boston, MA; daughter of Murray Luke, Jr. (a civil servant) and Evelyn (a homemaker; maiden name, Reid) Townsend; married Carlton I. Gilkes April 20, 1968 (divorced

March, 1971). *Ethnicity:* "African American." *Education:* Northeastern University, B.A., 1970, M.A., 1973, Ph.D., 1979; attended Boston University 1982-86. *Politics:* "Liberationist." *Hobbies and other interests:* Music, fiction.

ADDRESSES: Office—Department of Sociology, Colby College, Waterville, ME 04901-8847; fax: 207-872-3752.

CAREER: Boston University, Boston, MA, assistant professor of sociology, 1978-87; Colby College, Waterville, ME, professor of African-American studies and sociology, 1987—. Ordained Baptist minister; Union Baptist Church, Cambridge, MA, assistant pastor for special projects, 1982—; United Baptist Convention of Massachusetts, Rhode Island, and New Hampshire, parliamentarian and member of board of directors.

MEMBER: American Sociological Association, American Academy of Religion, National Association for the Advancement of Colored People, Delta Sigma Theta (golden life member).

WRITINGS:

"If It Wasn't for the Women . . .": Black Women's Experience and Womanist Culture in Church and Community, Orbis Books (Maryknoll, NY), 2001.

Contributor to books, including *Studying Congregations: A New Handbook,* edited by Nancy T. Ammerman, Jackson W. Carroll, and others, Abingdon Press (Nashville, TN), 1995; *W. E. B. Du Bois on Race and Culture: Philosophy, Politics, and Poetics,* Routledge (New York, NY), 1996; *One Nation under God? Religion in America,* edited by Marjorie Garber and Rebecca Walkowitz, Routledge, 1999; *The Courage to Hope,* edited by Quinton H. Dixie and Cornel West, Beacon Press (Boston, MA), 1999; and *African Americans and the Bible,* edited by Vincent L. Wimbush, Continuum (New York, NY), 2000. Contributor of articles, sermons, and reviews to periodicals, including *Annals of the American Academy of Political and Social Science, Trotter Review, Social Compass, Journal of the American Academy of Religion, Voices from the Third World, Journal of Religious Thought, Journal of Feminist Studies in Religion, Signs, Psychology of Women Quarterly,* and *Journal of Social Issues.*

WORK IN PROGRESS: Lots of Small Pieces: African-American Women and Their Community Work; That Blessed Book: The Bible and the African-American Cultural Imagination.

*   *   *

GIMÉNEZ CABALLERO, Ernesto 1899-1988
(Gecé)

PERSONAL: Born 1899, in Madrid, Spain; died 1988.

CAREER: Essayist, journalist, and artist. Instituto Cardenal Cisneros, Madrid, Spain, instructor; ambassador to Paraguay. *La Gaceta Literaria*, founder and editor, 1927-32.

WRITINGS:

Notas marruecas de un soldado, F. Beltrán (Madrid, Spain), 1923, reprinted, Planeta (Barcelona, Spain), 1983.

Los toros, las castañuelas y la Virgen, Caro Raggio (Madrid, Spain), 1927.

Carteles, Espasa-Calpe (Madrid, Spain), 1927.

Hércules jugando a los dados, La Nave (Madrid, Spain), 1928, reprinted, Libros del Innombrable (Zaragoza, Spain), 2000.

Yo, inspector de alcantarillas: epiplasmas, Biblioteca Nueva (Madrid, Spain), 1928.

Julepe de menta, Ciudad Lineal (Madrid, Spain), 1929.

Circuito imperial, Gaceta Literaria (Madrid, Spain), 1929.

Genio de España: exaltaciones a una resurrección nacional y del mundo, Gaceta Literaria (Madrid, Spain), 1932, reprinted, Planeta (Barcelona, Spain), 1983.

Manuel Azaña: profecías españolas, Gaceta Literaria (Madrid, Spain), 1932, reprinted, Turner (Madrid, Spain), 1975.

La nueva catolicidad: teoría general sobre el fascismo en Europa, en España, Gaceta Literaria (Madrid, Spain), 1933.

El Belén de Salzillo en Murcia (origen de los nacimientos en España), Gaceta Literaria (Madrid, Spain), 1934.

Arte y estado, 1935.

Exaltaciones sobre Madrid, Jerarquia (Madrid, Spain), 1937.

Conquista el Estado!, 1937, reprinted, J. M. Garrido (Burgos, Spain), 1998.

Espana y Franco, Los Combatientes (Guipúzcoa, Spain), 1938.

Roma madre, Jerarquia (Madrid, Spain), 1939.

El vidente, Talleres Tipográficos de Fe (Sevilla, Spain), 1939.

Camisa azul y Boina colorada, Talleres Tipográficos de Fe (Sevilla, Spain), 1939.

Los secretos de la Falange, Yunque (Barcelona, Spain), 1939.

Triunfo del 2 de mayo, E. Giménez (Madrid, Spain), 1939.

Hay Pirineos!, Nacional (Barcelona, Spain), 1939.

La Legión C. T. V., Los Combatientes (Madrid, Spain), 1939.

(Editor) Juan del Encina, *Égloga de Plácida y Victoriano, prededida de otras tres églogas introductorias*, Ebro (Zaragoza, Spain), 1940.

Lengua y literatura de España y su imperio, 1940.

Imperialismos en lucha mundial, Ibero-Itálica (Madrid, Spain), 1940.

La infantería española, Vicesecretaria de Educación Popular (Madrid, Spain), 1941.

Notas de un viaje con Franco a Cataluña, 1942.

Amor a Cataluña, Ruta (Madrid, Spain), 1942.

España nuestra; el libro de las juventudes españolas, Vicesecretaria de Educación Popular (Madrid, Spain), 1943.

La matanza de Katyn: visión sobre Rusia, E. Giménez (Madrid, Spain), 1943.

Despierta Inglaterra! Mensaje a Lord Holland, Toledo (Madrid, Spain), 1943.

El cine y la cultura humana, 1944.

Amor a Andalucía, Nacional (Madrid, Spain), 1944.

Madrid nuestro, Vicesecretaria de Educación Popular (Madrid, Spain), 1944.

Afirmaciones sobre Asturias, Encyclopedia de la Residencia Provincial (Oviedo, Spain), 1945.

Cine y político, Instituto de Estudios Políticos (Madrid, Spain), 1945.

Don Ernesto; o, El porcurador del pueblo en las cortes españolas, Ediciones Españolas (Madrid, Spain), 1947.

Dos americanos en Toledo, E. Giménez (Madrid, Spain), 1947.

Amor a Galicia, progenitora de Cervantes, Nacional (Madrid, Spain), 1947.

Amor a Méjico (a través de su cine), 1948.

Amor a Argentina; o, El genio de España en América, Nacional (Madrid, Spain), 1948.

Amor a Portugal, Cultura Hispánica (Madrid, Spain), 1949.

La Europa de Estrasburgo; visión española del problema europeo, Instituto de Estudios Políticos (Madrid, Spain), 1950.

Cervantes, E. Giménez (Madrid, Spain), 1951.

Norteamérica sonríe a España, 1952.

Palabras sobre Madrid, Instituto de Estudios Madrileños (Madrid, Spain), 1952.

San Isidro y Madrid; conferencia, 1953.

El genio antieconómico de España, 1954.

Curriculum vitae, 1957.

Maravillosa, Bolivia (clave de América), Cultura Hispánica (Madrid, Spain), 1957.

Revelación del Paraguay, Espasa-Calpe (Madrid, Spain), 1958.

Bahia de todos os santos e de todos os demônios, Publicações da Univerisdade da Bahia (Salvador, Brazil), 1958.

El dinero y España, A. Aguado (Madrid, Spain), 1964.

Genio hispánico y mestizaje, Nacional (Madrid, Spain), 1965.

Las mujeres de América, Nacional (Madrid, Spain), 1971.

Rizal, Publicaciones Españolas (Madrid, Spain), 1971.

Asunción, capital de América, Cultura Hispañica (Madrid, Spain), 1971.

Junto la tumba de Larra, 1971.

Cabra, la cordobesa: balcón poético de España, Publicaciones Españolas (Madrid, Spain), 1973.

El procurador del pueblo y su cronicón de España: secretos, revelaciones, disparos, Umbral (Madrid, Spain), 1975.

Cartageneras, Publicaciones Españolas (Madrid, Spain), 1975.

Don Quijote ante el mundo (y ante mí), Inter American University Press (San Juan, Puerto Rico), 1979.

Memorias de un dictador, Planeta (Barcelona, Spain), 1979.

Julepe de menta y otros aperitivos, Planeta (Barcelona, Spain), 1981.

Exaltación del matrimonio, 1936, Fundación Universitaria Española (Madrid, Spain), c. 1982.

Retratos españoles: bastante parecidos, Planeta (Barcelona, Spain), 1985.

E. Giménez Caballero, Editorial del Hombre (Barcelona, Spain), 1988.

Judios de patria España (silent film screenplay), 1922, published as *Jews of the Spanish Homeland,* Fil-

moteca Española/National Center for Jewish Film (Waltham, MA), 1994.

Visitas literarias de España, 1925-1928, Pre-Textos (Valencia, Spain), 1995.

Also author of *Paraguay y la hispanidad, La Falange, Hecha hombre,* and *Ante la tumba del catalanismo.* Several works originally published under pseudonym Gecé. Author's works have been translated into French and Portuguese.

SIDELIGHTS: Considered a representative prose writer of the generation coming of age after World War I, Ernesto Giménez Caballero was an essayist and journalist who taught in Madrid, Spain. A staunch Falangist who was loyal to the cause embraced by fascist leader Francisco Franco, Giménez Caballero was for a time ambassador to Paraguay. Maria T. Pao, writing in *Revista Canadiense de Estudios Hispanicos,* called the author "a central figure of avant-garde circles in Madrid," and added that throughout his career Giménez Caballero "simply could not remain still. His energy and eclecticism as a creative writer, literary critic, graphic artist, journal editor, movie and modern art enthusiast, and documentary film maker were legend among his peers."

According to Robert Havard, writing in *Modern Language Review,* Giménez Caballero's works are characterized by "the extremes of the spiritual-materialist [postwar] dilemma." Giménez Caballero is notable as author of "one of the most risqué works of the period and founder-editor of the corrosive avant-garde journal, *La Gaceta Literaria.*" The "risqué" work alluded to is the story collection *Yo, inspector de alcantarillas.* According to Havard, the stories in this collection "owe much to Freudian theory . . . with its metaphorical suggestion of investigating the lower recesses of the mind where unseemly matter is deposited. The narrator-inspector, who goes in search of his own *yo,* takes us down to subterranean levels where only the more daring of contemporary writers and artists . . . have dared to tread."

With *Carteles,* a collection of "graphic representations of writers and their works," Giménez Caballero "began the project of transforming the pictorial into text," according to Maria T. Pao in *Letras Peninsulares.* Pao described *Yo, inspector de alcantarillas* as "a book containing short narratives influenced by Freudian psychoanalysis followed by a section of 'Fichas textuales' in prose poetry and another of 'Composicion,' a series of brief texts based on word association. . . . The text replicates many aspects of [the concept of] 'Nochebuena,' including its first person narrator, its occurrence on Christmas Eve, food imagery, the interaction between the protagonist and servants, [and] a dichotomy between the narrator's internal and external self."

Sultana Wahnón, writing in *Fascism and Theatre,* postulated that "fascist aesthetics . . . found its fullest expression in Ernesto Giménez Caballero's *Arte y estado.*" As Wahnón stated, "in his system of fascist aesthetics, Ernesto Giménez Caballero theorized on all the arts, from architecture to theatre and music, in a half-speculative, half-political manner. *Arte y estado* is the text containing this system." Wahnón concluded, "there is one key that dominates all the aesthetic choices described in the book, and that is the idea of 'norm.'"

Among Giménez Caballero's many works is *Don Quijote, ante el mundo (y ante mi),* an historical bibliography that describes the many translations of Miguel Cervantes's now-classic novel.

BIOGRAPHICAL AND CRITICAL SOURCES:

BOOKS

Berghaus, Gunther, *Fascism and Theatre: Comparative Studies on the Aesthetics and Politics of Performance in Europe, 1925-1945,* Berghahn Books (Providence, RI), 1996.
Smith, Horatio, editor, *Columbia Dictionary of Modern European Literature,* Columbia University Press (New York, NY), 1947.
Ward, Philip, editor, *The Oxford Companion to Spanish Literature,* Oxford University Press (Oxford, England), 1978.

PERIODICALS

American Libraries, July-August, 1980, review of *Don Quijote ante el mundo (y ante mí),* p. 453.
Letras Peninsulares, fall-winter, 1997-98, Maria T. Pao, "Coming to His Senses: Physical Gratification in 'La Nochebuena de 1836' and Two Texts of the Spanish Avant-Garde," pp. 415-436.

Modern Language Review, October, 1998, Robert Havard, "Rafael Alberti, Maruja Mallo, and Giménez Caballero: Materialist Imagery in *Sermones y moradas* and the Issue of Surrealism," pp. 1007-1020.
Revista Canadiense de Estudios Hispánicos, Maria T. Pao, "Still(ed) Life: The Ekphrastic Prose Poems of Ernesto Giménez Caballero," pp. 469-492.
Revista de Filologia Hispanica, Dionisio Viscarri, "Literatura Prefascista y *La guerra de Marruecos,*" pp. 139-157.*

* * *

GOLD, Glen David 1964-

PERSONAL: Born 1964, in Hollywood, CA; married Alice Sebold (a writer), 2001. *Education:* University of California, Irvine, M.F.A., 1998.

ADDRESSES: Home—Long Beach, CA. *Agent*—c/o Author Mail, Hyperion Books, 77 West 66th St., New York, NY 10023.

CAREER: Novelist, screenwriter.

WRITINGS:

Carter Beats the Devil, Hyperion Books (New York, NY), 2001.

SIDELIGHTS: Glen David Gold is a journalist and screenwriter whose first published novel, *Carter Beats the Devil,* received excellent reviews. Gold's protagonist is none other than Charles Carter, a.k.a. Carter the Great, an illusionist whose skill rivaled that of Henry Houdini's. The story begins in 1923, a time when the United States was obsessed with magic acts. In an interview with *Bookreporter.com,* Gold explained, "Magic was especially potent from 1890 to 1920, which was also the rise of the assembly line and the explosion of technology in everyday life. I don't think that's a coincidence. The current take on Houdini is that he railed against the increasing discontent and sense of confinement that civilization bred. Magicians certainly blow the doors off reality, and that's still great fun to see. . . . As a society, we really wanted science to improve our lives, to dazzle us. We really didn't know what was or wasn't possible. But it also made people insecure and what they really wanted, at the end of the day, was a marvel that science couldn't explain."

Carter Beats the Devil begins with Carter at the top of his career and as the headliner for a San Francisco theater. In the audience is President Warren G. Harding, who is trying to imcrease his public support with his "Voyage of Understanding" tour. The president agrees to participate in the grand finale, complete with scimitars, a card table, a devil in black tights, and a lion named Baby. Just before the act is to begin, Harding confides something to Carter, and then he is diced up with swords and eaten by Baby. He reappears on-stage moments later, smiling and well. Of course, it is only magic, but when the President dies hours later, Secret Service agent Jack Griffith is sure Carter is the guilty party. Others thinks so too, including some political cronies who fear Harding was about to blow the whistle on his own scandal-ridden administration.

The plot is complex, historical personalities make appearances, and things are not what they seem. "Here is a book—a first novel no less—to blow you away. It seeks to stun and amaze and deceive and, always, to entertain, and it seldom misses a trick in 600 pulsating pages," wrote Peter Preston in *Guardian*. Mark Rozzo in the *Los Angeles Times* acknowledged that in *Carter Beasts the Devil*"Gold creates a foreboding, dreamlike aura of Americana."

To keep things rolling along, Gold has, he explains in the novel's epilogue, "subjected history to vanishes, immolations and other acts of misdirection." Mike Cavency, a renowned magician, wrote in his own *Carter the Great*, wrote: "I've been a practicing magician for over forty years, and Glen Gold has completely baffled me. *Carter Beats the Devil* is layered with accurate descriptions of strange-looking apparatuses, the distinct language used by magicians, and eccentric personalities that existed only during the heyday of vaudeville. It's a secret world that, by necessity, was closed to outsiders, and yet Gold's relentless research has allowed him to slowly untangle his tale of murder and intrigue in an environment that so accurately re-creates the Golden Age of Magic that one sometimes forgets that this story is simply a product of Glen Gold's devious mind."

BIOGRAPHICAL AND CRITICAL SOURCES:

BOOKS

Caveney, Mike, *Carter the Great*, Magic Words (Pasadena, CA), 1995.
Gold, Glen David, *Carter Beats the Devil*, Hyperion Books (New York, NY), 2001.

PERIODICALS

Atlanta Constitution, October 21, 2001, Mark Luce, review of *Carter Beats the Devil*, p. D5.
Booklist, July, 2001, Gavin Quinn, review of *Carter Beats the Devil*, p. 1948.
Christian Science Monitor, September 20, 2001, Ron Charles, review of *Carter Beats the Devil*, p. 16.
Daily Telegraph (London, England), August 4, 2001, Helen Brown, review of *Carter Beats the Devil*, p. 96.
Fortune, October 15, 2001, Erik Torkella, review of *Carter Beats the Devil*, p. 280.
Guardian (London, England), September 29, 2001, review of *Carter Beats the Devil*, p. 13.
Los Angeles Times, October 7, 2001, Mark Rozzo, review of *Carter Beats the Devil*, p. 10.
New York Times Book Review, October 30, 2001, Stephanie Zacharek, review of *Carter Beats the Devil*, p. 35.
New York Times, August 27, 2001, Janet Maslin, review of *Carter Beats the Devil*, p. PE6.
New Yorker, September 24, 2001, Ben Greenman, review of *Carter Beats the Devil*, p. 94.
People, October 15, 2001, Julie K.L. Dam, review of *Carter Beats the Devil*, p. 55.
Publishers Weekly, November 22, 2001, review *of Carter Beats the Devil*.
Sunday Telegraph (London, England), November 18, 2001, Julius Flynn, review of *Carter Beats the Devil*.
Sunday Times (London, England), October 21, 2001, Adam Lively, review of *Carter Beats the Devil*, p. D5.
Times, (London), September 5, 2001, James Eve, review of *Carter Beats the Devil*, p. 16; August 25, 2001, Amanda Craig, review of *Carter Beats the Devil*, p. 20.
Washington Post, September 2, 2001, Dennis Drabelle, review of *Carter Beats the Devil*, p. T05.

OTHER

Barnes & Noble Web site, http://www.barnesandnoble. com/ (February 5, 2002), " Glen David Gold."

BookReporter, http://www.bookreporter.com/ (December 2, 2001), Bob Ruggiero, interview with Glen David Gold.

Hyperion Books Web site, http://www.hyperionbooks. com/ (December 2, 2001), review of *Carter Beats the Devil.*

January Magazine, http://www.januarymagazine.com/ (December 2, 2001), Karen G. Anderson, review of *Carter Beats the Devil.*

Stuff, http://www.stuff.co.nz/ (December 2, 2001), Rosa Lay, review of *Carter Beats the Devil.**

*   *   *

GORDON, Thomas 1918-2002

OBITUARY NOTICE—See index for *CA* sketch: Born March 11, 1918, in Paris, IL; died August 26, 2002, in Los Angeles, CA. Psychologist, educator, and author. Gordon was a leading clinical psychologist and founder of Gordon Training International who gained acclaim for his work in conflict resolution. Before serving in the U.S. Army Air Force during World War II, he earned his bachelor's degree from DePauw University in 1939 and his master's degree from Ohio State in 1941. After leaving the military as a captain, he studied at the University of Chicago, where he graduated with a Ph.D. in 1949. Gordon taught at the University of Chicago for five years before joining Edward Glaser & Associates in California as a consultant in 1954. It was there that he developed his theories about conflict resolution. Going into private practice as a psychologist in 1958, he began counseling others on conflict resolution, and in 1968 he founded the Solana Beach, California-based Effectiveness Training, Inc., which later became Gordon Training International. Gordon's ideas about conflict resolution are expressed in his best-selling book *Parent Effectiveness Training: The No-Lose Way to Raise Responsible Children* (1970). He later applied the same principles used in parent-child relationships to educators in *T.E. T.: Teacher Effectiveness Training* (1974), businessmen in *Leader Effectiveness Training, L.E.T.: The No-Lose Way to Release the Productive Potential of People* (1983), salesmen in *Sales Effectiveness Training: The*

Breakthrough Method to Become Partners with Your Customers (1993; written with Carl D. Zaiss), and doctors in *Making the Patient Your Partner: Communication Skills for Doctors and Other Caregivers* (1995). For his groundbreaking work, Gordon was nominated in 1997, 1998, and 1999 for the Nobel Peace Prize, and he also received lifetime achievement awards from the American Psychological Foundation and the California Psychological Association.

OBITUARIES AND OTHER SOURCES:

BOOKS

Writers Directory, 16th edition, St. James Press (Detroit, MI), 2001.

PERIODICALS

Los Angeles Times, September 1, 2002, p. B18.
New York Times, September 6, 2002, p. A19.
Washington Post, September 2, 2002, p. B4.

*   *   *

GOULD, Lois 1932(?)-2002
(Lois Benjamin)

OBITUARY NOTICE—See index for *CA* sketch: Born c. 1932; died of cancer May 29, 2002, in New York, NY. Novelist. Gould gained fame for penning fiction that frankly portrays the emotional lives of women and addresses sexual issues. A graduate of Wellesley College, where she earned a bachelor's degree, she then embarked on a journalism career, working for such periodicals as the *New York Times* and the *Long Island Star Journal.* Her early publications, written under the name Lois Benjamin, included the nonfiction books *Sensible Childbirth: The Case against Natural Childbirth* (1962; written with Waldo L. Fielding) and *So You Want to Be a Working Mother!* (1966). After her first husband, novelist Philip Benjamin, died, she discovered that he had been having affairs with some of their friends. Gould, who later married psychiatrist Robert Gould, drew on her emotional distress from this experience tor write the novel *Such Good Friends* (1970), which involves a similar situation. The novel created a stir due to its frank portrayal of a woman's emotions and sexual desires, and it was adapted as a 1971 film directed by Otto Preminger. After her fiction debut, Gould continued to write novels involving women characters and difficult personal relationships, among them *Necessary Objects* (1972), *A Sea-Change* (1976), and *No Brakes* (1997). She also wrote about her relationship with her emotionally distant mother in *Mommy Dressing: A Love Story, after a Fashion* (1998). Although labeled by some as a feminist writer, Gould always maintained that she was simply trying to portray people's emotions in a truthful way. In addition to her books, she was a former editor at *McCall's,* the founder and editor of *Insider's Newsletter* (now *Look* magazine), and author of the "Hers" column in the *New York Times.*

OBITUARIES AND OTHER SOURCES:

BOOKS

American Women Writers: A Critical Reference Guide from Colonial Times to the Present, second edition, St. James Press (Detroit, MI), 2000.

PERIODICALS

Los Angeles Times, June 4, 2002, p. B11.
New York Times, May 29, 2002, p. C14.
Washington Post, June 2, 2002, p. C8.

*   *   *

GREATBATCH, Wilson 1919-

PERSONAL: Born September 6, 1919, in Buffalo, NY; son of Walter Plant (a building contractor) and Charlotte Margaret (Recktenwalt) Greatbatch; married Eleanor Wright, January 1, 1945; children: Warren Dee, John Leslie, Kenneth Alan, Anne Katherine. *Education:* Cornell University, B.E.E., 1950; University of Buffalo (New York), M.E.E., 1957. *Politics:* Republican. *Religion:* Presbyterian. *Hobbies and other interests:* Gardening.

ADDRESSES: Home—5935 Davison Rd., Akron, NY 14001. *Office*—Greatbatch Enterprises, Inc., 10510 Main St., Clarence, NY 14031. *Agent*—c/o Publicity Director, Prometheus Books, 59 John Glenn Dr., Amherst, NY 14228-2197.

CAREER: Engineer and inventor. Worked various jobs related to radio and electrical engineering, 1940s-50s; University of Buffalo, Buffalo, NY, assistant professor of electrical engineering, 1952-57; adjunct professor the University of Buffalo and Cornell University. Chronic Disease Research Institute, circuit designer, c. 1956. Wilson Greatbatch Ltd., Clarence, NY, founder, 1970—; Greatbatch Gen-Aid Ltd., founder, president, and research director. Adviser to Biophan Techologies, Rochester, NY; holder of more than 240 patents. *Military service:* U.S. Navy, 1940-45, dive bomber, rear gunner, and teacher in Navy radar school.

AWARDS, HONORS: National Inventors Hall of Fame inductee, Akron, OH, 1986; National Medal of Technology from President George Bush; named Western New York's Inventor of the Year, 1994; Lemelson-MIT Lifetime Achievement Award, 1996; cowinner, Fritz J. and Dolores H. Russ Prize, National Academy of Engineering, 2001; Gaudete Medal, St. Bonaventure University, 2001; honorary degrees from four universities.

WRITINGS:

The Making of the Pacemaker; Celebrating a Lifesaving Invention, Prometheus Press (Amherst, NY), 1999.

SIDELIGHTS: The critical moment in Wilson Greatbatch's invention of the pacemaker, according to an article in the *Technology Review,* came when the electrical engineer was in his lab at the University of Buffalo, New York, in 1956, using some early silicon transistors to build a circuit to help the nearby Chronic Disease Research Institute record fast heart sounds. When Greatbatch accidentally put the wrong resistor into the circuit, the sounds he heard were those of a normally beating heart. He had already been aware of the difficulty of a problem known as "heart block," which occurs when the heart's natural electrical impulses do not travel properly through tissue. As he recounts in his 1999 book *The Making of the Pacemaker: Celebrating a Life-saving Invention,* Greatbatch shared his discovery with William Chardack, chief of surgery at the Buffalo Veterans Administration Hospital, and on May 7, 1958, after working together for two years, the two men successfully implanted the first pacemaker model into a dog. The device shorted out after only four hours, however, because the dog's bodily fluids leaked past the electrical tape sealing the device.

Always one to learn from experience, Greatbatch recast the pacemaker in epoxy blocks. Within a year, the prototypes were lasting up to four months. Taber Instrument, Greatbatch's employer at the time, was hesitant to try it on humans, however, owing to the potential legal liability. Greatbatch left Taber and, with $2,000 of his own money, set out on his own to make fifty pacemakers in his barn workshop. Chardack then implanted the first of ten pacemakers in April, 1960. Minneapolis-based Medtronic licensed the pacemaker that same year and remains the top manufacturer of cardiac pacemakers.

As Greatbatch sought ways to extend the life of his pacemaker, he developed a corrosion-free lithium battery. The device went from working just two years to functioning up to ten years. In 1960 he established his own company, Greatbatch Enterprises, in Clarence, New York, which remains the world's largest manufacturer of implantable lithium batteries.

Greatbatch's first job after World War II was laying phone lines for the New York Telephone Company; in addition he was also a new husband. He decided to go to Cornell's School of Electrical Engineering but encountered difficulties in registering; Greatbatch solved this problem by using the ingenuity that would characterize his long career. "They wouldn't admit me at Cornell," he recalled. "There was room in the school, but no housing for nonresident students. So I went out to Danby, six miles south of Ithaca, and bought a farm. Then I came back and presented myself as a 'resident student.' I got in."

In an interview with Tracey Drury for *Business First of Buffalo,* Greatbatch said: "I don't get interested until people tell me things are impossible." His accident at the University of Buffalo may have led him directly to the invention of the pacemaker, but the idea for the device, Greatbatch told Drury, came to him much earlier. "I found out about the disease and knew I could fix it in 1951. I couldn't do anything for the pacemaker; it was before transistors. All we had were vacuum tubes and storage batteries, and it would have looked funny trying to sew a storage battery up inside of somebody," he noted.

Inventing the pacemaker is not the only story Greatbatch has to tell. He has been working since the late 1980s on a cure for AIDS and received an award in 1996 for a test-tube method he developed in the course of that research. Greatbatch's work with AIDS had stalled at the test tube stage by 2002. As he told Drury, "We've managed to block the replication . . . in test tubes, but we never got up to the animal level. We kept running into problems, and running out of money."

His more recent efforts to create nuclear fusion with a type of helium found only on the moon had him predicting that the trip to Mars, which now takes eight months with chemical rocket engines, will someday be made in a weekend using new fuels and nuclear fusion rockets.

As a proud member of in the Inventors Hall of Fame, Greatbatch attends the induction ceremony every year—on one condition. Louise Forsch, a member of the induction team in Akron, Ohio, told Drury that Greatbatch will attend only "if he can come to the schools and visit children. Every year we line up five schools, and he talks to the kids and tries to inspire them to get into scientific careers and tries to let them know it's not just for nerds."

Catherine Saint Louis interviewed Greatbatch for the *New York Times Magazine* column "What They Were Thinking," and he told her: "People often ask me what's been the most important accomplishment in my life. I have 240 patents now. But I think it's that I've had the opportunity to speak to over a thousand fourth-graders about the pacemaker. In 1960 I invented the implantable pacemaker. The problem with it was that it had a metal wire, so people who had a pacemaker couldn't get MRIs. This year we replaced the wire with a glass fiber. I tell them how it works, draw a picture, get down to the technical. When you hear how a pacemaker works for the first time, it sounds like a dream. But it's not. I think it's important to get them thinking."

In an interview with Jane Kwiatkowski for the *Buffalo News,* Greatbatch conveyed some predictions for the future: there will be clean, unlimited electrical power through nuclear fusion with helium-3; there will be entire implantable medical systems, not simply artificial hearts; and bioengineering contributions in molecular biology and its research into the structure of the human genome will lead to the development of drugs that are "rationally designed rather than from testing millions of jungle plants."

BIOGRAPHICAL AND CRITICAL SOURCES:

PERIODICALS

Buffalo News, April 25, 1999, Jane Kwiatkowski, "From a Scientist and Inventor, a New World of Possibilities," p. F2; January 14, 2001, Louise Continelli, "Father of Inventions Wilson Greatbatch to Be Honored for Greatest Contribution," p. B2; March 5, 2001, "Bona Names Four to Receive Gaudete Honor," p. B3; November 24, 2001, David Robinson, "Greatbatch Helps Develop New Type of Pacemaker," p. E1.

Business First of Buffalo, February 6, 1995, David Debo, "Greatbatch Takes Home Inventor Honors for Drug," p. 4; September 8, 1997, Tracey Drury, "Inventor Pursues the Unknown," p. 1.

Choice, June, 2001, I. Richman, review of *The Making of the Pacemaker: Celebrating a Life-saving Invention,* p. 1823.

New York Times, December 9, 2001, Catherine Saint Louis, "What They Were Thinking," p. 34.

Technology Review, September, 2001, "Setting the Pace: Wilson Greatbatch's Implantable Pacemakers," p. 96.

Washington Times, Kristina Stefanova, "Russ Prize Rewards Pacemaker's Creators," p. 10.

OTHER

Smithsonian Institution, Lemelson Center Invention Features, http://www.si.edu/.lemelson(March, 2002), John Adams, "Making Hearts Beat," February 5, 1999.

Wilson Greatbatch Technologies, Inc. Web site, http://www.greatbatch.com(March, 2002).

*   *   *

GRIFFITH, Thomas 1915-2002

OBITUARY NOTICE—See index for *CA* sketch: Born December 30, 1915, in Tacoma, WA; died from head injuries resulting from a fall March 16, 2002, in New York, NY. Journalist, editor, and author. Griffith was a former senior staff editor for *Time* magazine. Enduring a tough childhood, he was abandoned by his father and sent to a boarding school; nevertheless he went on to attend high school and college, graduating from the University of Washington in Seattle in 1936 and attending Harvard University from 1942 to 1943. Griffith started his journalism career as a crime reporter for the *Seattle Times,* where he worked from 1936 to 1942. He began his career at *Time* as a contributing editor before serving in a variety of other editorial positions at the magazine, becoming senior staff editor in 1963. Considered liberal in his politics by his fellow editors at the predominately conservative periodical, Griffith always maintained that his only goal was to publish a balanced magazine. During his stint at *Time* he oversaw such stories as Senator Joseph McCarthy's hunt for communists and the 1960 presidential elections and through his coverage of such events became respected for his evenhanded management. Griffith left *Time* in 1967 to work as the editor of *Life,* where he remained until 1972 when that magazine ceased to be a weekly. In addition to his editorial work, Griffith contributed articles to such publications as the *Atlantic* and *Fortune,* and he was the author of the books *The Waist-high Culture, How True* and *Harry and Teddy: The Turbulent Friendship of Press Lord Henry R. Luce and His Favorite Reporter, Theodore H. White.*

OBITUARIES AND OTHER SOURCES:

BOOKS

Who's Who in the Media and Communications, Marquis (Providence, NJ), 1997.

PERIODICALS

Los Angeles Times, March 19, 2002, p. B11.
New York Times, March 18, 2002, p. A25.
Washington Post, March 19, 2002, p. B7.

H

HACKLER, George 1948-

PERSONAL: Born June 24, 1948, in Stillwater, OK; son of Loyd and Norma Hackler; married Michelle Anne Perra (marriage ended); married Ellen Catherine Walsh November 26, 1982; children: (first marriage) Jason Loyd (deceased); (second marriage) two stepdaughters. *Education:* University of Texas—Austin, B.S., 1972. *Hobbies and other interests:* Travel, team rowing, fishing.

ADDRESSES: Home and office—P.O. Box 2445, Corrales, NM 87048. *E-mail*—ghack73586@aol.com.

CAREER: Alpine Avalanche, owner, editor, and publisher, 1972-76; Texas State Senate, press secretary for Senator Pete Snelson, 1976-78; El Paso Chamber of Commerce, El Paso, TX, business development officer, 1978; Independent Consultants, lobbyist in Washington, DC, 1978-81; Southwest Publications, Inc., owner, editor, and publisher, 1981-95, and founder of Corporate Press. Served as member of New Mexico Governor's advisory committee for economic development and at Governor's Economic Development and Tourism Conference; Private 100, founder. Volunteer teacher of English as a second language. *Military service:* U.S. Navy, 1966-68; served in Vietnam.

MEMBER: Latin American Association for Development (member of board of directors), Association of Commerce and Industry, New Mexico Economic Forum, New Mexico Amigos, New Mexico First (founding member), Quality New Mexico.

WRITINGS:

An Act of Faith: Twenty-five Golden Rules for Small Business Success, Cypress Group (Leawood, KS), 2002.

Columnist, *Alpine Avalanche,* 1973-75; columnist and editor, *New Mexico Business Journal,* 1981-95. Owner, publisher, and editor, *New Mexico Business Journal,* 1980-95.

WORK IN PROGRESS: Research on Spanish and Italian farmhouses.

SIDELIGHTS: George Hackler told *CA:* "My primary motivation for writing is a desire to inspire, insult, inform, or entertain. My writing has been influenced by Ernest Hemingway, William Faulkner—all the giants. My writing process is to write feverishly in a stream of consciousness, then edit and rewrite endlessly. My inspiration is my twenty-five years of experience in small business and the need to pass it along."

*   *   *

HALDON, John F.

PERSONAL: Male. *Education:* University of Birmingham, B.A., M.A., Ph.D.

ADDRESSES: Office—Centre for Byzantine Studies, Ottoman and Modern Greek Studies, University of Birmingham, Edgbaston, Birmingham B15 2TT, England. *E-mail*—HaldonJF@hhs.bham.ac.uk.

CAREER: Educator and author. University of Birmingham, Birmingham, England, reader in history.

WRITINGS:

Recruitment and Conscription in the Byzantine Army c. 550-950: A Study on the Origins of the Stratiotika, Österreichischen Akademie der Wissenschaften (Vienna, Austria), 1979.

Byzantine Praetorians: An Administrative, Institutional, and Social Survey of the Opsikion and Tagmata, c. 580-900, R. Habelt (Bonn, Germany), 1984.

(Translator, and author of introduction and commentary) Constantine VII Porphyrogenitus, *Three Treatises on Imperial Military Expeditions,* Österreichischen Akademie der Wissenschaften (Vienna, Austria), 1990.

Byzantium in the Seventh Century: The Transformation of a Culture, Cambridge University Press (New York, NY), 1990.

The State and the Tributary Mode of Production, Verso (New York, NY), 1993.

State, Army, and Society in Byzantium: Approaches to Military, Social, and Administrative History, 6th-12th Centuries, Variorum (Brookfield, VT), 1995.

Warfare, State, and Society in the Byzantine World, 565-1204, UCL Press (London, England), 1999.

Byzantium: A History, Tempus Publishing (London, England), 2000.

(With Leslie Brubaker) *Byzantium in the Iconoclast Era (c. 680-850): The Sources: An Annotated Survey,* Ashgate (Burlington, VT), 2001.

The Byzantine Wars: Battles and Campaigns of the Byzantine Era, Tempus Publishing (London, England), 2001.

Byzantium at War, Osprey (London, England), 2002.

Contributor to Virgil S. Crisafulli and John W. Nesbitt, editors, *The Miracles of St. Artemio: A Collection of Miracle Stories by an Anonymous Author of Seventh-Century Byzantium,* E. J. Brill (New York, NY), 1997.

SIDELIGHTS: John F. Haldon is a reader in history at the University of Birmingham, specializing in the history of the Byzantine Empire. In *Byzantine Praetorians: An Administrative, Institutional, and Social Survey of the Opsikion and Tagmata, c. 580-900,* Haldon examines the traditional stereotype of Byzantine

society as stodgy and institutionally inert, showing readers that, as Simon Franklin noted in the *English Historical Review,* there were chronic tensions in the system of imperial protection, that reflected tensions and changes in society. The forces assigned to protect the emperor were changeable, somewhat chaotic, and never firmly under control. Haldon examines the various imperial guards, analyzing their function, social makeup, recruitment, numbers, command structure, pay, and weapons. Franklin praised Haldon's meticulous documentation and his interpretation, writing that the book is a valuable and persuasive contribution to Byzantine studies.

In *Byzantium in the Seventh Century: The Transformation of a Culture,* Haldon discusses the major developments and events in Byzantine culture, society, and politics between the years of 610 to 717. During this time, ancient urban civilization collapsed, Islam became established, and culture and social structure changed. In the *Journal of Near Eastern Studies,* Paul M. Cobb wrote that the book "presents a sometimes speculative but highly attractive view of this culture in transition. . . . Haldon is successful in depicting not only the seventh-century Byzantine world, but also its worldview."

The Byzantine Wars: Battles and Campaigns of the Byzantine Era discusses the Byzantine wars against Persians, Arabs, Bulgars, and Normans, with an analysis of battle plans, military manuals of the time, and strategy and how the actions of the Byzantine generals led to victory or defeat. In *History Today,* Paul Stephenson praised Haldon's "close reading of the primary sources coupled with his personal knowledge of the sites," and commented, "The battle narratives flow nicely . . . and most are illustrated with comprehensible battle plans."

BIOGRAPHICAL AND CRITICAL SOURCES:

PERIODICALS

Catholic Historical Review, July, 2001, Stamatina McGrath, review of *The Miracles of St. Artemio: A Collection of Miracle Stories by an Anonymous Author of Seventh- Century Byzantium,* p. 486.
English Historical Review, December, 1987, Simon Franklin, review of *Byzantine Praetorians: An Administrative, Institutional, and Social Survey of*

the Opsikion and Tagmata, c. 580-900, p. 177; June, 1999, Peter Sarris, review of *Constantine VII Porphyrogenitus: Three Treatises on Imperial Military Expeditions,* p. 675.

History Today, December, 2001, Paul Stephenson, review of *The Byzantine Wars: Battles and Campaigns of the Byzantine Era,* p. 60.

Journal of Near Eastern Studies, October, 1995, Paul M. Cobb, review of *Byzantium in the Seventh Century: The Transformation of a Culture,* p. 302.

Science and Society, summer, 1997, Richard Duchesne, review of *The State and the Tributary Mode of Production,* p. 257.

Times Literary Supplement, November 23, 2001, Averil Cameron, review of *Byzantium: A History,* p. 21.*

*   *   *

HALE, Janice E(llen) 1948-

PERSONAL: Born April 30, 1948, in Fort Wayne, IN; daughter of Phale Dolfis (a pastor and state legislator) and Cleo (an early childhood educator; maiden name, Ingram) Hale; married Keith A. Benson, Sr. (divorced, 1992); children: Keith A., Jr. *Ethnicity:* "African American." *Education:* Spelman College, B.A., 1970; Interdenominational Theological Center, M.R.E., 1972; Georgia State University, Ph.D., 1974. *Politics:* Democrat. *Religion:* Baptist. *Hobbies and other interests:* Tennis.

ADDRESSES: Home—30336 Stratford Ct., Farmington Hills, MI 48331. *Office*—College of Education, Wayne State University, 5462 Gullen Mall, Room 213, Detroit, MI 48331; fax: 313-347-1890. *E-mail*—JaniceEHale@cs.com.

CAREER: Wayne State University, Detroit, MI, professor of education, 1991—. Educational consultant on the education of African-American children.

MEMBER: National Association for the Education of Young Children, American Educational Research Association, National Black Child Development Institute.

AWARDS, HONORS: Pulitzer Prize nominations and Anisfield-Wolf Award nominations, both 1994, both for *Unbank the Fire: Visions for the Education of African-American Children,* and both 2001, for *Learning while Black: Creating Educational Excellence for African-American Children;* John Hope Franklin Publication Prize nomination, 2001, for *Learning while Black.*

WRITINGS:

Black Children: Their Roots, Culture, and Learning Styles, Johns Hopkins University Press (Baltimore, MD), 1982.

Unbank the Fire: Visions for the Education of African-American Children, Johns Hopkins University Press (Baltimore, MD), 1994.

Learning while Black: Creating Educational Excellence for African-American Children, Johns Hopkins University Press (Baltimore, MD), 2001.

WORK IN PROGRESS: Research on school reform aimed at closing the achievement gap for African-American children.

*   *   *

HALL, Stacey A. 1957-

PERSONAL: Born October 9, 1957, in New York, NY. *Religion:* Baha'i.

ADDRESSES: Office—PerfectCustomers Unlimited, 2513 South Gessner Rd., Houston, TX 77098. *E-mail*—info@perfectcustomer.com.

CAREER: Entrepreneur, business consultant, and writer.

WRITINGS:

(With Jan Brogniez) *Attracting Perfect Customers: The Power of Strategic Synchronicity,* Berrett-Koehler (San Francisco, CA), 2001.

SIDELIGHTS: Stacey A. Hall told *CA:* "My book *Attracting Perfect Customers: The Power of Strategic Synchronicity* was influenced by two long-held 'truths' in my life: One—Work performed in the spirit of service is worship. Two—Marketing is having a company work in the best interests of the community which it serves."

BIOGRAPHICAL AND CRITICAL SOURCES:

OTHER

PerfectCustomers Unlimited Web site, http://perfectcustomer.com (March 12, 2003).

*   *   *

HAUSER, Gerald Dwight 1947-

(Wings Hauser)

PERSONAL: Born December 12, 1947, in Hollywood, CA; son of Dwight (a writer) and Geraldine Hauser; married Jane Boltenhouse (a singer), 1971 (marriage ended, 1973); married Cass Sperling (an author), 1974 (divorced, 1977); married Nancy Locke (an actress; marriage ended); married Dafna Galili, June 1, 1996; children: (first marriage) Bright; (second marriage) Cole.

ADDRESSES: Office—14126 Marquesas Way, Marina del Rey, CA 90292.

CAREER: Actor, producer, director, screenwriter, singer, and songwriter.

Film appearances include *First to Fight,* 1967; *Who'll Stop the Rain?,* United Artists, 1978; *Homework,* Jensen Farley, 1982; *Vice Squad,* AVCO-Embassy/Hemdale/Brent Walker, 1982; *Deadly Force,* Embassy, 1983; *Night Shadows,* Film Ventures, 1984; *A Soldier's Story,* Columbia, 1984; *Jo Jo Dancer, Your Life Is Calling,* Columbia, 1986; *3:15, the Moment of Truth,* Dakota Entertainment, 1986; *Tough Guys Don't Dance,* Cannon, 1987; *The Wind,* Omega, 1987; *Hostage,* Noble Entertainment, 1987; *No Safe Haven,* Overseas Filmgroup, 1987; *Dead Man Walking,* Metropolis/Hit

Films, 1988; *The Carpenter,* Cinepix/Capstone, 1988; *Nightmare at Noon,* Omega Entertainment, 1988; *Marked for Murder,* 1989; *The Siege of Firebase Gloria,* Fries Entertainment, 1989; *L.A. Bounty,* Noble Entertainment Group/Alpine Releasing Group, 1989; *Reason to Die,* 1989; *Street Asylum,* 1990; *Pale Blood,* 1990; *Living to Die,* 1990; *Exiled in America,* 1990; *Bedroom Eyes II,* 1990; *Beastmaster II: Through the Portal of Time,* 1991; *Wilding,* 1991; *The Killer's Edge,* 1991; *In Between,* 1991; *Frame Up,* 1991; *Coldfire,* 1991; *The Art of Dying,* 1991; *Mind, Body & Soul,* 1992; *Road to Revenge,* 1993; *Frame-Up II: The Cover-up,* 1993; *Watchers III,* 1994; *Tales from the Hood,* 1995; *Broken Bars,* 1995; *Original Gangstas,* Orion, 1996; *Victim of Desire,* 1996; *Life among the Cannibals,* 1996; *Skins,* 1998; *The Insider,* Buena Vista, 1999; *Clean and Narrow,* Mainline Releasing, 1999; *Savage Season,* 2001; *Irish Eyes,* Shooting Spree Films, 2002. Film work includes (associate producer) *Uncommon Valor,* Paramount, 1983; (director) *Living to Die,* 1990; (director) *Coldfire,* 1991; (director) *The Art of Dying,* 1991; (producer and director) *Skins,* 1998.

Television series appearances include *The Young and the Restless,* CBS, 1977-81; *The Last Precinct,* NBC, 1986; *Lightning Force,* syndicated, 1991; *Beverly Hills, 90210,* Fox, 1994-95. Appearances on TV movies includes *Ghost Dancing,* ABC, 1983; *Sweet Revenge,* CBS, 1984; *Perry Mason: The Case of the Scandalous Scoundrel,* NBC, 1987; *Out of Sight, Out of Mind,* syndicated, 1990; *Bump in the Night,* Starz!, 1991. Appearances on TV miniseries include *Aspen,* NBC, 1977, and *The Long Hot Summer,* NBC, 1985. Appearances on TV pilots include *Hear No Evil,* CBS, 1982; *Command 5,* ABC, 1985; *The Last Precinct,* NBC, 1986; *The Highwayman,* NBC, 1987. Appearances on episodic television include "Wave Goodbye," *Magnum, P.I.,* 1981; "Just a Small Circle of Friends," *The Fall Guy,* 1983; "Dead or Alive," *Hunter,* 1984; "The Big Squeeze" and "Blood, Sweat, and Cheers," *The A-Team,* NBC, 1985; "Reflections of the Mind," *Murder, She Wrote,* CBS, 1985; *Airwolf,* CBS, 1985; "F.N.G.," "The Big Bang," and "She Sells More than Sea Shells," *China Beach,* 1990; "The Cool Katt," *Hardball,* 1990; "Rewind," *China Beach,* 1991; "Night Fears," *Murder, She Wrote,* CBS, 1991; "Lessons Learned," *The Young Riders,* 1992; "Pretty in Black," "Stand on Your Man," and "Good Girls, Bad Girls," *Roseanne,* ABC, 1992; "Crime and Punishment" and "Lose a Job, Winnebago," *Roseanne,* ABC, 1993;

"Fort Hope," *Space Rangers,* 1993; "Love and Hate in Cabot Cove," *Murder, She Wrote,* CBS, 1993; *Route 66,* NBC, 1993; "Right Man, Wrong Time," *Walker, Texas Ranger,* CBS, 1994; "Brotherhood of the Bell," *Kung Fu: The Legend Continues,* 1995; *Marker,* UPN, 1995; "Sightings," *JAG,* CBS, 1996; "Track of a Soldier," *Murder, She Wrote,* CBS, 1996; "You Say It's Your Birthday: Part 1," *Beverly Hills, 90210,* Fox, 1996.

Recordings include *Your Love Keeps Me off the Streets,* RCA, 1975.

WRITINGS:

AS WINGS HAUSER

(With Nancy Locke) *No Safe Haven* (screenplay), Overseas Filmgroup, 1987.
Skins (screenplay; also known as *Gang Boys*), Spectrum Films, 1994.

Wrote theme song for *Vice Squad,* AVCO-Embassy/ Hemdale/Brent Walker, 1982.

SIDELIGHTS: While playing wingback on his high-school football team, Gerald Dwight Hauser earned the nickname "Wings," which was destined to remain with him into adulthood. During the 1980s, he established a reputation for playing dangerous, psychotic characters in the films *Vice Squad* (1982), *Tough Guys Don't Dance* (1987), and *L.A. Bounty* (1989). During the 1990s, he appeared on the popular television series *Roseanne* as the next-door neighbor.

Hauser cowrote the script for *No Safe Haven* (1987), in which he plays the role of protagonist Clete Harris. The film is an action thriller built around the theme of revenge, much in the style of the *Death Wish* movies from the 1970s. Together with his son Cole, Hauser made the film *Skins* (1994), in which the two men respectively play the hero and the villain. *Skins* is the story of neo-Nazi thugs who hold a city in terror, and single out a gay man for particularly severe mistreatment.

BIOGRAPHICAL AND CRITICAL SOURCES:

BOOKS

Contemporary Theatre, Film, and Television, Gale (Detroit, MI), Volume 33, 2001.

PERIODICALS

Video Review, December, 1989, Ed Hulse, review of *No Safe Haven,* p. 88.*

*   *   *

HAUSER, Wings
     See HAUSER, Gerald Dwight

*   *   *

HIBBEN, Frank Cummings 1910-2002

OBITUARY NOTICE—See index for *CA* sketch: Born December 5, 1910, in Lakewood, OH; died June 11, 2002, in Albuquerque, NM. Anthropologist, archaeologist, educator, and author. Hibben attended the University of New Mexico to study mountain lions and pursue a master's degree in zoology. After earning a doctorate in archaeology at Harvard University, he returned to New Mexico, where he spent his entire career. It was Hibben who conducted excavations of the Sandia Man Cave near Albuquerque in the late 1930s and discovered that human beings had lived there as long as 12,000 years before. His major contribution to anthropology was Sandia Man, one of the earliest-known human groups in North America. Hibben taught at the University of New Mexico for many years and served as the founding director of what is now the Maxwell Museum of Archaeology. He also established the Hibben Trust to help finance graduate students in archaeology and donated a substantial amount of money to build the Hibben Center, an annex to the museum. Hibben's books include *The Lost Americans, Treasure in the Dust,* and *Digging up America.* Outside the academy, Hibben was known as a hunter. As the chair of the New Mexico State Game and Fish Commission in the 1960s, he worked to introduce new species of wild game animals into the state. He also hunted for big game throughout the United States and elsewhere, including Africa, where he had conducted archaeological field research after World War II. Hibben's books on hunting include *Indian Hunts and Indian Hunters of the Old West* and *Under the African Sun: Forty-eight Years of Hunting the African Continent.*

OBITUARIES AND OTHER SOURCES:

PERIODICALS

Albuquerque Tribune, June 14, 2002, obituary by Frank Zoretich, p. A1.
Washington Post, June 21, 2002, p. 37.

*   *   *

HICKS, Carola 1941-

PERSONAL: Born 1941. *Education:* M.A., Ph.D., F.S.A.

ADDRESSES: Office—Newnham College, Cambridge CB3 9DF, England. *E-mail*—cmh19@cus.cam.ac.uk.

CAREER: Scholar, educator, and author. Institute of Continuing Education, University of Cambridge, England, staff tutor in art history; fellow of Newnham College.

WRITINGS:

(Editor) *England in the Eleventh Century,* Paul Watkins (Stamford, England), 1992.
Animals in Early Medieval Art, Edinburgh University Press (Edinburgh, Scotland), 1993.
Cambridgeshire Churches, Paul Watkins (Stamford, Englad), 1997.
Discovering Stained Glass, Shire Publications Ltd. (Princes Risborough, England), 1996.
Improper Pursuits: The Scandalous Life of Lady Di Beauclerk, Macmillan (London, England), 2001; published as *Improper Pursuits: The Scandalous Life of an Earlier Lady Diana Spencer,* St. Martin's Press (New York, NY), 2002.

SIDELIGHTS: Carola Hicks is the editor of *England in the Eleventh Century,* a collection of twenty interdisciplinary essays divided into four categories: government and society, the church, image and text, and the English language. She also edited *Cambridgeshire Churches* whose first part surveys church architecture from anglo-saxon to modern times. While the second part studies church decoration and contents.

Animals in Early Medieval Art examines the use of animal ornament in medieval art from the sixth to the eleventh centuries. Hicks considers animal motifs in sculpture, manuscripts, embroidery, and metalwork, including such masterpieces as the *Book of Kells,* the Sutton Hoo treasure, the Bayeaux Tapestry, St. Ninian's Hoard, and Pictish and Irish stonework. As Hicks notes, these artworks were influenced by Celtic, Germanic, and Mediterranean elements—a combination that led to a tradition of animal art that was stronger in the British Isles than anywhere else in Europe. Extrapolating from this art, Hicks also discusses the transmission of myths and images through societies and time.

In *Improper Pursuits: The Scandalous Life of Lady Di Beauclerk,* Hicks describes the life of Lady Diana Beauclerk, an aristocrat who became a successful and respected artist following a notorious divorce. Lady Beauclerk marries her lover and moves from the restrictions of life at court into London's cultural circles. In the *Times Literary Supplement,* Kevin Sharpe wrote, "Hicks's biography opens up a different life and world, one in which an aristocratic woman could make a respectable reputation as an artist and in which [after a scandalous affair] . . . [she] could effect a partial return from social exile."

BIOGRAPHICAL AND CRITICAL SOURCES:

PERIODICALS

Choice, July-August, 1996, review of *Animals in Early Medieval Art,* p. 1783.
English Historical Review, November, 1995, B. C. Barker-Benfield, review of *England in the Eleventh Century,* p. 1232; February, 2002, Leslie Mitchell, review of *Improper Pursuits: The Scandalous Life of Lady Di Beauclerk,* p. 200.

Speculum, January, 1998, Douglas MacLean, review of *Animals in Early Medieval Art,* p. 185.

Times Literary Supplement, November 23, 2001, Kevin Sharpe, "The Rehabilitation of Lady Di," p. 19.

*   *   *

HILL, Denise Nicholas
   See NICHOLAS, Denise

*   *   *

HILL, Hamlin (Lewis) 1932-2002

OBITUARY NOTICE—See index for CA sketch: Born November 7, 1931, in Houston, TX; died July 16, 2002, in Los Alamos, NM. Educator and author. Hill was an academic who wrote numerous books on his favorite subject, American author Mark Twain. A graduate of the University of Chicago where he earned his Ph.D. in 1959, Harris earned his bachelor's degree from the University of Houston and his master's degree from the University of Texas. His subsequent academic career took him all across the United States. During the 1960s he taught at the University of New Mexico, the University of Wyoming, and the University of Chicago, returning to the University of New Mexico in 1975 as a professor of English and, from 1979 to 1985, chairman of the department. Leaving that university in 1986, Hill concluded his career as head of the English department at Texas A&M University, where he retired in 1989. During the 1990s Hill lectured about Mark Twain around the world and was a visiting professor at the University of Budapest from 1989 to 1991. Among his many works on Twain are *Mark Twain and Elisha Bliss* (1964), *Mark Twain: God's Fool* (1975), and *Mark Twain's "Wapping Alice"* (1981). He also edited a number of Twain's books and correspondence.

OBITUARIES AND OTHER SOURCES:

BOOKS

Who's Who in America, 46th edition, Marquis (Wilmette, IL), 1990.

PERIODICALS

Chicago Tribune, July 26, 2002, section 2, p. 8.
New York Times, July 29, 2002, p. A21.
Washington Post, July 26, 2002, p. B6.

HOLMAN, J. Alan 1931-

PERSONAL: Born September 24, 1931, in Indianapolis, IN; son of Albert J. (a Bell Telephone Co. employee) and Catherine Pennington (a teacher) Holman; married Donna Goldsworthy (died); married Margaret Bishop, 1972; children: John Andrew, Robert Joseph, Raymond August, Michael Dale. *Ethnicity:* "White-European." *Education:* Franklin College (IN), B.A.; University of Florida—Gainesville, M.S., 1957, Ph.D., 1961. *Politics:* Independent. *Religion:* Protestant. *Hobbies and other interests:* Travel, fishing, photography, cinema.

ADDRESSES: Home—540 Linden St., East Lansing, MI 48823. *Office*—Rm. 302, Michigan State University Museum, East Lansing, MI 48824; fax: 517-432-2846. *E-mail*—holman@msu.edu.

CAREER: Michigan State University, East Lansing, professor of zoological and geological sciences, and Michigan State University Museum curator (emeritus) of vertebrate paleontology. *Military service:* U.S. Naval Reserve, 1953-55 (active duty); served as hospital corpsman; became third-class petty officer.

MEMBER: Society of Vertebrate Paleontology, Society for the Study of Amphibians and Reptiles, Michigan Academy of Science, Arts, and Letters.

WRITINGS:

(With Dirk Gringhuis) *Mystery Mammals of the Ice Age: Great Lakes Region* (juvenile), Hillsdale Educational (Hillsdale, MI), 1975.

Ancient Life of the Great Lakes Basin, University of Michigan Press (Ann Arbor, MI), 1995.

Pleistocene Amphibians and Reptiles in North America, Oxford University Press (New York, NY), 1995.

Pleistocene Amphibians and Reptiles in Britain and Europe, Oxford University Press (New York, NY), 1998.

Fossil Snakes of North America, Indiana University Press (De Kalb, IN), 2000.

In Quest of Great Lakes Ice-Age Vertebrates, Michigan State University Press (East Lansing, MI), 2001.

WORK IN PROGRESS: (With M. B. Holman) *Roadside Michigan: Geology, Biology, Archaeology,* for University of Michigan Press, 2002; *Fossil Frogs and*

Toads of North America, for Indiana University Press, 2003; *The Corner at the End of the Car Line;* research on "relict habitats for amphibians and reptiles of Michigan; Eocene reptile of England."

SIDELIGHTS: J. Alan Holman told *CA:* "I love to write about things that have fascinated me since I was ten years old. Experiences, education, travel, 'maturity' (I hope!) [are influences on my work]. [My writing process is] systematic and organized (I hope) with a little levity sometimes. Finally getting some self confidence at age sixty-five [has inspired me to write on the subjects I have chosen]."

*   *   *

HOPKINS, Lyman
    See RODNEY, Lester

*   *   *

HORST, Louis 1884-1964

PERSONAL: Born January 12, 1884, in Kansas City, MO; died January 23, 1964, in New York, NY; son of Conrad Horst (a musician) and Carolina Nickell; married Betty Cunningham (a dancer), November 29, 1909 (later separated; never divorced).

CAREER: Composer, piano accompanist, teacher, dance critic, and publisher. Denishawn Dance Company, accompanist and music director, 1915-25; Martha Graham Company, music director, 1926-48; Helen Tamiris, music director, 1927-30; Doris Humphrey and Charles Weidman, music director, 1927-32; *Dance Observer* magazine, founder and editor, 1934-64. Teaching experience included work at the Neighborhood Playhouse School of Theatre, 1928-64; Sarah Lawrence College, 1932-40; Bennington Summer School of Dance, 1935-45; American Dance Festival, 1948-63; and Juilliard School of Music, 1958-63. Also accompanist for theater companies and silent films in California, 1902-15.

AWARDS, HONORS: Capezio Award, 1955; honorary doctorate, Wayne State University, 1963; Creative Award, American Academy of Physical Education, 1964.

WRITINGS:

Pre-Classic Dance Forms, 1937, reprinted, [Princeton, NJ], 1987.
(With Carroll Russell) *Modern Dance Forms in Relation to Other Modern Arts,* [San Francisco, CA], 1961.

SIDELIGHTS: After being introduced to dance as a piano accompanist, Louis Horst was active during the formative years of modern dance as a music director, composer, teacher, and writer. He is credited with being one of the first composers to work closely with choreographers in the creative process. The son of German immigrants, Horst began playing piano for vaudeville shows and silent films when he was a teenager. He worked for ten years as music director of the Denishawn Dance Company in California, during which time he met dancer Martha Graham. Horst followed Graham to New York City in 1925, where they became collaborators and lovers. Graham would later say that her pioneering work with the Martha Graham Company would not have been possible without Horst's supportive, calming influence. Their most famous work together was *Primitive Mysteries,* which was inspired by ancient Native American rituals.

Because modern dance was largely ignored by mainstream dance publications at the time, Horst founded *Dance Observer,* a non-profit monthly that relied on talented but unpaid writers. By the late 1950s, he was known as an eccentric critic. This reputation was reinforced by his review of the Paul Taylor dance solo *Private Domain,* which consisted of a single page that was blank except for his initials "L. H."

Horst also worked extensively as a teacher, giving workshops and classes in dance composition. He focused on an understanding of pre-classical musical forms such as the minuet and discouraged improvisation. He wanted students to create recognizable themes and to treat the music as a frame for the dance. Working at several institutions, his students included choreographers, dancers, musicians, and actors. Horst wrote two books, *Pre-Classic Dance Forms* and, with co-author Carroll Russell, *Modern Dance Forms in Relation to Other Modern Arts.* He sought to show the theoretical differences between modern dance and ballet by defining a distinct understanding of movement rather than an emphasis on steps.

In 1992 Janet M. Soares, a former assistant to Horst who now teaches dance at Barnard College, published a comprehensive account of his life and career. Her biography *Louis Horst: Musician in a Dancer's World* is based in part on Horst's diaries. According to a writer for *Kirkus Reviews,* the book is particularly revealing about Horst's relationship with Graham. The critic recommended it as "a carefully chronicled, well-documented account of his life and work."

BIOGRAPHICAL AND CRITICAL SOURCES:

BOOKS

International Dictionary of Modern Dance, St. James Press (Detroit, MI), 1998.

PERIODICALS

Kirkus Reviews, April 15, 1992, review of *Louis Horst: Musician in a Dancer's World.**

*   *   *

HUMPHREY, Doris 1895-1958

PERSONAL: Born October 17, 1895, in Oak Park, IL; died December 29, 1958, in New York, NY; buried in Oak Park, IL; daughter of Horace Buckingham Humphrey (a composer and hotel manager) and Julia Ellen Wells (a musician); married Charles Francis Woodford, (a merchant seaman), June 7, 1932; children: Charles Humphrey Woodford. *Education:* Trained with Mary Wood Hinman; studied ballet with Josephine Hatlanek, Andres Pavley, and Serge Oukrainsky; attended Denishawn dance school beginning 1917.

CAREER: Dancer, choreographer, educator, and company artistic director. Founded dance school, Oak Park, IL, 1913; Denishawn Dance Company, dancer, c. 1917-27; Humphrey-Weidman School and Company, co-founder and dancer, 1928-45; José Limón Dance Company, artistic director, 1946-58; 92nd Street YMHA Dance Center, director, beginning 1947. Teaching included work at the Bennington College Summer School, Teachers College, and Perry-Mansfield Camp,

1930s; Connecticut College School of Dance, faculty member, 1948-58; Juilliard School of Music, faculty member, 1951-58; Juilliard Dance Theatre, director, 1954-58.

AWARDS, HONORS: Dance Magazine award, 1938; John Simon Guggenheim fellowship, 1949; Capezio Award, 1954.

WRITINGS:

The Art of Making Dances, Rinehart (New York, NY), 1959.
New Dance: An Unfinished Autobiography, introduced by John Martin, Dance Perspectives (New York, NY), 1966, edited and completed by Selma Jean Cohen as *Doris Humphrey: An Artist First,* Princeton Book Company (Pennington, NJ), 1995.
Doris Humphrey: The Collected Works, Dance Notation Bureau Press (New York, NY), 1978.

SIDELIGHTS: A key figure in the creation of modern dance, Doris Humphrey rebelled against the methods of her teachers to create a new style of dance reflecting personal experience. She left the prominent Denishawn Company in 1928 to create the Humphrey-Weidman School and Company with Charles Weidman in New York. After her own dancing career was ended by arthritis, Humphrey became, among other assignments, the artistic director of the José Limón Dance Company and a faculty member at Juilliard. One of her most important contributions to modern choreography is the development of the fall and recovery concept, which involves the loss of equilibrium and its emotional impact. Near the end of her life, Humphrey wrote what would become a standard text on choreography, *The Art of Making Dances.* Other writings by Humphrey appeared in *New Dance: An Unfinished Autobiography,* which was later completed by Selma Jean Cohen as *Doris Humphrey: An Artist First.* Much of Humphrey's choreography survives in printed form using Labanotation, in *Doris Humphrey: The Collected Works.*

At first, Humphrey doubted if she would realize her dream of becoming a performer. At age eighteen, she opened a dance school in Oak Park, Illinois when her father lost his job. After four years, however, the school's success allowed her to enter the Denishawn

School in Los Angeles. She studied, taught, and performed with Denishawn for ten years, during which time she began her first attempts at choreography. Eventually, however, Humphrey found herself at odds with the company's artistic goals. She was impatient with Denishawn's reliance on non-American influences and balked at an assignment to dance in the Zeigfield Follies. With fellow Denishawn dancer Charles Weidman, she left for New York City, where they formed their own school and company.

Prior to World War II, Humphrey specialized in creating ensemble pieces with sculptural effects. Two of her favorite themes were nature and the individual in society. Some of her earliest works are among her most important. *Color Harmony* (1928) was received as the first abstract modern ballet. *Water Study* (1928), one of her most influential works, is still performed regularly by dance students at colleges and universities. It uses the concepts that were central to Humphrey's work, including the use of breath rhythm, natural movement, and fall and recovery. *Water Study* is performed without music and uses some sixteen dancers to embody the movement of water. Jane Sherman, a former Denishawn and Humphrey-Weidman member, described it in *Dance* magazine as "a work that astounded critics and audiences alike with its synchronized, moving-wave forms, from calm lapping on a beach to a crashing tempest." Other notable dances by Humphrey are *The Shakers* (1931), which is also still performed, and *Day on Earth* (1947). The second piece, which represents the more intimate dances that Humphrey made later in her career, was considered a prime example of mid-twentieth century abstract dance.

Humphrey created theoretical descriptions for the basis of her choreography, the most influential being fall and recovery. "Humphrey found that all movement that stimulated kinesthetic and theatrical excitement arose within an arc between the body lying flat and the body standing erect," explained Sherman; "She called the pull of gravity between these two 'deaths' fall and recovery. And she believed that her theory reflected the pull within all of us as human beings—between our need for security and our urge to risk the unknown."

Despite the physical and financial difficulties it often presented, Humphrey was dedicated to her work. The title of her autobiography, *Doris Humphrey: An Artist First,* recalls that she once told her husband she was an artist first, a woman second. When she could no longer dance, that passion included teaching approaches to choreography. Her experiences as a teacher, including many years spent at the Connecticut College School of Dance and the Juilliard School of Music, were central to her book *The Art of Making Dances,* which she completed just prior to her death. Based on extensive teaching notes, it is considered the first text of its kind and is still widely read.

BIOGRAPHICAL AND CRITICAL SOURCES:

BOOKS

International Dictionary of Modern Dance, St. James Press (Detroit, MI), 1998.

PERIODICALS

Dance, October 1995, Jane Sherman, "Fall and Recovery: A Tribute to Doris Humphrey," p. 56.

OTHER

The Dance Works of Doris Humphrey (video).*

J-K

JAQUES-DALCROZE, Emile 1865-1950

PERSONAL: Original name Emile-Henri Jaques; born July 6, 1865, in Vienna, Austria; died July 1, 1950, in Geneva, Switzerland; son of Jules-Louis (a clockmaker's representative) and Julie Jaques. *Education:* Studied at the Geneva Conservatory (Geneva, Switzerland), 1877-83; studied music in Vienna and Paris, under Talbot, Fauré, Lavignac, Marmontel, Lussy, Graedener, Prosnitz, Fuchs, and Bruckner, 1884-91.

CAREER: Educator and composer. Geneva Conservatory, Geneva, Switzerland, professor of harmony, 1892-1910; ran a school in Hellerau, Germany, 1910-14; Institut Jaques-Dalcroze, Geneva, founder and director, 1914-50. Developed rhythmic training method known as Eurythmics; composed songs, choral works, operas, and operettas, including *Riquet à la houppe* (1883), *Onkel Dazumal* (1905), *Les jumeaux de Bergame* (1908), and *Sancho Pança* (1897); also composed for orchestra, chamber orchestra, and piano.

WRITINGS:

Le coeur chante: Impressions d'un musicien, [Geneva, Switzerland], 1900.

Vorschläge zur Reform des musikalischen Schulunterrichts, [Zurich, Germany], 1905.

La respiration et l'innervation musculaire, [Paris, France], 1906.

Méthode Jaques-Dalcroze, [Paris, France], 1906-07.

Rhythmische gymnastik, Sandoz, Jobin (Neuchâtel, Switzerland), 1907.

The Eurythmics of Jaques-Dalcroze, Constable (London, England), 1912.

La rythmique, [Lausanne, Switzerland], 1916-17.

Le rhythme, la musique et l'education, [Paris, France], 1919, translation by Harold F. Rubenstein published as *Rhythm, Music, and Education,* G. P. Putnam's Sons (New York, NY), 1921.

The Jaques-Dalcroze Method of Eurythmics, H. W. Gray (New York, NY), 1920.

Eurythmics, Art, and Education, translation by Frederick Rothwell (New York, NY), 1930.

Rhythmics Movement, [London, England], 1931.

Coordination et disordination des mouvements corporels: exercices pour l'harmonisation des actes moteurs spontanés et volontaires et le développement de la concentration, A. Leduc (Paris, France), 1935.

Métrique et rhythmique, H. Lemoine (Paris, France), 1937.

Souvenirs, notes et critiques, V. Attinger (Paris, France), 1942.

La musique et nous: notes de notre double vie, Perret-Gentil (Geneva, Switzerland), 1945.

Notes bariolées, [Geneva, Switzerland], 1948.

SIDELIGHTS: Emile Jaques-Dalcroze was an Austrian composer and educator who became internationally known as the creator of "eurythmics" (as it was called in English) during the early twentieth century. He developed a method of responding to music with the body that was designed to improve a student's appreciation of musical qualities such as rhythm, phrasing, and dynamics. The discipline was based on Jaques-Dalcroze's belief that a kinesthetic or whole-body experience of music would improve the individual's intellectual understanding and ability to perform music. Jaques-Dalcroze's writings, including the translations *Eurythmics, Art, and Education* and *Rhythm, Music, and Education,* are focused on teaching. As a composer, he was inspired by Swiss folk music and was considered a highly imaginative, talented artist.

During the 1890s Jaques-Dalcroze began creating movements which he called rhythmic gymnastics for his students at the Geneva Conservatory. His students moved and made music with their bodies in work that initially incorporated singing, breathing, walking, and beating time. Jaques-Dalcroze later connected music with movements such as lunging, skipping, pulling a partner, and carrying an imaginary weight. While he played at a keyboard, Jaques-Dalcroze asked his students to respond to changes in the music. Their steps often corresponded to rhythmic patterns, while the breath was connected to phrasing and dynamics.

Jaques-Dalcroze began giving lectures with demonstrations and in 1906 he published *Méthode Jaques-Dalcroze* in French and German. After the conservatory declined to let Jaques-Dalcroze offer classes in rhythmic gymnastics, he created a school in Hellerau, Germany in 1910. Two years later, the specially constructed school was expanded to include performance space where Jaques-Dalcroze produced Glück's *Orfeus.* His work at Hellerau involved hundreds of teachers and students, and course work included *solfège* (ear training), keyboard improvisation, music theory and practice, rhythmic gymnastics, Swedish gymnastics, dance, and anatomy. Jaques-Dalcroze did not equate eurythmics with dancing, but he taught numerous dancers as well as musicians; they included Marie Rambert, who worked with Nijinsky and the Ballet Russes, Michio Ita, Hanya Holm, Kurt Joos, and Mary Wigman. American dancers influenced by eurythmics included Ruth St. Denis and Doris Humphrey.

The Hellerau school closed at the start of World War I, when Jaques-Dalcroze criticized German militarism. He went to Geneva and continued to teach at the Institut Jaques-Dalcroze until his death in 1950. His method was also taught in special schools in London, Berlin, Vienna, Paris, New York, and Chicago, among others. The Institut Jaques-Dalcroze subsequently became a state-supported school and Jaques-Dalcroze's methods continue to be taught in countries aound the world.

BIOGRAPHICAL AND CRITICAL SOURCES:

BOOKS

Encyclopedia of World Biography, 2nd edition, Gale (Detroit, MI), 1998.
International Dictionary of Modern Dance, St. James Press (Detroit, MI), 1998.*

*   *   *

KEARNS, Josie 1954-

PERSONAL: Born October 21, 1954, in Flint, MI; daughter of James V. and Gladys (Randall) Kearns; married Joseph M. Matyzak July 18, 1981. *Education:* University of Michigan, B.A., B.S., M.F.A., 1994. *Hobbies and other interests:* Egyptology, memoir, science theory.

ADDRESSES: Home—120 Litchfield, Clinton, MI 49236. *Office*—3262 Angell Hall, University of Michigan, Ann Arbor, MI 48109. *E-mail*—jakearns@ umich.edu.

CAREER: University of Michigan, Ann Arbor, professor, 1994—. Ragdale Foundation, writer-in-residence, 1995-2002.

MEMBER: Associated Writing Programs.

AWARDS, HONORS: Fellow of National Endowment for the Arts; first prize, Poet Hunt Contest; four awards from Michigan Council for the Arts; three Hopwood Award from University of Michigan.

WRITINGS:

New Numbers (poetry chapbook), March Street Press, 1999, expanded edition, New Issues Press, 2000.

Author of nonfiction work *Life after the Line,* Wayne State University Press (Detroit, MI). Poetry represented in anthologies, including *Contemporary Michigan*

Poetry, Passages North, and *Boomer Girls.* Contributor of poetry to journals, including *Georgia Review* and *Iowa Review.*

WORK IN PROGRESS: *Art in America,* a novel; *The Theory of Everything,* a poetry collection.

SIDELIGHTS: Josie Kearns told *CA:* "In poetry, my focus has been looking at scientific ideas and bringing them to bear on human problems. Thus, physics has played an important role in using these terms and ideas for human problems, views, and ways of seeing the world. I use double-voiced pieces in the same way to look at two or more views of the same subject at the same time. The human condition of choices, failures, and successes is paramount to the ideas in mathematics and physics specifically. However, something like Drake's Equation—a complicated series of variables that may or may not help to determine the likelihood of life on other plants—has also been a touchstone for my poetry, as well as women inventors.

"The novel manuscript in progress is the result of looking at how artistic people survive in the world. Thus, I enjoy working in all kinds of groups in writing situations."

*   *   *

KELLER, Irene (Barron) 1927-2002

OBITUARY NOTICE—See index for CA sketch: Born January 13, 1927, in Falkirk, Scotland; died of lung cancer July 25, 2002, in Chicago, IL. Author. While Keller made her living as a copyeditor, she is perhaps best remembered for her books for children. Moving to the United States to marry an American, she worked in the classified ad department at the *Chicago Tribune* before dedicating herself to raising a family. However, during this time she also attended the University of Illinois at Chicago for two years, wrote poetry, and helped publish a poetry anthology titled *Port Chicago Poets.* In the 1960s she was an editorial assistant at Encyclopedia Britannica and then a proofreader at World Book, where she worked from 1969 until the late 1980s. Becoming a freelancer editor, she continued to do copyedit assignments for a number of publishers while also writing a series of children's stories, which were illustrated by her husband, Dick Keller. Keller

published nine books, many of which teach children proper manners and behavior, among them *The Thingumajig Book of Manners* (1981), *Buzzy the Bunny* (1981), *The Thingumajig Book of Do's and Don'ts* (1983), and *Benjamin Rabbit and the Stranger Danger* (1985).

OBITUARIES AND OTHER SOURCES:

PERIODICALS

Chicago Tribune, August 1, 2002, section 2, p. 9.

*   *   *

KELLER, William W(alton) 1950-

PERSONAL: Born 1950. *Education:* Princeton University, graduate; Cornell University, Ph.D.

ADDRESSES: *Agent*—c/o Author Mail, Cambridge University Press, 40 West 20th St., New York, NY 10011-4211.

CAREER: Congressional Office of Technology Assessment, analyst.

WRITINGS:

The Liberals and J. Edgar Hoover: Rise and Fall of a Domestic Intelligence State, Princeton University Press (Princeton, NJ), 1989.
Arm in Arm: The Political Economy of the Global Arms Trade, Basic Books (New York, NY), 1995.
(With Paul N. Duremus, Louis W. Pauly, and Simon Reich) *The Myth of the Global Corporation,* Princeton University Press, (Princeton, NJ), 1999.
(With Richard J. Samuels) *Crisis and Innovation in Asian Technology,* Cambridge University Press (New York, NY), 2002.

SIDELIGHTS: William W. Keller, an analyst for the former Congressional Office of Technology Assessment, has written several books exploring the political side of military and business development.

Keller's first book, *The Liberals and J. Edgar Hoover: Rise and Fall of a Domestic Intelligence State,* argues that while the FBI was criticized for its ultra-conservative focus, it actually grew up in the liberal political establishment; thus, the book concludes, the two political forces are necessarily intertwined. S. K. Hauser, in a review for *Choice,* felt that "This book offers a viewpoint that will be challenged by many. The text, however, is often tedious: the extensive accompanying footnotes are often more revealing."

Keller's next volume, *Arm in Arm: The Political Economy of the Global Arms Trade,* offers an analysis of post-Cold War armament. *Foreign Affairs* reviewer Eliot Cohen wrote that the book "is worth . . . a close reading." A reviewer for *Publishers Weekly* found the book "incisive and accessible."

Keller's *The Myth of the Global Corporation,* written with Paul N. Doremus, Louis W. Pauly, and Simon Reich, argues that despite the common thought, the spread of international businesses does not reflect a globalized economy. Bruce Kogut, writing for the *Harvard Business Review,* applauded Keller's views: "[The authors] see enormous differences among multinational companies, which they trace to the unique political and economic characteristics of their home countries. When it comes to corporate behavior, the authors show convincingly that nationality is destiny. This is a timely and brave book, given the widespread view that globalization means convergence among nations and companies toward common ways of doing things."

BIOGRAPHICAL AND CRITICAL SOURCES:

PERIODICALS

Choice, October, 1989, S. K. Hauser, review of *The Liberals and J. Edgar Hoover,* p. 378; April, 1996, J. W. Nordyke, review of *Arm in Arm,* p. 1362.
Foreign Affairs, March-April, 1996, Eliot A. Cohen, review of *Arm in Arm,* p. 147.
Harvard Business Review, January-February, 1999, Bruce Kogut, "What Makes a Company Global?" p. 165.
International Affairs, April, 1999, Gordon C. K. Cheung, review of *The Myth of the Global Corporation,* p. 415.

Nation, November 13, 1989, Diana R. Gordon, review of *The Liberals and J. Edgar Hoover,* p. 572.
National Review, May 5, 1989, Richard Gid Powers, review of *The Liberals and J. Edgar Hoover,* p. 47.
Publishers Weekly, September 25, 1995, review of *Arm in Arm,* p. 37.
Times Literary Supplement, January 22, 1999, Brian Hindley, "A Bogey and Its Myths," p. 28.*

*   *   *

KENT, Debra 1952-

PERSONAL: Married; children: two.

ADDRESSES: Home—Bloomington, IN. *Agent*—c/o Author Mail, Warner Books, 1271 Avenue of the Americas, New York, NY 10020.

CAREER: Writer.

WRITINGS:

(Editor) *The Kinsey Institute New Report on Sex: What You Must Know to Be Sexually Literate,* St. Martin's (New York, NY), 1990.
The Diary of V: The Affair, Warner Books (New York, NY) 2001.
The Diary of V: The Breakup, Warner Books (New York, NY) 2001.
The Diary of V: Happily Ever After, Warner Books (New York, NY) 2001.

Contributor of articles to magazines, including *Mademoiselle, Redbook, Cosmopolitan,* and *Family Circle.* Author of "Sex & the Body" column for *Seventeen.* Contributing editor, *Working Mother.*

ADAPTATIONS: The "Diary of V" series was adapted by Jeffrey Arch as a television series by NBC.

WORK IN PROGRESS: Contracted with Warner for two more books, not part of the "Diary of V" series.

SIDELIGHTS: As a veteran writer for women's magazines Debra Kent has explored the subjects of marriage, infidelity, sex, and family relationships for fifteen years. Her first work of fiction, *The Diary of V: The Affair,* is part comedy, part romance novel, as it follows the trials and titillations in the life of "V," an unhappily married psychotherapist living in the suburbs. The book, written as a series of journal entries, actually began in 1997 as a Web serial, or what Kent called a "weekly thing." In an online chat group associated with the *iVillage* Web site, Kent explained, "*V* got started when the editor of *Redbook* at the time, Kate White, called me and asked me if I would be interested in writing a weekly thing for *Redbook*'s new Web site." The site, *www.women.com,* had been getting seven million visitors every month.

The novel has spawned two sequels, *The Breakup* and *Happily Ever After?,* prompting Grade A Entertainment, which produces the popular television shows *The West Wing* and *Just Shoot Me,* to option *The Diary of V* to NBC as a half-hour series. The pilot, about a woman trying to juggle her career and family, was written by Jeffrey Arch, who wrote the story for *Sleepless in Seattle,* starring Tom Hanks and Meg Ryan. The original online version of *The Diary of V* differs slightly from the three print versions, which contain more complex plots, additional characters, and are "lighter and funnier and a bit more true to life," Kent explained. White, who first commissioned the electronic series, wrote in *Cosmopolitan* that she found each paperback "a delicious, funny, sexy, tantalizing page-turner." Kent "propels her heroine from crisis to crisis as relentlessly as any Victorian melodrama," wrote a *Publishers Weekly* contributor. *Romantic Times* reviewer Gerry Benninger called the book a "well-written, ultramodern novel."

Comparisons to the 1998 novel *Bridget Jones's Diary,* by British writer Helen Fielding, were unavoidable, as format (diary entries) and tone (comedic self-loathing) are similar. Kent's series "seems to be the American take on *Bridget Jones's Diary,* if Bridget was older and a suburban housewife writing in her journal," wrote Patty Engelmann in *Booklist,* "but Kent's heroine definitely has a quirky charm of her own." Addelaide Hayes, writing for *Bookreporter.com,* found the "wrenchingly candid" quality of "V's" journal entries distinguishing.

Kent's writing is considered to be spare, immediate, and uncensored. An entry from the third book in the series reflects a debilitating self-scrutiny, which is a theme recurrent not only in V's life but in the lives of many of Kent's readers. The story of "V" resonates with its readers because of its humor in the face of very real, and often unspoken, anxieties. One such concern is money. "I paid my bills. I have nothing left over. I guess I won't be getting those miracle fat pills after all," wrote Kent of the now-divorced "V" in a chapter excerpt printed on *Time Warner Bookmark.* "I hate being broke, especially in this neighborhood."

Kent, a contributing editor for *Working Mother,* is married and lives with her husband and two children in Bloomington, Indiana. "I'm inspired by mid-life suburbia," admitted Kent in an *iVillage* chat. She, like her heroine, lives in a Midwestern college town. Only one of her characters, Diana, is "total invention," she explained. "Everyone else is inspired by real life people. I would like to add that Jungian psychologists would say that every character in this book represents some aspect of myself. I don't know if that's true or not. If it's true that's pretty scary but I suppose there is a little bit of Diana and all the others inside me."

BIOGRAPHICAL AND CRITICAL SOURCES:

PERIODICALS

Atlanta Journal-Constitution, October 5, 2000, Don O'Briant, "*Diary of V* Expanding from Net to Paperback," p. D6.
Booklist, September 15, 2001, Patty Engelmann, review of *Diary of V: Happily Ever After?,* p. 204.
Publishers Weekly, April 23, 2001, review of *Diary of V: Happily Ever After?,* p. 55.

OTHER

Bookreporter.com, http://www.bookreporter.com (December 31, 2001).
Fenn Focus, http://www.hbfenn.com/ (April 1, 2002).
iVillage, http://magazines.ivillage.com/redbook/ "*Diary of V* Chat with Author Debra Kent," (April 1, 2002).
Romantic Times, http://www.romantictimes.com/ (December 31, 2001).
Time Warner Bookmark, http://www.twbookmark.com (December 31, 2001).*

KINGMA, Daphne Rose 1942-

PERSONAL: Born January 14, 1942, in Philadelphia, PA; daughter of Jan Willem (a professor of English literature) and Gezina (a professor of art; maiden name, Stuart) Kingma; married James D. Den Boer June 6, 1961 (divorced September, 1968); children: Megali. *Education:* Calvin College, Grand Rapids, MI, B.A., 1963; University of California—Santa Barbara, M.A., 1971. *Hobbies and other interests:* Dancing, art.

ADDRESSES: Home—P.O. Box 5244 Santa Barbara, CA 93150-5244. *Office*—2604 Stout Street, Denver, CO 80205. *Agent*—Al Lowman, Authors and Artists, West 44th Street, New York, NY. *E-mail*—daphnekingma@yahoo.com.

CAREER: Author, psychotherapist, television talk show guest, public speaker, and workshop leader. Frequent guest on *Oprah* and other television interview shows as an expert on relationships.

WRITINGS:

The Men We Never Knew: Women's Role in the Evolution of a Gender, Conari Press (Berkeley, CA), 1993.

The Breakup Bible: Why Relationships End and Living through the Ending of Yours (sound recording), Sounds True (Boulder, CO), 1995, published as *Coming Apart: Why Relationships End and How to Live through the Ending of Yours,* Conari Press (Berkeley, CA), 1998.

Weddings from the Heart: Contemporary and Traditional Ceremonies for an Unforgettable Wedding, Conari Press (Berkeley, CA), 1995.

Heart and Soul: Living the Joy, Truth, and Beauty of Your Intimate Relationship, MJF Books, (New York, NY), 1995.

Garland of Love: Daily Reflections on the Magic and Meaning of Love, Conari Press (Berkeley, CA), 1995.

To Have and to Hold: A Wedding Keepsake, Conari Press (Berkley, CA), 1997.

The Future of Love: The Power of the Soul in Intimate Relationships, Doubleday (New York, NY), 1998.

A Lifetime of Love: How to Bring More Depth, Meaning and Intimacy into Your Relationship, Conari Press (Berkeley, CA), 1998.

The Nine Types of Lovers: Why We Love the People We Do and How They Drive Us Crazy, Conari Press (Berkeley, CA), 1999.

The Book of Love, Conari Press (Berkeley, CA), 2001.

Finding True Love: The Four Essential Keys to Discovering the Love of Your Life, Conari Press (Berkeley, CA), 2001.

365 Days of Love, Conari Press (Berkeley, CA), 2002.

(With M. J. Ryan) *Attitudes of Gratitude in Love: Creating More Joy in Your Relationship,* Conari Press (Berkeley, CA), 2002.

True Love: How to Make Your Relationships Sweeter, Deeper and More Passionate, Conari Press (Berkeley, CA) 2003.

OTHER

(Author of introduction) Dawna Markova, *Random Acts of Kindness,* Conari Press (Berkeley, CA), 1993.

(Author of introduction) Alicia Alvrez, *On the Wings of Eros: Nightly Readings for Passion and Romance,* Conari Press (Berkeley, CA), 1995.

The Many Faces of Love: Exploring New Forms of Intimacy (sound recording), Sounds True (Boulder, CO), 2002.

WORK IN PROGRESS: A novel that will be a love story.

SIDELIGHTS: Daphne Kingma is a psychotherapist and writer who has published more than fifteen successful books on relationships. As she told *CA,* "I have written on the subject of love and relationships for many years because of my two and a half decades of work as a psychotherapist." In *The Book of Love,* Kingma offers advice on listening for the message under the words, walking a mile in your sweetheart's shoes, kindling the romance, tying up emotional loose ends, sharing your dreams, and holding each other in the light. Kingma has edited *The Book of Love* as a distillation of the best advice from two of her most successful books. It contains brief essays that explore the emotional and spiritual components of loving relationships. "With a distinctive style that is both lyrical and practical," wrote a reviewer for *Publishers Weekly,* "Kingma reminds readers of the importance of loving consciously (e.g. 'ask for what you need,' 'share your transcendent moments.'"

Kingma's message is one of acceptance of life as a precious gift to be cherished. This is what inspired her to begin writing. She told *CA* she began writing as an "expression of what I see and feel. The magic and tragic dimensions of life. Beauty and sorrow. When I was a child I had feelings that were 'inexpressible.'"

In *The Future of Love: The Power of the Soul in Intimate Relationships,* Kingma suggest turning away from issues of the personality to those of the soul in loving relationships. A *Publishers Weekly* contributor noted, "As she wisely makes clear, these soulful attributes can be present, or not, in myriad forms of relationship." In *The Nine Types of Lovers,* Kingma explores a set of nine personality traits derived from her twenty-five years of relationship counseling. In the author's analysis, successfully choosing a mate involves delving beneath the surface levels of compatibility and physical attraction. Kingma gives lovers a better understanding of the differences between them and their mates.

According to Kingma, not all relationships are good and some should simply end. In *Coming Apart: Why Relationships End and How to Live through the Ending of Yours,* Kingma offers a process and a way of examining relationships that is not only healing and helpful through the breakup process, but also provides a basis for using the breakup of a relationship to become a stronger person, one more able to love again.

BIOGRAPHICAL AND CRITICAL SOURCES:

PERIODICALS

Publishers Weekly, May 10, 1993, review of *The Men We Never Knew: Women's Role in the Evolution of a Gender,* p. 67; January 19, 1998, review of *The Future of Love: The Power of the Soul in Intimate Relationships,* p. 363; June 28, 1999, review of *How Deep Is Your Love,* p.70; February 5, 2001, review of *Finding True Love: The Four Essential Keys to Discovering the Love of Your Life,* p. 83.*

*   *   *

KITSON, Peter J.

PERSONAL: Male.

ADDRESSES: Agent—c/o Author Mail, Pickering & Chatto, 21 Bloomsbury Way, London WC1A 2TH, England.

CAREER: Writer. University of Dundee, Dundee, Scotland, professor.

WRITINGS:

(Editor) *Romantic Criticism, 1800-1825* ("Key Documents in Literary Criticism"), Batsford (Glasgow, Scotland), 1990.
(Editor with Thomas N. Corns) *Coleridge and the Armoury of the Human Mind: Essays on His Prose Writings,* Frank Cass (London, England), 1991.
(Editor with Tim Fulford) *Romanticism and Colonialism: Writing and Empire, 1780-1830,* Cambridge University Press (Cambridge, England), 1998.
(Editor with others) *The Year's Work In English Studies, Volume 76,* Blackwell Publishers (Oxford, England), 1998.
(Editor with Debbie Lee) *Slavery, Abolition, and Emancipation: Writings in the British Romantic Period,* Volume 1: *Black Writers,* Volume 2: *The Abolition Debate,* Volume 3: *The Emancipation Debate,* Volume 4: *Verse,* Volume 5: *Drama,* Volume 6: *Fiction,* Volume 7: *Medicine and Slavery,* Volume 8: *Theories of Race, and Index.* Pickering & Chatto (London, England), 1999.
(Editor with Tim Fulford) *Travels, Explorations, and Empires, 1770-1835: Travel Writings on North America, the Far East, the North and South Poles, and the Middle East,* four volumes, Pickering & Chatto (London, England), 2001.
(Editor) *Nineteenth-Century Travels, Explorations, and Empires: Writings from the Era of Imperial Consolidation, 1835-1910,* Pickering & Chatto (London, England), 2003.

WORK IN PROGRESS: With Tim Fulford, four more volumes in "Travels, Explorations, and Empires."

SIDELIGHTS: Peter J. Kitson is known for his compilations devoted to various aspects of life in late eighteenth- and early nineteenth-century England. *Coleridge and the Armoury of the Human Mind: Essays on His Prose Writings,* which Kitson edited with Thomas N. Corns, features essays from contributors such as John Beer, William Ruddick, and Kathleen Wheeler. Writing in the *Review of English Studies,* W. J. B. Owen accorded particular praise to Beer's analysis of Coleridge as a critic, declaring that "Beer offers a carefully documented historical survey of

Coleridge's progress from a political commentator, through his growing interest in the natural environment and his increasing attention to the psychology of literary creation." Owen also enjoyed Ruddick's essay, which considers Charles Lamb's response to Robert Southey's criticism of Coleridge's *Elia*. Owen deemed Ruddick's piece "subtle and revealing." In his appraisal, Owen concluded, "Readers of [*Coleridge and the Armoury of the Human Mind*] will not need to change greatly their overall view of Coleridge, but they will find some odd, and some familiar, corners of his mind illuminated."

After publishing the Coleridge volume, Kitson teamed with Tim Fulford in editing *Romanticism and Colonialism: Writing and Empire, 1780-1830,* which *Choice* reviewer D. Garrison ranked among studies "on the relationship between literature and cultural complexity." The book presents fifteen essays on subjects ranging from liberationist aspects of William Jones's *Hymns to Hindu Deities* to nationalistic tendencies in Romantic-era poetry. Among the notable essayists featured in the volume are Moira Ferguson, who examines Mary Butt Sherwood's *Dazee, the Recaptured Negro,* and Timothy Morton, who analyzes Robert Southey's sonnets on slavery. Brian Young declared in a *Review of English Studies* appraisal that "the contributors to [*Romantic Imperialism*] . . . are very determinedly engaged in placing Romanticism in a newly theorized terrain," and "are keen to establish a variety of post-colonial orders in which liberation and theory are somehow inextricably enmeshed." Terence Hoagwood, writing in the *Modern Language Review,* deemed *Romanticism and Colonialism* "an admirably eclectic collection of essays," and he affirmed it "makes . . . an informative and useful contribution to the field."

Kitson followed *Romanticism and Colonialism* with *Slavery, Abolition, and Emancipation: Writings in the British Romantic Period,* an eight-volume study that he edited with Debbie Lee. In this work, Kitson and Lee present writings ranging from conventional documents to literary creations in illuminating the British Empire's handling of slavery from approximately 1780 to the mid-1800s. Peter Fraser, writing in a review for the *Times Higher Education Supplement,* described *Slavery, Abolition, and Emancipation* as "impressively produced," and he stated that the entire series of eight volumes "deserves to be widely consulted." Howard

Temperley, meanwhile, wrote in the *Times Literary Supplement* of "the editors' intentions to remove barriers and encourage debate."

Kitson's subsequent writings include *Travels, Explorations, and Empires, 1770-1835: Travel Writings on North America, the Far East, the North and South Poles, and the Middle East,* a consideration of British travel during the Romantic Era. Fergus Fleming, writing in the *Times Literary Supplement,* appraised the study as "an ambitious anthology" acknowledging the amassing of such material as "a daunting task." Fleming added, "*Travels* does not pretend to be anything that it is not, and it delivers what it promises. Its extracts evoke the rawness of discovery in an age when vast portions of the atlas were blank and when large segments of the world's population lived in ignorance of each other."

BIOGRAPHICAL AND CRITICAL SOURCES:

PERIODICALS

Choice, April, 1999, D. Garrison, review of *Romanticism and Colonialism: Writing and Empire, 1780-1830,* p. 1460.

Modern Language Review, January, 2001, Terence Hoagwood, review of *Romanticism and Colonialism,* pp. 167-171.

Notes and Queries, September 1997, E. D. Mackerness, "Coleridge, Keats, and Shelley," pp. 416-418.

Review of English Studies, November, 1993, W. J. B. Owen, review of *Coleridge and the Armoury of the Human Mind: Essays on His Prose Writings;* November, 2001, Brian Young, review of *Romanticism and Colonialism,* pp. 551-556.

Times Higher Education Supplement, August 25, 2000, Peter Fraser, "Slave's Complaint Given Voice," p. 26.

Times Literary Supplement, October 22, 1999, Howard Temperley, "Slavery in Lakeland," p. 27; September 21, 2001, Fergus Fleming, "Armchair Adventures," pp. 3-4.*

*   *   *

KLEIN, Alexander 1918-2002

OBITUARY NOTICE—See index for CA sketch: Born November 12, 1918, in Szibo, Hungary; died August 13, 2002, in New York, NY. Businessman, educator, and author. Klein had a varied career but is likely to be remembered most for his spy thriller *The Counterfeit Traitor,* which was adapted as a 1962 movie starring William Holden. A Hungarian immigrant, Klein came to the United States when he was five years old and graduated from City College of the City University of New York in 1939. He embarked on a career as a screenwriter and speechwriter, working on combat-training films and documentaries during World War II. He subsequently worked in film and television for Henry Steele Commager, moving to vice president in charge of television for the J. D. Tarcher Advertising Agency in the early 1950s. During this time he was also a creative writing instructor at City College. In 1957 he cofounded the Arden House, a foreign-policy think tank, and from 1970 to 1975 was an adjunct professor at Fordham University. Although best remembered for *The Counterfeit Traitor,* Klein was the author of ten books and wrote over two hundred movie scripts. His books include *The Empire City* (1955), *The Double Dealers* (1959), *The Magnificent Scoundrels* (1961), and *The Pellet Woman* (1965); his movie scripts include *Shalom, Baby* (1975) and *The Savage.* Klein also edited the nonfiction works *Natural Enemies: Youth and Conflict of the Generations* (1970) and *Dissent, Power, and Confrontation* (1972).

OBITUARIES AND OTHER SOURCES:

PERIODICALS

New York Times, August 24, 2002, p. A13.
Washington Post, August 25, 2002, p. C6.

*   *   *

KNIGHT, Damon (Francis) 1922-2002

OBITUARY NOTICE—See index for *CA* sketch: Born September 19, 1922, in Baker, OR; died April 15, 2002, in Eugene, OR. Author. Knight was one of the giant figures of twentieth-century science-fiction literature, writing numerous award-winning novels and short stories as well as being a founder of the Science Fiction Writers of America and editor of the "Orbit" anthology series. He was also a highly respected critic and promoter of the genre. After briefly attending Salem Art Center from 1940 to 1941, Knight was an assistant editor for Popular Publications from 1943 to 1944 and again from 1949 to 1950. However, his passion was writing; he published his first short story in 1941 and his first novel, *Hell's Pavement,* in 1955. He went on to publish many more novels, including *Mind Switch* (1965), *The World and Thorinn* (1981), a trilogy composed of *CV, The Observers,* and *A Reasonable World* (1985-91), and *Humpty Dumpty: An Oval* (1996). One of his most famous short stories is "To Serve Man" (1950), which was turned into a *Twilight Zone* television episode, and many of his stories were collected in such books as *The Best of Damon Knight* (1974) and *God's Nose* (1991). Although Knight's writing was well regarded, he was most highly esteemed for his literary criticism, winning a Hugo Award in 1956 for his *In Search of Wonder: Essays on Modern Science Fiction.* He was also the author of a respected guide for writers titled *Creating Short Fiction* (1981). One of the original members of the writers group the Futurians, which included such luminaries Isaac Asimov and Frederic Pohl, Knight wrote about his colleagues in his memoir *The Futurians: The Story of the Science Fiction "Family" of the '30s That Produced Today's Top SF Writers and Editors* (1977). Knight worked hard throughout his life to support the work of his fellow sci-fi writers, cofounding the Milford Science Fiction Writers' Conference in Pennsylvania and teaching at the Clarion Workshop now held at Michigan State University, where he received an honorary doctorate in 1996.

OBITUARIES AND OTHER SOURCES:

PERIODICALS

Los Angeles Times, April 18, 2002, p. B13.
New York Times, April 17, 2002, p. A21.
Times (London, England), June 4, 2002.
Washington Post, April 20, 2002, p. B7.

*   *   *

**KOCH, Charlotte (Moskowitz) 1908(?)-2002
(Charles Raymond, a joint pseudonym)**

OBITUARY NOTICE—See index for *CA* sketch: Born c. 1908, in Syracuse, NY; died of complications from heart disease May 21, 2002, in Evanston, IL. Dancer, administrator, and author. Koch lived a colorful and active life from beginning to end. As a teenager she abandoned a conventional university education to tour as a modern dancer with the celebrated Martha Graham troupe. In the late 1920s Koch hitchhiked to Arkansas to attend a radical labor school called Commonwealth College; she then helped to operate the school. There she also met and married Raymond Koch, with whom she later wrote children's books under the joint pseudonym Charles Raymond. One of these novels, *Jud,* won a best juvenile novel award from the Friends of American Writers in 1968; other titles included *Up from Appalachia, The Trouble with Gus,* and *Enoch.* Koch also wrote nonfiction, including *Educational Commune: The Story of Commonwealth College* and a volume on nineteenth-century British hospital reformer Florence Nightingale. Koch remained active into her nineties, lastly as a volunteer at the Evanston Public Library in Illinois.

OBITUARIES AND OTHER SOURCES:

PERIODICALS

Chicago Tribune, June 22, 2002, obituary by Gregory Meyer, pp. 1-19.

* * *

KOKORIS, Jim 1958-

PERSONAL: Born 1958; married, wife's name, Anne; children: three sons. *Ethnicity:* "Greek." *Education:* University of Illinois—Champaign, B.A.

ADDRESSES: Home—La Grange Park, IL. *Agent*—c/o St. Martin's Press, 175 Fifth Avenue, New York, NY 10010.

CAREER: Advertising executive, 1982-90; Golin/ Harris Communications, vice president, 1990—.

WRITINGS:

The Rich Part of Life, St. Martin's (New York, NY), 2001.

Contributor of humor pieces to various publications, including *Chicago Sun-Times, Chicago Tribune,* and *Reader's Digest.* Humor columnist, *USA Weekend* magazine.

ADAPTATIONS: The Rich Part of Life was optioned for film by Columbia Pictures.

WORK IN PROGRESS: A second novel, titled *Sister North.*

SIDELIGHTS: While working as a marketing and public relations executive, Jim Kokoris put time aside to write his first novel before he turned forty-five, knowing that he would otherwise have run out of steam—and dreams. For his fortieth birthday, his wife gave him the unusual gift of a working visit at the celebrated Iowa Writers' Workshop Summer Festival in Iowa City. While there, Korkoris passed a draft of the novel among his colleagues. All were enthusiastic. He took that encouragement home with him and, five drafts and a year later, he had a novel, *The Rich Part of Life.*

Though there was a time when he had considered attending law school, Kokoris decided instead that he wanted to be a writer. "Right after college, I gave serious thought to going to California and writing for television. I always thought I would end up writing sit-coms. I visited California several times, but in the end never made the jump," he explained on his home page. "I wrote a lot in my profession however, marketing public relations, and for years that was enough. When I turned forty however, I realized that I wanted to try my hand at something completely different, lose myself in a whole new world. So rather than get a red Porsche, I spent my midlife crisis writing a novel."

Kokoris, a Greek American, spends a quarter of the year traveling for his work as a publicist. *The Rich Part of Life* was written in thirty-three states, on the floors of airports, in the back of taxi cabs, and between meetings with clients in rental cars. "I did over half my writing in airplanes while traveling for business," Kokoris told *Reader's Digest,* which excerpted the book. "It's a great place to focus: no phones, no TVs, and in-flight movies are easy to resist. Up in the air I'd get these weird creative spells, and then at night I'd write some more in my hotel room." One of his characters, a vampire named Sylvanius, was inspired by a man he noticed in line at the Nashville airport. "I was just at a point in writing the book where I felt it could use a bit more humor . . . and there he was. I plopped him right in."

The Rich Part of Life tells the story of an eccentric history professor who plays his deceased wife's lucky numbers and wins $190 million in the lottery. Smelling freshly risen money, a cast of suspicious characters begin to appear at the professor's doorstep, including far-flung family members and an ex with a strange claim of paternity. The narrative, told from the point of view of the professor's twelve-year-old son, reveals Kokoris's "subtle sense of humor—as sweet as it is wicked," wrote a *Publisher's Weekly* reviewer.

Eventually, Korkoris's agent placed the novel with a publisher. Not only was it his first novel, but it was also the first novel sold by his agent, Lynn C. Franklin, who normally handles works of nonfiction. And not only did he find a publisher but he also sold the movie rights to Columbia Pictures, to be produced, written, and directed by James Mangold. Many writers would flinch at someone else re-envisioning their story, but not Kokoris. "He paid good money," Kokoris told Neil Steinberg of the *Chicago Sun-Times,* "so he can do what he wants."

It is generally assumed that first novels tend to be autobiographical. "Like all writers, I guess there are bits and pieces of people I know in my characters," Kokoris noted on his Web site. "Certainly there is a little of my sons in the book. Their mother, my wife, is not a dead stripper though."

BIOGRAPHICAL AND CRITICAL SOURCES:

PERIODICALS

Chicago Sun-Times, July 1, 2001, Neil Steinberg, "One Man's Life Story Gets a New Title: Novelist."
Los Angeles Times, June 10, 2001, Mark Rozzo, review of *The Rich Part of Life,* p. 23.
Publishers Weekly, February 21, 2000, p. 14; April 16, 2001, review of *The Rich Part of Life,* p. 44.

OTHER

Booksense.com, http://www.booksense.com/ (December 31, 2001).
Cody's Books, http://www.codysbooks.com/ (March 27, 2002) Jim Kokoris, "Snapshots from the First Year."

Jim Kokoris Home Page, http://www.jimkokoris.com/ (March 27, 2002).
Marsh Agency Web site, http://www.marsh-agency.co.uk/ (March 27, 2002).
Reader's Digest Canada Web site, http://www.readersdigest.ca/ (March 27, 2002).*

*   *   *

KOOPERMAN, Evelyn L. 1945-

PERSONAL: Born November 28, 1945, in San Diego, CA; daughter of Ovide A. (a barber) and Elsie L. (a librarian; maiden name, Andersen) Roy; married Larry Robert Kooperman July 12, 1977. *Education:* San Diego State College (now University), B.A. (with high honors), 1968; University of California, Los Angeles, M.L.S., 1971. *Politics:* Democrat. *Hobbies and other interests:* Playing the cello.

ADDRESSES: Home—7579 Rowena St., San Diego, CA 92119. *Office*—San Diego Public Library, 820 E St., San Diego, CA 92101.

CAREER: San Diego Public Library, San Diego, CA, librarian, 1972—.

MEMBER: Congress of History of San Diego and Imperial Counties, San Diego Historical Society.

WRITINGS:

San Diego Trivia, Silver Gate Publications (San Diego, CA), 1989.
San Diego Trivia 2, Silver Gate Publications (San Diego, CA), 1993.

SIDELIGHTS: Evelyn L. Kooperman told *CA:* "In 1986 a local radio station contacted the San Diego Public Library, where I work, asking the librarians to submit seventy-five San Diego trivia questions that would be aired over the radio. I am a native San Diegan and have always been interested in local history, so I went to work and came up with 172 questions. Each one led to another, and the result was so addicting that I couldn't stop. I turned up so many tidbits about San Diego that I thought others would enjoy sharing the fun. I continued the research for another two years, adding over 600 more questions and expanding those I already had, and finally I had enough for a book. I was surprised and delighted that *San Diego Trivia* was a best-selling local book when it came out.

"Three years later a local game company asked if they could use my questions for a trivia game. For that I had to come up with hundreds of new questions. The work was completed in 1991 and was proclaimed by the mayor to be the 'Official Game of the City of San Diego.' After more research on each question I had enough material for a second book, *San Diego Trivia 2*."

L

LAINO, E. J. Miller 1948-

PERSONAL: Married; children: two daughters. *Education:* University of Massacusetts and Fitchburg State College.

CAREER: Poet. Has worked with youths as a substance abuse prevention specialist.

AWARDS, HONORS: American Book Award, for *Girl Hurt,* 1996.

WRITINGS:

Girl Hurt: Poems, Alice James (Farmington, ME), 1995.
(Editor with Robert Cording and Shelli Jankowski-Smith) *In My Life: Encounters With the Beatles,* Fromm (New York City), 1998.

Contributor to *American Poetry Review.*

SIDELIGHTS: Poet E. J. Miller Laino's *Girl Hurt: Poems* was called a "stunning debut collection" by a *Publishers Weekly* reviewer who felt Laino "is no one-theme, one-book poet." Laino wrote the title poem after reading a newspaper account of a young immigrant girl who tried to stop her father from committing suicide. "Hers is a defiant use of words, heartbreak that spins inside a vortex of anger," wrote Charlotte Mandel in *American Book Review.* Mandel said that throughout the poetry, "pain, sex, birth, and death inescapably intertwine." Laino's poems are autobiographical. Mandel wrote that "death ... does not equate with limbo or disappearance. Death is physical and violent, like the smashed flat body of a pet turtle that symbolizes the violent discord of her parents' marriage."

Laino reveals how she gave up her Down's syndrome baby, Rachel, in "Telling the Truth," because she "couldn't bear one more / wrong thing. . . . All my life I wanted to obey the rules / but they kept breaking. Like Huck Finn / on the raft, I knew I was going to hell. / So I committed one more sin." In another poem she envisions her aborted fetus as a "tadpole baby / swimming in a make believe space of sky." In "The Catholic Church Abolishes Limbo," she wrote, "Even after the church abolished Limbo, / I couldn't. / It gave me strange comfort / when I let a machine / suck a nine-week fetus / out of my body." Several poems address psychotherapy, including "Two Sisters, Three Therapy Sessions."

In the third and final section of *Girl Hurt,* Laino's shorter, lyrical poems speak of love and motherhood. In the final entry, "Lunar Eclipse," the author and her daughter, Jaime, contemplate their own lives while they watch the moon disappear, then reappear, as it moves across the sky. Cortney Davis, writing in *Prairie Schooner,* said: "Laino's poetic vision allows us to look through that 'high powered telescope,' examining the minutiae of reality with all its terrors and seeing, ultimately, our human beauty as we cling 'like angels' to our lives." Davis called Laino's poetry "sometimes tough, sometimes fragile and lyrical," observing that she is always in control "of a language that drives relentlessly toward transcendence."

Poet Martin Espada described Laino as a tough, honest poet. "She is liable to say anything. Her poems are startling from their frank treatment of sex and death to the abundance of hard, true metaphors. This is more than a confrontation of pain and fear, however. These poems celebrate survival, the durability of family, the liberation of unheard voices, especially female and working-class voices."

Laino coedited *In My Life: Encounters with the Beatles.* She and her co-editors were inspired to collaborate on the anthology when they discovered that Beatles music was incredibly poetic. They felt that the Beatles deserved to have a serious literary work that discussed their musical body of poetry. They solicited contributions from writers across the country and spent nearly three years preparing the book, coeditor Shelli Jankowski-Smith told the *South Bend Tribune* in an interview.

Included are fifty-six essays, memoirs, poems, and fiction by writers reflecting on the Fab Four. Timothy Leary's essay "Thank God for the Beatles" reveals Leary's experiences with the group while on LSD. A *Publishers Weekly* reviewer said this essay alone "justifies the price of admission." Composer Leonard Bernstein shares his sense of being overwhelmed when he first saw the Beatles on *The Ed Sullivan Show* on February 9, 1964. Other contributors include Allen Ginsburg, early Beatle Stuart Sutcliffe, poets Donald Hall and David Wojan, and music critic Greil Marcus. Many of the writers are less well known, and not all are complimentary. Gordon Flagg wrote in *Booklist* that the book is "an ardent yet thoughtful reminder of what it was like to be young during the heady days of Beatlemania."

In addition to writing, Laino has taught at the Key West Literary Seminar where she works to inspire new poets.

BIOGRAPHICAL AND CRITICAL SOURCES:

PERIODICALS

American Book Review, December, 1996, pp. 29-30.
Booklist, July 19, 1998.
Prairie Schooner, fall, 1997, pp. 189-192.

South Bend Tribune, December 27, 1998.
Publishers Weekly, November 27, 1995, p. 66; August 17, 1998, p. 60.*

* * *

LAKE, M. D.
    See SIMPSON, Allen

* * *

LAMBRECHT, Bill

PERSONAL: Male. *Education:* Illinois Wesleyan University, B.A., 1972; University of Illinois, Springfield, M.A., 1973. *Hobbies and other interests:* Fishing.

ADDRESSES: Home—Fairhaven, MD. *Office*—c/o St. Martin's Press, 175 Fifth Ave., New York, NY 10010.

CAREER: St. Louis Post-Dispatch, St. Louis, MO, Washington correspondent, 1984—. Co-founder, *Bay Weekly* (newspaper).

AWARDS, HONORS: Society of Professional Journalists Award, 1989, for "Trashing the Earth"; Raymond Clapper Award, 1989, for "Trashing the Earth," 1993, for "Broken Trust," and 1999, for a series on genetic engineering; Outstanding Alumni Award, University of Illinois, Springfield, 1996; multiple nominations for the Pulitzer Prize.

WRITINGS:

Dinner at the New Gene Café: How Genetic Engineering Is Changing What We Eat, How We Live, and the Global Politics of Food, St. Martin's Press (New York, NY), 2001.

WORK IN PROGRESS: A study of the global water supply.

SIDELIGHTS: Bill Lambrecht is a journalist who has long specialized in both political and environmental reportage. In his first book, he demonstrates how these issues are related; *Dinner at the New Gene Café: How Genetic Engineering Is Changing What We Eat, How We Live, and the Global Politics of Food* brings Lambrecht's years of researching and reporting on science, technology, business, agriculture, politics, and the environment to bear on the controversy over genetically modified organisms (GMOs).

Lambrecht's primary career has been as the Washington, D.C., correspondent for the *St. Louis Post-Dispatch.* St. Louis is the home of the Monsanto Company, a leading biotechnology corporation that found itself at the center of the debate over GMOs. Lambrecht's research, however, took him to thirteen different countries over a period of several years. Lambrecht labors to tell all sides of the story, including in the book interviews with Monsanto chairman Robert B. Shapiro, farmers who hope GMOs will rescue a faltering agricultural sector, and anti-GMO activists. Speaking to the *Pew Initiative on Food and Biotechnology Web site,* Lambrecht recalled, "You find people on both sides of the debate that wanted me to write more about their issues, but I had to be balanced and objective. . . . I write from the intersection of science and politics. I'm a journalist, not an advocate. I wrote this book to give people what they need to make choices about a transforming technology."

In fact, one of the major themes of Lambrecht's book is how little information the public currently has about GMOs, which do not have to be labeled as such under current U.S. government regulations. Lambrecht suggests that U.S. consumers lack the awareness of the sources of their food that other countries have developed, in part because they have not experienced the famines and scares familiar to Europe and other nations. A press release from Lambrecht's alma mater, Illinois Wesleyan University, quoted the journalist emphasizing the importance of better public awareness: "Food sustains life and my view is that people should know the origin of what they eat. In a few short years, a handful of companies have swiftly organized the beginning of the genetic transformation of our food supply. . . . It has enormous implications politically, economically and, in many countries, culturally." A reviewer for *Publishers Weekly* called *Dinner at the New Gene Café* an "indispensable history" of the GMO debate, remarking on the extensive testimony from major players in the GMO controversy and Lambrecht's balanced approach to the topic.

In an interview with Katherine Mieszkowski for *Salon. com,* Lambrecht said that his research has not led him to worry unduly about GMOs. "I have more concerns about pesticides and chemicals than I do about GMOs," he explained, "and if I'm hungry late some night and somebody sticks a bag of chips in front of me, I'm not about to pull my hand away at the prospect of there being a trace of modified ingredients in the bag." Instead, Lambrecht hopes that increased public awareness will lead to better uses of GMOs. He told Mieszkowski, "It sometimes seems that American consumers think their food grows in the back room of a grocery store. There's a disconnect between eating and where food comes from in this country that is not found in Europe and many parts of the world. In the U.S., we've become almost an island, and the sooner that companies realize that they're going to have accede to labeling, the quicker they will be able to get on to the types of genetic applications that they're promising, such as healthier food, even food that wards off disease."

Despite his objectivity, Lambrecht concludes that corporate interests have not been completely forthcoming about GMOs in the past, a policy that will have to change, in his view. In an Illinois Wesleyan University press release, Lambrecht asserted, "Big companies aligned with big government believe that they can use political muscle to achieve any end. But . . . it's my sense that the United States one day soon will join the debate raging around the world about genetically modified organisms and force companies to tell people on labels what it is they're doing to what we eat."

BIOGRAPHICAL AND CRITICAL SOURCES:

PERIODICALS

Library Journal, August, 2001, Irwin Weintraub, review of *Dinner at the New Gene Café,* p. 146.
Publishers Weekly, July 30, 2001, review of *Dinner at the New Gene Café,* p. 70.

OTHER

Illinois Wesleyan University Web site, http://www.iwu.edu/ (January 21, 2002), press release announcing a speech by Bill Lambrecht, with biography.
Pew Initiative on Food and Biotechnology Web Site, http://pewagbiotech.org/ (March 19, 2002), profile of Bill Lambrecht.

Salon.com, http://www.salon.com/ (October 19, 2001), Katherine Mieszkowski, "The Genetically Engineered Pause That Refreshes."

Washington Post Writers Group, http://www.postwritersgroup.com/ (October 7, 2001) Neal Pierce, "Biobelt St. Louis—Could It Be True?"*

*   *   *

LANGSTON, Douglas C. 1950-

PERSONAL: Born October 28, 1950, in San Antonio, TX; son of David Wall (a carpenter) and Theresa Marie (a homemaker; maiden name, Dymowski) Langston; married Kathleen M. Staggs (marriage ended); married Constance J. Whitesell, March, 1986; children: Nathaniel. *Ethnicity:* "White." *Education:* Stanford University, B.A., 1972; Princeton University, M.A., Ph.D. (religion); University of California—Irvine, M.A., Ph.D. (philosophy). *Politics:* Democrat. *Hobbies and other interests:* Softball, sailing, horses.

ADDRESSES: Home—867 Virginia Dr., Sarasota, FL 34234. *Office*—New College of Florida, 5700 Tamiami Trail, Sarasota, FL 34243. *E-mail*—langston@nvf.edu.

CAREER: New College of Florida, Sarasota, professor of philosophy, 1977—.

MEMBER: International Society for the Study of Medieval Philosophy, Society for Medieval and Renaissance Philosophy.

AWARDS, HONORS: Mellon fellow at Harvard University, 1980-81; Fulbright fellow at University of Helsinki, 1989.

WRITINGS:

God's Willing Knowledge, Pennsylvania State University Press (University Park, PA), 1986.
Conscience and Other Virtues: From Bonaventure to MacIntyre, Pennsylvania State University Press (University Park, PA), 2001.

WORK IN PROGRESS: Essays; research on stoic philosophy.

BIOGRAPHICAL AND CRITICAL SOURCES:

PERIODICALS

Theological Studies, September, 2002, Linda Hogan, review of *Conscience and Other Virtues: From Bonaventure to MacIntyre,* p. 630.

*   *   *

LAVACA, Pere
See TORRENT, Ferran

*   *   *

LAW, Cheukyiu
See LAW, Clara

*   *   *

LAW, Clara 1957-
(Clara Law Chuck-Yiu, Cheukyiu Law, Zhuoyao Luo)

PERSONAL: Born May 29, 1957, in Macao (now China); immigrated to Australia, 1990; married Eddie Ling-Ching Fong (a writer).

ADDRESSES: Agent—c/o Southern Star Film Sales, Level 10, 8 West St., North Sydney, New South Wales 2060, Australia.

CAREER: Director and writer. Film work as director includes *They Say the Moon Is Fuller Here,* 1985; *Wo ai tai kong ren,* 1988; *Pan Jin Lian zhi qian shi jin sheng,* East West Classics, 1989; *Ai zai taxiang de jijie,* 1990; *Yes! yi zu,* 1991; *Qiuyue,* International Film Circuit, 1992; *It's Now or Never,* 1992; *You Seng,* Northern Arts Entertainment, 1993; "Wonton Soup," *Erotique,* Odyssey Films, 1994; *Xi chu bawang,* 1994; *Floating Life,* Southern Star Films, 1996; and *The Goddess of 1967,* Fandango, 2000.

WRITINGS:

(With husband, Eddie Ling-Ching Fong) *Floating Life* (screenplay), Southern Star Films, 1996.
The Goddess of 1967 (screenplay), Fandango, 2000.

SIDELIGHTS: Born in Macao and raised in Hong Kong, filmmaker Clara Law immigrated to Australia as an adult. Her story is thus much like that of the Chan family in the screenplay of *Floating Life,* which she wrote with husband Eddie Ling-Ching Fong. Law also directed the film, in which the Chans, concerned over the impending Communist Chinese takeover of Hong Kong, flee to the freedom and wide-open spaces of Australia. As they discover, however, there might be just a bit too much freedom—with its attendant violence and lawlessness—for their tastes. And the spaces are perhaps too wide for their sensibilities as well: the subdivision in which they settle with their daughter, who already lives in Australia, is depicted as sterile and isolated in contrast to the crowded, invigorating bustle of Hong Kong.

With her 2000 film *The Goddess of 1967,* Law presented a much more complex tale, which is told in a more richly layered cinematic language. "Utterly postmodern in its story and style," wrote Deborah Young in *Variety,* "*The Goddess of 1967* is a sophisticated picture that could also gain a handhold on younger audiences able to relate to anarchic characters, loud rock, and [a] futuristic treatment of the Australian outback, where the action unfolds." The title refers to a car, the French Citroen DS, nicknamed "the goddess" by admirers. A wealthy Japanese computer hacker discovers one such vehicle for sale on the Internet, and eventually reaches an agreement with the seller, an Australian. He flies to Australia to finalize the purchase, but when he reaches the owner's home, he finds a man and a woman lying in a pool of blood. But not everyone in the house is dead: the beautiful blind niece of the dead man emerges and offers to take him to the car's actual owner, who lives in the outback, a distance of five days' drive. As Young notes, "It's not a bad premise to get the film rolling."

BIOGRAPHICAL AND CRITICAL SOURCES:

BOOKS

Contemporary Theatre, Film, and Television, Volume 35, Gale (Detroit, MI), 2001.
Women Filmmakers and Their Films, St. James Press (Detroit, MI), 1998.

PERIODICALS

Chicago Sun-Times, October 17, 2000, Bill Stamets, review of *The Goddess of 1967,* p. 35.

San Francisco Chronicle, August 4, 1999, Bob Graham, review of *Floating Life,* p. E3.
Variety, September 11, 2000, Deborah Young, review of *The Goddess of 1967,* p. 28.*

*   *   *

LEDWIDGE, Michael 1971-

PERSONAL: Born 1971; children: three. *Education:* Graduated from Manhattan College

ADDRESSES: Home—Kingsbridge, NY. *Office*—c/o Pocket Books, 1230 Avenue of the Americas, New York, NY 10020.

CAREER: Writer, 1999—. Also worked as a doorman and telephone repairperson.

WRITINGS:

The Narrowback, Atlantic Monthly Press (New York, NY), 1999.
Bad Connection, Pocket Books (New York, NY), 2001.
Before the Devil Knows You're Dead, Pocket Books (New York, NY), 2002.

ADAPTATIONS: George Clooney optioned *Bad Connection* for possible production as a feature film.

WORK IN PROGRESS: Another novel for Pocket Books.

SIDELIGHTS: Michael Ledwidge was a recent Manhattan College graduate working as a doorman to support his wife and baby when he began working on his first book, *The Narrowback* (1999). One of his former professors put him in contact with James Patterson, a fellow Manhattan College alumus and author. Ledwidge sent Patterson a section of *The Narrowback,* and Patterson helped him on the road to publication. Speaking to Scott Veale of the *New York Times,* Ledwidge said of Patterson, "I owe everything to him." Ledwidge soon found a job working as a telephone cable splicer for Verizon, a position he opted to continue even after the success of his second novel, *Bad Connection.*

In his novels, Ledwidge writes in the mode of hard-boiled noir crime fiction associated with Jim Thompson. In *The Narrowback,* he tells the story of ex-con Irish-American Tommy Farrell and his plan to rob a New York luxury hotel; "Narrowback" is an Irish term for Irish-Americans. Farrell does not know that one of his gang, Durkin, has joined in the scheme to get money for the Irish Republican Army (IRA), and when the man bolts with the cash Farrell's gang kills him. Only later does Farrell learn of his IRA connection, after Durkin's IRA associates start looking for revenge. Farrell, who dreams of moving out west and becoming an artist, instead hides out in the New York underground, trying to stay one step ahead of the IRA, the FBI, and a group of Albanian gangsters.

Critics generally found *The Narrowback* to be a strong debut from a first-time author. Writing for *Library Journal,* Michael Rogers called the book exciting, with an "easy, fluid style"; Rogers described the complex plot as "*The Usual Suspects* meets *The Devil's Own* meets *Reservoir Dogs.*" Though Erik Burns, reviewing the book for the *New York Times Book Review,* suggested that the novel is somewhat melodramatic, "relying . . . on hard-boiled clichés like booze, drugs, loose women, cheap bars and brutal murders," others thought Ledwidge's first effort more successful. A reviewer for *Publishers Weekly* called Ledwidge's prose "lean and mean," adding that the novel itself is a "well-executed debut"; David Pitt, in *Booklist,* said that although the book may lack depth, "most readers . . . will enjoy the chase."

Like many of his characters in *The Narrowback,* Ledwidge himself is Irish American. In his next book, *Bad Connection,* Ledwidge creates a protagonist who is even closer to home. Sean Macklin, the novel's hero, is an Irish-American telephone repairman, just like Ledwidge. Veale, in the *New York Times,* wrote, "Even as the book has been drawing good reviews, Mr. Ledwidge has continued working the 4 to midnight shift, spending about half his day underground. 'It's like detective work, poking around' in the maze of numbered phone lines, he said." Macklin does his own detective work in *Bad Connection,* which begins when he eavesdrops on a conversation that gives him insider information on the planned business merger of Chemtech and Allied Genesis. Hoping to provide a better life for his sick wife, he invests all his money in the deal and makes a small fortune. He begins taping the conversations, and he learns that Chemtech was involved in a series of murders in Central America. Concerned, Macklin gives the incriminating tapes to his brother Ray, a policeman in the South Bronx. But Ray, a corrupt cop, plans to use the tapes for blackmail; eventually both Macklin and his brother are on the hit lists of Chemtech and the mob.

With *Bad Connection,* Ledgwidge continued in the hard-boiled vein. Marilyn Stasio, reviewing the book for the *New York Times,* said that *Bad Connection* "stands on the solid foundation of noir suspense: the undoing of a basically decent man who makes one false move and whose every effort to reverse the damage sucks him deeper into the darkness he never saw coming." *BookBrowsers* reviewer Harriet Klausner compared *Bad Connection* to the noir film *The Conversation,* concluding that "Ledwidge shows plenty of abilities as he takes readers on a wild tour of New York that will gain him a lot of hard boiled crime fiction fans."

BIOGRAPHICAL AND CRITICAL SOURCES:

PERIODICALS

Booklist, October 15, 1998, David Pitt, review of *The Narrowback,* p. 406.
Kirkus Reviews, February 1, 2001, review of *Bad Connection,* p. 131.
Library Journal, September 1, 1998, Michael Rogers, review of *The Narrowback,* p. 215.
New York Times, May 6, 2001, Marilyn Stasio, "Crime," p. 30; August 12, 2001, Scott Veale, "Author and Telephone Repairman Finds Art in Imitating His Life," p. 4.
New York Times Book Review, March 21, 1999, Erik Burns, review of *The Narrowback,* p. 21.
Publishers Weekly, October 19, 1998, review of *The Narrowback,* p. 53; March 19, 2001, review of *Bad Connection,* p. 76; July 23, 2001, John F. Baker, "Pocket and the Phone Guy," p. 14.

OTHER

BookBrowser, http://www.bookbrowser.com/ (February 19, 2001), Harriet Klausner, review of *Bad Connection.*

Crime Time On-Line, http://www.crimetime.co.uk/ (August 23, 2001), Steve Holland, review of *The Narrowback.**

*   *   *

LEIDNER, Alan C.

PERSONAL: Male. *Education:* University of Virginia, Ph.D.

ADDRESSES: Office—Department of Classical and Modern Languages, University of Louisville, Louisville, KY 40292. *E-mail*—alan.leidner@louisville.edu.

CAREER: University of Louisville, Louisville, KY, professor of German.

WRITINGS:

(Editor) *Sturm and Drang,* Continuum (New York, NY), 1992.
(Editor with Helga S. Madland) *Space to Act: The Theater of J. M. R. Lenz,* Camden House (Columbia, SC), 1993.
The Impatient Muse: Germany and the Sturm und Drang, University of North Carolina Press (Chapel Hill, NC), 1994.
(With Karin A. Wurst) *Unpopular Virtues: The Critical Reception of J. M. R. Lenz,* Camden House (Columbia, SC), 1999.

SIDELIGHTS: Alan C. Leidner is a professor of German at the University of Louisville. He is also coeditor, with Helga S. Madland, of *Space to Act: The Theater of J. M. R. Lenz.* The volume of essays is the result of a 1991 University of Oklahoma International symposium on the work of writer Jakob Michael Reinhold Lenz who died mysteriously in Moscow in 1791. The book is divided into three parts: "The Nature of Lenz's Writings," "Lenz's Concept of Action," and "Performances, Adaptations, and Fiction." E. M. Batley wrote in *Modern Language Review* that the book's division into three sections fulfils "in fair measure" the aim of achieving "overall coherence. . . . Lenz's oeuvre, which includes poetry, prose narratives, and a range of essays on theology,

morality, and social issues, does not of course fit in its entirety into the frame set by the title, and comprehensiveness is therefore inevitably limited. On the other hand, comprehensive understanding of Lenz's dramaturgical thinking is achieved, most markedly in the middle section, on the concept of action." Batley felt the collection's "signal achievement, enhanced by the liberating essays of John Guthrie on Lenz's style of comedy, Richard Alan Korb on sex comedy, and Roman Graf on male homosocial desire, is that it shows Lenz to be emerging at last, strongly and clearly, from beneath the long shadow of Goethe's inhibiting judgement."

John Alexander wrote in *Rocky Mountain Review* that in the introduction to *The Impatient Muse: Germany and the Sturm und Drang,* Leidner takes exception to the view that this period was "simply a youthful precursor to Weimar Classicism" or a "mere extension of the European Enlightenment." Leidner writes that it can be better explained by an absence of political unity and the reaction of the literati to this situation. Alexander noted that this theory is the link between the book's seven chapters but felt the organization could have been better if the content were "more focused" and if the title "had reflected the content more accurately rather than simply reflecting a property of the age." Alexander concluded by calling *The Impatient Muse* "an original and sophisticated piece of scholarship" and an "elegantly written book."

BIOGRAPHICAL AND CRITICAL SOURCES:

PERIODICALS

Modern Language Review, January, 1996, E. M. Batley, review of *Space to Act,* pp. 251-252.
Rocky Mountain Review, February, 1995, John Alexander, review of *The Impatient Muse,* pp. 193-194.

OTHER

University of Louisville Web site, http://www.louisville.edu/~a0leid01/ (March 10, 2003), "Alan C. Leisner."

LERNER, Barron H. 1960-

PERSONAL: Born September 27, 1960 in Boston, MA; married, 1990; children: two. *Education:* University of Pennsylvania, A.B., 1982; Columbia College of Physicians and Surgeons, M.D., 1986; University of Washington, Seattle, M.A., 1992, Ph.D., 1996.

ADDRESSES: Home—P.O. Box 11. New York, NY 10032. *Office*—Columbia University, Department of Medicine, Black Building 1-101, 630 West 168th St., New York, NY 10032-3702; fax: (212) 305-6416. *E-mail*—bhl5@columbia.edu.

CAREER: Historian, internist, writer, educator, and scholar. Columbia University, New York, NY, instructor, 1989-91, Mailman School of Public Health, assistant professor of medicine and public health, 1993—; Presbyterian Hospital, assistant physician, 1989-91, attending physician, 1993-; University of Washington, Seattle, WA, Instructor, 1991-93. Director of Ethics Fellowship for Department of Medicine Housestaff.

MEMBER: American Association for the History of Medicine, Society of General Internal Medicine.

AWARDS, HONORS: Angelica Berrie Gold Foundation scholarship, 1993; Burroughs Wellcome Fund History of Medicine Award, 1997-99; Robert Wood Johnson generalist faculty scholarship, 1997-2001; National Library of Medicine Publication grant, 2001; Greenwall Foundation grant, 2001; Richard Shryock Medal; Jos. Garrison Parker prize; Arnold P. Gold award.

WRITINGS:

Contagion and Confinement: Controlling Tuberculosis along the Skid Row, Johns Hopkins University Press (Baltimore, MD), 1998.
The Breast Cancer Wars: Hope, Fear, and the Pursuit of a Cure in Twentieth-Century America, Oxford University Press (New York, NY), 2001.

Contributor to numerous medical and historical journals, magazines, and newspapers, including *Chest, American Journal of Public Health, Annals of Internal Medicine, Lancet,* and the *Washington Post;* editorial board member of *American Journal of Public Health, Annals of Internal Medicine, Bulletin of the History of Medicine, Journal of General Internal Medicine,* and *New England Journal of Medicine.*

SIDELIGHTS: Barron H. Lerner is a physician and an assistant professor of medicine and public health at Columbia University. He is also a historian whose areas of expertise include tuberculosis and detention and civil liberties issues concerning it; breast cancer and the history and ethics of its screening and treatment; and the history and ethical issues of public health. He writes and lectures on these and other subjects. Lerner's interest in breast cancer was intensified by his mother's struggle with the illness in 1977.

When writing about diseases, Lerner details the public-health and social-history aspects relating to the conditions. His book *Contagion and Confinement: Controlling Tuberculosis along the Skid Row* examines the social history of tuberculosis treatment in post-World War II Seattle, in the poor, transient population of "Skid Row." Seattle's many seasonal industries drew single, unskilled workers, and during the winter off-season they spent time in the flophouses, missions, and taverns of Skid Row. This area was notorious for its high rates of alcoholism and tuberculosis (TB). Most residents infected with TB did not complete their treatments and returned to their former hangouts, where they were likely to reinfect themselves or infect others.

With the end of World War II, Seattle received the deed of a vacant military hospital, and there they expanded the existing Firland Tuberculosis Sanatorium. During a three-month period in 1948, a massive chest X-ray screening effort of Seattle residents identified 402 TB victims who were admitted to Firland. The state of Washington adopted a quarantine policy for TB patients, and in 1949 Firland set up Ward 6, a locked detention ward.

Lerner's book examines the treatment of about two thousand patients who were detained in Ward 6 between 1949 and 1973. Social factors such as poor living conditions, working conditions, and nutrition were considered key risk factors for contracting TB, and in the 1950s Firland staff psychiatrist Thomas Holmes and medical sociologist Joan Jackson began studying the alcoholic TB patients from Skid Row. Alcoholism was seen as a medical illness, and its treatment was deemed essential, with on-site Alcoholics Anonymous meetings, vocational rehabilitation, and psychological support offered. Firland had the most aggressive involuntary detention policy in the country, and by the 1960s, half of all Skid Row alcoholics spent at least two weeks in Ward 6, whether they had the disease or not. They were detained without a legal process and could be held indefinitely. In 1965, a judge began hearing complaints by patients held in Ward 6, and an outpatient treatment program in Denver showed successful results, which eventually led to the closure of Firland and other TB sanatoriums.

The 1980s saw a resurgence of TB associated with HIV and homelessness, and TB was again considered a social disease. *New England Journal of Medicine* reviewer Daniel Wlodarczyk wrote that *Contagion and Confinement* "is exceedingly well referenced and uses primary sources extensively. It provides a chronology of the historical events that led to the rise and fall of the tuberculosis sanatorium and the abuses of civil liberties in the name of public health." Reviewer Richard A. Meckel observed in the *Journal of American History,* "Admirably, Lerner resists reducing control of TB in the antibiotic era to a narrative involving the progressive medicalization of a social problem. Instead, by describing the various psychiatric and social work interventions employed by Firland, he shows how medical and social interpretations of the disease were inexorably intertwined." A reviewer for the *Journal of the American Medical Association* described *Contagion and Confinement* as an "excellent, thoroughly researched, clearly-formulated book . . . the implications speak to TB prevention, and, indeed, to transmissible disease prophylaxis in general."

As its name declares, Lerner's *The Breast Cancer Wars: Hope, Fear, and the Pursuit of a Cure in Twentieth-Century America* provides a history of the diagnosis of breast cancer in the United States. *Library Journal* reviewer Martha E. Stone noted, "Lerner presents a remarkably readable understanding of distinctly American attitudes toward the disease and the ways in which American culture and society have influenced its treatment." "In a readable style with realms of research . . . Lerner describes the first battles: over surgical treatment for breast cancer, then over statistics versus clinical experience; over the biol-

ogy of individual cancers; over randomized controlled trials; and over the patient's role in deciding treatment," wrote *British Medical Journal* reviewer Janice Hopkins.

Using the acceptance and then discrediting of radical mastectomy surgery first practiced by surgeon William Halsted in the late nineteenth century, Lerner depicts the changes in treatment and perception of breast cancer. "The great strength of Barron Lerner's scrupulously documented new book lies in its account of the ways by which it finally came to be accepted that breast cancer, from the first phases of its development, is no longer the local disease that Halsted believed it to be," maintained *New York Review of Books* writer Sherwin B. Nuland.

In the 1960s George Crile supported less aggressive operations and did not agree with the cancer establishment's aggressive publicity campaign for early detection, believing it was the biology of the cancer, not how early it was diagnosed, that determined if a tumor would metastasize. Spearheaded by the women's movement of the 1970s, women began involving themselves in their treatment. Women journalists who developed breast cancer chronicled in the news media their process of self-education and battles with their doctors; First Lady Betty Ford and vice-president wife Happy Rockefeller also went public with their breast cancer fights. Women successfully organized for increased funding for breast cancer treatment and greater roles in their treatment decisions.

"Even as he tells the story of the breast cancer 'wars,' physician and medical historian Lerner directs attention to the dangers that arise from using military terms and thinking in a health-care context," pointed out *Booklist* reviewer William Beatty. "His impressively thorough, readably scholarly book may become the classic in the field," Beatty concluded. "Provocative and highly engaging, Lerner's book presents an important contribution to medical history," according to a *Publishers Weekly* critic; "moreover, he offers insights into areas that most books about breast health and disease do not probe." Shari Roan pointed out in a *Los Angeles Times* review that Lerner cautions against the overtreatment of breast cancer and "unrealistic expectations" in a treatment. Roan also praised Lerner: "The benefits of challenging conventional wisdom are on full display in this thorough historical account of breast cancer treatment in 20th century America.

Indeed, it becomes clear after just a few chapters that it was a mere handful of pioneers—doctors and patients—who refused to settle for the status quo and demanded scientific advances in the detection, treatment and prevention of breast cancer."

BIOGRAPHICAL AND CRITICAL SOURCES:

PERIODICALS

Booklist, May 1, 2001, William Beatty, review of *The Breast Cancer Wars: Hope, Fear, and the Pursuit of a Cure in Twentieth-Century America,* p. 1651.

British Medical Journal, July 14, 2001, Janice Hopkins, review of *The Breast Cancer Wars,* p. 115.

Journal of American History, June, 2000, Richard A. Meckel, review of *Contagion and Confinement: Controlling Tuberculosis along the Skid Row,* p. 294-296.

Journal of the American Medical Association, September 8, 1999, Harriet S. Meyer, Jonathan D. Eldredge, Robert Hogan, and Peter Baldwin, review of *Contagion and Confinement,* p. 996.

Journal of Health Politics, Policy, and Law, December, 2000, Scott Burris, review of *Contagion and Confinement,* p. 1168-1171.

Library Journal, May 15, 2001, Martha E. Stone, review of *The Breast Cancer Wars,* p. 152.

Los Angeles Times, July 23, 2001, Shari Roan, "Leaders in the Fight against Breast Cancer," p. S2.

New England Journal of Medicine, August 5, 1999, Daniel Wlodarczyk, review of *Contagion and Confinement,* pp. 459-460; November 1, 2001, Lundy Braun, review of *The Breast Cancer Wars,* p. 1354; June, 2000, Richard A. Meckel, review of *Contagion and Confinement,* pp. 459-461.

New York Review of Books, September 20, 2001, Sherwin B. Nuland, "'A Very Wide and Deep Dissection,'" pp. 51-53.

Publishers Weekly, April 16, 2001, review of *The Breast Cancer Wars,* p. 52.

Washington Post, May 22, 2001, review of *The Breast Cancer Wars,* p. T14.

Women's Review of Books, November, 2001, Judy Brady, "War without End?" p. 13.

OTHER

Columbia University Web site, http://chaos.cpmc.columbia.edu/ (December 31, 2001).

Society of Medicine, http://www.societyandmedicine.org/ (December 31, 2001).*

LESSARD, Bill 1966(?)-

PERSONAL: Born c. 1966. *Education:* Earned M.A., 1992.

ADDRESSES: Home—Yonkers, NY. *E-mail*—netslaves@hotmail.com.

CAREER: Time Warner, New York, NY, communications producer for Pathfinder, 1995-96; formerly employed by Prodigy and the Globe. Co-founder of NetSlaves.com (now Dotcom Scoop), 1998.

WRITINGS:

(With Steve Baldwin) *Netslaves: True Tales of Working the Web,* McGraw-Hill, 1999.

Netslaves was translated into French, Spanish, German, Japanese, Chinese, and Korean.

WORK IN PROGRESS: Will Code for Food: True Tales of the Great Web Wipeout.

SIDELIGHTS: Bill Lessard formerly worked for Prodigy and TimeWarner's Pathfinder, as well as for numerous Internet startups. Unhappy about the long hours, high stress, and the lack of profits, Lessard decided to locate others who shared his unhappy work experience. Together with coworker Steve Baldwin, Lessard founded *NetSlaves,* a webzine devoted to the stories of those who have been unsuccessful in Internet ventures, in 1998. Based on interviews conducted by the partners with Internet workers of all kinds, from the most humble of web designers to the wealthiest of entrepreneurs, *Netslaves* documents an industry with a gold rush mentality but little gold. "What's a good boom without a loud backlash?. . . ." asked Katharine Mieszkowski in an article on *NetSlaves* for *Fast Company.* "It's no surprise that the boom to end all booms—the explosion of Web startups and IPOs—has triggered a backlash. What is surprising is that the most entertaining complaints and caveats are coming from the Internet insiders."

In 1999 Baldwin and Lessard gathered together the best stories from their Webzine and published *Netslaves: True Tales of Working with the Web.* A

Publishers Weekly critic wrote that *Netslaves*'s "case studies of disgruntled tech support operators and HTML code writers make for bitterly funny reading." According to Meg Mitchell in *CIO Magazine,* the book's tales of working horror are "engaging, hilarious and tinged with despair." Dale F. Farris, writing in *Library Journal,* found *Netslaves* to be a "sobering inside look at what really goes on behind the closed doors of cyberspace." The *Publishers Weekly* critic concluded: "On the whole, this insider's look at the industry offers an amusing antidote to the media's chronic case of Internet hype."

BIOGRAPHICAL AND CRITICAL SOURCES:

PERIODICALS

CIO Magazine, June 1, 2000, Meg Mitchell, "Emancipation Proclamation."
Fast Company, July-August, 1999, Katharine Mieszkowski, "Backlash.com," p. 42.
Library Journal, November 1, 1999, Dale F. Farris, review of *Netslaves,* p. 98.
New York Times, March 23, 1999, Lisa Napoli, "Web-Weary Workers Find Outlets Online."
Publishers Weekly, October 18, 1999, review of *Netslaves,* pp. 62-63.
Seattle Weekly, March 25-31, 1999, John Whalen, "Netslaves."

OTHER

Dotcom Scoop Web site http://www.Dotcom Scoop. com/ (April 15, 2003).
Internetnews.com Web site, http://www.Internetnews. com/ (June 29, 2000), Ken Cimino, "Digital Disappointment: Horror Stories Haunt the Web."
NetSlaves Media Kit, http://www.disobey.com/ netslaves/ (February 3, 2000).

*   *   *

LEVY, Marc 1961-

PERSONAL: Born 1961, in France; children: Louis.

ADDRESSES: Home—London, England. *Agent*—c/o Publicity Director, Pocket Books, 100 Front St., Riverside, NJ 08075.

CAREER: Author. Former chief executive officer of architectural design firm in France.

WRITINGS:

Et si c'était vrai, Robert Laffont (Paris, France), 1999, translation published as *If Only It Were True,* Pocket Books (New York, NY), 2000.

ADAPTATIONS: Film rights to *If Only It Were True* have been bought by DreamWorks. *If Only It Were True* has been adapted for sound recording.

WORK IN PROGRESS: A novel set in New York and a collection of bedtime stories for children.

SIDELIGHTS: With the unexpected and almost immediate success of his debut novel *If Only It Were True,* Marc Levy gave up a career as an architect to devote all of his time to writing. Before publishing *If Only It Were True,* Levy was the chief executive officer of an architectural design firm in Paris, France. His interest in writing stemmed from the bedtime stories he thought up for his son Louis. Levy, a single father, would tell Louis a story every night to help him fall asleep. He enjoyed the challenge of making up stories and decided to write one down for his son to read when he grew up. Although he had no intention of having the book published when he began the project, Levy was persuaded by his sister to send the manuscript to the French publisher Robert Laffont, whose editors were impressed with the book and agreed to publish it. With the novel's success, both in France and abroad, Levy resigned from his architectural firm in 2000 and moved with his son to London, England, where he took up writing on a full-time basis.

If Only It Were True is set near San Francisco, where Levy once lived for several years. The plot revolves around the unusual love affair of Lauren Kline, a career-minded emergency room intern, and a renowned San Francisco architect named Arthur. When Lauren is in a serious car accident, she is left in a coma. While lying in the hospital bed, Lauren learns how to detach her spirit from her body. With this newfound ability, she roams the city, often returning to the apartment where she lived before the accident. When Arthur decides to move into this now-vacant apartment, he finds a crying, lonely Lauren in a closet. Unlike everyone else, he can actually see and communicate with her. The two fall in love, but the relationship falls into jeopardy when Lauren's family decides to take her off the life-support machine at the hospital and let her die. Arthur decides to steal Lauren's body from the hospital so he can keep her alive long enough to save her. As the story progresses, Lauren watches as Arthur studies medical journals and conducts paranormal research in an attempt to raise her from her coma.

Arthur's relationship with Lauren also makes him face some of his own past, especially his mother's death twenty years earlier. In the end, Arthur does find a way to cure Lauren, although she does not remember who he is when she awakes, and the two must learn to love one another again.

If Only It Were True received mixed reviews from critics. A *Kirkus Reviews* contributor felt the author's prose has "almost no sense of the urgencies of language or strivings for expression" and described the book as "flower-strewn, lyrical, and immensely predictable." But *Booklist* critic Patty Engelmann called the novel "a heartfelt journey into life's lessons," in addition to noting Levy's ability to create "well-developed characters." Carol DeAngelo of *School Library Journal* called Levy's effort a "feel-good story" that, in her opinion, would be "particularly popular with teen girls." And Kamila Shamsie in the *Times Literary Supplement* wrote that Levy's novel contains "all the ingredients for a rollicking romance/thriller, with the occasional touch of comedy."

BIOGRAPHICAL AND CRITICAL SOURCES:

PERIODICALS

Booklist, May 15, 2000, Patty Engelmann, review of *If Only It Were True,* p. 1730.
Entertainment Weekly, June 2, 2000, review of *If Only It Were True,* p. 74.
Europe, May, 2000, Ester Laushway, "Spielberg to Film French Novel," p. 36.
Kirkus Reviews, May 1, 2000, review of *If Only It Were True,* p. 568.
Publishers Weekly, November 1, 1999, John F. Baker, "Pardon My French: DreamWorks Buys Film Rights to a Novel by French Architect/Author

Levy," p. 18; April 10, 2000, review of *If Only It Were True,* p. 73; September 4, 2000, review of *If Only It Were True,* (sound recording).
School Library Journal, August, 2000, Carol DeAngelo, review of *If Only It Were True,* p. 212.
Times Literary Supplement, June 23, 2000, Kamila Shamsie, "Spirit Guidance," p. 24.
Variety, March 13, 2000, Alison James, "CEO Shows His 'True' Colors: Marc Levy to Become Full-time Writer," p. 16.

OTHER

Bookreporter.com, http://www.bookreporter.com/ (December 4, 2001), Erin Lenae Williams, review of *If Only It Were True.**

*   *   *

LHERMITTE, Thierry 1952-
  (Thierry Teil)

PERSONAL: Born November 24, 1952 in Boulogne-Billancourt, France.

ADDRESSES: Agent—c/o Le Splendid, 48 rue du Fbg. St. Martin, 75010 Paris, France.

CAREER: Actor, producer, director, and writer.

Film appearances include *L'an 01,* 1972; *Si vous n'aimez pas ca, n'en degoutez pas les autres,* SND, 1973; *Les valseuses,* Cinema 5 Distributing, 1974; *Que la fete commence,* Specialty Films, 1974; *F'comme Fairbanks,* 1976; *Des enfants gates,* Corinth Films, 1977; *Vous n'aurez pas l'Alsace et la Lorraine,* 1977; *Le dernier amant romantique,* 1978; *Sun Tan,* 1978; "Voleur de pneus," *Les heros n'ont pas froid aux oreilles,* 1978; *Les bronzes,* 1978; *Alors, heureux?,* 1979; *Les bronzes font du ski,* 1979; *Clara et les chics types,* 1980; *Les hommes preferent les grosses,* 1981; "Le prince voyageur," *Elle voit des nains partout!,* GEF, 1981; *L'annee prochaine . . . si tout va bien,* New World Pictures, 1981; *Le Pere Noel est une ordure,* 1982; *Legitime violence,* 1982; *Le prefere,* 1983; *Stella,* Hachette-Fox Productions, 1983; *La femme de mon pote,* European International, 1983; *La fiancee qui venait du froid,* 1983; *Un homme a ma taille,* 1983; *Papy fait de la resistance,* AMLF, 1983; *L'Indic,* 1983; *La smala,* 1984; *Les ripoux,* Orion, 1984; *Un ete d'enfer,* 1984; *Until September,* 1984; *Sac de noeuds,* 1985; *Les rois du gag,* 1985; *Le mariage du siecle,* 1985; *Nuit d'ivresse,* 1986; *Les freres petard,* 1986; *Dernier ete a Tanger,* 1987; *Fucking Fernand,* 1987; *Ripoux contre ripoux,* Interama Video, 1990; *La fete des peres,* 1990; *Les mille et une nuits,* Video Search of Miami, 1990; *Promotion Canape,* 1990; *Les secrets professionels du Dr. Apfelglueck,* 1991; *La Totale!,* Manuel Salvador, 1991; *Un piede in paradiso,* Lauren Film, 1991; *Le zebre,* Transeuro pa Video Entertainment, 1992; *Tango,* Cine Company, 1993; *Fanfan,* 1993; *L'ombre du doute,* Vertigo Films, 1993; *L'honneur de la tribu,* Neuf de Coeur, 1993; *La vengeance d'une blonde,* 1994; *Elles n'oublient jamais,* Video Search of Miami, 1994; *Grosse fatigue,* Miramax, 1994; *Un indien dans la ville,* Buena Vista, 1994; *Tous les jours dimanche,* AMLF, 1995; *Augustin,* 1995; *Ma femme me quitte,* 1996; *Fallait pas! . . .,* Lauren Film, 1996; *Les soeurs soleil,* NTV-PROFIT, 1997; *Comme des rois,* AB Films Distribution, 1997; *Quatre garcons pleins d'avenir,* 1997; *Marquise,* Video Search of Miami, 1997; *An American Werewolf in Paris,* Buena Vista, 1997; *Le diner de cons,* Lions Gate Films, 1998; *Le plus beau pays du monde,* Warner Bros., 1998; *Trafic d'influence,* PolyGram Film Distribution, 1999; *C'est pas ma faute,* Pathé, 1999; *Le prof,* Rezo Films, 2000; *Meilleur espoir feminin,* UGC-Fox Distribution, 2000; *Deuxieme vie,* UGC-Fox Distribution, 2000; *Le prince du Pacifique,* TF1 International, 2000; *Bon plan* (also known as *Great Idea*), United International Pictures, 2000; *Enfoires en 2000,* 2000; *Le placard* (also known as *The Closet*), 2001; *Le Roman de Lulu,* 2001; *La bande du drugstore* (also known as *Dandy*), 2002; *Une affaire privée* (also known as *A Private Affair*), Bac Films, 2002; *And Now. . . Ladies and Gentlemen,* Paramount Classics, 2002; *Effroyables jardin,* ICE3/UGC Images, 2003; *Mauvais esprit,* Pathé, 2003; and *Le Divorce,* Fox Searchlight Pictures, 2003.

Film work (as producer, unless otherwise noted) includes *Les secrets professionels du Dr. Apfelglueck,* 1991; *Un indien dans la ville,* Buena Vista, 1994; (associate producer) *Jungle2Jungle,* Buena Vista, 1997; *Charite biz'ness,* AMLF, 1999; *Les collegues,* AMLF, 1999; *C'est pas ma faute,* Pathé, 1999; and *Le prince du Pacifique,* TF1 International, 2000.

Episodic television appearances include "Le chat et la souris," *Sueurs froides,* 1988. Other television appearances include *L'ex-femme de ma vie,* 1989; *Les danseurs du Mozambique,* 1991; and *Deux justiciers dans la ville,* 1993.

WRITINGS:

(Adaptor, with others) *Un indien dans la ville* (screenplay adaptation; also known as *Little Indian, Big City; An Indian in the City; An Indian in Paris*), Buena Vista, 1994.
(With others) *Le prince du Pacifique* (also known as *The Prince of the Pacific*), TF1 International, 2000.

Other screenplays include (idea only) *C'est pas parce qu'on a rien à dire qu'il faut fermer sa gueuele,* 1975; *Sun Tan* (adaptation), 1978; *Les Bronzes* (also known as *French Fried Vacation*), 1978; *Les bronzes dont du ski,* 1979; *Le Pere Noël est une ordure,* 1982; *Nuit d'ivresse,* 1986; and *Les secrets professionels du Dr. Apfelglück,* 1991.

ADAPTATIONS: The Disney fiim *Jungle2Jungle,* Buena Vista, 1997, was based on Lhermitte's *Un indien dans la ville.*

SIDELIGHTS: Born in suburban Paris, Thierry Lhermitte founded a comedy troupe called La Splendid, one of the sketches of which became the basis for a movie. From there, Lhermitte's career flourished, and he has starred in dozens of films. Among these are several that have been remade in the United States: thus, as Frank Magiera observed in the Worcester, Massachusetts, *Telegram and Gazette,* "Before we had Arnold Schwarzenegger in *True Lies,* the French had Thierry Lhermitte in *La totale!* And before we had Steve Martin in *Mixed Nuts,* they had Thierry Lhermitte in *Le Pere Noël est une ordure,*" the screenplay of which Lhermitte also wrote.

When Lhermitte sold Disney the rights to remake the 1994 film *Un indien dans la ville,* which he cowrote—and which appeared in 1997 as *Jungle2Jungle,* starring Tim Allen—he included the stipulation that the French film receive a full U.S. release. Thus, in March 1996, *Un indien,* appearing under the English title *Little Indian, Big City,* opened at some 600 theatres nationwide.

The storyline is a classic tale of a "noble savage" taken to the city, only it is played as comedy and not as farce. In *Little Indian,* a Paris stockbroker (played by Lhermitte himself) travels to South America to find his estranged wife, and discovers that he has a son. The boy, raised in the Amazonian rain forest, is at home climbing trees and playing with wild animals, so it is as much a shock to him as to the father when circumstances require that the two return to Paris together.

Reviews of *Little Indian* were largely unfavorable, due in part to material that seemed to belie promotion of the movie as a "family picture." Bill Lohmann in the *Richmond Times-Dispatch* questioned whether anyone would agree with promotional material describing *Little Indian* as a "'warm-hearted family comedy' . . . . Unless you like the sight of a pigeon nailed to the side of an apartment building by an arrow. Or maybe a kid in a loin cloth taking a bite out of a snake's head." Such material, along with overt suggestions of budding sexuality on the part of the thirteen-year-old-boy, worked better with audiences in France and Europe—where the film was an enormous hit— than in America. Also problematic was the fact that the film had been dubbed into English rather than subtitled—another consequence of its promotion as a "family film," the reasoning being that children would not put up with a movie that had subtitles.

Much more successful critically was *Le prince du Pacifique*, released in English as *The Prince of the Pacific*. Another film starring and cowritten by Lhermitte, this one also plays on the differences between life in the pristine wilderness and the ways of the powerful European civilizations that invade them, but critics found it did so with much greater finesse. Set mostly during World War I, *The Prince of the Pacific* is the story of Captain Morsac, who is wounded on the battlefield in Morocco, and, after recovering, is sent to Tahiti to recruit Polynesians for the service of France. However, he finds the island ruled by a brutal French military governor, against whose authoritarian rule he ultimately organizes a resistance force.

BIOGRAPHICAL AND CRITICAL SOURCES:

BOOKS

Contemporary Theatre, Film, and Television, Gale (Detroit, MI), volume 35, 2001.

PERIODICALS

Boston Globe, March 22, 1996, Jay Carr, review of *Little Indian, Big City,* p. 50.

Dallas Morning News, March 23, 1996, Jane Sumner, review of *Little Indian, Big City,* p. C5.
New York Times, March 22, 1996, Janet Maslin, review of *Little Indian, Big City,* p. B6.
Richmond Times-Dispatch, March 23, 1996, Bill Lohmann, review of *Little Indian, Big City,* p. B7.
Telegram and Gazette (Worcester, MA), Frank Magiera, review of *Little Indian, Big City,* p. 3.
Variety, January 1, 2001, Lisa Nesselson, review of *The Prince of the Pacific,* p. 36.*

* * *

LIDDICOAT, Richard T(homas), Jr. 1918-2002

OBITUARY NOTICE—See index for CA sketch: Born March 2, 1918, in Kearsarge, MI; died July 23, 2002, in Los Angeles, CA. Gemologist and author. Liddicoat was considered by many to be the "dean of gemology" due to his leadership at the Gemological Institute of America and for inventing the grading system for diamonds that has become the standard. A graduate of the University of Michigan where he earned a master's degree in 1940, Liddicoat immediately headed to California to work at the Gemological Institute in Los Angeles. Except for the interruption of World War II, during which he served in the U.S. Navy as a weather officer on an aircraft carrier in the Pacific, he remained at the institute throughout his career. There he rose from assistant director of education to executive director in 1952, his position given the title of president after 1970. Although he retired in 1983 he continued to serve as chairman of the institute's executive board and was named chairman of the board for life in 1992. Liddicoat is credited with creating the "four C's" rating system for diamonds, which grades the gems according to color, cut, clarity, and carat weight. Along with Gemological Institute founder Robert M. Shipley, Liddicoat also led the way in creating a national education program for gemologists that has since spread to eight other countries. In addition, he was editor-in-chief of the institute's journal, *Gems and Gemology,* from 1952 until his death, and was a founding member of the board of directors of the Gem and Mineral Council of the Natural History Museum of Los Angeles County. Liddicoat was the author of *Handbook of Gem Identification* (1947), which has gone through numerous editions, the coauthor of *The Diamond Dictionary* (1960) and *The Jeweler's Manual* (1964; second edition, 1967), and editor of the *GIA Diamond*

Dictionary (1993). In recognition of his contributions, the mineral Liddicoatite was named in his honor.

OBITUARIES AND OTHER SOURCES:

BOOKS

Who's Who in America, 53rd edition, Marquis (New Providence, NJ), 1999.

PERIODICALS

Chicago Tribune, July 29, 2002, section 2, p. 7.
Los Angeles Times, July 26, 2002, p. B12.
New York Times, July 26, 2002, p. C15.
Times (London, England), August 5, 2002.
Washington Post, July 28, 2002, p. C6.

*   *   *

LLOYD, P(eter) J(ohn) 1937-

PERSONAL: Born June 20, 1937, in Manaia, New Zealand; son of Alfred Henry and May (McLeod) Lloyd; married Elizabeth Wallace Jones, December 21, 1965; children: Alison Jane Cui, Caroline May, Natalie Joy. *Education:* Victoria University of Wellington, B.A., 1958, M.A. (with first class honors), 1959; Duke University, Ph.D., 1962. *Hobbies and other interests:* Bush walking, fishing.

ADDRESSES: Home—6 McEvoy St., Kew, Victoria 3101, Australia. *Office*—Department of Economics, Faculty of Economics and Commerce, University of Melbourne, Parkville, Victoria 3010, Australia; fax: 61-03-844-6899. *E-mail*—pjlloyd@unimelb.edu.au.

CAREER: New Zealand Department of Statistics, research officer, 1959; Victoria University of Wellington, Wellington, New Zealand, lecturer, 1962-64, senior lecturer, 1964-65; Michigan State University, East Lansing, assistant professor, 1965-68, associate professor of economics, 1969; Australian National University, Canberra, Australian Capital Territory, Australia, senior research fellow, 1969, senior fellow, 1970-81, professorial fellow, 1981-83, faculty chair of

Research School of Pacific Studies, 1976, 1977; University of Melbourne, Parkville, Victoria, Australia, professor, 1983—, Ritchie Professor of Economics, 1995—, dean of Faculty of Economics and Commerce, 1988-93, director of Asian Business Centre, 1994-96, and Asian Economics Centre, 1997-99, acting director of Centre of Financial Studies, 2000-01. Australian-Japan Research Centre, member of research committee, 1986-88; University of Reading, member of editorial board of Trade Policy Research Centre, 1993-94. State of Victoria, Australia, member of Fulbright selection committee, 1990—. Australian Manufacturing Council, member, 1984-86; Industries Assistance Commission, associate commissioner, 1985-91; Australian Aid advisory council, member, 1998-2001; consultant to General Agreement on Tariffs and Trade, World Trade Organization, World Bank, Organization for Economic Cooperation and Development, and U.N. Conference on Trade and Development.

MEMBER: Australian Academy of the Social Sciences (fellow), Economic Society of Australia.

AWARDS, HONORS: Silver Award, *Review of International Economics,* 1995; Economics Award, New Zealand Institute of Economic Research, 2002; grants from Australian Research Council.

WRITINGS:

International Trade Problems of Small Nations, Duke University Press (Durham, NC), 1968.
Non-Tariff Barriers to Australian Trade, Australian National University Press (Canberra, Australian Capital Territory, Australia), 1973.
(With Herbert Grubel) *Intra-Industry Trade,* Macmillan (New York, NY), 1974.
(With Kerrin Vautier) *International Trade and Competition Policy: CER, APEC, and the WTO,* Institute of Policy Studies (Wellington, New Zealand), 1997.
International Trade Opening and the Formation of the Global Economy: Selected Essays, Edward Elgar Publishing (Northampton, MA), 1999.
(With Kerrin Vautier) *Promoting Competition in Global Markets: A Multi-national Approach,* Edward Elgar Publishing (Northampton, MA), 1999.
Intra-Industry Trade: Critical Writings in Economics, Edward Elgar Publishing (Northampton, MA), 2002.

Author of research monographs for New Zealand Institute of Economic Research, New Zealand Planning Council, and other organizations. Contributor to books, including *New Silk Roads: East Asia and World Textile Markets,* edited by K. Anderson, Cambridge University Press (New York, NY), 1992; *Development, Trade, and the Asia-Pacific: Essays in Honour of Lim Chong Yah,* edited by B. Kapur, E. Quah, and Hoon Hian Teck, Prentice-Hall (Englewood Cliffs, NJ), 1996; *Business, Markets, and Governments in Asia and the Pacific,* edited by Rong-I Wu, Routledge (New York, NY), 1998; *APEC: Challenges and Tasks for the Twenty-first Century,* edited by Ippei Yamazawa, Routledge, NY), 2000; and *Global Production and Trade in East Asia,* edited by Leonard K. Cheng and Henryk Kierzkowski, Kluwer Academic Publishers, 2001. Contributor to professional journals, including *European Economic Review, Applied Economics, World Economy, Asian Development Review, Review of International Economics, History of Political Economy, European Journal of Political Economy, World Trade Review, Journal of Policy Modeling,* and *Asia-Pacific Economic Literature.*

EDITOR

(And contributor) *Mineral Economics in Australia,* Allen & Unwin (Sydney, Australia), 1984.

(With Luigi Pasinetti) *Structural Change, Economic Interdependence, and World Development,* Macmillan (New York, NY), 1986.

(With Lim Chong-Yah; and contributor) *Singapore: Resources and Growth,* Oxford University Press (New York, NY), 1986.

(With Stephen King) *Economic Rationalism: Dead End or Way Forward?,* Allen & Unwin (Sydney, Australia), 1993.

(With Lynne Williams; and contributor) *International Trade and Migration in the APEC Region,* Oxford University Press (New York, NY), 1996.

(With Xiao-guang Zhang) *China in the Global Economy,* Edward Elgar Publishing (Northampton, MA), 2000.

(With Xiao-guang Zhang; and contributor) *Models of the Chinese Economy,* Edward Elgar Publishing (Northampton, MA), 2001.

(With John Nieuwenhuysen and Margaret Mead) *Growth with Equity,* Cambridge University Press (New York, NY), 2001.

(With Hyun-hoon Lee) *Frontiers of Research in Intra-Industry Trade,* Edward Elgar Publishing (Northampton, MA), 2002.

(With Herbert G. Grubel) *Intra-Industry Trade,* Edward Elgar Publishing (Northampton, MA), 2003.

Coeditor, *Economic Record,* 1977-82; corresponding editor, *Journal of Asian Economics,* 1994—; associate editor, *Australian Economic Review,* 1985—; coeditor of "Global Policy Review" edition of *World Economy,* 1998-2002; member of editorial board, *Singapore Economic Review,* 1994-95, and *Review of Development Economics,* 1999—; advisory editor, *Journal of the Korean Economy,* 2000—; member of editorial advisory council, *Pacific Economic Review,* 1997—.

WORK IN PROGRESS: Research on international trade theory and empirical research.

SIDELIGHTS: P. J. Lloyd told *CA:* "I write a lot because I am passionate about research in economics. That is what I most like to do at work. To me economics is a discipline that has a lot to say about the problems of managing economies, in both developed and developing countries. I have always believed that the only justification for the logic of economic theory is to enlighten us about real-world markets and real-world economies and, conversely, that the analysis of these real-world problems requires the logic and power of economic theory. Hence, I have tried throughout my career to combine work on economic theory and applied policy-oriented work. My specialization has been international economics, and this is rooted in microeconomic and general equilibrium theory.

"When it comes to the process of writing, I have never had difficulty putting pen to paper (as it were, in the age of desk computers). Typically I have thought about some policy problem and the relevant economic models, worked out some ideas and equations on paper, and just sat down to write at the keyboard."

BIOGRAPHICAL AND CRITICAL SOURCES:

PERIODICALS

New Zealand Economic Papers, December, 1997, Martin Richardson, review of *International Trade and Competition Policy: CER, APEC, and the WTO,* p. 229.

LOHF, Kenneth A. 1925-2002

OBITUARY NOTICE—See index for *CA* sketch: Born January 14, 1925, in Milwaukee, WI; died from complications from a stroke May 9, 2002, in New York, NY. Librarian and author. Lohf was a longtime librarian of rare books at Columbia University. Before attending college he served in India as a lieutenant in the U.S. Army Air Force. He then attended Northwestern University, where he received his bachelor's degree in 1949, followed by graduate work at Columbia University where he earned master's degrees in library science and English in 1952. Lohf became interested in collecting rare books while a graduate student and searching for books by Graham Greene for his master's thesis. He became an assistant librarian at Columbia in 1957, working in the rare book and manuscript library and becoming a librarian in 1967. During his tenure there, he doubled the library's collection of rare books and raised funds for a three million dollar renovation of the building before retiring in 1993. During his career Lohf published several scholarly books, including *The Jack Harris Samuels Library* (1974) and *The Centenary of John Masefield's Birth* (1978). He also edited a number of books and wrote poetry that was published in such collections as *XXX for Time* (1966), *Seasons* (1980), *Arrivals* (1987), *Fictions* (1990), *Places* (1992), *Poets in a War* (1995), *The Book of Twelve* (2000), and *East West* (2001).

OBITUARIES AND OTHER SOURCES:

PERIODICALS

New York Times, May 18, 2002, p. B15.

*   *   *

LONG, Elgen M. 1927

PERSONAL: Born 1927, in McMinneville, OR; son of Harry E. and Berniece Elsie (Tooney) Long; married Marie Kurlich (a consultant), May 12, 1946; children: Donna Marie Weiner, Harry Elgen. *Education:* University of California, Los Angeles, 1946-47; College of San Mateo, A.E. 1961. *Politics:* Democrat. *Hobbies and other interests:* Flying (holds world record for flying solo around the world over both poles), Amelia Earhart enthusiast and expert.

ADDRESSES: Home—18124 Wedge Parkway, Reno, NV 89511-8134.

CAREER: Author and pilot. Flying Tiger Line, Inc., Los Angeles, CA, radio operator, 1947-48, navigator, 1949-50; pilot, 1951-87; Federal Aviation Administration, air safety council, 1972. Director, Auto-Navigation, Inc.; partner, Woodside Investment Co. and Whalebone Music. *Military service:* U.S. Naval Reserve, 1942-46.

MEMBER: National Aeronautic Association, American Polar Society, Royal Canadian Airforce Association, Airline Pilots Association; Aircraft Owners and Pilots Association, Coronado Cays Yacht Club, Explorer's Club.

AWARDS, HONORS: Named First Citizen of San Mateo County, 1971; World Gold Air medal, Federation Aeronautique, 1971; Franklin Harris trophy, 1972; commendation from California State Assembly, 1971; received Key to the City of San Francisco, 1971; special award and trophy, Airline Pilots Association, 1973, Wright Bros. Memorial award, greater Los Angeles, 1972; FAI Gold Air Medal.

WRITINGS:

(With Marie K. Long) *Amelia Earhart: The Mystery Solved,* Simon & Schuster (New York, NY), 1999.

SIDELIGHTS: Former pilot Elgen M. Long and his wife, Marie K. Long, coauthored *Amelia Earhart: The Mystery Solved.* "They worked on this book for more than twenty-five years, traveling more than 100 thousand miles, and interviewing more than 100 sources," according to Andrea Higbie for the *New York Times Book Review.* The Longs write that Earhart and her navigator, Fred Noonan, went down in the Electra 100 miles from Howland Island as they attempted to fly around the world in 1937. They cite the causes for her disappearance as strong winds, insufficient fuel, an inoperable direction finder, and the fact that neither Earhart nor Noonan knew Morse Code. Higbie wrote, "the authors' intent is to recreate Earhart's life, career and death without taking 'poetic license,' a noble enterprise to be sure but one that turns dull rather quickly."

LONG — CONTEMPORARY AUTHORS • Volume 208

Carolyn See noted in her *Washington Post Book World* review that "there's absolutely nothing lurid, fancy or speculative here—no dastardly cannibals or suspicious Japanese lurking furtively about, no conspiracies, no hidden plots. This is a step-by-step reconstruction of Earhart's last flight. . . . Elgen and Marie Long are concerned with facts and nothing but the facts; their anti-glamour approach is so effective that by page 70 the reader has to fling the book down for awhile. Unless you're an utter old-time flying aficionado, the difference between 87 octane gas as opposed to 100, or the numerous frequencies used on early airplane radios . . . becomes too much to take."

In their work, the Longs provide an account of Earhart's life and career, including her marriage to publisher G. P. Putnam and document her first, aborted attempt at global flight. A *Publishers Weekly* reviewer said the information presented by the Longs "is convincing but less than startling," and concluded that they "present a complete picture of Earhart's fate and offer a tribute to her bravery and risk taking."

BIOGRAPHICAL AND CRITICAL SOURCES:

PERIODICALS

New York Times Book Review, January 2, 2000, Andrea Higbie, review of *Amelia Earhart.*
People Weekly, November 15, 1999, review of *Amelia Earhart,* p. 49.
Publishers Weekly, October 4, 1999, review of *Amelia Earhart,* p. 53.
Washington Post Book World, December 17, 1999, Carolyn See, "Earhart, Lost in the Details," p. C2.

*   *   *

LONG, Jeff

PERSONAL: Male. Education: College studies in anthropology, philosophy, and history.

ADDRESSES: Agent—c/o Author Mail, Simon & Schuster, 1230 Avenue of the Americas, New York, NY 10020.

CAREER: Novelist, historian, journalist, screenwriter, and stonemason.

AWARDS, HONORS: Western Writers of America Spur Award for best novel, 1994, for *Empire of Bones;* British Boardman-Tasker Award for Mountain Literature, 1993, for *The Ascent;* American Alpine Club's Literary Award, 1993, for *The Descent;* Texas Literary Award.

WRITINGS:

Outlaw: The True Story of Claude Dallas, William Morrow (New York, NY), 1985.
Angels of Light, Beech Tree Books, (New York, NY), 1987.
Duel of Eagles: The Mexican and U.S. Fight for the Alamo, William Morrow (New York, NY), 1990
The Ascent: A Novel, William Morrow (New York, NY), 1992.
Empire of Bones: A Novel of Sam Houston and the Texas Revolution, William Morrow (New York, NY), 1993.
The Descent: A Novel, Crown (New York, NY), 1999.
Year Zero: A Novel, Pocket (New York, NY), 2002.

Also author of foreword, *Mountain Journeys: Stories of Climbers and Their Climbs,* edited by James P. Vermeulen, Overlook Press (Woodstock, NY), 1989.

ADAPTATIONS: *Outlaw: The True Story of Claude Dallas* was adapted for the made-for-television movie *Manhunt for Claude Dallas,* 1986.

SIDELIGHTS: In a *Book Reporter* interview, Jeff Long related that after majoring in anthropology, philosophy, and history, he left college greatly unemployable. This status, Long realized, offered him the time and opportunity to try his hand at writing. So he took on summer jobs as a stonemason during the summers, saved his money, and wrote throughout the winters. Disregarding the typical advice that most writing teachers suggest, namely to write what you know about the most, Long decided he wanted to write about what he knew the least. "Life is an adventure," he said. "Writing should be, too."

With this philosophy, Long practically took up residence at his local university library and threw himself into the task of researching his topics.

198

"Ignorance is a wonderful, brute traveling companion if you know how to live with him," he told *Book Reporter* interviewer Joe Hartlaub. "The reward can be treasure chests filled with facts and details that can make your writing both credible and richly marbled."

Long's first published work, *Outlaw: The True Story of Claude Dallas,* tells the story of a young man who lived mostly by himself in the wild, in the remote mountain areas of Idaho and Nevada. Some people described him as a mountain man, a throwback to the nineteenth century era of trappers. Others saw him as a man who enjoyed killing and torturing animals. Dallas, at the age of thirty, gunned down two game wardens who were on his trail for poaching. It took almost a year and a half for police teams to find and eventually bring Dallas to trial.

Long's story covers both the brutal side of Dallas as well as the popular support he enjoyed from some who felt Dallas lived by a different set of rules than those posed by society. *Newsweek* reviewer Peter S. Prescott wrote that Long "assembled the bones of a good story," although Prescott wished that he had imbued it with "a vision that might make it significant."

Angels of Light, Long's first novel, is set in California's Yosemite Valley and follows the lives and passions of men who live for extended periods of time out in nature, as they attempt to climb the most difficult peaks in the park. During one episode, a small plane carrying a large cargo of marijuana crashes in the park; the men claim the booty, only to find themselves going down a path fraught with disaster. In a *Publishers Weekly* review, Sybil Steinberg wrote that other climbers would likely enjoy this story of "mythic properties," but she also stated that other readers might prefer that Long "strayed less often from the track of his story."

In *Duel of Eagles: The Mexican and U.S. Fight for the Alamo,* Long takes up a different historical perspective of the great battle at the Alamo, discarding the myths that have been created around this historical event. For his research, he dug into diaries, letters, and journals and came up with an account that sparked both intense criticism and praise. Long wanted to explore the ways that nations conquer territories and peoples. This perspective somewhat discouraged

Booklist's Steve Weingartner, who wrote that he couldn't tell whether "Long enjoyed what he was doing or hated it with a passion," due to the fact that Long brings up the seedier side of the mythologized characters that took part in this battle. For instance, Long points out that Sam Houston was addicted to opium, and that Jim Bowie looked at Texas as a great site in which to develop a slave trade. In conclusion, however, Weingartner found the book "rousing, grandly entertaining, and resolutely factual."

Long revisits his acquired passion for mountain climbing in *The Ascent: A Novel.* Long reaches back to his experiences in the 1970s, when he spent time climbing and leading tour groups in Tibet, to create a story about a group of Americans—eight men and two women—who attempt to climb the Tibetan side of Mt. Everest. Some of the characters in this story have experienced a previous climb that ended in disaster. Stanley Planton, writing in the *Library Journal,* highly recommended the book "for all libraries." Planton further stated that Long's story "reminds us that each person is the product of past choices."

Three years after completing his *Duel of Eagles,* Long published another historical study, *Empire of Bones: A Novel of Sam Houston and the Revolution,* this time zeroing in specifically on Houston and fictionalizing his story. Randolph B. Campbell, writing for the *Historian,* stated that although Texas history might need some revision, Long's novel "is revisionist 'overkill' and does a disservice to the process." However, John Eisenhower in the *Washington Post Book World* believed that due to the exhaustive research Long did for his nonfiction work *Duel of Eagles, Empire of Bones* was probably written with substantial truth behind it.

More recently, Long published *The Descent: A Novel,* whose title is a word play on his novel *The Ascent.* Instead of climbing up a mountain, the characters in *The Descent* discover horned and evil humanoids lurking in vast caverns inside the Earth. American forces are summoned to kill the beasts and their leader, Satan. Scientific expeditions set out to explore the creatures' caves, which spread out so far they eventually extend beneath the Pacific Ocean, to discover if these creatures are an unknown branch of humankind.

The Descent took Long years to develop, and Hartlaub noted that this time spent in research really shows.

"Literally every page of this novel demonstrates the meticulous work of a true craftsman," the reviewer maintained.

BIOGRAPHICAL AND CRITICAL SOURCES:

PERIODICALS

Booklist, July, 1990, Steve Weingartner, review of *Duel of Eagles: The Mexican and U.S. Fight for the Alamo,* p. 2066; May 15, 1992, Gilbert Taylor, review of *The Ascent: A Novel,* pp. 1662-1663; February 15, 1993, Gilbert Taylor, review of *Empire of Bones: A Novel of Sam Houston and the Revolution,* p. 1036; March 15, 1999, David Pitt, review of *The Descent: A Novel,* p. 1260.

Choice, December 1990, J. Tricamo, review of *Duel of Eagles,* pp. 693-694.

Historian, autumn, 1993, Randolph B. Campbell, review of *Empire of Bones,* pp. 156-157.

Journal of the Early Republic, fall, 1991, Dorman H. Winfrey, review of *Duel of Eagles,* pp. 434-436.

Kirkus Reviews, December 15, 1984, review of *Outlaw: The True Story of Claude Dallas,* p. 1189; April 15, 1987, review of *Angels of Light,* pp. 583-584; April 15, 1992, review of *The Ascent,* p. 489; June 1, 1999, review of *The Descent,* pp. 824-825.

Library Journal, January, 1985, Kenneth F. Kister, review of *Outlaw,* p. 97; July, 1990, Raymond L. Puffer, review of *Duel of Eagles,* p. 110; June 1, 1992, Stanley Planton, review of *The Ascent,* p. 177; March 15, 1993, Stanley Planton, review of *Empire of Bones,* p. 107; May 1, 1999, Alicia Graybill, review of *The Descent,* p. 110.

Los Angeles Times Book Review, May 12, 1985, Marty Lieberman, review of *Outlaw,* p. 4; March 21, 1993, Larry L. King, "Sam's Song," pp. 4, 8.

Newsweek, March 4, 1985, Peter S. Prescott, "Footnotes," p. 67B.

Publishers Weekly, December 7, 1984, review of *Outlaw,* p. 61; May 22, 1987, Sybil Steinberg, review of *Angels of Light,* p. 65; June 23, 1989, Genevieve Stuttaford, review of *Mountain Journeys: Stories of Climbers and Their Climbs,* p. 45; June 29, 1990, Genevieve Stuttaford, review of *Duel of Eagles;* April 13, 1992, review of *The Ascent,* p. 40; January 18, 1993, review of *Empire of Bones,* p. 450; May 24, 1999, review of *The Descent,* p. 64.

Southwestern Historical Quarterly, July, 1992, Paul Andrew Hutton, review of *Duel of Eagles,* pp. 134-135.

Texas Monthly, September, 1990, Suzanne Winckler, review of *Duel of Eagles,* pp. 34-37.

Washington Post Book World, March 14, 1993, John Eisenhower, "The President of Texas," p. 5.

OTHER

Book Reporter, http://www.bookreporter.com/ (September 15, 2001), Joe Hartlaub, "Author Profile: Jeff Long" (February 2, 2002), review of *The Descent.*

Random House Web site, http://www.randomhouse.com/ (February 2, 2002), "*The Descent,* Author Interview."*

*   *   *

LOSCH, Richard R. 1933-

PERSONAL: Born December 26, 1933, in Boston, MA. *Education:* Yale College, A.B., 1956; attended Berkeley Divinity School, Yale University, M.Div., 1959; North Carolina State University, M.Ed., 1990. *Religion:* Episcopalian. *Hobbies and other interests:* Computer programming, sculpture, shipbuilding.

ADDRESSES: Home—P.O. Box 1560, Livingston, AL 35470-1560. *Office*—c/o William B. Eerdmans, 255 Jefferson St. SE, Grand Rapids, MI 49503.

CAREER: Episcopal priest, 1959-69; secondary school teacher, 1966-85; computer programmer and consultant, 1985-86; St. Timothy's School, Raleigh, NC, principal, 1986-88, math instructor, 1988-89; Cape Fear Academy, Wilmington, NC, math instructor, 1989-93; University of West Alabama, Livingston, AL, math instructor, 1994-2000, assistant professor of statistics, 2001—; St. James' Episcopal Church, Livingston, AL, rector, 1994—.

MEMBER: Rotary International, Freemasonry, Boy Scouts of America, American Mensa.

AWARDS, HONORS: Silver Beaver, St. George Award, and Vigil Honor, all from Boy Scouts of America.

WRITINGS:

The Many Faces of Faith: A Guide to World Religions and Christian Traditions, William B. Eerdmans (Grand Rapids, MI), 2001.

SIDELIGHTS: Among author Richard R. Losch's primary writing duties prior to his first book publication was the contribution of a regular column to the newsletter of the Episcopal parish where he was the rector. In each article, Losch provided a summary of the history and tenets of major world religions and branches of Christianity aimed at educating reader with little knowledge of faiths outside their own. Losch's book *The Many Faces of Faith: A Guide to World Religions and Christian Traditions* extends his readership beyond his parish, providing an elementary introduction to world religion that, despite Losch's admitted "Christian perspective," attempts to present each in an objective, factual manner.

Christian traditions are covered in part two of the book, and encompass those of Roman Catholics, the Eastern Orthodox, Lutherans, Anglicans, Baptists, Mennonites, Quakers, Methodists, and others. Other religions discussed in the first section of the book include Hinduism, Judaism, Zoroastrianism, Buddhism, Islam, and Neopaganism. Losch also includes Mormonism, Jehovah's Witnesses, and Unitarian Universalism among non-Christian traditions, a decision of minor controversy due to the fact that many members of those sects consider their religion in line with Christianity. Losch focuses on clarifying theological terms and dispelling myths and misunderstandings, while discussing only the essential and distinguishing facets of each religion or denomination.

Reviews of Losch's work were mixed. A critic for *Publishers Weekly* found that *The Many Faces of Faith* contains a number of generalizations and misrepresentations of non-Christian faiths, particularly Mormonism and Islam. The reviewer concluded, "In the preface, Losch admits how little he knew about world religions before tackling this project. Many readers will wish he had taken the time to learn more." Ray Olson, reviewing *The Many Faces of Faith* for *Booklist,* had a more positive view of the book, remarking that "Losch purveys an awesome amount of information with maximal objectivity."

BIOGRAPHICAL AND CRITICAL SOURCES:

PERIODICALS

Booklist, August, 2001, Ray Olson, review of *The Many Faces of Faith,* p. 2055.
Publishers Weekly, July 30, 2001, review of *The Many Faces of Faith,* p. 81.

OTHER

Eerdmans Publishing Web site, http://www.eerdmans. com/ (October 7, 2001), book description for *The Many Faces of Faith.*
Richard R. Losch Home Page, http://members.telocity. com/rlosch/ (October 7, 2001).*

*   *   *

LOUIS, Cindi 1962-

PERSONAL: Born December 27, 1962, in Port Arthur, TX. *Education:* Lamar University, Beaumont, TX,

ADDRESSES: Home—P.O. Box 411366, Dallas, TX 75241. *Office*—c/o Author Mail, 7th Floor, HarperCollins Publishers, 10 East 53rd St., New York, NY 10022.

CAREER: Romance novelist.

MEMBER: Romance Noir Book Club (founder), The Writer's Block, Black Writers Alliance, Alpha Kappa Alpha.

WRITINGS:

Crazy Thing Called Love, Harper/Torch (New York, NY), 2001.
(With Brenda Jackson, Felicia Mason, and Kayla Perrin) *The Best Man,* St. Martin's (New York, NY), 2003.

SIDELIGHTS: Author Cindi Louis was a long-time fan of romance novels before she began her own writing career. Her love of the genre drew her to travel on a Romance Slam Jam cruise with some of her favorite authors. As she wrote on her Web site, her enthusiasm for the cruise led her husband to tell her, "As much as you read you should write." Not long afterwards she decided to start writing, and within a few years she had published her debut novel, *Crazy Thing Called Love.*

Louis's first book is set in her hometown of Port Arthur, Texas. Her heroine is Judge Jayda Tillman, a divorcee who has become soured on men after being burned by her ex-husband. Jayda has a reputation as a hanging judge who is cold as ice, a cover for her fragile self-confidence. Her love interest is Jason Mc-Neal, a criminal defense attorney and womanizer who moves into the apartment above Jayda, keeping her awake with his late-night activities. Both characters struggle against the feelings that develop, but when they are thrown together in a high-profile murder trial that puts Jayda in jeopardy, they give in to their passion.

Romance readers welcomed Louis's debut effort. Reviewer Martine Bates, writing for *Romance and Friends,* said, "Cindi Louis has written a delicious love story that reads like the work of a seasoned author." Reviewing the book for the online *Romance Reader,* Gwenolyn Osborne said that *Crazy Thing Called Love* "earned Cindi Louis a spot on my Emerging Authors List." Osborne cited Louis's humor and dialogue among her writing strengths, and noted that her work would help meet the need for more African-American romantic comedies. Summarizing the novel, critic Harriet Klausner wrote on *BookBrowser,* "Cindi Louis captivates fans of ethnic romances with a touch of the paranormal, intriguing court scenes, and a bit of suspense to sweeten a delectable love story." Klausner and other reviewers suggested that a subplot involving Jayda's friend Melissa Beacon would make a popular sequel to *Crazy Thing Called Love.*

Louis wrote on her Web site that she chose the romance genre because "I like happy ever after." Humor is also important to her, she said, "because life itself is serious enough."

BIOGRAPHICAL AND CRITICAL SOURCES:

PERIODICALS

Publishers Weekly, July 23, 2001, review of *Crazy Thing Called Love,* p. 56.

OTHER

BookBrowser, http://www.bookbrowser.com/ (July 25, 2001), Harriet Klausner, review of *Crazy Thing Called Love.*

Cindi Louis Web site, http://www.cindilouis.com/ (October 7, 2001).

Romance and Friends, http://www.geocities.com/romancebooks.geo/ (August, 2001), Martine Bates, review of *Crazy Thing Called Love.*

Romance Reader, http://www.theromancereader.com/ (October 7, 2001), Gwendolyn Osborne, review of *Crazy Thing Called Love.**

*   *   *

LOZA, Steven (Joseph)

PERSONAL: Male. *Education:* California State Polytechnic University, Pomona, B.A. (music), University of California, Los Angeles, M.A. (Latin American studies), Ph.D. (music), 1985.

ADDRESSES: Office—UCLA Department of Ethnomusicology, 405 Hilgard Ave., 2539 Schoenberg Hall, Los Angeles, CA 90095. *E-mail*—sloza@ucla.edu.

CAREER: University of Chile, School of Music, 1989; Kanda University of International Studies, Japan, 1996-97; University of California, Los Angeles, associate professor, then professor of ethnomusicology; UCLA Latin American Center, associate director, research, and director of music department. Latin jazz performer and producer; member, Grammy Awards National Screening Committee.

MEMBER: Latin Academy for Recording Artists.

WRITINGS:

Barrio Rhythm: Mexican American Music in Los Angeles, University of Illinois Press (Urbana, IL), 1993.

(Editor) *Selected Reports in Ethnomusicology 10: Musical Aesthetics and Multiculturalism in Los Angeles,* UCLA Ethnomusicology Publications (Los Angeles, CA), 1994.

Tito Puente and the Making of Latin Music, University of Illinois Press (Urbana, IL), 1999.

Author's work has been translated into Spanish.

SIDELIGHTS: In his academic career, Steven Loza has specialized in ethnomusicology, particularly the music of Latin America and its increasing popularity in the United States. Both as a university professor and as a member of the Grammy Awards National Screening Committee, Loza has had plenty of opportunity to witness the influence of Latin American rhythms on U.S. music culture, particularly in Los Angeles.

In 1993 Loza published *Barrio Rhythm: Mexican American Music in Los Angeles.* According to Raul Fernandez, writing in *American Quarterly,* "The reader who seeks to learn only about mariachi standards and *rancheras* will also discover the history of a delicious mixture of swing, bop, *danzones, huapangos, boleros,* rhythm and blues, rock and roll, mambo, tango" In short, this is the musical history of the twentieth century as seen through the eyes of Mexican-American musicians. Loza explores the complex effects of tradition and assimilation, and rural and urban settlement patterns, on the music of Mexican Angelenos. "This contextual analysis will certainly become one of the most cited models of urban ethnomusicology," wrote Kazadi wa Mukuna in *Choice.*

"When 'Barrio Rhythm' jumps to life," wrote Lynell George in the *Los Angeles Times Book Review,* "it's through the voices of those who bore witness." These voices include those of Lalo Guerrero, whose "Indian" features and heavy accent marked him as a Mexican singer, and barred him from crossing over into Anglo acceptance, and Andy Russell—born Andrés Rábago—who passed both physically and vocally into the musical mainstream. Their stories and their music "communicate more about the city we live in than any sun-bleached Beach Boy harmony," according to George.

From the lives of the diverse singers and groups that shaped Chicano music in Los Angeles, Loza turns to the story of one towering musical legend in *Tito Puente and the Making of Latin Music.* Drawing on numerous interviews with band members, collaborators, and music journalists, Loza brings out "El Rey's" (the King's) tremendous impact as a drummer and bandleader, while exploring the social and cultural forces that shaped him and his music. Clearly a fan, "Loza seems principally concerned with ensuring that Puente 'ranks with the Ellingtons and Beethovens,'" wrote G. Averill in *Choice.* As "the first major book on this master musician in English, Loza fleshes out the man behind the drum set," wrote Eugene Holley, Jr. in *Hispanic.* As Holley put it, he "goes beyond the public image of the ageless, white-haired percussion legend and reveals a tender and tough survivor," describing Puentes's early life in Harlem, his mentors such as Tito Rodriguez, and his Juilliard training, as well as including the recollections of friends and associates. While this background is a vital part, Puente's impact on American and Afro-Cuban music are also explored in full, as is his ability to span both the English-speaking and Spanish-speaking worlds. According to Holley, Puentes's successful mission to give percussion a leading voice in popular band music "is all documented in Loza's important book."

BIOGRAPHICAL AND CRITICAL SOURCES:

PERIODICALS

American Quarterly, September, 1994, Raul Fernandez, "Notes from East L.A.," pp. 441-447.
Choice, February, 1994, Kazadi wa Mukuna, review of *Barrio Rhythm,* p. 946; January, 2000, G. Averill, review of *Tito Puente and the Making of Latin Music,* p. 946.
Hispanic, December, 1999, Eugene Holley, Jr., "Five Decades of the King," p. 80.
Los Angeles Times Book Review, September 26, 1993, Lynell George, "The Music Moves the Streets," p. 12.
Publishers Weekly, June, 1999, review of *Tito Puente,* p. 69.

OTHER

Daily Bruin, http://www.dailybruin.ucla.edu/ (September 27, 1999), Teron Hide, "Not Just South of the Border."
University of Illinois Press Web site, http://www.press.uillinois.edu/ (February 14, 2002), review of *Tito Puente and the Making of Latin Music.**

*   *   *

LUNGE-LARSEN, Lise 1955-

PERSONAL: Born October 15, 1955, in Oslo, Norway; daughter of Asbørn (an antiquarian book dealer) and Berit (Evenrud) Lunge-Larsen; married Steven A. Kuross (an oncologist), August 19, 1978; children: Emily, Even, Erik. *Education:* Augsburg College, B.A., 1977; University of Minnesota, M.A. (applied linguistics), 1981. *Religion:* Lutheran.

ADDRESSES: Home—2011 Lakeview Dr., Duluth, MN 55803. *E-mail*—LLL@chartermi.net.

CAREER: Children's book author and storyteller, 1980—. College of St. Catherine, St. Paul, MN, instructor in English and director of English as a Second Language Program, 1981-87; Hamline University, St. Paul, MN, adjunct faculty member, 1982-90; University of Minnesota, Duluth, instructor in children's literature, 1990, 1994. Served on board of education, First Lutheran Church, Duluth.

MEMBER: Society of Children's Book Writers and Illustrators, Children's Literature Network.

AWARDS, HONORS: Minnesota Book Award, 2000, for *The Troll with No Heart in His Body, and Other Tales from Norway,* and 2002, for *Race of the Birkebeiners; The Legend of the Lady Slipper* was named a Great Lakes Book Award finalist; *The Troll with No Heart in His Body* was an American Library Association (ALA) notable book; *The Race of the Birkebeiners* was named an ALA and *Los Angeles Times* notable book of the year, was on the *Choice* list of books, and was among the Children's Book Committee at Bank Street College of Education best books of the year list.

WRITINGS:

(Reteller, with Margi Preus) *The Legend of the Lady Slipper: An Ojibwe Tale,* illustrated by Andrea Arroyo, Houghton (Boston, MA), 1999.

(Reteller) *The Troll with No Heart in His Body, and Other Tales of Trolls from Norway* (contains "The Three Billy Goats Gruff," "The Boy Who Became a Lion, a Falcon, and an Ant," "Butterball," "The Boy and the North Wind," "The White Cat in the Dovre Mountain," "The Sailors and the Troll," and "The Eating Competition"), illustrated by Betsy Bowen, Houghton (Boston, MA), 1999.

The Race of the Birkebeiners, illustrated by Mary Azarian, Houghton (Boston, MA), 2001.

Tales of the Hidden Folk: Stories of Fairies, Gnomes, Selkies, and Other Hidden Folk, illustrated by Beth Krommes, Houghton (Boston, MA), 2004.

WORK IN PROGRESS: Noah's New Clothes, Houghton (Boston, MA), 2004.

SIDELIGHTS: In the environs of Duluth, Minnesota, where Lise Lunge-Larsen makes her home, she is known fondly as "The Troll Lady" for as a storyteller and author she has focused on the tales of her native Norway, which are replete with trolls and other fantastic creatures. The daughter of an antiquarian bookseller in Oslo, Norway, Lunge-Larsen grew up literally immersed in literature for her home was the bookstore; yet she did not envision becoming a storyteller or author. "My parents' plan was that I should become a secretary then one day marry the boss!" she told *CA*. "All that changed when, during my last year in high school, I received the Crown Prince Harald Scholarship to Augsburg College in Minneapolis."

Although Lunge-Larsen planned to return to Norway after a year, she fell in love with Steve Kuross, a premed student. So she worked toward a bachelor's degree at Augsburg College and found a job in a children's library. "For the first time in my life, I was exposed to the writings of people like Dr. Seuss, A. A. Milne, Kenneth Graham, and C. S. Lewis," she recalled. "Now I was in love not just with Steve but with children's books as well and spent nearly thirty-two hours a week (on the job!) reading every book in the children's library." Lunge-Larsen discovered, however, that the library lacked some of her favorite stories: the Norse myths and sagas and the traditional tales collected by Norwegian folklorists Peter Christen Asbjørnsen and Jørgen Ingebretsen Moe. "I soon found myself telling anyone who would listen stories of trolls and other strange creatures from my own childhood, and in a short time found myself telling tales all over the state," she recalled to *CA*. According to Sheryl Jensen in *Area Woman* magazine, Lunge-Larsen is an expert storyteller: "From bellowing and roaring in the bass of a nasty troll hag to squealing and stammering like a terrified little boy, Lise uses her voice, her animated face, and her whirlwind of dynamic energy in a total body experience of storytelling."

After graduating with a bachelor's degree, Lunge-Larsen married Kuross. As a wedding gift, her father gave her a collection of troll stories in which he had written: "To Lise, with all my good wishes and the hope that even though she may forget her Norwegian, she will never forget her Norwegian trolls." She continued her work as a storyteller and earned a graduate degree in teaching English as a second language, with a minor in children's literature, writing her thesis on storytelling as a teaching tool. All the while, she was busy raising the couple's three children. Yet, as she remembered, "No matter what I did, storytelling and children's literature soon was involved."

In the early 1990s, with a quarter-century of storytelling experience behind her, Lunge-Larsen started committing her favorite Norwegian stories to paper. "I find that much of my writing goes back to the world I experienced as a child—a world full of trolls, mysterious hidden creatures, heroes and heroines who have to battle evil among men, trolls, and other hidden forces. I grew up in a landscape beautiful, haunting and alive and this very much shapes my experience of the world and now my writing. I am also interested in stories about that which is hidden from ordinary sight or knowledge, such as trolls or other hidden folk, or stories about how things got the way they are," she told *CA*. Thus it was natural that Lunge-Larsen should write *The Troll with No Heart in His Body, and Other Tales of Trolls from Norway,* a collection of eight folktales retold from Asbjørnsen and Moe's *Samlede eventyr* ("Collected Stories") and *Tales of the Hidden Folk: Stories of Fairies, Gnomes, Selkies, and Other Hidden Folk.* So, too, her interest in the capacity of people to rise above their normal abilities to accomplish the extraordinary led her to write *The Race of the Birkebeiners.* In this medieval Norwegian tale, based on a true story, the Birkebeiners—so named because they wear birch-bark leggings—save the infant Prince Hakon when they ski with the baby across the mountains in a blizzard to thwart assassins. Both Gillian Engberg in *Booklist* and *School Library Journal* critic Anne Chapman Callaghan praised this picture book for its compelling story, unambiguous language, and the woodcut illustrations by Caldecott award-winning illustrator Mary Azarian. "Mary had all kinds of offers and choices after her award," Lunge-Larsen told Jensen. "I felt honored that she wanted to illustrate my manuscript."

Lunge-Larsen has also teamed up with Margi Preus to retell a Native American tale, *The Legend of the Lady Slipper: An Ojibwe Tale,* about a girl who saves her village from illness. The only well person among her people, the girl battles through a snow storm to get medicinal herbs from a neighboring village. When her moccasins freeze to the ground on the return trip, she walks the rest of the way barefooted, leaving bloody footprints in the snow. In the spring, expecting to retrieve her moccasins, she finds in their place the pink-and-white shoe-shaped flowers known as lady slippers, or *ma-ki-sin waa-big-wann* in Ojibwe. Several reviewers found this first effort by Lunge-Larsen and Margi Preus notable, including *Booklist* contributor GraceAnne A. DeCandido, who described the retelling as "powerful"; and a *Publishers Weekly* critic praised the text and illustrations for their "unusual simplicity and fluidity." Writing in the *Bulletin of the Center for Children's Books,* Janice N. Harrington also praised the authors' style, particularly the use of nature metaphors and strong verbs, and she pointed out how the tale "smoothly integrates Ojibwe words and phrases into an accessible narrative."

Throughout her writing career, storytelling has given Lunge-Larsen an edge. "All those years of storytelling have given me an intuitive sense of what kinds of stories children love," she revealed to *CA*. "When I work, I spend a lot of time telling the story out loud to myself to find the right rhythm and pacing. Sometimes I even record it. But whenever I am stuck, all I have to do is tell the story to groups of children. Somehow, with the kids there, I always find the words I am looking for, the section that needs to be tightened, or the part that needs to be played up."

In a world full of hate and conflict, Lunge-Larsen gives hope through her stories of triumph by love. "To do battle with a troll is to learn to draw on the best of humanity," Lunge-Larsen wrote in *The Troll with No Heart.* "Despite the odds, good will triumph over evil, love over hatred"—and story over chaos. In conclusion, Lunge-Larsen told *CA*, "I love telling and writing stories. My thoughts are perhaps best expressed by this old saying: 'When the bond between heaven and earth is broken, even prayer is not enough. Only a story can mend it.'"

BIOGRAPHICAL AND CRITICAL SOURCES:

PERIODICALS

Area Woman (Duluth, MN), December-January, 2002, Sheryl Jensen, "The Troll Lady: Lise Lunge-Larsen," pp. 26-27, 68-69.
Booklist, April 15, 1999, GraceAnne A. DeCandido, review of *The Legend of the Lady Slipper: An Ojibwe Tale,* p. 1533; March 15, 2000, review of *The Troll with No Heart in His Body, and Other Tales of Trolls from Norway,* p. 1360; July, 2001, Gillian Engberg, review of *The Race of the Birkebeiners,* p. 2014.

Bulletin of the Center for Children's Books, July, 1999, Janice N. Harrington, review of *The Legend of the Lady Slipper,* pp. 394-395.

Horn Book, November, 1999, Roger Sutton, review of *The Troll with No Heart in His Body,* p. 748.

Kirkus Reviews, September 1, 2001, review of *The Race of the Birkebeiners,* p. 1295.

Publishers Weekly, April 12, 1999, review of *The Legend of the Lady Slipper,* p. 74; October 11, 1999, review of *The Troll with No Heart in His Body,* p. 76.

School Library Journal, September, 2001, Anne Chapman Callaghan, review of *The Race of the Birkebeiners,* p. 217.

*   *   *

LUO, Zhuoyao
    See LAW, Clara

*   *   *

LYON, Janet

PERSONAL: Female.

ADDRESSES: Office—Department of English, University of Illinois at Urbana-Champaign, 608 South Wright, Urbana, IL 61801; fax 217-333-4321. *E-mail*—jwlyon@uiuc.edu.

CAREER: University of Illinois at Urbana-Champaign, teacher of English and women's studies.

WRITINGS:

Manifestoes: Provocations of the Modern, Cornell University Press (Ithaca, NY), 1999.

Contributor to *Mina Loy: Poet and Person,* edited by Maeera Shreiber and Keith Tuma, National Poetry Foundation, 1997. Contributor to academic journals, including *New Literary History, Discourse, Differences,* and *Yale Journal of Criticism.*

WORK IN PROGRESS: A book on salons, modernity, and modernism.

BIOGRAPHICAL AND CRITICAL SOURCES:

PERIODICALS

Choice, November, 1999, K. Tölölyan, review of *Manifestoes: Provocations of the Modern,* p. 530.*

M

MAGGIO, Mike 1952-

PERSONAL: Born April 23, 1952, in New York, NY; son of Ignazio (a self-employed restaurateur) and Josephine (a homemaker) Maggio; married Amal Abou Eyada (a laboratory technologist), December 19, 1990; children: Fairuz Yasmine. *Education:* Queen's College, B.A. (cum laude), 1974; University of Southern California, M.A. (applied linguistics), 1980. *Politics:* "Democrat/Socialist." *Religion:* Muslim. *Hobbies and other interests:* Music, reading.

ADDRESSES: Home—1169 Cypress Tree Place, Herndon, VA 20170. *E-mail*—mikemaggio@aol.com.

CAREER: Bechtel, Herndon, VA, student advisor; Nextel, Herdnon, VA, systems support analyst; ELS Amman, Amman, Jordan, academic director. International Airports Projects, Jeddah, Saudi Arabia, scholarship coordinator; Teligent, Herndon, VA, I.T. trainer.

AWARDS, HONORS: Honorable mention, Water Poets Award, 1985; honorable mention, Gypsy Poetry Contest for Amnesty International, 1988; Chicago Poetry Society contest, honorable mention, 1992, second place, 1995.

WRITINGS:

Your Secret Is Safe with Me (poetry), Black Bear Publications, 1988.
Oranges from Palestine (poetry), Mardi Gras Press (Harvey, LA), 1996.

Sifting through the Madness (fiction), Sansip, 1999.

Contributor to *Intercultural Communication as an Integral Part of an ESL Program: The University of Southern California Experience,* NAFSA, 1986; and *A Game of Newspeak and Smokescreens: Did the U.S. Allow Iraq's Invasion of Kuwait?,* edited by Belinda Subraman, Vergen Press, 1992. Contributor of poetry to anthologies, including *Silent Explorations,* Laurel Press, 1981; *Still Life: Treasures of the Precious Moments,* New Worlds Unlimited, 1985; *Bedside Prayers: Prayers and Poems for When You Rise and Go to Sleep,* HarperSanFrancisco, 1997; and *For a Living: The Poetry of Work,* University of Illinois Press, 1995.

Contributor of articles, fiction, and poetry to periodicals, including *L.A. Weekly, New Press, International Educator, Landscapes of the Mind, Phoebe, Eratica, OnCue, Shattersheet, Element, Prophetic Voices, Jordan Times, Jerusalem Star, New Press, Windfall, Live Poets, Second Glance,* and *Sublime Odyssey.*

Translations of prose and poetry have appeared in *Freedom, Al-Awsat, Al-Watan, Jordan Times, Pig Iron World,* and *Pyramid Periodical.*

WORK IN PROGRESS: Why Do Men Have Nipples? (novel).

SIDELIGHTS: Mike Maggio told *CA:* "My primary motivation is to respond to contemporary society in all of its aspects. I think that current events influence my work, but often ideas come that have nothing to do with current events. My writing has changed as I have changed and matured. My experiences in life, particularly my experience living overseas for seven years, have greatly influenced me and have had a great change on my writing. I would also say that the environment around me reflects the kind of work I produce."

*   *   *

MAKEPEACE, Anne 1947-

PERSONAL: Born April 28, 1947, in CT; daughter of Roger and Elizabeth (Douglas) Makepeace. *Ethnicity:* "White, Anglo-Saxon Protestant." *Education:* Stanford University, B.A. (with honors), 1969, M.A. (education), 1971, M.A. (film), 1982.

ADDRESSES: Home—1763 Prospect, No. 1, Santa Barbara, CA 93103; fax: 212-560-2099. *E-mail*—AMakepeace@aol.com.

CAREER: Makepeace Productions, Inc., Santa Barbara, CA, president and director, c. 1992—. Film writer, producer, and director; Sundance Institute, writer/director fellow; Sundance Film Festival, juror, 2001.

MEMBER: American Film Institute, Writers Guild of America West, Film Arts Foundation, Independent Features Project, IDA.

AWARDS, HONORS: CINE Golden Eagle Awards, Council for International Nontheatrical Events, for *Whistle in the Wind, Moonchild, Night Driving, Ishi the Last Yahi, Baby, It's You,* and *Coming to Light: Edward S. Curtis and the North American Indians;* Wrangler awards, National Cowboy Hall of Fame, best feature screenplay, 1991, for *Thousand Pieces of Gold,* and best documentary screenplay, 1995 for *Ishi the Last Yahi;* Gold awards, Houston International Film Festival, for *Night Driving* and *Coming to Light;* Gold Hugo awards, Chicago International Film Festival, for *Moonchild* and *Ishi the Last Yahi;* National Educational Film Festival, Paramount Award, for best feature, for *Moonchild,* and best film award, for *Ishi the Last Yahi;* Chicago International Television Festival, Gold Plaque for *Baby, It's You* and Gold Hugo Award for *Coming to Light;* winner of Sundance

Feature Documentary Competitions for *Baby, It's You* and *Coming to Light;* Gold awards, Cindy Competition, for *Moonchild, Baby, It's You,* and *Coming to Light;* Red Ribbon, American Film Festival, first prize, Birmingham International Film Festival, and Chris Award, Columbus Film Festival, all for *Moonchild;* Munich Film Festival Award, for best American independent film, Native American Film Festival Award, for best documentary, and Emmy Award nomination, Academy of Television Arts and Sciences, all c. 1995, all for *Ishi the Last Yahi;* Bronze Apple Award, National Educational Media Network, Juror's Choice Award, Charlotte Film and Video Festival, and Whitney Biennial Award, 2000, all for *Baby, It's You;* grants from National Endowment for the Arts, National Endowment for the Humanities, Corporation for Public Broadcasting, Arizona Humanities Council, and California Council for the Humanities, c. 1999; Best Documentary Award, Telluride Mountain Film Festival, Academy Award nomination for best feature documentary, Academy of Motion Picture Arts and Sciences, and O'Connor Film Prize, American Historical Association, all 2000, all for *Coming to Light;* grants from Rockefeller Foundation and American Film Institute.

WRITINGS:

Edward S. Curtis: Coming to Light (also see below), National Geographic Society (Washington, DC), 2001.

DOCUMENTARY FILM SCREENPLAYS

(And director) *Moonchild,* Home Box Office, 1985.
(And director) *Whistle in the Wind,* USA Network, 1987.
"Thousand Pieces of Gold," *American Playhouse,* Public Broadcasting Service, 1992.
(And director) *Night Driving,* Showtime, 1993.
Ishi the Last Yahi, Public Broadcasting Service, 1995.
(And director) *Baby, It's You,* Public Broadcasting Service, 1998.
(And producer and director) *Coming to Light: Edward S. Curtis and the North American Indians,* Public Broadcasting Service, 2001.
(And producer and director) "The Making of IMAX Lewis and Clark," *National Geographic Explorer,* 2002.

WORK IN PROGRESS: Writing, producing, and directing *Robert Capa* and *Stories from the Field,* both documentaries, for Public Broadcasting Service.

BIOGRAPHICAL AND CRITICAL SOURCES:

PERIODICALS

Cineaste, summer, 2001, Johnny Lorenz, review of *Coming to Light: Edward S. Curtis and the North American Indians,* p. 214.

Library Journal, November 1, 1998, Marianne Eimer, review of *Baby, It's You,* p. 136; February 15, 2001, Stephen Rees, review of *Edward S. Curtis: Coming to Light,* p. 72.

Los Angeles, September, 1984, Eric Estrin, review of *Moonchild,* p. 58.

New York, May 4, 1992, John Leonard, review of *Thousand Pieces of Gold,* p. 62.

New York Times, June 2, 1998, Walter Goodman, "P.O. V.; *Baby, It's You,*" p. E7.

Petersen's Photographic, May, 2002, review of *Edward S. Curtis,* p. 41.

School Library Journal, February, 1983, Ben Harrison, review of *Moonchild,* p. 44.

Variety, November 30, 1992, Dennis Harvey, review of *Ishi the Last Yahi,* p. 75; February 9, 1998, Glenn Lovell, review of *Baby, It's You,* p. 74; April 17, 2000, Todd McCarthy, review of *Coming to Light,* p. 31.

*   *   *

MALMQVIST, N(ils) G(öran) D(avid) 1924-

PERSONAL: Born 1924. *Education:* Attended Uppsala University.

ADDRESSES: Office—Stockholm University, 106 91 Stockholm, Sweden.

CAREER: Stockholm University, Stockholm, Sweden, professor emeritus; sinologist; advisory board member for *Journal of Translation Studies* and *Renditions.* Nobel Prize in Literature, member of selection committee.

MEMBER: Academia Europaea (founding member), Swedish Academy, Royal Swedish Academy of Sciences, Royal Swedish Academy of Letters, History, and Antiquities, Royal Danish Academy of Sciences, History and Antiquities.

AWARDS, HONORS: Knighthood of the Northern Star; Royal Prize, Swedish Academy; Translation Prize, Royal Swedish Academy of Sciences; Gold Medal of Merit, H. M. King Karl XVI Gustav; Translation Prize, Swedish Writers Association; Elsa Thulin Medal for Translation; honorary doctorate, Stockholm University; honorary doctorate, Charles University; honorary fellow of the School of Oriental and African Studies.

WRITINGS:

Den Långa Floden. Utdrag ur Kinas Litteratur Genom Tre Årtusenden av Göran Malmqvist, Forum (Stockholm, Sweden), 1970.

Kinesiska är Inte Svårt, Aldus (Stockholm, Sweden), 1974.

(Editor) *Modern Chinese Literature and Its Social Context,* Institute för Orientalska Språk (Stockholm, Sweden), 1977.

A Selective Guide to Chinese Literature, 1990-1949, E. J. Brill (New York, NY), 1988-1990.

(Translator) Shang Ch'in, *The Frozen Torch: Select Prose Poems,* Wellsweep Press (London, England), 1992.

Claes Thell: Keramik: Östasiatiska Museet, 22 Oktober-28 November 1993, Östasiatiska Museet (Stockholm, Sweden), 1993.

Bernhard Karlgren: Ett Forskarporträtt, Norstedt (Stockholm, Sweden), 1995.

(Coeditor with Michelle Yeh) *Frontier Taiwan: An Anthology of Modern Chinese Poetry,* Columbia University Press (New York, NY), 2001.

SIDELIGHTS: N. G. D. Malmqvist, professor emeritus at Stockholm University, has been teaching Chinese in Europe and Australia for over forty years and has translated over thirty volumes and 200 literary pieces from Chinese. He has also played a large role in academic and social exchanges between Sweden and China and between the Western and Chinese cultures.

Malmqvist's translated works include *The Frozen Torch,* a selection of prose poems by Taiwan surrealist writer Shang Ch'in, whose work echoes predecessor Henri Michaux. In *World Literature Today* Philip F. Williams identified Shang Ch'in as a prominent Chinese author of the twentieth century, his more distinguished work acclimating "Western surrealism to a party mythicized Chinese setting in a convincing and unforced manner."

Malmqvist edited *Frontier Taiwan: An Anthology of Modern Chinese Poetry* with Michelle Yeh. *Frontier Taiwan* is a collection of modern Chinese poetry which tells the story of the transformation of Taiwan from a little-known island to an acclaimed economic power and a democracy. Included are 400 poems written in the twentieth century. A *Publishers Weekly* reviewer called the translations "solid, letting the work speak across cultures" and assessed the main impact of the book to be "sociopolitical, allowing connections between writers who might have had difficulty finding each other without this judicious letter of introduction."

BIOGRAPHICAL AND CRITICAL SOURCES:

PERIODICALS

Publishers Weekly, April 23, 2001, review of *Frontier Taiwan: An Anthology of Modern Chinese Poetry,* p. 74.
World Literature Today, autumn, 1993, Philip F. Williams, review of *The Frozen Torch: Select Prose Poems,* p. 890.

OTHER

Chinese University of Hong Kong Web site, http://www.cuhk.edu.hk/ (December 31, 2001), "Professor N. G. D. Malmqvist."*

*   *   *

MANDER, Anica Vesel 1934-2002

OBITUARY NOTICE—See index for *CA* sketch: Born October 21, 1934, in Sarajevo, Yugoslavia (now Bosnia and Herzegovina); died of breast cancer June 19, 2002, in Bolinas, CA. Historian, educator, publisher, editor, and author. Mander is remembered for the interviews she conducted with rape victims in Bosnia during the 1990s, interviews that led to the successful petition to classify rape as a war crime within the context of international law. Her visit to Bosnia represented a return to her native land, from which Mander had fled as a refugee at the age of seven. Mander's focus as a feminist academic centered on gender issues and racial equality. She taught at San

Francisco-area universities, including the University of San Francisco, beginning in 1965. In 1973 she was appointed a faculty member and coordinator of women's studies and feminist therapy at Antioch University West. Mander was also a publisher and founding editor of Moon Books, one of the first "feminist" publishing houses. Her books include *Blood Ties* and the nonfiction *Feminism as Therapy.*

OBITUARIES AND OTHER SOURCES:

PERIODICALS

Los Angeles Times, June 25, 2002, p. B11.
Washington Post, June 25, 2002, p. B6.

*   *   *

MANN, Janet 1960-

PERSONAL: Born July 26, 1960, in New York, NY; daughter of Irving and Joan Alice (Mann) Friedman. *Education:* Brown University, Sc.B. (with honors), 1983; University of Michigan, M.A., 1988, Ph.D., 1991.

ADDRESSES: Home—1523 Elliott Pl. NW, Washington, DC 20007. *Office*—Department of Biology, Georgetown University, Washington, DC 20057; fax: 202-687-5662. *E-mail*—mannj2@georgetown.edu.

CAREER: Georgetown University, Washington, DC, assistant professor, 1992-99, associate professor of biology and psychology, 1999—. Center for Advanced Study in the Behavioral Sciences, Palo Alto, CA, fellow, 1994-95; University of Western Australia, honorary visiting research fellow in anatomy and human biology, 1992-2000, adjunct professor, 2000—; University of New South Wales, honorary visiting fellow in biological sciences, 1998-2000; University of Maryland at Eastern Shore, special member of biology department, 2000-03; guest lecturer at colleges and universities, including University of Maryland at College Park, 1993 and 2000, University of California, Berkeley, and University of Victoria, 1996, University of North Carolina at Greensboro, 1998, Duke University, 2001, and University of Georgia. Dolphins of

Shark Bay Research Foundation, member of scientific advisory board, 1995—; Dolphins of Monkey Mia Research Foundation, member of board of directors and director of scientific advisory board, 1999—; scientific adviser or consultant to West Australian Conservation and Land Management, Shark Bay World Heritage Committee, and National Institute of Marine Fisheries. Participant in the making of eight natural history films for British and American television programs; guest on Australian television and radio programs.

MEMBER: International Society for Human Ethology, International Society for Behavioral Ecology, Animal Behavior Society, Human Behavior and Evolution Society, Marine Mammal Society, American Association for the Advancement of Science, American Association of University Professors, American Association of University Women, Sigma Xi.

AWARDS, HONORS: Jacob Javits fellow, U.S. Department of Education, 1986-90; Research Award, Michigan Psychological Association, 1987; Woodrow Wilson grant, 1989-90; grants from American Cetacean Society, 1991, Eppley Foundation for Research, 1993, 1997-98, Helen Brach Foundation, 1994-95, National Institute for Marine Fisheries, 1996, and National Science Foundation, 1997-2001; citation for outstanding science book of the year, *Choice,* 2001, for *Cetacean Societies: Field Studies of Dolphins and Whales.*

WRITINGS:

(Editor, with R. Connor, P. Tyack, and H. Whitehead, and contributor) *Cetacean Societies: Field Studies of Dolphins and Whales,* University of Chicago Press (Chicago, IL), 2000.

Contributor to books, including *The Adapted Mind,* edited by J. Barkow, L. Cosmides, and J. Tooby, Oxford University Press (New York, NY), 1992; and *The Biology of Traditions,* edited by D. Fragaszy and S. Perry, Cambridge University Press (New York, NY), in press. Contributor to periodicals, including *Marine Mammal Science, Behavioral and Brain Sciences, Trends in Ecology and Evolution, Family Systems, Ethology, Zoo Biology, Child Development, Animal Behavior, Behavioral Ecology,* and *Behaviour.*

SIDELIGHTS: Janet Mann told *CA:* "I've been studying wild bottlenose dolphin mothers and calves in Australia for thirteen years. My focus has been on maternal investment, calf development, and behavior. I have also studied mother-infant relationships in killer whales and primates."

*   *   *

MANN, Judith (W.) 1950-

PERSONAL: Born September 29, 1950, in Washington, DC; daughter of James H. (a lawyer) and Margaret (a politician and fund-raiser; maiden name, Blackwell) Mann; married David T. Konig (a college professor), November 9, 1975; children: Madeleine Blackwell, William James. *Ethnicity:* "Euro-American." *Education:* Mount Holyoke College, B.A., 1972; Washington University, St. Louis, MO, M.A., 1978, Ph.D., 1986. *Politics:* Democrat. *Religion:* Unitarian-Universalist. *Hobbies and other interests:* Sewing, travel, film, books.

ADDRESSES: Home—500 Lee Ave., Webster Groves, MO 63119. *Office*—Saint Louis Art Museum, 1 Fine Arts Dr., St. Louis, MO 63110; fax: 314-721-6172. *E-mail*—jmann@slam.org.

CAREER: Old Dominion University, Norfolk, VA, adjunct professor, 1986-87; Webster University, Webster Groves, MO, adjunct professor of art history, 1987-88; St. Louis Art Museum, St. Louis, MO, curatorial assistant, 1988-91, assistant curator, 1991-97, curator of early European art, 1997—. Washington University, St. Louis, MO, adjunct professor, 1989; University of Missouri—St. Louis, assistant professor, 1991-97. Lecturer at educational institutions, including College of William and Mary, American University in Paris, University of Tulsa, and Southeast Missouri State University; guest on media programs; public speaker.

MEMBER: International Center for Medieval Art, Sixteenth Century Studies Society, Renaissance Society of America, College Art Association, Italian Art Society, Association of Art Historians (England), Midwest Art History Society (president).

AWARDS, HONORS: Fellow of National Endowment for the Humanities, 1990; grants from National Endowment for the Arts, 1994, 2001.

WRITINGS:

Medieval Art in the Collection of the Saint Louis Art Museum, St. Louis Art Museum (St. Louis, MO), 1992.

Baroque into Rococo: Seventeenth- and Eighteenth-Century Italian Paintings, St. Louis Art Museum (St. Louis, MO), 1997.

(With Keith Christiansen) Orazio and Artemisia Gentileschi: Father and Daughter Painters in Baroque Italy, Metropolitan Museum of Art (New York, NY), 2001.

Contributor to books, including Gothic Sculpture in American Collections, edited by Dorothy Gillerman, Garland Publishing (New York, NY), 2002. Contributor to periodicals, including Art Bulletin, Sixteenth Century Journal, Studies in Iconography, and Apollo.

WORK IN PROGRESS: Artemisia Gentileschi and the Nature of Baroque Innovation, a monograph; editing Eroticism and Religious Art in the Seventeenth Century, with Caroline Straughan.

*   *   *

MARCHESE, John 1961-

PERSONAL: Born 1961; son of Tully Marchese (a construction worker).

ADDRESSES: Home—New York, NY, and Narrowsburg, NY. Agent—c/o Publicity Director, Riverhead Books, 375 Hudson St., New York, NY, 10014.

CAREER: Author and journalist. Professional trumpet player.

AWARDS, HONORS: National Magazine Award, for work with Philadelphia magazine.

WRITINGS:

Renovations: A Father and Son Rebuild a House and Rediscover Each Other, Riverhead Books (New York, NY), 2001.

Contributor of articles to many periodicals, including Premiere, Discover, Esquire, Rolling Stone, and the New York Times. Served as a contributing editor for Worth and Philadelphia magazines.

Author's works have appeared in collections, including The Best American Sports Writing and The Wall Street Journal Guide to Executive Style.

SIDELIGHTS: Near the end of his debut book, American freelance journalist and author John Marchese writes: "Like all sons, I am what I am both because of [my father] and despite him." Marchese came to that conclusion while writing the book Renovations: A Father and Son Rebuild a House and Rediscover Each Other. The book recounts Marchese's efforts to renovate his home in the rural New York town of Narrowsburg with the help of his father, a retired construction worker. It also describes how the two men mended the rift that had grown between them over the years.

When he turned forty, Marchese bought a home in the small town of Narrowsburg, New York. He was in the midst of what he described as a fit of midlife turmoil—drinking too much and not writing enough. He began to reevaluate his life because he had "missed the normal benchmarks of adulthood—college graduation, steady job, marriage, home ownership." So Marchese bought the home, in part as a way to get away on weekends from the fast-paced world of New York City. Marchese was glad to discover that the home needed many repairs, because he felt that his life "could be buoyed by the sheer busy-ness of work—work I'd never done before, work that seemed somehow more real than any I'd done." Because of his lack of experience with construction work, Marchese asked his father to help him. He also thought it would be a good way for the two to repair their relationship, which had grown distant. As he explains in the book, the two men were quite different. "As I entered midlife, I realized that my father and I shared a name and just about nothing else," Marchese wrote. "No one has ever told me, 'Oh, you're just like your father.' We had, each of us, built a wall between us, whether we meant to or not. I tried one day to make a list of things we had in common. It was a short list." Marchese's father, in his mid-seventies, is a blue-collar man with traditional values. "My father is not a particularly sentimental man, but his relationship with his work, I've come to realize, is strong and complex," Marchese wrote.

Renovations received positive reviews. *Booklist* reviewer David Pitt called Marchese's book "a memorable, sensitively written memoir, full of wisdom and . . . genuine humor." A reviewer for *Publishers Weekly* felt the author's "humor and self-deprecation . . . capture certain essentials about being a father and son." And J. Peder Zane of the *News Observer* wrote that the book "speaks to our concern that modern technology and contemporary thought are at odds with our basic humanity, that the great freedom and comforts we cherish distance us from our families, our selves and 'reality.'"

BIOGRAPHICAL AND CRITICAL SOURCES:

BOOKS

Marchese, John, *Renovations: A Father and Son Rebuild a House and Rediscover Each Other,* Riverhead Books (New York, NY), 2001.

PERIODICALS

Book, May, 2001, John Marchese, "Tearing down Walls," p. 55.
Booklist, April 1, 2001, David Pitt, review of *Renovations: A Father and Son Rebuild a House and Rediscover Each Other,* p. 1440.
Library Journal, June 1, 2001, Douglas C. Lord, review of *Renovations,* p. 193.
Philadelphia, May, 2001, Caroline Tiger, "See John Saw," p. 23.
Publishers Weekly, April 9, 2001, review of *Renovations,* p. 61.

OTHER

News Observer, http://cgi.newsobserver.com/ (June 17, 2001), J. Peder Zane, "A Son's Search." *

*   *   *

MARGOLICK, David

PERSONAL: Born in Putnam, CT. *Education:* Received degrees from University of Michigan and Stanford Law School.

ADDRESSES: *Home*—New York, NY. *Agent*—c/o Author Mail, Running Press, 125 South 22nd St., Philadelphia, PA 19103-4399.

CAREER: Writer and journalist. *New York Times,* New York, NY, legal reporter, 1981-86, national legal affairs editor and law columnist, 1987-96.

AWARDS, HONORS: Four-time Pulitzer Prize nominee.

WRITINGS:

Undue Influence: The Epic Battle for the Johnson & Johnson Fortune, William Morrow (New York, NY), 1993.
At the Bar: The Passions and Peccadilloes of American Lawyers, illustrated by Elliot Banfield, Simon & Schuster (New York, NY), 1995.
Strange Fruit: Billie Holiday, Café Society, and an Early Cry for Civil Rights, foreword by Hilton Als, Running Press (Philadelphia, PA), 2000.

Contributing editor, *Vanity Fair.*

SIDELIGHTS: While David Margolick was in law school he began writing for the *National Law Journal, American Lawyer,* and later for the *New York Times.* The central focus of much of that writing concerned the human side of the equation. During Margolick's tenure at The*New York Times,* he was nominated four times for the Pulitzer Prize.

Margolick's book *Undue Influence: The Epic Battle for the Johnson & Johnson Fortune* follows a three-year legal/family struggle that built to a seventeen-week "showdown" in New York County surrogate's court. According to Michelle Green in the *New York Times,* Margolick "followed this soap from start to finish, and he missed nary a shred of irony. Savvy and self-assured, he skillfully explicates a labyrinthine case." *Nation* reviewer John L. Hess noted that Margolick's "narrative of the trial is so gripping as to impel a reviewer to withhold mention of the outcome." And Shawn Tully in *Fortune* commended Margolick for "expertly [tracing] the Johnson saga," calling the book a "rich chronicle."

At the Bar: The Passions and Peccadilloes of American Lawyers is a collection of writings selected from the weekly column Margolick wrote for the *New York Times* between 1987 and 1994. According to a reviewer in *Publishers Weekly,* the book is written with "considerable skill, wit and an elegant turn of phrase." As a reviewer in the *New York Times* commented, "people like these, and stories about them, never go out of date; they are as deathless as the law itself."

According to a reviewer in *Publishers Weekly,* Margolick's book *Strange Fruit: Billie Holiday, Café Society, and an Early Cry for Civil Rights,* is replete with "thorough research and the smooth writing of a journalist." That reviewer called the book "a superb piece of cultural history." Focusing on the cultural history of "Strange Fruit," a 1930s "lynching ballad," Margolick discovered that its composer was a leftist Bronx schoolteacher named Abel Meeropol, although its authorship had been claimed by Blues singer Billie Holiday. Scott Schrake, a reviewer for the *Philadelphia City Paper,* called the book "a document of diverse voices" that is a "testament to the power of [Holiday's] talent." First performed in the late 1930s, "Strange Fruit" was considered by some to be a "rebuke of Congress" for failing to pass anti-lynching laws, according to Phil Nel at Kansas State University. Michael Sims called the book "cultural history at its best. Clear, literate, at once passionate and objective, it is quite a performance."

BIOGRAPHICAL AND CRITICAL SOURCES:

PERIODICALS

Book World, April 2, 1995, review of *At the Bar: The Passions and Peccadilloes of American Lawyers,* p. 6.

Financial Times of Canada, May 15,1993, Susan Smith, review of *Undue Influence: The Epic Battle for the Johnson & Johnson Fortune,* p. B21.

Fortune, May 31, 1993, Shawn Tully, review of *Undue Influence,* p. 167.

Library Journal, March 1, 2000, Nathan Ward, review of *Strange Fruit: Billie Holiday, Café Society, and an Early Cry for Civil Rights,* p. 107.

Nation, July 12, 1993, John L. Hess, review of *Undue Influence,* p. 76.

New Yorker, April 19, 1993, review of *Undue Influence,* p. 119.

New York Review of Books, June 24, 1993, Murray Kempton, review of *Undue Influence,* p. 49.

New York Times Book Review, March 14, 1993, Michelle Green, "The Band-Aid War," p. 7; April 30, 1995, review of *At the Bar: The Passions and Peccadilloes of American Lawyers,* p. 22.

Publishers Weekly, March 6, 1995, review of *At the Bar,* p. 67; February 14, 2000, Judy Quinn, "Hoping for 'Holiday Sales,'" p. 86; February 28, 2000, review of *Strange Fruit,* p. 76.

Washington Post Book World, April 2, 1995, Jeffrey T. Leeds, review of *At the Bar,* p. 6.

OTHER

All about Jazz, http://www.allaboutjazz.com/ (January 3, 2001), Vic Schermer, review of *Strange Fruit,* and "Author David Margolick on His New Book: *Strange Fruit,*"

Boston Herald, http://bostonherald.com (July 6, 2000), Larry Katz, "Bearing 'Strange Fruit': Author Examines Billie Holiday's Haunting Masterpiece and the Civil Rights Movement."

Jewish World Review, http://www.jewishworldreview.com/ (May 9, 2000), Robert Leiter, "Not So Black and White."

Kansas State University Web site, http://www.ksu.edu/english/nelp/ (April 9, 2000), Phil Nel, "What Art Can Do For Social Change."

Metrotimes, http://www.metrotimes.com/ (April 19, 2000), Eileen Murphy, review of *Strange Fruit.*

Nieman Foundation, http://www.nieman.harvard.edu/ (April 19, 2000), Bill Kovach, "Interview with David Margolick."

NonFiction Book Page, http://www.bookpage.com/ (April 19, 2000), Robert Fleming, review of *Strange Fruit.*

Philadelphia City Paper, http://www.cpcn.com/ (March 23, 2000), Scott Shrake, review of *Strange Fruit.*

Running Press Web site, http://www.runningpress.com/ (spring, 2000), review of *Strange Fruit.*

Weekly Wire, http://www.weeklywire.com/ (May 15, 2000), Michael Sims, "Ripe for Discovery: Recent Volume Tells Compelling Story of Tragic, Historic Jazz Tune."*

MARKFIELD, Wallace 1926-2002

OBITUARY NOTICE—See index for *CA* sketch: Born August 12, 1926, in Brooklyn, NY; died from complications from a heart attack May 24, 2002, in Roslyn, NY. Novelist. Markfield was a popular fiction writer whose unique ability to mix comedy and tragedy sometimes had critics comparing him to Irish author James Joyce. He graduated from Brooklyn College with a B.A. in 1947, and also attended graduate school at New York University for two years. One of his first jobs out of college was as a literary critic for *New Leader* magazine from 1954 to 1955, which was followed by ten years as a writer for the Anti-Defamation League in New York City. Markfield's first novel, *To an Early Grave* (1964), earned him wide praise and a Guggenheim fellowship; it was also adapted as the 1968 film *Bye Bye Braverman* starring George Segal and Jack Warden. Though Markfield was not prolific, he continued to publish quality novels such as *Teitelbaum's Widow* (1970) and *Radical Surgery* (1991), as well as the short-story collection *Multiple Orgasms* (1977). When he was not writing, he was teaching writing, and was an assistant professor at San Francisco State University from 1966 to 1968 and at Queens College of the City University of New York from 1971 to 1973.

OBITUARIES AND OTHER SOURCES:

PERIODICALS

Los Angeles Times, June 1, 2002, p. B19.
New York Times, May 31, 2002, p. C14.
Washington Post, June 2, 2002, p. C8.

*　　*　　*

MARTEL, Gordon

PERSONAL: Male. *Education:* Simon Fraser University, B.A. (honors), 1968; Fletcher School of Law & Diplomacy at Tufts University & Harvard University, M.A., 1969; University of Toronto, Ph.D., 1977.

ADDRESSES: Office—427 Library Bldg., University of Northern British Columbia, 3333 University Way, Prince George, BC V2N 4Z9, Canada. *E-mail*—martel@unbc.ca.

CAREER: Trent University, Peterborough, Ontario, Canada, assistant professor, 1977-81; Royal Roads Military College, Victoria, British Columbia, Canada, assistant professor, 1981-83, associate professor, 1983-87, professor, 1987-95; Simon Fraser University, Burnaby, British Columbia, Canada, adjunct professor of history, 1995—; DeMontfort University, Leicester, England, senior research fellow, 1995—; University of Northern British Columbia, Prince George, British Columbia, Canada, professor of history, 1995—.

WRITINGS:

(Editor) *Modern Germany Reconsidered, 1870-1945,* Routledge (New York, NY), 1992.
(Editor) *American Foreign Relations Reconsidered, 1890-1993,* Routledge (New York, NY), 1994.
Imperial Diplomacy: Rosebery and the Failure of Foreign Policy, McGill-Queen's University Press (Kingston, Ontario, Canada), 1986.
(Editor) *The Origins of the Second World War Reconsidered: The A. J. P. Taylor Debate after Twenty-five Years,* Allen and Unwin (Boston, MA), 1986, 2nd edition, 1999.
(Editor) *Studies in British Imperial History: Essays in Honour of A. P. Thornton,* St. Martin's Press (New York, NY), 1986.
The Origins of the First World War, Longman (New York, NY), 1987, 2nd edition, 1996.
(Editor) *The Times and Appeasement: The Journals of A. L. Kennedy, 1932-1939,* Cambridge University Press (Cambridge, England), 2000.

SIDELIGHTS: In *Imperial Diplomacy: Rosebery and the Failure of Foreign Policy,* Gordon Martel presents the first detailed examination of Lord Rosebery's foreign policy during the period when he was foreign secretary and prime minister. Drawing on the personal papers of politicians and diplomats, Martel discusses Rosebery's liberal principles and defense of the concept of the British Empire. The book includes an analysis of Rosebery's policies toward Egypt and Uganda, as well as his policies toward Russia and Germany. In *Choice*, a reviewer noted that the book is "pure diplomatic history with no reference to social, political, or cultural factors." In the *American Historical Review*, Briton C. Busch wrote that the book would be "of importance to any student of Rosebery and of power relationships in the 1880s and 1890s." D.

McLean, in the *English Historical Review,* described it as "sympathetic" and "thorough," as well as "well written and interesting to read," and commented that it "will, as claimed, become a standard authority on the diplomatic career of Lord Rosebery."

The Origins of the Second World War Reconsidered: The A. J. P. Taylor Debate after Twenty-five Years presents ten original essays by various scholars who provide commentary on Taylor's 1961 book *Origins of the Second World War.* In the *Times Educational Supplement,* Martin Fagg wrote, "Gordon Martel nimbly traverses the much-trodden territory of First World War origins." Keith Robbins commented in the *English Historical Review* that "students [of World War II] will find this book a useful and thorough introduction."

BIOGRAPHICAL AND CRITICAL SOURCES:

PERIODICALS

American Historical Review, October, 1986, Briton C. Busch, review of *Imperial Diplomacy: Rosebery and the Failure of Foreign Policy,* p. 923; April, 1987, review of *Studies in British Imperial History: Essays in Honour of A. P. Thornton,* p. 520; October, 1987, Gordon Wright, review of *The Origins of the Second World War Reconsidered: The A. J. P. Taylor Debate after Twenty-five Years,* p. 947.

Choice, June, 1986, J. H. Weiner, review of *Imperial Diplomacy,* p. 1590; January, 1987, C. P. Vincent, review of *The Origins of the Second World War Reconsidered,* p. 808.

Contemporary Review, April, 2000, James Munson, review of *The Origins of the Second World War Reconsidered,* p. 220; May, 2001, review of *The Times and Appeasement: The Journals of A. L. Kennedy, 1932-1939,* p. 319.

English Historical Review, April, 1987, Keith Robbins, review of *The Origins of the Second World War Reconsidered,* p. 446; January, 1989, D. McLean, review of *Imperial Diplomacy,* p. 244; October, 1989, Bernard Porter, review of *Studies in British Imperial History,* p. 1062.

European History Quarterly, October, 1989, Lothar Kettenacker, review of *The Origins of the Second World War Reconsidered,* p. 565.

Historical Journal, September, 1992, Niall Ferguson, review of *The Origins of the First World War,* p. 725.

History, February, 1988, Andrew Porter, review of *Imperial Diplomacy,* p. 174.

History Today, June, 1987, review of *Imperial Diplomacy,* p. 56.

International History Review, August, 1996, Wesley T. Wooley, review of *American Foreign Relations Reconsidered, 1890-1993,* p. 683.

Journal of Modern History, September, 1988, Agatha Ramm, review of *Imperial Diplomacy,* p. 585.

London Review of Books, June 21, 2001, Geoffrey Best, "Heiling Hitler", p. 13.

Slavonic and East European Review, October, 1994, Mary Fulbrook, review of *Modern Germany Reconsidered, 1870-1945,* p. 758.

Times Educational Supplement, December 11, 1987, Martin Fagg, review of *The Origins of the First World War,* p. 24.*

*   *   *

MARTIN, J(ulia) Wallis

PERSONAL: Daughter of Walter (a farmer) and Josephine Martin; married first husband, Chris (a banker; divorced); married second husband, Russell (a screenwriter); children: James.

ADDRESSES: Home—London, England. *Agent*—c/o Author Mail, St. Martin's Minotaur, 175 Fifth Ave., New York, NY 10010.

CAREER: Writer; editor for a South African publishing company.

AWARDS, HONORS: Edgar Allan Poe Award nominee, Mystery Writiers of America, for *A Likeness in Stone.*

WRITINGS:

A Likeness in Stone, St. Martin's Press (New York, NY), 1998.

The Bird Yard, St. Martin's Minotaur (New York, NY), 1999.

Dancing with the Uninvited Guest, Hodder & Stoughton (London, England), 2002, Thorndike Press (Waterville, ME), 2003.

Also author of *The Long Close Call,* a biography, *Gonda Betrix: Jumping to Success,* and a novella, *Mary Hibbert.*

ADAPTATIONS: A Likeness in Stone was adapted for the BBC. *The Long Close Call* was optioned for television.

SIDELIGHTS: English crime writer J. Wallis Martin's childhood, adolescence, and first marriage have provided ample material for her psychological thrillers. Her mother, Josephine, a manic depressive, was already married when she ran off with Walter Martin, the married man who fathered the author. Julia lived quietly enough with Josephine's parents until, at age eleven, her mother took her to live in an apartment in Warrington, England. "I ended up living in a very dreadful council flat on a very dreadful estate in the northwest of England with a suicidal, manic-depressive mother," recalled Martin in an interview with John Connolly for the *Irish Times.* Life continued to be dreadful; one day she came home from school to the sight of an ambulance preparing to take her mother to the hospital after she overdosed on Lithium. "It got to the stage where she couldn't walk, couldn't talk, couldn't function normally, and I found myself trying to cope with this woman at a time when a kid needs all the help she can get just to keep it together," Martin told Connolly.

When Martin was seventeen, her mother died of breast cancer at the age of forty-nine, and though the council gave the now-homeless teenager a small apartment, Martin soon left it behind. As she said in the *Irish Times* interview, "I remember looking out of the window and thinking: I have to walk away. What was I going to do, stay in Warrington for the rest of my life because someone had given me a place to live? I just had visions of myself in forty years still living in that building." Moving to Oxford, Martin found work as a waitress; she also wrote and submitted short stories, though only one was published during a five-year period.

When she was twenty-seven, Martin married her first husband, Chris, a banker who was fifteen years her senior. They moved to Johannesburg, South Africa, for what was to have been a six-month stay that stretched to seven years. She worked as a commissioning editor at a publishing company and wrote and published two books: *Gonda Betrix, Jumping to Success,* the biography of a South African showjumper, and *Mary Hibbert,* a novella. Martin hated the lawlessness and danger of the country and continually urged her husband to leave, but he brushed off her fears. Her son James was born while they were there. A six-week spate of violence, during which the family was the target of two attempted armed robberies on their home, was robbed at gunpoint in a restaurant, and had their car hijacked by armed men at a roadblock, culminated in a shootout in their house between gunmen attempting to enter during a dinner party and four armed Afrikanner guests. Two of the bandits were killed while the baby slept upstairs. Martin took little James and boarded a plane out of the country the next day.

Back in Oxford, her marriage over, Martin settled into a cheap apartment and started writing to support herself and her son. Though turned down several times, her first novel, *A Likeness in Stone,* was published in 1998. It delves into the relationships between a group of former college friends after the body of a young woman is discovered inside a house sunk beneath a reservoir. According to John Connolly in his *Irish Times* interview, it "marked the arrival of a spectacularly accomplished crime author."

The Bird Yard was Martin's next novel. Marilyn Stasio commented in the *New York Times Book Review* on the stifling atmosphere detailed so effectively in both of Martin's books: "[There are] claustrophobic images that Julia Wallis Martin likes to play with first in her debut novel . . . and now in the equally disturbing thriller *The Bird Yard.*" A *Publishers Weekly* reviewer called *The Bird Yard* "grim and intense." Detective Superintendent Parker searches for a killer after twelve-year-old Gary Maudsley's disappearance mirrors that of Joseph Coyne, who vanished five years earlier. Joseph's skeleton, dismembered as though in a ritualistic killing, is found in some remote woods, and Parker enlists criminal psychologist profiler Murray Hanson to help him find Gary. They discover that both boys, neglected by their parents, had worked for a pet shop owner and had connections with two other suspects: Douglas Byrne, a convicted pedophile, and Roly Barnes, a reclusive man who has created an aviary of exotic finches—the bird yard—in an abandoned house that attracts young boys. Parker and Hanson strain to discover Joseph's murderer, find Gary, and prevent the killing of a third boy, Brogan Healey, who seems to be straying down the same path that put the first two boys in the killer's clutches. Parker is spurred on in his quest because he has two young sons of his own and he fears for their safety.

"Like the bright little birds that beat against their cages, Brogan is a dear child caught in an 'atmosphere of rot and desolation' that Martin describes in all its horror," wrote Stasio. *Booklist* reviewers Jenny McLarin and Emily Melton, too, noted Martin's atmospheric detailing: "Particularly compelling are Martin's descriptions of the tiny, fragile, helpless birds and the young boys who so resemble them." Marianne Fitzgerald, writing in the *Library Journal,* compared Martin to Minette Walters, "writing about disturbing subject matter in intelligent and interesting prose. Lots of suspense and a surprising conclusion make *The Bird Yard* a good read."

Martin explained in the *Irish Times* interview that her inspiration for *The Bird Yard* came from a childhood experience: "When we lived on the council estate, my bedroom window looked out on a row of derelict houses. Someone had moved into one of those houses. He had attached mesh from the garden fence to the top of the house, opened all of the windows and he had filled the garden and the house with exotic finches, so the house was an extension of the aviary. Of course, the local kids were absolutely fascinated. He was a pedophile under twenty-four-hour surveillance, which we didn't know at the time."

The Long Close Call, Martin's third novel, takes a different tone than her first two books. A policeman whose father is in prison kills an armed man during a bank robbery and is stalked by the dead man's family. Martin found the idea for this story from her past, too. It is based on a meeting with an old boyfriend, now a policeman, whose father was in jail.

BIOGRAPHICAL AND CRITICAL SOURCES:

PERIODICALS

Booklist, August, 1999, Jenny McLarin and Emily Melton, review of *The Bird Yard,* p. 2035.
Library Journal, August, 1999, Marianne Fitzgerald, review of *The Bird Yard,* p. 146.

New York Times Book Review, December 12, 1999, Marilyn Stasio, review of *The Bird Yard,* p. 41.
Publishers Weekly, July 26, 1999, review of *The Bird Yard,* p. 66; November 1, 1999, review of *The Bird Yard,* p. 48.

OTHER

Crescent Blues Book Views, http://www.crescentblues. com/ (February 8, 2002), review of *The Bird Yard.*
Irish Times Web site, http://www.deadlypleasures.com/ (June, 2001), John Connolly, "Interview of Julia Wallis Martin."
St. Martin's Minotaur Books, http://www. minotaurbooks.com/ (February 8, 2002), profile of Julia Wallis Martin.*

*   *   *

MAXWELL, John C. 1947-

PERSONAL: Born 1947.

ADDRESSES: Home—Atlanta, GA. *Agent*—c/o Author Mail, Nelson Direct, P.O. Box 140300, Nashville, TN 37214-0300.

CAREER: Author and ordained minister; Skyline Wesleyan Church, San Diego, CA, senior pastor, 1995; Founder of INJOY Group and Equip.

WRITINGS:

Your Attitude: Key to Success, Here's Life Publishers (San Bernardino, CA), 1984.
Tough Questions—Honest Answers, Here's Life Publishers (San Bernardino, CA), 1985.
Be All You Can Be!, Victor Books (Wheaton, IL), 1987, revised edition, 2002.
The Communicator's Commentary: Deuteronomy, Word Books (Waco, TX), 1987.
Be a People Person, Victor Books (Wheaton, IL), 1989, revised edition, 1994.
The Winning Attitude, Here's Life Publishers (San Bernardino, CA), 1991, revised edition, T. Nelson Publishers (Nashville, TN), 1993.

Developing the Leader within You, T. Nelson Publishers (Nashville, TN), 1993.

Developing the Leaders around You, T. Nelson Publishers (Nashville, TN), 1995.

You Can't Be a Smart Cookie, If You Have a Crummy Attitude, Honor Books (Tulsa, OK), 1995.

(With Brad Lewis) *Your Family Time with God: A Weekly Plan for Family Devotions,* Christian Parenting Books (Elgin, IL), 1995.

Breakthrough Parenting, Focus on the Family Publishers (Colorado Springs, CO), 1996.

It's Just a Thought—But It Could Change Your Life: Life's Little Lessons on Leadership, Honor Books (Tulsa, OK), 1996.

Living at the Next Level: Insights for Reaching Your Dreams, T. Nelson Publishers (Nashville, TN), 1996.

Partners in Prayer, T. Nelson Publishers (Nashville, TN), 1996.

People Power: Life's Little Lessons on Relationships, Honor Books (Tulsa, OK), 1996.

(With Jim Dornan) *Becoming a Person of Influence: How to Positively Impact the Lives of Others,* T. Nelson Publishers (Nashville, TN), 1997.

The Success Journey, T. Nelson Publishers (Nashville, TN), 1997.

Your Bridge to a Better Future, T. Nelson Publishers (Nashville, TN), 1997.

The twenty-one Irrefutable Laws of Leadership: Follow Them and People Will Follow You, T. Nelson Publishers (Nashville, TN), 1998.

Think on These Things: Meditations for Leaders, Beacon Hill Press of Kansas City (Kansas City, MO), 1999.

The twenty-one Indispensable Qualities of a Leader: Becoming the Person that People Will Want to Follow, T. Nelson Publishers (Nashville, TN), 1999.

(With Dan Reiland) *The Treasure of a Friend,* J. Countryman Publishers (Nashville, TN), 1999.

Failing Forward: Turning Mistakes into Stepping-Stones for Success, T. Nelson Publishers (Nashville, TN), 2000.

The twenty-one Most Powerful Minutes in a Leader's Day: Revitalize Your Spirit and Empower Your Leadership, T. Nelson Publishers (Nashville, TN), 2000.

John C. Maxwell's Electronic Leadership Library (computer optical discs) Nelson Electronic (Nashville, TN), 2000.

Developing the Leader within You Workbook, T. Nelson Publishers (Nashville, TN), 2001.

(With Mark Littleton) *Leading as a Friend,* T. Nelson Publishers (Nashville, TN), 2001.

(With Jean Fischer) *Leading from the Lockers,* T. Nelson Publishers (Nashville, TN), 2001

(With Mark Littleton) *Leading Your Sports Team,* T. Nelson Publishers (Nashville, TN), 2001.

(With Mark Littleton) *Leading in Your Youth Group,* T. Nelson Publishers (Nashville, TN), 2001.

(With Monica Hall) *Leading at School,* T. Nelson Publishers (Nashville, TN), 2001.

The Power of Attitude, RiverOak Publishers (Tulsa, OK), 2001.

The Power of Influence, RiverOak Publishers (Tulsa, OK), 2001.

The Power of Leadership, RiverOak Publishers (Tulsa, OK), 2001.

The Power of Thinking Big, RiverOak Publishers (Tulsa, OK), 2001.

The Right to Lead: A Study in Character and Courage, J. Countryman Publishers (Nashville, TN), 2001.

The seventeen Indisputable Laws of Teamwork: Embrace Them and Empower Your Team, T. Nelson Publishers (Nashville, TN), 2001.

Leadership 101, T. Nelson Publishers (Nashville, TN), 2002.

Attitude 101, T. Nelson Publishers (Nashville, TN), 2002.

The seventeen Essential Qualities of a Team Player: Becoming the Kind of Person Every Team Wants, T. Nelson Publishers (Nashville, TN), 2002.

Running with the Giants: What Old Testament Heroes Want You to Know about Life and Leadership, Warner Books (New York, NY), 2002.

Your Road Map for Success, T. Nelson Publishers (Nashville, TN), 2002.

Thinking for a Change: Eleven Ways That Highly Successful People Approach Life and Work, Warner Books (New York, NY), 2003.

Also author of foreword, *Who Moved My Church? A Story about Discovering Purpose in a Changing Culture,* by Mike Nappa, RiverOak Publishers (Tulsa, OK), 2001.

ADAPTATIONS: Failing Forward: Turning Mistakes into Stepping-Stones for Success has been adapted for audio cassette.

SIDELIGHTS: John C. Maxwell has written over forty books, has founded several nonprofit and for-profit organizations, is an ordained minister, and is well known for his successful leadership conferences. He is a man who challenged himself to create a bridge between his Christian community and the business world by recording his own steps to realizing success. Now he teaches others how to do the same.

For almost twenty-years Maxwell has been writing books that tackle issues he has confronted over the years. His books have become so popular that they often spend weeks on the nation's bestseller lists. Maxwell's popularity as a writer is directly related to his own successful story. He gladly shares all he has learned in getting to where he is.

Although some of Maxwell's writing is specifically geared to the Christian family and religious practice, the majority of his books are directed to the business community, with a specific aim at business leaders. Of these, the most popular is *The twenty-one Irrefutable Laws of Leadership: Follow Them and People Will Follow You.* The basic premise of this book relates to creating successful working relationships with other people. Maxwell writes that anyone who wants to be a successful leader must be able to help other people develop their own skills, while maintaining a positive attitude and developing strong leadership skills such as charisma, courage, problem-solving abilities, and vision. As Dr. Terry van der Werff stated in a review of *The twenty-one Irrefutable Laws of Leadership* for the *Global Future Report,* "No one becomes a leader by reading a book." However, van der Werff added that solutions to a problem often come to light by looking at it through a different perspective. "Maxwell's book is a good place to begin."

At one time, both *The twenty-one Irrefutable Laws of Leadership* and the book that Maxwell published one year later were on the *Business Week* bestseller list. A book closely related to *The 21 Irrefutable Laws of Leadership* is his *The twenty-one Indispensable Qualities of a Leader: Becoming the Person That People Will Want to Follow.* In this work, Maxwell breaks down the character traits he believes make up the successful leader: commitment, discernment, generosity, initiative, passion, responsibility, and self-discipline. He covers each topic thoroughly, giving his readers definitions of each trait and illustrating with anecdotes. He also offers exercises that help readers improve areas in which they may be lacking. Kirk Charles reviewed book for *Black Enterprise* and recommended it to all, even those who were already in "quasi-

leadership" positions. Charles enjoyed the accessibility of *The twenty-one Indispensable Qualities of a Leader* and suggested that it might help take the reader to the next level of leadership.

In 2000, Maxwell published three books. One of them, *Failing Forward: How to Make the Most of Your Mistakes,* was reviewed in *Inc.,* by a writer who commented, "Maxwell obviously never met a failure he couldn't learn from." That seems to be the whole premise of the book, as he always manages to turn the proverbial lemon into lemonade. Maxwell offers fifteen steps toward making the best of a bad situation, and he offers real life examples of successful people and the challenges they overcame.

The twenty-one Most Powerful Minutes in a Leader's Day: Revitalize Your Spirit and Empower Your Leadership offers daily meditations for leaders based on Biblical truths and characters such as Jesus, Moses, and King Solomon. Although Maxwell, who comes from a religious background, has always relied upon a general Christian perspective in forming the bases of his teachings, in this book he makes more specific Christian references. Although Maxwell still addresses topics that have appeared in some of his prior publications, in *The 21 Most Powerful Minutes in a Leader's Day* he recommends the use of prayer to help readers put the ideas into practice.

During 2001 Maxwell published many books, but one stands out by virtue of its emphasis on teamwork rather than leadership. In *The seventeen Indisputable Laws of Teamwork: Embrace Them and Empower Your Team,* Maxwell suggests that teamwork is essential, whether the setting is the business world, a church, a sports team, a school, or a family. Although in the past Maxwell has often delivered the message that building a good team was a means of gaining success, in this book he puts teamwork at the forefront.

Marcia Ford, writing for *Publishers Weekly,* began her review of Maxwell's *The seventeen Indisputable Laws of Teamwork* by stating that "If John C. Maxwell is right, the next phase in management style will be team leadership." According to many business leaders, this is exactly what is needed. The old-school autocratic way of running an organization is witnessing an overhaul; or, as Maxwell puts it, there may be individuals who play the game, but when it comes to winning, it is the team that is awarded the championship.

Some of the teamwork laws, according to Maxwell, include the "Law of the Big Picture," which states that every member must be able to envision the goal; the "Law of the Niche," which states that there may be a lot of great potential in various team members, but they have to be in the spot that is right for them if they, and the team, are going to be successful; and the "Law of Mt. Everest," which proposes that each time the team achieves a goal, it must work a little harder to succeed at the next level. A reviewer for *Publishers Weekly* stated that it was quite obvious that "Maxwell has found a formula that works."

BIOGRAPHICAL AND CRITICAL SOURCES:

PERIODICALS

Christian Herald, April, 1985, review of *Your Attitude: Key to Success,* p. 52.
Black Enterprise, June, 2000, Kirk Charles, review of *The twenty-one Indispensable Qualities of a Leader: Becoming the Person That People Will Want to Follow,* p. 92.
Business Week, October 4, 1999, review of *The twenty-one Irrefutable Laws of Leadership: Follow Them and People Will Follow You,* p. 22
Inc., April 2000, "Viva la Difference," review of *Failing Forward: Turning Mistakes into Stepping-Stones for Success,* p. 153.
Library Journal, August, 2001, Barbara Hoffert, review of *The Success Journey: The Process of Living Your Dreams,* p. S76.
Planet IT, April 19, 2000, review of *Failing Forward.*
Publishers Weekly, July 10, 1995, review of *Your Family Time with God: A Weekly Plan for Family Devotions,* p. 29; August 30, 1999, review of *Think on These Things: Meditations for Leaders,* p. 75; July 2, 2001, Marcia Ford, "Leading Leaders," p. S18; July 23, 2001, review of *The 17 Indisputable Laws of Teamwork: Embrace Them and Empower Your Team,* p. 74.
Rapport March, 1992, review of *Be a People Person,* p. 41.
Washington Business Journal, February 16, 2001, review of *The twenty-one Irrefutable Laws of Leadership,* p. 39.

OTHER

Global Future Report, http://www.globalfuture.com/ (October 7, 2001), Dr. Terry van der Werff, review of *The twenty-one Irrefutable Laws of Leadership: Follow Them and People Will Follow You.**

McCLURE, Laura (K)athleen) 1959-

PERSONAL: Born December 26, 1959, in Wichita Falls, TX; married 1988; children: two. *Education:* Bard College, B.A. (languages and literature), 1982; St. John's College, M.A. (humanities), 1984; University of Chicago, M.A., 1986, Ph.D. (classical languages and literature), 1991.

ADDRESSES: Office—Department of Classics, 902 Van Hise Hall, 1220 Linden Dr., University of Wisconsin, Madison WI, 53706. *E-mail*—lmcclure@ facstaff.wisc.edu.

CAREER: University of Wisconsin, Madison, associate professor of classics, 1991—.

WRITINGS:

Rhetoric and Gender in Euripides: A Study of Sacrifice Actions (Ph.D. thesis), University of Chicago Press (Chicago, IL), 1991.
Spoken like a Woman: Speech and Gender in Athenian Drama, Princeton University Press (Princeton, NJ), 1999.
(Editor, with André Lardinois) *Making Silence Speak: Women's Voices in Greek Literature and Society,* Princeton University Press (Princeton, NJ), 2001.
(Editor) *Sexuality and Gender in the Classical World: Readings and Sources,* Blackwell Publishers (Malden, MA), 2002.

Contributor of articles to professional journals, including *Classical Philology, Classical World, Helios,* and *Classical Journal.* Contributor to collections, including *World Eras,* Volume 2: *Classical Greek Civilization, 800-323 BCE,* Gale (Detroit, MI), 2000.

Contributor of reviews to scholarly journals, including *Bryn Mawr Classical Review* and *Classical Philology.*

SIDELIGHTS: In her academic career, Laura McClure has written extensively on Ancient Greek drama, with a particular focus on the treatment of women. In *Spoken like a Woman: Speech and Gender in Athenian Drama,* McClure explores the ways in which female characters either uphold or subvert the traditional order. While in general it is men who hold forth on public policy in Greek plays, and women are relegated to political or sexual scheming, McClure "digs a bit deeper and examines plays by Aeschylus, Euripides, and Aristophanes that have women employing verbal genres associated with men to examine, critique, and even subvert Athenian democracy," wrote a reviewer for the *Seminary Co-op Bookstore Web site.*

In addition, she explores the subtleties of feminine and masculine speech patterns in these plays, "offering a useful, occasionally provocative overview of the politics of gendered diction," wrote D. Konstan in *Choice.* For Judith Fletcher, writing in the *Bryn Mawr Classical Review,* McClure's "unique contribution is an overriding theoretical approach which charts the common pattern of disruptive feminine discourse and its eventual necessary containment." Added Fletcher, "one of its most praiseworthy features is the happy marriage of sociolinguistics and literary analysis."

McClure followed up *Spoken like a Woman* by coediting *Making Silence Speak: Women's Voices in Greek Literature and Society.* The authors of this collection of essays attempt to recover the "voices" of ancient women, either through the few surviving letters or poetry by such women as Sappho, or through male-authored female characters in Homeric epics, fictional letters, dramas, and other sources. Even transvestite characters are examined for clues as to what it meant to speak like a woman. Obviously it is not always easy to tease out the real from the fictional in these sources. Noting that difficulty, Tim Whitmarsh wrote in the *Bryn Mawr Classical Review,* "Where *Making Silence Speak* succeeds most conspicuously is where, rather than confronting intractable sources with coercion, it homes in on the problems and issues raised in the process of 'making'; of *constructing,* gendered speaking subjects."

BIOGRAPHICAL AND CRITICAL SOURCES:

PERIODICALS

Choice, January, 2000, D. Konstan, review of *Spoken like a Woman: Speech and Gender in Athenian Drama,* p. 928.

OTHER

Bryn Mawr Classical Review, http://www.ccat.sas. upenn.edu/bmcr/ (July 2, 2000), Judith Fletcher,

review of *Spoken like a Woman;* (November 10, 2001) Tim Whitmarsh, review of *Making Silence Speak: Women's Voices in Greek Literature and Society.*

Princeton University Press, http://pup.princeton.edu/ (February 11, 2002), review of *Spoken like a Woman.*

Seminary Co-op Bookstore Web site, http://www.sem coop.com/ (February 11, 2002), review of *Spoken like a Woman.**

* * *

McCONNOCHIE, Mardi 1971-

PERSONAL: Born February 2, 1971, in Armidale, New South Wales, Australia. *Education:* University of Adelaide, B.A. (English literature; first class honors); University of Sydney, Ph.D.

ADDRESSES: Home—Sydney, Australia. *Agent*—c/o Author Mail, HarperCollins Publicity, P.O. Box 321, Pymble, NSW 2073, Australia.

CAREER: Novelist, playwright, scriptwriter, and editor.

WRITINGS:

Coldwater: A Novel, Doubleday (New York, NY), 2001.

Author of several plays produced in Australia; author of scripts for television series *Home and Away.*

SIDELIGHTS: Australian writer Mardi McConnochie produced her debut novel, *Coldwater,* in 2001, while she was completing her doctoral work at the University of Sydney. *Coldwater* drew attention from several reviewers, including Geoff Campbell, a contributor for the *Fort Worth Star-Telegram,* who called the novel "a spell-binding work of fiction." Campbell went on to write that *Coldwater* is a clear indication that McConnochie "has the tools and skill necessary for a long and illustrious writing career."

McConnochie's studies have included extensive research into the lives of Charlotte, Emily, and Anne Brontë, the famous literary siblings who published such works as *Jane Eyre, Wuthering Heights,* and *Agnes Grey* in the mid-1800s. In the fictional *Coldwater,* McConnochie paints a romanticized version of the Brontë sisters in their youth, though she changes their last name to Wolf. Instead of living in a Yorkshire parsonage, where the real Brontës grew up, McConnochie depicts Charlotte, Emily, and Anne Wolf growing up on an island penal colony off the coast of Australia, where their father is warden. The similarities between the Brontë sisters and the Wolf sisters extend beyond the names. Like the Brontës, all three Wolf sisters have literary aspirations, and pass their time by writing. McConnochie patterned all three characters on the research she conducted into the lives and careers of the Brontës. For example, Charlotte is more analytical and introspective than her sisters, characteristics scholars have attributed to Charlotte Brontë. McConnochie even includes an "historical note," in which she offers discussion about the Brontë sisters.

After McConnochie conceived the idea for *Coldwater,* she pitched it to Deb Futter, an editor for the Random House. Futter was impressed both by the idea and the completed manuscript, especially the way McConnochie developed the three sisters. "They're used as a kind of dark conceit in a book that is quite gothic and also utterly page-turning," Futter told John F. Baker of *Publishers Weekly.* On Futter's advice, the publisher bought the North American rights to the work. Several literary critics also noted McConnochie's re-imagined version of the Brontë sisters. "McConnochie's attempt at imaginative Brontë revisionism has some commendable aspects, notably her depiction of the siblings' different personalities," wrote a contributor for *Publishers Weekly.* "McConnochie spins a good yarn, and it is curiously fascinating to watch as she weaves so many elements of Brontana into her novel," Merle Rubin wrote in the *Los Angeles Times.* William Ferguson of the *New York Times Book Review* called the work a "clever mingling of history and fiction."

The novel begins in 1847 on the island of Coldwater, where the Wolf family has lived for some eight years. With little else to do, the Wolf sisters, who are surrounded by ocean and are thus the island's prisoners, begin to write novels, with the hope of getting them published so they can leave Coldwater. McConnochie

divides the narration among the three sisters, with the sensitive Charlotte carrying most of the load. In addition to running the penal colony with a ruthless hand, Edward Wolf, the girls' father, thwarts their literary aspirations.

The story takes a dramatic turn when Wolf decides to bring an Irish prisoner into the family home in an attempt to turn the man into a model prisoner. When Emily falls in love with this man, the family begins to splinter, with each sister choosing a different path. Ellen R. Cohen, writing for *Library Journal,* concluded that McConnochie wrote "the story of the Wolf girls with compassion and understanding."

BIOGRAPHICAL AND CRITICAL SOURCES:

PERIODICALS

Booklist, July, 2001, Kristine Huntley, review of *Coldwater,* p. 1982.
Fort Worth Star-Telegram, October 23, 2001, Geoff Campbell, "*Coldwater* Makes Splashy Debut, Plopping Brontës on Prison Island."
Library Journal, July, 2001, Ellen R. Cohen, review of *Coldwater,* p. 124.
Los Angeles Times, August 20, 2001, Merle Rubin, "Brontë Sisters in a Different Land, under a Different Name," p. E-3.
New York Times, September 23, 2001, William Ferguson, review of *Coldwater,* p. 24.
Publishers Weekly, September 18, 2000, John F. Baker, "Brontë Sisters in Australia," p. 18; July 23, 2001, review of *Coldwater,* p. 49.

OTHER

Australian Literature Gateway, http://www.austlit.edu.au/ (July 18, 2002) profile of Mardi McConnochie.
Sydney Morning Herald, http://www.smh.com.au/ (October 6, 2001), Catherine Keenan, "Giants Untouched by the Play in Their Shadow."*

*   *   *

McDONELL, Chris 1960-

PERSONAL: Born June 16, 1960, in Sarnia, Ontario, Canada; son of Alanson and Nora (a homemaker; maiden name, Hurley) McDonell; married Sue Gordon (a nurse), September 28, 1985; children: Quinn, Tara,

Isaac. *Ethnicity:* "Scottish/Irish." *Education:* University of Western Ontario, B.A. *Politics:* "Groucho Marxist." *Religion:* Christian.

ADDRESSES: Home—41 Gunn St., London, Ontario, Canada M6G 1C6.

CAREER: Writer.

WRITINGS:

(Compiler) *For the Love of Hockey: Hockey Stars' Personal Stories,* Firefly Books (Willowdale, Ontario, Canada), 1997, revised edition, 2001.

Hockey's Greatest Stars: Legends and Young Lions, Firefly Books (Toronto, Ontario, Canada), 1999.

Hockey All-Stars: The NHL Honor Roll, Firefly Books (Buffalo, NY), 2000.

(Compiler) *The Game I'll Never Forget: One hundred Hockey Stars' Stories,* Firefly Books (Willowdale, Ontario, Canada), 2002.

SIDELIGHTS: Chris McDonell's first book, *For the Love of Hockey: Hockey Stars' Personal Stories,* is a two-hundred-page collection of memories in the stars' own words. Hockey superstars like Gordie Howe and Brett Hull relate their often surprisingly inauspicious beginnings in the sport and write about what it was like to grow up playing the game. Others, like Paul Coffey and Bernie Geoffrion, reminisce about their active careers and the work habits that contributed to their success, while some comment on the highs and lows of being a professional athlete. These are not the memories of hockey's loyal fans. They are the very personal memories of the men who made their living on the ice.

In contrast, *Hockey's Greatest Stars: Legends and Young Lions* is McDonell's third-person commentary on the players he select as "greatest" within their specialties. His categorical sections distinguish among centers, wings, defense players, and goal tenders, and each section discusses the responsibilities of the position and the skills and talents required for success. McDonell's selections are drawn from hockey history and today's sports headlines. Each biographical entry summarizes a player's background and career, illustrated by color photographs, where available, or

archival photographs in black and white. McDonnell also adds a career analysis and list of statistics. A special feature of *Hockey's Greatest Stars* is a section in which McDonnell profiles a handful of rising stars who, he predicts, have the potential to become the "young lions" of tomorrow.

In *Hockey All-Stars: The NHL Honor Roll,* McDonnell profiles nearly three hundred players who have been cited for an outstanding season of performance in the National Hockey League by the Professional Hockey Writer's Association since the 1930-1931 season. The entries, in alphabetical order, are of approximately equal length, regardless of the player's legendary status or the duration of his career. Each entry features a career summary, one or more photographs, statistics, and personal recollections, from the player himself where possible, or from the team members or various sports writers. A summary chart includes a season-by-season list of all team members for both first and second all-star teams.

BIOGRAPHICAL AND CRITICAL SOURCES:

PERIODICALS

Library Journal, December, 1999, William O. Scheeren, review of *Hockey's Greatest Stars: Legends and Young Lions,* p. 146.

Resource Links, February, 2002, Michael Jung, review of *For the Love of Hockey: Hockey Stars' Personal Stories,* p. 43.

School Library Journal, May, 2000, Frances Reiher, review of *Hockey's Greatest Stars,* p. 195.

* * *

McDONOUGH, Jimmy 1960(?)-

PERSONAL: Born c. 1960.

ADDRESSES: Home—Amboy, WA. *Agent*—c/o Random House, Inc. c/o Random House Trade Publishing Group Publicity, 299 Park Avenue, New York, NY 10171.

CAREER: Biographer and journalist.

WRITINGS:

The Ghastly One: The Sex-Gore Netherworld of Andy Milligan, A Cappella (Chicago, IL), 2001.
Shakey: Neil Young's Biography, Villard Books (New York, NY), 2002.

Contributor to periodicals, including *Variety, Village Voice, Film Comment, Mojo, Spin,* and *Juggs.*

SIDELIGHTS: Veteran American journalist Jimmy McDonough's first two published books are both biographies of individuals known for their enigmatic personalities. His first work, published in 2001, is *The Ghastly One: The Sex-Gore Netherworld of Andy Milligan,* which examines the life of shock film-maker Andy Milligan (1929-1991). A year later McDonough published the long-awaited and highly anticipated *Shakey: Neil Young's Biography,* the first authorized biography of rock and roll legend Neil Young. The book, which McDonough actually began researching and writing in 1991, was held up in court for several years after Young, who originally supported the project, tried to use legal means to keep it from being published after it was completed in 1998. In addition to being a regular writer for the *Village Voice,* McDonough has contributed articles to *Variety, Film Comment, Mojo,* and *Spin.*

Some observers have called McDonough one of the most recognized music writers in America. "McDonough's writing is tough, probing, full of street-hustler style, yet hits with a cerebral impact," *Metro-Active Music's* Jonny Whiteside once wrote. McDonough employs his unique style in writing both his books. For example, in *The Ghastly One,* he describes Milligan as "one of those creatures who ride the midnight train," and "come from the land of the screaming skulls." In the book, McDonough explains that he was a fan of Milligan's films before he set out to write the book.

According to McDonough, filmgoers like himself are attracted to Milligan's movies in a similar fashion to the way people "gawk at car accidents, read lurid detective magazines, eyeball the dead two-headed baby in a jar." Milligan, who died of AIDS, shot almost thirty films between 1965 and 1988. Topics like sadism and misogyny are regularly explored in his films,

which include *The Naked Witch, The Orgy at Lil's Place, Torture Dungeon,* and *Depraved!* McDonough explains in his book that Milligan first gained attention when his 1965 film *Vapors* included scenes of male nudity and rendered a frank view of homosexuality.

While Milligan's films may have been known for their shock value, McDonough points out that they were not recognized for their technical craftsmanship. "Andy slapped his movies together with nary a thought for pacing, with dialogue that sounds like it was recorded through a tin can, and stories that suffer from holes you could drive a truck through," McDonough writes. "When Andy's movies are bad, there's nothing—*nothing*—worse. . . But scratch the dirty surface of Milligan's pictures and a very personal kind of poison seeps out of every frame."

Much of the *The Ghastly One* includes verbatim interviews that the author conducted with Milligan before his death. In addition to analyzing Milligan's films, McDonough also describes the film-maker's destructive lifestyle, which included many of the same elements he explored in his films. A number of literary critics praised *The Ghastly One,* including Mike Tribby of *Booklist,* who called it a "strangely fascinating story." A contributor for *Publishers Weekly* felt the work reveal Milligan as "a man who could be alternately brutally honest, obstructionist, deceitful and quite kind."

McDonough's decision to write a biography about Neil Young stemmed from an interview he conducted with the musician in 1989 for the *Village Voice.* The often-reclusive Young was so impressed with McDonough's subsequent story, he requested the writer pen the liner notes for a twenty-fifth anniversary anthology of his music. The success of this endeavor led to Young asking McDonough to write an authorized biography of his life and career. After sitting through five consecutive days of interviews with Young, McDonough set about the task of what eventually became an 800-page manuscript. Despite his initial approval of the work, Young hired several lawyers in late 1998 to block its publication. As a result, McDonough filed a $1.8 million lawsuit against Young, charging the musician with breach of contract. McDonough also sued to have the book published. McDonough won the case, which was heard in the Los Angeles County Superior Court, and the book was published in 2002.

BIOGRAPHICAL AND CRITICAL SOURCES:

PERIODICALS

Austin Chronicle, December 28, 2001, Marc Savlov, "Behind the Screens."
Book, May-June, 2002, Josh Karp, "Neil Young: Rockin' in the Free World," p. 23.
Booklist, August, 2001, Mike Tribby, review of *The Ghastly One: The Sex-Gore Netherworld of Andy Milligan,* p. 2073.
Entertainment Weekly, May 17, 2002, Troy Patterson, review of *Shakey: Neil Young's Biography.*
Publishers Weekly, July 23, 2001, review of *The Ghastly One: The Sex-Gore Netherworld of Andy Milligan,* p. 57.
Variety, May 8, 2000, Jonathan Bing and Janet Shprintz, "Young Pulls His Support from McDonough Bio," p. 4.

OTHER

Independent Publisher's Group, http://www.ipgbook.com/ (January 30, 2002).
MetroActive Music Web site, http://www.metroactive.com/ (November 2, 2000), Jonny Whiteside, "Broken Arrow: Neil Young's Biographer Goes to Court."
MTV News Online, http://www.mtv.com/news (May 2, 2000), John Gill, "Neil Young Sued by Bio Author."
PopMatters.com, http://www.popmatters.com/ (January 30, 2002), David Sanjek, review of *The Ghastly One: The Sex-Gore Netherworld of Andy Milligan.**

*   *   *

McGOWAN, Christopher 1942-

PERSONAL: Born March 30, 1942, in Beckenham, Kent, England; son of Wilfred Clarence (a baker) and Gwendoline Daisy (a homemaker; maiden name, Morphew) McGowan; married Liz Gregory, September 4, 1965; children: Claire Louise, Angela Kay. *Ethnicity:* "Anglo-Saxon." *Education:* Polytechnic College, London, England, B.S. (honors), 1965; Birkbeck College, University of London, Ph.D. (zoology), 1969.

ADDRESSES: Office—Royal Ontario Museum, 100 Queens Park, Toronto, Ontario, Canada M55 2C6. *Agent*—Anderson/Grinberg, 266 West 23rd St., No.3, New York, NY 10011. *E-mail*—scripta1@aol.com.

CAREER: Royal Ontario Museum, Department of Vertebrate Palaeontology, Toronto, Ontario, Canada, curatorial assistant, 1969-70, assistant curator, 1970-74, associate curator, 1974-80, curator, 1980—, department of palaeobiology, senior curator, 1994-2002; University of Toronto, Department of Zoology, Toronto, Ontario, Canada, associate professor, 1972-89, professor, 1990—.

MEMBER: Society for Experimental Biology, Society of Vertebrate Paleontology, The Palaeontological Society.

AWARDS, HONORS: Royal Ontario Museum grants, 1997, 1999, 2001; NSERC research grants, 1976-2003.

WRITINGS:

Evolutionary Trends in Longipinnate Ichthyosaurs, with Particular Reference to the Skull and Fore Fin, Royal Ontario Museum (Toronto, Ontario, Canada), 1972.
Differential Growth in Three Ichthyosaurs: Ichthyosaurus Communis, I. Breviceps, and Stenopterygius Quadriscissus, Royal Ontario Museum (Toronto, Ontario, Canada), 1973.
The Cranial Morphology of the Lower Liassic Latipinnate Ichthyosaurs of England, British Museum (London, England), 1973.
A Revision of the Latipinnate Ichthyosaurs of the Lower Jurassic of England, Royal Ontario Museum (Toronto, Ontario, Canada), 1974.
In the Beginning—: A Scientist Shows Why the Creationists Are Wrong, Prometheus (Buffalo, NY), 1983.
The Successful Dragons: A Natural History of Extinct Reptiles, Samuel Stevens (Toronto, Ontario Canada), 1983.
Dinosaurs, Spitfires, and Sea Dragons, Harvard University Press (Cambridge, MA), 1991.
Discover Dinosaurs: Become a Dinosaur Detective, illustrated by Tina Holdcroft, Addison-Wesley (Reading, MA), 1992.

Diatoms to Dinosaurs: The Size and Scale of Living Things, illustrated by Julian Mulock, Island Press for Shearwater Books (Washington, DC), 1994.

Make Your Own Dinosaur out of Chicken Bones: Foolproof Instructions for Budding Paleontologists, illustrated by Julian Mulock, HarperPerennial (New York, NY), 1997.

The Raptor and the Lamb: Predators and Prey in the Living World, Henry Holt (New York, NY), 1997.

A Practical Guide to Vertebrate Mechanics, illustrated by Julian Mulock, Cambridge University Press (New York, NY), 1999.

T. Rex to Go: Build Your Own from Chicken Bones, illustrated by Julian Mulock, HarperPerennial (New York, NY), 1999.

Dinosaur: Digging up a Giant, North Winds Press, 1999.

The Dragon Seekers: How an Extraordinary Circle of Fossilists Discovered the Dinosaurs and Paved the Way for Darwin, Perseus Publications (Cambridge, MA) 2001.

Also contributor of numerous articles to scholarly publications, including *Canadian Journal of Earth Science, Palaeobiology, Journal of Zoology, Journal of Vertebrate Palaeontology,* and publications of the Royal Ontario Museum.

SIDELIGHTS: As a researcher and senior curator in the department of palaeobiology at the Royal Ontario Museum, Christopher McGowan is a renowned expert in vertebrate biology of the Mesozoic era. He makes comparisons between living and extinct animals while presenting topics that range from size to intellect. In addition to exploring the natural history of the Mesozoic Era, McGowan draws on science and engineering to explain curiosities such as the similarities between extinct animals and modern machines.

In *The Dragon Seekers: How an Extraordinary Circle of Fossilists Discovered the Dinosaurs and Paved the Way for Darwin,* McGowan turns his attention to the early days of dinosaur hunting and the first paleontologists who hunted them. The book begins in 1811 on the cliffs of England's Dorset coast. Mary Anning, then a twelve year old hunting for fossil souvenirs to sell to tourists, found the skeletal remains of what she thought was a "sea dragon" but turned out to be the world's first ichthyosaur remains. Anning's discovery, according to McGowan, combined with other English fossilists to virtually begin dinosaur research and pave the way for Darwin's theory of evolution. McGowan notes that because of Anning's "humble station" and need to feed her family, she became one of the most productive fossilists of all time. She also possessed a natural scientific curiosity, and read everything she could from borrowed publications and made handwritten copies for her records.

In a review of the book for the *Los Angeles Times,* Paula Friedman wrote, "The descriptions of desolate digging sites in Lyme Regis and elsewhere in Britain, where fossilists often worked for long stints in near isolation, add an affecting lyrical beauty to McGowan's historical account. Depictions of the often-charged conflict between church and science, as well as those of the scientists sometimes unscrupulous practices, especially evident in fossil reconstruction, bring suspense to the plot line. And by dramatically bringing his tale to the edge of modernity, McGowan culminates his suspenseful buildup with the entrance of Charles Darwin himself."

The Raptor and the Lamb: Predators and Prey in the Living World explains that the predator-prey relationship is symbiotic and necessary in nature. Through a variety of examples the author examines the prey-predator on land, sea and air. A *Guardian* contributor noted, "Books like this, by stunning us with details we can measure, also alert us to how little we really know." Nancy Bent in *Booklist* wrote that "The subtle interactions between predator and prey, and how each is evolved to outwit the other, form the structure on which this clearly written narrative is based. . . . the author ties each example to the overall theme of natural selection at work."

In *Dinosaurs, Spitfires, and Sea Dragons* McGowan deals with questions of the mechanics ancient creatures used to move themselves through the air, in the sea, or on land. Using research disciplines methods including structural mechanics, aeronautics, and forensic biology, he reconstructs how the dinosaurs moved. Michael Taylor wrote in *New Scientist* that McGowan "has certainly found a new niche in what sometimes seem a hopelessly overcrowded dinosaur book market, not just because of the ichthyosaurs, but also because of its adult, reasonable, amiably balanced, and correctly open-ended approach to how we really develop our ideas about them."

BIOGRAPHICAL AND CRITICAL SOURCES:

PERIODICALS

Audubon, September, 1997, review of *The Raptor and the Lamb: Predators and Prey in the Living World,* p. 100.

Booklist, August, 1997, Nancy Bent, review of *The Raptor and the Lamb,* p. 1861; May 15, 2001, Gilbert Taylor, review of *The Dragon Seekers: How an Extraordinary Circle of Fossilists Discovered the Dinosaurs and Paved the Way for Darwin,* p. 1716.

Guardian (London, England), August 29, 1998, Tim Radford, review of *The Raptor and the Lamb,* p. 8.

Library Journal, July, 1997, Bruce D. Neville, review of *The Raptor and the Lamb,* p. 121.

Los Angeles Times, June 14, 2001, Paula Friedman, review of *The Dragon Seekers,* p. E3.

New Scientist, November 23, 1991, Michael Taylor, review of *Dinosaurs, Spitfires, and Sea Dragons,* p. 54.

Publishers Weekly, July 7, 1997, review of *The Raptor and the Lamb,* p. 61; May 7, 2001, review of *The Dragon Seekers,* p. 231.

Science, May 17, 1991, Kevin Padian, review of *Dinosaurs, Spitfires, and Sea Dragons,* p. 1006.

Whole Earth Review, summer, 1995, J. Baldwin, review of *Diatoms to Dinosaurs: The Size and Scale of Living Things,* p. 21.

*   *   *

McHENRY, Paul G(raham), Jr. 1924-2002

OBITUARY NOTICE—See index for *CA* sketch: Born January 23, 1924, in Chicago, IL; died of a heart and lung failure January 22, 2002, in Albuquerque, NM. Architect and author. McHenry was an authority on the construction of adobe homes. A student at the University of New Mexico when World War II began, he served in the U.S. Air Force as a tail gunner. After the war he completed his degree in business in 1948 and started a commercial construction company. When he decided to try building a home out of adobe bricks, he enjoyed the experience so much that he made it his life's passion. McHenry became an expert in building the structures, and eventually returned to school to earn a master's degree in architecture from his alma mater in 1974. He wrote three books on his favorite subject: *Adobe: Build It Yourself* (1972), *Adobe and Rammed-Earth Buildings: Design and Construction* (1984), and *The Adobe Story: A Global Treasure* (1996). Students from around the world visited him to learn his techniques, and he helped rewrite New Mexico building codes regarding earthen buildings. McHenry was also the founder of the nonprofit Earth Building Foundation.

OBITUARIES AND OTHER SOURCES:

PERIODICALS

Washington Post, February 4, 2002, p. B7.

*   *   *

McKITRICK, Eric Louis 1919-2002

OBITUARY NOTICE—See index for *CA* sketch: Born July 5, 1919, in Battle Creek, MI; died April 24, 2002, in New York, NY. Historian, educator, and author. McKitrick was a respected scholar of U.S. history. He served in the U.S. Army during World War II, after which he studied history at Columbia University, where he received his Ph.D. in 1959. After earning his doctorate, he taught briefly at Rutgers University before joining Columbia University in 1960. He became a professor of history there in 1965 and retired in 1989. McKitrick's first book, *Andrew Johnson and Reconstruction* (1960), was also his most highly praised work and received the John H. Dunning Prize from the American Historical Association. His other writings include *Slavery Defended: The Views of the Old South* and two books on which he collaborated with Stanley Elkins: *The Age of Federalism* (1993) and the edited work *The Hofstadter Aegis: A Memorial* (1974).

OBITUARIES AND OTHER SOURCES:

BOOKS

Who's Who in America, 55th edition, Marquis (New Providence, NJ), 2001.

PERIODICALS

New York Times, May 6, 2002, p. A23.
Washington Post, May 7, 2002, p. B6.

*   *   *

McMAHON, Darrin

PERSONAL: Male. *Education:* University of California, Berkeley, B.A., summa cum laude; Yale University, Ph.D., 1997.

ADDRESSES: Office—c/o Oxford University Press, 198 Madison Ave., New York, NY 10016.

CAREER: Mellon fellow, Society of Fellows in the Humanities, Columbia University, 1997-99; postdoctoral fellow, Remarque Institute, New York University, New York, 2000-01; postdoctoral fellow, Yale University, 2001—. Rockefeller junior visiting fellow at Institute für die Wissenschaften von Menschen, Vienna, 2001. New York director, Keythought LLC.; co-producer, writer, and researcher for PBS documentaries.

AWARDS, HONORS: Hans Gatzke prize.

WRITINGS:

Enemies of the Enlightenment: The French Counter-Enlightenment and the Making of Modernity, Oxford University Press (New York, NY), 2001.

WORK IN PROGRESS: In Pursuit: A History of Happiness in the Modern West, Grove-Atlantic Press (New York, NY), forthcoming.

SIDELIGHTS: In Darrin McMahon's book *Enemies of the Enlightenment: The French Counter-Enlightenment and the Making of Modernity,* Catholic opposition to the philosophy of Voltaire in the eighteenth century is consider as a forerunner of the modern American split between the political left and right, the "culture wars." McMahon's study runs counter to mainstream intellectual history by demonstrating the existence of substantial, vocal opposition to the philosophical movement called the Enlightenment. Those opposing Voltaire and the *philosophes* saw their influence as a threat to traditional values, especially the authority of the Church, and claimed that the philosophes could be as intolerant of dissidence as the authorities they condemned. McMahon suggests that the fears of Enlightenment opponents were born out in the French Revolution, when the idealism of revolutionaries gave way to violence.

In *Enemies of the Enlightenment* McMahon maintains that the force of the Counter-Enlightenment was influential in creating the course of Enlightenment thought; modern understanding of the Enlightenment is lacking without an awareness of the role of Counter-Enlightenment ideology. Moreover, McMahon suggests, the ideology of the Counter-Enlightenment did not disappear with the apparent triumph of the other side: factions in Europe and Latin America still evidence the currency of Counter-Enlightenment thought. More broadly, Counter-Enlightenment ideology has evolved into what political scientists term "the Right." As a reviewer for *Publishers Weekly* remarked, the book's "relevance to conservative-liberal tensions in the U.S. make it worthy of broad intellectual discussion."

BIOGRAPHICAL AND CRITICAL SOURCES:

PERIODICALS

Publishers Weekly, July 23, 2001, review of *Enemies of the Enlightenment: The French Counter-Enlightenment and the Making of Modernity,* p. 64.

OTHER

Columbia University Web site, http://www.columbia.edu/ (October 7, 2001).
Keythought.com, http://www.keythought.com/ (February 13, 2002).
Oxford University Press Web site, http://www.oup-usa.org/ (October 7, 2001).
Wall Street Journal Online, http://www.wsj.com/ (December 5, 2000), Darrin M. McMahon, "The Other Enlightenment, across the Channel."*

McMASTER, Susan 1950-

PERSONAL: Born August 11, 1950, in Toronto, Ontario, Canada; daughter of Gordon George and Betty Isobel Emily (Page) McClure; married Ian McMaster, July 5, 1969; children: Sarah Aven, Sylva Morel. *Education:* Carleton University, B.A., 1970, M.A. (journalism), 1980; Ottawa Teachers' College, elementary teaching certificate, 1971. *Religion:* Society of Friends (Quakers). *Hobbies and other interests:* Music, canoeing, horseback riding.

ADDRESSES: Home—43 Belmont Ave., Ottawa, Ontario K1S 0T9, Canada. *Office*—National Gallery of Canada, Publications, 380 Sussex Dr., P.O. Box 427, Stn. A., Ottawa, Ontario K1N 9N4, Canada. *E-mail*—ae414@freenet.carleton.ca.

CAREER: Poet, writer, editor, performance artist, and producer. Teacher, Edmonton public schools, Edmonton, Alberta, Canada, 1971-73; freelance editor and writer, 1973-89; National Gallery of Canada, Ottawa, Ontario, book editor, 1989—. *Branching Out,* founding editor, 1973-75, associate, 1975-80; cofounder, First Draft (intermedia performance art group), 1980-90; member of SugarBeat (music poetry group; now GeOde Music & Poetry), 1990—; editor-in-chief, *Vernissage.*

MEMBER: PEN International, League of Canadian Poets.

AWARDS, HONORS: Canada Council Explorations grant; Writers' Trust Fund grant.

WRITINGS:

POETRY

Seven Poems, Ouroboros (Ottawa, Ontario, Canada), 1983.
Dark Galaxies, Ouroboros (Ottawa, Ontario, Canada), 1986.
Lac Vert, 1985, illustrated by Irene Hofmann, Anthos Books (Perth, Ontario, Canada), 1987.
The Hummingbird Murders, Quarry Press (Kingston, Ontario, Canada), 1992.

Learning to Ride, illustrated by Robert Verrall, Quarry Press (Kingston, Ontario, Canada), 1994.
Uncommon Prayer: A Book of Dedications, Quarry Press (Kingston, Ontario, Canada), 1997.

POETRY; RECORDED

(With First Draft) *Wordmusic,* 1986.
First Draft at Carleton, 1992.
(Coauthor) *Dangerous Times,* 1996.
(With SugarBeat) *How Dandelions Prey,* 1998.
SugarBeat Music & Poetry, 1998.
Primate Wind, 1998.
(With GeOde Music & Poetry) *GeOde Music & Poetry,* 1999.

OTHER

(With Andrew McClure and Claude Dupuis) *Pass This Way Again: A Collection of Performance Poetry,* edited by B. P. Nichol, Underwhich Editions (Toronto, Ontario, Canada), 1983.
(With Andrew McClure and Colin Morton) *North/South: Performance Scores for One to Seven Speakers* (word/music scores), Underwhich Editions (Toronto, Ontario, Canada), 1987.
(Editor) *Dangerous Graces: Women's Poetry on Stage from "Fire Works!": A Celebration of Women's Theatre, Canadian Theatre Company* (poetry script anthology), Balmuir (Ottawa, Ontario, Canada), 1987.
(Editor, with Cathy Ford) Margaret Christakos and others, *Illegitimate Positions: Women and Language,* Feminist Caucus of the League of Canadian Poets (Toronto, Ontario, Canada), 1992.
(Editor) *Two Women Talking: Correspondence 1985-87, Erin Moure and Bronwen Wallace,* Feminist Caucus of the League of Canadian Poets (Ottawa, Ontario, Canada), 1993.
(Editor, with Colin Morton) *Bookware: Ottawa Valley Poets,* League of Canadian Poets (Ottawa, Ontario, Canada), 1994.
(Editor) *Siolence: Poets on Women, Violence, and Silence,* Quarry Women's Books (Kingston, Ontario, Canada), 1998.
(Editor) *Waging Peace: Poetry and Political Action,* Penumbra Press (Ottawa, Ontario, Canada), 2002.

Contributor to numerous anthologies, including *Celebrating Canadian Women: Poetry and Short Stories by and about Women,* Fitzhenry & Whiteside, 1989;

Capital Poets: An Ottawa Anthology, Ouroboros, 1989; *Labor of Love,* 1989; *When Is a Poem 2,* 1992; *Women and Violence,* League of Canadian Poets, 1993; *Poets in the Classroom,* Pembroke Press, 1995; and *Vintage 93,* Quarry Press. Contributing editor for magazines *ARC* and *Quarry.*

WORK IN PROGRESS: *How Chairs Pray,* for Quarry Press; *A Room at the Heart of Things,* for Vehicúle; *Waking Dreams, Bitter Prayers,* a poetry manuscript.

SIDELIGHTS: Susan McMaster is a poet and performance artist who has produced her work in a variety of media and venues. She also was a founding member of the intermedia group First Draft, which is composed of Canadian artists from a range of disciplines, including poets, writers, visual artists, and musicians. The group performed her poetry and "wordmusic" (spoken words set to music) around Canada and on the radio from 1981 to 1990. McMaster left First Draft in 1990 to become the poet for SugarBeat Music and Poetry, now known as GeOde Music and Poetry. Her poems are set to jazz, blues, contemporary, folk, and electro-acoustic musical styles. The group performs its original material at music festivals, galleries, clubs, the National Library, and other places around Canada. McMaster's poems and lyrics, set to music by such composers as David Parsons, John Armstrong, Quinn Redekop, and Mike Essoudry, have been performed by contemporary, jazz, and sound poetry groups as well as at theater and poetry workshops.

McMaster also combined contributions from seventeen Canadian women poets to produce the script *Dangerous Graces/Saving Sins,* presented at the month-long festival of women's theater, Fire Works!, and produced by the Greater Canadian Theatre Company. It was later published in book form as *Dangerous Graces: Women's Poetry on Stage from "Fire Works!": A Celebration of Women's Theatre,* Canadian Theatre Company.

Reviewer Heather Jones noted in *Canadian Literature,* that "The poems . . . work through the manifold frustrations of women's experience in patriarchy in order to realize women's empowerment through spirituality." The critic concluded, "Her skillful interweaving of woman-oriented themes and performance art makes *Dangerous Graces* an innovative example of alternative theater."

Among McMaster's published poetry is *Uncommon Prayer,* her fourth collection. According to Kim Fahner in *Canadian Book Review Annual,* this book "ably evokes 'God' as a creative force that is metaphorically transformed in the environment that surrounds us." Noting that McMaster's "dominant motif" in these verses is prayer, Fahner concluded that "McMaster's busy world that usually doesn't wait for anyone."

Learning to Ride contains poems chronicling the experience of taking horseback riding lessons as an adult. "Particularly well done are the poems describing the special relationship that develops between horse and rider," commented Sheila Martindale in *Canadian Book Review Annual.* Mary Dalton, in *Books in Canada,* found *Learning to Ride* a book that "delights in energy, verbs, the tension and speed of riding." Pointing out that the book includes a "useful glossary of terms" about horse riding that will assist readers, Pat Bolger said in *Canadian Materials* that this collection "will appeal to young readers who ride—or dream of doing so."

McMaster is also the editor of *Siolence: Poets on Women, Violence and Silence,* a collection of essays and poems from members of the Feminist Caucus of the League of Canadian Poets. These contributions stem from more than a decade of the League's presentations, readings, and discussions. Each of the book's fourteen sections is devoted to a different poet, and the essays discuss peace/violence and silence (siolence) in styles that range from philosophical to practical. "They are well informed, insightful and thought provoking," wrote Terry Vatrt in an Online *Canadian Materials* review.

In a statement on the *University of Toronto English Library* Web site, McMaster described her writing philosophy: "I tend toward the view that the very act of writing poetry drives the poetry perpetrator towards an essentially moral position, because the best poems, the ones that really communicate, that cut close to the bone for reader and writer alike, are the ones that are most true, most compassionate, most universal and thus most widely accepting, most unostentatious and empty of vanity, ego, self-seeking. I also think the nature of poetry is to travel to the depths, the edges, the margins, the exaltations. The rigour of this exploration tends to dissolve racism, sexism, classism, all forms of division and ego-protection." She added, "But I'd aim to write any kind of good poetry not through a set of rules, but by setting out on a quest for honesty and depth and fidelity to the craft. All that said, it's a quest not an arrival."

BIOGRAPHICAL AND CRITICAL SOURCES:

PERIODICALS

Books in Canada, November, 1994, Mary Dalton, review of *Learning to Ride,* p. 54.
Canadian Book Review Annual, 1994, p. 214; 1998, p. 233.
Canadian Literature, spring, 1991, Heather Jones, review of *Dangerous Graces: Women's Poetry on Stage from "Fire Works!": A Celebration of Women's Theatre, Canadian Theatre Company,* p. 185.
Canadian Materials, October, 1994, Pat Bolger, review of *Learning to Ride,* p. 175.

OTHER

Canadian Review of Materials Online, http://www.umanitoba.ca/cm/ (June 23, 2000), Terry Vatrt, review of *Siolence: Poets on Women, Violence, and Silence.*
Swifty.com, http://www.swifty.com/ (April 11, 2002), author profile.
University of Toronto English Library Web site, http://www.library.utoronto.ca/ (April 11, 2002), "Susan McMaster, Writing Philosophy."*

*　　　*　　　*

McPHEE, Jenny

PERSONAL: Daughter of John (an author) and Pryde (a photographer; maiden name, Brown) McPhee; married; children: two sons. *Education:* Williams College, Williamstown, MA.

ADDRESSES: Office—c/o Doubleday Publicity, 1540 Broadway, New York, NY 10036.

CAREER: Writer and translator.

WRITINGS:

(Translator with Martha McPhee) Pope John Paul II, *Crossing the Threshold of Hope,* Knopf (New York, NY), 1994.
(Translator) Paolo Maurensig, *Canone Inverso,* Henry Holt (New York, NY), 1998.
(Translator with Richard Fremantle) Franco Quadri, *Robert Wilson,* Rizzoli (New York, NY), 1998.
(With Laura McPhee and Martha McPhee) *Girls: Ordinary Girls and Their Extraordinary Pursuits,* Random House (New York, NY), 2000.
The Center of Things, Doubleday Publishing (New York, NY), 2001.

SIDELIGHTS: Jenny McPhee's father is the esteemed essayist John McPhee, and her sister Martha McPhee is an award-winning novelist. McPhee entered the world of publishing gradually, beginning as a translator. She later collaborated on a nonfiction book about the lives of American girls with Martha as well as with their sister Laura, a successful and prizewinning photographer. Then she struck out own her own, publishing her debut novel *The Center of Things* in 2001.

The McPhee sisters decided to embark on a study of the great things American girls were accomplishing after hearing so much bad news about girls' lives. Despite the media focus on the number of problems girls were facing, the sisters found that girls were also succeeding at everything from football, science, and investments, to chess, ballet, and music. McPhee told Jennifer Wolcott the *Christian Science Monitor,* "It wasn't as if we had to go searching. . . . Girls like this are everywhere. For every one we found, we could have found 50,000 more like her. We're just not used to celebrating our girls in this country."

Attempting to present a geographically diverse portrait, the McPhee sisters traveled the country seeking girls whose accomplishments stood out not because they were so unusual, but because they reflected the achievements of girls in general. In *Girls: Ordinary Girls and Their Extraordinary Pursuits,* they tell the stories of a teenage novelist, a seven-year-old competitive chess champion, a professional child harpist, and a New Yorker who works as a camp counselor in Bosnia. McPhee told a contributor to the *Christian*

Science Monitor, "I think all the time about these girls and what they accomplish. . . . Some of them have terrible troubles, but they don't let that stop them from putting all their energies into their interests."

Reviewers generally welcomed this contribution to literature about girls. Mary Carroll in *Booklist,* called the book "a celebration of young American women." Jean Hanff KoreLizt, reviewing *Girls* for *Harper's Bazaar,* described the book as "stunning," and "a nuanced, resonant snapshot of American girlhood at the turn of the millennium." Sandra Isaacson in*Library Journal* suggested that the girls chosen for the book are not so ordinary, but rather very talented and driven; and concluded: "This work is interesting but falls short of being dynamic because of its brevity." A reviewer for *Publishers Weekly,* however, maintained that "these endearing portraits of young athletes, artists and adventurers help expand the limits of the possible."

The release of *Girls* was shortly followed by the publication of McPhee's first novel, *The Center of Things. The Center of Things* tells the story of a single, plain, not-so-young tabloid reporter who becomes obsessed with Nora Mars, a former movie diva about whom she is assigned to write an obituary. The reporter, Marie Brown, is also obsessed with physics, an interest she indulges with "freelance intellectual" Marco Trentadue, whom she meets at the library. Meanwhile, her research into the life of Mars leads her to consider a tryst with the actress's third husband, Rex Mars. Among all these other longings, Marie reveals a desire to give up tabloid journalism and become a science writer.

A reviewer for *Publishers Weekly* said of *The Center of Things,* "It takes guts for a debut novelist to mix such disparate subjects as abstruse science, philosophy, movies, and the single life in New York City, but McPhee takes the risk with brio and acquits herself with élan." Dennis Overbye, reviewing the book for the *New York Times Book Review,* also found that the unusual combination worked: "McPhee . . . knows how to keep things light. All her cosmic vamping adds a teasing hint of intellectual relief to a tale of tangled lives that for all its complexity might seem a shade cartoonish told straight out." Judith Kicinski, in *Library Journal,* called McPhee "a talented, graceful, and often sardonic writer," saying that with *The Center of Things,* "John McPhee should be proud of his

daughter." The *Publishers Weekly* critic similarly noted the family connection, concluding, "While the McPhee name may be the initial drawing card here, the novel's off beat charm will distinguish Jenny McPhee as an accomplished writer with her own distinctive style."

BIOGRAPHICAL AND CRITICAL SOURCES:

PERIODICALS

Book, July, 2001, Beth Kephart, review of *The Center of Things,* p. 66.
Booklist, October 15, 1998, Bonnie Johnston, review of *Canone Inverso,* p. 400; November 1, 1998, Jack Helbig, review of *Robert Wilson,* p. 461; October 1, 2000, Mary Carroll, review of *Girls: Ordinary Girls and Their Extraordinary Pursuits,* p. 295; June 1, 2001, Kristine Huntley, review of *The Center of Things,* p. 1847.
Commonweal, January 13, 1995, Peter Steinfels, review of *Crossing the Threshold of Hope,* pp. 21-22.
Entertainment Weekly, August 17, 2001, Gillian Flynn, review of *The Center of Things,* p. 66.
Harper's Bazaar, October, 2000, Jean Hanff KoreLitz, "Family Portrait," p. 234.
Library Journal, October 1, 2000, Sandra Isaacson, review of *Girls: Ordinary Girls and Their Extraordinary Pursuits,* p. 130; July, 2001, Judith Kicinski, review of *The Center of Things,* p. 125.
New York Review of Books, Garry Willis, "The Tragic Pope," p. 4, 6-7.
New York Times Book Review, July 22, 2001, Dennis Overbye, "Quantum Fizz," p. 7.
People Weekly, August 27, 2001, synopsis of *The Center of Things,* p. 43.
Publishers Weekly, September 25, 2000, "Women and Girls of Stature," p. 107; June 11, 2001, review of *The Center of Things,* p. 55.
Times Literary Supplement, November 11, 1994, Peter Hebblethwaite, "Professor in Slippers," p. 32.
Washington Post, July 15, 2001, "Getting Physical," p. T4.

OTHER

Book Page Fiction Review, http://www.bookpage.com/ (October 7, 2001), Deborah Hopkinson, review of *The Center of Things.*

Calendar Live, http://www.calendarlive.com/ (September 2, 2001), Mark Rozzo, review of *The Center of Things.*

Christian Science Monitor Online, http://www. csmonitor.com/ (January 24, 2001), Jennifer Wolcott, "American Girls: 'We're Doing Just Great, Thanks.'"

Media Bistro, http://www.mediabistro.com/ (October 7, 2001), Diana Michele Yap, review of *The Center of Things.*

Rain Taxi, http://www.raintaxi.com/ (November 20, 2001), Rumaan Alam, review of *The Center of Things.*

Salon.com http://www.salon.com/ (October 7, 2001).

Zoetrope All Story, http://www.all-story.com/ (October 7, 2001)*.

*   *   *

MELE, Christopher

PERSONAL: Male. *Education:* University of Delaware, B.A. (political science), 1984, M.A. (political science), 1988; New School for Social Research, M.A. (sociology), 1991, Ph.D. (sociology), 1994.

ADDRESSES: Office—Department of Sociology, State University of New York, 430 Park Hall, Buffalo, NY 14260-4140. *E-mail*—cmele@acsu.buffalo.edu.

CAREER: Pace University, New York, NY, lecturer, 1989-90; Eugene Lang College of the New School for Social Research, New York, NY, lecturer, 1989-93; University of North Carolina, Wilmington, lecturer, 1993-94, assistant professor of sociology and anthropology, 1994-96; State University of New York at Buffalo, assistant professor of sociology, 1996—. Manuscript reviewer for Pine Forge Press, *Gender and Society,* 1996-97, and *Urban Affairs Review,* 1997; advisory board member for Wilmington Community Coalition, 1994-96, and CURE AIDS of Wilmington, 1994—; Wilmington Revitalization Initiative, member of grant-writing committee, 1995; Mema Project, Wilmington, NC, grant writer, 1995. Member of Project South and Puerto Rican Policy Institute.

MEMBER: American Sociological Association, Society for the Study of Social Problems.

AWARDS, HONORS: Grants from University of North Carolina Center for Teaching Excellence Course Development, 1994, University of North Carolina at Wilmington Faculty Summer Research Initiative, 1994, University of North Carolina, 1994, 1995, American Sociological Association/National Science Foundation, 1995, State University of New York at Buffalo, Research Development fund, 1997, University of New York at Buffalo, Julian Park Publication Fund, 1998, and Baldy Center for Law and Social Policy, 1998, 1999; College of Arts and Sciences Teaching Award, University of Buffalo, 2000.

WRITINGS:

Selling the Lower East Side: Real Estate, Culture, and Resistance in New York, University of Minnesota Press (Minneapolis, MN), 2000.

Contributor to books, including *Communities in Cyberspace,* edited by Peter Kollock and Marc Smith, Routledge, 1999; and *From Urban Village to East Village: The Battle for New York's Lower East Side,* edited by Janet Abu-Lughod and others, Blackwell, 1994.

Contributor to periodicals, including *Urban Affairs Review, Sociological Quarterly, Journal of Broadcast and Electronic Media, Journal of Community Practice, Rising East, Effective Teaching* (online), *Comparative Urban and Community Research,* and *Applied Social Research.* Editorial board member, *Journeys: The International Journal of Travel Studies.*

SIDELIGHTS: Sociologist, researcher, and professor Christopher Mele lived in the Lower East Side of New York City during the 1980s while a graduate student at the New School for Social Research. *Selling the Lower East Side: Culture, Real Estate, and Resistance in New York City* draws on his research while he was there and looks at the changes wrought in this area during the twentieth-century. During that time, the Lower East Side was transformed from an overcrowded ghetto populated by Eastern Europeans and other immigrants to a neighborhood chiefly occupied by Puerto-Ricans and blacks that then began to attract artists and other bohemian types with its affordable housing and studio spaces. The area eventually became the high-rent, trendily renamed East Village that glamorizes and commercializes the neighborhood's crime, poverty, noise, and drug-related social problems.

In the Online *Gotham Center for New York City History* Mele explained, "I am interested in examining the diverse ways the Lower East Side has been characterized since the late nineteenth century and how these characterizations have effected the area's development." He added, "In ways both intentional and unintentional, the dominant representations of the Lower East Side work their way into the various resistance tactics of local organizations and residents."

Sarah Ferguson noted in her *Village Voice* review of "Selling The Lower Eastside: Mele compiles an impressive wealth of archival data and historical surveys along with his own field research to illustrate how cultural representations have helped shape the political and economic development of the LES since the nineteenth century."

BIOGRAPHICAL AND CRITICAL SOURCES:

PERIODICALS

Library Journal, February 15, 2000, Deborah Bigelow, review of *Selling the Lower East Side: Culture, Real Estate, and Resistance in New York City,* p. 186.
Village Voice, March 28, 2000, Sarah Ferguson, "LES Is More," p. 62.

OTHER

Gotham Center for New York City History Web site, http://www.gothamcenter.org/ (February 8, 2002), "The Virtual Podium: Christopher Mele."

*   *   *

MENO, Joe 1975-

PERSONAL: Born 1975. *Education:* Attended Columbia College Chicago.

ADDRESSES: Home—Chicago, IL. *Office*—Columbia College Chicago, 624 South Michigan Ave., Room 1200 O, Chicago, IL. *Agent*—c/o Publicity Director, St. Martin's Press, 175 Fifth Ave., New York, NY 10010. *E-mail*—jmeno@colum.edu.

CAREER: Novelist. Columbia College Chicago, Chicago, IL, professor of fiction writing. Publisher of fiction zine *Sleepwalk;* worked as flower delivery truck driver and art therapy teacher at a juvenile detention center.

WRITINGS:

Tender as Hellfire (novel), St. Martin's Press (New York, NY), 1999.
How the Hula Girl Sings: A Novel, ReganBooks (New York, NY), 2001.

Contributor to literary magazines, including *Other Voices* and *Tri-Quarterly,* and to the *Playboy* Web site.

SIDELIGHTS: While still in his twenties novelist Joe Meno has already published two books and was labeled by some critics as a promising young author. A graduate of Columbia College Chicago, Meno wrote his debut novel, *Tender as Hellfire,* when he was just twenty-four. Two years later he published *How the Hula Girl Sings.* In both novels, Meno experiment with language, trying to keep the dialogue of his characters as close to everyday language as possible. The result, as some critics have noted, is a narration that includes numerous expletives and vulgarities. Meno explained this facet of his work in an interview with Melanie Masserant of the *Columbia Chronicle,* a Columbia College Chicago publication. "What I've learned in my short career as a writer is that taking big risks can have payoffs. I'm a firm believer in thinking big. It's important not to limit yourself as a writer." Meno also told Masserant that the writers he admires, such as Toni Morrison, Hubert Selby, Jr., and William Faulkner, have also used natural language in their writings.

Meno caught a professional break when an *Atlantic Monthly* editor discovered his manuscript for *Tender as Hellfire* while Meno was still an undergraduate at Columbia. The book, which a contributor for *Kirkus Reviews* called a "rambling and oddly good-natured debut," is narrated by an eleven-year-old boy named Dough Lunt. Dough, along with his brother Pill Bug, who is two years older, must move from their home in Duluth, Minnesota, after their truck-driving father is killed in an accident while smuggling a truckload of illegal cigarettes. The boys move to a trailer park home in the fictional plains town of Tenderloin. The story is the boys' coming-of-age tale, as they deal with the many trials and tribulations of living in the fictional trailer park. For instance, their funny names immediately put them at odds with the local kids, and they have to prove themselves physically on numerous occasions. They also have to deal with their mother's eccentric behavior, especially her communal sex life, while coming to grips with their own developing sexual desires. Despite the difficulties, the boys have each other to lean on, and they learn valuable lessons about themselves and life in general. "We had learned we didn't have a damn thing to lose, and no matter what we were caught doing, nothing could bring you down lower than the sad state you were already in," Dough declares at one point in the story.

Meno also created a number of secondary characters whom he paints with an extremely fine brush. Joy Malinowski of the *Philadelphia City Paper* called *Tender as Hellfire* "a satisfying story, with its small anti-heroes navigating proudly through any number of confusing, humiliating and horrifying situations." Likewise, a contributor for *Publishers Weekly* thought the book features "some of the liveliest characters just this side of believable that one is apt to meet in a contemporary novel." James Klise of *Booklist* called Meno "a writer with promise."

Several critics thought Meno improved upon his first effort with *How the Hula Girl Sings,* a tale about an ex-con named Luce Lemay who tries to pick up the fractured pieces of his life after being released from prison. Lemay has served three years in a state penitentiary for running over and killing a three-year-old child while fleeing from a liquor store he had just robbed. When he returns to his hometown of La Harpie, Illinois, "a place of quiet villainy and secret lust," Lemay finds that not only does his old girlfriend want nothing to do with a former convict, but the entire town continues to hold a grudge against him because of his past.

Meno sympathizes with Lemay's character, and he wants the reader to do the same. As the author explained to Masserant, the idea for *How the Hula Girl Sings* came from two separate experiences in his life. In 1999 Meno drove a flower delivery truck, and he was always haunted with the fear of running over a child and having to carry the burden of guilt associated with such a tragedy. The second experience was

when Meno taught art therapy at a detention center for juvenile sex offenders. Despite approaching the youths with initial prejudices, he said he ultimately felt some compassion for them. "Doing creative writing with them, I realized that it's a lot easier to be angry at these people and to think of them as nonhuman than to be aware of their humanity," he told Masserant. "In a sense, they are completely haunted by what they have done. They are haunted by the sense of their future and are stuck in time by this event in their lives. They are having an impossible time forgiving themselves."

In the book Lemay fits this description—a man continuously at odds with himself and society for what he did in his past: "They gave me back my full Christian name and my own clothes and three miserable old Viceroy Golds," Lemay says when leaving prison. "They gave me back my full name and the life I had lost, but still that baby carriage rolled on cold through my head. It rocked and wavered right past me as I wandered out of those penitent iron gates and back to being a sovereign man." Lemay finds some hope when he begins to romance a waitress named Charlene, but the townspeople, including her father and former fiancé, do not approve of their relationship. When their narrow-mindedness pushes the townspeople to take violent action against Lemay, he is forced to confront his own violent past he is trying to run from. To make matters worse, a man named Toreador is set on seeing Lemay dead because Lemay beat him up while the two were in prison together. In the violent climax, Lemay finds out just how far people can take a grudge.

How the Hula Girl Sings. received positive reviews. Masserant felt Meno maintains "his position as a poignant voice in fiction." A contributor for *Publishers Weekly* thought the novel "should bolster Meno's reputation" as a writer, noting that "Meno has a poet's feel for small-town details . . . and he's a natural storyteller with a talent for characterization." "Fans of hard-boiled pulp fiction will particularly enjoy this novel," wrote Dowling Brendan, reviewing the book for *Booklist.*

BIOGRAPHICAL AND CRITICAL SOURCES:

PERIODICALS

Booklist, March 1, 1999, James Klise, review of *Tender as Hellfire,* p. 1156; August, 2001, Dowling Brendan, review of *How the Hula Girl Sings,* p. 2089.

Kirkus Reviews, January 15, 1999, review of *Tender as Hellfire,* p. 91.

Library Journal, October 15, 1999, Dan Bogey, review of *Tender as Hellfire,* p. 132; March 1, 1999, Jim Dwyer, review of *Tender as Hellfire,* p. 110.

Publishers Weekly, January 18, 1999, review of *Tender as Hellfire,* p. 326; July 23, 2001, review of *How the Hula Girl Sings,* p. 47.

OTHER

Columbia Chronicle Online, http://www.ccchronicle.com/ (November 26, 2001), Melanie Masserant, "Faculty Author to Read Excerpts from Dark Novel."

On Milwaukee, http://www.onmilwaukee.com/ (September 7, 2001), "Chicago's Meno Reads from Edgy New Novel."

Philadelphia City Paper, http:// www.citypaper.net/ (June 17, 1999), Joy Malinowski, review of *Tender as Hellfire.**

* * *

MERCER, Joan Bodger 1923-2002
(Joan Bodger)

OBITUARY NOTICE—See index for *CA* sketch: Born August 31, 1923, in San Francisco, CA; died of cancer July 4, 2002, in Tofino, British Columbia, Canada. Storyteller, educator, consultant, editor, and author. Mercer filled her life with children and books. She directed a nursery school in Nyack, New York where the state's first "head-start" program was launched in the early 1960s. She taught children's literature and storytelling at the Bank Street College of Education, then went to the State Library of Missouri as a consultant to the Children's Division and later became a children's book editor for publisher Random House. Moving to Toronto, Canada in the early 1970s, Mercer became a Gestalt therapist and a professional storyteller, and was a founding member of the board of directors of the Storytellers School of Toronto. Mercer was described by those who knew her as an adventurer, curious to solve mysteries and probe beneath the surface of what she read. A trip to England to explore first hand the settings of children's stories by Kenneth Grahame, Rudyard Kipling, and others resulted in her first book, *How the Heather Looks: A Joyous Journey*

to the British Sources of Children's Books. Mercer, who published under the name Joan Bodger, also wrote several children's books, including *Clever-Lazy: The Girl Who Invented Herself, Belinda's Bell,* and *The Forest Family.* Her autobiography, *The Crack in the Teacup: The Life of an Old Woman Steeped in Story,* was published in 2000.

OBITUARIES AND OTHER SOURCES:

BOOKS

Mercer, Joan Bodger, *The Crack in the Teacup: The Life of an Old Woman Steeped in Story,* McClelland & Stewart (Toronto, Ontario, Canada), 2000.

PERIODICALS

National Post, July 6, 2002, obituary by Dan Yashinsky, p. B11.
School Library Journal, September, 2002, obituary by Kathy Ishizuka, p. 25.

* * *

MILLER, Geoffrey F. 1965-

PERSONAL: Born 1965, in Cincinnati, OH. *Education:* Columbia University; 1987; Stanford University, Ph.D., 1993; postdoctoral study at University of Sussex.

ADDRESSES: Home—Surrey, England. *Office*—Centre for Economic Learning and Social Evolution, Department of Economics, University College London, Gower St., London WC1E 6BT, England.

CAREER: Evolutionary psychologist. Centre for Economic Learning and Social Evolution, University College, London, England, currently senior research fellow. University of California at Los Angeles, Los Angeles, CA, visiting associate professor; Max Planck Institute of Psychological Research, Munich, Germany, research scientist.

WRITINGS:

The Mating Mind: How Sexual Choice Shaped the Evolution of Human Nature, Doubleday (New York, NY), 2000.
(editor)*Treatment of Integral Equations by Numerical Methods,* Academic Press (San Diego, CA), 1997.

Also contributor to various radio and television series on human biology and evolution.

SIDELIGHTS: Geoffrey F. Miller, an American cognitive psychologist teaching at University College, London. His career is devoted to the study of evolutionary psychology. As Miller said in an Online interview for *Edge,* "My goal at this point really is to take evolutionary psychology the next step, and to apply standard of evolutionary theory as much as possible to explain the whole gamut of the human mind, human emotions, human social life, human sexual behavior as much as possible." He added, "Another thing I'm interested in at the moment is trying to create more cooperation between evolutionary psychology and behavior genetics, especially for understanding the mind, and distinguishing between parts of the mind that are truly universal, where everybody's got the same structure, versus parts of the mind where there's significant variability between people, and where some of that variability is genetic."

In the interview, Miller also commented, "All of psychology, anthropology, the humanities, political science, economics in the 20th century, developed without any understanding of how sexual selection could have shaped human behavior. It was just not on the table as an idea. Everything that we are, every aspect of human nature, had to be explained through survival selection—natural selection. And that imposed such serious restrictions on what we could explain—it seemed easy to explain tool making; it seemed hard to explain music. It seemed easy to explain parenting, but hard to explain courtship. All that's changed now. We've got from biology some powerful new principals about sexual selection that are just ripe for applying to human nature. That's what I'm trying to do."

Miller did research on evolutionary robotics, genetic algorithms, and simulations of sexual selection and dynamical games between predators and prey while an NationalScienceFedration-NATO postdoctoral student at the University of Sussex. As a research scientist at the Center for Adaptive Behavior and Cognition at Max Planck Institute in Munich, his concentration was on modeling human judgment and decision-making. His work at the Center for Economic Learning and Social Evolution at University College, London, which is Europe's largest center for game theory and experimental economics, involves applications of sexual-selection theory and signaling theory to understanding human cognition, motivation, communication, and economic behavior.

His book, *The Mating Mind: How Sexual Choice Shaped the Evolution of Human Nature,* advances the controversial concept that sexual selection, Darwin's "other" idea besides natural selection, explains the evolution of human creativity. According to *CogWeb* reviewer Timothy Horvath, "Miller has a go at the conundrum of why people devote massive amounts of time, energy, and emotion to endeavors with little obvious survival value. He argues that the explanation has been woefully overlooked: sexual selection theory, the idea that ultimately it doesn't matter who survives, the only survival worth anything in evolutionary time is that which lasts long enough for procreation." Horvath concluded, "Miller's arguments are compelling, and must be reckoned with by any scholar trying to bring evolutionary explanations to bear on the arts."

In his book Miller argues that every human characteristic indicates some kind of fitness for mating. "Miller's main claim to our attention," said *New York Times Book Review* critic Ian Tattersall, "lies in his assertion that 'the human mind's most distinctive features, such as our capacities for language, art, music, ideology, humor, and creative intelligence,' are due more or less exclusively to mate choice." A *Publishers Weekly* reviewer called *The Mating Mind* an "enjoyable book" and noted that "Miller provides an articulate and memorable case for the role of sexual selection in determining human behaviors." Gilbert Taylor reflected in a *Booklist* review that "the series of scenarios he presents on how sexual selection proclivities may have favored the expressive and self-revealing aptitudes of the human mind prove most thought provoking."

BIOGRAPHICAL AND CRITICAL SOURCES:

PERIODICALS

Booklist, May 1, 2000, Gilbert Taylor, review of *The Mating Mind: How Sexual Choice Shaped the Evolution of Human Nature,* p. 1631.
New York Times Book Review, June 11, 2000, Ian Tattersall, review of *The Mating Mind.*
Publishers Weekly, April 17, 2000, review of *The Mating Mind,* p. 60.

OTHER

CogWeb, http://cogweb.ucla.edu/ (May 20, 2002), Timothy Horvath, "Our Tales Are Our Tails: Miller Revives Darwin's 'Other' Dangerous Idea."

Edge, http://edge.org/ (February 8, 2002), John Brockman, "Sexual Selection and the Mind: A Talk with Geoffrey Miller."

Science News Books, http://www.sciencenewsbooks. org/ (May 20, 2002).

Keplers, http://www.keplers.com/ (May 20, 2002).*

*　　*　　*

MILLER, Kit 1956(?)-

PERSONAL: Born c. 1956, in Nevada; married; two children.

ADDRESSES: Home—Carson City, NV. *Agent*—c/o Author Mail, Great Basin Publishing, 6185 Franktown Rd., Carson City, NV 89704.

CAREER: Photographer, writer, and producer. Photographs have been exhibited and published in periodicals, including *New York Times, San Francisco Chronicle,* and *Native People's Magazine.*

WRITINGS:

Inside the Glitter: Lives of Casino Workers, Great Basin Publishing (Carson City, NV), 2000.

SIDELIGHTS: An experienced and highly regarded photographer, Kit Miller has covered the street children of Brazil and other stories around the world, publishing her work in such periodicals as the *New York Times* and the *Washington Post.* But in her home state of Nevada, she found a story that was not getting much attention and decided to address it. Miller believes a shift is happening in labor migration, from the traditional farms and factories, to the glitzy gambling capitals of Las Vegas and Reno. *Inside the Glitter: Lives of Casino Workers* brings out the stories of the maids and mechanics, the waiters and bartenders, and the other service workers who keep these towns running while remaining essentially invisible to the tourists and gamblers. "Miller's subjects are never made into icons, however, symbols of troubling social problems rather than fully-fleshed human beings," wrote Annelise Orleck in the *Women's Review of Books.*

Each of the subjects gets an on-the-job photo and one off-duty photo, as well as a personal profile. Their stories are compelling and often entertaining. There is the "serving wench" at the Excalibur who misses the old days when organized crime ran the city, and she could make $300 a night in tips. There is the Vietnamese refugee who arrived in Reno penniless and a year later is dealing blackjack at the Comstock casino. And there are surprises, like the bellman who has discovered eighteen plant species in his spare time as an amateur botanist. In an interview *Holt Uncensored,* Miller said she'd been "chasing the exotic" in places like Brazil. "Then I came back to Nevada and found a not-so-different 'other' in my back yard—a huge population that's rarely been seen or acknowledged." Or as some of the workers themselves told her, "Geez, it's about time someone talked to us."

BIOGRAPHICAL AND CRITICAL SOURCES:

PERIODICALS

Women's Review of Books, May, 2000, Annelise Orleck, "Supporting Cast," pp. 22-23.

OTHER

High Country News, http://www.hcn.org/ (October 2, 1995), review of *Inside the Glitter.*

Holt Uncensored, http://www.greatbasinweb.com/holt. html (August 11, 2000), "Sleeper of the Summer: 'Inside the Glitter.'"

Las Vegas Review-Journal, http://www.lvrj.com/ (January 21, 1997), Joan Whitely, "Glimpses behind the Glitter."*

*　　*　　*

MILLER, Randolph Crump 1910-2002

OBITUARY NOTICE—See index for *CA* sketch: Born October 1, 1910, in Fresno, CA; died of cancer June 13, 2002, in New Haven, CT. Minister, educator, consultant, editor, and author. Miller, an ordained priest of the Protestant Episcopal church, devoted his life to religious education. He was a professor of divinity at Yale University for some thirty years beginning in 1952, and was named the Horace Bushnell Professor of Christian Nurture in 1964. He was also the editor of the nondenominational journal *Religious Education* from 1958 to 1978; he continued as managing editor of that journal from 1982 until 1993. Miller was a visiting professor at universities and seminaries throughout the world and a consultant to the National Council of Protestant Episcopal Churches. He had also served as the vicar of a church in Albany, California, in the 1940s. Miller wrote or edited more than twenty books. He was the author of *The American Spirit in Theology, Live until You Die, This We Can Believe,* and other volumes. His edited titles include *What Is the Nature of Man?, Empirical Theology: A Handbook,* and *Theologies of Religious Education.*

OBITUARIES AND OTHER SOURCES:

PERIODICALS

Chronicle of Higher Education, June 28, 2002, p. A37.
Plain Dealer (Cleveland, OH), June 17, 2002, p. B5.
Washington Post, June 17, 2002, p. B4.

* * *

MITCHELL, Nancy

PERSONAL: Born in Kingsport, TN; married John Mitchell (a commercial airline pilot); children: Jenny; stepchildren: Dave, Tom, Mike, Susan, Kathy. *Education:* University of Colorado, Boulder.

ADDRESSES: Home—Fremont, CA *Office*—Lightstream Publications, P.O. Box 3229, Fremont, CA 94539. *E-mail*—nancyr@thegrid.net.

CAREER: Writer and founder of Lightstream Publications. Pan American World Airways, flight attendant.

MEMBER: Fremont Council PTA (newsletter editor), Peralta District PTA (treasurer), Freemont Public Schools (superintendent's parent advisory committee).

WRITINGS:

"THE CHANGING EARTH" TRILOGY

Earth Rising: Disaster Strikes the Bay Area, Lightstream Books (Fremont, CA), 1999.
Raging Skies: Catastrophe in the East Bay, Lightstream Books (Fremont, CA), 1999.
Global Warning: Attack on the Pacific Rim, Lightstream Books (Fremont, CA), 1999.

WORK IN PROGRESS: The Time Riders, an e-book; (with Laura Mordaunt) *Fit at 55-Plus: Weight Loss and Fitness for the Rest of Your Life,* true stories of people who have lost weight and improved their health through methods both ancient and modern.

SIDELIGHTS: Nancy Mitchell is the author of "The Changing Earth" trilogy, a series of young adult novels combining her interest in disaster preparedness with her interest in creating a fictional protagonist who is physically handicapped. Drawing on her experiences as the parent of a wheelchair-bound daughter, as well as on a great deal of research, Mitchell's trilogy confronts the possibility of ecological disaster in the near future, and the ways in which a group of teenagers might react to earthquakes, floods, and terrorist threats. Reviewing *Global Warning: Attack on the Pacific Rim,* in *School Library Journal,* Jana R. Fine wrote that "the author does successfully portray teens in a positive light, working to solve each crisis." Rather than wait for publishers to accept her books, Mitchell formed Lightstream Books to publish them herself. She has also made herself available to San Francisco Bay Area schools to discuss creative writing and the mechanics of getting published.

BIOGRAPHICAL AND CRITICAL SOURCES:

PERIODICALS

School Library Journal, October, 1999, Jana R. Fine, review of *Global Warning,* pp. 154, 156.

OTHER

Lightstream Publications Web site, http://www.lightstreampubs.com/ (June 26, 2002).
Society of Children's Book Writers & Illustrators Web site, http://www.scbwinorca.org/ (February 11, 2002), "Nancy Mitchell."*

MOHAR, Bojan 1956-

PERSONAL: Born September 21, 1956, in Yugoslavia (now Slovenia); married Marina Blatnik, 1982; children: Nika, Daša. *Education:* Earned Ph.D., 1986.

ADDRESSES: Office—Department of Mathematics, University of Ljubljana, 1000 Ljubljana, Slovenia. *E-mail*—bojan.mohar@uni-lj.si.

CAREER: University of Ljubljana, Ljubljana, Slovenia, professor of mathematics, 1980—.

MEMBER: Engineering Academy of Slovenia.

AWARDS, HONORS: Slovene National Prize for Science, 1990.

WRITINGS:

(With Andrej Vitek, Vladimir Batagelj, Marc Martinec, and others) *Problems in Programming: Experience through Practice,* John Wiley & Sons (New York, NY), 1991.

(With Carsten Thomassen) *Graphs on Surfaces,* Johns Hopkins University Press (Baltimore, MD), 2001.

*   *   *

MONROE, Steve 1961-

PERSONAL: Born 1961.

ADDRESSES: Home—Chicago, IL. *Agent*—c/o Publicity Director, Hyperion Books, 77 West 66th St., 11th Floor, New York, NY 10023.

CAREER: Author. Grubb & Ellis, Chicago, real estate broker. Former newspaper reporter.

WRITINGS:

'57, Chicago (novel), Talk Miramax Books/Hyperion (New York, NY), 2001.

'46, Chicago (novel), Talk Miramax Books/Hyperion (New York, NY), 2002.

SIDELIGHTS: Unlike writers who toil for years before obtaining financial security, Chicago-based Steve Monroe succeeded almost immediately after publishing his debut novel, *'57, Chicago.* Monroe wrote the book while working as a real estate broker, finishing it after three years. Talk Miramax Books accepted it for publication and also bought screenplay rights, with plans of making Monroe's story into a motion picture.

According to critic Richard Wallace in the *San Francisco Chronicle, '57, Chicago* is "a throwback novel" in which Monroe "pays dubious homage to the pulp noir thrillers of yesteryear." The fictional tale is set in the world of bookies and gambling in 1957 Chicago. Once a gambler himself, Monroe explained in an interview with *New City Chicago.com* that he wrote the book in his spare time because he wanted to "put a bookie through the hell that I've been through." In fact, many of the characters in Monroe's book are bookies, including Al Kelley, who plays a significant role. Kelley is an honest bookie whose ethics are tested after he loses big money on an NCAA basketball game. In an attempt to win some of his money back, Kelley gets involved in the betting on a heavyweight boxing match between Junior "the Hammer" Hamilton and "Tomcat" Gordon, two other main characters in the novel. Hamilton, who is black and an up-and-coming fighter, is trained by an ex-con named Eddie "The Lip" Lipranski, who promotes the match in an attempt to jump-start his career. Lipranski thinks Hamilton can beat Gordon, who is white and the local heavyweight contender. However, a number of local bookies, including Kelley, want to fix the fight so that Gordon wins. Although Lipranski and Hamilton initially refuse to go along with the plan, they are ultimately corrupted by the lure of money.

Monroe created a number of secondary characters, including mobsters, boxing commissioners, Lipranski's sexy girlfriend, and a wheelchair-bound police detective named Jack who uses the fixed fight as a way to nab a mob chief he has been trying to catch for a long time. A number of subplots surround the match, and the story comes to a climax with an unexpected plot twist when the fighters step into the ring.

A number of critics lauded 157 Chicago, including Jerry Gladman of the *Toronto Sun,* who felt that Monroe manages "to cook up enough of a plot twist" to take "this crackling first effort to a higher plain." Gladman, in fact, was one of the critics who felt

Monroe was able to draw an authentic picture of 1957 Chicago. The book "resonates with authentic dialogue" and has "very believable characters," according to Gladman. "Monroe does a credible job of capturing the gritty feel of 1957 Chicago's seamier side," wrote a contributor for *Publishers Weekly*. Bill Ott, who reviewed the book for *Booklist*, felt that the author had filled the story with "fascinating detail on how to run a sports book." In addition, Ott commended Monroe's dialogue, which he felt "crackles with authenticity." Even critics who found fault with Monroe's novel had kind words for its ability to entertain readers. "Despite its shortcomings, *'57, Chicago* offers brisk and undemanding entertainment," Mahinder Kingra wrote in a review for the *Baltimore City Paper*.

Monroe's second novel, *'46, Chicago,* was published in 2002 and revolves around the "policy rackets, an illegal numbers game."

BIOGRAPHICAL AND CRITICAL SOURCES:

PERIODICALS

Booklist, February 15, 2001, Bill Ott, review of *'57, Chicago*, p. 1119.
Kirkus Reviews, February 1, 2001, review of *'57, Chicago*, p. 135.
New York Times, July 29, 2001, Tom Beer, review of *'57, Chicago*.
Publishers Weekly, March 12, 2001, review of *'57, Chicago*, p. 63.
San Francisco Chronicle, April 29, 2001, Richard Wallace, review of *'57, Chicago*, p. 83.
Toronto Sun, July 24, 2001, Jerry Gladman, "Thriller Delivers Knockout Punch."

OTHER

Baltimore City Paper Online, http://www.citypaper. com/ (August 31, 2001), Mahinder Kingra, review of *'57, Chicago*.
Newcity Chicago, http://www.newcitychicago.com/ (August 31, 2001), "Street Smart Chicago: Lit 50: Who Really Books in Chicago."
Powels.com, http://www.powels.com/ (August 31, 2001), Adrienne Miller, review of *'57, Chicago*.*

MOORE, T. M. 1949-

PERSONAL: Born 1949; married, wife's name Susie; children: four. *Religion:* Christian.

ADDRESSES: Home—Phillipi, WV. *Office*—c/o InterVarsity Press, P.O. Box 1400, Downers Grove, IL 60515.

CAREER: Poet, writer, and theologian. President, Chesapeake Theological Seminary, Baltimore, MD; consultant, Prison Fellowship, Reformed Theological Seminary, and Scripture Union.

WRITINGS:

(With D. James Kennedy) *Chain Reaction!: Changing the World from Where You Are*, Word Books (Waco, TX), 1985.
Celtic Flame: The Burden of Patrick, XLibris (Philadelphia, PA), 2000.
Disciplines of Grace: From Spiritual Routine to Spiritual Renewal, InterVarsity Press (Downers Grove, IL), 2001.
Ecclesiastes: Ancient Wisdom When All Else Fails, InterVarsity Press (Downers Grove, IL), 2001.
Preparing Your Church for Revival, Christian Focus Publications (Geanies House, Fearn, Scotland), 2001
The Psalms for Prayer, Baker Book House (Grand Rapids, MI), 2002
I Will Be Your God: How God's Covenant Enriches Our Lives, Presbyterian & Reformed Publishing Company (Phillipsburg, NJ), 2002.

SIDELIGHTS: A former teacher, T. M. Moore has turned to full-time writing to explore and express his views on Christian theology. One of his earliest books in wide distribution is *Celtic Flame: The Burden of Patrick*, a study of St. Patrick that includes Moore's renderings of Patrick's ancient manuscripts. Moore portrays a Patrick free from the mythology and legend that dominates modern knowledge of the Irish icon, linking him back to his history as one of the first Celtic Fathers.

Moore made another foray into translation with *Ecclesiastes: Ancient Wisdom When All Else Fails.* rewriting the Hebrew text of Qoheleth in rhymed iambic pentameter and accompanying it with annotations from other early wise men. A reviewer for *Publishers Weekly*, quoted on the InterVarsity Press Web site, said about the book, "Biblical studies so rarely produces something totally new that when it does happen, it's a revelation." Several theologians commented on the relevance of *Ecclesiastes* in Moore's rendering. David S. Castle, a religion teacher, wrote of the book, "Moore gives us what the Teacher gave his generation: a broken heart with an open mind. . . . For what was true in ancient Israel is likewise the same in our post-modern culture, and Moore deftly pleads for the sanctity of that simple message not to go unguarded."

With 2001's *Disciplines of Grace: From Spiritual Routines to Spiritual Renewal*, Moore offers readers a guidebook to living a Christian spiritual life, advocating familiar practices like fasting, prayer, and Bible study in tandem with meditation and chanting. Moore draws from Christian thinkers including the Celtic church of St. Patrick, Tertullian, and Jonathan Edwards. He also provides questions for further study. Many readers commented on the practical value of the book. Several theologians endorsed the book on the *InterVarsity Press Web site:* Luder G. Whitlock, Jr., president of the Reformed Theological Seminary, wrote, "If you want to grow spiritually, this is as helpful a guide as you will find." A reviewer for *Publishers Weekly* suggested that Moore's "to-do list" of spiritual exercises would likely overwhelm the average reader, adding that "his long list of shoulds sounds a bit too much like a works-based theology." Others, including Whitney T. Kuniholm, found the book helpful and clear: Whitney said of *Disciplines of Grace,* "This is a practical guide for catching a fresh wind in your walk with God."

BIOGRAPHICAL AND CRITICAL SOURCES:

PERIODICALS

First Things, March, 2001, review of *Celtic Flame,* p. 64.
Publishers Weekly, July 30, 2001, *Disciplines of Grace: From Spiritual Routines to Spiritual Renewal,* p. 81.

OTHER

InterVarsity Press Web site, http://www.gospelcom.net/cgi-ivpress/ (October 7, 2001).*

MORGAN, Berry 1919-2002

OBITUARY NOTICE—See index for *CA* sketch: Born c. May 19, 1919, in Port Gibson, MS; died from complications of a series of strokes June 19, 2002, in Charles Town, WV. Educator and author. Morgan was a teacher of creative writing, first at Northeast Louisiana University in the 1970s, then later at American University, the Catholic University of America, and George Washington University, all located in Washington, D.C. Funded by a Houghton Mifflin literary fellowship in the 1960s, he began what was intended to be a trilogy of novels. The first volume, *Pursuit,* relates a bizarre tale of obsession and lunacy revolving around a southern plantation and an adjoining town not unlike the community where Morgan herself grew up. The next volume, described alternately as a novel and a collection of stories and titled *The Mystic Adventures of Roxie Stoner,* features the titular character as a townswoman serving the plantation family of *Pursuit* as a nanny. Morgan's fiction was well received by some critics for its exploration of the human spirit. Some of her stories were also published in the *New Yorker.*

OBITUARIES AND OTHER SOURCES:

BOOKS

Contemporary Literary Criticism, Volume 6, Gale (Detroit, MI), 1976.
Dictionary of Literary Biography, Volume 6: *American Novelists since World War II, Second Series,* Gale (Detroit, MI), 1980, pp. 241-243.

PERIODICALS

Washington Post, June 27, 2002, p. B6.

*   *   *

MURPHY, Patrick J. 1946-

PERSONAL: Born December 17, 1946; son of Ernest J. and Carol May (Woitowitz) Murphy; married Kay Cleary (an actuary), April 23, 1992; children: Jennifer Jean. *Education:* Portland State University, B.S.

(general studies), 1973; San Francisco Theological Seminary, M.Div., 1976; Florida State University, M.A. (English), Ph.D. coursework. *Politics:* Democrat.

ADDRESSES: Home—3612 Monmouth Ct., Tallahassee, FL 32308. *E-mail*—PJMurph@aol.com.

CAREER: U.S. Navy, enlisted man and civil servant (electronics), 1967-71, 1982-86; Simco Electronics, electronic engineer, 1986-97.

WRITINGS:

Way below E, White Pine Press (Fredonia, NY), 1995.

Contributor of more than fifty short stories to journals, including *New Orleans Review, Tampa Review, Buffalo Spree, Hawaii Pacific Review, Cream City Review, Gamut, Sycamore Review,* and *Hawaii Review.* Contributor to *100% Pure Florida Fiction* (anthology), University Press of Florida.

N

NASS, Sharyl J(eanne) 1966-

PERSONAL: Born November 15, 1966, in Watertown, WI; daughter of William (a dairy farmer) and Jeanne (a registered nurse; maiden name, Schultz; later surname, Goeglein) Nass; married Eric J. Costello (an electrical engineer), May 13, 2000; children: Elisa Kady. *Education:* University of Wisconsin— Madison, B.S. (with highest distinction), 1989, M.S., 1991; Georgetown University, Ph.D. (with distinction), 1996.

ADDRESSES: Home—Catonsville, MD. *Office*— National Academy of Sciences, 2101 Constitution Ave. N.W., Washington, DC 10418. *E-mail*—snas@nas.edu.

CAREER: Max Planck Institute, Freiburg, Germany, research fellow, 1992-93; Johns Hopkins University, Baltimore, MD, research scientist, 1997-99, lecturer in cancer biology, 1999-2000; National Academy of Sciences, Washington, DC, study director for National Cancer Policy Board, Institute of Medicine, 1999—, program officer, 1999-2001, senior program officer, 2001—. University of Maryland, guest lecturer at School of Nursing, 2001.

MEMBER: American Association for Cancer Research (associate member of council, 1999-2002, American Association for the Advancement of Science, Johns Hopkins University Postdoctoral Association (vice president, 1998-99), Sigma Xi.

AWARDS, HONORS: Heinrich-Hertz-Stiftung fellow in Germany, 1992-93; grant from National Cancer Institute, 1997; scholarship from American Association for Cancer Research, 1999; grant from Breast Cancer Research Foundation, 1999-2000.

WRITINGS:

(Editor, with M. Patlak, I. C. Henderson, and J. C. Lashof) *Mammography and Beyond: Developing Technologies for the Early Detection of Breast Cancer; A Non-Technical Summary,* National Academy Press (Washington, DC), 2001.

Contributor of articles and reviews to periodicals, including *Women's Health Advances Today, Managed Care and Cancer, Nature Medicine, Mammalian Genome, BioTechniques, Breast Cancer Research and Treatment, Cancer Research, Oncogene,* and *Current Genomics.*

WORK IN PROGRESS: Large-scale science and cancer research; research on mammography and breast cancer screening.

SIDELIGHTS: Sharyl J. Nass told *CA:* "I enjoy combining my writing skills with my passion for science to make scientific and medical topics accessible to the non-expert. I also find it very rewarding to gather the small pieces of a puzzle and then put them together in the big picture through my writing."

*　　*　　*

NICHOLAS, Denise 1944-

PERSONAL: Born July 12, 1944, in Detroit, MI (some sources say Delaware); daughter of Otto Nicholas and Louise Carolyn Burgen; married Gilbert Moses (a theater artistic director), 1964 (divorced, 1965); married Bill Withers (a singer; divorced); married Jim Hill (a sportscaster), 1981. *Education:* Attended University of Michigan, 1962-64; University of Southern California, B.A. in drama, 1987; trained for the stage with Paul Mann and Lloyd Richards; studied dance with Louis Johnson and voice with Kristan Linklater at the Negro Ensemble Company.

ADDRESSES: Agent—c/o Paul Kohner, Inc., 9300 Wilshire Blvd., Suite 555, Beverly Hills, CA 90212.

CAREER: Actress, writer, and producer. Appeared in productions with Media Forum Players, CA, and at Old Reliable Theatre Tavern, New York City; member of original acting company, Negro Ensemble Company, New York City, 1967-68; artist-in-residence, Oklahoma Summer Arts Institute, 1987-88; acting teacher, University of Southern California, 1987-89; founding member, Free Southern Theatre, New Orleans, LA; founder and co-owner, Masai Films, Inc., Hollywood, CA; producer, *Artists and Athletes against Apartheid: A Benefit,* Beverly Wilshire Hotel; producer, *The Media Forum Presents,* Wilshire Ebell Hotel. Chair, *Fourth Annual American Airlines/Jet Celebrity Tennis Classic,* United Negro College Fund Super Tennis Week, 1978; secretary, Negro Ensemble Company; works with Neighbors of Watts, Inc. (an organization for the care of children); and worked as a secretary for J. Walter Thompson. Sometimes works under name Denise Nicholas-Hill.

Film appearances include *Blacula,* American International Pictures, 1972; *The Soul of Nigger Charley,* Paramount, 1973; *Mr. Ricco,* Metro-Goldwyn-Mayer, 1975; *Let's Do It Again,* Warner Bros., 1975; *A Piece of the Action,* Warner Bros., 1977; *Capricorn One,* Warner Bros., 1978; *Marvin and Tige,* Lorimar, 1983; *Ghost Dad,* 1990; *Ritual,* Gotham Entertainment, 2000. Film work includes work as producer of short films, all with Masai Films: *Navy Junior R.O.T.C.* and *Welcome Aboard,* both for the U.S. Navy; *Aquarius,* for Mattel Electronics; *The Road Rapper,* for the California Department of Highways; also *Doing Business in Nigeria.*

Television series appearances include *Room 222,* ABC, 1969-74; *Baby, I'm Back,* CBS, 1978; *In the Heat of the Night,* 1989-94. Also appeared in *Yes, Inc.,* PBS. TV movie appearances include *Five Desperate Women,* ABC, 1971; *Ring of Passion,* 1978; *Jacqueline Susann's Valley of the Dolls,* 1981; *Supercarrier,* 1988;

Mother's Day, 1989; *On Thin Ice: The Tai Babilonia Story,* NBC, 1990; *In the Heat of the Night: A Matter of Justice,* CBS, 1994; *In the Heat of the Night: Who Was Geli Bendl?,* CBS, 1994; *In the Heat of the Night: By Duty Bound,* CBS, 1995; *In the Heat of the Night: Grow Old along with Me,* CBS, 1995; *The Rockford Files: Murder and Misdemeanors,* CBS, 1997. Appearances on TV miniseries include *The Sophisticated Gents,* NBC, 1981. Appearances on TV specials include *Battle of the Network Stars IV,* 1978; *The Big Stuffed Dog,* 1980; *And the Children Shall Lead,* PBS, 1985; *Heart and Soul,* 1989; *The Nineteenth Annual Black Filmmakers Hall of Fame,* 1992. Appearances on TV pilots include *Jacqueline Susann's "Valley of the Dolls,"* CBS, 1981. Also appeared in *Over Here, Mr. President,* HBO. Appearances on episodic television include "To Catch a Roaring Lion," *It Takes a Thief,* ABC, 1968; "Eye of the Storm," *The F.B.I.,* ABC, 1969; "Logoda's Heads," *Night Gallery,* 1971; "A Community of Victims," *Police Story,* 1975; "Substitute Mother," *Diff'rent Strokes,* NBC, 1980; "I Witness," *Magnum, P.I.,* 1984; "Birthday Blues," *The Cosby Show,* 1989; "Plates," *B.L. Stryker,* 1990; "Here's to Old Friends," *A Different World,* NBC, 1990; "My Dinner with Mark," *Hangin' with Mr. Cooper,* ABC, 1992; *Storytime,* PBS, 1994; "A Kiss Is Just a Kiss," *The Parent 'Hood,* The WB, 1995; "One Degree of Separation" and "Never Can Say Goodbye," *Living Single,* Fox, 1997. Also appeared in *N.Y. P.D.,* ABC; *Rhoda,* CBS; *Marcus Welby, M.D.,* ABC; *One Day at a Time,* CBS; *The Paper Chase,* CBS; *The Love Boat,* ABC; *Masquerade,* ABC; and *Benson,* ABC.

Stage appearances include *Viet Rock,* Martinique Theatre, 1966; *The Song of the Lusitanian Bogey,* Negro Ensemble Company, St. Mark's Playhouse, New York City, 1967; *Summer of the Seventeenth Doll,* Negro Ensemble Company, St. Mark's Playhouse, 1968; *Kongi's Harvest,* Negro Ensemble Company, St. Mark's Playhouse, 1968; *Daddy Goodness,* Negro Ensemble Company, St. Mark's Playhouse, 1968; *Ceremonies in Dark Old Men,* Negro Ensemble Company, Pocket Theatre, New York City, 1968 then St. Mark's Playhouse, 1969; *Dame Lorraine,* Los Angeles Actors Theatre, Los Angeles, CA, 1982; *Long Time Since Yesterday,* New Federal Theatre, New York City, 1985; *The Ohio State Murders,* American Repertory Theatre, Hasty Pudding Theatre, Cambridge, MA, 2000. Also appeared in *Their Eyes Were Watching God,* Oklahoma Summer Arts Institute; in *Poetry Show,* Judson Poets Theatre, New York City; and in *Buses,* University of

Southern California. Major tours include *In White America,* Free Southern Theatre, U.S. cities, 1964; *Three Boards and a Passion,* U.S. cities, 1966. Also appeared in *Purlie Victorious, The Rifles of Senora Carrar, Does Man Help Man?,* and *Shadow of a Gunman,* all Free Southern Theatre, U.S. cities; in *An Evening of Afro-American Poetry and Song,* Free Southern Theatre, U.S. cities; and assistant stage manager, *Waiting for Godot,* Free Southern Theatre, U.S. cities. Appeared in *An American Daughter,* Los Angeles Theatre Works, on National Public Radio.

MEMBER: Actors' Equity Association, Screen Actors Guild, American Federation of Television and Radio Artists, Academy of Television Arts and Sciences, Academy of Motion Picture Arts and Sciences, Women in Film.

AWARDS, HONORS: CEBA awards for excellence for advertising and communications, 1981, 1982; Cultural Artist of the Year, Harvard University Harvard Foundation, 1995; five National Association for the Advancement of Colored People (NAACP) Image Awards; two Los Angeles Emmy Awards for *Voices of Our People: In Celebration of Black Poetry.*

WRITINGS:

The Denise Nicholas Beauty Book (nonfiction), Cornerstone Library (New York, NY), 1971.
In the Heat of the Night (various episodes), CBS, 1991-94.

Author of the play *Buses,* contributor to *The National Black Drama Anthology: Eleven Plays from America's Leading African-American Theatres,* edited by Woodie King, Applause (New York, NY), 1995.

SIDELIGHTS: Though she was raised in Michigan, Denise Nicholas was intimately involved with the civil rights struggles of the American South in the 1960s, where she worked as a member of a traveling theater troupe. The troupe, the Free Southern Theater, was racially integrated, and put on free plays for black and integrated audiences throughout the South—highly dangerous work at the time. Nicholas later told Michael J. Bandler, as reported in the Cleveland, Ohio, *Plain Dealer,* that members of the Free Southern

Theater had been shot at, bombs had been thrown at the stage, and troupe members were arrested. She herself had been terrified in New Orleans when a policeman pointed a gun at her head and threatened to "blow my brains out if I took another step."

With this background, it is hardly a surprise that much of Nicholas's writing is concerned, in one way or another, with civil rights and integration. Her play *Buses* is an imagined interaction between two women separated by nearly a century: Mary Ellen Pleasant, a freed slave who became known as the "mother of civil rights" for her work in San Francisco during the 1860s, and Rosa Parks, renowned for her refusal to move to the back of a segregated bus in the 1950s.

Nicholas went from her work in the Free Southern Theater to a role on the television show *Room 222,* in which she became one of the first black female stars of an episodic TV program. Her career suffered a setback after the end of the show in the mid-1970s, and she went through a period of depression heightened by alcohol and pill abuse, several failed marriages (including one to singer Bill Withers), and the unsolved murder of her half-sister at New York's La-Guardia Airport.

Her life had already begun to turn around, however, by the time a major career break came in 1990, when she was invited to join the cast of *In the Heat of the Night.* The idea came from Carroll O'Connor, star and executive producer, who suggested that they add the character of Harriet DeLong, a black councilwoman in the fictional town of Sparta, Mississippi. His wife Nancy knew Nicholas from their work on several Los Angeles charities, and soon she became a permanent part of the show.

Eventually DeLong and O'Connor's character, the formerly bigoted Sheriff Bill Gillespie, engaged in a May-December interracial romance, and in 1994 the characters married. In the South that Nicholas had known thirty years earlier, such a romance—not to mention the wedding—would have been scandalous, and could have gotten both participants killed. By 1994, however, television was filled with far more controversial material, but some viewers still objected.

Nicholas not only appeared on *Heat,* but had written half a dozen episodes as of mid-1994, and collaborated with O'Connor on another episode. In the mid-1990s, she was also reportedly working on a screenplay that, according to N. F. Mendoza in the *Los Angeles Times,* "incorporates her favorite aspects of film: politics and romance." Said Nicholas, "Now the thing to do is to convince the industry that it's a general talent I have and that I can write for other things. That's the thing about this business, you're always convincing other people you can do things other than what you are doing at that moment."

BIOGRAPHICAL AND CRITICAL SOURCES:

BOOKS

Contemporary Theatre, Film, and Television, volume 32, Gale (Detroit, MI), 2000.

PERIODICALS

Detroit News, January 15, 1993, Kevin Ransom, "*Buses* Drives Denise Nicholas to More Writing," p. C9.
Jet, July 9, 1981, "Denise Nicholas-Hill Has Success in Perspective," p. 61; August 6, 1990, "Denise Nicholas: *Ghost Dad* Star Tells of Experience with Ghost of Slain Sister," pp. 58-59; February 17, 1992, "Actress Denise Nicholas Directs *Heat* Episode on Black Woman's Fight to Vote," p. 6; May 9, 1994, "Denise Nicholas and Carroll O'Connor Wed on TV Drama *In the Heat of the Night,*" pp. 54-57.
Los Angeles Times, January 16, 1994, N. F. Mendoza, "With an Eye on . . . *In the Heat of the Night*'s Denise Nicholas Finds the Positive in Past and Present," p. 80.
Plain Dealer (Cleveland, OH), January 19, 1993, Michael J. Bandler, "Denise Nicholas Finding Her Life Going Full Circle," p. C4.*

* * *

NICHOLAS-HILL, Denise
See NICHOLAS, Denise

* * *

NIELSEN, Helen Berniece 1918-2002
(Kris Giles)

OBITUARY NOTICE—See index for *CA* sketch: Born October 23, 1918, in Roseville, IL; died June 22, 2002, in Prescott, AZ. Landlord, artist, drafter, scriptwriter,

and author. Nielsen's largest audience may have been the viewers who saw her scripts enacted as episodes of such popular television series as *Alcoa Theater, Alfred Hitchcock Presents,* and *Perry Mason.* From the 1950s through the 1970s, however, Nielsen also published nearly twenty mystery novels and short-story collections, her work appreciated by readers and critics alike because she provided sufficient clues to enable the astute reader to solve the mystery. Many of Nielsen's novels were set in southern California, where she lived, but she occasionally took her readers abroad to Denmark or to Greece. Nielsen believed that characterization is a vital element in fiction, and she was often complimented by critics for creating characters realistic enough to believe in yet unusual enough to set them apart from the ordinary. Nielsen's novels include *Gold Coast Nocturne,* which was later adapted as the 1954 screenplay *Blackout* and *The Fifth Caller,* which was later broadcast as a television movie, as well as *A Killer in the Street, Shot on Location, The Severed Key,* and *The Brink of Murder.* Her writings also appeared in anthologies; some of her work appeared under the pseudonym Kris Giles. During her career as a writer Nielsen also owned and managed an apartment house; during World War II she worked as a freelance artist and as a drafter for various engineering companies.

OBITUARIES AND OTHER SOURCES:

PERIODICALS

Los Angeles Times, June 29, 2002, p. B20.

* * *

NIELSEN, Jerri 1951-

PERSONAL: Born 1951, in Salem, OH; daughter of Phil (a builder) and Lorine (a psychologist) Cahill; married Jay Nielsen (a physician), 1974 (divorced 1998); children: Julia, Benjamin, Alex. *Education:* Ohio University, B.A. (zoology); Medical College of Ohio, M.D., 1977.

ADDRESSES: Agent—c/o Publicity Director, Hyperion Books, 77 West 66th St., 11th Floor, New York, NY 10023.

CAREER: Physician in general practice for more than twenty years.

WRITINGS:

(With Maryanne Vollers) *Ice Bound: A Doctor's Incredible Battle for Survival at the South Pole,* Talk Miramax Books/Hyperion (New York, NY), 2001.

SIDELIGHTS: Most readers are intrigued by stories about living on the edge or meeting the challenges offered by remote destinations. Dr. Jerri Nielsen's story is no exception. Having taken a job at a U.S. base in Antarctica, the furthest thing from Nielsen's mind was that she would diagnose herself with breast cancer and perform biopsies on her own breast with the aid of an Internet connection to medical specialists in faraway Denver, Colorado. But that is exactly what happened to her. The story of her ordeal and personal battle is found in *Ice Bound: A Doctor's Incredible Battle for Survival at the South Pole.*

Isabel Vincent, writing in the *National Post,* concurred that the book is "an extraordinary story of courage and survival." Gloria Maxwell, reviewing it in *Library Journal,* called the book "an absolutely riveting account of hardship and perseverance." Jane S. Drabkin, reviewing *Ice Bound* in *School Library Journal,* described it as "an engrossing story in an unforgiving setting . . . a story of growth, endurance, teamwork, and survival." Jo Ann Rosenfeld, writing in the *British Medical Journal,* said, "It is an adventure tale in the true sense as Jerri Nielsen travels through more than just geography and finds herself at the end." Stephanie Papa, writing in *Library Journal,* remarked, "No matter what the passage, Nielsen mesmerizes readers as she carries them along for a ride of a lifetime."

Nielsen, cancer-free in 2002, planned to start a hospital in Africa or work in emergency rooms in Anchorage, Alaska.

BIOGRAPHICAL AND CRITICAL SOURCES:

PERIODICALS

British Medical Journal, April 14, 2001, Jo Ann Rosenfeld, review of *Ice Bound: A Doctor's Incredible Battle for Survival at the South Pole,* p. 935.

Entertainment Weekly, February 18, 2000, p. 79; February 23, 2001, p.156
Geographical, March, 2001, "Sub-zero Heroine," p. 114.
Library Journal, April 1, 2001, Stephanie Papa, review of *Ice Bound,* p. 122; June 1, 2001, Gloria Maxwell, review of *Ice Bound: A Doctor's Incredible Battle for Survival at the South Pole,* p. 250.
MacLean's, March 19, 2001, "Fighting for Her Life," p. 47.
National Post, February 24, 2001, Isabel Vincent, "Very Dramatic. And Very Cold," p. B12.
Newsweek International, October 18, 1999, Anna Kuchment, "At Last, a Long Winter's End," p. 5; May 14, 2001, Vibhuti Patel, "Facing Death on the Ice," p. 60.
New York Times Book Review, February 4, 2001, Katherine Bouton, "The Doctor Who Came in from the Cold," p. 7.
Oprah, February, 2001, Cathleen Medwick, "Phenomenal Woman: Dr. Jerri Nielsen."
People Weekly, November 1, 1999, Bill Hewitt, "Prison at Earth's End: Confronted with the Specter of Cancer, a Brave Woman Comes Home from the Pole," p. 132.
Publishers Weekly, February 7, 2000, John F. Baker, "Antarctic Rescue Story Bought"; January 8, 2001, review of *Ice Bound: A Doctor's Incredible Battle for Survival at the South Pole,* p. 64; February 5, 2001, "Bound for Success" p. 24; May 7, 2001, review of *Ice Bound,* p. 49.
R & D, February 7, 2000, Jenny Gavacs and Victoria K. Sicaras, "Camera Brings Digital Imaging to the South Pole" p. 190.
School Library Journal, May, 2001, Jane S. Drabkin, review of *Ice Bound: A Doctor's Incredible Battle for Survival at the South Pole,* p. 178.
United Press International, Pamela Hess, "National Guard Poised for Antarctic Rescue."
U.S. News & World Report, February 12, 2001, Rachel K. Sobel, "She's a South Pole Survivor," p. 16.

OTHER

Nationwide Speakers Bureau, Inc., Web site, http://www.nationwidespeakers.com/ (September 15, 2001).
New York Daily News Web site, http://www.nydailynews.com/ "South Pole Doctor Who Beat Cancer Says She Feels All Alone,"(January 10, 2001).

PR Newswire, http://tbutton.prnewswire.com/ (May 9, 2001).

Tribune News Service, http://www.philly.com/ (March 28, 2001).*

*   *   *

NIELSEN, Leslie 1926-

PERSONAL: Born February 11, 1926, in Regina, Saskatchewan, Canada; son of Ingvard (an officer of the Royal Canadian Mounted Police) and Maybelle Nielsen; nephew of Jean Hersholt (an actor); married Monica Boyar, 1950 (marriage ended, 1955); married Barbaree Eari (marriage ended); married Alisande Ullman, 1958 (marriage ended, 1973); married Brooks Oliver, 1981 (divorced, 1983); children: (third marriage) two. *Education:* Attended Victoria High School, Edmonton, Alberta; attended Academy of Radio Arts, Toronto, Ontario; studied at Neighborhood Playhouse, New York, NY.

ADDRESSES: Agent—Bresler, Kelly, and Associates, 11500 West Olympic Blvd., Suite 510, Los Angeles, CA 90064-1529.

CAREER: Actor, producer, and writer. Worked as a radio announcer in Canada; appeared in television commercials, including those for British Columbia Lottery Corp., 1997, and Better Hearing Institute, 1998.

Film appearances include *The Battle of Gettysburg,* Metro-Goldwyn-Mayer, 1955; *Forbidden Planet,* Metro-Goldwyn-Mayer, 1956; *The Opposite Sex,* Metro-Goldwyn-Mayer, 1956; *Ransom!,* Metro-Goldwyn-Mayer, 1956; *The Vagabond King,* Paramount, 1956; *Hot Summer Night,* Metro-Goldwyn-Mayer, 1957; *Tammy and the Bachelor,* Universal, 1957; *The Sheepman,* Metro-Goldwyn-Mayer, 1958; *Night Train to Paris,* Twentieth Century-Fox, 1964; *Dark Intruder,* Universal, 1965; *Harlow,* Paramount, 1965; *Beau Geste,* Universal, 1966; *The Plainsman,* Universal, 1966; *Counterpoint,* Universal, 1967; *Gunfight in Abilene,* Universal, 1967; *The Reluctant Astronaut,* Universal, 1967; *Rosie!,* Universal, 1967; *Dayton's Devils,* Cue, 1968; *How to Steal the World,* Metro-Goldwyn-Mayer, 1968; *Change of Mind,* Cinerama, 1969; *ADA,* 1969; *How to Commit Marriage,*

Cinerama, 1969; *The Resurrection of Zachary Wheeler,* Vidtronics, 1971; *The Poseidon Adventure,* Twentieth Century-Fox, 1972; *And Millions Will Die,* Columbia, 1973; *Threshold: The Blue Angels Experience,* Ambassador, 1975; *Project: Kill,* Stirling Gold, 1976; *Day of the Animals,* Film Ventures, 1977; *Viva Knievel!,* Warner Bros., 1977; *Sixth and Main,* National Cinema, 1977; *Grand Jury,* 1977; *The Amsterdam Kill,* Columbia, 1978; *City on Fire,* Avco-Embassy, 1979; *Airplane!,* Paramount, 1980; *Prom Night,* Avco-Embassy, 1980; *The Creature Wasn't Nice,* Creature Features, 1981; "Something to Tide You Over," *Creepshow,* Warner Bros., 1982; *Wrong Is Right,* Columbia, 1982; *Foxfire Light,* 1982; *Airplane II: The Sequel,* 1982; *The Home Front,* 1984; *The Patriot,* Crown International, 1986; *Soul Man,* New World, 1986; *Home Is Where the Hart Is,* Atlantic, 1987; *Nuts,* Warner Bros., 1987; *The Naked Gun: From the Files of Police Squad!,* Paramount, 1988; *Dangerous Curves,* Lightning Pictures, 1988; *Repossessed,* New Line Cinema, 1990; *All I Want for Christmas,* Paramount, 1991; *The Naked Gun 2-1/2: The Smell of Fear,* Paramount, 1991; *Surf Ninjas,* New Line Cinema, 1993; *Naked Gun 33 1/3: The Final Insult,* Paramount, 1994; *Digger,* Paramount Home Video, 1994; *S.P.Q.R. 2000 e 1/2 anni fa,* Laurenfilm, 1994; *Dracula: Dead and Loving It,* Sony Pictures Entertainment, 1995; *Rent-a-Kid,* Republic Pictures, 1995; *Spy Hard,* Buena Vista, 1996; *Mister Magoo,* Buena Vista, 1997; *Family Plan,* Initial Entertainment Group, 1997; *Wrongfully Accused,* Warner Bros., 1998; *Camouflage,* Hope Street Entertainment, 1999; *Pirates: 3D Show,* 1999; *2001: A Space Travesty,* 2000; *Kevin of the North,* CLT-UFA International, 2000; and *Men with Brooms,* 2002. Film work includes (producer) *Repossessed,* New Line Cinema, 1990; and (executive producer) *Spy Hard,* Buena Vista, 1996; (executive producer) *2001: A Space Travesty,* 2000.

Appearances on television pilots include *Hawaii Five-0,* CBS, 1968; *Deadlock,* NBC, 1969; *Trial Run,* NBC, 1969; *Incident in San Francisco,* ABC, 1971; *They Call It Murder,* NBC, 1971; *Amanda Fallon,* NBC, 1973; *The Letters,* ABC, 1973; *S.W.A.T., Parts 1 and 2,* 1975; *Institute for Revenge,* NBC, 1979; *Happiness Is a Warm Clue,* NBC, 1979; *Twilight Theater II,* NBC, 1982; *Prime Times,* NBC, 1983; and *Blade in Hong Kong,* CBS, 1985.

Appearances on episodic television include *Magnavox Theater,* CBS, 1950; "Hannah," *Actors' Studio,* CBS, 1950; "Roman Holiday," *Suspense,* CBS, 1950; "The

Survivors," *Studio One*, CBS, 1950; "The Second Class Passenger," *Suspense*, CBS, 1950; "Never Murder Your Grandfather," *Stage 13*, CBS, 1950; "Sentence of Death," *The Trap*, CBS, 1950; "The Luck of Guldeford," *Ford Theater*, NBC, 1950; "Zone Four," *Studio One*, CBS, 1950; "A Child Is Crying," *Lights Out*, NBC, 1950; "Home for Christmas," *The Web*, CBS, 1950; "Prescription for Death," *The Clock*, CBS, 1950; "The Touch of a Stranger," *Philco Television Playhouse*, NBC, 1950; "Spectre of Alexander Wolff," *Studio One*, CBS, 1950; "The Last Cruise," *Studio One*, CBS, 1950; "The Brush Off," *Suspense*, CBS, 1950; "The Philadelphia Story," *Robert Montgomery Presents the Lucky Strike Hour*, NBC, 1950; "The Best Years," *Ford Theater*, NBC, 1951; "You Killed Elizabeth," *The Web*, CBS, 1951; "The Devil Takes a Bride," *Sure As Fate*, CBS, 1951; "The Magic Wire," *Starlight Theater*, CBS, 1951; "The Foggy Night Visitor," *Suspense*, CBS, 1951; "The Lost Will of Dr. Kant" and "Mrs. Manifold," *Lights Out*, NBC, 1951; "Lover's Leap," *Armstrong Circle Theater*, NBC, 1951; "Death Sabre," *Suspense*, CBS, 1951; "Flame-Out," *Armstrong Circle Theater*, NBC, 1951; "October Story," *Goodyear Playhouse*, NBC, 1951; "The Sisters," *Philco Television Playhouse*, NBC, 1951; "After the Fact," *The Web*, CBS, 1952; "20,000 Leagues under the Sea," "Black Planet" and "Appointment to Mars," *Tales of Tomorrow*, ABC, 1952; "Crown of Shadows," *Goodyear Playhouse*, NBC, 1952; "The Man in 308," *Armstrong Circle Theater*, NBC, 1952; "My Eyes Have a Cold Nose," *Workshop*, syndicated, 1952; *Crime Syndicated*, CBS, 1952; "For Worse," *Armstrong Circle Theater*, NBC, 1952; "Death Trap," *Lights Out*, NBC, 1952; "A Kiss for Cinderella," *Kraft Television Theatre*, NBC, 1952; "The Diary," *Short, Short Drama*, NBC, 1952; "Boomerang," *Danger*, CBS, 1952; "Another Chance," *Tales of Tomorrow*, ABC, 1953; "The Rumor," *Goodyear Playhouse*, NBC, 1953; "Second-hand Sofa," *Robert Montgomery Presents*, NBC, 1953; "Candle in a Bottle," *Armstrong Circle Theater*, NBC, 1953; "The Missing Night," *Danger*, CBS, 1953; "A Story to Whisper" and "The Beard," *Armstrong Circle Theater*, NBC, 1953; "Twenty-four Men to a Plane," *Medallion Theatre*, CBS, 1953; "The Psychological Error," *Danger*, CBS, 1953; "The Ohio Prison Story" and "The Case of the Yankee II," *The Man behind the Badge*, CBS, 1954; "Dark Possession," "A Guest at the Embassy," "The Man Who Owned the Town," and "Castles in Spain," *Studio One*, CBS, 1954; "The Scarlet Letter," *Kraft Television Theatre*, NBC, 1954; "The Good Morrow," *Love Story*, The Du Mont Network, 1954; "End of a Mission," *Robert Montgom-*

ery Presents, NBC, 1954; "The Right Hand Man," *Playhouse 90*, CBS, 1958; "The Two Million Dollar Defense," *Alfred Hitchcock Presents*, CBS, 1958; "The Velvet Alley," *Playhouse 90*, CBS, 1959; "Nora," *General Electric Theater*, CBS, 1959; "Incident below the Brazos," *Rawhide*, CBS, 1959; "Any Friend of Julie's," *The Alcoa Hour/Alcoa Theatre*, ABC, 1959; "The Swamp Fox" and "The Swamp Fox: Brother against Brother," *Walt Disney Presents*, ABC, 1959; "The Swamp Fox: Tory Vengeance," "The Swamp Fox: Day of Reckoning," "The Swamp Fox: Redcoat Strategy" and "The Swamp Fox: A Case of Treason," *Walt Disney Presents*, ABC, 1960; "Three Thousand Suspects," *The Untouchables*, ABC, 1960; "Total Recall," *Moment of Fear*, NBC, 1960; "The Twisted Image," *Thriller*, NBC, 1960; "Journal of Hope," *General Electric Theater*, CBS, 1960; "Down the Long Night," *Naked City*, ABC, 1960; "The Jeremy Dow Story," *Wagon Train*, NBC, 1960; "A Fury Slinging Flame," *Route 66*, CBS, 1960; "The Swamp Fox: A Woman's Courage" and "The Swamp Fox: Horses for Greene," *Walt Disney Presents*, ABC, 1961; "Willy's Millionaire," *The Islanders*, ABC, 1961; "Ambition," *Alfred Hitchcock Presents*, NBC, 1961; "Poor Little Kangaroo Rat," *Route 66*, CBS, 1962; "The Long Ride Home," *The Virginian*, NBC, 1962; "He Thought He Saw an Albatross," *Ben Casey*, ABC, 1963; "Exercise in a Shark Tank," *Channing*, ABC, 1963; "One Step Down," *Kraft Suspense Theatre*, NBC, 1963; "The Glass Tightrope," *The Fugitive*, ABC, 1963; "The Magic Shop," *Alfred Hitchcock Presents*, CBS, 1964; "Survival," *The Defenders*, CBS, 1964; "Tiger Left, Tiger Right," *The Fugitive*, ABC, 1964; "The Warrior," *The Nurses*, CBS, 1964; "Ryker," *The Virginian*, NBC, 1964; "The Brian Conlin Story," *Wagon Train*, ABC, 1964; "Mountain of the Dead," *Daniel Boone*, NBC, 1964; "Death on Wheels," *The Defenders*, CBS, 1965; "Do You Trust Our Doctor?" "She Loves Me, She Loves Me Not," "The Life Machine," "Toast the Golden Couple," "Wives and Losers," "Welcome Home, Dear Anna," "A Little Child Shall Lead Them," "Hour of Decision" and "Aftermath," *Dr. Kildare*, NBC, 1965; "The Creature," *Voyage to the Bottom of the Sea*, ABC, 1965; "The Green Felt Jungle," *Kraft Suspense Theatre*, NBC, 1965; "A War of Nerves," *Ben Casey*, ABC, 1965; "The Kingdom of McComb," *The Loner*, CBS, 1965; "Sink U-116," *Convoy*, NBC, 1965; "The Night of the Double-edged Knife," *The Wild, Wild West*, CBS, 1965; "The Laramie Road," *The Virginian*, NBC, 1965; "Pound of Flesh," *The F.B.I.*, ABC, 1965; "When Hell Froze" and "Guilty or Not Guilty," *Bob Hope Presents the Chrysler Theater*, NBC, 1966; "Steve, Boy Bohemian," *The Farmer's*

Daughter, ABC, 1966; "No Drums, No Trumpets," *The Virginian,* NBC, 1966; "The Last Safari," *Run for Your Life,* NBC, 1966; "Code Name Heraclitus," *Bob Hope Presents the Chrysler Theater,* NBC, 1967; "A Thief Is a Thief Is a Thief," *It Takes a Thief,* ABC, 1967; "The Unseen Wound," *Bonanza,* NBC, 1967; "The Deep End," *Judd, for the Defense,* ABC, 1967; "The Beast That Walks like a Man," *Cimarron Strip,* CBS, 1967; "The Fortress," *The Virginian,* NBC, 1967; "The Seven Wonders of the World Affair," *The Man from U.N.C.L.E.,* NBC, 1968; "Magnificent Seven," *It Takes a Thief,* ABC, 1968; "Wild Heart," *The World of Disney,* NBC, 1968; "Time of the Jackals," *Gunsmoke,* CBS, 1969; "Town of No Exit," *The Big Valley,* ABC, 1969; "The Long Ride Home," *The Virginian,* NBC, 1969; "The Other Kind of Spy," *The Name of the Game,* NBC, 1970; "Phantom of What Opera?" *Night Gallery,* NBC, 1971; *Monty Nash,* syndicated, 1971; "A Question of Fear," *Night Gallery,* NBC, 1971; "Silent Target," *Sarge,* NBC, 1971; *Bearcats,* CBS, 1971; "Conspiracy," *Medical Center,* CBS, 1971; "Lady in Waiting," *Columbo,* NBC, 1971; "Deal with the Devil," *The Mod Squad,* ABC, 1972; "Last Target," *Assignment: Vienna,* ABC, 1972; "The Ringbanger," *M*A*S*H,* CBS, 1973; "Legion of the Lost" and "Before I Die," *The Streets of San Francisco,* ABC, 1973; "The Obituary," *The Evil Touch,* syndicated, 1973; "Fool's Gold," *The F.B.I.,* ABC, 1973; "The Killing Defense," *Barnaby Jones,* CBS, 1973; "Valley of the Damned," *Cannon,* CBS, 1973; "The Voyage," *The Evil Touch,* syndicated, 1974; "One Last Shot," *The Streets of San Francisco,* ABC, 1974; "We Hang Our Own," *Hawaii Five-0,* CBS, 1974; "Jacknife," *Manhunter,* CBS, 1974; "The Man Who Couldn't Forget," *Cannon,* CBS, 1974; "The Over-the-Hill Blues," *Ironside,* NBC, 1974; "Loser Takes All," *Kojak,* CBS, 1974; "S.W.A.T.," *The Rookies,* ABC, 1975; "Barbary House," "Flight to Orion," "The Brothers Cain" and "Full Circle," *Kung Fu,* ABC, 1975; *Lucas Tanner,* NBC, 1975; "The Outlaw Cats of Colossal Cave," *The World of Disney,* NBC, 1975; "The Man Who Died Twice," *Cannon,* CBS, 1975; "Identity Crisis," *Columbo,* NBC, 1975; "The Slave Ship," *Swiss Family Robinson,* ABC, 1975; "The Running Man," *S.W.A.T.,* ABC, 1976; "Dear Beverly," *The Love Boat,* ABC, 1977; "The Search," *Lucan,* ABC, 1977; "The Class Underachiever," *What Really Happened to the Class of '65? NBC,* 1978; "A Selfless Love," *The Love Boat,* ABC, 1978; "Salem," *Fantasy Island,* ABC, 1978; "Treasure," *Fantasy Island,* ABC, 1979; "Doubtful Target," *Vega$,* ABC, 1979; *The Love Boat,* ABC, 1979; *Fantasy Island,* ABC, 1980; *The Chisholms,* CBS, 1980; "Romiet and Julio," *The Littlest Hobo,*

syndicated, 1980; *Aloha Paradise,* ABC, 1981; "Crossroads," *Hotel,* ABC, 1985; "My Johnny Lies over the Ocean," *Murder, She Wrote,* CBS, 1985; "Aftershocks," *Finder of Lost Loves,* ABC, 1985; "Marionettes, Inc.," *The Ray Bradbury Theater,* HBO, 1985; "A Letter to the President," *227,* NBC, 1985; "Dead Man's Gold," *Murder, She Wrote,* CBS, 1986; "Gift of Life," *Highway to Heaven,* NBC, 1987; "Just Mona and Me," *Who's the Boss,* ABC, 1987; "Fatal Confession," *Father Dowling Mysteries,* NBC, 1987; "Marry Me, Mona," *Who's the Boss,* ABC, 1988; *The Comedy Company,* 1988; *Saturday Night Live,* NBC, 1989; "One Flew out of the Cuckoo's Nest," Parts 1 and 2, *The Golden Girls,* NBC, 1992; "God, Girls, and Herman," *Herman's Head,* Fox, 1993; *Someone Like Me,* NBC, 1994; "Manhunt," *Due South,* CBS, 1994; "All the Queen's Horses," *Due South,* CBS, 1996; *Kate and Orbie,* PBS, 1996; *Golf 2000 with Peter Jacobsen,* syndicated, 1998; "Call of the Wild," Parts 1 and 2, *Due South,* CBS, 1999; *So Graham Norton,* 2000; and "Leslie Nielsen: Naked Laughter," *Biography,* Arts and Entertainment, 2000. Also appeared in "Ages of Man," "Bo 'n' Sam," and "Families," all episodes of *The Love Boat,* ABC; appeared in *Justice,* NBC; and *Pulitzer Prize Playhouse,* ABC.

Appearances on TV series include *The New Breed,* ABC, 1961-62; *Channing,* ABC, 1963-64; *Peyton Place,* ABC, 1965; *The Bold Ones: The Law Enforcers,* NBC, 1969; *The Bold Ones: The Lawyers,* NBC, 1969-70; *Bracken's World,* NBC, 1969-71; *The Explorers,* syndicated, 1972; *Police Squad! ABC,* 1982; *Shaping Up,* ABC, 1984; and *Pumper Pups,* 2000. Appearances on TV miniseries include *Backstairs at the White House,* NBC, 1979, and *Race for the Bomb,* CBC, 1986.

Appearances on TV movies include *See How They Run,* NBC, 1964; *Shadow over Elveron,* NBC, 1968; *Companions in Nightmare,* NBC, 1968; *The Aquarians,* NBC, 1970; *Hauser's Memory,* NBC, 1970; *Night Slaves,* ABC, 1970; *The Invaders,* NBC, 1970; *Snatched,* ABC, 1973; *Can Ellen Be Saved?,* ABC, 1974; *Brinks: The Great Robbery,* CBS, 1976; *Little Mo,* NBC, 1978; *Riel,* CBC, 1979; *OHMS,* CBS, 1980; *Cave-In!,* NBC, 1983; *The Night the Bridge Fell Down,* NBC, 1983; *Reckless Disregard,* Showtime, 1985; *Striker's Mountain,* 1985; *Nightstick,* 1987; *Chance of a Lifetime,* NBC, 1991; *Harvey,* CBS, 1996; and "Safety Patrol," *The Wonderful World of Disney,* ABC, 1998. Also appeared in *Death of a Salesman.*

Appearances on TV specials include *Murder among Friends,* Showtime, 1982; *Cinemax Comedy Experiment: The Canadian Conspiracy,* Cinemax, 1986; *Super Bloopers and New Practical Jokes,* NBC, 1989; *People Magazine on TV,* CBS, 1989; *The 14th Annual Circus of the Stars,* CBS, 1989; *Starathon '90 Weekend with the Stars for Cerebral Palsy,* syndicated, 1990; *National Lampoon's Comedy Playoffs,* Showtime, 1990; *Naked Gun 2-1/2: Looking down the Barrel of Comedy,* HBO, 1991; *All New Circus of the Stars and Side Show,* CBS, 1991; *ABC Presents Krofft Late Night,* ABC, 1991; *The Unknown Marx Brothers,* The Disney Channel, 1993; *Masters of Illusion: The Wizards of Special Effects,* 1994; *Bob Hope's Birthday Memories,* NBC, 1994; *Circus of the Stars Goes to Disneyland,* CBS, 1994; *ABC's World's Funniest Commercials,* ABC, 1994; *Mr. Willowby's Christmas Tree,* CBS, 1995; *Television's Comedy Classics,* CBS, 1997; and *Savage Garden,* 1997. Also narrator of National Geographic Society specials.

Appearances in awards presentation ceremonies include *The Third Annual American Comedy Awards,* ABC, 1989; *The Third Annual International Rock Awards,* ABC, 1991; *Cybermania '94: The Ultimate Gamer Awards,* 1994; *The Twenty-second Annual People's Choice Awards,* 1996. Other television appearances include *The Albertans,* 1979; *The Railway Dragon,* 1988; *Memories of M*A*S*H,* 1991; and *Santa Who?,* 2000.

Stage appearances include *Darrow,* U.S. cities, 1979, and *Clarence Darrow: A One Man Play,* Canadian cities, 1996. Recordings include the videos *Leslie Nielsen's Bad Golf Made Easier,* 1993; *Bad Golf My Way,* 1994; and *Leslie Nielsen's Stupid Little Golf Video,* 1998. Sound recordings include *The Naked Truth* (see also below), 1993. Also appeared in Muppets music video "She Drives Me Crazy."

AWARDS, HONORS: Emmy Award nomination, outstanding lead actor in a comedy series, 1981, for *Police Squad!;* Special Award, male comedy star of the year, ShoWest Convention, National Association of Theatre Owners, 1989; shared MTV Movie Award nomination, best kiss (with Priscilla Presley), 1991, for *Naked Gun 2-1/2: The Smell of Fear.*

WRITINGS:

Leslie Nielsen: The Naked Truth, Pocket Books (New York, NY), 1993.
(With Henry Beard) *Leslie Nielsen's Stupid Little Golf Book* (humor), Doubleday (New York, NY), 1995.
Bad Golf My Way (humor), Doubleday (New York, NY), 1996.
(With Alan Shearman) *2001: A Space Travesty* (screenplay), Columbia TriStar, 2000.

SIDELIGHTS: Once a "serious" actor with countless screen credits to his name, Leslie Nielsen changed his image entirely with an appearance in the 1980 spoof *Airplane.* As the producers guessed, and the public soon realized, there was something inherently hilarious about the idea of an ultra-respectable-looking, silver-haired senior white male—the type who might be a bank president or a senator—making an absolute fool of himself.

Since that time, Nielsen has transformed that role into a full-scale persona, reflected in his appearances as Lt. Frank Drebin in the TV series *Police Squad* and the highly successful *Naked Gun* film spinoffs, as well as in several books. In the first of these, a 1993 mock autobiography called *The Naked Truth,* "Nielsen's consistently high obnoxiousness level and relentless pace keep things moving," according to a reviewer in *Publishers Weekly.*

Nielsen followed *The Naked Truth* with two send-ups of the traditional golf instruction manual, *Leslie Nielsen's Stupid Little Golf Book* and *Bad Golf My Way.* (The title of the latter is a parody of golfing legend Jack Nicklaus's *Golf My Way.*) Wrote Alex Tresniowski in *People Weekly,* "Most weekend golfers own at least a dozen instruction books, collected as gifts and usually barely skimmed," but *Bad Golf My Way*—a spinoff of a humorous instructional video— deserved more attention. Among the gems offered by Nielsen and coauthor Henry Beard, formerly of the *National Lampoon,* is the idea of "picking up any ball within six feet of the hole," according to a reviewer in *Publishers Weekly,* "then arguing that it was yours."

In addition to his books, Nielsen cowrote the screenplay of *2001: A Space Travesty,* in which he stars as a U.S. marshal sent to the planet Vegan to investigate a conspiracy to clone President Bill Clinton. "I had a tendency in my early days," Nielsen told the *Orange County Register,* "and I see it more and more with today's young actors and actresses, to strive toward something of significance. It's a feeling that you have something important to do. That you have a calling. That you're the Second Coming. That you need only to walk out on a stage for people to realize you are truly a genius. I think back to that attitude I used to have and I cringe. I know now that acting is acting, whether it's comedy or drama. It's all the same. Playing Frank Drebin is no different than playing Hamlet, and that's the truth."

BIOGRAPHICAL AND CRITICAL SOURCES:

PERIODICALS

Library Journal, April 15, 1995, Jim Paxman, review of *Leslie Nielsen's Stupid Little Golf Book,* p. 76.

Modern Maturity, July-August, 1998, Carmine De-Sena, "Ad Lib" (interview), p. 18.

New York Times, August 25, 1993, Richard Sandomir, "An Actor Revels in Silly Films and (Oops!) Noises," p. B3.

Orange County Register (Orange County, California), March 17, 1994, Barry Koltnow, "Leslie Nielsen Doesn't Miss Being Taken Seriously in Film."

People, July 17, 1996, Alex Tresniowski, review of *Bad Golf My Way,* pp. 32-33; September 7, 1998, "Dumb and Getting Dumber" (interview), p. 144.

Publishers Weekly, June 5, 1993, review of *The Naked Truth* (audio), p. 35; February 27, 1995, review of *Leslie Nielsen's Stupid Little Golf Book,* p. 93; May 6, 1996, review of *Bad Golf My Way,* p. 63.

Saturday Night, May, 1993, Brian Preston, "The Perfect Idiot" (interview), pp. 32-34.

Time, December 8, 1997, Joel Stein, "Q&A: Leslie Nielsen," p. 111.

Washington Post, June 28, 1991, Tom Shales, "Leslie Nielsen: The Insane Story," p. D1.*

*   *   *

NORRIS, Pamela

PERSONAL: Female.

ADDRESSES: Agent—c/o New York University Press, 838 Broadway, 3rd Floor, New York, NY 10003-4812.

CAREER: Writer. Teacher of English in London, Paris, and Zagreb, Croatia.

WRITINGS:

(Editor) *Sound the Deep Waters: Women's Romantic Poetry in the Victorian Age,* Little, Brown (Boston, MA), 1992.

(Editor) *Come Live with Me and Be My Love,* Little, Brown (Boston, MA), 1993.

(Editor) Jane Austen, *Pride and Prejudice,* C. E. Tuttle (Rutland, VT), 1993.

(Editor) *Between the Apple-Blossom and the Water: Women Writing about Gardens,* Little, Brown (Boston, MA), 1994.

(Editor) *Through the Looking Glass Window Shines the Sun: An Anthology of Medieval Poetry and Prose,* Little, Brown (Boston, MA), 1995.

Eve: A Biography, New York University Press (New York, NY), 1999, published as *The Story of Eve,* Picador (London, England), 1999.

SIDELIGHTS: Pamela Norris has edited works primarily by women, and she has also written a celebrated book on the biblical Eve. Norris's first editorial achievement resulted in the poetry compilation *Sound the Deep Waters: Women's Romantic Poetry in the Victorian Age.* This 1992 collection features poems by nineteenth-century American and British women poets, including Elizabeth Barrett Browning, Emily Dickinson, Ella Wheeler Wilcox, and Emily and Anne Brontë. The tone of the poems ranges from lighthearted to sad. Also included among the verses are fifty-two beautiful paintings of classical figures by Victorian men and women. The paintings of Dante Gabriel Rossetti appear with his sister's and wife's poetry. A reviewer for *Publishers Weekly* stated, "Romantic souls too shy to write a sentimental line to their loved ones on Valentine's Day may choose to proffer their compact and marvelously illustrated treasury instead."

Following *Sound the Deep Waters,* Norris edited works by Jane Austen, including Austen's classic novel *Pride and Prejudice,* as well as medieval poetry and prose and writings by women about gardens. Norris's book on Eve, which was published in the United States in 1999 as *Eve: A Biography,* attempts to explain the myths that surround Eve. Did Eve help or destroy humankind when she made the fateful decision to take a bite of the forbidden apple that led her and Adam to be ejected from the Garden of Eden into a harsh life filled with pain and death, but also with knowledge and independence? Was she tempted by Satan in the form of the snake or was it Eve's own decision to defy the word of God? Norris addresses these questions and discusses the connection between women and snakes as it became a common practice in the Middle Ages to illustrate a woman's head on a serpent's body. She also suggests that the story of Adam and Eve is hardly unique; the basic elements of their story are found in many European stories. She also compares Adam and Eve to an old Sierra Leone story about a couple named Adamu and Ifu. In this story, Ifu is seduced by a long, red, spotted snake.

In *Eve: A Biography* Norris also explores the mysterious woman mentioned in the first chapter of Genesis. This woman, Lilith, was Adam's first wife who left Adam and went on to create notoriety when she involved herself with a group of demons in the Red Sea. Eve differs from Lilith in that Eve was created from Adam's rib and her legend goes on to affect the world like no other. After her departure from the Garden of Eden, Eve disappears from the scriptures and is replaced by her daughters, including the wife of Noah, Sarah, Rebekah, Rachel, and Hannah. When Eve's name is mentioned later, she has become a symbol of everything that is considered wrong with women. She is also blamed for all the suffering of men. This mistaken belief was clearly seen in the writings of classical authors who treated evil women as typical of their sex and good women as the exceptions. Norris disproves these beliefs, but she does not blame Adam or men in general for their treatment of women. Instead, she continues to focus on the theme that women should not be ashamed to be the daughters of Eve. *Times Literary Supplement* contributor Helen Cooper notes, "*The Story of Eve* charts the history-long struggle and symbiosis between those two inseparable myths: woman the bringer of death; woman the origin of life."

BIOGRAPHICAL AND CRITICAL SOURCES:

PERIODICALS

Booklist, February 1, 1992, Ray Olson, review of *Sound the Deep Waters: Women's Romantic Poetry in the Victorian Age,* p. 1005.
Economist, December 12, 1998, "Adam and Eve: She Started It," p. 6.
Publishers Weekly, January 1, 1992, review of *Sound the Deep Waters,* p. 45.
Times Literary Supplement, March 19, 1999, Helen Cooper, "A Glimpse of Paradise," pp. 3-4.*

*   *   *

NOSSITER, Adam 1961-

PERSONAL: Born 1961; married. *Education:* Graduated from Harvard University (French history).

ADDRESSES: Home—2828 Coliseum St., New Orleans, LA 70115.

CAREER: Journalist. *Atlanta Journal-Constitution,* Atlanta, GA, journalist; *New York Times,* New York, NY, journalist, 1995-97.

WRITINGS:

Of Long Memory: Mississippi and the Murder of Medgar Evers, Addison-Wesley (Reading, MA), 1994.
The Algeria Hotel: France, Memory, and the Second World War, Houghton Mifflin (Boston, MA), 2001.

SIDELIGHTS: Adam Nossiter grew up in Paris, where his father was stationed as a correspondent. He returned to America and studied French history at Harvard, then worked as a reporter for the *Atlanta Journal-Constitution.* In 1991, he left his job there to spend time writing his first book.

Of Long Memory: Mississippi and the Murder of Medgar Evers examines the retrial of the murderer of civil rights activist Medgar Evers. In December of 1990, Byron de la Beckwith was indicted for the 1963 murder; in 1964, he had been released after two hung juries failed to convict him, even though the evidence was overwhelming that he had committed the crime. Beckwith escaped because at that time in Mississippi, racist attitudes ensured that no white person would be convicted for the murder of an African American. However, times changed, and at the retrial, justice was done. The book examines the careers of Evers, Beckwith, Mississippi governor Bill Waller, district attorney

Bobby DeLaughter, Medgar Evers's brother Charles, and the white supremacist movement in Mississippi over the three decades between the trials. In the *Washington Post Book World,* Marilyn Chandler McEntyre wrote, "Each story provides a different angle of vision on America's high tolerance for bigotry." A *Kirkus Reviews* writer called Nossiter "a perceptive, observant journalist," and described the book as "well-researched, fluidly written, and thoughtful."

Of Loving Memory helped Nossiter get a job as a journalist with the *New York Times,* where he worked for two years before beginning his next book, *The Algeria Hotel: France, Memory, and the Second World War.* Over the next three years, he traveled to Bordeaux, Vichy, and Paris, researching events that occured there during World War II. Vichy was the capital of Marshal Philippe Petain's government, which collaborated with the Nazis during that war, but this unsavory history has largely been swept under the rug and ignored by its citizens and historical society alike. Rather, citizens selectively remember how many Jewish people they saved from the Nazis, or remember small details rather than the whole. Regarding a day of mass hangings, people who were present recall German officers gorging on fresh cherries or the accordion music that played throughout the executions rather than the executions themselves. The historical society focuses on architecture from pre-Nazi eras; in the whole town, there is only one little-known plaque acknowledging any of the unsavory events of the collaborationist government era.

Before writing his book, Nossiter interviewed French people from all parts of society about the region's history and the collaborationist government. The book first examines the trial of Maurice Papon, who was charged with crimes against humanity for assisting in the deportation of Jews from Vichy to Nazi concentration camps. Next, it explores the town of Vichy and its collective attempt to forget and deny the era; and third, it discusses the execution of almost one hundred men in the town of Tulle by German troops. Nossiter examines the rationalizations and justifications that French people have used to ignore their participation in the Nazi death machine. In *Newsweek International,* Christopher Dickey wrote, "This is not a polemic, nor a dry analytic history. It's an elegantly written and deeply troubling portrait of humanity touched by enormous inhumanity." Lucy Hughes-Hallett wrote in the *Sunday Times,* "Nossiter's book is a study of the way that memories, individual and collective, accom-

modate intolerable historical fact." In the *Daily Telegraph,* Allan Massie wrote, "Memory is really Nossiter's forte: what people choose to recall and what to forget, what they are unable to recall or to forget."

BIOGRAPHICAL AND CRITICAL SOURCES:

PERIODICALS

Booklist, June 1, 2001, Jay Freeman, review of *The Algeria Hotel: France, Memory, and the Second World War,* p. 1832.
Business and Society Review, summer, 1994, review of *Of Long Memory: Mississippi and the Murder of Medgar Evans,* p 76.
Daily Telegraph (London, England), August 18, 2001, Allan Massie, "What Do You Do When You Lose a War?"
Kirkus Reviews, April 1, 1994, review of *Of Long Memory,* p. 463.
Library Journal, June 1, 1994, p. 130; June 1, 2001, Michael F. Russo, review of *The Algeria Hotel,* p. 186.
New York Times, August 12, 2001, "France's Dark Years," p. 4; August 1, 2002, p. B7.
New York Times Book Review, July 24, 1994, p. 16; July 15, 2001, Christopher Caldwell, "France's Native Disgrace," p. 9.
Newsweek International, August 27, 2001, Christopher Dickey, "Recollecting World War II," p. 50.
Publishers Weekly, April 11, 1994, review of *Of Long Memory,* p. 46; June 25, 2001, review of *The Algeria Hotel,* p. 64.
San Francisco Chronicle, August 26, 2001, John McMurtrie, "France's Painful Past," p. 80.
Sunday Times (London, England), August 19, 2001, Lucy Hughes-Hallett, "Learning to Live with Lessons of Collaboration," p. 40.
Washington Post, July 8, 2001, Susie Linfield, "What Lies Beneath," p. T04.
Washington Post Book World, July 10, 1994, review of *Of Long Memory,* p. 11.

OTHER

Sudouest http://www.sudouest.com/ (February 6, 2003), Dominique Richard, "Regard d'un journaliste americain."
Welcome to the Best of New Orleans!, http://www/bestofneworleans.com/ (December 2, 2001), Jason Berry, "A&E Feature: Collaborative Effort."*

O

o huigin, sean 1942-

PERSONAL: Born 1942, in Brampton, Canada.

ADDRESSES: Agent—c/o Author Mail, Black Moss Press, 2450 Byng Rd., Windsor, Ontario, Canada M8W 3E8.

CAREER: Poet and writer.

AWARDS, HONORS: Canada Council Children's Literature Prize, 1983, for *The Ghost Horse of the Mounties.*

WRITINGS:

Poe-Tree: A Simple Introduction to Experimental Poetry, Black Moss Press (Windsor, Ontario, Canada), 1978.

The Inks and the Pencils and the Looking Back, Coach House Press (Toronto, Ontario, Canada), 1978.

The Trouble with Stitches, illustrated by Anthony LeBaron, Black Moss Press (Windsor, Ontario, Canada), 1981.

Scary Poems for Rotten Kids, illustrated by Anthony LeBaron, Black Moss Press (Windsor, Ontario, Canada), 1982.

Pickles, Street Dog of Windsor, illustrated by Phil McLeod, Black Moss Press (Windsor, Ontario, Canada), 1982.

Well, You Can Imagine (contains the essay "Poe-Tree"), illustrated by John Fraser, edited by Edward Pickersgill, Black Moss Press (Windsor, Ontario, Canada), 1983.

The Story's Dream, Black Moss Press (Windsor, Ontario, Canada), 1983.

The Ghost Horse of the Mounties, illustrated by Barry Moser, Black Moss Press (Windsor, Ontario, Canada), 1983, D. R. Godine (Boston, MA), 1991.

The Dinner Party, illustrated by Maureen Paxton, Black Moss Press (Windsor, Ontario, Canada), 1984.

Blink, Black Moss Press (Windsor, Ontario, Canada), 1984.

The Granny Poems (based on memoirs written by Anna Rosina Koch), Black Moss Press (Windsor, Ontario, Canada), 1984.

Atmosfear, illustrated by Barbara Di Lella, Black Moss Press (Windsor, Ontario, Canada), 1985.

I'll Belly Your Button in a Minute, Black Moss Press (Windsor, Ontario, Canada), 1985.

The Nightmare Alphabet, Black Moss Press (Windsor, Ontario, Canada), 1987.

Pickles and the Dog Nappers, Black Moss Press (Windsor, Ontario, Canada), 1988.

Monsters He Mumbled, Black Moss Press (Windsor, Ontario, Canada), 1989.

King of the Birds, Black Moss Press (Windsor, Ontario, Canada), 1992.

A Dozen Million Spills and Other Disasters, illustrated by John Fraser, Black Moss Press (Windsor, Ontario, Canada), 1993.

ADAPTATIONS: Scary Poems for Rotten Kids, was adapted for laser optical disc, Discis Books (Buffalo, NY), 1993.

SIDELIGHTS: During the 1980s and early 1990s, Canadian poet and writer sean o huigin made a name for himself by writing popular children's poetry collections. The poet struck a cord with grade school children by writing about their concerns and interests in a humorous way. When he conducted numerous poetry readings and workshops at schools throughout North America, he was able to see firsthand the reactions his work elicited. Dealing with such inherently interesting topics as bodily functions, childhood fears, and mysterious phenomena, his work might easily get giggles and moans from children, while arousing the "gag reflex" of adults. His early essay *Poe-Tree: A Simple Introduction to Experimental Poetry,* based on work with students in Toronto schools, testifies to his interest in extending the boundaries of poetry for children and was dubbed "good fun" for students and teachers by *Books in Canada* contributor Lorne R. Hill. Stylistically, o huigin's poetry resembles that of e e cummings in its use of little or no punctuation and few capital letters.

The majority of o huigin's poems deal with dark topics lightened with humor. Written for middle-grade readers, *Scary Poems for Rotten Kids* depicts the various monsters that may inhabit a child's room and nightmares and, according to Barbara McGinn in *School Library Journal,* compares favorably in fun, originality, and fright factor to *Nightmares* by Jack Prelutsky. *Canadian Children's Literature* reviewer Lisa MacNaughton also praised the work, citing its versatility and calling it an "excellent entrance into the world of print and language." In a similar vein, o huigin wrote *The Dinner Party,* in which grotesque characters eat even more disgusting food. As if this collection were not frightening enough, o huigin followed it shortly with the cautionary tale in verse *Atmosfear.* In this work he personifies air pollution as a monster that would destroy the world. This poem was republished four years later in the ten-poem collection *Monsters He Mumbled.* In this companion volume to *Scary Poems for Rotten Kids,* o huigin presents an array of gruesome creatures.

The poet made a departure from his previous work with a couple of books about a stray dog named Pickles: *Pickles, Street Dog of Windsor* and *Pickles and the Dog Nappers.* In the first volume, a narrator tells in verse and prose of his various encounters with the savvy and personable black-and-white hound. While remarking that the book has a "thin story line," *Canadian Materials* reviewer Gudrun Wight nevertheless praised the work for being "sensitive and original." The subsequent book about Pickles contains a better

developed plot, according to some reviewers. Joanne Robertson, for one, called it an "imaginative and entertaining yarn" in her *Canadian Materials* assessment.

While most of o huigin's poems are short, his most celebrated work is the 1983 narrative poem *The Ghost Horse of the Mounties.* In this piece, based on a real storm-caused stampede in 1874 of 250 horses used by the Royal Canadian Mounted Police, a lost horse searches for his rider. They are finally reunited as ghosts, and the pair forever rides with new Mountie cadets. When this work won the Canada Council Children's Literature Prize, it became the first children's poetry book to do so.

As his essay on experimental poetry suggests, o huigin tried out new versification techniques, including how a poem appears on the page. For example, in *Blink: A Strange Book for Children* he tells of a young girl whose eyes each see something different, and the verse telling what she sees runs in parallel columns down the page, one for each eye. Though the format baffled some readers, who wondered how to read it aloud, a *Quill and Quire* reviewer found the comparison from one eye to the other "delightful" and predicted that teachers could use *Blink* as a springboard for lessons on a variety of scientific topics dealing with perception.

BIOGRAPHICAL AND CRITICAL SOURCES:

BOOKS

Children's Literature Review, Volume 75, Gale (Detroit, MI), 2002.

PERIODICALS

Books in Canada, March, 1979, Lorne R. Hill, review of *Poe-Tree: A Simple Introduction to Experimental Poetry,* p. 23; December, 1984, Mary Ainslie Smith, review of *Blink,* p. 12; November, 1985, Mary Ainslie Smith, review of *Atmosfear,* p. 37; October, 1988, Ray Filip, review of *The Nightmare Alphabet,* p. 10; March, 1994, Rhea Tregebov, review of *A Dozen Million Spills and Other Disasters,* p. 48.

Canadian Children's Literature, Number 42, 1986, reviews of *Ghost Horse of the Mounties, Scary Poems for Rotten Kids, The Trouble with Stitches,* and *Well, You Can Imagine,* p. 58; Number 42, 1986, Gwyneth Evans, "sean o huigin's Children's Verse," pp. 62-64; Numbers 57-58, 1990, Lisa MacNaughton, review of *Scary Poems for Rotten Kids,* pp. 111-113.

Canadian Materials, May, 1984, Gudrun Wight, review of *Pickles, Street Dog of Windsor,* p. 193; January, 1985, Fran Newman, review of *Blink*; March, 1985, Fran Newman, review of *The Dinner Party,* p. 87; January, 1986, Patricia Fry, review of *Atmosfear,* p. 31; March, 1986, Grace E. Funk, review of *I'll Belly Your Button in a Minute!* p. 86; May, 1987, Joanne Robertson, review of *Pickles and the Dog Nappers*; March, 1990, Gwen Maguire, review of *Monsters He Mumbled*; September, 1994, Theo Hersh, review of *A Dozen Million Spills and Other Disasters.*

Children's Book Review Service, September, 1991, Neldo Mohr, review of *The Ghost Horse of the Mounties,* p. 10.

Emergency Librarian, May, 1990, Joan McGrath, review of *Monsters He Mumbled,* pp. 58-59.

Horn Book Guide, fall, 1991, Bridget Bennett, review of *The Ghost Horse of the Mounties,* p. 319.

Quill and Quire, November, 1984, review of *Blink,* pp. 12-13; December, 1989, Fred Boer, review of *Monsters He Mumbled,* p. 22; February, 1994, Janet MacNaughton, review of *A Dozen Million Spills and Other Disasters,* p. 38.

School Library Journal, December, 1983, Barbara McGinn, review of *Scary Poems for Rotten Kids,* 68.

*   *   *

OLSON, Kirby 1956-

PERSONAL: Born September 16, 1956, in Mason City, IA; son of Arne L. (a professor of kinesiology) and Joanna (a first-grade teacher; maiden name, Wilson) Olson; married Riikka Lahdensvo, August 4, 1998; children: Lola, Tristan Tommy. *Ethnicity:* "White." *Education:* Evergreen State College, B.A., 1979; University of Washington, Seattle, Ph.D., 1994. *Politics:* "Wildly fluctuating." *Religion:* Lutheran. *Hobbies and other interests:* Badminton, humor.

ADDRESSES: Home—24 Crestwood Dr., Delhi, NY 13753. *Office*—Evenden 707, State University of New York—Delhi, 13753. *E-mail*—kirbyolson2@hotmail. com.

CAREER: University of Washington, Seattle, acting instructor, 1994-95; University of Tampere, Tampere, Finland, assistant professor, 1995-2000; State University of New York—Delhi, Delhi, NY, assistant professor, 2001—.

WRITINGS:

Comedy after Postmodernism, Texas Tech University Press (Lubbock, TX), 2001.
Gregory Corso: Doubting Thomist, Southern Illinois University Press, 2002.

WORK IN PROGRESS: Andrei Codrescu and the Open Society; research on the role of humor in contemporary society.

SIDELIGHTS: Kirby Olson told *CA:* "My primary motivation for writing is a desire to improve the standing of humorists. My work is particularly influenced by postmodernism, especially Lyotard. I am Lutheran, with roots in St. Augustine. I feel that humor is a much neglected aspect of Christian spirituality."

*   *   *

ONG, Han 1968-

PERSONAL: Born 1968, in Manila, Philippines; immigrated to the United States in 1984.

ADDRESSES: Agent—Farrar, Strauss & Giroux, 19 Union Square West, New York, NY 10003.

CAREER: Playwright and novelist.

AWARDS, HONORS: Kesselring Prize, 1993; MacArthur fellowship, 1997; grants from National Endowment for the Arts, New York State Council on the Arts, New York City Department of Cultural Affairs, Rockefeller Foundation, and ART/NY.

WRITINGS:

PLAYS

Symposium in Manila, produced at Joseph Papp Public
  Theater/NYSF, New York, NY, 1991.
Reasons to Live, produced at Magic Theater, San
  Francisco, CA, 1992.
Bachelor Rat, produced at Thick Description Play-
  house, San Francisco, CA, 1992.
Corner Store Geography, produced at Joseph Papp
  Public Theater/NYSF, New York, NY, 1992.
The L.A. Plays, produced at American Repertory
  Theatre, Boston, MA, 1993.
(With Jessica Hagedorn) *Airport Music,* produced at
  Joseph Papp Public Theater/NYSF, New York, NY,
  1994.
Play of Father and Junior, produced at Solo Mio
  Festival, San Francisco, CA, 1995.
The Chang Fragments, produced at Joseph Papp
  Public Theater/NYSF, New York, NY, 1996.
Middle Finger, produced at Joseph Papp Public
  Theater/NYSF, New York, NY, 1997.
Watcher, produced at Mark Taper Forum New Works
  Festival, Los Angeles, CA, 1998.
Mysteries, produced by Ma-Yi Theatre Company, New
  York, NY, 2001.
Swoony Planet, produced by Ma-Yi Theatre Company,
  New York, NY, 2001.

OTHER

Fixer Chao, Farrar, Strauss & Giroux (New York, NY),
  2001.

SIDELIGHTS: Having a dozen plays produced and a
well-reviewed novel published before turning thirty,
Han Ong bega n his career at a full run. *The L.A.
Plays,* staged in 1993, brought Ong to national
attention. In an interview with John Lahr in the *New
Yorker,* Ong explained that the Asian Americans he
creates in his plays are far from the stereotypical
portrait of Asian Americans he sees in the media.
"Most Asian life is neutered by the unspoken critical
mandate to portray Asians as good, hardworking
people. . . . I'm looking for characters like Greg and
Broos, who neither seek to be identified with blacks or
Asians nor aspire to enter the white world. That in-
betweenness is what interests me."

Ong, who calls himself "the perpetual immigrant,"
came to the United States from the Philippines in 1984
and claims that he has been thinking in English for
only five years. (He dropped out of high school and
earned an equivalency degree). In 1994, Ong collaborated with Jessica Hagedorn to present *Airport
Music* at the Public Theater in New York. "It's about
immigration," Ong explained to Lahr, "Jessica and I
are both from the Philippines. So it's about coming to
the States when the Philippines was considered home,
and what home means. It's about recreating the idea
of home recreating itself in a new country."

Ong wrote *Middle Finger* as a commission for New
York's Public Theater in 1997; after artistic differences
with the Public Theater Ong put the project away and
swore off theater altogether. New York's Ma-Yi theater
company resuscitated the project and it finally went
into production. In an interview with Lenora Inez
Brown in *American Theater,* Ong talked about the
project and his views on contemporary theater. "In the
fall of 1996, the Public had a concept of connecting
classics to modern theater. I personally have no interest in adaptation—to me it is not as rewarding as
original work. . . . but I was really broke."

Ong applied to the Public Theater for a position as
playwright-in-residence. They responded instead with
a commission for the adaptation series. Ong wanted to
explore Frank Wedekind's *Spring Awakening.* "The
more I read, the more engrossed I became," he told
Brown. "But two things were against it. Number one,
it wasn't my first choice. Number two, it was a very,
very good play. But as I reread I saw one flaw, the
boys in *Spring Awakening* speak as if they're on a
podium, mouthing essayic defenses against
authoritarianism. One way to approach this is to find a
language suitable to boys—you know, gross and
adolescent—and see if the audience is still able to get
on their side."

The result was *Middle Finger,* where the author sets
Filipino Catholic schoolboys on the brink of manhood,
discovering who they are as society enforces who they
should be. Jakob knows the secret of life: play life
hard and fast; there are no big secrets to waste time
pondering. His best friend Lunga, on the other hand,
isn't sure if life's mysteries have an answer. But their
parochial teachers and upstanding parents are determined to hold their feet to the fire.

Ong made his debut as a novelist with the highly acclaimed *Fixer Chao.* It is a satire of the shallow and

over-privileged New York wealthy. The protagonist is William Narciso Paulinha, a Filipino male prostitute who is offered the opportunity to escape his wretched existence by Shem C, a writer bent on revenge owing to his lack of success. At Shem's insistence, William assumes the role of Master Chao, a feng shui expert, and the two begin to rob New York's super wealthy of both their money and their well-being by "fixing" their homes. As William moves through the class spectrum of Manhattan, he offers sardonic and keen observations about social, racial, and cultural distinctions and privileges. Heath Madom, writing in *Library Journal*, noted "Ong's strong writing keeps the plot moving at a good pace, and his abilities as a playwright serve him well in rendering excellent dialog." Janet Maslin of the *New York Times*, desribed *Fixer Chao* as "an inventively malevolent debut novel . . . vivid. . . . Ong has a gift for quick acerbic caricatures and piercing observations about contemporary culture." Amy Benfer, writing in *Salon.com* called *Fixer Chao* "Extremely satisfying and even moving. . . . An unrelenting aria of high bitchiness and scathing satire." One thing puzzled Han Ong about the glowing reception of his debut novel. As he told an *Advocate* interviewer, "Reviewers persist in labeling it a satire. For me, it's just the way people behave."

BIOGRAPHICAL AND CRITICAL SOURCES:

BOOKS

Asian-American Almanac, Gale (Detroit, MI), 1995.

PERIODICALS

Advocate, August 14, 2001, article on Han Ong, p. 89.
American Theatre, February, 2001, Lenora Inez Brown, interview with Han Ong, p. 29.
Back Stage, May 17, 1996, David Sheward, review of *The Chang Fragments*, p. 23.
Lambda Book Report, September, 2001, Jim Gladstone, review of *Fixer Chao*, p. 20.
Library Journal, February 15, 2001, Heath Madom, review of *Fixer Chao*, p. 61.
Los Angeles Times, April 29, 2001, Mark Rozzo, review of *Fixer Chao*, p. 22.
Nation, September 26, 1994, Hal Gelb, review of *Airport Music*, p. 321.

New Statesman & Society, November 19, 1993, Sheridan Morley, review of *The L.A. Plays*, p. 41.
New York Times Book Review, April 29, 2001, Kera Bolonik, review of *Fixer Chao*, p. 20.
New York Times, October 20, 1993, p. B3; May 9, 1994, Stephen Holden, review of *Airport Music*, p. B3; May 13, 1996, Vincent Canby, review of *The Chang Fragments*, p. B4; April 5, 2001, Janet Maslin, review of *Fixer Chao*, p. B9.
New Yorker, April 26, 1993, John Lahr, review of *The L.A. Plays*, p. 112.
Publishers Weekly, January 15, 2001, W. S. Gilbert, review of *Fixer Chao*, p. 37; March 12, 2001, review of *Fixer Chao*, p. 61.
Review of Contemporary Fiction, fall, 2001, Paul Maliszewski, review of *Fixer Chao*, p. 204.
Spectator (London, England), Aleks Sierz, review of *The L.A. Plays*, p. 58.
Variety, May 17, 1993, Markland Taylor, review of *The L.A. Plays*, p. 109; May 16, 1994, Matt Wolf, review of *The L.A. Plays*, p. 34.
Washington Post, April 26, 2001, Jonathan Yardley, review of *Fixer Chao*, p. C02.

OTHER

Salon.com, http//www.salon.com/ (April 19, 2001), Amy Benfer, review of *Fixer Chao*.*

* * *

OSOKINA, Elena A(leksandrovna) 1959-

PERSONAL: Born March 2, 1959, in Podel'sk, USSR (now Russia); daughter of Alexander A. and Anna P. (Sobakina) Osokin; married Sergei V. Semitchev, August 15, 1980 (deceased); married Richard M. Lang, October 11, 1996; children: (first marriage) Anna S.; (second marriage) Clio A. *Education:* Moscow State University, B.A. and M.A., both 1981, Ph.D., 1987. *Hobbies and other interests:* Swimming.

ADDRESSES: Home—257 Elm St., 3rd Floor, Oberlin, OH 44074. *Office*—Department of History, 316 Rice Hall, Oberlin College, 10 North Professor St., Oberlin, OH 44074; fax: 440-775-6910. *E-mail*—elena.osokina@oberlin.edu.

CAREER: Moscow State University, Moscow, Russia, junior research fellow, 1988-90; Hoover Institution on War, Revolution, and Peace, visiting scholar, 1993; Woodrow Wilson Center for International Scholars, visiting scholar at Kennan Institute for Advanced Russian Studies, 1993-94, and University of North Carolina—Chapel Hill, 1995-96; Harvard University Davis Center for Russian Studies, fellow, 2000-01; Oberlin College, visiting assistant professor of history, 2001—. Russian Academy of Sciences, research fellow at Institute of Russian History, 1991-95, senior research associate, 1991-2002; Maison des Sciences de l'homme, Paris, France, scholar, 1996, 1999; Donaueschingen Academy, visiting lecturer, 1997; guest lecturer at other institutions in the United States and elsewhere, including University of Aberdeen, University of Helsinki, and University of Toronto.

MEMBER: History and Computing.

AWARDS, HONORS: Honorary degree from Moscow State University, 1981; International Research and Exchanges Board fellowship, 1993; Fulbright fellow, 1995-96.

WRITINGS:

The Hierarchy of Consumption: Life under the Stalinist Rationing System, 1928-1935 (in Russian), Moscow Open State University (Moscow, Russia), 1993.
Behind Stalin's Plenty: Distribution and Market in the Supply of the Population during Industrialization, 1927-1941 (in Russian), Rosspen (Moscow, Russia), 1998.
Our Daily Bread: Socialist Distribution and the Art of Survival in Stalin's Russia, 1927-1941, M. E. Sharpe (Armonk, NY), 2001.

Contributor to books, including *Contending with Stalinism: Soviet Power and Popular Resistance in the 1930s,* edited by Lynne Viola, Cornell University Press. Contributor of articles to Russian, French, German, and U.S. periodicals, including *Soviet and Post-Soviet Review, Russian Studies in History,* and *Social History.*

WORK IN PROGRESS: A book on Soviet art sales under Stalin, completion expected c. 2004.

OSTERMAN, Paul

PERSONAL: Male. *Education:* Oberlin College, B.A. (history), 1968; Massachusetts Institute of Technology, Ph.D. (economics/urban studies and planning), 1976.

ADDRESSES: Office—Sloan School of Management, 50 Memorial Drive, E52-586, Cambridge, MA 02142. *E-mail*—osterman@mit.edu.

CAREER: Massachusetts Institute of Technology, Sloan School of Management, Cambridge, MA, professor of human resources and management.

WRITINGS:

Getting Started: The Youth Labor Market, M.I.T. Press (Cambridge, MA), 1980.
(Editor) *Internal Labor Markets,* M.I.T. Press (Cambridge, MA), 1984
Employment Futures: Reorganization, Dislocation, and Public Policy, Oxford University Press (New York, NY), 1988.
Workforce Policies for the 1990s, Economic Policy Institute (Washington, DC), 1989.
(With Thomas A. Kochan) *The Mutual Gains Enterprise: Forging a Winning Partnership among Labor, Management, and Government,* Harvard Business School Press (Cambridge, MA), 1994.
Broken Ladders: Managerial Careers in the New Economy, Oxford University Press (New York, NY), 1996.
Securing Prosperity: The American Labor Market: How It Has Changed and What to Do about It, Princeton University Press (Princeton, NJ), 1999.
(With Thomas A. Kochan, Richard M. Locke, and Michael J. Piore) *Working in America,* MIT Press (Cambridge, MA), 2001.
Gathering Power: The Future of Progressive Politics in America, Beacon Press (Boston, MA), 2003.

SIDELIGHTS: Paul Osterman's book, *Securing Prosperity: The American Labor Market; How It Has Changed and What to Do about It,* is based on the premise that rises in the American economy during the 1990s were accompanied by significant changes in labor practices. According to Osterman, there are three things wrong with the U.S. labor market: declining job security, widening disparity between the rich and poor, and a growth in various forms of contingent employment such as temporary workers and contract workers. Since World War II, says Osterman, companies have become progressively less committed to their employees than in the past, and this has increased job mobility. This trend, as the decline of unions attest, has also shifted the balance of power between employees and management in favor of management. Finally, survey data shows that the implementation of high-performance work systems has increased worker skills and responsibility levels, to the benefits of the companies; yet companies have not shared the gains with workers and have even used these gains to layoff workers. Writing in *Labour & Industry,* Mark Wooden said that *Securing Prosperity* "makes a compelling read. The writing is very lucid and easy to understand, and the key arguments are supported by the judicious use of statistics. In short, most of *Securing Prosperity* makes good sense."

Working in America is a broad history of labor in the U.S. since World War II. It traces today's labor-market policy and laws back to the New Deal and to a second wave of social regulation that began in the 1960s. The book looks at who is working, what workers do, and how much job security workers enjoy. Osterman's contribution addresses the persistence of a large low-wage sector, worsening inequality in earnings, employees' lack of voice in the workplace, and the need of employers to maximize flexibility if they are to survive in an increasingly competitive market.

Osterman's theory for revisions in the job market is laid out in *The Mutual Gains Enterprise: Forging a Winning Partnership among Labor, Management, and Government.* The author suggests that the U.S. economy will be best served not only by the competitiveness of its firms but also the working conditions and standards of living enjoyed by its workers.

Broken Ladders: Managerial Careers in the New Economy focuses on the workplace transformation affecting managerial employees. After Word War II, managers typically followed career paths built around "internal" labor markets. Once employed by the company, workers enjoyed pay increases, promotions and job security, and in turn they remained loyal to the company. As economic change and organizational changed in the 1990s, however, managers experienced career insecurities as shareholders called for more

profitable companies. In *Employment Futures,* the author argues that current industrial policy gives job security to a core group of workers. They rely on "peripheral" workers (part-time, temporary, and sub-contracted labor) to absorb the necessary work force adjustments. Osterman thinks these policies are bound to fail and he look toward Sweden and Germany for viable alternatives. Industrial relations in these countries, he writes, combine a high level of employment security with a great deal of flexibility to deploy workers within the company. Government policy plays a key role in shaping and supporting the system through advanced employment services and youth job training programs.

BIOGRAPHICAL AND CRITICAL SOURCES:

PERIODICALS

Academy of Management Review, July, 2000, Joseph T. Mahoney, Gloria Harrell-Cook, review of *Securing Prosperity: The American Labor Market: How It Has Changed and What to Do about It,* p.674.
Administrative Science Quarterly, March, 1998, Michael B. Arthur, review of *Broken Ladders: Managerial Careers in the New Economy,* p. 193.
Booklist, September 1, 1999, David Rouse, review of review of *Securing Prosperity,* p. 48
British Journal of Industrial Relations, June, 1995, David Metcalf, review of *Mutual Gains Enterprise: Forging a Winning Partnership among Labor, Management, and Government,* p. 300; September, 1998, John Godard, review of *Change at Work,* pp. 501-503.
Business Horizons, March-April, 1990, Alfred Diamant, review of *Employment Futures: Reorganization, Dislocation, and Public Policy,* pp. 85-86.
Choice, March 1981, review of *Getting Started: The Youth Labor Market,* p. 994; July-August 1984, *Internal Labor Markets,* p. 1647; February 1989, H. Harris, review of *Employment Futures,* p. 978; April 1997, review of *Broken Ladders,* p. 1382-1383; January, 2000, R. M. Whaples, review of *Securing Prosperity,* p. 979.
Comparative Labor Law & Policy Journal, fall, 1997, Paula Voos, review of *Change at Work,* p. 127.
Contemporary Sociology, July, 1982, W. Norton Grubb, review of *Getting Started,* pp. 449-450; January, 1985, James Baron, review of *Internal Labor Markets,* p. 63; May, 1990, Charles M. Tol-

bert II, review of *Employment Futures,* p. 383; September, 1995, Linda Markowitz, review of *Mutual Gains Enterprise,* p. 677; May, 1998, Vicki Smith, review of *Broken Ladders,* p. 260; January, 2001, Arne L. Kalleberg, review of *Securing Prosperity,* p. 9.

Economic Books, September 1984, review of *Internal Labor Markets,* p.65.

Government Finance Review, June, 2000, Scott Diaz, review of *Securing Prosperity,* p.47.

Human Resource Planning, March, 1995, Douglas M. McCabe, review of *Mutual Gains Enterprise,* p. 45-46.

Industrial and Labor Relations Review, January, 1982, review of *Getting Started,* p. 285; January, 1985, Thomas H. Patten Jr., review of *Internal Labor Markets,* p. 293; October, 1989, Susan N. Houseman, review of *Employment Futures,* p. 1721; January, 1998, Daniel J. B. Mitchell, review of *Change at Work,* p. 336; January, 2001, Daniel J. B. Mitchell, review of *Securing Prosperity,* p. 382.

Journal of Economic Issues, September, 1990, Irwin L. Herrnstadt, review of *Workforce Policies for the 1990s: A New Labor Market Agenda,* p. 913.

Journal of Economic Literature, March, 1985, Lawrence Kahn, review of *Internal Labor Markets,* pp. 140-142; December, 1989, Michael Curme, review of *Employment Futures,* p. 1721.

Journal of Policy Analysis & Management, spring, 1990, Stephen E. Baldwin, *Employment Futures: Reorganization, Dislocation, and Public Policy,* p. 277.

Labour & Industry, December, 1999, Mark Wooden, review of *Securing Prosperity,* p. 175.

Library Journal, December 1, 1980, Harry Frumerman, review of *Getting Started,* p. 2494; October 1, 1994, Joan A. Traugott, review of *Mutual Gains Enterprise,* p. 90; September 1, 1999, Harry Frumerman, review of *Securing Prosperity,* p. 208.

Monthly Labor Review, July, 1989, Richard M. Devens Jr., review of *Employment Futures,* pp. 46-47; March, 1995, Markley Roberts, review of *Mutual Gains Enterprise,* p. 67; June, 2000, Michael Wald, review of *Securing Prosperity,* p. 42.

National Productivity Review, spring, 1995, review of *Mutual Gains Enterprise,* p. 127.

Psychology Today, September, 1982, Bernard Lefkowitz, review of *Getting Started,* p. 12.

Reason, November, 1991, Karl Zinsmeister, review of *The Urban Underclass,* p. 58.

Science, May 19, 1989, George Farkas, review of *Employment Futures: Reorganization, Dislocation, and Public Policy,* pp. 837-838.

Sloan Management Review, fall, 1999, Judith Maas, review of *Securing Prosperity,* p. 96.

Southern Economic Journal, January, 1985, Robert J. Gitter, review of Internal *Labor Markets,* p. 951.

Spectrum, fall, 1995, Michal Smith-Mello, review of *Mutual Gains Enterprise,* pp. 48-49.

Today's Education, April, 1981, Nancy R. Needham, review of *Getting Started,* p. 84.

Work and Occupations, February, 1998, Paul Hirsch, review of *Broken Ladders,* p. 115; November, 2000, Vicki Smith, review of *Securing Prosperity,* p. 524.

OTHER

MIT Press Web site, http://mitpress,mit.edu/ (January 12, 2002).

*   *   *

OWENS, Janis E(llen) 1960-

PERSONAL: Born August 25, 1960, in Marianna, FL; daughter of Roy Junior (a preacher and insurance salesman) and Martha (a homemaker; maiden name, Rice) Johnson; married Wendel Ray Owens (a production technician), January 19, 1980; children: Emily Ellen, Abigail Lee, Mary Isabel. *Ethnicity:* "White." *Education:* University of Florida, B.A. (English), 1983. *Politics:* "New Deal Democrat." *Religion:* "Christian/Pentecostal." *Hobbies and other interests:* Environmentalism, advocacy for the mental ill and for dyslexia awareness.

ADDRESSES: Home—Newberry, FL. *Agent*—Joy Harris Agency, 156 Fifth Ave., New York, NY 10010. *E-mail*—janiseowens@juno.com.

CAREER: Novelist.

AWARDS, HONORS: Chautauqua South Fiction Award, best novel, 2000, for *My Brother Michael.*

WRITINGS:

My Brother Michael, Pineapple Press (Englewood, FL), 1997.

Myra Sims, Pineapple Press (Englewood, FL), 1999.

The Schooling of Claybird Catts, HarperCollins (New York, NY), 2003.

ADAPTATIONS: Film rights to *My Brother Michael* and *Myra Sims* were sold to Citadel Films.

SIDELIGHTS: Janis E. Owens is the author of three novels in the "Catts" series, centered on a working-class north Florida family. Civil War historian Gabriel Catts narrates *My Brother Michael,* which begins at a funeral for the title character and delves into a triangle involving the deceased's wife, Myra Sims, whom Gabriel had always loved. In the opinion of a *Publishers Weekly* reviewer, the prose sometimes tends toward the sentimental, but Owens's "fine writing and the ring of her natural voice will carry readers along like a tale told on a porch on a sultry Southern night."

The second entry in the series, *Myra Sims,* tells essentially the same story, this time from the woman's point of view. According to a *Publishers Weekly* contributor, the author's ambitious attempt to refigure her previous tale reveals a few flaws in the narrative; nevertheless, Owens still has "a remarkable talent for touching the heart of a tale and endowing the circumstances of humble lives with dignity." The third novel in the "Catts" series is *The Schooling of Claybird Catts.* Claybird, the son of Myra and Michael Catts, is trying to get back to his life as usual after the devastating loss of his father when a stranger, his Uncle Gabriel, enters his life. Claybird and Uncle Gabe become best friends and Gabriel begins to fill the hole left by Michael's death until Claybird discovers a family secret that threatens everything he knows and loves.

Owens told *CA:* "Probably the greatest influence on my writing was my grandmother, who was a poet herself, and one of those wonderful, magical, southern grannies, the kind who put you to bed every night with a story, usually a Bible story, though she also offered Latin and Greek myths. I think she made me understand at an early age two of the greatest aims of literature: to entertain and instruct. My father was a Pentecostal preacher when I was very small (later an insurance salesman), and I grew up sitting in church at least three times a week—and usually more—listening to sermons that were preached Pentecostal-style, with great dramatic renderings of right and wrong and the decline and fall of man, and his possible redemption.

"I'd have to say that my greatest motivation to write is that I'm miserable when I don't, along with a pressing need I have to tell the stories that I grew up with, stories of life in the working-class South, Florida-style, a land that is rapidly changing, disappearing before our very eyes.

"I really consider myself, above all, a storyteller, and my favorite writers are the great lyrical southern writers—Truman Capote and Katherine Anne Porter, Tennessee Williams, James Dickey, and the like—though I also like English novelists and their very crisp manners. Point of fact is: I'll read anything—a cookbook or a newspaper or a grocery list—as long as it's well written."

BIOGRAPHICAL AND CRITICAL SOURCES:

PERIODICALS

Florida Times-Union, August 3, 1997, Ann Hyman, "First-time Author Hits with Panhandle Tale," p. F4.
Library Journal, December, 1996, Susan C. Colegrove, review of *My Brother Michael,* p. 146.
Publishers Weekly, January 20, 1997, review of *My Brother Michael,* p. 394; December 21, 1998, review of *Myra Sims,* p. 54.
Tampa Tribune (Tampa, FL), March 28, 1998, "Writer Credits Fevered Dream as Inspiration for Successful Book," p. 4.

OTHER

HarperCollins Web site, http://www.harpercollins.com/ (February 10, 2003).

P

PACELLE, Mitchell

PERSONAL: Male.

ADDRESSES: Home—Brooklyn, NY. *Office*—c/o Wiley Publishers, 605 Third Ave., New York, NY 10158.

CAREER: Reporter for *Wall Street Journal.*

AWARDS, HONORS: Business Reporting Award, New York Press Club, 1999; finalist, Gerald Loeb Award, 1999, for Distinguished Business and Financial Journalism; nominee, Pulitzer Prize for journalism.

WRITINGS:

Empire: A Tale of Obsession, Betrayal, and the Battle for an American Icon, Wiley Publishers (New York, NY), 2001.

Also contributor of articles on real estate and business issues, including the collapse of the Long-Term Capital Management Hedge Fund, to newspapers.

SIDELIGHTS: Mitchell Pacelle made a name for himself in business journalism, winning honors for reporting on investments, business deals, and other seemingly dry topics. His first book, however, is a biography of the world-famous Empire State Building, and its story is far from dry. *Empire: A Tale of Obses-*sion, Betrayal, and the Battle for an American Icon is a window into the New York real estate industry and its major players, such as Leona Helmsely and Donald Trump.

The focus of *Empire* is on the battle for controlling ownership of the Empire State Building that took place throughout the 1980s and 1990s. The story begins when Henry Helmsley (husband to Leona) and Lawrence Wein buy and sell the building in 1961. Prudential then buys the building, but leases it to a group of investors, including Helmsley and Peter Malkin, for a 114-year period at what would eventually become a ridiculously low price. When the Helmsley fortunes began to fall apart—capped by the imprisonment of Leona Helmsley for tax evasion—they attempt to sell the property and Japanese billionaire Hideki Yokoi steps in. Yokoi, the central figure of Pacelle's story, buys the building in 1991, although it may have been secretly purchased by his illegitimate daughter Kiiko Nakahara and her husband, French investment banker Jean-Paul Renoir, who for a time partnered with Donald Trump to remake the New York landmark. Trump owns the land on which the building sits, but has no control over the building itself because of the long lease to Helmsley and Malkin. Pacelle suggests that Trump conspired with both Yokoi and Renoir to break the lease. Several of the principal figures in the book ultimately go to prison, others are accused of crimes, fall seriously ill, or die, further complicating the status of the building, which remains in doubt.

Pacelle's *Empire* was well received as a study of New York real estate with real-life soap opera elements. A reviewer for *Publishers Weekly* wrote that Pacelle "has great fun with the bizarre cast of characters, who plot and connive against one another in what reads like a cross between film noir and a Harold Robbins novel." Robert McNatt, writing for *Business Week,* suggested that Pacelle raises questions about the evolution of property ownership and development in New York. McNatt said *Empire* "gives the reader an overview of one of the greatest urban generators of wealth: real estate."

BIOGRAPHICAL AND CRITICAL SOURCES:

PERIODICALS

Publishers Weekly, July 23, 2001, review of *Empire: A Tale of Obsession, Betrayal, and the Battle for an American Icon,* p. 57.

OTHER

Business Week Online, http://www.businessweek.com/ (November 19, 2001), Robert McNatt, "Street Fight for a Skyscraper."
Wiley Publications Web site, http://www.wiley.com/ (October 7, 2001).*

*   *   *

PALOMBO, Joseph 1928-

PERSONAL: Born July 18, 1928, in Cairo, Egypt; married August 3, 1958; wife's name Dorothy D.; children: Karen Palombo Visser. *Ethnicity:* "Caucasian." *Education:* New School for Social Research, B.A., 1954; Yale University, M.A. (philosophy), 1957; University of Chicago, M.A. (social work), 1959; Chicago Institute for Psychoanalysis, certificate in child therapy, 1969.

ADDRESSES: Home—626 Homewood Ave., No. 307, Highland Park, IL 60038; fax: 847-432-0957. *E-mail*—jpalombo2@aol.com.

CAREER: United Charities of Chicago, Chicago, IL, caseworker for Family Service Bureau, 1959-65; North Shore Mental Health Association, Northfield, IL,

psychiatric social worker, 1965-70; Chicago Institute for Psychoanalysis, Chicago, IL, faculty member in Child and Adolescent Psychoanalytic Therapy Program, 1970—, administrative director of Child Therapy Program and coordinator of continuing education, 1970-78, administrative director of Barr-Harris Center for the Study of Separation and Loss during Childhood, 1976-78. Association for Family Living, psychiatric social worker, 1962-68; private practice of psychotherapy, 1968—; Rush-Presbyterian-St. Luke's Medical Center, research associate in pediatrics, 1994-95, associate director of Rush Neurobehavioral Center at Rush Children's Hospital, 1995-97, research coordinator, 1997—. University of Chicago, lecturer and leader of summer institutes, 1970-82; Institute for Clinical Social Work, Chicago, founding dean, 1981-92, faculty member, 1992—; Loyola University of Chicago, faculty member, 1982-84, instructor, 1994-95; Institute for Contemporary Psychoanalysis, corresponding member, 2000—.

MEMBER: Academy of Certified Social Workers, Association of Child Psychotherapists (past president), National Association of Social Workers, National Academies of Practice in Social Work (founding member), Illinois Society for Clinical Social Work.

AWARDS, HONORS: D.H.L., Institute for Clinical Social Work, 1999; Lifetime Achievement Award, National Membership Committee on Psychoanalysis for Clinical Social Work, 2001.

WRITINGS:

Learning Disorders and Disorders of the Self in Children, W. W. Norton (New York, NY), 2001.

Contributor to books, including *The Borderline Patient: Emerging Concepts in Diagnosis, Psychodynamics, and Treatment,* edited by J. S. Grotstein, M. Solomon, and J. A. Lang, 1987; *Narration and Therapeutic Action: The Construction of Meaning in Psychoanalytic Social Work,* edited by J. R. Brandell, Haworth Press (New York, NY), 1996; *The Handbook of Infant, Child, and Adolescent Psychotherapy,* Jason Aronson Press (NJ), Volume 1: *A Guide to Diagnosis and Treatment,* 1995, Volume 2: *New Directions in Integrative Treatment,* 1997; and *Understanding, Diagnosing, and Treating AD/HD in Children and*

Adolescents: An Integrative Approach, Volume 3, edited by J. A. Incorvaia, B. S. Mark-Goldstein, and D. Tesmer, Jason Aronson Press, 1999. Contributor of articles and reviews to periodicals, including *American Journal of Orthopsychiatry, Annual of Psychoanalysis, Child and Adolescent Social Work Journal, Psychoanalytic Inquiry, Adolescent Psychiatry, Progress in Self Psychology, Psychoanalytic Social Work,* and *Journal of Analytic Social Work.*

*   *   *

PALUMBI, Stephen R.

PERSONAL: Married Mary Roberts (a physician); children: two. *Education:* University of Washington, Ph.D. (marine ecology).

ADDRESSES: Office—Stanford University, Department of Biological Sciences, Hopkins Marine Station, Ocean View Blvd., Pacific Grove, CA 93950. *E-mail*—spalumbi@stanford.edu.

CAREER: Stanford University, Stanford, CA, professor of biology; Palumbi Lab, Pacific Grove, CA, director; Harvard University, Cambridge, MA, professor of biology; Harvard Museum of Comparative Zoology, curator of invertebrates.

WRITINGS:

(Editor with Joan D. Ferraris) *Molecular Zoology: Advances, Strategies, and Protocols,* Wiley-Liss (New York, NY), 1996.
The Evolution Explosion: How Humans Cause Rapid Evolutionary Change, Norton (New York, NY), 2001.

SIDELIGHTS: Stephen R. Palumbi is a professor of biology at Stanford University. He is director of the Palumbi Lab, a facility for students and post-doctoral fellows who study genetics, evolution, population biology, and systematics of marine and terrestrial organisms. In *The Evolution Explosion: How Humans Cause Rapid Evolutionary Change,* Palumbi examines how humans have influenced evolution through the past several thousand years, starting with Paleolithic

hunters who, by cooperating with wolves and favoring certain traits, unknowingly steered the evolution of dogs. He continues with a discussion of humans ten thousand years ago, who, without any knowledge of genetics or evolution, began breeding and hybridizing plants and animals, selecting for traits they wanted in cattle, pigs, potatoes, and other plants.

Palumbi makes it clear that evolution is still happening today, and he suggests that it can be observed over years, not millennia. For example, in the past fifty years, Pacific Northwest salmon have evolved to be only two-thirds the size of their ancestors five decades ago. The reason: fishermen in the area have selectively killed big fish rather than small ones, so smaller ones survive to procreate and produce more small fish. In another example, Palumbi describes a person with AIDS as an evolutionary arms race in which HIV viruses adapt to the victim's immune system as well as to the drugs used to fight them. In order to stop the disease, researchers must discover not only new drugs that will fight the virus but, more importantly, how to curtail the virus's ability to rapidly evolve resistant forms. The same battle against resistance is being waged by farmers, who continually try new methods to control insects in their crops. As rapidly as new controls are developed, the insects adapt to them and become resistant, requiring a whole new generation of pesticides to be developed. According to Carl Zimmer in the *New York Times,* Palumbi "does an excellent job of showing how man-made evolution is not only real but relevant." In *Publishers Weekly,* a reviewer commented that the book "is a straightforward overview for the lay reader of the dangerous real-life significance of evolution."

In *Molecular Zoology: Advances, Strategies, and Protocols,* Palumbi and coeditor Joan D. Ferraris present papers from a January 1995 symposium. The articles examine contemporary tools in molecular biology and outline new areas of biological research. Maureen K. Krause wrote in *BioScience* that "Biologists who already use molecular tools will find *Molecular Zoology* an invaluable reference source." In *Science,* Rodney L. Honeycutt noted, "All the authors in this book demonstrate a clear understanding of natural systems and relate their research to the broader issues in evolutionary biology that deal with the diversity of organisms and the explanation of natural phenomena."

BIOGRAPHICAL AND CRITICAL SOURCES:

PERIODICALS

BioScience, March, 1997, Maureen K. Krause, review of *Molecular Zoology: Advances, Strategies, and Protocols,* p. 194.

Booklist, May 1, 2001, Donna Seaman, review of *The Evolution Explosion: How Humans Cause Rapid Evolutionary Change,* p. 1649.

Nature, August 9, 2001, Jerry A. Coyne, review of *The Evolution Explosion,* p. 586.

New York Times Book Review, May 27, 2001, Carl Zimmer, "Unsafe for Any Species," p. 14.

Publishers Weekly, May 7, 2001, review of *The Evolution Explosion,* p. 232.

Science, January 3, 1997, Rodney L. Honeycutt, review of *Molecular Zoology,* p. 36.

OTHER

W.W. Norton Web site, http://www.wwnorton.com/ (December 2, 2001).*

*   *   *

PANCHYK, Richard 1970-

PERSONAL: Born March 30, 1970, in Jackson Heights, NY; son of Robert and Katherine Panchyk; married Caren Prommersberger (an editor); children: Matthew, Elizabeth. *Education:* Adelphi University, B.A. (anthropology), 1992; University of Massachusetts, M.A. (anthropology), 1994, graduate studies, 1994-96. *Politics:* Independent.

ADDRESSES: Agent—Gannett Fleming, 1 Penn Plaza, Ste. 2222, New York, NY 10119. *E-mail*—panchyk@ yahoo.com.

CAREER: Author. University of Massachusetts, Cambridge, MA, teaching assistant, 1993-95; Pocumtuck Valley Memorial Association's Indian House, Deerfield, MA, teacher, 1994-95; Macmillan Publishing, New York, NY, freelance editor, 1995-96; Gannett Fleming Engineers and Architects, New York, NY, marketing coordinator, 1996—.

WRITINGS:

FOR ADULTS; NONFICTION

(With Katherine Panchyk) *The CADD Department: A Guide to Its Successful Organization and Management,* Van Nostrand Reinhold (New York, NY), 1991.

Birth Index for Buda Jewry: Covering the Years 1820-52, 1868 for Neolog Jews in Buda (Budapest). Hungary: An Alphabetical Listing by Father's Surname, with a Cross-Index of Mother's Surnames, Avotaynu, Inc. (Teaneck, NJ), 1995.

Obuda Census of 1850: Index and Complete Census, Avotaynu, Inc. (Teaneck, NJ), 1996.

(With mother, Katherine Panchyk) *CAD Management: The Definitive Guide to Systems Set-up, Maintenance, and Efficiency,* Kluwer Academic Press (Boston, MA), 1998.

Mako and Battonya (Hungary) Vital and Census Records, 1824-1880, Avotaynu (Bergenfield, NJ), 1998.

FOR CHILDREN; NONFICTION

(With Matthys Levy) *Engineering the City: How Infrastructure Works, Projects and Principles for Beginners,* Chicago Review Press (Chicago, IL), 2000.

Archeology for Kids: Uncovering the Mysteries of Our Past: twent-five Activities, Chicago Review Press (Chicago, IL), 2001.

World War II for Kids, forewords by Bill Clinton and John McCain, Chicago Review Press (Chicago, IL), 2002.

Folk Art for Kids, Chicago Review Press (Chicago, IL), 2003.

Some of Panchyk's work has been translated into Japanese and Portuguese.

WORK IN PROGRESS: Working on a children's picture book as well as more "for Kids" ideas.

SIDELIGHTS: Richard Panchyk told *CA:* "I knew I wanted to be a writer when I was in second grade. It helped that as a child, I read voraciously. Besides fiction, my favorite books were about history or science.

The books I liked best were packed with information and photos and did not talk down to me. Well, now everything has come full circle and it turns out that I am writing the kind of book I would have loved as a child. *Archeology for Kids* and *World War II for Kids* are part of a series of books that have the same format—about 160 pages, lots of photos and drawings, and suggested activities to flesh out the subject matter even further.

"What I enjoy so much about writing these books is the challenge of taking a topic and making it accessible and fun for kids to read about. For my World War II book, I interviewed about twenty people and included their stories in the book. I also obtained original letters written between soldiers and their families back in the States. All of this helped me achieve an authentic feeling that can transport kids back in time. I enjoy presenting material in an original way and letting kids read original documents and understand what people actually have to say about their experiences.

"I have always had an interest in teaching, and have taught elementary age kids as well as college students. I find that writing for kids is even more rewarding. I find that a well-written kids' nonfiction book can also serve as a primer for adults, especially teachers. I like books that serve as a springboard by igniting your interest and inviting you to read further into the subject."

As Panchyk further explained to *CA,* he is most interested in writing children's nonfiction books that both inspire and educate, often using real anecdotes and actual documents to convey the immediacy of his descriptions. In his very first book for children, *Engineering the City: How Infrastructure Works, Projects and Principles for Beginners,* which he coauthored with Matthys Levy, Panchyk presents a compilation of infrastructure stories, including an overview of the history of infrastructure evolution from the earliest times to modern-day complexities, such as running railroads, building bridges, and telecommunications technology. Also included in the book are activities for children, with accompanying step-by-step instructions.

BIOGRAPHICAL AND CRITICAL SOURCES:

PERIODICALS

Booklist, February 15, 2001, Roger Leslie, review of *Engineering the City: How Infrastructure Works,*

Projects and Principles for Beginners, p. 1126; January 1, 2002, Susan Dove Lempke, review of *Archeology for Kids: Uncovering the Mysteries of Our Past: twenty-five Activities,* p. 854.

Gifted Child Today, spring, 2001, "Investigate Infrastructures in Our World," p. 46.

Publishers Weekly, August 26, 2002, "World War II Remembered," p. 71.

School Library Journal, December, 2001, Patricia Manning, review of *Archeology for Kids,* p. 169.

Science Activities, winter, 2002, Donald E. Myers, review of *Engineering the City,* p. 44.

*   *   *

PATERNOT, Stephan 1974-

PERSONAL: Born March 21, 1974, in San Francisco, CA. *Education:* Cornell University, B.A. (computer science and business), 1996.

ADDRESSES: Home—New York, NY. *Agent*—c/o J. Wiley, 605 Third Avenue, New York, NY 10158-0012. *E-mail*—website@paternot.com.

CAREER: Author, actor, and filmmaker. *theglobe.com,* New York, NY, founder/co-chief executive office, 1994-2000, vice chairman, 2000-01.

AWARDS, HONORS: New York Avignon Film Festival finalist, for *Shutter.*

WRITINGS:

(With Andrew Essex) *A Very Public Offering: A Rebel's Story of Business Excess, Success, and Reckoning,* J. Wiley (New York, NY), 2001.

SIDELIGHTS: While he was a freshman at Cornell University in 1992, Stephan Paternot met Todd Krizelman, a fellow student who was as introverted as Paternot, and who shared Paternot's fascination with computer games and his curiosity about the uprising computer resource called the Internet. Two years later, they sat in Cornell's student union trying to convince other computer programmers and graphic artists to help them launch a Web site. So began their notoriously fast-streaking success—and soon-to-be failure—in the dot.com world.

To chronicle his adventures, Paternot has written a combination memoir and insider's view of a computer start-up company, *A Very Public Offering: A Rebel's Story of Business Excess, Success, and Reckoning*. Paternot has come to represent everything that went right—and everything that went wrong—in the volatile, fast-paced Internet start-up craze of the 1990s. At age twenty he had a dream. By age twenty-six that dream was over.

Paternot began his quest as a young student struggling to maintain passing grades while plunging into the Internet world. He talked family and friends into investing $15,000, with which he bought computer equipment and set up a small office near Cornell University. He stayed close to his alma mater in order to tap into the talent pool of Web-savvy Cornell graduates.

Paternot's dream was to create a Web site that would be visited by people from all over the world. The site would combine attractive graphics and advertising and would be interactive. People could go to this site, check for messages, chat, and play games. His vision was to make the Web site a kind of online entertainment spot, which he hoped would eventually attract one hundred million users each month. In April 1995, the first month that the Web site went live, Paternot calculated that the site, which he named *theglobe.com*, received over 44,000 hits.

Paternot worked long hours to keep the site functioning. When the workload became too heavy for him and his partner, Krizelman, they enticed some of their fellow classmates to join them, offering a steady supply of pizza in place of salaries. In 1997, when the company moved to New York City, Paternot employed 115 people and had major financial backers such as David Horowitz, founder of MTV Networks; Robert Halperin, former president of Raychem; David Duffield, CEO of PeopleSoft; and Michael Egan, former chairman of Alamo Rent-a-Car, who alone reportedly invested twenty million dollars in *theglobe.com* right before Paternot and his partner decided to go public with their stock.

Theglobe.com quickly became a popular Internet site. At the site, visitors could play interactive games, create personal Web pages, and launch into e-commerce.

Feeling confident that the future success of the site was all but guaranteed, on Friday, November 13, 1998 Paternot placed the company's stock on the NASDAQ stock exchange. Paternot and others watching Internet stocks witnessed *theglobe.com* "inadvertently becoming the benchmark for Internet frenzy when its stock soared a then-record 606%," explained a reviewer for *Business Week*. Suddenly, Paternot and his partner were each worth $97 million. However, as a reviewer for *Publishers Weekly* observed, "fortune can turn quickly: less than two years later, *theglobe.com*'s stock price plummeted close to zero," at which point Paternot and Krizelman were singled out by the media as "global poster boys of Internet excess."

Commenting on Paternot's memoir, Rob Walker wrote in the *New York Times*, "Maybe because of his limited experience of life generally and business in particular, Paternot seems to have no real insight into the weird hothouse environment that made Theglobe's I.P.O. a landmark event." Instead, Walker stated, "he goes on at some length [in his memoir] about his briefly euphoric high life: Manhattan nightclubs were 'mindblowing.' Flying in a private jet was 'phenomenal.'" Walker commented that at the end of the book, Paternot informs his readers he has left *theglobe.com* in the hands of a new administration. In fact, as Walker noted, the Web site's stock is no longer listed and the Web site itself "closed its doors on August 15, 2001," as stated at the site's home page.

A reviewer from *Business Week* commented, "Paternot blames investors, bankers, and the press for the vortex that eventually sucked the life out of his company. But theglobe.com wasn't the victim of outside forces: It fell apart because it didn't have a fundamental business plan or strong vision that could be defended." The reveiwer concluded that if Paternot had known what he wanted to do and how people would best be served by the Internet, he might have succeeded.

Neil Barsky, writing for the *Wall Street Journal*, noted in his review of *A Very Public Offering*, "Mr. Paternot is now pursuing a film career. His partner is thinking of going to business school." Barsky added that in his book Paternot "makes the past several years seem like little more than an innocent detour." Commenting on Paternot's new direction in the film industry, Paul Durman, the London *Sunday Times*, stated that Paternot hopes to star in the film version of his book, which Paternot has described as "Rocky meets the Net."

Studying to be an actor. Paternot also made two small independent films, *Wholey Moses* and *Shutter,* the latter which was a finalist at New York's Avignon Festival.

Dennis McCafferty interviewed Paternot for *careerbuilder.com.* McCafferty noted that others considering becoming involved in an Internet start-up company should "check out the workplace before leaping aboard. The questions you should consider are many-faceted, reflecting not just pay, but quality of life." "My experience is all about people taking risks because of their passion," Paternot told McCafferty, "But I don't see this as the end. It's time to examine what went wrong and build upon it."

BIOGRAPHICAL AND CRITICAL SOURCES:

PERIODICALS

Business Week, September 10, 2001, "Witless Dot-Com," p. 22E6.
Guardian (London, England), September 2, 1999, Hamish Mackintosh, "Working It Out: Global Warmer," p. 4.
Interview, February, 1999, Amy Harmon, "Stephan Paternot & Todd Krizelman," p. 42.
Los Angeles Times, February 7, 2000, Charles Piller, "Internet: Young Co-Founders Defend Their Tenure, Company's Performance Despite a Precipitous Decline in Stock Price," p. C1.
Publishers Weekly, July 23, 2001, review of *A Very Public Offering: A Rebel's Story of Business Excess, Success, and Reckoning,* p. 59.
Sunday Times (London, England), August 5, 2001, "Theglobe Stops Spinning," p. 2.
Times (London, England), November 26, 1997, Chris Ward, "Bonanza as Globe Turns Supernova," p. 19; January 29, 2000, Adam Jones, "Internet Duo Quit as Shares Tumble," p. 26.
Wall Street Journal, August 27, 2001, Neil Barsky, "How to Become a Millionaire, without Any Profits," p. A13.

OTHER

Careerbuilder.com, http://www.careerbuilder.com/ (April 19, 2002), Dennis McCafferty, "Confessions of a Dot-Com Has-Been."

Cornell Chronicle, http://www.news.cornell.edu/ Chronicle/ (March 9, 2000), Linda Myers, "CU Dot-Com Founders Discuss Industry Ups and Downs March 14."
IMDB, http://us.imdb.com/ (February 10, 2003), biography of Stephan Paternot.
New York Times on the Web, http://www.nytimes.com/ (November 4, 2001), Rob Walker, "Flash in the Pan."
Salon.com, http://www.salon.com/ (August 22, 2001), Katharine Mieszkowski, "Dumb, Dumber, and theglobe.com."
Stephan Paternot Web site, http://www.paternot.com/ (April 19, 2002).*

*   *   *

PEAD, Greg
See SERIOUS, Yahoo

*   *   *

PEARL, Matthew 1975(?)-

PERSONAL: Born c. 1975, in New York. *Education:* Harvard University, graduated (summa cum laude), 1997; Yale Law School, graduated, 2000.

ADDRESSES: Home—Cambridge, MA. *Agent*—c/o Author Mail, Random House, 1745 Broadway, New York, NY 10019. *E-mail*—matthew@thedanteclub.com

CAREER: Harvard University, Cambridge, MA, teaching fellow in literature, c. 2000—.

AWARDS, HONORS: Dante Prize, Dante Society of America, 1998.

WRITINGS:

(Editor, and author of introduction) Dante Alighieri, *Inferno,* translated by Henry Wadsworth Longfellow, Modern Library (New York, NY), 2003.
The Dante Club (novel), Random House (New York, NY), 2003.

WORK IN PROGRESS: Another literature-inspired nineteenth century murder mystery, for Random House.

SIDELIGHTS: "If [Matthew Pearl] isn't the emerging enfant terrible of American literature, I can't imagine who is," Mark Shechner wrote in the *Buffalo News* shortly after Pearl's first novel, *The Dante Club,* was published. Within weeks of publication, Pearl's book had reached eleventh place on the *New York Times* bestseller list.

The Dante Club is based on an actual club of the same name which met in Cambridge, Massachusetts in the mid-nineteenth century to translate and study Italian poet Dante Alighieri's works. This club—which included the poets Henry Wadsworth Longfellow and James Russell Lowell, publisher J. T. Fields, and Harvard scholar Oliver Wendell Holmes, Sr. (father of Oliver Wendell Holmes, Jr., the Supreme Court justice)—first came to Pearl's attention when he took a class on Dante as an undergraduate at Harvard University. Pearl, who was majoring in English and American literature, was so enthralled with Dante that he wanted to switch majors to Romance Languages, but this would have made it difficult for him to graduate in time. Instead, Pearl's professor, Lino Pertile, suggested that Pearl write his senior thesis on the Dante Club. Pearl did, and the work earned him the Dante Prize from the Dante Society of America (the current incarnation of the former Dante Club).

After graduating from Harvard University, summa cum laude, Pearl went to Yale Law School to study intellectual property law, but his love for Dante kept coming back to haunt him. Halfway through his time at Yale, Pearl began to write a novel based on the Dante Club. The historical club, its members, and its work—helping Longfellow to prepare his first-ever American translation of Dante's *Divine Comedy*—provide the background for Pearl's fictional invention, a murder mystery where the killer's methods are based on the punishments that Dante describes for sinners in the *Inferno,* the first part of the *Divine Comedy.* It is up to the members of the Dante Club, just about the only people in the United States at that time who were familiar with the *Divine Comedy,* to help find the killer.

Pearl recognizes the inherent humor in the idea of a group of scholars investigating gruesome murders, and at points in the book he uses this to provide "some welcome comic relief," Mark Rozzo noted in a review in the *Los Angeles Times.* However, many other reviewers thought that the strongest parts of the book were the "nicely grisly" descriptions of the tortures, which "are well spaced and delivered to characters about whom we care nothing at all," James R. Kincaid wrote in the *New York Times.*

"There was a part of me that wanted to re-create what I found so extraordinary in Dante: putting poets into a journey of confronting evil," Pearl explained to David Mehegan of the *Boston Globe.* "That is what the 'Inferno' is: two poets, Dante and Virgil, travel through hell and confront violence and evil. I wanted the Dante Club to go through their own descent."

BIOGRAPHICAL AND CRITICAL SOURCES:

PERIODICALS

Booklist, November 15, 2002, Kristine Huntley, review of *The Dante Club,* p. 577.
Boston Globe, March 3, 2003, David Mehegan, review of *The Dante Club.*
Buffalo News (Buffalo, NY), February 16, 2003, review of *The Dante Club.*
Esquire, March, 2003, Adrienne Miller, review of *The Dante Club,* p. 78.
Kirkus Reviews, November 15, 2002, review of *The Dante Club,* p. 1650.
Library Journal, December, 2002, Laurel Bliss, review of *The Dante Club,* p. 180.
Los Angeles Times, February 9, 2003, Mark Rozzo, review of *The Dante Club,* p. R14.
New York Times, February 7, 2003, Janet Maslin, review of *The Dante Club,* p. E34; March 2, 2003, James R. Kincaid, review of *The Dante Club,* p. 6.
People, February 17, 2003, Julie K. L. Dam, review of *The Dante Club,* p. 43.
Publishers Weekly, April 17, 2000, John F. Baker, "Dante Scholars in Murder Mystery," p. 16; October 7, 2002, review of *The Dante Club,* p. 50; February 3, 2003, review of the audio version of *The Dante Club,* p. 24.
Star-Ledger (Newark, NJ), February 16, 2003, Alice K. Turner, review of *The Dante Club,* p. 4.

OTHER

Dante Club Web site, http://www.thedanteclub.com (March 5, 2003).
Pages, http://www.ireadpages.com/ (March 5, 2003), interview with Matthew Pearl.*

PENCE, Caprial A. 1963-

PERSONAL: Born July 4, 1963, in Pasco, WA; daughter of Patrick (a studio potter) and Artheen Hopper (self-employed) Horsley; married John Pence (a chef) September 8, 1985; children: Alexander Savannah. *Education:* Culinary Institute of America, A.O.S., 1984.

ADDRESSES: Office—Caprial and John's Kitchen, 1608 South East Bybee, Portland, OR 97202. *E-mail*—caprial@caprial.com.

CAREER: Chef, cookbook author, and television chef. Fuller's Restaurant, chef, Seattle, WA, 1987-92; Caprial's Bistro, Portland, OR, co-owner, 1992—; Caprial and John's Kitchen, Portland, OR, co-owner, 2002—; Host, *Caprial's Café,* The Learning Channel, and *Cooking with Caprial and John,* Public Broadcasting Service.

MEMBER: International Association of Culinary Professionals, Oregon Women's Forum, Women Chefs and Restaurateurs.

AWARDS, HONORS: James Beard Foundation award, 1990, for best chef, Pacific Northwest.

WRITINGS:

Caprial's Seasonal Kitchen, Graphic Arts Publishing Center (Portland, OR), 1988.
Caprial's Café, Ten Speed Press (Berkeley, CA), 1994.
Cooking with Caprial, Ten Speed Press (Berkeley, CA), 1996.
Caprial's Bistro Style Cuisine, photographs by Edward Gowans, Ten Speed Press (Berkeley, CA), 1997.
(With Mark Dowers) *Caprial's Soup and Sandwiches,* Ten Speed Press (Berkeley, CA), 1998.
Caprial's Bistro, Ten Speed Press (Berkeley, CA), 1999.
Caprial Cooks for Friends, Ten Speed Press (Berkeley, CA), 2000.
(With Melissa Carey) *Caprial's Desserts,* Ten Speed Press (Berkeley, CA), 2001.
Caprial and John's Kitchen, Ten Speed Press (Berkeley, CA), 2002.

SIDELIGHTS: Chef Caprial A. Pence demonstrates her command of her craft both by cooking for patrons at her own restaurants, Caprial's Bistro and Caprial and John's Kitchen, in Portland, Oregon, her many cookbooks and through her television shows, *Caprial's Café* and *Cooking with Caprial and John,* the latter co-hosted with her husband, John. "Pence . . . has a friendly, down-to-earth style that comes across in her books . . . as well as in her popular PBS television series," *Library Journal* reviewer Judith C. Sutton said.

Caprial's Desserts, which Pence wrote with her pastry chef, Melissa Carey, shows how to make sixty-seven standard recipes, such as angel food cake, berry pie, and flourless chocolate cake, and then offers variations on those themes. The book illustrates completed desserts, and how to perform such basics as layering and frosting cakes, making puff pastry, and rolling pie dough; Pence also includes eight pages of advice on kitchen tools and ingredients. Michael Hastings wrote in the *Winston-Salem Journal,* "*Caprial's Desserts* well represents the recent trend of American restaurant desserts toward the homey and simple sweets that everyone's grandmother used to make. But we would recommend it only to experienced bakers or those who don't mind making a recipe a couple of times to perfect it."

In *Caprial Cooks for Friends,* would-be chefs can attempt a range of dishes: wild mushroom tarte tatinas appetizers, John's barbecued ribs with secret cure and mange barbecue sauce, coconut-shrimp stew—even corn dogs and chocolate birthday cake. Sutton wrote, "With casual entertaining in mind, she includes make-ahead tips for most of the recipes, as well as boxes on such subjects as cocktails, centerpieces, and 'When to Call for Help: Times a Caterer Can Lend a Hand.'" Mark Knoblauch wrote in *Booklist,* "Most of the recipes will delight the cook looking for new ideas for simple, easily prepared dishes that will nevertheless intrigue even the most sophisticated guest."

Said a *Publishers Weekly* reviewer of *Caprial's Soups and Sandwiches,* a joint venture between Pence and Mark Dower, one of her restaurant chefs, "[They] have accomplished the seemingly impossible: they've taken a familiar topic like soups and sandwiches and managed to come up with surprises. The caveat is that these are not soups or sandwiches that can be slapped together using what's on hand—they require special ingredients and forethought—but the process yields culinary rewards." These are favorites served at her restaurant and include red seafood chowder, salmon club sandwich, roasted chicken tortilla wrap, lamb stew with wild mushrooms and figs, and tomato and tomatillo soup with chilies and chicken meatballs. It also includes recipes for breads, stocks, and spreads.

Caprial's Bistro-Style Cuisine offers recipes for main dishes such as pepper-crusted salmon with green sauce and five-spice roasted duck and delicious desserts.

BIOGRAPHICAL AND CRITICAL SOURCES:

PERIODICALS

Booklist, June 1, 2000, Mark Knoblauch, review of *Caprial Cooks for Friends,* p. 1828.
Library Journal, February 15, 1996, Judith C. Sutton, review of *Cooking with Caprial: American Bistro Favorites,* p. 170; June 15, 1998, Judith C. Sutton, review of Caprial's *Bistro-Style Cuisine,* p. 102; February 15, 1999, Judith C. Sutton, review of *Caprial's Soups and Sandwiches,* p. 178; May 15, 2000, Judith C. Sutton, review of *Caprial Cooks for Friends,* p. 121; November 15, 2001, Judith C. Sutton, review of *Caprial's Desserts,* p. 94.
Publishers Weekly, December 21, 1998, review of *Caprial's Soups and Sandwiches,* p. 60; May 15, 2000, review of *Caprial Cooks for Friends,* p. 113.
Travel & Leisure, April 1997.
Winston-Salem Journal (Winston-Salem, NC), March 6, 2002, Michael Hastings, "Dessert Basics: Standards Less Easy to Embellish than Chef-Writer Predicts," p. E2.

*   *   *

PENNING-ROWSELL, Edmund 1913-2002

OBITUARY NOTICE—See index for *CA* sketch: Born March 16, 1913, in London, England; died March 4, 2002. Wine expert, journalist, and author. Penning-Rowsell was a well-known oenophile who wrote a regular column on wine for the London *Financial Times.* Born to well-to-do parents, he was forced to abandon his formal education when a worldwide economic depression put the family in financial

straights during the 1930s. Finding a job in the library for the *Morning Post,* he worked there from 1930 to 1935. What followed was an unremarkable career in publishing with the company Frederick Muller. During World War II Penning-Rowsell was a corporal in the British Signal Corps, and then returned to work for Muller before becoming a sales manager for B. T. Batsford during the 1950s. Penning-Rowsell eventually worked as a publishing director for Hulton Press, a position he enjoyed but ultimately lost in 1963 when the publisher replaced him with a family member. The abrupt loss of his job led to better things, however, when Penning-Rowsell turned his love of wines into a new career. A member, and later chairman, of the Wine Society, he had become an expert on the subject and found work writing a column on wine for the *Financial Times.* His columns were innovative for their time, setting a new style in wine writing: rather than simply describing wines and the experience of wine-drinking as earlier writers had, Penning-Rowsell counseled readers on which wines were superior and which vintages to buy. He published some of his advice in the books *Red, White, Rosé* and *The Wines of Bordeaux;* he also edited *Château Latour: The History of a Great Vineyard, 1331-1992.*

OBITUARIES AND OTHER SOURCES:

BOOKS

Who's Who 2000, St. Martin's Press (New York, NY), 2000.

PERIODICALS

Independent (London, England), March 7, 2002, p. 6.
Times (London, England), March 5, 2002.

*   *   *

PERANI, Judith

PERSONAL: Female. *Education:* University of California at Berkeley, B.A. (art history), 1968; Indiana University, M.A. (art history), 1970, Ph.D., 1977.

ADDRESSES: Office—438 Seigfred Hall, Ohio University, Athens, OH 45701. *E-mail*—perani@ohio.edu.

CAREER: Author and educator. Ohio University, Athens, OH, professor of art history and faculty member in African Studies Program.

WRITINGS:

(With Craig Kinzelman) *Sacred and Secular Art of West Africa* (museum catalog), Trisolini Gallery (Athens, OH), 1976.

(With Lisa Aronson) *Nigerian Textiles: Evolution of Surface Design* (museum catalog), Trisolini Gallery (Athens, OH), 1979.

(With Elizabeth Bunsen Chokr) *Art of the Congo River Basin* (museum catalog), Trisolini Gallery (Athens, OH), 1983.

(With Marilyn Hunt-Nishi) *Ritual Art of the Sepik River: The Solomon Collection* (museum catalog), Trisolini Gallery (Athens, OH), 1984.

(With Mark Fleming) *Yoruba Art of West Africa* (museum catalog), Parkersburg Art Center (Parkersburg, WV) and Trisolini Gallery (Athens, OH), 1986.

(With Marilyn Hunt-Nishi) *Art of the Sepik River and the Papuan Gulf: An Exhibition of New Guinea Art* (museum catalog), Parkersburg Art Center (Parkersburg, WV) and Trisolini Gallery (Athens, OH), 1987.

(With Fred T. Smith) *The Visual Arts of Africa: Gender, Power, and Life-Cycle Rituals,* Prentice-Hall (Upper Saddle River, NJ), 1998.

(With Norma H. Wolff) *Cloth, Dress, and Art Patronage in Africa,* Berg (Oxford, England), 1999.

Contributor to *History, Design, and Craft in West African Strip-woven Cloth,* National Museum of African Art, 1992.

SIDELIGHTS: Judith Perani, a professor of art history at Ohio University, published two books about African art in the late 1990s. The first, *The Visual Arts of Africa: Gender, Power, and Life-Cycle Rituals,* which she coauthored with Kent State University art historian Fred T. Smith, is a textbook for college art students. The book discusses the history and development of various art forms in Africa, including sculpture, architecture, textiles, ceramics, and painting. Perani coauthored her most recent book, *Cloth, Dress, and Art Patronage in Africa,* with anthropologist Norma H. Wolff. The book explores the role that cloth plays in African art.

Perani taught both undergraduate and graduate courses in art history at the college level for nearly thirty years. As her writings suggest, the focus of her work is African art, and more specifically the art of West Africa and Central Africa. In her courses, Perani covers the social, economic, religious, and political elements that influence African art. Perani has made many research trips to Africa, particularly to Nigeria, whose art has been her main focus. In fact, Perani first developed her interest in African art during a trip to Sierra Leone as a member of the Peace Corps after graduating from college. "While in Sierra Leone, I developed a keen interest in African art. My active participation with the Peace Corps became the foundation of my career as a professor of art history," Perani said in an interview with Dora Oduoi posted on the *Ohio University Web site.*

Perani also explained to Oduoi why she feels that studying art is important, especially for those seeking information about a particular society or culture. "Art can be used as a concrete entry to explore a people's values, philosophy, and religious beliefs. Also, art can aid in the reconstruction of a people's early history," Perani said. This is particularly true, she maintained, of the study of African art. "Overall, the study of African art places more emphasis on the way art functions and the purpose for which it was made," Perani told Oduoi. Perani has used her expertise on the subject to put together several exhibitions of African art at various American galleries over the years. For example, she received permission to gather more than seventy pieces of Yoruba art from various private collections to be displayed at the Parkersburg Art Center in Parkersburg, West Virginia, and the Trisolini Gallery in Athens, Ohio, in 1986.

According to Perani, *The Visual Arts of Africa* took three years to complete, largely because of the arduous task of collecting data and obtaining authorization from various museums and private art collections to include their artworks in the book. The text is broken up into sections based on different geographic regions of Africa and on how art varies in each region. The important artistic traditions of each region are highlighted, and the authors explain how each has its own unique art patronage system. Some of the artists represented in the book include Vincent Kofi, Lamidi Fakeye, and Uche Okeke. The book also includes 360 illustrations of artworks, as well as a bibliography for those who wish to do further research on the topic.

According to Barbara E. Frank, who reviewed the book for *African Arts,* the work introduces "students to a diversity of African creative expression" more completely "than previous sources." However, Frank continued, the "writing style is somewhat uneven, with well-written passages linked by awkward transitions."

In *Cloth, Dress, and Art Patronage in Africa,* Perani explores the role that cloth plays in African art. She and coauthor Wolff call cloth "the most important two-dimensional art form in Africa," as it "dresses the body, packages artifacts and defines space." The authors explain the ancient craft of cloth-making, which continuously adapts to changes, particularly when new textiles are imported into a culture. They also say that few materials play as important a role as cloth does in a culture's creative expression, because it "defines ethnic identity and social status, articulates sacred and secular boundaries, and acts as a measure of value."

BIOGRAPHICAL AND CRITICAL SOURCES:

PERIODICALS

African Arts, July, 1993, Elisha P. Renne, "History, Design, and Craft in West African Strip-woven Cloth," pp. 30-31, 83; spring, 1999, Barbara E. Frank, review of *The Visual Arts of Africa: Gender, Power, and Life-Cycle Rituals,* pp. 14-16.
Choice, January, 2000, A. F. Roberts, review of *Cloth, Dress, and Art Patronage in Africa,* p. 977.

OTHER

Ohio University Web site, http://www.ohiou.edu/ (March 12, 2002), profile of Dr. Judith Perani, including interview with Dora Oduoi.*

*   *   *

PHELAN, Jay

PERSONAL: Male. *Education:* University of California, Los Angeles, B.A.; Yale University, M.A.; Harvard University, Ph.D. (biology), 1995.

ADDRESSES: Home—Box 951606, Los Angeles, CA 90095. *Office*—Biology Department, 405 Hilgard Avenue, Box 951361, University of California, Los Angeles, Los Angeles, CA 90095-1361. *E-mail*—jay@ucla.edu.

CAREER: University of California, Los Angeles, biology professor.

WRITINGS:

(With Terry Burnham) *Mean Genes: From Sex to Money to Food: Taming Our Primal Instincts,* Perseus Publishing (Cambridge, MA), 2000.

SIDELIGHTS: At the University of California, Los Angeles Web site of faculty members, where students rate their professors, Jay Phelan earns a solid 8.5 out of a possible score of ten. Overall opinion is that, as teachers go, Phelan is great, but his exams are grueling. With graduate degrees from both Yale and Harvard, and research interests in the genetic roots of human behavior, the evolutionary genetics of aging, and the relationship between heterozygosity and developmental stability, attractiveness, and physical symmetry, Phelan may have earned the right to give tough final exams, no matter how much his students complain.

If Phelan's students are disappointed in their grades at the end of a semester, and they try to allay their woes by going to the nearest bar, they might want to read Phelan's book, first. *Mean Genes: From Sex to Money to Food: Taming our Primal Instincts* offers an underlying explanation of feelings and primal motivations. According to Phelan's study, the human brain evolved in an environment much different from that of modern society. We are, therefore, predisposed to actions that are inappropriate in many contemporary contexts. For example, the scarcity of food that characterized many ancient settings promoted a certain type of eating behavior that, though genetically present in modern man or woman, may be inappropriate to the environment of modern America, in which food is more than abundantly available during all seasons of the year. In other words, the tendency of people to eat too much, Phelan suggests, may be traceable to ancient peoples' adaptations to harsh winters, which often meant long periods without food.

In this book, Phelan examines issues that confront most modern populations: money, violence, addictions, physical appearance, and the search for abstract things such as love and happiness. He and coauthor Terry Burnham provide a means for people to examine their own lives, in order to be more aware of the conflicts between behavior the brain might direct and behavior that is more appropriate. In other words, Phelan believes that if people understand their own genetically-motivated behavioral drives they can offset such drives through corrective action.

Why do people overeat? Why do they drink too much? Why do they gamble? Why can't they save money? And where does their image of physical beauty come from? These are some of the more interesting questions that *Mean Genes* attempts to answer. Whatever the modern dilemma, Phelan continually offers the same suggestion: learn about your genes. Learn how alcohol affects the brain; why caffeine affects your energy level; why hope makes everything seem endlessly possible.

A reviewer for *Skeptical Inquirer,* Daniel Grassam found *Mean Genes* to be "both enjoyable and educational." Grassam acknowledged the scientific study that informs Phelan and Burnham's book and commended the authors for translating these findings into "a book for the general reader." Fiona Cowie also enjoyed the book, and, in her review for *American Scientist,* she stated her reasons. "Unlike much pop sociobiological fare, these speculations about our psyches' evolutionary trajectories are well-peppered with interesting cross-cultural and cross-species comparisons." Cowie also praised the authors for their well-documented research, which, although not included in the book, is available at their Web site, http://www.meangenes.org.

BIOGRAPHICAL AND CRITICAL SOURCES:

PERIODICALS

American Scientist, January, 2001, Fiona Cowie, "Ask Darwin's Grandma," p. 72.
Booklist, August, 2000, Gilbert Taylor, review of *Mean Genes: From Sex to Money to Food: Taming Our Primal Instincts,* p. 2078.

Choice, April, 2001, M. Pilati, review of *Mean Genes: From Sex to Money to Food: Taming Our Primal Instincts,* p. 1535.
Library Journal, October 1, 2000, Elizabeth Goeters, review of *Mean Genes: From Sex to Money to Food: Taming Our Primal Instincts,* p. 126.
Los Angeles Times, October 19, 2000, Rosie Mestel, "Next Time You Pig out, Blame It on the Genes."
New York Times Books, December 31, 2000, Erica Goode, "Back to the Stone Age."
Publishers Weekly, August 14, 2000, review of *Mean Genes: From Sex to Money to Food: Taming Our Primal Instincts,* p. 334.
Skeptical Inquirer, May 2001, Daniel Grassam, "Self Help from Science," p. 61.

OTHER

Book Page, http://www.bookpage.com/ (September 15, 2001), Clay Stafford, "Academic Authors Are Comfortable in Their Genes."
Evolution's Voyage, http://www.evoyage.com/ (March 1, 2002).
Gene Watch, http://www.gene-watch.org/ (March 1, 2002).
Mean Genes Web site, http://www.meangenes.org (September 15, 2001).
Perseus Books Group Web site, http://www. perseusbooksgroup.com/ (March 1, 2002).*

*   *   *

PICCIONI, Giuseppe 1953-

PERSONAL: Born July 2, 1953, in Ascoli Piceno, Italy.

ADDRESSES: Agent—c/o 01 Rai Cinema & Studio Canal Distribution S.r.l., Piazza Adriana, 12, 00193 Rome, Italy.

CAREER: Director and screenwriter. Work as film director includes *Il Grande Blek,* 1987; *Chiedi la luna,* Titanus, 1991; *Condannato a nozze,* 1993; *Cuori al verde,* 1996; *Fuori dal mondo,* Entertech Releasing, 1999; *Luci dei miei occhi,* 01 Distribution, 2001. Film appearances include *Il Cielo e sempre piu blu,* 1995.

AWARDS, HONORS: Italian National Syndicate of Film Journalists Promotional Silver Ribbon, 1988, for *Il Grande Blek;* A.F.I. Fest Audience Award and Grand Jury Prize, Chicago International Film Festival Golden Hugo, Montreal World Film Festival Special Grand Prize of the Jury, and David di Donatello Award for Best Screenplay, all 1999, and Mons International Festival of Love Films Audience Award, 2000, all for *Not of This World;* Venice Film Festival Sergio Trasatti Award, 2001, for *Light of My Eyes.*

WRITINGS:

(With Gualtiero Rosella and Lucia Zei) *Fuori dal mondo* (screenplay, also known as *Not of This World*), Entertech Releasing, 1999.
(With Umberto Contarello and Linda Ferri) *Luce dei miei occhi* (also known as *Light of My Eyes*), Rai Cinema, 2001.

Author of screenplays, including *Il Grande Blek,* 1987; *Chiedi la luna* (also known as *Ask for the Moon*), Titanus, 1991; *Condannato a nozze* (also known as *Condemned to Wed*), 1993; and *Cuori al verde* (also known as *Love, Money, and Philosophy* and *Penniless Hearts*), 1996.

SIDELIGHTS: Not of This World, which Italian film director Giuseppe Piccioni cowrote and directed, is the story of three characters: Catarina, a nun who finds an abandoned baby; Ernesto, the laundromat owner who may be the baby's father; and Teresa, the young girl who, as the viewer discovers, is the baby's mother. Catarina finds the baby wrapped in a blanket, and a glance at a dry-cleaning tag on the blanket leads her to the establishment owned by Ernesto, a man so married to his work that he has seemingly lost all feeling for his fellow humans.

This act of sleuthing on the part of Catarina is only the beginning of a process whereby the characters unfold with subtlety before the viewers' eyes. A single scene of Teresa flinching as she hugs her stepfather, for instance, reveals volumes regarding the background of abuse and pain that led her to unwed pregnancy and the abandonment of her baby. Likewise a photograph of Ernesto with his arm around a woman, uncovered accidentally by Catarina, tells much about who he once was.

Beneath Piccioni's subtext is a still deeper layer, wherein lies the central relationship of the tale: that between Ernesto and Catarina. This is "Not a romance in any conventional sense," as Deborah Hornblow pointed out in the *Hartford Courant,* yet it "nevertheless plays like one as . . . two individuals nearly unconscious of their own desires, are pulled together like magnets." Things can only go so far, of course, given the fact of Catarina's vows, yet the viewer is led to the sense that she is ambivalent about those vows, and reluctant to let go of the baby once her maternal instinct has been awakened.

In *Light of My Eyes,* another film directed and cowritten by Piccioni, circumstances once again bring characters together. This time, a good-natured driver named Antonio almost hits a young girl named Lisa, and as a result meets her emotionally distant mother, Maria. A romance between Antonio and Maria ensues, but though she remains cold to him, he agrees to pay her debt to a small-time gangster, Saverio, by serving as chauffeur to the loan shark.

BIOGRAPHICAL AND CRITICAL SOURCES:

BOOKS

Contemporary Theatre, Film, and Television, volume 33, Gale (Detroit, MI), 2001.

PERIODICALS

Hartford Courant (Hartford, CT), June 29, 2001, Deborah Hornblow, review of *Not of This World,* p. D6.
New York Times, February 25, 2000, Elvis Mitchell, review of *Not of This World,* p. B33.
Variety, December 2, 1991, Derek Elley, review of *Ask for the Moon,* p. 90; November 1, 1993, David Rooney, review of *Condemned to Wed,* p. 44; April 1, 1996, David Rooney, review of *Penniless Hearts,* p. 56; April 5, 1999, David Rooney, review of *Not of This World,* p. 34; September 17, 2001, David Rooney, review of *Light of My Eyes,* p. 25.
Village Voice, February 29, 2000, Nico Baumbach, review of *Not of This World,* p. 118.*

PICCOLI, (Jacques Daniel) Michel 1925-

PERSONAL: Born December 27, 1925, in Paris, France; son of Henri Piccoli; married Eleno Eleonore Hirt (divorced); married Juliette Greco (an actress and singer), 1966 (divorced, 1977); married Ludivine Clerc, 1978; children: (first marriage) Anne-Cordelia.

ADDRESSES: Agent—c/o Gemini Films, 34 Blvd. Sebastopol, 75004 Paris, France.

CAREER: Actor, director, writer, and producer. Film appearances include *Sortileges,* Mage Films, 1944; *Le point du jour,* 1949; *Le parfum de la dame en noir,* Les Films Corona, 1949; *Sans laisser d'adresse,* Corona, 1951; *Terreur en Oklahoma,* 1951; *Torticola contre Frankensberg,* 1952; *Saint-Tropez, devoir et vacances,* 1952; *Chicago Digest,* 1952; *Interdit de sejour,* 1953; *Destinees,* Arlan, 1953; *French Cancan,* United Motion Picture Organization, 1955; *Tout chante autour de moi,* Les Films Marceau, 1955; *Ernst Thaelmann—Fuehrer seiner Klasse,* 1955; *Les mauvaises rencontres,* 1955; *Marie-Antoinette reine de France,* Rizzoli Film, 1955; *La mort en ce jardin,* Bauer International, 1956; *Les sorcieres de Salem,* Kingsley International, 1957; *Nathalie,* Times, 1957; *Tabarin,* Mayfair, 1957; *Rafles sur la ville,* Ellis Films, 1958; *Les copains du Dimanche,* 1958; *La bete a l'affut,* 1959; *La dragee haute,* 1959; *Le bal des espions,* 1960; *Le rendez-vous,* 1961; *Le vergini di Roma,* United Artists, 1961; *Le doulos,* Pathe Contemporary Films, 1961; *Le chevelure,* 1961; *Le jour et l'heure,* Metro-Goldwyn-Mayer, 1962; *Fumee, histoire et fantaisie,* 1962; *Climats,* 1962; *Le mepris,* Embassy, 1963; *Le journal d'une femme de chambre,* Rialto, 1964; *La chance et l'amour,* 1964; *Paparazzi,* 1964; *Bardot et Godard,* 1964; *Masquerade,* United Artists, 1965; *Lady L,* Metro-Goldwyn-Mayer, 1965; *Tentazioni proibite,* Indipenti Regionali, 1965; *Les ruses du diable,* 1965; *Marie Soleil,* 1965; *De l'amour,* Goldstone Film Enterprises, 1965; *Le coup de grace,* 1965; *Compartiment tueurs,* Seven Arts, 1965; *Cafe Tabac,* 1965; *La guerre est finie,* Brandon Films, 1966; *Les creatures,* New Yorker, 1966; *Paris brule-t-il?,* Paramount, 1966; *La voleuse,* 1966; *La curee,* Royal Films International, 1966; *Les demoiselles de Rochefort,* Miramax, 1967; *Belle de jour,* Allied Artists, 1967; *Un homme de trop,* United Artists, 1967; *Mon amour, mon amour,* Les Films Marceau, 1967; *Dom Juan,* 1967; *Charles,* Heartbeat, 1968; *Benjamin,* 1968; "Invite au vernis-

sage," *La prisonniere,* Avco Embassy, 1968; *Dillinger e morto,* 1968; *Diabolik,* Paramount Home Video, 1968; *La chamade,* Lopert, 1968; *La voie lactee,* UMC Pictures, 1969; *Topaz,* Universal, 1969; *L'invitata,* 1969; *Les choses de la vie,* Columbia, 1969; *L'invasion,* 1970; *L'udienza,* 1971; *La poudre d'escampette,* Libra Films International, 1971; *Max et les ferrailleurs,* 1971; *Liza,* Horizon, 1972; *La decade prodigieuse,* Levitt/Pickman, 1972; *Themroc,* Libra, 1972; *La femme en bleu,* 1972; *Cesar et Rosalie,* Orion, 1972; *Le charme discret de la bourgeoisie,* Twentieth Century-Fox, 1972; *L'attentat,* 1972; *La grande bouffe,* Abkco Films, 1973; *Les Films 13,* 1973; *Les noces rouges,* New Line Cinema, 1973; *Grandeur nature,* Dimension, 1973; *Touche pas a la femme blanche,* Video Search of Miami, 1974; *Le fantome de la liberte,* Twentieth Century-Fox, 1974; *Vincent, Francois, Paul . . . et les autres,* Joseph Green, 1974; *Le trio infernal,* New Line Cinema, 1974; *Leonor,* New Line Cinema, 1975; *Sept morts sur ordonnance,* Hispano Foxfilm, 1975; *Der Dritte Grad,* 1975; *One Way or Another,* 1976; *L'ultima donna,* Columbia, 1976; *Mado,* Joseph Green, 1976; *Rumson,* 1976; *Rene la canne,* 1976; *F comme Fairbanks,* 1976; *L'imprecateur,* 1977; *Des enfants gates,* Corinth Films, 1977; *La part du feu,* 1977; *L'etat sauvage,* Interama Video, 1978; *Le sucre,* 1978; *Strauberg ist da,* 1978; *La petite fille en velours bleu,* 1978; *Giallo napoletano,* 1978; *Le saut dans le vide,* 1979; *Salto nel vuoto,* Summit, 1979; *Der Preis fuers Ueberleben,* 1979; *Le mors aux dents,* 1979; *Le divorcement,* 1979; *La citta delle donne,* 1980; *Atlantic City,* Paramount, 1980; *La fille prodigue,* Gaumont, 1981; *Une etrange affaire,* 1981; *Espion, leve-toi,* 1981; *Oltre la porta,* Orion, 1982; *Une chambre en ville,* 1982; *Que les gros salaires levent le doigt!!!,* 1982; *Passion,* United Artists, 1982; *La passante du Sans-Souci,* Libra Cinema 5, 1982; *Gli occhi, la bocca,* Triumph Releasing, 1982; *La nuit de Varennes,* Triumph Releasing, 1982; *Il generale dell'armata morte,* 1982; *Le prix du danger,* Astral Video, 1983; *Le matelot 512,* 1984; *Viva le vie!,* Union Generale Cinematographique, 1984; *La diagonale du fou,* International Spectrafilm, 1984; *Success Is the Best Revenge,* 1984; *Mon beau-frere a tue ma soeur,* 1985; *Peril en la demeure,* Triumph, 1985; *Partir, revenir,* 1985; *Weda'an Bonapart,* 1985; *La puritaine,* 1986; *Le Paltoquet,* 1986; *Mauvais sang,* Win-Star Cinema, 1986; *Y'a bon les blancs,* 1987; *La rumba,* 1987; *L'homme voile,* 1987; *Maladie d'amour,* 1987; *Das Weite Land,* BetaFilm, 1987; *Blanc de Chine,* 1987; *Los negros tambien comen,* 1988; *La Revolution Francaise,* 1989; *The Monkey People,* 1989; *Milou en Mai,* 1989; *Martha et Moi,* 1990; *La belle noiseuse*, MK2 Diffusion, 1991; *Le voleur d'enfants*, 1991; *Les Equilibristes*, 1991; *Das Schicksal des Freiherrn von Leisenbohg*, 1991; *Contre l'oubli*, 1991; *Le bateau de Lu*, 1991; *Le bal des cassepieds*, 1992; *From Time to Time*, 1992; *Le souper*, Mainstream, 1992; *La vie crevee*, 1992; *Leonard Wilde*, Archipel, 1992; *La cavale des fous*, 1993; *Paul*, Rupture, 1993; *L'ange noir*, 1994; *Train de nuit*, 1994; *Adam, al'Mohager*, 1994; *Bete de scene*, 1994; *Les cent et une nuits*, Cinema Village, 1995; *The Universe of Jacques Demy*, 1995; *Deux fois cinquante ans de cinema francais*, 1995; *Beaumarchais, l'insolent*, New Yorker, 1996; *Party*, JMM Invest, 1996; *Tykho Moon*, 1996; *Compagna di viaggio*, Atisbador, 1996; *The Bunuel Paradox*, 1997; *Genealogies d'un crime*, Strand Releasing, 1997; *Simoom: A Passion in the Desert*, Fine Line Features, 1998; *Rien sur Robert*, Rezo Films, 1999; *Libero burro*, Twentieth Century-Fox Italia, 1999; *Paris Tombuctu*, Anola Films, 1999; *Les acteurs*, Bac Films, 2000; *A proposito de Bunuel*, 2000; *Tout va bien, on s'en va*, Rezo Films, 2000; *Nouvel ordre mondial . . . quelque part en Afrique*, 2000; *Paris a tout prix*, 2001; *Yadon ilaheyya*, 2001; *Ja rentre a la maison*, 2001; and *La petite Lili*, 2003.

Film work includes (coproducer) *Themroc*, Libra, 1972; (coproducer) *Der Dritte Grad*, 1975; (producer) *L'etat sauvage*, Interama Video, 1978; (producer) *Il generale dell'armata morte*, 1982; (director) *Contre l'oubli*, 1991; (director) *Train de nuit*, 1994; (director) *Alors voila*, Rezo Films, 1997; (and director) *La plage noire*, Gemini Films, 2001.

Appearances on episodic television include "Louis-Charles, mon amour," *Sueurs froides*. Other television appearances include *Michel Piccoli lit Andre de Richaud*, 1977; *Lecture*, 1978; *La confusion des sentiments*, 1979; *La fausse suivante*, 1985; *La ruelle au clair de lune*, 1987; *Le conte d'hiver*, 1988; *Les grandes familles*, 1989; and *Toedliches Geld*, 1995. Stage appearances include *Phedre*, Theatre Nationale Populaire.

AWARDS, HONORS: Cannes Film Festival Best Actor Award, 1980, for *Salto nel vuoto;* Berlin International Film Festival Silver Berlin Bear, 1982, for *Une etrange affaire;* German Gold Film Award, 1988, for *Das Weite Land;* Shanghai International Film Festival Golden Goblet, 1997, for *Compagna di viaggio;* Venice Film Festival Bastone Bianco Award, 1997, for *Alor voila*.

WRITINGS:

(With Alain Lacombe) *Dialogues egoistes* (autobiography), O. Orban (Paris, Frane), 1976.

SCREENPLAYS

Il generale dell'armata morte (also known as *General of the Dead Army*), Radiotelevisione Italiana, 1982.
Train de nuit, PRV, 1994.
Alors voila, Rezo Films, 1997.
(With Ludivine Clerc) *La plage noire* (also known as *The Black Beach*), Gemini Films, 2001.

SIDELIGHTS: A veteran actor with more than 150 films to his credit, Michel Piccoli has also written several screenplays and a book. His screenplays include explorations of totalitarianism, repression, and democratization—or at least the patina thereof—in central and eastern Europe. This interest on Piccoli's part long predates the end of communist rule in eastern Europe, as a look at 1982's *Il generale dell'armata morte* reveals. The story is based on a novel by Albanian writer Ismael Kadare that places the brutality of Albania's Stalinist regime in stark relief. In the film, an Italian general combs the barren, cold mountains in the north of Albania looking for the bodies of soldiers killed in a past war.

A similar air of unreality pervades *La plage noire*, made nearly two decades later. Set in what Lisa Nesselson of *Variety* called "an unspecified but creepy land," the story seems to suggest that the end of totalitarian rule in countries long used to the grip of an iron hand results not in true freedom, but in an even deeper repression. In the film, a character named A—another touch of unreality, this one recalling that great prophet of totalitarianism, Franz Kafka—remains in his homeland after the nation's dictatorship is overthrown. His French wife, Sylvie, returns to Paris, leaving A and their daughter Joyce ultimately stranded in a country that in actuality is being convulsed by a new reign of terror. The plage noire, or "black beach," of the title is an actual location, A's childhood home, but also serves as an apt metaphor for a world in which things that are supposed to be pleasant turn out instead to be hellish.

BIOGRAPHICAL AND CRITICAL SOURCES:

BOOKS

Contemporary Theatre, Film, and Television, volume 34, Gale (Detroit, MI), 2001.
International Dictionary of Films and Filmmakers, Volume 3: *Actors and Actresses*, St. James Press (Detroit, MI), 1996.

PERIODICALS

Variety, May 28, 2001, Lisa Nesselson, review of *The Black Beach,* p. 27.*

*   *   *

PICKERING, Samuel F(rancis), Jr. 1941-

PERSONAL: Born September 30, 1941, in Nashville, TN; married, wife's name Vicki; children: three. *Education:* Sewanee, The University of the South, B.A., 1963; Cambridge University, B.A., 1965, M.A., 1970; Princeton University, Ph.D. (English), 1970.

ADDRESSES: Home—Storrs, CT. *Office*—Department of English, Box U-4025, University of Connecticut, 215 Glenbrook Road, Storrs, CT 06269-4025. *E-mail*—samuel.pickering@uconn.edu.

CAREER: Montgomery Bell Academy, Nashville, TN, instructor, 1965-66; Dartmouth College, Hanover, NH, assistant professor, 1970-78; University of Western Australia, Crawley, research associate, 1993-94; University of Connecticut, Storrs, professor, 1978—; author and book reviewer.

AWARDS, HONORS: National Endowment for the Humanities fellowship, 1974; American Council of Learned Societies grant, 1976.

WRITINGS:

ESSAY COLLECTIONS

A Continuing Education, University Press of New England (Hanover, NH), 1985.
The Right Distance, University of Georgia Press (Athens, GA), 1987.
May Days, University of Iowa Press (Iowa City, IA), 1988.
Still Life, University Press of New England (Hanover, NH), 1990.
Let It Ride, University of Missouri Press (Columbia, MO), 1991.

Trespassing, University Press of New England (Hanover, NH), 1994.
Walkabout Year: Twelve Months in Australia, University of Missouri Press (Columbia, MO), 1995.
Living to Prowl, University of Georgia Press (Athens, GA), 1997.
The Blue Caterpillar and Other Essays, University Press of Florida (Gainesville, FL), 1997.
Deprived of Unhappiness, Ohio University Press (Athens, OH), 1998.
A Little Fling and Other Essays, University of Tennessee Press (Knoxville, TN), 1999.
The Last Book, University of Tennessee Press (Knoxville, TN), 2001.

OTHER

The Moral Tradition in English Fiction, 1785-1850, University Press of New England (Hanover, NH), 1976.
John Locke and Children's Books in Eighteenth-Century England, University of Tennessee Press (Knoxville, TN), 1981.
Moral Instruction and Fiction for Children, University of Georgia Press (Athens, GA), 1993.

Also coeditor of *Children's Literature,* 8 volumes, Yale University Press, 1979-81. Contributor to numerous magazines and journals.

SIDELIGHTS: Samuel F. Pickering is a professor at the University of Connecticut and the author of eleven essay collections. He has also authored numerous scholarly works, book reviews, and over two hundred journal and magazine articles. He is "a much sought after speaker," noted Janie Franz for *Critique,* popular in the lecture circuit "mostly for his wit and his writing expertise, but sometimes for his inadvertent connection with Hollywood." Franz is referring to the fact that while teaching at Montgomery Bell Academy, a boys' prep school in Tennessee, Pickering so influenced one of his students, Tom Schulman, that when Schulman grew up, he wrote a screenplay based on Pickering. The name of the movie is *Dead Poets' Society,* and the character that actor Robin Williams plays in this movie, although fictionalized, was brought to life by Schulman's memories of Pickering.

Pickering is known best, outside of his classroom, as the creator of such imaginary characters as Slubey Carts, Proverbs Goforth, Googoo, and Loppie, all of whom live in the fictionalized city of Carthage, Tennessee. These characters tend to pop up in the middle of Pickering's essays about common things in life like grading papers, raising children, or listening to conversations at a local cafe. In a review of *The Last Book,* a *Publishers Weekly* writer said, "Pickering has the natural essayist's intimate yet distanced take on the world."

Many of the essays in Pickering's first collection, *A Continuing Education,* are about Pickering's experience as a teacher. The collection marks Pickering as a man who can laugh at himself and at other people who take themselves too seriously. He is also noted as a writer who focuses on the small details in life. As quoted in a review for *Booklist,* Pickering stated that the little things "are about all most people have." George Core in *Sewanee Review* quoted Pickering as saying, "I told curious friends in the university that I wrote the essay as an exercise in gilding the mundane."

In *The Right Distance,* Pickering reminisces about his Tennessee boyhood. "His Tennessee background provides a steady supply of amusing stories," wrote a reviewer for *Kirkus Reviews.* One of the more amusing tales involves Pickering, as a young boy, rushing through a meal, only later to discover that he had eaten his pet rooster. A reviewer for *Publishers Weekly,* like many other critics, praised Pickering's writing in this collection for its "informal but flawlessly crafted prose."

Many of the essays contained in *May Days* were inspired by a trip Pickering took with his wife, Vicki, and their children to Nova Scotia, Canada, where Vicki's grandparents once ran a farm. While visiting the now nonfunctioning farmland, Pickering went up to the attic and browsed through old trunks filled with scrapbooks, letters, and diaries. He then reconstructed the life of Margaret Fuller Jones, Pickering's wife's grandmother, creating images that he hoped his young daughter would appreciate one day. A reviewer for *Kirkus Reviews* referred to the essays in this collection as "refreshing little gems."

Pickering wrote *Still Life* at about the same time that reporters began to hound him, wanting to know how it felt to have part of his life retold in *Dead Poets' Society.* When people asked about his life, he supposedly told them they should read his current book for

answers. Barbara Scotto, in the *Wilson Library Bulletin,* wrote that in the essays in *Still Life* Pickering's "sense of voice is so compelling that it seems he has allowed the reader to enter his thoughts, to wander there with him." In this collection, Pickering reflects on his sudden notoriety, as well as his role in the community as he becomes a member of the school board, and his emotions as he responds to the death of his mother. *Library Journal* reviewer Martin J. Hudacs noted that Pickering's essays are "revealing and entertaining pieces of literature."

In 1995 Pickering took a sabbatical from teaching and traveled with his wife and children to Australia. He published his account of that experience in *Walkabout Year: Twelve Months in Australia.* Some of the essays in this collection reflect on his children's adjustment—or lack of it—to Australian schools. Most of the essays, however, refer to Pickering's own fascination with the flora and fauna of the Outback. George M. Jenks wrote in *Library Journal* that the essays contain "nuggets of wisdom . . . and glimpses of the thoughts of a middle-aged man in a foreign . . . world." Alice Joyce, writing for *Booklist,* said the collection is "distinguished by its warmly rendered, entertaining observations that leave a satisfying afterglow."

Pickering is well known for mixing fact with fiction in order to emphasize some of the familiar Southern culture in which he grew up. It is in *Living to Prowl* that his slight leaning toward fiction comes most alive, as he walks down the streets of his imaginary version of the city of Carthage. In a review for *AB Bookman's Weekly,* a reviewer wrote, "Pickering's imaginary Tennesseans are unusual in American literature: they are fictional characters existing outside the novel or short story form." There is a real city of Carthage, to which Pickering also refers, recounting stories about his family. Pickering also often jumps from the fictional town of Carthage in the midst of a conversation between his made-up characters to the conversations of real people, forcing readers to let go of a rational string of thought. The reviewer from *AB Bookman's Weekly* commented that Pickering's "essays have an elliptical structure that allows him to mix detailed observations of daily life . . . together with evocations of fictional lives and readings. . . . He knows just how far to follow a meandering line, just when to come back."

Several elements tie all of Pickering's essay collections together: his sense of humor, his focus on the ordinary, and his meandering from one topic to another more serious one with a few completely made-up characters thrown in at odd moments. "Pickering's essays," wrote a *Publishers Weekly* writer in a review of *The Blue Caterpillar and Other Essays,* "are like balls in a pinball machine, rolling from target to target with no apparent logic." As Jeff Gundy observed in *Georgia Review,* Pickering's writing "is charming, funny, incessantly inventive, and always entertaining." Although his musings center on similar, ordinary themes, Gundy said, "when Pickering gets done with the ordinary, there's nothing ordinary about it." As a reviewer for *Kirkus Reviews* wrote in a review of *A Little Fling and Other Essays,* Pickering "knows just how to coax from the ordinary the kind of sustained nourishment that imbues life with significance."

BIOGRAPHICAL AND CRITICAL SOURCES:

PERIODICALS

AB Bookman's Weekly, May 18, 1998, review of *Living to Prowl,* pp. 1359-1360.

Best Sellers, February, 1986, Riaz Hussain, review of *A Continuing Education,* pp. 427-428.

Bloomsbury Review, May, 1997, review of *The Blue Caterpillar and Other Essays,* p. 22.

Booklist, October 15, 1985, review of *A Continuing Education,* p. 294; January 1, 1988, review of *The Right Distance,* p. 731; May 15, 1994, Roland Wulbert, review of *Trespassing,* p. 1646; November 15, 1995, Alice Joyce, review of *Walkabout Year,* p. 531.

Choice, April, 1977, review of *The Moral Tradition in English Fiction 1785-1850,* p. 202; February, 1982, review of *John Locke and Children's Books in Eighteenth-Century England,* p. 767.

Georgia Review, fall, 2000, Jeff Gundy, review of *A Little Fling and Other Essays,* pp. 567-569.

Kirkus Reviews, July 1, 1987, review of *The Right Distance,* p. 979; May 1, 1988, review of *May Days,* p. 680; March 15, 1994, review of *Trespassing,* p. 62; July 15, 1998, review of *Deprived of Unhappiness,* p. 1022; August 1, 1999, review of *A Little Fling and Other Essays,* p. 1206.

Library Journal, June 15, 1990, Martin J. Hudacs, review of *Still Life,* p. 117; May 1, 1994, Judy Minken, review of *Trespassing,* p. 104; November 1, 1995, George M. Jenks, review of *Walkabout Year,* p. 97; March 15, 1997, Janice Braun, review of *The Blue Caterpillar and Other Essays,* p. 64.

Modern Language Review, April, 1979, K. J. Fielding, review of *The Moral Tradition in English Fiction 1785-1850,* pp. 421-422.

New York Times Book Review, August 3, 1997, N. Graham Newsmith, review of *The Blue Caterpillar and Other Essays,* p. 17.

Publishers Weekly, July 31, 1987, review of *The Right Distance,* p. 64; April 18, 1994, review of *Trespassing,* p. 54; October 16, 1995, review of *Walkabout Year,* p. 55; February 10, 1997, review of *The Blue Caterpillar and Other Essays,* p. 79; August 3, 1998, review of *Deprived of Unhappiness,* p. 69; July 23, 2001, review of *The Last Book,* p. 66.

Sewanee Review, October, 1985, George Core, review of *A Continuing Education,* p. R92; October, 1988, Pat C. Hoy II, review of *May Days,* p. 688, and *The Right Distance,* pp. 692-693; July, 1992, Martin Lebowitz, review of *Let It Ride,* p. R60.

Southern Humanities Review, winter, 1984, review of *John Locke and Children's Books in Eighteenth-Century England,* pp. 77-78.

Times Literary Supplement, June 24, 1977, A. O. J. Cockshut, review of *The Moral Tradition in English Fiction 1785-1850,* p. 756; May 7, 1982, Pat Rogers, review of *John Locke and Children's Books in Eighteenth-Century England,* p. 500.

Virginia Quarterly Review, spring, 1982, review of *John Locke and Children's Books in Eighteenth-Century England,* p. 56; summer, 1988, review of *A Continuing Education,* p. 106; autumn, 1988, review of *May Days,* p. 140; autumn, 1993, review of *Moral Instruction and Fiction for Children 1749-1820,* p. 118.

Washington Post Book World, July 29, 1990, review of *Still Life,* p. 13.

William and Mary Quarterly, July, 1994, Melvin Yazawa, review of *Moral Instruction and Fiction for Children 1749-1820,* p. 577.

Wilson Library Bulletin, September, 1990, Barbara Scotto, review of *Still Life,* p. 119; November, 1994, Michael Tubridy, review of *Trespassing,* p. 134.

OTHER

Critique Magazine, http://www.etext.org/Zines/ Critique/ (October 7, 2001), Janie Franz, "Sam Pickering."*

PISIER, Marie-France 1944-

PERSONAL: Born May 10, 1944, in Dalat, Indochina (now Vietnam); father, a French government official.

ADDRESSES: Agent—Laurent Gregoire, Intertalent, 5 rue Clement-Marot, 75008 Paris, France.

CAREER: Actress, director, and writer. Film appearances include *Qui ose nous accuser?*, 1961; *Les Saintes nitouches,* 1962; "Antoine et Colette," *L'Amour a vingt ans,* 1962, released in the United States by Embassy, 1963; *La Morte d'un tueur,* 1963; *Les Yeux cernes,* 1964; *Le Vampire de Duesseldorf,* 1965; *L'Ecume des jours,* 1967; *Non sta bene rubare il tesoro,* 1967; *Trans-Europ-Express,* Trans American, 1968; *Baisers voles,* Lopert, 1969; *Paulina s'en va,* 1969; *Le Journal d'un suicide,* 1972; *Feminin-Feminin,* 1973; *Celine et Julie vont en bateau,* Les Films Christian Fachner, 1974; *Le Fantome de la liberte,* 1974; *Souvenirs d'en France,* AMLF, 1975; *Barocco,* Films la Boetie, 1976; *Serail,* Contemporary, 1976; *Cousin, Cousine,* Les Films Pomerey/Gaumont, 1976; *Le Corps e mon ennemi,* AMLF, 1976; *The Other Side of Midnight,* Twentieth Century-Fox, 1977; *Les Apprentis sorciers,* Backstreet/Institut National de L'Audiovisuel/Buffalo, 1977; *Les Soeurs Brontë,* Gaumont, 1979; *French Postcards,* Paramount, 1979; *La Banquiere,* Gaumont, 1980; *L'Amour en fuite,* Les Films du Carosse, 1980; *Miss Right,* IAP/Sony Video Software, 1981; *Chanel Solitaire,* United Film Distribution, 1981; *L'As des as,* Gaumont, 1982; *Hot Touch,* Astral/Trans-Atlantic Enterprises, 1982; *Der Zauberberg,* Franz Seitz Filmproduktion/Gaumont/Opera Film Produzione/Zweites Deutsches Fernsehen, 1982; *Boulevard des assassins,* 1982; *AMLF/World Marketing,* 1983; *Le Prix du danger,* Brent Walker Film Distributors/Union Generale Cinematographique, 1983; *Union Generale Cinematographique,* 1984; *44 ou les recits de la nuit,* 1985; *Parking,* A.M., 1985; *L'Inconnu de Vienne,* SFP, 1986; *L'Oeuvre au noir,* Union Generale Cinematographique/Twentieth Century-Fox, 1988; *La Note bleue,* 1991; *Francois Truffaut: Portraits voles,* 1993; *Pourquoi maman est dans mon lit?,* 1994; *Tous les jours dimanche,* 1995; *Le Fils de Gascogne,* 1995; *La Gazelle,* 1996; *Marion,* 1997; *Pourquoi pas moi?,* Cinema Mondo, 1999; *La Patinoire,* Interama Video, 1999; *Le Temps retrouve,* Kino International, 1990; *Sur un air d'autoroute,* United International Pictures, 2000; *Combat d'amour en songe,* Gemini Films, 2000; *Inch'Allah dimanche,* 2001; and *Comme un avion,* 2002.

Appearances on television miniseries include *The French Atlantic Affair,* ABC, 1979; *Scruples,* CBS, 1980; and *Les Marmottes,* 1998. Appearances on episodic television include "Le Fetichiste," *Temoignages.* Other television appearances include *Les Gens de mogador,* 1972; *Der Stille Ozean,* 1982; *Une Maman dans la ville,* 1992; *La Verite est un vilain defaut,* 1995; *Notre homme,* 1995; *Une femme sur mesure,* 1997; *Un jeune Francais,* 2000; and *La Couleur du mensonge,* 2001. Television work as director includes *Le Bal du gouverneur,* 1990.

AWARDS, HONORS: Cesar Award for Best Supporting Actress, 1976, for *Cousin, cousine,* 1977, for *Barocco.*

WRITINGS:

(With Jacques Rivette, Eduardo du Gregorio, Juliet Berto, Dominique LaBourier, and Bulle Ogier) *Celine et Julie Vont en bateau* (screenplay, also known as *Celine and Julie Go Boating* and *Phantom Ladies over Paris*), Les Films Christian Fachner, 1974.

(With François Truffaut, Jean Aurel, and Suzanne Schiffman) *L'Amour en fuite* (screenplay, also known as *Love on the Run*), Les Films du Carosse, 1980.

Le Bal du gouverneur (screenplay, also known as *The Governor's Party;* based on her novel by the same name—see below) France 3 Cinema, 1990.

Comme un avion (screenplay, also known as *Like an Airplane*), Rezo Films, 2002.

NOVELS

Le bal du gouverneur, Bernard Grasset (Paris, France), 1984.

Je n'ai aime que vous, Bernard Grasset (Paris, France), 1986.

Le deuil du printemps, Bernard Grasset (Paris, France), 1997.

SIDELIGHTS: Referring to the director with whom Marie-France Pisier shared screenwriting credit for *Celine and Julie Go Boating,* Royal S. Brown in *Cineaste* wrote that "Of the various French directors that one can place within that loosely defined group known as The New Wave, Jacques Rivette is certainly one of the least well-known in the United States." Brown went on to note that while others such as François Truffaut were gaining mainstream acceptance, Rivette "remained the true independent, if not totally underground, filmmaker." It is certainly hard, when reading Brown's summary of the film's "plot," to find evidence suggesting that the film—which he judged as Rivette's masterpiece—would be likely to find acceptance with any popular audience, particularly in the United States. For instance, Brown described the characters played by Pisier, Bulle Ogler, and Barbet Schroeder as ghoulish figures who live "within the foreboding confines of a large, shuttered brick mansion set beneath the level of a street improbably named the Rue du Nadir des Pommes (Apples' Nadir Street). . . . Like refugees from a Pirandello play, they find themselves trapped in a double narrative taken from two different works by Henry James."

By contrast, Pisier's own *Like an Airplane,* which she wrote and directed a quarter century after her work with Rivette, seems straightforward if a bit complex. In the story, a doctoral candidate named Lola has a tempestuous relationship with a lawyer, Simon, while her little brother Guillaume develops a crush on a girl in his high-school class. Meanwhile, their mother, Claire (played by Pisier herself), pretends to go on vacation so that she can secretly recuperate from a double mastectomy. Somewhat less complicated, if only slightly, is 1979's *Love on the Run,* directed by Truffaut, which concerns a proofreader named Antoine. Having divorced his wife, he meets Colette (Pisier), the girl he loved as a teenager, who has just purchased a copy of an autobiographical novel he has recently published. Still, there are more complications, since Antoine is already in love with a third woman, a record-seller named Sabine.

BIOGRAPHICAL AND CRITICAL SOURCES:

BOOKS

Contemporary Theatre, Film, and Television, volume 34, Gale (Detroit, MI), 2001.

PERIODICALS

Cineaste, summer, 1998, Royal S. Brown, review of *Celine and Julie Go Boating,* pp. 30-31.
Variety, February 18, 2002, Lisa Nesselson, review of *Like an Airplane,* p. 36.*

POTOK, Chaim 1929-2002
(Herman Harold Potok)

OBITUARY NOTICE—See index for *CA* sketch: Born Herman Harold Potok on February 17, 1929, in New York, NY; died of brain cancer July 23, 2002, in Merion, PA. Novelist. Potok published nearly twenty books, and was best known for his novels *The Chosen, The Promise,* and *My Name Is Asher Lev* although he also wrote nonfiction and children's books. Born to Polish-Jewish immigrants and groomed to become a Talmudic scholar, Potok decided instead to become a writer. He graduated summa cum laude from Yeshiva University and in 1954 was ordained a Conservative rabbi. After serving as an army chaplain in Korea, he earned a Ph.D. in philosophy from the University of Pennsylvania. He published his first novel, *The Chosen,* in 1967; it was nominated for a National Book Award, adapted as a motion picture in 1982, and adapted for the stage as a musical in the late 1980s and a play in 2002. Potok wrote of Jewish culture from an insider viewpoint, often focusing on the inevitable conflicts that arise between secular artistic impulses and deeply held, culturally based Jewish beliefs. Several of his novels, among them *The Promise* (1969), *My Name Is Asher Lev* (1972), the mystical *The Book of Lights* (1981), and *Davita's Harp* (1985), received mixed critical reviews as a result of his return to this theme. Potok also taught at several colleges, including the University of Pennsylvania, Bryn Mawr College, and Johns Hopkins University. His 1999 children's story "Moon" won the O. Henry Award, while his last book, a collection of three novellas titled *Old Men at Midnight,* was published in 2001. He also worked with violinist Isaac Stern on Stern's critically respected autobiography, *My First Seventy-nine Years,* published in 1999.

OBITUARIES AND OTHER SOURCES:

PERIODICALS

Baltimore Sun, July 24, 2002.
Guardian (London, England), July 31, 2002, p. 18.
Los Angeles Times July 24, 2002 p. B11.
New York Times, July 24, 2002, p. A17.
Philadelphia Daily News, July 24, 2002, p. 31.
Times (London, England) July 26, 2002 p. 31.
Washington Post, July 24, 2002, p. B05.

POTOK, Herman Harold
    See POTOK, Chaim

*   *   *

POWELL, Jane
    See BURCE, Suzanne Lorraine

*   *   *

PURKISS, Diane 1961-

PERSONAL: Born 1961. *Education:* University of Queensland, B.A. (honors); Merton College, Oxford, Ph.D.

ADDRESSES: Office—Keble College, Parks Rd., Oxford OX1 3PG, England. *E-mail*—diane.purkiss@keble.ox.ac.uk.

CAREER: Keble College, Oxford, England, fellow and tutor; Exeter University, Exeter, England, professor of English.

WRITINGS:

(Editor with Clare Brant) *Women, Texts, and Histories: 1575-1760,* Routledge (New York, NY), 1992.
(Editor) *Renaissance Women: The Plays of Elizabeth Cary: The Poems of Aemilia Lanyer,* Pickering and Chatto (Brookfield, VT), 1994.
The Witch in History: Early Modern and Twentieth-Century Representations, Routledge (New York, NY), 1996.
At the Bottom of the Garden: A Dark History of Fairies, Hobgoblins, and Other Troublesome Things, New York University Press (New York, NY), 2000, published as *Troublesome Things: A History of Fairies and Fairy Stories,* 2000.

SIDELIGHTS: Diane Purkiss is a fellow and tutor of English at Keble College, Oxford. Her research areas include Milton, Renaissance drama, the English Civil War, and the supernatural in the early modern period. Purkiss's book *At the Bottom of the Garden: A Dark History of Fairies, Hobgoblins, and Other Trouble-some Things* discusses the history and anthropology of fairies. Backing up her history with intensive scholarly research, Purkiss shows that in the past, fairies were regarded with fear and dread, as frightening beings from another world who could steal or kill children, abduct young men, cause illness or blindness, or rape human women. Later, in the seventeenth century, people began regarding them as beings who could bring luck or wealth to those they favored. In the nineteenth and early twentieth century, their image changed, and they were seen as pure, childlike beings that represented innocence and light. A *Publishers Weekly* reviewer wrote, "Although fairies are a popular subject among New Age readers today, Purkiss's book is better suited for serious researchers of popular beliefs and culture." In the London *Sunday Times,* Lucy Hughes-Hallett wrote that the book is "both splendidly scholarly and breezily accessible," and called it "a monstrous, magnificent fairy ride." In the *Times,* Michele Roberts praised it as "an elegantly written and witty book" Sara Maitland wrote in *Spectator* that the book was "accessible without being simplistic" and "both illuminating and enormous fun."

The Witch in History: Early Modern and Twentieth-Century Representations examines a variety of documents on witches and witchcraft to determine how witches have been regarded during different periods in history. Purkiss examines records of witchcraft trials and shows how some women used fantasies of witchcraft to feel more empowered in their daily lives. She also studies witches as depicted in the works of Shakespeare, Jonson, and others, and shows how these authors not only drew upon popular images of witches, but also reshaped them. In addition, she also surveys contemporary witchcraft practitioners and examines their feminist version of witchcraft's long history in European culture. As Alison Lurie wrote in the *New York Review of Books,* Purkiss "avoids the problem of the confusing, fragmentary, and probably biased records of the witchcraft trials by putting aside any attempt to find out what 'really happened' and concentrating on what people *thought* happened, both then and now."

BIOGRAPHICAL AND CRITICAL SOURCES:

PERIODICALS

Ariel, July, 1998, Wendy Schissel, review of *The Witch in History: Early Modern and Twentieth-Century Representations,* p. 198.

Contemporary Review, spring, 1997, Chris Arthur, review of *The Witch in History,* p. 158.

Eighteenth-Century Life, May, 1998, Michael Hunter, "Witchcraft and the Decline of Belief," p. 139.

Journal of Women's History, winter, 1999, Heather Lee Miller, review of *The Witch in History,* p. 232.

New York Review of Books, October 23, 1997, Alison Lurie, "Bothered and Bewildered," p. 48.

Notes and Queries, September, 1993, Isobel Grundy, review of *Women, Texts, and Histories: 1575-1760s,* p. 366.

Publishers Weekly, February 5, 2001, review of *At the Bottom of the Garden: A Dark History of Fairies, Hobgoblins, and Other Troublesome Things,* p. 78.

Renaissance Quarterly, summer, 1998, Brian P. Levack, review of *The Witch in History,* p. 655.

Review of English Studies, February, 1995, Jacqueline Pearson, review of *Women, Texts, and Histories,* p. 89.

Sixteenth Century Journal, spring, 1994, Robert C. Evans, review of *Women, Texts and Histories,* p. 210; winter, 1997, Kathryn A. Edwards, review of *The Witch in History,* p. 1433.

Spectator, January 6, 2001, Sara Maitland, "Haunters of the Margins," p. 25.

Sunday Telegraph (London, England), December 17, 2000, Lucy Hughes-Hallett, "Fairies Could Be Dangerously, Seductively Beautiful, or Repulsively, Hairily Naked," p. 38; December 24, 2000, Richard Davenport-Hines, "The Tooth Fairy Had Fangs," p. 15.

Times (London, England), November 29, 2000, Michele Roberts, "Enchanting Visions of Fairyland," p. 14; December 17, 2000, p. 38; January 20, 2001, "Fairies Don't Just Live at the Bottom of the Garden," p. 12.

Times Literary Supplement, June 22, 2001, Andrew Wawn, "Farewell Rewards and Fairies," p. 36.

OTHER

Dr. Diane Purkiss Web site, http://senior.keble.ox.ac.uk/fellows (February 11, 2003).*

Q-R

QUINN, Rob 1972-

PERSONAL: Born January 9, 1972; son of James P. (in sales) and Donna S. (an administrative assistant) Quinn. *Education:* West Chester University, B.A. (with honors) 1996.

ADDRESSES: Office—Chelsea House Publishers, 1974 Sproul Rd., Broomall, PA 19008. *E-mail*—rob_quinn@ chelseahouse.com.

CAREER: Author. Chelsea House Publishers, Broomall, PA, Web site copywriter and editor.

WRITINGS:

Oscar de la Hoya, Chelsea House (Philadelphia, PA), 2001.

Contributor of articles to *Philadelphia Inquirer.*

WORK IN PROGRESS: A novel.

BIOGRAPHICAL AND CRITICAL SOURCES:

PERIODICALS

Book Report, November, 2001, Sandra L. Morton, review of *Oscar de la Hoya,* p. 72.
Horn Book Guide, fall, 2001, Jeanne M. Chapman, review of *Oscar de la Hoya,* p. 409.

RADICHKOV, Yordan Dimitrov 1929-

PERSONAL: Born October 6, 1929, in Kalimanitsa, Mikhaylovgrad, Bulgaria; son of Dimiter Traykov Radichkov (a farmer and mason) and Mladena Vasileva Filipova (a midwife and farmer); married Suzi Markova Garti; children: Dumiter, Roza. *Education:* Attended high school in Berkovitsa, Bulgaria.

CAREER: Narodna mladezh (title means "National Youth"), newspaper correspondent, 1951, editor, 1952-55; *Vecherni novini* (title means "Evening News"), editor, 1955-59; Bulgarian Cinematography Company, scenario board, 1959-62; *Literaturen front* (title means "Literary Front"), writer, beginning 1950s, editor, 1962-69. Adviser to Council on Cultural Treasures, 1971.

MEMBER: Union of Bulgarian Writers, from 1962 (deputy chairman, 1986-90).

AWARDS, HONORS: Honored cultural worker, 1974; Grinzane Cavur, international prize for literature; silver plate award, *Cinema Internacionale,* and Prize for contemporary cinematographic expression, Festival of Bulgarian Films in Varna, both for *Goreshto pladne;* International Movie Festival, Atlanta, Georgia, 1974, best foreign director; International Movie Festival, San Remo, Italy, gold medal for best actor; Special Prize of the Jury, International Festival in Toulon, France, 1975, for *Posledno lyato.*

WRITINGS:

Gorda Stara planina (title means "The Proud Balkan Range"), Narodna mladezh (Sofia, Bulgaria), 1956.

Sértseto bie za khorata: Sotochinski razkazi (title means "The Heart Beats for the People: Stories from Sotochino"), Narodna mladezh (Sofia, Bulgaria), 1959.

Prosti rétse: Razkazi (title means "Simple Hands"), Narodna mladezh (Sofia, Bulgaria), 1961.

Obérnato nebe: Razkazi (title means "The Sky Upside Down"), Narodna mladezh (Sofia, Bulgaria), 1962.

Planinsko tsvete: Razkazi (title means "A Mountain Flower"), Profizdat (Sofia, Bulgaria), 1964.

Sharena cherga: Razkazi za detsa (title means "A Multicolored Rug"), Narodna mladezh (Sofia, Bulgaria), 1964, enlarged edition, Otechestvo (Sofia, Bulgaria), 1987.

Goreshto pladne Narodna mladezh (Sofia, Bulgaria), 1965, translated by Peter Tempest as *Hot Noon*, Sofia Press (Sofia, Bulgaria), 1973.

Svirepo nastroenie (title means "Violent Mood"), Bélgarski pisatel (Sofia, Bulgaria), 1965.

Neosvetenite dvorove: Pétepis za Sibir (title means "Unlit Courtyards"), Bélgarski pisatel (Sofia, Bulgaria), 1966.

Vodoley (title means "Aquarius"), Narodna mladezh (Sofia, Bulgaria), 1967.

Kozyata brada: Noveli (title means "Goat's Beard"), Bélgarski pisatel (Sofia, Bulgaria), 1967.

Vyatérét na spokoystvieto: Noveli (title means "The Wind of Calm"), Narodna mladezh (Sofia, Bulgaria), 1968.

Nie, vrabchetata (title means "We, the Sparrows"), Narodna mladezh (Sofia, Bulgaria), 1968.

Baruten bukvar (title means "The Gunpowder ABC Book"), Bélgarski pisatel (Sofia, Bulgaria), 1969.

Kozheniyat pépesh (title means "The Leather Melon"), Khristo G. Danov (Plovdiv, Bulgaria), 1969.

Skalni risunki: Noveli (title means "Rock Drawings"), Bélgarski pisatel (Sofia, Bulgaria), 1970.

Choveshka proza (title means "Human Prose"), Khristo G. Danov (Plovdiv, Bulgaria), 1971.

Plyava i zérno (title means "Chaff and Grain"), Bélgarski pisatel (Sofia, Bulgaria), 1972.

Yanuari: Zimna poema (title means "January: A Winter Poem"), 1973.

Kak taka? (title means "How Come?"), G. Bakalov (Varna, Bulgaria), 1974.

Malko otechestvo (title means "Small Fatherland"), Dérzhavno voenno izdatelstvo (Sofia, Bulgaria), 1974.

Vsichki i nikoy: Roman (title means "Everybody and No One"), Otechestven front (Sofia, Bulgaria), 1975.

Spomeni za kone: Noveli (title means "Memories about Horses"), Bélgarski pisatel (Sofia, Bulgaria), 1975.

Shest malki matryoshki i edna golyama: Noveli (title means "Six Small Matryoshkas and a Big One"), G. Bakalov (Plovdiv, Bulgaria), 1977.

Lazaritsa: Piesa v 4 sezona (title means "Lazarus Treed: A Play in Four Seasons"), translated by E. J. Czerwinski as *Lazarus Treed*, in *Slavic and East European Arts*, 5, summer, 1987.

Sumatokha. Yanuari. Lazaritsa: Piesi (title means "Commotion"), Bélgarski pisatel (Sofia, Bulgaria), 1978.

Prashka: Roman (title means "Sling"), Khristo G. Danov (Plovdiv, Bulgaria), 1979.

Luda treva (title means "Wild Grass"), Bélgarski pisatel (Sofia, Bulgaria), 1980.

Malka severna saga (title means "A Small Northern Saga"), Bélgarski pisatel (Sofia, Bulgaria), 1980.

Pedya zemya (title means "A Span of Land"), Profizdat (Sofia, Bulgaria), 1980.

Opit za letene: Piesi (title means "Attempt to Fly"), Bélgarski pisatel (Sofia, Bulgaria), 1982.

Nezhnata spirala (title means "The Tender Spiral"), Bélgarski pisatel (Sofia, Bulgaria), 1983.

Po vodata: Noveli (title means "On the Water"), Narodna mladezh (Sofia, Bulgaria), 1983.

Verblyud: Razkazi i noveli, G. Bakalov (Plovdiv, Bulgaria), 1984.

Izpadnali ot karutsata na boga (title means "Things That Have Fallen off God's Cart"), BZNS (Sofia, Bulgaria), 1984.

Skakalets (title means "Grasshopper"), Profizdat (Sofia, Bulgaria), 1984.

Koshnitsi: Piesa (title means "Baskets"), Bélgarski pisatel (Sofia, Bulgaria), 1985.

Skandinavtsite: Razkazi (title means "Scandinavians"), Bélgarski pisatel (Sofia, Bulgaria), 1985.

Tenekienoto petle: Noveli (title means "The Little Tin Rooster"), Partizdat (Sofia, Bulgaria), 1985.

Noev kovcheg: Roman (title means "Noah's Ark"), Bélgarski pisatel (Sofia, Bulgaria), 1988.

Khora i svraki (title means "People and Magpies"), Narodna mladezh (Sofia, Bulgaria), 1990.

Svirepo nastroenie, Khristo Botev (Sofia, Bulgaria), 1992.

Malki zhabeshki istorii, Khemus (Sofia, Bulgaria), 1994.

Smokove v livadite, Pechatnitsa-izd-vo (Plovdiv, Bulgaria), 1995.

Literaturnata ornitsa: Interviuta, Balkani (Sofia, Bulgaria), 1999.

Avtostradata, Fakel (Sofia, Bulgaria), 1999.

Svirepo nastroenie, Anubis (Sofia, Bulgaria), 2000.
Pupavo vreme, Fakel (Sofia, Bulgaria), 2000.
Izbrano, Anubis (Sofia, Bulgaria), 2000.

PLAYS

Sumatokha, 1965.
Zhelyaznoto Momche (title means "The Iron Boy"),
    1968
Yanuari (title means "January"), 1968.

MOTION PICTURES

Goreshto pladne, (screenplay), Studiya za igralni filmi,
    1966.
Privérzaniyat balon (screenplay; title means "The Tied
    Balloon"), Studiya za igralni filmi, 1967.
Posledno lyato (screenplay; title means "Last
    Summer"), Studia za igralni filmi, 1974.

Contributor to periodical publication *Sévremennik.*

SIDELIGHTS: Yordan Radichkov is best known for
his surreal stories and dramas, in which he continually
works to protect his natural environment and reinvigo-
rate his cultural environment. Radichkov's absurdist,
grotesque narratives at first found only a popular audience, but by the 1990s, Radichkov became a world-
renowned author, playwright, and screenwriter.

Lyubomira Parpulova-Gribble wrote in *Dictionary of
Literary Biography:* "Radichkov's works did not
comply with the rules of the so-called method of
socialist realism, which many official literary critics
tried to enforce." Thus, Radichkov revolutionized
Bulgarian fiction.

Radichkov was raised in the small village of Kalimanitsa, in the Mikhaylovgrad district of Bulgaria. According to Parpulova-Gribble, his upbringing made
him sensitive to wildlife preservation and other
environmental themes, particularly in the 1990s.

Radichkov, who received some formal education at
the high school in Berkovitsa, became a reporter for
Narodna mladezh in 1951. He was quickly promoted
to editor, and moved to the city of Sofia, where he

was an editor for a larger paper, *Vecherni novini.* Four
years later, Radichkov moved to the Scenario Board of
the Bulgarian Cinematography Company, where he
became involved in writing motion pictures. Three
years after that, he edited the *Lituraturen front.*

During this period, Radichkov also began to publish
collections of his stories, including *Sertseto bie za
khorata: Sotochinski razkazi, Prosti retse, Obernato
nebe,* and *Planinsko tsvete.* In these early volumes,
Radichkov remained within traditional Bulgarian literary bounds. But this changed, beginning with *Svirepo
natroenie.* In that collection, stories depict a bizarre
world in which pigs fly through space, dogs can eat
stories, and wolves and sheep graze peacefully side by
side. Parpulova-Gribble commented: "His narratives
are open and can sustain several different interpretations, which is a typical feature of mythical discourse."

Through this open-ended, folk-mythological style,
Radichkov criticized political movements and ecological policy. Through surrealism, Radichkov opened up
possibilities for literary and political revolution.
Though Radichkov gradually began to guide readers,
this open-interpretation style remained one of his most
enduring qualities.

As Parpulova-Gribble pointed out, Radichkov also
contributed significantly to Bulgarian dramatic
literature. Again, he pushed the "rules," but reaction
was positive. In *Lazaritsa,* for example, the audience
watches a peasant named Lazar hiding in a pear tree
from his vicious dog after he tried to shoot it and
missed. For a full year, Lazar sits in the tree and
wonders what went wrong. The play was a hit.
"Perhaps there was some special affinity to theater
hidden within the fiction writer that enabled him to
produce these unique plays," Parpulova-Gribble wrote,
noting that Radichkov's son was a theater director, his
daughter a drama critic.

Scenarios he provided for films such as *Goreshto
plande, Priverzaniyat balon,* and *Posledno lyato,* some
of which he based on his own stories, led to major
international awards for his fellow Bulgarian
filmmakers.

Eventually, Radichkov drew praise for his literary
contributions; he was granted various international
awards for his work along with appointments to

Bulgarian cultural establishments. In 1971, Radichkov became an advisor to the Council for Cultural Treasures, and in 1974 he became an "honored cultural worker." His surreal, mythical style of writing, which initially disturbed and even frightened some readers, eventually became his best achievement.

BIOGRAPHICAL AND CRITICAL SOURCES:

BOOKS

Dictionary of Literary Biography, Volume 181: *South Slavic Writers since World War II,* Gale (Detroit, MI), 1997, pp. 270-274.*

*　　　*　　　*

RAYMOND, Charles
See KOCH, Charlotte (Moskowitz)

*　　　*　　　*

RIBA, Carles 1893-1959

PERSONAL: Born December 23, 1893, in Barcelona, Spain; died July 12, 1959, in Barcelona, Spain; son of Antoni and Adela (Bracons) Riba; married Clementina Arderiu (a poet). *Education:* Attended University of Barcelona.

CAREER: Poet, literary critic, translator, and professor. University of Barcelona, Barcelona, Spain, professor of Greek; Bernat Metge Foundation, Barcelona, Spain, director.

WRITINGS:

Primer llibre d'Estances, La Revista (Barcelona, Spain), 1919, republished as *Estances,* Observador (Barcelona, Spain), 1991.
Carles Riba, prologue by M. de Montoliu, Edicions Lira (Barcelona, Spain), 1923, revised edition, edited by Jaime Bofill y Ferro, 1938.
Tres suites, Edicions de la Rosa dels Vents (Barcelona, Spain), 1937, new edition, edited by Jordi Malé i Pegueroles, Edicions 62 (Barcelona, Spain), 1993.

Elegies de Bierville, Santiago de Xile (Buenos Aires, Argentina), 1942, new edition, Edicions 62 (Barcelona, Spain), 1994, translation by J. L. Gili published as *Elegies de Bierville/Bierville Elegies* (bilingual edition, English and Catalan), Dolphin (Oxford, England), 1995.
Elegies de Bierville; Salvatge cor; Altre poemes, Observador (Barcelona, Spain), 1942, new edition, 1991.
Del joc i del foc, Editorial Selecta (Barcelona, Spain), 1946, republished in a bilingual Spanish/Catalan edition as *Del juego y del fuego,* Spanish translation by José Augustin Goytisolo, prologue by Jaume Pont, Edicions del Mall (Barcelona, Spain), 1987.
L'ingenu amor: edició definitiva illustrada amb cinc gravats sobre boix a tot color, Ll. Sibils (Barcelona, Spain), 1948.
Les aventures d'En Perot Marrasqui, Editorial Selecta (Barcelona, Spain), 1950, new edition, Observardor (Barcelona, Spain), 1991.
Salvatge cor: sonets, Óssa (Barcelona, Spain), 1952, translation by J. L. Gili published as *Salvatge cor/ Savage Heart* (bilingual edition, English and Catalan), Dolphin (Oxford, England), 1993.
Més els poemes: notes sobre poetes i poesia, J. Horta (Barcelona, Spain), 1957.
Esbós de tres oratoris: Els tres reis d'Orient: Llàtzer, el ressuscitat: El fill Pròdig, Ossa Menor (Barcelona, Spain), 1957.
Poems of Carles Riba (bilingual edition, English and Catalan), English translation by J. L. Gili, Dolphin (Oxford, England), 1964, revised edition, 1970.
Obres completes, two volumes, Ediciones 62 (Barcelona, Spain), 1965, new edition, edited and introduced by Enric Sullà, 1992.
Versions de Hölderlin, preface by Gabriel Ferrater, Edicions 62 (Barcelona, Spain), 1971.
Antologia poetica, prologue by Joan Triadú, Proa (Barcelona, Spain), 1979, new edition, edited by Enric Sullà, Edicions 62 (Barcelona, Spain), 1982.
Esbossos de versions de Rilke, edited by Enric Sullà, Edicions 62 (Barcelona, Spain), 1984.
Papers de joventut, Generalitat de Catalunya (Barcelona, Spain), 1987.
Cartes d'Alemanya i Grecia, edited by Carles-Jordi Guardiola, Edicions de la Magrana (Barcelona, Spain), 1987.
Cantares d'amor e d'amigo, edited by Xosé Lois Garcia, Ediciós do Castro (Sada, A Coruña, Spain), 1990.

Centenari Carles Riba, 1893-1993, edited by Joan Triadú, Generalitat de Catalunya (Barcelona, Spain), 1993.

JUVENILE

Sis Joans, Sabadell (Barcelona, Spain), 1928, new edition, Observador (Barcelona, Spain), 1991.

Les aventures d'en Perot Marrasquí, Editorial Selecta (Barcelona, Spain), 1947.

Seis Juanes, Editorial Juventud (Barcelona, Spain), 1951.

(Translator) Jean de Brunhoff, *Babar i la vella senyora,* Ayma (Barcelona, Spain), 1957.

(Adaptor) Homer, *Las aventuras de Ulises,* illustrated by Fina Rifà, La Galera (Barcelona, Spain), 1993.

ESSAY COLLECTIONS

Escolis, i altres articles, La Revista (Barcelona, Spain), 1921.

Els marges, Observador (Barcelona, Spain), 1927, new edition, 1991.

Per comprendre, 1927-1935, La Revista (Barcelona, Spain), 1937, new edition, Observador (Barcelona, Spain), 1991.

Resum de literatura llatina, Editorial Barcino (Barcelona, Spain), 1933.

Resum de literatura grega, Editorial Barcino (Barcelona, Spain), 1937.

Llegendari català, Editorial Catalana (Barcelona, Spain), 1950.

Llengua i literatura, edited by Joaquim Molas, Edicions 62 (Barcelona, Spain), 1965.

Clàssics i moderns, edited by Joaquim Molas, Edicions 62 (Barcelona, Spain), 1979.

Carles Riba en els seus millors escrits, M. Arimany (Barcelona, Spain), 1984.

Sobre poesia i sobre la meva poesia, edited by Enric Sullà, Empúries (Barcelona, Spain), 1984.

Polítics i intellectuals i altres assaigs, Observador (Barcelona, Spain), 1991.

Súnion: antologia comentada, La Magrana (Barcelona, Spain), 1995.

TRANSLATOR

Virgil, *Las Bucòliques,* [Barcelona], 1911.

Homer, *L'odissea,* Editorial Catalana (Mallorca, Spain), 1919, new edition, Edicions de la Magrana (Barcelona, Spain), 1993.

(And editor) Xenophon, *Obres socràtiques menors: Economia, Convit, Defensa de Sòcrates,* Fundació Bernat Metge (Barcelona, Spain), 1924.

A. Gudeman, *Historia de la literature latina,* Editorial Labor (Barcelona, Spain), 1926.

(And editor) Plutarch, *Vides parelleles,* Fundació Bernat Metge (Barcelona, Spain), 1926, republished as *Alejandro y César: vidas paralelas,* introduction by E. Valentí Fiol, Salvat Editores (Barcelona, Spain), 1970.

Xenophon, *Els Due Mil,* Fundació Bernat Metge (Barcelona, Spain), 1927.

(And editor) Xenophon, *Records de Sòcrates,* Fundació Bernat Metge (Barcelona, Spain), 1929.

Aeschylus, *Tragèdies,* Fundació Bernat Metge (Barcelona, Spain), 1932.

Sophocles, *Tragèdies* (bilingual edition, Greek and Catalan), Fundació Bernat Metge (Barcelona, Spain), 1951.

Edgar Allan Poe, *Els assassinates del carrer de la morgue,* Editorial Selecta (Barcelona, Spain), 1953.

Constantine Cavafy, *Poemes de Kavafis,* Editorial Teide (Barcelona, Spain), 1962.

Euripedes, *Tragèdies,* edited and introduced by Carles Miralles, Curial (Barcelona, Spain), 1977.

Joseph Bédier, *El romanç de Tristany i Isolda,* Edicions dels Quaderns Crema (Barcelona, Spain), 1981.

Also wrote prologues for a Catalan translation of the fables of Jean de La Fontaine, and for *Anthologia Poetica,* by Joan Maragall, 1954.

ADAPTATIONS: Riba's poetry has been set to music by Francesc Taverna-Bech and Alan Rawsthorne.

SIDELIGHTS: Carles Riba was a poet, literary critic, translator, and professor of Greek. He was an important voice for Catalan literature, encouraging discussions between Catalan and Castilian writers and introducing Catalan culture to other parts of the world. Writing in *World Literature Today,* Janet Pérez stated, "[Riba] is important above all in the normalization of Catalan language and expression."

Riba was born in Barcelona and studied law and literature at the University of Barcelona. He went into exile in 1939 to France, returning to Barcelona in 1943. After translating classical works for the Bernat Metge Foundation, he eventually became its director.

Riba's first book of criticism, *Escolis, i altres articles,* was a declaration of his adherence to the classical and distinctly anti-modernist "Noucentisme" movement of Eugenie d'Ours. Besides critical work, Riba wrote well-received children's stories and a varied body of translations ranging from Greek tragedy to the works of Edgar Allan Poe.

Riba's primary form of writing, however, was poetry. By the 1920s he had established a positive reputation as a poet, following the publication of his first poetry collection, *Primer llibre d'Estances. Tres suites,* a collection of thirty poems written in sonnet form published in 1937, confirmed Riba as a master poet. Pérez noted that early inspirations for Riba's verse came from classical sources, while his later verse was influenced by French symbolism.

Elegies de Bierville is cited by many critics as Riba's finest poetry collection. The work reflects upon his experience of exile in Bierville, France, during the Spanish Civil War. It explores themes of physical isolation and spiritual deprivation, and ultimately recognition of a Christian God. Two later works expand on religious themes, *Salvatge cor: sonets* and *Esbós de tres oratoris: Els tres reis d'Orient: Llàtzer, el ressuscitat: El fill Pròdig.* Riba experimented with alternative forms of poetry in other works, as in *Del joc i del foc,* in which he uses the Japanese tanka form.

Riba's works have been translated into twelve languages. A poetry prize has also been established in his name.

BIOGRAPHICAL AND CRITICAL SOURCES:

BOOKS

Guardiola, Carles-Jordi, *Carles & Clementina: àlbum de Carles Riba i Clementina Arderíu,* La Magrana (Barcelona, Spain), 1993.
Montero, Xesús Alonso, *Carles Riba e Galicia: homenaxe no I centenario do seu nacemento,* Galaxia (Vigo, Spain), 1993.

PERIODICALS

Catalan Review, June, 1987, Graciel la Edo i Baste, "Erotisme i temps a *Salvatge cor* de Carles Riba," pp. 101-110; Volume 6, 1992, Manuel Duran,

"Carles Riba on Josep Carner: Four Studies (1914-1929)," pp. 431-454; Volume 8, 1994, Jordi Male i Pergueroles, "Una tipologia poetica de Carles Riba als *Escolis,*" pp. 245-264.
Journal of Catalan Studies, 2000, Isidor Mari i Mayans, "Rilke i l'orfisme a les *Elegies de Bierville,*" p. n/a.
Llengua & Literatura, Volume 1, 1986, Jaume Medina, "El lexic poetic de Carles Riba: Index de frequencies de mots," pp. 305-359.
Nueva Estfeta, May, 1983, Jimenez Martos, "Riba y cunqueiro, poesia litoral," pp. 75-78.
Quimera, Volume 125-126, 1994, Birute Ciplijauskaite, "Aclimatacion de la tanka: Carles Riba y Alejandro Duque Amusco," pp. 66-69.
Romance Languages Annual, 1990, Yolanda Gamboa, "Botticelli's *Primavera* and Riba's *Elegies de Bierville* as 'The Allegory of Love,'" pp. 406-409.
World Literature Today, spring, 1985, Janet Pérez, review of *Obras Completas,* p. 258.

OTHER

Lletra, http://www.uoc.edu/lletra/ (September 15, 2002), "Carles Riba."*

*   *   *

RICHTER, Roland Suso 1961-

PERSONAL: Born 1961, in Marburg, Germany.

ADDRESSES: Agent—c/o Dimension Films/Miramax Films, 375 Greenwich Street, New York, NY 10013.

CAREER: Director, producer, and writer. Film work includes (director, unless otherwise noted) *Überfluessig,* 1982; (and editor) *Kolp,* 1983; *Nur Frauen, kein Leben,* 1985; (editor) *Der Krieg meines Vater,* 1985; (unit manager) *Land der Vater, Land der Sohne,* 1988; *Dagobert,* 1994; *14 Tage lebenslaenglich,* Nil Film Art and Entertainment, 1997; (and producer) *Sara Amerika,* 1999; *After the Truth,* Helkon, 1999; *Eine Handvoll Gras,* Bavaria Film International, 2000; *Der Tunnel,* 2000; and *The I Inside,* Miramax, 2003. Work as television director includes *Alles ausser Mord— Mann im Mond,* 1993; *Svens Geheimnis,* 1994; *Polizeiruf 10—Samstags, wenn Krieg ist,* 1994; *Das*

Phantom—Die Jagd nach Dagobert, 1994; *Alles ausser Mord—Im Namen der Nelke*, 1994; *Risiko Null—Der Tod steht auf dem Speiseplan*, 1995; *Buddies—Leben auf der Ueberholspur*, 1997; and *Die Bubi Scholz Story*, 1998.

AWARDS, HONORS: Youth Video Prize, 1986, for *Kolp;* Erich Kaestner Prize and Banff Television Festival Rocky Award, both 1996, both for *Seven's Secret;* Bavarian Television Award, 1998, for *The Bubi Scholz Story;* Bavarian Television Award, Coachella Valley Festival of Festivals Best Overall Film Award, Montreal World Film Festival People's Choice Award, St. Louis International Film Festival Audience Choice Award and International Film Award, all 2001, and Portland International Film Festival Audience Award for Best Film, 2002, all for *Der Tunnel.*

WRITINGS:

Sara Amerika (screenplay), Helkon Media AG, 1999.

Also composer for *Kolp*, 1983.

SIDELIGHTS: In addition to his extensive work as a director, German filmmaker Roland Suso Richter wrote the screenplay for his 1999 film *Sara Amerika*. The latter is an ensemble piece involving four characters whose lives converge in the exuberant, chaotic atmosphere of Germany in the early 1990s, after the fall of the Berlin Wall and the reunification of the country. Pervading the story, however, is the image of another country, referred to in the title: the film actually begins in the real-life Saxon town of Amerika, and concludes in America itself.

Sara of the title has grown up in East Germany, but is the daughter of a black American soldier she never met. She leaves her hometown, where she works in a factory, and travels to Berlin for an abortion. There she meets a fast-talking city boy named Jo, who in turn introduces her to Hans. Hans, a German who has worked as interpreter for the U.S. Army in Berlin for fourteen years, thinks of himself as an American even though he has never visited the United States. The three friends eventually are joined by a fourth, Stanislav, who they meet in what was once the Soviet sector of East Berlin.

Eventually the ensemble ends up in the United States for what Lisa Nesselson of *Variety* described as a "far-fetched" ending to the movie; however, she concluded, the film's "emotional truth feels spot-on." Nesselson also called *Sara Amerika* a "haunting, playfully structured" story.

BIOGRAPHICAL AND CRITICAL SOURCES:

BOOKS

Contemporary Theatre, Film, and Television, volume 34, Gale (Detroit, MI), 2001.

PERIODICALS

Variety, February 13, 1985, review of *Kolp*, p. 19; November 15, 1999, Lisa Nesselson, review of *Sara Amerika*, p. 92.*

*   *   *

RIESMAN, David, Jr. 1909-2002

OBITUARY NOTICE—See index for *CA* sketch: Born September 22, 1909, in Philadelphia, PA; died May 10, 2002, in Binghamton, NY. Sociologist, attorney, educator, and author. Riesman was the coauthor of the influential 1950 book *The Lonely Crowd: A Study of the Changing American Character*, which helped make sociology a popular subject in the United States. Although he later became a sociologist, Riesman began his career as an attorney, having received his law degree in 1934 from Harvard University. After passing the Bar in both Massachusetts and Washington, D.C., he worked as a law clerk for Associate U.S. Supreme Court Justice Louis Brandeis and then for a Boston law firm. In 1937 he joined the University of Buffalo faculty as a law professor, remaining until 1941. Passing the New York Bar exam, he moved on to Columbia University Law School and became deputy assistant district attorney for New York County from 1942 to 1943. During World War II Riesman was an executive at the Sperry Gyroscope Company; after the war he switched to sociology after his writings on civil liberties drew attention from the University of Chicago. He was a professor of social sciences at the

University of Chicago during the late 1940s and through the 1950s, joining the Harvard University faculty in 1958 where he remained until his retirement in 1980. Riesman's *The Lonely Crowd,* coauthored with Nathan Glazer and Reuel Denney, was initially intended to be only for academics, but its message about U.S. society made it an unexpected bestseller. In it, the authors explain that U.S. society during the 1950s was in a conformist state, prompting some readers—inspired by the social unrest of the 1960s—to interpret the work as a call for nonconformity. Riesman held that *The Lonely Crowd* should not be taken to mean that all people were conformists: individuals are much too complex for such generalities. Significantly, Riesman's *The Lonely Crowd* initiated a period of self-analysis among Americans that continued into the twenty-first century. The author followed his first book with *Faces in the Crowd: Individual Studies in Character and Politics* (1952), written with Glazer, and *Individualism Reconsidered, and Other Essays* (1954). In his subsequent books Riesman turned more to the subject of academia, writing on such subjects as student power, the decrease in faculty power, and the effect of politics on educational institutions in such works as *The Academic Revolution* (1968; written with Christopher Jencks) and *On Higher Education: The Academic Enterprise in an Era of Rising Student Consumerism* (1980).

OBITUARIES AND OTHER SOURCES:

BOOKS

Writers Directory, 16th edition, St. James Press (Detroit, MI), 2001.

PERIODICALS

Los Angeles Times, May 12, 2002, p. B16.
New York Times, May 11, 2002, p. B15.
Times (London, England), May 30, 2002.
Washington Post, May 12, 2002, p. C9.

*   *   *

RIGGS, Stephanie 1964-

PERSONAL: Born September 14, 1964, in Phoenix, AZ; daughter of Ben and Ann Riggs. *Education:* Pepperdine University, B.A., 1985. *Hobbies and other interests:* Playing the piano.

ADDRESSES: Home—1044 Lincoln St., Denver, CO 80203.

CAREER: KSEE/KNTV, Fresno, CA, and Lincoln, NE, news anchor and reporter, 1987-92; KOVR, Sacramento, CA, news anchor and reporter 1992-94; WKRC, Cincinnati, OH, news anchor and reporter, 1994-96; KCNC, Denver, CO, news anchor and reporter, 1996-2002. Member of Governor of Colorado's committee on early childhood care and education; board member of the Leukemia Society in Colorado.

AWARDS, HONORS: Russell L. Cecil Medical Journalism Award, 1996, for a documentary on teens overcoming arthritis; Colorado Broadcasters Association "Citizen of the Year" award for community service, 1996, 2000; Emmy Award for "best journalistic enterprise," 1997, for a news investigation on Colorado Child Care; Clarion Award, 1998, for in-depth coverage of child care investigation; Emmy Award, 1999, for documentary *Latinos in Colorado: One Family's Journey;* Emmy Award, 2000, National Headliner Award, 2001, and Gracie Award, American Women in Radio and Television, 2001, all for documentary *Embracing a Dream: The Legacy of Oumar Dia;* Colorado Black Journalist Award, 2001; Edward R. Murrow Award, 2002, for *Never Sell Yourself Short;* Emmy Awards, 2002, for best documentary and writing and for best television anchor.

WRITINGS:

Never Sell Yourself Short, illustrated by Bill Youmans, A. Whitman (Morton Grove, IL), 2001.

SIDELIGHTS: Filmmaker and reporter Stephanie Riggs's book, *Never Sell Yourself Short,* is a real-life account of fourteen-year-old Josh, a boy who is living with dwarfism. Included in the book are photos of Josh at home and at play, as well as information about dwarfism and the Little People of America—a nonprofit association that offers support, education, and more information on dwarfism for little people and their families.

Riggs told *CA:* "I have made a career out of giving children a voice. They remind us how we should never judge a person on the outside but on the inside! How we treat each other is all that matters when you come right down to it."

BIOGRAPHICAL AND CRITICAL SOURCES:

PERIODICALS

Booklist, September 1, 2001, Ilene Cooper, review of *Never Sell Yourself Short,* p. 101.

Bulletin of the Center for Children's Books, January, 2002, review of *Never Sell Yourself Short,* p. 184.

School Library Journal, November, 2001, Pamela K. Bomboy, review of *Never Sell Yourself Short,* p. 150.

*   *   *

RINEHART, Steven

PERSONAL: Male. *Education:* University of Iowa, M.F.A.

ADDRESSES: Home—New York, NY. *Agent*—c/o Publicity Director, Doubleday, 280 Park Ave., New York, NY 10017.

CAREER: Writer and teacher.

AWARDS, HONORS: National Endowment for the Arts, fellowship, 1995; James Michener fellowship.

WRITINGS:

Kick in the Head (short stories), Doubleday (New York, NY), 2000.

Also a contributor to *Harper's, GQ, Story,* and *Ploughshares.*

WORK IN PROGRESS: Built in a Day, forthcoming, 2003.

SIDELIGHTS: Steven Rinehart grew up in a military family overseas, then attended college in Hawaii and Iowa. His debut publication is a collection of stories titled *Kick in the Head.* Christine DeZelar-Tiedman, reviewing the book in *Library Journal,* called it "an engaging debut collection of short stories." A reviewer

in *Publishers Weekly* stated, "In applying chaos theory to the emotional life of modern men, he reveals with striking clarity their lingering failures and small triumphs."

Rinehart has taught fiction writing at New York University and is a graduate of the University of Iowa Writers' Workshop.

BIOGRAPHICAL AND CRITICAL SOURCES:

PERIODICALS

Library Journal, June 1, 2000, Christine DeZelar-Tiedman, review of *Kick in the Head,* p. 206.

Publishers Weekly, April 3, 2000, review of *Kick in the Head,* p. 64.

OTHER

Random House Web site, http://www.randomhouse.com/ (February 5, 2003).

University of Iowa, http://www.uiowa.edu/ (June 6, 2000).*

*   *   *

ROADS, Michael J. 1937-

PERSONAL: Born April 14, 1937, in England; son of Herbert (a farmer) and Vera (Clark) Roads; married Treenie Barker, October 4, 1958; children: Duncan, Adrian, Russell, Tracey.

ADDRESSES: Home—Queensland, Australia. *Office*—P.O. Box 778, Nambour, Queensland 4560, Australia; fax: 61-75442-3040. *Agent*—Carolyn Silver and James Silver, Silver Literary Agency, 3029 Prospect Ave., Cleveland, OH 44115. *E-mail*—roadsway@optusnet.com.au.

CAREER: Farm worker in Cambridgeshire, England, 1952-64; dairy and beef farmer in Tasmania, Australia, 1964-76; writer, 1976—. Worked as consultant to Eco-Farming. Homeland Foundation, past member; Roadsway Re*treats, presenter of seminars and public lectures on organic farming and metaphysical experiences in Australia, the United States and Canada, and elsewhere around the world, 1990—.

WRITINGS:

A Guide to Organic Gardening in Australia, 1976.

A Guide to Organic Living in Australia, M. Fisher Bookshop (Launceston, Australia), 1977.

Talking with Nature: Sharing the Energies and Trees, Plants, Birds, and Earth, illustrated by Genevieve Wilson, revised edition, H. J. Kramer (Tiburon, CA), 1987.

The Natural Magic of Mulch, 1989.

Journey into Nature: A Spiritual Adventure, H. J. Kramer (Tiburon, CA), 1990.

Simple Is Powerful: Anecdotes for a Complex World, H. J. Kramer (Tiburon, CA), 1992.

Journey into Oneness: A Spiritual Odyssey, H. J. Kramer (Tiburon, CA), 1994.

Into a Timeless Realm, H. J. Kramer (Tiburon, CA), 1995.

Getting There (novel), Hampton Roads Publishing (Charlottesville, VA), 1998.

The Magic Formula, SilverRoads Publishing (Cleveland, OH), 2003.

Roads' books have been widely translated.

WORK IN PROGRESS: More books; research on "true prosperity and abundance."

SIDELIGHTS: Michael J. Roads told *CA:* "I have spent all my life as an outdoors man, from a child delving into the mysteries of a hidden, silent nature. On leaving school at fifteen, I worked on my father's farm in Cambridgeshire in England. I found that these rather challenging years of innocently connecting with nature were in direct contrast with the control and manipulation of agriculture.

"At age twenty-one I married Treenie, the smartest thing I ever did! In my mid-twenties, following the death of my father, Treenie and I and our two sons moved to Tasmania, the island state of Australia. Here, intending to be a beef grazier, I met with the implacable resistance of nature. A plague of army-worm caterpillars devastated both the pastures and the beef herd in the very first year, forcing me to become a dairy farmer for economic survival.

"This began a whole new education for me. I quickly came to realize that normal, traditional farming techniques were in direct conflict with nature, so for the next decade I became an observer and student of nature. During this time I became a pioneer in the eco-farming movement, applying my techniques and observations on my own land. The soil health was soon reflected in the superior pasture, which in turn passed on its benefits to the cattle. But this was no longer my only focus.

"During the decade of creating change in the land, I learned to become attuned to the spirit of the land, to the silent whispers of nature, and within me grew an inner vision. I saw that humanity and nature had become separated, and I realized that this was not in the natural order of things. I felt within myself an inner longing to powerfully and knowingly reconnect with nature. In this way I felt I would find my own self.

"My years on the farm gave birth to two practical books, *A Guide to Organic Gardening in Australia* and *A Guide to Organic Living in Australia.* Both became Australian best-sellers. However, with a desire for personal and spiritual growth, Treenie and I sold the farm and embarked on a year's journey around Australia with our (now four) children. The culmination of this odyssey was for us to become founder members of the Homeland Foundation, a community originally based on the Findhorn Foundation in Scotland. For us both it was a time of challenge, inner growth, and change.

"Four years later, we left the community to continue our inner journey in our own way. At this time I became a consultant for Eco-Farming. This lasted for two years, until a nationwide drought brought the consultancy to a standstill. Once more I turned to writing, setting out my experiences with an inner mystical nature, while daily I worked on empowering my conscious spiritual connection with nature. I learned to cross the membrane separating the material (physical) from the intangible (metaphysical), and writing became my creative outlet, my love in action.

"The first of my mystical adventures is titled *Talking with Nature: Sharing the Energies and Trees, Plants, Birds, and Earth.* The next book, *Journey into Nature:*

A Spiritual Adventure, continues the theme, going deeper into the inner realms of nature. *Simple Is Powerful: Anecdotes for a Complex World* is what people call an 'everyone's book.' It is not deeply metaphysical like the others. It is a book of anecdotes from our life that have been very simple yet powerful experiences. My third book in a quartet, *Journey into Oneness: A Spiritual Odyssey,* goes more deeply into my metaphysical experiences. The last book in the quartet, *Into a Timeless Realm,* is based on a mystical experience I had in 1977, an experience that took me many years to come to terms with.

"In 1990 Treenie and I started giving seminars in Switzerland and the United States. This rapidly expanded, and we have now given seminars and five-day retreats in many countries, including Australia, South Africa, the Netherlands, Germany, Belgium, Denmark, Austria, England, Canada, and Mexico. We now concentrate on the five-day retreats, and the demand is growing each year.

"I have now turned my writing skills toward the mass market, yet I have retained my New Age theme. My first novel, *Getting There,* is the story of a man, deeply embittered by life, as he searches for meaning and purpose in his daily struggle for existence."

BIOGRAPHICAL AND CRITICAL SOURCES:

PERIODICALS

East West, March, 1988, review of *Talking with Nature: Sharing the Energies and Trees, Plants, Birds, and Earth,* p. 90.
Publishers Weekly, August 14, 1987, John Mutter, review of *Talking with Nature,* 1987.

OTHER

Roadsway Web site, http://www.michaelroads.com (March 14, 2003).

*   *   *

ROBERTS, Jon H. 1947-

PERSONAL: Born November 7, 1947, in Wichita, KS; son of Robert E. (in business) and Anna (Belle) Roberts; married August 12, 1978; wife's name, Sharon W; children: Jeffrey R. *Education:* University of Missouri—Columbia, A.B., 1969; Harvard University, Cambridge, MA, M.A., 1970, Ph.D., 1980.

ADDRESSES: Home—221 Doty St., Waltham, MA 02452. *Office*—Boston University, 226 Bay State Rd., Boston, MA 02215; fax: 617-353-2557. *E-mail*—roberts1@bu.edu.

CAREER: Harvard University, Cambridge, MA, assistant professor of history, 1980-85; University of Wisconsin—Stevens Point, assistant professor, 1985-88, associate professor, 1988-95, professor of history, 1995-2001; Boston University, Boston, MA, professor of history, 2001—.

WRITINGS:

Darwinism and the Divine in America, University of Wisconsin Press (Madison, WI), 1988.
(With James Turner) *The Sacred and the Secular University,* Princeton University Press (Princeton, NJ), 2001.

WORK IN PROGRESS: Research on psychology and American Protestant theology, 1870-1940.

BIOGRAPHICAL AND CRITICAL SOURCES:

PERIODICALS

America, April 8, 2000, Peter Heinegg, review of *The Sacred and the Secular University,* p. 36.
Isis, December, 2000, Stanley M. Guralnick, review of *The Sacred and the Secular University,* p. 772.

*   *   *

ROBERTSON, Cliff(ord Parker, III) 1925-

PERSONAL: Born September 9, 1925, in La Jolla, CA; son of Clifford Parker and Audrey (Willingham) Robertson; married Cynthia Stone, 1957 (divorced, 1959); married Dina Merrill (an actress), December 21, 1966 (divorced, 1986); children: (first marriage) Stephanie; (second marriage) Heather. *Education:* Studied at the Actors Studio. *Religion:* Presbyterian. *Hobbies and other interests:* Sailplane and airplane piloting, tennis, skiing.

ADDRESSES: Agent—International Creative Management, 8942 Wilshire Blvd., Beverly Hills, CA 90211.

CAREER: Actor, director, and writer. Former adjunct professor at Antioch College. Blacklisted by Hollywood for exposing corruption, 1979-82, but later commended by the Hollywood industry, Screen Actors Guild, and the *Congressional Record;* also appeared in commercials for AT&T during the mid-1980s, and radio commercials for Union Bank in the late 1990s. Adjunct professor at Antioch College, Antioch, OH.

Stage appearances include *Late Love,* National Theatre, New York City, 1953, and *Orpheus Descending,* New York City, 1957. Also appeared in *Mr. Roberts, The Lady and the Tiger,* and *The Wisteria Trees.* Stage work includes (director) *The V.I.P.s,* 1981.

Film appearances include *Corvette K-225,* 1943; *Picnic,* Columbia, 1955; *Autumn Leaves,* Columbia, 1956; *The Girl Most Likely,* Universal, 1957; *The Naked and the Dead,* Warner Bros., 1958; *Gidget,* Columbia, 1959; *Battle of the Coral Sea,* Columbia, 1959; *As the Sea Rages,* Columbia, 1960; *All in a Night's Work,* Paramount, 1961; *The Big Show,* Twentieth Century-Fox, 1961; *The Interns,* Columbia, 1962; *Underworld, U.S.A.,* Columbia, 1962; *My Six Loves,* Paramount, 1963; *PT-109,* Warner Bros., 1963; *Sunday in New York,* Metro-Goldwyn-Mayer, 1963; *The Best Man,* United Artists, 1964; *633 Squadron,* United Artists, 1964; *Up from the Beach,* Twentieth Century-Fox, 1965; *Love Has Many Faces,* Columbia, 1965; *Masquerade,* United Artists, 1965; *The Honey Pot,* United Artists, 1966; *Charly,* Cinerama/Selmur Films, 1968; *The Devil's Brigade,* United Artists, 1968; *Too Late the Hero,* Cinerama, 1970; *The Great Northfield,* Minnesota Raid, Universal, 1972; *J. W. Coop,* Columbia, 1972; *Alfred Hitchcock,* 1973; *Ace Eli and Rodger of the Skies,* Twentieth Century-Fox, 1973; *Man on a Swing,* Paramount, 1974; *Three Days of the Condor,* Paramount, 1975; *Out of Season,* Athenaeum, 1975; *Midway,* Universal/Mirisch Corporation, 1976; *Shoot,* Avco Embassy, 1976; *Obsession,* Columbia, 1976; *Fraternity Row,* Paramount, 1977; *Dominique,* Subotsky, 1978; *The Pilot,* New Line Cinema, 1979; *Class,* Orion Films, 1983; *Brainstorm,* Metro-Goldwyn-Mayer/United Artists, 1983; *Star '80,* Warner Bros., 1983; *Shaker Run,* New Line Home Video, 1985; *Malone,* Orion, 1987; *Wild Hearts Can't Be Broken,* Buena Vista, 1991; *Wind,* TriStar, 1992; *Renaissance*

Man, Buena Vista, 1994; *Pakten,* Kushner-Locke International, 1995; *Escape from L.A.,* Paramount, 1996; *Melting Pot,* A-Pix Entertainment, 1997; *Assignment Berlin,* Hallmark Entertainment, 1998; *Family Tree,* Independent Artists, 1999; *Falcon Down,* 2000; *Paranoid,* 2000; *Spider-Man,* 2002; and *Thirteenth Child: Legend of the Jersey Devil, Volume I,* 2002.

Film work includes (director and producer) *J. W. Coop,* Columbia, 1972; (director) *Morning, Winter, and Night,* Xanadu Films, 1977; and (director) *The Pilot,* New Line Cinema, 1979. Television work includes (director and executive producer), *Hunters in the Sky.* Recordings include *Running on Empty* (narrator; video documentary).

Television series appearances include *Rod Brown of the Rocket Rangers,* CBS, 1953-54, and *Falcon Crest,* CBS, 1983-84. Appearances on TV miniseries include *Washington: Behind Closed Doors,* ABC, 1977; *The Key to Rebecca,* syndicated, 1985; *Ford: The Man and the Machine,* syndicated, 1987; *Judith Krantz's Dazzle,* CBS, 1995; *With God on Our Side: The Rise of the Religious Right,* PBS, 1996. Appearances on TV movies include *The Sunshine Patriot,* NBC, 1968; *Man without a Country,* ABC, 1973; *A Tree Grows in Brooklyn,* 1974; *My Father's House,* ABC, 1975; *Return to Earth,* ABC, 1976; *Overboard,* NBC, 1978; *Two of a Kind,* CBS, 1982; *Dreams of Gold: The Mel Fisher Story,* CBS, 1986; and *Dead Reckoning,* USA Network, 1990.

Appearances on episodic television include *Short Dramas,* NBC, 1953; *Treasury Men in Action,* ABC, 1954; *Robert Montgomery Presents,* NBC, 1954; *Philco TV Playhouse,* NBC, 1955; "A Fair Shake," *The U.S. Steel Hour,* CBS, 1956; "The Days of Wine and Roses," *Playhouse 90,* CBS, 1958; "The Liam Fitzmorgan Story," *Wagon Train,* NBC, 1958; "The Underground Railway," *The Untouchables,* ABC, 1959; "The Man Who Knew Tomorrow," *The U.S. Steel Hour,* CBS, 1960; "Ballad for a Badman," *Outlaws,* 1960; "The Two Worlds of Charlie Gordon," *The U.S. Steel Hour,* CBS, 1961; "A Hundred Yards over the Rim," *The Twilight Zone,* CBS, 1961; "The Story of Connie Masters," *Outlaws,* 1961; "Man on the Mountaintop," *The U.S. Steel Hour,* CBS, 1961; "The Dark Sunrise of Griff Kincaid," *Outlaws,* 1962; "The Dummy," *The Twilight Zone,* CBS, 1962; "The Galaxy Being," *The Outer Limits,* ABC, 1963; "The Game," *Bob Hope*

Presents the Chrysler Theatre, NBC, 1965; "Come Back Shame" and "It's the Way You Play the Game," *Batman,* ABC, 1966; "The Great Escape" and "The Great Train Robbery," *Batman,* ABC, 1968; *Front Page Challenge,* 1975; *Take Charge!,* PBS, 1988; *First Flights,* Arts and Entertainment, 1991; and "Joyride," *The Outer Limits,* 1999. Also appeared in *Alcoa Theatre,* NBC; *Studio One,* CBS; *Alcoa Premiere,* ABC; and *Philco-Goodyear Hour.*

Appearances on TV specials include *The Screen Actors Guild Fiftieth Anniversary Celebration,* 1984; *An All-Star Party for "Dutch" Reagan,* 1985; *Galapagos: My Fragile World,* TBS/PBS, 1986; *Ghosts of '87,* PBS, 1988; *William Holden: The Golden Boy,* Cinemax, 1989; *Medal of Honor: True Stories of America's Greatest War Heroes,* syndicated, 1990-91; *Life and Death of a Dynasty,* PBS, 1991; *Wings as Eagles,* ABC, 1994; *Earthwinds,* Discovery Channel, 1995; *Intimate Portrait: Stephanie Powers,* Lifetime, 1999; *Joan Crawford: The Ultimate Movie Star,* 2002.

MEMBER: Screen Actors Guild, Directors Guild of America, Writers Guild of America, Bath and Tennis Club Palm Beach, Maidston Club (East Hampton, NY), River Club (New York City), Brook Club (New York City), Players, Wings Club.

AWARDS, HONORS: Emmy Award for best actor, 1966, for "The Game," *Bob Hope Presents the Chrysler Theatre;* Academy Award for best actor, 1968, NBR Award for best actor, National Board of Review, and Golden Globe nomination for best motion picture actor in a drama, both 1969, all for *Charly;* Theatre World Award, 1970, for *Orpheus Descending;* congressional recognition for exposing Hollywood corporate studio corruption, 1979; Sharples Aviation Award, AOPA, 1983; Wallace Award, American Scottish Foundation, 1984; Advertising Age Award, 1985; Lifetime Achievement Award, Long Island Film Festival, 1988; Special Achievement Award for acting, Florida Film Festival, 1998; honorary doctorate of Fine Arts from Bradford College, 1981, MacMurray College, 1986, and Susquehanna University, 1988. President John F. Kennedy personally chose Robertson to portray him in *PT-109.*

WRITINGS:

J. W. Coop (screenplay), Columbia, 1972.
(With Robert P. Davis) *The Pilot* (screenplay), New Line Cinema, 1979.

(With Michael Maryk) *Thirteenth Child: Legend of the Jersey Devil, Volume I* (screenplay), Alex Mendoza & Associates, 2002.

Also author of the play *The V.I.P.s,* 1981. Robertson reportedly wrote a sequel to *Charly* in the 1990s.

SIDELIGHTS: Actor Cliff Robertson's own biography might well be the subject of a movie. The son of a father who loved partying and women much more than he cared for his son and wife—the elder Robertson was married half a dozen times in an era when divorce was uncommon—young Robertson was adopted and raised by his grandmother after his own mother died of a ruptured appendix when he was two years old. Consciously disavowing the negative role model set for him by his father, he grew up with a strong work ethic, and as a child even lied about his age so that he could get a job delivering papers.

In 1955, the young Robertson appeared in the film *Picnic* as the clean-cut Kansan who loses his girlfriend, Kim Novak, to his old buddy William Holden. His career entered high gear in the early 1960s, when no less a figure than President John F. Kennedy personally chose Robertson to play him in *PT 109,* which dramatizes Kennedy's wartime service. Against the advice of his agent, who told him that playing a mentally retarded man would spell the end of his career, Robertson took the title role in *Charly,* an adaptation of Daniel Keyes's moving novella *Flowers for Algernon,* and walked away with the Academy Award for best actor in 1968.

Four years later, Robertson wrote, produced, directed, and starred in *J. W. Coop.* At the outset of the film, Coop is released from prison after eight years, and intends to return to work as a professional rodeo cowboy. But as the overly confident Coop discovers, much has changed in the world since the early 1960s, and he finds himself bewildered by the society he encounters.

J. W. Coop was well received, and Robertson went on to create a second project, *The Pilot,* in which he played Mike Hagan, a successful commercial flyer who tries to hide his alcoholism. The year of *The Pilot*'s release in 1979, however, found Robertson embroiled in a scandal that would ultimately confer even greater status on the actor, but which in the short run all but brought his career to a halt.

In 1976, Columbia Pictures president David Begelman forged Robertson's name in order to cash a check for $10,000, made out to Robertson by the studio. Robertson only found out about this much later, when the Internal Revenue Service (IRS) contacted him, demanding payment of taxes on the money, which Robertson did not even know he had earned. He reported Begelman, and in what many regard as a typical Hollywood response to a problem, the film industry took swift action—against Robertson. While Begelman received a slap on the wrist, Robertson was blacklisted throughout Hollywood, and could get no work between 1979 and 1982. As for Begelman, the studio head went on to MGM/United Artists, but several failures led him to leave and form his own production company. When that company failed, too, he shot and killed himself in August 1995. The scandal involving Robertson is the subject of David McClintick's 1982 book, *Indecent Exposure: A True Story of Hollywood and Wall Street.*

Ultimately Robertson returned to favor, with successful roles such as his portrayal of *Playboy*'s Hugh Hefner in *Star '80.* The incident, however, only confirmed his suspicions of Hollywood: Robertson is famous for his refusal to move to Los Angeles, a fact that brought an end to his marriage to actress Dina Merrill, and he has chosen instead to reside on Long Island.

Ever the independent, Robertson reportedly wrote a sequel to *Charly,* the rights to which he had purchased long before. In 1996, he told *People* that he intended to make the picture, but needed to raise $4.6 million to do so. In 2002, he appeared in, and wrote the screenplay for, a film made for an even smaller budget—just $1.5 million. Released just in time for Halloween, *Thirteenth Child: Legend of the Jersey Devil* takes as its premise a centuries-old folk tale regarding a horned, cloven-hoofed demonic figure that is said to roam the Pine Barrens of southern New Jersey. Supposedly the devil was the child of a woman named Mother Leeds, who already had twelve children, and who cursed the thirteenth, born in 1735. In the film, Robertson plays Mr. Shroud, an old man who lives alone in the Pine Barrens as part of a pact with the devil.

By contrast, Robertson himself is famed for his refusal to make a pact with the real-life devils of fame and fortune. "I've lived long enough to learn," he told

Luaine Lee of the Knight Ridder/Tribune News Service, ". . . where the top of the totem pole should be. To me it's my kids, family, a kind of a religion, and a sense of self."

BIOGRAPHICAL AND CRITICAL SOURCES:

BOOKS

Contemporary Theatre, Film, and Television, volume 32, Gale (Detroit, MI), 2000.
Crist, Judith, and Shirley Sealy, *Take 22: Moviemakers on Moviemaking,* Viking (New York, NY), 1984.
International Dictionary of Films and Filmmakers, Volume 3: *Actors and Actresses,* St. James Press (Detroit, MI), 1996.
McClintick, David, *Indecent Exposure: A True Story of Hollywood and Wall Street,* Morrow (New York, NY), 1982.

PERIODICALS

Christian Science Monitor, May 5, 2000, "A Man with a Moral Mission: Hollywood Stories" (interview), p. 19.
Knight Ridder/Tribune News Service, August 5, 1996, Luaine Lee, "Cliff Robertson Still Breaking Hollywood's Rules," p. 805.
New York Times, October 13, 2002, Margo Nash, review of *Thirteenth Child: Legend of the Jersey Devil, Volume I,* p. 11.
Record (Bergen County, NJ), October 25, 2002, John Curran, review of *Thirteenth Child,* p. A12.*

*   *   *

RODDAM, Franc(is George) 1946-

PERSONAL: Born April 29, 1946, in Stockton-on-Tees, England; son of Vincent Nicholson and Ellen Maud (Canavan) Roddam; married Carina Mary Cooper (a director; marriage ended); married Barbara Margaret Deehan (a television producer); children: Annie Canavan, Patrick Michael.

ADDRESSES: Agent—Robert Stein, William Morris Agency, Beverly Hills, CA 90211; c/o Union Pictures, 36 Marshall St., London W1, England.

CAREER: Director, writer, and producer. Film work includes (director, unless otherwise noted) *Birthday,* 1969; *Quadrophenia,* World Northal, 1979; *The Lords of Discipline,* Paramount, 1983; *The Bride,* Columbia, 1985; "Liebestod"/*Tristan und Isolde* sequence, *Aria,* Virgin Vision, 1987; *War Party,* Hemdale, 1988; and *K2,* 1991. Television series work as creator and executive producer includes *Auf Wiedersehen, Pet,* Central TV, 1983-86 and 2002, and *Making Out,* BBC, 1987. Other television work as executive producer includes *Dogs,* Arts and Entertainment, 1993. Television miniseries work includes (producer and director) *Moby Dick,* The Learning Channel, 1998, and (director) *Cleopatra,* ABC, 1999. Work as director of TV specials includes *Mini,* BBC, 1973; *The Family,* BBC, 1974; *Dummy,* ATV, 1977; and *Catastrophe: Airships,* syndicated, 1978. TV movie work includes (executive producer) *Deadly Voyage,* HBO, 1993. Appearances on TV specials include *Thar She Blows! The Making of "Moby Dick,"* USA Network, 1998.

WRITINGS:

(Creator) *Auf Wiedersehen, Pet* (television series), Central TV, 1983-86, 2002.
Moby Dick (television miniseries), The Learning Channel, 1998.

SCREENPLAYS

(With Dave Humphries, Martin Stellman, and Pete Townsend) *Quadrophenia,* World Northal, 1979.
Rain Forest, Twentieth Century-Fox, 1981.
American Dreams, Paramount, 1983.
Aria ("Tristan und Isolde," *Liebestod* sequence only), Virgin Vision, 1987.

SIDELIGHTS: Franc Roddam's most famous work as a director and cowriter was 1979's *Quadrophenia.* The film, which guitarist and songwriter Pete Townsend of the Who helped write, is particularly memorable for its music, including songs by the Who themselves, as well as classic recordings of the 1950s and 1960s by artists such as the Ronettes, Gene Vincent, and Booker T. and the MGs. Set in London in 1964, the story centers around the conflict between mods, who wear zoot suits, ride motor scooters, and listen to The Who, and rockers, who wear leather jackets, ride motorcycles, and favor the rockabilly of the 1950s.

Protagonist Jimmy Cooper works in a dead-end job, but finds meaning in his role as a mod, yet a series of events force him to question that meaning. "I don't give a monkey's [expletive] about mods and rockers," his former friend Kevin, who has fallen in with the rockers, tells Jimmy. But Jimmy replies, "I don't wanna be the same as everybody else. That's why I'm a mod, see? I mean, you gotta be somebody, ain't ya?" Observed John Soeder in the Cleveland, Ohio, *Plain-Dealer,* "There you have it—the tricky struggle between individuality and conformity that keeps *Quadrophenia* ringing true."

Roddam's other work as writer and director includes a TV version of *Moby Dick* that Tony Scott in *Variety* praised thus: "The action-filled miniseries serves well as an 1840s ocean adventure; director Roddam deftly sails his craft close to the wind." John Carman of the *San Francisco Chronicle* was less favorable in his review, but singled out for praise its portrayal of "the raucous life aboard a nineteenth-century sailing ship—the hazing, the pest-infected food, the quick tempers and rough comradeship."

In the world of British television, Roddam is most noted for his work as creator of the series *Auf Wiedersehen, Pet,* which aired in the mid-1980s and was revived again in 2002. Set in the industrial town of Middleborough, the pilot for the renewed series centers around an attempt to dismantle the city's transport bridge and sell it to Native Americans in Arizona.

BIOGRAPHICAL AND CRITICAL SOURCES:

BOOKS

Contemporary Theatre, Film, and Television, volume 34, Gale (Detroit, MI), 2001.

PERIODICALS

Boston Globe, May 20, 1988, Michael Blowen, review of *Aria,* p. 35; October 30, 1988, Richard Dyer, review of *Aria,* p. B10.
Commentary, March, 1980, Richard Grenier, review of *Quadrophenia,* pp. 69-70.
Film Comment, May-June, 1988, Michael Walsh, review of *Aria,* pp. 76-77.

Financial Times, May 1, 2002, Graham McCann, review of *Auf Wiedersehen, Pet,* p. 16.

Los Angeles Times, April 15, 1988, review of *Aria,* p. 1; April 18, 1991, Jon Matsumoto, review of *Quadrophenia,* p. 9; April 27, 2001, Randy Lewis, review of *Quadrophenia,* p. F18.

Melody Maker, February 1, 1997, Simon Price, review of *Quadrophenia,* p. 19.

New York, March 16, 1998, John Leonard, review of *Moby Dick,* pp. 62-63.

New York Times, March 13, 1998, Caryn James, review of *Moby Dick,* p. B27; October 12, 2001, Janet Maslin, review of *Quadrophenia,* p. E26.

Northern Echo (Darlington, England), September 20, 2001, Steve Pratt, "Oz and the Boys Hug the Limelight" (profile), p. 3; April 27, 2002, Steve Pratt, "Where's Wor Bridge Going, Pet?" (profile), p. 10; May 20, 2002, "TV Hit Creator in 'Ugly' Town Row" (profile), p. 5.

Plain Dealer (Cleveland, OH), June 15, 2001, John Soeder, review of *Quadrophenia,* p. 7.

San Francisco Chronicle, May 16, 1988, Joshua Kosman, review of *Aria,* p. F1; March 13, 1998, John Carman, review of *Moby Dick,* p. C1.

Time, May 2, 1988, Richard Corliss, review of *Aria,* p. 79.

Variety, March 9, 1998, Tony Scott, review of *Moby Dick,* p. 38.

Video Business, August 27, 2001, Samantha Clark, review of *Quadrophenia,* p. 21.

Video Store, September 30-October 6, 2001, Andrew Melomet, review of *Quadrophenia,* p. 27.*

*   *   *

RODNEY, Lester 1911-
(Benjamin Brewster, Lyman Hopkins)

PERSONAL: Born April 17, 1911, in New York, NY; son of Max (a salesman) and Isabelle (a milliner; maiden name, Cotton) Rodney; married, 1946; wife's name, Clare; children: Amy, Ray. *Education:* Attended Syracuse University.

ADDRESSES: Home—2137 Skycrest Dr., Walnut Creek, CA 94595.

CAREER: Journalist. *Brooklyn Daily Eagle,* stringer, 1920s; worked as a chauffeur and shipping clerk; *Daily Worker,* New York, NY, reporter, sports editor, 1936- 42, 1946-57; *Santa Monica Evening Outlook,* Santa Monica, CA, feature writer, religion editor, special sections editor, 1946-47; worked for an advertising agency in Beverly Hills, CA, 1947-63; *Long Beach Independent Press-Telegram,* feature writer, 1964-74. *Military service:* U.S. Army, 1942-46, served with the Fifty-second Field Hospital in the South Pacific; became sergeant.

AWARDS, HONORS: Honorary lifetime member, Baseball Writers Association of America; Pacific Coast Press Club awards, 1971 and 1973, for daily religion columns, and 1972, for op-ed; Bill Hunter Memorial Award for Excellence, 1973; recognized as California's number one tennis player in the eighty-five-and-older division.

WRITINGS:

(Under pseudonym Benjamin Brewster) *The First Book of Baseball,* Watts (New York, NY), 1950.
(Under pseudonym Lyman Hopkins) *The Real Book about Baseball,* Doubleday (Garden City, NY), 1951, revised edition, 1962.

Contributor to periodicals, including *Negro Digest* and *In These Times;* wrote column "On the Scoreboard" for *Daily Worker.*

SIDELIGHTS: Lester Rodney was a sportswriter and editor for nearly two decades with the *Daily Worker,* the newspaper of the American Communist Party. He wrote about sports but is most well known as an advocate of the integration of sports, in particular major league baseball, and a critic of the capitalist constraints that prevented minorities and the working class from having a share of the American sports dream.

Rodney was the third of four children born to Max and Isabelle (Cotton) Rodney, first-generation Jewish immigrants. Like many families, the Great Depression hit the Rodneys hard. Max, a silk salesman, turned to selling auto parts, and the family moved from Manhattan to the Bensonhurst section of Brooklyn. Rodney enjoyed playing street ball as a child and ran track and played basketball in high school. On his thirteenth birthday, his parents surprised him with a reserved seat ticket for opening day at Ebbets Field, home of the Brooklyn Dodgers. The year Rodney graduated from high school, his younger brother Ira died when a truck struck and killed him while he was roller skating in the street. Rodney's mother, a milliner, opened a hat shop in Newark, New Jersey and commuted daily in order to bring in some income. Even with some scholarship money, Rodney was unable to finish at Syracuse University, although he later took a few night courses. One of the courses was in journalism; during high school Rodney had covered school sports for the *Brooklyn Daily Eagle,* and he developed a knack for the genre.

Rodney read the *Daily Worker* "out of curiosity" and wrote to the editors with some ideas for the paper. In an interview with Paul Buhle and Michael Fermanowsky of the University of California's Oral History Program, he said that he was "just modestly suggesting how to improve their sports section and the importance of it, and I made the mistake of having a return address. I immediately was summoned in." Management wasn't sure there was a place for regular sports reporting. Space was limited, reader interest was an unknown, and the paper's communist ideology gave sports reporting a secondary priority at best. When they gave Rodney a chance, however, his weekly sports reports increased circulation and interest, with six out of seven respondents favoring its continuation, and he was offered a full-time position. There were skeptics, but the paper and Rodney thrived. Sports was taking up more and more column inches in daily newspapers, and the readers of the *Daily Worker,* mostly European and Jewish immigrants, benefited from an increased understanding, not only of their new country, but also of its national pastimes.

Rodney's sports section was never more than three pages, and during the Korean War it consisted only of the last page. He began by covering industrial league and union league games and began writing about mainstream sports and players when his readers clearly wanted more. About half of his coverage was of the soccer, baseball, and basketball leagues sponsored by the Trade Union Athletic Association in which his readers were participants, and the other half was about spectator sports. Rodney's columns enjoyed increased popularity, and in 1938 Yankee third baseman Red Rolfe agreed to write an article following each of the World Series games he played in that October. It was a first, as players were generally thought to be

incapable of communicating their own ideas. Rolfe was a "tough New England democrat with a small 'd', " Rodney told Buhle and Fermanowsky. He was also a graduate of Dartmouth College and was immediately successful as a journalist.

By the time Rodney joined the *Daily Worker,* nearly all major sports except baseball had been integrated, and he immediately began calling for an end to discrimination against black baseball players. In 1937 Rodney printed a challenge made by Negro League pitcher Leroy "Satchel" Paige to the New York Yankees to play one game against Paige's All-Stars at Yankee Stadium. The challenge went unanswered, however, even though the Yankee roster included the likes of Joe DiMaggio and Lou Gehrig. In addition to addressing the segregation issue, Rodney wrote about betting scandals, violence in college football, and the realities of pro boxing. He was a diligent researcher, and his regular column, *On the Score Board,* was a source of pertinent and well-rounded sports reporting.

Rodney served nearly four years with the U.S. Army in the South Pacific. When he returned to the *Worker* in 1946, he had additional help from Nat Low, who had handled the sports section while Rodney was overseas, and Bill Mardo, both of whom shared Rodney's passion about the injustices and discrimination to be found in sports. For a time, Rodney had the freedom to report on issues other than sports, and he went to Washington, D.C., where he covered Senate hearings on returning black veterans. In 1946 baseball was finally integrated with Jackie Robinson's first groundbreaking game with the Dodgers at Ebbets Field. Robert Klein wrote in the *Dictionary of Literary Biography* that "Rodney's position on segregation in baseball was clearly and uncompromisingly articulated. Because of the comparatively low circulation and unpopular politics of the *Worker,* however, his role as one of the first to excoriate in print the sixteen club owners for their racial intransigence was only belatedly recognized." "Historian Jules Tygiel," said Klein, ". . . documents Rodney's tenacious efforts to publicize (and unabashedly politicize) Robinson's difficulties as well as his progress. Rodney and the *Worker,* Tygiel argues, have been unfairly overlooked regarding the beneficial effects their reportorial and political coverage had on the integration of baseball, especially during the decade or so leading up to Robinson's barrier-breaking season."

When trends shifted away from participant team sports, Rodney decried the lack of open space, such as vacant lots, where amateurs could play ball. He also continued to write about limited participation in professional sports based on race or economic status. But the 1950s brought a new threat: anticommunist sentiment that resulted in the lost jobs and liberties of people associated with communism, including those who had worked at the Party paper. Rodney was unable to publish his *The First Book of Baseball* under his own name, and so used the pseudonym Benjamin Brewster. He used another pseudonym, Lyman Hopkins, for his second, *The Real Book about Baseball.* His books are fact-filled but also include the kind of writing readers of his columns had come to expect. His emphasis is on the fact that the big stars of many nationalities and all races can work together successfully as a team.

When Althea Gibson became the first black player to compete in the National Tennis Championships, Rodney wrote about the event. "Present in the article," said Klein, "are his characteristically gentle, unerring reminders of the damaging effects of wrongs only recently righted and the inevitable restraints on human achievement they represent, as well as his sure grasp of the sport he is examining." When white boxer Jack Dempsey was praised as being a better fighter than "Brown Bomber" Joe Louis, Rodney brought out the statistics and compared the matches of both, proving that Louis was the superior boxer.

Rodney covered the 1956 Winter Olympic Games in Italy, writing about the harmony of the games between the many nations and personal pieces on American champions, including skier Art Devlin and skaters Tenley Albright and Dick Button. In his last years at the *Daily Worker,* Rodney wrote about racial integration and covered stories in Clinton, Tennessee and Montgomery, Alabama, where he reported on the observation of the first anniversary of the Montgomery bus boycott. He resigned from both the newspaper and the Communist Party in 1957.

Rodney, his wife Clare, and their children, relocated to California in 1958, and Rodney worked for one year at the *Santa Monica Evening Outlook.* "I said I worked for the Brooklyn *Eagle,* and they didn't even know that the Brooklyn *Eagle* had gone out of business." He also used the name Les Rodney instead of Lester Rodney, which he said "didn't fool the Red Squad attorney." His next position was with a Beverly Hills ad agency, and his last, from 1964 until his retirement in 1974, was writing features for the *Long Beach Independent Press-Telegram.* Kelly E. Rusinack, a contributor to *Jackie Robinson: Race, Sports, and the American Dream,* said that Rodney "helped to further legitimize sports as a social concern, and purposely gave a voice to the opinions of athletes formerly considered to be stupid and shallow. . . . Rodney's efforts, sincerity, and fair reporting earned him the respect of athletes he interviewed, as well as of other journalists, black and white."

BIOGRAPHICAL AND CRITICAL SOURCES:

BOOKS

Dictionary of Literary Biography, Volume 241: *American Sportswriters and Writers on Sport,* Gale (Detroit, MI), 2001, pp. 232-239.
Dorinson, Joseph, and Joram Warmund, editors, *Jackie Robinson: Race, Sports, and the American Dream,* M. E. Sharpe (Armonk, NY), 1998.
Rader, Benjamin, *Baseball: A History of America's Game,* University of Illinois Press (Urbana and Chicago, IL), 1992.
Tygiel, Jules, *Baseball's Great Experiment: Jackie Robinson and His Legacy,* Vintage (New York, NY), 1983, pp. 36-37.

PERIODICALS

In These Times, October, 1977, Mark Naison, "Sports for the (Daily) worker," pp. 12-14.
Journal of Sports History, spring, 1974, D. Q. Voight, "Reflections on Diamonds: American Baseball and American Culture," pp. 3-25.
Village Voice, June 10, 1997, Peter Duffy, "Red Rodney—The American Communist Who Helped Liberate Baseball," p. 122.

OTHER

Buhle, Paul, and Michael Fermanowsky, "Baseball and Social Conscience" (interview), Oral History Program, University of California, Los Angeles (Los Angeles, CA), 1984.*

*   *   *

ROGERS, Fred McFeely 1928-2003

OBITUARY NOTICE—See index for *SATA* sketch: Born March 20, 1928, in Latrobe, PA; died of stomach cancer February 27, 2003, in Pittsburgh, PA. Television host, educator, minister, author. Rogers was best known as the soft-spoken, gentle host of children's program, *Mister Rogers' Neighborhood,* which, at the time of Rogers death, was the longest running program on Public Broadcasting Service (PBS). Rogers, an ordained Presbyterian minister, first began his career in children's television in the mid-1950s as executive producer of *Children's Corner,* the predecessor of the long-running *Mister Rogers* show. For more than thirty years, Rogers' broadcasts assured children of their self-worth; every episode of *Mister Rogers' Neighborhood* ended with the phrase, "I like you just the way you are." The recipient of two Peabody Awards, four Emmy Awards, and lifetime acheivement awards from both the National Academy of Television Arts and Sciences and the TV Critics Association, Rogers was presented with the Presidential Medal of Freedom, the nation's highest civilian honor, in 2002. Rogers wrote more than two hundred songs, many of which were used on his television program, and was the author of books for children, including his "Let's Talk about It" and "First Experience" series. He also wrote books for adults on topics such as parenting.

OBITUARIES AND OTHER SOURCES:

PERIODICALS

Los Angeles Times, February 28, 2003, Elaine Woo, "Fred Rogers: 1928-2003; It's a Sad Day in This Neighborhood," p. 1A.
New York Times, February 28, 2003, Daniel Lewis, "Fred Rogers, Host of 'Mister Rogers' Neighborhood,' Dies at 74."
Philadelphia Inquirer, February 28, 2003, Art Carey, "Mr. Rogers Was Tutor, Friend for the Ages."
Star Tribune (Minneapolis, MN), February 28, 2003, Neal Justin, "Mr. Rogers Dies of Stomach Cancer at 74."

*   *   *

ROLL, Charles W(eissert), Jr. 1928-2002

OBITUARY NOTICE—See index for *CA* sketch: Born July 26, 1928, in Trenton, NJ; died from coronary and vascular complications May 12, 2002, in Lawrenceville, NJ. Polltaker and author. Roll was an expert on public-opinion polls that helped predict elections. Educated at Princeton University, where he earned an A.B. in 1950, and Columbia University, where he received his master's degree in 1953, Roll served in the U.S. Army until 1956. He became study director for the famous Gallup Organization in 1958, remaining there until 1977. During this time, he devised ways to figure out which people were most likely to vote, and developed several polling methods that increased the accuracy of forecasting public opinion. Until the early 1990s Roll was the director of the highly respected Pennsylvania Poll for the *Pittsburgh Post-Gazette.* He was also the author of two books written with A. H. Cantril: *Hopes and Fears of the American People* (1971) and *Polls: Their Use and Misuse in Politics* (1972; revised, 1980).

OBITUARIES AND OTHER SOURCES:

PERIODICALS

New York Times, May 23, 2002, p. C14.

*   *   *

ROSENBERG, Otto 1927-2001

PERSONAL: Born April 28, 1927, in East Prussia; died July 4, 2001, in Berlin, Germany; married twice; children: (second marriage) seven.

CAREER: Writer and activist. Founder, Sinti Union of Berlin and Organization for German Sinti and Roma.

WRITINGS:

(With Ulrich Enzensberger) *A Gypsy in Auschwitz,* London House (London, England), 1999.

SIDELIGHTS: Otto Rosenberg was born a Sinto Gypsy in East Prussia in 1927, and was raised by his grandparents when his parents separated. With about ten other families, he and his grandmother lived in a convoy of horse-drawn caravans, selling handcrafts and telling fortunes, until 1936, when the Sinti and Roma Gypsies were rounded up and forced to settle in Marzahn, a small area outside Berlin. Almost a thousand Gypsies were kept at Marzahn by the German authorities, who wanted to keep them out of sight during the 1936 Olympics.

Rosenberg attended a small school in the Marzahn camp, and learned about Roman Catholicism from a priest who visited the camp. He later said this faith helped him during the ordeals he would soon endure at the hands of the Nazis. Rosenberg also met anthropologist Robert Ritter and his assistant, Eva Justin, whom he liked because they often fed him. In 1938, most of the men in the camp were sent to the Sachsenhausen concentration camp. In 1943, when Rosenberg was fifteen, he and other Gypsies, including his grandmother, were taken to the Auschwitz-Birkenau concentration camp, where they were beaten, starved, and where many of them were murdered and cremated in huge ovens.

While at Auschwitz, Rosenberg met the infamous Josef Mengele, a physician who used the inmates of the camp as subjects in horrific experiments. Rosenberg noted that Mengele, despite his evil deeds, had a pleasant demeanor, often laughing, and Rosenberg found it hard to hate him even though he knew what Mengele was doing.

In 1944 Rosenberg and other prisoners considered strong enough to work were sent to Buchenwald concentration camp. Rosenberg's grandmother, left behind, was murdered by the Nazis. Rosenberg was subsequently moved to Camp Dora and then to Bergen-Belsen concentration camp. Russian soldiers liberated the prisoners in 1945. After six years of slavery, Rosenberg went to Berlin to find work and claim the small sum that the government was providing for survivors of the Holocaust. However, explained the author of a London *Times* obituary, the authorities told him, "You are not a Berliner. . . . You are a Gypsy, a wanderer," and refused to give him any reparations. Rosenberg, in response, started associations for Gypsy people and became an activist on their behalf, asking for war reparations for them.

In the 1970s, Rosenberg founded the Sinti Union of Berlin as well as the Organization for German Sinti and Roma. He spoke at schools, youth groups, and universities about his experiences during the war. According to Eric Pace in his *New York Times* obituary, Rosenberg once said, "I was very young and healthy,

and always fit for work. I was probably very lucky, and protected by God. The weaker ones died in the hospital or were beaten to death with guns."

Rosenberg retained the prisoner identity number that had been tattooed on his arm by the Nazis for the remainder of his life. He did not have it removed, but instead had an angel tattooed over it as a symbol of good triumphing over evil. According to a *Chicago Tribune* obituary writer, the journal *History Today* praised Rosenberg's autobiography as "a haunting account of the author's life."

BIOGRAPHICAL AND CRITICAL SOURCES:

PERIODICALS

Booklist, December 1, 1999, review of *A Gypsy in Auschwitz,* p. 683.

OBITUARIES:

PERIODICALS

Chicago Tribune, July 5, 2001, "Otto Rosenberg, 74: German Gypsy who Wrote of Life in Auschwitz," p. 9.
Los Angeles Times, July 13, 2001, "Otto Rosenberg: Gypsy Survived Nazi Death Camps," p. B14.
New York Times, July 1, 2001, Eric Pace, "Otto Rosenberg, 74, Gypsy Who Survived Auschwitz," p. B9.
Times (London, England) August 2, 2001, "Otto Rosenberg: Reminding the World of the Holocaust's Gypsy Victims," p. 19.*

*　　　*　　　*

ROSS, Mark C.

PERSONAL: Male.

ADDRESSES: Agent—c/o Author Mail, Hyperion, 77 West 66th St., 11th Floor, New York, NY 10023.

CAREER: Safari guide in Kenya, 1986—. Also worked summers as a forest firefighter in Montana, Wyoming, and Washington.

WRITINGS:

Dangerous Beauty: Life and Death in Africa; True Stories from a Safari Guide, Hyperion (New York, NY), 2001.

SIDELIGHTS: Mark Ross is an American safari guide in Africa. On March 1, 1999, he and four clients were camped in Uganda, where they were hoping to find endangered mountain gorillas. Instead, they found danger in the form of Rwandan rebels, who were sneaking across the border from the Congo. The rebels killed two of Ross's clients, as well as six other tourists.

Ross explores both his love of Africa and his firsthand experience of the continent in the book, which includes stories of his experiences in Kenya, Tanzania, Zimbabwe, and Uganda. He explains how he finds animals, how he moves through the bush, and how he teaches his clients some of these skills. He describes dangerous elephant charges, meetings with lions, and encounters with cheetahs and Cape buffalo, as well as spectacular, massive migrations of wildebeest and zebras. In addition, he tells the story of the horrific events in March, 1999, and their consequences. In an article in *Canoe,* Jane van der Voort wrote, "He is obviously in the right line of work as he guides, babysits, scolds and shares with safari tourists the wonders of cheetah cubs and the thrill of a predator's kill."

BIOGRAPHICAL AND CRITICAL SOURCES:

PERIODICALS

Booklist, July, 2001, Nancy Bent, review of *Dangerous Beauty,* p. 1962.
New York Times Book Review, September 30, 2001, Naomi Max, review of *Dangerous Beauty,* p. 20.
Publishers Weekly, June 18, 2001, review of *Dangerous Beauty,* p. 70.

OTHER

Dangerous Beauty Web site, http://www.fsbassociates.com/ (December 2, 2001).
Canoe, http://www.canoe.ca/ (December 2, 2001), Jane van der Voort, review of *Dangerous Beauty.*
Soul to Spirit, http://www.soultospirit.com/ (December 2, 2001).**

ROSSI, Hozy (Joe) 1965-

PERSONAL: Born 1965. *Education:* University of Hawaii, B.A., 1987; Washington University, M.A., 1997.

ADDRESSES: Home—San Francisco, CA. *Office*—1045 Sansome St., Ste. 304, San Francisco, CA 94111.

CAREER: KHET, Honolulu, HI, producer/writer; Manoa Center for Oral History, Manoa, HI, field interviewer; eNature.com, San Francisco, CA, news producer.

AWARDS, HONORS: Discover Great New Writers selection, Barnes and Noble, for *Appointment with Il Duce.*

WRITINGS:

Appointment with Il Duce, Welcome Rain Publishers (New York, NY), 2001.

Contributor of poetry to anthologies, including *Bamboo Ridge,* and the University of Hawaii's *Hawaii Review.*

SIDELIGHTS: Hozy Rossi spent three years working on his first novel, *Appointment with Il Duce.* It is the story of Beppe Arpino, a poor, young Italian boy who becomes a talented cellist under the guidance of Father Vincenzo, but who would rather be a dentist. After Father Vincenzo mysteriously dies, Beppe goes to Naples to pursue a career in dentistry. He apprentices with Dr. Puzo, who is an eccentric man, and he falls in love with Angelina Perelli. As Beppe grows older the fascists gain power in Italy, and he finds himself having to take sides. Reviewing the novel for *Booklist,* Kathleen Hughes claimed, "*Appointment with Il Duce* is an enjoyable and often silly, but quick and satisfying read."

BIOGRAPHICAL AND CRITICAL SOURCES:

PERIODICALS

Booklist, April 1, 2001, Kathleen Hughes, review of *Appointment with Il Duce,* p. 1454.
Publishers Weekly, May 21, 2001, review of *Appointment with Il Duce,* p. 81.

OTHER

Honolulu Star Bulletin, http://starbulletin.com/ (January 30, 2002), Gary C. W. Chun, "One Quote Leads to a Quirky First Novel."

New York Times on the Web, http://www.nytimes.com/ (October 7, 2001), William Ferguson, review of *Appointment with Il Duce.**

*   *   *

RUSHFIELD, Richard

PERSONAL: Male. *Education:* Educated in Santa Monica, CA.

ADDRESSES: Home—Southern California. *Office*—9056 Santa Monica Blvd, Ste. 101, West Hollywood, CA 90060.

CAREER: Novelist, journalist, and trend-spotter. Monkey Zero, Los Angeles, CA, cofounder; former political consultant.

WRITINGS:

On Spec: A Novel of Young Hollywood, St. Martin's (New York, NY), 2000.

Contributor to periodicals, including *Vanity Fair* and *Details.*

SIDELIGHTS: American author Richard Rushfield earned critical praise with his debut effort, *On Spec: A Novel of Young Hollywood,* which was published in 2000. A former field organizer for U.S. President Bill Clinton, Rushfield grew up and continues to live near Hollywood, California. He and Adam Leff own a "cultural futurist" firm; their company strives to understand every aspect of culture in the present and what that will lead to in the future. Rushfield and Leff also coauthor *Vanity Fair*'s trend-spotting column, "Intelligence Report."

As the title of his book suggests, Hollywood, otherwise known as Tinseltown, plays a major role in *On Spec.* While fictional, the book is very critical of the Hollywood lifestyle and especially the film business. A contributor for *Publishers Weekly* described *On Spec* as a "swift and humorous trip behind the Hollywood facade." In addition to writing the book, Rushfield has also made public remarks about his disdain for both Hollywood and the film business.

After *On Spec* was published, Rushfield discussed the issue with Trisha Kirk, a writer for University of California Los Angeles's *Daily Bruin.* "The book is about a town where young people come and everyone tries to make it in a business where nobody really knows anything," he explained. "Everyone is grasping at straws and trying to get a place up the ladder by schmoozing and conniving anyway they can, and out of this schmoozing comes movies." The title of *On Spec* refers to the many speculative screenplays that circulate between development agents and film producers. The story revolves around one such screenplay and its author, Stu Bluminvitz. Bluminvitz, a recent graduate of Reed College, lives with his parents in Hollywood. His main goal in life is to become a film writer. The story begins with him trying to find a buyer for his first script, titled "Kennel Break," which is about two men trying to break a girlfriend's dog out of the pound. The plot follows the script as it circulates between an agent, a producer, and a studio head, who decide to make it into a movie. However, by the time the film actually makes it into theaters, it has been altered into a high-budget thriller about a couple of international jewel thieves who have a pet dinosaur. During this excruciating process, the young Bluminvitz is pushed further and further away from production, and is eventually thrown off the movie set. Ultimately the film is an unsuccessful bomb, a fact the studio's power players blame on the poor script and its writer. Instead of using a single, more traditional narrator, Rushfield concocts a narrative that is taken from a series of memos, journal entries, fragments from magazine articles, a police blotter, and computer messages.

Numerous literary critics lauded Rushfield's unabashed account of the Hollywood process. "Rushfield employs a scathing cynicism that spares no one," the *Publishers Weekly* critic wrote. Referring to *On Spec* as a "scabrously funny first novel," Eden Ross Lipson of the *New York Times Book Review* went on to describe the work as "a cautionary tale about Hollywood and a contemporary take on a morality play, or rather, script." Lipson also thought Rushfield has "complete command of his intricate plot." Jay A. Fernandez, who reviewed the book for the *Washington Post,* believed readers would "love it." George Needham of *Booklist* called the work "solid entertainment."

BIOGRAPHICAL AND CRITICAL SOURCES:

PERIODICALS

Booklist, March 1, 2000, George Needham, review of *On Spec: A Novel of Young Hollywood,* p. 1195.

Entertainment Weekly, May 12, 2000, Clarissa Cruz, review of *On Spec,* p. 72.

New York Times Book Review, April 2, 2000, Eden Ross Lipson, "The Treatment," p. 22.

Publishers Weekly, February 14, 2000, review of *On Spec,* p. 176.

Washington Post Book World, April 2, 2000, Jay A. Fernandez, "Close up and Personal," p. 9.

OTHER

Daily Bruin Online, http://www.dailybruin.ucla.edu/ (May 11, 2002), Trisha Kirk, "Novel Takes Candid Look at Race for Fame in Hollywood."

Monkey Zero, http://www.monkeyzero.net/ (February 13, 2003).

New City Chicago, http://www.newcitychicago.com/ (May 11, 2002), Ellen Fox, "Tinseltown Tarnish."*

*   *   *

RUSSELL, Fred(erick McFerrin) 1906-2003

PERSONAL: Born August 27, 1906, in Nashville, TN; died January 26, 2003; son of John E. (a journalist) and Mabel (McFerrin) Russell; married Katherine Wyche Early, November 2, 1933; children: four. *Education:* Attended Vanderbilt University.

CAREER: Journalist and sportswriter. Worked as a soda jerk and for a title company in Nashville, TN, 1920s; admitted to the Bar of Tennessee, 1927; *Nash-*

ville Banner, Nashville, TN, reporter, columnist and sports editor, 1928-98; *Tennessean,* Nashville, TN, sportswriter, beginning 1998; National Football Foundation and Hall of Fame, chairman of honors committee, 1967-92; Heisman Trophy committee, southern chairman, 1946-92; Football Writers Association, president, 1960-61.

AWARDS, HONORS: Grantland Rice Award, 1955; College Football Centennial Award, 1969; writing award, Golf Writers Association of America, 1972; U.S. Olympic Committee award for distinguished journalism, 1976; Distinguished American Award, National Football Foundation and Hall of Fame, 1980; Amos Alonzo Stagg Award, American Football Coaches Association, 1981; National Turf Writers Association Award, 1983; Red Smith Award, Associated Press Sports Editors, 1984; inducted into Tennessee Sports Hall of Fame, 1974 and National Sportscasters and Sportswriters Hall of Fame, 1988; Grantland Rice sports writing scholarship established in 1956 renamed the Fred Russell-Grantland Rice sports writing scholarship by Vanderbilt University/Thoroughbred Racing Association, 1986; Fred Russell Baseball Press Box dedicated by Vanderbilt University, 2001.

WRITINGS:

(Editor with Maxwell Benson) *Fifty Years of Vanderbilt Football,* privately printed (Nashville, TN), 1938.

I'll Go Quietly, McQuiddy (Nashville, TN), 1944.

I'll Try Anything Twice, McQuiddy (Nashville, TN), 1945.

Funny Thing about Sports, McQuiddy (Nashville, TN), 1945.

(With George Leonard) *Vol Feats, Nashville Banner* (Nashville, TN), 1950.

Bury Me in an Old Press Box: Good Times and Life of a Sportswriter, Barnes (New York, NY), 1957.

(With George Leonard) *Big Bowl Football: The Great Postseason Classics,* Ronald (New York, NY), 1963.

The Libel Case of Wally Butts vs. the Saturday Evening Post (collection of articles), Nashville Banner (Nashville, TN), 1963.

Also author of column "Sideline" for *Nashville Banner;* regular contributor to *Saturday Evening Post,* 1939-62.

SIDELIGHTS: Fred Russell, considered one of the most beloved sportswriters in the South, was a man who literally never retired and wrote more than 12,000 columns for four generations of fans. Russell won many awards for his accomplishments, and Vanderbilt University's Grantland Rice sports writing scholarship, established in the name of another great sportswriting alumni in 1956, was renamed the Fred Russell-Grantland Rice sports writing scholarship in 1986 when the award received an endowment from the Oaklawn Jockey Club on behalf of the Thoroughbred Racing Association.

Russell was born in Nashville, Tennessee, but he spent his first thirteen years in Wartrace, a small town his journalist father thought would provide a better environment for bringing up his children. In 1920 the family returned to Nashville, however, and Russell attended Duncan Preparatory School. After graduation he worked as a soda jerk and saved for an education at Vanderbilt. He studied law and later passed the Bar exam, but he was more impressed by English courses, particularly a freshman class taught by Edwin Mimes. Russell worked for a title company until it was sold, leaving him unemployed. He applied to the *Nashville Banner,* and owner and publisher Jimmy Stahlman gave him a choice of jobs, as a cub reporter at six dollars a week, or on the classified desk at four times that amount. Russell chose the reporting job.

Russell was at the *Banner* less than a year when, at age twenty-four, he became sports editor. It was a time of sports legends like Babe Ruth in baseball, Knute Rockne and Red Grange in football, Bobby Jones in golf, Johnny Weismueller in swimming, and Jack Dempsey in boxing. Just as there were great athletes, there were great writers to immortalize them, including Rice, Paul Gallico, and many others. William J. Plott noted in *Dictionary of Literary Biography* that "humor permeated Russell's writing and his speech. . . . Most of Russell's daily 'Sideline' pieces were 'notes' columns, a trade expression for columns that are a smorgasbord of short news items, jokes, and humorous anecdotes. Russell also loved carefully crafting practical jokes, some of which required elaborate preparation."

Stories were not confined to Tennessee sports, and Russell wrote many articles about Purdue and Kansas. He served on various committees and for forty-six years was southern chairman of the committee that selected the Heisman Trophy winner. He was not only president of the Football Writers Association, he was a charter member, along with Tom Siler, sports editor of the *Knoxville News-Sentinel.* Both men contributed to national magazines, Siler to *Colliers,* and Russell to the *Saturday Evening Post,* beginning with his first assignment in 1949 and his last when the magazine shut down in the 1960s.

Not all of Russell's writing was about sports. In 1936 he covered the kidnaping of Alice Speed Stoll of Louisville, Kentucky. Her kidnapper, Thomas H. Robinson, Jr., and Russell had been classmates at Vanderbilt, and Russell was able to get an exclusive interview with Robinson before his conviction. In one particular instance Russell drew on his background in law in writing a series of articles about the *Wally Butts vs. the Saturday Evening Post* libel trial. The *Post* was sued by the former University of Georgia football coach over an article alleging that Butts and Paul "Bear" Bryant of the University of Alabama had conspired to fix a game. The *Banner* sent Russell to Atlanta to cover the trial, and when it was over the newspaper collected his articles and published them. Plott noted that Blackie Sherrod, sports editor of the *Dallas Morning News,* "said Russell covered the libel trial much like Damon Runyon covered murder trials. The idea of a sportswriter being sent to cover a judicial event of national interest was a source of pride for other sportswriters. . . . His prose indicated that he had little problem switching from the world of sports to that of law. Indeed, his attention to details and perceptions of human nature were often evident in his coverage. Russell rarely displayed verse or high metaphor, but his stories and columns usually captured the essence of the subject in clear, easily digested language."

When Wilma Rudolph, the star of the 1960 Olympic Games, died in 1994, Russell, who had covered the Tennessee athlete's amazing career, delivered her eulogy. When the *Banner* folded, Russell hardly missed a beat. He wrote his last column for the *Banner* on February 19, 1998 and his first at his new spot at the *Tennessean* on April 2. Randy Horick wrote in *Nashville Scene* that Russell "witnessed the reshaping of the entire sports landscape, from college football teams that didn't offer scholarships to athletic departments that are run like corporations; from an era of unpretentious baseball players to a time of millionaire media stars; from the days of cold type and Western Union to real-time, all-the-time information. Russell died in 2003."

BIOGRAPHICAL AND CRITICAL SOURCES:

BOOKS

Dictionary of Literary Biography, Volume 241: *American Sportswriters and Writers on Sport,* Gale (Detroit, MI), 2001, pp. 251-258.

Russell, Fred, *Bury Me in an Old Press Box: Good Times and Life of a Sportswriter,* Barnes (New York, NY), 1957.

PERIODICALS

Nashville Scene, March 26, 1998, Randy Horick, "The Time of His Life: How Fred Russell Got the Story," pp. 22-32.

New York Times, April 27, 1980, "Russell, Sports Columnist, Is Cited by Football Hall," p. S10.

Sports Illustrated, March 2, 1998, "Fred Russell's Banner Career," p. 22.

Vanderbilt Magazine, spring, 1995, Nelson Bryan, "70 Years in the Making," pp. 6-9.

Wall Street Journal, November 27, 1992, Frederick C. Klein, "On Sports: An Old-time Scribe," p. A7.*

*   *   *

RYAN, Kay 1945-

PERSONAL: Born 1945.

ADDRESSES: Office—60 Taylor Dr., Fairfax, CA, 94930.

CAREER: Poet.

AWARDS, HONORS: Lenore Marshall Poetry Prize finalist, American Academy of Poets, 1995; Union League Civic and Arts Poetry Prize, *Poetry* magazine, 2000; two-time winner of Pushcart Prize.

WRITINGS:

Dragon Acts to Dragon Ends, Taylor Street Press (Fairfax, CA), 1983.

Strangely Marked Metal: Poems, Copper Beech Press (Providence, RI), 1985.

Flamingo Watching: Poems, Copper Beech Press (Providence, RI), 1994.

Elephant Rocks, Grove Press (New York, NY), 1996.

Say Uncle: Poems, Grove Press (New York, NY), 2000.

Contributor of poetry to various publications, including the *New Yorker, Atlantic Monthly, New Republic,* and *Paris Review.* Also contributor to *The Best American Poetry,* 1995.

SIDELIGHTS: American poet Kay Ryan has published five volumes of poetry since 1983, the year her debut effort, *Dragon Acts to Dragon Ends,* appeared in print. Ryan's first major work was *Strangely Marked Metal,* published in 1985, and it has been followed by the critically acclaimed collections *Flamingo Watching, Elephant Rocks,* and *Say Uncle.*

In addition to earning several literary awards, Ryan has also won the praise of many literary critics, a number of whom have compared her work to the verse of Emily Dickinson. "Kay Ryan is one contemporary poet whose work exemplifies the old humanist notion that poetry can both delight and instruct. Ryan is a poet of ideas, of pragmatic philosophical reflection, and the pleasure of it is we hardly even know we're being taught," wrote critic Andrew Frisardi in *Poetry.* Ryan's poetry "is cause for celebration," wrote George Bradley, reviewing *Flamingo Watching* for *Yale Review.* "Her poetry is vivid and peculiar, flexible and flamboyant, sinuous and exact."

Ryan realized at an early age that she wanted to become a poet. In an interview with *Entertainment Weekly,* she explained that she began to appreciate her gift for language "when I was twelve and able to use language in such a way as to cause a grown-up to spit a mouthful of milk across the dinner table in an uncontrollable expression of amusement." Today, however, she aspires to more than spilled milk. "I would like to have my poems burned into the code of the universe," she said in the same interview.

Critics began taking notice of Ryan's gift for language with the publication of *Strangely Marked Metal.* In the book's title poem, Ryan asks, "Where were the tablets before Moses?" Her answer: "Perhaps / they are all the strangely marked metals / which we cannot resist reading as fiercely / as we can because they are so beautiful." The subjects of her musings include the ancient Greeks and Egyptians, Marianne Moore, and herself. Calling the book "a delight to read," R. Whitman of *Choice* described Ryan as an "engaging and engaged poet" with a "subtle and accurate" ear.

Many of the poems in *Elephant Rocks* are compressed, with brief lines and short stanzas. For example, in the poem "Intention," Ryan writes: "Intention doesn't sweeten. / It should be picked young / and eaten. Sometimes only hours / separate the cotyledon / from the wooden plant. / Then if you want to eat it, / you can't." A *Publishers Weekly* reviewer felt that *Elephant Rocks* contains a "careful observation of the external world of sensation" as well as a "faithful documentation of the inner world of thought." In *Booklist,* Elizabeth Millard described Ryan as "remarkably dexterous at slanting the poetic light upon common places."

The poems in *Say Uncle,* Ryan's fifth published book, also have short lines, most of them no more than six syllables long. For example, in the poem "Blunt," Ryan writes, "If we could love / the blunt / and not / the point / we would / almost constantly / have what we want." Other poem titles include "The Fabric of Life," "Agreement," "The Old Cosmologists," and "The Pass." Most critics lauded *Say Uncle,* including David Yezzi of *Poetry.* "Kay Ryan's diminutive poems resemble pastilles, lemon drops hard enough to cut your lip on. The sweetness derives from their gently musical, amusing surfaces, the tang from a rueful world view," Yezzi wrote. Peter Davison, reviewing the work for the *Atlantic Monthly,* observed that it contains "precise, epigrammatic poems" with "hook-and-eye rhymes." The *Publishers Weekly* reviewer concluded that Ryan's verse seeks "compression, consonance, cute rhymes, and moral lessons."

BIOGRAPHICAL AND CRITICAL SOURCES:

BOOKS

Directory of American Poets and Fiction Writers, Poets & Writers (New York, NY), 1997-98.

PERIODICALS

Antioch Review, fall, 1996, Daniel McGuiness, review of *Elephant Rocks,* p. 496.
Atlantic Monthly, October, 2000, Peter Davison, review of *Say Uncle,* p. 136.
Booklist, April 1, 1996, Elizabeth Millard, review of *Elephant Rocks,* p. 1340.
Choice, December, 1985, R. Whitman, review of *Strangely Marked Metal,* p. 606.
Entertainment Weekly, June 29, 2001, "Books: The It List," p. 90.
Georgia Review, fall, 2000, Paul Lake, review of *Say Uncle,* p. 584.
Library Journal, August, 1994, Christine Stenstrom, review of *Flamingo Watching,* p. 91; February 1, 2001, Ann K. van Buren, review of *Say Uncle,* p. 100.
New Yorker, December 16, 1996, Benoit van Innis, review of *Elephant Rocks,* p. 108.
Poetry, May, 1997, Andrew Frisardi, review of *Elephant Rocks,* p. 101; May, 2001, David Yezzi, review of *Say Uncle,* p. 103.
Publishers Weekly, March 18, 1996, review of *Elephant Rocks,* p. 67; July 24, 2000, review of *Say Uncle,* p. 82.
Yale Review, July, 1995, George Bradley, review of *Flamingo Watching,* p. 170; April, 2001, Rachel Hadas, review of *Say Uncle,* p. 170.

OTHER

Salon.com, http://www.salonmag.com/ (September 15, 2001)*.

* * *

RYDER, Frederick Bushnell 1871-1936
(Jack Ryder)

PERSONAL: Born November 16, 1871, in Oberlin, OH; died of a heart attack June 5, 1936. *Education:* Williams College, graduated, 1892.

CAREER: Sportswriter. Cofounder of a preparatory school for boys, Columbus, OH, 1890s; worked briefly on a cattle boat; Ohio State University, Columbus, football coach; *Commercial-Tribune,* Cincinnati, OH, columnist, 1904; *Cincinnati Enquirer,* Cincinnati, sportswriter and editor, 1904-36. Founder of the Baseball Writers Association of America, 1908. *Military service:* U.S. Army, served during Spanish-American War.

WRITINGS:

AS JACK RYDER

(Editor) Edward Michael Ashenback, *Humor among the Minors: True Tales from the Baseball Bush,* Donohue (Chicago, IL), 1911.

Also author of column "Ginger Jar" for Cincinnati *Commercial-Tribune;* contributor to *Spalding's Official Baseball Guide,* various annuals.

SIDELIGHTS: Frederick Bushnell Ryder, who was known as Jack Ryder, spent his entire sportswriting career in Cincinnati, Ohio, where he covered the Cincinnati Reds baseball team. Lee Allen wrote in *The Cincinnati Reds: An Informal History* that "breakfast in Cincinnati was plump sausage and barnyard-fresh eggs, strong, fragrant coffee, and Jack Ryder's column," and said that Ryder "always spiced up his columns with gentle sarcasm, sly digs, and subtle quips about life in general."

Ryder was born in Ohio but raised in New England. His father, a Congregational minister, was also a professor of theology at Andover Academy in Massachusetts. Ryder graduated from Phillips Exeter Academy in Exeter, New Hampshire and Williams College, where he played guard on the football team. He and his brother Robert founded and managed a preparatory school for boys in Columbus, Ohio for several years until 1898, when Ryder worked on a cattle boat for his passage so that he could travel in Europe. He returned to the United States and joined the U.S. Army during the Spanish-American War but was never sent further than Florida and Alabama.

The brothers both pursued journalism careers. Robert began as an editorial writer for the *Ohio State Journal,* and Ryder, after one year of coaching football at Ohio State University, joined the staff of the *Commercial-Tribune* in Cincinnati, where in 1904 he began writing

his column "Ginger Jar." In December of the same year, he moved to the *Cincinnati Enquirer,* where he succeeded Ren Mulford as baseball reporter and editor. The Reds were playing in League Park, also known as the Palace of the Fans, and in 1909 Redlands Field opened. (It was renamed Crosley Field in 1934.) The team was unspectacular during the first part of the century, but Ryder always found positive things to say in his column and often injected humor into his writing, called "florid" and "typical of the era" by James B. Dworkin in *Dictionary of Literary Biography.* Dworkin wrote that Ryder's writing "was filled with the droll words and catchphrases of early baseball: *foozle* for an error, *bingles* for hits. Ryder strove for color and irony as well as a clever introduction."

Two of Ryder's favorite targets were New York Giants pitcher Christy Mathewson, who joined the Reds in 1916 as a player-manager, and Giants manager John J. McGraw. On August 7, 1908, McGraw refused to postpone a game with the Reds after rain had soaked the field, thinking that his team would easily win. McGraw miscalculated, and the Giants' loss cost them first place in the National League standings. In typical Ryder style, he wrote in the next day's column that "Mr. John J. McGraw thought he was cutting into a fine, ripe cantaloupe this afternoon and was much surprised to find a lemon of the sourest variety."

Ryder was sometimes able to include both Mathewson and McGraw in the same column. After Mathewson joined the Reds, he and Giants manager McGraw were taken to court for playing a Sunday game in violation of the Sabbath laws. The case was dismissed, and the judge complimented the managers for entertaining the soldiers who sat in the stands. Ryder wrote that "as a comment on the hypocrisy of human nature, however, it was necessary for him to announce that he let them off because the money taken in at the gate was paid by the fans to hear the alleged sacred concert which preceded the game, and not to see the contest. It's a queer world!" Allen said Ryder wrote about the Reds "as if he were describing the gallant battle of the titans, but still gave the impression that his tongue was in his cheek." Although Ryder later tempered his style, he once wrote that "a man who can crack out such a hit, with the bases full, is entitled to all the candy, cigars, booze, household goods, and other paraphernalia that comes to the four-base hitter on the home lot." Allen, who for a time was an unpaid assistant to Ryder, went on to become a writer, researcher, and baseball historian.

As one of the organizers of the Baseball Writers Association of America (BBWAA), Ryder served on the rules committee and helped write the guidelines that defined the group's goals of fairness, uniform scoring, simplified rules, better facilities for reporters, and the regulation of box scores. The first meeting of the BBWAA was held in New York City, and Ryder was elected spokesperson of a committee to approach the two major leagues with proposals.

In selecting the National League's Most Valuable Player of the 1924 season, a controversy erupted when Ryder failed to include in the list of nominees top hitter Rogers Hornsby of St. Louis, who had hit .424 that year. Instead, the award went to Brooklyn pitcher Dazzy Vance. The next year Ryder was replaced by Tom Swope from the rival *Cincinnati Post.* Hornsby biographer Charles C. Alexander noted that in 1962, the BBWAA "awarded Hornsby 'a silver bat' . . . retroactively recognizing him as the National League's Most Valuable Player for 1924 and finally undoing Jack Ryder's dirty work."

Ryder was a strong proponent of playing by the rules and living by the decisions of umpires. In 1924 when St. Louis Cardinals manager Branch Rickey postponed three games in a row because of threatening weather which never came to pass, Ryder, who knew that Hornsby had suffered an injury, said the games had been called off "due to cold feet. Umpires and not club owners should decide such matters." He pulled no punches in writing his opinions. When Pittsburgh's Fred Clarke contested three games in 1911, Ryder called him "a fancy protester." He was blunt in writing that Rube Benton, who was known to come to the mound after bouts of drinking, "will pitch for the Reds if he puts in an appearance by game time." In 1913 Ryder interviewed the new Reds player-manager Joe Tinker, who blasted owner August Herrmann for the team's poor performance. Herrmann responded that Tinker's comments were a violation of baseball etiquette. Ryder allowed Tinker to use his column for his reply, in which he stated that there was no law that required that only positive statements be made about the management of the club.

The 1934 season found the Cardinals, led by pitcher Dizzy Dean and his brother Paul, winning forty games, just five short of the Pennant. At the beginning of the season, Ryder downplayed the brothers' abilities and the chances of the team leading the League, but by its close, he was enthusiastic in his praise of the Deans. Ryder's Reds came in last, and he made excuses for

their abysmal finish. When they won, wrote Dworkin, "Ryder's enthusiasm poured over into his prose: 'Red stood out all over the place during the super-heated matinee yesterday on the sun-baked turf of Crosley Field. The countenances of the athletes glistened under the violent rays of Old Sol, an umpire had to be removed in a parboiled condition, and our boys climaxed an afternoon of brilliant hue by soaking the Cardinals.'"

Throughout his career Ryder persisted in using archaic terms, like "tallies" instead of runs, "hard blows" instead of hits, and "frames" or "rounds" rather than innings. His lingo was criticized in particular by Stanley Woodward of the *New York Herald Tribune,* although Woodward eventually dropped it. "Ryder remained unfazed," said Dworkin. "He may have been a dinosaur, but he was still popular and respected by his readers and by most of his peers. If Damon Runyon, Westbrook Pegler, Paul Gallico, and other 'Golden Age' writers were stretching the genre, while still others like John Lardner and Frank Graham were giving it new respectability, Ryder seemed willing to 'stand the gaff,' as he might have put it."

Ryder died of a heart attack in 1936. His paper wrote in tribute that he "worked as hard at each game as did the players, rejoicing when the Reds won and sorrowing when they lost. . . . As a news getter, he had no peer. His convictions were strong, and he did not hesitate to state them by mouth or in print."

BIOGRAPHICAL AND CRITICAL SOURCES:

BOOKS

Alexander, Charles C., *Rogers Hornsby: A Biography,* H. Holt (New York, NY), 1995.

Allen, Lee, *The Cincinnati Reds: An Informal History,* Putnam (New York, NY), 1948, pp. 241-243.

Dictionary of Literary Biography, Volume 241: *American Sportswriters and Writers on Sport,* Gale (Detroit, MI), 2001, pp. 259-265.

Eskenazi, Gerald, *The Lip: A Biography of Leo Durocher,* Morrow (New York, NY), 1993, pp. 54-59, 65.

Fleming, G. H., *The Unforgettable Season,* Holt, Rinehart and Winston (New York, NY), 1981, pp. 68, 69, 71, 95, 118, 158, 177-178, 180, 257, 290, 296.

Fleming, G. H., *The Dizziest Season: The Gashouse Gang Chases the Pennant,* Morrow (New York, NY), 1984, pp. 8, 76, 102, 134-135, 196, 260-261.

James, Bill, *The Bill James Historical Baseball Abstract,* Villard (New York, NY), 1985, pp. 73-74.

James, Bill, *Whatever Happened to the Hall of Fame?: Baseball, Cooperstown, and the Politics of Glory,* Simon and Schuster (New York, NY), 1995, p. 143.

Pietrusza, David, *Judge and Jury: The Life and Times of Judge Kenesaw Mountain Landis,* Diamond Communications (South Bend, IN), 1998, p. 258.

Spink, Alfred H., *The National Game,* Southern Illinois University Press (Carbondale, IL), 2000, pp. 350-351.

White, Edward G., *Creating the National Pastime: Baseball Transforms Itself, 1903-1953,* Princeton University Press (Princeton, NJ), 1996, p. 161.*

*   *   *

RYDER, Jack
    See RYDER, Frederick Bushnell

S

S., Tayeb
See DJAOUT, Tahar

*   *   *

SAGASTIZÁBAL, Patricia 1953-

PERSONAL: Born December 31, 1953, in Buenos Aires, Argentina; daughter of Rodolfo Oliveri (a journalist) and Catalina Costavega (an agronomic engineer); married Leandro de Sagastizábal (a history professor and publisher), December 23, 1977; children: Francisco, Hernán. *Ethnicity:* Hispanic. *Education:* Universidad Nacional de Buenos Aires (law).

*ADDRESSES: Home—*Buenos Aires, Argentina. *Agent—*Guillermo Schavelzon, Rodríguez Peña 2067, 3A, Buenos Aires, Argentina C1021ABQ.

CAREER: Lawyer and writer. Has also worked as an actress and theater director and as the coordinator of cultural and sports activities at a private university.

AWARDS, HONORS: Premio la Nación de Novela, *Lanación* (newspaper), 1999, for *Un Secreto para Julia.*

WRITINGS:

En Nombre de dios (title means "In the Name of God"), Editorial Sudamericana (Buenos Aires, Argentina), 1997.

Un Secreto para Julia, Editorial Sudamericana (Buenos Aires, Argentina), 1999, English translation by Asa Zatz published as *A Secret for Julia,* W. W. Norton (New York, NY), 2001.

WORK IN PROGRESS: Estados mentales (novel) and *La Cantante de tango* (novel).

SIDELIGHTS: Patricia Sagastizábal is a native of Buenos Aires, Argentina. Born in 1953, she personally witnessed the horrors and violence of a repressive government throughout her youth and into her adulthood. In a *Los Angeles Times* review of Sagastizábal's second novel, *A Secret for Julia,* Merle Rubin wrote about a time still fresh in the memories of most observers, both American and Argentinian: "Not all that long ago, in Argentina in the 1970s, people who criticized the government were summarily arrested, imprisoned, interrogated, tortured and, in many cases, killed. The mothers of those who had 'disappeared' held vigils, standing for hours in all kinds of weather holding signs and pictures of their children." Television news programs into the 1980s were full of the reality of repression.

Sagastizábal was trained as a lawyer but practiced only for a short time. In 1997, after working for several years at a private university, she published her first novel, *En Nombre de dios* ("In the Name of God"), the story of a Spanish Jesuit who is sent to the Americas at the beginning of the seventeenth century to convert the Indians. Antonio Ruiz eventually must decide whether to choose violence in order to defend his adopted land and its inhabitants, the Guarani Indians.

The first chapter of *A Secret for Julia* is full of intrigue: in a family-run restaurant in the Bloomsbury neighborhood of London, a man is arrested by Interpol. It is reported—not by the police but in the stories that circulate about his arrest—that he is from Argentina. Using a narrator, Mercedes Beecham, the story reads like a personal diary, according to the publisher. Beecham lives in London with her teenage daughter Julia but still suffers from memories of the horrible past she endured in Argentina. Julia's major concern is finding out the identity of her father, information that her mother is reluctant to share with her. Rubin wrote, "The squeamish reader need not run for cover: Sagastizábal does not place undue emphasis on the grisly details of torture. But she does achieve a strong, almost visceral, effect through her powerful evocation of her heroine's thoughts and actions: her fear, her anger, her determination and her courage." Writing for *Book*, Beth Kephart observed, "Like a story whispered under the cover of night, [*A Secret for Julia*] is harrowing and compelling. This is a book of rare authenticity that will leave readers sympathetic to the loneliness of the exile." The book won Argentina's prestigious Premio La Nación de Novela in 1999. In addition to its publication in Argentina and the United States, the novel was also published in Spain, Israel, and Holland.

Sagastizábal told *CA* that, when she was a child, her grandfather used to tell "very detailed and thrilling tales about his work" as a militant of Argentina's Radical Party. "In a quiet tone, without even moving a muscle of his face," he would narrate accounts of horrifying atrocities committed on Argentina's frontier in the late nineteenth century. Seven-year-old Sagastizábal listened "with my eyes wide open, breathless, and fascinated. Therefore, the adventures that awoke my interest in fantasy were not only Robin Hood's or the fantastic fables of *The Thousand and One Nights*. Reality operated in me as an incentive because my understanding could not seize it, and I remained confused and full of unanswered questions. I wanted—I was such a dreamer—to solve the intrigues that were in every one of those mysterious situations."

An actress in her younger days, Sagastizábal is sometimes asked by friends why she no longer pursues that vocation. She disagrees, telling them: "When I write, I perform, because I get angry, I laugh, and I get dirty with my characters, and their wounds hurt me."

BIOGRAPHICAL AND CRITICAL SOURCES:

PERIODICALS

Book, September 2001, Beth Kephart, review of *A Secret for Julia*, p. 77.
Booklist, July 2001, Elsa Gaztambide, review of *A Secret for Julia*, p. 1983.
Library Journal, August 2001, Lawrence Olszewski, review of *A Secret for Julia*, p. 166.
Los Angeles Times, September 3, 2001, Merle Rubin, "*Secret* Skillfully Weaves Repression into a Fictional Tale of Courage," p. E-3.
Ms., October-November, 2001, Daisy Hernandez, review of *A Secret for Julia*, p. 69.

*　　*　　*

SALMON, André 1881-1969

PERSONAL: Born October 4, 1881, in Paris, France; died 1969; married Jeanne Blazy-Escarpette, July 13, 1909 (died, 1949); married October 29, 1953; second wife's name Leo.

CAREER: Poet, art critic, novelist, and journalist. *Vers et prose* (journal), co-founder. *Military service:* Served in French infantry during World War I.

AWARDS, HONORS: Grand Prize for Poetry, Academie Française, 1964.

WRITINGS:

Les clés ardentes (poetry; title means "The Burning Keys"), [France], 1905.
Poèmes, Vers et prose (Paris, France), 1905.
Les Féeries (poetry; title means "Enchantments"), Les Soins de vers et prose (Paris, France), 1907.
Le Calumet (poetry), H. Falque (Paris, France), 1910.
La jeune peinture française, Société des Trente (Paris, France), 1912.
(With Guy Dollian) *Histoires de boches*, Société littéraire de France (Paris, France), 1917.
(With Enzo Manfredini) *Quelques dessins de guerre*, Renaissance du Livre (Paris, France), 1917.

Le Chass'bi: notes de campagne en Artois en et Argonne in 1915, Perrin (Paris, France), 1917.

Monstres choisis, Nouvelle Revue Française (Paris, France), 1918, reprinted, Gallimard (Paris, France), 1968.

Prikaz (poetry), La Sirène (Paris, France), 1919, reprinted, Debresse (Paris, France), 1956.

Moeurs de la famille Poivre (novel), Kundig (Geneva, Switzerland), 1919.

Le manuscript trouvé dans un chapeau (verse and prose), Société Littéraire de France (Paris, France), 1919, reprinted, Fata Morgana (Montpellier, France), 1983.

(With others) *Catalogue des éditions d'art,* Kundig (Geneva, Switzerland), 1919.

La jeune sculpture française, Messein (Paris, France), 1919.

(With others) *Ballade du pauvre Macchabé mal enterré* (poetry), Bernouard (Paris, France), 1919.

(With Yves Blanc) *Le long de la route* (poetry), La Belle Édition (Paris, France), 1919.

(Author of preface) *Émile-Othon Friesz: vingt-six reproductions de peintures et dessins,* Nouvelle Revue Française (Paris, France), 1920.

L'art vivant (title means "Living Art"), Crès (Paris, France), 1920.

La négresse du Sacré-Coeur, Nouvelle Revue Française (Paris, France), 1920, reprinted, Gallimard (Paris, France), 1968, translation by Slater Brown published as *The Black Venus,* Macaulay (New York, NY), 1929.

C'est une bellie fille!: chronique du vingtième siècle, A. Michel (Paris, France), 1920.

Bob et Bobette en ménage (novel), A. Michel (Paris, France), 1920.

La livre et la bouteille (title means "The Book and the Bottle"), C. Bloch (Paris, France), 1920.

Des indépendants au Louvre, L'Europe Nouvelle (Paris, France), 1920.

L'érotisme l'art contemporain, Librarie des Arts Décoratifs (Paris, France), c. 1920.

Coleur du temps, 1920.

L'age de l'humanité, Nouvelle Revue Française (Paris, France), 1921.

L'amant des amazones, La Banderole (Paris, France), 1921.

L'entrepreneau d'illuminations, Nouvelle Revue Française (Paris, France), 1921.

Peindre (poetry), La Sirène (Paris, France), 1921.

La révélation de Seurat, Éditions Sélection (Brussels, Belgium), 1921.

Ventes d'amour (poetry), Bernouard (Paris, France), 1921.

Tendres canailles, Nouvelle Revue Française (Paris, France), 1921.

Propos d'atelier (title means "Studio Talk"), third edition, Crès (Paris, France), 1922.

(With Rene Saunier) *Natchalo: Le commencement scenes e la revolution russe* (three-act play; produced in Paris, France, 1922), Imprimiteur de l'illustration (Paris, France), 1922.

(With others) *Les princesses de Cythère: chronique libertine de l'histoire,* J. Fort (Paris, France), 1922.

Cézanne, Stock (Paris, France) 1923.

Archives du club des onze (novel), G. & A. Mornay (Paris, France), 1923.

(Editor) Marcel Schwob, *Le livre de Monelle,* Stock (Paris, France), 1923.

(With René Saunier) *Deux hommes, une femme* (three-act play), Hébertot (Paris, France), 1923.

John Storrs and Modern Sculpture (in English), Sociétè Anonyme (New York, NY), 1923.

La collection particulière de M. Paul Poret: exposée du 26 avril au 12 mai, Barbazanges (Paris, France), 1923.

(Author of text) *André Derain: 26 reproductions de peintures,* Nouvelle Revue Française (Paris, France), 1924.

(With Emmanuel Bourcier and Henri Béraud) *L'affaire Landru,* A. Michel (Paris, France), 1924.

Une orgie à Saint-Pétersbourg, Sagittaire (Paris, France), 1925.

(With Maurice Utrillo) *Gouaches d'Utrillo,* Quatre Chemins (Paris, France), 1925.

Vielle garnison, F. Paillart (Abbeville, France), 1925.

(With others) *Friesz, oeuvres (1901-1927): cinquante reproductions en phototypie,* Chroniques du Jour (Paris, France), 1926.

Modigliani, sa vie et son oeuvre, Quatre Chemins (Paris, France), 1926, translation by Dorothy and Randolph Weaver published as *Modigliani, a Memoir,* Putnam (New York, NY), 1961.

Créances, 1905-1910; Les clés ardentes; Féeries; Le calumet, Nouvelle Revue Française (Paris, France), 1926.

Metamorphoses de la harpe et de la harpiste (poetry), Cahiers Libres (Paris, France), 1926.

Venus dans la balance (poetry) Quatre Chemins (Paris, France), 1926.

(With others) *Poèmes,* Chroniques du Jour (Paris, France), 1926.

(With Pierre Charbonnier) *Les noces exemplaires de Mie Saucée; ou, Les nouvelles métamorphoses de*

Mm. Quasi, Total, Agénor de Jussieu et frère Gavier sous les controle et presidence de l'homme qui bêche, Fanfare de Montparnasse (Paris, France), 1926.

Jacques Lipchitz, L'Art d'aujourd'hui (Paris, France), 1926.

Henri Rousseau dit le douanier, Crès (Paris, France), 1927, translation by Paul Colacicchi published as *Henri Rousseau,* Oldbourne Press (London, England), 1963.

(With Serge Gladky) *Synthèse du costume théatral,* Théatre Mondial (Paris, France), 1927.

Léopold Gottlieb, Écrivains Réunis (Paris, France), 1927.

Le drapeau noir, Cité des Livres (Paris, France), 1927.

(With others) *Friesz, oeuvres (1901-1927),* Chroniques du Jour (Paris, France), 1927.

Tout l'or du monde, Sagittaire (Paris, France), 1927.

Max Jacob: poète, peintre, mystique, et l'homme de qualité, R. Girard (Paris, France) 1927.

(With Albert Besnard) *Exposition Albert Besnard: pastels, aquarelles et dessings, gravures,* Galerie Marcel Guiot (Paris, France), 1927.

Kisling, Chroniques du Jour (Paris, France), 1928.

Art russe moderne, Laville (Paris, France), 1928.

Carreaux, 1918-1921; Prikaz; L'age de l'humanité; Le livre et la bouteille, Gallimard (Paris, France), 1928.

(With Marc Chagall) *Chagall,* Chroniques du Jour (Paris, France), 1928.

Donat vainqueur; ou, Les panathénées du le arrondissement, Delpeuch (Paris, France), 1928.

(With Carlos Mérida) *Images de Guatemala,* Quatre Chemins (Paris, France), 1928.

André Derain, Chroniques du Jour (Paris, France), 1929.

(With Oscar Fabrés) *Montparnasse: bars, cafés, dancings,* Bonjour (Paris, France), 1929, published as *Montparnasse,* A. Bonne (Paris, France), 1950.

(With Geo London and Fernand Divoire) *Roman d'un crime,* Portiques (Paris, France), 1929.

(With others) *Maurice Maeterlinck,* Figuière (Paris, France), 1929.

(With others) *Les sept péchés capitaux,* Kra (Paris, France), 1929.

Portraits, Ganymed (Berlin, Germany), 1929.

(With Paul Morand) *Marcel Vertès,* H. Babou (Paris, France), 1930.

Léopold-Levy, Triangle (Paris, France), 1930.

Saints de glace, NRF (Paris, France), 1930.

(Coauthor of text) *Clément Redko,* Éditions Ars (Paris, France), 1930.

Voyages au pays des voyantes, Portiques (Paris, France), 1931.

Comme un homme, Figuière (Paris, France), 1931.

Caporal Valentine, Emile-Paul Frères (Paris, France), 1932.

(Coauthor) Raymond Falcou, *Histoire de ma vie,* M. de Hartoy (Paris, France), 1933.

L'affaire Dreyfus, Emile-Paul Frères (Paris, France), 1934.

Le secret de Barataud, Emile-Paul Frères (Paris, France), 1934.

Troubles en Chine, Debresse (Paris, France), 1935.

(With Francesco Messina) *Francesco Messina,* Chroniques du Jour (Paris, France), 1936.

(With Raymond Cogniat) *Peintres instinctifs: naissance de l'expressionism* (catalog), [Paris, France], 1936.

Saint André (poetry), Gallimard (Paris, France), 1936.

Le jour et le nuit, Ilse de Lerins (Sainte-Marguerite de la Mer, France), 1937.

Propos d'atelier, Excelsior (Paris, France), 1938.

Le vagabond de Montparnasse: vie en more du peintre Amadeo Modigliani, [Paris, France], 1939.

Odeur de poésie, R. Laffont (Marseille, France), 1944.

L'air de la butte, Nouvelle France (Paris, France), 1945.

(With Charles Samson) *Images du vieus Paris,* Heures Claires (Paris, France), 1951.

(With Max Jacob) *Histoire du roi Kaboul ler et du Marmiton Gauwain,* Amis de Max Jacob (Paris, France), 1951.

(Editor with André Berry) *Victor Hugo tel qu'en lui—meme enfin,* Tambourinaire (Paris, France), 1952.

Les étoiles dans l'encrier (poetry), Gallimard (Paris, France), 1952.

(With Geneviève Gallibert) *Geneviève Gallibert,* Arc-en-Ciel (Paris, France), 1952.

(With Reinhold Kalnins) *Kalnins,* Gizard (Paris, France), 1953.

(With Jacob and Leon-Paul Fargue) *Vingt-six dessins de Roger Wild,* Tambourinaire, 1953.

Stanislas Stückgold, 1868-1933, Les Gémeaux (Paris, France), 1954.

Souvenir sans fin (memoirs; title means "Endless Memories"), Gallimard (Paris, France), 1955-61, Volume 1: *Première epoque (1903-1908);* Volume 2: *Deuxième epoque (1908-1920);* Volume 3: *Trosième epoque (1920-1940).*

(With P. Berger) *André Salmon,* P. Seghers (Paris, France), 1956.

Sylvère; ou, La vie moquée (novel), Gallimard (Paris, France), 1956.

Le Fauvisme, Aimery Somogy (Paris, France), 1956.

*Chroniques d'anjou: recueilliés et publiés pour la so-
ciété de l'histoire de France,* Renouard (Paris,
France), 1956.

Le vie passionnée de Modigilani, Intercontinentale du
livre (Paris, France), 1957, reprinted, Seghers
(Paris, France), 1979.

Vocalises, Seghers (Paris, France), 1957.

Originaux, extravagants et visionnaires, Oeuvres Libres (Paris, France), 1957.

*Séquences: anthologie permanente de poésie française
contemporaine,* Jean Grassin (Paris, France), 1958.

La terreur noire: chronique du mouvement libertaire
(title means "The Black Terror: Chronicle of the
Libertarian Movement"), J. J. Pauvert (Paris,
France), 1959, reprinted, 1973.

(With Mikou Bertrand) *Fériale, Debresse-poésie* (Paris,
France), 1960.

Henri Rousseau, A. Somogy (Paris, France), 1962.

(With Claude Venard) *Claude Venard,* Galerie Roma-
net (Paris, France), 1962.

Le Monocle a deux coups, J. J. Pauvert (Paris, France),
1968.

Créances, 1905-1910; suivie de Carreaux, 1918-1921,
Gallimard (Paris, France), 1968.

Modigliani: le roman de Montparnasse, Presses Se-
lecte (Montréal, Quebec, Canada), 1968.

(With others) *Orlando Pelayo,* La Ville (Paris, France),
1992.

(With others) *Maurice de Vlaminck: suivi de Maurice
Utrillo,* Mercure de France (Paris, France), 1999.

(With Marilena Pronesti and Pierre Lexert) *Les dessins
d'un poète: André Salmon, ses copains et les myths
d'une génération d'artists,* Region Autonome
Vallee d'Aoste (Aoste, Italy), 1999.

Also author of *Correspondence* and (with Albert
Acremant) *Garçon!—de quoi écire!* (play).

Contributor to *Elie Lascaux,* Galerien Alfred Flech-
theim, Berlin (Düsseldorf, Germany), 1930; contributor to periodicals, including *L'Intrasigeant.*

SIDELIGHTS: An associate of such twentieth-century
artists and writers as Pablo Picasso, Max Jacob, and
Guillame Apollinaire, André Salmon also made a name
for himself as a modernist poet, art critic, and novelist.

A native of Paris, France, Salmon throughout his
career divulged little about his personal years save for
his three-volume memoirs *Souvenirs sans fin.* His

father was a sculptor turned engraver, and at age
sixteen Salmon left with his family for St. Petersburg,
Russia, where by 1900 the young man was employed
as a clerk in the French consulate. Salmon returned to
France to fulfill his military service, which lasted until
1902. "He later dated his 'birth to poetry' from 1903,
when he began to frequent the literary circles of *La
Plume,*" according to essayist Anthony Levi in *Guide
to French Literature: 1789 to the Present.*

It was amid the artistic milieu created by *La Plume*
that Salmon first began publishing his poetry, inspired
as he was by the symbolists France Viele-Griffin, Stuart Merill, and Jean Moreas. As Levi noted, Salmon
became close friends with Paul Fort, with whom he
founded the review *Vers et prose,* "and greatly
influenced Apollinaire, of whom Max Jacob used
frequently to say that Salmon was the true teacher."
Salmon's artistic group centered on the young Picasso,
and some of Salmon's early poetry reflected the
painter's style, characterized by a sense of play in the
verses. Like his peers Picasso, Jacob, and composer
Igor Stravinsky, Salmon "was keen on popular culture,
and he not infrequently incorporated bits of, or allusions to, popular tunes and lyrics in his work," Levi
stated.

Salmon married in July 1909; that same year he began
publishing art criticism for *L'Intrasigeant,* where he
defended cubism. Eager to earn a steady income,
Salmon parlayed his art writing into general journalism, reporting on such events as the Tour de France
bicycle race. The travel involved in the newspaper
trade inspired at least one poem, "Romancero du
voyageur." World War I interrupted Salmon's writing
career; he served in the French infantry, an experience
Levi explained compelled the writer to "burst into
poetic activity, publishing two poems with epic qualities" that were inspired by fall of Russian Czar
Nicholas II in 1917: "Prikaz" and "L'Age de
humanite." Referring to "Prikaz," Levi noted that the
"epic quality" of the poem's sixteen cantos "depends
on so complicated a series of cumulative effects
achieved in part by switches of register from the colloquial to the solemn, in part through syntactical paral-
lelism, rhythmic variety, sonorous names, and mixtures
of prose and poetic effects."

While a original voice, according to Levi, Salmon's
tenure as a poet was limited. "Time quickly passed
him by," said the essayist. "The cubist painters reacted

against the symbolism with which Salmon had started off, and the oppressive Russia of his St. Petersburg days had been forgotten while he was still writing about it." Still, "it would be wrong to dismiss Salmon as a poet," Levi added. "Among the frivolities, witticisms, and pieces of flabby or flagging inspiration, he published some very fine poems indeed."

BIOGRAPHICAL AND CRITICAL SOURCES:

BOOKS

Levi, Anthony, *Guide to French Literature: 1789 to the Present,* St. James Press (Detroit, MI), 1992.
Salmon, André, *Souvenir sans fin,* Gallimard (Paris, France), 1955-61, Volume 1: *Première epoque (1903-1908);* Volume 2: *Deuxième epoque (1908-1920);* Volume 3: *Trosième epoque (1920-1940).*

PERIODICALS

Cahiers Bleus, autumn, 1981, "André Salmon 1881-1969."
Nouvelle Revue Française, June, 1969, Jean Foulain, "André Salmon," pp. 1181-1183.*

*   *   *

SALVATORES, Gabriele 1950-

PERSONAL: Born July 30, 1950, in Naples, Italy.

ADDRESSES: Agent—c/o Medusa Film S.P.A., 422-424 Via Aurelia Antica, Rome 00165, Italy.

CAREER: Director and author of screenplays. Film work as director includes *Sogno di una notte d'estate,* 1983; *Kamikazen ultima notte a Milano,* 1987; *Marrakech Express,* 1989; *Strada Blues,* 1990; *Turne,* 1990; *Mediterraneo,* Miramax, 1991; *Puerto escondido,* 1992; *Sud,* 1993; *Nirvana,* Miramax, 1997; *Denti,* Cecchi Gori Distribuzione, 2000; *Calcutta Chromosome* (not released), 2000; *Un Altro mondo e possibile,* 2001; *Amnesia,* 2002; and *Io non ho paura,* 2002. Film appearances include *La vera vita di Antonio H.,* 1994, and *Il cielo e sempre piu blu,* 1995.

AWARDS, HONORS: Italian National Syndicate for Film Journalists Silver Ribbon for Best Director, 1992, for *Mediterraneo;* Giffoni Film Festival François Truffaut Award, 1995; Venice Film Festival Digital Award special mention, 2002, for *Denti.*

WRITINGS:

(With Enzo Monteleone) *Puerto escondido,* Colorado Film Production, 1992.
(With Franco Bernini and Angelo Pasquini) *Sud* (also known as *South*), Colorado Film Production, 1993.
(With Pino Cacucci and Gloria Corica) *Nirvana,* Miramax, 1997.
Denti (based on a novel by Domenico Starnone; also known as *Teeth*), Cecchi Gori Distribuzione, 2000.
(With Andrea Garello) *Amnesia,* Medusa Produzione, 2002.

Other screenplays, either as writer or cowriter, include *Sogno di una notte d'estate,* 1983, *Kamikazen ultima notte a Milano,* 1987, and *Turne,* 1990.

SIDELIGHTS: Acclaimed for his directorial work in the 1991 film *Mediterraneo,* Gabriele Salvatores has written or cowritten the scripts for several of his motion pictures. A common theme in Salvatores's directoral work, according to Janet Stobart in the *Los Angeles Times,* is the theme of the loser as hero. "I have [losers] in my films because they're friends," the Italian filmmaker told Stobart. "That's the problem, I feel great affection for losers."

Typical of such characters is the protagonist of 1992's *Puerto escondido,* a banker from Milan who has accidentally witnessed the murder of a policeman. Afraid he may be next, he flees to Mexico, where he winds up in what Salvatores has called "a sort of Casablanca," a place Stobart described as "peopled by end-of-the-line characters who live by their wits."

During the mid to late 1990s, Salvatores's writing confronted a variety of surreal themes. In 1997's *Nirvana,* for instance, Solo, the persona of a computer video game, acquires a consciousness through the action of a virus. Solo begs its designer, Jimi, to "kill" it, even as Jimi himself is haunted by questions regarding the fate of his estranged girlfriend, Lisa.

Only slightly less bizarre is *Denti*—released in English as *Teeth*—whose protagonist, Antonio, is obsessed with the size of what David Rooney in *Variety* called his "generous dental endowments." There unfolds a story centering around teeth and dentists' chairs, a "squirm-inducing run of blood-drenched dental tampering," as Rooney put it.

With *Amnesia* in 2002, Salvatores seemed to be returning to more traditional fare, though the storyline is certainly far from uncomplicated. In much the same fashion as Quentin Tarantino's *Pulp Fiction,* the tale is split in two, and concerns events involving two different groups of characters over the same period of time.

BIOGRAPHICAL AND CRITICAL SOURCES:

BOOKS

Contemporary Theatre, Film, and Television, volume 34, Gale (Detroit, MI), 2001.

PERIODICALS

Los Angeles Times, June 13, 1992, Janet Stobart, "Director Continues Winning Way Movies" (profile), p. 13.
Variety, September 21, 1983, review of *Sogno di una notte d'estate,* pp. 24-25; March 1, 1993, Deborah Young, review of *Puerto escondido,* p. 56; November 1, 1993, Deborah Young, review of *South,* p. 45; March 6, 1995, David Rooney, review of *Nirvana,* p. 47; September 18, 2000, David Rooney, review of *Teeth,* p. 36; March 11, 2002, David Rooney, review of *Amnesia,* pp. 32-33.*

*   *   *

SANDOR, Marjorie

PERSONAL: Female. *Education:* University of California—Davis, B.A., 1979; University of Iowa, M.F.A., 1984.

ADDRESSES: Office—238 Moreland Hall, Oregon State University, Corvallis, OR 97331-5302. *E-mail*—msandor@orst.edu.

CAREER: University of Florida, Gainesville, professor, 1988-94; Oregon State University, Corvallis, professor, literature and creative writing, 1994—.

AWARDS, HONORS: Rona Jaffe Foundation Award, 1998, for short fiction; Oregon Book Award for literary nonfiction, 2000.

WRITINGS:

A Night of Music: Stories, Ecco Press (New York, NY), 1989.
The Night Gardener, Lyons Press (New York, NY), 1999.
Portrait of My Mother, Who Posed Nude in Wartime: Stories, Sarabande (Louisville, KY), 2003.

Work has been anthologized in *Best American Short Stories 1985* and *1988, America and I: Stories by American-Jewish Women, The Best of Beacon 1999,* and *Pushcart Prize XIII.* Contributor of short fiction to periodicals, including *Georgia Review, New York Times Magazine, Southern Review, Shenandoah,* and *House Beautiful.*

SIDELIGHTS: Marjorie Sandor is an award-winning author of short stories and essays. In *A Night of Music,* Sandor published tales about dreamers. In such stories as "The Gittel," a mother's tale of warning to her daughter, in which a young Jewish woman cannot fathom the realities of Nazi Germany; in "Victrola," about a Mexican child's growing awareness of her mother's mystery; and in "The Bonbon Man," where a girl's vivid imagination changes her vision of her southern California town. The stories garnered praise for their technique and emotive qualities. Writing in the *New York Times Book Review,* Robert Minkoff praised the "fresh perspective," "honest imagination," and skill that is apparent in Sandor's work. A *Publishers Weekly* reviewer described the stories as "rich in pathos and joy, skillful in technique," while Mary Soete of *Library Journal* found the title story to be "enchanting."

A decade passed before Sandor released her next book-length publication, *The Night Gardener,* a collection of twenty linked memoirs. In it she considers her parents and her childhood in California, and a family friend referred to as Uncle Maury; she ponders on her marriage and family life in Boston, Florida, and Oregon; and she recounts taking up fly fishing and her unexpected falling in love with another man, which ultimately leads to her divorce from her husband. The work caught the attention of critics. *Library Journal* reviewer Gina Kaiser noted Sandor's "engaging style," while *Booklist* commentator Donna Seaman found several of the "essays" to be "fresh, funny, and thoughtful." "Although some of the pieces are more engrossing than others," maintained a *Publishers Weekly* critic, "[*The Night Gardener*] is a thoughtful collection by a talented writer."

BIOGRAPHICAL AND CRITICAL SOURCES:

PERIODICALS

Booklist, September 15, 1999, Donna Seaman, review of *The Night Gardener,* p. 216.

Kirkus Reviews, August 1, 1999, review of *The Night Gardener,* pp. 1210-1211.

Library Journal, December, 1989, Mary Soete, review of *A Night of Music,* p. 175; October 15, 1999, Gina Kaiser, review of *The Night Gardener,* p. 71.

New York Times Book Review, January 21, 1990, Robert Minkoff, review of *A Night of Music,* p. 20.

Publishers Weekly, September 1, 1989, Sybil Steinberg, review of *A Night of Music,* p. 74; August 16, 1999, review of *The Night Gardener,* p. 69.

*   *   *

SANTANA, Dharmi 1914-2002
(Sri Swami Satchidananda)

OBITUARY NOTICE—See index for CA sketch: Born December 22, 1914, in Chettipalayam, India; died of a thoracic aneurysm August 19, 2002, in Madras, India. Religious leader, educator, and author. Santana, better known as Sri Swami Satchidananda, was a highly influential guru in America beginning in the 1960s, and helped to provide some spiritual underpinnings to the turbulent counterculture movement. Born and raised in India, he worked in his father's car import business and as a cameraman. However, when his wife died five years after their marriage, he began a spiritual quest that led him to Swami Sivananda, who became his mentor. Joining the Divine Life Society, he studied raja and hatha yoga and became a professor in those arts at the Yoga Vedanta Forest Academy in the Himalayas. He then journeyed to Sri Lanka, where he opened branches of the Divine Life Society and lectured throughout Malaysia, India, Hong Kong, and Japan during the 1950s and early 1960s. Invited to the United States in 1966 by pop artist Peter Max, he traveled to New York City. In New York Satchidananda broke with Divine Life and established the Integral Yoga Institute (now called Integral Yoga International), an organization that seeks to unify the various disciplines of yoga and to teach it to others. While in New York he gained many loyal adherents, including such celebrities as Carole King, George Harrison, and Mia Farrow. Indian culture, spiritualism, and music were popular among many in the United States during the 1960s, a fact that was demonstrated when the guru was invited to open the Woodstock Festival in 1969 with his blessing; he became known thereafter as the "Woodstock Guru." Continuing his work, Satchidananda founded Yogaville-West in California and Yogaville-East in Connecticut, and in 1986 he founded a temple in Virginia called the Light of Truth Universal Shrine (LOTUS). He is also credited with having an influence on modern medicine through his advocacy of diet, exercise, and meditation for better health. He was the author of several books on religion, philosophy, and yoga, including *Integral Yoga Hatha* (1970), *Living Yoga: The Value of Yoga in Today's Life* (1977), *Peace Is within Our Reach* (1985), *The Living Gita: The Complete Bhagavad Gita: A Commentary for Modern Readers* (1988), and *Heart to Heart: Sure Success in Married Life* (1999).

OBITUARIES AND OTHER SOURCES:

BOOKS

Religious Leaders of America, Gale (Detroit, MI), 1999.

PERIODICALS

Los Angeles Times, August 25, 2002, p. B19.

New York Times, August 21, 2002, p. C17.

Times (London, England), August 28, 2002.

Washington Post, August 24, 2002, p. B7.

SANTOSUOSSO, Antonio 1936-

PERSONAL: Born July 20, 1936, in Taurasi, Italy; married, 1964; children: two. *Education:* University of Toronto, B.A., 1968, M.A. 1969, Ph.D. (history), 1972.

ADDRESSES: Home—55 Balcarres Road, London, Ontario, Canada N5X 2H6.

CAREER: University of Western Ontario, London, Ontario, Canada, lecturer, 1971-72, assistant professor, 1972-74, associate professor, 1974-81, professor of history, 1981—; *The Newcomers,* Nielsen-Ferns, television consultant, 1976-80.

MEMBER: Renaissance Society of America; Renaissance Society of Canada.

WRITINGS:

The Bibliography of Giovanni Della Casa: Books, Readers and Critics, 1537-1975, L. S. Olschki (Florence, Italy), 1979.
Vita di Giovanni Della Casa, Bulzoni (Rome, Italy), 1979.
Soldiers, Citizens, and the Symbols of War: From Classical Greece to Republican Rome, 500-167 B.C., Westview Press (Boulder, CO), 1997.
Storming the Heavens: Soldiers, Emperors, and Civilians in the Roman Empire, Westview Press (Boulder, CA), 2001.

Contributor to numerous scholarly journals.

SIDELIGHTS: Antonio Santosuosso is a professor of history at the University of Western Ontario where he specializes in the cultural history of sixteenth-century Italy. His first two published works focused on Giovanni Della Casa, a Catholic bishop and writer, whom John F. D'Amico, writing for the *Journal of Modern History,* referred to as "one of the great sixteenth-century Italian exponents of the ideal gentleman."

In *Vita di Giovanni Della Casa,* Santosuosso reveals details of the Italian bishop's life, reflecting on one of Della Casa's more famous works, *Galateo* published in 1558, a study, wrote D'Amico, of "the more

rudimentary aspects of grace." "Like many of his contemporaries," D'Amico observed, "[Della Casa] chose the ecclesiastical life as the means of achieving security even though he had no real religious sensitivities." Della Casa's book was used by young men of the sixteenth century as a guide on how to make it up the ranks of society. In *Church History* Barbara McClung Hallman noted that *Galateo* "became the handbook for gentility in most of Europe."

The Bibliography of Giovanni Della Casa: Books, Readers and Critics, 1537-1975 is a thoroughly researched bibliography of all of Della Casa's works and correspondences, as well as a list of critical studies. "The European-wide reputation of Della Casa," wrote D'Amico, "clearly emerges through this bibliography." *Galateo* was translated into several different languages. Bonner Mitchell, a reviewer for the *Catholic Historical Review,* found that Santosuosso showed "much interest in social and economic history as well as in intellectual, and in interpreting Della Casa's rather elusive character and the social significance of his writings, he makes selective and imaginative use of current theories in psychology, sociology, and other social sciences."

Santosuosso compiled a study of war tactics in his *Soldiers, Citizens, and the Symbols of War: From Classical Greece to Republican Rome, 500-167 B.C.* J. P. Adams praised this work in *Choice* for its bibliography, which he found "extensive, up-to-date, and well chosen." In this book, Santosuosso examines the impact of warfare on the culture of ancient Rome and Greece, how the concepts of warfare changed between the fifth and second centuries B.C., and why these Greece and Rome triumphed over their eastern neighbors in Persia. Another topic that Santosuosso develops is that of the role of the warrior as it relates to the average private citizen of the time. He also shows how the symbols of war were used as propaganda to promote the values of Western societies.

A *Publishers Weekly* reviewer called *Storming the Heavens: Soldiers, Emperors, and Civilians in the Roman Empire* a "fascinating sequel" to *Soldiers, Citizens, and the Symbols of War,* noting that in *Storming the Heavens,* "Santosuosso traces the rise and fall of the Roman Empire via the rise and fall of the Roman army." Santosuosso reveals that as the Roman Empire expanded, the military forces on the outer edges of the empire often felt less allegiance to Rome and in some cases actually turned against the capital city in an attempt to overthrow the current leaders and claim power for themselves. The *Publishers Weekly* reviewer praised Santosuosso's "crackling prose and lively narrative." Lawrence Okamura, writing for the *Journal of Military History,* stated, "Reading Santosuosso's book is like attending a well-prepared, animated, but judicious lecture. The author writes clear, robust prose; his narrative, mixing action and analysis, moves swiftly, free of ponderous jargon."

BIOGRAPHICAL AND CRITICAL SOURCES:

PERIODICALS

Catholic Historical Review, January, 1981, Bonner Mitchell, reviews of *Vita Di Giovanni Della Casa* and *The Bibliography of Giovanni Della Casa,* p. 132.
Choice, May, 1998, J. P. Adams, review of *Soldiers, Citizens, and the Symbols of War: From Classical Greece to Republican Rome, 500-167 B.C.,* p. 1584.
Church History, September, 1984, Barbara McClung Hallman, review of *The Bibliography of Giovanni Della Casa,* p. 438.
Journal of Military History, April, 2002, Lawrence Okamura, review of *Storming the Heavens: Soldiers, Emperors, and Civilians in the Roman Empire,* pp. 542-543.
Journal of Modern History, September, 1980, John F. D'Amico, reviews of *Vita di Giovanni Della Casa* and *The Bibliography of Giovanni Della Casa,* pp. 536-538.
Publishers Weekly, July 30, 2001, review of *Storming the Heavens,* pp. 75-76.*

*   *   *

SATCHIDANANDA, Sri Swami
See SANTANA, Dharmi

*   *   *

SCHICKLER, David

PERSONAL: Male. *Education:* Georgetown University, B.A. (international relations); Columbia University, M.F.A. (creative writing), 1995.

ADDRESSES: Home—New York, NY. *Agent*—Jennifer Carlson, Henry Dunow Literary Agency, 22 West 23rd St., 5th Floor, New York, NY 10010.

CAREER: Writer of fiction and screenplays. Taught English and drama at a Vermont boarding school and a private school in Rochester, NY.

WRITINGS:

Kissing in Manhattan, Dial Press (New York, NY), 2001.

His stories have appeared in the *New Yorker* and *Tin House.*

ADAPTATIONS: Short story "The Smoker" has been optioned for possible movie production by Scott Rudin.

WORK IN PROGRESS: Working on a screenplay of "Telling It All to Otis" for Robert Redford's Wildwood Enterprises. Also working on a new novel.

SIDELIGHTS: Novelist David Schickler told Catherine McWeeney in an interview for *Bold Type* that he always wanted to know what New York City was all about. He lived there while attending Columbia University but did not have enough time or money to enjoy the city. After completing his M.F.A. at Columbia, he was "stone broke" and so he had to move away. He was raised in upper New York state, and that is where he went to earn some money as a high school teacher and to write. Due to the success of his debut novel, *Kissing in Manhattan,* he now lives in his favorite neighborhood in New York's Upper West Side, just blocks away from the fictional setting of his book.

Kissing in Manhattan, which consists of eleven connected short stories, is sometimes referred to as a "novel in stories." "I was seeking magic, humor and bliss in my own life," Schickler told W. S. Gilbert for *Publishers Weekly,* "so I created a world that offers those graces to its inhabitants." Schickler noted he wanted the stories in his book to "testify to the dark but welcoming soul of New York City." One thing his characters in the various stories have in common is the place where they live, the Preemption apartment building, which leans toward the mystical. One other common element is that all the characters are searching for love.

"The first chapter of *Kissing in Manhattan,*" wrote a reviewer for the *Washington Post,* "is a comic masterpiece, a perfectly pitched portrait of urban absurdity." Throughout the novel, Schickler switches from humor to hate to depravity, and back to love and the lighter side of life. "Is *Kissing in Manhattan,* with its women who want to be 'devoured' and its men who want to 'have' them, objectionable?" asked the *Washington Post* critic. "Absolutely. But somehow, it also works." It is Schickler's good writing and "the force of his imagination" that keeps the novel together and makes it worth reading, stated this reviewer.

In an attempt to "create a mosaiclike picture of a community," wrote Michiko Kakutani for the *New York Times,* Schickler has created "overlapping portraits of individuals linked by a shared sense of loneliness and alienation." These characters include Hannah Glorybrook, a woman who attracts men to her home, makes them take off their clothes, then locks them out of her apartment; Rally McWilliams, who is searching for her soul mate in all the wrong places; Patrick Rigg, a Wall Street trader, who always carries a gun with him and collects women who allow him to tie them up; and James Branch, an accountant who confides all his worries and problems to the elevator as it takes him up to his floor. "The story of James Branch," Schickler told McWeeney, "is the reason I wrote *Kissing in Manhattan.* James's story is the story I really wanted to write . . . I had to create a Manhattan where a guy talking to an elevator can make some empathetic and absurd sense."

Kissing in Manhattan was described by Wayne Janes for the *Toronto Sun* as being "weirdly charming and funny, in the way *The X-Files* is funny. Strange happenings drop like boulders into the stream of ordinary events." Brandon M. Stickney stated for the online review *Bookreporter.com:* "Schickler employs darkness, mythology, Middle Ages mysticism, medieval rites of passage and bestiality to portray a modern New York full of profoundly lonely thirtysomethings finding love and redemption in the oddest of circumstances."

Schickler's has hinted that his James Branch character is likely to be written into more stories. Other characters who might see more details of their vivid fictional lives exposed are Rook, Sender, and Harmony Button. Movie-goers as well as readers may be able to enjoy more of these characters, since Schickler's publisher has signed him to a two-book contract and movie producers have optioned rights to several of Schickler's stories and characters.

Schickler made enough money from *Kissing in Manhattan* to devote his full attention to writing. However, he told Nicholas Wroe of the *Guardian* that he considered returning to teaching, "Perhaps a day a week, just to be around more people during the day." However, he clarified that the most important thing to him "about writing is turning everybody and everything else off for four or five hours a day."

BIOGRAPHICAL AND CRITICAL SOURCES:

PERIODICALS

Booklist, April 15, 2001, Kristine Huntley, review of *Kissing in Manhattan,* p. 1537.
Library Journal, July, 2001, Nancy Pearl, review of *Kissing in Manhattan,* p. 128.
New York Times, June 29, 2001, Michiko Kakutani, "The Unconventional and the Unloved in an Urban Mosaic," p. E38.
New York Times Book Review, June 24, 2001, Jennifer Schuessler, "Tie Me Up! Tie Me Down!" p. 11.
Newsweek, June 26, 2000, "The Writer," p. 6.
People, July 9, 2001, review of *Kissing in Manhattan,* p. 45.
Publishers Weekly, January 15, 2001, W. S. Gilbert, "First Novels That Bloom in the Spring, Tra-la," p. 37; April 23, 2001, review of *Kissing in Manhattan,* p. 45.
Toronto Sun, Wayne Janes, "Kissing behind Closed Doors."
U.S. News & World Report, June 18, 2001, Marc Silver, review of *Kissing in Manhattan,* p. 58.
Washington Post, July 8, 2001, review of *Kissing in Manhattan,* p. T07.

OTHER

Bold Type, http://www.randomhouse.com/boldtype/ (June, 2001), Catherine McWeeney, "A Conversation with David Schickler."

Bookreporter.com, http://www.bookreporter.com/ (April 19, 2002), Brandon M. Stickney, review of *Kissing in Manhattan.*
Guardian Unlimited, http://books.guardian.co.uk/ (March 23, 2002), Nicholas Wroe, "The Dreamer of Manhattan."*

*   *   *

SEIDMAN, Harold 1911-2002

OBITUARY NOTICE—See index for *CA* sketch: Born July 2, 1911, in New York, NY; died of prostate cancer August 20, 2002, in Washington, DC. Public administrator, educator, journalist, and author. Seidman worked for what is now called the U.S. Bureau of the Budget for nearly twenty-five years, first as an analyst and government corporation specialist, then as assistant director of organization and management. He focused his attention on federal programs that were administered by private companies, nonprofit organizations, or other agencies selected by the government. Seidman' realm of concern was accountability, especially when the oversight of the programs was passed along to these third-party agencies instead of being retained by the federal agency funding them. One of Seidman's books most widely known books, *Politics, Position, and Power: The Dynamics of Federal Organization,* went through five editions following its appearance in 1970 and was still in use as a college textbook at the time of its author's death. Seidman begun his career as a journalist for the *Nation,* and in the 1930s he investigated labor union corruption in New York City under Mayor Fiorello LaGuardia. In retirement Seidman became a scholar at the National Academy of Public Administration, a senior fellow of the Center for the Study of American Government at Johns Hopkins University, and a guest scholar at the Brookings Institution. He also taught political science at the University of Connecticut from 1971 to 1984. In 2001 Seidman received the Keeper-of-the-Flame Award of the American Society for Public Administration and the National Academy of Public Administration.

OBITUARIES AND OTHER SOURCES:

PERIODICALS

Washington Post, August 22, 2002, obituary by Adam Bernstein, p. B6.

OTHER

Government Executive, http://www.govexec.com/ (August 21, 2002), obituary by Jason Peckenpaugh.

*   *   *

SERIOUS, Yahoo 1953-
(Greg Pead)

PERSONAL: Original name Greg Pead (changed name in 1979) July 27, 1953; born in Hunter Valley, New South Wales, Australia; married Lulu Pinkus (a writer and producer), January 22, 1989. *Education:* Attended National Art School, Australia.

ADDRESSES: Office—12-33 East Crescent, McMahon's Point, New South Wales 2060, Australia.

CAREER: Actor, director, producer, and writer. Formerly worked as a tire fitter. Film appearances include *Young Einstein,* Warner Bros., 1988; *Reckless Kelly,* Warner Bros., 1993; and *Mr. Accident,* Metro-Goldwyn-Mayer, 2000. Film work as producer and director includes *Young Einstein* (also editor, supervisor, and cowriter of song "Great Big Brain"), Warner Bros., 1988; *Reckless Kelly* (also supervising editor; involved with music design and visual design concepts), Warner Bros., 1993; and *Mr. Accident,* Metro-Goldwyn-Mayer, 2000. Also produced and directed the documentary *Coaltown.* Television appearances include segments on MTV, 1989. Created television series *Lifestyle.*

AWARDS, HONORS: Celebrated Filmmaker Award, Harvard University Hasty Pudding Club, 1988, for *Young Einstein.* Honorary doctor of letters, University of Newcastle, 1996.

WRITINGS:

Young Einstein (screenplay), Warner Bros., 1988.
Reckless Kelly (screenplay), Warner Bros., 1993.
Mr. Accident (screenplay), Metro-Goldwyn-Mayer, 2000.

Also wrote the screenplay for documentary *Coaltown*. Wrote a series of segments for MTV, 1989.

SIDELIGHTS: Australian actor Yahoo Serious (born Greg Pead) won a large following at home and abroad with his 1988 film *Young Einstein,* but his wacky brand of Australian humor received a less enthusiastic response in the United States. Roger Ebert, for instance, called *Young Einstein* "a one-joke movie, and I didn't laugh much the first time." According to Jim Delmont of the *Omaha World-Herald,* who noted that Serious hoped to cash in on the success of fellow Australian Paul Hogan and his *Crocodile Dundee* films, "My guess is that *Einstein* won't travel as well as *Crocodile Dundee* but will make enough money to finance another project or two for Yahoo."

One aspect of *Young Einstein* that reviewers found problematic was the fact that it takes place in some sort of alternate universe that plays on the facts of the real world. The story takes place in 1905, when the real Albert Einstein introduced his theory of relativity, but in Serious's portrayal, Einstein is an off-the-wall Aussie who discovers how to split the atom while trying to introduce bubbles to beer. He also invents the electric guitar and rock 'n' roll, neither of which existed in 1905, and falls in love with a young girl named Marie Curie. In actuality, Einstein and Curie were contemporaries and fellow scientists, but they were married to other people.

These complications, combined with the fact that American reviewers did not warm to Serious's zany humor, spelled doom for *Einstein,* which, despite a huge promotional effort, disappeared from theaters within just a few days. Still, even as some critics tended to pan the movie, others commented on the appeal of its star. For example, Delmont wrote that "The silly film is a pastiche of wild ideas but is full of energy and has a likeable central character." According to Ralph Novak in *People Weekly,* "Serious is energetic (he did his own stunts) and good-looking (think of the young Dean Stockwell with his hair standing straight out)."

Reckless Kelly in 1993 and *Mr. Accident* in 2000, both of which Serious wrote and made as he had *Einstein,* received similar press. Like its predecessor, *Reckless Kelly* takes as its basis a real person, Australian outlaw Ned Kelly, but places him in a surreal alter-universe.

Mr. Accident, on the other hand, is a purely fictional story that nonetheless takes place in a strange funhouse world where, for instance, the Sydney Opera House is the Sydney Egg House, "the biggest free-range egg enterprise in the country."

According to David Stratton in *Variety,* "Serious hasn't learned from the great comedians, beginning with Buster Keaton, that this kind of frantic farce is best played out against a realistic background." He went on to note that "It's a pity, because in many ways Serious is able to devise near-classical sequences." In addition, like many a reviewer before, Stratton commented on the likeability of Serious himself, if not of his products: "The star displays an appealing persona, with his unkempt red hair and his sweetly naive disposition."

BIOGRAPHICAL AND CRITICAL SOURCES:

BOOKS

Contemporary Theatre, Film, and Television, volume 33, Gale (Detroit, MI), 2001.

PERIODICALS

Chicago Sun-Times, August 4, 1989, Roger Ebert, review of *Young Einstein,* p. 41.
Entertainment Weekly, September 23, 1994, Steve Simels, review of *Reckless Kelly,* p. 77; January 26, 2001, Erin Podolsky, review of *Mr. Accident,* p. 80.
Interview, July, 1989, Brad Kessler and Brad Guice, "Get Serious," p. 32.
Melody Maker, October 7, 1989, Mark Salisbury, review of *Young Einstein,* p. 49; October 14, 1989, Mark Salisbury, "Immedia: Yahoo Serious," p. 46.
New York Times, July 30, 1989, Myra Forsberg, "The Name's Serious. Yahoo Serious" (profile), p. H21; August 4, 1989, Caryn James, review of *Young Einstein,* p. B5; February 25, 1990, Caryn James, review of *Young Einstein,* p. H32.
Omaha World-Herald, August 4, 1989, Jim Delmont, review of *Young Einstein,* p. 26.
People Weekly, August 21, 1989, Ralph Novak, review of *Young Einstein,* pp. 13-14.

Premiere, August, 1989, Nancy Griffin and Enrico Ferorelli, "Is He Serious?" (profile), pp. 56-59.

Us, August 21, 1989, "Getting Serious," p. 34; September 4, 1989, Chris Chase, review of *Young Einstein,* p. 63.

USA Today, December 27, 1989, review of *Young Einstein,* p. D2.

Variety, October 12, 1988, review of *Young Einstein,* p. 18; January 25, 1989, Blake Murdoch, "Yahoo Serious' *Einstein* Taking Oz by Storm," p. 5; April 12, 1993, David Stratton, review of *Reckless Kelly,* p. 76; September 11, 2000, David Stratton, review of *Mr. Accident,* p. 23.

Video Business, December 11, 2000, Irv Slifkin, review of *Mr. Accident,* p. 16.

Video Review, April, 1990, Robert Christgau and Carola Dibbell, review of *Young Einstein,* p. 68.

Village Voice, August 15, 1989, J. Hoberman, review of *Young Einstein,* p. 69.

Washington Post, August 5, 1989, Richard Harrington, review of *Young Einstein,* p. C1; April 12, 1990, Rita Kempley, review of *Young Einstein,* p. C7.

OTHER

Yahoo Serious Web site, http://www.yahooserious.com (October 29, 2002).*

* * *

SEWARD, Robert (Allen) 1942-

PERSONAL: Born June 7, 1942, in Oakland, CA; son of Odis L. and Marcia C. (Potter) Seward. *Education:* San Francisco State University, B.A., 1965; postgraduate work at the University of Stockholm, 1967; University of Oregon, Ph.D., 1979.

ADDRESSES: *Office*—Faculty of International Studies, Meiji Gakuin University, 1518 Kamikurata-cho, Totuska-ku, Yokohama 244-8539, Japan; fax: 81-45-863-2265.

CAREER: University of New Mexico, Albuquerque, NM, assistant professor, 1977-80; Wharton School, Philadelphia, PA, associate director of analysis center, 1980-82; Courant Institute, New York University, New York, NY, sponsored research administrator, 1982-87; Meiji Gakuin University, Yokohama, Japan, professor of international studies, 1987—.

WRITINGS:

Radio Happy Isles: Media and Politics at Play in the Pacific, University of Hawaii Press (Honolulu, HI), 1999.

SIDELIGHTS: In *Radio Happy Isles: Media and Politics at Play in the Pacific,* Robert Seward presents an anecdotal account of the influence of radio in the Pacific Islands. Avoiding a dry, factual, theoretical analysis, Seward prefers instead to focus on the social aspects of radio. Much more influential than other mediums, radio has played an important role in the culture of the Pacific.

Seward particularly focuses on PACNEWS, the news service in the Pacific—how it came to be, and the opportunity it presents listeners to knowing what is happening in their own region of the world. Lissant Bolton, in the *Journal of Pacific History,* wrote that the book "is valuable, both in providing a broad account of the development of radio in the region, and in drawing attention to the impact that the medium, and especially the news it communicates, is having on the Pacific."

BIOGRAPHICAL AND CRITICAL SOURCES:

PERIODICALS

Choice, September, 1999, J. A. Lent, review of *Radio Happy Isles: Media and Politics at Play in the Pacific,* p. 134.

Contemporary Pacific, fall, 2001, Adria L. Imada, review of *Radio Happy Isles,* p. 594.

Journal of Pacific History, December, 2000, Lissant Bolton, review of *Radio Happy Isles,* p. 332.

Oceania, September, 2001, Jennifer Deger, review of *Radio Happy Isles,* p. 84.

Pacific Affairs, fall, 2000, Michael Goldsmith, review of *Radio Happy Isles,* p. 477.*

* * *

SHAMSIE, Kamila 1973-

PERSONAL: Born 1973, in Karachi, Pakistan; daughter of Muneeza Shamsie (a writer and editor) *Education:* Hamilton College, B.A.; University of Massachusetts, M.F.A.

ADDRESSES: Office—Hamilton College, 198 College Hill Rd., Clinton, NY 13323.

CAREER: Writer. Hamilton College, Clinton, NY, creative writing teacher.

WRITINGS:

In the City by the Sea, Penguin (New York, NY), 1998.
Salt and Saffron, Bloomsbury USA (New York, NY), 2000.
Kartography, Bloomsbury (London, England), 2002.

SIDELIGHTS: Though she was born in Pakistan, Kamila Shamsie's first novel was written in English, the result of an upbringing and education that is dexterously chronicled in her 1998 debut, *In the City by the Sea.* Shamsie, like the protagonist Hasan, was born in Karachi, one of Pakistan's largest cities, and actual events from her childhood—the writer was born in 1973—play an integral role in the turmoil of the young character's life. At the age of eleven, Hasan leads a pleasant life as the well-loved son of educated, liberal parents. His father is an attorney, while his artist mother runs a gallery. Both the father and an uncle, the popular head of a political party, have been educated at elite English universities—a legacy, in part, of Pakistan's former colonial ties to the British Empire—and rose to prominence after Pakistan gained independence in 1947.

This idyllic era suddenly ends when Hasan's uncle, Salman mamoo, is placed under house arrest after a political upheaval. When Shamsie was still a toddler, liberal Pakistan president Zulfiqar Ali Bhutto was arrested and jailed after a 1977 military coup. Martial law was declared, and a dictatorship remained in place for several years until his daughter, Benazir Bhutto, became the first female leader elected to head a Muslim country. As the events of *In the City by the Sea* unfold, the young Hasan understands only some of the drama. The family is harassed, his mother's gallery is forced to close, but they are finally granted permission to visit their uncle's house.

Hasan attends an English-language school, Karachi Grammar, and shortly after the arrest of his uncle, he waits as a participant in one of its interminable elocu-tion assemblies. Here, students contest one another in standard recitations culled from the classics of English poetry and prose. As he awaits his turn, however, Hasan thinks about the poem on a magazine page his mother has bookmarked; he secretly visits her desk every morning before school to look at it, where he "found a new water-coloured fingerprint on the page." He shocks the assembly when he recites "Some Advice to Those Who Will Serve Time in Prison," by a Turkish dissident writer, instead of his scheduled oration.

In the City by the Sea also chronicles another decisive factor in Hasan's upset life: his guilt over the death of a neighbor boy who had been flying a kite on a roof. Hasan believes the boy was trying to impress him, a situation that touches upon some of Karachi's keen class divisions. He is also enamored of the thirteen year old who lives next door, Zehra, who can translate some of the tumult outside their sheltered Karachi neighborhood for his understanding. Real-life political leader Zulfiqar Ali Bhutto was executed two years later, and a military dictatorship fostered even greater turmoil for the country over the next several years. "This is the first novel of our generation," declared Rehan Ansari in *Himal,* explaining that the generation of his parents came of age in the 1960s, a time of liberalization and progress in Pakistan that ended with the 1977 coup. "People of my generation, urban, from Karachi and Lahore professional families . . . have not recovered from dictatorship, segregation and Islamisation."

Other reviews of *In the City by the Sea* were similarly positive. "This is a richly complicated tapestry, but Shamsie weaves the many bright threads skilfully and humourously," declared *Times Literary Supplement* writer Sarah Curtis, who saw the rooftop death episode as the attempt by one boy to escape the terror of the ground. "It is Shamsie's understanding of the partiality of Hasan's comprehension, the reliance of children on magical means to will away what they do not want to happen, that makes this book memorable."

In *Salt and Saffron,* a Pakistani woman, Aliya, tells the story of her family history. Trying to reconcile the present, and its more progressive nature, with the past, and its history of tradition, Aliya must also deal with class distinction—the salt (ordinary people), and the saffron (the elite). Reviewing the book for *World Literature Today,* Bruce King wrote, "This is . . . a novel about social divisions and the way they are often constructed on a past that no one really knows. . . . *Salt and Saffron* is too much of a good thing." A *Publishers Weekly* review called *Salt and Saffron* "clever, witty and inventive," and wrote that it "resonates more deeply than its lighthearted tone would suggest."

BIOGRAPHICAL AND CRITICAL SOURCES:

PERIODICALS

Booklist, September 1, 2000, GraceAnne A. DeCandido, review of *Salt and Saffron*, p. 67.
Himal, June 25, 1999.
Library Journal, September 15, 2000, Jo Manning, review of *Salt and Saffron*, p. 114.
Massachusetts Review, spring, 1998.
Publishers Weekly, August 28, 2000, review of *Salt and Saffron*, p. 55.
Times Literary Supplement, December 18, 1998.
World Literature Today, summer, 2000, Bruce King, review of *Salt and Saffron*, p. 588.*

*   *   *

SHIPNUCK, Alan 1973-

PERSONAL: Born 1973; married: wife's name, Frances. *Hobbies and other interests:* Golf, basketball, skiing, backpacking, reading, cinema.

ADDRESSES: Home—453 Sixth St., New York, NY 11215.

CAREER: Sports Illustrated, New York, NY, writer, 1994—

WRITINGS:

Bud, Sweat, and Tees: A Walk on the Wild Side of the PGA Tour, Simon and Schuster (New York, NY), 2001.

SIDELIGHTS: Alan Shipnuck is a writer for *Sports Illustrated*. His book *Bud, Sweat, and Tees: A Walk on the Wild Side of the PGA Tour* tells the story of Rich

Beem, a former cell phone salesperson who won golf's Kemper Open in 1999. The win was unexpected, as Beem was unknown in golf, and the book follows his first year on the PGA Tour, as well as his conflict-filled relationship with his caddy, Steve Duplantis. Scott Veale wrote in the *New York Times* that Shipnuck describes "the harsh Darwinian calculus for a rookie's survival on the tour, in particular the grueling schedule and the scramble for supporters and endorsements." Shipnuck describes both Beem and Duplantis's self-doubts, conflicts, and successes, culminating in the Kemper Open win and the ensuing flurry of media attention and endorsement money.

In the *Washington Times*, Barker Davis described the book as "an irresistible read" and noted that Shipnuck "captures every unforgettable moment in minute detail." In *Booklist*, Bill Ott commented that the book "will gladden the heart of every golfer who would rather play than practice." A *Publishers Weekly* reviewer wrote that Shipnuck portrays the two men "as flawed, likeable people who struggle like the rest of us, with imperfect results." Lance Cagle wrote in *eGolf Weekly*, "The chapter on the Kemper Open might be the most honest and uninhibited version of what it is like to contend in a professional golf tournament ever published."

BIOGRAPHICAL AND CRITICAL SOURCES:

PERIODICALS

Booklist, December 15, 2000, Bill Ott, review of *Bud, Sweat, and Tees: A Walk on the Wild Side of the PGA Tour*, p. 779.
New York Times Book Review, March 25, 2001, Scott Veale, review of *Bud, Sweat, and Tees*, p. 23.
Publishers Weekly, November 27, 2000, review of *Bud, Sweat, and Tees*, p. 65.
Washington Times, April 12, 2001, Barker Davis, "Shipnuck Captures Life on the PGA Tour," p. 2.

OTHER

eGolf Weekly, http://www.egolfweekly.com/ (December 2, 2001), Lance Cagle, review of *Bud, Sweat, and Tees*.

Golf Online.com, http://www.golfonline.com/ (December 2, 2001), Brian Egeston, review of *Bud, Sweat, and Tees.*

Sports Illustrated Online http://www.si.com/ (February 17, 2003), Alan Shipnuck archive.*

* * *

SIJIE, Dai 1954-

PERSONAL: Born 1954, in Fujian, China; immigrated to France, 1984.

ADDRESSES: Agent—c/o Author Mail, Knopf Publishing, 299 Park Ave., 4th Fl., New York, NY 10171.

CAREER: Film director and writer. Director of films, such as *Le temple de la montagne,* 1984, *Chine, ma douleur,* 1989, and *La mangeur de lune,* 1994.

AWARDS, HONORS: Prix Jean Vigo, 1989, for *Chine, ma douleur;* special jury prize, Prague Film Festival, 1994, for *La mangeur de lune.*

WRITINGS:

Balzac and the Little Chinese Seamstress (originally published as *Balzac et la petite tailleuse chinoise*), translation by Ina Rilke, Knopf (New York, NY), 2001.

(And director) *Le Onzième* (also known as *The Eleventh Child*), Max Films (Montreal, QC, Canada), 2001.

SIDELIGHTS: Dai Sijie's novel *Balzac and the Little Chinese Seamstress* tells the story of two teenagers who are sent to a remote mountain village in China. Their families are in disgrace, and the boys are to be "re-educated" with ideas and attitudes that are acceptable to the Communist Party's Cultural Revolution. The villagers are not welcoming to the boys, and the narrator gets in trouble because he has a violin, which the villagers think is some kind of toy. When he explains that it is a musical instrument, the villagers want to destroy it as a symbol of capitalism. The two

boys lie, saying the violin is acceptable to the Communists, and to "prove" this they play a Mozart sonata, which they say is titled "Mozart Is Thinking of Chairman Mao."

Sentenced to hard labor in the village, the boys have to carry around human and animal manure to fertilize the mountain fields. One spark of hope lightens their existence: the village headman assigns them to go to another village to watch movies and then come home and tell him the stories they've seen. Their storytelling skills are their key to a tolerable existence in the village.

On another trip outside their little village, they meet a beautiful but uneducated seamstress, and the narrator's friend Luo falls in love with her. When they discover that an old friend has a supply of forbidden Western literature, the boys steal the books so they can read them to the seamstress and thus win her love. Although the boys gain hope from the books' stories of free people, the stories also make them chafe even more at their imprisonment in the re-education camp; it is a mixed blessing, and may not leave them better off in the long run.

In the *San Francisco Chronicle,* David Wiegand wrote that Sijie, like the boys, was sent to a Chinese re-education camp in the 1970s, and noted that the book "brilliantly reflects [Dai Sijie's] Chinese upbringing and his more recent understanding of Western culture and literature." Michael Dirda wrote in the *Washington Post,* "This is a funny, touching, sly and altogether delightful novel, an older man's 'memoir' of some episodes in his youth that fundamentally altered his life." In the London *Times,* Alex Clark called *Balzac and the Little Chinese Seamstress* "a highly original and sweetly charming tale, despite its grim subject matter." A *Publisher's Weekly* reviewer wrote, "The warmth and humor of Sijie's prose and the clarity of Rilke's translation distinguish this slim first novel, a wonderfully human tale." In the *Spectator,* Paul Tebbs called the novel "a jewel of world literature."

BIOGRAPHICAL AND CRITICAL SOURCES:

PERIODICALS

Booklist, September 15, 2001, Elsa Gaztambide, review of *Balzac and the Little Chinese Seamstress,* p. 196.

Boston Herald, October 21, 2001, p. 49.

Christian Science Monitor, February 5, 1993, David Sterritt, review of *Chine, ma douleur,* p. 14.

Economist, August 11, 2001, "From Mainland to Mainstream."

French Review, May, 2001, Nathalie Cornelius, review of *Balzac et la petite tailleuse chinoise,* p. 1285.

Kirkus Reviews, August 1, 2001, review of *Balzac and the Little Chinese Seamstress,* p. 1046.

New York Times, March 19, 1990, Caryn James, review of *Chine, ma douleur,* p. C17; January 29, 1993, Caryn James, review of *Chine, ma douleur,* p. C6; October 18, 2001, Alan Riding, "Adopting a Country, then Crashing its Best-seller List," p. E2.

New York Times Book Review, September 16, 2001, Brooke Allen, "A Suitcase Education," p. 24.

Publishers Weekly, August 27, 2001, review of *Balzac and the Little Chinese Seamstress,* p. 51.

San Francisco Chronicle, October 28, 2001, David Wiegand, "Painful truths," p. 3.

Spectator, June 30, 2001, p. 43.

Sunday Times (London, England), July 15, 2001, p. 44.

Times (London, England), June 23, 2001, Francis Gilbert, "Culture Shock," p. 20.

Times Literary Supplement, July 20, 2001, Justin Hill, "The Teller of Films," p. 22.

Wall Street Journal, September 7, 2001, Jamie James, review of *Balzac and the Little Chinese Seamstress,* p. W13.

Washington Post, September 9, 2001, Michael Dirda, review of *Balzac and the Little Chinese Seamstress,* p. T15.*

* * *

SIMMS, Michael 1954-

PERSONAL: Born April 6, 1954, in Houston, TX; son of Harry (an attorney) and Jane (a real estate agent) Simms; married September 29, 1985; wife's name Eva-Maria (a psychologist); children: Nicholas, Lea. *Education:* Attended School of Irish Studies, Dublin, Ireland, 1974; Southern Methodist University, B.A., 1976; University of Iowa, M.F.A., 1978.

ADDRESSES: Office—Autumn House Press, 219 Bigham St., Pittsburgh, PA 15211. *E-mail*—simms@duq.edu.

CAREER: Southern Methodist University, Dallas, TX, faculty member, 1979-85; Michael Simms Real Estate, managing partner. Autumn House Press, Pittsburgh, PA, executive director, 1998—; International Poetry Forum, member of board of directors, 1998—. Duquesne University, faculty member, 1996-2000; Carnegie-Mellon University, poet-in-residence, 1998. Southwestern Pennsylvania Regional Planning Commission, member, 1986-95.

WRITINGS:

Notes on Continuing Light (poetry), Blue Buildings, 1981.

Longman Dictionary of Poetic Terms, Longman (New York, NY), 1985.

Migration (poetry), Breitenbush, 1985.

The Fire-eater (poetry), Del Rogers, 1989.

SIDELIGHTS: Poet and educator Michael Simms commented to *CA:* "I believe in the pure, clear word."

* * *

SIMPSON, Allen 1934-
(M. D. Lake)

PERSONAL: Born 1934. *Hobbies and other interests:* Playing piano.

ADDRESSES: Home—Minneapolis, MN. *Agent*—c/o Author Mail, Avon Books, 10 East 53rd St., New York, NY 10022. *E-mail*—mdlake1234@aol.com.

CAREER: Minnesota University, Minneapolis, MN, professor of Scandinavian languages and literature; writer. *Military service:* U.S. Marines.

AWARDS, HONORS: American Mystery Award for best original paperback, 1992, for *Poisoned Ivy;* Agatha Awards, 1994, for "Kim's Game."

WRITINGS:

UNDER PSEUDONYM M. D. LAKE; "PEGGY O'NEILL" MYSTERY NOVELS

Amends for Murder, Avon (New York, NY), 1989.
Cold Comfort, Avon (New York, NY), 1990.

A Gift for Murder, Avon (New York, NY), 1992.
Poisoned Ivy, Avon (New York, NY), 1992.
Murder by Mail, Avon (New York, NY), 1993.
Grave Choices, Avon (New York, NY), 1995.
Once upon a Crime, Avon (New York, NY), 1995.
Flirting with Death, Avon (New York, NY), 1996.
Ties of Blood, Avon (New York, NY), 1997.
Midsummer Malice, Avon (New York, NY), 1997.
Death Calls the Tune, Avon (New York, NY), 1999.

Work represented in anthologies, including *Funny Bones.*

SIDELIGHTS: Allen Simpson uses the pseudonym M. D. Lake to author various mystery novels featuring heroine Peggy O'Neill, who works in law enforcement at an American university. Lake introduced O'Neill to readers in 1989 with *Amends for Murder,* and in the ensuing years he has produced ten more novels featuring the resourceful character who was described, in a *Publishers Weekly* review, as "clever and winning."

Prior to writing, Lake conducted courses in Scandinavian languages and literature. "I taught at the University of Minnesota for twenty-seven years, before taking early retirement to write full-time," he told a *Crescent Blues* interviewer. But in a *Minnesota Daily* interview, he also revealed that he turned to writing as a means of venting a murderous desire. "I wanted to murder somebody, and I wrote a novel," he admitted. "So out of what I consider to be a real tragedy came my writing career."

In the *Crescent Blues* interview, Lake disclosed that he created the O'Neill character following discussions with Regan Metcalf, an acquaintance who worked as a campus cop. "I was incredibly impressed," he said, "since I'd never seen a woman doing the kinds of things Regan did—especially alone, outside, in the middle of the night." He added, "The routine things [O'Neill] does and sees on her patrols, I got from Regan and from a few other cops I spent time with later."

In *Amends for Murder* the heroine investigates the demise of an English professor presumed murdered during a burglary. During the course of her work, however, O'Neill learns that the killing may have been planned by one of several suspicious campus figures.

A *Publishers Weekly* critic called *Amends for Murders* "implausible," and Kathleen Maio, in her *Wilson Library Bulletin* assessment, contended that O'Neill is "just not believable the way she is." But an *Armchair Detective* reviewer deemed O'Neill "lively and likable."

Among Lake's earlier "O'Neill" mysteries is *Cold Comfort,* in which O'Neill agrees to investigate the death of a friend's brother. The police have determined that the death was a suicide, but O'Neill soon finds evidence of mayhem. She also makes the acquaintance of several seamy individuals, including a CIA agent and a pornography peddler. *Armchair Detective* reviewer Allen J. Hubin proclaimed the volume "pleasant enough."

The next "O'Neill" mystery, *A Gift for Murder,* concerns treachery within a campus writing collective. A *Publishers Weekly* critic, in reviewing *A Gift for Murder,* described O'Neill as a "campus cop with a . . . talent for stumbling onto murder victims." The following novel, *Poisoned Ivy,* involves O'Neill with an unappealing dean who is targeted for murder. A *Publishers Weekly* reviewer affirmed that "it is great fun trailing around with [O'Neill] as she digs up the dirt."

In an ensuing tale, *Murder by Mail,* O'Neill probes the death of an individual suspected of sending racist hate mail. Gail Pool, in her *Wilson Library Bulletin* appraisal, deemed the book "sturdy and thoughtful," and a *Publishers Weekly* reviewer noted that O'Neill is "as clever and winning as ever." *Grave Choices,* meanwhile, finds O'Neill investigating the murder of a painter/professor on campus. *Armchair Detective* critic Catherine M. Nelson summarized this book as an "enjoyable read."

In the next O'Neill case, *Once Upon a Crime,* the intrepid crime solver becomes involved in danger while on medical leave. A *Library Journal* critic called *Once upon a Crime* "the best O'Neill yet." A later tale, *Midsummer Malice,* concerns the murder of a blackmailer. In this book, as a *Publishers Weekly* critic observed, Lake "keeps the tension high."

Although Lake has become an established novelist in the years since he published his first mystery novel, he told a *Sisters in Crime* interviewer that writing remains an arduous process. "Writing can be fun," he said, "but it's also hard work, lonely, and—for me, anyway—nerve-wracking." He added, "I never know where the creativity comes from or if its going to continue to come, and that's stressful."

BIOGRAPHICAL AND CRITICAL SOURCES:

PERIODICALS

Armchair Detective, fall, 1991, Allen J. Hubin, review of *Cold Comfort,* p. 407; winter, 1993, Marvin Lachman, review of *Amends for Murder,* p. 54; spring, 1996, Catherine M. Nelson, review of *Grave Choices,* pp. 233-234.

Library Journal, July, 1995, review of *Once upon a Crime,* p. 152.

Publishers Weekly, September 22, 1989, review of *Amends for Murder,* p. 48; February 3, 1992, review of *Poisoned Ivy;* November 23, 1992, review of *A Gift for Murder,* p. 58; October 25, 1993, review of *Murder by Mail,* pp. 56-57; November 10, 1997, review of *Midsummer Malice,* p. 71.

Wilson Library Bulletin, December, 1989, Kathleen Maio, review of *Amends for Murder,* pp. 116-117; February, 1994, Gail Pool, review of *Murder by Mail,* pp. 66-67.

OTHER

Crescent Blues, http://www.crescentblues.com/ (June 17, 2001), interview with M. D. Lake.

Minnesota Daily, http://www.mndaily.com/ (June 17, 2001), "Dial M. D. Lake for Murder."

Mystery Net, http://www.mysterynet.com/ (June 17, 2001), "Twilight Lane on Mystery Net."

Sisters in Crime, http://www.sinc-ic.org/ (April, 1999), Louise Guardino, interview with M. D. Lake.*

*   *   *

SIMPSON, Brooks D.

PERSONAL: Male. *Education:* University of Wisconsin—Madison, Ph.D., 1989.

ADDRESSES: Office—Department of History, Arizona State University, Tempe, AZ 85287. *E-mail*—Brooks. simpson@asu.edu.

CAREER: Educator, editor, and author. Arizona State University, professor of history.

WRITINGS:

(Editor, with Leroy P. Graf and John Muldowny) *Advice after Appomattox: Letters to Andrew Johnson, 1865-1866,* University of Tennessee Press (Knoxville, TN), 1987.

Let Us Have Peace: Ulysses S. Grant and the Politics of War and Reconstruction, 1861-1868, University of North Carolina Press (Chapel Hill, NC), 1991.

America's Civil War, Harlan Davidson (Wheeling, IL), 1996.

The Political Education of Henry Adams, University of South Carolina Press (Columbia, SC), 1996.

(Editor, with David W. Blight) *Union and Emancipation: Essays on Politics and Race in the Civil War Era,* Kent State University Press (Kent, OH), 1997.

(Editor) *Think Anew, Act Anew: Abraham Lincoln on Slavery, Freedom, and Union,* Harlan Davidson (Wheeling, IL), 1998.

The Reconstruction Presidents, University of Kansas Press (Lawrence, KS), 1998.

(With Mark Grimsley) *Gettysburg: A Battlefield Guide,* University of Nebraska Press (Lincoln, NE), 1999.

(Editor, with Jean V. Berlin) *Sherman's Civil War: Selected Correspondence of William T. Sherman, 1860-1865,* University of North Carolina Press (Chapel Hill, NC), 1999.

Ulysses S. Grant: Triumph over Adversity, 1822-1865, Houghton Mifflin (Boston, MA), 2000.

(Editor, with Mark Grimsley) *The Collapse of the Confederacy,* University of Nebraska Press (Lincoln, NE), 2001.

SIDELIGHTS: U.S. historian Brooks D. Simpson has written and edited a number of scholarly volumes that give insight into the political and military aspects of the American Civil War era. Simpson is a professor of history at Arizona State University, and has been publishing his work since the late 1980s, beginning with *Advice after Appomattox: Letters to Andrew Johnson, 1865-1866.* This critically praised book, which Simpson coedited with Leroy P. Graf and John Muldowny, contains correspondence and advice directed to U.S. President Andrew Johnson during America's postwar Reconstruction period. Throughout the 1990s Simpson continued to produce related projects, including *America's Civil War, Union and Emancipation: Essays on Politics and Race in the Civil War Era, The Reconstruction Presidents,* and *Gettysburg: A Battlefield Guide.* In 2000 Simpson published *Ulysses S. Grant: Triumph over Adversity, 1822-1865,* a biography covering the upbringing and military exploits of America's eighteenth president. Simpson, an admirer of Grant, had previously written about the Union's military hero in *Let Us Have Peace: Ulysses S. Grant and the Politics of War and Reconstruction, 1861-1868,* as well as in several other volumes. In most cases, literary critics have lauded Simpson's efforts, including his historiography and writing ability.

After the conclusion of the U.S. Civil War, President Johnson had to decide on ways to rebuild the shattered South, and he courted the advice of several close friends and colleagues in order to help him in the process. In *Advice after Appomattox,* Simpson and his coeditors compiled the letters that these men wrote to Johnson over the course of about one year, in 1865. The men, including Ulysses S. Grant, Chief Justice Salmon P. Chase, journalists Carl Schurz and Benjamin C. Truman, and friend Harry M. Watterson, provided Johnson with varying expertise and viewpoints. Robert G. Mangrum, in the *Journal of Southern History,* explained that Simpson provided brief introductions about each man in an effort to "'present to the reader, as they did to President Johnson, the opportunity to evaluate differing opinions on the attitudes and conditions of the post-Appomattox South.'" Critics, including Michael Les Benedict in *Journal of American History,* who felt Simpson has contributed "insightful introductory essays," praised the book. J. Mushkat of *Choice* believed the editors put together an "excellent compilation of contemporary documents," which describe "the nature and ambiguities of postwar southern life." Mangrum was also impressed with the effort. "This volume will be of great value to historians and students of the post-Civil War era concerning attitudes and problems in the disrupted South," he wrote.

Simpson's next effort, *Let Us Have Peace,* concentrates on Grant's political development between 1861 and 1868, which was the year he was elected president.

The period includes his time as a general in the Union army, during which Simpson believes he began thinking in political as well as military terms. *Choice*'s J. P. Sanson quoted Simpson as saying, "'Grant was both soldier and politician for military and civil policy were inevitably intertwined.'" Simpson examines the relationships Grant had with presidents Abraham Lincoln and Johnson, Secretary of War Edwin Stanton, and other politicians of the period. The book also looks at Grant's views on Reconstruction and the freed slaves. Sanson felt Simpson does an admirable job looking at material that other historians had already written about. "Other historians have touched on this aspect of Grant's career, but Simpson's work surpasses them all," Sanson wrote. Calling the book "well written," W. Walter Wicker, who reviewed the book for *Library Journal,* went on to write that it fills "a void in our understanding" of Grant. Simpson further examines Grant's life in both *The Reconstruction Presidents* and *Ulysses S. Grant.* In the former, Simpson discusses how Reconstruction policies evolved during the terms of four presidents, beginning with Lincoln and Johnson, moving through Grant's eight years in office, and culminating with the presidency of Rutherford B. Hayes. According to Simpson, each president approached rebuilding the South differently. Grant, for example, did little to secure the rights of former slaves, because he thought doing so would undermine the support for his presidency in the South. Simpson paints Reconstruction as a failure that ultimately died during Hayes's presidency. Again, critics lauded Simpson's work. Calling it "an excellent study of presidential decision making," Michael Les Benedict of the *American Historical Review* praised the author's "concise analytic narrative." Benedict concluded that *The Reconstruction Presidents* would "be consulted not only by specialists but by anyone interested in the history of the Civil War, American race relations, and American government." Reviewer M. Morrison of *Choice* felt the book provides "a needed corrective to Reconstruction historiography."

In *Ulysses S. Grant,* which a contributor for *Publishers Weekly* called "an eminently informed and finely balanced portrait," Simpson attempts to separate Grant from the many caricatures that have dogged his legacy. As he tracks Grant's "triumph over adversity," Simpson does not leave out Grant's many shortcomings, but he does give the Civil War hero more credit than many historians have tended to do. Included in the book is a discussion of Grant's upbringing in rural Ohio and his enrollment at the Military Academy, his business failures and tours of military duty, and especially the Civil War, which saw Grant rise to take command of the entire Union Army. Despite the common notion that Grant was a military butcher who lacked compassion for human life, Simpson paints the man as someone who actually hated warfare and saw it as a necessary evil. He quotes Grant as having said that war was "at all times a sad and cruel business . . . and nothing but imperative duty could induce me to engage in its work or witness its horrors." The work earned praise from most critics, though some felt Simpson goes too far in praising Grant. John Carver Edwards of *Library Journal* called the work "a finely nuanced view of Grant" that contains an "excellent afterword." Although he believed Simpson does "a masterly job for the most part," Robert V. Remini of the *New York Times Book Review* did find some shortcomings. "Unfortunately, what Simpson fails to do in this book is adequately place Grant in the context of his times," Remini wrote. "The narrative is too tightly focused on its subject." David E. Long of the *Civil War Times* felt "every section of Simpson's book contains labored generalizations that the author constructs to defend his hero."

Simpson has also written several volumes focusing solely on various aspects of the Civil War, including *America's Civil War* and *Gettysburg: A Battlefield Guide,* the latter of which he coauthored with Mark Grimsley. He also coedited *Sherman's Civil War: Selected Correspondence of William T. Sherman, 1860-1865* with Jean V. Berlin. In *America's Civil War,* part of the "Harlan Davidson American History" series, Simpson cites a number of primary and secondary sources, and uses them to describe the political, social and military aspects of the war. Critic G. T. Edwards of *Choice* said Simpson refers to the Civil War as the "'central event of American history.'" Simpson divides the war into several distinct phases. In his view, the crucial moment of the war was the fall of Atlanta in September of 1864, because of the political ramifications the event caused in the South. In Simpson's concluding chapter, titled "Why the Union Won," he theorizes about causes that led to the fall of the Confederacy. Included in the book are a number of maps and a bibliographic essay. G. T. Edwards called the book "a lively and interpretive history." Mary A. DeCredico of the *Journal of Southern History* enjoyed Simpson's "fast-paced narrative that included some good analysis and current historiography." However, DeCredico felt Simpson has not presented anything "dramatically new," and that the work lacks "detail on certain key issues."

BIOGRAPHICAL AND CRITICAL SOURCES:

PERIODICALS

American Historical Review, December, 1999, pp. 1675-1676; June, 2002, Michael B. Ballard, review of *The Collapse of the Confederacy,* p. 883; February, 2001, Michael Fellman, review of *Ulysses S. Grant: Triumph over Adversity, 1822-1865,* p. 174.

American History, August, 2000, Eric Ethier, review of *Ulysses S. Grant,* p. 68.

American Spectator, June, 2000, John A. Barnes, review of *Ulysses S. Grant,* p. 73.

Biography, winter, 2001, Peter J. Parish, review of *Ulysses S. Grant,* p. 329.

Choice, April, 1992, p. 1291; September, 1996, p. 199; July-August, 1998, pp. 1742, 1917; January, 1999, p. 956; September, 2000, N. J. Hervey, review of *Ulysses S. Grant,* p. 206.

Civil War History, March, 2001, Joan Waugh, review of *Ulysses S. Grant,* p. 71.

Civil War Times, May, 2000, p. 10.

Journal of American History, December, 1991, pp. 1094-1095; March, 1998, p. 1515.

Journal of Southern History, November, 1989, p. 734; May, 1997, pp. 410-411; November, 2002, Emory M. Thomas, review of *The Collapse of the Confederacy,* p. 962.

Journal of Military History, October, 2001, Steven E. Nash, review of *The Collapse of the Confederacy,* p. 1103.

Library Journal, October 15, 1991, p. 96; June 15, 1998, p. 96; December, 1999, p. 152.

New York Times Book Review, March 12, 2000.

Publishers Weekly, January 10, 2000, p. 53.

Times Higher Education Supplement, June 15, 2001, Brian Holden Reid, review of *Ulysses S. Grant,* p. 32.*

*   *   *

SINGTON, David

PERSONAL: Male. *Education:* Trinity College, Cambridge, B.S., 1981.

ADDRESSES: Agent—c/o Author Mail, Princeton University Press, 41 William St., Princeton, NJ 08540. *E-mail*—david.sington@tvdox.com.

CAREER: Science journalist and documentary film-maker; BBC Television, senior producer.

AWARDS, HONORS: Walter Sullivan Award for Excellence in Science Journalism, American Geophysical Union, for television series *Earth Story,* 1999; Sigma XI, The Scientific Research Society, honorary member, 2000.

WRITINGS:

BOOKS

(With Simon Lamb) *Earth Story: The Shaping of Our World,* Princeton University Press (Princeton, NJ), 1998.

Also wrote and produced three documentary films, including *Traces of Guilt, The Man Who Made up His Mind,* and *The Man Who Moved the Mountains;* and wrote and produced *Earth Story* (an eight part television series), BBC (England), 1998.

WORK IN PROGRESS: A follow-up television series for the BBC.

SIDELIGHTS: Science writer David Sington is the first non-American and the first broadcast journalist to win the Walter Sullivan Award for Excellence in Science Journalism, which he received in 1999 for his television series *Earth Story.* Singington, who graduated from Trinity College, Cambridge in 1981 with a degree in natural sciences, began his career in 1983 writing science programs for radio. He later joined BBC-TV, where he worked in production and eventually became senior producer. Among his respected documentary films are *Traces of Guilt,* which explores the use of science in criminal detective work; *The Man Who Made up His Mind,* which traces Gerald Edelman's theory of the brain; and *The Man Who Moved the Mountains,* which examines the life and thought of a New Zealand geologist who developed an innovative theory of earthquakes.

For his eight-part television series *Earth Story,* which took thirty months to film, Singington traveled across the globe to focus on sites pertinent to the program's exploration of earth processes. The first episode introduces the concept of geologic time and shows how geologists obtain data from rocks that provide information about the past. The next episodes provide more detail on plate tectonics, mantle convection, and the behavior of the earth's crust. The series then goes on to show how these processes have affected the earth's climate and evolution.

The American Geophysical Union honored *Earth Story* as a work that "makes geophysical science accessible and interesting to the general public" when it bestowed upon Singington its Walter Sullivan Award for Excellence in Science Journalism in 1999. The identically titled companion book to the series, which Singington co-wrote with Simon Lamb, also impressed readers with its detailed information and engaging style. Among the book's more interesting themes is its explanation of how earth features that appear to be distinct, such as earthquakes, volcanoes, glaciers, and weather, are actually related parts of one complex interlinked system. The book also argues that geological activity was a precondition for the development of life, and that life on earth has seriously affected the earth's geological activity. Reviewers admired *Earth Story*'s lucidity, organization, and vivid prose. *Booklist*'s Gilbert Taylor commended the book as "a splendidly concise presentation of how plate tectonics became the orthodox theory that explained a lengthy portion of the earth's history." A *Publishers Weekly* reviewer deemed it a "compelling and accessible account [that] merits sustained attention." Singington planned a follow-up series to *Earth Story* for the BBC.

BIOGRAPHICAL AND CRITICAL SOURCES:

PERIODICALS

Booklist, September 1, 1998, p. 45.
Choice, March, 1999, M. A. Wilson, review of *Earth Story: The Shaping of Our World,* p. 1292.
Library Journal, October 15, 1998, p. 93.
Publishers Weekly, August 17, 1998, p. 33.*

*　　　*　　　*

SINHA, Indra 1950-

PERSONAL: Born 1950, in India; son of Bhagvati Prasad and Irene Elizabeth (Phare) Sinha; married Viktoria Jane Yvette, September 9, 1978; children: Tara, Dan, Samuel. *Education:* Mayo College, Ajmer,

Rajasthan, India; Oakham School, Pembroke College, Cambridge, B.A. *Hobbies and other interests:* Travel, reading, cybertravel, folk music, butterflies.

ADDRESSES: *Agent*—c/o Author Mail, Penguin Putnam, 375 Hudson St., New York, NY 10014. *E-mail*—bear@cybergypsies.com.

CAREER: Author. The Creative Business, advertising copywriter, 1976-79; Ogilvy & Mather, advertising copywriter, 1980-83; Collett, Dickenson, Pearce & Partners, advertising copywriter, 1984-95. Worked for Amnesty International.

AWARDS, HONORS: Voted by his peers as one of the top ten copywriters in the United Kingdom.

WRITINGS:

(Translator) *The Love Teachings of Kama Sutra: With Extracts from Koka shastra, Ananga ranga, and Other Famous Indian Works on Love,* Crescent (New York, NY), 1980.
(Editor, and translator) *The Great Book of Tantra: Translations and Images from the Classic Indian Texts with Commentary,* Destiny (Rochester, VT), 1993.
The Cybergypsies: A True Tale of Lust, War, and Betrayal on the Electronic Frontier, Viking (New York, NY), 1999.
Tantra: The Cult of Ecstasy, Hamlyn (London, England), 2000.

SIDELIGHTS: Indra Sinha was one of England's top copywriters before turning to writing full time. He has worked for Amnesty International and wrote of the problems of the Kurds in the Middle East and the Bhopal chemical disaster. His *The Love Teachings of Kama Sutra: With Extracts from Koka shastra, Ananga ranga, and Other Famous Indian Works on Love* is a translation from the original Sanskrit and was the first such translation to be accompanied by erotic Indian miniatures. Sinha and his wife collected many of the paintings in India, obtaining them from shops and private collections.

In *The Cybergypsies: A True Tale of Lust, War, and Betrayal on the Electronic Frontier,* Sinha provides an account of his cyberaddiction, which began in the 1980s. Linton Weeks wrote in *Washington Post Book World* that the book "is a clever, inspired tale of the pre-World Wide Web days when folks communicated via bulletin boards, companies charged hourly access fees, and mad hackers roamed the phone lines. . . . With Sinha as participant/guide, we tour the spooky electronic underworld and the equally eerie real world. And we delve into the most complex network of all—the human imagination." As "Bear," Sinha frequented bulletin boards and MUDs (multiuser dungeons) for ten years. Hester Lacey wrote in the *Independent on Sunday* that for Sinha, the "real hook was in role-playing fantasy worlds so finely conceived that they seemed real. 'It was fascinating, almost like a therapy,' he says now. 'An actor in a workshop could try out lots of different roles. For a writer it's even more tantalizing—you're having to improvise the character. I invented lots of them. It was absolutely as real as my real life—there's no question about it. Once you're in it, it's as real as anything around you.'"

Sinha spent hours each day on sites like *Vortex* and *Shades,* where he created up to fifty roles. Characters with whom he communicated included witches, pornographers, virus writers, and people with atom bomb plans for sale. *Booklist* reviewer Benjamin Segedin wrote that "like Thomas de Quincey's classic *Confessions of an English Opium Eater,* Sinha's book reveals an exotic subculture." At one point, while commuting one hundred miles a day to London, he came home to spend most of the night at the keyboard. When Sinha could focus only on his cyberlife, his marriage was threatened, and the responsibility for the house and children fell to his wife. Mary Elizabeth Williams wrote in the *New York Times Book Review* that when Sinha "speaks plainly" about his addiction and how it distanced him from his family, "he tells an absorbing and strange story. But too often he writes an overeager prose that puts the reader off." The per-hour charges for Sinha's online time added up, and he wrote *Cybergypsies,* in part, to recover the fifty thousand pounds his addiction had cost. Sinha quit *Shades* and his job simultaneously, on his forty-fifth birthday, to concentrate on his writing.

"Narrated with wit and moments of literary flair in the nonlinear style of the Internet itself, this book amounts to a sort of architectural dig," wrote a *Publishers Weekly* reviewer. *Time* reviewer Anita Hamilton called *Cybergypsies* an "engaging memoir."

BIOGRAPHICAL AND CRITICAL SOURCES:

PERIODICALS

Booklist, September 15, 1999, Benjamin Segedin, review of *The Cybergypsies,* p. 202.
Entertainment Weekly, August 20, 1999, p. 120.
Independent on Sunday, May 2, 1999, p. 4.
New York Times Book Review, September 26, 1999, p. 21.
Publishers Weekly, July 5, 1999, review of *The Cybergypsies,* p. 46.
Time, September 13, 1999, Anita Hamilton, review of *The Cybergypsies,* p. 77.
Washington Post Book World, August 29, 1999, p. 9.*

*   *   *

SINKANKAS, John 1915-2002

OBITUARY NOTICE—See index for *CA* sketch: Born May 15, 1915, in Paterson, NJ; died of heart and lung ailments May 17, 2002, in San Diego, CA. Gemologist, minerologist, lapidary, and author. Sinkankas was an internationally renowned gemologist who wrote books that have become standard reference sources for those in his profession. He received his bachelor's degree from New Jersey State Teachers College (now William Paterson College of New Jersey) in 1936, then joined the U.S. Navy as a pilot from 1936 until 1961. While in the service, Sinkankas continued a lifelong interest in gems by taking correspondence courses from the Gemological Institute of America; he also received further training at the University of California at San Diego. Sinkankas published his first book on gems in 1955: *Gem Cutting: A Lapidary's Manual.* From there he continued to write about the subject. Many of his books have becomes standards in the field, among them the three-volume *Gemstones of North America* (1959, 1976, 1993) and *Emeralds and Other Beryls* (1981). Among his other works are *Standard Catalogue of Gems* (1968), *Beryl* (written with Peter G. Read; 1986), *Gemology: An Annotated Bibliography* (1993), *Humboldt's Travels in Siberia (1837-1842): The Gemstones by Gustav Rose* (1994), and the edited work *Earth Science Studio Handbook of Minerals* by Helmuth Boegel (1971). Sinkankas was such an influential figure in the field of gemology that in 1984 a new phosphate mineral was named after him—sin-

kankasite; some of his lapidary work is also displayed at the Smithsonian Institute. His private reference collection of over 10,000 books was sold to the Gemological Institute of America in 1988.

OBITUARIES AND OTHER SOURCES:

BOOKS

Writers Directory, 16th edition, St. James Press (Detroit, MI), 2001.

PERIODICALS

Los Angeles Times, June 7, 2002, p. B12.
New York Times, June 16, 2002, p. A23.
Washington Post, June 8, 2002, p. B7.

*   *   *

SJOSTEDT, Ulf (Georg) 1935-

PERSONAL: Born April 7, 1935, in Karistad, Sweden; married Brita Karang in 1970 (divorced, 1985); children: Katarina. *Education:* Studied graphics and photography at Konstindustriskolan, Göteborg, Sweden, 1959-62; Institute of Higher Marketing Education, Göteborg, graduate degree, 1973.

ADDRESSES: Home—Valnotsgatan 6, S-426 74 V. Frolunda, Sweden.

CAREER: Photographer. Tryckare (publishing company), Göteborg, Sweden, employee, 1962-64; *Nordisk Tidskrift för Fotografi* (magazine), editor, 1964-66; *Hasselblad Magazine,* editor-in-chief, 1967-75; Victor Hasselblad AB (photo equipment company), Göteborg, advertising manager, 1969-82, regional sales manager, 1983-91, Hasselblad *FORUM,* editor, 1994—. *Exhibitions:* Works included in permanent collections at Fotografiska Museet, Moderna Museet, Stockholm, at Varmlands Museum, Karlstad, Sweden, and Boras Museum, Sweden. Solo exhibitions include *Swedish Artisans* at the Historical Museum, Göteborg, 1966, *Pictures* at Pentax Gallery, London, England, Instituto Fotografico, Buenos Aires, Argentina, 1982, and Lycksele Konstforening, Sweden, 1990. Group exhibitions include *Two Generations* at the Art Museum, Göteborg, 1961, *Fantastic Photography in Europe,* Fondacion Joan Miró, Barcelona, Spain, 1976, and *Naturfotografi i Sverige,* Hasselblad Center, Göteborg, 1992. *Military service:* Swedish Army Infantry, Falun and Stockholm, 1957-59.

AWARDS, HONORS: Municipal Culture Award, Göteborg, 1967; Welinder Award, Swedish Photographers Association, 1967; Swedish Authors Fund Award, 1972, 1976, 1979, 1982, 1985, 1989, 1993.

WRITINGS:

Min Bilderbok, [Göteborg, Sweden], 1961.
Modern Reklam, text by Lars Foxe, [Göteborg, Sweden], 1967.
En Bok om Några Vanner, ([Göteborg, Sweden], 1971.
Katarina: Stina och Sommaren, [Göteborg, Sweden], 1976.
Sjön Suger, text by Bengt Petersen, [Göteborg, Sweden], 1976.
Mina Mest Subjektiva Bilder, [Alingsås, Sweden], 1979.
Den Fotografiska Bilden, Spektra [Halmstad, Sweden], 1979.
Barn på Bild, [Halmstad, Sweden], 1981.
Foto på Resaw, [Halmstad, Sweden], 1981.
Nya Bilder, Fotografiska Museet I Moderna Museet [Stockholm, Sweden], 1981.
(Photo-illustrator) Svenungson, Erland, *Vid Stranden,* [Göteborg, Sweden], 1981.
Fotokomposition, [Halmstad, Sweden], 1984.
Färgfotografi, [Halmstad, Sweden] 1990.
Poetisk Bilderbok, [Göteborg, Sweden], 1994.
Fotografiskt Bildtänkande, [Halmstad, Sweden], 1994.

Contributor to numerous publications, including *Petersen's Photographic, Foto,* and *Nuova Fotografia.*

SIDELIGHTS: A *Contemporary Photographers* writer noted that Ulf Sjöstedt has often been called Sweden's "best-known amateur photographer," even though he has shot professionally since 1950. The writer suggested, "In spite of a very prolific photographic activity, Sjöstedt has succeeded in preserving the amateur's curiosity and delight in experiment."

In a *Contemporary Photographers* entry, Sjöstedt said, "Most of my pictures are documentary, but, as photography can be used in many different ways, I am more interested in creative photography, in what Professor Otto Steinert called 'subjective photography.' Painters, draughtsmen, and graphic artists can use their media in order to capture a man's mood or his experience, and so can the photographer. It is true that photography has not yet produced a Leonardo, a Rembrandt or a Picasso, but be sure there will be one, someday."

Sjöstedt has maintained beginner's enthusiasm while working professionally as the head of a drawing department for a publishing company, and as an editor of several photo journals, including *Hasselblad Magazine* and *Nordisk Tidskrift för Fotografi.* An experienced lecturer, he has published more than one dozen books, including *Min Bilderbok, Modern Reklam, Katarina: Stina och Sommaren,* and *Sjon Suger.* Sjöstedt has also contributed articles on photography to many journals.

In an article Sjöstedt wrote in *Petersen's Photographic,* titled, "In Search of Great Themes, Windows and Walls," the photographer remarked, "Many photographers have trouble finding things to shoot. Actually there's good subject matter everywhere. You just have to know when—and where—to look for it." The *Contemporary Photographers* writer said, "Much of what he does can be classified as family and holiday photos."

Sjöstedt's better-known works are photographs from the 1970s that convey a 1950s aesthetic—the '50s were a period of widespread subjective photography. An admirer of the work of Russian constructivists Aleksandr Rodchenko and Wassily Kandinsky, Sjöstedt applies these artists' theories of geometrical composition to his own "subjective" photos.

Other areas of interest include birches, which Sjöstedt considers a symbol of Sweden; romanticism; and the sea, a symbol of his new home, the West Coast. He participates in exhibitions internationally.

BIOGRAPHICAL AND CRITICAL SOURCES:

BOOKS

Contemporary Photographers, third edition, St. James Press (Detroit, MI), 1996.

Wigh, Leif, *Fotograferna och det Svenska landskappet* (exhibition catalogue), Fotografiska Museet: Fyra Förläggare (Stockholm, Sweden), 1982.*

*   *   *

SLAVICEK, Milivoj 1929-

PERSONAL: Born October 24, 1929, in Cakovec, Medjimurje, Croatia; son of Mato (a lawyer) and Dragica Slavicek. *Education:* University of Zagreb, B.A., 1954.

ADDRESSES: Agent—c/o Krscanska Sadasnjost, Marulicev trg 14, 41000 Zagreb, Croatia.

CAREER: Poet. Has worked as a salesman, a teacher, and a librarian.

MEMBER: Omladinski literarni kruzok (Youth Literary Circle), University of Zagreb.

AWARDS, HONORS: Several Croatian literary awards.

WRITINGS:

Zaustavljena pregrst, Mladost (Zagreb, Croatia), 1954.
Daleka pokrajina, Lykos (Zagreb, Croatia), 1957.
Modro vece, Zora (Zagreb, Croatia), 1959.
Predak, Naprijed (Zagreb, Croatia), 1963.
Noc'ni autobus ili naredni dio cjeline, Zora (Zagreb, Croatia), 1964.
Soneti, pjesme o ljubavi i ostale pjesme, Ogranak Matice hrvatske (Cakovec, Croatia), 1967.
Purpurna pepeljara, naime to i to, Naprijed (Zagreb, Croatia), 1969.
Poglavlje, Razlog (Zagreb, Croatia), 1970.
Naslov sto ga nikad nec'u zaboraviti, Veselin Maslesa (Sarajevo, Bosnia), 1974.
Otvoreno radi (eventualnog) preuredjenja, Alfa-August Cesarec (Zagreb, Croatia), 1978.
Trinaesti pejzaz, Znanje (Zagreb, Croatia), 1981.
Teror/Terror Biblioteka Biskupic (Zagreb, Croatia), 1981.
Sjaj ne/svakodnevnice Naprijed (Zagreb, Croatia), 1987.
Nastanjen uvijek Krscanska sadasnjost (Zagreb, Croatia), 1990.

COLLECTIONS

Izmedju: Izbor pjesama Bagdala (Krusevac), 1965.
Izabrane pjesme, Nakladni zavod Matice hrvatske (Zagreb, Croatia), 1987.

EDITIONS IN ENGLISH

Silent Doors (selected poems), translated by Branko Gorjup and Jeanette Lynes, Exile Editions (Toronto, Ontario, Canada), 1988.

Poetry has also appeared in English translation in anthologies, including *Contemporary Yugoslav Poetry,* edited by Vasa D. Mihailovich, Iowa University Press (Iowa City, IA), 1977, and in periodicals, including *Bridge, Journal of Croatian Studies,* and *Exile.*

OTHER

(Editor) *A Collection of Modern Croatian Verse,* Hrvatski centar P.E.N. Cluba (Zagreb, Croatia), 1965.
(Editor) *Wewnetrzne morze. Antologia poezji chorwackiej XX wieku,* Wydawnictwo Literackie (Krakow, Poland), 1982.

SIDELIGHTS: With its aberrant and individualistic nature Milivoj Slavicek's poetry pronounces its rebellion against politically sanctioned literature. The seeming simplicity of his poetry is a political statement and a celebration of the individual perspective as opposed to the collective viewpoint. His innovative use of language further reveals his individuality.

Although the majority of Slavicek's poetry suggests his defense of individuality, the political pressures of 1950s Yugoslavia strongly dictated the forms and functions of literature. Under these pressures, Slavicek occasionally subordinated his talents by writing on acceptable themes in acceptable forms. As Aida Vidan at Harvard University, writing in the *Dictionary of Literary Biography,* commented: "Although Slavicek's first verses announced the arrival of a potentially interesting contributor to the Croatian literary scene, it should be noted that not all of his early poems are of equal quality. The pressure of political factors in Yugoslavia in the 1950s and the demand for an optimistic, collective viewpoint in literature made Slavicek occasionally succumb to themes and forms not well suited to his talent." Vidan identified two of Slavicek's early works, Zaustavljena pregrst ("The Restrained Armful," 1954) and Daleka pokrajina ("A Far Away Province," 1957), as his most politically docile. Vidan wrote that "even in these one can find poems such as 'Pusim lulu, drzim je prstima, i gledam u dim' ('I smoke my pipe, hold it in my fingers, and look at the smoke') that announce Slavicek's typical simplicity, or cycles such as 'Vode' ('Waters'), a group of six sonnets in which the author experiments with this traditional form."

Slavicek's early poems display his affinity for commonplace elements that refute Romantic themes. According to Vidan: "This tendency deepens and becomes more prominent as Slavicek matures, gradually transforming the somewhat sentimental overtones of his early poems into the tongue-in-cheek attitude or even openly voiced sarcasm and irony in his later works." What Vidan called Slavicek's "tendency toward a 'democratic' expression in verse" has prompted a stir among his critics. As Vidan indicated: "Some critics have seen this approach as a deliberate statement, stressing Slavicek's conscious and (in the later period) consistent avoidance of both poetic devices and poetic language."

According to Vidan, sound experimentation "remains for the most part foreign to [Slavicek's] style." The result of this, Vidan asserted, is that "much of his poetry comes close to 'spilling' into prose, and it is only in the correlation and juxtaposition of phrases and syntactic units that one can recognize poetic principles at work." Vidan went on to say: "On the lexical level it is not only that Slavicek brings urban colloquial expressions into his verse, but that he also refuses to use romantically colored nature vocabulary in the fashion typical for most of his predecessors and contemporaries. Nature, in its concrete manifestations, is absent from Slavicek's poetry. On the rare occasions when it is mentioned, it is mostly viewed from an urban environment as something distant, almost symbolic."

Slavicek's refusal to romanticize nature derives from the fact that his central focus has been humanity. As Vidan maintained: "Because Slavicek's primary concern is with humanity, he observes nature exclusively in relation to human existence, to which it remains secondary. As specific as Slavicek can be about urban landscapes, he remains distant and abstract in his rare evocations of images from nature. This can be observed, for example, in the poem 'Rijeka i ja smo u neprijateljstvu' ('The River and I are in a State of Enmity') from the collection *Modro vece* (*Blue Evening,* 1959). In eleven rebellious verses, in which Slavicek calls for and celebrates individuality, the motif of the river is used as a metaphor for everything that is mainstream, obedient and unchallenging. Throughout the poem the river remains an abstract notion and is stripped of any specific attributes." In Vidan's view, *Modro vece* is an important collection of poetry not only for what the poems reveal about Slavicek's relation to nature and humanity but also because of the courage Slavicek exhibits by rejecting common forms. Vidan, however, stresses a greater significance: "In addition, his preoccupation with the position of the common person in the alienating conditions of twentieth-century, civilization clearly takes a central position in this book. Even the title of one of its poems, 'Vrijeme je da se dogadja napokon Covjek' ('It Is Time for the Man to Finally Happen'), is enough to indicate this concern."

Vidan concluded by addressing Slavicek's work as a whole: "From Slavicek's first book of poetry to the most recent, certain themes and techniques recur. Moreover, the author quite often brings the works of previous years into his new collections, thereby encouraging the reader to disregard the chronology and to read the poems not as separate entities but rather in relation to one another. It could even be argued that they are to be perceived as different chapters of a single text whose logic does not depend on a temporal sequence. The tone that connects different chapters of Slavicek's oeuvre is one of simplicity, resistance, and protest, which is what makes this poetry 'with a mission' or 'poetry of detail' so recognizable."

BIOGRAPHICAL AND CRITICAL SOURCES:

BOOKS

Dictionary of Literary Biography, Volume 181: *South Slavic Writers Since World War II,* Gale (Detroit, MI), 1997, pp. 327-331.*

SLAVIN, Neal 1941-

PERSONAL: Born August 19, 1941, in Brooklyn, NY; *Education:* Cooper Union, New York, NY, B.F.A., 1963; studied Renaissance painting and sculpture, Lincoln College, Oxford University, England, 1961.

ADDRESSES: Home—62 Greene Street, New York, NY 10012. *Agent*—Barbara von Schreiber, 315 Central Park West, New York, NY 10025.

CAREER: Photographer, educator, and film director. Freelance photographer and graphic artist since 1963; Manhattanville College, Purchase, NY, instructor of photography, 1970-74; Queen's College, instructor, 1972; Cooper Union, instructor, 1972-74; School of Visual Arts, New York, NY, instructor, 1973. Director of the motion picture *Focus* (Paramount Classics), 2001. *Exhibitions:* Works included in permanent collections at Metropolitan Museum of Art, New York, NY; Museum of Modern Art, New York, NY, and the University of Maryland, Baltimore, MD. Solo exhibitions include Underground Gallery, New York, 1967, Focus Gallery, San Francisco, CA, 1972; Akron Art Institute, Akron, OH, 1980; and National Museum of Photography, Bradford, Yorkshire, England, 1986. Group exhibitions include *Rooms,* Museum of Modern Art, New York, NY, 1976; *Aspects of the '70s,* DeCordova Museum, Lincoln, MA, 1980; and *The History of Color Photography,* at *Photokina '86,* Cologne, Germany. *Military service:* United States Army Reserve, 1963-64.

AWARDS, HONORS: Fulbright Photography fellowship, 1968; National Endowment for the Arts grants, 1972, 1976; Creative Artists Public Service Award, 1977.

WRITINGS:

Portugal, afterword by Mary McCarthy, Lustrom Press (New York, NY), 1971.
When Two or More Are Gathered Together, Farrar, Straus & Giroux (New York, NY), 1976.
(Illustrator, with Charles Mikolaycak) Earlene Long, *Johnny's Egg,* Addison-Wesley (Reading, MA), 1980.
Britons, Aperture (New York, NY), 1986.

SIDELIGHTS: New York-based photographer and film director Neal Slavin produces volumes of commercial photography, creating images for book jackets and magazine covers, completing photo essays appearing in such major magazines as *New York* and *Geo,* and directing television commercials.

He has also undertaken his own photography projects, including *Portugal* (1971), a chronicle of a people under dictatorship, which share common sociological themes but display a variety of technical skills.

He has published several books of his photos. *Portugal,* for which Slavin received the first-ever Fulbright grant for photography in 1968, is a study in black-and-white film, using a 35-millimeter camera. A *Contemporary Photographers* writer said, "The resulting sequence of images, a revealing and highly personal interpretation of his subject, showed Slavin to be adept at the small-camera documentary mode as defined by Cartier-Bresson and redefined by Robert Frank."

When Two or More Are Gathered Together is a lengthy series of formal, full-color portraits of American social and business groups. Slavin set out to demonstrate how members of a group signal their shared identity. Because uniforms and accessories are often important to group allegiance, Slavin wanted to work with color film and emphasize physical presentation.

In *Britons,* a collection of group portraits, Slavin captures British club members, drinking buddies, co-workers, and choirs. He used a large Polaroid camera to photograph his subjects, including members of the Distressed Gentlefolks Aid Association and the Duke and Duchess of Devonshire.

In 1991, Slavin launched production company Slavin/Schaffer Films, with partner Perry Schaffer. In 1997, Slavin bought out Schaffer and renamed his one-director company Carros Pictures. Under the Carros name, Slavin directed several Procter & Gamble Sunny Delight beverage spots and others. In an interview published in *Shoot,* Slavin explained, "I had reached the point in life where things were going well, but I was not having fun. We had 10 people . . . and I went to bed worrying about running a company instead of running a project."

Slavin directed his first motion picture, *Focus,* based on the 1945 novel by Arthur Miller. Interested in film directing for several decades before he tried his hand at it, Slavin had dreamed of bringing to life Miller's novel upon first reading it as an art student at Cooper Union in New York City. He read it fifteen times before undertaking the directing project.

The movie, starring William H. Macy and Laura Dern, tells of Lawrence Newman, a weak Everyman, whose new, horn-rimmed glasses cause people to think him Jewish and react harshly. He lives with his sick mother. *Focus,* which tracks the effects of anti-Semitism, the ruthless power of perception, and one humble man's search for truth and compassion, is set in New York during World War II.

Dennis Harvey wrote in *Variety,* "Shot in Toronto, [*Focus*] does an OK job evoking the period on modest means." Daniel Egan observed in *Film Journal International,* "Although presented with sympathy and taste, these are themes which inevitably carried more weight in the past. . . . At best, *Focus* will win a certain amount of respectful reviews and almost no viewers."

"Anti-Semitism was still a taboo subject then," Slavin told Gary Arnold in a *Washington Times* interview and discussion of Miller's novel. "Even the Jews didn't want to talk about it. As the years went on, the book's metaphor encompassed other kinds of racism, prejudice and hatred. I was struck with it relevancy to the civil rights movement during my college period. Now, so soon after the (September, 2001) terrorist attacks, it becomes even more part and parcel of the realities we face."

BIOGRAPHICAL AND CRITICAL SOURCES:

BOOKS

Contemporary Photographers, third edition, St. James Press (Detroit, MI), 1996.

Hard af Segerstad, Ulf, Sune Jonsson, and Ake Sidwall, *Tusen och en bild* (exhibition catalogue), Moderna Museet/Fotografiska museet (Stockholm, Sweden), 1978.

Honnef, Klaus, and Evelyn Weiss, *Documenta 6, Band 2* (exhibition catalogue), [Kassel, Germany], 1977.

Sammlung Gruber: Photographie des 20. Jahrhunderts (exhibition catalogue), City of Cologne (Cologne, Germany), 1984.

Weiermair, Peter, *Photographie als Kunst 1879-1979/ Kunst als Photographie 1949-79* (exhibition catalogue), two volumes, Allerheiligenpresse (Innsbruck, Austria), 1979.

PERIODICALS

Film Journal International, October, 2001, Daniel Egan, review of *Focus,* pp. 57-58.

Shoot, September 19, 1997, Reginald Oberlag, "Neal Slavin Opens Carros Pictures as Solo Shop," pp. 7-8.

Time, December 15, 1986, review of *Britons,* p. 89.

Variety, April 2, 2001, Dana Harris, "Par Classics Hones in on Slavin's Focus," p. 44.

Variety, October 15, 2001, Dennis Harvey, review of *Focus,* p. 40.

Washington Times, November 17, 2001, Gary Arnold, "Director of New Film Finds Focus Late in Life," p. 5.

OTHER

PopMatters, http://www.popmatters.com/ (May 7, 2002), Cynthia Fuchs, "Interview with Neal Slavin."*

*   *   *

SMALL, Hugh 1943-

PERSONAL: Born 1943.

ADDRESSES: Agent—c/o Author Mail, St. Martin's Press, 175 Fifth Ave., New York, NY 10010.

CAREER: Writer.

WRITINGS:

Florence Nightingale: Avenging Angel, St. Martin's Press (New York, NY), 1999.

SIDELIGHTS: Florence Nightingale is the stuff of legend, the angelic figure nursing British soldiers and writing letters to their families during the Crimean

War in the 1850s. Hugh Small's revisionist book, *Florence Nightingale: Avenging Angel,* probes the reasons for her retreat into invalidism after her return to England. He concludes that she was stricken with remorse over her failure to prevent as many as 14,000 deaths in the camp she ran in Scutari (now Uskudar, across the Bosporus from Istanbul, Turkey). Small uses several sources not tapped by other biographers, particularly letters that had not been included in the original Nightingale papers.

With little experience, Nightingale volunteered for service in the Crimea at the age of thirty-four. She was appointed to run a field hospital at Scutari only because she had influential friends. A particular supporter was the wife of Secretary of War Sidney Herbert, who set out to help Nightingale prove that it was acceptable for women to nurse men. On the job, Nightingale was a tireless worker but was thought to be bossy and abrasive. At the hospital, she directed a number of other women in the nursing of over 2,500 soldiers, in filthy, overcrowded conditions. Blocked drains lay under the hospital, and Nightingale did nothing to have them cleaned up; meanwhile, deaths at Scutari exceeded those in other hospitals, and during the winter of 1854-55 around 5,000 men died.

The image of the "Lady with the Lamp," Small says, is belied by the unnecessary suffering and deaths, which occurred under Nightingale's watch. Statistics reveal that three out of eight of her patients did not survive their stays in the hospital. Small indicates that Nightingale was also implicated in the political wrangling between Queen Victoria and Prime Minister Palmerston over control of the army. Yet Nightingale was lionized upon her return to England and claimed to have proved that women were fit caretakers of men.

To her credit, when Nightingale studied figures compiled by a Royal Commission of Inquiry, she set out to reveal the truth. She concluded that a significant drop in deaths at Scutari occurred after her watch when a government doctor had decided to clean the hospital's toilets and sewers, precautions she had not taken. But a government coverup silenced her concerns. Remorseful, she had a brief breakdown, then took to her bed for most of the remainder of her life. She wrote that her life had been "a tissue of mistakes." Small concludes that repressed guilt caused Nightingale to hide herself; yet even from her sickbed, she wrote let-

ters and articles encouraging environmental cleanups and succeeded in directing pioneering public health campaigns.

Critics found Small's book a valuable addition to scholarship on Nightingale, if somewhat harsh in tone. Jane Ridley in the *Spectator* noted that the book "is really more polemic than biography," but found the story "gripping." Margaret Van Dangens reported in the *New York Times Book Review* that "at times [Small] sacrifices clarity for rhetoric . . . Nightingale is driven, tormented, messianic and interesting." A *Publishers Weekly* critic found Small's book an "abrasive exploration" of Nightingale's life, marked by a "dryly academic . . . presentation" but called the story "interesting for its insights into public health issues."

BIOGRAPHICAL AND CRITICAL SOURCES:

PERIODICALS

Booklist, November 1, 1999, William Beatty, review of *Florence Nightingale: Avenging Angel,* p. 496.

English Historical Review, September, 2000, Mark Bostridge, review of *Florence Nightingale,* p. 1008.

Historian, spring, 2001, Mary Ann Bradford Burnam, review of *Florence Nightingale,* p. 695.

Isis, June, 2001, Julie Fairman, review of *Florence Nightingale,* p. 412.

Journal of Women's History, summer, 2000, Lorraine Netrick Abraham, review of *Florence Nightingale,* p. 232.

New York Times Book Review, January 16, 2000, Margaret Van Dagens, review of *Florence Nightingale.*

NWSA Journal, summer, 2001, Anne O. Dzamba, review of *Florence Nightingale,* p. 178.

Publishers Weekly, November 1, 1999, review of *Florence Nightingale,* p. 64.

Spectator, October 24, 1998, Jane Ridley, "Thou Wast Not Born for Death, Immortal Bird," p. 47.

Victorian Studies, summer, 2001, Joann C. Wilterquist, review of *Florence Nightingale,* p. 690.*

*　　*　　*

SMELIANSKII, Anatolii M.
　　See SMELIANSKY, Anatoly

SMELIANSKY, Anatoly
(Anatolii M. Smelianskii)

PERSONAL: Male. *Education:* USSR Academy of Sciences All-Union, Ph.D.

ADDRESSES: Office—A.R.T./MXAT Institute, Loeb Drama Center, 64 Brattle St., Cambridge, MA 02138.

CAREER: Russian theater scholar, lecturer, and critic. Moscow Art Theatre, 1980—, began as literary director, became associate artistic director, 1996; Moscow Art Theatre School for Academic Studies, became dean, 1986, became head, 2000; Institute for Advanced Theatre Training, Harvard University, Cambridge, MA, associate director. Russian Union of Theatremakers, board secretary; American-Soviet Theatre Initiative, founding member. Lecturer at universities, including, Yale, Carnegie Mellon, Columbia, Princeton, and Georgetown in the United States; the Sorbonne in France, and Oxford and Cambridge in England.

AWARDS, HONORS: National awards for artistic excellence, including Distinguished Artsmaker of Russia.

WRITINGS:

Mikhail Bulgakov v Khudozhestvennom teatre, Iskusstvo (Moscow, Russia), 1986, translation by Arch Tait published as *Is Comrade Bulgakov Dead?: Mikhail Bulgakov at the Moscow Art Theatre,* Routledge (New York, NY), 1993.
The Russian Theatre after Stalin ("Cambridge Studies in Modern Theatre" series), revised edition, translation from the Russian by Patrick Miles, Cambridge University Press (Cambridge, England), 1999.

Also author of *Our Collocutors: Russian Classics on Stage;* editor-in-chief of a seven-volume revised *Complete Works of Konstantin Stanislavsky,* Iskusstvo, 1988-1995, and *The Moscow Art Theatre Encyclopedia.* Columnist for the *Moscow New Weekly* (all Russian-language writings).

SIDELIGHTS: Anatoly Smeliansky is a scholar of Russian theater and a leader of its institutions, as well as an international lecturer. He is the author of many Russian-language books, several of which have been translated for English-speaking readers. Among these is *Is Comrade Bulgakov Dead?: Mikhail Bulgakov at the Moscow Art Theatre,* called a "soulful book . . . a labor of love, respect, and empathy for its subject," by *Choice* reviewer S. Golub. Bulgakov died on March 10, 1940. The next morning a call came directly from Stalin's office asking for confirmation of his death. Vera Gottlieb noted in *Theatre Research International* that this anecdote, "and hence the title . . . exemplifies both the significance of Bulgakov in his contemporary Russia—and his vulnerability."

By 1930, Bulgakov's plays were banned, and he wrote to Stalin asking for any theatrical employment, even as a stagehand. Stalin told him to apply to the Moscow Art Theatre (MAT), and by May of that year, Bulgakov found himself in the position of assistant director in the same theater that had previously censored his work under political pressure. Stalin supported MAT, its directors, and its actors, but on condition that his policies be legitimized in their creative works. Stalin approved some of Bulgakov's plays and ordered others, such as *Molière* (also known as *A Cabal of Hypocrites*), to be withdrawn. Bulgakov's later satire *The Master and the Margarita,* which was published posthumously, about a writer who receives favors from the devil, seems obviously inspired by his relationship with Stalin.

In *Slavic Review,* Nicholas Rzhevsky commented on a chapter "dealing with *Batum.* Bulgakov's play about the young Stalin has long been a puzzle and a challenge to Bulgakov readers for its apparent capitulation of his most cherished principles. Smelianskii convincingly argues in terms of text and context that the play was ultimately subversive and evoked themes of history, Antichrist, the Devil and repression quite different from the usual hagiography of the times."

Smeliansky completed the volume before 1985 and needed only to add newly archived material. Gottlieb said that the integrity of Smeliansky "as critic, theatre historian, biographer, and analyst has not required an ungainly scramble to 'rewrite' in the face of the radical changes in Russia since 1986." Smeliansky documents Bulgakov's writing career, his relationships with the Moscow Art Theatre, Stanislavsky, Nemirovich-Danchenko, Stalin and the Party, and the performances, critics, and audiences of the time.

"Like Bulgakov's own writing, Smeliansky's discourse is rich in comic discoveries and the intellectual freedom of inquiry that have outlasted countless censors," wrote Joel Schechter in *American Theatre.* "Theatre historians, and superb historians like Smeliansky, now vindicate Bulgakov's determination to write about Soviet life as he saw it and suffer the consequences."

The Russian Theatre after Stalin is Smeliansky's study of Russian theatre since 1953, and Smeliansky personally knows most of the artists he discusses. The book is divided into time periods. "The Thaw" is the Kruschev era, during which artists, sometimes incorrectly, felt that were working in a more open environment. "The Frosts" is the period from Brezhnev to Chernenko, and "The Black Box" refers to the period from 1985 to 1997. Smeliansky concentrates on four directors—Yury Lyubimov, Oleg Yefremov, Georgy Tovstonogov, and Anatoly Efros. Writing in *American Theatre,* Daniel Mufson called this "an engaging and useful account of Russia's most important directors for the last half century."

Mufson wrote that "it's hard not to notice some nostalgia for the elevated status that 'spiritual activity' once had in Soviet Russia and for the sense that artists were playing a role vital to society. Smeliansky reiterates the conventional wisdom that theatre under Soviet rule occupied a privileged place as one of the few spheres where public gatherings were permitted; the government tolerated a degree of dissent and criticism in the theatre so long as it confined itself within given parameters and employed an 'Aesopian' technique of suggesting veiled parallels between contemporary society and the allegedly discrete world depicted on stage." Mufson said "the breadth of [Smeliansky's] knowledge and his intimacy with the material manifests itself throughout the book." Golub called the study "a 'must read' for those in the field, offered by one of the few people with the opportunity, intelligence, maturity, and good sense to write it."

BIOGRAPHICAL AND CRITICAL SOURCES:

PERIODICALS

American Theatre, July, 1994, Joel Schechter, "Save a Seat for Comrade Stalin," pp. 68-69; December, 1999, Daniel Mufson, "From Russia with Love," p. 77.

Choice, September, 1994, S. Golub, review of *Is Comrade Bulgakov Dead?: Mikhail Bulgakov at the Moscow Art Theatre,* p. 125; January, 2000, S. Golub, review of *The Russian Theatre after Stalin,* pp. 947-948.

Library Journal, December, 1993, review of *Is Comrade Bulgakov Dead?,* p. 129.

New Theatre Quarterly, February, 1995, Edward Braun, review of *Is Comrade Bulgakov Dead?,* p. 94.

Slavic Review, summer, 1995, Nicholas Rzhevsky, review of *Is Comrade Bulgakov Dead?,* pp. 442-443.

Theatre Research International, summer, 1995, Vera Gottlieb, review of *Is Comrade Bulgakov Dead?,* p. 167.

Theatre Survey, November, 2000, Felicia Hardison Londre, review of *The Russian Theatre after Stalin,* p. 120.

Times Literary Supplement, March 24, 2000, Donald Rayfield, review of *The Russian Theatre after Stalin,* p. 23.*

*   *   *

SMITH, Martha Nell 1953-

PERSONAL: Born May 14, 1953, in San Angelo, TX; daughter of Earl Wesley (an attorney) and Hattie (Mozelle) Smith; married Timothy Lee Higginbotham, August 2, 1975 (divorced, September 8, 1982); partner of Marilee Lindemann. *Education:* Rutgers University, B.A. (magna cum laude), 1977, M.A., 1982, Ph.D., 1985. *Politics:* Democrat.

ADDRESSES: Office—Department of English, University of Maryland, 3101 Susquehanna Hall, College Park, MD 20742.

CAREER: Writer. Rutgers University, New Brunswick, NJ, assistant director of writing program, 1985-86; University of Maryland, College Park, assistant professor, 1986-92, associate professor, 1992-98, associate director of graduate English, 1990-94; professor of English, 1998—. Director, Maryland Institute for Technology in the Humanities, 1999—.

MEMBER: Association for Computers and the Humanities, Emily Dickinson International Society (founder), European Society for Textual Scholarship,

Free State Justice, Modern Languages Association, National Gay and Lesbian Task Force, National Leadership Honor Society, National Organization of Women, Northeastern Modern Languages Association, Omicron Delta Kappa, Society for Textual Scholarship.

AWARDS, HONORS: Woodrow Wilson Foundation fellowship, 1984; Bill Casey Award, 1987, 1988; American Council of Learned Societies grant, 1988; National Endowment for the Humanities fellowship, 1990; Networked Association fellowship, 1994.

WRITINGS:

Rowing in Eden: Rereading Emily Dickinson, University of Texas Press (Austin, TX), 1992.

(With Suzanne Juhasz and Christanne Miller) *Comic Power in Emily Dickinson,* University of Texas Press (Austin, TX), 1993.

(Editor, with Ellen Louis Hart) *Open Me Carefully: Emily Dickinson's Intimate Letters to Susan Huntington Dickinson,* Paris Press (Ashfield, MA), 1998.

Letters to Susan Huntington Dickinson, Paris Press (Ashfield, MA), 1998.

Contributor to *The Emily Dickinson Handbook,* edited by Gudrun Grabher, Roland Hagenbüchle, and Cristanne Miller, University of Massachusetts Press, 1999. Contributor to *Cambridge Companion to Emily Dickinson,* edited by Wendy Martin, Cambridge University Press, 2002. Also contributed to more than thirty journal articles on topics such as humanities computing, Emily Dickinson, and textual studies.

ADAPTATIONS: Open Me Carefully: Emily Dickinson's Intimate Letters to Susan Huntington Dickinson was adapted for stage by Madeleine Olnek.

WORK IN PROGRESS: Dickinson Electronic Archives; The Life of Susan Dickinson; Emily Dickinson: A User's Guide; Companion to Emily Dickinson; a volume of essays on humanities computing, digital studies, and the future of humanities work and publication.

SIDELIGHTS: Martha Nell Smith is an English professor and writer who was described by Christopher Benfey in a *New York Review of Books* essay as "a

ubiquitous and influential feminist scholar of [Emily] Dickinson's work." Smith's first book, *Rowing in Eden: Rereading Emily Dickinson,* was described by Heather Kirk Thomas in *American Literature* as a "fine dialogic study [that] investigates Dickinson's intense devotion to her sister-in-law, Susan Gilbert Dickinson." Thomas declared that "this scholarly study breaks new ground," and she concluded that it "raises important questions about artistic intent and creative cooperation in Dickinson's 'Letter[s] to the World.'" Another reviewer, Paula Uruburu, called *Rowing in Eden* an "original and provocative study" and affirmed, in her *Belles Lettres* assessment, that Smith "convincingly answers those who continue to ask why Dickinson did not publish more while she was alive." P. J. Ferlazzo, meanwhile, wrote in *Choice* that *Rowing in Eden* serves as "a well-argued and insightful reinterpretation of the poet."

Smith's other publications include *Open Me Carefully: Emily Dickinson's Intimate Letters to Susan Huntington Dickinson,* which she edited with Ellen Louis Hart. In a *New York Times Book Review* appraisal, Renee Tursi observed that Smith and Hart "wisely let these letters speak for themselves," and she contended that the book provides "a fresh and overdue context" for appreciating Dickinson's verse.

Smith told *CA:* "My work on Emily Dickinson's manuscripts and American poetry eventually led to the production of the *Dickinson Electonic Archives* and to the establishment of the Maryland Institute for Technology in the Humanities. Work in humanities computing, contextualized as it is by publishing crises for humanities scholarship, promises not only alternative, sustainable new models for publication of humanities work but also promises to change the way humanists work."

BIOGRAPHICAL AND CRITICAL SOURCES:

PERIODICALS

American Literature, December, 1993, Heather Kirk Thomas, review of *Rowing in Eden: Rereading Emily Dickinson,* pp. 796-797.

Belles Lettres, fall, 1993, Paula Uruburu, review of *Rowing in Eden,* pp. 54-55.

Choice, June, 1993, P. J. Ferlazzo, review of *Rowing in Eden,* p. 1628.

New York Review of Books, April 8, 1999, Christopher Benfey, "The Mystery of Emily Dickinson," pp. 39-44.

New York Times Book Review, December 13, 1998, Renee Tursi, "Two Belles of Amherst," p. 20.

Women's Review of Books, November 1999, Catherine R. Stimpson, review of *Open Me Carefully.*

*   *   *

SOHN, Amy 1973-

PERSONAL: Born 1973, in Brooklyn, NY. *Education:* Brown University, B.A.

ADDRESSES: Home—Brooklyn, NY. *Agent*—c/o Author Mail, Simon & Schuster, 1230 Avenue of the Americas, New York, NY 10020.

CAREER: Professional storyteller. Writer of column, "Female Trouble," for *New York Press;* Writer of "Naked City" column in *New York* magazine.

WRITINGS:

Run Catch Kiss, Villard Books (New York, NY), 1998.
Sex and the City: Kiss and Tell, Pocket Books (New York, NY), 2002.

Contributor of articles to *Playgirl* and *Details.*

SIDELIGHTS: Amy Sohn's *Run Catch Kiss* is a "hip first novel," declared reviewer Yvonne Crittenden in the *Toronto Sun,* "a recognizably autobiographical take on her own career writing about sex and the single girl in New York in the '90s." Sohn, who writes a column called "Naked City" for *New York* magazine, has created a novel about modern urban life among the Gen-Xers—a novel replete with graphic sexual misadventures and humor—that in may ways echoes her own column.

Protagonist Ariel Steiner travels to New York City after graduating from Brown University with hopes of setting herself up as a stage actress. Her hopes are frustrated, however, and she becomes an office temporary employee "and dating lots of freaks and losers," explained Kathleen Hughes in her *Booklist* review of the novel. Finally, she turns to writing as a release from the drudgery of her life. She writes a humorous piece recounting one of her lackluster dates and mails it to a New York paper. The editors enjoy the material so much that they offer Steiner a weekly column about her problems seeking good sex on the streets, in the bars, and in the offices of New York City. "This is convenient for Ariel," wrote Beth Gibbs in her *Library Journal* review, "because she goes through men faster than dead-end temp jobs." Soon Steiner is encountering and writing about her brief associations with "minor rock stars, heroin addicts, bipolar ex-temple-youth-group members, and lesbian beat reporters," observed *Boston Phoenix* reviewer Devra First, all of which are fictional stories she creates for her column. These "fabrications," explained Daniel Rietz in his *New York Times Book Review* critique of the novel, "once uncovered, prompt a city-wide media scandal." Steiner slowly comes to the realization that she is actually looking for the same thing that generations of women have sought before her: a normal, nice man who is a good lover and an understanding partner.

In general, reviewers enjoyed Sohn's novel. First compared Sohn's work to the hit television program *Friends* because of its concentration on the lives of "single urban twentysomethings," with the exception that it replaces the interaction with lots of casual sex. However, she added, the novel is in some ways disappointing: "It might engage your prurient interest, but what's the good of that when your heart's not in it? It's rather, as a friend pointed out, like bad sex itself: a fine one-night stand of a read." Other reviewers were more complimentary. "Sohn's writing, with its graphic sex, can be smug or comical," wrote the *Publishers Weekly* reviewer, "but she's best when imperious snugglebunny Ariel lets her guard down and confronts her humiliations with honesty and pluck." Gibbs praised Sohn's "witty language," and Hughes concluded by calling the book "a funny, honest, and enjoyable read."

BIOGRAPHICAL AND CRITICAL SOURCES:

PERIODICALS

Booklist, June 1, 1999, p. 1798.
Boston Phoenix, July 29-August 5, 1999.

Library Journal, June 15, 1999, p. 106.
New York Times Book Review, July 25, 1999, p. 16.
Publishers Weekly, May 31, 1999, p. 64.
Toronto Sun, August 29, 1999.*

*   *   *

SOLINGER, Rickie 1947-

PERSONAL: Born 1947. *Education:* Earned Ph.D. (history).

ADDRESSES: Home—Boulder, CO. *Office*—WAKEUP/ARTS 1017 Maxwell Ave., Boulder, CO 80304. *E-mail*—rsolinger@mochamail.com.

CAREER: Historian and writer.

MEMBER: Women United for Justice, Community, and Family (cofounder).

AWARDS, HONORS: Women's Caucus winner from Popular Culture Association, Emily Toth Award from American Culture Association, *New York Times Book Review* Notable Book of the Year, and Lerner-Scott Award from Organization of American Historians, all 1992, all for *Wake up Little Susie: Single Pregnancy and Race before Roe v. Wade;* Prelinger Award, 2001.

WRITINGS:

Wake up Little Susie: Single Pregnancy and Race before Roe v. Wade, Routledge (New York, NY), 1992.
The Abortionist: A Woman against the Law, Free Press (New York, NY), 1994.
(Editor) *Abortion Wars: A Half Century of Struggle, 1950-2000,* University of California Press (Berkeley, CA), 1998.
Beggars and Choosers: How the Politics of Choice Shapes Adoption, Abortion, and Welfare in the United States, Hill and Wang (New York, NY), 2001.

Contributor to books, including *Bad Mothers,* edited by Molly Ladd-Taylor and Lauri Umansky, 1998. Also contributor to periodicals, including *Gender and History, Feminist Studies,* and *Social Justice.*

WORK IN PROGRESS: A study of *King versus Smith,* the first welfare case ever heard by the U.S. Supreme Court.

SIDELIGHTS: Rickie Solinger describes herself as an independent scholar who writes regular book reviews and copyedits manuscripts for various publishing companies. She also does extensive research and has published several books that focus on issues of reproductive and economic justice for women. She took up this theme for her first book, *Wake up Little Susie: Single Pregnancy and Race before Roe v. Wade,* and collaborated with a group of artists to create room-sized art installations that give viewers a visual representation of her studies of women's reproductive rights. These installations have traveled all over the United States and have been shown in galleries on college campuses. She also created a photographic exhibition, titled "The Faces of Women in Poverty: Strength, Dignity, Determination," which she has displayed at various sites in Colorado. Also in connection with her work, Solinger is a founder of Women United for Justice, Community, and Family, a coalition based in Boulder, Colorado that is committed to welfare justice. Furthermore, she often speaks to groups on issues of poverty, welfare, and economic justice.

The title of Solinger's *Wake up Little Susie* refers to the once-popular 1958 song by the Everly Brothers that subtly suggested a sexual liaison between a young man and woman who then fall asleep together while on a date. The young man is trying to awaken the woman by relating his fears that they are going to be in trouble when they have to face their parents. Solinger takes this theme one step further, jumping to the foregone conclusion that not only did Susie and her boyfriend have sex, but also that she is pregnant. Susie, in Solinger's case, represents any young woman who may have found herself unmarried and with child. The author, after scouring reference material that she gathered about this issue during the twenty years between 1945 and 1965, discovered that there were striking differences between the treatments of middle-class, white pregnant teenagers and poor, black pregnant teenagers.

In *Wake up Little Susie* Solinger reports that, prior to 1945, unwed mothers were ostracized. They were considered bad girls, whether or not they were products of upper-class or working-class families, or if they were from black or white ethnic groups. However, after World War II, Solinger found a distinct gap formed between the races, which was produced by a shift in social attitude. Suddenly, white unwed mothers were enticed to offer their babies for adoption, thus increasing the white population by producing children for otherwise childless marriages. On the other hand, stereotypes of black sexual promiscuity spread, leaving young, African-American, unwed mothers labeled as using their pregnancies as an excuse to gain welfare benefits. Solinger argues that this dual classification was the direct result of low birth rates in the white baby adoption market and high birth rates among African Americans, which produced a fear in many white people that African Americans would overpopulate the country.

Deirdre English, reviewing *Wake up Little Susie* for the *Los Angeles Times Book Review,* found Solinger's conclusions "timely and perceptive," despite all the changes in attitude, government regulations, and publicity of positive role models of single mothers since the 1960s. English referred to such common contemporary slurs still present in commentary about unwed mothers, such as "'slut' to 'black matriarch,' 'man-hating feminist' to 'welfare cheat,' 'unwed baby' . . . to 'bastard.'" English then turned to Solinger's book and pointed out some differences that exist between the attitudes of the 1960s and today. She related how Solinger reports that, prior to the 1960s, unwed mothers were usually expelled from high school by law. Social workers, under the popular influence of Freudian theories, believed that young girls got pregnant out of anger and rebellion against their parents. Solinger gives an example of one young man, who, upon being told by his girlfriend that she was pregnant, replied, "God help me, I'm ashamed of you." Whereas white girls were encouraged, and sometimes tricked, into giving their babies away for adoption, Solinger found that "one African-American woman who tried to give her baby to a hospital for adoption was arrested for desertion." The pressures placed upon both races when faced with unwanted pregnancies led to a rise in illegal abortions, which in turn spurred a campaign for abortion reform, which culminated with the landmark Supreme Court decision on *Roe v. Wade* in 1972.

Solinger's next book, *The Abortionist: A Woman against the Law,* relates the experiences of Ruth Barnett, an abortionist who lived in Portland, Oregon,

between 1918 and 1968. Solinger contends that it was the law that prohibited abortions, not "back-street abortionists," that endangered women's lives prior to the legalization of the practice. Barnett was a legitimate doctor with a successful business. She performed forty thousand abortions without causing medical complications. However, after World War II, political pressures and needs for sensational newspaper stories began to mount, and Barnett was continuously hounded. Many women were forced to seek out less professional abortionists, or attempted to abort their fetuses themselves, when doctors such as Barnett became inaccessible. This practice led to serious injury and sometimes death. A writer for *Kirkus Reviews* described Ruth Barnett as a "compelling character" and recommended Solinger's book as an introduction to "the underdocumented history of illegal abortion" and "women's reproductive rights."

Solinger's *Beggars and Choosers: How the Politics of Choice Shapes Adoption, Abortion, and Welfare in the United States* takes the issues of unwed mothers, abortion, and race one step further. In it, Solinger takes on what some reviewers have called a feminist history of public policy on the issue of abortion since *Roe v. Wade.* One of Solinger's main themes in *Beggars and Choosers* is the change in attitude toward abortion as reflected in a shift in word selection from "abortion rights" to the less dramatic "woman's choice." Embedded in this re-phrasing is the underlying assumption, Solinger contends, that some women make good choices and other woman make bad ones. Often, Sollinger writes, this opens the door for economic and racial presumptions, causing perceived disparities between women of different socio-economic groups and races. She believes that women need to reintroduce the concept of abortion as a right.

Beggars and Choosers was recommended for women's rights advocates by Mary Jane Brustman, who reviewed the book in *Library Journal.* Brustman stated that despite the fact that there are many books that deal with the topic of "choice," Solinger's "juxtaposition of choice and class" make this book "insightful reading." Likewise, the book was also recommended by a reviewer for *Publishers Weekly,* who called it "a provocative read for any modern feminist."

BIOGRAPHICAL AND CRITICAL SOURCES:

PERIODICALS

Booklist, September 1, 1994, William Beatty, review of *The Abortionist: A Woman against the Law,* pp.

10-11; July, 2001, Mary Carroll, review of *Beggars and Choosers: How the Politics of Choice Shapes Adoption, Abortion, and Welfare in the United States*, p. 1959.

Journal of Social History, winter, 1993, Susan Harari, review of *Wake up Little Susie: Single Pregnancy and Race before Roe v. Wade*, pp. 393-395.

Kirkus Reviews, August 1, 1994, review of *The Abortionist: A Woman against the Law*, p. 1063.

Library Journal, August, 2001, Mary Jane Brustman, review of *Beggars and Choosers*, p. 138.

Los Angeles Times Book Review, June 14, 1992, Deirdre English, review of *Wake up Little Susie*, pp. 1, 8.

Nation, July 6, 1992, Eileen Boris, review of *Wake up Little Susie*, pp. 24-26; January 30, 1995, Leora Tanenbaum, review of *The Abortionist*, pp. 142-144.

Publishers Weekly, September 5, 1994, review of *The Abortionist*, p. 102; July 30, 2001, review of *Beggars and Choosers*, p. 71.*

*   *   *

SOLOMON, Evan

PERSONAL: Male. *Education:* McGill University, M.A..

ADDRESSES: Office—CBC, P.O. Box 500, Station A, Toronto, Ontario M5W 1E6, Canada. *E-mail*—futureworld@toronto.cbc.ca.

CAREER: South China Morning Post, reporter; *Shift*, cofounder and editor-in-chief, 1992-1998; Canadian Broadcasting Corporation, host of Newsworld's *Hot Type* and *Futureworld;* contributor to television, radio, and print media; consultant.

AWARDS, HONORS: Named one of the "100 Canadians to Watch," by *Macleans*, 1997.

WRITINGS:

Crossing the Distance (novel), McClelland & Stewart (Toronto, Ontario, Canada), 1999.

Columnist for *National*; contributor to periodicals.

WORK IN PROGRESS: A screenplay tentatively titled *The Deadline;* a second novel.

SIDELIGHTS: Well known among Canadian viewers as host of two popular television programs for the Canadian Broadcasting Corporation (CBC), journalist Evan Solomon attracted significant notice with the publication of his first book, *Crossing the Distance.* The novel is the story of two brothers: Jake, the host of a Jerry Springer-style television show, and Theo, an ecoterrorist hiding from the police. Each brother is suspected of a murder—Jake for the shooting of his lover, a Toronto media critic, and Theo for the tree-spiking death of a British Columbia logger. The novel follows many twists and turns as the fugitive brothers acknowledge their shared past and their present differences, culminating in Jake's decision to abandon his lucrative television career.

Crossing the Distance met with mixed reviews. *Indigo Review*'s Bronwyn Drainie found Theo a "cardboard villain," and complained that the novel "could have been a much more complex exploration of the values and pitfalls of political commitment in an age of cool media manipulation." Yet she also praised Solomon's sharp satirical stance and biting humor.

This ironic approach, Solomon told *January Magazine* interviewer Linda Richards, is "designed to reflect that channel-surfing mentality of very serious and very . . . engaged in the events you see . . . and then two seconds later you're looking at Seinfeld or something and laughing. . . . Walking down the street of engagement and disengagement. Cycling through those." Yet Solomon emphasized that *Crossing the Distance*, while often satirical and funny, is also a serious novel about familial love and the archetypal theme of redemption. "It strikes me that storytelling has always been a sacred thing," he said. This interest in the ritual power of narrative, Solomon explained, led him to pursue a Master's degree in religious studies at McGill University; this experience confirmed the young writer's reverence for story as a means of cultural expression.

Indeed, Solomon sees all writing as, at root, storytelling, and this approach characterizes his journalism as well as his fiction. "As an editor," he told Richards, "running a magazine was about documenting a story at a certain time and a certain place." As cofounder and editor-in-chief of *Shift*, a magazine about media, entertainment, and technology, Solomon had the opportunity to document "fearless people who were telling stories," such as the Dalai Lama. During Solomon's seven years with the magazine, it developed from a small fiction publication into a successful journal with a staff of thirty-three people. Solomon left his editorial post in 1998 to work full-time on his own writing. He completed a screenplay which he describes as a "dark comedy," tentatively titled *The Deadline;* it is about a writer with severe writer's block. He was also at work on a second novel.

Solomon, who has worked as a reporter in Asia and Europe, is host of CBC's *Hot Type* and *Futureworld,* programs that explore new trends in media, culture, and technology. He is a regular columnist on CBC's news-magazine, *National,* and contributes to several other television, radio, and print media. He was twice nominated for a Gemini Award as host of *Futureworld,* which received a Gemini Award for best Lifestyle Information Series, and he was listed by *Maclean's* magazine as one of the "100 Canadians to Watch." Solomon is also a consultant on issues relating to new technologies and culture.

BIOGRAPHICAL AND CRITICAL SOURCES:

OTHER

Indigo Review, http://www.indigo.ca/ (November 15, 2002), review of *Crossing the Distance.*
January Magazine, http://www.januarymagazine.com/ (November 15, 2002), interview with Evan Solomon.*

*   *   *

SOLOMONSON, Katherine M.

PERSONAL: Female. *Education:* Stanford University, Ph.D.

ADDRESSES: Office—Department of Architecture, University of Minnesota, Room 145F Arch 0811, 89 Church Street SE, Minneapolis, MN 55455. *E-mail*—solom003@umn.edu.

CAREER: Stanford University, professor; University of Minnesota, Minneapolis, associate professor of architecture.

MEMBER: Society of Architectural Historians.

WRITINGS:

The Chicago Tribune Tower Competition: Skyscraper Design and Cultural Change in the 1920s, Cambridge University Press (New York, NY), 2001.

Assistant editor of *Buildings of the United States* (Society of Architectural Historians book series).

SIDELIGHTS: Katherine M. Solomonson is an associate professor of architecture at the University of Minnesota. In *The Chicago Tribune Tower Competition: Skyscraper Design and Cultural Change in the 1920s,* she provides an in-depth look at the 1922 *Chicago Tribune*-sponsored competition to design "the most beautiful skyscraper in the world," according to Richard Longstreth in *American Studies International.* Of the 1,800 original participants, only 263 architects actually submitted drawings, and the entries were widely discussed in the architectural press in the United States and other countries. At the time, the *Chicago Tribune* published a book that provided illustrations of all the entries, and according to Longstreth, the competition was "probably the most famous staged for the design of a building ever conducted in the United States," with the exception of the 1792 competition to design the Capitol building in Washington, D.C.

At the time of the contest, skyscrapers were entering a new development phase, undergoing changes in image, scale, and form. Many competition entries reveal that architects had still not grasped the concepts of skyscraper design. On the other hand, some entrants, notably those from northern Europe, came up with innovative designs. Notably, the winning design had little influence on future architecture, while the second-place entry provided a template for American skyscrapers for the next ten years.

In addition to discussing the entries and the architecture of the time, Solomonson also considers such issues as city planning, urban design, community, the relationship between corporate symbolism and individual artistic integrity, and historicity versus modernity. She also examines the role of the *Chicago Tribune* in striking a balance between aesthetics and mass appeal. Longstreth praised Solomonson for her discussion of broader issues, as well as her "range of material presented in a rigorous and engaging narrative." In *Choice,* P. Kaufman commented that the book contains "the most complete scholarly coverage" of both the contest and the resulting building itself, while David Soltesz in *Library Journal* noted the work is "the first well-rounded examination of this important episode in the development of the urban skyline." Witold Rybczynski wrote in the *Times Literary Supplement* that Solomonson "understands the issues and writes engagingly not only about the competition itself, but about the architectural and commercial culture—both European and American—that formed its backdrop."

BIOGRAPHICAL AND CRITICAL SOURCES:

PERIODICALS

American Studies International, October, 2001, Richard Longstreth, review of *The Chicago Tribune Tower Competition: Skyscraper Design and Cultural Change in the 1920s,* p. 88.
Choice, October, 2001, P. Kaufman, review of *The Chicago Tribune Tower Competition,* p. 300.
Library Journal, May 15, 2001, David Soltesz, review of *The Chicago Tribune Tower Competition,* p. 118.
Times Literary Supplement, November 2, 2001, Witold Rybczynski, review of *The Chicago Tribune Tower Competition,* p. 13.*

*   *   *

SOMMER, Jason

PERSONAL: Male. *Education:* Brandeis University, B.A.; Stanford University, M.A.; St. Louis University, Ph.D. *Religion:* Jewish.

ADDRESSES: Home—8349 Big Bend Blvd., St. Louis, MO 63119-3136.

CAREER: Professor and poet. Fontbonne College, St. Louis, MO, professor of English and poet-in-residence, 1985—. Also taught at St. Louis University, Webster University, and University College, Dublin.

WRITINGS:

(Translator) Gabriel Rosenstock, *Portrait of the Artist as an Abominable Snowman: Selected Poems,* Forest Books (Boston, MA), 1989.
Lifting the Stone (poems), Forest Books (Boston, MA), 1991.
Other People's Troubles (poems), University of Chicago Press (Chicago, IL), 1997.

SIDELIGHTS: Jason Sommer's first collection of poems, *Lifting the Stone,* is an exploration of myth and legend, especially those based on Judaic and Biblical sources. Writing in the first person and drawing on the tradition of the Midrash, Sommer expands and explores ancient Jewish tales with a personal, modern diction. Typical first lines, such as "With me out cold on the kitchen floor" and "I have something to say that I will say here" open into what M. Butovsky, writing for *Choice,* described as "fresh and compelling readings of human experience" and "richly satisfying patterns of thought and feeling." Helpful notes provide the reader with the cultural and historical context of the tales and poems.

Sommer is the son of a Holocaust survivor, and in his second book, *Other People's Troubles,* he writes about the Holocaust, about how history marks people's lives, and about how we can live with the horrors of history. His characters are Holocaust survivors who "speak through" him or to him; he records their stories in poems that are both troubling and telling.

BIOGRAPHICAL AND CRITICAL SOURCES:

PERIODICALS

Choice, January, 1992, p. 748.
New Republic, May 31, 1980, p. 26; July 19, 1980, p. 34.
Ploughshares, winter, 1997, H. L. Hix, review of *Other People's Troubles,* p. 217.
Prairie Schooner, fall, 2000, Marcus Cafagna, review of *Other People's Troubles,* p. 177.*

SONNEMAN, Eve 1950-

PERSONAL: Born January 14, 1950, in Chicago, IL; *Education:* University of Illinois, Urbana, IL, B.F.A., 1967; University of New Mexico, Albuquerque, M.A., 1969.

ADDRESSES: Home—684 Avenue of the Americas, New York, NY 10010. *Agent*—Castelli Graphics, 4 East 77th Street, New York, NY 10021; Rudiger Schottle, Martiusstrasse 7, 8 Munich 40, Germany; Texas Gallery, 2439 Bissonet, Houston, TX; Galerie Farideh Cadot, 11 rue du Jura, 75013 Paris, France.

CAREER: Freelance photographer, since 1969. Cooper Union for the Advancement of Science and Art, New York, lecturer, 1970-71, 1975-78, 1985; Rice University, Houston, visiting artist, 1971-72; City University of New York, lecturer, 1972-75; School of Visual Arts, New York, lecturer, 1975-89. *Exhibitions:* Works included in permanent collections at Museum of Modern Art, New York, NY; Metropolitan Museum of Art, New York, NY; Princeton University, Princeton, NJ; Art Institute of Chicago, Chicago, IL; Museum of Fine Arts, Houston, TX; de Menil Foundation, Houston, TX; Centre Georges Pompidou, Paris, France; Bibliothèque Nationale, Paris, France; Rheinisches Landesmuseum, Bonn, Germany; National Gallery of Australia, Canberra, Australia; Museum of Contemporary Art, Los Angeles, CA; National Gallery of Australia, Canberra, Australia; Center for Creative Photography, Tucson, AZ; Dallas Museum of Fine Arts, Dallas, TX; San Francisco Museum of Modern Art, San Francisco, CA; Le Nouveau Musée, Lyon, France; Fondation Cartier pour l'art contemporain, Paris, France; and Toppan Museum, Tokyo, Japan. Solo exhibitions include *A Survey,* Cooper Union, New York, NY (traveled to the Media Center, Rice University, Houston, TX, 1971), 1970; Art Museum of South Texas, Corpus Christi, 1972; Whitney Museum Art Resources Center, New York, NY, 1973; *Coney Island Series,* The Texas Gallery, Houston, 1974; *Subway Series,* The Texas Gallery, Houston, 1975; Bard College, Annandale-on-Hudson, New York, NY, 1976; *Observations:—Mile in the Sky,* Castelli Gallery, New York, NY, 1976; *New Work,* Artemisia Gallery, Chicago, IL, 1977; *New Work,* Galerie Farideh Cadot, Paris, France, 1977; *New Work,* The Texas Gallery, Houston, 1977; *New Work,* Diane Brown Gallery, Washington, DC, 1977; *A Survey,* College of Wooster,

OH, 1977; *New Work,* Castelli Gallery, New York, NY, 1978; *Color Work,* Thomas Segal Gallery, Boston, MA, 1979; Three Americans, Moderna Museet, Stockholm, Sweden (with Lewis Baltz and Mark Cohen; traveled to the Aalborg Künstmuseum, Denmark, and Künstpavillionen, Esbjerg, Denmark, Tranegarden, Gentofte, Copenhagen, Denmark, and Henie-Onstad Museum, Oslo, Norway, 1980), 1979; *Color Work,* Rudiger Schottle Gallery, Munich, Germany, 1979; *Color Work,* Le Nouveau Musée, Lyon, France, 1980; *Five-Year Color Show,* Contemporary Arts Center, New Orleans, LA (traveled to the Contemporary Arts Center, Cincinnati, OH), 1980: *Work from 1968-78,* Minneapolis Institute of Arts, Minneapolis, MN, 1980; *New Work and Polaroids,* Galerie Farideh Cadot, Paris, France, 1980; The Texas Gallery, Houston, 1980; *Polaroid Work,* Young Hoffman Gallery, Chicago, IL, 1980; *New Work,* Francoise Lambert Gallery, Milan, Italy, 1980; *New Work: New York,* Castelli Gallery, New York, NY, 1980; *Future Memories,* Cirrus Gallery, Los Angeles, CA, 1981; *Work from 1968-78,* Tucson Museum of Art, Tucson, AZ, 1981; Galerie Peter Noser, Zurich, Switzerland, 1981; Burton Gallery, Toronto, Ontario, Canada, 1981; Locus Solus, Genoa, Italy, 1981; Leo Castelli Gallery, New York, NY, 1982; The Texas Gallery, Houston, 1982; Hudson River Museum, New York, NY, 1982; Cirrus Gallery, Los Angeles, CA, 1982; Galerie Farideh Cadot, Paris, France, 1983; The Photographers' Gallery, London, England, 1983; Musée de Toulon, Toulon, France, 1983; Centre Georges Pompidou, Paris, France, 1984; Leo Castelli Gallery, New York, NY, 1984; Schloss Mickeln, Düsseldorf, Germany, 1984; Gloria Luria Gallery, Miami, FL, 1984; Mattingly Baker Gallery, Dallas, TX, 1984; Santa Barbara Art Museum, CA, 1984; The Texas Gallery, Houston, 1984; Museum of Modern Art, San José, Costa Rica, 1985; Galerie Peter Noser, Zurich, Switzerland, 1985; Gloria Luria Gallery, Miami, FL, 1985; Galleria Francoise Lambert, Milan, Italy 1985; Galerie Imago, Cologne, Germany 1985; Gallery for Fine Photography, New Orleans, LA, 1985; Castelli Graphics, New York, NY, 1986; Tyler School of Art, Philadelphia, PA, 1986; Peter Noser Galerie, Zurich, Switzerland, 1988; Elizabeth Galasso Gallery, Ossining, NY, 1988; A Gallery for Fine Photography, New Orleans, LA, 1989; Cirrus Gallery, Los Angeles, CA, 1989; Jones Troyer Fitzpatrick Gallery, Washington, DC, 1989; Lieberman & Saul Gallery, New York, 1989; Gloria Luria Gallery, Miami, FL, 1990; Zabriskie Gallery, New York, NY, 1990; Grand Central Terminal, New York, NY, 1991; Charles Cowles Gallery, New York, NY, 1992; Jones Troyer Fitzpatrick Gallery, Washington, DC, 1993;

Cirrus Gallery, Los Angeles, CA, 1993, and The Art Museum of New Mexico, Albuquerque, 1995. Group exhibitions include *Recent Acquisitions,* Museum of Modern Art, New York, NY, 1969, *Bookworks,* Museum of Modern Art, New York, NY, 1977, *Mirrors and Windows: American Photography since 1960,* Museum of Modern Art, New York, NY (toured the United States, 1978-80), 1978, *Attitudes: American Photography in the 1970s,* Santa Barbara Museum of Art, Santa Barbara, CA, 1979; *One of a Kind,* Corcoran Gallery of Art, Washington, D.C., 1980; *Counterparts: Form and Emotion in Photographs,* Metropolitan Museum of Art, New York, NY (traveled to the Contemporary Arts Center, Cincinnati, OH; Dallas Museum of Fine Art, Dallas, TX; San Francisco Museum of Modern Art, San Francisco, CA: Corcoran Gallery, Washington, DC), 1982; *Photography in America 1910-83,* Tampa Museum, Tampa, FL, 1983; *Exposed and Developed,* National Museum of American Art, Washington, DC, 1984; *Rare Books of the Twentieth Century,* Bibliothèque Nationale, Paris, France, 1985; *Photography and Painting 1946-86,* Los Angeles County Museum of Art, Los Angeles, CA, 1987; *Saletta Conumale de Sposizone,* Françoise Lambert Galleria, Milan, Italy, 1988; *Le SAGA 88-FIAC Editions,* Grand Palais, Paris, France, 1988; *Artist Books,* Victoria and Albert Museum, London, England, 1989; *The Imaginary Library,* National Gallery of Canada, Ottawa, Ontario, Canada, 1991; National Museum of Women in the Arts, Washington, DC, 1991; *Illuminations,* Museum of Modern Art at Pfizer Inc., New York, NY, 1992; *Contemporary Collection,* Centre Georges Pompidou, Paris, France, 1992; *A Private Collection,* Galerie Cadot, Paris, France, 1993; and *Flowers,* Museum of Modern Art, New York, NY, 1994.

AWARDS, HONORS: Boskop Foundation grant, New York, 1969; National Endowment for the Arts awards, 1972, 1978; Institute for Art and Urban Resources grant, New York, 1977; Polaraid Corporation grant for work in Polavision, 1978; Polaroid Corporation grants, 1988, 1989; Fondation Cartier pour l'Art Contemporain, Paris, France, 1989.

WRITINGS:

Real Time, 1968-1974, Printed Matter (New York, NY), 1976.
Roses Are Read, text by Klaus Kertess, Editions Génération (Colombes, France), 1982.
America's Cottage Gardens, text by Patricia Thorpe, Random House (New York, NY), 1990.
Where Birds Live, Random House (New York, NY), 1992.
(With Lawrence Weiner) *How to Touch What,* Power-House (New York, NY), 2000.

SIDELIGHTS: New York photographer and painter Eva Sonneman is best known for her photographic pairs, or diptychs, which she began creating while a graduate student at the University of New Mexico. More than thirty museum collections worldwide house her creations.

Poet David Shapiro wrote, "She is a painterly photographer [who] reminds us that photography, as with Man Ray and Rodchenko, must never be denigrated as mere materiality."

Sonneman, in an interview with Rick Cunniff in *artcritical.com,* explained that her photography and paining approaches differ. "In photography I'm very interested in a tiny moment of gesture or innuendo and of change," said Sonneman, who began taking photographs in her late teens. "In painting I'm trying to grasp a larger universal feeling about nature, atmosphere, color, which is a much broader issue."

Her early black-and-white diptychs depicted sequential events or items juxtaposed. A writer noted in *Contemporary Photographers,* "Her work characteristically contains pairs or quartets of images having some formal or thematic relationship to one another."

Sonneman's professional breakthrough came in 1971 at the Young Photographers exhibition at New York's Museum of Modern Art. Sonneman, during that time, experimented further with shifting perspective, chronology, and the juxtaposition of color and black-and-white images. Her "Coney Island" series exemplifies this process, presenting beach and street scenes, positioned within a quadruple image; *Observations:—Mile in the Sky,* a one-woman show of diptychs taken at the World Trade Center during the bicentennial festivities, followed in 1976.

In 1980 she presented paired works shot in Europe and the United States over two years. The *Contemporary Photographers* writer commented, "They demonstrate that photography need not be either a cold document of reality or a poetic evocation of the world processed through the photographer's manipulative intelligence."

Sonneman has written four books of photographic work: *Real Time, Roses Are Read, America's Cottage Gardens, Where Birds Live,* and, with Lawrence Wiener, *How to Touch What: An Artists Book.*

Where Birds Live studies birds in flight and related aviary matters. Ben Lifson wrote in *Artforum,* "As a photographer Sonneman is an able and often an affecting maker of lyrical sketches. . . . Indeed, in her earliest street work the figures often have the look of rapid, deft brushwork. In *Where Birds Live,* the strongest pictures in this style are of birds themselves." In *How to Touch What: An Artists Book,* Sonneman collaborates with Weiner, known for his conceptualism and trademark lettering on walls.

BIOGRAPHICAL AND CRITICAL SOURCES:

BOOKS

Contemporary Photographers, third edition, St. James Press (Detroit, MI), 1996.
Eve Sonneman, exhibition catalogue, text by Jeffrey Deitch (San Jose, Costa Rica), 1985.
Eve Sonneman: Work from 1968-81 (exhibition catalogue), text by Bruce Kurtz (New York, NY), 1982.
Gauss, Kathleen McCarthy, and Andy Grundberg, *Photography and Art 1946-1986* (exhibition catalogue), [Los Angeles, CA], 1987.
Green, Jonathan, *American Photography: A Critical History, 1945 to the Present,* H. N. Abrams (New York, NY), 1984.
Rosenblum, Naomi, *A History of Women Photographers,* Abbeville Press (New York, NY), 1994.
Rosenblum, Naomi, *A World History of Photography,* Abbeville Press (New York, NY), 1984.
Szarkowski, John, *Mirrors and Windows: American Photography since 1960* (exhibition catalogue), Museum of Modern Art (New York, NY), 1978.

PERIODICALS

Artforum International, summer, 1993, Ben Lifson, "Where Birds Live," pp. 102-103.

OTHER

Artcritical.com, http://www.artcritical.com/ (summer, 2002), Rick Cunniff, "Studio Visit, Eve Sonneman Interview."
Bruce Silverstein Web site, http://www.brucesilverstein.com/ (spring, 2002), Eve Sonneman/Diptych Exhibit Description.*

* * *

SPINK, J(ohn) G(eorge) Taylor 1888-1962

PERSONAL: Born November 6, 1888, in St. Louis, MO; died following a heart attack December 7, 1962; son of Charles Claude (a publisher) and Marie (Taylor) Spink; married Blanche Keene, April 15, 1914; children: two.

CAREER: Publisher. Worked variously as a stock boy for the Rawlings Sporting Goods Company, as a copy boy in the sports department of the *St. Louis Post-Dispatch,* and as correspondent for the *New York Morning Telegraph; Sporting News,* 1903-62, publisher, 1914-62.

AWARDS, HONORS: Bill Slocum Memorial Award, Baseball Writers Association of America, 1962, for "long and meritorious service to baseball"; J. G. Taylor Spink Award for outstanding baseball writing was created in his honor by Baseball Writers Association of America; Spink was its first recipient in 1962.

WRITINGS:

Judge Landis and Twenty-five Years of Baseball, Crowell (New York, NY), 1947.
(Compiler with Paul A. Rickart and Ray J. Naymer) *Daguerreotypes: Hall of Fame Members and Other Immortals,* C. C. Spink (St. Louis, MO), 1961.

Author of *Sporting News Record Book.* Columns included "Three and One—Looking Them over with J. G. Taylor Spink" and "Looping the Loops."

SIDELIGHTS: For nearly fifty years, J. G. Taylor Spink was publisher of the *Sporting News,* often referred to as the "Bible of Baseball," a main source of news, features, statistics, and opinion for fans, umpires, owners, and the sports media. Spink's paternal grandfather, William Spink, had been a legislator in Canada, and his grandmother, Frances Woodbury Spink, came to the United States during the Civil War and raised their eight children, including Charles, Spink's father, and his uncles, Billy and Al. Al launched the *Sporting News* two years before Spink was born, and Charles, who had been homesteading in South Dakota, came to St. Louis to manage the startup. After he married Marie Taylor, her father, a businessman, invested in the new publication. Charles was assisted by statistician Ernest J. Lanigan in making the paper a success. They started by publishing minor league statistics, the first step in their entrenchment in the world of baseball.

Spink became involved in the family business while still in grammar school when his father gave him the task of selling four copies of the paper each week. He doubled his quota and sold copies of the *Saturday Evening Post* as well. He had little interest in school, and when he was in the tenth grade, his parents allowed him to drop out, whereupon he worked for the Rawlings Sporting Goods Company as a stock boy and for the *St. Louis Post-Dispatch* as a copy boy. His father let him experience the working world for one year before bringing him into the family business, over which Charles now had control. Al, who had become financially depleted in his attempt to promote a theatrical production, was forced to sell his stock to his brother. In 1899 Charles added the *Sporting Goods Dealer* to their publications list, a trade magazine that was very profitable. Two toy-focused publications were established then sold to another publisher.

Spink was expected to work seven days a week and wrote for both the *Sporting News* and the *Sporting Goods Dealer.* In 1909 he began to publish the *Sporting News Record Book.* He also worked part-time as the St. Louis correspondent for the *New York Morning Telegraph,* a theatrical paper edited by former lawman Bat Masterson, for which he covered stage productions when they came to town. What he longed for was to be the official scorer for the World Series, but he was unqualified and not yet old enough. His persistence in continually making this request of American League president Byron "Ban" Johnson paid

off, particularly in view of the support the League had received from Charles when it was newly formed. Spink held the position for ten years.

Immediately after Spink's wedding to Blanche Keene, Charles died, and at the age of twenty-five, Spink found himself head of the family business. At the time, the paper employed only two correspondents hired by Charles: W. H. Rankin, who wrote from New York, and H. G. Merrill, who covered the minor leagues from Wilkes-Barre, Pennsylvania. Spink hired enough new correspondents to cover each of the major league teams. He also reversed the paper's position of covering the rogue Federal League which later collapsed in 1915. The *Sporting Life,* the country's only other national baseball weekly, ceased publication in 1917.

Times were difficult for the *Sporting News.* World War I siphoned off players and readers, and circulation dropped. When Spink heard that U.S. soldiers stationed in Europe were passing around copies of the paper, he convinced American League president Johnson to buy and distribute 150,000 copies to the troops overseas. Club owners added 25,000 copies, and Spink increased the number by another 5,000 with the 1917 Christmas issue. The price of the paper had to be raised twice due to wartime shortages, but the *Sporting News* survived.

Spink was involved in the scandal that surrounded the defeat of the Chicago White Sox by the Cincinnati Reds in the 1919 World Series. He cooperated fully with Johnson in investigating allegations that the win was the result of a fix—that White Sox ballplayers had been paid by professional gamblers to lose the series. The eight accused men, dubbed the "Black Sox," were eventually acquitted, but they still were banned from baseball by the newly appointed first baseball commissioner Kenesaw Mountain Landis. When the dust settled baseball emerged cleansed, and the popularity of the *Sporting News* became stronger than ever. But Landis never quite forgave Spink for his alliance with Johnson during the troubles with the Sox. In 1921 he removed Spink from his position as scorer for the World Series. Spink remained friendly to Landis in print until the 1923 World Series, when an editorial in the *Sporting News* questioned his giving the proceeds of a tie game to charity. Landis responded publicly to the paper's outrage, and the paper retorted. It also continued to be financially successful, due in part to the increased interest in baseball because of players like Babe Ruth.

The popularity of the *Sporting News* widened even more when Spink hired baseball writers from all over the country to contribute their regional coverage. Many of these articles were little more than reprints of pieces that had run in their local papers, but because the *Sporting News* was national nearly all of the writing was fresh to its readers.

In 1931 Edgar G. Brands became editor of the paper and thereafter wrote all editorial opinion for the *Sporting News*. One of his first positions was that major league teams would never play at night. However, when the Cincinnati Reds played the first night game in 1935, the paper gave the new practice the editorial stamp of approval. "Spink and Brands were no crusaders, especially if circulation was at stake," wrote Steven P. Gietschier in *Dictionary of Literary Biography*. "Instead, they often used their editorial space to pick at frivolous matters, such as asking fans to return home-run balls hit into the stands because 'baseballs cost money' or suggesting that scorecard printers should put the name of the home team at the bottom of the scorecard instead of at the top."

Landis and the paper continued to exchange barbs, but in 1941, when A. G. Spalding and Brothers Company made the decision to stop publication of their annual baseball guide, Landis agreed to give Spink the contract. When World War II broke out, Spink and the leagues and club owners collaborated in sending out a special overseas tabloid edition of the *Sporting News* to the men and women serving in Europe and the Pacific. Circulation of this issue reached nearly one million during the World Series. Spink printed letters of appreciation in the paper and added coverage of army and navy baseball. In order to make the paper more desirable to fans of sports other than baseball, Spink began covering college and professional football in the fall of 1942. Before the year had ended, he added hockey and basketball. The tabloid format had been so popular in the overseas edition that he used it for the stateside edition.

With the end of World War II, attendance at games surged, and baseball got a huge boost, as did the circulation of the *Sporting News* when veterans who had received it while on duty returned as loyal readers. Spink continued to support the owners of the major league clubs when Jorge Pasqual and his brother tried to convince players to join a third major league in Mexico and when Boston labor organizer Robert Mur-

phy tried to unionize players as the American Baseball Guild. However, the paper's editorials did reflect problems that needed to be addressed.

From 1942 the *Sporting News* had taken a stand against integrating the major leagues. The position was that it would be difficult for black players and would also compromise Negro League ball. When Jackie Robinson was signed to play with the Montreal Royals, the farm club of the Brooklyn Dodgers, in 1945, the paper editorialized that he was being unfairly placed in competition with younger players, would be expected to demonstrate skills beyond his ability, and would be "confronted with the . . . social rebuffs and the competitive heartaches which are inevitable for a Negro trail-blazer." Further the *Sporting News* criticized white players who reacted negatively to the signing, calling these responses "unsportsmanlike, and, above all else, un-American." The *Sporting News* followed Robinson through his second spring training and declared that he was ready for the big leagues, even though Dodgers manager Branch Rickey held back with his intentions. When Robinson was transferred to Brooklyn, the newspaper covered the event with a full article reflecting its approval. Later that year the *Sporting News* awarded Robinson the Rookie of the Year Award.

By the 1950s Spink had earned such a reputation that other sportswriters wrote about him in other publications. "Spink's personality and work habits fairly begged for such treatment," noted Gietschier. "He was regarded as a character, the living embodiment of the stereotypical publisher: gruff, demanding, competitive, impatient, and dedicated to getting the story. Most of those who exalted Spink had weathered his personal and professional demeanor firsthand when they had been asked to write for the *Sporting News*. Taking an assignment from Spink and then completing it to his specifications and on his deadline was often an exasperating, exhausting, and frustrating ordeal. Writers did not shy away, though, perhaps because Spink, for all his bluster, demanded of them their best work." "He insisted always that his publications be as perfect as mind, ingenuity, and hard work could make them," wrote Spink's assistant Carl T. Felker in *Taylor Spink: The Legend and the Man*. His work ethic resulted in many scoops for the paper, and his inside information sometimes prevented events from occurring, as when Spink told Stan Musial in 1958 that the St. Louis Cardinals were planning to trade him. Musial threatened to retire, and his trade was canceled.

By 1961 Spink's health was failing. He suffered from emphysema, but he continued to put in long hours at his office and brought his work home with him. Although many in the business felt that he was deserving of being named to the Baseball Hall of Fame, journalists were not eligible for this honor. Since the Hall of Fame would not change its rules, the Baseball Writers Association of America (BBWAA) did the next best thing by giving Spink the Bill Slocum Memorial Award for his service to baseball in January 1962. After the World Series that same year, the BBWAA established the J. G. Taylor Spink Award for outstanding baseball writing, which is presented annually at the Hall of Fame ceremony. Spink was the first recipient.

Spink, who was spending the winter in Arizona, was too ill to accept the Slocum Award. He sent his son, Charles Claude Johnson Spink, to New York for the presentation. His son also took over as president, treasurer, and publisher of his father's company, while Spink assumed the title of chairman of the board. On December 7, Spink called in to check on the progress of the issue coming to deadline. A few hours later, he died of a heart attack. Felker wrote his full obituary in the next issue, and said, in part, that "by any standard of measurement, Taylor Spink was a great personality. In whatever field of action he had been placed, he would have been a leader by the sheer force of his character, his ability, and his extraordinary energy. Circumstances made him a publisher, with baseball as his chief arena. And in that field, he was unique, without a peer."

BIOGRAPHICAL AND CRITICAL SOURCES:

BOOKS

Dictionary of Literary Biography, Volume 241: *American Sportswriters and Writers on Sport,* Gale (Detroit, MI), 2001, pp. 274-282.

Felker, Carl T., *Taylor Spink: The Legend and the Man,* Sporting News (St. Louis, MO), 1973.

Reidenbaugh, Lowell, *The Sporting News First Hundred Years, 1886-1986,* Sporting News (St. Louis, MO), 1985.

PERIODICALS

Saturday Evening Post, June 20, 1942, Stanley Frank, "Bible of Baseball."

Sporting News, May 21, 1936, Ernst J. Lanigan, "The *Sporting News* Spans Half a Century with Baseball," pp. 1A, 6A; March, 1966, Frederick G. Lieb, "80 Candles Dot the *Sporting News* Cake," pp. 21-24.

Sports Illustrated, February, 1961, Gerald Holland, "Taylor Spink Is First-Class," pp. 58-66.

University of Missouri Bulletin, May 3, 1951, J. G. Taylor Spink, "Sports Writing and Editing: An Address, 43rd Annual Journalism Week, School of Journalism, University of Missouri."

Sporting News, December 22, 1962, Carl T. Felker, "J. G. Taylor Spink, 1882-1962," pp. 13-16, 20.*

*   *   *

STANFORD, Craig (Britton) 1956-

PERSONAL: Born 1956. *Education:* University of California—Berkeley, Ph.D, 1990.

ADDRESSES: Office—Department of Anthropology, University of Southern California, Los Angeles, CA 90089-0032; *E-mail*—stanford@usc.edu.

CAREER: University of Southern California, Los Angeles, CA, professor of anthropology, 1992—. Taught at University of Michigan.

AWARDS, HONORS: University of Southern California Raubenheimer Junior Faculty award, 1996; Phi Kappa Phi Recognition award, 2000.

WRITINGS:

The Capped Langur in Bangladesh: Behavioral Ecology and Reproductive Tactics, Karger (New York, NY), 1991.

Chimpanzee and Red Colobus: The Ecology of Predator and Prey, Harvard University Press (Cambridge, MA), 1998.

The Hunting Apes: Meat Eating and the Origins of Human Behavior, Princeton University Press (Princeton, NJ), 1999.

Significant Others: The Ape-Human Continuum and the Quest for Human Stature, Basic Books (New York, NY), 2001.

Meat-Eating and Human Evolution, Oxford University Press (New York, NY), 2001.

SIDELIGHTS: Craig Stanford based his first book, *The Capped Langur in Bangladesh: Behavioral Ecology and Reproductive Tactics,* on his Ph.D. thesis on the capped langur (Presbytis pileata) of Bangladesh, an animal largely unknown before Stanford's study. The eight chapters cover the langurs' behavior, population fluctuations and feeding patterns. For more than fifteen months Stanford studied five social groups of langurs in the same area for 2,000 hours. In his review for *American Anthropologist,* Thomas Struhsaker acknowledged the study's importance to understanding langurs specifically and Colobinae in general. But he cited several problems with the book. He felt Stanford should have differentiated between chemically different plant foods, "for example, ripe versus unripe fruit," as did many publications. He also called Stanford's citation of the literature inaccurate: "This becomes especially important when Stanford attempts to compare his results with other studies and develop a synthesis." In one instance, according to Struhsaker, Stanford says no published information on leadership behavior in arboreal forest monkeys exists; he later cites three works that have that information. Stanford followed this book with a study of primates, *Chimpanzee and Red Colobus: The Ecology of Predator and Prey.*

In *The Hunting Apes: Meat Eating and the Origins of Human Behavior,* Stanford argues that hunting large animals shaped human social behavior and intelligence. Taking studies on fossil records and contemporary hunters, and his own on chimpanzees, he addresses the "Man the Hunter" model from the 1960s which field research and feminist anthropology in the 1970s refuted. Stanford synthesizes some of the new research to reaffirm the "Man the Hunter" idea. Meat sharing, he claims, may represent "the essential recipe for the expansion of the human brain." Males, he adds, also exchange food for mating opportunities. He concludes that "the ability to make use of meat for nutritional purposes is facilitated in a social primate by a relatively high degree of intelligence, because of the complexities of sharing the meat of other animals." The book is written for general readers.

According to Deborah L. Manzolillo in the *Times Literary Supplement,* Stanford's book is too comprehensive, its arguments flawed. Manzolillo found Stanford's explanation of the hunting techniques of chimpanzee communities "puzzling" because he doesn't explain how female chimpanzees, who rarely hunt, transport food. She wrote, "Individually, most of the examples Stanford gives are based in fact, and lead to sensible arguments. But fitting them together is problematic. Perhaps he would have been more successful if he had pared down the scope of his book, while at the same time pursing some of his arguments more fully and providing more detail to back them up." A *Publishers Weekly* critic, on the other hand, found the book's arguments suitable for general readers: "Stanford's ideas, while controversial, are amply documented by behavioral studies of non-human primates, anthropological studies of a number of human societies and archeological studies of early and pre-humans."

BIOGRAPHICAL AND CRITICAL SOURCES:

PERIODICALS

American Anthropologist, December, 1992.
American Journal of Human Biology, May-June, 2002, Curtis W. Marean, review of *Meat-Eating and Human Evolution,* p. 411.
Booklist, June 1, 2001, Ray Olson, review of *Significant Others: The Ape-Human Continuum and the Quest for Human Stature,* p. 1807.
Choice, December, 2001, M. S. Grace, review of *Significant Others,* p. 712; February, 2002, M. J. O'Brien, review of *Meat-Eating and Human Evolution,* p. 1086.
Los Angeles Times, December 9, 2001, Douglas Foster, review of *Significant Others,* p. R-5.
Psychology Today, November-December, 2001, review of *Significant Others,* p. 77.
Publishers Weekly, February 8, 1999.
Times Literary Supplement, May 7, 1999.*

*   *   *

SUSANNA (i NADAL), Àlex 1957-

PERSONAL: Born 1957, in Barcelona, Spain.

ADDRESSES: Agent—Columna Edicions, Provença 260, 6A, 08008 Barcelona, Spain.

CAREER: Poet.

AWARDS, HONORS: Premio Miguel de Palol, 1980, for *Memoria del cos.*

WRITINGS:

POETRY

Abandonada ment, Susanna (Barcelona, Spain), 1977.

Memoria del cos, La Gaia Ciencia (Barcelona, Spain), 1980.

El dies antics, Edicions del Mall (Barcelona, Spain), 1982.

De l'home quan no hi veu, Edicions del Mall (Barcelona, Spain), 1982.

El darrer sol, Edicions Proa (Barcelona, Spain), 1985.

(With Jaime Bofil y Ferro) *Poetes Catalans moderns* (criticism), Columna (Barcelona, Spain), 1986.

(Editor, with Fina Figuerolo and Rosa Planella), *El Noucentisme* (criticism), Columna (Barcelona, Spain), 1986.

Palau d'hivern, Columna (Barcelona, Spain), 1987.

(With Joan Maragall i Noble, Rafael Santos Torroella, and Antoni Mari), *Figuracions: del 25 d'octubre al 20 de novembre de 1988: Sala Pares* (exhibition catalogue), Sala Pares, (Barcelona, Spain), 1988.

Quadern venecia, Destino (Barcelona, Spain), 1989.

(Editor) *Homenatge a T. S. Eliot* (criticism), Acta-Fundacion per a les Idees i les Arts (Barcelona, Spain), 1989.

Les anelles dels anys, Ediciones Proa (Barcelona, Spain), 1991.

(With Jauma Vidal-Alcover, Montse Palau, and Magi Sunyer i Molne), *Antollogicia poetica,* Columna (Barcelona, Spain), 1991.

(With Jordi Maragall i Noble, Jordi Llimona, and J. Serra Llimona), *J. Serra Llimona,* Ediciones Mayo (Barcelona, Spain), 1991.

(With Pere Garcia-Fons and Jordi Pere Cerda) *Garcia-Fons,* Columna Edicions (Barcelona, Spain), 1992.

(With Tomàs Garcés and Joan Triadù) *Tomàs Garcés,* Generalitat de Catalunya (Barcelona, Spain), 1992.

Boscos i ciudats, Columna (Barcelona, Spain), 1994.

Quadern de Fornells (novel), Columna Edicions (Barcelona, Spain), 1995.

(Editor) Jordi Sarsanedas, *Mites* (novel), illustrated by Albert Rafols-Casamada and Maria Girona, Columna (Barcelona, Spain), 1995.

(With N. Galià) *N. Galià,* Columna (Tarragona, Spain), 1995.

Àlex Susanna, Generalitat de Catalunya (Barcelona, Spain), 1996.

Entering the Cold: Translations from the Catalan, translated by members of the European Network for the Translations of Contemporary Poetry, Poetry Ireland (Dublin, Ireland), 1998.

Quadern d'ombres, Ediciones de Bronce, (Barcelona, Spain), 1999.

Suite de Gelida, Edicions Proa (Barcelona, Spain), 2001.

Casas y cuerpos, Fundacion Jorge Guillen (Vallodolid, Spain), 2001.

Author of prologue to *Las acacias salvajes* by Maria Manent, 1986.

BIOGRAPHICAL AND CRITICAL SOURCES:

PERIODICALS

Insula, May, 1985, Antonio Jiménez Millán, "Sobre poesía catalana actual: La obra de Alex Susanna," pp. 1, 12.*

*   *   *

SUTCLIFFE, Jane 1957-

PERSONAL: Born May 25, 1957, in Providence, RI; daughter of Chester and Clarice (Bergeron) McCormick; married Skip Sutcliffe, (an engineer) May 30, 1981; children: John, Michael. *Education:* University of Connecticut, B.A., 1979; Pennsylvania State University, M.S., 1980. *Religion:* Episcopal.

ADDRESSES: Home—128 Eaton Rd., Tolland, CT 06084. *E-mail*—jane872@aol.com.

CAREER: Author.

MEMBER: Society of Children's Book Writers and Illustrators.

AWARDS, HONORS: Patriotic Feature of the Year, *Highlights for Children,* for article "The Tree That Saved History."

WRITINGS:

Babe Didrikson Zaharias, All-around Athlete, Carolrhoda Books (Minneapolis, MN), 2000.

Jesse Owens, Carolrhoda Books (Minneapolis, MN), 2000.

Paul Revere, Lerner Books (Minneapolis, MN), 2002.

Amelia Earhart, Lerner Books (Minneapolis, MN), 2002.

Helen Keller, Carolrhoda Books (Minneapolis, MN), 2002.

Milton Hershey, Lerner Books (Minneapolis, MN), 2003.

Chief Joseph of the Nez Perce, Lerner Books (Minneapolis, MN), 2003.

Contributor of articles to various periodicals, including *Appleseeds, Boys' Life,* and *Highlights for Children.*

WORK IN PROGRESS: Picture book biographies of Sacagawea, St. Paul, and Tom Thumb; an early reader biography of John F. Kennedy.

SIDELIGHTS: Jane Sutcliffe told *CA:* "I grew up in Providence, Rhode Island, in the days when library fines were a penny. One of my earliest memories was my weekly trip to the local library with my father. I've loved books ever since. My childhood was fairly average. In fact, it was so average, all my friends had pretty much the same childhood. We all went to the same school, and attended the same church on Sundays. Our mothers all called us home to supper at the same time. On weekends we visited grandmothers and aunties who spoke a different language when they didn't want us to understand.

"To live any differently seemed exciting and exotic to me. I began to read biographies, just to get a peek at how other people lived day to day, in different times and places. When I was ten or eleven, I spent a whole year reading nothing but biographies. I was never interested in sports much, with one exception—the Olympics. Everything about the Olympics appealed to me—the competition, the glory, the pageantry, the honor. So I guess it was no accident that, years later, when I became a children's writer, my first two books were biographies of Olympic athletes. I was doing my research even then."

Sutcliffe went on to say that although she was interested in writing and even went to college and obtained a communications degree, she did not begin writing until after she had her two sons, John and Michael. "Having children just unlocked my creative spirit. That's why I dedicated my first book to them."

BIOGRAPHICAL AND CRITICAL SOURCES:

PERIODICALS

Horn Book Guide, fall, 2001, Cindy Lombardo, review of *Jesse Owens,* p. 399.

School Library Journal, June, 2000, Jean Gaffney, review of *Babe Didrikson Zaharias: All-around Athlete,* p. 137.

*   *   *

SUTCLIFFE, Katherine 1952-

PERSONAL: Born September 20, 1952, in Texas; married; husband's name, Neil (a geologist); children: Bryan, Rachel, Lauren, Jennifer. *Hobbies and other interests:* Raising and showing Arabian horses, travel.

ADDRESSES: Agent—Evan Fogelman, Fogelman Literary Agency, 7515 Greenville Ave., Suite 712, Dallas, TX 75231; fax: 214-361-9553. *E-mail*—katherine@katherinesutcliffe.net.

CAREER: Writer. Computer personnel headhunter; *As the World Turns* and *Another World,* consultant head writer; freelance writer, 1982—.

MEMBER: Romance Writers of America.

AWARDS, HONORS: Romantic Times Reviewer's Choice Award, twice; Affaire de Coeur Favorite Author of the Year; Romance Writers of America Write Touch Readers Award for Best Historical of the Year, 2000; Dorothy Parker Award for Best Romantic Suspense and Long Contemporary, Francis Reader's Award for Best Romantic Suspense, Romance Writers of America Kiss of Death's Daphne du Maurier Award for Best

Single Title Romantic Suspense, all 2001, all for *Darkling I Listen; Romantic Times* Career Achievement Award for Historical Storyteller of the Year, 2002.

WRITINGS:

Desire and Surrender, Avon Books (New York, NY), 1985.
Windstorm, Avon Books (New York, NY), 1987.
A Heart Possessed, Topaz/Penguin (New York, NY), 1988.
Renegade Love, Avon Books (New York, NY), 1988.
A Fire in the Heart, Avon Books (New York, NY), 1990.
Shadow Play, Avon Books (New York, NY), 1991.
Dream Fever, Jove Books (New York, NY), 1991.
My Only Love, Jove Books (New York, NY), 1994.
Once a Hero, Jove Books (New York, NY), 1995.
Miracle, Berkley (New York, NY), 1996.
Devotion, Jove Books (New York, NY), 1997.
Jezebel, Jove Books (New York, NY), 1997.
Hope and Glory, Jove Books (New York, NY), 1998.
Whitehorse, Jove Books (New York, NY), 1999.
Notorious, Jove Books (New York, NY), 2000.
Darkling I Listen, Jove Books (New York, NY), 2001.
Fever, Sonnet Books (New York, NY), 2001.
Bad Moon Rising, Sonnet Books (New York, NY), 2003.

Contributor to *Moonglow,* Berkley (New York, NY), 1998.

ADAPTATIONS: Darkling I Listen was optioned for film.

WORK IN PROGRESS: Hot August Moon, due in July 2003.

SIDELIGHTS: Katherine Sutcliffe is an award-winning writer of romance and suspense. Her writing has been called rich and sensual with vivid imagery by a *Publishers Weekly* critic in a review of *Once a Hero.*

An only child, Sutcliffe was raised mainly by her grandmother, and never knew her father. She spent much of her childhood alone, as she wrote at her Web site, "holed up with my best friends: books, notebooks, pencils. When I wasn't reading, I was writing. Wrote my first book at age 13."

After graduating from high school, Sutcliffe was living alone, working at a motorcycle dealer until the shop went out of business. She had no money for food, so she walked five miles to a pizza restaurant and sat at a back booth, writing stories on paper napkins and waiting for the patrons to leave. She would take the uneaten pizza off their plates and eat it during her long walk home. Eventually she decided to go to business school, and then moved to Dallas, Texas, where she met her husband Neil. In 1982 Sutcliffe quit her job as a headhunter for a computer personnel company, deciding that she would try to write. Three years later she sold her first book, *Desire and Surrender,* to Avon Books.

Most of Sutcliffe's historical novels are set in the eighteenth and nineteenth centuries. Sutcliffe told an interviewer for the German Web site *Die romantische Bücherecke,* "I've always imagined that I was born in the wrong century. The 19th century, especially the Victorian era, has a very strong pull on me. Perhaps I lived a former life during that period."

Sutcliffe, whose favorite author is horror novelist Stephen King, often incorporates dark or supernatural elements into her novels. For example, in *Love's Illusion* she uses the story of the nineteenth-century murderer known as "Jack the Ripper," but made the murderer a vampire instead of a mortal human being. In addition, her female characters are often tormented souls with many weaknesses, in contrast to the more pure and sunny characters other romance novelists employ. Sutcliffe told the interviewer: "My characters must do a lot of soul searching to understand their motives for behaving as they do, and once they come to grips with what is troubling them . . . they get over their angst and put it behind them. . . . I guess the whole process of writing is a sort of catharsis for me."

Sutcliffe's novels have received mixed reviews, with some critics finding the darkness and heaviness of some of her historical novels a bit tedious, while others have found her work to be compelling and suspenseful. *Publishers Weekly* reviewer Penny Kaganoff noted that *A Heart Possessed* has "a suspenseful, intricate plot," while Mary K. Chelton, a *Library*

Journal reviewer, said the book tells "a dramatic story . . . longer on atmosphere and mystery than romance." *Love's Illusion* was called "captivating" and an "outstanding romance" by Kaganoff. *Booklist* reviewer Diana Tixier praised the "tightly twisted plot" of *Notorious,* calling the book a "compelling historical romance." *Devotion* was praised as "flawlessly plotted and written" by a *Publishers Weekly* critic.

Sutcliffe intends to move away from historical romance and write more contemporary romantic suspense, moving more into mainstream fiction with the hopes of appealing to a wider audience. She is also considering writing horror. In her interview for *Die romantische Bücherecke* Sutcliffe said, "Writing is absolutely the best career, in my opinion, for raising a family. I've always been home with [my children] and therefore allowed to take any time I needed to participate in their wonderful lives."

BIOGRAPHICAL AND CRITICAL SOURCES:

PERIODICALS

Booklist, January 15, 1995, Denise Perry Donavin, review of *Miracle,* p. 896; September 15, 1998, Melanie Duncan, review of *Moonglow,* p. 213; February 1, 1999, Diana Tixier Herald, review of *Hope and Glory,* p. 966; September 15, 2000, Diana Tixier, review of *Notorious,* p. 228.

Library Journal, May 15, 1996, Mary K. Chelton, review of *A Heart Possessed,* p. 50.

Publishers Weekly, April 1, 1988, Penny Kaganoff, review of *A Heart Possessed,* p. 81; March 3, 1989, Penny Kaganoff, review of *Love's Illusion,* p. 99; February 2, 1990, Penny Kaganoff, review of *A Fire in the Heart,* p. 79; February 8, 1991, review of *Shadow Play,* p. 54; October 11, 1991, review of *Dream Fever,* p. 59; May 2, 1994, review of *Once a Hero,* p. 303; January 8, 1996, review of *Devotion,* p. 65; September 8, 1997, review of *Jezebel,* p. 73; January 4, 1999, review of *Hope and Glory,* p. 87; May 28, 2001, review of *Fever,* p. 57; August 27, 2001, review of *Darkling I Listen,* p. 62.

OTHER

Die romantische Bücherecke, http://www.die-buecherecke.de/ (March, 2000), Angela W., "Interview with Katherine Sutcliffe."

Katherine Sutcliffe, http://www.katherinesutcliffe.net/ (August 11, 2002).

T

TAGG, Christine Elizabeth 1962-

PERSONAL: Born May 25, 1962, in Yorkshire, England; daughter of George (an engineer) and Margaret (Plowright) Tagg; partner of Michael Ellwand (an antique dealer); children: Suzy Rae Ellwand. *Politics:* "Try to avoid them." *Religion:* Church of England. *Hobbies and other interests:* Swimming, reading, horses, breeding guinea pigs, 1950s design.

ADDRESSES: Home—Casatina, 32 The Spinney, Sandal, Wakefield, West Yorkshire, England. *E-mail*—casatina32@hotmail.com.

CAREER: Children's book author. Ridings Shopping Centre, Wakefield, England, secretary, 1985-97. Volunteer for Riding for the Disabled Association.

WRITINGS:

Who Will You Meet on Scary Street?, illustrated by Charles Fuge, Little, Brown (Boston, MA), 2001.
Silly Stories, Templar Publishing (Dorking, England), 2001.
Monster Stories, Templar Publishing (Dorking, England), 2001.
Metal Mutz!, illustrated by David Ellwand, Templar Publishing (Dorking, England), 2001, Candlewick Press (Cambridge, MA), 2003.
Buzz Off, I'm Busy ("BusyBugz" series), illustrated by Bill Bolton, Templar Publishing (Dorking, England), 2002.

When I'm Big ("BusyBugz" series), illustrated by Bill Bolton, Silver Dolphin Books (San Diego, CA), 2002.
Home Sweet Home ("BusyBugz" series), illustrated by Bill Bolton, Silver Dolphin Books (San Diego, CA), 2002.
Little Owl in the Snow, illustrated by Stephanie Boey, Templar Publishing (Dorking, England), 2002.

SIDELIGHTS: Christine Elizabeth Tagg told *CA:* "On my seventh birthday I was given a typewriter. It was the best present I ever received. Over the years, my 'typewriters' have gotten more sophisticated, but the thrill of putting words on a page has never diminished.

"Following the birth of my daughter, Suzy Rae, I gave up work to care for her and began working on a few children's story ideas. At this time I also joined a creative writing group which gave me confidence and inspiration. Shortly afterwards, Templar Publishing gave me the opportunity to work on a number of projects, and one of these was *Scary Streets*. I haven't looked back since.

"As a child, I loved the work of C. S. Lewis, Enid Blyton, and Dr. Seuss. I have recently rediscovered Beatrix Potter's charming tales. I love to read to Suzy, and we enjoy anything by Alan Ahlberg and Babette Cole, also the poetry of Roger McGough, Edward Lear, and Spike Milligan.

"I am always searching for characters and situations to put them in, usually as I stroll around the supermarket. I work mainly in the morning when Suzy is in school or late evening and into the night. I find that tea and toast goes very well with the blank page. Writing can be a lonely and often frustrating business, but it is addictive and the development of one good idea keeps me on a creative high for days.

"I would advise any young aspiring writers to keep at it, join a writing group and let your stories be heard. If you believe you have an original style and worthwhile ideas, one day someone else will, too. Publishing success eluded me in the early days, but I never considered giving up. To see your first book in print is a fantastic feeling. I'm doing what I love, getting paid for it and, of course, writing for children is the perfect excuse to never quite grow up."

BIOGRAPHICAL AND CRITICAL SOURCES:

PERIODICALS

Booklist, September 15, 2001, Ilene Cooper, review of *Who Will You Meet on Scary Street?,* p. 237.
Observer (London, England), October 28, 2001, Stephanie Merritt, review of *Metal Mutz!,* p. 16.
Times Educational Supplement, October 26, 2001, Ted Dewan, review of *Metal Mutz!,* p. 22.*

* * *

TANNER, Norman P. 1943-

PERSONAL: Born February 26, 1943, in Woking, Surrey, England; son of John Basil (a lawyer) and Agnes Emily (Tolhurst) Tanner. *Ethnicity:* "English." *Education:* Attended Ampleforth College, 1956-61; Jesuit novice, 1961-63; Heythrop College, licentiate, 1966; Oxford University, B.A., 1969, M.A., 1974, Ph.D., 1974; Gregorian University (Rome), B.Th, 1976. *Religion:* Roman Catholic.

ADDRESSES: Office—Campion Hall, Oxford OX1 1QS, England. *E-mail*—norman.tanner@campion.ox.ac.uk.

CAREER: Ordained Roman Catholic Priest, 1976; Farm Street parish, London, England, assistant priest, 1977-78; Oxford University, Oxford, England, 1978—,

teacher of history, 1978—, theology, 1989—, research lecturer, 1997—, senior tutor (Dean of Studies) of Campion Hall, 1981-97. Visiting professor of Church councils and/or Church history at Hekima College, Catholic University of East Africa, Nairobi, Kenya, 1991, 1996, 1999, 2001, Chishawasha National Seminary, Harare, Zimbabwe, 1991, 1996, 2000, Cedara College, near Pietermaritzburg, South Africa, 1991, Vidyajyoti Theological College, Delhi, India, 1996, 1999, St. Augustine College, Johannesburg, South Africa, 1999, St John Vianney Seminary, Pretoria, South Africa, 1999, Jnana Deepa Vidyapeeth, Pune, India, 1999, 2001, Centre Sèvres, Paris, France, 2000, Gregorian University, Rome, Italy, 2000, 2002, College General, Penang, Malaysia, 2001, and Sanata Dharma University, Yogyakarta, Indonesia, 2001.

MEMBER: Royal Historical Society (fellow), Ecclesiastical History Society, Catholic Theological Association of Great Britain.

WRITINGS:

(Editor) *Heresy Trials in the Diocese of Norwich, 1428-31,* Royal Historical Society (London, England), 1977.
The Church in Late Medieval Norwich, 1370-1532, Pontifical Institute of Mediaeval Studies (Toronto, Ontario, Canada), 1984.
(Editor) *Decrees of the Ecumenical Councils,* two volumes, Georgetown University Press (Washington, DC), 1990.
(Editor) *Kent Heresy Proceedings, 1511-12,* Kent Archaeological Society/Sutton Publishing (Maidstone, England), 1997.
The Councils of the Church: A Short History, Crossroad (New York, NY), 2001.
Is the Church too Asian?: Reflections on the Ecumenical Councils, Dharmaram Publications (Bangalore, India), 2002.
(Coauthor) *History of Vatican II,* volume four, edited by G. Alberigo and J. Komonchak, Orbis/Peeters (Maryknoll, NY), 2002.

Contributor to books, including *A History of Religion in Britain,* edited by S. Cilley and W. J. Sheils, Blackwell (Oxford, England), 1994; *Norwich Cathedral: Church, City, and Diocese, 1096-1996,* edited by I. Atherton and others, Hambledon Press (London,

England), 1996; *Christian Theology,* edited by Adrian Hastings, Oxford University Press (New York, NY), 2000; and *A History of Pastoral Care,* edited by G. Evans, Cassell (New York, NY), 2000; and to periodicals, including *Heythrop Journal, African Ecclesial Review,* and *Hekima Review.*

WORK IN PROGRESS: As editor with Shannon McSheffrey, *Lollards of Coventry, 1486-1522,* Royal Historical Society/Cambridge University Press, 2003; various journal articles and chapters in books.

SIDELIGHTS: Norman P. Tanner is a Jesuit priest, educator, and the author or editor of a number of books, including *Decrees of the Ecumenical Councils.* Tanner was interviewed by a writer for *Hekima Review,* the journal of Hekima College's Jesuit School of Theology in Nairobi, Kenya, where he was teaching a course in medieval Church history. Tanner has visited and taught courses on church history and the councils around the world. He told the interviewer, "My life is best described as a nomadic scholar, a writer, and teacher."

The interviewer asked Tanner why he had become so interested in Church history, and particularly the councils. Tanner said that he has always enjoyed history, majoring in both history and Church history all through his studies. He wrote his doctorate on popular religion in medieval Norwich and taught medieval Church history after his ordination.

"During this teaching, I became interested in the councils of the Church, starting with the medieval ones. I realised, and was appalled, that the great councils of the Middle Ages were effectively unavailable to students. The original decrees of the councils existed in Latin, but there were no translations of most of them into English—which was the only language that most students could manage."

Tanner noted that he made the decision to provide not only English translations but also the original texts on facing pages, "since translations are always imperfect, and for these important documents students have a right to be able to refer to the original texts." Tanner added that "for the purpose of sales, it would be better to include all the ecumenical councils of the Church, therefore the early and later councils (Nicaea I to Constantinople IV; Trent, Vatican I, and Vatican II), as well as the medieval ones."

The Greek and Latin versions had been published in 1973 as *Conciliorum Oecumenicorum Decreta,* and the editors agreed to their reproduction in Tanner's volumes. Thirty Jesuits, including Tanner, spent eight years completing the English translations, and Tanner spent another two years editing 2,500 pages before they were published. He had spent time in Rome in the 1970s studying for the priesthood and a short period for his "tertianship" in Denver, Colorado in 1991, but after the publication of these volumes, he was invited to lecture in many countries, and has done so with the support of the Church and Oxford University.

Tanner said that "the ecumenical councils are of great importance, they have been at the centre of the Church's life and thought from early times to the present day. They contain a rich mixture of theology, Church history, and canon law. Almost every aspect of Christian life, indeed of human nature, may be found in them. I am the only person anywhere, so far as I know, who teaches a course on all the councils together, and it seems to me well worthwhile to share with others this treasury of our Christian past."

A one-volume overview is presented in Tanner's *The Councils of Churches: A Short History,* for which "every theologian is indebted," noted Lawrence S. Cunningham in *Commonweal.* Cunningham called the book "superb." It covers all of the major councils, from Nicaea to Vatican II, divided into three sections. Tanner notes that not all of the twenty-one councils were clearly ecumenical, particularly the medieval ones, which were called "general councils of the West" by Pope Paul VI in a letter to Cardinal Willebrands. Cunningham concluded by saying that "given Tanner's fine style, his command of the conciliar tradition, and the importance of councils both as a history and as potential instruments for future church reform and ecumenical activity, this volume is a must read."

BIOGRAPHICAL AND CRITICAL SOURCES:

PERIODICALS

America, February 23, 1991, Ladislas Orsy, review of *Decrees of the Ecumenical Councils,* p. 219.
American Historical Review, June, 1985, Richard W. Pfaff, review of *The Church in Late Medieval Norwich, 1370-1532,* p. 665.

Atlantic, July, 1991, Charles R. Morris, review of *Decrees of the Ecumenical Councils,* p. 105.

Commonweal, October 12, 1990, Lawrence S. Cunningham, review of *Decrees of the Ecumenical Councils,* p. 590; September 28, 2001, Lawrence S. Cunningham, review of *The Councils of the Church: A Short History,* p. 26.

English Historical Review, April, 1987, R. B. Dobson, review of *The Church in Late Medieval Norwich, 1370-1532,* p. 477.

Hekima Review, May, 2001, "An Interview with Norman Tanner SJ."

Journal of Religion, October, 1992, Michael Cameron, review of *Decrees of the Ecumenical Councils,* p. 642.

*   *   *

TAYLOR, Drew Hayden 1962-

PERSONAL: Born July 1, 1962, in Curve Lake Reserve, Ontario, Canada. *Ethnicity:* Ojibway. *Education:* Seneca College of Applied Arts and Technology, Diploma (honors) in radio/television broadcasting, 1980-82.

ADDRESSES: Home—5 Mitchell Ave., Toronto, Ontario M6J 1C1, Canada. *E-mail*—DhTaylor1@Yahoo.com.

CAREER: Worked variously as a writer, director, playwright, and author; has also worked in journalism and television industries and served as researcher, consultant, casting, production assistant, and publicity agent on numerous television shows and documentaries.

AWARDS, HONORS: Chalmers Award for Best Play for Young Audiences, 1992, for *Toronto At Dreamer's Rock;* Best Drama, Canadian Authors Association Literary Award, 1992, for *The Bootlegger Blues;* Native Playwrights First Prize award, University of Alaska-Anchorage, 1996, for *The Baby Blues;* Dora Mavor Moore Award for Outstanding New Play (Small Theatre Division), 1996, for *Only Drunks and Children Tell the Truth;* James Buller Award for Best Playwright, Centre for Indigenous Theatre, 1997; Native Playwrights First Prize award, University of Alaska-Anchorage, 1997, for *Pranks* (later titled

AlterNATIVES); Best Live Short Subject Second Place award, American Indian Film Institute Awards, 1999, for *The Strange Case of Bunny Weequod;* British Columbia Millenium Award for "one of the best books published in the Province of British Columbia," 2000.

WRITINGS:

PLAYS

Toronto at Dreamers Rock (produced in Wikwemikong, Manitoulin Island, Ontario, Canada), 1989, Fifth House Publishers (Saskatoon, Saskatchewan, Canada), 1990.

Education Is Our Right, produced in Wikwemikong, Manitoulin Island, Ontario, Canada, 1990.

Talking Pictures, produced in Wikwemikong, Manitoulin Island, Ontario, Canada, 1990.

The Bootlegger Blues (produced in Wikwemikong, Manitoulin Island, Ontario, Canada, 1990), Fifth House Publishers (Saskatoon, Saskatchewan, Canada), 1991.

Someday (produced in Wikwemikong, Manitoulin Island, Ontario, Canada, 1991), Fifth House Publishers (Saskatoon, Saskatchewan, Canada), 1993.

A Contemporary Gothic Indian Vampire Story, produced in Saskatoon, Saskatchewan, Canada, 1992.

The All-Complete Aboriginal Show Extravaganza, produced in Montreal, Quebec, Canada, 1994.

The Baby Blues (produced at Arbour Theatre Festival, 1995), Talonbooks (Vancouver, British Columbia, Canada), 1998.

Girl Who Loved Her Horses (produced in Toronto, Ontario, Canada, 1995), published in anthology *Voices: Being Native in Canada,* University of Saskatchewan Press (Saskatoon, Saskatchewan, Canada), 1992.

Only Drunks and Children Tell the Truth (produced in Toronto, Ontario, Canada, 1996), Talonbooks (Vancouver, British Columbia, Canada), 1998.

Kilometres, produced in Canning, Nova Scotia, Canada, 1999.

AlterNATIVES (originally titled *Pranks*; produced at Bluewater Theatre/Lighthouse Theatre, 1999), Talonbooks (Vancouver, British Columbia, Canada), 2000.

Toronto@DREAMERSROCK.com, produced in Wikwemikong, Manitoulin Island, Ontario, Canada, 1999.

The Boy in The Treehouse, produced in Winnipeg, Manitoba, Canada, 2000.

The Buz'gem Blues, Talonbooks (Vancouver, British Columbia, Canada), 2002.

NONFICTION

Funny, You Don't Look like One: Observations of a Blue-eyed Ojibway, Theytus Books (Penticon, British Columbia, Canada), 1998.

Further Adventures of a Blue-eyed Ojibway: Funny, You Don't Look like One II, Theytus Books (Penticon, British Columbia, Canada), 1999.

Furious Observations of a Blue-eyed Ojibway: Funny, You Don't Look like One III, Theytus Books (Penticon, British Columbia, Canada), 2002.

Also author of short stories and prose; contributor of satirical commentaries to numerous newspapers and publications.

WORK IN PROGRESS: Two movie scripts and several new plays.

SIDELIGHTS: Drew Hayden Taylor grew up on the Ojibway Curve Lake reservation in Ontario, Canada. He writes screenplays, television scripts, short stories, plays, and essays and has a diploma in radio and television broadcasting from the Seneca College of Applied Arts and Technology. Taylor is a well-known playwright throughout North America; his plays focus on the modern-day life of Native Americans and they tour throughout Canada and the United States.

Taylor's play *Someday* is adapted from his short story that appeared on the front page of the Toronto *Globe & Mail,* the only time fiction has appeared there. The story is based on the Canadian social policy that allowed the Children's Aid Society to remove Native children from their parents and give the infants to white families. David Prosser from *Books in Canada* called *Someday,* "an engaging play." A poor Ojibway woman named Anne, wins the lottery and uses her winnings to find her eldest daughter, Grace, who was taken from Anne as a baby and raised by a white family. Darleen Golken, a reviewer from *Canadian Materials,* wrote, "Taylor endows his characters with charm, humour and wit. . . . The dialogue flows smoothly and resonates with the emotional integrity of the characters." Judith Zivoanovic from *Canadian Literature* agreed, "This play will not overwhelm its readers or audience with emotion, but it will engage them through realistic dialogue, action and characters, perhaps prompting a new level of understanding."

Taylor's first play in his "Blues" series is *The Bootleggers Blues,* which takes place on a reservation during a powwow weekend. Martha is a good Christian woman who bought too much beer for her church's fundraiser. Shortly after the fundraiser she discovers that she cannot return the beer, so in order for her to get rid of it, she turns to bootlegging. Ann Jansen from *Books in Canada* wrote that "*Bootlegger Blues* relies on broad physical humour, underwear scenes, and puns to keep its enging revving. . . . the energy is high, the beer starts to sell, and even the most stuffed shirt character finally figures out how to go with the flow." Beverly Yhap, reviewing for *Quill & Quire,* also found the story playful, "Taylor mines his characters' idiosyncrasies and attitudes for laughs that come from recognition rather than ridicule."

Taylor told *CA:* "Though I am primarily a playwright, I am also a short story writer, scriptwriter, as well as a journalist because often times I come across a story or idea that does not fit the structure of a play, or specifically a television show, or even an essay. Also, I like to think of my self as a literary slut—I like to 'write' around because variety is the spice of life and it provides me the opportunity to express myself in so many different ways. It's like flexing different muscles for different jobs.

"And, as a Native writer, I find that part of my mission, if I can call it a mission, is to provide a window or bridge between the Native and non-Native cultures hopefully through my writing, using large helpings of humour as the catalyst. I long ago discovered it doesn't take much talent to depress or anger somebody, but it takes a wee bit more ability to make somebody laugh. And since nobody really likes being preached to, humour allows you to sneak in a message or two when the audience or reader doesn't realize they are being taught something."

BIOGRAPHICAL AND CRITICAL SOURCES:

PERIODICALS

Books in Canada, Volume 11, number 6, David Prosser, "Unpunctually Yours," p. 35; Volume 21, number 1, Ann Jansen, "Dramatic Histories," p. 29.

Canadian Literature, spring, 1995, Judith Zivanovic, review of *Someday,* p. 184.

Canadian Materials, Volume 21, number 4, Darleen Golke, review of *Someday,* p. 157.

Essays on Canadian Writing, fall, 1998, Robert Nunn, "Hybridity and Mimicry in the Plays of Drew Hayden Taylor," p. 95.

Quill & Quire, Volume 58, number 1, Beverly Yhap, review of "The Bootlegger Blues," p. 28.

OTHER

Canadian Theatre Encyclopedia, http://www.canadiantheatre.com/ (June 23, 2000), "Drew Hayden Taylor."*

*   *   *

TAYLOR, Robert Allan 1958-

PERSONAL: Born May 2, 1958, in McKeesport, PA; son of George R. and Genniveve Taylor; married, December 18, 1999, wife's name Virginia Joan. *Education:* University of South Florida, B.A., 1983, M.A., 1985; Florida State University, Ph.D. in history, 1991. *Religion:* Episcopalian.

ADDRESSES: Office—Florida Institute of Technology, 150 West University Blvd., Melbourne, FL 32901-6975. *E-mail*—rotaylor@fit.edu.

CAREER: University of South Alabama, visiting instructor of history, 1990-91; Indian River Community College, adjunct instructor of history, 1992-99; Florida Atlantic University, adjunct instructor of history, 1992-96; Florida Institute of Technology, Melbourne, adjunct professor, 1997-99, assistant professor, 1999-2001, associate professor of history, 2001—. *Military service:* U.S. Naval Reserves, 1975-1977.

MEMBER: Organization of American Historians, Southern Historical Association, Florida Historical Society (vice president, 2000—), Brevard County, FL, Historical Commission, Tebeau-Field Library of Florida History (board of directors, 2000—).

AWARDS, HONORS: Volunteer Service Award, 1997; Executive Director's Award, 1999, Tebeau-Field Library of Florida History.

WRITINGS:

(Editor with Lewis N. Wynne) *This War So Horrible: The Civil War Diary of Hiram Smith Williams,* University of Alabama Press (Tuscaloosa, AL), 1993.

(Editor) *A Pennsylvanian in Blue: The Civil War Diary of Thomas Beck Walton,* White Mane (Shippensburg, PA), 1995.

Rebel Storehouse: Florida in the Confederate Economy, University of Alabama Press (Tuscaloosa, AL), 1995.

World War II in Fort Pierce, Arcadia Press (Charleston, SC), 1999.

(Editor with Ann Blomquist) *This Cruel War: The Civil War Letters of Grant and Malinda Taylor,* Mercer University Press (Macon, GA), 2000.

(With Lewis N. Wynne) *Florida in the Civil War,* Arcadia Press (Charleston, SC), 2001.

Also contributed article, "The Frogmen in Florida: U.S. Navy Combat Demolition Training in Fort Pierce, 1943-46," published in *Florida Historical Quarterly,* winter, 1997.

WORK IN PROGRESS: Florida: An Illustrated History, for Hippicrene Press; *Florida and Civil War Generalship: A Study in Command,* for Mercer University Press (Macon, GA); *Fort Pierce's Naval Amphibious Training Base, 1943-46; The 40th Alabama Volunteer Infantry.*

SIDELIGHTS: Robert A. Taylor has taught history at the collegiate level for several institutions and has written several books, mostly about the U.S. Civil War, as well as articles that chronicle the role of Fort Pierce, Florida, and its naval amphibious training base during World War II.

Taylor co-edited *This Cruel War: The Civil War Letters of Grant and Malinda Taylor, 1986-1865* with Ann K. Bloomquist, a descendent of this west central Alabama couple. According to *Journal of Southern History's* David Carlson, *"This Cruel War* offers an important look at one southern family's personal, patriotic, emotional, and spiritual evolution during the Civil War."

The collection of more than 160 letters includes thirty-two from Malinda to her husband. Private Grant Taylor joined the Confederate army in 1862 at age thirty-four to avoid the shame of being conscripted, leaving his wife and four children to tend the family farm on which he owned no slaves. As part of the 40th Alabama regiment, Taylor fought in several major battles, including the defense of Vicksburg, Lookout Mountain and Missionary Ridge in Tennessee, the Atlanta campaign, and action around Mobile, Alabama.

Taylor's letters, however, address more than his fighting experiences. Carlson said, "He tries to guide Malinda through a move to a new home, failing crops, unscrupulous neighbors, greedy substitutes, the birth of a child, the burning of the family kitchen, and the death of friends and family." The couple's correspondence also demonstrates their strong Christian convictions, which uphold them amid the strain of Taylor's long absence and other ordeals.

Civil War History reviewer James S. Humphreys wrote, "While concern for loved ones at home and descriptions of camp and combat are not unusual in Civil War soldiers' correspondence, a few of the letters of the Taylors go beyond the ordinary. . . . *This Cruel War* ranks as a significant addition to the large corpus of Civil War correspondence." One of the letters describes Taylor's opposition to the Confederate Congress's decision in spring, 1865, to deploy black slaves as soldiers; had the Confederates won, the slaves would have been freed after the war, and Taylor thought it was "outrageous" for blacks to be freed for fighting to keep slavery.

Carlson praised the editing, calling it easy for modern readers while maintaining original spellings and sentence structure, but he criticized the footnoting as ineffective. Still, he said the work "offers important insights into the battlefield and home front, husband and wife, father and family during the Civil War that deserve further study."

Taylor's *Rebel Storehouse: Florida in the Confederate Economy* examines Florida's significance as a supplier to the Confederate army. Because no important battles were fought in Florida and its capital was the only Confederate one Union troops did not capture, the state was able to produce large amounts of food and other supplies for the rest of the Confederacy. Farmers in Florida planted crucial crops of corn, and the Confederate government bought oranges and other citrus fruits as well as sugar and molasses. Cattle was an especially important export as other sources in the South were cut off, and production from several salt works along the Gulf coast was probably Florida's most vital economic contribution.

Civil War History reviewer William Warren Rogers, Jr. felt that "some might hope for a more lively account of the subject, and a greater focus on individuals as providers would help," but added, "These objections do not detract from the contribution that has been made. The Southern economy, as with the homefront generally, has received less attention than is warranted."

BIOGRAPHICAL AND CRITICAL SOURCES:

PERIODICALS

American Historical Review, December 1996, Larry Schweikart, review of *Rebel Storehouse: Florida in the Confederate Economy,* pp. 1627-1628.
Civil War History, September, 1994, J. Tracy Power, review of *This War So Horrible: The Civil War Diary of Hiram Smith Williams,* pp. 264-267; June 1997, William Warren Rogers, Jr., review of *Rebel Storehouse: Florida in the Confederate Economy,* pp. 158-159; March, 2001, James S. Humphreys, review of *This Cruel War: The Civil War Letters of Grant and Malinda Taylor, 1986-1865,* p. 88.
Historian, fall, 1996, Lex Renda, review of *Rebel Storehouse: Florida in the Confederate Economy,* p. 161.
Journal of American History, March, 1996, Samuel C. Hyde Jr., review of *Rebel Storehouse: Florida in the Confederate Economy,* pp. 1579-1580.
Journal of Southern History, February, 1997, Marion B. Lucas, review of *Rebel Storehouse: Florida in the Confederate Economy,* pp. 176-177; November 1994, Mark Grimsley, review of *This Cruel War: The Civil War Letters of Grant and Malinda Taylor, 1986-1865,* pp. 821-822; November, 2001, David Carlson, review of *This Cruel War: The Civil War Letters of Grant and Malinda Taylor, 1986-1865,* p. 868.*

*   *   *

TAYLOR, Sheila Ortiz 1939-

PERSONAL: Born September 25, 1939, in Los Angeles, CA; daughter of John Santray Taylor (a lawyer and musician) and Juanita Shrode Chase (a homemaker); married John Clendenning, 1971 (divorced); married J. L. Lewis (a school librarian), March 16, 1991; children: Andrea, Jessica. *Education:* University of California—Los Angeles, B.A., 1963, M.A., 1964, Ph.D., 1973. *Politics:* Democrat. *Religion:* "Pantheist."

ADDRESSES: Office—English Dept., Florida State University, Tallahassee, FL 32306-1580. *E-mail*—sotaylor@English.fsu.edu.

CAREER: Florida State University, Tallahassee, professor of English, 1973—.

MEMBER: Modern Language Association, Associated Writing Programs.

AWARDS, HONORS: Money for Women award, Barbara Deming Memorial Fund, 1995, for *Imaginary Parents;* Dr. Martin Luther King, Jr. Distinguished Service Award, Florida State University, 1997; fine arts grant, State of Florida, 1998.

WRITINGS:

Faultline (novel; also see below), Naiad Press (Tallahassee, FL), 1982.
Spring Forward/Fall Back (novel), Naiad Press (Tallahassee, FL), 1985.
Slow Dancing at Miss Polly's (poetry), Naiad Press (Tallahassee, FL), 1989.
Southbound (novel; sequel to *Faultline*), Naiad Press (Tallahassee, FL), 1990.
Imaginary Parents (memoir), University of New Mexico Press (Albuquerque, NM), 1996.
Coachella (novel), University of New Mexico Press (Albuquerque, NM), 1998.

WORK IN PROGRESS: The novels *Extranjera* and *Assisted Living; Roxana, the Fortunate Mistress,* a screenplay.

*　　*　　*

TAYLOR, William Howland 1901-1966

PERSONAL: Born May 31, 1901, in New Bedford, MA; died January 6, 1966, at Sands Point Nursing Home, Port Washington, Long Island, NY; married Anne Kay Hocking; children: Stephen Howland, William Hocking. *Education:* Dartmouth College, graduated 1923.

CAREER: Sportswriter. Reporter for *New Bedford Standard,* New Bedford, MA, *Fall River News,* Fall River, MA, and *Boston Herald,* Boston, MA, 1923-27; *New York Herald Tribune,* New York, NY, yachting editor, 1927-42. *Yachting,* 1923-64, began as freelance contributor, associate editor, 1945, managing editor, 1951; Yachting Publishing Corporation, vice president. *Military service:* U.S. Navy, 1942-45, executive officer and commanding officer of USS *PC 598,* 1943, 1944, commanded a PC submarine chaser in the Pacific and served aboard a tanker; became lieutenant commander and executive officer of USS *Kennebec.*

AWARDS, HONORS: Pulitzer Prize, 1935, for coverage of America's Cup races of 1934.

WRITINGS:

(With Others) *Yachting in North America along the Atlantic and Pacific and Gulf Coasts and on the Great Lakes and on the Western and Canadian Lakes and Rivers,* edited by Eugene V. Connett, Van Nostrand (New York, NY), 1948.
(Editor) *Just Cruising,* Van Nostrand (New York, NY), 1949.
(Editor) *On and Off Soundings,* Van Nostrand (New York, NY), 1951.
Outboards at Work, Outboard Marine International (Nassau, Bahamas), 1958.
(With Herbert L. Stone) *The America's Cup Races,* Van Nostrand (New York, NY), 1958.
(With Stanley Rosenfeld) *The Story of American Yachting, Told in Pictures,* photographs by Morris Rosenfeld, Appleton-Century-Crofts (New York, NY), 1958.

Work represented in *Best Sports Stories 1951: A Panorama of the 1950 Sports Year,* edited by Irving T. Marsh and Edward Ehre, E. P. Dutton (New York, NY), 1951, *The Encyclopedia of Sports,* third revised edition, edited by Frank G. Menke, Barnes (New York, NY), 1963, and *The Best from Yachting,* Scribners (New York, NY), 1967; contributor to periodicals, including *True, House & Garden, Publishers Weekly,* and *New York Times Magazine.*

SIDELIGHTS: William Howland Taylor was a respected writer on the subject of yachting and yacht racing and was the first sportswriter to win the Pulitzer Prize for his coverage of the America's Cup races of 1934 between the American defender *Rainbow* and the British contender *Endeavor* off Newport Beach, Rhode Island. Although Taylor was already well known in the world of yachting for the quality and accuracy of his writing, with the Pulitzer his fame spread beyond the niche in which he had set the standard. He was the author and editor of a variety of books on yachting, and wrote about the great yachtsmen of his time and in history, including Sir Thomas Lipton, Tom Sopwith, and Captain Charlier Barr, and about boat builders and designers, such as W. Starling Burgess and Nathanael Greene Herreshoff. Robert Cole noted in *Dictionary of Literary Biography* that Taylor "wrote about the great boats, with names such as *Yankee, Rainbow, Endeavour,* and *America,* as though they were racehorses."

Taylor was born in the coastal fishing town of New Bedford, Massachusetts. His ancestors had been whalers and seamen, and Taylor soon learned to sail various kinds of boats. After graduating from Dartmouth College (and before he joined the staff of the *New York Herald Tribune* as yachting editor in 1927), Taylor worked as a reporter for a number of Massachusetts papers, including the *Boston Herald.* He stayed in New York for fifteen years, then joined the U.S. Navy. After returning to civilian life, he continued to contribute to the *New York Herald Tribune.* On July 27, 1944, Taylor published the first piece he had written since he began his Navy career.

During the 1920s and 1930s, Taylor contributed articles to *Yachting* magazine. After leaving the U.S. Navy in 1945, he joined the *Yachting* staff full time as an associate editor, and in 1951 he was named managing editor, a position he held until illness forced him to cut back on his responsibilities. He often covered the America's Cup races, yachting's premiere racing event, for the periodical. Taylor's prizewinning coverage was of the 1934 race between *Endeavor,* a J. Class challenger from England, and *Rainbow,* the American defender. Sentiment held that the *Endeavor* would win, based on her superior design, and that the trophy that had been held by the New York Yacht Club would go back with the British crew. But the *Rainbow* won, sailed by a crew led by Harold S. Vanderbilt.

On September 25, 1934, the *New York Herald Tribune* ran Taylor's account of the last race in the series. Cole called the article "exceptional as an example of Taylor's prose: clear, straightforward explanations of a different and technical sport. For Taylor the America's Cup races were the epitome of the sport. He was less concerned about the millions spent in earning or defending it than in the goodwill it generated." Many years later, in 1962, Taylor's "The Day We Thought the Cup Was Lost" was published in *Yachting.*

Among Taylor's books is *The Story of American Yachting, Told in Pictures.* The volume, for which Taylor collaborated with Stanley Rosenfeld, features hundreds of photographs from the collection of Morris Rosenfeld, Stanley's father. The authors provide a narrative of the lives of yachtsmen from the mid-nineteenth to the twentieth century and examine the appeal of their sport. Taylor felt the attraction to be "the sense of power and authority that comes from command" and the "communion" experienced by the men on a boat as they work together to overcome the elements. In the same year he published *The America's Cup Races* with Herbert L. Stone, also a *Yachting* editor, a history of the international competition.

Beginning in 1964, Taylor began to suffer a serious of strokes, and he died in 1966. Cole said that the writer of Taylor's *New York Times* obituary described him as "a big easygoing, quiet-spoken pipe smoker whose relish for the life of the sea came to him naturally. Throughout his life he developed an intimate knowledge of seamanship. Stanley Rosenfeld . . . agreed, calling Taylor 'a man of wholesome good humor and unstinting energy, tempered with the benefit of his wealth of yachting lore and experience.'" The year after Taylor's death, *Yachting* published *The Best from Yachting,* which contains several of Taylor's pieces, including "Just Cruisin'," which Cole called "a short, charming essay that reveals Taylor's love for sailing."

BIOGRAPHICAL AND CRITICAL SOURCES:

BOOKS

Dictionary of Literary Biography, Volume 241: *American Sportswriters and Writers on Sport,* Gale (Detroit, MI), 2001, pp. 298-302.

O'Connor, Dennis, and Michael Levitt, *The America's Cup,* St. Martin's Press (New York, NY), 1998.

OBITUARIES:

PERIODICALS

New York Times, January 8, 1966.*

TEIL, Thierry
See LHERMITTE, Thierry

* * *

TENNESON, Joyce 1945-

PERSONAL: Born May 29, 1945, in Boston, MA. *Education:* Regis College, B.A. 1967, George Washington University, M.A., 1969; Antioch College, Ph. D., 1978.

ADDRESSES: Office—1915 Biltmore Street, N.W., Washington, DC 20009; 114 West 27th Street, New York, NY 10001.

CAREER: Independent photographer, Washington, DC, 1971-83; Corcoran School of Art, Washington, DC, and Northern Virginia Community College, professor of art, 1971-83; freelance portrait, fashion, and magazine photographer, Washington, DC and New York, NY, 1983—.

MEMBER: Society for Photographic Education, College Art Association of America.

AWARDS, HONORS: Ford Foundation grant, 1979; District of Columbia Commission on the Arts grant, 1982; Infinity Award, International Center for Photography, 1989; named Photographer of the Year, Woman in Photography, 1990.

WRITINGS:

(Editor) *In-Sights: Self-portraits by Women,* text by Patrician Meyer Spacks, David R. Godine (Boston, MA), 1978.
Transformations, Little, Brown (Boston, MA), 1983.
Joyce Tenneson—Photography, David R. Godine (Boston, MA), 1985.
Au Dela—Joyce Tenneson, Contrejer (Paris, France), 1989.
Illuminations, Little, Brown (Boston, MA), 1997.
Wise Women, Little, Brown (Boston, MA), 2002.

SIDELIGHTS: Raised on the grounds of a convent, where her parents worked, Joyce Tenneson has been noted for the otherworldly quality of her photographic images. Nudes and semi-nudes draped in white gowns, disembodied limbs against a white linen background, her early work suggested the mysteries of birth and death, and rebirth. In her more recent work Tenneson has moved toward full portraits, less mysterious but psychologically more complex. "Human beings stripped of all but the lightest raiment dwell serene, contemplative and melancholy," noted a *Publishers Weekly* reviewer of *Transformations.* Tenneson told an interviewer with the *Florida Times Union,* "I see my portraits as an extension of the work I have always done—an attempt to penetrate and reveal emotional essences."

Tenneson's portraits tend to be of women, whether in comic, erotic, or otherworldly poses. "The fact that I was surrounded by a female culture has also marked me," she told an interviewer for *Photo Insider.* "Not only the convent, but my mother had nine sisters who lived nearby." Her first book, *Insights: Self-Portraits by Women,* which she edited, predated the current interest in female photographers' images of themselves. And in *Wise Women,* Tenneson celebrates the enigmatic power and beauty of women aged sixty-five to one-hundred.

BIOGRAPHICAL AND CRITICAL SOURCES:

PERIODICALS

Florida Times Union, November 7, 1997, Sharon Weightman, "Photographer at Lectern," p. 28.
People, February 11, 1985, Campbell Geeslin, review of *Photographs,* p. 12.
Publishers Weekly, January 4, 1993, review of *Transformations,* p. 68.

OTHER

Photoinsider, http://www.photoinsider.com/ (May 6, 2002).*

* * *

THIELEN, Benedict 1903-1965

PERSONAL: Born April 29, 1903, in Newark, New Jersey; died 1965; son of Henry J. (a banker) and Theodora (Prieth) Thielen; married Virginia Berresford (a painter), June 20, 1930 (divorced, 1949); married Helen Close, July 9, 1949; children: Charles Close (stepson). *Education:* Princeton University, B.A., 1923, M.A., 1924. *Hobbies and other interests:* Scuba diving, marine biology.

CAREER: Writer, 1932-65.

WRITINGS:

Deep Streets, Bobbs-Merrill (Indianapolis, IN), 1932.
Women in the Sun, Bobbs-Merrill (Indianapolis, IN), 1935.
Dinosaur Tracks and Other Stories, Secker and Warburg (London, England), 1937.
Stevie, Dial (New York, NY), 1941.
The Lost Men, Appleton-Century (New York, NY), 1946.
Friday at Noon, Holt (New York, NY), 1947.

Contributor of stories to magazines, including *New Yorker, Harper's Bazaar, Scribner's, Town and Country, Esquire, Atlantic Monthly, Yale Review,* and *London Mercury.* Stories also appear in anthologies.

SIDELIGHTS: Benedict Thielen was born in Newark, New Jersey in 1903, the son of banker Henry J. Thielen, a German who had immigrated to the United States at age twenty, and Theodora Prieth Thielen, whose father was also a German immigrant. Thielen grew up with his parents and widowed maternal grandmother. When he was sixteen, he entered Princeton University. His mother died in 1923, and his father in 1928. After his parents' deaths, Thielen was taken in by a wealthy uncle, Lothar Faber, whose family manufactured pencils. Faber's family was large and eccentric, and Thielen used his observations of their vivid and funny personalities as the basis for many of his fictional characters.

After earning both a bachelor's degree and a master's degree at Princeton, Thielen traveled widely, spending a year and a half in Paris and five years traveling through southern France, England, Italy, Germany, Belgium, Switzerland, Austria, Greece, and Yugoslavia. He married Virginia Berresford, a painter, on July 20, 1933, and moved with her to New York City, where they lived until 1940. They subsequently divided their time between Key West and Martha's Vineyard. In 1949, they were divorced; shortly thereafter, Thielen married Helen Close. Although they did not have children, he raised Close's son from an earlier marriage as his own.

Thielen was a disciplined writer: at Key West he worked every day in an attic; at Martha's Vineyard, in a small shack separate from the main house. When he was not working, he indulged his hobbies of scuba diving and marine biology.

Thielen's first novel, *Deep Streets,* explores the effect of city life on characters who live vain, empty, and deluded lives. According to Eric W. Carlson in the *Dictionary of Literary Biography,* critics praised "its lively, natural dialogue, its genuine feeling for nature and music, and its sardonic treatment of the futility of attempting to escape from the urban to the primitive in nature." He followed this with a collection of stories, *Dinosaur Tracks and Other Stories.*

Stevie is a satiric comedy starring Stevie, who is an "honest businessman," the book's narrator, Joe, and their wives, who appear in eleven amusing situations in which they reveal themselves to be "perfectly dreadful people," as Thielen explains in his introduction to the book. He commented, "Stevie and his pals are, it seems to me, the corned-beef-and-cabbage, the beer, the weeds, the burlesque shows of this existence, and as such I like them and like to report their doings."

Thielen's next work, *The Lost Men,* examines the intimate relationship between man and nature and the impact of man's past upon his present. *The Lost Men* tells the story of three jobless World War I veterans who are caught up in the violent hurricane of Labor Day 1935. Some of the veterans survive the storm, while others are either washed away from their inadequate shelters or "baptized" by the hurricane waters with a new view of life. "Out of the tragedy of spiritual and social lostness there emerges the epic theme of survival and rebirth of the spirit of man," Carlson wrote in *Arizona Quarterly.* He continues, "Thielen can use vivid and colorful language to the point of brillance . . . his description seeks . . . to represent nature as felt reality, nature transformed through some experienced realization of eye and mind." Another hurricane, this one in 1938 on Martha's Vineyard, inspired Thielen to write "A House by the Sea," an essay penned shortly after Thielen's new house was swept off its foundation and moved by the ocean and winds a half mile away.

Friday at Noon is a more complex book, with a complicated series of relationships among characters, each of whom is seen from the point of view of all the others. Several important themes run throughout the book, including materialism, artistic idealism, social democracy, and emotional domination. Carlson wrote, "Thielen here makes effective use of leitmotifs, symbolism, contrast of the subjective and the objective, past and present, interacting characters, and the subtle revelation of mood and motive." In the *Princeton University Library Chronicle* Carlson described *Friday at Noon* and Thielen's serious fiction, "If one function of literature is to expand our sympathy and understanding by sensitizing us to a larger range of values, then Thielen's work fulfills that purpose in the highest degree."

Summing up Thielen's career, Carlson noted, "Thielen was 'a voice of his time' in the rich variety of his characters and themes," and wrote, "His voluminous journals (1920s to 1965) and letters . . . further represent the wide range of human values that inform Thielen's fiction."

BIOGRAPHICAL AND CRITICAL SOURCES:

BOOKS

Dictionary of Literary Biography, Volume 102: *American Short Story Writers, 1910-1945,* Series II, Gale (Detroit, MI), 1991, pp. 307-318.
Warfel, Harry R., *American Novelists of Today,* American Book Co., 1951.

PERIODICALS

Arizona Quarterly, Volume 1, number 6, Eric W. Carlson, "Thielen's *The Lost Men:* A Study in Organic Form," pp. 239, 243, 245.
Princeton University Library Chronicle, spring, 1952, Eric W. Carlson, "Benedict Thielen: An Introduction and a Check List," pp. 148-150.*

*   *   *   *

TIERNO, Philip M(ario), Jr. 1943-

PERSONAL: Born June 5, 1943, in Brooklyn, NY; son of Philip M. and Phyllis (Tringone) Tierno; married Josephine Martinez, April 2, 1967; children: Alexandra Lorraine, Meredith Anne. *Education:* Brooklyn College of Pharmacy, Long Island University, B.S., 1965; New York University, M.S., 1974, Ph.D., 1977.

ADDRESSES: Home—102 Harbor Cove, Piermont, NY 10960. *Office*—Dept. of Microbiology, Tisch Hospital 374, New York University Medical Center, 550 1st Ave., New York, NY 10016. *E-mail*—philip. tierno@med.nyu.edu.

CAREER: Lutheran Medical Center, Brooklyn, NY, microbiologist, 1965-66; Veterans Administration Hospital, Bronx, NY, chief research microbiologist of the hemodialysis unit, 1966-70; Goldwater Memorial Hospital, New York University Medical Center, Franklin D. Roosevelt Island, NY, director of microbiology, 1970-81; Maimonides Medical Center, Brooklyn, associate, microbiologist, 1970-79; Tisch Memorial Hospital, New York University Medical Center, director of microbiology department, 1981—; New York University Medical School, associate professor of microbiology and pathology, 1981—. Adjunct assistant professor at City University of New York, 1974-76, and Bloomfield College, Bloomfield, NJ, 1975-82; consultant to the State of New York's Office of the Attorney General, National Institutes of Health, College of American Pathologists, City of New York Department of Health; New York City Mayor's Task Force on Bioterrorism 2001—; Foundation for Scientific Research in the Public Interest, Staten Island, NY, founder, 1985. Member of civic and community boards and commissions.

MEMBER: AAAS, New York Academy of Scientists, American Academy of Microbiology, American Public Health Association, National Registry of Microbiologists, American Society for Microbiology, Optimists (vice president, Norwood chapter, 1978-95), Phi Sigma, Alpha Epsilon Delta.

AWARDS, HONORS: Named among Knights of Malta, Sovereign Military and Hospitaler Order of Saint John of Jerusalem, 1986.

WRITINGS:

The Secret Life of Germs: Observations and Lessons of a Microbe Hunter, Pocket Books (New York, NY), 2001.
Protect Yourself against Bioterrorism, Simon & Schuster (New York, NY), 2002.

Also contributor of articles to numerous professional scientific and medical journals and also to text books.

SIDELIGHTS: Philip M. Tierno, Jr. is a microbiologist and investigator who promoted the use of safer menstrual products after the relationship between toxic shock syndrome and dioxins in tampons came to be understood in the 1980s. He has also been involved with AIDS research and is an expert on the dangers of germs, from the common cold to the microscopic beginnings of such deadly newsmakers as E. coli, Lyme disease, encephalitis, mad cow, and anthrax.

Tierno has been frequently interviewed about his research involving germs, and in a *New Republic* article, Hanna Rosin noted that he "may deserve the blame for starting the hysteria. A few years ago, he began swabbing taxis, pay phones, movie theater seats, and restaurant chairs and publishing the results in the newspapers. Tierno himself wipes the receivers of public phones with alcohol swabs, uses paper towels to open the doors of rest rooms, and never rides the subway." A *Seattle Times* article carried Tierno's advice on the fungal infections, parasites, and diseases that can be picked up by humans from their turtles, birds, cats, and dogs. In avoiding unnecessary disease, Tierno stresses the importance of hand washing. "If you've been only the most casual of hand washers until now, you won't be after reading this book," commented Beth Woodard in the *Winston-Salem Journal.*

Tierno offers specific advice in his *The Secret World of Germs: Observations and Lessons from a Microbe Hunter* on food safety and other tips for maintaining health and minimizing contact with germs in and outside the home. He also includes information on how bacteria and viruses are transmitted, as well as the results of some of his field samplings in New York, including those from the engagement ring counter at the upscale Tiffany's. The volume is also a history of how we have come to understand germs over time, beginning with the biblical emphasis on cleanliness.

Tierno also writes about the role of germs in such illnesses as heart disease and ulcers. He notes that the overprescribing of antibiotics resulted in antibiotic-resistant germs becoming more virulent. *Library Journal*'s Elizabeth Williams noted that Tierno "offers a broad overview of the impact of these microbes on the world today." "This germ primer brings the bug

into focus while setting even the most jittery hypochondriac's mind at ease," wrote a *Publishers Weekly* reviewer.

Tierno includes a chapter on germ warfare in *The Secret Life of Germs,* and his *Protect Yourself against Bioterrorism* is an entire volume dedicated to the explanation of anthrax and other diseases that could potentially be used against the populace and a guide to protection and preparedness. After the anthrax scare of 2001, Tierno was on call to serve the New York City Mayor's Task Force on Bioterrorism. Francis Ma of the Syracuse, New York *Post-Standard* covered Tierno's address at Cazenovia College and reported that "Tierno said part of getting over the fear of bioterrorism is education and knowledge." Tierno spoke about anthrax and past outbreaks, how people become infected, and of a new vaccine that has been developed at the Louis Pasteur Institute in Paris, France. He explained how our filtering systems, chlorination, and treatment plants would render impotent any anthrax added to the U.S. water supply.

Tierno was the guest of a *CNN.com* chat in which participants asked him a number of questions relating to anthrax. Tierno explained the different forms of the disease, the investigation, and future risks from anthrax and smallpox: "I think that the governmental bodies are so alert to what's going on throughout America, so many new plans have been put into effect, so many surveillance systems are operating, I think that we would be able to readily identify any new threat or any new disease that might be perpetrated on us."

In concluding the chat, Tierno pointed out that the late Howard Hughes was obsessed with the fear that a germ would kill him. Tierno said that "without germs, man could not exist on this planet. There would be no food, oxygen, nitrates, no recycling of organic matter, so life could continue. In the beginning was the germ, and we came afterward, believe it or not. Man has accomplished something extraordinary, by being able to explore the gargantuan potential of germs. We are now for the first time harnessing their power for the good of all mankind. In fact, using germs we can accomplish some of the biggest problems facing mankind, disease, hunger, and pollution."

BIOGRAPHICAL AND CRITICAL SOURCES:

PERIODICALS

Booklist, December 15, 2001, William Beatty, review of *The Secret Life of Germs: Observations and Lessons of a Microbe Hunter,* p. 690.

Library Journal, January, 2002, Elizabeth Williams, review of *The Secret Life of Germs,* p. 147.

New Republic, November 10, 1997, Hanna Rosin, "Don't touch This: America's Obsession with Germs," p. 24.

New York Post, November 22, 2001, "Spore Deaths May Have Been Missed," p. 7.

Post-Standard (Syracuse, NY), April 11, 2002, Francis Ma, "Ready to Respond to Terror: Lecturer Tells Cazenovia College Audience That U.S. Needs to Be Prepared to Win 'the Wars of the Future,'" p. 7.

Publishers Weekly, December 10, 2001, review of *The Secret Life of Germs,* p. 61.

Seattle Times, June 27, 1999, "You Share a Lot with Your Pets—Including Risk of Infection," p. L4.

Winston-Salem Journal, January 13, 2002, Beth Woodard, "Book on Germs Will Have You Reaching for the Soap," p. A20.

OTHER

CNN.com, http://www.cnn.com/ (November 8, 2001), chat with Tierno.

*   *   *

TILLIS, Steve

PERSONAL: Married: wife's name, Adrienne Baker; children: Sam, Hannah. *Education:* University of California—Berkeley, Ph.D. (dramatic art).

ADDRESSES: Home—Pleasanton, CA. *Office*—Center for Theater Arts, University of California, Berkeley, CA 94720.

CAREER: University of California, Berkeley, lecturer in theater arts.

WRITINGS:

Toward an Aesthetics of the Puppet: Puppetry as a Theatrical Art, Greenwood Press (Westport, CT), 1992.

Rethinking Folk Drama, Greenwood Press (Westport, CT), 1999.

Contributor to periodicals, including *Theatre Topics.*

BIOGRAPHICAL AND CRITICAL SOURCES:

PERIODICALS

Theatre Journal, May, 1994, p. 301.*

*   *   *

TOBIN, James 1918-2002

OBITUARY NOTICE—See index for *CA* sketch: Born March 5, 1918, in Champaign, IL; died after a stroke March 11, 2002, in New Haven, CT. Economist, educator, and author. Tobin was a respected economist who won the 1981 Nobel Prize in Economic Science. He received his M.A. from Harvard University in 1940 before joining the U.S. Navy and serving on a destroyer in the South Pacific; he was also a lieutenant for the U.S. Naval Reserve until 1955. After World War II Tobin returned to Harvard and earned his Ph.D. in 1947. He remained at Harvard as a junior fellow for the next three years before moving on to Cambridge University, where he would spend the rest of his academic career and served as chairman of the department of economics from 1968 to 1969 and again from 1974 to 1978. Tobin was considered an apostle of John Maynard Keynes, believing that government fiscal and monetary policies could be used to benefit the economy. As such, he was on the opposite side of monetarists who held that the control of a nation's money supply was the best way to control the economy. His theories impressed President John F. Kennedy, who in 1960 invited Tobin to serve on his council of economic advisors, which Tobin did from 1961 to 1962, continuing as a consultant until 1968. Tobin won the Nobel Prize for his work on the Portfolio Selection Theory, which analyzes how changes in the stock market affect consumer spending and investment habits. A prolific writer, he edited and contributed to many books on economics, was a former editor of the journals *Econometrica* and *Review of Economic Studies,* and wrote several books, among them the four-volume *Essays in Economics, The New Economics: One Decade Older,* and *Full Employment and Growth: Further Keynesian Essays on Policy.*

OBITUARIES AND OTHER SOURCES:

BOOKS

Writers Directory, 16th edition, St. James Press (Detroit, MI), 2001.

PERIODICALS

Chicago Tribune, March 13, 2002, section 2, p. 9.
Los Angeles Times, March 13, 2002, p. B10.
New York Times, March 13, 2002, p. A25.
Times (London, England), March 14, 2002.
Washington Post, March 13, 2002, p. B6.

*   *   *

TOOMING, Peter 1939-

PERSONAL: Born June 1, 1939, in Rakvere, Estonia; married Sirje Ong, 1963; children: Lee. *Education:* Attended State University of Tartu, 1968-74.

ADDRESSES: Home—Harju 1-7, Tallinn 200 001, Estonia.

CAREER: Photographer, cinematographer, and documentary filmmaker. Producer of films and television productions; director of documentary films. Founded Lee (photo gallery), 1993. *Exhibitions:* Works included in permanent collections of Municipal Museum, Tallinn, Estonia; Photography Museum, Siauliai, Lithuania; Australian Photographic Society; Bibliothèque Nationale, Paris, France; and other institutions. Solo exhibitions include *Selected Photos,* University of Kaunas, Kaunas, Lithuania, 1967; *A Summer's Story,* Kiek in de Kök, Tallinn, 1972; *One Day's Story,* Kiek in de Kök, 1977; *Selected Photos,* Urania-Schaufenstergalerie, Vienna, Austria, 1980; *Nude and Nature,* Kiek in de Kök, 1984; and *Sun Games,* Kiek in de Kök, 1992. Group exhibitions include *Fotoforum 73,* Ruzomberok, Czechoslovakia, 1973; *Stodom,* Dom Kultury ROH, Pribor, Czechoslovakia, 1980; and *The Memory of Images,* Stadgalerie im Sophienhof, Kiel, Germany, 1993.

MEMBER: Stodom.

AWARDS, HONORS: Award for best cinematography, Film Festival of Tallinn, 1980; first prize, Rakvere Film Festival, 1983; special prize, Film Festival of Tallinn, 1986; special prize, Nature Film Festival, 1993.

WRITINGS:

25 Fotot, Eesti Raamat (Tallinn, Estonia), 1975.
Rakvere, Eesti Raamat (Tallinn, Estonia), 1976.
Fotolood, Eesti Raamat (Tallinn, Estonia), 1979.
Peatu, meenuta, Eesti Raamat (Tallinn, Estonia), 1980.
Saaremaa, Eesti Raamat (Tallinn, Estonia), 1982.
Foto! Foto? Foto . . . , [Tallinn, Estonia], 1983.
Sina, jogi, [Tallinn, Estonia], 1984.
Sketches from the Past of Estonian Photography, 1840-1940, [Tallinn, Estonia], 1986.
Silvery Way, [Tallinn, Estonia], 1990.
Fifty-five Years Later: Virumaa, Huma (Tallinn, Estonia), 1993.
Highway Attracts, Huma (Tallinn, Estonia), 1993.
Fifty-five Years Later: Saaremaa, Huma (Tallinn, Estonia), 1994.

Contributor to periodicals, including *Fotografie.*

WORK IN PROGRESS: A History of Estonian Photography.

SIDELIGHTS: Peter Tooming is an Estonian photographer and filmmaker who is known for his poetic imagery, even with regard to his photojournalism. Tooming developed an interest in photography in the 1960s, when the medium found increasing favor among artists in the Soviet Union's Baltic republics. A *Contemporary Photographers* critic attributed this rise in the popularity of photography in the Baltic states to "the historic artistic culture of the region and its folk art tradition," and Tooming is identified as "an outstanding figure in this significant cultural transformation in . . . Estonia."

In the ensuing years, as Tooming developed proficiency as a photojournalist, his art changed from "emotional symbolism to a kind of vital authenticity," according to the *Contemporary Photographers* contributor. Even in his photojournalism, however, Tooming has continued to practice a relatively refined artistry. The *Contemporary Photographers* writer affirmed that he has "not entirely renounced poetic arrangements," and acknowledged "a certain aesthetic quality regarding man's relationship with nature."

Tooming has also won acclaim as a cinematographer and documentary filmmaker. In 1980 he won the prize for best cinematographer at the Film Festival of

Tallinn, and in 1986 he received a special prize at the same festival. In addition, he secured a special prize at the 1993 Nature Film Festival held in Sundsvall, Sweden.

BIOGRAPHICAL AND CRITICAL SOURCES:

BOOKS

Contemporary Photographers, 3rd edition, St. James Press (Detroit, MI), 1996.*

*   *   *

TORRENT, Ferran 1951-
   (Pere Lavaca)

PERSONAL: Born May 30, 1951, in Sedaví, Valencia, Spain. *Education:* Earned law degree.

ADDRESSES: Agent—c/o Author Mail, Columna Edicions, Provenca 333, Barcelona 8037, Spain.

CAREER: Novelist, journalist, and author of screenplays. Formerly worked as a lawyer and a commercial representative. Frequently appears on radio and television.

AWARDS, HONORS: Premio Sant Jordi, 1994, for *Gràcies per la pronina.*

WRITINGS:

(With Josep Lluís Seguí; as Pere Lavaca) *La gola del llop* (novel), Federació d'Entitats Culturals del País Valencià (Valencia, Spain), 1983.
No emprenyeu el comissari (novel; title means "Don't Annoy the Commissioner"), Eliseu Climent /3i4 (Valencia, Spain), 1984.
Penja els guants, Butxana! (novel; title means "Hang up Your Gloves, Butxana!"), Quaderns Crema (Barcelona, Spain), 1985.
Un negre amb un saxo (novel; title means "Black Guy with a Saxophone"), Quaderns Crema (Barcelona, Spain), 1987.

Cavall i rei (novel; title means "Knight and King"), Quaderns Crema (Barcelona, Spain), 1989.
L'any de l'embotit (novel; title means "The Year of the Salted Meat"), Quaderns Crema (Barcelona, Spain), 1992.
Gràcies per la propina (semiautobiographical novel; title means, "Thanks for the Tip"), Columna (Barcelona, Spain), 1994.
Tocant València (travel; title means "Playing Valencia"), Aigua de Mar (Altea, Spain), 1995.
La mirada del tafur (novel; title means "The Look of the Card Shark"), Columna (Barcelona, Spain), 1997.
L'illa de l'holandès (novel; title means "The Dutchman's Island"), Columna (Barcelona, Spain), 1999.
Living l'Havana (travel), Columna (Barcelona, Spain), 1999.
Cambres d'acer inoxidable (novel; title means "Chambers of Stainless Steel"), Columna (Barcelona, Spain), 2000.
Societat limitada (novel), Columna/Bromera (Barcelona and Alzira, Spain), 2002.

Contributor to books, including *Semental, estimat Butxana,* Columna (Barcelona, Spain), 1997.

Author's works have been translated into Spanish and French.

ADAPTATIONS: Un negre amb un saxo was adapted as a film directed by Francesc Bellmunt; *Gràcies per la propina* was adapted as a film.

SIDELIGHTS: Ferran Torrent has won critical and popular acclaim for his series of detective novels set in his native Valencia. Infusing the novels with turbulent local politics and the native Valencian language—a dialect of Catalan—Torrent has effectively transplanted the quintessentially American gumshoe genre into eastern Spain. In addition to his work as a novelist, Torrent also works as a scriptwriter and journalist, and is a well-known radio personality.

Torrent was born in Sedaví, in the historic county of l'Horta near the city of Valencia. During winter evenings before the fireplace and summer nights on the porch, the young Torrent would attempt to entertain his family with stories. While attending a Jesuit high school, he discovered the work of Agatha Christie and Edgar Allan Poe, and decided to dedicate himself to writing. Cinema became his second love, and its influences can be discerned in his fiction.

After beginning professional life as a lawyer and businessman, Torrent collaborated in 1983 with Josep Lluís Seguí on the novel *La gola del llop*, using the pseudonym Pere Lavaca. The following year he struck out on his own, releasing the detective novel *No emprenyeu el comissari* under his own name. The novel was a commercial success due in part to the popularity of its lead characters, journalist Hèctor Barrera and Detective Butxana. Torrent continued with the characters in his next two novels, *Penja els guants, Butxana!* (1985) and *Un negre amb un saxo* (1987), the latter which was adapted as a film directed by Francesc Bellmunt. Although the author has noted that transplanting the American detective noir to Valencia is difficult due the genre's complicated conventions, his approach has been to integrate Valencia's colorful and troubled social and political scene into the plots.

Torrent continues to write new novels for the series every few years, more recent installments including 2000's *Cambres d'acer inoxidable*. Land development and the tortured politics behind it are explored in Torrent's 2002 novel, *Societat limitada*. As the city explodes with money and ambitious government building projects, a rice farmer from Albufera threatens to upset the game by refusing to play along. In a review in *Avui*, Joan Josep Isern called the novel Torrent's best to date, combining "to perfection dialogue, interior monologues, rapid changes in the point of view and a special humorous accent in the moments when the narrators voice is heard."

A non-series novel, Torrent's semi-autobiographical *Gràcies per la propina* won the Premio Sant Jordi in 1994 before it was made into a movie. Some critics have maintained that *Gràcies per la propina* marks a turning point in the author's literary style due to its increasing sophistication. He has also worked extensively as an essayist and travel writer, and has written two plays and various screenplays for radio and film.

The fact that Torrent writes exclusively in Valencian Catalan necessarily places him in the forefront of the so-called "normalization" process. The movement seeks to reassert Valencia's native tongue in commerce,

government, and art after centuries of official neglect. The author has been publically cited for his contribution to this effort.

BIOGRAPHICAL AND CRITICAL SOURCES:

PERIODICALS

Avui (Barcelona, Spain), February 21, 2002, Joan Josep Isern, review of *Societat limitada.*

OTHER

Association of Writers in the Catalan Language Web site, http://www.escriptors.com/ (June, 2002), "Ferran Torrent."*

* * *

TOWNSEND HALL, Brenda P.

PERSONAL: Female.

ADDRESSES: Home—Au Village, Ansan, 32270, France. *E-mail*—brendahall@compuserve.com.

CAREER: Novelist.

MEMBER: World Romance Writers, Romance Writers of America (president of local chapter), Association of Electronically Published Romance Authors.

WRITINGS:

Where's Michelle?, RFI West Inc., 2000.
Without a Clue, RFI West Inc., 2002.

WORK IN PROGRESS: A mystery series set in Great Britain with the principal female protagonist from Los Vegas and the principal male character a member of British CID.

SIDELIGHTS: Brenda P. Townsend Hall told *CA:* "My primary motivation for writing is a compelling need to create. I love British mysteries—especially those with continuing characters—as well as TV police drama, and cop/lawyer shows such as *Law and Order.* My writing process always starts with a simple 'What if?' and grows from there. When I first started writing, I wrote straight romance novels. Now, I'm more interested in creating complicated mystery or suspense plots. I continue to have a certain amount of romance in my work, but it's no longer the main ingredient. In fact, the first book in the series I'm currently working on will not end 'happily ever after.'"

*　　*　　*

TREMBLAY, Florent A(lexander Joseph) 1933-

PERSONAL: Born July 12, 1933, in St. Angele, Quebec, Canada; son of Arthur and Claire (Plourde) Tremblay; married Simonne Chiasson, July 21, 1973; children: Natalie, Jean-Sébastien. *Education:* University of Montreal, B.A., 1956; Université Laval, B.Ed., 1958; John Carroll University, M.A., 1961; Catholic University of America, Ph.D., 1968. *Religion:* Roman Catholic. *Hobbies and other interests:* Church organist. Reading history, researching medieval manuscripts, writing, gardening, and travelling.

ADDRESSES: Home—805 Chemin des Ormes, L'Acadie, Quebec, Canada J2Y IC3. *Office*—Canadian Forces Language School, BFC St. Jean, St. Jean-sur-Richelieu, Quebec, Canada J0J 1RO. *E-mail*—florent_tremblay@hotmail.com.

CAREER: Immigration-Quebec, director of language programs, 1968-71; Université Laval, Quebec City, Quebec, professor of applied linguistics, 1968-72; Bureau des Langues, Ottawa, Ontario, coordinator of French as a second language, 1972-73; McGill University, Montreal, Quebec, applied linguistics, 1978-82; Royal Military College of Canada, St. Jean-sur-Richelieu, Quebec, professor of French language and literature, 1977-2002; Canadian Forces Language School, scholar-in-residence, 1995—. *Military service:* Canadian National Defence, Army Reserve, 1956-77, coordinator of North Atlantic Treaty Organization (NATO) schools in Europe, 1973-77, program director at Royal Military College, St. Jean, Quebec, 1977-95; became major; received special service medal and distinguished conduct medal.

MEMBER: Comité International de Recherche sur l'Histoire Bibliographique des Langues Occidentales (co-president), Association Canadienne Française pour l'Avancement des Sciences, Canadian Learned Societies, Modern Language Association of America, Societé des Études Anciennes du Québec, Societé des Études Médiévales du Québec; Ordre des Linguistes-Conseils du Québec, Association du Royal 22e Regiment, Phi Delta Kappa.

AWARDS, HONORS: Listed among Authors of the Year, Canadian Learned Societies, 1992; Medaille d'Or de la Renaissance Française pour le Rayonnement de la Culture Française, French Government, 1988; Premio "Lettora antica," The Vatican, 2001.

WRITINGS:

La Méthod situationnelle en Français-langue d'usage, Centre de linguistique appliquée, Cap-Rouge (Quebec, Canada), 1972.

Bibliotheca Lexicologiae Medii Aevi, Volume 1: *Classics and Education in the Middle Ages,* Volumes 2-3: *Lexicons in the Middle Ages,* Volume 4: *Grammars in the Middle Ages,* Volume 5: *The Rise of Vernacular Languages,* Volume 6: *The Influence of Vulgar Latin,* Volumes 7-8: *Lexicographical Manuscripts,* Volumes 9-10: *Author, Geographical, Abbreviation, Title, Chronological, and Incipits Index,* Edwin Mellen (Lewiston, NY), 1989-90.

Bibliotheca grammaticorum, Volume 1: *Antiquity: Circa 2000 ante Christum-circa 200 ante Christum,* two books, Volume 2: *The Classical Period: Circa 200 ante Christum-circa 200 post Christum,* two books, Volume 3: *Roman Decadence: Circa 100 post Christum-circa 500 post Christum,* two books, Volume 4: *The Middle Ages: circa 6th to the End of the 15th Century,* two books, Volume 5: *The Renaissance: ca. 1450-ca. 1790,* two books, Volume 6: *The Modern Period: Circa 1790-Present,* three books, Volume 7, book 1: *Index of Titles: Ca. 2000 ante Christum-ca. 1990 post Christum,* Volume 7, book 2: *Index of Authors: Ca. 2000 ante Christum-ca. 1990 post Christum,* Edwin Mellen (Lewiston, NY), 1996.

Repertorium siglorum: Acronyms and Abbreviations in Philology and Related Subjects / sigles et abréviations en études anciennes et dans les sujets connexes, Edwin Mellen (Lewiston, NY), 2002.

Contributor of about fifty articles to scholarly journals.

WORK IN PROGRESS: A Latin-Middle English dictionary based on the unpublished manuscript *Medulla Grammatice* of the Harley collection in the British Museum Library, London, England.

SIDELIGHTS: Florent A. Tremblay told *CA:* "Two scholars have particularly influenced my research and my publications. Dr. Robert T. Meyer, my mentor during all my doctoral studies at Catholic University of America, told me about manuscripts and incunabula preserved in the vaults of the British Museum, in London, and in the Archives of the Bibliotheque Nationale, in Paris. He also encouraged me to go into researching the evolution of lexicology and 'grammatical thought.' And the late Dr. Rodrigue LaRue, the editor of the great *Clavis Auctorum Graecorum et Latinorum,* introduced me to the world of classical bibliography.

"I have visited most of the great libraries of the western world, have looked through books by the thousands, have written short summaries and prepared files by the tens of thousands, have given them a chronological order, computerized them, sorted and rearranged them in a non-stop-type of history before publication. They have become the twenty-five books of my *Bibliotheca.*"

*   *   *

TRIPP, Paul 1916-2002

OBITUARY NOTICE—See index for *CA* sketch: Born February 20, 1916, in New York, NY; died August 29, 2002, in New York, NY. Actor, television producer and director, business executive, lyricist, and writer. Although Tripp never described himself as an educator, he is remembered as a pioneer in the field of children's educational television. His most lasting achievement was likely the orchestrated story he wrote, in collaboration with composer George Kleinsinger, and titled *Tubby the Tuba.* The story of a lonely tuba relegated by his size and clumsiness to play a monotonous "oompah" harmony yet longing for a melody he can call his own, *Tubby the Tuba* was hailed not only for its timeless message of perseverance and triumph over adversity but for what it taught millions of small children about the instruments of the orchestra. The story, originally recorded by Tripp in the 1940s, was subsequently translated into several languages and presented in concert by the world's leading conductors. Tripp was also a leader in the early days of children's television programming. He produced, directed, and wrote the award-winning TV series *Mr. I. Magination,* in which, dressed as an engineer on a miniature train, he drew young viewers into imaginative stories from the past as well as into the classics of literature. Tripp's later television series included *On the Carousel,* which earned him an Emmy Award in the 1950s, and *Birthday House.* Despite his television work, Tripp's primary occupation was that of a lyricist; he is credited with the publication of at least 600 songs and the release of some thirty children's albums. He also penned the script and lyrics for the 1966 feature film *The Christmas That Almost Wasn't,* in which he also starred. His stage appearances included tours as Benjamin Franklin in *1776* and in the solo show *Will Rogers, U.S.A.* In the 1960s Tripp served as president and director of Fantasy Music Publishing. He also wrote children's books, including *The Strawman Who Smiled by Mistake* and *The Tail That Went Looking.*

OBITUARIES AND OTHER SOURCES:

PERIODICALS

Los Angeles Times, September 2, 2002, obituary by Myrna Oliver, p. B11.
New York Times, September 1, 2002, obituary by William H. Honan, p. L34.
Times (London, England), September 4, 2002.
Washington Post, September 3, 2002, p. B6.

*   *   *

TYERMAN, Christopher 1953-

PERSONAL: Born May 22, 1953. *Education:* M.A., D.Phil., F.R.Hist.S.

ADDRESSES: Office—Faculty of Modern History, Hertford College, University of Oxford, Broad Street, Oxford OX1 3BD, England.

CAREER: Hertford College, Oxford, Oxford, England, lecturer in modern history.

WRITINGS:

England and the Crusades, 1095-1588, University of Chicago Press (Chicago, IL), 1988.

Who's Who in Early Medieval England, 1066-1272, Shepheard Walwyn (London, England), 1996, Stackpole Books (Mechanicsburg, PA), 2001.

The Invention of the Crusades, Macmillan (Basingstoke, England), 1998.

A History of Harrow School, 1324-1991, Oxford University Press (New York, NY), 2000.

SIDELIGHTS: Christopher Tyerman is a British author of several books documenting the history of Medieval England and the Crusades. In *England and the Crusades, 1095-1588* he discusses the second and third Crusades, Lord Edward's expedition, the English who fought for the Teutonic Knights in the Baltic wars, the Lollard crusaders, and the transition of crusading principles and actions into the Tudor period.

Nearly a third of Tyerman's book deals with the period following 1272. Instead of the traditional focus on economic, colonial, ecclesiastical, and military perspectives, the author concentrates on how the Crusades influenced various aspects of English society and domestic and international politics. He discusses the positions and activities of the English kings between 1154 and 1327, all of whom took the cross. He also provides considerable detail about the lives of English crusaders and compares individuals at all social levels. "References are exemplary, as are the index and bookmaking," wrote J. W. Alexander in *Choice. Times Literary Supplement* contributor Norman Housley noted that Tyerman "has done the job not only thoroughly but brilliantly. It is hard to believe that any important aspect of the subject has been omitted. . . . The attention to detail is meticulous, and the author's use of the sources critical and astute." Housley's only quarrels with Tyerman's work were that its author both "displays an almost obsessional mistrust of the papacy's crusading goals and motives" and "is curiously wary of committing himself on the main developments which shaped the course of the crusading movement." Although Housley maintained that these faults detract from the book's overall

perspective, he added that, "For all that, [*England and the Crusades*] remains a highly impressive study, deserving rich praise." A reviewer noted in *Virginia Quarterly Review* that Tyerman "sheds new light on a complex and bloody period in English history."

The first part of Tyerman's *The Invention of the Crusades* is a reprint of a 1995 article he wrote for *English Historical Review* titled "Were There Any Crusades in the Twelfth Century?" The middle section of the book covers the period between c. 1200 and 1500. It was during this time that the Crusade was fully defined and all Christians were able to take vows. Tyerman examines how societies received crusading and how canon law was applied in secular courts. The final section covers historical accounts of the Crusade to the present time, including the large number provided by various historians as to who participated in crusading campaigns. Tyerman observes that historians are influenced by their own views and time.

In *A History of Harrow School, 1324-1991,* Tyerman has written the first history of England's most famous public school after Eton. Using the school's archives, Tyerman reveals the significance Harrow has played in British history. Known as a school for the wealthy, the school has witnessed many changes from the promises of virtually every new headmaster to de-emphasize the classics and spend more time on math, science, history, and foreign languages, to the end of the tradition of "fagging"—the bullying of new students. Michael V. C. Alexander wrote in *History: Review of New Books,* that *A History of Harrow School, 1324-1991* "will serve as a model for future educational historians."

BIOGRAPHICAL AND CRITICAL SOURCES:

PERIODICALS

American Historical Review, June, 1990, p. 799.
Catholic Historical Review, July, 1989, p. 486.
Choice, February, 1989, p. 992.
Contemporary Review, March, 2001, review of *A History of Harrow School, 1324-1991,* p. 187.
English Historical Review, June, 1990, p. 449.
History: Review of New Books, spring, 1989, p. 114; spring, 2001, review of *A History of Harrow School, 1324-1991,* p. 116.

Journal of Church and State, winter, 1990, p. 136.

Journal of Interdisciplinary History, autumn, 1989, p. 284.

Religious Book News, December, 1988, p. 3.

Religious Studies Review, July, 1990, p. 266.

Spectator, February 11, 1989, p. 38; December 16, 2000, review of *A History of Harrow School, 1324-1991,* p. 87.

Speculum, October, 1990, p. 1069.

Times Educational Supplement, November 24, 2000, Peter Gordon, review of *A History of Harrow School, 1324-1991,* p. S23.

Times Literary Supplement, November 18, 1988, p. 1276; September 4, 1998; February 16, 2001, J. H. C. Leach, review of *A History of Harrow School, 1324-1991,* p. 29.

Virginia Quarterly Review, spring, 1989, p. 43.

V

VONARBURG, Élisabeth 1947-
(Sabine Verreault, a pseudonym)

PERSONAL: Born August 5, 1947, in Paris France; immigrated to Quebec, Canada, in 1973; daughter of Rene (a military officer) and Jeanne (a pharmacist; maiden name, Morche) Ferron-Wehrlin; married Jean-Joel Vonarburg, December 15, 1969 (divorced January, 1990). *Education:* University of Dijon, B.A., 1969, M.A. (with honors), 1969, Agregation de Lettres Modernes, 1972; Universite Laval, Ph.D., 1987. *Hobbies and other interests:* Reading, music, movies, cats, skiing, good food, and bad puns.

ADDRESSES: Home and office—Chicoutimi, Quebec, Canada. *E-mail*—evarburg@royaume.com.

CAREER: High school teacher in Chalon-sur-Saone, France, 1972-73; Universit´ du Quebec a Chicoutimi, assistant lecturer in literature, 1973- 81; Université du Quebec a Rimouski, assistant lecturer in literature and creative writing, 1983-86; Université Laval, Quebec, Quebec, teacher of creative writing in science fiction, 1990. Worked as a singer and songwriter, 1974-82; Aluminum Co. of Canada, technical translator from English to French, 1976-77; Radio-Canada, weekly science-fiction columnist, 1993-95. Editor of Quebecois science-fiction and fantasy magazine *Solaris,* 1976-91, contributing editor and literary editor, 1999—.

MEMBER: SFSF Boréal, Science Fiction Canada, Science Fiction and Fantasy Writers of America (SFWA), Writer's Union of Canada (TWUC), Union de Écrivaines et Écrivaines Québecois (UNEEQ), INFINI (France).

Élisabeth Vonarburg

AWARDS, HONORS: Grand Prix de la SF francaise, Prix Rosny Aine, and Quebec's Prix Boreal, all 1982, all for *Le Silence de la Cité* Canadian Aurora Award, 1991, for *Histoire de la Princesse et du Dragon;* Canadian Aurora Award, 1992, for *Ailleurs et au Japon;* Canadian Aurora Award, Grand Prix de la SF quebecoise, Prix Boreal, Philip K. Dick Special Runner-up Award, and Tiptree Award finalist, all 1993, all for *Chroniques du Pays des Meres;* Philip K. Dick Award finalist, 1995, for *The Reluctant Voyagers;* Grand Prix de la SF quebecoise and Prix Boreal, both 1997, both for *Tyranael I & II;* Quebec's Prix du Conseil du Statut de la Femme, 1998.

WRITINGS:

Lœil de la nuit (stories), Editions du Preambule, 1980.

Le Silence de la Cité (novel), Denoël (Paris, France), 1981, translation by Jane Brierley published as *The Silent City,* Press Porcepic (Toronto, Ontario), 1990, Bantam (New York, NY), 1992.

Janus (stories), Denoel, 1984.

Comment écrire des histoires: guide de l'explorateur (title means "How to Write Stories: An Explorer's Guide"), Editions La Lignee, 1986, 3rd edition, 1996.

Histoire de la Princesse et du Dragon (children's novella), Quebec/Amerique (Montreal, Quebec), 1990.

Ailleurs et au Japon (stories), Quebec/Amerique, 1991.

Chroniques du Pays des Meres (novel), Quebec/Amerique, 1992, translation by Brierley published as *In the Mother's Land,* Bantam, 1992, published as *The Maerlande Chronicles,* Beach Holme, Victoria, British Columbia, 1992.

Les Voyageurs malgre eux, Canada Quebec/Amerique, 1992, translation by Jane Brierley published as *Reluctant Voyagers,* Bantam (New York, NY), 1995.

Les Contes de la Chatte Rouge (young adult novel), Quebec/Amerique, 1993.

Contes et Legendes de Tyranaël (young adult novel), Quebec/Amerique, 1994.

Reluctant Voyagers, Tesseract Books, 1995.

Le Jeu de la Perfection, Editions Alire, 1996.

Le Reves de la Mer, Editions Alire, 1996.

L'Autre Rivage, Editions Alire, 1997.

La Mer Allee Avec Le Soleil, Editions Alire, 1997.

Mon Frere L'Ombre, Editions Alire, 1997.

Le Lever du Recit: Poesie, Les Herbes Rouges, 1999.

La Maison au Bord de la Mer (stories), Editions Alire (Quebec, Canada), 2000.

Slow Engines of Time (stories), Tesseract Books (Edmonton, Canada), 2001.

Author of the screenplay *Le Silence de la Cite.* Contributor to anthologies. Contributor to periodicals, including *Tomorrow Speculative Fiction, Solaris, Estuaire, Faerie, Arcade, Stop, XYZ, Le Sabord, Moebius,* and *La Presse.*

TRANSLATOR

Tanith Lee, *La Tombe de naissance* (novel; title means "The Birthgrave"), Marabout, 1976.

James Tiptree, Jr. *Par-Dela les Murs du monde* (novel; title means "Up the Walls of the World"), Denoël, 1979.

Chelsea Quinn Yarbro, *Fausse Aurore* (novel; title means "False Dawn"), Denoel, 1979.

Ian Watson, *Chronomachine lente* (stories; title means "A Very Slow Time Machine"), Lattes (Paris. France), 1981.

Jayge Carr, *L'Abime de Leviathan* (novel; title means "Leviathan's Deep"), Albin-Michel (Paris, France), 1982.

Tanith Lee, *Le Jour, la nuit* (novel; title means "Day by Night"), Albin-Michel (Paris, France), 1982.

Jack L. Chalker, *Le Diable vous emportera* (novel; title means" And the Devil Will Drag You Under"), Albin-Michel(Paris, France), 1983.

R. A. Lafferty, *Le Livre d'or de Lafferty* (stories), Presses Pocket (Paris), 1984.

Jack Williamson, *Le Livre d'or de Jack Williamson* (stories), Presses Pocket, 1988.

(And editor) Marion Zimmer Bradley, *Le Livre d'or de Marion Zimmer Bradley* (stories), Presses Pocket, 1992.

(And editor) Anne McCaffrey, *Le Livre d'or de Anne McCaffrey* (stories), Presses Pocket, 1992.

Gerald Nicosia, *Memory Babe: Une biographie critique de Jack Kerouac* (title means "Jack Kerouac: A Critical Biography"), Quebec/Amerique, 1994.

Guy Gavriel Kay, *La Tapisserie de Fionavar* (title means"The Fionavar Tapestry"), Quebec/Amerique, Volume I: *L'Arbre de l'Ete* ("The Summer Tree"), 1994, Volume II: *Le Feu vagabond* ("The Wandering Fire"), 1995, Volume III: *La Route obscure* ("The Darkest Road"), 1995.

Marion Zimmer Bradley, *La Chute d'Atlantis* (title means "The Fall of Atlantis"), Presses Pocket, 1996.

Guy Gavriel Kay, *Les Lions d' Al Rassan* (novel; title means "The Lions of Al-Rassan"), L' Atalante (France), Alire (Quebec), 1999.

Guy Gavriel Kay, *La Mosaïque Sarantine* (novel; title means "The Sarantine Mosaic"), Books 1 and 2:

Voice vers Serance ("Sailing to Sarantium") and *Le Seigneur des Empereurs* ("Lord of Emperors"), Buchet-Chastel (France), 2000.

WORK IN PROGRESS: Reine de Memoire ("Queen of Memory"), a two-book uchronic fantasy.

SIDELIGHTS: Élisabeth Vonarburg began writing science fiction in 1964, and since then has become one of the genre's leading female contributors and spokespersons. She organized the first Quebecois SF convention in 1979, before publishing her first novel, *Le Silence de la Cité* (*The Silent City*), in France in 1981. A story about a doomed world, and a city in which only a small number of humans still survive, *Le Silence de la Cité* tells of Elisa, a unique child born with powers of rejuvenation. When the human race faces a virus set to render the male gender extinct, Elisa must make a choice about her future, and the future of humanity.

In *Chroniques du Pays des Meres* (*In the Mother's Land; The Maerland Chronicles*) Vonarburg again depicts a world in decline where survivors come together to create a new social structure. During this time, Lisbei, a young thinker, begins an archaeological dig and unearths a historical artifact, one which she uses to challenge the new establishment in an attempt to initiate change.

Les Voyageurs Malgre Eux (*Reluctant Voyagers*), Vonarburg's third novel, is about a Montreal woman who stumbles on to the trail of an underground revolutionary movement. Like her first two novels, *Les Voyageurs Malgre Eux* depicts the world we know, but not quite as we know it. As Vonarburg once told the *Financial Post,* the book features "a mythical Quebec where history developed very differently."

In addition to these and other novels for readers both adult and young adult audiences, Vonarburg has published short stories and poems in collections, anthologies, and periodicals, and often translates the work of other French and French-Canadian authors. Vonarburg herself is one of only a few SF writers in Quebec to have had work translated into English. She once told the *Financial Post* that, having immigrated to Quebec from France, she believes her work offers a unique take on Quebec's regional perspective. "I don't

see Canada/Quebec as they do, as it relates to my history," she commented. "Quebec [in my books] doesn't really exist, it's a phantasm. That's a very individual way of seeing Quebec."

AUTOBIOGRAPHICAL ESSAY:

Élisabeth Vonarburg contributed the following autobiographical essay to *CA:*

A BLUE HOUSE

Way back then, in the mid-Eighties, at a Canadian SF convention taking place in Vancouver, there was a panel on "what is a professional writer?" The Important American Guest Writer told us in no uncertain terms that a Professional Writer was a writer who had an Agent, published many Books, and above all made Money with *his* writing. I was seething at the back of the audience, with a Canadian friend and colleague. *Sotto voce,* delinquently, we agreed that a true writer was someone who had organized her or his life in order to write, period. Now, some fifteen years later, I still agree with us, of course. Making choices in one's life, accepting the consequences of those choices, and living with them day in day out, yes. In another universe, I am a professor at some French University, or in Chicoutimi, or elsewhere; I teach Literature, I publish learned, opaque articles, I have a car, I vacation in Cancun, Greece, or wherever, I worry about having enough money for my retirement—I mean, I do have vacations and reasonable prospects of retirement. And I have never written a word of fiction, that type of writing having been a fad of my silly youth. In this other universe, as I see it from this one, and as far as I (only I) am concerned, I am dead. *A writer is someone who's organized her life in order to write.*

But is it not potentially the same for any artist who is passionate about what she's doing? And not only for any artist but for *anyone* who is passionate, etc.? So what specifically makes a *writer?*

Two years ago, I was teaching again, as a temp, at the Chicoutimi University, "Creative Writing." Thirty-six twentysomethings, two or three of whom perhaps did want to write, some of whom had never written a personal letter in their life, most of whom had been forced to write a three-page story in three hours in high school—and none of them had a clue. They were so lost they didn't even have *questions*. After teaching that course twice, *I* had a lot more questions than before, which is good because I don't have many answers about writing. If any, they are of the biodegradable kind, subject to change without much notice.

Still, one answer did coalesce at the time: *A writer is not someone who has ideas, imagination, a unique point of view on the world. These, everyone has. A writer is someone who has a certain kind of relationship with* words— *not the written word only, but all words. Someone who loves words, the very concept of words, their forms, sounds, rhythms, history, mutable meanings. Someone for whom words are not merely tools but exist in their own right, like living beings. But even more than that, it is someone who, through some quirk of her circumstances, has come to channel her whole being-in-the-world through words.*

And stories. Someone who tells herself stories all the time, who feels the impulse, the desire, need, obsession, perversion, to tell stories. Someone for whom the whole universe is a story, and herself a part of it, engaged in a constant dialogue with it, at once telling and being told. Not for "money, fame and the love of women," as Balzac once said—women or men, same thing: that deep impulse to tell needs neither the love of others nor their acknowledgement, it just needs to be. It is there.

We humans are storytellers anyhow—some of us more than others, that's all. And when I ask myself (as I have been asked so many times) "among all the things you could write, why do you write science fiction, fantasy or poetry?," what comes naturally to me is a story.

*

Once upon a time, there was a little girl who lived in a box. It was small, but it was nice. Mommy and Daddy lived there too. They worked at their Store but they came to see the little girl now and then during the day, because the Store was just on the other side of one of the appartment's doors. The store was a Pharmacy. Mommy was a Pharmacist—that meant she talked nice to a lot of people who came to tell her

The author's parents, René and Jeanne Ferron-Wehrlin, on a picnic near Saint-Florentin, France, c. 1958

things about themselves, and she concocted magic potions for them in the back of the Store. Daddy had been a soldier in three wars, and now he helped Mommy with the Pharmacy, but everybody thought *he* was the Pharmacist, which Mommy didn't like much but she said nothing because she loved Daddy. And at bedtime, they told the little girl wonderful stories.

In a way, both Mommy and Daddy *were* stories that the little girl told herself during the day, waiting for them to appear. Mommy came from a very, very far away place, a lost place, called Indochina, where she had been born from the daughter of a native Princess and had lived until she had somehow escaped from it and her nasty adoptive father just before the Second War. She had brought some strange and wonderful things from there, like ivory and jade little women who played the flute; sometimes she prepared weird but mouth-watering meals which had nothing to do with chicken and fries, the Sunday's usual fare. And sometimes she even spoke in the tongue of that place, a funny, sing-songy language. She'd taught one word of it to the little girl: it sounded like *O-Zoï-Oï*, and it meant something like "The Sky is Falling !"

Daddy was a different kind of story. For more than a year, after the little girl was born, the box had been elsewhere, in another, less far away country called

Germany, and only Mommy lived in the box with her then, although the little girl did not see her very often either because Mommy was an important person there, with the Oc-cu-pa-tion Ar-my, and a lot of soldiers and other people were doing her bidding all day. But every night, before going to sleep, Mommy showed the little girl a picture of a man whom she told her was "Daddy," and she made the little girl say good-night to the picture and kiss it. One day, Mommy took the little girl away from Germany. When they arrived in Paris, at the train-station, there was a man waiting for them, and Mommy told the little girl: "There is your Daddy, say hello to him!" The little girl was quite disturbed: this man was obviously not the real Daddy! He had way too many dimensions, and he moved on his own! And he *talked* to her!

After a while, the little girl let herself be persuaded to talk back, in German first, then in French, for she then spoke both; and she ended up loving the three-dimensional Daddy very much—he played with her more than Mommy did, because he had a little more time. But at the back of her mind, from then on, there was always some vague distrust, or at least some wonder, about what was real, and what was not.

She was two, three, then four, going on five. And she was very lonely when Mommy or Daddy were not with her. She saw little of the other children in and around the appartment block, and she did not go to school yet. All she had were her few toys, the stories she told herself all day long, and the ones her parents told her at bedtime. She knew those by heart, she could almost *read* them too—but not quite. She just knew that those small, regular squiggles on the page were *words,* like the ones people spoke, but better, because these ones told stories. She also knew there was something called *writing,* that transformed sounds in those strange images that were words—but that kind of magic was still beyond her.

Until one afternoon, when she was entertaining herself alone, as usual, in the big bedroom she shared with her parents. She was playing with her wooden cubes, the ones Mommy had given her, with the *letters* and *numbers* and images on each brightly colored face. Mommy had been teaching her the letters and numbers. They had one-syllable names (except Double-You) and were somehow supposed to be like the image on their face of the cube but were obviously not, since there really was no resemblance whatsoever between M and the house, "maison," pictured on M's yellow face.

Age five, with her mother, on vacation in Thenon-les-Bains, Leman Lake, France, 1952

And so the little girl was playing with the cubes, in various arrangements. The combinations she preferred were the ones in which the images told a sort of story, the longer, the better.

What happened that day? I really don't remember. But at some point, the story goes, while she was chanting the sounds of the letters to go with the story, something . . . clicked. No other way to describe it. Click. She *got it.* The way the letters and the sounds played with one another to make *words,* and *she* could take the letters and make them make words. She could *write words.* And she did. She wrote "Mama" and "Papa," and then at some point she wrote her first story, and it was sheer fantasy, (and horrible spelling), because with her wooden cubes she wrote the equivalent of *maison bleue,* blue house.

I had never seen a blue house. There were no blue houses where we lived, only all shades-of-grey ugly cement buildings, or all-shades-of-dirty ugly red-brick houses. Blue houses simply *did not exist.* And yet one existed there, somehow, in front of me on the carpet, one that had not existed before—and I was the one who had made it.

I too could do magic!!!

I do perfectly remember the exhilaration, the sense of incredible power—and the wonder.

"How could I not become a writer after all this—and a writer of SF and Fantasy?" I rhetorically ask myself with forty-forty hindsight.

*

But nothing is as simplistically cause-and-effect in life, and it would be downright bad in a story, wouldn't it? Those things should be treated more like . . . genes: a predisposition to become this or that, which the environment plays upon. And boy, did the environment play! But we can skip ahead a few chapters, since that part of the story is quite typical: lonely childhood, picked upon at school, books my only friends—and there were *lots* of books at home, every kind *but* science fiction and fantasy (if one excepts romances, but what did I know of that then?). Anyway, it was not a question of reality versus fantasy. I lived among words, period. Words were life.

Was I determined from then on to become a writer? Noooooo. Not *at all.* But I did notice my parents' ooohs and aaaahs every time I wrote something. I learned quickly which side of my toast was buttered—especially since the oohs and aaaahs were much less enthusiastic when I drew or painted something, although I liked that much better. So from about my seventh year on, the drawing and painting fell slowly by the wayside, and I wrote . . . I wrote poetry, the rhyming kind. But at fifteen I realized I wanted another relationship with space and time than the one allowed by the poetry I had been taught. I played a while with free verse, but it seemed awfully . . . soft, amorphous—and way too emotional and personal. Without being aware of it, I wanted more *distance.* I wanted to tell real untrue stories.

Concurrently with my poetry, I had already begun dabbling in fiction, actually. For instance, I rewrote the ending of the Alamo story: I loved the John Wayne movie, but I wanted Bowie and Travis to survive and become pals. Also, at long last, I had a friend at school, a girl as crazy as I was: we encouraged one another, and at fifteen or so I did begin to write a novel. No preparation at all, just paper and pen, let's *go!* And it went well, although from the very first sentence the narrator who told the story of the me-character did it first person, past tense, said he was a boy, and he took a lot of place in the story thereafter. Still, it was fun to see oneself through him and him through what he saw of the me-character; I could revisit some cherished moments of my adolescence, try to capture sensations and feelings and places, and yes, it did work for a while. Somewhere near the last third of the story, though, as I was beginning to tell myself I should think of how it would end, my main protagonist, the girl whom everybody loved, still perversely insisted on being unhappy and border-line suicidal. In fact, the only way it could end was for her to kill herself. I was furious. I had confusedly thought writing would give me some sort of control, at least over my imaginary life, and it was turning out to be the other way around! I buried the unfinished, contrary, terrifying thing in a drawer and swore off writing main-lit. forever.

And as chance, serendipity, fate, destiny and/or the Author would have it, this is when I discovered science fiction, fantasy, and all these interesting, not-quite-legit literary beasties that roamed outside the box. That's when the little girl escaped the boxes—increasingly bigger, but still boxes—that she had inhabited after the one with the wooden cubes. Especially her teenage girl's box, this gloomy, narrow space that filled her with inchoate despair because it continuously exuded these words, silently uttered day after day by everyone and everything around her: "It is like this, it has always been like this, and it will always be like this."

But it was not true!

Science fiction was showing me that the Universe was much bigger, wilder, and wondrouser than I had been taught by my beloved teachers, and even by my beloved books. It *was* like this, yes, and it *had been* like this for a very long time, but it did not *have to be* like this forever.

Oh brave new world!

I do not mean I became a science fiction writer right then and there. But the fix was in. The next year, I would leave home to be all by myself for the first time in my life, a student at Dijon University. It would be the mid-Sixties, and a lot, my friend, would be blowing in the wind.

*

I would also have been writing science fiction in my closet for a year, ever since the Big Meaningful Dream

With her father, age five

from which had sprung, almost fully-dressed, a galloping, multigenerational science fiction saga which would become the five books of my series "Tyranaël" more than thirty years later. It was a very simple dream. In the daily diary I kept that last year at home and dropped after a few months at the university, utterly bored and depressed by my so-called real life, I wrote only two lines about this dream, and to this day I have no recollection of its images: words are all that are left of it. "A huge planet, entirely covered twice a year by a universal tide, during a universal eclipse, but nobody dies."

Though my journal says nothing of that dream afterwards and I don't remember exactly how things evolved from there, I very soon had a canvas of stand-alone but interlinked stories all contributing to an over-arching storyline—from the very beginning, I thought big. I began to draw maps and invent various languages, creatures, societies, and two whole planets.

The entire story was there from the beginning. Details changed over time, of course, as I came to understand more and more about it, myself, and the craft of writing. Of the two thousand pages I wrote and rewrote obsessively for ten years, only two hundred have passed without modifications from one draft to the next. But the basic impulse never changed, the original design, the original need. And in some way, everything I have written since (and will ever write, I am beginning to suspect), is inscribed in that ur-story.

During the mostly horrid university years, while I went to the required classes, wrote the required papers, passed the required exams and got the required degrees, I lived *there,* on my Tyranaël planet. Writing was breathing, was freedom, and, at last, power— writing *Science Fiction,* which was *so* not about boring and ugly little me (as my first abortive mainstream novel had been)! Wondrous creatures, magnificent landscapes, fateful destinies, deep mysteries, and world-shattering revelations, a whole cosmos was mine, entirely of my own devising. I was, let's not mince words, God.

From sixteen on, I learned writing with that grand, multigenerational story. That is, I learned to read what I had written, and then rewrite and reread and rewrite. . . . Ten years later, after writing the fourth version (all two thousand pages of it), having left the motherland and living in Chicoutimi, I would be able to admit at last that however far away in space and time, that story was and always had been all about me, my past and present life—what else could writing be about than what we know or think we know best, ourselves? But I also knew by then that this was much more than the mere, me-myself-and-I of the here-and-now. That "I," my Self, was Legion—touched by and always touching others, family, friends, my society, my time, the whole world, present, past *and future,* and all its places and cultures and stories, and on and on to the wonderfully endless, the endlessly wonderful Cosmos—the one I had not created but that I could recreate as I pleased and, doing so, could endlessly question.

That is the inquisitive little girl in me, and she will never stop being curious. I put her, again and again, in my stories, either as a child or as a grown-up, but always, my characters are asking *why,* or *how,* or *what for.* There were so many mysteries in my childhood! So many strange happenings: one day I learned that I had three half-sisters, much older than me, as they came to visit. My father had had other children, another family, another life of which I knew nothing! I learned later that my mother had also been married before. And I was told many colourful family stories, on both sides. My parents were for me heroes in a novel—both their lives had been tortured, adventurous, and romantic, vaulting two or three continents and, for my father, two centuries (he was born in 1898). But those stories were not fixed. They changed subtly over time, and above all they were full of holes that no one ever volunteered to fill and that I was discouraged to ask about—a far-away look, an averted face, the length of a silence, oh I was exquisitely atuned to those, like all children. I learned not to ask—and to make up stories instead to fill in the gaps. Trusting that someday, somehow, all would be revealed at last. But it never was. And I will never know what is real and what reinvented in what I was told. Not "lies"—different versions of one forever elusive tale.

Age sixteen, Sergines, France, 1963

My parents are dead now. And so they will forever be characters in a story of which they were the unreliable narrators. But their stories now belong wholly to me. I can ask all the questions I want and give all the answers I need—since I have learned, sometimes with painful and sometimes with glorious results, to refrain from not asking questions.

It must be one of the main reasons why science fiction rang such a resonant chord inside me when I discovered it. The main drive behind science fiction is a question: "What if . . . ?" What would happen if one of the tame givens of our consensual reality were *different*? And that key, for me, opened *everything*. It was not about "escapism" or "a good read" or Being Wonderfully Weird and Marginal (although it certainly helped: I was sixteen, after all). I read some of those books with the same exaltation as I read Camus or Kierkegaard or Sartre at the time: it was about life, my life and human life, here and now, in this world, in this time; it was about humans become as gods through science and technology—and whether they were worthy of it. It was about what "being human" could mean. It was about change, metamorphosis, transcendance—and the price to pay. And it was about the Other who is not always Us. Yes, all that was disguised, sometimes so exotically that I could lose myself for a moment—and that was fine!—but mostly the metaphors were strong enough, clear enough; the meaning always came through.

*

I have always been a voracious reader, since I was six or seven years old. In high school, I took to literature like the proverbial fish to water. I am talking about the pre-Sixties in France here, before mass education kicked in. I got a classical education in a girls-only *lycée* that catered mostly to the "future elite of the nation" (that's what the female principal reminded us of during the trimesterly reviews). Small groups, devoted and stern teachers (all women), and long days of work, five days a week. I do not regret it one bit. The social interactions were hell, but I loved learning. And there was some narcissistic pleasure to be derived from my scholarly successes, especially in the writing department. Lit. teachers usually love students who love reading and writing. And did I read! Some teachers even thought I read too much, and too indiscriminately. Not because I was reading science fiction—I wasn't then—but because at fifteen I devoured Simone de Beauvoir's, Camus' and Sartre's philosophy even more than their fiction. The keepers of the box worried about their little inmate—with the best intentions, certainly. Somehow, I have trouble understanding why, I had been pegged as a "difficult" student, a troublemaker. Poor little me, who wanted nothing more than to be loved and accepted, and who was so apt at conforming—I mean, I could write alexandrines in my sleep! But I couldn't quell my damnable curiosity and my logical contrariness: "Yes, but . . ." or "No, but . . ." had somehow become my

mantras somewhere along the line in high school, and have remained so ever since.

When SF happened to me, I read it with the same voracious appetite as I'd read the Classics and Moderns. In 1963, a French book tangential to the genre lent to me by an older male friend had brought it to my awareness. It was *Dawn of the Magicians*, by Louis Pauwels and Jacques Bergier. They argued very convincingly that science fiction was the only literature of the future. To find more about the authors they quoted, I rummaged through used books bins, I spent all my monthly allowance on SF books new and old, and when I had gone through all I could buy in French (around 1965: not as many translations then) I brushed up on my English, a lot, in order to read books in the original.

Science Fiction and the folksingers of the Sixties—Pete Seeger, Bob Dylan, Joan Baez, Leonard Cohen: to them I owe being able to speak and write in two languages—inhabiting two different realities at once, a very science-fictional (we say "sfnal") experience. But I loved knowing other languages anyway. After some shaky beginnings in my first high school year, I delighted in learning English, Latin, and then Greek; to this day I regret not having learned Spanish. In our circle at school, my friends and I spoke and wrote a private *sabir* made up in equal parts of all those languages. This was magic. This was power. It certainly gave me a peculiar point of view on the linguistic problems in Quebec and in Canada when I came to live there! But it also made me very aware of the importance of language in the building of one's world-view—and even more so when inventing a whole new world, be it human and dominantly female in the future as in *In the Mothers' Land*, or humanoid but alien in "Tyranaël." It also made me appreciate science fiction even more: where else would have I found such concerns in the mainstream fiction of the time? (Or even elsewhere: at the University, later, we were not told about Chomsky or the Sapir-Whorf hypothesis. . . .)

Still, by the end of the Sixties, I was beginning to feel vaguely disappointed, not really understanding why, by the science fiction I still read as intensively as ever. It seemed more and more to be about cowboys and Indians in space, shootouts, conquest, war, and destruction—in space. I was still writing my own stuff, though, the Tyranaël stories; it was a kind of addiction by then. Actually I didn't as much *write* the stories as explore and build the world around them in more and more minute details, with maps and dictionaries and repertories and what not. I was in grave danger of no longer *writing*, just . . . doodling. But There Came Ursula Le Guin.

Oh, I'd loved Sturgeon, and Simak, and Cordwainer Smith, and Jack Vance. And around 1968 I discovered with joy and awe and glee the two Harlan Ellison's New Wave anthologies, *Dangerous Visions*, which broke new ground both thematically and stylistically. And there had been a smattering of stories by women: Catherine Moore, and especially Judith Merril—not so much her own stories, except "That Only a Mother," but the SF anthologies she edited and that I found now and then in secondhand bookstores. I had indeed begun to hear new voices, but I was not really *aware* that their newness for me, their deep resonance, was somehow linked to their femaleness. So I can say that the one who really gave me permission to write what I wanted to write was Ursula Le Guin with *The Left Hand of Darkness*. (Me and about a zillion others women writers in my generation. But I was the one and only freak in the whole world who loved and read science fiction at the time, of course.) However, the two others who gave me permission were men, which only reflects the realities of the genre then. Frank Herbert, with *Dune* (1970): hey, it is *allowed* to write a big, more than two hundred page long SF novel! and Tolkien, a bit later (1972): hey, it is *allowed* to build a world by playing with invented languages and names!

With its beautifully grim and provocative depiction of the planet Winter and its potentially ambisexed inhabitants, its deeply human characters (both alien and human) engaged in strange but meaningful relationships, its effortless merging of science and myth and its elegant prose, Le Guin's book was a revelation. Yes, this was what I had wanted to read. Yes, this was how I wanted to write: with total committment to both writing and subject matter, not for facile entertainment, testosteroned power trips, or conformity to the dominant world-views but for beauty, for self-exploration, for knowledge, for wisdom. And not for answers, but for questions. New ways of asking old questions—and if I was very, very lucky, new questions.

*

The feminist aspect of this new awareness became more specific after 1970. It was not the birth of my political conscience, I already had acquired one, especially after the events of 1968, a turning point for me as well as for many young adults in France and elsewhere. But from then on feminism would orient my political awareness in all domains. I was now married, to begin with—to my own surprise. Love, a husband, all that relational stuff, I had thought very early that it would never be at the center of my existence—or even at its periphery! I had resigned myself to and found many pleasures in being a loner, as most girls do who are not pretty enough to be forgiven for being bright—even today, alas. But even the experience of being married in 1969, in the midst of the counterculture thing, was not the prime cause of my becoming a feminist. Science fiction was.

For there was an explosion of female science fiction authors in the Seventies: not only Le Guin but Joanna Russ, Suzy McKee Charnas, Pamela Sargent, and many, many others. (An "explosion" for me because I lived in France until 1973; there was a very definite timelag in translations then, and the original books were hard to get.) I became a feminist more through their science-fiction than with the texts of the Grand Old Canonical Feminist Mothers, which I read much, much later. Women writers of SF, yes, those were the ones who wrote what I wanted to read, asked what I wanted to understand. Even though there was that American author who was getting in his stride at the time, James Tiptree, Jr., the one man who allowed me to entertain some hope for male SF writers.

In 1978, with the rest of the SF world community, I learned that a woman was James Tiptree, Jr. and had been deliberately playing the alias card for ten years. Witness to the sometimes quite unpleasant upheavals provoked by this revelation, I gathered all the Tiptree stories I had on my shelves and reread them all. And suddenly, gee, it was so *obvious* that she was a woman!

"When It Changed" is a striking feminist short story by Joanna Russ. Well, for me, that's When It Changed forever. For I had had no inkling whatsoever before that a woman was James Tiptree, Jr. All I knew when I read the stories as they were published under the Tiptree alias was that they resonated with me much more deeply than most stories written by other male writers at the time. I could only compare their effect on me to that of Ted Sturgeon's stories—but even stronger. After all, Sturgeon's main body of work, what I had read of it, dated back to the '40s, '50s and

Receiving the Dagon Prize with Norbert Spehner, Longueuil, Quebec, 1978

'60s; whereas Tiptree wrote *now,* with a sensibility more directly linked to the world I was experiencing as a young adult. That they in fact belonged to the same generation (Sturgeon born in 1918, Tiptree in 1915), I didn't know at the time; their life stories were very different—and Tiptree, indeed, had begun writing and publishing quite late in her life. At any rate, what the Tiptree Incident changed for me, the lasting cognitive dissonance it introduced in my thinking, was that feminism and related subjects ceased once and for all to be possible *answers* for me. Going far beyond the old saw of "feminine" and "masculine" writing, it all became another huge question mark—and a new way of approaching science fiction's fundamental query, "What is to be human?"

I was still a closet writer in 1978. I still did not see myself as a writer either, did not dare think of myself in that way. The mystique was still very much alive. Still, there was a glimmer of something to which I secretly clung in spite of myself. A French writer I admired, a man I admired, Pierre Versins (author of the first French encyclopedia of SF and Utopia), reading the final version of "Tyranaël" circa 1976, had told me: "You have in you many stories to tell yet." He had even wanted to get the novel published at the time

by L'Age d'Homme, a then prestigious Swiss publisher—thank God it fell through. But his comment, and his friendship, were a tremendous boost whenever I had the blues. We do have several fathers in our lives.

*

So I was a closet SF storyteller, at least. But no longer a closet SF afficionada. In 1974, I had linked with the then-nascent Quebecois SF community, gathered around the fanzine *Requiem.* Despite its title, it published SF as well as what we call "Fantastique" in French. I was then a temp teaching literature at the Chicoutimi University; *Requiem*'s editor and publisher, Norbert Spehner, who was a very busy full-time teacher in a Longueuil college as well as a busy family man, was quite willing to unload most of his literary editing job on me about 1976; I would become the official literary editor in 1979, as the fanzine would change its name to *Solaris.* In 1976, I had finished the fourth and what I thought to be the last draft of "Tyranaël". People had read bits and pieces of it, a few (Norbert among them) the whole thing, and they were quite enthusiastic about it. It had become a sort of running gag among us: the great SF novel sitting in a drawer. Dared to produce a short story after writing at such unconscionable lengths, I did manage to write something short—still linked somehow to "Tyranaël," although as in a parallel universe, independently of the novel's storylines. In 1979, it was translated as "High Tide" in a Maxim Jakubowsky anthology published at the same time in the UK and in France—my first professionally published story was also a translated one, perhaps a harbinger of things to come but I certainly did not see it that way then: it was more like a fluke, or at least a most excellent joke.

OK, I could apparently write short stuff. *Requiem* organized an annual short story contest. My first try in 1977 was the first version of "Le Pont du froid," later translated as "Cold Bridge." The members of the *Requiem* jury found the story interesting but too opaque and too long. I rewrote it—*adding* about six or seven pages. Upon which Norbert exclaimed: "There, you see, now that you've shortened it, it works great!" A priceless lesson in narrative strategies . . . and I was so proud that it was not related to "Tyranaël"! It came from a conversation with my then husband, a physicist whose master's degree has been about vacuum (an endless subject of hilarity between us). To make a vacuum in a laboratory, you must reach very low temperatures. At very low temperatures, the dance of the atoms slows down. From there on to speculate that at cold enough temperatures movement would cease altogether, there was a step easily made by a sfnal mind. But as I recall, what immediately came to me was a sort of oxymoronic impulse: the movement of *matter* would stop, and so the *mind* would somehow be free to move anywhere across the universe. (I was still a dualist at the time—hard not to be when one is born in Descartes' country. This would become a question too, which I tested in "Cogito.") How I went from "across the universe" to "across the universes" plural, must have been linked to "Tyranaël": the parallel universes motif was already in there. The brainstorming specific to science fiction then took over, and I ended up with the idea of a machine (unexplained, really), the Bridge, and Voyagers who are trained in monastery-like Centers to jump from one universe to another.

The theme was not original, of course: it's been one of the staples of science fiction for decades, the source of endless variations. I love it because it is an apt image of life as well as of writing, and a useful trans-generic device. My variation was the idea of a universe-hopping process that is completely unreliable, and thus "useless," unexploitable in capitalistic terms, while somehow dependent on the individual Voyager's inner evolution—a metaphor both of dreaming and psychoanalysis. Or of writing. Megalomaniac as ever, I immediately felt I had a frame for several Voyagers' stories there and I wrote a list of stories-to-write, among which that of a "reluctant Voyager." Then I put the list in a file with other outlines and forgot it.

My second try at the *Requiem* prize, in 1978, "L'œil de la nuit" ("The Eye of the Night," not translated) won that year. To my relative dismay, it also had its origin in "Tyranaël"—was in fact the very last story of the series, although one of the stand-alones that could really stand alone. As synchronicity would have it, a colleague of Norbert, who owned a small publishing house, Le Préambule, asked him then to become the chief editor of a new SF line, "Chroniques du Futur." Norbert began making the rounds of would-be authors. Suddenly motivated, I trotted out my stories-to-write file and began churning out one story after the other—none about the Bridge, though. One was even not SF but "fantastique." They were published as a collection, my first, and well received by critics in the field and

out of it. Gee, it even won a regional award; what I liked best was the $500 check, I confess.

I was pleased, of course. But I still didn't see myself as a writer. It was all a fluke, or a game—it still is a game, fortunately, since I have learned in the meantime that games are serious business in which you don't take *yourself* seriously. Besides, about 1978 and for a few years after that, I was almost more interested in being a singer and a songwriter: I had been at it since the early Seventies, on an amateur basis, but it was suddenly becoming more than a lark: I had won a singing contest, I was on the local, then the national, radio, I got gigs in various places around Quebec. . . . I see now that writing songs was a way for me to keep on writing poetry, which I had stopped doing altogether a few years before. It filled a deeply-felt need. I am often told I write very visual stories, and I guess it is partially true, but the last editing is always done for the ear, not for the eye or "the message"—and so is my poetry.

Still, fiction-writing-wise, I hadn't been idle after "finishing" "Tyranaël" in 1976. I had been working on and off on another SF project, mostly after reading a novel by Charles Maine, *Alph* (1972): five hundred years in the future, only women having survived and still surviving quite well, they discover a cryogenized male and basically fall over themselves in order to have his baby, which will be the beginning of a New, Better, Heterosexually Reproductive Era. I am being unfair to Charles Maine, it's slightly more complex than that—but not by much, and anyway it's how I read it then that impelled me to begin what would in time become *In the Mothers' Land*. I was incensed by Maine's book, as I recall. First, the verisimilitude of the whole plot seemed shaky to me from a sfnal point of view: after five centuries of homoeroticism, homosociety, and parthogenesis, why would one woman immediately fall in love with the reborn male (a male baby is created from the man's DNA) and then want to mate with him in the antique manner? And how could *one* male be, so to speak, up to the task afterwards for a whole society? Second, and more to the point, the unexamined subtextual masculinist assumptions of this plot were just too much for me. At about the same time, 1978, I had read Suzy McKee Charnas's *Walk to the End of the World* and its sequel, *Motherlines,* which also posits a postapocalyptic world, with on the one hand women's enslavement and abuse and on the other separatist groups of Amazonish Free Women—much harder-hitting and more thought-provoking books for all their unrelenting grimness. Each writer writes with other writers in her field, an endless, fecund conversation: all this, the Tiptree Incident and what I was experiencing as a woman at the time, coalesced into another big project, a trilogy, no less, that would explore my own version of a women-only, or a women-mainly, postapocalyptic future, the postapocalyptic setting being the usual expedient tabula rasa.

*

A Lot Was Revealed at the end of the first book, but I still didn't want to do the grand boring explanation tour. I decided to go visual, cinematic even, and splice in short takes of a larger story, in the form of bursts of images seen on a screen by the main protagonist. I at least had to know what the larger story was, didn't I? It was around 1981 then, my collection had been published, several people were pestering me for a short story. . . . I thought that writing one as a stand-alone would neatly serve a dual purpose and I set out to do just that.

After a week, I had about eighty pages. OK, it wanted to be a novella. After two weeks, I had twice as many pages—I knew I had a novel on my hands. Unexpected, uninvited, infuriating in some bizarre way because I still believed much more in writing as control than as a dance between control and trust. But I wrote it, sometimes letting it write itself, and learning a lot in the process—as always. After a month or so I ended up with a three hundred page novel, *Le Silence de la Cité*—later *The Silent City*.

Now what to do with it? My then-husband, who had always been very supportive of my writing, told me to send it to various publishers in Quebec, and in France. Of the three publishers I sent the MS to, French Denoël answered "yes" the fastest (a telegram!). They had "Présence du Futur," the grand old SF line that had given me so many great SF books to read. What a thrill that my first novel should be published there! The editor at the time was Élisabeth Gille, whom I had met in various SF conventions in France and who, intrigued by pieces of "Tyranaël" I had sent her, wanted to see something else, more publishable, that is, shorter. Well, there was something else, and she wanted it. We negotiated some changes—we saw eye

to eye on all of them—and the book was published in 1981. It won the French Grand Prix de la SF in 1982. Two books, two awards: I lived a charmed life. I was beginning to think that I would keep on writing, and perhaps being published.

I did write several versions of the new SF trilogy, or at least of the two first books. But Élisabeth Gilles, and I am forever grateful to her for that, kept rejecting them with cogent arguments which always echoed the misgivings crowding in on me just after I'd sent her yet another version. But as publishing was not my main goal, this wasn't too much of a downer. I felt I was learning the craft. Then ordinary life got the better of me, and the writing took a back seat. After almost fifteen years of marriage, and despite remaining good friends, my husband and I had changed a lot, and we had drifted apart. I acknowledged that fact in 1982 and called it quits. I was by myself again, with a part-time university job that was becoming less and less reliable as a source of income—and absolutely no desire to embark on a serious academic "career" (I am not good in hierarchical power structures where I have no say about who will have direct power over me, and how). The Eighties were going to be rough, on every account.

Around 1984, another story collection was published by Denoël, *Janus*. There were a few stories belonging to the "Bridge Cycle" and others were set in Baïblanca, a fictitious city in a world predating that of *Silent City*, complete with both metamorphs—shapechangers— and "artefacts": artificially created organic "statues" that are really a new breed of people. It got good reviews again. I decided that a way of surviving financially while still writing would be to go back to school: try for a Ph.D. at Laval University, in Quebec City. Not to get yet another degree to further a career I neither had nor wanted, but simply because I had good prospects of obtaining several respectably sized grants for at least three or four years running—and that just to think about writing and science fiction! At first it was to be "Women and Science Fiction," then a new program was launched at Laval U. in 1985, Creative Writing. I did qualify for it and switched with secret glee since I would be studying . . . my own writing.

*

One had to write a theoretical thesis *and* a fiction that somehow illustrated the ideas and theories put forward in the first part (what an odd concept!). I would do

Vonarburg, 1982

both in one fell swoop: a fictional character from another universe, a young woman studying to be a Voyager, would undergo her final test in a parallel near future of our world. She would choose as her cover identity that of a student working on her master's at Laval University, a study of the fiction of Élisabeth Vonarburg, an obscure SF author presumed dead in a political riot during Quebec's turbulent Nineties. She would keep a journal, in which she would enter her various academic essays and articles on Vonarburg, each using a different critical approach—narratology, psychocritique, sociology, semiotics, and whatnot, all the academic sacred cows of the day. In the end, since we all have doubles in other universes, she would understand that Vonarburg was her double in that particular universe and by doing so she would pass her final exam with flying colours.

I was fortunate enough to have a really good supervisor, who didn't know much about SF but had no literary preconceptions, liked the kind of SF I wrote, and let me mostly run amok, only intervening exactly when and where necessary. She barely complained while I

sent her, machine gun like, about two thousand pages of text over six months. She read it all and just said in the end: "Now, make five hundred pages out of it, with a bibliography." I did, concocting a very serious-looking and partially bogus bibliography, containing stories or books I or others had not written—yet. Oh, it was fun.

Or was it? A dark, savage kind of fun, mostly. I remember that period as one of terrible angst. The usual questions, made mandatory by the exercise itself, were killing me: What is writing? Why do I write? Why do I write science fiction? What kind of a writer am I? Will I keep on being a writer? What *use* being a writer? *Who am I?* At some point, I had the impression that I had stopped writing fiction altogether, until I realized that over a three-year period, I had published almost a dozen short stories—perhaps one of the most prolific periods in my life.

There was another reason yet for the angst: I had pulled a Tiptree on myself, sort of.

In the early Eighties, I was still temp-teaching on and off, and sometimes teaching creative writing, in various universities. I was experimenting along with my students. In 1985, I tried a neo-surrealist *collage* technique. Diverse poems or texts are cut into words, or lines, pinches of them are put in small plastic bags, then later spread right side up on the desk, one after the other, and you wait for the not so random electricity of meaning to zap them together (I should say "magnetism," as in Philippe Soupault's "Les chants magnétiques"; the source lines, or combinations of words in poetry, are of course always heavily reworked afterwards.) It's a bit like Tarot cards, or the I Ching. Or the ink blot test! I came to use it on an irregular basis to get a deeper reading of my inner states—and thus to write my poetry.

In 1985, it produced a story that resembled nothing I had done before ("Ailleurs et au Japon," not translated) but in which I thought I saw absolutely everything my writing was about—influences, styles, themes. Yet, the friends who read it unanimously told me it was something completely new. Half-jokingly, one of them suggested sending it under a pseudonym to the editor of the other Quebecois SF magazine, *imagine . . .,* who had systematically rejected every story I had sent him, even those Denoël had published later in *Janus.* I tended to suspect less than good faith on his part: we didn't get along well personally, and *Solaris* and *imagine . . .* were, despite various lip services by all, rivals as well.

I sent the story, under a pseudonym—a female one, though: "Sabine Verreault," an anagram of my name less the letters b-o-g, which meant God in Russian—I chose to see it as a sign!—with an accompanying letter establishing the kind of bogus identity I thought would entice him: an academic (he was one), a rather cerebral lit. professor dabbling in fiction (he was one too).

He gobbled it up. He loved it. Still, he wrote me back, it was a bit too complex and experimental a story for his usual readers; could I do something more mainstream SF?

Sure. I churned out another story, not using the random method, ("The Sleeper in the Crystal," very loosely derived from a song of mine, itself vaguely linked to "Tyranaël") and sent it almost by return mail—I, who never could fill a writing order! He loved it again. He was obviously delighted to have discovered a New Author, and a woman to boot, who could jump through hoops on demand. Now, how about a novella, something around eighty pages?

I proceeded to do so, using the same *collage* technique as in the first text, and wrote "Mané, Thékel, Pharès" (not translated). The friends who were my trial readers had already been worried with the second story; even more so with the novella: to them, it was so obviously from Vonarburg that it would be recognized at once, and then what? But no: the editor's enthusiasm didn't wane. He published all three stories, saluting a new, formidable author; and Sabine Verreault was nominated for that year's main Quebecois SF award.

I couldn't do that to my friends on the jury, so I outed Sabine to them. And to *imagine . . .*'s editor. To this day his argument has been two-pronged; (a) those texts were not Vonarburg's kind of stories, and (b) even if they were for those in the know, the effect of the para-text (the pseudonym and the letters we exchanged) naturally made him read them as different.

And to this day I can't decide otherwise: after all, isn't that what Tiptree pulled on the whole SF community—and on me?

But then, I thought anxiously to myself at the time, if I can write differently just by using a pseudonym—who am I, really? As a writer *and* as a person? Fortunately, the work I did for the Ph.D. helped me solve those questions, at least for a while. Sabine was, in many ways, the return of the repressed; she was less eager to seduce or coddle her readers, more "literary" in her style, less encumbered with plot, darker and more openly violent in her themes and writing. Finally, in 1987 (the year I obtained my Ph.D.), Sabine and I wrote a story together, ("To Die, a Little"), which we co-signed; after that, Sabine reintegrated my self, having taught me a priceless lesson and helped me get out of a box of my own devising.

*

The thinking I did for my Ph.D. had two other major consequences. First, it reconnected me with *Tyranaël*. Rereading parts of it to study them, I could feel that something was still responding in me; the magic was still there; the landscape, the characters, the stories, all still talked to me. It was not merely a narcissistic, guilty pleasure to indulge in secret and never let out in the light of day. It was central to my writing as well as to my understanding of myself; it was a matrix. And perhaps, just perhaps, I would one day be able to write it as it deserved to be written, without betraying it. Sometimes, in the innocence/ignorance of youth, you find truths that you rediscover again, the hard way, when you're older. It's also true of writing: when you don't know you're not supposed to do something, you just do it, and it works, and you don't ask why. Later, you don't know why it worked: you have to learn, painstakingly, to do in full awareness what you did effortlessly, unself-consciously, way back then. Still, eight years would pass before I tackled "Tyranaël" again, once and for all.

Another consequence of the Ph.D. was to show me what was wrong with the feminist SF trilogy I had tried to write from '78 to '85. I now knew how to write it! But I didn't then. Ordinary life and its demands, again. Survival. I was relying more on translations than on teaching now to keep me afloat, and although translating is the next best thing to writing for a writer (especially translating works that you like), it eats up the time one would otherwise dedicate to writing. The impetus for writing—writing novel-length fiction, I mean—came from another quarter entirely.

Some time in the first half of the Eighties, I had received a phone call from a Montreal translator, Jane Brierley. Asked to translate some Quebecois short stories for an anthology published in Toronto, she'd been given free rein as to whom she would translate, she liked my stories, could she translate a few of them?

As I said: I live a charmed life. When one knows how difficult it generally is to find a good translator! (There are translation grants in Canada, though, which helps a lot once you have a publisher.) I gave Jane the go-ahead, gladly, and there began a friendly and fecund collaboration that greatly changed my literary trajectory. From then on I would be published in English. For a non-English-speaking SF writer, that was and still is a kind of Holy Grail. SF, for better and for worse, speaks English (and especially American English). Unless you've been translated, you have no chance whatsoever to be included in the collective creation that is science fiction (and I am not even talking about making a living at it!). Your work doesn't register. It simply doesn't exist. Which I could have lived with quite easily since I did exist after all in the little box of French-speaking SF, both in Quebec and in France. But serendipity, again, would have it otherwise.

In 1979, I organized the first Quebecois SF convention in Chicoutimi. Unchastised, I went at it again three times, in 1982, 1988, and 1999. In 1982, it coincided with the International Francophone Convention. International meant there were people from Europe, from the States, and from Canada. I knew that the fabled Judith Merril, SF writer and anthologist extraordinaire, lived in Toronto. This was the New World, the Land of Opportunity: I invited her. She accepted. She came. She danced all night. I fell in love. With luck, you may also have several mothers in your life, women who bring you into a new world. Le Guin certainly was one. Judith was another. I still am not sure what she saw in my writing or in me—I had only one translated story at the time, "High Tide." But when she edited the first Canadian SF anthology, *Tesseracts*, in 1985, she asked me for a story. It didn't have to be an original one. Jane Brierley exquisitely translated "Home by the Sea," one of my favourites—the first story in which I had been able to portray a mother and a daughter. And Judy gave it the lead in the anthology. Because she really liked it, she said. I was thunderstruck. Being acknowledged by a living legend sometimes does that to you.

The story was well received. And the people at Press Porcépic, the *Tesseracts* publisher, asked me if I had anything novel-length. Well, I did have a novel—which Jane then proceeded to translate as *The Silent City*. That was in 1988. In 1990, it would be published in the U.K. by The Women's Press. I was thrilled. At last it would be available in English to the readership I most wanted to reach: women.

*

Then, in 1991, by some twist of fate I haven't elucidated yet, I found myself with a high-powered American agent and a three-books contract with Bantam—without having done a thing to get them. *The Silent City* would be the first book, in 1992; did I have anything else in the works? I said "yes," although strictly speaking it wasn't true; but there was that postapocalyptic feminist novel I'd floundered at during the early Eighties, and I was ready now to write it—or it was ready to be written, same difference. It took a year, with a peculiar effect of feedback since Jane Brierley was translating it as it was written, part by part, and I changed things after revising the English version, and so on and so forth—Jane was getting rather frazzled in the end! But *In the Mother's Land* was published at the same time in English and in French, a first ever in Canadian SF, I was told. The third book I didn't worry too much about: something would come to me. And it did: a dream I had in the basement bedroom my friend Norbert Spehner kept for me at his Montreal home. Cross-pollinated with those Bridge/ Voyagers story outlines I had put away in a drawer in the Seventies, several other dreams I had kept for years and some already published stories which I put through the grinder, it would become what I consider half-jokingly my "post-modernist quebecois novel," *Reluctant Voyagers* (1995).

Then, as suddenly as my "American career" had begun, it ended: Bantam dropped me (as many other, bigger writers) due to savage reorganizations in the wake of its takeover by a German megacorp. After that, about a dozen of my translated short stories were still published in Canada, in the yearly *Tesseract* anthologies, and also in the States, in *Amazing* and especially thanks to the editor of *Tomorrow*, Algis Budrys (another of my living legends!).

I still regard the whole episode as another kind of fluke, a wonderful learning opportunity, but above all I am grateful that it connected me —at least poten-

Élisabeth Vonarburg, 1995, Montreal, Quebec

tialy—with the audience I craved, the women readers and writers. For among the awards bestowed on *In the Mother's Land* (for instance, the Philip K. Dick Jury's Special Award), the novel was short-listed for the Tiptree Award. "It's an honor just to be nominated" is supposed to be a hypocritical cliché, but I swear it wasn't for me. Considering the influence Tiptree had on my life and writing, it was an almost unimaginable happenstance. I remember thinking half-jokingly: "Well, I can die now!" In the wake of that acknowledgement, I connected with the community of women SF writers in the States by attending the twentieth anniversary of their annual convention, Wiscon—where I met, or met again, with my heroes: Le Guin, Merril, Charnas, et al.

Science fiction and fantasy are not like other genres: they can be intensely personal in that writers, readers, publishers, editors, reviewers, artists, and just-fans constantly have opportunities to meet and talk and argue and speculate. Somehow, science fiction and

fantasy are like one huge story collectively told, infinitely mutable, almost like a living organism. It is also true, of course, of the rest of literature, but this essence is concentrated in sometimes dizzying densities in the science fiction microcosm. I know this because I am also part of "the rest of literature," through the various writers' associations I belong to in Canada. Nowhere have I felt a sense of camaraderie comparable to the one I feel, even after all this time, among the SF community. It can be explained away, of course, by the Ghetto Syndrome—something the SF afficionados either rail against or proudly defend. But part of it also comes from deeply-shared worldviews and quirks, be it relentless questioning, distrust of consensual reality, the quest for the Other, or the good old "sense of wonder" when looking at the Universe.

I call myself a writer now—a female writer (*écrivaine*, which is linguistically iffy in French, even today. Ah well. Being a feminist is having a pebble in one shoe you can never take off anyway). I am a woman-who-writes, even though I still don't really know what that means. But it's OK. If I *knew* this, or anything else for that matter, I would not write. A writer is also, it seems, someone who writes because she or he does not *know*. How nicely Socratic. I do not *know* what is reality or fiction, reality or dream—I'm quite happy circulating from one to the other and back without having to flash a passport every time. I do not *know* what a woman or a man or a human being is, what is Same and what is Other, but I am quite happy to explore and entertain some fancy ideas about what they *could* be.

Now, is that creating what wasn't there before or discovering what is there for all eternity? I do not know. Either. Both. Why not? Who's to judge? I'm not sitting in the lap of Ultimate Reality. None of us are. We fumble around, in creative misunderstanding at best, trying to dance, to keep a balance. I am a dreamer whose dreams become words, become books, whose books go in some readers' hands and then in their minds, and some readers tell me, or write me, that they dream of my words, of my worlds. What the heck is happening here? I am not sure—but I like it.

Now something has happened in the world that has made me question my craft once more in anguish. Another Fall. We humans keep falling and falling again. Which means we get up again and again—some of us do, at least. I stopped writing—I was in the last part of a two-parts fantasy novel which I had been writing in pure bliss during the whole summer of 2001 when the towers fell in Manhattan. But we must do what we can and know how to do, each in one's little space-time, each with one's little talent. For various accidental reasons, I became a writer and I must write, it is as simple as that. Writing is breathing to me and I must breathe—it is as simple as that.

For a while, I didn't breathe much, just passed words to and fro, the words of others mostly, to console, educate, enlighten, renew bounds. I hoped my own words would come back to me. I would breathe again, I had to believe that. I am a creature of words, I must believe in words. And now they're back—I'm back in the blue house. It's as simple as that.

BIOGRAPHICAL AND CRITICAL SOURCES:

PERIODICALS

Booklist, March 1, 1996, review of *Les Voyagers Malgre Eux,* p. 1126.
Financial Post, May 20, 1995, Shlomo Schwartzberg, "Winning the Battle of Strange Worlds," p. 28.
Lettres Quebecoises, fall, 1997, review of *Tyranaël III,* p. 35; spring, 1998, review of *Tyranaël IV,* p. 33; summer, 1999, review of *Silence de la Cit´* p. 31.
Lurelu, spring-summer, 1995, review of *Contes de Tyranaël,* p. 40; December, 1997-March, 1998, review of *Contes de la Chatte Rouge,* p. 78.
Nuit Blanche, summer, 1997, review of *Reves de la Mer,* p. 17; fall, 1997, review of *Tyranaël II* and *Tyranaël III,* p. 11; fall, 1998, review of *Tyranaël IV,* p. 13.
Prarie Fire, winter, 1995, "Going Home to Baiblanca: Homage to Élisabeth Vonarburg," p. 88.
Saturday Night, December, 1999, "A Strange Trip into Tomorrow," p. 76.
SF Chronicle, April 1997, review of *Tesseracts 9,* p. 74; June, 2001, review of *Slow Engines of Time,* p. 39.
Tribune Books (Chicago, IL), February 3, 2002, review of *Slow Engines of Time,* p 10.
Utopian Studies, spring, 1999, Philip Abbott, "Northern Dreamers: Interviews with Famous Science-Fiction, Fantasy, and Horror Writers," p. 325.
Video-Presse, June, 1995, "Élisabeth Vonarburg," p. 22.

OTHER

Feminist Science Fiction, Fantasy, & Utopia Web site, http://www.feministsf.org/ (July 4, 2002).
Official Élisabeth Vonarburg Web site http://www.sfwa.org/ (June 9, 2001).*

W

WAGNER, Nike 1945-

PERSONAL: Born September 6, 1945, in Weberlingen, Germany; daughter of Wieland (a stage producer) and Gertrud (a choreographer) Wagner; married Jean Launay (divorced) married Jürg Stenzel (a musicologist), October 1991; children: Louise. *Education:* Northwestern University, Ph.D., 1980.

ADDRESSES: Home—Walfishgasse 12, 1010 Vienna, Austria. *E-mail*—nikewagner@utanet.at

CAREER: Musicologist and cultural critic.

MEMBER: Deutsche Academies für Sprache und Dichtung, Pen Club (Austria).

WRITINGS:

The Wagners: The Dramas of a Musical Dynasty, translated by Ewald Osers and Michael Downes, Princeton University Press (Princeton, NJ), 2001.
Wagner Theater, Insel Verlag (Frankfurt, Germany), 1998.
Traumtheater: Szenarien der Moderne, Insel Verlag (Frankfurt, Germany) 2001.

Also author of *Geist und Geschlecht,* a literary criticism of Karl Kraus, and *Terre étrangère: Création au Théâtre des amandiers,* [Nanterre, France], 1984.

SIDELIGHTS: Nike Wagner is a musicologist and cultural critic based in Vienna. She is also the great-granddaughter of Richard Wagner and is passionately involved in her family saga. *The Wagners: The Dramas of a Musical Dynasty* is the intertwined story of the Wagner family, the operas of Richard Wagner, and the Bayreuth Festival, which the extended family of Richard Wagner has presided over since it opened in 1876.

Nike Wagner begins her family history with her great-grandfather, Richard, who started the dynasty. She sees him as a man of musical talent but believes he has reprehensible political views. His 1850 essay, "Jewishness in Music," she explains, is a study in anti-Semitism. His wife Cosima, the daughter of Franz Liszt, was strong, single-minded, nationalistic, anti-Semitic, and devoted to her husband. She was largely responsible for creating the Wagner legend after his death in 1883. At the beginning of the twentieth century, Cosima went so far as to declare her daughter Isolde illegitimate to insure her son Seigfried's ascendancy to the family throne.

When the Third Reich took power in the 1930s Sigfreid was in control of Bayreuth and his English wife Winifred ran the family estate Wahnfried and became a close friend of Adolf Hitler. After the war there was a growing rivalry between Wieland, Nike's father, and her uncle Wolfgang, who jointly controlled the festival. Wieland began producing acclaimed avant-garde interpretations of the Wagner canon and, if he had not died young, Nike Wagner believes her father would have become one of the great operatic directors of the twentieth century. Nike Wagner is hoping to control the Bayreuth festival one day.

Nike Wagner says that Richard Wagner always divided the outside world into friends and enemies, and that this has become the family norm. In *The Wagners: The Dramas of a Musical Dynasty* she concludes that "The traces of this Wagnerian manner can be seen clearly in the behavior of the individual family members: self glorifying egos permit themselves astonishing liberties in word and deed, solidarities become antagonisms, and conflicts broaden into vendetta. The rejection and expulsion of weaker members of the family, particularly women, become preferable to the attempt at integration, and the selfish gestures, the divisive action and the polarization of enemies are accepted strategies of survival."

The Wagners is partly a manifesto for change at Bayreuth—Wagner believes that her uncle's old-fashioned productions are not in tune with the times. As she told Margarette Driscoll in the London *Sunday Times,* "In other opera houses in Germany you can see much better performances. . . . Saying 'Yes, yes, Herr Wagner', is no way to run a theater." However, she admits, "I'm schizophrenic on this. Such is the subterranean power of family. On the one hand I believe art is above such things, it doesn't recognise family bonds. But knowing our history, knowing how much blood, sweat and tears went into building Wahnfried and the opera house I can't help but feel a family member should be responsible."

BIOGRAPHICAL AND CRITICAL SOURCES:

BOOKS

Wagner, Nike, *The Wagners: The Dramas of a Musical Dynasty,* translated by Ewald Osers and Michael Downes, Princeton University Press (Princeton, NJ), 2001.

PERIODICALS

Booklist, March 15, 2001, Alan Hirsch, review of *The Wagners,* p. 1343.
Daily Telegraph (London, England), January 13, 2001, Michael White, review of *The Wagners,* p. 6.
Economist, May 9, 1998, review of *Wagner Theater,* p. 84.
Financial Times (London, England), January 13, 2001, Andrew Clark, review of *The Wagners,* p. 5.

Herald (Glasgow, Scotland), February 17, 2001, Conrad Wilson, review of *The Wagners,* p. 19.
Library Journal, March 1, 2001, review of *The Wagners,* p. 96.
New York Times Book Review, May 20, 2001, John Rockwell, "Lords of the 'Ring': Wagner's Great-granddaughter Sees Her Family Mirrored in the Operas," p. 36.
New York Times, August 27, 2000, Bernard Holland, "More Cracks in the Walls of Valhalla," p. AR23; May 20, 2001, John Rockwell, "Lords of the Ring," p. 36.
New York Review of Books, August 9, 2001, Joseph Kerman, review of *The Wagners,* p. 37.
Opera News, April, 2001, Rudolph S. Rauch, review of *The Wagners,* p. 104.
Publishers Weekly, March 26, 2001, review of *The Wagners,* p. 78.
Sunday Telegraph (London, England), January 21, 2001, Michael Kennedy, review of *The Wagners,* p. 16.
Sunday Times (London, England), January 14, 2001, Margarette Driscoll, profile of the Wagner family and the Bayreuth Festival, p. 6.
Times (London, England), January 17, 2001, Roger Boyes, review of *The Wagners,* p. 14.
Times Literary Supplement, May 4, 2001, Patrick Carnergy, review of *The Wagners,* p. 11.
Wall Street Journal, August 9, 2001, Paul Levy, "A Ring around the Ring."*

*   *   *

WATERS, James E. 1922-2002

OBITUARY NOTICE—See index for *CA* sketch: Born June 29, 1922, in Michigan City, IN; died from diabetes-related complications March 2, 2002, in Phoenix, AZ. Journalist and author. Waters was a longtime reporter for the Associated Press who helped cover the Watergate Scandal of the early 1970s. He attended Pierce College in Los Angeles and Arizona State University before joining the Associated Press in 1943, working in offices in New York City, Washington, D.C., Los Angeles, Philadelphia, Phoenix, and Columbus. Waters went into semi-retirement in 1984 and began writing a syndicated garden column. An award-winning horticulturalist, he was named a Master Gardener by the University of Arizona in 1995 and was the author, with collaborator Balbir Backhaus, of *Shade and Color with Water: Conserving Plants* (1992).

OBITUARIES AND OTHER SOURCES:

BOOKS

Writers Directory, 16th edition, St. James Press (Detroit, MI), 2001.

PERIODICALS

Washington Post, March 8, 2002, p. B6.

*   *   *

WEATHERFORD, Carole Boston 1956-

PERSONAL: Born February 13, 1956, in Baltimore, MD; daughter of Joseph Alexander and Carolyn Virginia (Whitten) Boston; married Ronald Jeffrey Weatherford (a writer), February 2, 1985; children: one daughter, one son. *Education:* American University, B.A., 1977; University of Baltimore, M.A., 1982; University of North Carolina—Greensboro, M.F.A. *Politics:* Democrat. *Religion:* Methodist.

ADDRESSES: Home and office—3313 Sparrowhawk Dr., High Point, NC 27265-9350.

CAREER: English teacher at public schools in Baltimore, MD, 1978; American Red Cross, Baltimore, MD, field representative in Blood Services Department, 1978-79; *Black Arts Review* (radio talk show), creator, producer, and host, 1979; Art Litho Co., Baltimore, MD, account executive, 1981; National Bar Association, Washington, DC, director of communications, 1981-85; B & C Associates, Inc., High Point, NC, vice president and creative director, 1985-88; freelance writer and publicist, 1988—. Publicist and consultant to Black Classic Press, 1985—, and *Chronicle,* 1990—; consultant to Dudley Products Co. and local schools.

MEMBER: North Carolina Writers Network (vice president, 1996-97), Phi Kappa Phi, Delta Sigma Theta, Alpha Kappa Alpha.

AWARDS, HONORS: North Carolina Writers Network, winner of Black Writers Speak Competition, 1991, and Harperprints Chapbook Competition, 1995, both

for *The Tan Chanteuse;* fellow, North Carolina Arts Council, 1995; Carter G. Woodson Book Award, elementary category, National Council for the Social Studies, 2001, for *The Sound that Jazz Makes;* Furious Flower Poetry Prize.

WRITINGS:

Remember Me, African American Family Press (New York, NY), 1994.

My Favorite Toy, Writers and Readers Publishing (New York, NY), 1994.

The Tan Chanteuse (poetry for adults), 1995.

Juneteenth Jamboree (novel), illustrated by Yvonne Buchanan, Lee & Low Books (New York, NY), 1995.

Me and My Family Tree, illustrated by Michelle Mills, Black Butterfly (New York, NY), 1996.

Grandma and Me, illustrated by Michelle Mills, Black Butterfly (New York, NY), 1996.

Mighty Menfolk, illustrated by Michelle Mills, Black Butterfly (New York, NY), 1996.

Sink or Swim: African-American Lifesavers of the Outer Banks, Coastal Carolina Press (Wilmington, NC), 1999.

(With husband, Ronald Jeffrey Weatherford) *Somebody's Knocking at Your Door: AIDS and the African-American Church,* Haworth Pastoral Press (Binghamton, NY), 1999.

The Tar Baby on the Soapbox, Longleaf Press at Methodist College, 1999.

The Sound That Jazz Makes (poetry), illustrated by Eric Velasquez, Walker and Co. (New York, NY), 2000.

The African-American Struggle for Legal Equality in American History, Enslow Publishers (Berkeley Heights, NJ), 2000.

Princeville: The 500-Year Flood, illustrated by Douglas Alvord, Coastal Carolina Press (Wilmington, NC), 2001.

Sidewalk Chalk: Poems of the City, illustrated by Dimitrea Tokunbo, Wordsong/Boyds Mills Press (Honesdale, PA), 2001.

African American Lawyers, Enslow Publishers (Berkeley Heights, NJ), 2002.

Jazz Baby (stories in verse), illustrated by Laura Freeman, Lee & Low Books (New York, NY), 2002.

Remember the Bridge: Poems of a People, Philomel Books (New York, NY), 2002.

Contributor of articles and poetry to magazines and newspapers, including *Essence, Christian Science Monitor,* and *Washington Post.*

SIDELIGHTS: The writings of Carole Boston Weatherford, wrote Heather Ross Miller in her review of *Juneteenth Jamboree* for the *African American Review,* "are remarkably forthright celebrations, a colorful assembly of African American tradition, pride, and love." *Juneteenth Jamboree* is the story of a tradition, the celebration of the day in 1865 when Texas slaves learned of their emancipation. It had taken more than two long years for the word to reach them. In Weatherford's novel, young Cassandra has recently moved to Texas and has never heard of "Juneteenth," despite the fact that it became a legal holiday in that state in 1980. She witnesses the elaborate preparations with the eyes of a newcomer and feels the excitement rising in her community without understanding, at first, what it means. Gradually, Cassandra and the reader learn the significance of this historic celebration, its importance amplified by the jubilant crowds, the parades and dances, and the picnic that all bring the community together. "Weatherford does an excellent job," commented Carol Jones Collins in *School Library Journal,* of introducing the reader to this holiday. A *Publishers Weekly* contributor remarked that the "enthusiastic text allows readers to discover— and celebrate—the holiday along with Cassandra."

Sidewalk Chalk: Poems of the City is an expression of pride, according to a reviewer for the *Bulletin of the Center for Children's Books.* Weatherford celebrates the city in twenty vignettes of urban life as a child might experience it. Her poems evoke the spirit of the neighborhood and the daily activities of the people who live there—jumping rope on the sidewalk, getting a haircut, going to the laundromat or to church. "The overall tone of the collection is upbeat and positive," *Booklist* contributor Kathy Broderick remarked. The *Bulletin* reviewer acknowledged some inconsistency in the quality of the poems but described them as "vivid snapshots of city life."

The Sound That Jazz Makes is a celebration in rhyme of American music and its roots in African-American history. Weatherford's short poems and the paintings of award-winning artist Eric Velasquez depict a musical journey from the drumbeats of Africa to the drumbeats of rap music in the streets of the city. Poet and illustrator lead the reader from the work-chants of the cotton fields to the plaintive laments of the blues echoing through the Mississippi delta, to the celebrations of gospel, the sweet rhythms of the swing era, and the bold harmonies of the nightclubs of Harlem. Weatherford's poems, according to *Booklist* contributor Bill Ott, "possess a flowing rhythm that younger readers [in particular] will respond to eagerly." A *Publishers Weekly* reviewer found the rhymes to be "at odds with" the rhythms of the very music the book is intended to honor, but in *Black Issues Book Review,* critic Khafre Abif described *The Sounds That Jazz Makes* as "a soft poetic journey of rhythm" in which the "words are as seamless as the rhythm's growth" from primitive drumbeats into one of the most far-reaching musical movements of modern times.

Remember the Bridge: Poems of a People is a celebration of the men and women who contributed to African-American history from the earliest times to the present day. Weatherford writes of the great and the not so great: the leaders whose names are familiar to everyone and the people whose names were never known. For these latter people she creates fictional profiles, exploring in her poetry how it must have felt to be sold into slavery or showcasing, for instance, the diversity of African Americans in a wide array of occupations. As with previous collections, critical response was mixed. A *Publishers Weekly* reviewer appreciated the free-verse poems but was less satisfied with the metered rhymes, and found the chronological narrative somewhat "confusing." A contributor to *Kirkus Reviews,* on the other hand, claimed that Weatherford "brilliantly summarizes . . . a complete timeline" of history. The last poem in *Remember the Bridge* is titled "I Am the Bridge," perhaps an allusion that this book, this poet, and every individual can be a part of what the *Kirkus Reviews* writer called "a bridge toward understanding and acceptance."

BIOGRAPHICAL AND CRITICAL SOURCES:

PERIODICALS

African American Review, spring, 1998, Heather Ross Miller, review of *The Tan Chanteuse* and *Juneteenth Jamboree,* pp. 169-171.
American Visions, December-January, 1995, Yolanda Robinson Coles, review of *Juneteenth Jamboree,* p. 37.

Black Issues Book Review, September, 2000, Khafre Abif, review of *The Sound That Jazz Makes,* p. 81.

Booklist, December 15, 1999, Carolyn Phelan, review of *Sink or Swim: African-American Lifesavers of the Outer Banks,* pp. 783-784; August, 2000, Bill Ott, review of *The Sound That Jazz Makes,* p. 2133; September 15, 2001, Kathy Broderick, review of *Sidewalk Chalk: Poems of the City,* p. 224.

Bulletin of the Center for Children's Books, October, 2001, review of *Sidewalk Chalk,* p. 81.

Children's Book & Play Review, March, 2001, AnnMarie Hamar, review of *The Sound that Jazz Makes,* p. 23.

Georgia Review, summer, 1997, Ted Kooser, review of *The Tan Chanteuse,* p. 375.

Kirkus Reviews, December 1, 2001, review of *Remember the Bridge: Poems of a People,* p. 1691.

Publishers Weekly, October 30, 1995, review of *Juneteenth Jamboree,* p. 61; May 15, 2000, review of *The Sound That Jazz Makes,* p. 115; September 17, 2001, review of *Sidewalk Chalk,* p. 82; December 24, 2001, review of *Remember the Bridge,* p. 62.

School Library Journal, January, 1996, Carol Jones Collins, review of *Juneteenth Jamboree,* p. 97; July, 2000, Ginny Gustin, review of *The Sound That Jazz Makes,* p. 99.*

*   *   *

WEAVER, Sylvester L(aflin) 1908-2002

OBITUARY NOTICE—See index for *CA* sketch: Born December 21, 1908, in Los Angeles, CA; died of pneumonia March 15, 2002, in Santa Barbara, CA. Television executive and author. Weaver was involved in television in its early years and is credited with helping to shape how the industry is run today. He graduated from Dartmouth College with a bachelor's degree in 1930 and spent his early years as a writer, producer, and radio program director for the Columbia Broadcast System, Inc. (CBS). He served in the U.S. Navy during World War II and was an executive for Young & Rubicam and American Tobacco through the 1940s. In 1949 he joined the National Broadcast Company, Inc. (NBC) as vice president in charge of television; he later became vice chair, president, and then chair. Weaver had high hopes for television, seeing it as a way to help spread culture and the arts to average citizens. On the business end he was instrumental in restructuring how programming was paid for; instead of having company sponsors determine programming as had been done in radio, the television network took over programming and sold time to advertisers. Weaver also kept *Meet the Press* on the air when it was in danger of being canceled, launched comedian Sid Caesar's *Your Show of Shows,* and created the *Today* and *Tonight* news talk shows and the *Wide Wide World* series. Weaver was replaced by Robert Sarnoff, son of NBC's owner, in 1955. Although he was made chairman of the board at the network, Weaver resigned the following year. He moved on to other ventures, such as an early attempt at running a cable television company and heading Intercept TV, a subscription channel that focused on the arts. In his later years he also devoted time to charitable organizations, serving as chair of the American Heart Association from 1959 to 1963 and board member and president of the Muscular Dystrophy Association during the 1960s and 1970s. Weaver, who received a Peabody Award and two Emmy Awards for his television work, was the coauthor of 1994's *The Best Seat in the House: The Golden Years in Radio and Television.*

OBITUARIES AND OTHER SOURCES:

BOOKS

Writers Directory, 14th edition, St. James Press (Detroit, MI), 1999.

PERIODICALS

Los Angeles Times, March 18, 2002, pp. A1, A12.
New York Times, March 18, 2002, p. A25.
Washington Post, March 18, 2002, p. B6.

*   *   *

WHITEHEAD, Paxton 1937-

PERSONAL: Born October 17, 1937, in East Malling, Kent, England; son of Charles Parkin (a lawyer) and Louise (Hunt) Whitehead; married Patricia Gage (an actress), January 2, 1971 (divorced); married Katherine Robertson; children: (second marriage) Sarah, Charles.

ADDRESSES: Office—Abrams Artists, 9200 West Sunset Blvd., Los Angeles, CA 90069-3502. *Agent*—Barna Ostertag Agency, 501 Fifth Ave., New York, NY 10017.

CAREER: Actor and director. Shaw Festival, Niagara-on-the-Lake, Ontario, Canada, artistic director, 1967-77.

Stage appearances include *The Epilogue,* The Old Stagers Theatre, Canterbury, England, 1949; *All for Mary,* Devonshire Park, Eastbourne, England, 1956; *Hamlet,* Royal Shakespeare Company, Stratford, England, 1958; *Gallows Humor,* Gramercy Arts Theatre, New York City, 1961; *One Way Pendulum,* East 74th Street Theatre, New York City, 1961; *The Affair,* Henry Miller's Theatre, 1962; *A Doll's House,* Theatre Four, New York City, 1963; *Henry V,* American Shakespeare Festival, Stratford, CT, 1963; *King Lear,* American Shakespeare Festival, Stratford, 1963; *Beyond the Fringe,* John Golden Theatre, New York City, 1964; *The Country Wife,* Front Street Theatre, Memphis, TN, 1964; *My Fair Lady,* Front Street Theatre, 1964; *The Rivals,* Charles Playhouse, Boston, MA, 1964; *The Entertainer,* Hartford Stage Company, Hartford, CT, 1965; *Major Barbara,* Playhouse in the Park, Cincinnati, OH, 1965; *Heartbreak House,* Manitoba Theatre Center, Winnipeg, Ontario, Canada, 1965; *The Public Eye,* Manitoba Theatre Center, 1965; *The Importance of Being Earnest,* Manitoba Theatre Center, 1965; *The Importance of Being Earnest,* Canadian Players, Toronto, Ontario, Canada, 1966; *Misalliance,* Shaw Festival, Niagara-on-the-Lake, Ontario, Canada, 1966; *The Apple Cart,* Shaw Festival, 1966; *Arms and the Man,* Shaw Festival, 1967; *Major Barbara,* Shaw Festival, 1967; *Heartbreak House,* Shaw Festival, 1968; *The Chemmy Circle,* Shaw Festival, 1968; *Charley's Aunt,* Studio Arena Theatre, Buffalo, NY, 1968; *Chemin de Fer,* Mark Taper Forum, Los Angeles, 1969; *Hudson West Theatre,* New York City, 1969; *The Doctor's Dilemma,* Shaw Festival, 1969; *The Guardsman,* Shaw Festival, 1969; *Forty Years On,* Shaw Festival, 1970; *The Chemmy Circle,* Arena Stage, Washington, DC, 1970; *Heartbreak House,* Goodman Memorial Theatre, Chicago, IL, 1970; *The Brass Butterfly,* Chelsea Theatre Center, New York City, 1970; *Candida,* Longacre Theatre, New York City, 1970; *Habeas Corpus,* Martin Beck Theatre, New York City, 1975; *The Philanderer,* Shaw Festival, 1971; *Tonight at 8:30,* Shaw Festival, 1971; *You Never Can Tell,* Shaw Festival, 1973; *Fanny's First Play,* Shaw Festival, 1973; *Charley's Aunt,* Shaw Festival, 1974; *The Devil's Disciple,* Shaw Festival, 1975; *Arms and the Man,* Shaw Festival, 1976; *The Apple Cart,* Shaw Festival, 1976; *The Millionairess,* Shaw Festival, 1976; *Thark,* Shaw Festival, 1977; *The Crucifer of Blood,* Helen Hayes Theatre, New York City, 1978; *Travesties,* Manitoba Theatre Centre, 1979; *The Trials of Oscar Wilde,* The Citadel Theatre, Edmonton, Ontario, Canada, 1980; *Thark,* Philadelphia Drama Guild, 1980; *Twelfth Night,* Philadelphia Drama Guild, 1980; *Camelot,* State Theatre, New York City, 1980; *The Pirates of Penzance,* Ahmanson Theatre, Los Angeles, 1981; *The Miser,* Old Globe Theatre, San Diego, CA, 1982; *Heartbreak House,* Theatre Royal, London, 1983; *The Rivals,* Old Globe Theatre, San Diego, 1983; *Noises Off,* Brooks Atkinson Theatre, New York City, 1983-85; *Richard III,* Old Globe Theatre, San Diego, 1985; *Much Ado about Nothing,* Old Globe Theatre, San Diego, 1986; *Out of Order,* Paper Mill Playhouse, Millburn, NJ, 1997; *The Mask of Moriarty,* Paper Mill Playhouse, 1998; *Rocky Horror Picture Show,* Tiffany Theater, Hollywood, CA, 1998; *A Song at Twilight,* Mirage Theater Company, Lucille Lortel Theater, New York City, 2000; and *Shadows of the Evening,* Mirage Theater Company, Lucille Lortel Theater, 2000. Also appeared in *A Little Hotel on the Side; King Lear,* Manitoba Theatre Centre; and Neil Simon's *London Suite.*

Major tours include *Hamlet,* Royal Shakespeare Company, Moscow and Leningrad, Russia, 1958; *The Grass Is Greener,* Royal Shakespeare Company, United Kingdom cities, 1959; *Pygmalion,* Royal Shakespeare Company, U.K. cities, 1960; *Beyond the Fringe,* U.S. cities, 1963; *The Bed before Yesterday,* U.S. cities, 1976; and *Camelot,* U.S. cities, 1980-81. Also toured with the Andrew McMaster Company, United Kingdom cities, 1957.

Stage work as director includes *The Circle,* Shaw Festival, 1967; *The Chemmy Circle,* Shaw Festival, 1968; *A Flea in Her Ear,* Charles Playhouse, 1969; *Forty Years On,* Shaw Festival, 1970; *The Secretary Bird,* Main Stage, Vancouver, British Columbia, Canada, 1970; *The Chemmy Circle,* Main Stage, Vancouver, 1971; *The Sorrows of Frederick,* Main Stage, Vancouver, 1971; *Misalliance,* Shaw Festival, 1972; *Getting Married,* Shaw Festival, 1972; *Charley's Aunt,* Shaw Festival, 1972; *Widowers' Houses,* Shaw Festival, 1973; *Arms and the Man,* Main Stage, Vancouver, 1973; *Misalliance,* Walnut Street Theatre,

Philadelphia, PA, then Old Globe Theatre, San Diego, 1982; *The Real Thing,* Seattle Repertory Theatre, WA, 1986; and *Beyond the Fringe,* Old Globe Theatre, San Diego, 1986.

Film appearances include *Riel,* 1979; *Back to School,* Orion, 1986; *Jumping Jack Flash,* 1986; *Baby Boom,* 1987; *Rover Dangerfield,* 1991; *Nervous Ticks,* 1992; *My Boyfriend's Back,* 1993; *The Adventures of Huck Finn,* 1993; *Rocket Man,* Buena Vista, 1997; *Wakko's Wish,* 1999; *The Duke,* Buena Vista Home Video, 1999; and *Kate and Leopold,* Miramax, 2001.

Appearances on television series include *Marblehead Manor,* 1987; *Mad about You,* NBC, 1992-99; *Simon,* The WB, 1995; *The Real Adventures of Johnny Quest,* TBS, 1996. Appearances in TV movies include *Chips, the War Dog,* The Disney Channel, 1990; *Child of Darkness, Child of Light,* USA Network, 1991; *Boris and Natasha,* Showtime, 1992; *12:01,* Fox, 1993; *Where Are My Children?,* ABC, 1994; *Trick of the Eye,* CBS, 1994; and *London Suite,* NBC, 1996. Also appeared in *The First Night of Pygmalion,* CBC.

Appearances on episodic television include *Hart to Hart,* ABC, 1982-83; "Foiled Again," *Magnum, P.I.,* CBS, 1982; "Beneath the Surface," *The A Team,* NBC, 1986; *The Alan King Show,* CNN, 1986; *Silver Spoons,* NBC, 1986; "The Grand Old Lady," *Murder, She Wrote,* CBS, 1989; *Dinosaurs,* ABC, 1991; "The Troubles," *Law & Order,* NBC, 1991; *Almost Home,* ABC, 1993; "The Therapy Episode" and "The Sleep Clinic," *Ellen,* ABC, 1995; *Lush Life,* Showtime, 1996; "Caroline and the Cat Dancer," *Caroline in the City,* NBC, 1996; "The Parent Trap," *Ellen,* ABC, 1996; "A Lilith," *Frasier,* NBC, 1996; *Early Edition,* CBS, 1997; "The One with Rachel's Crush" and "The One with Joey's Dirty Day," *Friends,* NBC, 1998; and "Noel," *The West Wing,* NBC, 2000. Also appeared in *3rd Rock from the Sun* and *Brothers.*

Appearances on TV specials include *Lady Windermere's Fan,* CBC, 1966; *The Wit and World of GBS,* BBC and CBC, 1971; *The National Dream,* CBC, 1973; *The Village Wooing,* CBC, 1974; *America Picks the All-Time Favorite Movies,* ABC, 1988; *Tales from the Hollywood Hills: The Old Reliable,* PBS, 1988; *Hale the Hero,* Arts and Entertainment, 1992; and *Monster in My Pocket: The Big Scream,* ABC, 1992. Appearances on TV miniseries include *The National Dream,* 1974; *An Inconvenient Woman,* ABC, 1991; and *LIBERTY! The American Revolution,* PBS, 1997.

WRITINGS:

(Translator and adaptor, with Suzanne Grossman) Georges Feydeau, *Chemin de fer,* Samuel French (New York, NY), 1968.
(With Suzanne Grossman) *A Flea in Her Ear,* produced at the Music Center, Los Angeles, CA, 1982.

Other plays with Grossman include *The Chemmy Circle,* 1968, and *There's One in Every Marriage,* 1972.

SIDELIGHTS: Although British-born actor Paxton Whitehead has appeared in numerous films and television productions, his principal career has been on the stage. Likewise his writings, collaborative works with Suzanne Grossman, are stage plays rather than film scripts.

Whitehead, who has lived in the United States since 1960, noted in an interview with Ira J. Bilowit for *Back Stage* that stage actors are held in much higher regard in the land of his birth than in his adopted homeland. Naturally, this has put him in an awkward position, since, as he commented, "I have been fortunate to be able to support myself, and subsequently my family, with work that has been primarily on stage. Television and film have had small influence on my life and income." Certainly this is true of his writing, but in the 1990s he began to have more film roles, including an appearance in the time-travel romantic comedy *Kate and Leopold.*

BIOGRAPHICAL AND CRITICAL SOURCES:

BOOKS

Contemporary Theatre, Film, and Television, Volume 33, Gale (Detroit, MI), 2001.

PERIODICALS

Back Stage, December 21, 1990, Ira J. Bilowit, "Making a Living on the Stage" (profile), p. 26.
Los Angeles Magazine, July, 1982, Dick Lochte, review of *A Flea in Her Ear,* p. 253.*

WHITELAW, Billie 1932-

PERSONAL: Born June 6, 1932, in Coventry, England; daughter of Gerry and Frances Mary (Williams) Whitelaw; married Peter Vaughan (divorced); married Robert Muller; children: a son.

ADDRESSES: Agent—Joy Jameson Ltd., 7 West Easton Place Mews, London SW1, England.

CAREER: Actress. Stage appearances include *Pink String and Sealing Wax*, Princes Theatre, Bradford, England, 1950; *Hotel Paradiso*, Winter Garden Theatre, 1956; *Progress to the Park*, Theatre Royal, Stratford, England, 1960, then Saville Theatre, London, 1961; *England, Our England*, Princes Theatre, 1962; *A Touch of the Poet*, Dublin Festival, then Venice Festival, 1962; *Play*, National Theatre Company, Old Vic Theatre, London, 1964; *The Dutch Courtesan*, National Theatre Company, Chichester Festival, 1964; *Othello*, National Theatre Company, Chichester Festival, 1964; *The Dutch Courtesan*, Old Vic Theatre, 1964; *Hobson's Choice*, Old Vic Theatre, 1965; *Trelawny of the Wells*, Chichester Festival, later Old Vic Theatre, 1965; *After Haggerty*, Royal Shakespeare Company, Criterion Theatre, London, 1971; *Not I*, Royal Court Theatre, London, 1973, again, 1975; *Alphabetical Order*, Hampstead Theatre Club, then May Fair Theatre, both London, 1975; *Footfalls*, Royal Court Theatre, 1976; *Molly*, Comedy Theatre, London, 1978; *Happy Days*, Royal Court Theatre, 1979; *The Greeks*, Aldwych Theatre, London, 1980; *Passion Play*, Aldwych Theatre, 1981, then National Theatre, London, 1982; *Rockabye*, La Mama Etc. Theatre, New York City, 1982; *Tales from Hollywood*, National Theatre, 1983. Also appeared with the National Theatre Company in *Othello*, and in *Hobson's Choice*, Moscow and Berlin, 1965. Appeared in productions of Samuel Beckett's plays *Rockabye, Enough,* and *Footfalls*, New York City, 1984. Major tours include *Where There's a Will . . .*, British cities, 1954.

Film appearances include *The Fake*, 1953; *The Sleeping Tiger*, 1954; *Companions in Crime*, 1954; *Room in the House*, 1955; *Small Hotel*, 1957; *Miracle in Soho*, 1957; *Carve Her Name with Pride*, 1958; *Gideon's Day*, 1958, released in the United States as *Gideon of Scotland Yard*, 1959; *The Flesh and the Fiends*, 1959; *Breakout*, 1959; *Bobbikins*, 1960; *Hell Is a City*, 1960; *Make Mine Mink*, 1960; *The Devil's Agent*, 1961; *Mr. Topaze*, 1961; *No Love for Johnnie*, 1961; *Payroll*, Allied Artists, 1961; *The Comedy Man*, 1961; *Charlie Bubbles*, Regional, 1968; *Twisted Nerve*, National General, 1969; *The Adding Machine*, 1969; *Leo the Last*, 1970; *Start the Revolution without Me*, Warner Bros., 1970; *Eagle in a Cage*, National General, 1971; *Gumshoe*, Columbia, 1972; *Frenzy*, Universal, 1972; *Night Watch*, Avco Embassy, 1973; *The Omen*, Twentieth Century-Fox, 1976; *The Water Babies* 1978; *Leopard in the Snow*, 1978; *An Unsuitable Job for a Woman*, 1981; *The Dark Crystal*, Universal, 1982; *Tangier*, 1982; *Slayground*, Universal, 1984; *Shadey*, 1985; *Murder Elite*, 1985; *The Chain*, 1985; *Maurice*, 1987; *The Dressmaker*, 1988; *The Krays*, 1990; *Freddie as F.R.O.7*, 1992; *Deadly Advice*, 1993; *Skallagrigg*, 1994; *Jane Eyre*, Miramax, 1996; *The Lost Son*, Artisan Entertainment, 1999; *Quills*, Fox Searchlight, 2000.

Television movie appearances include *No Trams to Lime Street*, 1959; *Lena, O My Lena*, 1960; *Dr. Jekyll and Mr. Hyde*, 1968; *Follow the Yellow Brick Road*, 1972; *Poet Game*, 1972; *A Tale of Two Cities*, 1980; *Camille*, CBS, 1984; *Jamaica Inn*, 1985; *The Secret Garden*, CBS, 1987; *The Fifteen Streets*, 1989; *Lorna Doone*, 1990; *The Cloning of Joanna May*, Arts and Entertainment, 1992; *Duel of Hearts*, TNT, 1992; *The Last of the Blonde Bombshells*, HBO, 2000; *A Dinner of Herbs*, 2000. Also appeared in *A World of Time; The Withered Arm; Happy Days; The Serpent Son; Lady of the Camellias; The Pity of It All; You and Me; Resurrection; Wessex Tales; The Fifty-Pound Note; Supernatural; Eustace and Hilda;* and *Haunted Man.* Appearances on TV series include *Dixon of Dock Green*, 1955; *Time Out for Peggy*, 1958; *Born to Run*, 1997. Appearances on TV miniseries include *Napoleon and Love*, 1974; *Private Schultz*, 1981; *Imaginary Friends*, 1987; *Firm Friends*, 1992; *Merlin*, NBC, 1998; *Changing Stages*, 2000. Appearances on TV specials include *A Murder of Quality*, PBS, 1991; *The Canterbury Tales*, HBO Family, 1999; *Shooting the Past*, PBS, 1999. Also appeared in a WNET documentary on the creation of Samuel Beckett's play *Rockabye; Three Plays by Samuel Beckett;* and *The Oresteia of Aeschylus.* Appearances on episodic television include "One Moment of Humanity," *Space: 1999*, 1976.

AWARDS, HONORS: British Academy of Film and Television Arts (BAFTA) Film awards for Best Supporting Actress for *Charlie Bubbles* and for *Twisted*

Nerve, 1969; National Society of Film Critics Awards, USA, NSFC Award for Best Supporting Actress for *Charlie Bubbles,* 1969; Fantasporto International Fantasy Film Award for Best Actress for *The Krays,* 1991.

WRITINGS:

Billie Whitelaw . . . Who He? (autobiography), St. Martin's Press (New York, NY), 1996.

SIDELIGHTS: Despite the humorous sound of the title, *Billie Whitelaw . . . Who He?* is anything but light reading. After all, British actress Whitelaw worked closely with Samuel Beckett, one of the twentieth century's most complex playwrights, and she is noted for her mastery of Beckett's particularly challenging later plays. Discussing Beckett, who wrote many of his short works especially for her, Whitelaw wrote, "He was concerned with my character's movements, not the words . . . he was interested in something other than the text."

Though a reviewer in *Publishers Weekly* called *Billie Whitelaw . . . Who He?* "an invaluable guide for the Beckett actor or director," Beckett's is not the only distinguished name that crops up on the pages of Whitelaw's autobiography. Among others are actors Laurence Olivier and Albert Finney (with whom she admitted having an affair, though she refused to disclose the identity of other famous lovers), as well as playwrights John Osborne and Harold Pinter.

According to Jack Helbig in *Booklist,* "Whitelaw is most vivid when she describes her most difficult moments." There were plenty of these, as a passage from the book illustrates: "I've heard people say: 'She's only a child, she'll get over it, children don't mind.' Well, children do mind, and they don't get over it. I minded like hell my father having cancer and dying horribly. I minded the air raids"—the Nazis heavily bombed Whitelaw's hometown of Coventry during World War II—"and the fear they instilled in me. I minded being sent away from home. I minded the curtains being drawn, and living in darkness lit by just one sad electric bulb. I minded having no money, and having to fight to keep myself warm and clean. I minded the struggle to light a fire, and being surrounded by dirty dishes."

No wonder, then, that as an adult Whitelaw has been involved in efforts to combat child abuse. Among the other pains she suffered was her son's bout with meningitis, yet *Billie Whitelaw . . . Who He?* is about much more than its author's personal struggles. Helbig concluded that the book's "lighter, less focused moments . . . will greatly amuse film and theater aficionados."

BIOGRAPHICAL AND CRITICAL SOURCES:

BOOKS

Contemporary Theatre, Film, and Television, Volume 34, Gale (Detroit, MI), 2001.

PERIODICALS

American Theatre, July-August, 1996, Irene Worth, review of *Billie Whitelaw . . . Who He?,* pp. 56-57.
Booklist, April 1, 1996, Jack Helbig, review of *Billie Whitelaw . . . Who He?,* p. 1337.
Films in Review, September/October 1996, John Nangle, "An Interview with Billie Whitelaw," pp. 89-91.
Library Journal, March 1, 1996, Douglas McClemont, review of *Billie Whitelaw . . . Who He?,* p. 80.
Publishers Weekly, April 8, 1996, review of *Billie Whitelaw . . . Who He?,* p. 50.*

*   *   *

WICK, Walter

PERSONAL: Born in CT. *Education:* Paier College of Art, Hamden, CT, graduated, 1973.

ADDRESSES: Agent—c/o Author Mail, Scholastic Books, 557 Broadway, New York, NY 10012.

CAREER: Writer and photographer. Worked as a lab technician and photographer's assistant, Hartford, CT; photographer for *Discover, Psychology Today,* and *Games.*

WRITINGS:

(With Jean Marzollo) *I Spy Little Numbers,* Scholastic (New York, NY), 1992.

(With Jean Marzollo) *I Spy Christmas,* Scholastic (New York, NY), 1992.

(With Jean Marzollo) *I Spy a Book of Picture Riddles,* Scholastic (New York, NY), 1992.

(With Jean Marzollo) *I Spy Fun House: A Book of Picture Riddles,* Scholastic (New York, NY), 1993.

(With Jean Marzollo) *I Spy Mystery: A Book of Picture Riddles,* Scholastic (New York, NY), 1993.

(With Jean Marzollo) *I Spy Fantasy: A Book of Picture Riddles,* Scholastic (New York, NY), 1994.

Veo Navidad, Scholastic (New York, NY), 1995.

(With Jean Marzollo) *I Spy School Days: A Book of Picture Riddles,* Scholastic (New York, NY), 1995.

(With Jean Marzollo) *I Spy More than Meets the Eye,* Scholastic (New York, NY), 1996.

(With Jean Marzollo) *I Spy Spooky Night,* Scholastic (New York, NY), 1996.

(With Jean Marzollo) *I Spy Challenger: A Book of Picture Riddles,* Scholastic (New York, NY), 1997.

(With Jean Marzollo) *I Spy Super Challenger,* Scholastic (New York, NY), 1997.

A Drop of Water: A Book of Science and Wonder, Scholastic (New York, NY), 1997.

Walter Wick's Optical Tricks, Scholastic (New York, NY), 1998.

(With Jean Marzollo) *I Spy Little Animals,* Scholastic (New York, NY), 1998.

(With Jean Marzollo) *I Spy Little Wheels,* Scholastic (New York, NY), 1998.

(With Jean Marzollo) *I Spy Gold Challenger,* Scholastic (New York, NY), 1998.

(With Jean Marzollo) *I Spy Little Christmas,* Scholastic (New York, NY), 1999.

(With Jean Marzollo) *I Spy Treasure Hunt,* Scholastic (New York, NY), 1999.

(With Jean Marzollo) *I Spy Little Numbers,* Scholastic (New York, NY), 1999.

(With Jean Marzollo) *I Spy Spooky Mansion,* Scholastic (New York, NY), 1999.

(With Jean Marzollo) *I Spy Little Letters,* Scholastic (New York, NY), 2000.

(With Jean Marzollo) *I Spy Extreme Challenger,* Scholastic (New York, NY), 2000.

(With Jean Marzollo) *I Spy Junior: Puppet Playhouse,* (CD-ROM), Scholastic (New York, NY), 1999.

(With Jean Marzollo) *I Spy Year-round Challenger,* Scholastic (New York, NY), 2001.

(With Jean Marzollo) *I Spy Little Bunnies,* Scholastic (New York, NY), 2001.

(With Jean Marzollo) *I Spy Treasure Hunt,* Scholastic (New York, NY), 2001.

Can You See What I See?: Pictures Puzzles to Search and Solve, Scholastic (New York, NY), 2002.

(With Jean Marzollo) *I Spy Ultimate Challenger,* Scholastic (New York, NY), 2003.

SIDELIGHTS: Walter Wick is best known for his collaborative effort with Jean Marzollo on the "I Spy" series of picture riddles for children. In almost twenty different titles, critics point out, Wick's exceptional photographs sumptuously illustrate this series of visual exploration books for children grades one to seven. In addition to his work on the "I Spy" series, Wick has also created several titles on his own, including *Walter Wick's Optical Tricks* and *A Drop of Water: A Book of Science and Wonder* and *Can You See What I See?*

The "I Spy" books' format includes a short riddle by Marzollo, and an accompanying photograph from Wick, normally chock full of objects referred to in the riddle. The intended result is to inspire a child to hunt within the photograph for the objects in the riddle. This will prove invaluable for children as it assists their learning of shapes, colors, numbers, and other visual phenomena. The cleverness of the text and inviting photography make books in the series popular for children of many ages. The focus of each book is slightly different. *I Spy Mystery* includes dramatic lighting, many ominous masks, and views through keyholes. *I Spy Fun House* presents clowns, fun-house mirrors, and musician's props.

While the early books were geared primarily toward a younger audience, some of the later books, such as *I Spy Gold Challenger* and *I Spy Super Challenger,* are written for a slightly higher level of reader and the material is suitably more challenging. *Walter Wick's Optical Tricks* and *A Drop of Water: A Book of Science and Wonder* represent a break from the "I Spy" format and rely more on visual trickery and scientific fact respectively. In *Optical Tricks,* Wick uses his highly developed style of detail-driven photography to trick the eyes and mind. Some images appear to change before your very eyes as Wick introduces the reader to several anomalies of visual perception. Daniel J. Brabander of *Horn Book* described Wick's technique by saying that "Wick's elegant yet bold style of photography is ideally suited for the task of visual deception."

A Drop of Water focuses upon the analysis of water as it changes properties and appearance from vapor, to frost, to even forming a mini-prism. Wick relies upon the use of extreme magnification and stop-action technology to capture water in its many fascinating forms. While the book was well received, some critics felt that the descriptions of the photographs are too brief to accurately describe the illustrated transformations. Carolyn Angus of *School Library Journal* wrote, "Wick clearly shows that science and art both offer ways to observe the world around us. However, the visuals may stimulate a level of curiosity that will not be satisfied by the brief text."

In 2002, Wick published *Can You See What I See?*, another puzzle book for young readers. However, in this case, while the puzzles may seem simple, each rhyme ends with a challenge to discover the puzzle within the puzzle, or a maze. *School Library Journal*'s Marianne Saccardi wrote that "Wick's fans will relish his explanation of his work at the end of the book and may even find some puzzle-solving hints. This is 'I Spy' and much more!" A *Publishers Weekly* reviewer noted that "These pages are nearly guaranteed to keep kids happily occupied for hours and coming back for return visits."

BIOGRAPHICAL AND CRITICAL SOURCES:

PERIODICALS

Booklist, November 1, 1992; May 15, 1993; January 1, 1999; October 1, 1997; September 15, 1996; December 1, 1994; December 1, 1995.
Bulletin of the Center for Children's Books, November 1992.
Horn Book, March, 1997; September, 1998.
Los Angeles Times Book Review, October 20, 1996.
New York Times, May 18, 1997.
New York Times Book Review, November 15, 1998.
New Yorker, December 13, 1993.
Publishers Weekly, January 6, 1992; April 19, 1993; August 23, 1993; October 17, 1994; July 24, 1995; July 1, 1996; June 29, 1998; January 7, 2002, review of *Can You See What I See?: Pictures Puzzles to Search and Solve,* p. 63.
School Library Journal, April, 1992; April, 1993; October, 1994; October, 1995; March, 1997; October, 1997; March, 2002, Marianne Saccardi, review of *Can You See What I See?: Pictures Puzzles to Search and Solve,* p. 223.

OTHER

Walter Wick Web site, http://www.walterwick.com (December 1, 2002).
Scholastic Web site, http://www.scholastic.com (October 8, 2002).*

*   *   *

WIFFEN, Joan 1922(?)-

PERSONAL: Born c. 1922; married M. A. Wiffen (an electronics technician, deceased); children: Christopher, Judith. *Hobbies and other interests:* Paleontology.

ADDRESSES: Home—138 Beach Rd., Haumoana, Hawke's Bay, New Zealand.

CAREER: Hawkes Bay Museum, New Zealand, honorary curator of paleontology; lecturer.

AWARDS, HONORS: Honorary science doctorate, Massey University, 1994; C.B.E., 1995, for services to science.

WRITINGS:

Valley of the Dragons: The Story of New Zealand's Dinosaur Woman, Random Century (Glenfield, New Zealand), 1991.

SIDELIGHTS: Joan Wiffen is a self-trained amateur paleontologist who, together with her husband, pioneered dinosaur hunting in New Zealand. She has been nicknamed "the dragon lady" by professional paleontologists for her discovery of four previously unknown sea creatures, as well as of several dinosaur fossils, in a country most scientists once believed was too small a land mass to support such animals. New Zealand is not quite as big as the state of Colorado, and its turbulent geological history includes having been submerged under the ocean more than once. In an article by Jack McClintock for *Discover,* Wiffen claimed she was "too ignorant" to know better. Without the benefit of a college education, she relied on her scientific curiosity and her natural instincts, which eventually led to her fossil discoveries.

As a mother of two children, Wiffen became interested in dinosaurs after reading about them to her children. Already an avid rock collector, it was an easy transition for her to begin looking for fossils. Her curiosity grew stronger with each small find, and soon her library included a small collection of books that specialized in the history of reptiles. The more she read, the more she became convinced of the possibility that dinosaurs could have once lived in New Zealand. Her research confirmed her theory when she discovered that there existed evidence that New Zealand once had forests that dated back to the Jurassic period.

About eighty-five million years ago, New Zealand was part of what is referred to as Gondwana, a large mass of land that included South America, Africa, and Australia. The land mass broke apart eventually, leaving New Zealand cut off from all other land masses. Although most paleontologists never considered the possibility that dinosaurs could have existed in New Zealand, Wiffen saw no reason that the large creatures could not have wandered through the forest regions while it was still a part of the super continent of Gondwana.

Due to the instability of New Zealand's land mass caused by frequent earthquakes, which caused the entire island to sink several times beneath the ocean, fossils were very difficult to find. However, Wiffen got lucky one day and discovered an old oil field map in the back of a toy store. The map showed places near a riverbed where fossils had been found. Wiffen was quick to gather around her a group of friends whom she infected with her enthusiasm. Soon they were all exploring the riverbed, where Wiffen claims they found fossils in approximately one in every fifty stones.

It would not be until 1980 that she would find her first exciting fossil, however, a species of mosasaur, which, according to McClintock, is a "massive carnivorous marine reptile that grew to be as long as 45 feet." This particular fossil represents a new genus of a "specific, separate, unknown lineage of mosasaur." Its discovery has made Wiffen famous, but she did not stop there. She has since discovered three other marine reptiles that were previously unknown to scientists.

Wiffen's fossil finds included more than marine reptiles. Her husband brought home a chunk of petrified wood in which Wiffen thought she saw a bone fragment. She did not think too much about it until she and her husband were visiting a museum in Australia. There she recognized a similar fossil, which turned out to be a bone from a dinosaur. Upon arriving home, Wiffen verified that she indeed had a dinosaur bone in her hand. The scientific community did not eagerly respond to Wiffen's discovery at first. They merely assumed that if she did have a dinosaur fossil, it must have washed up on New Zealand's shores from Australia. However, after much research, Wiffen's discoveries have been verified and have been included in many textbooks on the subject. She has also written her own book on her discoveries called *Valley of the Dragons: The Story of New Zealand's Dinosaur Woman*.

BIOGRAPHICAL AND CRITICAL SOURCES:

PERIODICALS

Discover, June, 2000, Jack McClintock, "Romancing the Bone," p. 84.*

OTHER

Enchanted Learning, http://www.enchantedlearning. com/ (September 16, 2001).
HarperCollins Web site, http://www.harpercollins.co. nz/ (March 14, 2002).
Royal Society of New Zealand Web site, http://www. rsnz.govt.nz/ (January 3, 1998).*

*   *   *

WILLIAMS, Jerome 1926-2002

OBITUARY NOTICE—See index for *CA* sketch: Born July 15, 1926, in Toronto, Ontario, Canada; died after surgery June 7, 2002, in Annapolis, MD. Oceanographer, physicist, environmentalist, educator, administrator, consultant, and author. For more than thirty years Williams taught oceanography at the U.S. Naval Academy in Annapolis, Maryland where he also studied marine pollution and other topics related to the sea. He was active in several scientific research bodies, including as vice president and executive director of the Estuarine Research Federation, as president of the Atlantic Estuarine Research Society, and as a consultant to the Environmental Protection Agency and the Marine Technology Society. Early in his career Williams worked as a researcher for the Chesapeake Bay Institute and as a marine physicist for Vitro Laboratories. In his later years he devoted some of his spare time to community activities, as an officer and performer with the Colonial Players and as the chair of the Anne Arundel County Commission for Culture and the Arts. Williams produced several scientific volumes, including *Oceanography: An Introduction to the Marine Sciences* (1962), *Optical Properties of the Sea* (1970), *Introduction to Marine Pollution Control* (1979) and the 1972 children's book *Oceanography: A First Book.*

OBITUARIES AND OTHER SOURCES:

PERIODICALS

Washington Post, June 23, 2002, p. C8.

*   *   *

WILLIAMS, Joe
    See WILLIAMS, Joseph Peter

*   *   *

WILLIAMS, Joseph Peter 1889-1972
    (Joe Williams)

PERSONAL: Born December 10, 1889, in Memphis, TN; died of intestinal cancer February 14, 1972, in Pine Brook, NJ; son of Edward Metcalfe (a cotton broker) and Anne Elizabeth (Connolly) Williams; married Helen Schauman, October 17, 1914; married Emma Herbers, June 23, 1934; children: (first marriage) Charles Edward, Louise Adelaide; (second marriage) Joseph Peter, Curtis Michael. *Education:* Attended Christian Brothers College.

CAREER: Sportswriter. *Commercial Appeal,* Memphis, TN, reporter, drama critic, and cartoonist, 1910-16; *Cleveland News,* Cleveland, OH, reporter, and movie critic, 1916-27; Scripps-Howard Newspapers, sports

director, 1927-31; *New York Telegram* (renamed *New York World Telegram and Sun*), New York, NY, sports editor and columnist, 1927-64; *Joe Williams* (newsletter), publisher, 1964-72; *Morning Telegraph,* columnist, 1964-72.

AWARDS, HONORS: Knighted, first class, Order of the White Rose of Finland, for involvement in the Finland War Relief program.

WRITINGS:

Joe Williams's TV-Boxing Book, Van Nostrand (New York, NY), 1954.
The Joe Williams Baseball Reader: The Glorious Game from Ty Cobb and Babe Ruth to the Amazing Mets: Fifty Years of Baseball Writing by the Celebrated Newspaper Columnist, edited by Peter Williams, Algonquin (Chapel Hill, NC), 1989.

Also author of column "Lottie Lee" for the *Commercial Appeal;* contributor to periodicals, including *Sporting News, Sport,* and *Judge.* Work represented in anthologies, including *Sports Extra,* edited by Stanley Frank, Barnes (New York, NY), 1944; *Best Sports Stories 1951: A Panorama of the 1950 Sports Year,* edited by Irving T. Marsh and Edward Ehre, Dutton (New York, NY), 1951; *Best Sport Stories 1953: A Panorama of the 1952 Sports Year,* edited by Irving T. Marsh and Edward Ehre, Dutton (New York, NY), 1953; *Best Sports Stories 1957: A Panorama of the 1956 Sports Year,* edited by Irving T. Marsh and Edward Ehre, Dutton (New York, NY), 1957; *The Second Fireside Book of Baseball,* edited by Charles Einstein, Simon and Schuster (New York, NY), 1958; *The Fireside Book of Boxing,* edited by W. C. Heinz, Simon and Schuster (New York, NY), 1961; *Notre Dame Football,* edited by Gene Schoor, Funk and Wagnalls (New York, NY), 1962; and *The Phillies Reader,* edited by Richard Orodenker, Temple University Press (Philadelphia, PA), 1996.

Some of Williams's papers are held at the Department of English, Community College of Morris, Randolph, NJ.

SIDELIGHTS: Joseph Peter "Joe" Williams wrote about sports for over half a century, first in Memphis, Tennessee, and later in New York City. He was one of the first writers to cover sports in a realistic and critical manner, and his "scoops" included Babe Ruth's "called shot" home run and other major stories. Williams was born in Memphis, where he attended local schools and Christian Brothers College. His son, Peter Williams, who edited a collection of his father's writings, said his father and uncle Bill spent their free time swimming in the Wolf River and at Red Elm Park. Williams also worked for a short time as a boxer at the Phoenix Athletic Club, but he soon chose to cover the sport rather than participate. Memphis was a thriving sports city at the time, and Williams did his first sportswriting for the local *Commercial Appeal* in 1910, selling individual pieces about school and amateur sports. He accepted a full-time job covering sports, but also worked as a drama reviewer, sometime cartoonist, and columnist for the question-and-answer column "Lottie Lee." In 1914 he married Helen Schauman, and the couple had two children.

Williams next took a job at the *Cleveland News* because of a case of mistaken identity. He approached *News* reporter Tom Terrell for an interview, thinking him to be Cleveland infielder Terry Turner, and Terrell went along with the interview as though he were the player. He later apologized to Williams for the joke and offered him a job in 1916. Williams got his first scoop while covering the Cleveland Indians in 1923. He was in New Orleans for an exhibition game with the St. Louis Browns and was given the hotel room that had been reserved for the team's manager Lee Fohl. When a telephone call came for Fohl, Williams took it and learned that Browns first baseman George Sisler needed eye surgery, which would end his season and perhaps his career.

The Scripps-Howard Newspaper chain tapped Williams to be their sports director in 1927, and in the same year he became the sports editor and a columnist with the *New York Telegram,* where he remained until 1964. Williams was able to expand his writing to features, such as his 1929 profile of baseball commissioner Judge Kenesaw Mountain Landis. The *Telegram* merged twice, with the *New York World* in 1931 and with the *New York Sun* in 1950, and Williams enjoyed a national readership as he covered the sports greats of the day. Bill Knight noted in *Dictionary of Literary Biography* that Williams "revealed his simultaneous admiration for athletes and his reluctance to anoint them as heroes." Nevertheless, Williams was an admirer of Mordecai "Three-Finger" Brown, Shoeless Joe Jackson, and Babe Ruth.

Williams was the first to report on Ruth's famous "called shot" during the World Series game against the Cubs in Chicago on October 1, 1923. He reported that Ruth, with two strikes against him, pointed a finger at the center field fence and then hit a home run over that exact spot. Other sportswriters later noted Ruth's call, but only after reading Williams's account. Ruth himself denied (but eventually accepted) the legend, and Williams later conceded that Ruth was probably holding up the finger as an indication that he had one strike left. Williams could also be very vocal when he disagreed with something, as when bottles (often thrown onto the field by angry fans) were replaced at baseball games with paper cups. He said the change was made by "pansy reformers." Williams's next big Ruth scoop came in 1935, when he reported that Ruth had given Yankees owner Colonel Jacob Ruppert the ultimatum of either replacing manager Joe McCarthy with Ruth or having Ruth leave the team for good. When Ruth died in 1948, Williams was asked to be a pallbearer at his service, but he hesitated because of the emotion surrounding the event and eventually declined.

Many of the top sportswriters of the time used "leg men," who covered events and phoned in the details, which the writers then developed into stories. Williams wrote only from his own experience, covering the people and games in person. Knight wrote that he "enjoyed beating others to stories, using his insider access, and expressing insight on behalf of fans. No matter the subject or deadline, he could write with precision and pacing." He also had no problem with disagreeing with the *Wall Street Journal* in 1949 when the financial newspaper claimed baseball had no potential for profit. Williams lauded the sport as a business venture, noting the clubs that were showing a profit and the multimillion-dollar sales of franchises.

In his more dramatic moments, the richness of his writing voice came though. As Knight noted, "Williams experimented with various stylistic effects, with varying degrees of success. Sometimes his effective use of quotes enlivens interviews and reads similarly to literary dialogue. At other times he intrudes into his own material, letting himself become a character in the column, or writes in the first person in such an undisciplined way that readers could be distracted from the topic by the obstacle the author becomes."

Of the six columns Williams wrote each week, his Monday pieces were a melange of unrelated musings and short items. In his autobiography *Bury Me in an Old Press Box,* Fred Russell wrote that Williams was "a genius at weaving the fragments together smoothly, injecting wise-cracks and barbs." Williams also wrote Heywood Broun's opinion column when Broun was unable to do so. He founded a hole-in-one golf tournament for charity in the name of the *World Telegram,* the yearly naming of the most valuable high school baseball player in New York, and Scripps-Howard's college football coaching award. Knight wrote that "baseball and its subjects always seemed to encourage Williams to more elaborate descriptions in his prose. . . . Ty Cobb was 'an egoist with a brain' and John McGraw 'a black-haired, pasty-faced Irishman to whom roughhouse tactics were merely a part of the trade.' Garry Hermann of the Cincinnati Reds—bankrupted by 'conviviality'—'was a cross between Bacchus and Falstaff.'"

After baseball, Williams most enjoyed writing about boxing, and his *Joe Williams's TV-Boxing Book,* with a foreword by Bob Hope, was a good seller. A *Sporting News* reviewer called it "rich in dramatic incident, incredible scandal, historical episode, and humorous anecdotes." Williams also wrote a subscription newsletter that focused mainly on horse racing and, after being forced out by Scripps-Howard management after the death of Roy Howard in 1964, a weekly column for the *Morning Telegraph.* He suffered a series of strokes and succumbed to intestinal cancer in 1972.

BIOGRAPHICAL AND CRITICAL SOURCES:

BOOKS

Alvarez, Mark, editor, *The Perfect Game,* Taylor (Dallas, TX), 1993.

Chandler, Happy, *Heroes, Plain Folks, and Skunks,* Bonus Books (Chicago, IL), 1989.

Considine, Bob, *It's All News to Me: A Reporter's Deposition,* Meredith Press (New York, NY), 1967.

Creamer, Robert, *Babe: The Legend Comes to Life,* Simon and Schuster (New York, NY), 1974.

Dictionary of Literary Biography, Volume 241: *American Sportswriters and Writers on Sport,* Gale (Detroit, MI), 2001.

Gelfand, Louis I., and Harry E. Heath, *Modern Sportswriting,* Iowa State University Press (Ames, IA), [n.d.].

Mead, Chris, *Champion: Joe Lewis, Black Hero in White America,* Scribners (New York, NY), 1985, pp. 132-133, 161, 205.

Murrow, Edward R., *This I Believe,* Simon and Schuster (New York, NY), 1952.

Robinson, Jackie, *My Own Story,* Greenberg (New York, NY), 1948.

Russell, Fred, *Bury Me in an Old Press Box,* Barnes (New York, NY), 1957.

PERIODICALS

Memphis Press-Scimitar, August 20, 1949, John Rogers, "Joe Williams, Back Home, Tells Stories of Past, Discusses Sports of Present" (interview).

Nine, fall, 1995, Peter Williams, "When Chipmunks Become Wolves: The Scapegoating of Sportswriter Joe Williams by His Peers," pp. 51-61.

Sporting News, August 22, 1940, J. G. Taylor Spink, "Three and One" (interview); November 17, 1954, J. G. Taylor Spink, "*TV-Boxing* Rich in Drama, Humor."*

*   *   *

WILSON, Larry 1930-

PERSONAL: Born 1930, in Louisville, KY. *Education:* Graduate of University of Minnesota.

ADDRESSES: Home—Minneapolis, MN. *Agent*—c/o Author Mail, Simon & Schuster, 1230 Avenue of the Americas, New York, NY 10020.

CAREER: Entrepreneur and training and management specialist. Founded Wilson Learning Corporation, 1965; founded Pecos River Learning Centers, 1983 (later became Pecos River Change Management Division of Aon Consulting Worldwide).

AWARDS, HONORS: Named Senior Fellow in Education and Alumni of the Year, University of Minnesota, both 1984; Ambassador of Free Enterprise, Sales and Marketing Executives International Academy of Achievements, 1991.

WRITINGS:

(With Spencer Johnson) *The One-Minute Salesperson: The Quickest Way to More Sales with Less Stress,* Morrow (New York, NY), 1984.

(With Hersch Wilson) *Changing the Game: The New Way to Sell,* Simon & Schuster (New York, NY), 1987.
(With Hersch Wilson) *Stop Selling, Start Partnering: The New Thinking about Finding and Keeping Customers,* Omneo (Essex Junction, VT), 1994.
(With Hersch Wilson) *Play to Win!: Choosing Growth over Fear in Work and Life,* Bard Press (Austin, TX), 1998.

Also wrote *Changing the Game Together: Inventing the Company That Will Put You out of Business,* Aon Consulting, with Hersch Wilson.

SIDELIGHTS:

Larry Wilson's writings and work as a business consultant are based on helping individuals and organizations embrace change and positive motivation to stimulate growth. Wilson founded Wilson Learning Corporation and Pecos River Learning Centers, which became the Pecos River Change Management Division of Aon Consulting Worldwide.

Wilson's first book, *The One-Minute Salesperson,* was written with Spencer Johnson. It tells readers that feeling good about yourself is essential to being an effective, successful salesperson. The book links feeling good about yourself to feeling good about your work, and ties liking that work with wanting to help people. An audio tape based on the book features Socratic dialogues between "Every Salesperson Who Has Lost His Enthusiasm" and "Selected Professionals Who Are Fulfilled." A *Publishers Weekly* critic called the material "best suited to psyching up the sagging salesperson" but of value to newcomers to the profession as well.

Subsequent books by Wilson have been coauthored with his son Hersch Wilson, who works as a senior vice president at Pecos River Change Management. Their 1998 title *Play to Win!: Choosing Growth over Fear in Work and Life* is based on concepts used by Pecos River in work with some 500,000 clients. It urges readers to focus on thriving instead of just surviving. This involves emotional and spiritual growth, as well as acceptance of new ideas. Sections of the book include a "two-minute drill" with the steps "stop, challenge, and choose," and the search for "Lov-

ing Service." Writing for *Booklist,* David Rouse likened the author's approach to Abraham Maslow's theory of self-actualization. Rouse described the book as "presented effectively in low-key, straightforward fashion."

BIOGRAPHICAL AND CRITICAL SOURCES:

PERIODICALS

Booklist, August 1998, p. 1941.
Publishers Weekly, October 1987, p. 58; August 24, 1998, p. 43.*

*   *   *

WINCKLER, Martin 1955-

PERSONAL: Born Marc Zaffran, 1955 (some sources say 1953), in Algiers, Algeria; married; children: eight. *Education:* Earned M.D., 1977.

ADDRESSES: Home—Le Mans, France. *Agent*—c/o Publicity Director, Seven Stories Press, 140 Watts St., New York, NY 10013.

CAREER: Writer and translator. Retired general medical practitioner.

AWARDS, HONORS: Prix du Livre Inter, for *The Case of Dr. Sachs.*

WRITINGS:

La Vacation, Paul Otchakovsky-Laurens (Paris, France), 1989.
La Maladie de Sachs, Paul Otchakovsky-Laurens (Paris, France), 1998, translation by Linda Asher published as *The Case of Dr. Sachs,* Seven Stories Press (New York, NY), 2001.

Contributor of essays on social and medical issues to periodicals. Translator into French of the works of Richard Powers, Patrick Macnee, and Nicholson Baker. *La Maladie de Sachs* has been translated into ten languages.

ADAPTATIONS: Movie version of *The Case of Dr. Sachs,* directed by Michel Deville, won first prize at the Chicago Film Festival, 2001.

SIDELIGHTS: Martin Winckler's first published work, *La Vacation,* introduces Dr. Bruno Sachs, a doctor who performs legal abortions at his clinic on Tuesday, Thursdays, and Fridays. Davida Brautman, reviewing *La Vacation* in the *French Review,* noted that it is a "new novel," that is, it uses "thought processes to communicate the dissatisfaction of the protagonist (and of the narrator) throughout the novel." Brautman commented that Winckler "has chosen an extremely delicate, controversial subject."

Winckler returned to his protagonist Dr. Sachs in *The Case of Doctor Sachs,* published in French as *La Maladie de Sachs.* Iain Bamforth, reviewing the novel in the *British Medical Journal,* called the work "a big, operatic, engaging book." Bamforth also observed, "*La Maladie de Sachs* unfolds in that grey area between the privacy of the doctor's surgery and a writer's need to develop a book through the lives of its characters." F. Gonzalez-Crusse, reviewing *The Case of Doctor Sachs* in the *Washington Post Book World,* commented: "The book unfolds with unflagging bravura; it is finely written and inconceivable as the work of anyone other than a practicing physician. . . . his words, simple and unpretentious, move us deeply."

Born Marc Zaffran in French Algeria, Winckler is a former doctor who stopped practicing medicine to devote his time to writing. He draws from several years of experience as a general practitioner in writing his books. Tony Miksanek, a reviewer for the *Journal of the American Medical Association,* noted that *The Case of Doctor Sachs*'s protagonist "is a compassionate general practitioner who works in a small French town" and that the story "is narrated primarily by the doctor's patients and acquaintances." In a *Publishers Weekly* interview with the author, Herbert R. Lottman noted that "the real Bruno Sachs is not him, but his father." Another reviewer in *Publishers Weekly* described the book as a "journal . . . made up of discrete chapters or vignettes." William Beatty, writing in *Booklist,* called Winckler's "imagination and skill . . . remarkable." Jim Dwyer, reviewing the novel in *Library Journal,* "highly recommended" the book, which he described as "a realistic romance, and a fascinating character study."

BIOGRAPHICAL AND CRITICAL SOURCES:

PERIODICALS

Booklist, September 15, 2000, William Beatty, review of *The Case of Dr. Sachs,* p. 220.
British Medical Journal, December 12, 1998, Iain Bamforth, review of *La Maladie de Sachs,* p. 1666.
French Review, March, 1991, Davida Brautman, review of *La Maladie de Sachs,* pp. 728-729.
Journal of the American Medical Association, December 27, 2000, Tony Miksanek, review of *The Case of Dr. Sachs,* p. 3186.
Library Journal, September 15, 2000, Jim Dwyer, review of *The Case of Dr. Sachs,* p. 115.
New England Journal of Medicine, March 8, 2001, Elena M. Massarotti, review of *The Case of Dr. Sachs,* p. 778.
Publishers Weekly, September 25, 2000, review of *The Case of Dr. Sachs,* p. 89; October 30, 2000, Herbert R. Lottman, "Martin Winckler: Notes of a French Doctor," p. 41.
Washington Post Book World, November 19, 2000, F. Gonzalez-Crussi, "The Healing Art," p. 3.

OTHER

French Culture, http://www.frenchculture.org/ (September 16, 2001).
University of Wisconsin—Madison Web site, http://wiscinfo.wisc.edu/ (September 16, 2001).

* * *

WIND, Yoram (Jerry) 1938-

PERSONAL: Born March 27, 1938, in Haifa, Israel; immigrated to United States, 1964; married; wife's name, Vardina; children: two. *Education:* Hebrew University, Jerusalem, Israel, B.Soc.Sc, 1961, M.A., 1963; Stanford University, Ph.D., 1966.

ADDRESSES: Office—University of Pennsylvania, Wharton School of Business, 3620 Locust Walk, Rm. 1040, Philadelphia, PA 19104-6373. *E-mail*—windj@wharton.upenn.edu.

CAREER: University of Pennsylvania, Wharton School of Business, Philadelphia, PA, assistant professor of marketing and international business, 1967-70, associate professor of marketing, 1970-73, professor of marketing, 1973—, Lauder Professor, 1983—.

MEMBER: American Marketing Association, American Association of Public Opinion Research, American Psychological Association, Strategic Management Society, London Market Research Society.

AWARDS, HONORS: Alpha Kappa Psi Foundation awards, 1973, 1976; Attitude Research Hall of Fame, 1984; Charles Coolidge Parlin award, 1985; First Faculty Impact award, Wharton Alumni Association, 1993; AMA/Irwin Distinguished Educator award, 1993; Paul D. Converse award, 1996.

WRITINGS:

(With Ronald E. Frank and William F. Massy) *Market Segmentation,* Prentice-Hall (Englewood Cliffs, NJ), 1972.

(With Frederick E. Webster) *Organizational Buying Behavior,* Prentice-Hall (Englewood Cliffs, NJ), 1972.

(With Paul E. Green) *Multiattribute Decisions in Marketing: A Measurement Approach,* Dryden Press (Hinsdale, IL), 1973.

(Editor, with Francesco M. Nicosia) *Behavioral Models for Market Analysis: Foundations for Marketing Action,* Dryden Press (Hinsdale, IL), 1977.

Product Policy: Concepts, Methods, and Strategy, Addison-Wesley (Reading, MA), 1981.

(Editor, with Vijay Mahajan and Richard N. Cardozo) *New-Product Forecasting: Models and Applications,* D.C. Heath (Lexington, MA), 1981.

(Editor, with Vijay Mahajan) *Innovation Diffusion Models of New Product Acceptance,* Ballinger (Cambridge, MA), 1986.

(With Jeremy Main) *Driving Change: How the Best Companies Are Preparing for the Twenty-first Century,* Free Press (New York, NY), 1997.

(Editor, with Vijay Mahajan and Eitan Muller) *New-Product Diffusion Models,* Kluwer Academic (Boston, MA), 2000.

(With Vijay Mahajan) *Digital Marketing: Global Strategies from the World's Leading Experts,* Wiley (New York, NY), 2001.

(With Vijay Mahajan) *Convergence Marketing: Running with the Centaurs,* Prentice-Hall (Upper Saddle River, NJ), 2002.

SIDELIGHTS: Yoram Wind has written or edited many marketing management textbooks and trade books. Wind's 1981 text, *Product Policy: Concepts, Methods, and Strategy,* is designed for advanced marketing students and takes a "holistic view" of product management problems, according to John Myers in the *Journal of Marketing.* Myers commented that the book leans "toward the methodology of conjoint analysis in the treatment of various issues." *Product Policy* is divided into four sections: foundations, methods and processes of new product development, managerial problems with existing products, and a conclusion. The book thoroughly covers such subjects as the art of marketing research, product classification and position, product portfolios in multi divisional corporations, new product development systems, product design, and procedures for test marketing. Although Myers felt that the author could have added review questions at the ends of chapters and that he showed a few biases in favor of conjoint analysis, he asserted that the book's "strengths lie in the holistic treatment and a concern for integrating several related issues from the literature." Myers felt that a teacher would find the Wind book useful "to present a coherent treatment of the product policy question."

Driving Change: How the Best Companies Are Preparing for the Twenty-first Century was called "the best written of all the change books out there" by Paul B. Brown in *Bookpage,* and a *Publishers Weekly* critic noted that "managers trying to cope with an endlessly changing marketplace will find comfort in this study." In his review of *Driving Change,* Brown admitted that the idea that change is inevitable in business could be considered a trite observation. "But to completely dismiss the observation is to miss the point," he added. Companies have realistic concerns, stated Brown, about the modern business environment, with its "steadily shifting landscape." He appreciated Yoram and Main's handling of this issue: "Instead of presenting a magic 'silver bullet' solution . . ., the authors are more than content to present what could be called snapshots of the evolution." They focus on the successful formulas used by several big-name companies, such as AT&T, Xerox, and VISA, to cope with fast-changing market niches and consumer needs and instant communications. Pioneer Hi-Bred, for example, has used the information superhighway to connect some 35,000 consultants via global net links. According to a reviewer for *Publishers Weekly,* "The book's approach, which allows readers to find ideas that are likely to work for them and their companies, is useful."

BIOGRAPHICAL AND CRITICAL SOURCES:

PERIODICALS

Bookpage, March, 1998, Paul B. Brown, "Change Is Good . . . Really," p. 16.
Choice, April, 1982, review of *New-Product Forecasting,* pp. 1105-1106.
Contemporary Sociology, September, 1987, Eric M. Leifer, review of *Innovation Diffusion Models of New Product Acceptance,* p. 764.
Interfaces, May-June, 1989, Michael J. C. Martin, review of *Innovation Diffusion Models of New Product Acceptance,* p. 92.
Journal of Marketing, summer, 1981, Vithala R. Rao, review of *Product Policy,* pp. 200, 203-205.
Publishers Weekly, November 17, 1997, review of *Driving Change,* p. 46.
Technological Forecasting & Social Change, September, 1987, Joseph P. Martino, review of *Innovation Diffusion Models of New Product Acceptance,* p. 225.*

* * *

WISE, Michael Z. 1957-

PERSONAL: Born 1957.

ADDRESSES: Agent—c/o Author Mail, Princeton Architectural Press, 37 East Seventh St., New York, NY 10003.

CAREER: Journalist and nonfiction writer. Former central European correspondent for Reuters and the *Washington Post.*

WRITINGS:

Capital Dilemma: Germany's Search for a New Architecture of Democracy, Princeton Architectural Press (New York, NY), 1998.

SIDELIGHTS: Michael Z. Wise makes use of his experience as an overseas correspondent and expertise in German culture and history to create a study of Berlin as the capital of a reunified and ardently democratic Germany. While after World War II West Germany had shifted its federal operations to Bonn, which then-chancellor Konrad Adenauer called "a city without a past," the dismantling of the Berlin Wall led to a move to reunify the capital city as well. *Capital Dilemma* details how an awareness of the Nazi legacy influenced the planning of Berlin's federal buildings.

While many of the buildings erected during Hitler's reign were destroyed during the war, he left his mark on a whole school of architecture: the "classical style." Russian dictator Josef Stalin's desire to shape East Berlin into his own image is another historic element contemporary Germans want to offset through a new architecture. But the desire for architecture which sends a democratic message can pose onerous difficulties for architects trying to design buildings for large public use. As Wise quotes one contemporary Berlin architect: "Everything that has a stone facade and a large door is regarded here, in this paranoid situation, as a fascist building." If one tries to imagine Washington, D.C., without stone facades or large doors, it is easy to see how hobbling such restrictions might be.

In efforts to democratize not only the architectural style of Berlin but the process of choosing architectural designs, the German government "sought to make sure that any such controversy would eventually focus on questions of taste rather than politics. It handled the decision-making process in an open, competitive, and deliberate manner. In important instances, winning bids (perhaps not surprisingly) were awarded to prominent non-German architects who could hardly be accused of politically incorrect designs or ambitions," according to *Foreign Policy* essayist Gebhard Schweigler. Also not surprisingly, those questions of taste have been hotly contested. For instance, for the dome of one new government building its architect supplied what *New York Times Book Review* contributor Martin Filler called a "tragi-comic array of 26 alternative dome proposals—none very good— . . . before a consensus was reached [which] speaks volumes about the enervating effect of design by committee."

Reviewers were impressed with Wise's research, much of which was in the form of interviews with current parliamentarians and architects. Filler called *Capital*

Dilemma "insightful and admirably concise," and concluded that "one hopes that a decade from now Wise will get back to Berlin for a similarly clear-eyed and sharp-witted reappraisal" of the current plans. A contributor to *Publishers Weekly* dubbed the work a "concise and accessible study of a deeply complicated issue," and Schweigler called *Capital Dilemma* a "fascinating analysis of politics, architecture, the burdens of history, and the search for national self-image."

BIOGRAPHICAL AND CRITICAL SOURCES:

PERIODICALS

Foreign Policy, summer, 1998, Gebhard Schweigler, review of *Capital Dilemma,* pp. 145-149.
New York Times Book Review, August 30, 1998, Martin Filler, "Edifice Complex," p. 15.
Publishers Weekly, May 4, 1998, pp. 198-199.*

*   *   *

WISEMAN, Carter (Sterling) 1945-

PERSONAL: Born October 8, 1945, in New York, NY; son of Mark Huntington Wiseman and Eleanor Carter Wood; married Eileen Condon, October 19, 1985; children: Emma, Owen, Damian. *Education:* Yale University, B.A., 1968; Columbia University, M.A., 1972.

ADDRESSES: Office—Yale Alumni Magazine, P.O. Box 1905, New Haven, CT 06509-1905. *E-mail*—carter.wiseman@yale.edu.

CAREER: Associated Press, New York, NY, newsman, 1972-74; *Newsweek,* New York, NY, associate editor, 1974-77; *Horizon* magazine, New York, NY, senior editor, 1977-79; *Portfolio* magazine, New York, NY, managing editor, 1979-80; *New York* magazine, architectural critic, 1980-96; *Yale Alumni Magazine,* New Haven, CT, editor, 1986—. Contributing editor, *ArtNews.* MacDowell Colony, Peterborough, NH, president, 1999. *Military service:* U.S. Army, 1968-71.

MEMBER: Yale Club of New York.

AWARDS, HONORS: Special citation award, American Institute of Architects, 1984; Loeb fellow, Harvard University, 1985; Interpretive Writing award, Society of Silurians, 1985; Institute Honor award, American Institute of Architects, 1987; Roger Starr award, Citizens Housing and Planning Counsel, 1987, 1990.

WRITINGS:

I. M. Pei: A Profile in American Architecture, H. N. Abrams (New York, NY), 1990.
Shaping a Nation: Twentieth-Century American Architecture and Its Makers, Norton (New York, NY), 1998.

SIDELIGHTS: Carter Wiseman, for many years the respected architecture critic for *New York* magazine, has written two books on twentieth-century architecture. In *I. M. Pei: A Profile in American Architecture,* Wiseman portrays the modernist architect who was responsible for many important structures, such as the East Building of the National Gallery of Art in Washington, D.C., the John F. Kennedy Library in Boston, the Jacob Javits Convention Center in New York, and the pyramidal entrance to the Louvre Museum in Paris. Pei, born in China, is described as both practical and idealistic, both egotistical and humble, and both tactful and political with prospective commission donors. Pei's tendency to go over-budget, along with some of his other faults, are pointed out along with his virtues. According to Blair Kamin in the Chicago *Tribune Books,* Wiseman's coverage of the actual architecture, which "lacks the conceptual heft needed to put Pei's work into perspective," is less appealing than his portrait of Pei as a person. Still, Kamin called the book "lucid" and appreciated the interviews with Pei, his family, and his associates, as well as the 375 illustrations. A reviewer in *Newsweek* also praised the portrayal of Pei's "charisma, patience and determination."

Wiseman's second book was welcomed by many critics as a well-written and appealing look at the history of twentieth-century architecture. *Shaping a Nation: Twentieth-Century American Architecture and Its Makers* covers such important American architects as Louis Sullivan, Frank Lloyd Wright, Pei, Louis Kahn, and Frank Gehry. It also deals with the architects' reactions to the culture and the cultural ramifications of the architecture. Wiseman puts into perspective a number of trends in architecture, including the Arts and Crafts movement, modernism, the growth of the preservation movement, post-modernist revivals, and more recent influences of the computer on architectural design. The author reveals his attitude toward building design in the introduction: "I believe that serious architecture should be buildable, useful and beautiful."

A reviewer in the *Economist* liked the book for being "undogmatic" and especially appreciated Wiseman's coverage of little-known architects such as Raymond Hood, the designer of Rockefeller Center. In *Booklist*, Donna Seaman praised the book's readability, calling it a "well-told tale"; she also pointed out that Wiseman fully appreciates both the aesthetic and cultural meanings of the architecture he describes. He explains the forces at work in the culture which produced romantic, early twentieth-century buildings, the "pristine visions" of Frank Lloyd Wright, and the minimalist creations of architects like Mies van der Rohe.

Robert Campbell in the *New York Times Book Review* called *Shaping a Nation* "about as good a summary of American architecture of this century as anyone is likely to write." The reviewer thought that Wiseman avoids some pitfalls of a typical book of this sort: namely, he does not set up one paradigm (such as the "march of progress") as a model for the history of architecture, nor does he simply present an encyclopedic look at America's architectural past. Rather, he contextualizes architecture by bringing in many writers and theorists who comment on the culture at large vis-à-vis the architects who were designing the buildings in a particular era. According to Campbell, this gives the book "a quality of intellectual and social narrative that raises it above the level of merely factual history."

Campbell pointed out some factual errors in the book but said that they are "few and minor." His major criticisms of *Shaping a Nation* were that some of the terms Wiseman uses (such as "romantic" and "rationalist") need more explanation or refinement and that the author tries to pack in too much information: "[He] seems never to have met a fact he didn't want to include." Campbell, however, felt that the book was a valuable contribution to the field, one which would "send . . . people out" to "inhabit [architecture's] spaces, sense its scale and its materiality, [and] know it in its setting."

BIOGRAPHICAL AND CRITICAL SOURCES:

PERIODICALS

Booklist, January 1 & 15, 1998, Donna Seaman, review of *Shaping a Nation,* p. 762.
Tribune Books (Chicago, IL), December 2, 1990, Blair Kamin, "Modernism and More," p. 9.
Economist, August 22, 1998, "An Ace Fills the Straight," p. 68.
Los Angeles Times Book Review, November 25, 1990, Charles Lockwood, "Giving Shelter," p. 26.
Newsweek, December 10, 1990, review of *I. M. Pei,* p. 84.
New York Times Book Review, April 12, 1998, Robert Campbell, "American Blueprint."

OTHER

Norton Web site, http://www.wwnorton.com/ (November 13, 1998).*

*   *   *

WOLF, Joan

PERSONAL: Born in Bronx, NY; married; husband's name, Joseph; children: Jay, Pam. *Education:* Hunter College, M.A. *Hobbies and other interests:* Horses, New York Yankees fan, University of Connecticut men's and women's basketball teams fan.

ADDRESSES: Home—Milford, CT. *Agent*—c/o Warner Books, Inc., Time and Life Building, 1271 Avenue of the Americas, New York, NY 10020. *E-mail*—JoanWolf190@aol.com.

CAREER: Writer. Cardinal Spellman High School, Bronx, NY, former English teacher.

MEMBER: Author's Guild, Novelists, Inc.

WRITINGS:

A Kind of Honor, J. Curley and Associates (South Yarmouth, MA), 1980.
A London Season, J. Curley and Associates (South Yarmouth, MA), 1980.

A Difficult Truce, J. Curley and Associates (South Yarmouth, MA), 1981.

The American Duchess, J. Curley and Associates (South Yarmouth, MA), 1982.

The Counterfeit Marriage, J. Curley and Associates (South Yarmouth, MA), 1982.

Lord Richard's Daughter, J. Curley and Associates (South Yarmouth, MA), 1983.

The Divided Sphere, Floating Island Publications (Floating Island Station, CA), 1985.

The Rebel and the Rose, Signet (New York, NY), 1986.

The Road to Avalon, NAL Books (New York, NY), 1988.

The Arrangement, Thorndike Press (Thorndike, ME), 1988.

Born of the Sun, New American Library (New York, NY), 1989.

The Edge of Light, NAL Books (New York, NY), 1990.

Daughter of the Red Deer, Dutton (New York, NY), 1991.

The Horsemasters, Dutton (New York, NY), 1993.

The Reindeer Hunters, Dutton (New York, NY), 1994.

The Guardian, Wheeler Publications (Rockland, MA), 1997.

Golden Girl, Warner Books (New York, NY), 1999.

No Dark Place, HarperCollins Publishers (New York, NY), 1999.

The Poisoned Serpent, HarperCollins Publishers (New York, NY), 2000.

Royal Bride, Warner Books (New York, NY), 2001.

Silverbridge, Warner Books (New York, NY), 2002.

High Meadow, Warner Books (New York, NY), 2003.

SIDELIGHTS: Historical romance novelist Joan Wolf was born in the Bronx, but has lived in Milford, Connecticut for over twenty years. Wolf taught creative writing to high school students before becoming a full-time writer. She noted at her Web site that teaching sharpened her critical skills, and editing students' work aided her in improving her own writing.

In *The Road to Avalon,* set in England after the Roman occupation, Wolf presents her version of the King Arthur legend. Uther Pendragon is a Roman king; his wife Igraine is a Celtic princess, and their son Arthur, conceived while Igraine was still married to her first husband, has been raised in secret by Morgan, daughter of the magician Merlin. Although Morgan is Arthur's half-aunt, the two are in love with each other, though they cannot show that love in public. Arthur

marries Celtic princess Gwynhwyfar, but keeps his secret relationship with Morgan. In *Publishers Weekly,* Sybil Steinberg praised Wolf's characterization, noting that the book "captures—and enriches—the tragic sweep of romance and idealism inherent in the Arthurian tale." In *Kirkus Reviews,* a reviewer noted, "Wolf interestingly paints Arthur as a Roman Briton, and imaginatively intuits the course of a number of ancient battles."

The Road to Avalon is the first book in a trilogy, which includes *Born of the Sun* and *The Edge of Light.* In *Born of the Sun,* Niniane a British princess, and Ceawlin, the son of a Saxon king, are married in an attempt to form an alliance between their mutually hostile tribes. Trouble breaks out when in a duel the illegitimate Ceawlin accidentally kills his half-brother, the legitimate heir to their father's throne, and the lovers must flee for their lives. Eventually they return in triumph, amid conspiracy and conflict. In *Booklist,* Margaret Flanagan wrote that the book encompasses both "a grand adventure and a tender love story." "The plotting is excellent and the main characters and their love story appealing," reported Ann Mills in *Library Journal.* "*Born of the Sun* [is] a clear, precise description of life among the Saxons and Celts," said Brian Jacomb in a review of *The Edge of Light* for the *Washington Post Book World.*

The Edge of Light is set during a turbulent period in English history, the eighth century, when the country was a patchwork of warring kingdoms and factions, and Danish invaders pillaged the coasts. Jacomb wrote, "Wolf's descriptions of a long-ago, mostly rural England are colorful, her portrait of what life was like in those days convincing."

Daughter of the Red Deer, set in prehistoric southern France, features a conflict between the Tribe of the Horse, whose drinking water supply has become fouled, killing their women, and the Tribe of the Red Deer. In order to replace the women who have died, the men of the Tribe of the Horse kidnap women from the Tribe of the Red Deer. This larger conflict is personified by the tormented love between Mar, a leading man in the Tribe of the Horse, who falls in love with Alin, a priestess from the Red Deer clan. In *School Library Journal,* Carol Clark summed up the book as "fascinating reading." "A quick-moving, enchanting tale," wrote Denise Blank in *Booklist,* noting that the book "holds a powerful modern message concerning the battle of the sexes." A *Kirkus Reviews* critic called the book "post-feminist prehistory . . . well researched and thought out."

The Reindeer Hunters, described by Louise Titchener in the *Washington Post Book World* as "a fine addition to the growing genre of prehistories," is set in southern France at the time when the last Ice Age ended and warming weather changed the migration patterns of the reindeer. The action centers on Nardo and Alane, favored son and daughter of two "horsemaster" tribes, who marry to cement an alliance of their tribes against the invading "horse-eater" tribes. Their tribes, though allied, are different—Alane's is patrilineal, focusing power on men, and Nardo's is matrilineal, passing down power through the maternal line. Their private cultural clashes about marriage and the proper place of men and women are a running theme through the novel. "Now this is what a prehistorical should be!" commented Pat Monaghan in *Booklist.* "With assured plotting, pacing and characterization," wrote a *Publishers Weekly* reviewer, "Wolf . . . again convincingly imagines prehistoric people and events."

No Dark Place and *The Poisoned Serpent* are set in the medieval era and share a hero in Hugh de Leon. *The Poisoned Serpent* "serves up history and intrigue in equal measure," wrote a *Publishers Weekly* critic, who called the novel "engaging." Ilene Cooper, in a review of the audio version of *The Poisoned Serpent* for *Booklist,* called it a "well-constructed, well-set, and very satisfying tale."

Royal Bride also won Wolf critical praise. Set in a small canton named Jura, a neighbor of Austria, the novel is a tale of romance and political intrigue. "Wolf is fast becoming a household name among Regency fans," said a *Publishers Weekly* reviewer, who found the book to balance "sympathetic insight with captivating political suspense." Noting the novel's "charming . . . intelligent heroine" and "politically astute hero," Kristin Ramsdell in *Library Journal* called *Royal Bride* "a witty, fast-paced" tale.

Wolf stated in Peggy J. Jaegly's *Romantic Hearts: A Personal Reference for Romance Readers,* "Character is the element of a novel that interests me most. . . . Romance is the genre where character reigns supreme. Action by itself and for itself I find surprisingly dull. It is the deeper motivations of the people who do the action that interest me."

BIOGRAPHICAL AND CRITICAL SOURCES:

BOOKS

Jaegly, Peggy J., *Romantic Hearts: A Personal Reference for Romance Readers,* 3rd edition, Scarecrow Press (Lanham, MD), 1997.

PERIODICALS

Booklist, October 1, 1994, Pat Monaghan, review of *The Reindeer Hunters,* p. 240; October 1, 1999, Diana Tixier Herald, review of *Golden Girl,* p. 347; May 1, 2000, Ilene Cooper, review of *The Poisoned Serpent,* p. 1626.

Kirkus Reviews, June 15, 1988, review of *The Road to Avalon,* p. 858; September 1, 1991, review of *Daughter of the Red Deer,* p. 1117.

Library Journal, October 15, 1988, Beth Ann Mills, review of *The Road to Avalon,* p. 105; July, 1989, Beth Ann Mills, review of *Born of the Sun,* p. 111; June 15, 1990, Patricia Altner, review of *The Edge of Light,* p. 138; September 15, 1991, Beth Ann Mills, review of *Daughter of the Red Deer,* p. 115; April 1, 1993, Beth Ann Mills, review of *The Horsemasters,* p. 133; September 15, 1994, Mary Ellen Elsbernd, review of *The Reindeer Hunters,* p. 93; November 15, 1996, Kristin Ramsdell, review of *The Deception,* p. 52; May 15, 1998, Kristin Ramsdell, review of *The Gamble,* p. 76; May 1, 2000, Barbara Hoffert, review of *The Poisoned Serpent,* p. 158; February 15, 2001, Kristin Ramsdell, review of *Royal Bride,* p. 155.

Publishers Weekly, May 9, 1986, review of *The Rebel and the Rose,* p. 251; June 10, 1988, Sybil Steinberg, review of *The Road to Avalon,* p. 70; June 16, 1989, Sybil Steinberg, review of *Born of the Sun,* p. 56; June 15, 1990, Sybil Steinberg, review of *The Edge of Light,* p. 56; January 25, 1991, Penny Kaganoff, review of *Born of the Sun,* p. 53; September 6, 1991, review of *Daughter of the Red Deer,* p. 96; March 15, 1993, review of *The Horsemasters,* p. 69; September 12, 1994, review of *The Reindeer Hunters,* p. 80; October 14, 1996, review of *The Deception,* p. 81; March 3, 1997, review of *The Guardian,* p. 71; September 15, 1997, review of *The Arrangement,* p. 73; September 13, 1999, review of *Golden Girl,* p. 79; April 17, 2000, review of *The Poisoned Serpent,* p. 55; January 13, 2001, review of *Royal Bride,* p. 56.

School Library Journal, June, 1992, Carol Clark, review of *Daughter of the Red Deer,* p. 150; October, 2000, Claudia Moore, review of *The Poisoned Serpent,* p. 194.

Voice of Youth Advocates, June, 1990, review of *The Road to Avalon,* p. 138; December, 2000, John Charles and Joanne Morrison, review of *No Dark Place,* p. 320.

Washington Post Book World, September, 1990, Brian Jacomb, review of the *The Edge of Light,* p. 9; January 22, 1995, Louise Titchener, review of *The Reindeer Hunters,* p. 11.

OTHER

Joan Wolf Web site, http://www.joanwolf.com/ (July 2, 2002).*

*   *   *

WOLF, Michele

PERSONAL: Born in Denville, NJ; daughter of Sheldon Wolf and Dorothy Shapiro Yospe; married Sanford Herzon (a high school science teacher), August 5, 2001. *Education:* Boston University, B.S. (public communication; summa cum laude); Columbia University, M.S. (journalism).

ADDRESSES: Home—4615 North Park Ave., No. 810, Chevy Chase, MD 20815-4514. *E-mail*—michele wolf@juno.com.

CAREER: Chevy Chase, MD, writer and editor, 1987—; Simon & Schuster, New York, NY, copy editor; Charles Scribner's Sons, New York, NY, associate copy editor; *Harper's Bazaar,* New York, NY, associate editor; Boston Ballet, Boston, MA, publicist. Administrative staff, Bread Loaf Writers' Conference, 1990-92.

MEMBER: PEN American Center, Poetry Society of America, American Society of Journalists and Authors.

AWARDS, HONORS: Chapbook series prize, *Painted Bride Quarterly,* 1995, for *The Keeper of Light,*; Anna Davidson Rosenberg Award for poems on the Jewish experience, Judah L. Magnes Museum, 1997, for poem "Trees"; Anhinga Prize for Poetry, Anhinga Press, 1997, for *Conversations during Sleep.*

WRITINGS:

The Keeper of Light, Painted Bride Quarterly Poetry Chapbook Series, 1995.

Conversations during Sleep, Anhinga Press (Tallahassee, FL), 1998.

Contributor to anthologies, including *Clockpunchers: Poetry of the American Workplace,* Partisan Press; *Beyond Lament: Poets of the World Bearing Witness to the Holocaust,* Northwestern University Press; *I Am Becoming the Woman I've Wanted, If I Had a Hammer: Women's Work,* and *When I Am an Old Woman I Shall Wear Purple,* all Papier-Mache Press; and *Out of Season,* Amagansett Press. Contributor of poetry to periodicals, including *Poetry, Hudson Review, Boulevard, Antioch Review, Painted Bride Quarterly, Confrontation, Poet Lore, Southern Poetry Review,* and others.

WORK IN PROGRESS: "The Great Tsunami" (poetry).

SIDELIGHTS: Michele Wolf told *CA:* "I strive for lyrical poems with a narrative base and a strong emphasis on lucid imagery and the interplay of sounds, always trying to fully use the aesthetic capacities of language. To me, a poem, no matter what its subject—emotional bonds, mortality, adversity, bliss—is an act of discovery and connection. At its end, both the writer and the reader should arrive at a place they assumed they had known, only to find it has been transformed."

*   *   *

WOLFMAN, Judy 1933-

PERSONAL: Born July 25, 1933, in Washington, DC; married Al Wolfman (a broadcaster), June 21, 1957; children: Barry, Scott, Ellen. *Education:* Pennsylvania State University, B.S., 1955; certification in elementary education, 1972; certificate in early childhood education, 1972, master's equivalency, 1972.

ADDRESSES: Home—2770 Hartford Rd., York, PA 17402. *E-mail*—jbwolfman@juno.com.

CAREER: Author, professional storyteller, and creative writing teacher. York City School District, York, PA, teacher, 1968-93; Pennsylvania State University, York, adjunct professor for two years; York College of Pennsylvania, York, adjunct professor, 1993—; Western Maryland College, adjunct professor, 1999—. Back Mt. Nursery School, Dallas, PA, former owner and operator for three years; Little People Day Care School, Hanover, PA, owner and administrator for one year; former head teacher for Wellington Child Development Center for one year. Creative writing classes instructor at summer camps, 1998—. Founder and coach of York College Storytelling Troupe.

MEMBER: Society for Children's Book Writers and Illustrators, National Storytelling Network, National Education Association, Penn Writers, Pennsylvania Association of School Retirees, Pennsylvania State Education Association, Mid-Atlantic Storytellers, York Writers, York Tellers.

AWARDS, HONORS: First place in the Bartels Children's Playwriting Contest, 1988, for *Red vs. the Wolf;* "Book of the Year," Agricultural Education in Wisconsin, and Notable Books List, Pennsylvania Library Association, both 1999, both for *Life on a Pig Farm.*

WRITINGS:

Red vs. the Wolf (play), Pioneer Drama (Denver, CO), 1989.

The Real Life of Red Riding Hood (musical), Pioneer Drama (Denver, CO), 1998.

Life on a Pig Farm, photographs by David Lorenz Winston, Carolrhoda Books (Minneapolis, MN), 1998.

The Golden Goose, Pioneer Drama (Denver, CO), 2001.

Life on a Goat Farm, photographs by David Lorenz Winston, Carolrhoda Books (Minneapolis, MN), 2002.

Life on a Cattle Farm, photographs by David Lorenz Winston, Carolrhoda Books (Minneapolis, MN), 2002.

Life on a Horse Farm, photographs by David Lorenz Winston, Carolrhoda Books (Minneapolis, MN), 2002.

Life on a Crop Farm, photographs by David Lorenz Winston, Carolrhoda Books (Minneapolis, MN), 2002.

Life on a Chicken Farm, Carolrhoda Books (Minneapolis, MN), 2003.

Life on a Sheep Farm, Carolrhoda Books (Minneapolis, MN), 2003.

Life on a Dairy Farm, Carolrhoda Books (Minneapolis, MN), 2003.

Life on an Apple Orchard, Carolrhoda Books (Minneapolis, MN), 2003.

Contributor of articles, plays, scripts, poetry, and nonfiction to various periodicals and anthologies, including *Mel White's Readers Theatre Anthology,* Meriwhether Publishing, 1992.

WORK IN PROGRESS: Not My Time, a holocaust survivor's story.

SIDELIGHTS: Judy Wolfman told *CA:* "Even thought I dabbled in writing as a kid, it wasn't until I began working that writing became a part of my life. I did freelance work for magazines and newspapers, and wrote a column as part of my job as an extension home economist that appeared in five county newspapers. My first attempt at a children's play was published, and I soon began writing short stories and articles for children's magazines. My retirement from teaching provided the time I needed to 'really' write—books, more plays, theater scripts, sketches, finger plays, poems, articles, and stories.

"In addition to writing, I enjoy working with young people, helping them to get their creative juices flowing and putting their ideas into written form. My writing classes continue to grow, as they are offered at a variety of summer camps and libraries. Showing slides as I present author talks helps more children become aware of the writing process and book development. It's rewarding to hear students express their interest in writing, and hopes of being published, after hearing what is involved.

"Discipline has become important to me in establishing a writing schedule, and I try to keep to that schedule. Usually, I'm at the computer by 9:00, and work until 1:00. My afternoons are free to run errands or perform domestic chores. Thanks to my writers' critique group, I'm able to express myself better, write tighter, and appeal to my audience. Their comments and suggestions have been invaluable. Anyone desiring to write needs to enjoy reading, and study many books and writing styles. Analyzing other people's writing helps me recognize what works and what doesn't. And, without a dictionary and Thesaurus, I'd be lost! They are truly the tools of a writer.

"My first effort at whatever I'm writing is strictly 'free-flowing,' in which words come from my head, down my arm, into my fingers and into the keyboard. I'm not concerned at that time with perfection, although I try to select the right words. Later, I read what I wrote and edit myself. I let that sit a while, then read it out aloud and do another edit. Finally, I print it out, set it aside for a final read and edit. It takes a long time to complete an article, story, or book. But, it's all worthwhile when readers say, 'Wow! That was interesting.'"

BIOGRAPHICAL AND CRITICAL SOURCES:

PERIODICALS

Booklist, October 15, 1998, Lauren Peterson, review of *Life on a Pig Farm,* p. 420; November 15, 2001, Ellen Mandel, review of *Life on a Cattle Farm,* p. 569.
Horn Book Guide, spring, 1999, Jackie C. Horne, review of *Life on a Pig Farm,* p. 117.
School Library Journal, March, 1999, Lee Bock, review of *Life on a Pig Farm,* p. 202; November, 2001, Carolyn Janssen, review of *Life on a Cattle Farm* and *Life on a Goat Farm,* p. 153; January, 2002, Eldon Younce, review of *Life on a Horse Farm,* p. 128.

*   *   *

WOODWELL, William H., Jr.

PERSONAL: Married, wife's name, Kim; children: Nina (deceased), Josie, Dean.

ADDRESSES: Home—Maurertown, VA. *Agent*—c/o University Press of Mississippi, 3825 Ridgewood Road, Jackson, MS 39211-6492.

CAREER: Freelance writer and editor.

WRITINGS:

(Editor with Janette M. Woodwell) *A Watershed Primer for Pennsylvania: A Collection of Essays on Watershed Issues,* Pennsylvania Environmental Council (Pittsburgh, PA), 1999.
Coming to Term: A Father's Story of Birth, Loss, and Survival, University Press of Mississippi (Jackson, MS), 2001.

Also the author of "Choosing the President: The Citizen's Guide to the 2000 Election." Contributor to periodicals, including the *Washington Post.*

SIDELIGHTS: American writer William H. Woodwell, Jr. earned critical praise for his 2001 book, *Coming to Term: A Father's Story of Birth, Loss, and Survival,* a personal account of his wife's problematic experience delivering twins in 1997, and the sadness that followed when one of the babies died. The book, which a contributor for *Publishers Weekly* called "a riveting, poignant, often piercing account," describes wife Kim Woodwell's battle with a condition called pre-eclampsia, which is often fatal to pregnant women and their babies. The condition forced Kim to give birth to the couple's twin daughters almost four months before they were due. Kim survived the experience, as did Josie, the larger of the two babies. However, Nina, who weighed a little more than a pound, died two days after being born. A freelance writer and editor whose work has appeared in the *Washington Post,* Woodwell decided to write a book about his family's ordeal as a way to give expression to his own emotions as well as to help others in the same situation. He explained this decision in the book. "As time went on . . . I came to feel that this story had meaning beyond our family. I was so affected and so moved by what had happened to us—the experience had forced me to think anew about so many of my assumptions, so many things I felt like I had already figured out—that I imagined it might somehow affect others in a similar way," he writes in the book. The book is filled with detailed descriptions of the couple's reaction when learning of Kim's condition, as well as the birth experience. After the girls were born, hooked up to ventilators and hanging onto life, Woodwell was forced to realize that he could do nothing to help them survive. "Their hearts beat on like nothing's wrong. Kim says they sound like horses," Woodwell writes. "It's hard enough coming into the world the way most of us do. For them, it will be that much more of a surprise, that much more of a shock. Fact is, we're essentially powerless to help them now, except to keep them in there as long as we can." Throughout much of the book, Woodwell focuses on Josie's long struggle for life. She spent four months in the hospital before she was able to come home. The only lasting effect of Josie's early life troubles is a condition called hemiplegia, a form of paralysis, which causes her to wear a brace on her left leg. Throughout the entire ordeal, from the time Kim went into the hospital, until Josie came home, Woodwell kept a journal, in which he jotted down his thoughts and fears. He used these notes when writing *Coming to Term*, which was critically praised for its frank portrayal of the family's traumatic experience. Charlotte Bruce Harvey, writing in the *Brown Alumni Magazine*, felt the book revealed Woodwell's "growth from a young man fearful of parenthood and uncertain of his own utility on this planet, to a father awed by his tiny daughter's resourcefulness and will to live." Harvey went on to write that Woodwell "tells this story plainly, without self-congratulation or self-pity." In late 2000, before the book was even published, Woodwell's wife gave birth to a healthy son named Dean. During the birth, Kim Woodwell showed no sign of the condition that had threatened her life during her earlier pregnancy.

BIOGRAPHICAL AND CRITICAL SOURCES:

PERIODICALS

Brown Alumni Magazine, January/February, 2002, Charlotte Bruce Harvey, "Josie's Song."
Publishers Weekly, July 30, 2001, review of *Coming to Term: A Father's Story of Birth, Loss, and Survival,* p. 75.
Washington Post, August 24, 1999, William H. Woodwell, Jr., "A Deadly Pregnancy," p. Z10.

OTHER

About.com, http://specialchildren.about.com/ (May 6, 2002), Donald R. Mattison, review of *Coming to Term: A Father's Story of Birth, Loss, and Survival.*

Paternity Angel, http://www.paternityangel.com/ (April 12, 2002).
UVA Top News Daily, (March 13, 2002), http://www.virginia.edu/ Mary Jane Gore, review of *Coming to Term: A Father's Story of Birth, Loss, and Survival.**

* * *

WOOLLEY, Lisa 1960-

PERSONAL: Born July 18, 1960, in Peoria, IL; daughter of Gene (a carpenter and pilot) and Phyllis (an office manager; maiden name, Grandberg) Woolley; married Larry T. Shillock (a professor of English), October 13, 1990; children: Robin. *Education:* Augustana College, B.A., 1982; University of Minnesota, M.A., 1990, Ph.D., 1993. *Religion:* Lutheran/Episcopalian. *Hobbies and other interests:* Birdwatching.

ADDRESSES: Home—563 East King St., Chambersburg, PA 17201. *Office*—Wilson College, 1015 Philadelphia Ave., Chambersburg, PA 17201. *E-mail*—lwoolley@wilson.edu.

CAREER: Wilson College, Chambersburg, PA, associate professor of English, 1993—.

MEMBER: Modern Language Association, Society for the Study of Midwestern Literature, Midwest Modern Language Association, Conococheague Audubon Society (president, 1999-2001).

WRITINGS:

American Voices of the Chicago Renaissance, Northern Illinois University Press (DeKalb, IL), 2000.

Contributor to periodicals, including *MELUS* and *Langston Hughes Review.*.

WORK IN PROGRESS: Research on urban ecocriticism and on Richard Wright.

* * *

WOOTSON, Alice (G.) 1937-

PERSONAL: Born July 14, 1937, in Pittsburgh, PA; daughter of Robert Randolph (a steel worker) and Lorena (a homemaker; maiden name, Fleming) Greenhowe; married Isaiah Wootson (a teacher), September

3, 1960. *Education:* Cheyney State University, B.S. and M.Ed.; University of Pennsylvania, reading specialist certification; also attended Temple University, Ambler, and Goddard College. *Religion:* Baptist. *Hobbies and other interests:* Crafts, sewing, writing poetry, listening to music.

ADDRESSES: Office—P.O. Box 18832, Philadelphia, PA 19119. *E-mail*—agwwriter@email.com.

CAREER: School teacher in Chester and Philadelphia, PA, 1964-92; writer. Also works as a reading specialist. Member of a local dance group.

MEMBER: Romance Writers of America, Pennsylvania Poetry Society, New Jersey Romance Writers, Philadelphia Writers Conference, Mad Poets, Poets' Roundtable, VFRW.

WRITINGS:

ROMANCE NOVELS

Snowbound with Love, BET Books (Washington, DC), 2000.
Dream Wedding, BET Books (Washington, DC), 2001.
Home for Christmas, BET Books (Washington, DC), 2001.
Trust in Me, BET Books (Washington, DC), 2002.
To Love Again, BET Books (Washigton, DC), in press.

WORK IN PROGRESS: Research on the U.S. Civil War era in Fredericksburg, VA.

SIDELIGHTS: Alice Wootson told *CA:* "My primary motivation for writing is that I have these people in my head prodding me, asserting themselves, making a pure nuisance of themselves. The only way to quiet them is to tell their stories. I am a voracious reader, as were my parents and grandparents. My reading appetite is quite eclectic. I try to emulate excellent writing. There are so many writers whom I admire that I can't name them.

"My writing process is to turn on my computer immediately, make a large cup of tea, and write for three or four hours or as long as I can stay in the story. Often I read about a story that triggers a big 'what if' and sends me off on a new story.

"I write romance because, in a world with so much sadness, I like to write stories with happy endings. I have addressed some social issues within several of my stories. *Home for Christmas* features a hero, Jeffrey, who starts a program based on one initiated by National Football League star Warrick Dunn to put homeless families into their own homes. *Trust in Me* has a hero who goes back to his old, impoverished neighborhood and opens a community center for the kids, and Marc in *To Love Again* gets involved in the Big Brothers program. My overall goal is to tell a story well enough so that the reader considers reading my book time well spent."

*   *   *

WUCKER, Michele 1969-

PERSONAL: Born 1969, in Kansas City, MO. *Education:* Rice University, B.A.; Columbia University School of International Affairs, M.A.

ADDRESSES: Agent—c/o Author Mail, Farrar, Straus & Giroux, 19 Union Square W., New York, NY 10001.

CAREER: World Policy Institute, New York, NY, senior fellow, 2001—. *Milwaukee Sentinel,* Milwaukee, WI, reporter; *Listín USA,* foreign editor; *International Financing Review,* Latin America bureau chief.

WRITINGS:

Why the Cocks Fight: Dominicans, Haitians, and the Struggle for Hispaniola, Hill and Wang (New York, NY), 1999.

Contributor of articles to periodicals, including *Boston Globe, Christian Science Monitor, Newsday, Newsweek, World Policy Journal, Haiti Insight, Nando Times, NACLA Report on the Americas,* and *In These Times.*

SIDELIGHTS: Freelance journalist Michele Wucker lived for a number of years in the Dominican Republic and reported on the coup in Haiti in 1991. Based on these first-hand experiences, she wrote her first book about the countries of Haiti and the Dominican

Republic, which share the space of the single island of Hispaniola in the Caribbean. *Why the Cocks Fight: Dominicans, Haitians, and the Struggle for Hispaniola,* published in 1999, is more than just a journalistic account of the author's own experiences. It covers five centuries of the island's history, showing how the conflict between the divided cultures on the island developed.

The cockfight reference in the title of Wucker's book is a metaphor for the often contentious relationship between the Spanish-speaking and mixed-race Dominicans and the black, French-speaking Haitians. The limited resources of the land they share lends to their wary and oftentimes violent reactions to one another. Violence and poverty, the author points out, has led numerous people from both sides of the island to migrate to the United States. For example, Miami and New York counted among their populations a million Haitian immigrants in 1994. Twelve and one-half percent of the island's entire population, Wucker tells us, immigrated to the United States in the last twenty years. Numbers like these give these communities significant political power in the United States, making the events of Hispaniola relevant to Americans.

In addition to statistics and historical facts, Wucker mixes in colorful anecdotes and images of people from both cultures living on the island today. Wucker interviews a Haitian cane cutter who knows no other way of life than to work seventy hours a week for just pennies an hour. She also talks to a number of immigrants in the United States. According to Patrick Markee in the *New York Times Book Review,* one particularly memorable street life scene closes the book. The author describes a carnival that takes place annually on the outskirts of Santo Domingo, the capital of the Dominican Republic. The author shows us that some of the barrier walls can come down as both Haitian and Dominicans dance side-by-side during this celebratory time.

Moments such as continued to be rare, however, and the theme of racism is explored in depth in *Why the Cocks Fight.* In addition to being of different races, the two peoples of Hispaniola have long suffered conflict over the issue of immigration from Haiti to the Dominican Republic. The Dominican government continued to purchase thousands of Haitians each year to work as sugar cane cutters. The conditions these laborers work in barely surpassed slave labor with

minuscule pay, poor conditions, and few legal rights. IN additin, the natives of the Dominican Republic treat them with disdain, calling them *braceros* and marginalizing them to segregated communities on the outskirts of town.

A reviewer for *Publisher's Weekly* praised the Wucker's "insightful treatment of many cultural issues, particularly the politicized nature of language, to which she brings an understanding of Creole, Spanish and French."

BIOGRAPHICAL AND CRITICAL SOURCES:

PERIODICALS

Booklist, December 15, 1998, Vanessa Bush, review of *Why the Cocks Fight: Dominicans, Haitians, and the Struggle for Hispaniola,* p. 712.
Library Journal, December 1998, review of *Why the Cocks Fight,* p. 134.
New York Times Book Review, May 2, 1999, Patrick Markee, "History as a Cockfight," p. 22.
Publishers Weekly, December 21, 1998, review of *Why the Cocks Fight,* p. 40.*

* * *

WURMSER, David

PERSONAL: Male. *Education:* Johns Hopkins University, B.A., M.A., Ph.D.

ADDRESSES: Agent—c/o Author Mail, AEI Press, 1150 17th St. NW, Washington, DC 20036.

CAREER: American Enterprise Institute, Washington, DC, research fellow and director in Middle Eastern studies.

WRITINGS:

(Editor, with Kenneth M. Jensen) *Is It Feasible to Negotiate Chemical and Biological Weapon Control?,* United States Institute of Peace (Washington, DC), 1990.

(Editor, with Kenneth M. Jensen) *The Meaning of Munich Fifty Years Later,* United States Institute of Peace (Washington, DC), 1990.

Tyranny's Ally: America's Failure to Defeat Saddam Hussein, foreword by Richard Pearle, American Enterprise Institute (Washington, DC), 1999.

SIDELIGHTS: David Wurmser is a Middle East specialist with the American Enterprise Institute and the author of *Tyranny's Ally: America's Failure to Defeat Saddam Hussein.* U.S. attacks against the Iraqi despot have essentially had no effect on his power. A large-scale effort, Operation Desert Fox, took place over four days in December 1998. Hundreds of Tomahawk cruise missiles were fired at targets that proved to have little strategic value, and the operation was a failure. The decision to bomb Iraq was considered by some as a distraction from the debate over the impeachment of President Bill Clinton. Following Operation Desert Fox, a low-level air campaign continued as Saddam Hussein's forces persisted in challenging no-fly zones.

Writing prior to the 2003 U.S. invasion of Iraq, Wurmser argues that even if efforts to remove Saddam Hussein were successful, Iraq's basic structure would not change; another Saddam-like ruler would step in to preserve the power structure. Wurmser supports the Iraqi National Congress (INC), that is working from a safe haven in the north and has tried to combine opposition groups. The INC failed in its 1995 effort to take positions held by Saddam Hussein, largely because the United States backed off on its pledge of support. Wurmser contends that the INC holds the most promise for insurgency. *Commentary* reviewer Bret Louis Stephens noted that given the history of the area, Wurmser's proposals are not very encouraging. "Still," wrote Stephens, "whatever its problems, Wurmser's path is at least a path, as opposed to the aimless wandering represented by the Clinton policy. And it has the undeniable merit . . . of being consonant with the principles—an end to tyranny, the forthright promotion of freedom—we have successfully stood for elsewhere around the world."

BIOGRAPHICAL AND CRITICAL SOURCES:

PERIODICALS

Commentary, July, 1999, Bret Louis Stephens, review of *Tyranny's Ally,* pp. 86-88.*

*   *   *

WURZBURGER, Walter 1920-2002

OBITUARY NOTICE—See index for *CA* sketch: Born March 29, 1920, in Munich, Germany; immigrated to the United States, 1938; naturalized citizen; died April 16, 2002, in New York, NY. Rabbi, educator, and author. Wurzburger came to the United States as Nazi attacks on Jews were intensifying and enrolled at Yeshiva University, from which he graduated and was ordained an Orthodox rabbi. He followed with both a master's degree and doctorate from Harvard University. He served congregations in Massachusetts, Toronto, Canada, and New York, retiring in 1994 from Congregation Shaaray Tefila in Lawrence, New York. From 1962 until 1988 Wurzburger was editor of *Tradition,* an Orthodox journal, and from 1967 until March of 2002 he was part of the philosophy faculty at Yeshiva University. Wurzburger wrote *Ethics of Responsibility: Pluralistic Approaches to Covenantal Ethics* in 1994 and *God Is Proof Enough* in 2000. His first book considers whether Halakhah (Jewish law) allows people to make choices based on other ethical systems, which Wurzburger argued it did if such systems were based on "religiously significant issues." His second book focuses on belief. For many years Wurzburger was president of the Synagogue Council of America, an umbrella agency for Conservative, Orthodox, and Reform Jewish groups.

OBITUARIES AND OTHER SOURCES:

PERIODICALS

Los Angeles Times, April 19, 2002, p. B15.
New York Times, April 18, 2002, p. A25.
Washington Post, April 20, 2002, p. B7.

Y-Z

YING, Hu 1962-

PERSONAL: Born January 2, 1962, in Beijing, China. *Ethnicity:* "Chinese." *Education:* Peking University, B.A., 1984; Bryn Mawr College, M.A., 1988; Princeton University, Ph.D., 1992. *Hobbies and other interests:* Pottery.

ADDRESSES: Office—University of California—Irvine, Irvine, CA 92717.

CAREER: University of California—Irvine, Irvine, CA, faculty member, 1994—. Institute for Advanced Study, member, 2002-03.

MEMBER: AAS.

WRITINGS:

Tales of Translation: Composing the New Woman in China, 1898-1918, Stanford University Press (Stanford, CA), 2000.

*   *   *

YOUNG, Donald J. 1930-

PERSONAL: Born 1930.

ADDRESSES: Office—Fort MacArthur Military Museum Association, 3601 Gaffey Street, P.O. Box 27777, San Pedro, CA 90731.

CAREER: Military writer. Director of Fort MacArthur Military Museum, San Pedro, CA.

WRITINGS:

The Lion's Share, Avranches (Aptos, CA), 1990.
December 1941: America's First Twenty-five Days at War, Pictorial Histories (Missoula, MT), 1992.
The Battle of Bataan: A History of the Ninety-Day Siege and Eventual Surrender of 75,000 Filipino and United States Troops to the Japanese in World War II, McFarland (Jefferson, NC), 1992.
First Twenty-four Hours of War in the Pacific, Burd Street Press (Shippensburg, PA), 1998.

SIDELIGHTS:

Donald J. Young has written accounts of World War II that put major events under a magnifying glass. In *The Battle of Bataan: A History of the Ninety-Day Siege and Eventual Surrender of 75,000 Filipino and United States Troops to the Japanese in World War II,* he re-examines the Allied defense of the Bataan peninsula from December 1941 to April 1942. His analysis in the *First Twenty-four Hours of War in the Pacific* is limited, chronologically and geographically, to show how the events of December 7, 1941, were linked to early Japanese domination in the Pacific theater.

The defeat of U.S.-Filipino troops at Bataan was the largest surrender in U.S. military history and a terrible chapter in the country's military annals. The Allied troops on Bataan outnumbered their Japanese attackers but were unprepared and unequipped to protect their position. The Filipinos who made up three-quarters of the forces often had less than a month's training; and they were then asked to fight with inadequate supplies of ammunition, fuel, and machinery. During the course of fighting these soldiers also faced terrible conditions that led to diseases such as dysentery and malaria, as well as starvation.

The Battle of Bataan reveals that U.S. accounts of the battle have underemphasized the courage, ingenuity, and suffering of the Filipino army in the desperate months on Bataan. Young provides information gathered during twelve years of research, including interviews with Ambrosio Pena, a retired chief historian for the Philippine Army. The account also includes fifty photographs, twenty-nine hand-drawn maps, and a poem by Lt. Henry G. Lee, who died on a Japanese prison ship.

Young's work was welcomed for its thoroughness and insight. In the *Military Review,* W. D. Bushnell, a retired colonel in the U.S. Marine Corps, called it "a remarkably comprehensive and evenhanded history." Bushnell commended the book as "The complete story of a terrible battle filled with astonishing human suffering and sacrifice. Young brings the heroes and cowards, victory and despair, sacrifice and escape to life with stark clarity and vivid description." *Library Journal*'s Michael Coleman wrote that the account "brings together all facets of the story."

In a review for *Choice,* C. J. Weeks offered a different view of the book. The reviewer agreed that Young does a good job of showing the parts played by the Filipino army and the U.S. military, but felt that there are important omissions. Weeks suggested that the Japanese side of the story is missing and that a tactical focus avoids the question "How could such a disaster have been permitted to occur and who was responsible for it?"

In *First Twenty-four Hours of War in the Pacific* Young takes a narrower focus, reviewing the events of December 7, 1941, except for the bombing of Pearl Harbor. This includes happenings in Hong Kong, Malaya, the Philippines, Wake Island, and Washington, D.C., that show how the Japanese quickly established air superiority in the Pacific due to strength and luck. The greatest emphasis is placed on the ruin of American air forces in the Philippines within hours of receiving reports on Pearl Harbor. *Booklist*'s Roland Green explained that such information would "rate only cursory mention in larger works" and that *First Twenty-four Hours of War in the Pacific* "remedies the oversimplification of other accounts." A *Publishers Weekly* reviewer noted that "concentration on a single theater diminishes reader confusion." The book was further described as "a narrative that successfully walks the edge of entropy, while the limited focus also offers case studies in the fog and friction of modern conflict."

BIOGRAPHICAL AND CRITICAL SOURCES:

PERIODICALS

Booklist, September 1, 1998, Roland Green, review of *First Twenty-four Hours of War in the Pacific,* p. 63.

Choice, May, 1993, C. J. Weeks, review of *The Battle of Bataan,* p. 1526.

Library Journal, January, 1993, MIchael Coleman, *The Battle of Bataan,* p. 144.

Military Review, May, 1994, W. D. Bushnell, *The Battle of Bataan,* p. 76.

Publishers Weekly, August 3, 1998, review of *First Twenty-four Hours of War in the Pacific,* p. 67.*

* * *

YOUNGE, Gary 1969-

PERSONAL: Born 1969, in Stevenage, Hertfordshire, England. *Education:* Graduated from City University, London, England, 1993.

ADDRESSES: Home—London, England. *Agent*—c/o Author Mail, University Press of Mississippi, 3825 Ridgewood Rd., Jackson, MS 39211.

CAREER: Guardian, London, England, columnist.

AWARDS, HONORS: Guardian First Book Award, for *No Place like Home: A Black Briton's Journey through the American South.*

WRITINGS:

No Place like Home: A Black Briton's Journey through the American South, Picador (London, England), 1999, University Press of Mississippi (Jackson, MS), 2002.

BIOGRAPHICAL AND CRITICAL SOURCES:

PERIODICALS

Sunday Times, October 10, 1999, review of *No Place like Home: A Black Briton's Journey through the American South,* p. 38.

Times Educational Supplement, October 15, 1999, Reva Klein, review of *No Place like Home,* p. C10.

Times Literary Supplement, January 7, 2000, Martin Fletcher, review of *No Place like Home,* p. 27.*

* * *

ZAFFRAN, Marc
See WINCKLER, Martin

* * *

ZANZOTTO, Andrea 1921-

PERSONAL: Born October 10, 1921, in Pieve di Soligo, Italy; son of Giovanni (a miniature and landscape painter) and Carmela Zanzotto; married, 1959; wife's name, Marisa; children: Giovanni, Fabio. *Education:* University of Padua, laureate in literature, 1942.

ADDRESSES: Home—Pieve di Soligo, Italy. *Agent*—c/o Mondadori, Via Mondadori 1, Segrate, Milan 20090 Italy.

CAREER: Poet, translator, and literary critic, 1951—. Traveled and worked at menial jobs in France and Switzerland, late 1940s. Elementary school teacher and administrator in Pieve di Soligo, Italy, c. 1948-75.

AWARDS, HONORS: San Babila prize, 1950; Premio Saint-Vincent, 1950, for *Dietro il paesaggio;* Premio Viareggio, 1979; honoris causa degree, University of

Venice, 1982; Premio Librex-Montale for poetry, 1983, for *Fosfeni;* Premio Feltrinelli, Accademia dei Lincei, 1987, for poetry; prize of the city of Münster, for European poetry and its translations, 1993; Premio di poesia Pandolfo, 1998.

WRITINGS:

Dietro il paesaggio, Mondadori (Milan, Italy), 1951.
Elegia e altri versi, Meridiana (Milan, Italy), 1954.
Vocativo, Mondadori (Milan, Italy), 1957, revised edition, 1981.
IX Ecloghe, Mondadori (Milan, Italy), 1962.
Sull'altopiano: Racconti e prose, 1942-1954, Neri Pozza (Venice, Italy), 1964.
La beltà, Mondadori (Milan, Italy), 1968.
Gli sguardi i fatti e senhal, Bernardi (Pieve di Soligo, Italy), 1969.
A che valse? Versi, 1938-1942, Scheiwiller (Milan, Italy), 1970, enlarged edition published as *Poesie, 1938-1972,* edited by Stefano Agosti, Mondadori (Milan, Italy), 1973, 2nd enlarged edition published as *Poesie, 1938-1986,* edited by Giorgio Luzzi, L'Arzanà (Turin, Italy), 1987.
Pasque, Mondadori (Milan, Italy), 1973.
Selected Poetry, edited and translated by Ruth Feldman and Brian Swann, Princeton University Press (Princeton, NJ), 1975.
Filò: per il Casanova di Fellini, Ruzante (Venice, Italy), 1976, revised edition published as *Filò e altre poesie,* Lato Side (Rome, Italy), 1981, 2nd revised edition published as *Filò,* Mondadori (Milan, Italy), 1988, translation by John P. Welle and Ruth Feldman published as *Peasants Wake for Fellini's Casanova and Other Poems,* University of Illinois Press (Urbana, IL), 1997.
Il galateo in bosco, Mondadori (Milan, Italy), 1978.
Circhi e cene/Circuses and Suppers (bilingual edition), translated by Beverly Allen, Plain Wrapper (Verona, Italy), 1979.
Mistieròi Poemetto dialettale veneto, Castaldi (Feltre, Italy), 1979.
(Author of introduction) Franco Fortini, *Una obbedienza: 18 poesie 1969-1979,* San Marco dei Giustiniani (Genoa, Italy), 1980.
(Editor, with Nico Naldini) *Pasolini: Poesie e pagine ritrovate,* Lato Side (Rome, Italy), 1980.
Fosfeni, Mondadori (Milan, Italy), 1983.
Idioma, Mondadori (Milan, Italy), 1986.
Opere, Volume 1, Mondadori (Milan, Italy), 1987, 2nd edition, 1998.
Racconti e prose, Mondadori (Milan, Italy), 1990.

Fantasie di avvicinamento, Mondadori (Milan, Italy), 1991.

Aure e disincanti: nel Novecento letterario, Mondadori (Milan, Italy), 1994.

Sull'altopiano e prose varie, Pozza (Vicenza, Italy), 1995.

Lievi voci, api inselvatichite, with photographs by Guido Piacentini, Stamperia Bentivoglio (Bologna, Italy), 1995.

Meteo, Donzelli (Rome, Italy), 1996.

Il mio viaggio: poesie scelte (1987-1995), Marsilio (Venice, Italy), 1996.

Ligonàs, Premio di poesia Pandolfo (Florence, Italy), 1998.

Le poesie e prose scelte, edited by Stefano dal Bianco and Gian Mario Villalta, Mondadori (Milan, Italy), 1999.

(With Geno Pampaloni and Sandro Veronesi) *Nel caldo cuore del mondo: lettere sull'Italia,* Liberal libri (Florence, Italy), 1999.

TRANSLATOR

Michel Leiris, *Età d'uomo e Notti senza notte,* Mondadori (Milan, Italy), 1966.

George Bataille, *Nietzsche, il culmine e il possibile,* Rizzoli (Milan, Italy), 1970.

George Bataille, *La letteratura e il male,* Rizzoli (Milan, Italy), 1973.

Honoré de Balzac, *La ricerca dell'assoluto,* Garzanti (Milan, Italy), 1975.

Honoré de Balzac, *Il medico di campagna,* Garzanti (Milan, Italy), 1977.

Contributor of poetry and essays to anthologies and collections, including *I metodi attuali della critica in Italia,* edited by Maria Corti and Cesare Segre, RAI (Turin, Italy), 1970; *From Pure Silence to Impure Dialogue: A Survey of Post-War Italian Poetry, 1945-1965,* edited and translated by Vittoria Bradshaw, Las Américas (New York, NY), 1971; *Francesco Petrarca's Rime,* edited by Guido Bezzola, Rizzoli (Milan, Italy), 1976; *Pasolini: Cronaca giudiziaria, persecuzione, morte,* edited by Laura Betti, Garzanti (Milan, Italy), 1977; *Federico Fellini's La città delle donne,* Garzanti (Milan, Italy), 1980; *The New Italian Poetry: 1945 to the Present: A Bilingual Anthology,* edited and translated by Lawrence R. Smith, University of California Press (Berkeley, CA), 1981; *Pier Paolo Pasolini: L'opera e il suo tempo,* edited by Guido

Santato, CLUEP (Padua, Italy), 1983; *Naldini's Nei campi di Friuli,* All'Insegna del Pesce d'Oro (Milan, Italy), 1984; and *Poesia e nichilismo,* Il melangolo (Genoa, Italy), 1998. Contributing writer for Federico Fellini's films *Casanova,* 1976, and *E la nave va,* 1983. Contributor to periodicals, including *Verri.*

SIDELIGHTS: "Andrea Zanzotto," wrote *World Literature Today* critic John P. Welle, "is often described as the major voice of the so-called fourth generation of modern Italian poets." Zanzotto's writing career, which began in the 1940s while the poet was serving with the Italian Resistance during World War II, "is informed by the main currents of modern European thought—the philosophy of Martin Heidegger, the psychoanalytic theory of Jacques Lacan and recent developments in linguistics, structuralism and semiotics," Welle observed.

Zanzotto has worked most of his professional life as a schoolteacher in his native town of Pieve di Soligo, and many of his poems reflect his chosen semirural lifestyle. "A creative innovator and a brilliantly inspired verbal experimenter, Zanzotto has a style, an idiom, and a timbre altogether his own," stated *World Literature Today* contributor G. Singh. Welle noted in the *Dictionary of Literary Biography* that, starting with Zanzotto's first poetry collection, *Dietro il paessagio,* his "native landscape provides a springboard for an exploration of inner space. . . . The recurring symbols of sun, moon, grass, snow, mother, and child depict the flux of the seasons and the fluidity of subjectivity."

Zanzotto also creates new forms of language in order to involve the reader in the process of exploring his native country. "In Zanzotto's early works, his mastery of the materiality of language was such that standard languages were not the only system within which he worked," declared *American Book Review* contributor Glenn Mott. "He has used palimpsests, ideograms, hieroglyphics, and typographical layout, embracing lexical registers from the high toned *lingua aulica* . . . to the language of commercial media (jingles, slogans, Benetton's), scientific language from the Latin, archaisms, neologisms, and dialect. From this he has created an amusing linguistic frontier on the verge of disorder."

Perhaps Zanzotto's best-known experiment with language occurred in his collaboration with film director Federico Fellini in the film *Casanova.* The poet's contributions were later published under the title *Filò: per il Casanova di Fellini,* published in English as *Peasants Wake for Fellini's Casanova and Other Poems.* "Zanzotto was to write two poems in an imaginary pseudo-archaic Venetian dialect: a nursery rhyme, somewhere between a rigmarole and a lullaby," explained Guido Almansi in the *Times Literary Supplement,* ". . . and a litany to accompany the emergence of the head of a woman from the slimy bed of the Grand Canal." Patricia M. Gathercole in *World Literature Today* said of *Peasants Wake,* "The volume is a multilingual edition, thought-provoking in its treatment of life's mysteries and both varied and highly imaginative in its conception."

BIOGRAPHICAL AND CRITICAL SOURCES:

BOOKS

Beverly, Allen, *Andrea Zanzotto: The Language of Beauty's Apprentice,* University of California Press (Berkeley, CA), 1989.
Dictionary of Literary Biography, Volume 128: *Twentieth-Century Italian Poets,* Gale (Detroit, MI), 1993, pp. 354-359.

PERIODICALS

American Book Review, January-February, 1999, Glenn Mott, "Botanist of Grammars," pp. 24, 26.
Chelsea, Volume 29, 1998, R. Watson, review of *Peasants Wake for Fellini's Casanova and Other Poems,* pp. 240-245.
Hudson Review, winter, 1977, Vernon Young, "Poetry Chronicle," pp. 619-630.
Library Journal, April 15, 1976, Marilyn Schneider, review of *Selected Poetry of Andrea Zanzotto,* p. 1024.
Publishers Weekly, May 26, 1997, review of *Peasants Wake for Fellini's Casanova and Other Poems,* p. 82.
Times Literary Supplement, October 31, 1975, Franco Fortini, "The Wind of Revival," p. 1308; August 18, 1978, Guido Almansi, "Verbal Folly," p. 936; October 2, 1987, Peter Hainsworth, "A Dying Race," p. 1083; February 23, 1990, Gian Luigi Beccaria and Peter Hainsworth, "The Most Recent Phase in Andrea Zanzotto's Vast Output of Poetry," p. S15.

World Literature Today, summer, 1981, F. J. Jones, review of *Poesie (1938-1972),* p. 455; spring, 1984, John P. Welle, review of *Fosfeni,* pp. 253-254; summer, 1984, John P. Welle, "From Babel to Pentecost: The Poetry of Andrea Zanzotto," pp. 377-379; summer, 1987, John P. Welle, review of *Idioma,* p. 434; spring, 1989, John P. Welle, review of *Filò,* p. 294; spring, 1990, Vinio Rossi, review of *Andrea Zanzotto: The Language of Beauty's Apprentice,* p. 294; winter, 1992, John P. Welle, review of *Gli sguardi i fatti e senhal,* p. 115; spring, 1995, Patricia M. Gathercole, review of *Aure e disincanti nel Novecento letterario,* p. 342; autumn, 1997, Patricia M. Gathercole, review of *Peasants Wake for Fellini's Casanova and Other Poems,* p. 771; autumn, 2000, G. Singh, review of *Le poesie e prose scelte,* p. 876.*

*   *   *   *

ZISSER, Eyal 1960-

PERSONAL: Born April 3, 1960, in Haifa, Israel; son of Yosef (a businessman) and Derora (Goldenberg) Zisser; married Shirley Sharon, June 16, 1986; children: Liron, Lilach, Toam. *Nationality:* Israeli. *Ethnicity:* "Jewish." *Education:* Tel Aviv University, B.A., 1985, M.A., 1988, Ph.D., 1992. *Religion:* Jewish.

ADDRESSES: Home—Beit Shamay 10, Ramat Hasharon, 47278, Israel. *Office*—Moshe Dayan Center for Middle Eastern Studies, Tel Aviv University, Ramat Aviv, 69978, Israel. *E-mail*—zisser@post.tau.ac.il.

CAREER: Educator. Tel Aviv University, Tel Aviv, Israel, research fellow, 1992-98, lecturer, 1993-98, senior research fellow, 1998—; Cornell University, Ithaca, NY, visiting assistant professor, 1995-96; Washington Institute for Near East Policy, visiting researcher, 1996; senior lecturer of Middle Eastern and African History, 1998—.

WRITINGS:

Syria under Asad—At a Crossroads, HaKibutz Hameuhad (Tel Aviv, Israel), 1999.

Lebanon—The Challenge of Independence, I. B. Tauris (London, England), 2000.

Asad's Legacy, Syria in Transition, New York University Press (New York, NY), 2000.

Contributor to books, including *Middle East Contemporary Survey* (annual), Westview Press (Boulder, CO), 1991-2001; *Regional Security Regimes: Israel and Its Neighbors,* edited by Efraim Inbar, State University of New York Press (Albany, NY), 1995; *Religious Radicalism in the Greater Middle East,* edited by Bruce Maddy-Weitzman and E. Inbar, Frank Cass (London, England), 1997; *Islam and Democracy in the Arab World,* edited by Meir Litvak, Kav Adom (Tel Aviv, Israel), 1997; *Minorities and State in the Arab World,* edited by Gabriel Ben-Dor and Orfa Bangio, Lynne Reinner (New York, NY), 1998; *Modern Syria: From Ottoman Rule to Pivotal Role in the Middle East,* edited by Moshe Ma'oz, Joseph Ginat, and Onn Winckler, Sussex Academic Press (Brighton, England), 1999; and *Review Essays in Israel Studies,* edited by Laura Zittrain-Eizenberg and Neil Caplan, State University of New York Press, 2000. Contributor to journals, including *New Republic, Washington Quarterly, Middle East Quarterly, Japanese Institute of Middle East Economics Review,* and *Orient.*

*   *   *

ZMUDA, Bob 1949-

PERSONAL: Born 1949, in Chicago, IL.

ADDRESSES: Agent—c/o Author Mail, Warner Books, 1271 Avenue of the Americas, New York, NY 10020.

CAREER: Comedian; television and film producer; *Comic Relief,* HBO, creator; *Man on the Moon (film),* co-executive producer, 1999.

AWARDS, HONORS: Emmy Award; Cable ACE Award.

WRITINGS:

(With Matthew Scott Hansen) *Andy Kaufman Revealed! Best Friend Tells All,* Little, Brown (Boston, MA), 1999.

SIDELIGHTS: Though television and film producer Bob Zmuda has numerous credits to his name, most notably as creator of the popular *Comic Relief* shows for HBO, the work he did with innovative comedian Andy Kaufman is arguably his greatest claim to fame. Zmuda, who had grown up in a working-class Polish-American family in Chicago, moved to New York City to pursue a career in comedy after developing a taste for the type of political street theater the Yuppie group used to satirize Chicago politics at the 1968 democratic convention. Zmuda met Kaufman in New York in 1972, befriending the influential comic and becoming his writer and collaborator through a career that included Kaufman's role as Latka in the popular sit-com *Taxi,* several appearances on *Saturday Night Live,* and contests in which the comedian wrestled attractive young women. Zmuda helped Kaufman develop the controversial character of Tony Clifton, an offensive lounge singer, and even played Clifton in an elaborate hoax that Kaufman hoped to pull on the media. Privy to many of Kaufman's most notorious pranks, Zmuda was considered well qualified to pen his friend's biography, *Andy Kaufman Revealed! Best Friend Tells All.*

The book, which Zmuda coauthored with Matthew Scott Hansen, fulfills part of a promise Zmuda made Kaufman as the comedian lay dying of lung cancer in 1984. As Zmuda explained to Betsy Sherman in a *Boston Globe* interview, Kaufman feared that he would be remembered only as the sweet and silly Latka and not as a comedian who took considerable creative risks. Zmuda's book, the publication of which coincided with the release of the biographical film *Man on the Moon,* for which Zmuda served as co-executive producer and which was also part of Kaufman's dying wish, was intended to set the record straight. "There's an Andy Kaufman mystique that I'm concerned about perpetuating" in the book and the film, the author told Sherman. "Yet at the same time, I realize that this is the record now. . . . I want [these works] to show the real guy."

Critics appreciated the book's timeliness, and generally enjoyed its portrayal of the innovative comic, who fooled his friends into thinking that his death may have been another of his trademark hoaxes—a prank to which Zmuda alludes, which reads "Kaufman, if you're still alive, I'll kill you." A reviewer for *Publishers Weekly* found the book a "highly absorbing memoir" that reveals some interesting secrets about its eccentric subject. *Booklist*'s Mike Tribby heaped similar praise on the book, calling it "thoroughly entertaining [and] illuminating." Though *New York Times Book Review* writer Lance Gould felt that the book fails to reveal much that was new about its subject, he pointed out that it is nevertheless an "often hilarious tribute" to Kaufman.

As creator of HBO's *Comic Relief* specials, Zmuda helped the network raise over $50 million for America's homeless. The popularity of *Comic Relief* led to the 1995 NBC tribute, *Comic Salute to Andy Kaufman,* which in turn helped convince producers that an audience existed for the biographical film that followed. Having fulfilled his dual obligation to his friend, Zmuda feels he has revealed the man behind the elaborate act. As he said in the *Boston Globe* interview, "I think there's a greater appreciation of Andy if you know the whole story."

BIOGRAPHICAL AND CRITICAL SOURCES:

BOOKS

Zmuda, Bob, and Matthew Scott Hanson, *Andy Kaufman Revealed! Best Friend Tells All,* Little, Brown (Boston, MA), 1999.

PERIODICALS

Booklist, September 15, 1999, Mike Tribby, review of *Andy Kaufman Revealed! Best Friend Tells All,* p. 214.

Boston Globe, December 19, 1999, Betsy Sherman, "Channeling Andy with 'Man on the Moon,'; Bob Zmuda Tries to Let the Real Kaufman Out," p. N7.

Esquire, March, 1998, Ronn Rosenbaum, "The Return of Andy Kaufman," p. N58.

New York Times Book Review, September 26, 1999, Lance Gould, review of *Andy Kaufman Revealed! Best Friend Tells All,* p. 21.

Publishers Weekly, August 9, 1999, "It's Andy Time," p. 226; August 16, 1999, review of *Andy Kaufman Revealed! Best Friend Tells All,* p. 69.*